Stanley Gibbons
Commonwealth St

Southern & Central Africa

1st edition 2011

STANLEY GIBBONS LTD
London and Ringwood

By Appointment to Her Majesty The Queen
Stanley Gibbons Ltd, London
Philatelists

Published by Stanley Gibbons Ltd
Editorial, Publications Sales Offices
and Distribution Centre:
7 Parkside, Christchurch Road, Ringwood,
Hants BH24 3SH

British Library Cataloguing in
Publication Data.
A catalogue record for this book is available
from the British Library.

Errors and omissions excepted
the colour reproduction of stamps is only as
accurate as the printing process will allow.

ISBN-10: 0-85259-823-8
ISBN-13: 978-0-85252-823-8

Item No. R 2978-11

Printed by
Stephens & George, Wales

Contents

Stanley Gibbons Holdings Plc

Stanley Gibbons Limited, Stanley Gibbons Auctions
399 Strand, London WC2R OLX
Tel: +44 (0)207 836 8444
Fax: +44 (0)207 836 7342
E-mail: help@stanleygibbons.com
Website: www.stanleygibbons.com
for all departments, Auction and Specialist Stamp Departments.

Open Monday–Friday 9.30 a.m. to 5 p.m. Shop. Open Monday–Friday 9 a.m. to 5.30 p.m. and Saturday 9.30 a.m. to 5.30 p.m.

Stanley Gibbons Publications Gibbons Stamp Monthly and Philatelic Exporter
7 Parkside, Christchurch Road, Ringwood, Hampshire BH24 3SH.
Tel: +44 (0)1425 472363
Fax: +44 (0)1425 470247
E-mail: help@stanleygibbons.com
Publications Mail Order.
FREEPHONE 0800 611622

Monday–Friday 8.30 a.m. to 5 p.m.

Stanley Gibbons (Guernsey) Limited
18–20 Le Bordage, St Peter Port, Guernsey GY1 1DE.
Tel: +44 (0)1481 708270
Fax: +44 (0)1481 708279
E-mail: investment@stanleygibbons.com

Stanley Gibbons (Jersey) Limited
18 Hill Street, St Helier, Jersey, Channel Islands JE2 4UA.
Tel: +44 (0)1534 766711
Fax: +44 (0)1534 766177
E-mail: investment@stanleygibbons.com

Benham Collectibles Limited
Unit K, Concept Court, Shearway Business Park
Folkestone Kent CT19 4RG
E-mail: benham@benham.com

Fraser's
(a division of Stanley Gibbons Ltd)
399 Strand, London WC2R OLX
Autographs, photographs, letters and documents
Tel: +44 (0)207 836 8444
Fax: +44 (0)207 836 7342
E-mail: sales@frasersautographs.com
Website: www.frasersautographs.com

Monday–Friday 9 a.m. to 5.30 p.m. and Saturday 10 a.m. to 4 p.m.

Stanley Gibbons Publications Overseas Representation
Stanley Gibbons Publications are represented overseas by the following

Australia *Renniks Publications PTY LTD*
Unit 3 37-39 Green Street, Banksmeadow, NSW 2019, Australia
Tel: +612 9695 7055
Website: www.renniks.com

Canada *Unitrade Associates*
99 Floral Parkway, Toronto, Ontario M6L 2C4, Canada
Tel: +1 416 242 5900
Website: www.unitradeassoc.com

Germany *Schaubek Verlag Leipzig*
Am Glaeschen 23, D-04420 Markranstaedt, Germany
Tel: +49 34 205 67823
Website: www.schaubek.de

India *Trustin Philatelic*
96 Richmond Road, Bangalore 560 025, India
Tel: +9180 222 11 555/ 22 97 516
Tel: +9180500 49500
Email: trustin@vsnl.net

Italy *Ernesto Marini S.R.L.*
V. Struppa, 300, Genova, 16165, Italy
Tel: +3901 0247-3530
Website: www.ernestomarini.it

Japan *Japan Philatelic*
PO Box 2, Suginami-Minami, Tokyo 168-8081, Japan
Tel: +81 3330 41641
Website: www.yushu.co.jp

Netherlands also covers Belgium Denmark, Finland & France *Uitgeverij Davo BV*
PO Box 411, Ak Deventer, 7400 Netherlands
Tel: +315 7050 2700
Website: www.davo.nl

New Zealand *House of Stamps*
PO Box 12, Paraparaumu, New Zealand
Tel: +61 6364 8270
Website: www.houseofstamps.co.nz

New Zealand *Philatelic Distributors*
PO Box 863
15 Mount Edgecumbe Street
New Plymouth 4615, New Zealand
Tel: +6 46 758 65 68
Website: www.stampcollecta.com

Norway *SKANFIL A/S*
SPANAV. 52 / BOKS 2030
N-5504 HAUGESUND, Norway
Tel: +47-52703940
E-mail: magne@skanfil.no

Singapore *C S Philatelic Agency*
Peninsula Shopping Centre #04-29
3 Coleman Street, 179804, Singapore
Tel: +65 6337-1859
Website: www.cs.com.sg

South Africa *Peter Bale Philatelics*
P O Box 3719, Honeydew, 2040, South Africa
Tel: +27 11 462 2463
Tel: +27 82 330 3925
E-mail: balep@iafrica.com

Sweden *Chr Winther Sorensen AB*
Box 43, S-310 20 Knaered, Sweden
Tel: +46 43050743
Website: www.ifsda.org/i/dealer.php?mid=2100&asscd=SE

USA *Regency Superior Ltd*
229 North Euclid Avenue
Saint Louis, Missouri 63108, USA

PO Box 8277, St Louis, MO 63156-8277, USA
Toll Free Tel: (800) 782-0066
Tel: (314) 361-5699
Website: www.RegencySuperior.com
Email: info@regencysuperior.com

General Philatelic Information and Guidelines to the Scope of Stanley Gibbons Commonwealth Catalogues

These notes reflect current practice in compiling the Stanley Gibbons Commonwealth Catalogues.

The Stanley Gibbons Stamp Catalogue has a very long history and the vast quantity of information it contains has been carefully built up by successive generations through the work of countless individuals. Philately is never static and the Catalogue has evolved and developed over the years. These notes relate to the current criteria upon which a stamp may be listed or priced. These criteria have developed over time and may have differed somewhat in the early years of this catalogue. These notes are not intended to suggest that we plan to make wholesale changes to the listing of classic issues in order to bring them into line with today's listing policy, they are designed to inform catalogue users as to the policies currently in operation.

PRICES

The prices quoted in this Catalogue are the estimated selling prices of Stanley Gibbons Ltd at the time of publication. They are, unless it is specifically stated otherwise, for examples in fine condition for the issue concerned. Superb examples are worth more; those of a lower quality considerably less.

All prices are subject to change without prior notice and Stanley Gibbons Ltd may from time to time offer stamps below catalogue price. Individual low value stamps sold at 399 Strand are liable to an additional handling charge. Purchasers of new issues should note the prices charged for them contain an element for the service rendered and so may exceed the prices shown when the stamps are subsequently catalogued. Postage and handling charges are extra.

No guarantee is given to supply all stamps priced, since it is not possible to keep every catalogued item in stock. Commemorative issues may, at times, only be available in complete sets and not as individual values.

Quotation of prices. The prices in the left-hand column are for unused stamps and those in the right-hand column are for used.

A dagger (†) denotes that the item listed does not exist in that condition and a blank, or dash, that it exists, or may exist, but we are unable to quote a price.

Prices are expressed in pounds and pence sterling. One pound comprises 100 pence (£1 = 100p).

The method of notation is as follows: pence in numerals (e.g. 10 denotes ten pence); pounds and pence, up to £100, in numerals (e.g. 4.25 denotes four pounds and twenty-five pence); prices above £100 are expressed in whole pounds with the '£' sign shown.

Unused stamps. Great Britain and Commonwealth: the prices for unused stamps of Queen Victoria to King George V are for lightly hinged examples. Unused prices for King Edward VIII, King George VI and Queen Elizabeth issues are for unmounted mint.

Some stamps from the King George VI period are often difficult to find in unmounted mint condition. In such instances we would expect that collectors would need to pay a high proportion of the price quoted to obtain mounted mint examples. Generally speaking lightly mounted mint stamps from this reign, issued before 1945, are in considerable demand.

Used stamps. The used prices are normally for stamps postally used but may be for stamps cancelled-to-order where this practice exists.

A pen-cancellation on early issues can sometimes correctly denote postal use. Instances are individually noted in the Catalogue in explanation of the used price given.

Prices quoted for bisects on cover or large piece are for those dated during the period officially authorised.

Stamps not sold unused to the public (e.g. some official stamps) are priced used only.

The use of 'unified' designs, that is stamps inscribed for both postal and fiscal purposes, results in a number of stamps of very high face value. In some instances these may not have been primarily intended for postal purposes, but if they are so inscribed we include them. We only price such items used, however, where there is evidence of normal postal usage.

Cover prices. To assist collectors, cover prices are quoted for issues up to 1945 at the beginning of each country.

The system gives a general guide in the form of a factor by which the corresponding used price of the basic loose stamp should be multiplied when found in fine average condition on cover.

Care is needed in applying the factors and they relate to a cover which bears a single of the denomination listed; if more than one denomination is present the most highly priced attracts the multiplier and the remainder are priced at the simple figure for used singles in arriving at a total.

The cover should be of non-philatelic origin; bearing the correct postal rate for the period and distance involved and cancelled with the markings normal to the offices concerned. Purely philatelic items have a cover value only slightly greater than the catalogue value for the corresponding used stamps. This applies generally to those high-value stamps used philatelically rather than in the normal course of commerce. Low-value stamps, e.g. ¼d. and ½d., are desirable when used as a single rate on cover and merit an increase in 'multiplier' value.

First day covers in the period up to 1945 are not within the scope of the system and the multiplier should not be used. As a special category of philatelic usage, with wide variations in valuation according to scarcity, they require separate treatment.

Oversized covers, difficult to accommodate on an album page, should be reckoned as worth little more than the corresponding value of the used stamps. The condition of a cover also affects its value. Except for 'wreck covers', serious damage or soiling reduce the value where the postal markings and stamps are ordinary ones. Conversely, visual appeal adds to the value and this can include freshness of appearance, important addresses, old-fashioned but legible hand-writing, historic town-names, etc.

The multipliers are a base on which further value would be added to take account of the cover's postal historical importance in demonstrating such things as unusual, scarce or emergency cancels, interesting routes, significant postal markings, combination usage, the development of postal rates, and so on.

Minimum price. The minimum catalogue price quoted is 10p. For individual stamps prices between 10p. and 95p. are provided as a guide for catalogue users. The lowest price charged for individual stamps or sets purchased from Stanley Gibbons Ltd is £1

Set prices. Set prices are generally for one of each value, excluding shades and varieties, but including major colour changes. Where there are alternative shades, etc., the cheapest is usually included. The number of stamps in the set is always stated for clarity. The prices for sets containing *se-tenant* pieces are based on the prices quoted for such combinations, and not on those for the individual stamps.

Varieties. Where plate or cylinder varieties are priced in used condition the price quoted is for a fine used example with the cancellation well clear of the listed flaw.

Specimen stamps. The pricing of these items is explained under that heading.

Stamp booklets. Prices are for complete assembled booklets in fine condition with those issued before 1945 showing normal wear and tear. Incomplete booklets and those which have been 'exploded' will, in general, be worth less than the figure quoted.

Repricing. Collectors will be aware that the market factors of supply and demand directly influence the prices quoted in this Catalogue. Whatever the scarcity of a particular stamp, if there is no one in the market who wishes to buy it cannot be expected to achieve a high price. Conversely, the same item actively sought by numerous potential buyers may cause the price to rise.

All the prices in this Catalogue are examined during the preparation of each new edition by the expert staff of Stanley Gibbons and repriced as necessary. They take many factors into account, including supply and demand, and are in close touch with the international stamp market and the auction world.

Commonwealth cover prices and advice on postal history material originally provided by Edward B Proud.

GUARANTEE

All stamps are guaranteed originals in the following terms:

If not as described, and returned by the purchaser, we undertake to refund the price paid to us in the original transaction. If any stamp is certified as genuine by the Expert Committee of the Royal Philatelic Society, London, or by BPA Expertising Ltd, the purchaser shall not be entitled to make any claim against us for any error, omission or mistake in such certificate.

Consumers' statutory rights are not affected by the above guarantee.

The recognised Expert Committees in this country are those of the Royal Philatelic Society, 41 Devonshire Place, London W1G, 6JY, and BPA Expertising Ltd, PO Box 1141, Guildford, Surrey GU5 0WR. They do not undertake valuations under any circumstances and fees are payable for their services.

ACKNOWLEDGEMENTS

We are grateful to individual collectors, members of the philatelic trade and specialist societies and study circles for their assistance in improving and extending the Stanley Gibbons range of catalogues. The addresses of societies and study circles relevant to this volume are:

Bechuanalands and Bostwana Society
Membership Secretary – Mr. N. Midwood
69 Porlock Lane, Furzton,
Milton Keynes MK4 1JY

Cape and Natal Study Circle
Secretary – Mr. J. Dickson, Lismore House,
Great Lane, Shepton Beauchamp,
Somerset TA19 0LJ

Orange Free State Study Circle
Secrertary – Mr. J.R. Stroud
28 Oxford Street, Burnham-on-Sea,
Somerset TA8 1LQ

Rhodesian Study Circle
Membership Secretary – Mr. R.G. Barnett
2 Cox Ley, Hatfield Heath,
Bishop's Stortford CM22 7ER

South African Collectors' Society
General Secretary – Mr. C. Oliver
Telephone 020 8940 9833

Transvaal Study Circle
Secretary – Mr. J. Woolgar
132 Dale Street, Chatham, Kent
ME4 6QH

MARGINS ON IMPERFORATE STAMPS

Superb | Very fine | Fine | Average | Poor

GUM

Unmounted | Very lightly mounted | Lightly mounted | Mounted/ large part original gum (o.g.). | Heavily mounted small part o.g.

CENTRING

Superb | Very fine | Fine | Average | Poor

CANCELLATIONS

Superb | Very fine | Fine | Average | Poor

Superb | Very fine

Fine | Average | Poor

CONDITION GUIDE

To assist collectors in assessing the true value of items they are considering buying or in reviewing stamps already in their collections, we now offer a more detailed guide to the condition of stamps on which this catalogue's prices are based.

For a stamp to be described as 'Fine', it should be sound in all respects, without creases, bends, wrinkles, pin holes, thins or tears. If perforated, all perforation 'teeth' should be intact, it should not suffer from fading, rubbing or toning and it should be of clean, fresh appearance.

Margins on imperforate stamps: These should be even on all sides and should be at least as wide as half the distance between that stamp and the next. To have one or more margins of less than this width, would normally preclude a stamp from being described as 'Fine'. Some early stamps were positioned very close together on the printing plate and in such cases 'Fine' margins would necessarily be narrow. On the other hand, some plates were laid down to give a substantial gap between individual stamps and in such cases margins would be expected to be much wider.

An 'average' four-margin example would have a narrower margin on one or more sides and should be priced accordingly, while a stamp with wider, yet even, margins than 'Fine' would merit the description 'Very Fine' or 'Superb' and, if available, would command a price in excess of that quoted in the catalogue.

Gum: Since the prices for stamps of King Edward VIII, King George VI and Queen Elizabeth are for 'unmounted' or 'never hinged' mint, even stamps from these reigns which have been very lightly mounted should be available at a discount from catalogue price, the more obvious the hinge marks, the greater the discount.

Catalogue prices for stamps issued prior to King Edward VIII's reign are for mounted mint, so unmounted examples would be worth a premium. Hinge marks on 20th century stamps should not be too obtrusive, and should be at least in the lightly mounted category. For 19th century stamps more obvious hinging would be acceptable, but stamps should still carry a large part of their original gum—'Large part o.g.'—in order to be described as 'Fine'.

Centring: Ideally, the stamp's image should appear in the exact centre of the perforated area, giving equal margins on all sides. 'Fine' centring would be close to this ideal with any deviation having an effect on the value of the stamp. As in the case of the margins on imperforate stamps, it should be borne in mind that the space between some early stamps was very narrow, so it was very difficult to achieve accurate perforation, especially when the technology was in its infancy. Thus, poor centring would have a less damaging effect on the value of a 19th century stamp than on a 20th century example, but the premium put on a perfectly centred specimen would be greater.

Cancellations: Early cancellation devices were designed to 'obliterate' the stamp in order to prevent it being reused and this is still an important objective for today's postal administrations. Stamp collectors, on the other hand, prefer postmarks to be lightly applied, clear, and to leave as much as possible of the design visible. Dated, circular cancellations have long been 'the postmark of choice', but the definition of a 'Fine' cancellation will depend upon the types of cancellation in use at the time a stamp was current—it is clearly illogical to seek a circular datestamp on a Penny Black.

'Fine', by definition, will be superior to 'Average', so, in terms of cancellation quality, if one begins by identifying what 'Average' looks like, then one will be half way to identifying 'Fine'. The illustrations will give some guidance on mid-19th century and mid-20th century cancellations of Great Britain, but types of cancellation in general use in each country and in each period will determine the appearance of 'Fine'.

As for the factors discussed above, anything less than 'Fine' will result in a downgrading of the stamp concerned, while a very fine or superb cancellation will be worth a premium.

Combining the factors: To merit the description 'Fine', a stamp should be fine in every respect, but a small deficiency in one area might be made up for in another by a factor meriting an 'Extremely Fine' description.

Some early issues are so seldom found in what would normally be considered to be 'Fine' condition, the catalogue prices are for a slightly lower grade, with 'Fine' examples being worth a premium. In such cases a note to this effect is given in the catalogue, while elsewhere premiums are given for well-centred, lightly cancelled examples.

Stamps graded at less than fine remain collectable and, in the case of more highly priced stamps, will continue to hold a value. Nevertheless, buyers should always bear condition in mind.

The Catalogue in General

Contents. The Catalogue is confined to adhesive postage stamps, including miniature sheets. For particular categories the rules are:

(a) Revenue (fiscal) stamps or telegraph stamps are listed only where they have been expressly authorised for postal duty.
(b) Stamps issued only precancelled are included, but normally issued stamps available additionally with precancel have no separate precancel listing unless the face value is changed.
(c) Stamps prepared for use but not issued, hitherto accorded full listing, are nowadays foot-noted with a price (where possible).
(d) Bisects (trisects, etc.) are only listed where such usage was officially authorised.
(e) Stamps issued only on first day covers or in presentation packs and not available separately are not listed but may be priced in a footnote.
(f) New printings are only included in this Catalogue where they show a major philatelic variety, such as a change in shade, watermark or paper. Stamps which exist with or without imprint dates are listed separately; changes in imprint dates are mentioned in footnotes.
(g) Official and unofficial reprints are dealt with by footnote.
(h) Stamps from imperforate printings of modern issues which occur perforated are covered by footnotes, but are listed where widely available for postal use.

Exclusions. The following are excluded:

(a) non-postal revenue or fiscal stamps;
(b) postage stamps used fiscally (although prices are now given for some fiscally used high values);
(c) local carriage labels and private local issues;
(d) bogus or phantom stamps;
(e) railway or airline letter fee stamps, bus or road transport company labels or the stamps of private postal companies operating under licence from the national authority;
(f) cut-outs;
(g) all types of non-postal labels and souvenirs;
(h) documentary labels for the postal service, e.g. registration, recorded delivery, air-mail etiquettes, etc.;
(i) privately applied embellishments to official issues and privately commissioned items generally;
(j) stamps for training postal officers.
(k) Telegraph stamps

Full listing. 'Full listing' confers our recognition and implies allotting a catalogue number and (wherever possible) a price quotation.

In judging status for inclusion in the catalogue broad considerations are applied to stamps. They must be issued by a legitimate postal authority, recognised by the government concerned, and must be adhesives valid for proper postal use in the class of service for which they are inscribed. Stamps, with the exception of such categories as postage dues and officials, must be available to the general public, at face value, in reasonable quantities without any artificial restrictions being imposed on their distribution.

For errors and varieties the criterion is legitimate (albeit inadvertent) sale through a postal administration in the normal course of business. Details of provenance are always important; printers' waste and deliberately manufactured material are excluded.

Certificates. In assessing unlisted items due weight is given to Certificates from recognised Expert Committees and, where appropriate, we will usually ask to see them.

Date of issue. Where local issue dates differ from dates of release by agencies, 'date of issue' is the local date. Fortuitous stray usage before the officially intended date is disregarded in listing.

Catalogue numbers. Stamps of each country are catalogued chronologically by date of issue. Subsidiary classes are placed at the end of the country, as separate lists, with a distinguishing letter prefix to the catalogue number, e.g. D for postage due, O for official and E for express delivery stamps.

The catalogue number appears in the extreme left-column. The boldface Type numbers in the next column are merely cross-references to illustrations.

Once published in the Catalogue, numbers are changed as little as possible; really serious renumbering is reserved for the occasions when a complete country or an entire issue is being rewritten. The edition first affected includes cross-reference tables of old and new numbers.

Our catalogue numbers are universally recognised in specifying stamps and as a hallmark of status.

Illustrations. Stamps are illustrated at three-quarters linear size. Stamps not illustrated are the same size and format as the value shown, unless otherwise indicated. Stamps issued only as miniature sheets have the stamp alone illustrated but sheet size is also quoted. Overprints, surcharges, watermarks and postmarks are normally actual size. Illustrations of varieties are often enlarged to show the detail. Stamp booklet covers are illustrated half-size, unless otherwise indicated.

Designers. Designers' names are quoted where known, though space precludes naming every individual concerned in the production of a set. In particular, photographers supplying material are usually named only where they also make an active contribution in the design stage; posed photographs of reigning monarchs are, however, an exception to this rule.

CONTACTING THE CATALOGUE EDITOR

The editor is always interested in hearing from people who have new information which will improve or correct the Catalogue. As a general rule he must see and examine the actual stamps before they can be considered for listing; photographs or photocopies are insufficient evidence.

Submissions should be made in writing to the Catalogue Editor, Stanley Gibbons Publications at the Ringwood office. The cost of return postage for items submitted is appreciated, and this should include the registration fee if required.

Where information is solicited purely for the benefit of the enquirer, the editor cannot undertake to reply if the answer is already contained in these published notes or if return postage is omitted. Written communications are greatly preferred to enquiries by telephone or e-mail and the editor regrets that he or his staff cannot see personal callers without a prior appointment being made. Correspondence may be subject to delay during the production period of each new edition.

The editor welcomes close contact with study circles and is interested, too, in finding reliable local correspondents who will verify and supplement official information in countries where this is deficient.

We regret we do not give opinions as to the genuineness of stamps, nor do we identify stamps or number them by our Catalogue.

TECHNICAL MATTERS

The meanings of the technical terms used in the catalogue will be found in our *Philatelic Terms Illustrated*.

References below to (more specialised) listings are to be taken to indicate, as appropriate, the Stanley Gibbons *Great Britain Specialised Catalogue* in five volumes or the *Great Britain Concise Catalogue*.

1. Printing

Printing errors. Errors in printing are of major interest to the Catalogue. Authenticated items meriting consideration would include: background, centre or frame inverted or omitted; centre or subject transposed; error of colour; error or omission of value; double prints and impressions; printed both sides; and so on. Designs *tête-bêche*, whether intentionally or by accident, are listable. *Se-tenant* arrangements of stamps are recognised in the listings or footnotes. Gutter pairs (a pair of stamps separated by blank margin) are not included in this volume. Colours only partially omitted are not listed. Stamps with embossing omitted are reserved for our more specialised listings.

Printing varieties. Listing is accorded to major changes in the printing base which lead to completely new types. In recess-printing this could be a design re-engraved; in photogravure or photolithography a screen altered in whole or in part. It can also encompass flat-bed and rotary printing if the results are readily distinguishable.

To be considered at all, varieties must be constant.

Early stamps, produced by primitive methods, were prone to numerous imperfections; the lists reflect this, recognising re-entries, retouches, broken frames, misshapen letters, and so on. Printing technology has, however, radically improved over the years, during which time photogravure and lithography have become predominant. Varieties nowadays are more in the nature of flaws and these, being too specialised for this general catalogue, are almost always outside the scope.

In no catalogue, however, do we list such items as: dry prints, kiss prints, doctor-blade flaws, colour shifts or registration flaws (unless they lead to the complete omission of a colour from an individual stamp), lithographic ring flaws, and so on. Neither do we recognise fortuitous happenings like paper creases or confetti flaws.

Overprints (and surcharges). Overprints of different types qualify for separate listing. These include overprints in different colours; overprints from different printing processes such as litho and typo; overprints in totally different typefaces, etc. Major errors in machine-printed overprints are important and listable. They include: overprint inverted or omitted; overprint double (treble, etc.); overprint diagonal; overprint double, one inverted; pairs with one overprint omitted, e.g. from a radical shift to an adjoining stamp; error of colour; error of type fount; letters inverted or omitted, etc. If the overprint is handstamped, few of these would qualify and a distinction is drawn. We continue, however, to list pairs of stamps where one has a handstamped overprint and the other has not.

Varieties occurring in overprints will often take the form of broken letters, slight differences in spacing, rising spaces, etc. Only the most important would be considered for listing or footnote mention.

Sheet positions. If space permits we quote sheet positions of listed varieties and authenticated data is solicited for this purpose.

De La Rue plates. The Catalogue classifies the general plates used by De La Rue for printing British Colonial stamps as follows:

VICTORIAN KEY TYPE

Die I

1. The ball of decoration on the second point of the crown appears as a dark mass of lines.
2. Dark vertical shading separates the front hair from the bun.
3. The vertical line of colour outlining the front of the throat stops at the sixth line of shading on the neck.
4. The white space in the coil of the hair above the curl is roughly the shape of a pin's head.

Die II

1. There are very few lines of colour in the ball and it appears almost white.
2. A white vertical strand of hair appears in place of the dark shading.

3. The line stops at the eighth line of shading.
4. The white space is oblong, with a line of colour partially dividing it at the left end.

Plates numbered 1 and 2 are both Die I. Plates 3 and 4 are Die II.

GEORGIAN KEY TYPE

Die I

A. The second (thick) line below the name of the country is cut slanting, conforming roughly to the shape of the crown on each side.
B. The labels of solid colour bearing the words "POSTAGE" and "& REVENUE" are square at the inner top corners.
C. There is a projecting "bud" on the outer spiral of the ornament in each of the lower corners.

Die I

A. The second line is cut vertically on each side of the crown.
B. The labels curve inwards at the top.
C. There is no "bud" in this position.

Unless otherwise stated in the lists, all stamps with watermark Multiple Crown CA (w **8**) are Die I while those with watermark Multiple Crown Script CA (w **9**) are Die II. The Georgian Die II was introduced in April 1921 and was used for Plates 10 to 22 and 26 to 28. Plates 23 to 25 were made from Die I by mistake.

2. Paper

All stamps listed are deemed to be on (ordinary) paper of the wove type and white in colour; only departures from this are normally mentioned.

Types. Where classification so requires we distinguish such other types of paper as, for example, vertically and horizontally laid; wove and laid bâtonné; card(board); carton; cartridge; glazed; granite; native; pelure; porous; quadrillé; ribbed; rice; and silk thread.

Wove paper

Laid paper

Granite paper

Quadrillé paper

Burelé band

The various makeshifts for normal paper are listed as appropriate. The varieties of double paper and joined paper are recognised. The security device of a printed burelé band on the back of a stamp, as in early Queensland, qualifies for listing.

Descriptive terms. The fact that a paper is handmade (and thus probably of uneven thickness) is mentioned where necessary. Such descriptive terms as "hard" and "soft"; "smooth" and "rough"; "thick", "medium" and "thin" are applied where there is philatelic merit in classifying papers.

Coloured, very white and toned papers. A coloured paper is one that is coloured right through (front and back of the stamp). In the Catalogue the colour of the paper is given in italics, thus:

black/*rose* = black design on rose paper.

Papers have been made specially white in recent years by, for example, a very heavy coating of chalk. We do not classify shades of whiteness of paper as distinct varieties. There does exist, however, a type of paper from early days called toned. This is off-white, often brownish or buffish, but it cannot be assigned any definite colour. A toning effect brought on by climate, incorrect storage or gum staining is disregarded here, as this was not the state of the paper when issued.

"Ordinary" and "Chalk-surfaced" papers. The availability of many postage stamps for revenue purposes made necessary some safeguard against the illegitimate re-use of stamps with removable cancellations. This was at first secured by using fugitive inks and later by printing on paper surfaced by coatings containing either chalk or china clay, both of which made it difficult to remove any form of obliteration without damaging the stamp design.

This catalogue lists these chalk-surfaced paper varieties from their introduction in 1905. Where no indication is given, the paper is "ordinary".

The "traditional" method of indentifying chalk-surfaced papers has been that, when touched with a silver wire, a black mark is left on the paper, and the listings in this catalogue are based on that test. However, the test itself is now largely discredited, for, although the mark can be removed by a soft rubber, some damage to the stamp will result from its use.

The difference between chalk-surfaced and pre-war ordinary papers is fairly clear: chalk-surfaced papers being smoother to the touch and showing a characteristic sheen when light is reflected off their surface. Under good magnification tiny bubbles or pock marks can be seen on the surface of the stamp and at the tips of the perforations the surfacing appears "broken". Traces of paper fibres are evident on the surface of ordinary paper and the ink shows a degree of absorption into it.

Initial chalk-surfaced paper printings by De La Rue had a thinner coating than subsequently became the norm. The characteristics described above are less pronounced in these printings.

During and after the Second World War, substitute papers replaced the chalk-surfaced papers, these do not react to the silver test and are therefore classed as "ordinary", although differentiating them without recourse to it is more difficult, for, although the characteristics of the chalk-surfaced paper remained the same, some of the ordinary papers appear much smoother than earlier papers and many do not show the watermark clearly. Experience is the only solution to identifying these, and comparison with stamps whose paper type is without question will be of great help.

Another type of paper, known as "thin striated" was used only for the Bahamas 1s. and 5s. (Nos. 155a, 156a, 171 and 174) and for several stamps of the Malayan states. Hitherto these have been described as "chalk-surfaced" since they gave some reaction to the silver test, but they are much thinner than usual chalk-surfaced papers, with the watermark showing clearly. Stamps on this paper show a slightly 'ribbed' effect when the stamp is held up to the light. Again, comparison with a known striated paper stamp, such as the 1941 Straits Settlements Die II 2c. orange (No. 294) will prove invaluable in separating these papers.

Glazed paper. In 1969 the Crown Agents introduced a new general-purpose paper for use in conjunction with all current printing processes. It generally has a marked glossy surface but the degree varies according to the process used, being more marked in recess-printing stamps. As it does not respond to the silver test this presents a further test where previous printings were on chalky paper. A change of paper to the glazed variety merits separate listing.

Green and yellow papers. Issues of the First World War and immediate postwar period occur on green and yellow papers and these are given separate Catalogue listing. The original coloured papers (coloured throughout) gave way to surface-coloured papers, the stamps having "white backs"; other stamps show one colour on the front and a different one at the back. Because of the numerous variations a grouping of colours is adopted as follows:

Yellow papers

(1) The original *yellow* paper (throughout), usually bright in colour. The gum is often sparse, of harsh consistency and dull-looking. Used 1912–1920.

(2) The *white-backs*. Used 1913–1914.

(3) A bright lemon paper. The colour must have a pronounced greenish tinge, different from the "yellow" in (1). As a rule, the gum on stamps using this lemon paper is plentiful, smooth and shiny, and the watermark shows distinctly. Care is needed with stamps printed in green on yellow paper (1) as it may appear that the paper is this lemon. Used 1914–1916.

(4) An experimental *orange-buff* paper. The colour must have a distinct brownish tinge. It is not to be confused with a muddy yellow (1) nor the misleading appearance (on the surface) of stamps printed in red on yellow paper where an engraved plate has been insufficiently wiped. Used 1918–1921.

(5) An experimental *buff* paper. This lacks the brownish tinge of (4) and the brightness of the yellow shades. The gum is shiny when compared with the matt type used on (4). Used 1919–1920.

(6) A *pale yellow* paper that has a creamy tone to the yellow. Used from 1920 onwards.

Green papers

(7) The original "green" paper, varying considerably through shades of blue-green and yellow-green, the front and back sometimes differing. Used 1912–1916.

(8) The *white backs*. Used 1913–1914.

(9) A paper blue-green on the surface with *pale olive* back. The back must be markedly paler than the front and this and the pronounced olive tinge to the back distinguish it from (7). Used 1916–1920.

(10) Paper with a vivid green surface, commonly called *emerald-green*; it has the olive back of (9). Used 1920.

(11) Paper with *emerald-green* both back and front. Used from 1920 onwards.

3. Perforation and Rouletting

Perforation gauge. The gauge of a perforation is the number of holes in a length of 2 cm. For correct classification the size of the holes (large or small) may need to be distinguished; in a few cases the actual number of holes on each edge of the stamp needs to be quoted.

Measurement. The Gibbons *Instanta* gauge is the standard for measuring perforations. The stamp is viewed against a dark background with the transparent gauge put on top of it. Though the gauge measures to decimal accuracy, perforations read from it are generally quoted in the Catalogue to the nearest half. For example:

Just over perf 12¾ to just under 13¼	= perf 13
Perf 13¼ exactly, rounded up	= perf 13½
Just over perf 13¼ to just under 13¾	= perf 13½
Perf 13¾ exactly, rounded up	= perf 14

However, where classification depends on it, actual quarter-perforations are quoted.

Notation. Where no perforation is quoted for an issue it is imperforate. Perforations are usually abbreviated (and spoken) as follows, though sometimes they may be spelled out for clarity. This notation for rectangular stamps (the majority) applies to diamond shapes if "top" is read as the edge to the top right.

P 14: perforated alike on all sides (read: "perf 14").

P 14×15: the first figure refers to top and bottom, the second to left and right sides (read: "perf 14 by 15"). This is a compound perforation. For an upright triangular stamp the first figure refers to the two sloping sides and second to the base. In inverted triangulars the base is first and the second figure to the sloping sides.

P 14–15: perforation measuring anything between 14 and 15: the holes are irregularly spaced, thus the gauge may vary along a single line or even along a single edge of the stamp (read: "perf 14 to 15").

P 14 *irregular*: perforated 14 from a worn perforator, giving badly aligned holes irregularly spaced (read: "irregular perf 14").

P *comp(ound)* 14×15: two gauges in use but not necessarily on opposite sides of the stamp. It could be one side in one gauge and three in the other; or two adjacent sides with the same gauge. (Read: "perf compound of 14 and 15".) For three gauges or more, abbreviated as "P 12, 14½, 15 *or compound*" for example.

P 14, 14½: perforated approximately 14¼ (read: "perf 14 or 14½"). It does *not* mean two stamps, one perf 14 and the other perf 14½. This obsolescent notation is gradually being replaced in the Catalogue.

Imperf: imperforate (not perforated)

Imperf×P 14: imperforate at top ad bottom and perf 14 at sides.

P 14×*imperf*: perf 14 at top and bottom and imperforate at sides.

Such headings as "P 13×14 (*vert*) and P 14×13 (*horiz*)" indicate which perforations apply to which stamp format—vertical or horizontal.

Some stamps are additionally perforated so that a label or tab is detachable; others have been perforated for use as two halves. Listings are normally for whole stamps, unless stated otherwise.

Imperf×perf

Other terms. Perforation almost always gives circular holes; where other shapes have been used they are specified, e.g. square holes; lozenge perf. Interrupted perfs are brought about by the omission of pins at regular intervals. Perforations merely simulated by being printed as part of the design are of course ignored. With few exceptions, privately applied perforations are not listed.

In the 19th century perforations are often described as clean cut (clean, sharply incised holes), intermediate or rough (rough holes, imperfectly cut, often the result of blunt pins).

Perforation errors and varieties. Authenticated errors, where a stamp normally perforated is accidentally issued imperforate, are listed provided no traces of perforation (blind holes or indentations) remain. They must be provided as pairs, both stamps wholly imperforate, and are only priced in that form.

Stamps imperforate between stamp and sheet margin are not listed in this catalogue, but such errors on Great Britain stamps will be found in the *Great Britain Specialised Catalogue*.

Pairs described as "imperforate between" have the line of perforations between the two stamps omitted.

Imperf between (horiz pair): a horizontal pair of stamps with perfs all around the edges but none between the stamps.

Imperf between (vert pair): a vertical pair of stamps with perfs all around the edges but none between the stamps.

Imperf between (vertical pair)

Imperf horizontally (vertical pair)

Where several of the rows have escaped perforation the resulting varieties are listable. Thus:

Imperf vert (horiz pair): a horizontal pair of stamps perforated top and bottom; all three vertical directions are imperf—the two outer edges and between the stamps.

Imperf horiz (vert pair): a vertical pair perforated at left and right edges; all three horizontal directions are imperf—the top, bottom and between the stamps.

Straight edges. Large sheets cut up before issue to post offices can cause stamps with straight edges, i.e. imperf on one side or on two sides at right angles. They are not usually listable in this condition and are worth less than corresponding stamps properly perforated all round. This does not, however, apply to certain stamps, mainly from coils and booklets, where straight edges on various sides are the manufacturing norm affecting every stamp. The listings and notes make clear which sides are correctly imperf.

Malfunction. Varieties of double, misplaced or partial perforation caused by error or machine malfunction are not listable, neither are freaks, such as perforations placed diagonally from paper folds, nor missing holes caused by broken pins.

Types of perforating. Where necessary for classification, perforation types are distinguished.

These include:

Line perforation from one line of pins punching single rows of holes at a time.

Comb perforation from pins disposed across the sheet in comb formation, punching out holes at three sides of the stamp a row at a time.

Harrow perforation applied to a whole pane or sheet at one stroke.

Rotary perforation from toothed wheels operating across a sheet, then crosswise.

Sewing machine perforation. The resultant condition,

clean-cut or rough, is distinguished where required.

Pin-perforation is the commonly applied term for pin-roulette in which, instead of being punched out, round holes are pricked by sharp-pointed pins and no paper is removed.

Mixed perforation occurs when stamps with defective perforations are re-perforated in a different gauge.

Punctured stamps. Perforation holes can be punched into the face of the stamp. Patterns of small holes, often in the shape of initial letters, are privately applied devices against pilferage. These (perfins) are outside the scope except for Australia, Canada, Cape of Good Hope, Papua and Sudan where they were used as official stamps by the national administration. Identification devices, when officially inspired, are listed or noted; they can be shapes, or letters or words formed from holes, sometimes converting one class of stamp into another.

Rouletting. In rouletting the paper is cut, for ease of separation, but none is removed. The gauge is measured, when needed, as for perforations. Traditional French terms descriptive of the type of cut are often used and types include:

Arc roulette (percé en arc). Cuts are minute, spaced arcs, each roughly a semicircle.

Cross roulette (percé en croix). Cuts are tiny diagonal crosses.

Line roulette (percé en ligne or *en ligne droite).* Short straight cuts parallel to the frame of the stamp. The commonest basic roulette. Where not further described, "roulette" means this type.

Rouletted in colour or coloured roulette (percé en lignes colorées or *en lignes de coleur).* Cuts with coloured edges, arising from notched rule inked simultaneously with the printing plate.

Saw-tooth roulette (percé en scie). Cuts applied zigzag fashion to resemble the teeth of a saw.

Serpentine roulette (percé en serpentin). Cuts as sharply wavy lines.

Zigzag roulette (percé en zigzags). Short straight cuts at angles in alternate directions, producing sharp points on separation. US usage favours "serrate(d) roulette" for this type.

Pin-roulette (originally *percé en points* and now *perforés trous d'epingle*) is commonly called pin-perforation in English.

4. Gum

All stamps listed are assumed to have gum of some kind; if they were issued without gum this is stated. Original gum (o.g.) means that which was present on the stamp as issued to the public. Deleterious climates and the presence of certain chemicals can cause gum to crack and, with early stamps, even make the paper deteriorate. Unscrupulous fakers are adept in removing it and regumming the stamp to meet the unreasoning demand often made for "full o.g." in cases where such a thing is virtually impossible.

The gum normally used on stamps has been gum ararbic until the late 1960s when synthetic adhesives were introduced. Harrison and Sons Ltd for instance use *polyvinyl alcohol,* known to philatelists as PVA. This is almost invisible except for a slight yellowish tinge which was incorporated to make it possible to see that the stamps have been gummed. It has advantages in hot countries, as stamps do not curl and sheets are less likely to stick together. Gum arabic and PVA are not distinguished in the lists except that where a stamp exists with both forms this is indicated in footnotes. Our more specialised catalogues provide separate listing of gums for Great Britain.

Self-adhesive stamps are issued on backing paper, from which they are peeled before affixing to mail. Unused examples are priced as for backing paper intact, in which condition they are recommended to be kept. Used examples are best collected on cover or on piece.

5. Watermarks

Stamps are on unwatermarked paper except where the heading to the set says otherwise.

Detection. Watermarks are detected for Catalogue description by one of four methods: (1) holding stamps to the light; (2) laying stamps face down on a dark background; (3) adding a few drops of petroleum ether 40/60 to the stamp laid face down in a watermark tray; (4) by use of the Stanley Gibbons Detectamark, or other equipment, which work by revealing the thinning of the paper at the watermark. (Note that petroleum ether is highly inflammable in use and can damage photogravure stamps.)

Listable types. Stamps occurring on both watermarked and unwatermarked papers are different types and both receive full listing.

Single watermarks (devices occurring once on every stamp) can be modified in size and shape as between different issues; the types are noted but not usually separately listed. Fortuitous absence of watermark from a single stamp or its gross displacement would not be listable.

To overcome registration difficulties the device may be repeated at close intervals *(a multiple watermark),* single stamps thus showing parts of several devices. Similarly, a *large sheet watermark* (or *all-over watermark*) covering numerous stamps can be used. We give informative notes and illustrations for them. The designs may be such that numbers of stamps in the sheet automatically lack watermark: this is not a listable variety. Multiple and all-over watermarks sometimes undergo modifications, but if the various types are difficult to distinguish from single stamps notes are given but not separate listings.

Papermakers' watermarks are noted where known but not listed separately, since most stamps in the sheet will lack them. Sheet watermarks which are nothing more than officially adopted papermakers' watermarks are, however, given normal listing.

Marginal watermarks, falling outside the pane of stamps, are ignored except where misplacement caused the adjoining row to be affected, in which case they may be footnoted.

Watermark errors and varieties. Watermark errors are recognised as of major importance. They comprise stamps intended to be on unwatermarked paper but issued watermarked by mistake, or stamps printed on paper with the wrong watermark. Varieties showing letters omitted from the watermark are also included, but broken or deformed bits on the dandy roll are not listed unless they represent repairs.

Watermark positions. The diagram shows how watermark position is described in the Catalogue. Paper has a side intended for printing and watermarks are usually impressed so that they read normally when looked through from that printed side. However, since philatelists customarily detect watermarks by looking at the back of the stamp the watermark diagram also makes clear what is actually seen.

Illustrations in the Catalogue are of watermarks in normal positions (from the front of the stamps) and are actual size where possible.

Differences in watermark position are collectable varieties. This Catalogue now lists inverted, sideways inverted and reversed watermark varieties on Commonwealth stamps from the 1860s onwards except where the watermark position is completely haphazard.

Great Britain inverted and sideways inverted watermarks can be found in the *Great Britain Specialised Catalogue* and the *Great Britain Concise Catalogue*.

Where a watermark comes indiscriminately in various positions our policy is to cover this by a general note: we do not give separate listings because the watermark position in these circumstances has no particular philatelic importance.

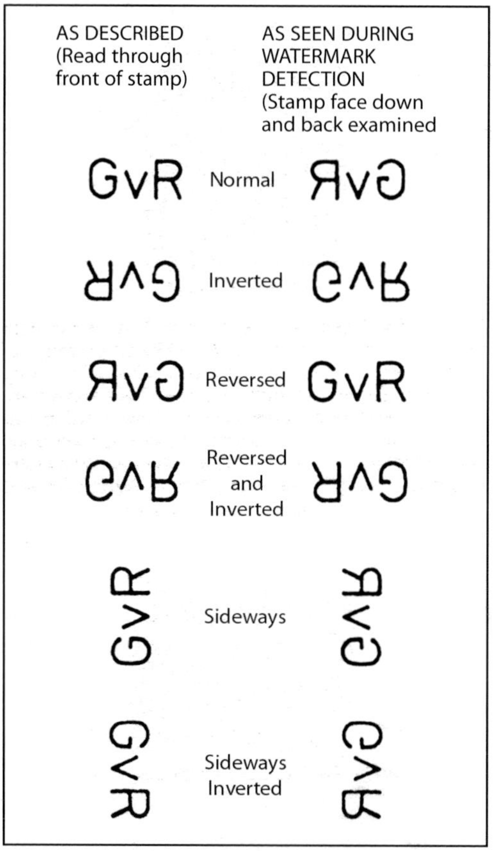

Standard types of watermark. Some watermarks have been used generally for various British possessions rather than exclusively for a single colony. To avoid repetition the Catalogue classifies 11 general types, as under, with references in the headings throughout the listings being given either in words or in the form ("W w **9**") (meaning "watermark type w **9**"). In those cases where watermark illustrations appear in the listings themselves, the respective reference reads, for example, W **153**, thus indicating that the watermark will be found in the normal sequence of illustrations as (type) **153**.

The general types are as follows, with an example of each quoted.

W	*Description*	*Example*
w **1**	Large Star	St. Helena No. 1
w **2**	Small Star	Turks Is. No. 4
w **3**	Broad (pointed) Star	Grenada No. 24
w **4**	Crown (over) CC, small stamp	Antigua No. 13
w **5**	Crown (over) CC, large stamp	Antigua No. 31
w **6**	Crown (over) CA, small stamp	Antigua No. 21
w **7**	Crown CA (CA over Crown), large stamp	Sierra Leone No. 54
w **8**	Multiple Crown CA	Antigua No. 41
w **9**	Multiple Script CA	Seychelles No. 158
w **9***a*	do. Error	Seychelles No. 158a
w **9***b*	do. Error	Seychelles No. 158b
w **10**	V over Crown	N.S.W. No. 327
w **11**	Crown over A	N.S.W. No. 347

CC in these watermarks is an abbreviation for "Crown Colonies" and CA for "Crown Agents". Watermarks w **1**, w **2** and w **3** are on stamps printed by Perkins, Bacon; w **4** onwards on stamps from De La Rue and other printers.

w **1**
Large Star

w **2**
Small Star

w **3**
Broad-pointed Star

Watermark w **1**, *Large Star*, measures 15 to 16 mm across the star from point to point and about 27 mm from centre to centre vertically between stars in the sheet. It was made for long stamps like Ceylon 1857 and St. Helena 1856.

Watermark w **2**, *Small Star* is of similar design but measures 12 to 13½mm from point to point and 24 mm from centre to centre vertically. It was for use with ordinary-size stamps such as Grenada 1863–71.

When the Large Star watermark was used with the smaller stamps it only occasionally comes in the centre of the paper. It is frequently so misplaced as to show portions of two stars above and below and this eccentricity will very often help in determining the watermark.

Watermark w **3**, *Broad-pointed Star*, resembles w **1** but the points are broader.

w **4**
Crown (over) CC

w **5**
Crown (over) CC

Two *Crown (over) CC* watermarks were used: w **4** was for stamps of ordinary size and w **5** for those of larger size.

w **6**
Crown (over) CA

w **7**
CA over Crown

Two watermarks of *Crown CA* type were used, w **6** being for stamps of ordinary size. The other, w **7**, is properly described as *CA over Crown*. It was specially made for paper on which it was intended to print long fiscal stamps: that some were used postally accounts for the appearance of w **7** in the Catalogue. The watermark occupies twice the space of the ordinary Crown CA watermark, w **6**. Stamps of normal size printed on paper with w **7** watermark show it *sideways*; it takes a horizontal pair of stamps to show the entire watermark.

w **8**
Multiple Crown CA

w **9**
Multiple Script CA

Multiple watermarks began in 1904 with w **8**, *Multiple Crown CA,* changed from 1921 to w **9**, *Multiple Script CA*. On stamps of ordinary size portions of two or three watermarks appear and on the large-sized stamps a greater number can be observed. The change to letters in script character with w **9** was accompanied by a Crown of distinctly different shape.

It seems likely that there were at least two dandy rolls for each Crown Agents watermark in use at any one time with a reserve roll being employed when the normal one was withdrawn for maintenance or repair.

Both the Mult Crown CA and the Mult Script CA types exist with one or other of the letters omitted from individual impressions. It is possible that most of these occur from the reserve rolls as they have only been found on certain issues. The MCA watermark experienced such problems during the early 1920s and the Script over a longer period from the early 1940s until 1951.

During the 1920s damage must also have occurred on one of the Crowns as a substituted Crown has been found on certain issues. This is smaller than the normal and consists of an oval base joined to two upright ovals with a circle positioned between their upper ends. The upper line of the Crown's base is omitted, as are the left and right-hand circles at the top and also the cross over the centre circle.

Substituted Crown

The *Multiple Script CA* watermark, w **9**, is known with two errors, recurring among the 1950–52 printings of several territories. In the first a crown has fallen away from the dandy-roll that impresses the watermark into the paper pulp. It gives w **9a**, *Crown missing*, but this omission has been found in both "Crown only" (*illustrated*) and "Crown CA" rows. The resulting faulty paper was used for Bahamas, Johore, Seychelles and the postage due stamps of nine colonies

w **9a**: Error, Crown missing

w **9b**: Error, St. Edward's Crown

When the omission was noticed a second mishap occurred, which was to insert a wrong crown in the space, giving w **9b**, St. Edward's Crown. This produced varieties in Bahamas, Perlis, St. Kitts-Nevis and Singapore and the incorrect crown likewise occurs in (Crown only) and (Crown CA) rows.

w **10**
V over Crown

w **11**
Crown over A

Resuming the general types, two watermarks found in issues of several Australian States are: w **10**, *V over Crown*, and w **11**, *Crown over A*.

w **12**
Multiple St. Edward's Crown Block CA

w **13**
Multiple PTM

The *Multiple St. Edward's Crown Block CA* watermark, w **12**, was introduced in 1957 and besides the change in the Crown (from that used in Multiple Crown Script CA, w **9**) the letters reverted to block capitals. The new watermark began to appear sideways in 1966 and these stamps are generally listed as separate sets.

The watermark w **13**, *Multiple PTM*, was introduced for new Malaysian issues in November 1961.

w **14**
Multiple Crown CA Diagonal

By 1974 the two dandy-rolls the "upright" and the "sideways" for w **12** were wearing out; the Crown Agents therefore discontinued using the sideways watermark one and retained the other only as a stand-by. A new dandy-roll with the pattern of w **14.** *Multiple Crown CA Diagonal,* was introduced and first saw use with some Churchill Centenary issues.

The new watermark had the design arranged in gradually spiralling rows. It is improved in design to allow smooth passage over the paper (the gaps between letters and rows had caused jolts in previous dandy-rolls) and the sharp corners and angles, where fibres used to accumulate, have been eliminated by rounding.

This watermark had no "normal" sideways position amongst the different printers using it. To avoid confusion our more specialised listings do not rely on such terms as "sideways inverted" but describe the direction in which the watermark points.

w **15**
Multiple POST OFFICE

During 1981 w **15.** *Multiple POST OFFICE* was introduced for certain issues prepared by Philatelists Ltd, acting for various countries in the Indian Ocean, Pacific and West Indies.

w **16**
Multiple Crown Script CA Diagonal

A new Crown Agents watermark was introduced during 1985, w **16**, *Multiple Crown Script CA Diagonal.* This was very similar to the previous w **14**, but showed "CA" in script rather than block letters. It was first used on the omnibus series of stamps commemorating the Life and Times of Queen Elizabeth the Queen Mother.

6. Colours

Stamps in two or three colours have these named in order of appearance, from the centre moving outwards. Four colours or more are usually listed as multicoloured.

In compound colour names the second is the predominant one, thus:

orange-red = a red tending towards orange;
red-orange = an orange containing more red than usual.

Standard colours used. The 200 colours most used for stamp identification are given in the Stanley Gibbons Stamp Colour Key. The Catalogue has used the Stamp Colour Key as standard for describing new issues for some years. The names are also introduced as lists are rewritten, though exceptions are made for those early issues where traditional names have become universally established.

Determining colours. When comparing actual stamps with colour samples in the Stamp Colour Key, view in a good north daylight (or its best substitute; fluorescent "colour matching" light). Sunshine is not recommended. Choose a solid portion of the stamp design; if available, marginal markings such as solid bars of colour or colour check dots are helpful. Shading lines in the design can be misleading as they appear lighter than solid colour. Postmarked portions of a stamp appear darker than normal. If more than one colour is present, mask off the extraneous ones as the eye tends to mix them.

Errors of colour. Major colour errors in stamps or overprints which qualify for listing are: wrong colours; one colour inverted in relation to the rest; albinos (colourless impressions), where these have Expert Committee certificates; colours completely omitted, but only on unused stamps (if found on used stamps the information is footnoted) and with good credentials, missing colours being frequently faked.

Colours only partially omitted are not recognised, Colour shifts, however spectacular, are not listed.

Shades. Shades in philately refer to variations in the intensity of a colour or the presence of differing amounts of other colours. They are particularly significant when they can be linked to specific printings. In general, shades need to be quite marked to fall within the scope of this Catalogue; it does not favour nowadays listing the often numerous shades of a stamp, but chooses a single applicable colour name which will indicate particular groups of outstanding shades. Furthermore, the listings refer to colours as issued; they may deteriorate into something different through the passage of time.

Modern colour printing by lithography is prone to marked differences of shade, even within a single run, and variations can occur within the same sheet. Such shades are not listed.

Aniline colours. An aniline colour meant originally one derived from coal-tar; it now refers more widely to colour of a particular brightness suffused on the surface of a stamp and showing through clearly on the back.

Colours of overprints and surcharges. All overprints and surcharges are in black unless stated otherwise in the heading or after the description of the stamp.

7. Specimen Stamps

Originally, stamps overprinted SPECIMEN were circulated to postmasters or kept in official records, but after the establishment of the Universal Postal Union supplies were sent to Berne for distribution to the postal administrations of member countries.

During the period 1884 to 1928 most of the stamps of British Crown Colonies required for this purpose were overprinted SPECIMEN in various shapes and sizes by their printers from typeset formes. Some locally produced provisionals were handstamped locally, as were sets prepared for presentation. From 1928 stamps were punched with holes forming the word SPECIMEN, each firm of printers using a different machine or machines. From 1948 the stamps supplied for UPU distribution were no longer punctured.

Stamps of some other Commonwealth territories were overprinted or handstamped locally, while stamps of Great Britain and those overprinted for use in overseas postal agencies (mostly of the higher denominations) bore SPECIMEN overprints and handstamps applied by the Inland Revenue or the Post Office.

De La Rue & Co. Ltd.

Bradbury, Wilkinson & Co. Ltd.

Waterlow & Sons Ltd.

Great Britain overprints

Some of the commoner types of overprints or punctures are illustrated here. Collectors are warned that dangerous forgeries of the punctured type exist.

The *Stanley Gibbons Commonwealth Catalogues* record those Specimen overprints or perforations intended for distribution by the UPU to member countries. In addition the Specimen overprints of Australia and its dependent territories, which were sold to collectors by the Post Office, are also included.

Various Perkins Bacon issues exist obliterated with a "CANCELLED" within an oval of bars handstamp.

Perkins Bacon "CANCELLED" Handstamp

This was applied to six examples of those issues available in 1861 which were then given to members of Sir Rowland Hill's family. 75 different stamps (including four from Chile) are recorded with this handstamp although others may possibly exist. The unauthorised gift of these "CANCELLED" stamps to the Hill family was a major factor in the loss of the Agent General for the Crown Colonies (the forerunner of the Crown Agents) contracts by Perkins Bacon in the following year. Where examples of these scarce items are known to be in private hands the catalogue provides a price.

For full details of these stamps see *CANCELLED by Perkins Bacon* by Peter Jaffé (published by Spink in 1998).

All other Specimens are outside the scope of this volume.

Specimens are not quoted in Great Britain as they are fully listed in the Stanley Gibbons *Great Britain Specialised Catalogue*.

In specifying type of specimen for individual high-value stamps, "H/S" means handstamped, "Optd" is overprinted and "Perf" is punctured. Some sets occur mixed, e.g. "Optd/Perf". If unspecified, the type is apparent from the date or it is the same as for the lower values quoted as a set.

Prices. Prices for stamps up to £1 are quoted in sets; higher values are priced singly. Where specimens exist in more than one type the price quoted is for the cheapest. Specimen stamps have rarely survived even as pairs; these and strips of three, four or five are worth considerably more than singles.

8. Luminescence

Machines which sort mail electronically have been introduced in recent years. In consequence some countries have issued stamps on flourescent or phosphorescent papers, while others have marked their stamps with phosphor bands.

The various papers can only be distinguished by ultraviolet lamps emitting particular wavelengths. They are separately listed only when the stamps have some other means of distinguishing them, visible without the use of these lamps. Where this is not so, the papers are recorded in footnotes or headings.

For this catalogue we do not consider it appropriate that collectors be compelled to have the use of an ultraviolet lamp before being able to identify stamps by our listings. Some experience will also be found necessary in interpreting the results given by ultraviolet. Collectors using the lamps, nevertheless, should exercise great care in their use as exposure to their light is potentially dangerous to the eyes.

Phosphor bands are listable, since they are visible to the naked eye (by holding stamps at an angle to the light and looking along them, the bands appear dark). Stamps existing with or without phosphor bands or with differing numbers of bands are given separate listings. Varieties such as double bands, bands omitted, misplaced or printed on the back are not listed.

Detailed descriptions appear at appropriate places in the listings in explanation of luminescent papers; see, for example, Australia above No.363, Canada above Nos. 472 and 611, Cook Is. above 249, etc.

For Great Britain, where since 1959 phosphors have played a prominent and intricate part in stamp issues, the main notes above Nos. 599 and 723 should be studied, as well as the footnotes to individual listings where appropriate. In general the classification is as follows.

Stamps with phosphor bands are those where a separate cylinder applies the phosphor after the stamps are printed. Issues with "all-over" phosphor have the "band" covering the entire stamp. Parts of the stamp covered by phosphor bands, or the entire surface for "all-over" phosphor versions, appear matt. Stamps on phosphorised paper have the phosphor added to the paper coating before the stamps are printed. Issues on this paper have a completely shiny surface.

Further particularisation of phosphor – their methods of printing and the colours they exhibit under ultraviolet – is outside the scope. The more specialised listings should be consulted for this information.

9. Coil Stamps

Stamps issued only in coil form are given full listing. If stamps are issued in both sheets and coils the coil stamps are listed separately only where there is some feature (e.g. perforation or watermark sideways) by which singles can be distinguished. Coil stamps containing different stamps *se-tenant* are also listed.

Coil join pairs are too random and too easily faked to permit of listing; similarly ignored are coil stamps which have accidentally suffered an extra row of perforations from the claw mechanism in a malfunctioning vending machine.

10. Stamp Booklets

Stamp booklets are now listed in this catalogue.

Single stamps from booklets are listed if they are distinguishable in some way (such as watermark or perforation) from similar sheet stamps.

Booklet panes are listed where they contain stamps of different denominations *se-tenant*, where stamp-size labels are included, or where such panes are otherwise identifiable. Booklet panes are placed in the listing under the lowest denomination present.

Particular perforations (straight edges) are covered by appropriate notes.

11. Miniature Sheets and Sheetlets

We distinguish between "miniature sheets" and "sheetlets" and this affects the catalogue numbering. An item in sheet form that is postally valid, containing a single stamp, pair, block or set of stamps, with wide, inscribed and/or decorative margins, is a miniature sheet if it is sold at post offices as an indivisable entity. As such the Catalogue allots a single MS number and describes what stamps make it up. The sheetlet or small sheet differs in that the individual stamps are intended to be purchased separately for postal purposes. For sheetlets, all the component postage stamps are numbered individually and the composition explained in a footnote. Note that the definitions refer to post office sale—not how items may be subsequently offered by stamp dealers.

12. Forgeries and Fakes

Forgeries. Where space permits, notes are considered if they can give a concise description that will permit unequivocal detection of a forgery. Generalised warnings, lacking detail, are not nowadays inserted, since their value to the collector is problematic.

Forged cancellations have also been applied to genuine stamps. This catalogue includes notes regarding those manufactured by "Madame Joseph", together with the cancellation dates known to exist. It should be remembered that these dates also exist as genuine cancellations.

For full details of these see *Madame Joseph Forged Postmarks* by Derek Worboys (published by the Royal Philatelic Society London and the British Philatelic Trust in 1994) or *Madame Joseph Revisited* by Brian Cartwright (published by the Royal Philatelic Society London in 2005).

Fakes. Unwitting fakes are numerous, particularly "new shades" which are colour changelings brought about by exposure to sunlight, soaking in water contaminated with dyes from adherent paper, contact with oil and dirt from a pocketbook, and so on. Fraudulent operators, in addition, can offer to arrange: removal of hinge marks; repairs of thins on white or coloured papers; replacement of missing margins or perforations; reperforating in true or false gauges; removal of fiscal cancellations; rejoining of severed pairs, strips and blocks; and (a major hazard) regumming. Collectors can only be urged to purchase from reputable sources and to insist upon Expert Committee certification where there is any kind of doubt.

The Catalogue can consider footnotes about fakes where these are specific enough to assist in detection.

Abbreviations

Printers

A.B.N. Co.	American Bank Note Co, New York.
B.A.B.N.	British American Bank Note Co. Ottawa
B.D.T.	B.D.T. International Security Printing Ltd, Dublin, Ireland
B.W.	Bradbury Wilkinson & Co, Ltd.
Cartor	Cartor S.A., La Loupe, France
C.B.N.	Canadian Bank Note Co, Ottawa.
Continental	Continental Bank Note Co. B.N. Co.
Courvoisier	Imprimerie Courvoisier S.A., La-Chaux-de-Fonds, Switzerland.
D.L.R.	De La Rue & Co, Ltd, London.
Enschedé	Joh. Enschedé en Zonen, Haarlem, Netherlands.
Format	Format International Security Printers Ltd., London
Harrison	Harrison & Sons, Ltd. London
J.W.	John Waddington Security Print Ltd., Leeds
P.B.	Perkins Bacon Ltd, London.
Questa	Questa Colour Security Printers Ltd, London
Walsall	Walsall Security Printers Ltd
Waterlow	Waterlow & Sons, Ltd, London.

General Abbreviations

Alph	Alphabet
Anniv	Anniversary
Comp	Compound (perforation)
Des	Designer; designed
Diag	Diagonal; diagonally
Eng	Engraver; engraved
F.C.	Fiscal Cancellation
H/S	Handstamped
Horiz	Horizontal; horizontally
Imp, Imperf	Imperforate
Inscr	Inscribed
L	Left
Litho	Lithographed
mm	Millimetres
MS	Miniature sheet
N.Y.	New York
Opt(d)	Overprint(ed)
P or P-c	Pen-cancelled
P, Pf or Perf	Perforated
Photo	Photogravure
Pl	Plate
Pr	Pair
Ptd	Printed
Ptg	Printing
R	Right
R.	Row
Recess	Recess-printed
Roto	Rotogravure
Roul	Rouletted
S	Specimen (overprint)
Surch	Surcharge(d)
T.C.	Telegraph Cancellation
T	Type
Typo	Typographed
Un	Unused
Us	Used
Vert	Vertical; vertically
W or wmk	Watermark
Wmk s	Watermark sideways

(†) = Does not exist

(–) (or blank price column) = Exists, or may exist, but no market price is known.

/ between colours means "on" and the colour following is that of the paper on which the stamp is printed.

Colours of Stamps

Bl (blue); blk (black); brn (brown); car, carm (carmine); choc (chocolate); clar (claret); emer (emerald); grn (green); ind (indigo); mag (magenta); mar (maroon); mult (multicoloured); mve (mauve); ol (olive); orge (orange); pk (pink); pur (purple); scar (scarlet); sep (sepia); turq (turquoise); ultram (ultramarine); verm (vermilion); vio (violet); yell (yellow).

Colour of Overprints and Surcharges

(B.) = blue, (Blk.) = black, (Br.) = brown, (C.) = carmine, (G.) = green, (Mag.) = magenta, (Mve.) = mauve, (Ol.) = olive, (O.) = orange, (P.) = purple, (Pk.) = pink, (R.) = red, (Sil.) = silver, (V.) = violet, (Vm.) or (Verm.) = vermilion, (W.) = white, (Y.) = yellow.

Arabic Numerals

As in the case of European figures, the details of the Arabic numerals vary in different stamp designs, but they should be readily recognised with the aid of this illustration.

٠	١	٢	٣	٤	٥	٦	٧	٨	٩
0	1	2	3	4	5	6	7	8	9

Features Listing

An at-a-glance guide to what's in the Stanley Gibbons catalogues

Area	Feature	Collect British Stamps	Stamps of the World	Thematic Catalogues	Comprehensive Catalogue, Parts 1-22 (including Commonwealth and British Empire Stamps and country catalogues)	Great Britain Concise	Specialised catalogues
General	SG number	√	√	√	√	√	√
General	Specialised Catalogue number						√
General	Year of issue of first stamp in design	√	√	√	√	√	√
General	Exact date of issue of each design				√	√	√
General	Face value information	√	√	√	√	√	√
General	Historical and geographical information	√	√	√	√	√	√
General	General currency information, including dates used	√	√	√	√	√	√
General	Country name	√	√	√	√	√	√
General	Booklet panes				√	√	√
General	Coil stamps				√		√
General	First Day Covers	√				√	√
General	Brief footnotes on key areas of note	√	√	√	√	√	√
General	Detailed footnotes on key areas of note				√	√	√
General	Extra background information				√	√	√
General	Miniature sheet information (including size in mm)	√	√	√	√	√	√
General	Sheetlets				√		
General	Stamp booklets				√	√	√
General	Perkins Bacon "Cancelled"				√		
General	PHQ Cards	√				√	√
General	Post Office Label Sheets					√	
General	Post Office Yearbooks	√				√	√
General	Presentation and Souvenir Packs	√				√	√
General	*Se-tenant* pairs	√			√	√	√
General	Watermark details - errors, varieties, positions				√	√	√
General	Watermark illustrations	√			√	√	√
General	Watermark types	√			√	√	√
General	Forgeries noted				√		√
General	Surcharges and overprint information	√	√	√	√	√	√
Design and Description	Colour description, simplified		√	√			
Design and Description	Colour description, extended	√			√	√	√
Design and Description	Set design summary information	√	√	√	√	√	√
Design and Description	Designer name				√	√	√
Design and Description	Short design description	√	√	√	√	√	√

Area	Feature	Collect British Stamps	Stamps of the World	Thematic Catalogues	Comprehensive Catalogue, Parts 1-22 (including Commonwealth and British Empire Stamps and country catalogues)	Great Britain Concise	Specialised catalogues
Design and Description	Shade varieties				√	√	√
Design and Description	Type number	√	√		√	√	√
Illustrations	Multiple stamps from set illustrated	√			√	√	√
Illustrations	A Stamp from each set illustrated in full colour (where possible, otherwise mono)	√	√	√	√	√	√
Price	Catalogue used price	√	√	√	√	√	√
Price	Catalogue unused price	√	√	√	√	√	√
Price	Price - booklet panes				√	√	√
Price	Price - shade varieties				√	√	√
Price	On cover and on piece price				√	√	√
Price	Detailed GB pricing breakdown	√			√	√	√
Print and Paper	Basic printing process information	√	√	√	√	√	√
Print and Paper	Detailed printing process information, e.g. Mill sheets				√		√
Print and Paper	Paper information				√		√
Print and Paper	Detailed perforation information	√			√	√	√
Print and Paper	Details of research findings relating to printing processes and history						√
Print and Paper	Paper colour	√	√		√	√	√
Print and Paper	Paper description to aid identification				√	√	√
Print and Paper	Paper type				√	√	√
Print and Paper	Ordinary or chalk-surfaced paper				√	√	√
Print and Paper	Embossing omitted note						√
Print and Paper	Essays, Die Proofs, Plate Descriptions and Proofs, Colour Trials information						√
Print and Paper	Glazed paper				√	√	√
Print and Paper	Gum details				√		√
Print and Paper	Luminescence/Phosphor bands - general coverage	√			√	√	√
Print and Paper	Luminescence/Phosphor bands - specialised coverage						√
Print and Paper	Overprints and surcharges - including colour information	√	√	√	√	√	√
Print and Paper	Perforation/Imperforate information	√	√		√	√	√
Print and Paper	Perforation errors and varieties				√	√	√
Print and Paper	Print quantities				√		√
Print and Paper	Printing errors				√	√	√
Print and Paper	Printing flaws						√
Print and Paper	Printing varieties				√	√	√
Print and Paper	Punctured stamps - where official				√		
Print and Paper	Sheet positions				√	√	√
Print and Paper	Specialised plate number information						√
Print and Paper	Specimen overprints (only for Commonwealth & GB)				√	√	√
Print and Paper	Underprints					√	√
Print and Paper	Visible Plate numbers	√			√	√	√
Print and Paper	Yellow and Green paper listings				√		√
Index	Design index	√			√	√	

International Philatelic Glossary

English	*French*	*German*	*Spanish*	*Italian*
Agate	Agate	Achat	Agata	Agata
Air stamp	Timbre de la poste aérienne	Flugpostmarke	Sello de correo aéreo	Francobollo per posta aerea
Apple Green	Vert-pomme	Apfelgrün	Verde manzana	Verde mela
Barred	Annulé par barres	Balkenentwertung	Anulado con barras	Sbarrato
Bisected	Timbre coupé	Halbiert	Partido en dos	Frazionato
Bistre	Bistre	Bister	Bistre	Bistro
Bistre-brown	Brun-bistre	Bisterbraun	Castaño bistre	Bruno-bistro
Black	Noir	Schwarz	Negro	Nero
Blackish Brown	Brun-noir	Schwärzlichbraun	Castaño negruzco	Bruno nerastro
Blackish Green	Vert foncé	Schwärzlichgrün	Verde negruzco	Verde nerastro
Blackish Olive	Olive foncé	Schwärzlicholiv	Oliva negruzco	Oliva nerastro
Block of four	Bloc de quatre	Viererblock	Bloque de cuatro	Bloco di quattro
Blue	Bleu	Blau	Azul	Azzurro
Blue-green	Vert-bleu	Blaugrün	Verde azul	Verde azzuro
Bluish Violet	Violet bleuâtre	Bläulichviolett	Violeta azulado	Violtto azzurrastro
Booklet	Carnet	Heft	Cuadernillo	Libretto
Bright Blue	Bleu vif	Lebhaftblau	Azul vivo	Azzurro vivo
Bright Green	Vert vif	Lebhaftgrün	Verde vivo	Verde vivo
Bright Purple	Mauve vif	Lebhaftpurpur	Púrpura vivo	Porpora vivo
Bronze Green	Vert-bronze	Bronzegrün	Verde bronce	Verde bronzo
Brown	Brun	Braun	Castaño	Bruno
Brown-lake	Carmin-brun	Braunlack	Laca castaño	Lacca bruno
Brown-purple	Pourpre-brun	Braunpurpur	Púrpura castaño	Porpora bruno
Brown-red	Rouge-brun	Braunrot	Rojo castaño	Rosso bruno
Buff	Chamois	Sämisch	Anteado	Camoscio
Cancellation	Oblitération	Entwertung	Cancelación	Annullamento
Cancelled	Annulé	Gestempelt	Cancelado	Annullato
Carmine	Carmin	Karmin	Carmín	Carminio
Carmine-red	Rouge-carmin	Karminrot	Rojo carmín	Rosso carminio
Centred	Centré	Zentriert	Centrado	Centrato
Cerise	Rouge-cerise	Kirschrot	Color de ceresa	Color Ciliegia
Chalk-surfaced paper	Papier couché	Kreidepapier	Papel estucado	Carta gessata
Chalky Blue	Bleu terne	Kreideblau	Azul turbio	Azzurro smorto
Charity stamp	Timbre de bienfaisance	Wohltätigkeitsmarke	Sello de beneficenza	Francobollo di beneficenza
Chestnut	Marron	Kastanienbraun	Castaño rojo	Marrone
Chocolate	Chocolat	Schokolade	Chocolate	Cioccolato
Cinnamon	Cannelle	Zimtbraun	Canela	Cannella
Claret	Grenat	Weinrot	Rojo vinoso	Vinaccia
Cobalt	Cobalt	Kobalt	Cobalto	Cobalto
Colour	Couleur	Farbe	Color	Colore
Comb-perforation	Dentelure en peigne	Kammzähnung, Reihenzähnung	Dentado de peine	Dentellatura e pettine
Commemorative stamp	Timbre commémoratif	Gedenkmarke	Sello conmemorativo	Francobollo commemorativo
Crimson	Cramoisi	Karmesin	Carmesí	Cremisi
Deep Blue	Blue foncé	Dunkelblau	Azul oscuro	Azzurro scuro
Deep bluish Green	Vert-bleu foncé	Dunkelbläulichgrün	Verde azulado oscuro	Verde azzurro scuro

English	*French*	*German*	*Spanish*	*Italian*
Design	Dessin	Markenbild	Diseño	Disegno
Die	Matrice	Urstempel. Type, Platte	Cuño	Conio, Matrice
Double	Double	Doppelt	Doble	Doppio
Drab	Olive terne	Trüboliv	Oliva turbio	Oliva smorto
Dull Green	Vert terne	Trübgrün	Verde turbio	Verde smorto
Dull purple	Mauve terne	Trübpurpur	Púrpura turbio	Porpora smorto
Embossing	Impression en relief	Prägedruck	Impresión en relieve	Impressione a relievo
Emerald	Vert-eméraude	Smaragdgrün	Esmeralda	Smeraldo
Engraved	Gravé	Graviert	Grabado	Inciso
Error	Erreur	Fehler, Fehldruck	Error	Errore
Essay	Essai	Probedruck	Ensayo	Saggio
Express letter stamp	Timbre pour lettres par exprès	Eilmarke	Sello de urgencia	Francobollo per espresso
Fiscal stamp	Timbre fiscal	Stempelmarke	Sello fiscal	Francobollo fiscale
Flesh	Chair	Fleischfarben	Carne	Carnicino
Forgery	Faux, Falsification	Fälschung	Falsificación	Falso, Falsificazione
Frame	Cadre	Rahmen	Marco	Cornice
Granite paper	Papier avec fragments de fils de soie	Faserpapier	Papel con filamentos	Carto con fili di seta
Green	Vert	Grün	Verde	Verde
Greenish Blue	Bleu verdâtre	Grünlichblau	Azul verdoso	Azzurro verdastro
Greenish Yellow	Jaune-vert	Grünlichgelb	Amarillo verdoso	Giallo verdastro
Grey	Gris	Grau	Gris	Grigio
Grey-blue	Bleu-gris	Graublau	Azul gris	Azzurro grigio
Grey-green	Vert gris	Graugrün	Verde gris	Verde grigio
Gum	Gomme	Gummi	Goma	Gomma
Gutter	Interpanneau	Zwischensteg	Espacio blanco entre dos grupos	Ponte
Imperforate	Non-dentelé	Geschnitten	Sin dentar	Non dentellato
Indigo	Indigo	Indigo	Azul indigo	Indaco
Inscription	Inscription	Inschrift	Inscripción	Dicitura
Inverted	Renversé	Kopfstehend	Invertido	Capovolto
Issue	Émission	Ausgabe	Emisión	Emissione
Laid	Vergé	Gestreift	Listado	Vergato
Lake	Lie de vin	Lackfarbe	Laca	Lacca
Lake-brown	Brun-carmin	Lackbraun	Castaño laca	Bruno lacca
Lavender	Bleu-lavande	Lavendel	Color de alhucema	Lavanda
Lemon	Jaune-citron	Zitrongelb	Limón	Limone
Light Blue	Bleu clair	Hellblau	Azul claro	Azzurro chiaro
Lilac	Lilas	Lila	Lila	Lilla
Line perforation	Dentelure en lignes	Linienzähnung	Dentado en linea	Dentellatura lineare
Lithography	Lithographie	Steindruck	Litografía	Litografia
Local	Timbre de poste locale	Lokalpostmarke	Emisión local	Emissione locale
Lozenge roulette	Percé en losanges	Rautenförmiger Durchstich	Picadura en rombos	Perforazione a losanghe
Magenta	Magenta	Magentarot	Magenta	Magenta
Margin	Marge	Rand	Borde	Margine
Maroon	Marron pourpré	Dunkelrotpurpur	Púrpura rojo oscuro	Marrone rossastro
Mauve	Mauve	Malvenfarbe	Malva	Malva
Multicoloured	Polychrome	Mehrfarbig	Multicolores	Policromo
Myrtle Green	Vert myrte	Myrtengrün	Verde mirto	Verde mirto
New Blue	Bleu ciel vif	Neublau	Azul nuevo	Azzurro nuovo
Newspaper stamp	Timbre pour journaux	Zeitungsmarke	Sello para periódicos	Francobollo per giornali

English	*French*	*German*	*Spanish*	*Italian*
Obliteration	Oblitération	Abstempelung	Matasello	Annullamento
Obsolete	Hors (de) cours	Ausser Kurs	Fuera de curso	Fuori corso
Ochre	Ocre	Ocker	Ocre	Ocra
Official stamp	Timbre de service	Dienstmarke	Sello de servicio	Francobollo di
Olive-brown	Brun-olive	Olivbraun	Castaño oliva	Bruno oliva
Olive-green	Vert-olive	Olivgrün	Verde oliva	Verde oliva
Olive-grey	Gris-olive	Olivgrau	Gris oliva	Grigio oliva
Olive-yellow	Jaune-olive	Olivgelb	Amarillo oliva	Giallo oliva
Orange	Orange	Orange	Naranja	Arancio
Orange-brown	Brun-orange	Orangebraun	Castaño naranja	Bruno arancio
Orange-red	Rouge-orange	Orangerot	Rojo naranja	Rosso arancio
Orange-yellow	Jaune-orange	Orangegelb	Amarillo naranja	Giallo arancio
Overprint	Surcharge	Aufdruck	Sobrecarga	Soprastampa
Pair	Paire	Paar	Pareja	Coppia
Pale	Pâle	Blass	Pálido	Pallido
Pane	Panneau	Gruppe	Grupo	Gruppo
Paper	Papier	Papier	Papel	Carta
Parcel post stamp	Timbre pour colis postaux	Paketmarke	Sello para paquete postal	Francobollo per pacchi postali
Pen-cancelled	Oblitéré à plume	Federzugentwertung	Cancelado a pluma	Annullato a penna
Percé en arc	Percé en arc	Bogenförmiger Durchstich	Picadura en forma de arco	Perforazione ad arco
Percé en scie	Percé en scie	Bogenförmiger Durchstich	Picado en sierra	Foratura a sega
Perforated	Dentelé	Gezähnt	Dentado	Dentellato
Perforation	Dentelure	Zähnung	Dentar	Dentellatura
Photogravure	Photogravure, Heliogravure	Rastertiefdruck	Fotograbado	Rotocalco
Pin perforation	Percé en points	In Punkten durchstochen	Horadado con alfileres	Perforato a punti
Plate	Planche	Platte	Plancha	Lastra, Tavola
Plum	Prune	Pflaumenfarbe	Color de ciruela	Prugna
Postage Due stamp	Timbre-taxe	Portomarke	Sello de tasa	Segnatasse
Postage stamp	Timbre-poste	Briefmarke, Freimarke, Postmarke	Sello de correos	Francobollo postale
Postal fiscal stamp	Timbre fiscal-postal	Stempelmarke als Postmarke verwendet	Sello fiscal-postal	Fiscale postale
Postmark	Oblitération postale	Poststempel	Matasello	Bollo
Printing	Impression, Tirage	Druck	Impresión	Stampa, Tiratura
Proof	Épreuve	Druckprobe	Prueba de impresión	Prova
Provisionals	Timbres provisoires	Provisorische Marken. Provisorien	Provisionales	Provvisori
Prussian Blue	Bleu de Prusse	Preussischblau	Azul de Prusia	Azzurro di Prussia
Purple	Pourpre	Purpur	Púrpura	Porpora
Purple-brown	Brun-pourpre	Purpurbraun	Castaño púrpura	Bruno porpora
Recess-printing	Impression en taille douce	Tiefdruck	Grabado	Incisione
Red	Rouge	Rot	Rojo	Rosso
Red-brown	Brun-rouge	Rotbraun	Castaño rojizo	Bruno rosso
Reddish Lilac	Lilas rougeâtre	Rötlichlila	Lila rojizo	Lilla rossastro
Reddish Purple	Poupre-rouge	Rötlichpurpur	Púrpura rojizo	Porpora rossastro
Reddish Violet	Violet rougeâtre	Rötlichviolett	Violeta rojizo	Violetto rossastro
Red-orange	Orange rougeâtre	Rotorange	Naranja rojizo	Arancio rosso
Registration stamp	Timbre pour lettre chargée (recommandée)	Einschreibemarke	Sello de certificado lettere	Francobollo per raccomandate
Reprint	Réimpression	Neudruck	Reimpresión	Ristampa
Reversed	Retourné	Umgekehrt	Invertido	Rovesciato

English	French	German	Spanish	Italian
Rose	Rose	Rosa	Rosa	Rosa
Rose-red	Rouge rosé	Rosarot	Rojo rosado	Rosso rosa
Rosine	Rose vif	Lebhaftrosa	Rosa vivo	Rosa vivo
Roulette	Percage	Durchstich	Picadura	Foratura
Rouletted	Percé	Durchstochen	Picado	Forato
Royal Blue	Bleu-roi	Königblau	Azul real	Azzurro reale
Sage green	Vert-sauge	Salbeigrün	Verde salvia	Verde salvia
Salmon	Saumon	Lachs	Salmón	Salmone
Scarlet	Écarlate	Scharlach	Escarlata	Scarlatto
Sepia	Sépia	Sepia	Sepia	Seppia
Serpentine roulette	Percé en serpentin	Schlangenliniger Durchstich	Picado a serpentina	Perforazione a serpentina
Shade	Nuance	Tönung	Tono	Gradazione de colore
Sheet	Feuille	Bogen	Hoja	Foglio
Slate	Ardoise	Schiefer	Pizarra	Ardesia
Slate-blue	Bleu-ardoise	Schieferblau	Azul pizarra	Azzurro ardesia
Slate-green	Vert-ardoise	Schiefergrün	Verde pizarra	Verde ardesia
Slate-lilac	Lilas-gris	Schierferlila	Lila pizarra	Lilla ardesia
Slate-purple	Mauve-gris	Schieferpurpur	Púrpura pizarra	Porpora ardesia
Slate-violet	Violet-gris	Schieferviolett	Violeta pizarra	Violetto ardesia
Special delivery stamp	Timbre pour exprès	Eilmarke	Sello de urgencia	Francobollo per espressi
Specimen	Spécimen	Muster	Muestra	Saggio
Steel Blue	Bleu acier	Stahlblau	Azul acero	Azzurro acciaio
Strip	Bande	Streifen	Tira	Striscia
Surcharge	Surcharge	Aufdruck	Sobrecarga	Soprastampa
Tête-bêche	Tête-bêche	Kehrdruck	Tête-bêche	Tête-bêche
Tinted paper	Papier teinté	Getöntes Papier	Papel coloreado	Carta tinta
Too-late stamp	Timbre pour lettres en retard	Verspätungsmarke	Sello para cartas retardadas	Francobollo per le lettere in ritardo
Turquoise-blue	Bleu-turquoise	Türkisblau	Azul turquesa	Azzurro turchese
Turquoise-green	Vert-turquoise	Türkisgrün	Verde turquesa	Verde turchese
Typography	Typographie	Buchdruck	Tipografia	Tipografia
Ultramarine	Outremer	Ultramarin	Ultramar	Oltremare
Unused	Neuf	Ungebraucht	Nuevo	Nuovo
Used	Oblitéré, Usé	Gebraucht	Usado	Usato
Venetian Red	Rouge-brun terne	Venezianischrot	Rojo veneciano	Rosso veneziano
Vermilion	Vermillon	Zinnober	Cinabrio	Vermiglione
Violet	Violet	Violett	Violeta	Violetto
Violet-blue	Bleu-violet	Violettblau	Azul violeta	Azzurro violetto
Watermark	Filigrane	Wasserzeichen	Filigrana	Filigrana
Watermark sideways	Filigrane couché liegend	Wasserzeichen	Filigrana acostado	Filigrana coricata
Wove paper	Papier ordinaire, Papier uni	Einfaches Papier	Papel avitelado	Carta unita
Yellow	Jaune	Gelb	Amarillo	Giallo
Yellow-brown	Brun-jaune	Gelbbraun	Castaño amarillo	Bruno giallo
Yellow-green	Vert-jaune	Gelbgrün	Verde amarillo	Verde giallo
Yellow-olive	Olive-jaunâtre	Gelboliv	Oliva amarillo	Oliva giallastro
Yellow-orange	Orange jaunâtre	Gelborange	Naranja amarillo	Arancio giallastro
Zig-zag roulette	Percé en zigzag	Sägezahnartiger Durchstich	Picado en zigzag	Perforazione a zigzag

Gibbons
Stamp
Monthly
Stamp of Christ
Past
NEW ZEA
Win
£249.95
Gibbons
Stamp
Monthly
The first stamps of
Queensland
150 years old and never more desirable
QUEENSLAND
SIX PENCE

Guide to Entries

A **Country of Issue** – When a country changes its name, the catalogue listing changes to reflect the name change, for example Namibia was formerly known as South West Africa, the stamps in Southern Africa are all listed under Namibia, but split into South West Africa and then Namibia.

B **Country Information** – Brief geographical and historical details for the issuing country.

C **Currency** – Details of the currency, and dates of earliest use where applicable, on the face value of the stamps.

D **Illustration** – Generally, the first stamp in the set. Stamp illustrations are reduced to 75%, with overprints and surcharges shown actual size.

E **Illustration or Type Number** – These numbers are used to help identify stamps, either in the listing, type column, design line or footnote, usually the first value in a set. These type numbers are in a bold type face – **123**; when bracketed (**123**) an overprint or a surcharge is indicated. Some type numbers include a lower-case letter – **123a**, this indicates they have been added to an existing set.

F **Date of issue** – This is the date that the stamp/set of stamps was issued by the post office and was available for purchase. When a set of definitive stamps has been issued over several years the Year Date given is for the earliest issue. Commemorative sets are listed in chronological order. Stamps of the same design, or issue are usually grouped together, for example some of the New Zealand landscapes definitive series were first issued in 2003 but the set includes stamps issued to May 2007.

G **Number Prefix** – Stamps other than definitives and commemoratives have a prefix letter before the catalogue number.
Their use is explained in the text: some examples are A for airmail, D for postage due and O for official stamps.

H **Footnote** – Further information on background or key facts on issues.

I **Stanley Gibbons Catalogue number** – This is a unique number for each stamp to help the collector identify stamps in the listing. The Stanley Gibbons numbering system is universally recognized as definitive.

Where insufficient numbers have been left to provide for additional stamps to a listing, some stamps will have a suffix letter after the catalogue number (for example 214a). If numbers have been left for additions to a set and not used they will be left vacant.

The separate type numbers (in bold) refer to illustrations (see **E**).

J **Colour** – If a stamp is printed in three or fewer colours then the colours are listed, working from the centre of the stamp outwards (see **R**).

K **Design line** – Further details on design variations

L **Key Type** – Indicates a design type on which the stamp is based. These are the bold figures found below each illustration, for example listed in Cameroon, in the West Africa catalogue, is the Key type A and B showing the ex-Kaiser's yacht *Hohenzollern*. The type numbers are also given in bold in the second column of figures alongside the stamp description to indicate the design of each stamp. Where an issue comprises stamps of similar design, the corresponding type number should be taken as indicating the general design. Where there are blanks in the type number column it means that the type of the corresponding stamp is that shown by the number in the type column of the same issue. A dash (–) in the type column means that the stamp is not illustrated. Where type numbers refer to stamps of another country, e.g. where stamps of one country are overprinted for use in another, this is always made clear in the text.

M **Coloured Papers** – Stamps printed on coloured paper are shown – e.g. "brown/*yellow*" indicates brown printed on yellow paper.

N **Surcharges and Overprints** – Usually described in the headings. Any actual wordings are shown in bold type. Descriptions clarify words and figures used in the overprint. Stamps with the same overprints in different colours are not listed separately. Numbers in brackets after the descriptions are the catalogue numbers of the non-overprinted stamps. The words "inscribed" or "inscription" refer to the wording incorporated in the design of a stamp and not surcharges or overprints.

O **Face value** – This refers to the value of each stamp and is the price it was sold for at the Post Office when issued. Some modern stamps do not have their values in figures but instead it is shown as a letter, for example Great Britain use 1st or 2nd on their stamps as opposed to the actual value.

P **Catalogue Value** – Mint/Unused. Prices quoted for Queen Victoria to King George V stamps are for lightly hinged examples.

Q **Catalogue Value** – Used. Prices generally refer to fine postally used examples. For certain issues they are for cancelled-to-order.

Prices
Prices are given in pence and pounds. Stamps worth £100 and over are shown in whole pounds:

Shown in Catalogue as	Explanation
10	10 pence
1.75	£1.75
15.00	£15
£150	£150
£2300	£2300

Prices assume stamps are in 'fine condition'; we may ask more for superb and less for those of lower quality. The minimum catalogue price quoted is 10p and is intended as a guide for catalogue users. The lowest price for individual stamps purchased from Stanley Gibbons is £1.

Prices quoted are for the cheapest variety of that particular stamp. Differences of watermark, perforation, or other details, often increase the value. Prices quoted for mint issues are for single examples, unless otherwise stated. Those in *se-tenant* pairs, strips, blocks or sheets may be worth more. Where no prices are listed it is either because the stamps are not known to exist (usually shown by a †) in that particular condition, or, more usually, because there is no reliable information on which to base their value.
All prices are subject to change without prior notice and we cannot guarantee to supply all stamps as priced. Prices quoted in advertisements are also subject to change without prior notice.

R **Multicoloured** – Nearly all modern stamps are multicoloured (more than three colours); this is indicated in the heading, with a description of the stamp given in the listing.

S **Perforations** – Please see page xi for a detailed explanation of perforations.

A Country of issue

Bangladesh

B Country Information

In elections during December 1970 the Awami League party won all but two of the seats in the East Pakistan province and, in consequence, held a majority in the National Assembly. On 1 March 1971 the Federal Government postponed the sitting of the Assembly with the result that unrest spread throughout the eastern province. Pakistan army operations against the dissidents forced the leaders of the League to flee to India from where East Pakistan was proclaimed independent as Bangladesh. In early December the Indian army moved against Pakistan troops in Bangladesh and civilian government was re-established on 22 December 1971.

From 20 December 1971 various Pakistan issues were overprinted by local postmasters, mainly using handstamps. Their use was permitted until 30 April 1973. These are of philatelic interest, but are outside the scope of the catalogue.

C Currency

(Currency. 100 paisa = 1 rupee)

D Illustration

L **17**

E Illustration or Type number

F Date of issue

1978 (8 Mar). No. *L* 57 surch with Type *L* **16**. Chalky paper.
L63 L **14** 25c. on 2½c. ultramarine, green and buff .... 75 1·75

(Des A. G. Mitchell. Litho Harrison)

G Number prefix

1981 (3 June). P 14½.
L64 L **17** 5c. multicoloured 10 10
L65 10c. multicoloured 10 10
L66 20c. multicoloured 15 15
L67 30c. multicoloured 25 25
L68 40c. multicoloured 30 30
L69 50c. multicoloured 30 45
L64/9 *Set of 6* .... 1·00 1·25

H Footnote

Issues for the Government Life Insurance Department were withdrawn on 1 December 1989 when it became the privatised Tower Corporation.

(Des G. R. Bull and G. R. Smith. Photo Harrison)

I Stanley Gibbons catalogue number

1959 (2 Mar). Centenary of Marlborough Province. T **198** and similar horiz designs. W **98** (sideways). P 14½×14.
772 2d. green 30 10
773 3d. deep blue 30 10
774 8d. light brown .... 1·25 2·25
772/4 *Set of 3* .... 1·60 2·25

J Colour

K Design line

Designs:—3d. Shipping wool, Wairau Bar, 1857; 8d. Salt industry, Grassmere.

L Key type column

1915 (12 July). Stamps of German Kamerun. Types *A* and *B*, surch as T **1** (Nos. B1/9) or **2**. (Nos. B10/13) in black or blue.
B1 A 1½d. on 3pf. (No. k7) (B.) .... 13·00 42·00
a. Different fount "d" £150 £350

340 **41** 2d. purple (1903) £350 £325
341 **28** 3d. bistre-brown (1906) £700 £600
342 **37** 4d. blue and chestnut/*bluish* (1904) £300 £350
a. Blue and yellow-brown/bluish £300 £350

M Coloured papers

N Surcharges and overprints

1913 (1 Dec). Auckland Industrial Exhibition. Nos. 387aa, 389, 392 and 405 optd with T **59** by Govt Printer, Wellington.
412 **51** ½d. deep green .... 20·00 55·00
413 **53** 1d. carmine .... 25·00 48·00
a. "Feather" flaw £225
414 **52** 3d. chestnut £130 £250
415 6d. carmine £160 £300
412/15 *Set of 4* £300 £600

These overprinted stamps were only available for letters in New Zealand and to Australia.

O Face value

P Catalogue value – Mint

Q Catalogue value – Used

(Des Martin Bailey. Litho Southern Colour Print)

R Multicoloured stamp

2008 (2 July). Olympic Games, Beijing. T **685** and similar diamond-shaped designs. Multicoloured. Phosphorised paper. P 14½.
3056 50c. Type **685** .... 1·00 85

S Perforations

Botswana
formerly Bechuanaland

Before the 1880s the only Europeans in the area which became Bechuanaland were scattered hunters and traders, together with the missionaries who were established at Kuruman as early as 1816.

Tribal conflicts in the early years of the decade led to the intervention of Boers from the Transvaal who established the independent republics of Goshen and Stellaland.

STELLALAND

The Boer republic of Stellaland was proclaimed towards the end of 1882. A postal service was organised from the capital, Vryburg, and stamps were ordered from a firm in Cape Town. These were only valid within the republic. Until June 1885 mail to other parts of South Africa was sent through Christiana, in the Transvaal, and was franked with both Stellaland and Transvaal stamps.

No date stamps or obliterators were used by the Stellaland Post Office. Stamps were pen-cancelled with the initials of a postal official and the date.

PRICES FOR STAMPS ON COVER

The issues of Stellaland are very rare on cover.

1 Arms of the Republic

(Litho by Van der Sandt, de Villiers & Co., Cape Town)

1884 (29 Feb). P 12.

No.	Type	Description	Unused	Used
1	1	1d. red	£180	£325
		a. Imperf between (horiz pair)	£3750	
		b. Imperf between (vert pair)	£4000	
2		3d. orange	28·00	£325
		a. Imperf between (horiz pair)	£750	
		b. Imperf between (vert pair)	£1700	
		c. Imperf vert (horiz pair)	£1100	
3		4d. olive-grey	26·00	£350
		a. Imperf between (horiz pair)	£650	
		b. Imperf between (vert pair)	£1800	
4		6d. lilac-mauve	28·00	£350
		a. Imperf between (horiz pair)	£1300	
		b. Imperf between (vert pair)	£1500	
5		1s. green	65·00	£700

In 1884 the British Government, following appeals from local chiefs for protection, decided to annex both Goshen and Stellaland. A force under Sir Charles Warren from the Cape reached Vryburg on 7 February 1885 and continued to Mafeking, the principal town of Goshen.

On 30 September 1885 Stellaland and other territory to the south of the Molopo River was constituted the Crown Colony of British Bechuanaland. A protectorate was also proclaimed over a vast tract of land to the north of the Molopo.

Stellaland stamps continued to be used until 2 December 1885 with external mail, franked with Stellaland and Cape of Good Hope stamps, postmarked at Barkly West and Kimberley in Griqualand West.

1885 (Oct). Handstamped "Twee" sideways in violet-lake.

No.	Type	Description	Unused	Used
6	1	2d. on 4d. olive-grey	£3500	

On 2 December 1885 Cape of Good Hope stamps overprinted "British Bechuanaland" were placed on sale at the Vryburg post office.

BRITISH BECHUANALAND

CROWN COLONY

PRICES FOR STAMPS ON COVER

Nos. 1/8	*from* × 12
No. 9	*from* × 80
Nos. 10/21	*from* × 8
Nos. 22/8	*from* × 10
No. 29	*from* × 10
No. 30	*from* × 10
Nos. 31/2	*from* × 12
Nos. 33/7	*from* × 20
Nos. 38/9	*from* × 25

British
Bechuanaland
(1)

BRITISH
BECHUANALAND
(2)

1885 (3 Dec)–**87**. Stamps of Cape of Good Hope ("Hope" seated) optd with T **1**, by W. A. Richards & Sons, Cape Town.

No.	Description	Unused	Used
	(a) Wmk Crown CC (No. 3) or Crown CA (others)		
1	½d. grey-black (No. 40a) (R.)	27·00	30·00
	a. Opt in lake	£4250	£5000
	b. Opt double (Lake+Black)	£750	
2	3d. pale claret (No. 43)	40·00	55·00
	a. No dot to 1st "i" of "British"	£700	
3	4d. dull blue (No. 30) (2.6.87)	80·00	80·00
	*(b) Wmk Anchor (Cape of Good Hope. Type **13**)*		
4	½d. grey-black (No. 48*a*) (24.12.86)	10·00	23·00
	a. Error. "ritish"	£2500	
	b. Opt double	£3250	
5	1d. rose-red (No. 49)	20·00	9·00
	a. Error. "ritish"	£4000	£2250
	b. No dot to 1st "i" of "British"	£350	£275
	c. Opt double	†	£2000
6	2d. pale bistre (No. 50)	40·00	8·00
	a. Error. "ritish"	£7000	£3750
	b. No dot to 1st "i" of "British"	£650	£250
	c. Opt double	†	£1800
	w. Wmk inverted	†	£700
7	6d. reddish purple (No. 52)	£150	38·00
	a. No dot to 1st "i" of "British"	£1800	£700
8	1s. green (No. 53) (26.11.86)	£300	£170
	a. Error. "ritish"	£21000	£14000

Nos. 1/8 were overprinted from settings of 120. The missing "B" errors are believed to have occurred on one position for one of these settings only. The 'No dot to 1st "i"' variety occurs on R. 10/3 of the left pane.

Overprints with stop after "Bechuanaland" are forged.

1888 (19 Jan). No. 197 of Great Britain optd with T **2**, by D.L.R.

No.	Description	Unused	Used
9	½d. vermilion	1·25	1·25
	a. Opt double	£2500	
	s. Handstamped "SPECIMEN"	85·00	

3

4

5

(Typo D.L.R.)

1888 (19 Jan).

No.	Type	Description	Unused	Used
		*(a) Wmk Orb (Great Britain Type **48**). P 14*		
10	3	1d. lilac and black	20·00	3·00
11		2d. lilac and black	90·00	2·25
		a. Pale dull lilac and black	90·00	23·00
12		3d. lilac and black	6·00	5·50
		a. Pale reddish lilac and black	80·00	22·00
13		4d. lilac and black	50·00	2·50
14		6d. lilac and black	60·00	2·50
		(b) Wmk Script "V R" (sideways, reading up). P 13½		
15	4	1s. green and black	30·00	8·50
16		2s. green and black	55·00	48·00
17		2s.6d. green and black	65·00	70·00
18		5s. green and black	£100	£150
19		10s. green and black	£200	£350
		(c) Two Orbs (sideways). P 14×13½		
20	5	£1 lilac and black	£850	£750
21		£5 lilac and black	£3750	£1600
10s/21s H/S "SPECIMEN" *Set of 12*			£950	

Nos. 10/21 were produced by overprinting a series of "Unappropriated Die" designs originally produced by the Board of Inland Revenue for use as Great Britain fiscal stamps.

Several values are known on blued paper. No. 11*a* is the first printing of the 2d. (on safety paper?) and has a faded appearance.

When purchasing Nos. 20/21 in used condition beware of copies with fiscal cancellations cleaned off and bearing forged postmarks.

For No. 15 surcharged "£5" see No. F2.

(**6**) (**7**) Curved foot to "2"

1888 (Sept–20 Nov). Nos. 10/11 and 13/15 surch as T **6** or **7**, by P. Townshend & Co., Vryburg.

No.	Type	Description	Unused	Used
22	**3**	1d. on 1d. lilac and black	7·50	6·50
23		2d. on 2d. lilac and black (R.)	42·00	3·50
		a. Pale dull lilac and black (No. 11a)	£110	50·00
		b. Curved foot to "2"	£300	£150
		c. Surch in green	†	£4000
25		4d. on 4d. lilac and black (R.) (20.11)	£400	£500
26		6d. on 6d. lilac and black	£140	12·00
		a. Surch in blue	†	£13000
28	**4**	1s. on 1s. green and black	£190	85·00

Nos. 23c and 26a are from two sheets of surcharge trials subsequently put into stock and used at Vryburg (2d.) or Mafeking (6d.) during 1888–89.

It should be noted that, in addition to its curved foot, the "2" on No. 23b is distinctly shorter than the "d".

A single example of No. 23c with the 'curved foot to "2"' variety has been recorded.

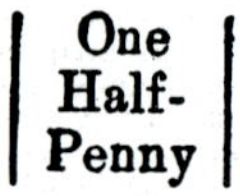

(**8**)

1888 (8 Dec). No. 12a surch with T **8**, by P. Townshend & Co, Vryburg.

No.	Type	Description	Unused	Used
29	**3**	½d. on 3d. pale reddish lilac and black	£225	£275
		a. Broken "f" in "Half"	£15000	

No. 29 was produced from a setting of 60 (12×5).

No. 29a shows the letter "f" almost completely missing and occurs on R. 5/11 of the setting. Five examples are known, one being in the Royal Collection.

Errors of spelling on this surcharge are bogus. The normal surcharge has also been extensively forged.

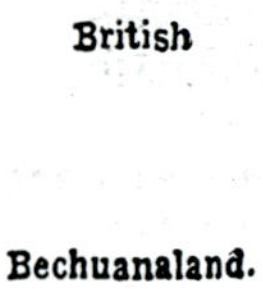  

(**9**) (**10**) (**11**)

1888 (27 Dec). No. 48a of Cape of Good Hope (wmk Anchor) optd with T **9**, by P. Townshend & Co, Vryburg.

No.	Type	Description	Unused	Used
30		½d. grey-black (G.)	3·25	30·00
		a. Opt "Bechuanaland British"	£2500	
		ab. "British" omitted	£5500	
		b. Opt double, one inverted, inverted opt "Bechuanaland British"	£2500	
		ba. Opt double, one inverted, inverted "British" omitted	£5500	
		c. Opt double, one vertical	£850	
		ca. *Se-tenant* with stamp without opt	£8000	

No. 30 was produced using a setting of 30 (6×5).

The overprint was misplaced upwards on at least one pane, giving the overprint "Bechuanaland British" (No. 30a) on rows 1 to 4 and "British" omitted on row 5 (No. 30ab). "British" was also omitted on R. 5/1 of the setting on some sheets only.

On one pane on which the overprint was applied double, one inverted, the inverted overprint was misplaced downwards, giving No. 30b on rows 7 to 10 and "British" omitted (No. 30ba) on row 6.

Normal "n" Inverted "u"

1891 (Nov). Nos. 49a/50 of Cape of Good Hope (wmk Anchor), optd with T **10**, reading upwards.

No.	Type	Description	Unused	Used
31		1d. carmine-red	10·00	13·00
		a. Horiz pair, one without opt	£16000	
		b. Optd "Bechuanaland. British"		
		c. "Bechuanaland" omitted	£2500	
		d. Inverted "u" for 2nd "n"	£180	£200
32		2d. bistre (*shades*)	4·25	2·25
		a. No stop after "Bechuanaland"	£300	£325
		b. Inverted "u" for 2nd "n"	£275	£275
31s/2s		H/S "SPECIMEN" *Set of* 2	£130	

The overprint on Nos. 31 and 32 was of 120 impressions in two panes of 60 (6×10). That on No. 32 was applied both by a stereo plate and by a forme made up from loose type. No. 31 was overprinted only with the latter. No. 32a is from the stereo overprinting (left pane, R. 3/3), 31d and 32b are from the typeset overprinting (left pane, R. 10/4).

A single example of No. 31 with "British" omitted is known; it is in the Royal Philatelic Collection.

See also Nos. 38 and 39.

1891 (1 Dec)–**1904**. Nos. 172, 200, 205, 208 and 211 of Great Britain optd with T **11**, by D.L.R.

No.	Type	Description	Unused	Used
33		1d. lilac	7·00	1·50
34		2d. grey-green and carmine	19·00	4·00
35		4d. green and purple-brown	3·00	60
		a. Bisected (2d.) (on cover) (11.99)	†	£2500
36		6d. purple/*rose-red*	5·50	2·00
37		1s. dull green (7.94)	13·00	16·00
		a. Bisected (6d.) (on cover) (12.04)	†	—
33/7		*Set of* 5	42·00	22·00
33s/6s		H/S "SPECIMEN" *Set of* 4	£170	

No. 35a was used at Palapye Station and No. 37a at Kanye, both in the Protectorate.

1893 (Dec)–**95**. As Nos. 31/2, but T **10** reads downwards.

No.	Type	Description	Unused	Used
38		1d. carmine-red	3·00	2·25
		b. "British" omitted	£3750	£3750
		c. Optd "Bechuanaland. British"	£1400	£1500
		d. Inverted "u" for 2nd "n"	£140	£150
		e. No dots to "i" of "British"	£140	£150
		f. "s" omitted	£550	£550
		g. Opt reading up, no dots to "i" of "British"	£4000	
39		2d. bistre (12.3.95)	7·50	2·50
		a. Opt double	£1400	£700
		b. "British" omitted	£850	£500
		c. "Bechuanaland" omitted	—	£550
		d. Optd "Bechuanaland. British"	£450	£250
		e. Inverted "u" for 2nd "n"	£250	£150
		f. No dots to "i" of "British"	£250	£150
		g. Opt reading up, no dots to "i" of "British"	£4250	

The same typeset overprint was used for Nos. 38 and 39 as had been employed for Nos. 31 and 32 but applied the other way up; the inverted "u" thus falling on the right pane, R. 1/3. The no dots to "i" variety only occurs on this printing (right pane, R. 1/4). Some sheets of both values were overprinted the wrong way up, resulting in Nos. 38g. and 39g.

No. 38f. developed gradually on right pane R. 10/8. The variety is not known on Nos. 31, 32 or 39.

On 16 November 1895 British Bechuanaland was annexed to the Cape of Good Hope and ceased to have its own stamps, but they remained in use in the Protectorate until superseded in 1897. The Postmaster-General of Cape Colony had assumed control of the Bechuanaland postal service on 1 April 1893 and the Cape, and subsequently the South African, postal authorities continued to be responsible for the postal affairs of the Bechuanaland Protectorate until 1963.

BECHUANALAND PROTECTORATE

PRICES FOR STAMPS ON COVER TO 1945

Nos.	40/51	*from* × 10
Nos.	52/71	*from* × 6
Nos.	72/82	*from* × 5
Nos.	83/98	*from* × 4
Nos.	99/110	*from* × 6
Nos.	111/17	*from* × 10
Nos.	118/28	*from* × 4
Nos.	129/31	*from* × 10
Nos.	D1/3	*from* × 50
Nos.	D4/6	*from* × 60
No.	F1	*from* × 5
No.	F2	—
No.	F3	*from* × 5

This large area north of the Molopo River was proclaimed a British Protectorate on 30 September 1885 at the request of the native chiefs.

A postal service using runners was inaugurated on 9 August 1888 and Nos. 40 to 55 were issued as a temporary measure with the object of assessing the cost of this service

(**12**) 15½ mm (**13**)

13a Small figure "1" (R. 7/2)

13b Small figure "1" (R. 10/2)

Normal "2"

Curved foot to "2" (42b)

1888 (Aug). No. 9 optd with T **12** and Nos. 10/19 surch or optd only as T **13** by P. Townshend & Co. Vryburg.

No.	Type	Description	Unused	Used
40	–	½d. vermilion	9·00	45·00
		a. "Protectorate" double	£350	
		s. Handstamped "SPECIMEN"	90·00	
41	3	1d. on 1d. lilac and black	14·00	15·00
		a. Small figure "1" (R. 7/2, 10/2)	£425	£500
		b. Space between "1" and "d" (R. 10/9)	£650	
42		2d. on 2d. lilac and black	32·00	17·00
		b. Curved foot to "2"	£850	£550
43		3d. on 3d. pale reddish lilac and black	£170	£225
44		4d. on 4d. lilac and black	£425	£450
		a. Small figure "4"	£5000	£5000
45		6d. on 6d. lilac and black	90·00	50·00
46	4	1s. green and black	£110	55·00
		a. First "o" omitted	£6500	£3750
		s. Handstamped "SPECIMEN"	£110	
47		2s. green and black	£600	£1000
		a. First "o" omitted	£18000	
48		2s.6d. green and black	£550	£950
		a. First "o" omitted	£18000	
49		5s. green and black	£1300	£2250
		a. First "o" omitted	£25000	
50		10s. green and black	£4250	£6500

Nos. 40/5 were produced from a basic setting of 120 (12×10) on which a faulty first "o" in "Protectorate" occurred on R. 5/12. For Nos. 46/50 the setting was reduced to 84 (12×7) and on many sheets the first "o" on R. 5/12 failed to print.

There were two distinct printings made of No. 40, the first in 1888 and the second in 1889. The overprint setting used for the first printing was broken up and had to be remade for the second. The first printing used a matt ink which produces a cleaner impression than the second, which is printed with a black glossy ink giving a distinctly muddy appearance.

There are a number of smaller than normal "1"s in the setting, usually identifiable by the upper serif of the "1" which is pointed and slopes sharply downwards at the left. R. 7/2 and 10/2 are quite distinct and are as shown.

The normal space between "1" and "d" measures 1 mm. On No. 41b it is 1.7 mm.

It should be noted that, like No. 23b, the "2" on No. 42b is distinctly shorter than the "d" and has a distinctive curl to the upper part of the "2", not present on No. 23.

A single example of No. 50 with the first "o" omitted is known; it is in the Royal Philatelic Collection.

Nos. 40/50 were first placed on sale in Vryburg on 23 June 1888. The August issue date refers to the start of the Runner Post.

See also Nos. 54/5.

1888 (10 Dec). No. 25 optd with T **12** by P. Townshend & Co., Vryburg.

No.	Type	Description	Unused	Used
51	3	4d. on 4d. lilac and black	£100	50·00

Bechuanaland

Protectorate.

(**14**)

Protectorate

Fourpence

(**15**)

1888 (27 Dec). No. 48a of Cape of Good Hope (wmk Anchor), optd with T **14** by P. Townshend & Co., Vryburg.

No.	Description	Unused	Used
52	½d. grey-black (G.)	4·75	55·00
	a. Opt double	£475	£750
	ab. Ditto, one reading "Protectorate Bechuanaland"	£1200	
	ac. Ditto, one reading "Bechuanaland" only	£2500	
	b. "Bechuanaland" omitted	£1800	
	c. Optd "Protectorate Bechuanaland"	£1000	£1000

1889 (Mar). No. 9 surch with T **15** by P. Townshend & Co., Vryburg.

No.	Description	Unused	Used
53	4d. on ½d. vermilion	35·00	5·00
	a. "rpence" omitted (R. 9/2)	†	£6000
	b. "ourpence" omitted (R. 9/2)	£10000	
	c. Surch (T **15**) inverted	†	£4000
	cb. Ditto. "ourpence" omitted	†	£16000
	s. Handstamped "SPECIMEN"	£140	

The lines of the surcharge are normally 6 mm apart, but 5 mm and 4.5 mm spacings are known.

Examples of No. 53c are postmarked "679" (Tati).

The surcharge is known printed in green, due to faulty cleaning of the inking roller. All examples known were cancelled at Shoshong. (*Price £1500 used*).

Protectorate

(**16**) 15 mm

Protectorate

(**17**) 19 mm

1890. No. 9 optd.

No.	Type	Description	Unused	Used
54	16	½d. vermilion	£180	£200
		a. Type **16** inverted	80·00	£110
		b. Type **16** double	£110	£170
		c. Type **16** double and inverted	£600	£750
		d. Optd "Portectorate" inverted	£19000	
		w. Wmk inverted		
55	17	½d. vermilion	£225	£425
		a. Type **17** double	£1500	£1600
		b. Optd "Protectorrte"		
		c. Optd "Protectorrte" double	£19000	

These were trial printings made in June 1888 (No. 55) and subsequently (No. 54) which were later issued.

The 15 mm measurement of the overprint on No. 54 should not be relied on as a sole diagnostic, since the overprint on a few positions within the setting of No. 40 similarly measure 15 mm. No. 54 is a cleaner, more even overprint and the out of line letters so frquently encountered on No. 40, especially the raised 'P' of 'Protectorate' and its consequent greater separation from the first 'r' are not found on this stamp.

In June 1890 the Bechuanaland Protectorate and the Colony of British Bechuanaland came under one postal administration and the stamps of British Bechuanaland were used in the Protectorate until 1897.

BRITISH

BECHUANALAND

(**18**)

BECHUANALAND
PROTECTORATE

(**19**)

1897. No. 61 of Cape of Good Hope (wmk Anchor), optd as T **18**.

(a) Lines 13 mm apart, bottom line 16 mm long, by Taylor & Marshall, Cape Town

No.	Description	Unused	Used
56	½d. yellow-green (July?)	2·50	17·00

(b) Lines 13½ mm apart bottom line 15 mm long, by P. Townshend & Co, Vryburg

No.	Description	Unused	Used
57	½d. yellow-green (April)	35·00	95·00
	a. Opt double, one albino inverted	£225	

(c) Lines 10½ mm apart, bottom line 15 mm long, by W. A. Richards & Sons, Cape Govt Printers

No.	Description	Unused	Used
58	½d. yellow-green (July?)	17·00	65·00

Although issued only in the Protectorate, the above were presumably overprinted "BRITISH BECHUANALAND" because stamps bearing this inscription were in use there at the time.

1897 (Oct)–**1902**. Nos. 172, 197, 200, 202, 205 and 208 of Great Britain (Queen Victoria) optd with T **19** by D.L.R.

No.	Description	Unused	Used
59	½d. vermilion	1·50	2·25
60	½d. blue-green (25.2.02)	1·40	3·50
61	1d. lilac	4·00	75
62	2d. grey-green and carmine	8·50	3·50
63	3d. purple/*yellow* (12.97)	5·50	8·50
64	4d. green and purple-brown	22·00	20·00
65	6d. purple/*rose-red*	23·00	11·00
59/65 *Set of 7*		60·00	45·00
59s/65s Optd or H/S (No. 60s) "SPECIMEN" *Set of 7*		£250	

BECHUANALAND PROTECTORATE

(**20**)

BECHUANALAND
PROTECTORATE

(**21**)

1904 (29 Nov)–**13**. Nos. 216, 218/19, 230 and 313/14 (Somerset House ptgs) of Great Britain (King Edward VII) optd with T **20**, by D.L.R.

No.	Description	Unused	Used
66	½d. blue-green (3.06)	2·75	2·00
67	½d. yellowish green (11.08)	3·75	3·50

68		1d. scarlet (4.05)	9·50	30
		s. Optd "SPECIMEN"	60·00	
69		2½d. ultramarine	10·00	7·00
		a. Stop after "P" in "PROTECTORATE"	£1000	£1300
70		1s. deep green and scarlet (10.12)	50·00	£150
		a. Opt double, one albino	£225	
71		1s. green and carmine (1913)	55·00	£120
		s. Optd "SPECIMEN"	£100	

No. 69a occurs on R. 5/9 of the lower pane.

1912 (Sept)–**14**. No. 342 of Great Britain (King George V, wmk Crown) optd with T **20**.

72		1d. scarlet	2·75	60
		a. No cross on crown	£150	75·00
		b. Aniline scarlet (No. 343) (1914)	£190	95·00

1913 (1 July)–**24**. Stamps of Great Britain (King George V) optd.

(a) Nos. 351, 357, 362, 367, 370/1, 376, 379, 385 and 395 (wmk Simple Cypher, T **100***) optd with T* **20**

73		½d. green (*shades*)	1·25	1·50
74		1d. scarlet (*shades*) (4.15)	2·75	75
		a. Carmine-red (1922)	32·00	3·25
75		1½d. red-brown (12.20)	6·50	2·50
		a. Opt double, one albino	£275	
76		2d. reddish orange (Die I)	10·00	3·25
		a. Orange (Die I) (1921)	20·00	3·00
		aw. Wmk inverted		
77		2d. orange (Die II) (1924)	42·00	2·75
78		2½d. cobalt-blue	3·50	26·00
		a. Blue (1915)	22·00	23·00
79		3d. bluish violet	6·00	12·00
80		4d. grey-green	6·50	27·00
81		6d. reddish purple (*shades*)	8·50	23·00
		a. Opt double, one albino	£275	
82		1s. bistre	17·00	32·00
		a. Bistre-brown (1923)	40·00	32·00
		b. Opt double, one albino	£300	
		s. Optd *"SPECIMEN"*	80·00	
73/82 *Set of* 9			55·00	£110

(b) With T **21**

(i) Waterlow printings (Nos. 399 and 401) (1914–15)

83		2s.6d. deep sepia-brown (1.15)	£140	£275
		a. Re-entry (R. 2/1)	£1400	£2000
		b. Opt double, one albino	£300	
84		5s. rose-carmine (1914)	£160	£375
		a. Opt double, one albino	£375	
83s/4s Optd *"SPECIMEN" Set of* 2			£275	

(ii) D.L.R. printings (Nos. 407/8 and 409) (1916–19)

85		2s.6d. pale brown (7.16)	£120	£250
		a. Re-entry (R. 2/1)	£1200	£1800
86		2s.6d. sepia (1917)	£130	£225
		a. Opt treble, two albino		
		b. Re-entry (R. 2/1)	£1400	£1700
87		5s. bright carmine (8.19)	£300	£425
		a. Opt double, one albino	£450	

(iii) B.W. printings (Nos. 414 and 416) (1920–23)

88		2s.6d. chocolate-brown (7.23)	90·00	£160
		a. Major re-entry (R. 1/2)	£2500	
		b. Opt double, one albino	£550	
		c. Opt treble, two albino	£550	
89		5s. rose-carmine (7.20)	£110	£275
		a. Opt treble, two albino	£375	
		b. Opt double, one albino		

Examples of Nos. 83/9 are known showing a forged Lobatsi postmark dated "6 MAY 35" or "6 MAY 39".

1925 (July)–**27**. Nos. 418/19, 421, 423/4, 426/a and 429 of Great Britain (wmk Block Cypher, T **111**) optd with T **20**.

91		½d. green (1927)	1·50	1·75
92		1d. scarlet (8.25)	2·00	70
		w. Wmk inverted	£300	
93		2d. orange (Die II)	1·75	1·00
94		3d. violet (10.26)	4·75	25·00
		a. Opt double, one albino	£200	
		w. Wmk inverted	£200	
95		4d. grey-green (10.26)	6·50	55·00
		a. Printed on the gummed side		
96		6d. reddish purple (*chalk-surfaced paper*) (12.25)	65·00	95·00
97		6d. purple (*ordinary paper*) (1926)	50·00	55·00
98		1s. bistre-brown (10.26)	9·00	24·00
		w. Wmk inverted	£325	£300
91/8 *Set of* 8			£130	£225

No. 94w. also usually shows the variety, opt double, one albino.

22 King George V, Baobab Tree and Cattle drinking

22a Windsor Castle

Extra flagstaff (Plate "1" R. 9/1)

Short extra flagstaff (Plate "2" R. 2/1)

Lightning conductor (Plate "3" R. 2/5)

Flagstaff on right-hand turret (Plate "5" R. 7/1)

Double flagstaff (Plate "6" R. 5/2)

(Des from photo by Resident Commissioner, Ngamiland, Recess Waterlow)

1932 (12 Dec). Wmk Mult Script CA. P 12½.

99	**22**	½d. green	2·50	30
		a. Imperf between (horiz pair)	£25000	
100		1d. scarlet	1·50	25
101		2d. brown	1·50	30
102		3d. ultramarine	3·50	3·75
103		4d. orange	3·50	8·50
104		6d. purple	4·50	6·50
105		1s. black and olive-green	3·75	7·00
106		2s. black and orange	24·00	60·00
107		2s.6d. black and scarlet	22·00	45·00
108		3s. black and purple	42·00	50·00
109		5s. black and ultramarine	95·00	£100
110		10s. black and brown	£190	£200
99/110 *Set of* 12			£350	£425
99s/110s Perf "SPECIMEN" *Set of* 12			£350	

Examples of most values are known showing a forged Lobatsi postmark dated "6 MAY 35" or "6 MAY 39".

1935 (4 May). Silver Jubilee. Wmk Mult Script CA. P 11×12.

111	**22a**	1d. deep blue and scarlet	1·75	6·50
		a. Extra flagstaff	£250	£450
		b. Short extra flagstaff	£450	
		c. Lightning conductor	£375	
		d. Flagstaff on right-hand turret	£475	
		e. Double flagstaff	£475	

No.		Description	Un	Used
112		2d. ultramarine and grey-black	2·00	6·50
		a. Extra flagstaff	£120	£200
		b. Short extra flagstaff	£180	£250
		c. Lightning conductor	£150	£225
113		3d. brown and deep blue	4·00	7·00
		a. Extra flagstaff	£160	£275
		b. Short extra flagstaff	£225	
		c. Lightning conductor	£180	£275
114		6d. slate and purple	9·00	7·00
		a. Extra flagstaff	£180	£225
		b. Short extra flagstaff	£200	
		c. Lightning conductor	£200	£225
111/14 *Set of* 4			15·00	24·00
111s/14s Perf "SPECIMEN" *Set of* 4			£120	

22b King George VI and Queen Elizabeth

23 King George VI, Baobab Tree and Cattle drinking

(Des and recess D.L.R.)

1937 (12 May). Coronation. Wmk Mult Script CA. P 14.

No.	Type	Description	Un	Used
115	**22b**	1d. scarlet	45	40
116		2d. yellow-brown	60	1·00
117		3d. bright blue	60	1·25
115/17 *Set of* 3			1·50	2·40
115s/17s Perf "SPECIMEN" *Set of* 3			£110	

(Recess Waterlow)

1938 (1 Apr)–**52**. Wmk Mult Script CA. P 12½.

No.	Type	Description	Un	Used
118	**23**	½d. green	3·75	3·75
		a. Light yellowish green (1941)	12·00	9·50
		b. Yellowish green (4.43)	12·00	4·75
		c. Deep green (4.49)	4·50	12·00
119		1d. scarlet	75	50
120		1½d. dull blue	12·00	2·00
		a. Light blue (4.43)	1·00	1·00
121		2d. chocolate-brown	75	50
122		3d. deep ultramarine	1·00	2·50
123		4d. orange	2·00	3·50
124		6d. reddish purple	7·00	3·00
		a. Purple (1944)	4·25	2·50
		ab. "A" of "CA" missing from wmk	†	—
125		1s. black and brown-olive	4·75	8·50
		a. Grey-black & olive-green (21.5.52)	22·00	35·00
126		2s.6d. black and scarlet	14·00	18·00
127		5s. black and deep ultramarine	38·00	28·00
		a. Grey-black & dp ultram (10.46)	75·00	60·00
128		10s. black and red-brown	25·00	32·00
118/28 *Set of* 11			85·00	90·00
118s/28s Perf "SPECIMEN" *Set of* 11			£300	

Bechuanaland

(**24**)

1945 (3 Dec). Victory. Stamps of South Africa optd with T **24**. Inscr alternately in English and Afrikaans.

No.	Type	Description	*Un pair*	*Used pair*	*Used single*
129	**55**	1d. brown and carmine	75	1·50	10
130	**56**	2d. slate-blue and violet	50	1·50	10
131	**57**	3d. deep blue and blue	50	1·75	10
		a. Opt omitted (in vert pair with normal)	£14000		
129/31 *Set of* 3			1·60	4·25	25

No. 131a comes from a sheet on which the overprint was displaced downwards so that it is omitted from stamps in the top row and shown on the sheet margin at foot.

24a King George VI

26 King George VI and Queen Elizabeth

24c Queen Elizabeth II as Princess and Princess Margaret

24d The Royal Family

(Recess Waterlow)

1947 (17 Feb). Royal Visit. Wmk Mult Script CA. P 12½.

No.	Type	Description	Un	Used
132	**24a**	1d. scarlet	10	10
133	**24b**	2d. green	10	10
134	**24c**	3d. ultramarine	10	10
135	**24d**	1s. mauve	10	10
132/5 *Set of* 4			35	30
132s/5s Perf "SPECIMEN" *Set of* 4			£120	

24e King George VI and Queen Elizabeth

24f

(Des and photo Waterlow (T **24e**) design recess; name typo B.W. (T **24f**)

1948 (1 Dec). Royal Silver Wedding. Wmk Mult Script CA.

No.	Type	Description	Un	Used
136	**24e**	1½d. ultramarine	30	10
137	**24f**	10s. black	40·00	48·00

24g Hermes Globe and Forms of Transport

24h Hemispheres Jet-powered Vickers Viking airliner and Steamer

24i Hermes and Globe

24j UPU Monument

(Recess Waterlow (T **24g**, **24j**). Designs recess name Typo B.W. (T **24h**, **24i**)

1949 (10 Oct). 75th Anniv of Universal Postal Union. Wmk Mult Script CA.

No.	Type	Description	Un	Used
138	**24g**	1½d. blue (P 13×14)	30	1·25
139	**24h**	3d. deep blue (P 11×11½)	1·50	2·50
140	**24i**	6d. magenta (P 11×11½)	60	4·75
141	**24j**	1s. olive (P 13½×14)	60	1·50
138/41 *Set of* 4			2·75	9·00

24k Queen Elizabeth II

(Des and eng B.W. Recess D.L.R.)

1953 (3 June). Coronation. Wmk Mult Script CA. P 13½×13.

No.	Type	Description	Un	Used
142	**24k**	2d. black and brown	1·50	30

25 Queen Elizabeth II, Baobab Tree and Cattle drinking

26 Queen Victoria, Queen Elizabeth II and Landscape

(Des from photo by Resident Commissioner, Ngamiland. Recess Waterlow)

1955 (3 Jan)–**58**. Wmk Mult Script CA. P 13½×14.

No.	Type	Description	Unused	Used
143	**25**	½d. green	50	30
144		1d. rose-red	80	10
145		2d. red-brown	1·25	30
146		3d. ultramarine	3·00	2·50
		a. Bright ultramarine (16.1.57)	13·00	4·50
146*b*		4d. red-orange (1.12.58)	11·00	12·00
147		4½d. blackish blue	1·50	35
148		6d. purple	1·25	60
149		1s. black and brown-olive	1·25	1·00
150		1s.3d. black and lilac	14·00	9·50
151		2s.6d. black and rose-red	12·00	10·00
152		5s. black and violet-blue	15·00	16·00
153		10s. black and red-brown	38·00	18·00
143/53 *Set of 12*			90·00	65·00

(Photo Harrison)

1960 (21 Jan). 75th Anniv of Bechuanaland Protectorate. W w **12**. P 14½×14.

No.	Type	Description	Unused	Used
154	**26**	1d. sepia and black	40	50
155		3d. magenta and black	40	30
156		6d. bright blue and black	40	50
154/6 *Set of 3*			1·10	1·10

(New Currency. 100 cents = 1 rand)

1c (27)   1c (I)   1c (II)   2½c (I)   2½c (II)

3 (I)   3 (II)   3 (III)   5c (I)   5c (II)   R1 (I)   R1 (II)

2½c

Spaced "c" (R. 10/3)

3½c Normal   3½c Bold "c"

The Bold "c" variety occurs on the Type II surcharge (R. 9/3) and Type III (R. 7/3).

1961. Nos. 144/6a and 148/53 surch as T **27** by South African Govt Printer, Pretoria.

No.	Type	Description	Unused	Used
157	**25**	1c. on 1d. rose-red (Type I)	30	10
		a. Type II (6 June)	40	10
158		2c. on 2d. red-brown	30	10
159		2½c. on 2d. red-brown (Type I)	30	10
		a. Type II (26 July)	85	2·00
		b. Vert pair, one without surch	£11000	
160		2½c. on 3d. bright ultramarine	4·50	8·00
		a. Spaced "c" (R. 10/3)	£100	
161		3½c. on 4d. red-orange (Type I)	50	2·75
		a. Wide surch (I)	18·00	32·00
		b. Type II	2·25	10·00
		ba. Bold "c" (Type II)	£110	£160
		c. Wide surch (II)	65·00	90·00
		d. Type III (6 June)	20	60
		da. Bold "c" (Type III)	10·00	18·00
162		5c. on 6d. purple (Type I)	65	1·50
		a. Type II (12 May)	20	10
163		10c. on 1s. black and brown-olive	20	10
		a. Horiz pair, righthand stamp without surch	£8000	
164		12½c. on 1s.3d. black and lilac	65	20
165		25c. on 2s.6d. black and rose-red	1·50	50
166		50c. on 5s. black and violet-blue	2·00	2·25
167		1r. on 10s. black & red-brown (Type I)	£425	£140
		a. Type II (surch at bottom left) (17 Mar)	15·00	18·00
		b. Type II (surch at foot, either to right or central) (Apr)	15·00	10·00
157/67b *Set of 11*			23·00	19·00

Nos. 161/c occur from the same printing, each sheet containing thirty-three examples of Type I, five of Type I with wide spacing, nineteen of Type II and three of Type II with wide spacing. The wide surcharge measures 9½ mm overall (with "C" spaced 1½ mm from "½") and comes on 8 of the 10 stamps in the last vertical row. The surcharge on the remainder of the sheet varies between 8½ and 9½ mm.

No. 163a was caused by a shift of the surcharge so that the last vertical row on the sheet is without "10 c".

A later printing of the 12½c. on 1s.3d. was from a fresh setting of type, but is insufficiently different for separate listing. Later printings of the 10c. and 25c. were identical to the originals.

28 African Golden Oriole

29 Hoopoe

30 Scarlet-chested Sunbird

31 Yellow-rumped Bishop

32 Swallow-tailed Bee Eater

33 African Grey Hornbill

34 Red-headed Weaver

35 Brown-hooded Kingfisher

36 Woman Musician

37 Baobab Tree

38 Woman grinding maize

39 Bechuana Ox

40 Lion

41 Police Camel Patrol

(Des P. Jones (1c. to 12½c.). Photo Harrison)

1961 (2 Oct). T **28/41**. W w **12**. P 14½×14 (25, 50c.) or 14×14½ (others).

No.	Type	Description	Unused	Used
168	**28**	1c. yellow, red, black and lilac	1·50	50
169	**29**	2c. orange, black and yellow-olive	2·00	4·50

170	**30**	2½c. carmine, green, black and bistre	1·75	10
171	**31**	3½c. yellow, black, sepia and pink....	2·50	4·75
172	**32**	5c. yellow, blue, black and buff......	3·25	1·00
173	**33**	7½c. brown, red, black and apple-green..	2·25	2·25
174	**34**	10c. red, yellow, sepia & turquoise-green..	2·25	60
175	**35**	12½c. buff, blue, red and grey-black.	18·00	6·00
176	**36**	20c. yellow-brown and drab............	3·75	4·00
177	**37**	25c. deep brown and lemon............	4·75	2·25
178	**38**	35c. deep blue and orange..............	4·00	4·25
179	**39**	50c. sepia and olive..........................	2·75	2·50
180	**40**	1r. black and cinnamon..................	9·00	2·50
181	**41**	2r. brown and turquoise-blue.......	24·00	13·00
168/81 *Set of 14*		....	75·00	42·00

41a Protein Foods

41b Red Cross Emblem

(Des M. Goaman. Photo Harrison)

1963 (4 June). Freedom from Hunger. W w **12**. P 14×14½.

182	**41a**	12½c. bluish green..	30	15

(Des V. Whiteley. (Litho B.W.)

1963 (2 Sept). Red Cross Centenary. W w **13**. P 13½.

183	**41b**	2½c. red and black..	20	10
184		12½c. red and blue..	40	50

41c Protein Foods

(Des R. Granger barrett. Photo Harrison)

1964 (23 April). 400th Birth Anniv of William Shakespeare. W w **12**. P14×14½.

185	**41c**	12½c. light brown..	15	15

INTERNAL SELF-GOVERNMENT

42 Map and Gaberones Dam

(Des Mrs. M. Townsend, adapted V. Whiteley. Photo Harrison)

1965 (1 Mar). New Constitution. W w **12**. P 14½×14.

186	**42**	2½c. red and gold...	30	10
		w. Wmk inverted...	18·00	3·75
187		5c. ultramarine and gold................................	30	40
188		12½c. brown and gold......................................	40	40
189		25c. green and gold...	45	55
186/9 *Set of 4*		....	1·25	1·25

42a ITU Emblem

(Des M. Goaman. Litho Enschedé)

1965 (17 May). I.T.U. Centenary. W w **12**. P11×11½.

190	**42a**	2½c. red and bistre-yellow..............................	20	10
191		12½c. mauve and brown..................................	45	30

42b ICY Emblem

1965 (25 Oct). International Co-operation Year. W w **12**. P 12½.

192	**42b**	1c. reddish purple and turquoise-green..	10	45
193		12½c. deep bluish green and lavender....	60	55

42c Sir Winston Churchill and St. Paul's Cathedral in wartime

(Des Jennifer Toombs. Photo Harrison)

1966 (24 Jan). Churchill Commemoration. Printed in black, cerise and gold with background in colours stated. W w **12**. P14.

194		1c. new blue	20	2·00
195		2½c. deep green...	35	10
196		12½c. brown	70	35
197		20c. bluish violet...	75	55
194/7 *Set of 4*		....	1·75	2·75

43 Haslar Smoke Generator

(Des V. Whiteley. Photo Harrison)

1966 (1 June). Bechuanaland Royal Pioneer Corps. T **43** and similar horiz designs. W w **12**. P 14½.

198		2½c. Prussian blue, red and light emerald	25	10
199		5c. brown and light blue..................................	30	20
200		15c. Prussian blue, rosine and emerald	1·00	25
201		35c. buff, blackish brown, red and green......	30	1·00
198/201 *Set of 4*		....	1·60	1·25

Designs:—5c. Bugler; 15c. Gun-site; 35c. Regimental cap badge.

INDEPENDENCE

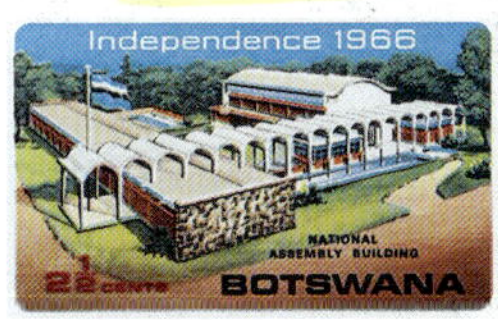

47 National Assembly Building

(Des R. Granger Barrett. Photo Harrison)

1966 (30 Sept). Independence. T **47** and similar horiz designs. Multicoloured. P 14½.

202		2½c. Type **47**...	15	10
		a. Imperf (pair)..	£425	
203		5c. Abattoir Lobatsi...	20	10
204		15c. National Airways Douglas DC-3...............	65	20
205		35c. State House, Gaberones............................	40	30
202/5 *Set of 4*		....	1·25	55

REPUBLIC OF BOTSWANA
(51)

1966 (30 Sept). Nos. 168/81 of Bechuanaland optd as T **51**.

206		1c. yellow, red, black and lilac..................	25	10
207		2c. orange, black and yellow-olive.........	30	1·75
208		2½c. carmine, green, black and bistre.......	30	10
209		3½c. yellow, black, sepia and pink..............	1·25	20
		a. Yellow, black, sepia and flesh................	5·00	1·50
210		5c. yellow, blue, black and buff................	1·50	1·50

211	7½c. brown, red, black and apple-green	50	1·75
	a. Yellow background		£1600
212	10c. red, yellow, sepia & turquoise-green	1·00	20
213	12½c. buff, blue, red and grey-black	2·00	2·75
214	20c. yellow-brown and drab	20	1·00
215	25c. deep brown and lemon	20	2·00
216	35c. deep blue and orange	30	2·25
217	50c. sepia and olive	20	70
218	1r. black and cinnamon	40	1·25
219	2r. brown and turquoise-blue	60	2·50
206/19 *Set of* 14		8·00	16·00

No. 209*a* was a special printing produced to make up quantities. It does not exist without the overprint.

No. 211a shows the background in yellow instead of apple-green and may have come from a trial printing. Most known examples come from first day covers.

52 Golden Oriole

66 Students and University

(Des D. M. Reid-Henry. Photo Harrison)

1967 (3 Jan). Birds. Vert designs as T **52**. Multicoloured. P 14×14.

220	1c. Type **52**	30	15
	a. Error. Wmk **105** of Malta	†	£800
221	2c. Hoopoe	60	70
222	3c. Groundscraper Thrush	55	10
223	4c. Cordon-bleu ("Blue Waxbill")	55	10
224	5c. Secretary Bird	55	10
225	7c. Yellow-billed Hornbill	60	1·00
226	10c. Burchell's Gonolek ("Crimson-breasted Shrike")	60	15
227	15c. Malachite Kingfisher	7·50	3·00
228	20c. African Fish Eagle	7·50	2·00
229	25c. Go-away Bird ("Grey Loerie")	4·00	1·50
230	35c. Scimitar-bill	6·00	2·25
231	50c. Comb Duck	2·75	2·75
232	1r. Levaillant's Barbet	5·00	3·50
233	2r. Didric Cuckoo	7·00	17·00
220/33 *Set of* 14		38·00	30·00

A used copy of the 20c. has been seen with the pale brown colour missing, resulting in the value (normally shown in white) being omitted.

The 1, 2, 4, 7 and 10c. values exist with PVA gum as well as gum arabic.

(Des V. Whiteley. Photo Harrison)

1967 (7 Apr). First Conferment of University Degrees. P 14×14½.

234	**66**	3c. sepia, ultramarine and light orange-yell	10	10
235		7c. sepia, ultram & lt greenish bl	10	10
236		15c. sepia, ultramarine and rose	10	10
237		35c. sepia, ultramarine and light violet	20	20
234/7 *Set of* 4			30	30

67 Bushbuck

(Des G, Vasarhelyi. Photo Harrison)

1967 (2 Oct). Chobe Game Reserve. T **67** and similar horiz designs. Multicoloured. P 14.

238	3c. Type **67**	10	20
239	7c. Sale Antelope	15	30
240	35c. Fishing on Chobe River	90	1·10
238/40 *Set of* 3		1·00	1·40

70 Arms of Botswana and Human Rights Emblem

(Litho D.L.R.)

1968 (8 Apr). Human Rights Year. T **70** and similar horiz designs showing Anniv of Botswana and Human Rights emblem arranged differently. P 13½×13.

241	3c. multicoloured	10	10
242	15c. multicoloured	25	45
243	25c. multicoloured	25	60
241/3 *Set of* 3		50	1·00

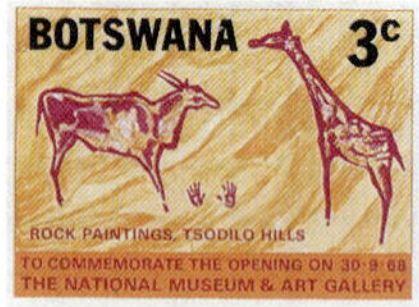

73 Eland and Giraffe Rock Paintings, Tsodilo Hills

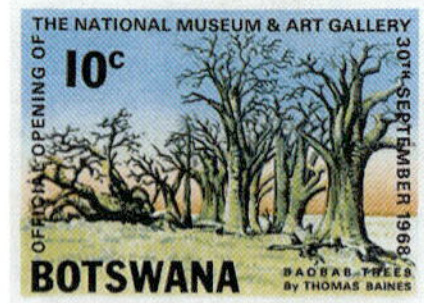

75 "Baobab Trees" (Thomas Baines)

76 National Museum and Art Gallery

(Litho D.L.R.)

1968 (30 Sept). Opening of National Museum and Art Gallery. T **73/6** and similar multicoloured design. P 12½ (7c.), 12½×13½ (15c.), or 13×13½ (others).

244	3c. Type **73**	20	20
245	7c. Girl wearing ceremonial beads (30×48 mm)	25	40
246	10c. Type **75**	25	30
247	15c. Type **76**	40	1·50
244/7 *Set of* 4		1·00	2·25
MS248 132×82 mm. Nos. 244/7. P 13		1·00	2·25

77 African Family, and Star over Village

(Des Mrs M. E. Townsend, adapted J. Cooter. Litho Enschedé)

1968 (11 Nov). Christmas. P 13×14.

249	**77**	1c. multicoloured	10	10
250		2c. multicoloured	10	10
251		5c. multicoloured	10	10
252		25c. multicoloured	15	50
249/52 *Set of* 4			30	70

78 Scout, Lion and Badge in Frame

(Des D.L.R. Litho Format)

1969 (21 Aug). 22nd World Scout Conference, Helsinki. T **78** and similar multicoloured designs. P 13½.

253	3c. Type **78**	30	30
254	15c. Scouts cooking over open fire (*vert*)	35	1·00
255	25c. Scouts around camp fire	35	1·00
253/5 *Set of* 3		90	2·00

81 Woman, Child and Christmas Star

82 Diamond Treatment Plant, Orapa

(Des A. Vale, adapted V. Whiteley. Litho Harrison)

1969 (6 Nov). Christmas. P 14½×14.

256	**81**	1c. pale blue and chocolate	10	10
257		2c. pale yellow-olive and chocolate	10	10
258		4c. yellow and chocolate	10	10
259		35c. chocolate and bluish violet	20	20
256/9 *Set of 4*			30	30
MS260 86×128 mm. Nos. 256/9. P 14½ (*shades*)			70	1·10

(Des J.W. Litho Harrison)

1970 (23 Mar). Developing Botswana. T **82** and similar designs. Multicoloured. P 14½×14 (3c., 7c.) or 14×14½ (others).

261	3c. Type **82**	70	20
262	7c. Copper-nickel mining	95	20
263	10c. Copper-nickel mine, Selebi–Pikwe (horiz)	1·25	15
264	35c. Orapa diamond mine, and diamonds (horiz)	2·75	1·25
261/4 *Set of 4*		5·00	1·60

83 Mr. Micawber (*David Copperfield*)

(Des V. Whiteley. Litho Walsall)

1970 (6 July). Death Centenary of Charles Dickens. T **83** and similar horiz designs. Multicoloured. P 11.

265	3c. Type **83**	25	10
266	7c. Scrooge (*A Christmas Carol*)	25	10
267	15c. Fagin (*Oliver Twist*)	45	40
268	25c. Bill Sykes (*Oliver Twist*)	70	60
265/8 *Set of 4*		1·50	1·00
MS269 114×81 mm. Nos. 265/8		2·75	4·00

84 U.N. Building and Emblem

(Des J. Cooter. Litho Walsall)

1970 (24 Oct). 25th Anniv of United Nations. P 11.

270	**84**	15c. bright blue, chestnut and silver	70	30

85 Crocodile

(Des A. Vale. Litho Questa)

1970 (3 Nov). Christmas. T **85** and similar horiz designs. Multicoloured. P 14.

271	1c. Type **85**	10	10
272	2c. Giraffe	10	10
273	7c. Elephant	15	15
274	25c. Rhinoceros	60	80
271/4 *Set of 4*		80	1·00
MS275 128×90 mm. Nos. 271/4		1·00	3·00

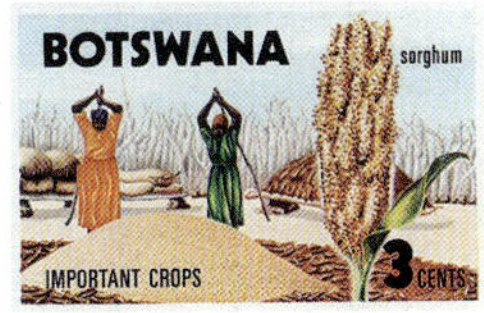

86 Sorghum

(Des J.W. Litho Questa)

1971 (6 April). Important Crops. T **86** and similar horiz designs. Multicoloured. P 14.

276	3c. Type **86**	15	10
277	7c. Millet	20	10
278	10c. Maize	20	10
279	35c. Groundnuts	70	1·00
276/9 *Set of 4*		1·10	1·10

87 Map and Head of Cow

88 King bringing Gift of Gold

(Des A. Vale, adapted L. Curtis. Litho Harrison)

1971 (30 Sept). Fifth Anniv of Independence. T **87** and similar vert designs inscr "PULA" (local greeting). P 14½×14.

280	3c. black, brown and apple-green	10	10
281	4c. black, new blue and pale blue	10	10
282	7c. black and red-orange	20	15
283	10c. multicoloured	20	15
284	20c. multicoloured	55	2·50
280/4 *Set of 5*		1·00	2·75

Designs:—4c. Map and cogs; 7c. Map and zebra; 10c. Map and sorghum stalk crossed by tusk; 20c. Arms and map of Botswana.

(Des A. Vale. Litho Questa)

1971 (11 Nov). Christmas. T **88** and similar vert designs. Multicoloured. P 14.

285	2c. Type **88**	10	10
286	3c. King bearing frankincense	10	10
287	7c. King bearing myrrh	10	10
288	20c. Three Kings behold the star	35	65
285/8 *Set of 4*		40	75
MS289 85×128 mm. Nos. 285/8		1·00	3·50

89 Orion

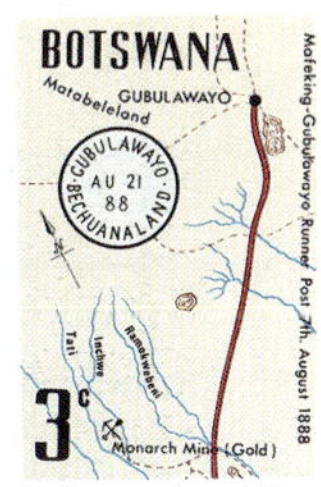

90 Postmark and Map

(Des R. Granger Barrett. Litho Questa)

1972 (24 Apr). "Night Sky". T **89** and similar vert designs. P 14.

290	3c. turquoise-blue, black and red	1·00	40
291	7c. dull blue, black and yellow	1·25	85
292	10c. dull green, black and orange	1·40	1·00
293	20c. deep violet-blue, black and blue-green	2·00	3·50
290/3 *Set of 4*		5·00	5·25

Constellations:—7c. The Scorpion; 10c. The Centaur; 20c. The Cross.

(Des M. Bryan. Litho A. & M.)

1972 (21 Aug). Mafeking–Gubulawayo Runner Post. T **90** and similar vert designs. Multicoloured. P 13½×13.

294	3c. Type **90**	30	10
	a. Imperf (vert pair)	£500	
295	4c. Bechuanaland stamp and map	30	35
296	7c. Runners and map	45	50

297	20c. Mafeking postmark and map	1·10	1·50
294/7	*Set of 4*	2·00	2·25

MS298 84×216 mm. Nos. 294/7 vertically *se-tenant*, forming a composite map design ..... 11·00 15·00
a. Pale buff (background) omitted £700

For these designs redrawn smaller with changed inscriptions see Nos. 652/6.

91 Cross, Map and Bells

92 Thor

(Des M. Bryan. Litho Questa)

1972 (6 Nov). Christmas. Vert designs each with Cross and Map as T **91**. Multicoloured. P 14.

299	2c. Type **91**	10	75
300	3c. Cross, map and candle	10	10
301	7c. Cross, map and Christmas tree	15	25
302	20c. Cross, map, star and holly	40	85
299/302	*Set of 4*	60	1·75
MS303	96×119 mm. Nos. 299/302	1·25	3·50

(Des Edna Elphick. Litho Questa)

1973 (23 Mar). IMO/WMO Centenary. T **92** and similar designs showing Norse myths. Multicoloured. P 14.

304	3c. Type **92**	20	10
305	4c. Sun God's chariot (horiz)	25	15
306	7c. Ymir, the frost giant	30	15
307	20c. Odin and Sleipnir (horiz)	75	70
304/7	*Set of 4*	1·40	1·00

93 Livingstone and River Scene

94 Donkey and Foal at Village Trough

(Des G. Vasarhelyi. Litho Walsall)

1973 (10 Sept). Death Centenary of Dr. Livingstone. T **93** and similar horiz designs. Multicoloured. P 13½.

308	3c. Type **93**	20	10
309	20c. Livingstone meeting Stanley	90	90

(Des M. Bryan. Litho Questa)

1973 (3 Dec). Christmas. T **94** and similar multicoloured designs. P 14.

310	3c. Type **94**	10	10
311	4c. Shepherd and flock (horiz)	10	10
312	7c. Mother and child	10	10
313	20c. Kgotla meeting (horiz)	40	85
310/13	*Set of 4*	55	1·00

95 Gaborone Campus

(Des. M. Bryan, adapted P. Powell. Litho Questa)

1974 (8 May). Tenth Anniv of University of Botswana, Lesotho and Swaziland. T **95** and similar horiz designs. Multicoloured. P 14.

314	3c. Type **95**	10	10
315	7c. Kwaluseni Campus	10	10
316	20c. Roma Campus	15	20
317	35c. Map and flags of the three countries	20	35
314/17	*Set of 4*	35	55

96 Methods of Mail Transport

(Des. M. Bryan. Litho J.W.)

1974 (29 May). Centenary of Universal Postal Union. T **96** and similar horiz designs. Multicoloured. P 14.

318	2c. Type **96**	55	35
319	3c. Post Office, Palapye, circa 1889	55	35
320	7c. Bechuanaland Police Camel Post, circa 1900	95	70
321	20c. Hawker Siddeley H.S.748 and de Havilland D.H.9 mail planes of 1920 and 1974	2·75	2·50
318/21	*Set of 4*	4·25	3·50

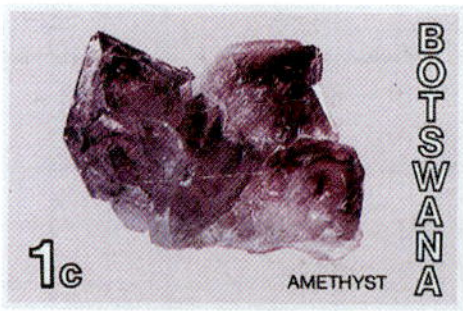

97 Amethyst

98 *Stapelia variegata*

(Des M. Bayliss, adapted PAD Studio. Photo Enschedé)

1974 (1 July). Botswana Minerals. T **97** and similar horiz designs. Multicoloured. P 14×13.

322	1c. Type **97**	60	2·50
323	2c. Agate—"Botswana Pink"	60	2·50
324	3c. Quartz	65	80
325	4c. Copper nickel	70	60
326	5c. Moss agate	70	1·00
327	7c. Agate	80	1·25
328	10c. Stilbite	1·60	65
329	15c. Moshaneng Banded Marble	2·00	4·00
330	20c. Gem diamonds	4·00	4·50
331	25c. Chrysotile	5·00	2·50
332	35c. Jasper	5·00	5·50
333	50c. Moss quartz	4·50	7·00
334	1r. Citrine	7·50	10·00
335	2r. Chalcopyrite	20·00	20·00
322/35	*Set of 14*	48·00	55·00

(Des M. Bryan. Litho Questa)

1974 (4 Nov). Christmas. T **98** and similar vert designs showing flowers. Multicoloured. P 14.

336	2c. Type **98**	20	40
337	7c. *Hibiscus lunarifolius*	30	20
338	15c. *Ceratotheca triloba*	45	1·00
339	20c. *Nerine laticoma*	60	1·25
336/9	*Set of 4*	1·40	2·50
MS340	85×130 mm. Nos. 336/9	2·00	4·25

99 President Sir Seretse Khama

100 Ostrich

(Des M. Bryan, adapted G. Vasarhelyi. Photo Enschedé)

1975 (24 Mar). Tenth Anniv of Self-Government. P 13½×13.

341	**99**	4c. multicoloured	10	10
342		10c. multicoloured	15	10

343	20c. multicoloured	25	25
344	35c. multicoloured	45	50
341/4 *Set of 4*		85	85
MS345 93×130 mm. Nos. 341/4		1·00	1·50

(Des M. Bryan. Litho Questa)

1975 (23 June). Rock Paintings, Tsodilo Hills. T **100** and similar horiz designs. Multicoloured. P 14.

346	4c. Type **100**	60	10
347	10c. White Rhinoceros	1·00	10
348	25c. Spotted Hyena	2·00	55
349	35c. Scorpion	2·00	1·10
346/9 *Set of 4*		5·00	1·60
MS350 150×150 mm. Nos. 346/9		12·00	7·50

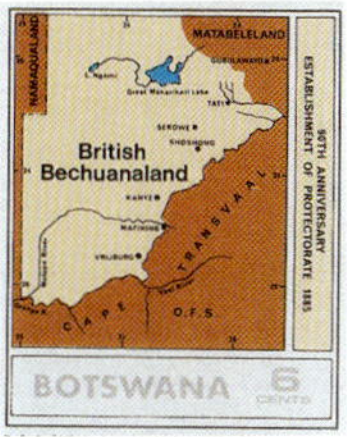

101 Map of British Bechuanaland, 1885

102 *Aloe marlothii*

(Des M. Bryan, adapted G. Vasarhelyi. Litho Harrison)

1975 (13 Oct). Anniversaries. T **101** and similar multicoloured designs. P 14×14½ (25c.) or 14½×14 (others).

351	6c. Type **101**	30	20
352	10c. Chief Khama, 1875	40	15
353	25c. Chiefs Sebele, Bathoen and Khama, 1895 (horiz)	80	75
351/3 *Set of 3*		1·40	1·00

Events:—6c. 90th Anniv of Protectorate; 10c. Centenary of Khama's Accession; 25c. 80th Anniv of Chiefs' visit to London.

(Des M. Bryan. Litho Questa)

1975 (3 Nov). Christmas. T **102** and similar vert designs showing aloes. Multicoloured. P 14½.

354	3c. Type **102**	20	10
355	10c. *Aloe lutescens*	40	20
356	15c. *Aloe zebrine*	60	1·50
357	25c. *Aloe littoralis*	75	2·50
354/7 *Set of 4*		1·75	3·75

103 Drum

(Des M. Bryan. Litho Questa)

1976 (1 Mar). Traditional Musical Instruments. T **103** and similar horiz designs. Multicoloured. P 14.

358	4c. Type **103**	15	10
359	10c. Hand Piano	20	10
360	15c. Segankuru (violin)	25	50
361	25c. Kudu Signal Horn	30	1·25
358/61 *Set of 4*		80	1·75

104 One Pula Note

(Des M. Bryan from banknotes by D.L.R. Litho Questa)

1976 (28 June). First National Currency. T **104** and similar horiz designs. Multicoloured. P 14.

362	4c. Type **104**	15	10
363	10c. Two pula note	20	10
364	15c. Five pula note	35	20
365	25c. Ten Pula note	45	45
362/5 *Set of 4*		1·00	70
MS366 163×107 mm. Nos. 362/5		1·00	3·50

(New Currency. 100 thebe = 1 pula)

1t (Type I)	1t (Type II)
2t (I)	2t (II)
4t (I)	4t (II)
5t (I)	5t (II)
15t (I)	15t (II)
20t (I)	20t (II)

(Surch in letterpress by Govt Printer, Pretoria (Type I), or in lithography by Enschedé (Type II))

1976 (23 Aug)–**77**. Nos. 322/35 surch as T **105**.

367	1t. on 1c. Type **97** (I)	2·00	70
	a. Type II Surch (15.7.77)	2·50	80
368	2t. on 2c. Agate—"Botswana Pink" (I)	2·00	1·75
	a. Type II Surch (15.7.77)	2·50	80
369	3t. on 3c. Quartz (surch at top right) (Gold)	1·50	60
	a. Surch at bottom right (17.10.77)	50·00	15·00
370	4t. on 4c. Copper nickel (I)	2·50	40
	a. Type II Surch (15.7.77)	2·75	80
371	5t. on 5c. Moss agate (I)	2·50	40
	a. Type II Surch (15.7.77)	2·75	70
372	7t. on 7c. Agate (surch at top right)	1·25	2·75
	a. Surch at bottom right (3.8.77)	60·00	20·00
373	10t. on 10c. Stilbite	1·25	80
374	15t. on 15c. Moshaneng Banded Marble (I) (Gold)	4·25	3·25
	a. Type II Surch (15.7.77)	7·00	1·50
375	20t. on 20c. Gem diamonds (I)	7·50	80
	a. Type II Surch (15.7.77)	9·00	1·50
376	25t. on 25c. Chrysotile	5·00	1·25
377	35t. on 35c. Jasper	4·00	5·00
378	50t. on 50c. Moss quartz (surch at top right)	5·50	9·00
	a. Surch at bottom right (17.10.77)	£275	70·00
379	1p. on 1r. Citrine (surch at top right)	6·00	9·50
	a. Surch at bottom left (10.10.77)	80·00	40·00
380	2p. on 2r. Chalcopyrite (Gold)	8·00	11·00
367/80 *Set of 14*		48·00	42·00
367a/75a *Set of 6*		24·00	5·50

Nos. 369a, 372a, 378a and 379a come from a second Pretoria printing on a small stock returned from the Crown Agents. By the time the stamps arrived in Pretoria the surcharge type for the 3t., 7t., 50t. and 1p. had been dispersed and when it was reset the position of the value figures was changed.

No. 368 with a much larger "2t" surcharge is believed to be a postal forgery.

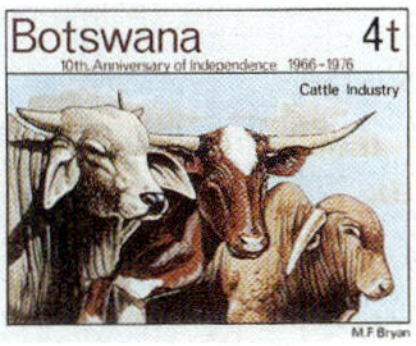

106 Botswanan Cattle

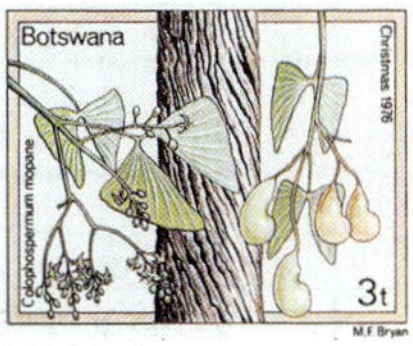

107 *Colophospermum mopane*

(Des M. Bryan. Litho Questa)

1976 (30 Sept). Tenth Anniv of Independence. T **106** and similar multicoloured designs. P 14.

381	4t. Type **106**	15	10
382	10t. Antelope, Okavango Delta (vert)	20	10
383	15t. Schools and pupils	20	40
384	25t. Rural weaving (vert)	20	50
385	35t. Miner (vert)	75	85
381/5 *Set of 5*		1·40	1·75

Nos. 381/5 were printed on sand-grained paper which has an uneven surface.

(Des M. Bryan. Litho J.W.)

1976 (1 Nov). Christmas. T **107** and similar horiz designs showing trees. Multicoloured. P 13.

386	3t. Type **107**	15	10
387	4t. *Baikiaea plurijuga*	15	10
388	10t. *Sterculia rogersii*	20	10
389	25t. *Acacia nilotica*	45	50
390	40t. *Kigelia africana*	75	1·25
386/90 *Set of 5*		1·50	1·75

108 Coronation Coach

(Des M. Bryan, adapted G. Vasarhelyi. Litho Cartor)

1977 (7 Feb). Silver Jubilee. T **108** and similar horiz designs. Multicoloured. P 12.

391	4t. Queen and Sir Seretse Khama	10	10
392	25t. Type **108**	20	15
393	40t. The Recognition	35	90
391/3 *Set of 3*		60	1·00

Nos. 391/3 have matt, almost invisible gum.

109 African Clawless Otter

(Des M. Bryan. Litho Questa)

1977 (7 June). Diminishing Species. T **109** and similar horiz designs. Multicoloured. P 14.

394	3t. Type **109**	4·25	40
395	4t. Serval	4·25	40
396	10t. Bat-eared Fox	4·75	40
397	25t. Temminck's Ground Pangolin	11·00	2·00
398	40t. Brown Hyena	13·00	7·50
394/8 *Set of 5*		32·00	9·50

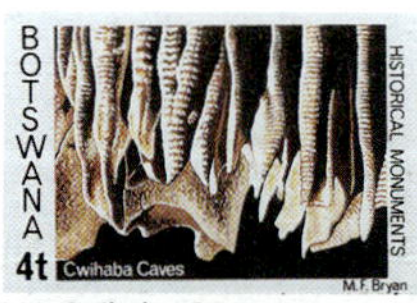

110 Cwihaba Caves

(Des M. Bryan. Litho J.W.)

1977 (22 Aug). Historical Monuments. T **110** and similar horiz designs. Multicoloured. P 14.

399	4t. Type **110**	20	10
400	5t. Khama Memorial	20	10
401	15t. Green's Tree	30	40
402	20t. Mmajojo Ruins	30	45
403	25t. Ancient morabaraba board	30	50
404	35t. Matsieng's footprint	40	60
399/404 *Set of 6*		1·50	2·00
MS405 154×105 mm. Nos. 399/404		2·50	3·25

111 *Hypoxis nitida*

112 Little Black Bustard

(Des M. Bryan. Litho Questa)

1977 (7 Nov). Christmas. T **111** and similar vert designs showing lilies. Multicoloured. P 14.

406	3t. Type **111**	15	10
407	5t. *Haemanthus magnificus*	15	10
408	10t. *Boophane disticha*	20	10
409	25t. *Vellozia retinervis*	40	55
410	40t. *Ammocharis coranica*	55	1·25
406/10 *Set of 5*		1·25	1·75

(Des M. Bryan. Photo Harrison)

1978 (3 July). Birds. Vert designs as T **112**. Multicoloured. P 14×14½ (1 to 20t.) or 14 (25t. to 5p.).

411	1t. Type **112**	70	1·25
412	2t. Marabou Stork	90	1·25
413	3t. Green Wood Hoopoe	70	85
414	4t. Carmine Bee Eater	2·00	1·00
415	5t. African Jacana	1·00	40
416	7t. African Paradise Flycatcher	1·00	3·00
417	10t. Bennett's Woodpecker	2·00	60
418	15t. Red Bishop	1·50	3·00
419	20t. Crowned Plover	1·75	2·00
420	25t. Giant Kingfisher	70	3·00
421	30t. White-faced Whistling Duck	70	70
422	35t. Green Heron	70	3·25
423	45t. Black-headed Heron	1·00	3·00
424	50t. Spotted Eagle Owl	5·00	4·50
425	1p. Gabar Goshawk	2·50	4·50
426	2p. Martial Eagle	3·00	8·00
427	5p. Saddle-bill Stork	5·50	16·00
411/27 *Set of 17*		27·00	48·00

113 Tawana making Karos

(Des M. Bryan. Litho Questa)

1978 (11 Sept). Okavango Delta. T **113** and similar horiz designs. Multicoloured. P 14.

428	4t. Type **113**	10	30
429	5t. Tribe localities	10	10
430	15t. Bushmen collecting roots	25	40
431	20t. Herero woman milking	35	70
432	25t. Yei poling "mokoro" (canoe)	40	60
433	35t. Mbukushu fishing	45	1·75
428/33 *Set of 6*		1·50	3·25
MS434 150×98 mm. Nos. 428/33		1·50	3·75

Nos. 428/34 were printed on sand-grained paper which has an uneven surface.

114 *Caralluma lutea*

115 Sip Well

(Des M. Bryan. Litho J.W.)

1978 (6 Nov). Christmas. Flowers. T **114** and similar vert designs. Multicoloured. P 14.

435	5t. Type **114**	35	10
436	10t. *Hoodia lugardii*	50	15
437	15t. *Ipomoea transvaalensis*	90	55
438	25t. *Ansellia gigantea*	1·10	70
435/8 *Set of 4*		2·50	1·40

(Des M. Bryan. Litho Questa)

1979 (30 Mar). Water Development. T **115** and similar vert designs. Multicoloured. P 14.

439	3t. Type **115**	10	10
440	5t. Watering pit	10	10
441	10t. Hand dug well	15	10
442	25t. Windmill	20	30
443	40t. Modern drilling rig	40	55
439/43 *Set of 5*		80	1·00

116 Pottery

(Des M. Bryan. Litho Questa)

1979 (11 June). Handicrafts. T **116** and similar vert designs. Multicoloured. P 14½×14.

444	5t. Type **116**	10	10
445	10t. Clay modelling	10	10
446	25t. Basketry	20	25
447	40t. Beadwork	40	50
444/7	*Set of 4*	70	80
MS448	123×96 mm. Nos. 444/7	1·00	2·50

117 1885 British Bechuanaland 1d. Stamp and Sir Rowland Hill

(Des M. Bryan. Litho Secura, Singapore)

1979 (27 Aug). Death Centenary of Sir Rowland Hill. T **117** and similar horiz designs showing stamps and Sir Rowland Hill. Multicoloured. P 13½.

449	5t. Type **117**	20	10
450	25t. 1932 Bechuanaland Protectorate 2d.	45	50
451	45t. 1967 2c.definitive	55	1·25
449/51	*Set of 3*	1·10	1·60

118 Children Playing

119 *Ximenia caffra*

(Des K. Mosinyi (5t.), M. Bryan (10t.). Litho Questa)

1979 (24 Sept). International Year of the Child. T **118** and similar multicoloured design. P 14.

452	5t. Type **118**	20	10
453	10t. Child playing with doll (vert)	30	20

(Des M. Bryan. Litho Questa)

1979 (12 Nov). Christmas. Fruit. T **119** and similar vert designs. Multicoloured. P 14.

454	5t. Type **119**	10	10
455	10t. *Sclerocarya caffra*	20	20
456	15t. *Hexalobus monopetalus*	35	35
457	25t. *Ficus soldanella*	45	45
454/7	*Set of 4*	1·00	1·00

120 Flap-necked Chameleon

(Des M. Bryan. Litho Security Printers (M), Malaysia)

1980 (3 Mar). Reptiles. T **120** and similar horiz designs. Multicoloured. P 13½.

458	5t. Type **120**	30	10
459	10t. Leopard Tortoise	30	15
460	25t. Puff Adder	50	65
461	40t. White-throated Monitor	60	2·50
458/61	*Set of 4*	1·50	3·00

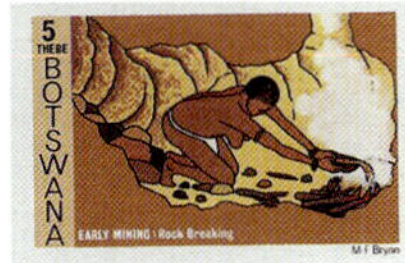

121 Rock Breaking

(Des M. Bryan. Litho Secura, Singapore)

1980 (7 July). Early Mining. T **121** and similar horiz designs. Multicoloured. P 13½.

462	5t. Type **121**	25	15
463	10t. Ore hoisting	30	15
464	15t. Ore transport	70	60
465	20t. Ore crushing	75	90
466	25t. Smelting	80	90
467	35t. Tools and products	1·00	1·75
462/7	*Set of 6*	3·50	4·00

122 "Chiwele and the Giant"

(Des W. Battiss. Litho Questa)

1980 (8 Sept). Folktales. T **122** and similar multicoloured designs. P 14 (5t.), 14×13½ (45t.) or 14½×14 (others).

468	5t. Type **122** (35×22 mm)	10	10
469	10t. "Kgori is not deceived" (28×37 mm)	15	10
470	30t. "Nyambi's wife and Crocodile" (28×37 mm)	45	45
471	45t. "Clever Hare" (44×27 mm)	60	60
468/71	*Set of 4*	1·10	1·10

123 Game watching. Makgadikgadi Pans

(Des M. Bryan. Litho Govt Printer, Pretoria)

1980 (6 Oct). World Tourism Conference, Manila. P 14.

472	**123**	5t. multicoloured	45	20

124 *Acacia gerrardii*

125 Heinrich von Stephan with Bechuanaland 1949 3d. and Botswana 1974 3c. UPU Anniversary Commemoratives

(Des M. Bryan. Litho Govt Printer, Pretoria)

1980 (3 Nov). Christmas. Flora. T **124** and similar vert designs. Multicoloured. P 14×13½.

473	5t. Type **124**	10	10
474	10t. *Acacia nilotica*	20	10
475	25t. *Acacia erubescens*	45	30
476	40t. *Dichrostachys cinerea*	70	70
473/6	*Set of 4*	1·25	1·00

(Des M. Bryan. Litho Govt Printer, Pretoria)

1981 (7 Jan). 150th Birth Anniv of Heinrich von Stephan (founder of UPU). T **125** and similar horiz design showing Von Stephan and UPU anniversary commemoratives. Multicoloured. P 14.

477	6t. Type **125**	50	30
478	20t. Bechuanaland 1949 6d. and Botswana 1974 7c	1·25	2·25

126 *Anax imperator* (dragonfly)

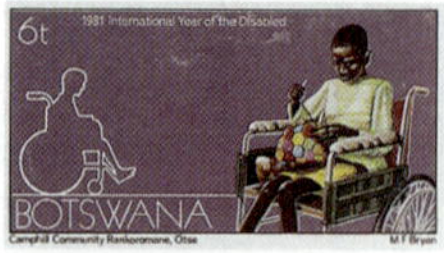

127 Camphill Community Ramkoromane, Otse

(Des M. Bryan. Litho Govt Printer, Pretoria)

1981 (23 Feb). Insects. T **126** and similar vert designs. Multicoloured. P 14.

479	6t. Type **126**	15	10
480	7t. *Sphodromantis gastrica* (mantid)	15	20
481	10t. *Zonocerus elegans* (grasshopper)	15	20
482	20t. *Kheper nigroaeneus* (beetle)	25	50
483	30t. *Papilio demodocus* (butterfly)	35	70
484	45t. *Acanthocampa belina* (moth larva)	40	1·10
479/84 *Set of 6*		1·25	2·50
MS485 180×89 mm. Nos. 479/84		3·00	8·50

(Des M. Bryan. Litho Govt Printer, Pretoria)

1981 (6 Apr). International Year for Disabled Persons. T **127** and similar horiz designs. Multicoloured. P 14.

486	6t. Type **127**	20	10
487	20t. Resource Centre for the Blind, Mochudi	55	35
488	30t. Tlamelong Rehabilitation Centre, Tlokweng	75	45
486/8 *Set of 3*		1·40	80

128 Woman reading Letter

129 Sir Seretse Khama and Building

(Des Petra Rouendaal. Litho Govt Printer, Pretoria)

1981 (8 June). Literacy Programme. T **128** and similar vert designs. Multicoloured. P 14.

489	6t. Type **128**	20	10
490	7t. Man filling in form	20	15
491	20t. Boy reading newspaper	60	35
492	30t. Child being taught to read	80	45
489/92 *Set of 4*		1·60	90

(Des G. Vasarhelyi. Litho Format)

1981 (13 July). First Death Anniv of President Sir Seretse Khama. T **129** and similar horiz designs. Multicoloured. P 14.

493	6t. Type **129**	15	10
494	10t. Seretse Khama and building (different)	25	15
495	30t. Seretse Khama and Botswana flag	40	45
496	45t. Seretse Khama and building (different)	55	70
493/6 *Set of 4*		1·25	1·25

25t

(130)

131 Traditional Ploughing

1981 (1 Sept). Nos. 417 and 422 surch as T **130**.

497	25t. on 35t. Green Heron	2·50	2·00
498	30t. on 10t. Bennett's Woodpecker	2·50	2·00

(Des K. Mosinyi. Litho Format)

1981 (21 Sept). Cattle Industry. T **131** and similar horiz designs. Multicoloured. P 14½.

499	6t. Type **131**	10	10
500	20t. Agricultural show	30	50
501	30t. Botswana Meat Commission	35	60
502	45t. Vaccine Institute, Botswana	50	1·00
499/502 *Set of 4*		1·10	2·00

132 *Nymphaea caerulea*

133 "Cattle Post Scene" (Boitumelo Golaakwena)

(Des M. Bryan. Litho Govt Printer, Pretoria)

1981 (11 Nov). Christmas. Flowers. T **132** and similar vert designs. Multicoloured. P 14.

503	6t. Type **132**	20	10
504	10t. *Nymphoides indica*	25	10
505	25t. *Nymphaea lotus*	60	90
506	40t. *Ottelia kunenensis*	80	2·25
503/6 *Set of 4*		1·60	3·00

(Litho Govt Printer, Pretoria)

1982 (15 Feb). Children's Art. T **133** and similar horiz designs. Multicoloured. P 14.

507	6t. Type **133**	40	10
508	10t. "Kgotla Meeting" (Reginald Klinck)	50	15
509	30t. "Village Water Supply" (Keromemang Matswiri)	1·75	1·25
510	45t. "With the Crops" (Kennedy Balemoge)	1·75	3·00
507/10 *Set of 4*		4·00	4·00

134 Common Type

(Des K. Mosinyi and V. Moremi. Litho Govt Printer, Pretoria)

1982 (3 May). Traditional Houses. T **134** and similar horiz designs. Multicoloured. P 14.

511	6t. Type **134**	40	15
512	10t. Kgatleng type	50	15
513	30t. North Eastern type	2·00	1·10
514	45t. Sarwa type	2·00	3·00
511/14 *Set of 4*		4·50	4·00

135 African Masked Weaver

(Des M. Bryan. Photo Harrison)

1982 (2 Aug). Birds. T **135** and similar multicoloured designs. P 14×14½ (1t. to 10t.) or 14½×14 (others).

515	1t. Type **135**	80	1·75
516	2t. Lesser Double-collared Sunbird	90	1·75
517	3t. Red-throated Bee Eater	1·00	1·75
518	4t. Ostrich	1·00	1·75
519	5t. Grey-headed Gull	1·00	1·75
520	6t. African Pygmy Goose	1·00	40
521	7t. Cattle Egret	1·00	15
522	8t. Lanner Falcon	2·50	1·75
523	10t. Yellow-billed Stork	1·00	20
524	15t. Red-billed Pintail (horiz)	2·75	25
525	20t. Barn Owl (horiz)	5·50	3·50
526	25t. Hammerkop (horiz)	3·25	70
527	30t. South African Stilt (horiz)	3·75	90
528	35t. Blacksmith Plover (horiz)	3·75	80
529	45t. Senegal Wattled Plover (horiz)	3·75	1·75
530	50t. Helmet Guineafowl (horiz)	4·75	2·50
531	1p. Cape Vulture (horiz)	9·00	12·00
532	2p. Augur Buzzard (horiz)	11·00	17·00
515/32 *Set of 18*		48·00	45·00

136 *Coprinus comatus*

137 President Quett Masire

(Des Gillian Condy. Litho Mardon Printers Ltd, Zimbabwe)

1982 (2 Nov). Christmas. Fungi. T **136** and similar vert designs. Multicoloured. P 14½.

533	7t. Type **136**	2·50	20
534	15t. *Lactarius deliciosus*	3·75	65
535	35t. *Amanita pantherina*	6·00	2·00
536	50t. *Boletus edulis*	7·50	8·00
533/6	*Set of 4*	18·00	9·75

(Des G. Vasarhelyi. Litho Questa)

1983 (14 Mar). Commonwealth Day. T **137** and similar horiz designs. Multicoloured. P 14.

537	7t. Type **137**	10	10
538	15t. Native dancers	15	20
539	35t. Melbourne conference centre	45	55
540	45t. Meeting of Heads of State, Melbourne.	55	80
537/40	*Set of 4*	1·00	1·50

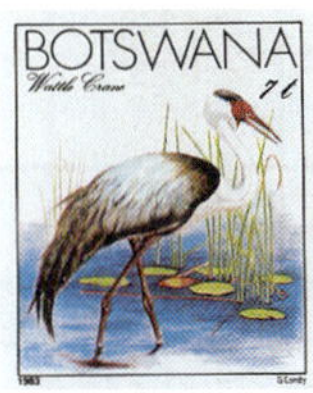

138 Wattled Crane

139 Wooden Spoons

(Des Petra Rouendaal (50t.), Gillian Condy (others). Litho Mardon Printers Ltd, Zimbabwe)

1983 (19 Apr). Endangered Species. T **138** and similar vert designs. Multicoloured. P 14×14½.

541	7t. Type **138**	3·00	55
542	15t. *Aloe lutescens*	2·50	80
543	35t. Roan Antelope	3·00	3·25
544	50t. Ivory Palm (*Hyphaene ventricosa*)	3·50	7·00
541/4	*Set of 4*	11·00	10·50

(Des M. Bryan. Litho Mardon Printers Ltd, Zimbabwe)

1983 (20 July). Traditional Artifacts. T **139** and similar vert designs. Multicoloured. P 14½.

545	7t. Type **139**	25	10
546	15t. Personal ornaments	45	30
547	35t. Ox-hide milk bag	75	65
548	50t. Decorated knives	1·00	1·10
545/8	*Set of 4*	2·25	1·90
MS549	**145** 115×102 mm. Nos. 545/8	4·25	5·00

140 *Pantala flavescens*

141 Sorting Diamonds

(Des Beverley Boudreau. Litho Mardon Printers Ltd, Zimbabwe)

1983 (7 Nov). Christmas. Dragonflies. T **140** and similar horiz designs. Multicoloured. P 14½×14.

550	6t. Type **140**	85	10
551	15t. *Anax imperator*	1·75	50
552	25t. *Trithemis arteriosa*	2·00	85
553	45t. *Chlorolestes elegans*	2·75	4·75
550/3	*Set of 4*	6·50	5·50

(Des M. Kahn. Litho Mardon Printers Ltd, Zimbabwe)

1984 (19 Mar). Mining Industry. T **141** and similar multicoloured designs. P 14½.

554	7t. Type **141**	2·00	50
555	15t. Lime kiln	2·00	75
556	35t. Copper-nickel smelter plant (vert)	3·25	3·25
557	50t. Stockpiled coal (*vert*)	3·75	10·00
554/7	*Set of 4*	10·00	12·00

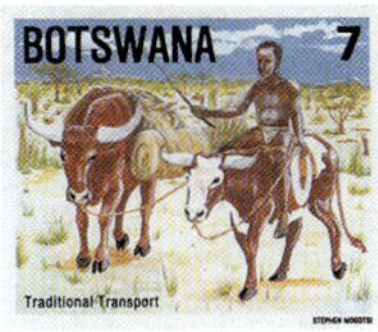

142 Riding Cattle

(Des S. Mogotsi. Litho Mardon Printers Ltd, Zimbabwe)

1984 (18 June). Traditional Transport. T **142** and similar horiz designs. Multicoloured. P 14½×14.

558	7t. Type **142**	20	10
559	25t. Sledge	65	60
560	35t. Wagon	85	1·50
561	50t. Two wheeled donkey cart	1·25	4·50
558/61	*Set of 4*	2·75	6·00

143 Avro 504 Aircraft

(Des V. Larsson. Litho Mardon Printers Ltd, Zimbabwe)

1984 (8 Oct). 40th Anniv of International Civil Aviation Organization. T **143** and similar horiz designs, each with ICAO emblem. Multicoloured. P 14½×14.

562	7t. Type **143**	75	20
563	10t. Westland Wessex trimotor	1·00	35
564	15t. Junkers Ju 52/3m	1·40	95
565	25t. de Havilland D.H.89B Dominie	2·00	1·75
566	35t. Douglas DC-3	2·25	3·50
567	50t. Fokker F.27 Friendship	2·50	7·00
562/7	*Set of 6*	9·00	12·00

144 *Papilio demodocus*

145 Seswaa (meat dish)

(Des M. Kahn. Litho Mardon Printers Ltd, Zimbabwe)

1984 (5 Nov). Christmas. Butterflies. T **144** and similar horiz designs. Multicoloured. P 14½×14.

568	7t. Type **144**	2·00	30
569	25t. *Byblia anvatara*	3·25	1·50
570	35t. *Danaus chrysippus*	3·50	3·00
571	50t. *Graphium taboranus*	4·75	11·00
568/71	*Set of 4*	12·00	14·00

No. 570 is incorrectly inscribed "Hypolimnas misippus".

(Des K. Mosinyi. Litho Mardon Printers Ltd, Zimbabwe)

1985 (18 Mar). 5th Anniv of Southern African Development Co-ordination Conference. Traditional Foods. T **145** and similar vert designs. Multicoloured. P 14½.

572	7t. Type **145**	50	10
573	15t. Bogobe (cereal porridge)	75	35
574	25t. Madila (soured coagulated cows milk)..	1·00	55
575	50t. Phane (caterpillars)	1·50	2·25
572/5	*Set of 4*	3·25	2·75
MS576	117×103 mm. Nos. 572/5	7·00	10·00

146 1885 British Bechuanaland Overprint on Cape of Good Hope ½d.

147 Bechuanaland Border Police, 1885–95

(Des D. Finlay and J. Hodgson. Litho Mardon Printers Ltd, Zimbabwe)

1985 (24 June). Centenary of First Bechuanaland Stamps. T **146** and similar designs. P 14½.

577	7t. black, grey-black and orange-vermilion	1·00	20
578	15t. black, deep brown and greenish yellow	1·75	50
579	25t. black and bright scarlet	2·25	80
580	35t. black, ultramarine and gold	2·50	2·00
581	50t. multicoloured	2·75	3·75
577/81	*Set of 5*	9·00	6·50

Designs: Vert—15t.1897 Bechuanaland Protectorate overprint on G.B. 3d.; 25t. Bechuanaland Protectorate 1932 1d. definitive. Horiz—35t. Bechuanaland 1965 Internal Self-Government 5c.; 50t. Botswana 1966 Independence 2½c.

(Des V. Larsson. Litho Mardon Printers Ltd, Zimbabwe)

1985 (5 Aug). Centenary of Botswana Police. T **147** and similar horiz designs. Multicoloured. P 14½×14.

582	7t. Type **147**	2·25	50
583	10t. Bechuanaland Mounted Police, 1895–1902	2·50	50
584	25t. Bechuanaland Protectorate Police, 1903–66	3·50	2·00
585	50t. Botswana Police, from 1966	5·50	7·50
582/5	*Set of 4*	12·00	9·50

148 *Cucumis metuliferus*

149 Mr. Shippard and Chief Gaseitsiwe of the Bangwaketse

(Des Audrey Renew. Litho Mardon Printers Ltd, Zimbabwe)

1985 (4 Nov). Christmas. Edible Wild Cucumbers. T **148** and similar horiz designs. Multicoloured. P 14½×14.

586	7t. Type **148**	1·25	10
587	15t. *Acanthosicyos naudinianus*	2·25	70
588	25t. *Coccinia sessifolia*	3·50	1·25
589	50t. *Momordica balsamina*	5·00	9·50
586/9	*Set of 4*	11·00	10·50

(Des A. Campbell. Litho Mardon Printers Ltd. Zimbabwe)

1985 (30 Dec). Centenary of Declaration of Bechuanaland Protectorate. T **149** and similar vert designs. Multicoloured. P 14×14½.

590	7t. Type **149**	35	10
591	15t. Sir Charles Warren and Chief Sechele of the Bakwena	70	45
592	25t. Revd. Mackenzie and Chief Khama of the Bamangwato	1·25	85
593	50t. Map showing Protectorate	2·75	6·50
590/3	*Set of 4*	4·50	7·00
MS594	130×133 mm. Nos. 590/3	13·00	15·00

150 Halley's Comet over Serowe

(Des L. Hutchings. Litho Mardon Printers Ltd, Zimbabwe)

1986 (24 Mar). Appearance of Halley's Comet. T **150** and similar horiz designs. Multicoloured. P 14½×14.

595	7t. Type **150**	80	15
596	15t. Comet over Bobonong at sunset	1·50	70
597	35t. Comet over Gomare at dawn	2·00	1·50
598	50t. Comet over Thamaga and Letlhakeng	2·25	3·75
595/8	*Set of 4*	6·00	5·50

151 Milk Bag

(Des B. Mazebedi. Litho Mardon Printers Ltd, Zimbabwe)

1986 (23 June). Traditional Milk Containers. T **151** and similar vert designs. Multicoloured. P 14½.

599	8t. Type **151**	30	10
600	15t. Clay pot and calabashes	45	30
601	35t. Wooden milk bucket	75	65
602	50t. Milk churn	1·00	1·40
599/602	*Set of 4*	2·25	2·25

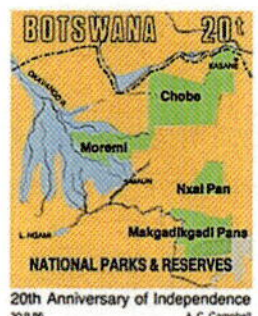

152 Map showing National Parks and Reserves

153 *Ludwigia stogonifera*

(Des K. Bogatsu, A. Campbell, I. Marshall and K. Mosinyi. Litho Govt Printer, Pretoria)

1986 (30 Sept). 20th Anniv of Independence. Sheet 100×120 mm, containing T **152** and similar vert designs. Multicoloured. P 14.

MS603	20t. Type **152**; 20t. Morupule Power Station; 20t. Cattle breeding in Kgalagadi; 20t. National Assembly Building	3·75	2·50

(Des Julia Cairns. Litho Mardon Printers Ltd, Zimbabwe)

1986 (3 Nov). Christmas. Flowers of Okavango. T **153** and similar vert designs. Multicoloured. P 14×14½.

604	8t. Type **153**	1·25	10
605	15t. *Sopubia mannii*	2·25	1·10
606	35t. *Commelina diffusa*	3·50	3·00
607	50t. *Hibiscus diversifolius*	4·00	12·00
604/7	*Set of 4*	10·00	14·00

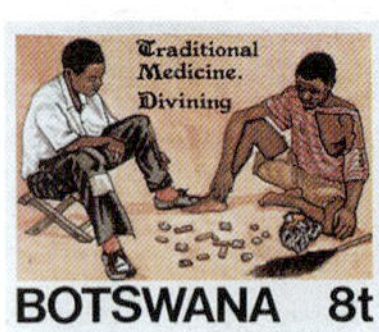

154 Divining

3t

(155)

156 Oral Rehydration Therapy

(Des K. Mosinyi. Litho Mardon Printers Ltd, Zimbabwe)

1987 (2 Mar). Traditional Medicine. T **154** and similar horiz designs. Multicoloured. P 14½×14.

608	8t. Type **154**	80	10
609	15t. Lightning prevention	1·50	80
610	35t. Rain making	2·25	2·50
611	50t. Blood letting	2·75	8·50
608/11	*Set of 4*	6·50	10·50

1987 (1 Apr). Nos. 520, 523 and 530 surch as T **155**.

612	3t. on 6t. African Pygmy Goose	1·75	75

613	5t. on 10t. Yellow-billed Stork	1·75	1·25
614	20t. on 50t. Helmet Guineafowl (horiz)	3·25	1·40
612/14	*Set of 3*	6·00	3·00

(Des A. Nunoo. Litho Govt Printer, Pretoria)

1987 (1 June). UNICEF Child Survival Campaign. T **156** and similar vert designs. Multicoloured. P 14.

615	8t. Type **156**	35	10
616	15t. Growth monitoring	60	55
617	35t. Immunization	1·25	2·00
618	50t. Breast feeding	1·50	5·00
615/18	*Set of 4*	3·25	7·00

157 Cape Fox

158 *Cyperus articulatus*

(Des P. Huebsch. Photo Harrison)

1987 (3 Aug). Animals. T **157** and similar horiz designs. Multicoloured. P 14.

619	1t. Type **157**	10	1·25
620	2t. Lechwe	50	1·75
621	3t. Zebra	15	1·25
622	4t. Duiker	15	1·75
623	5t. Banded Mongoose	20	1·75
624	6t. Rusty-spotted Genet	20	1·75
625	8t. Hedgehog	30	10
626	10t. Scrub Hare	30	10
627	12t. Hippopotamus	4·00	4·00
628	15t. Suricate	2·50	2·25
629	20t. Caracal	70	65
630	25t. Steenbok	70	1·50
631	30t. Gemsbok	1·50	1·50
632	35t. Square-lipped Rhinoceros	2·50	3·00
633	40t. Mountain Reedbuck	1·75	1·50
634	50t. Rock Dassie	90	1·75
635	1p. Giraffe	2·50	4·00
636	2p. Tsessebe	2·50	5·50
637	3p. Side-striped Jackal	3·75	8·00
638	5p. Hartebeest	6·00	9·00
619/38	*Set of 20*	28·00	48·00

(Des Julia Cairns. Litho National Printing & Packaging, Zimbabwe)

1987 (26 Oct). Christmas. Grasses and Sedges of Okavango. T **158** and similar vert designs. Multicoloured. P 14×14½.

639	8t. Type **158**	40	10
640	15t. Broomgrass	60	40
641	30t. Cyperus alopurcides	1·25	75
642	1p. Bulrush Sedge	2·50	5·75
639/42	*Set of 4*	4·25	6·25
MS643	88×99 mm. Nos. 639/42	4·25	5·75
	a. 30t. value imperf vert	40·00	

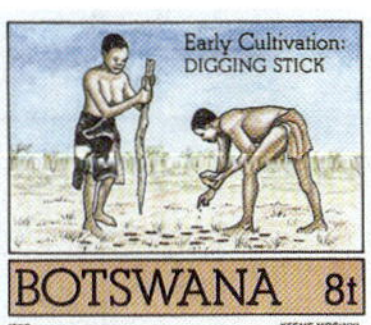

159 Planting Seeds with Digging Stick

160 Red Lechwe at Water-hole

(Des K. Mosinyi. Litho National Printing & Packaging, Zimbabwe)

1988 (14 Mar). Early Cultivation. T **159** and similar horiz designs. Multicoloured. P 14½×14.

644	8t. Type **159**	40	10
645	15t. Using iron hoe	60	35
646	35t. Wooden ox-drawn plough	1·00	1·00
647	50t. Villagers working on lesotla (Communal field)	1·40	2·00
644/7	*Set of 4*	3·00	3·00

(Des P. Augustinus. Litho National Printing & Packaging, Zimbabwe)

1988 (6 June). Red Lechwe. T **160** and similar horiz designs. Multicoloured. P 14½×14.

648	10t. Type **160**	90	15
649	15t. Red Lechwe and early morning sun	1·75	65
650	35t. Female and calf	2·50	1·75
651	75t. Herd on the move	3·75	8·50
648/51	*Set of 4*	8·00	10·00

161 Gubulawayo Postmark and Route Southwards to Tati

162 Pope John Paul II and Outline Map of Botswana

(Des M. Bryan, adapted Lucy Phalayagae. Litho National Printing & Packaging, Zimbabwe)

1988 (22 Aug). Centenary of Mafeking-Gubulawayo Runner Post. Designs as Nos. 294/8, but redrawn smaller with changed inscription as in T **161**. Multicoloured. P 14½.

652	10t. Type **161**	35	10
653	15t. Bechuanaland 1888 6d. on 6d. stamp and route from Tati southwards	55	30
654	30t. Runners and twin routes south from Shoshong	95	75
655	60t. Mafeking postmark and routes to Bechuanaland and Transvaal	1·60	2·75
652/5	*Set of 4*	3·00	3·50
MS656	81×151 mm. Nos. 652/5 vertically *se-tenant*, forming a composite map design	9·00	9·50

(Des P. Lodoen. Litho National Printing & Packaging, Zimbabwe)

1988 (13 Sept). Visit of Pope John Paul II. T **162** and similar vert designs. Multicoloured. P 14×14½.

657	10t. Type **162**	2·00	20
658	15t. Pope John Paul II	2·25	30
659	30t. Pope giving blessing and outline map	2·75	70
660	80t. Pope John Paul II (different)	3·50	4·00
657/60	*Set of 4*	9·50	4·50

163 National Museum and Art Gallery

164 *Grewia flava*

(Des G. Mattsson and T. Sandberg (8t.), A. Campbell (15t.), K. Bogatsu (30t.), T. Sandberg (60t.). Litho National Printing & Packaging, Zimbabwe)

1988 (30 Sept). 20th Anniv of National Museum and Art Gallery, Gaborone. T **163** and similar vert designs. Multicoloured. P 14½.

661	8t. Type **163**	15	10
662	15t. Pottery	20	25
663	30t. Blacksmith's buffalo bellows	35	40
664	60t. Children and mobile museum van	70	1·00
661/4	*Set of 4*	1·25	1·60

(Des Verena Blomberg-Ermatinger. Litho National Printing & Packaging, Zimbabwe)

1988 (31 Oct). Flowering Plants of South-eastern Botswana. T **164** and similar vert designs. Multicoloured. P 14×14½.

665	8t. Type **164**	20	10
666	15t. *Cienfuegosia digitata*	30	25
667	40t. *Solanum seaforthianum*	60	55
668	75t. *Carissa bispinosa*	1·00	1·40
665/8	*Set of 4*	1·90	2·00

165 Basket Granary

(Des K. Mosinyi. Litho National Printing & Packaging, Zimbabwe)

1989 (13 Mar). Traditional Grain Storage. T **165** and similar vert designs. Multicoloured. P 14×14½.

669	8t. Type **165**	75	10
670	15t. Large letlole granary	1·25	40
671	30t. Pot granary	2·00	60
672	60t. Two types of serala	2·75	2·25
669/72 *Set of* 4		6·00	3·00

The use of different paper stocks led to a wide range of shades in this issue.

166 Female Red-throated Heron with Eggs

(Des P. Augustinus. Litho Harrison)

1989 (5 July). Slaty Egret. T **166** and similar horiz designs. Multicoloured. P 15×14.

673	8t. Type **166**	55	15
674	15t. Chicks in nest	75	40
675	30t. Red-throated Heron in flight	1·00	75
676	60t. Pair building nest	1·40	2·25
673/6 *Set of* 4		3·25	3·25
MS677 119×89 mm. Nos. 673/6		3·25	3·75

167 "My Work at Home" (Ephraim Seeletso)

168 *Eulophia angolensis*

(Litho Govt Printer, Pretoria)

1989 (4 Sept). Children's Paintings. T **167** and similar multicoloured designs. P 14.

678	10t. Type **167**	35	10
679	15t. "My Favourite Game" (hopscotch) (Neelma Bhatia) (vert)	50	35
680	30t. "My Favourite Toy" (clay animals) (Thabo Habana)	75	70
681	1p. "My School Day" (Thabo Olesitse)	2·00	3·25
678/81 *Set of* 4		3·25	4·00

(Des Julia Cairns. Litho Govt Printer, Pretoria)

1989 (30 Oct). Christmas. Orchids. T **168** and similar vert designs. Multicoloured. P 14.

682	8t. Type **168**	90	10
683	15t. *Eulophia hereroensis*	1·50	60
684	30t. *Eulophia speciosa*	2·00	1·00
685	60t. *Eulophia petersii*	3·50	7·00
682/5 *Set of* 4		7·00	8·00

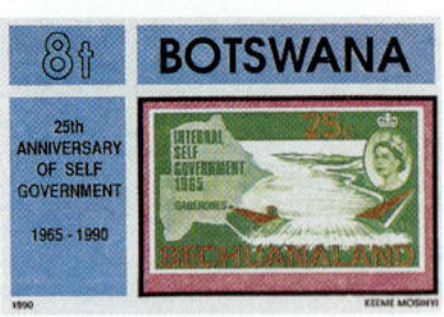

169 Bechuanaland 1965 New Constitution 25c. Stamp (25th anniv of Self-Government)

(170)

(Des K. Mosinyi. Litho National Printing & Packaging, Zimbabwe)

1990 (5 Mar). Anniversaries. T **169** and similar horiz designs. P 14½.

686	8t. multicoloured	70	15
687	15t. multicoloured	75	50
688	30t. multicoloured	3·75	1·60
689	60t. black, new blue and yellow-ochre	3·75	7·00
686/9 *Set of* 4		8·00	8·25

Designs:—15t. Casting vote in ballot box (25th anniv of First Elections); 30t. Outline map and flags of Southern African Development Coordination Conference countries (10th anniv); 60t. Penny Black (150th anniv of first postage stamp).

1990 (27 Apr). Nos. 619, 624 and 627 surch as T **170**.

690	10t. on 1t. Type **157**	60	20
	a. Surch double	†	—
691	20t. on 6t. Rusty-spotted Genet	1·00	80
692	50t. on 12t. Hippopotamus	3·50	3·50
690/2 *Set of* 3		4·50	4·00

See also Nos. 725/8.

171 Telephone Engineer

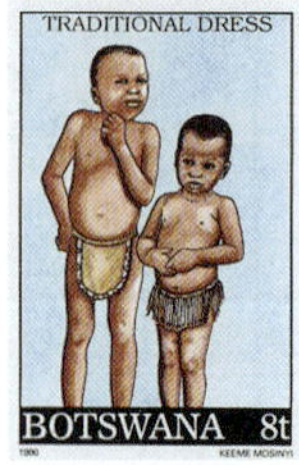

172 Young Children

(Des M. Kahn. Litho National Printing & Packaging, Zimbabwe)

1990 (3 May). "Stamp World London 90" International Stamp Exhibition. T **171** and similar vert designs. Multicoloured. P 14½.

693	8t. Type **171**	35	10
694	15t. Transmission pylon	65	40
695	30t. Public telephone	1·00	75
696	2p. Testing circuit board	3·00	6·50
693/6 *Set of* 4		4·50	7·00

(Des K. Mosinyi. Litho National Printing & Packaging, Zimbabwe)

1990 (1 Aug). Traditional Dress. T **172** and similar vert designs. Multicoloured. P 14½.

697	8t. Type **172**	45	10
698	15t. Young woman	80	40
699	30t. Adult man	1·40	70
700	2p. Adult woman	3·50	6·50
697/700 *Set of* 4		5·50	7·00
MS701 104×150 mm. Nos. 697/700		8·00	10·00
	a. 30t. and 2p. imperf vert		

173 *Acacia nigrescens*

174 Children running in front of Car

(Des Gillian Condy. Litho National Printing & Packaging, Zimbabwe)

1990 (30 Oct). Christmas. Flowering Trees. T **173** and similar vert designs. Multicoloured. P 14×14½.

702	8t. Type **173**	60	10
703	15t. *Peltophorum africanum*	95	35
704	30t. *Burkea Africana*	1·75	75
705	2p. *Pterocarpus angolensis*	3·75	7·50
702/5 *Set of* 4		6·25	8·00

(Des B. Heman-Ackah. Litho National Printing & Packaging, Zimbabwe)

1990 (7 Dec). First National Road Safety Day. T **174** and similar horiz designs. Multicoloured. P 14½.

706	8t. Type **174**	2·50	30
707	15t. Careless overtaking	3·00	1·00
708	30t. Cattle on road	3·75	2·75
706/8 *Set of* 3		8·25	3·50

175 Cattle

176 Children

(Des B. Mazebedi. Litho Questa)

1991 (4 Mar). Rock Paintings. T **175** and similar horiz designs. Multicoloured. P 14.

709	8t. Type **175**	2·25	40
710	15t. Cattle, drying frames and tree	2·75	85

711	30t. Animal hides	3·25	1·50
712	2p. Family herding cattle	6·00	10·00
709/12	*Set of* 4	13·00	11·50

Nos. 709/12 were printed on sand-grained paper which has an uneven surface.

(Des H. Methorst. Litho National Printing & Packaging, Zimbabwe)

1991 (3 June). National Census. T **176** and similar vert designs. Multicoloured. P 14.

713	8t. Type **176**	1·50	20
	a. Perf 14½	5·50	20
714	15t. Village	3·25	60
	a. Perf 14½	2·00	55
715	30t. School	2·25	1·00
	a. Perf 14½	2·25	90
716	2p. Hospital	8·00	11·00
	a. Perf 14½	8·00	11·00
713/16	*Set of* 4	12·50	11·50

177 Tourists viewing Elephants

178 *Harpagophytum procumbens*

(Des P. Lodoen. Litho Govt Printer, Pretoria)

1991 (30 Sept). African Tourism Year. Okavango Delta. T **177** and similar multicoloured designs. P 14 (2p.) or 14×14½ (others)

717	8t. Type **177**	1·75	70
718	15t. Crocodiles basking on river bank	2·00	90
719	35t. African Fish Eagles and de Havilland DHC-7 Dash Seven aircraft	4·25	3·25
720	2p. Okavango wildlife (26×44 mm)	6·00	9·00
717/20	*Set of* 4	12·50	12·50

(Des Gillian Condy. Litho Govt Printer, Pretoria)

1991 (4 Nov). Christmas. Seed Pods. T **178** and similar vert designs. Multicoloured. P 14.

721	8t. Type **178**	60	10
722	15t. *Tylosema esculentum*	1·00	40
723	30t. *Abrus precatorius*	1·75	80
724	2p. *Kigelia africana*	4·50	8·50
721/4	*Set of* 4	7·00	8·75

1992 (9 Mar). Nos. 621, 624 and 627 surch as T **170**.

725	8t. on 12t. Hippopotamus	1·50	70
	a. Surch triple	†	—
726	10t. on 12t. Hippopotamus	1·50	70
727	25t. on 6t. Rusty-spotted Genet	1·25	1·50
728	40t. on 3t. Zebra	2·25	4·00
725/8	*Set of* 4	6·00	6·25

179 *Cacosternum boettgeri*

180 Air-conditioned Carriages

(Des Julia Cairns. Litho Govt Printer, Pretoria)

1992 (23 Mar). Climbing Frogs. T **179** and similar multicoloured designs. P 14.

729	8t. Type **179**	75	30
730	10t. *Hyperolius marmoratus angolensis* (vert)	75	30
731	40t. *Bufo fenoulheti*	2·50	1·50
732	1p. *Hyperolius sp* (vert)	5·00	7·00
729/32	*Set of* 4	8·00	8·25

(Des P. Lodoen. Litho Harrison)

1992 (29 June). Deluxe Railway Service. T **180** and similar multicoloured designs. P 14.

733	10t. Type **180**	1·50	40
734	25t. Diesel locomotive No. BD001 (vert)	2·25	80
735	40t. Carriage interior (vert)	2·50	1·25
736	2p. Diesel locomotive No. BD028	3·75	7·50
733/6	*Set of* 4	9·00	9·00
MS737	127×127 mm. Nos. 733/6	13·00	13·00

181 Cheetah

(Des Judith Penny. Photo Harrison)

1992 (3 Aug). Animals. T **181** and similar horiz designs. Multicoloured. P 14½×14.

738	1t. Type **181**	40	2·00
739	2t. Spring Hare	40	2·00
740	4t. Blackfooted Cat	50	2·00
741	5t. Striped Mouse	50	1·75
742	10t. Oribi	65	10
743	12t. Pangolin	1·25	3·00
744	15t. Aardwolf	1·25	40
745	20t. Warthog	1·25	40
746	25t. Ground Squirrel	1·25	20
747	35t. Honey Badger	1·50	30
748	40t. Common Mole Rat	1·50	30
749	45t. Wild Dog	1·50	30
750	50t. Water Mongoose	1·50	35
751	80t. Klipspringer	2·50	2·50
752	1p. Lesser Bushbaby	2·50	2·50
753	2p. Bushveld Elephant Shrew	3·50	4·50
754	5p. Zorilla	5·50	8·00
755	10p. Vervet Monkey	8·00	12·00
738/55	*Set of* 18	32·00	38·00

182 Boxing

(Litho Harrison)

1992 (7 Aug). Olympic Games, Barcelona. T **182** and similar vert designs. Multicoloured. P 14×15.

756	10t. Type **182**	60	10
757	50t. Running	1·50	50
758	1p. Boxing (different)	2·00	2·50
759	2p. Running (different)	2·50	5·00
756/9	*Set of* 4	6·00	7·25
MS760	87×117 mm. Nos. 756/9	6·00	8·00

183 *Adiantum incisum*

184 Helping Blind Person (Lions Club International)

(Des Gillian Condy. Litho National Printing & Packaging, Zimbabwe)

1992 (23 Nov). Christmas. Ferns. T **183** and similar vert designs. Multicoloured. P 14½.

761	10t. Type **183**	40	10
762	25t. *Actiniopteris radiata*	70	35
763	40t. *Ceratopteris cornuta*	1·00	55
764	1p.50 *Pellaea calomelanos*	3·00	7·00
761/4	*Set of* 4	4·50	7·25

(Des Ann Nilsson. Litho National Printing & Packaging, Zimbabwe)

1993 (29 Mar). Charitable Organizations in Botswana. T **184** and similar multicoloured designs. P 14.

765	10t. Type **184**	80	20
766	15t. Nurse carrying child (Red Cross Society) (horiz)	90	40
767	25t. Woman watering seedling (Ecumenical Decade)	90	50
768	35t. Deaf children (Round Table) (horiz)	1·25	1·50

769	40t. Crowd of people (Rotary International)	1·25	1·75
770	50t. Hands at prayer (Botswana Christian Council) (horiz)	1·50	2·50
765/70	*Set of 6*	6·00	6·25

185 Bechuanaland Railways Class "6" Locomotive No. 1

186 Long-crested Eagle

(Des P. Lodoen. Litho Harrison)

1993 (24 May). Railway Centenary. T **185** and similar horiz designs. Multicoloured. P 15×14.

771	10t. Type **185**	75	40
772	40t. Class "19" locomotive No. 317	1·40	75
773	50t. Class "12" locomotive No. 256	1·40	90
774	1p.50 Class "7" locomotive No. 71	2·00	5·00
771/4	*Set of 4*	5·00	6·25
MS775	190×100 mm. Nos. 771/4	5·00	7·00

(Des J. Leath. Litho National Printing & Packaging, Zimbabwe)

1993 (30 Aug). Endangered Eagles. T **186** and similar vert designs. Multicoloured. P 14½.

776	10t. Type **186**	70	35
777	25t. Short-toed Eagle	1·25	65
778	50t. Bateleur	1·60	1·75
779	1p.50 Secretary Bird	2·50	6·50
776/9	*Set of 4*	5·50	8·25

187 *Aloe zebrina*

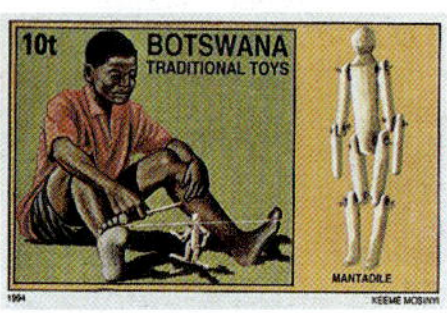

188 Boy with String Puppet

(Des Gillian Condy. Litho National Printing & Packaging, Zimbabwe)

1993 (25 Oct). Christmas. Flora. T **187** and similar vert designs. Multicoloured. P 14×14½.

780	12t. Type **187**	40	10
781	25t. *Croton megalobotrys*	60	25
782	50t. *Boophane disticha*	85	70
783	1p. *Euphoria davyi*	1·25	3·50
780/3	*Set of 4*	2·75	4·00

(Des K. Mosinyi. Litho National Printing & Packaging Zimbabwe)

1994 (28 Mar). Traditional Toys. T **188** and similar horiz designs. Multicoloured. P 14½.

784	10t. Type **188**	20	10
785	40t. Boys with clay cattle	45	30
786	50t. Boy with spinner	50	50
787	1p. Girls playing in make-believe houses	1·10	3·00
784/7	*Set of 4*	2·00	3·50

189 Interior of Control Tower, Gaborone Airport

10t■
(**190**)

(Des M. McArthur. Litho National Printing & Packaging, Zimbabwe)

1994 (30 June). 50th Anniv of International Civil Aviation Organization. T **189** and similar multicoloured designs. P 14½.

788	10t. Type **189**	40	10
789	25t. Crash tender	75	40
790	40t. Loading supplies onto Boeing 747 (vert)	1·00	85
791	50t. Control tower, Gaborone (vert)	1·00	1·75
788/91	*Set of 4*	2·75	2·75

1994 (1 Aug). No. 743 surch with T **190** by Govt Printer, Pretoria.

792	10t. on 12t. Pangolin	8·50	75

191 Lesser Flamingos at Sua Pan

192 *Ziziphus mucronata*

(Des P. Lodoen. Litho National Printing & Packaging, Zimbabwe)

1994 (26 Sept). Environment Protection. Makgadikgadi Pans. T **191** and similar multicoloured designs. P 14×14½ (vert) or 14½×14 (horiz).

793	10t. Type **191**	1·00	40
794	35t. Baobab trees (horiz)	50	40
795	50t. Zebra and palm trees	65	80
796	2p. Map of area (horiz)	3·00	6·00
793/6	*Set of 4*	4·75	6·75

(Des Gillian Condy. Litho National Printing & Packaging, Zimbabwe)

1994 (24 Oct). Christmas. Edible Fruits. T **192** and similar vert designs. Multicoloured. P 14×14½.

797	10t. Type **192**	25	10
798	25t. *Strychnos cocculoides*	40	30
799	40t. *Bauhinia petersiana*	60	70
800	50t. *Schinziphyton rautonenii*	70	1·40
797/800	*Set of 4*	1·75	2·25

193 Fisherman with Bow and Arrow

194 Boys watering Horses (FAO)

(Des B. Mazebedi. Litho National Printing & Packaging, Zimbabwe)

1995 (3 Apr). Traditional Fishing. T **193** and similar horiz designs. Multicoloured. P 14½.

801	15t. Type **193**	35	20
802	40t. Men in canoe and boy with fishing rod	60	45
803	65t. Fisherman with net	80	90
804	80t. Fisherman with basket fish trap	1·00	2·00
801/4	*Set of 4*	2·50	3·25

(Des M. McArthur. Litho National Printing & Packaging Zimbabwe)

1995 (16 Oct). 50th Anniv of United Nations. T **194** and similar vert designs. Multicoloured. P 14½.

805	20t. Type **194**	20	10
806	50t. Schoolchildren queuing for soup (WFP)	35	30
807	80t. Policeman carrying out hut census (UNDP)	1·00	1·00
808	1p. Weighing baby (UNICEF)	70	2·00
805/8	*Set of 4*	2·00	3·00

195 Brown Hyena

196 *Adenia glauca*

(Des Judith Penny. Litho Questa)

1995 (6 Nov). Endangered Species. Brown Hyena. T **195** and similar horiz designs. Multicoloured. P 14½.

809	20t. Type **195**	45	60
	a. Strip of 4. Nos. 809/12	3·00	4·50
810	50t. Pair of Hyenas	65	75

811	80t. Hyena stealing ostrich eggs	1·10	1·50
812	1p. Adult Hyena and cubs	1·25	2·25
809/12	*Set of* 4	3·00	4·50

In addition to separate sheets of 50 Nos. 809/12 were also available in sheets of 16 (4×4) with the stamps arranged *se-tenant* both horizontally and vertically.

(Des Gillian Condy. Litho National Printing & Packaging, Zimbabwe)

1995 (27 Nov). Christmas. Plants. T **196** and similar vert designs. Multicoloured. P 14.

813	20t. Type **196**	35	10
814	50t. *Pterodiscus ngamicus*	60	30
815	80t. *Sesamothamnus lugardii*	1·00	1·00
816	1p. *Fockea multiflora*	1·10	2·00
813/16	*Set of* 4	2·75	3·00

(**197**)

Different "2"
(R. 7/5, 8/5, 9/5)

1996 (12 Feb). Nos. 738/40 surch as T **197**.

817	20t. on 2t. Spring Hare	1·00	30
	a. Different "2"	8·00	2·25
818	30t. on 1t. Type **181**	1·25	30
819	70t. on 4t. Blackfooted Cat	2·00	3·25
817/19	*Set of* 3	3·75	3·50

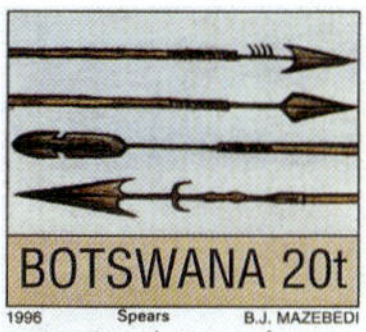

198 Spears

(Des B. Mazebedi. Litho National Printing & Packaging, Zimbabwe)

1996 (25 Mar). Traditional Weapons. T **198** and similar horiz designs. Multicoloured. P 14½×14.

820	20t. Type **198**	20	10
821	50t. Axes	35	30
822	80t. Shield and knobkerries	55	65
823	1p. Knives and sheaths	60	1·50
820/3	*Set of* 4	1·50	2·25

199 Child with Basic Radio

(Des P. Lodoen. Litho National Printing & Packaging, Zimbabwe)

1996 (3 June). Centenary of Radio. T **199** and similar vert designs. Multicoloured. P 14×14½.

824	20t. Type **199**	25	10
825	50t. Radio Botswana's mobile transmitter	40	30
826	80t. Police radio control	1·50	1·10
827	1p. Listening to radio	70	1·75
824/7	*Set of* 4	2·50	3·00

200 Olympic Flame, Rings and Wreath

(Des R. Andersson. Litho Govt Printer, Pretoria)

1996 (19 July). Centenary of Modern Olympic Games. T **200** and similar vert designs. Multicoloured. P 14.

828	20t. Type **200**	40	10
829	50t. Pierre de Coubertin (founder of modern Olympics)	60	30
830	80t. Map of Botswana with flags and athletes	1·50	1·00
831	1p. Ruins of ancient stadium at Olympia	1·00	1·60
828/31	*Set of* 4	3·25	2·50

201 Family Planning Class (Botswana Family Welfare Association)

202 *Adansonia digitata* Leaf and Blossom

(Des K. Mosinyi. Litho National Printing and Packaging, Zimbabwe)

1996 (23 Sept). Local Charities. T **201** and similar vert designs. Multicoloured. P 14½.

832	20t. Type **201**	20	10
833	30t. Blind workers (Pudulogong Rehabilitation Centre)	20	15
834	50t. Collecting seeds (Forestry Association of Botswana)	30	30
835	70t. Secretarial class (YWCA)	40	70
836	80t. Children's day centre (Botswana Council of Women)	50	80
837	1p. Children's village, Tlokweng (SOS Children's village)	60	1·50
832/7	*Set of* 6	2·00	3·25

(Des Gillian Condy. Litho National Printing and Packaging, Zimbabwe)

1996 (4 Nov). Christmas. T **202** and similar vert designs showing parts of life cycle for Adansonia digitata. Multicoloured. P 14.

838	20t. Type **202**	25	10
839	50t. Fruit	40	25
840	80t. Tree in leaf	60	75
841	1p. Tree with bare branches	70	1·60
838/41	*Set of* 4	1·75	2·40

203 Tati Hotel

204 Steam Locomotive, Bechuanaland Railway, 1897

(Des M. Smith. Litho National Printing and Packaging, Zimbabwe)

1997 (21 Apr). Francistown Centenary. T **203** and similar horiz designs. Multicoloured. P 14½×14.

842	20t. Type **203**	15	10
843	50t. Railway Station	75	35
844	80t. Company Manager's House	60	80
845	1p. Monarch Mine	1·00	1·60
842/5	*Set of* 4	2·25	2·50

(Des P. Lodoen. Litho National Printing and Packaging, Zimbabwe)

1997 (12 July). Railway Centenary. T **204** and similar vert designs. Multicoloured. P 14×14½.

846	35t. Type **204**	40	20
847	50t. Elephants crossing railway line	60	35
848	80t. First locomotive in Bechuanaland, 1897	70	45
849	1p. Beyer-Garratt type steam locomotive No. 352	75	75
850	2p. Diesel locomotive No. BD339	1·00	1·75
851	2p.50 Fantuzzi container stacker	1·25	2·25
846/51	*Set of* 6	4·25	5·25

205 Pel's Fishing Owl

205a Prince Philip with carriage

(Des Helena Schüssel. Litho Enschedé)

1997 (4 Aug). Birds. T **205** and similar multicoloured designs. P 13½×13 (vert) or 13×13½ (horiz).

852	5t. Type **205**	70	1·25
853	10t. Gymnogene (horiz)	70	1·25
854	15t. Meyer's Parrot	75	1·25
855	20t. Harlequin Quail (horiz)	80	1·25
856	25t. Marico Sunbird (horiz)	80	1·25
857	30t. Kurrichane Thrush (horiz)	85	1·25
858	40t. Redheaded Finch	90	80
859	50t. Buffalo Weaver	1·00	50
860	60t. Sacred Ibis (horiz)	1·25	1·00
861	70t. Cape Shoveler (horiz)	1·25	1·00
862	80t. Greater Honeyguide (horiz)	1·25	1·00
863	1p. Woodland Kingfisher (horiz)	1·50	1·00
864	1p.25 Purple Heron	2·00	1·75
865	1p.50 Yellow-billed Oxpecker (horiz)	2·00	2·25
866	2p. Shaft-tailed Whydah	2·25	2·50
867	2p.50 White Stork	2·75	3·00
868	5p. Sparrowhawk	4·00	4·50
869	10p. Spotted Crake	6·50	8·00
852/69	*Set of* 18	27·00	30·00

No. 861 is inscribed "Shoveller" in error.

(Des N. Shewring (No. **MS**876), D. Miller (others). Litho Questa (No. **MS**876), Cartor (others))

1997 (22 Sept). Golden Wedding of Queen Elizabeth and Prince Philip. Multicoloured T **205a** and similar vert designs. W w **14**. P 13.

870	35t. Type **205a**	20	55
	a. Horiz pair. Nos. 870/1	40	1·10
871	35t. Queen Elizabeth with binoculars	20	55
872	2p. Queen Elizabeth with horse team	90	1·50
	a. Horiz pair. Nos. 872/3	1·75	3·00
873	2p. Prince Philip and horse	90	1·50
874	2p.50 Queen Elizabeth and Prince Philip	1·10	1·50
	a. Horiz pair. Nos. 874/5	2·10	3·00
875	2p.50 Princess Anne and Prince Edward	1·10	1·50
870/5	*Set of* 6	4·00	6·25
MS876	110×70 mm. 10p. Queen Elizabeth and Prince Philip in landau (horiz). Wmk sideways. P 14×14½	4·00	5·50

Nos. 870/1, 872/3 and 874/5 were each printed together, *se-tenant*, in horizontal pairs throughout the sheets.

206 *Combretum zeyheri*

207 Baobab Trees

(Des Gillian Condy. Litho National Printing and Packaging, Zimbabwe)

1997 (10 Nov). Christmas. Plants. T **206** and similar vert designs. Multicoloured. P 14.

877	35t. Type **206**	45	10
878	1p. *Combretum apiculatum*	1·00	35
879	2p. *Combretum molle*	1·75	1·90
880	2p.50 *Combretum imberbe*	2·00	2·75
877/80	*Set of* 4	4·75	4·50

(Des A. Campbell. Litho National Printing and Packaging, Zimbabwe)

1998 (23 Mar). Tourism (1st series). T **207** and similar multicoloured designs. P 14½.

881	35t. Type **207**	25	15
882	1p. Crocodile	50	45
883	2p. Stalactites (vert)	95	1·10
884	2p.50 Tourists and rock paintings (vert)	1·25	1·60
881/4	*Set of* 4	2·75	3·00

See also Nos. 899/902.

207a Princess Diana, 1990

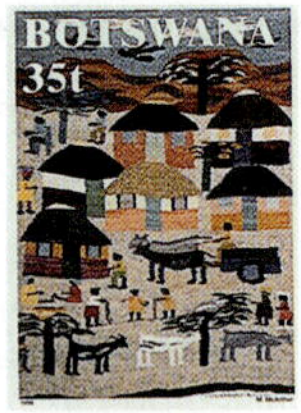

208 "Village Life" (tapestry)

(Des D. Miller. Litho Cartor)

1998 (1 June). Diana, Princess of Wales Commemoration. T **207a** and similar vert designs. Multicoloured. W w **14**. P 13.

885	35t. Type **207a**	25	15
886	1p. In green hat, 1992	40	35
887	2p. In white blouse, 1993	75	1·10
888	2p.50 With crowd, Cambridge, 1993	90	1·50
885/8	*Set of* 4	2·10	2·75
MS889	145×70 mm. As Nos. 885/8, but each with a face value of 2p.50	3·00	3·75

(Des M. McArthur. Litho Enschedé)

1998 (28 Sept). Botswana Weavers. T **208** and similar multicoloured designs. P 14×13½.

890	35t. Type **208**	30	15
891	55t. Weaver dyeing threads	40	20
892	1p. "African wildlife" (tapestry)	1·40	1·00
893	2p. Weaver at loom	1·50	2·25
890/3	*Set of* 4	3·25	3·25
MS894	68×58 mm. 2p.50, "Elephants" (tapestry) (horiz). P 13½×14	3·00	3·75

209 *Ficus ingens*

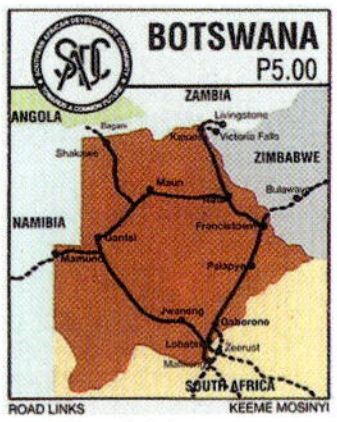

210 Road Map

(Des Gillian Condy. Litho Oriental Press, Bahrain)

1998 (30 Nov). Christmas. Plants. T **209** and similar vert designs. Multicoloured. P 13×13½.

895	35t. Type **209**	45	10
896	55t. *Ficus pygmaea*	65	20
897	1p. *Ficus abutilifolia*	1·25	55
898	2p.50 *Ficus sycomorus*	2·00	3·00
895/8	*Set of* 4	4·00	3·50

(Des A. Campbell. Litho Enschedé)

1999 (24 May). Tourism (2nd series). Multicoloured designs as T **207**. P 13½×14 (horiz) or 14×13½ (vert).

899	35t. Rock painting of men and cattle	85	25
900	55t. Expedition at salt pan	1·25	30
901	1p. Rock painting of elephant and antelope (vert)	1·50	1·40
902	2p. Tourists under Baobab tree (vert)	1·60	2·50
899/902	*Set of* 4	4·75	4·00

(Des K. Mosinyi. Litho National Printing and Packaging, Harare)

1999 (17 Aug). Southern African Development Community Day. Sheet 77×84 mm. P 14½.

MS903	**210** 5p. multicoloured	3·75	4·00

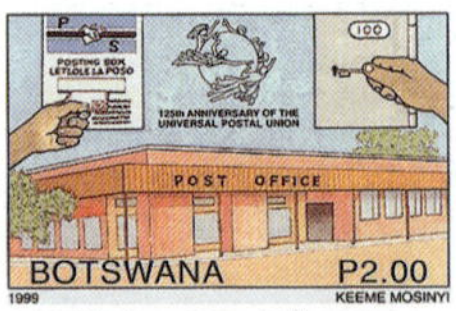

211 Modern Post Office

212 Mpule Kwelagobe winning Contest

(Des K. Mosinyi. Litho National Printing and Packaging, Zimbabwe)

1999 (9 Oct). 125th Anniv of Universal Postal Union. P 14½.

904	**211**	2p. multicoloured	2·00	2·00

(Des Seasky Design Studio. Litho Southern Colour Print, Dunedin)

1999 (1 Dec). Mpule Kwelagobe ("Miss Universe 1999"). T **212** and similar multicoloured designs. P 14½.

905	35t. Type **212**	35	10
906	1p. In traditional dress (horiz)	75	30
907	2p. In traditional dancing costume with lion	1·10	60
908	2p.50 Wearing "Botswana" sash (horiz)	1·25	75
909	15p. With leopard in background (horiz)	7·00	12·00
905/9 *Set of 5*		9·50	12·00
MS910 175×80 mm. Nos. 905/9		9·50	12·00

213 Saddle-bill Stork and Limpopo River

(Des SeaSky Design. Litho Southern Colour Print, Dunedin)

2000 (5 Apr). Scenic Rivers. T **213** and similar multicoloured designs. P 14.

911	35t. Type **213**	60	20
912	1p. Hippopotamuses in water lilies (vert)	1·00	60
913	2p. African Skimmer and makoro (dugout canoe)	1·75	1·75
914	2p.50 African elephant at sunset, Chobe River (vert)	2·00	2·50
911/14 *Set of 4*		4·75	4·50

214 Mopane Moth

(Des Donna McKenna. Litho Cartor)

2000 (19 July). Moths. T **214** and similar diamond-shaped designs. Multicoloured. P 12½.

915	35t. Type **214**	15	10
916	70t. Wild Silk Moth	25	20
917	1p. Crimson Speckled Footman ("Tiger Moth")	35	30
918	2p. African Lunar Moth	65	60
919	15p. Speckled Emperor Moth	4·75	9·00
915/19 *Set of 5*		5·50	9·00
MS920 175×135 mm. Nos. 915/19		7·50	10·00

No. **MS**920 is in the shape of a moth.

215 Mother reading Medicine Label with Child ("Protect Your Children")

(Des B. Pearce and K. Mosinyi. Litho Southern Colour Print, Dunedin)

2000 (23 Aug). United Nations Literacy Decade. T **215** and similar horiz designs. Multicoloured. P 12.

921	35t. Type **215**	20	10
922	70t. Adult literacy class ("Never Too Old To Learn")	30	20
923	2p. Man smoking next to petrol pump ("Be Aware Of Danger")	75	1·10
924	2p.50 Man at Automatic Teller Machine ("Be Independent")	90	2·00
921/4 *Set of 4*		1·90	3·00

Nos. 921/4 were each printed with *se-tenant* label (45×10 mm) at foot inscribed with the Botswana Post logo and the theme of the stamp.

216 Pres. Sir Seretse Khama

217 Doctor giving Eye Test

(Des Karen Odiam. Litho and embossed Southern Colour Print, Dunedin)

2000 (29 Sept). Chiefs and Presidents. T **216** and similar designs. P 14.

925	35t. black, orange-red and gold	50	10
926	1p. multicoloured	75	40
927	2p. multicoloured	1·25	1·40
928	2p.50 multicoloured	1·50	2·25
925/8 *Set of 4*		3·50	3·75

Designs: Horiz (60×40 mm)—35t. Chiefs Sebele I of Bakwena, Bathoen I of Bangwaketse and Khama III of Bangato, 1895 Vert (as T **216**)—2p. Pres. Sir Ketumile Masire; 2p.50, Pres. Festus Mogae.

(Des C. Abbott. Litho Cartor)

2000 (3 Nov). Airborne Medical Service. T **217** and similar vert designs. Multicoloured. P 13×13½.

929	35t. Type **217**	30	10
	a. Horiz strip of 4. Nos. 929/32 plus label.	3·25	3·75
930	1p. Medical team and family	65	40
931	2p. Cessna 502 over canoes	1·25	1·40
932	2p.50 Donkeys and mule cart on airstrip	1·50	2·25
929/32 *Set of 4*		3·25	3·75

Nos. 929/32 were printed either in sheets of one value or as *se-tenant* horizontal strips of four stamps with a central label showing the flight network. The borders along the bottom of the strip form a composite design.

218 Hippopotamus

(Des G. Ryan. Litho Enschedé)

2000 (6 Dec). Wetlands (1st series) Okavango Delta. T **218** and similar multicoloured designs. P 13½×14 (horiz) or 14×13½ (vert).

933	35t. Type **218**	50	20
934	1p. Tiger Fish and Tilapia	55	30
935	1p.75 Painted Reed Frog and Wattled Crane (vert)	1·50	1·50
936	2p. Pels Fishing Owl and Vervet Monkey (vert)	1·75	1·75
937	2p.50 Nile Crocodile, Sitatunga and Red Lechwe	1·75	1·75
933/7 *Set of 5*		5·50	5·00
MS938 175×80 mm. Nos. 933/7. P 13½		6·50	6·50

See also Nos. 958/63, 994/9 and 1009/14.

2001 (1 Feb). "HONG KONG 2001" Stamp Exhibition. No. **MS**938 optd with exhibition logo on sheet margin.

MS939 175×80 mm. Nos. 933/7	6·00	7·00

219 Diamonds

(Des D. Gunson. Litho Southern Colour Print, Dunedin)

2001 (1 Feb). Diamonds. T **219** and similar diamond-shaped designs. Multicoloured. Self-adhesive. Roul 9 (die-cut perf 10 around designs).

940	35t. Type **219**	70	35
941	1p.75 JCB in open-cast mine	1·75	2·00

942 2p. Quality inspector 2·00 2·25
943 2p.50 Diamonds in jewellery 2·50 3·00
940/3 *Set of 4* 6·25 7·00

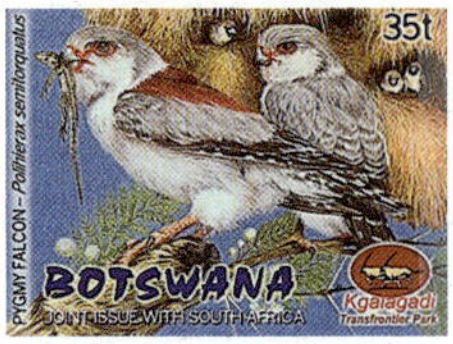

220 African Pygmy Falcon

221 Shallow Basket

(Des Karen Odiam. Litho Cartor)

2001 (12 May). Kgalagadi Transfrontier Wildlife Park. Joint Issue with South Africa. T **220** and similar horiz designs. Multicoloured. P 13.

944 35t. Type **220** 1·50 45
945 1p. Leopard 1·00 75
946 2p. Gemsbok 1·60 2·25
947 2p. Bat-eared Fox 1·60 2·25
944/7 *Set of 4* 5·25 5·25
MS948 115×80 mm. Nos. 945 and 947 2·50 3·00

(Des C. Abbott. Litho Enschedé)

2001 (30 July). Traditional Baskets. T **221** and similar vert designs. Multicoloured. P 13½.

949 35t. Type **221** 20 15
950 1p. Tall basket 35 25
951 2p. Woman weaving 60 85
952 2p.50 Spherical basket 65 95
949/52 *Set of 4* 1·60 2·00
MS953 177×92 mm. Nos. 949/52 2·00 3·50

222 Boys by River at Sunset

(Des Typeface. Litho B.D.T)

2001 (28 Sept). Scenic Skies. T **222** and similar horiz designs. Multicoloured. P 13½.

954 50t. Type **222** 35 15
955 1p. Woman with baby at sunset 60 25
956 2p. Girls carrying firewood at sunset 90 75
957 10p. Traditional village at sunset near huts 3·50 4·50
954/7 *Set of 4* 4·75 5·00

(Des G. Ryan. Litho Enschedé)

2001 (12 Dec). Wetlands (2nd series). Chobe River. Multicoloured designs as T **218**. P 13½×14 (horiz) or 14×13½ (vert).

958 50t. Water Moniter and Carmine Bee-eater 65 20
959 1p.75 Buffalo 75 60
960 2p. Savanna Baboons (vert) 90 1·00
961 2p. Lion (vert) 1·10 1·40
962 3p. African Elephants in river 2·25 2·25
958/62 *Set of 5* 5·00 5·00
MS963 175×80 mm. Nos. 958/62. P 13½ 5·00 5·00

223 Black Mamba

224 Mbukushu Pots

(Des P. Lodoen. Litho Enschedé)

2002 (22 Mar). Snakes. T **223** and similar multicoloured designs. P 14×13½ (horiz) or 13½×14 (vert).

964 50t. Type **223** 45 15
965 1p.75 Spitting Cobra (vert) 70 45
966 2p.50 Puff Adder 80 1·40
967 3p. Boomslang (vert) 1·00 1·75
964/7 *Set of 4* 2·75 3·25

(Des B. Mazebedi. Litho B.D.T.)

2002 (31 May). Botswana Pottery. T **224** and similar horiz designs. Multicoloured. P 13½.

968 50t. Type **224** 45 10
969 2p. Sekgatla pots 80 75
970 2p.50 Setswana pots 90 1·10
971 3p. Kalanga pots 1·10 1·50
968/71 *Set of 4* 3·00 3·00

225 Queen Elizabeth in Evening Dress and Commonwealth Emblem

226 Tree Squirrel

(Litho Cartor)

2002 (25 July). Golden Jubilee. T **225** and similar multicoloured design. P 13.

972 55t. Type **225** 65 15
973 2p. Queen Elzabeth with bouquet (vert) 1·75 2·00

(Des Judith Greenwood Penny. Photo Enschedé)

2002 (5 Aug). Mammals. T **226** and similar multicoloured designs. Chalk-surfaced paper. P 13½.

974 5t. Type **226** 10 30
975 10t. Black-backed Jackal 15 30
976 20t. African Wild Cat 20 40
977 30t. Slender Mongoose (horiz) 30 40
978 40t. African Civet (horiz) 50 50
a. Glazed, ordinary paper (20.11.05) 1·25 75
979 55t. Elephant 1·75 50
980 90t. Reedbuck 60 50
981 1p. Kudu 70 50
982 1p.45 Waterbuck 1·00 1·00
983 1p.95 Sable (horiz) 1·50 1·50
984 2p.20 Sitatunga (horiz) 1·50 1·50
985 2p.75 Porcupine (horiz) 1·50 1·50
986 3p.30 Serval (horiz) 1·60 1·75
987 4p. Antbear (horiz) 2·00 2·50
988 5p. Bushpig (horiz) 2·25 2·75
989 15p. Chakma Baboon 5·00 7·00
974/89 Set of 16 18·00 21·00

227 Tebelopele (councelling and testing centres) Symbol

228 Lentswe la Baratani ("Hill of Lovers")

(Des B. Mazebede. Litho Govt Printer, Pretoria)

2002 (1 Dec). AIDS Awareness. T **227** and similar vert designs. Multicoloured. P 14.

990 55t. Type **227** 60 15
991 1p.10 AIDS ribbon and mother and baby badge 1·10 40
992 2p.75 Hands and male gender symbol 1·75 2·25
993 3p.30 Orphans with foster parent 1·90 2·50
990/3 *Set of 4* 4·75 4·75

(Des G. Ryan. Litho Enschedé)

2002 (18 Dec). Wetlands (3rd series). The Makgadikgadi Pans. Multicoloured designs as T **218**. P 13½×14 (horiz) or 14×13½ (vert).

994 55t. Aardwolf 50 15
995 1p.10 Blue Wildebeest and Zebra 1·00 30
996 2p.50 Zebra (vert) 1·75 1·40
997 2p.75 Flamingo (vert) 2·25 2·50
998 3p.30 Pelican in flight 2·50 3·00
994/8 *Set of 5* 7·25 6·50
MS999 175×80 mm. Nos. 994/8. P 13½ 7·25 8·00

(Des U. Nermark. Litho Enschedé)

2003 (27 Mar). Natural Places of Interest. T **228** and similar multicoloured designs. P 13½.

1000	55t. Type **228**	35	15
1001	2p.20 Sand dunes	1·00	90
1002	2p.75 Moremi Waterfalls (vert)	1·50	2·00
1003	3p.30 Gcwihaba Cave	1·75	2·50
1000/3	Set of 4	4·25	4·50

229 Ngwale

230 San People with Birds (Cg' Ose Ntcox'o)

(Des Dr. M. Sctshogo. Litho Cartor)

2003 (12 Nov). Beetles. T **229** and similar horiz designs. Multicoloured. P 13.

1004	55t. Type **229**	40	15
1005	2p.20 Kgomo-ya-buru	1·10	80
1006	2p.75 Kgomo-ya-pula	1·40	1·75
1007	3p.30 Lebitse	1·75	2·25
1004/7	*Set of 4*	4·25	4·50
MS1008	69×59 mm. 5p.50 Kgaladuwa	5·00	5·50

(Des G. Ryan. Litho Enschedé)

2003 (23 Dec). Wetlands (4th series). The Limpopo River. Multicoloured designs as T **218**. P 13½×14 (horiz) or 14×13½ (vert).

1009	55t. Giraffe	70	35
1010	1p.45 Black Eagle and Nile Crocodile (vert)	1·50	85
1011	2p.50 Ostrich (vert)	2·00	1·50
1012	2p.75 Klipspringer	1·60	1·75
1013	3p.30 Serval Cat	1·90	2·25
1009/13	*Set of 5*	7·00	6·00
MS1014	175×80 mm. Nos. 1009/13. P 13½	7·00	8·00

(Litho Enschedé)

2004 (29 Apr). Kuru Art Project. T **230** and similar vert designs. Multicoloured. P 14.

1015	55t. Type **230**	35	20
1016	1p.45 Tree with gum (Nxaedom Qhomatca)	75	55
1017	2p.75 Tree with berries (Nxaedom Qhomatca)	1·10	1·60
1018	3p.30 Snake (Qgoma Ncokg'o)	1·50	2·00
1015/18	*Set of 4*	3·25	4·00

231 Masimo (working the land)

232 Child posting Letter

(Des K. Mosinyi. Litho B.D.T)

2004 (30 June). Traditional Life Styles. T **231** and similar horiz designs. Multicoloured. P 14.

1019	80t. Type **231**	50	25
1020	2p.10 Kgotla (village meeting place)	1·25	85
1021	3p.90 Moraka (cattle post)	1·75	2·25
1022	4p.70 Legae (compound within village)	2·25	3·00
1019/22	*Set of 4*	5·25	5·75

(Des P. Lodoen. Litho B.D.T)

2004 (9 Oct). World Post Day. T **232** and similar vert designs. Multicoloured. P 14×14½.

1023	80t. Type **232**	45	25
1024	2p.10 Children sharing a letter	1·00	85
1025	3p.90 Post man	1·60	2·25
1026	4p.70 Woman reading letter	2·00	3·00
1023/6	*Set of 4*	4·50	5·75

233 Peregrine Falcon (Angola)

234 *Pterodiscus speciosus*

(Des Anja Denker. Litho Enschedé)

2004 (9 Oct). First Joint Issue of Southern Africa Postal Operators Association Members. Sheet 170×95 mm containing T **233** and similar hexagonal designs showing national birds of Association Members. Multicoloured. P 14.

MS1027 40t. Type **233**; 50t. Two African Fish Eagles in flight (Zambia); 60t. Two African Fish Eagles perched (Zimbabwe); 70t. Bar-tailed Trogon (Malawi) (inscribed "apaloderma vittatum"); 80t. Purple-crested Turaco ("Lourie") (Swaziland); 1p. African Fish Eagle (Namibia); 2p. Stanley ("Blue") Crane (South Africa); 5p. Cattle Egret (Botswana) 13·00 14·00

The 70t. value stamp is not inscribed with the country of which the bird is a national symbol.

(Litho Cartor)

2004 (8 Dec). Christmas. Flowers. T **234** and similar vert designs. Multicoloured. P 13.

1028	80t. Type **234**	50	25
1029	2p.10 *Bulbine narcissifolia*	95	60
1030	3p.90 *Bulbiana hypogea*	1·75	2·25
1031	4p.70 *Hibiscus micranthus*	2·25	3·00
1028/31	*Set of 4*	5·00	5·50

235 Blackbeard's Store, Phalatswe

236 Cowpeas ("beans")

(Des Mike Smith. Litho BDT)

2005 (21 Mar). Historical Buildings. T **235** and similar horiz designs. Multicoloured. P 15×14.

1032	80t. Type **235**	45	25
1033	2p.10 Primary School	85	60
1034	3p.90 Telegraph Office, Phalatswe	1·60	2·25
1035	4p.70 Magistrate's Court, Phalatswe	2·00	3·00
1032/5	*Set of 4*	4·50	5·50

(Des Ann Gollifer. Litho Enschedé)

2005 (15 June). Edible Crops. T **236** and similar vert designs. Multicoloured. P 14.

1036	80t. Type **236**	40	20
1037	2p.10 Pearl millet	80	55
1038	3p.90 Sorghum	1·10	2·25
1039	4p.70 Watermelon	1·75	3·00
1036/9	*Set of 4*	4·00	5·50

237 Black-footed Cat with Prey

238 Namaqua Dove

(Des Roger Gorringe. Litho Cartor)

2005 (25 Oct). Endangered Species. Black-footed Cat (*Felis nigripes*). T **237** and similar horiz designs. Multicoloured. P 13½.

1040	80t. Type **237**	45	20
1041	2p.10 Black-footed cat	85	60

1042	3p.90 With cub	1·60	2·00
1043	4p.70 In close-up	2·00	2·75
1040/3	*Set of 4*	4·50	5·00
MS1044	160×185 mm. Nos. 1040/3, each ×2	7·00	8·50

(Des Anja Denker. Litho BDT)

2005 (20 Dec). Christmas. Doves and Pigeons. T **238** and similar vert designs. Multicoloured. P 14½×15.

1045	80t. Type **238**	50	20
1046	2p.10 Red-eyed dove	95	60
1047	3p.90 Laughing doves (pair)	1·75	2·25
1048	4p.70 Green pigeons (pair)	2·25	3·00
1045/8	*Set of 4*	5·00	5·50

80t

(238a)

P2-10

(238b)

2006 (26 Apr). Nos. 980 and 983 surch as T **238a/b**.

1048a	80t. on 90t. Reedbuck	75	35
	ab. Surch inverted		
1048b	2p.10 on 1p.95 Sable (horiz)	1·25	1·25

239 Nembwe

240 Oxen

(Des Tim Liversedge. Litho Enschedé)

2006 (30 May). Okavango Fish. T **239** and similar horiz designs. Multicoloured. P 13½×14.

1049	80t. Type **239**	50	40
1050	2p.10 Tiger fish	1·25	85
1051	3p.90 Pike	1·75	2·00
1052	4p.70 Spotted squeaker	2·25	2·75
1049/52	*Set of 4*	5·25	5·50

(Des Keeme Mosinyi. Litho Enschedé)

2006 (4 Sept). Tswana Cattle. T **240** and similar vert designs. Multicoloured. P 14×13½.

1053	1p.10 Type **240**	40	35
1054	2p.60 Cows and calves	85	75
1055	4p.10 Bulls	1·25	2·00
1056	4p.90 Horn shapes	1·50	2·25
1053/6	*Set of 4*	3·50	4·75

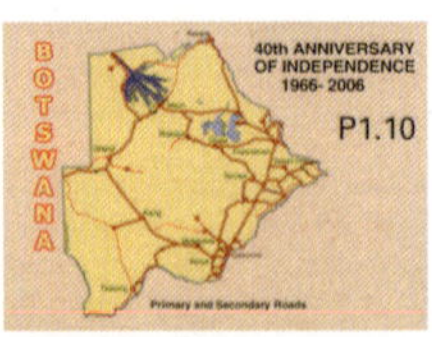

241 Road Map

(Des Lucy Phalaagae. Litho Enschedé)

2006 (29 Sept). 40th Anniv of Independence. T **241** and similar horiz designs showing maps of Botswana. Multicoloured. P 13½×14.

1057	1p.10 Type **241**	75	45
1058	2p.60 Population distribution	95	90
1059	4p.10 Mines and coal resources	2·50	2·50
1060	4p.90 National parks and game reserves	2·75	3·00
1057/60	*Set of 4*	6·25	6·25
MS1061	109×85 mm. Nos. 1057/60	7·00	8·00

Nos. 1057/**MS**1061 were expected to be issued on 29 September 2006, but did not go on sale at post offices until 19 October. First day covers, prepared in advance, were cancelled with the original date.

242 *Hyphaene petersiana*

243 Pied Kingfisher

(Des Gillian Condy. Litho Enschedé)

2006 (1 Dec). Christmas. Trees. T **242** and similar vert designs. Multicoloured. P 14×13½.

1062	1p.10 Type **242**	45	30
1063	2p.60 *Phoenix reclinata*	1·00	70
1064	4p.10 *Hyphaene petersiana*	1·50	2·00
1065	4p.90 *Phoenix reclinata*	1·75	2·50
1062/5	*Set of 4*	4·25	5·00

(Des Gwithie Kirby. Litho Enschedé)

2007 (13 Mar). Kingfishers. T **243** and similar vert designs. Multicoloured. P 14×13½.

1066	1p.10 Type **243**	60	45
1067	2p.60 Malachite kingfisher	1·40	1·00
1068	4p.10 Woodland kingfisher	2·00	2·25
1069	4p.90 Brown-hooded kingfisher	2·50	3·00
1066/9	*Set of 4*	6·00	6·00

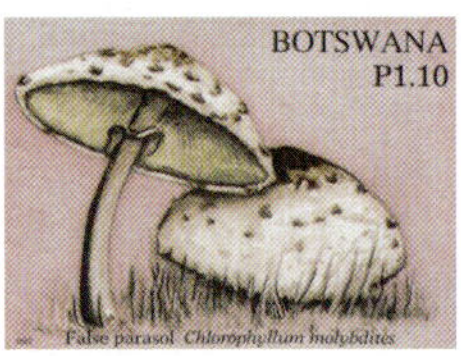

244 *Chlorophyllum molybdites* (false parasol)

245 Nyala (pair) (Malawi)

(Des Ann Gollifer. Litho Enschedé)

2007 (31 July). Fungi. T **244** and similar horiz designs. Multicoloured. P 13½×14.

1070	1p.10 Type **244**	40	30
1071	2p.60 *Phlebopus sudanicus* (bushveld bolete)	90	80
1072	4p.10 *Ganoderma lucidum* (laquered bracket fungus)	1·50	1·75
1073	4p.90 *Geastrum triplex* (collared earthstar)	1·75	2·00
1070/3	*Set of 4*	4·00	4·25

(Des Anja Denker. Litho and die-stamped Enschedé)

2007 (9 Oct). Second Joint Issue of Southern Africa Postal Operators Association Members. T **245** and similar square designs showing national animals of association members. Multicoloured. P 14.

1074	1p.10 Type **245**	40	30
1075	2p.60 Nyala (Zimbabwe)	90	80
1076	4p.10 Oryx (Namibia)	1·50	1·75
1077	4p.90 African buffalo (Zambia)	1·75	2·00
1078	5p.50 Burchell's zebra (Botswana)	2·25	2·50
1074/8	*Set of 5*	6·00	6·50
MS1079	135×170 mm. Nos. 1074/9	7·00	7·50

Miniature sheets containing similar designs were also issued by Malawi, Namibia, Zambia and Zimbabwe. Zambia also issued sheet stamps.

246 Students and Tutor (University of Botswana Library)

(Des Jack Mazebedi. Litho Austrian State Ptg Wks)

2007 (13 Oct). 25th Anniv of University of Botswana. T **246** and similar horiz designs. Multicoloured. P 14.

1080	1p.10 Type **246**	35	30
1081	2p.60 Farmers and Sir Seretse Khama (first Botswana President) (BUCA campus appeal)	75	70
1082	4p.10 Researcher, village and wetland (Okavango Research)	1·25	1·50
1083	4p.90 Students and university buildings ('Infrastructure; old and new')	1·75	2·00
1080/3	*Set of* 4	3·50	4·00

247 Mimosa Sapphire (*Iolaus mimosae mimosae*)

248 Traditional Dancer (Boitshepo Lesego)

(Des Philip Huebsch. Litho Enschedé)

2007 (1 Nov). Butterflies. T **247** and similar horiz designs. Multicoloured. P 13½×14.

1084	10t. Type **247**	10	10
1085	20t. Bushveld orange-tip (*Colotis pallene*)	10	10
1086	30t. African monarch (*Danaus chrysippus aegyptius*)	10	10
1087	40t. Common black-eye (*Gonatomyrina gorgias gorgias*)	15	20
1088	50t. Brown playboy (*Virachola antalus*)	25	30
1089	1p. Sapphire (*Lolaus silas*)	50	55
1090	(1p.10) Scarlet tip (*Colotis* (C) *danae annae*)	55	60
1091	2p. Large blue emperor (*Charaxes bohemani*)	65	70
1092	(2p.60) Dwarf blue (*Oraidium barberae*)	70	75
1093	3p. Apricot playboy (*Virachola dinochares*)	80	85
1094	4p. Blue pansy (*Junonia oenone oenone*)	90	95
1095	5p. Black-striped hairtail (*Anthene amarah amarah*)	1·10	1·25
1096	10p. Natal barred blue (*Spindasis natalensis*)	2·25	2·40
1097	20p. Foxy charaxes (C.) (*jasius saturnus*)	4·50	4·75
1084/97	*Set of* 14	11·50	12·00

No. 1090 was inscr 'Standard Postage A' and sold for 1p.10. No. 1092 was inscr 'Standard Postage B' and sold for 2p.60.

(Adapted Paul Melenhurst. Litho Austrian State Ptg Wks)

2008 (28 Mar). Artists in Botswana. T **248** and similar multicoloured designs showing winning entries in stamp design competition. P 14.

1098	1p.10 Type **248**	35	30
1099	2p.60 Baobab tree (Philip Huebsch)	75	70
1100	4p.10 Girl playing with dolls (Giel Kgamane)	1·25	1·40
1101	4p.90 Donkeys tired after hard work (Tineni Kepaletswe) (horiz)	1·60	2·00
1102	5p.50 Donkeys in the city (Andrew Jones) (horiz)	1·90	2·40
1098/1102	*Set of* 5	5·25	6·00

249 Hunter and Guide facing Bull Elephant

250 Athletes

(Des Philip Huebsch. Litho Austrian State Ptg Wks, Vienna)

2008 (20 June). Elephants in Botswana. T **249** and similar vert designs. Multicoloured. P 14.

1103	1p.10 Type **249**	75	45
1104	2p.60 Tourists photographing female elephant with baby from dugout canoe	1·50	90
1105	4p.10 Villagers chasing crop raiding elephant	2·25	2·25
1106	4p.90 Elephant-back safari in Okavango Delta	2·50	2·75
1103/6	*Set of* 4	6·25	5·75

(Des Keeme Mosinyi and Ulf Nermark. Litho Southern Colour Print, New Zealand)

2008 (8 Aug). Olympic Games, Athens. T **250** and similar vert design. Multicoloured. P 14.

1107	1p.10 Type **250**	45	40
1108	2p.60 Boxers	80	85

251 Pitse Ya Naga Launch

252 Plaque for "The No. 1 Ladies Detective Agency" and Precious Ramotswe

2008 (29 Sept). 40th Anniv of Botswana National Museum. T **251** and similar multicoloured designs. P 14.

1109	1p.10 Type **251**	35	30
1110	2p.60 Botanical Garden (vert)	65	60
1111	4p.10 New Museum Galleries	1·25	1·25
1112	4p.90 Rock painting, Tsodilo Hills	1·60	2·00
1113	5p.50 Official opening (vert)	1·75	2·25
1109/13	Set 5	5·00	5·75

(Des Ulf Nermark. Litho Southern Colour Print, New Zealand)

2008 (30 Oct). Events of Botswana 2008. T **252** and similar multicoloured designs. P 14.

1114	4p.10 Type **252** (Botswana Movie Premiere of "The No. 1 Ladies Detective Agency")	1·25	1·25
1115	4p.90 Heart within heart (launch of Heart Foundation) (vert)	1·60	1·75
1116	5p.50 DTC Building (launch of Diamond Trading Company Botswana)	1·90	2·25
1114/16	*Set of* 3	4·25	4·75

253 *Gymnopleurus humanus* (small green dung beetle)

254 Lesser Flamingo

(Des Nancy Horenburg. Litho Enschedé)

2008 (1 Dec). Beetles of Botswana. T **253** and similar horiz designs. Multicoloured. P 14×13.

1117	1p.10 Type **253**	60	40
1118	2p.60 *Cheilomenes lunata* (lunate ladybird)	1·25	90
1119	4p.10 *Pachnoda sinuata* (garden fruit chafer)	1·75	1·90
1120	4p.90 *Eleodes sp.* (darkling beetle)	2·00	2·25
1117/20	*Set of* 4	5·00	5·00

(Des Mary Lane-Jones. Litho Austrian State Ptg Wks, Vienna)

2009 (5 June). Threatened Birds of Botswana. T **254** and similar multicoloured designs. P 14.

1121	1p.10 Type **254**	55	40
1122	2p.60 Grey crowned crane (horiz)	1·25	90
1123	4p.10 Wattled crane (horiz)	1·60	1·75
1124	4p.90 Blue crane (horiz)	1·90	2·25
1121/4	*Set of* 4	4·75	4·75

255 Boy and Girl reading ('Education')

(Des Karin Malan. Litho Austrian State Ptg Wks, Vienna)

2009 (11 Sept). Children of Botswana. T **255** and similar multicoloured designs. P 14.

1125	1p.10 Type **255**	45	40
1126	2p.60 Boy washing hands under tap ('Sanitation') (vert)	90	80
1127	4p.10 Giving girl oral vaccine ('Inoculation') (vert)	1·50	1·60
1128	4p.90 Woman with children ('Orphan Care')	1·75	2·00
1125/8	*Set of* 4	4·25	4·25

256 Southern Cross over Tsodilo World Heritage Site and Giraffes

(Des Paul Melenhorst. Litho Austrian State Ptg Wks, Vienna)

2009 (18 Nov). Night Skies. T **256** and similar horiz designs. Multicoloured. P 13½.

1129	1p.10 Type **256**	45	40
1130	2p.60 Meteorite over Okavango Delta and Ju/'hoansi firing arrows	90	80
1131	4p.10 Moon, Jupiter and Venus over central Kalahari and three Setswana women	1·50	1·60
1132	4p.90 Solar eclipse over Setswana village and trickster lion from Naro story	1·75	2·00
1129/32	*Set of* 4	4·25	4·25

257 Honey Bee alighting on Flower

(Des G. Condy. Litho Enschedé)

2010 (25 Mar). Honey Bees. T **257** and similar horiz designs. Multicoloured. P 14×13½.

1133	1p.10 Type **257**	35	30
1134	2p.60 Two bees on honeycomb	75	70
1135	4p.10 Bee's nest in tree	1·25	1·40
1136	4p.90 Bee gathering pollen from flower	1·60	1·75
1133/5	*Set of* 3	3·50	3·75

258 Player, Football, Botswana Flag and Zakumi Mascot

2010 (9 Apr). Third Joint Issue of Southern Africa Postal Operators Association Members. World Cup Football Championship, South Africa. T **258** and similar circular designs, each showing Zakumi mascot, different silhouettes of players on football and the national flag of a member country. Multicoloured. P 13½.

1137	1p.10 Type **258**	10	10
1138	2p.60 Namibia	70	75
1139	3p. South Africa	80	85
1140	4p. Zimbabwe	90	95
1141	4p.10 Malawi	1·00	1·10
1142	4p.90 Swaziland	1·40	1·50
1143	5p.50 Mauritius	1·50	1·75
1144	6p.60 Lesotho	1·75	1·90
1145	8p.20 Zambia	2·25	2·40
1137/45	*Set of* 9	9·25	10·00
MS1146	188×167 mm. As Nos. 1137/45 but with gold foil background	9·25	10·00

Nos. 1137/45 and the stamps within **MS**1146 were each perforated in a circle contained within an outer perforated square.

Stamps from **MS**1146 have a shiny gold background; the sheet stamps have a matt gold background.

Similar designs were issued by Lesotho, Malawi, Mauritius, Namibia, South Africa, Swaziland, Zambia and Zimbabwe.

259 Family watching Television ('Coal for National Power Grid')

(Des Philip Huebsch. Litho Austrian State Ptg Wks, Vienna)

2010 (8 Oct). Energy Sources and Uses. T **259** and similar multicoloured designs. P 14.

1147	2p.60 Type **259**	70	75
1148	4p.10 Woman using mobile phone and solar panel ('Solar Power Voltaic Panels')	1·00	1·10
1149	5p.50 Diesel locomotive	1·50	1·75
1150	6p.10 Compact fluorescent light bulb ('CFLs Save Money and Energy') (horiz)	1·75	1·90
1147/50	*Set of* 4	4·50	5·00

STAMP BOOKLETS

B **1**

1989 (1 Dec)–**92**. Covers as Type B **1** printed in blue on coloured card, each showing different stamp and postal logo. Stapled.

SB1	20t. booklet containing 2t. (No. 620) in block of 10 (white cover)	1·00
SB2	40t. booklet containing 2t. (No. 620) in block of 20 (white cover)	1·25
SB3	50t. booklet containing 5t. (No. 623) in block of 10 (claret cover)	1·25
SB4	80t. booklet containing 8t. (No. 625) in block of 10 (grey cover)	1·60
	a. Containing 8t. on 12t. (No. 725) (1992)	
SB5	1p. booklet containing 5t. (No. 623) in block of 20 (claret cover)	1·75
SB6	1p. booklet containing 10t. (No. 626) in block of 10 (cinnamon cover)	1·75
	a. Containing 10t. on 1t. (No. 690) (1990)	
	b. Containing 10t. on 12t. (No. 726) (1992)	
SB7	1p.50 booklet containing 15t. (No. 628) in block of 10 (pink cover)	2·50
SB8	1p.60 booklet containing 8t. (No. 625) in block of 20 (grey cover)	2·75
	a. Containing 8t. on 12t. (No. 725) (1992)	
SB9	2p. booklet containing 10t. (No. 626) in block of 20 (cinnamon cover)	3·00
	a. Containing 10t. on 1t. (No. 690) (1990)	
	b. Containing 10t. on 12t. (No. 726) (1992)	
SB10	2p. booklet containing 20t. (No. 629) in block of 10 (pale blue cover)	3·00
	a. Containing 20t. on 6t. (No. 691) (1990)	
SB11	13p. booklet containing 15t. (No. 628) in block of 20 (pink cover)	4·00
SB12	3p. booklet containing 30t. (No. 631) in block of 10 (lemon cover)	4·00
SB13	4p. booklet containing 20t. (No. 629) in block of 20 (pale blue cover)	4·50
SB14	4p. booklet containing 40t. (No. 633) in block of 10 (pale green cover)	4·50
	a. Containing 40t. on 3t. (No. 728) (1992)	
	b. Error. Containing 50t. on 12t. (No. 692) (1990).	
SB15	6p. booklet containing 30t. (No. 631) in block of 20 (lemon cover)	7·00
SB16	8p. booklet containing 40t. (No. 633) in block of 20 (pale green cover)	9·00
	a. Containing 40t. on 3t. (No. 728) (1992)	

The booklets of twenty are larger, 81×69 mm.

No. SB14b, which was produced in error, has the face value of the booklet amended in manuscript.

B **2**

1993 (4 Oct)–**94**. Covers as Type B **2** printed in black on coloured card, each showing different stamp with postal logo. Stapled.

SB17	1p. booklet containing 10t. (No. 742) in strip of 10 (yellow cover)	1·25
	a. Containing 10t. on 12t. (No. 792)(1994)	1·25
SB18	1p.20 booklet containing 12t. (No. 743) in strip of 10 (pale orange cover)	1·50
SB19	1p.50 booklet containing 15t. (No. 744) in strip of 10 (orange cover)	1·75
SB20	2p. booklet containing 10t. (No. 742) in block of 20 (yellow cover)	2·00
	a. Containing 10t. on 12t. (No. 792) (1994)	2·00
SB21	2p. booklet containing 20t. (No. 745) in strip of 10 (white cover)	2·00
SB22	2p.40 booklet containing 12t. (No. 743) in block of 20 (pale orange cover)	9·00
SB23	2p.50 booklet containing 25t. (No. 746) in strip of 10 (pink cover)	2·25
SB24	3p. booklet containing 15t. (No. 744) in block of 20 (orange cover)	2·50
SB25	3p.50 booklet containing 35t. (No. 747) in strip of 10 (green cover)	4·00
SB26	4p. booklet containing 20t. (No. 745) in block of 20 (white cover)	3·50
SB27	4p. booklet containing 40t. (No. 748) in strip of 10 (blue cover)	3·50
SB28	4p.50 booklet containing 45t. (No. 749) in strip of 10 (pale rose-lilac cover)	3·75
SB29	5p. booklet containing 25t. (No. 746) in block of 20 (pink cover)	4·00
SB30	5p. booklet containing 50t. (No. 750) in strip of 10 (grey cover)	4·00
SB31	7p. booklet containing 35t. (No. 747) in block of 20 (green cover)	4·75
SB32	8p. booklet containing 40t. (No. 748) in block of 20 (blue cover)	5·00
SB33	9p. booklet containing 45t. (No. 749) in block of 20 (pale rose-lilac cover)	5·50
SB34	10p. booklet containing 50t. (No. 750) in block of 20 (grey cover)	6·00

The booklets of twenty are larger, 75×80 mm.

1996. Covers as Nos. SB17 and SB21 cut down to 75×40 mm. Stamps attached by selvedge.

SB35	1p. booklet containing 5t. and 15t. (Nos. 741 and 744) each in strip of 5 (yellow cover)	
SB36	1p. booklet containing 20t. (No. 809) in strip of 5 (white cover)	

Nos. SB35/6 were issued from machines at Gaborone and Francistown Main Post Offices. They were subsequently replaced by booklets with plain white covers containing 1p. worth of current stamps attached by the selvedges.

B **3**

2002 (29 Apr)–**04**. Covers as Type B **3**. Stamps attached by selvedge.

SB37	5p. booklet containing 50t. (No. 954) in strip of 10	40·00
SB38	5p. booklet containing 50t. (No. 958) in strip of 10	40·00
SB39	5p. booklet containing 50t. (No. 964) in strip of 10	40·00
SB40	5p. booklet containing 50t. (No. 968) in strip of 10	40·00
SB41	5p. booklet containing 55t. (No. 972) in strip of 10	40·00
SB42	5p. booklet containing 55t. (No. 979) in strip of 10	40·00
SB43	5p. booklet containing 55t. (No. 990) in strip of 10	40·00
SB44	5p. booklet containing 55t. (No. 994) in strip of 10	40·00
SB45	5p. booklet containing 55t. (No. 1000) in strip of 10 (2003)	40·00
SB46	5p. booklet containing 55t. (No. 1004) in block of 10 (2003)	40·00
SB47	5p. booklet containing 55t. (No. 1009) in strip of 10 (2003)	40·00
SB48	5p. booklet containing 55t. (No. 1015) in strip of 10 (2004)	40·00

Nos. SB41/8 sold for 5p.50.

No. SB45 has been reported with the pane in block of 10 (2×5).

POSTAGE DUE STAMPS

BECHUANALAND PROTECTORATE (D **1**)

BECHUANALAND
PROTECTORATE
(D **2**)

1926 (1 Jan). Nos. D9/10 and D13 of Great Britain, optd with Types D **1** or D **2** (2d.).

D1	½d. emerald (wmk sideways - inverted)	11·00	£120
D2	1d. carmine	11·00	75·00
D3	2d. agate	11·00	90·00
D1/3 *Set of 3*		30·00	£250

The watermark shows Crown to the left of GvR on D1 and to the right of GvR on D2/3, *as seen from the back of the stamp*.

D **3**

Normal

Large "d."
(R. 9/6, 10/6)

2d. Serif on "d" (R. 1/6)

(Typo D.L.R.)

1932 (12 Dec)–**58**. Ordinary paper. Wmk Mult Script CA. P 14.

D4	D **3**	½d. sage-green	6·00	60·00
D5		1d. carmine	7·00	9·00
		a. Chalk-surfaced paper (27.11.58)	1·50	28·00
D6		2d. violet	9·00	60·00
		a. Large "d"	£150	
		b. Serif on "d"	£225	
		c. Chalk-surfaced paper (27.11.58)	1·75	22·00
		ca. Large "d"	40·00	
		cb. Serif on "d"	55·00	
D4/6c *Set of 3*			8·50	80·00
D4s/6s Perf "SPECIMEN" *Set of 3*			90·00	

No. D6a/b first occurred on the 1947 printing.

1c (I) (Small)

1c (II) (Large)

1961 (14 Feb). Surch as T **27**. Chalk-surfaced paper (Nos. D7/8).

D7	D **3**	1c. on 1d. (Type I)	25	50
		a. Type II (Apr)	15	1·75
		ab. Double surch	£275	
		ac. Ordinary paper	18·00	60·00
D8		2c. on 2d. (Type I)	25	1·50
		a. Large "d"	9·00	
		b. Serif on "d"	15·00	

	c. Type II	15	2·00
	ca. Large "d"	6·50	
	cb. Serif on "d"	12·00	
	d. Ordinary paper. Type II	£140	£150
	da. Large "d"	£650	
D9	5c. on ½d.	20	60
D7/9	*Set of* 3	45	2·40

1961 (15 Nov). As Type D **3** but values in cents. Chalk-surfaced paper. Wmk Mult Script CA. P 14.

D10	1c. carmine	30	2·00
D11	2c. violet	30	2·00
D12	5c. green	50	2·00
D10/12	*Set of* 3	1·00	5·50

REPUBLIC OF

BOTSWANA

(D **4**)

1967 (1 Mar). Nos. D10/12 optd with Type D **4**.

D13	1c. carmine	15	1·75
D14	2c. violet	15	1·75
D15	5c. green	20	1·75
D13/15	*Set of* 3	45	4·75

(Des and litho B.W.)

1971 (9 June). P 13½.

D16	D **5**	1c. carmine	1·10	3·25
D17		2c. bluish violet	1·40	3·50
D18		6c. sepia	1·75	5·50
D19		14c. blue-green	2·00	7·50
D16/19		*Set of* 4	5·50	18·00

(Des M. Bryan. Litho Govt Printer, Pretoria)

1977 (18 Apr)–**84**. P 12½.

D20	D **6**	1t. black and vermilion (1978)	1·25	2·75
		a. Black and bright orange (1980)	1·75	3·00
		b. Perf 14 (1982?)	1·00	2·75
D21		2t. black and emerald	40	3·25
		a. Perf 14 (5.8.81*)	1·00	3·25
D22		4t. black and red	40	3·25
		a. Perf 14 (28.9.81*)	1·00	3·25
D23		10t. black and deep ultramarine	40	3·00
		a. Perf 14 (7.3.84)	1·00	3·00
D24		16t. black and chestnut	65	3·75
		a. Perf 14 (7.3.84)	1·25	3·75
D20/24		*Set of* 5	2·75	14·50
D20b/24a		*Set of* 5	4·75	14·50

*First supplies of Nos. D20b, D21a and D22a were sent to Botswana in June 1981. The dates quoted for the 2t. and 4t. are earliest known dates of use. Early use of the 1t. has yet to be identified.

Nos. D20b/4a are on white paper. A subsequent printing in September 1988 was on poorer grade paper. Stamps perforated 14 measure 24 mm across from perforation to perforation.

Two Types of Nos. D25/9 (Zimbabwe ptgs):—

Type I

Type II

Type I. Grass sparse. No shading dots on zebra. Zebra's right ear has right edge missing.

Type II. Grass thicker. Shading dots on zebra. Right ear almost complete.

(Litho National Printing & Packaging, Zimbabwe)

1989 (1 Apr)–**96**. P 14½.

D25	D **6**	1t. black and reddish orange (I)	30	1·00
		a. Type II. Perf 14 (1993)	60	1·25
		ab. Perf 14½	10	20
D26		2t. black and emerald (I)	30	1·00
		a. Type II. Perf 14 (1993)	60	1·25
		ab. Perf 14½	10	20
D27		4t. black and bright scarlet (I)	30	1·00
		a. Type II. Perf 14 (1993)	60	1·25
		ab. Perf 14½	10	20
D28		10t. black and deep ultramarine (I)	35	1·00
		a. Type II. Perf 14 (1993)	60	1·25
		ab. Perf 14½	15	20
D29		16t. black and reddish brown (I)	50	1·25
		a. Type II. Perf 14 (1993)	70	1·50
		ab. Perf 14½	25	35
D25/9		*Set of* 5	1·60	4·75
D25a/9a		*Set of* 5	2·50	5·75

Nos. D25a/9a measure 26 mm across from perforation to perforation.

POSTAL FISCAL STAMPS

The following stamps issued for fiscal purposes were each allowed to be used for postal purposes for a short time. No. F2 was used by the public because the word "POSTAGE" had not been obliterated and No. F3 because the overprint did not include the words "Revenue only" as did the contemporary fiscal overprints for Basutoland and Swaziland.

Bechuanaland		**Bechuanaland**
Protectorate	**£5**	**Protectorate.**
(F **1**)	(F **2**)	(F **3**)

1910 (July). No. 266a of Transvaal optd with Type F **1** by Transvaal Govt Ptg Wks, Pretoria.

F1	6d. black and brown-orange (Bl-Blk)	£170	£350

No. F1 was supplied to Assistant Commissioners in January 1907 for revenue purposes. The "POSTAGE" inscription was not obliterated, however, and the stamp is known postally used for a period of a year from July 1910.

1918. No. 15 surch with Type F **2** at top.

F2 **4** £5 on 1s. green and black (F.C. £800)

1921. No. 4b of South Africa optd with Type F **3**, in varying positions.

F3	1d. scarlet	42·00	£130
	a. Opt double, one albino	£160	

Lesotho

Stamps of CAPE OF GOOD HOPE were used in Basutoland from about 1876, initially cancelled by upright oval with framed number type postmarks of that colony. Cancellation numbers known to have been used in Basutoland are 133 (Quthing), 156 (Mafeteng), 210 (Mohaleshoek), 277 (Morija), 281 (Maseru), 317 (Thlotse Heights) and 688 (Teyateyaneng).

From 1910 until 1933 the stamps of SOUTH AFRICA were in use. Stamps of the Union provinces are also known used in Basutoland during the early years of this period and can also be found cancelled-to-order during 1932–33.

The following post offices and postal agencies existed in Basutoland before December 1933. Stamps of Cape of Good Hope or South Africa with recognisable postmarks from them are worth a premium. For a few of the smaller offices or agencies there are, as yet, no actual examples recorded. Dates given are those generally accepted as the year in which the office was first opened.

- Bokong (1931)
- Butha Buthe (1907)
- Jonathan's (1927)
- Khabos (1927)
- Khetisas (1930)
- Khukhune (1933)
- Kolonyama (1914)
- Kueneng (1914)
- Leribe (1890)
- Mafeteng (1874)
- Majara (1912)
- Makhoa (1932)
- Makoalis (1927)
- Mamathes (1919)
- Mapoteng (1925)
- Marakabeis (1932)
- Maseru (1872)
- Maseru Rail (1915?)
- Mashai (1929)
- Matsaile (1930)
- Mekading (1914)
- Mofokas (1915)
- Mohaleshoek (1873)
- Mokhotlong (1921)
- Morija (1884)
- Motsekuoa (1915)
- Mount Morosi (1918)
- Mphotos (1914)
- Peka (1908)
- Phamong (1932)
- Pitseng (1921)
- Qachasnek (1895)
- Qalo (1923?)
- Quthing (1882)
- Rankakalas (1933)
- Roma Mission (1913)
- Sebapala (1930)
- Seforong (1924)
- Sehlabathebe (1921)
- Sekake (1931)
- Teyateyaneng (1886)
- Thaba Bosigo (1913)
- Thabana Morena (1922)
- Thabaneng (1914)
- Thaba Tseka (1929)
- Thlotse Heights (1872)
- Tsepo (1923)
- Tsoelike (1927)
- Tsoloane (1918)

For further details of the postal history of Basutoland see *The Cancellations and Postal Markings of Basutoland/Lesotho* by A. H. Scott, published by Collectors Mail Auctions (Pty) Ltd, Cape Town, from which the above has been, with permission, extracted.

PRICES FOR STAMPS ON COVER TO 1945	
Nos. 1/19	*from* × 5
Nos. 11/14	*from* × 6
Nos. 15/17	*from* × 10
Nos. 18/28	*from* × 6
Nos. 29/31	*from* × 10
Nos. O1/4	*from* × 4
Nos. D1/2	*from* × 25

CROWN COLONY

1 King George V, Nile Crocodile and Mountains

(Recess Waterlow)

1933 (1 Dec). Wmk Mult Script CA. P 12½.

1	**1**	½d. emerald	1·00	1·75
2		1d. scarlet	75	1·25
3		2d. bright purple	1·00	80
4		3d. bright blue	75	1·25
5		4d. grey	2·25	7·00
6		6d. orange-yellow	2·25	1·75
7		1s. red-orange	3·00	4·50
8		2s.6d. sepia	32·00	50·00
9		5s. violet	60·00	80·00
10		10s. olive-green	£170	£180
1/10 *Set of* 10			£250	£300
1s/10s Perf "SPECIMEN" *Set of* 10			£300	

Diagonal line by turret (Plate 2A R. 10/1 and 10/2)

Dot to left of chapel (Plate 2B R. 8/3)

Dot by flagstaff (Plate 4 R. 8/4)

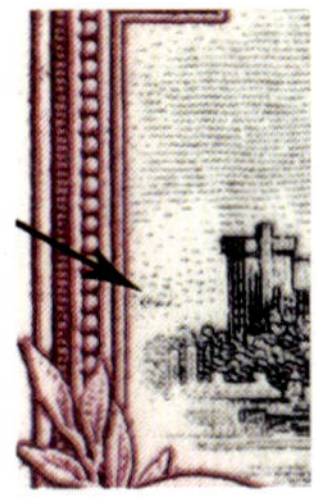

Dash by turret (Plate 4 R. 3/6)

1935 (4 May). Silver Jubilee. As Nos. 111/14 of Botswana. P 13½×14.

11	1d. deep blue and carmine	55	3·00
	f. Diagonal line by turret	£140	£200
12	2d. ultramarine and grey	65	3·00
	f. Diagonal line by turret	£140	£200
	g. Dot to left of chapel	£225	£300
	i. Dash by turret	£275	
13	3d. brown and deep blue	3·75	7·00
	g. Dot to left of chapel	£225	£325
	h. Dot by flagstaff	£325	
	i. Dash by turret	£350	
14	6d. slate and purple	3·75	7·00
	g. Dot to left of chapel	£425	
	h. Dot by flagstaff	£350	£400
	i. Dash by turret	£375	
11/14 *Set of* 4		8·00	18·00
11s/14s Perf "SPECIMEN" *Set of* 4		£140	

1937 (12 May). Coronation. As Nos. 115/17 of Botswana, but printed by D.L.R. P 14.

15	1d. scarlet	35	1·25
16	2d. bright purple	50	1·25
17	3d. bright blue	60	1·25
15/17 *Set of* 3		1·25	3·25
15s/17s Perf "SPECIMEN" *Set of* 3		£110	

2 King George VI, Nile Crocodile and Mountains

1d. Tower flaw (R. 2/4)

(Recess Waterlow)

1938 (1 Apr). Wmk Mult Script CA. P 12½.

18	**2**	½d. green	30	1·25
19		1d. scarlet	50	70
		a. Tower flaw	£170	£190
20		1½d. light blue	40	50
21		2d. bright purple	30	60
22		3d. bright blue	30	1·25

23	4d. grey	1·50	3·75
24	6d. orange-yellow	2·50	1·50
25	1s. red-orange	2·50	1·00
26	2s.6d. sepia	16·00	8·50
27	5s. violet	40·00	9·50
28	10s. olive-green	40·00	20·00
18/28	*Set of* 11	90·00	45·00
18s/28s	Perf "SPECIMEN" *Set of* 11	£300	

Basutoland

(**3**)

1945 (3 Dec). Victory. Stamps of South Africa, optd with T **3**, inscr alternately in English and Afrikaans.

			Un pair	*Used pair*	*Used single*
29	**55**	1d. brown and carmine	50	80	10
30	**56**	2d. slate-blue and violet	50	60	10
31	**57**	3d. deep blue and blue	50	85	15
29/31		*Set of* 3	1·40	2·00	30

4 King George VI

5 King George VI and Queen Elizabeth

6 Queen Elizabeth II as Princess, and Princess Margaret

7 The Royal Family

(Recess Waterlow)

1947 (17 Feb). Royal Visit. Wmk Mult Script CA. P 12½.

32	**4**	1d. scarlet	10	10
33	**5**	2d. green	10	10
34	**6**	3d. ultramarine	10	10
35	**7**	1s. mauve	15	10
32/5		*Set of* 4	40	30
32s/5s		Perf "SPECIMEN" *Set of* 4	£120	

1948 (1 Dec). Royal Silver Wedding. As Nos. 136/7 of Botswana.

36	1½d. ultramarine	20	10
37	10s. grey-olive	45·00	48·00

1949 (10 Oct). 75th Anniv of Universal Postal Union. As Nos. 138/41 of Botswana.

38	1½d. blue	20	1·50
39	3d. deep blue	2·00	2·00
40	6d. orange	1·00	5·00
41	1s. red-brown	50	1·40
38/41	*Set of* 4	3·25	9·00

1953 (3 June). Coronation. As No. 120 of Botswana.

42	2d. black and reddish purple	40	40

8 Qiloane

9 Orange River

10 Mosuto

11 Basuto household

12 Maletsunyane Falls

13 Herd-boy playing lesiba

14 Pastoral scene

15 Aeroplane over Lancers Gap

16 Old Fort, Leribe

17 Mission Cave House

18 Mohair (Shearing Angora Goats)

½d. ■

(**19**)

(Recess D.L.R.)

1954 (18 Oct)–**58**. T **8/18** Wmk Mult Script CA. P 11½ (10s.) or 13½ (others).

43	**8**	½d. grey-black and sepia	40	10
44	**9**	1d. grey-black and bluish green	30	10
45	**10**	2d. deep bright blue and orange	1·00	10
46	**11**	3d. yellow-green and deep rose-red	1·50	30
		a. Yellow-green and rose (27.11.58)	10·00	2·00
47	**12**	4½d. indigo and deep ultramarine	1·25	15
48	**13**	6d. chestnut and deep grey-green	1·75	15
49	**14**	1s. bronze-green and purple	1·75	30
50	**15**	1s.3d. brown and turquoise-green	25·00	8·50
51	**16**	2s.6d. deep ultramarine and crimson	25·00	11·00
		a. Brt ultram & crimson-lake (27.11.58)	80·00	23·00
52	**17**	5s. black and carmine-red	10·00	11·00
53	**18**	10s. black and maroon	32·00	26·00
43/53		*Set of* 11	90·00	50·00

1959 (1 Aug). No. 45 surch with T **19**, by South African Govt Ptr, Pretoria.

54	½d. on 2d. deep bright blue and orange	10	15

20 "Chief Moshoeshoe I" (engraving by Delangle)

21 Council house

22 Mosuto horseman

(Des from drawings by James Walton. Recess Waterlow)

1959 (15 Dec). Basutoland National Council. T **20/2**. W w **12**. P 13×13½.

55	3d. black and yellow-olive	60	10
56	1s. carmine and yellow-green	60	20
57	1s.3d. ultramarine and red-orange	80	45
55/7	*Set of 3*	1·75	65

(New Currency. 100 cents = 1 rand)

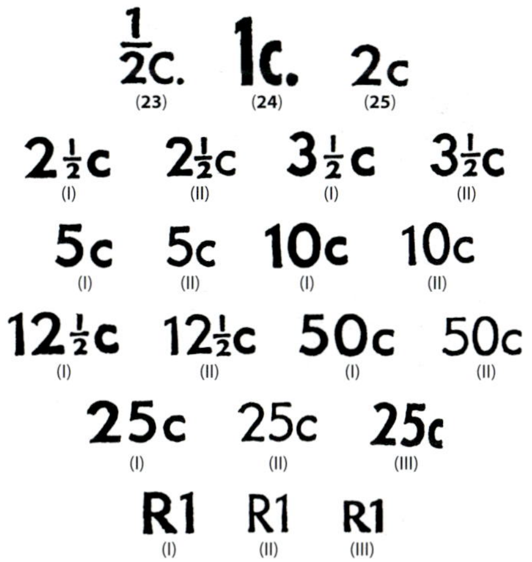

1961 (14 Feb). Nos. 43/53 surch with T **23** (½c.), **24** (1c.) or as T **25** (others) by South African Govt Printer, Pretoria.

58	½c. on ½d. grey-black and sepia	10	30
	a. Surch double	£550	
59	1c. on 1d. grey-black and bluish green	10	10
60	2c. on 2d. deep bright blue and orange	60	1·00
	a. Surch inverted	£160	
61	2½c. on 3d. yellow-green and rose (Type I)	10	10
	a. Type II (central on vignette)	10	10
	ab. Type II (higher to left, fraction dropped)	20	15
	b. Type II inverted	†	£2000
62	3½c. on 4½d. indigo and deep ultram (Type I)	20	10
	a. Type II	1·75	6·50
63	5c. on 6d. chestnut and deep grey-green (Type I)	30	10
	a. Type II	20	10
64	10c. on 1s. bronze-green and purple (Type I)	20	10
	a. Type II	£130	£150
65	12½c. on 1s.3d. brown and turq-green (Type I)	7·50	2·50
	a. Type II	5·50	2·50
66	25c. on 2s.6d. bright ultramarine and crimson-lake (Type I)	1·00	60
	a. Type II	42·00	12·00
	b. Type III	50	1·50
67	50c. on 5s. black and carmine-red (Type I)	4·00	3·00
	a. Type II	3·50	3·75
68	1r. on 10s. black and maroon (Type I)	45·00	23·00
	a. Type II	24·00	55·00
	b. Type III	24·00	23·00
58/68b	*Set of 11*	32·00	27·00

Examples of the 2c. surcharge are known in a fount similar to Type **24** (*Price £200 unused*).

26 Basuto Household

(Recess D.L.R.)

1961–63. As Nos. 43/53 but values in cents as in T **26**. Wmk Mult Script CA. P 13½ or 11½ (1r.).

69	½c. grey-black and sepia (as ½d.) (25.9.62)	20	20
	a. Imperf (pair)	£350	
70	1c. grey-blk and bluish grn (as 1d.) (25.9.62)	20	40
71	2c. dp brt blue and orange (as 2d.) (25.9.62)	2·75	1·40
72	2½c. yellow-green and deep rose-red (14.2.61)	1·50	60
	a. Pale yellow-green & rose-red (22.5.62)	14·00	1·75
73	3½c. indigo and dp ultram (as 4½d.) (25.9.62)	30	1·50
74	5c. chestnut and deep grey-green (as 6d.) (10.8.62)	60	75
75	10c. bronze-green and pur (as 1s.) (22.10.62)	30	40
76	12½c. brown and turquoise-green (as 1s.3d.) (17.12.62)	21·00	10·00
77	25c. deep ultramarine and crimson (as 2s.6d.) (25.9.62)	6·50	6·50
78	50c. black and carmine-red (as 5s.) (22.10.62)	18·00	19·00
79	1r. black and maroon (as 10s.) (4.2.63)	55·00	24·00
	a. Black and light maroon (16.12.63)	80·00	38·00
69/79	*Set of 11*	95·00	60·00

1963 (4 June). Freedom from Hunger. As No. 182 of Botswana.

80	12½c. reddish violet	40	15

1963 (2 Sept). Red Cross Centenary. As Nos. 183/4 of Botswana.

81	2½c. red and black	20	10
82	12½c. red and blue	80	60

1964. As Nos. 70, 72, 74, 76 and 78, but W w **12**.

84	1c. grey-black and bluish green (11.8.64)	10	20
86	2½c. pale yellow-green and rose-red (10.3.64)	15	25
88	5c. chestnut and deep grey-green (10.11.64)	30	50
90	12½c. brown and turquoise-green (10.11.64)	8·00	1·50
92	50c. black and carmine-red (29.9.64)	7·25	11·00
84/92	*Set of 5*	14·00	12·00

SELF-GOVERNMENT

28 Mosotho Woman and Child

29 Maseru Border Post

1965 (10 May). New Constitution. T **28/9** and similar horiz designs. Multicoloured. W w **12**. P 14×13½.

94	2½c. Type **28**	20	10
	w. Wmk inverted	50·00	17·00
95	3½c. Type **29**	35	20
96	5c. Mountain scene	35	20
	w. Wmk inverted	29·00	17·00
97	12½c. Legislative Buildings	60	70
94/7	*Set of 4*	1·40	1·10

1965 (17 May). I.T.U. Centenary. As Nos. 190/1 of Botswana.

98	1c. orange-red and bright purple	15	10
99	20c. light blue and orange-brown	50	30

1965 (25 Oct). International Co-operation Year. As Nos. 192/3 of Botswana.

100	½c. reddish purple & turquoise-green	10	65
101	12½c. deep bluish green and lavender	45	35

1966 (24 Jan). Churchill Commemoration. Printed in black, cerise, gold and background in colours stated. As Nos. 194/7 of Botswana.

102	1c. new blue	15	1·25
103	2½c. deep green	50	10
104	10c. brown	75	40
105	22½c. bluish violet	1·25	1·25
102/5	*Set of 4*	2·40	2·75

INDEPENDENT KINGDOM

King Moshoeshoe II, 4 October 1966–November 1990 (deposed)

33 Moshoeshoe I and Moshoeshoe II

FDC

(Des and photo Harrison)

1966 (4 Oct). Independence. P 12½×13.

106	**33**	2½c. light brown, black and red	10	10

107	5c. light brown, black and new blue	10	10
108	10c. light brown, black and emerald	15	10
109	20c. light brown, black and bright purple	20	15
106/9 *Set of 4*		45	30

LESOTHO
(**34**)

35 "Education Culture and Science"

1966 (1 Nov). Stamps of Basutoland optd as T **34**.

A. On Nos. 69/71 and 73/9 (Script CA wmk)

110A	½c. grey-black and sepia	10	10
111A	1c. grey-black and bluish green	10	10
112A	2c. deep bright blue and orange	60	10
114A	3½c. indigo and deep ultramarine	30	10
115A	5c. chestnut and deep grey-green	10	10
116A	10c. bronze-green and purple	10	10
117A	12½c. brown and turquoise-green	4·50	35
118A	25c. deep ultramarine and crimson	30	20
119A	50c. black and carmine-red	80	1·25
120A	1r. black and maroon	1·40	5·00
	a. "LSEOTHO" (R. 4/2)	75·00	
	b. Opt double	£160	
	ba. Ditto. "LSEOTHO" (R. 4/2)		
110A/20A *Set of 10*		7·50	6·50

B. On Nos. 84/92 and unissued 1r. (wmk w 12)

111B	1c. grey-black and bluish green	10	10
113B	2½c. pale yellow-green and rose-red	50	10
115B	5c. chestnut and deep grey-green	20	10
117B	12½c. brown and turquoise-green	30	20
119B	50c. black and carmine-red	70	50
120B	1r. black and maroon	65	75
	a. "LSEOTHO" (R. 4/2)	48·00	60·00
111B/20B *Set of 6*		2·00	1·40

(Des V. Whiteley. Litho D.L.R.)

1966 (1 Dec). 20th Anniv of U.N.E.S.C.O. P 14½×14.

121	**35**	2½c. orange-yellow and emerald-green	10	10
122		5c. light green and olive	15	10
123		12½c. light blue and red	35	15
124		25c. red-orange and deep greenish blue	60	75
121/4 *Set of 4*			1·10	50

36 Maize

37 Moshoeshoe II

(Des and photo Harrison)

1967 (1 Apr). Designs as T **36/7**. No wmk. P 14½×13½ (2r.) or 13½×14½ (others).

125	½c. bluish green and light bluish violet	10	10
126	1c. sepia and rose-red	10	10
127	2c. orange-yellow and light green	10	1·25
128	2½c. black and ochre	10	10
129	3½c. chalky blue and yellow	10	30
130	5c. bistre and new blue	20	10
131	10c. yellow-brown and bluish grey	10	10
132	12½c. black and red-orange	20	10
133	25c. black and bright blue	55	20
134	50c. black, new blue and turquoise	4·50	1·75
135	1r. multicoloured	65	75
136	2r. black, gold and magenta	1·00	1·75
125/36 *Set of 12*		6·25	5·50

Designs: Horiz as T **36**—1c. Cattle; 2c. Agaves (wrongly inscr "Aloes"); 2½c. Basotho Hat; 3½c. Merino Sheep ("Wool"); 5c. Basotho Pony; 10c. Wheat; 12½c. Angora Goat ("Mohair"); 25c. Maletsunyane Falls; 50c. Diamonds; 1r. Arms of Lesotho.

See also Nos. 147/59.

46 Students and University

(Des V. Whiteley. Photo Harrison)

1967 (7 Apr). First Conferment of University Degrees. P 14×14½.

137	**46**	1c. sepia, ultramarine and light yellow-orange	10	10
138		2½c. sepia, ultramarine and light greenish blue	10	10
139		12½c. sepia, ultramarine and rose	10	10
140		25c. sepia, ultramarine and light violet	15	15
137/40 *Set of 4*			30	30

47 Statue of Moshoeshoe I

(Des and photo Harrison)

1967 (4 Oct). First Anniv of Independence. T **47** and similar triangular designs. P 14½×14.

141	2½c. black and light yellow-green	10	10
142	12½c. multicoloured	25	15
143	25c. black, green and light ochre	35	25
141/3 *Set of 3*		65	40

Designs:—12½c. Lesotho flag; 25c. Crocodile (national emblem).

50 Lord Baden-Powell and Scout Saluting

(Des V. Whiteley. Photo Harrison)

1967 (1 Nov). 60th Anniv of Scout Movement. P 14×14½.

144	**50**	15c. multicoloured	20	10

51 W.H.O. Emblem and World Map

(Des G. Vasarhelyi. Photo Harrison)

1968 (7 Apr). 20th Anniv of World Health Organization. T **51** and similar horiz design. P 14×14½.

145	2½c. blue, gold and carmine-red	15	10
	a. Gold (emblem) omitted		
146	25c. multicoloured	45	60

Design:—25c. Nurse and child.

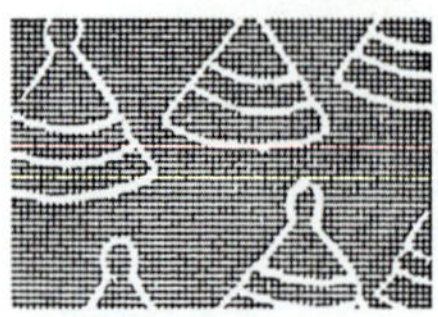
53 Basotho Hat

54 Sorghum

1968–69. As Nos. 125/36 and T **54**, but wmk **53** (sideways on 2r.).

147	½c. bluish green and light bluish violet (26.11.68)	10	10
	a. Blue-green and violet (30.9.69)	2·25	2·25
148	1c. sepia and rose-red (26.11.68)	10	10

149	2c. orange-yellow and light green (26.11.68)	10	10
	a. Orange-yellow and yellow-green (30.9.69)	1·00	1·25
150	2½c. black and ochre (21.10.68)	15	10
	a. Black and yellow-ochre (30.9.69)	1·00	1·00
151	3c. chocolate, green and yellow-brown (1.8.68)	15	15
152	3½c. chalky blue and yellow (26.11.68)	15	10
153	5c. bistre and new blue (22.7.68)	60	10
154	10c. yellow-brown and pale bluish grey (26.11.68)	15	10
155	1½c. black and red-orange (30.9.69)	60	35
156	25c. black and bright blue (30.9.69)	1·50	1·00
157	50c. black, new blue and turquoise (30.9.69)	11·00	3·75
158	1r. multicoloured (26.11.68)	1·50	2·75
159	2r. black, gold and magenta (30.9.69)	8·00	13·00
147/59	*Set of* 13	21·00	19·00

55 Running Hunters

(Des Jennifer Toombs. Photo Harrison)

1968 (1 Nov). Rock Paintings. T **55** and similar designs. W **53** (sideways on 5c., 15c.). P 14×14½ (5c., 15c.) or 14½×14 (others).

160	3c. yellow-brown. light blue-green and blackish green	20	10
161	3½c. greenish yellow, yellow-olive and sepia	25	10
162	5c. Venetian red, yellow-ochre and blackish brown	25	10
163	10c. yellow, rose and deep maroon	35	10
164	15c. light buff, pale olive-yellow and blackish brown	50	30
165	20c. yellow-green, greenish yellow and blackish brown	60	55
166	25c. yellow, orange-brown and black	65	75
160/6	*Set of* 7	2·50	1·75

Designs: Horiz—3½c. Baboons; 10c. Archers; 20c. Eland; 25c. Hunting scene. Vert—5c. Javelin throwing; 15c. Blue Cranes.

62 Queen Elizabeth II Hospital

(Des C. R. Househam and G. Drummond. Litho P.B.)

1969 (11 Mar). Centenary of Maseru (capital). T **62** and similar horiz designs. Multicoloured. W **53** (sideways). P 14×13½.

167	2½c. Type **62**	10	10
168	10c. Lesotho Radio Station	10	10
169	12½c. Leabua Jonathan Airport	35	10
170	25c. Royal Palace	25	15
167/70	*Set of* 4	65	30

66 Rally Car passing Mosotho Horseman

(Des P. Wheeler. Photo Harrison)

1969 (26 Sept). Roof of Africa Car Rally. T **66** and similar horiz designs. W **53**. P 14.

171	2½c. yellow, mauve and plum	15	10
172	12½c. cobalt, greenish yellow and olive-grey	20	10
173	15c. blue, black and mauve	20	10
174	20c. black, red and yellow	20	10
171/4	*Set of* 4	65	30

Designs:—12½c. Rally car on mountain road; 15c. Chequered flags and mountain scenery; 20c. Map of rally route and Rally Trophy.

71 Gryponyx and Footprints

75 Moshoeshoe I, when a Young Man

(Des Jennifer Toombs. Photo Harrison)

1970 (5 Jan). Prehistoric Footprints (1st series). T **71** and similar designs. W **53** (sideways*). P 14×14½ (3c.) or 14½×14 (others).

175	3c. pale brown, yellow-brown and sepia	90	70
176	5c. dull purple, pink and sepia	1·10	30
	w. Wmk hat pointing right	3·25	
177	10c. pale yellow, black and sepia	1·40	35
178	15c. olive-yellow, black and sepia	2·00	2·25
179	25c. cobalt and black	2·75	2·25
175/9	*Set of* 5	7·25	5·25

Designs: (60×23 mm)—3c. Dinosaur footprints at Moyeni. (40×24 mm)—10c. Plateosauravus and footprints; 15c. Tritylodon and footprints; 25c. Massospondylus and footprints.

*The normal sideways watermark shows the hat pointing left, *when seen from the back of the stamp.*

See also Nos. 596/8.

(Des G. Vasarhelyi. Litho D.L.R.)

1970 (11 Mar). Death Centenary of King Moshoeshoe I. T **75** and similar vert design. W **53**. P 13½.

180	2½c. pale green and magenta	10	10
181	25c. pale blue and chesnut	20	20

Design:—25c. Moshoeshoe I as an old man.

77 U.N. Emblem and "25"

(Des V. Whiteley. Litho Questa)

1970 (26 June). 25th Anniv of United Nations. T **77** and similar horiz designs. W **53** (sideways). P 14½×14.

182	2½c. light pink, light blue and maroon	10	10
183	10c. multicoloured	10	10
184	12½c. brown-red, cobalt and drab	10	25
185	25c. multicoloured	15	65
182/5	*Set of* 4	30	60

Designs:—10c. U.N. Building; 12½c. "People of the World"; 25c. Symbolic Dove.

78 Basotho Hat Gift Shop, Maseru

(Des G. Drummond. Litho Questa)

1970 (27 Oct). Tourism. T **78** and similar horiz designs. Multicoloured. W **53** (sideways). P 14.

186	2½c. Type **78**	10	10
187	5c. Trout fishing	20	10
188	10c. Pony trekking	25	10
189	12½c. Skiing	50	10
190	20c. Holiday Inn, Maseru	40	50
186/90	*Set of* 5	1·25	70

79 Maize

(Des Harrison. Litho Questa)

1971 (4 Jan). As Nos. 147/58 but in new format omitting portrait of Moshoeshoe II, as in T **79**. 4c. and 2r. in new designs. W **53** (sideways* except 2r.). P 14.

191	½c. blue-green and light bluish violet	10	10
192	1c. brown and orange-red	10	10
193	2c. yellow and green	10	10
	w. Wmk top of hat to right		
194	2½c. black, olive-green and yellow-ochre	10	10
195	3c. brown, green and yellow-ochre	10	10
196	3½c. indigo and yellow	10	10
196*a*	4c. multicoloured (1.4.71)	20	10
	aw. Wmk top of hat to right		
197	5c. yellow-brown and pale blue	15	10
198	10c. orange-brown and grey-blue	15	10
199	12½c. chocolate and yellow-orange	25	30
200	25c. slate and pale bright blue	60	40
201	50c. black, pale blue and turquoise-green	6·00	4·50
202	1r. multicoloured	1·25	1·75
203	2r. yellow-brown and ultramarine	70	2·25
191/203 *Set of* 14		8·50	8·50

Designs: Horiz—4c. National flag. Vert—2r. Statue of Moshoeshoe I.

*The normal sideways watermark shows top of hat to left, as seen from the back of the stamp.

For 2r. value without watermark see No. 401.

80 Lammergeier

(Des R. Granger Barrett. Litho J.W.)

1971 (1 Mar). Birds. T **80** and similar vert designs. Multicoloured. W **53**. P 14.

204	2½c. Type **80**	2·50	20
205	5c. Bald Ibis	3·50	2·50
206	10c. Rufous Rockjumper	3·50	2·00
207	12½c. Blue Bustard	3·75	3·50
208	15c. Painted Snipe	4·25	4·50
209	20c. Golden-breasted Bunting	4·25	4·50
210	25c. Ground Woodpecker	4·75	4·50
204/10 *Set of* 7		24·00	19·00

81 Lionel Collett Dam

(Des G. Drummond. Litho J.W.)

1971 (15 July). Soil Conservation. T **81** and similar horiz designs. Multicoloured. W **53** (sideways). P 14.

211	4c. Type **81**	10	10
212	10c. Contour ridges	10	10
213	15c. Earth dams	25	10
214	25c. Beaver dams	35	35
211/14 *Set of* 4		70	50

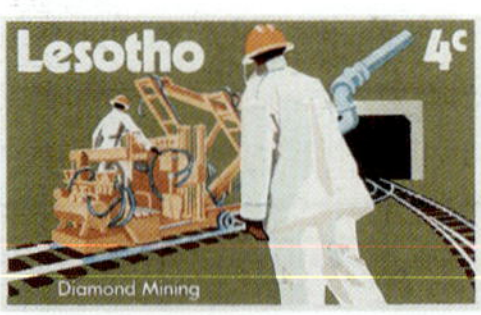

82 Diamond Mining

(Des J.W. Litho Questa)

1971 (4 Oct). Development. T **82** and similar horiz designs. Multicoloured. W **53** (sideways). P 14.

215	4c. Type **82**	75	40
216	10c. Pottery	30	10
217	15c. Weaving	45	60
218	20c. Construction	55	1·50
215/18 *Set of* 4		1·90	2·25

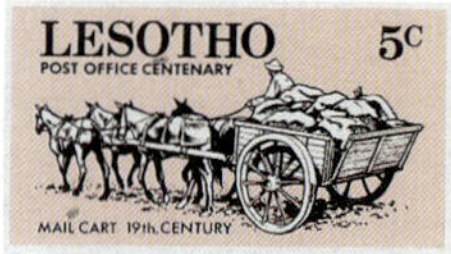

83 Mail Cart

(Des D. B. Picton-Phillips. Litho Questa)

1972 (3 Jan). Post Office Centenary. T **83** and similar designs. W **53** (sideways on 5, 10 and 20c.). P 14×13½ (15c.) or 13½×14 (others).

219	5c. pale pink and black	15	20
220	10c. multicoloured	15	10
221	15c. pale drab, light blue and black	20	15
222	20c. multicoloured	30	90
219/22 *Set of* 4		70	1·10

Designs: Horiz—10c. Postal bus; 20c. Maseru P.O. Vert—15c. Cape of Good Hope 4d. stamp of 1876.

84 Sprinting

(Des J.W. Litho Questa)

1972 (1 Sept). Olympic Games, Munich. T **84** and similar vert designs. Multicoloured. W **53**. P 14.

223	4c. Type **84**	15	10
	w. Wmk inverted		
224	10c. Shot putting	20	10
225	15c. Hurdling	30	10
226	25c. Long-jumping	35	55
223/6 *Set of* 4		90	70

85 "Adoration of the Shepherds" (Matthias Stomer)

(Des and litho J.W.)

1972 (1 Dec). Christmas. W **53** (sideways). P 14.

227	**85**	4c. multicoloured	10	10
228		10c. multicoloured	10	10
229		25c. multicoloured	15	20
227/9 *Set of* 3			30	30

86 WHO Emblem

O.A.U.
10th Anniversary
Freedom in Unity
(**87**)

(Des J. Cooter. Litho Questa)

1973 (7 Apr). 25th Anniv of WHO. W **53** (sideways). P 13½.

230	**86**	20c. greenish blue and yellow	30	30

1973 (25 May). Tenth Anniv of OAU. Nos. 194 and 196a/8 optd with T **87** by Govt Printer, Maseru.

231	2½c. black, olive-green and yellow-ochre	10	10
232	4c. multicoloured	10	10
	a. Horiz pair, one without opt	£150	
233	5c. yellow-brown and pale blue	10	10
234	10c. orange-brown and grey-blue	15	15
231/4 *Set of* 4		35	35

88 Basotho Hat and WFP Emblem

(Des locally; adapted J. Cooter. Litho Format)

1973 (1 June). Tenth Anniv of World Food Programme. T **88** and similar horiz designs. Multicoloured. W **53** (sideways). P 13½.

235	4c. Type **88**	10	10
236	15c. School feeding	20	15
237	20c. Infant feeding	20	20
	a. Imperf (pair)	£250	
238	25c. "Food for Work"	25	25
235/8	*Set of 4*	65	60

89 *Aeropetes tulbaghia*

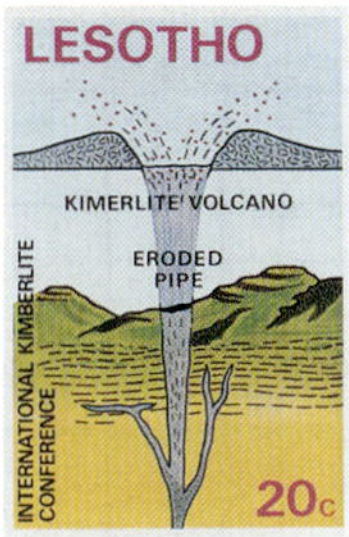

90 Kimberlite Volcano

(Des A. Mcloed; artwork G. Drummond. Litho Questa)

1973 (3 Sept). Butterflies. T **89** and similar horiz designs. Multicoloured. W **53** (sideways). P 14.

239	4c. Type **89**	85	10
240	5c. *Papilio demodocus*	95	50
241	10c. *Cynthia cardui*	1·50	50
242	15c. *Precis hierta*	2·75	1·75
243	20c. *Precis oenone*	2·75	1·75
244	25c. *Danaus chrysippus*	3·00	2·75
245	30c. *Colons evenina*	3·00	3·75
239/45	*Set of 7*	13·50	10·00

(Des PAD Studio. Litho Questa)

1973 (1 Oct). International Kimberlite Conference. T **90** and similar multicoloured designs. W **53** (sideways on 10 and 15c.). P 13½.

246	10c. Map of diamond mines (horiz)	2·00	50
247	15c. Kimberlite-diamond rock (horiz)	2·25	2·25
248	20c. Type **90**	2·25	2·50
249	30c. Diamond prospecting	3·75	7·00
246/9	*Set of 4*	9·00	11·00

Type **90** is incorrectly inscribed "KIMERLITE VOLCANO".

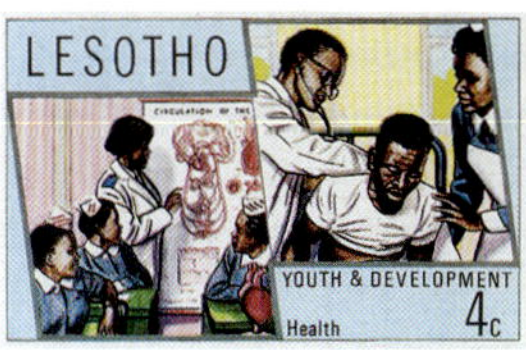

91 "Health"

92 Open Book and Wreath

(Des R. Granger Barrett. Litho Questa)

1974 (18 Feb). Youth and Development. T **91** and similar horiz designs. Multicoloured. W **53** (sideways). P 13½.

250	4c. Type **91**	10	10
251	10c. "Education"	15	10
252	20c. "Agriculture"	20	10
253	25c. "Industry"	30	20
254	30c. "Service"	30	25
250/4	*Set of 5*	85	55

(Des PAD Studio. Litho Questa)

1974 (8 Apr). Tenth Anniv of U.B.L.S. T **92** and similar vert designs. Multicoloured. W **53**. P 14.

255	10c. Type **92**	15	10
256	15c. Flags, mortar-board and scroll	20	20
257	20c. Map of Africa	25	25
258	25c. King Moshoeshoe II capping a graduate	25	65
255/8	*Set of 4*	75	1·00

93 Senqunyane River Bridge, Marakabei

94 UPU Emblem

(Des J. Cooter. Litho Questa)

1974 (26 June). Rivers and Bridges. T **93** and similar horiz designs. Multicoloured. W **53** (sideways). P 14½.

259	4c. Type **93**	10	10
260	5c. Tsoelike River and bridge	10	10
261	10c. Makhaleng River Bridge	20	10
262	15c. Seaka Bridge, Orange/Senqu River	35	35
263	20c. Masianokeng Bridge, Phuthiatsana River	40	40
264	25c. Mahobong Bridge, Hlotse River	45	45
259/64	*Set of 6*	1·50	1·25

(Des R. Granger Barrett. Litho Enschedé)

1974 (6 Sept). Centenary of Universal Postal Union. T **94** and similar horiz designs. W **53** (sideways). P 13½×13.

265	4c. light emerald and black	10	10
266	10c. orange, greenish yellow and black	15	10
267	15c. multicoloured	20	60
268	20c. multicoloured	45	85
265/8	*Set of 4*	0·80	1·40

95 Siege of Thaba-Bosiu

96 Mamokhorong

(Des Jennifer Toombs. Litho Enschedé)

1974 (25 Nov). 150th Anniv of Establishment of Thaba-Bosiu as Capital. T **95** and similar multicoloured designs. W **53** (sideways on 4 and 5c.). P 12½×12 (4 and 5c.) or 12×12½ (others).

269	4c. Type **95**	10	10
270	5c. The wreath-laying	10	10
271	10c. Moshoeshoe I (vert)	25	10
272	20c. Makoanyane, the warrior (vert)	90	55
269/72	*Set of 4*	1·25	65

(Des PAD Studio. Litho Questa)

1975 (25 Jan). Basotho Musical Instruments. T **96** and similar horiz designs. Multicoloured. W **53** (sideways). P 14.

273	4c. Type **96**	10	10
274	10c. Lesiba	10	10
275	15c. Setolotolo	15	20
276	20c. Meropa	15	20
273/6	*Set of 4*	40	45
MS277	108×92 mm. Nos. 273/6	1·00	2·00

97 Horseman in Rock Archway

98 Morena Moshoeshoe I

(Des J. Cooter. Litho Questa)

1975 (15 Apr). Sehlabathebe National Park. T **97** and similar horiz designs. Multicoloured. W **53** (sideways). P 14.

278	4c. Type **97**	30	10
279	5c. Mountain view through arch	30	10
280	15c. Antelope by stream	50	45
281	20c. Mountains and lake	50	50

282	25c. Tourists by frozen waterfall	65	75
278/82	*Set of 5*	2·00	1·60

(Des G. Vasarhelyi. Litho Questa)

1975 (10 Sept). Leaders of Lesotho. T **98** and similar vert designs. W **53**. P 14.

283	3c. black and light blue	10	10
284	4c. black and light mauve	10	10
285	5c. black and pink	10	10
286	6c. black and light grey-brown	10	10
287	10c. black and light claret	10	10
288	15c. black and light orange-red	20	20
289	20c. black and dull green	25	30
290	25c. black and azure	25	40
283/90	*Set of 8*	1·00	1·10

Designs:—4c. King Moshoeshoe II; 5c. Morena Letsie I; 6c. Morena Lerotholi; 10c. Morena Letsie II; 15c. Morena Griffith; 20c. Morena Seeiso Griffith Lerotholi; 25c. Mofumahali Mantsebo Seeiso, OBE.

The 25c. also commemorates International Women's Year.

99 Mokhibo Dance

(Des PAD Studio. Litho Questa)

1975 (17 Dec). Traditional Dances. T **99** and similar horiz designs. Multicoloured. W **53** (sideways). P 14×14½.

291	4c. Type **99**	15	10
292	10c. Ndlamo	20	10
293	15c. Baleseli	35	75
294	20c. Mohobelo	40	1·25
291/4	*Set of 4*	1·00	1·75
MS295	111×100 mm. Nos. 291/94	3·75	3·50

100 Enrolment

(Des L. Curtis. Litho Questa)

1976 (20 Feb). 25th Anniv of the Lesotho Red Cross. T **100** and similar horiz designs. Multicoloured. W **53** (sideways). P 14.

296	4c. Type **100**	50	10
297	10c. Medical aid	70	10
298	15c. Rural service	1·00	1·25
299	25c. Relief supplies	1·40	2·50
296/9	*Set of 4*	3·25	3·50

101 Tapestry

102 Football

(Des V. Whiteley Studio. Litho Format)

1976 (2 June). Multicoloured designs as T **101**. W **53** (sideways* on 2 to 50c.). P 14.

300	2c. Type **101**	10	35
	w. Wmk top of hat to right	—	40·00
301	3c. Mosotho horseman	20	30
302	4c. Map of Lesotho	1·50	10
	w. Wmk top of hat to right		
303	5c. Lesotho Brown diamond	75	1·00
	w. Wmk top of hat to right		
304	10c. Lesotho Bank	30	10
305	15c. Lesotho and OAU flags	2·00	1·00
306	25c. Sehlabathebe National Park	60	35
307	40c. Pottery	60	1·00
308	50c. Prehistoric rock art	2·75	2·00
309	1r. King Moshoeshoe II (vert)	60	1·75
300/9	*Set of 10*	8·00	7·00

*The normal sideways watermark shows top of hat to left when seen from the back of the stamp.

For 25c., 40c.and 50c. values on unwatermarked paper, see Nos. 398/400.

(Des P. Powell. Litho Questa)

1976 (9 Aug). Olympic Games, Montreal. T **102** and similar vert designs. Multicoloured. W **53**. P 14.

310	4c. Type **102**	15	10
311	10c. Weightlifting	15	10
312	15c. Boxing	35	35
313	25c. Throwing the discus	50	80
310/13	*Set of 4*	1·00	1·25

103 "Rising Sun"

104 Telephones, 1876 and 1976

(Des L. Curtis. Litho Questa)

1976 (4 Oct). Tenth Anniv of Independence. T **103** and similar vert designs. Multicoloured. W **53**. P 14.

314	4c. Type **103**	10	10
315	10c. Open gates	10	10
316	15c. Broken chains	40	20
317	25c. Britten Norman Islander aircraft over hotel	50	35
314/17	*Set of 4*	1·00	55

(Des and litho J.W.)

1976 (6 Dec). Telephone Centenary. T **104** and similar horiz designs. Multicoloured. W **53** (sideways). P 13.

318	4c. Type **104**	10	10
319	10c. Early handset and telephone-user, 1976	15	10
320	15c. Wall telephone and telephone exchange	25	20
321	25c. Stick telephone and Alexander Graham Bell	45	50
318/21	*Set of 4*	85	75

105 *Aloe striatula*

(Des D. Findlay. Litho Walsall)

1977 (14 Feb). Aloes and Succulents. T **105** and similar vert designs. Multicoloured. W **53** (inverted). P 14.

322	3c. Type **105**	25	10
323	4c. *Aloe aristata*	25	10
324	5c. *Kniphofia caulescens*	25	10
325	10c. *Euphorbia pulvinata*	35	10
326	15c. *Aloe saponaria*	1·00	30
327	20c. *Caralluma lutea*	1·00	50
328	25c. *Aloe polyphylla*	1·25	70
322/8	*Set of 7*	4·00	1·60

106 Large-toothed Rock Hyrax

(Des D. Findlay. Litho Questa)

1977 (25 Apr). Endangered Species. T **106** and similar horiz designs. Multicoloured. W **53** (sideways). P 14.

329	4c. Type **106**	3·50	30
330	5c. Cape Porcupine	3·50	75
331	10c. Zorilla (polecat)	3·50	30
332	15c. Klipspringer	11·00	2·50
333	25c. Chacma Baboon	12·00	3·75
329/33	*Set of* 5	30·00	6·75

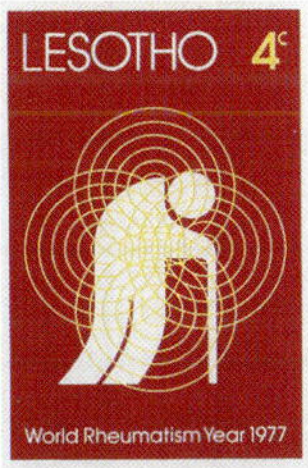

107 "Rheumatic Man"

(Des C. Abbott. Litho Questa)

1977 (4 July). World Rheumatism Year. T **107** and similar vert designs showing the "Rheumatic Man". W **53**. P 14.

334	4c. yellow and red	10	10
335	10c. new blue and deep blue	15	10
336	15c. yellow and blue-green	30	10
337	25c. orange-red and black	40	45
334/7	*Set of* 4	85	55

Designs:—10c. Man surrounded by "pain"; 15c. Man surrounded by "chain"; 25c. Man supporting globe.

108 Small-mouthed Yellowfish

(Des D. Findlay. Litho Questa)

1977 (28 Sept). Fish. T **108** and similar horiz designs. Multicoloured. W **53** (sideways). P 14.

338	4c. Type **108**	30	10
339	10c. Mudfish	45	10
340	15c. Rainbow Trout	70	35
341	25c. Barnard's Mudfish	80	60
338/41	*Set of* 4	2·00	1·00

(**109**)

110 Black and White Heads

1977 (7 Dec*). No. 198 surch with T **109** by Govt Printer, Maseru.

342	3c. on 10c. yellow-brn & pale bluish grey..	1·00	1·00
	a. Top obliterating bar short at left (R.2/5)	14·00	
	b. Top obliterating bar short at right (R.5/5)	14·00	
	w. Wmk top of hat to right		

*Earliest known date of use.
Nos. 342a/b occur on the upper pane.

(Des Jennifer Toombs. Litho Walsall)

1977 (12 Dec). Decade for Action to Combat Racism. T **110** and similar vert designs. W **53**. P 14.

343	4c. chocolate and mauve	10	10
344	10c. chocolate and light new blue	10	10
345	15c. chocolate and light orange	15	15
346	25c. chocolate and light turquoise-green	25	25
343/6	*Set of* 4	55	45

Designs:—10c. Jigsaw pieces; 15c. Cogwheels; 25c. Handshake.

(Des D. Findlay. Litho Questa)

1978 (13 Feb). Flowers. Vert designs similar to T **105**. Multicoloured. W **53**. P 14.

347	2c. Papaver aculeatum	10	50
348	3c. Diascia integerrima	10	50
349	4c. Helichrysum trilineatum	10	10
350	5c. Zaluzianskya maritima	10	10
351	10c. Gladiolus natalensis	15	10
352	15c. Chironia krebsii	20	40
353	25c. Wahlenbergia undulata	35	1·00
354	40c. Brunsvigia radulosa	65	2·00
347/54	*Set of* 8	1·50	4·00

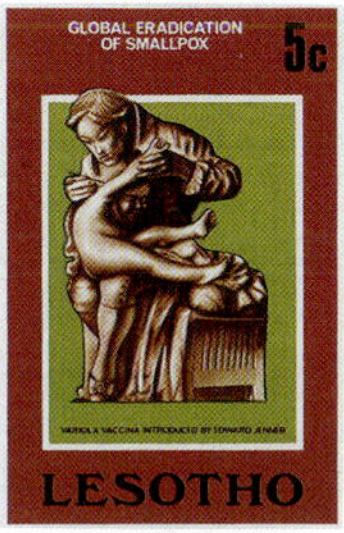

111 Edward Jenner performing Vaccination

112 Tsoloane Falls

(Des G. Hutchins. Litho J.W.)

1978 (8 May). Global Eradication of Smallpox. T **111** and similar vert design. Multicoloured. W **53**. P 13.

355	5c. Type **111**	25	35
356	25c. Head of child and WHO emblem	75	90
	w. Wmk inverted	5·00	

(Des Kobus De Beer Art Studio. Litho Questa)

1978 (28 July). Waterfalls. T **112** and similar vert designs. Multicoloured. W **53**. P 14.

357	4c. Type **112**	15	10
358	10c. Qiloane Falls	25	10
359	15c. Tsoelikana Falls	35	60
360	25c. Maletsunyane Falls	55	1·75
357/60	*Set of* 4	1·10	2·25

113 Wright *Flyer III*, 1903

114 *Orthetrum farinasum*

(Des L. Curtis. Litho Harrison)

1978 (9 Oct). 75th Anniv of Powered Flight. T **113** and similar horiz design. W **53** (sideways). P 14½×14.

361	5c. black, brown-ochre and new blue	15	30
362	25c. multicoloured	40	60

Design:—25c. Wilbur and Orville Wright.

(Des D. Findlay. Litho Questa)

1978 (18 Dec). Insects. T **114** and similar vert designs. Multicoloured. W **53**. P 14.

363	4c. Type **114**	10	10
364	10c. *Phymateus viridipes*	20	10
365	15c. *Belonogaster lateritis*	30	55
366	25c. *Sphodromantis gastrica*	50	90
363/6	*Set of* 4	1·00	1·40

115 Oudehout branch in flower

116 Mampharoane

(Des D. Findlay. Litho Questa)

1979 (26 Mar). Trees. T **115** and similar vert designs showing branches in flower. Multicoloured. W **53**. P 14.

367	4c. Type **115**	10	10
368	10c. Wild Olive	15	10
369	15c. Blinkblaar	30	80
370	25c. Cape Holly	55	1·50
367/70	*Set of* 4	1·00	2·25

(New Currency. 100 lisente = 1(ma)loti)

(Des D. Findlay. Litho Questa)

1979 (1 June). Reptiles. T **116** and similar horiz designs. Multicoloured. P 14.

A. No wmk

371A	4s. Type **116**	10	10
372A	10s. Qoaane	20	10
373A	15s. Leupa	30	80
374A	25s. Masumu	60	1·50
371A/4A	*Set of* 4	1·10	2·25

B. W **53** *(sideways)*

371B	4s. Type **116**	20	10
372B	10s. Qoaane	30	10
373B	15s. Leupa	50	70
374B	25s. Masumu	80	1·50
371B/4B	*Set of* 4	1·60	2·10

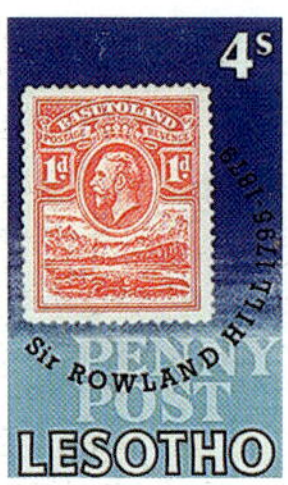

117 Basutoland 1933 1d. Stamp

118 Detail of painting "Children's Games" by Breughel

(Des J.W. Litho Format)

1979 (22 Oct). Death Centenary of Sir Rowland Hill. T **117** and similar vert designs showing stamps. P 14.

375	4s. multicoloured	10	10
376	15s. multicoloured	30	20
377	25s. black, yellow-orange and olive-bistre	40	30
375/7	*Set of* 3	70	50
MS378	118×95 mm. 50s. multicoloured	60	80

Designs:—15s. Basutoland 1962 ½c. definitive; 25s. Penny Black; 50s. 1972 15c. Post Office Centenary commemorative.

(Des C. Abbott. Litho Questa)

1979 (10 Dec). International Year of the Child. T **118** and similar vert designs showing details of the painting "Children's Games" by Brueghel. W **53**. P 14.

379	4s. multicoloured	10	10
380	10s. multicoloured	10	10
381	15s. multicoloured	15	15
379/81	*Set of* 3	30	30
MS382	113×88 mm. 25s. multicoloured (horiz) (wmk sideways)	55	45

119 Beer Strainer, Broom and Mat

(Des Kobus de Beer Art Studio. Litho Walsall)

1980 (18 Feb). Grasswork. T **119** and similar horiz designs. Multicoloured. W **53** (sideways). P 14.

383	4s. Type **119**	10	10
384	10s. Winnowing Basket	10	10
385	15s. Basotho Hat	20	40
386	25s. Grain storage	35	65
383/6	*Set of* 4	60	1·00

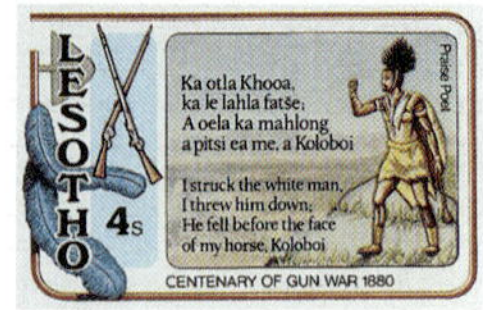

120 Praise Poet

(Des BG Studio. Litho Walsall)

1880 (6 May). Centenary of Gun War. T **120** and similar horiz designs. Multicoloured. P 14.

387	4s. Type **120**	15	10
388	5s. Leretholi (commander of Basotho Army)	15	10
389	10s. Ambush at Qalabane	20	10
390	15s. Snider and Martini-Henry rifles	60	55
391	25s. Map showing main areas of action	70	1·25
87/91	*Set of* 5	1·60	1·75

121 Olympic Flame, Flags and Kremlin

(**122**)

(Des G. Vasarhelyi. Litho Format)

1980 (20 Sept). Olympic Games, Moscow. T **121** and similar horiz designs. Multicoloured. P 14½.

392	25s. Type **121**	25	25
	a. Horiz strip of 5. Nos. 392/6	1·10	1·10
393	25s. Doves, flame and flags	25	25
394	25s. Football	25	25
395	25s. Running	25	25
396	25s. Opening ceremony	25	25
392/6	*Set of* 5	1·10	1·10
MS397	110×85 mm. 1m.40, Ancient and modern athletes carrying Olympic torch	1·10	1·25

Nos. 392/6 were printed together, *se-tenant*, in horizontal strips of 5 throughout the sheet.

A further series for the Moscow Olympics, printed by Walsall, showing 4s. Javelin, 10s. Sprinting, 15s. Marathon and 25s. Football, was prepared, but not issued.

1980. As Nos. 203 and 306/8, but without wmk.

398	25c. Sehlabathebe National Park	75	2·00
399	40c. Pottery	2·00	5·50
400	50c. Prehistoric rock art	2·75	5·00
401	2r. Statue of Moshoeshoe I (yellow-brown and ultramarine)	70	2·25
398/401	*Set of* 4	5·50	13·00

Two opt types of No. 409:

Type I. Cancelling bars centred on depth of "M1" (stamps surcharged in individual panes of 25 and from the righthand panes of those surcharged in sheets of 50 (2 panes 5×5)).

Type II. Lower cancelling bar aligns with foot of "M1" (stamps from left hand panes of those surcharged in sheets of 50).

1980 (20 Oct)–**81**. As Nos. 300/5, 309 and 398/401 surch as T **122** or with new figures of value (5s. (No. 410A), 6, 75s., 1 and 2m.).

A. By typo (locally)

(a) W **53** *(sideways on 2, 3, 6, 10, 40, 60 and 75s.)*

402A	2s. on 2c. Type **101**	10	30
	w. Wmk top of hat to right	5·50	
403A	3s. on 3c. Mosotho horseman	20	30
404A	6s. on 4c. Map of Lesotho	†	—
	a. Surch double	†	—
	b. Albino surch	†	—
405A	10s. on 10c. Lesotho Bank	80	10
405cA	25s. on 25c. Sehlabathebe National Park	3·25	5·00
406A	40s. on 40c. Pottery	45	50
407A	50s. on 50c. Prehistoric rock art	2·50	2·25
408A	75s. on 15c. Lesotho and OAU flags	80	1·00
409A	1m. on 1r. King Moshoeshoe II (I) (Sil.)	80	1·25
	a. Surch double		
	b. Surch inverted		
	c. Surch double, one inverted	55·00	
	d. Opt Type II	3·75	4·00

(b) No wmk

410A	5s. on 6s. on 5c. Lesotho Brown diamond	35·00	10
	a. Third surch (Basotho hat and "5s.") double	35·00	
	b. Basotho hat and "5s." surch albino	25·00	

	c. Basotho hat and "5s." omitted	25·00	
	d. Basotho hat and "5s." surch treble	40·00	
	e. Basotho hat and "5s." surch treble, one inverted	45·00	
	f. Second surch ("6s." and bars) albino	20·00	
412A	25s. on 25c. Sehlabathebe National Park	12·00	30
	a. Surch double	12·00	
	b. Surch triple		
	c. Surch quadruple		
413A	40s. on 40c. Pottery	2·50	4·50
414A	50s. on 50c. Prehistoric rock art	30·00	55
	a. Surch double, one inverted	30·00	
	b. Surch quadruple, one inverted	35·00	
	c. Surch omitted (in pair with normal)		
417A	2m. on 2r. Statue of Moshoeshoel	80	1·60
402A/17A *Set of* 14		15·00	16·00

B. By Litho (London)

(a) W **53** *(sideways on 2, 3, 6, 10, 40, 50 and 75s.)*

402B	2s. on 2c. Type **101**	10	30
403B	3s. on 3c. Mosotho horseman	20	30
404B	6s. on 4c. Map of Lesotho	1·00	30
405B	10s. on 10c. Lesotho Bank	5·00	6·00
406B	40s. on 40c. Pottery	45	50
407B	50s. on 50c. Prehistoric rock art	1·25	55

(b) No wmk

410B	5s. on 5c. Lesotho Brown diamond	60	10
411B	10s. on 10c. Lesotho Bank	10	10
412B	25s. on 25c. Sehlabathebe National Park	25	30
415B	75s. on 15c. Lesotho and OAU flags	1·50	1·25
416B	1m. on 1r. King Moshoeshoe II (Blk. and Sil.)	80	1·50
417B	2m. on 2r. Statue of Moshoeshoe I	80	1·75
402B/17B *Set of* 12		11·00	11·00

No. 410A is a further surcharge on No. 410B. Initially sheets of No. 410B were locally surcharged "6s.", but this was later obliterated by a Basotho hat emblem and a further "5s." surcharge added, both in typography.

The surcharge on No. 416 is similar to that on No. 409 but has the cancelling bars printed in black and the new face value in silver.

On each value except the 5s. and 1m. stamps, the design of the surcharge on the local printing is identical to that on the London printing. Stamps from the local printing can easily be identified from those of the London printing as indentations are clearly visible on the reverse of stamps with the typographed surcharge.

It is believed that the local surcharges were not placed on general sale before 1 December 1980. No. 410A did not appear until 20 January 1981.

Nos. 412Ab/c occurred in the same sheet which contained 5 examples of the triple surcharge, 5 of a partial quadruple surcharge and 40 with complete quadruple surcharge.

123 Beer Mug

124 Queen Elizabeth the Queen Mother and Prince Charles

(Des G. Vasarhelyi (No. **MS**422), Kobus de Beer Art Studio (others). Litho Format (No. **MS**422), Questa (others))

1980 (20 Nov). Pottery. T **123** and similar horiz designs. Multicoloured. W **53** (sideways). P 14.

418	4s. Type **123**	10	10
419	10s. Beer brewing pot	10	10
420	15s. Water pot	15	15
421	25s. Pot shapes	25	30
418/21 *Set of* 4		50	50
MS422	150×110 mm. 40s.×4 Wedgwood plaques of Prince Philip; Queen Elizabeth II; Prince Charles; Princess Anne (each 22×35 mm). P 14×14½	50	90

No. **MS**422 was issued to commemorate the 250th birth anniversary of Josiah Wedgwood.

(Des G. Vasarhelyi. Litho Format)

1980 (1 Dec). 80th Birthday of Queen Elizabeth the Queen Mother. T **124** and similar multicoloured designs. P 14½.

423	5s. Type **124**	25	25
	a. Horiz strip of 3. Nos. 423/5	1·25	1·25
424	10s. Queen Elizabeth the Queen Mother	25	25
425	1m. Basutoland 1947 Royal Visit 2d. commemorative and flags (54×44 mm)	90	90
423/5 *Set of* 3		1·25	1·25

Nos. 423/5 were printed together, *se-tenant*, in horizontal strips of 3 throughout small sheets of nine stamps.

125 Lesotho Evangelical Church, Morija

(Des G. Vasarhelyi. Litho Format (75s., 1m.50), Harrison (others))

1980 (8 Dec). Christmas. T **125** and similar horiz designs. Multicoloured. No wmk (75s.) or W **53** (others). P 14×14½.

426	4s. Type **125**	10	10
427	15s. St. Agnes' Anglican Church, Teyateyaneng	10	10
428	25s. Cathedral of Our Lady of Victories, Maseru	15	10
429	75s. University Chapel, Roma	45	50
426/9 *Set of* 4		65	60
MS430	110×85 mm. 1m.50, Nativity scene (43×29 mm). No wmk. P 14½	50	80

126 "Voyager" Satellite and Jupiter

127 Greater Kestrel

(Des G. Vasarhelyi. Litho Format)

1981 (15 Mar). Space Exploration. T **126** and similar horiz designs. Multicoloured. P 13½×14.

431	25s. Type **126**	30	25
	a. Horiz strip of 5. Nos. 431/5	1·40	
432	25s. "Voyager" and Saturn	30	25
433	25s. "Voyager" passing Saturn	30	25
434	25s. "Space Shuttle" releasing satellite	30	25
435	25s. "Space Shuttle" launch	30	25
431/5 *Set of* 5		1·40	1·10
MS436	111×85 mm. 1m.40, Saturn	1·40	1·00

Nos. 431/5 were printed together, *se-tenant*, in horizontal strips of 5 throughout the sheet.

No. **MS**436 exists imperforate from stock dispersed by the liquidator of Format International Security Printers Ltd.

(Des G. Vasarhelyi. Litho Format)

1981 (20 Apr). Birds. Multicoloured designs as T **127**. With imprint date. P 14½.

437	1s. Type **127**	15	40
	a. Perf 13 (12.81)	55	30
438	2s. Speckled Pigeon (horiz)	15	40
	a. Perf 13 (12.81)	65	30
439	3s. South African Crowned Crane	20	40
440	5s. Bokmakierie Shrike	20	40
	a. Perf 13 (12.81)	90	30
441	6s. Cape Robin Chat	30	10
442	7s. Yellow Canary	30	10
443	10s. Red-billed Pintail (horiz)	40	10
	a. Perf 13 (12.81)	90	30
444	25s. Malachite Kingfisher	1·00	15
445	40s. Yellow-tufted Malachite Sunbird (horiz)	1·25	55
446	60s. Cape Longclaw (horiz)	1·50	1·00
447	75s. Hoopoe (horiz)	1·50	85
448	1m. Red Bishop (horiz)	1·50	75
449	2m. Egyptian Goose (horiz)	1·00	1·50
450	5m. Lilac-breasted Roller (horiz)	1·25	4·00
437/50 *Set of* 14		9·75	9·50

Imprint dates: "1981", Nos. 437/50; "1982", Nos. 437/43.

Nos. 437/50 exist imperforated and as progressive proofs from stock dispersed by the liquidator of Format International Security Printers Ltd.

For these stamps watermarked w **14** see Nos. 500/13.

128 Wedding Bouquet from Lesotho

(Des J.W. Litho Format)

1981 (22 July). Royal Wedding. T **128** and similar vert designs. Multicoloured. P 14.

451	25s. Type **128**	10	10
	a. Booklet pane. No. 451×3 plus printed label	50	
	b. Booklet pane. Nos. 451/3 plus printed label	50	
452	50s. Prince Charles riding	20	25
	a. Booklet pane. No. 452×3 plus printed label	55	
453	75s. Prince Charles and Lady Diana Spencer.	30	50
	a. Booklet pane. No. 453×3 plus printed label	70	
451/3 *Set of 3*		55	75

Nos. 451/3 also exist imperforate from a restricted printing (price for set of 3 £5.50 mint).

Booklet panes Nos. 451a/3a exist part perforated from stock dispersed by the liquidator of Format International Security Printers Ltd.

129 Prince Charles and Lady Diana Spencer

(Des G. Vasarhelyi. Litho Format)

1981 (5 Sept). Royal Wedding (2nd issue). Sheet 115×90 mm. P 14½.

MS454	**129** 1m.50 multicoloured	1·00	1·25

No. **MS**454 also exists imperforate from a restricted printing (price £4 mint).

130 "Santa planning his Annual Visit"

131 Duke of Edinburgh, Award Scheme Emblem and Flags

(Des G. Vasarhelyi. Litho Format)

1981 (5 Oct). Christmas. Paintings by Norman Rockwell (6 to 60s.) or Botticelli (1m.25). T **130** and similar multicoloured designs. P 13½.

455	6s. Type **130**	15	10
456	10s. "Santa reading his Mail"	20	10
457	15s. "The Little Spooners"	25	20
458	20s. "Raleigh Rockwell Travels"	25	25
459	25s. "Ride 'em Cowboy"	25	30
460	60s. "The Discovery"	30	1·00
455/60 *Set of 6*		1·25	1·75
MS461	111×85 mm. 1m.25, "Mystic Nativity" (48×31 mm). P 13½×14	1·10	1·10

(Des G. Vasarhelyi. Litho Format)

1981 (5 Nov). 25th Anniv of Duke of Edinburgh Award Scheme. T **131** and similar multicoloured designs. P 14½.

462	6s. Type **131**	10	10
463	7s. Tree planting	10	10
464	25s. Gardening	25	20
465	40s. Mountain climbing	40	40
466	75s. Award Scheme emblem	70	75
462/6 *Set of 5*		1·40	1·40
MS467	111×85 mm. 1m.40, Duke of Edinburgh (45×30 mm)	1·25	1·25

132 Wild Cat

(Des G. Vasarhelyi. Litho Format)

1982 (15 Jan). Wildlife. T **132** and similar multicoloured designs. P 13½ (6, 25s.) or 14½ (others).

468	6s. Type **132**	1·25	30
469	20s. Chacma Baboon (44×31 mm)	2·00	70
470	25s. Eland	2·50	75
471	40s. Cape Porcupine (44×31 mm)	3·25	1·75
472	50s. Oribi (44×31 mm)	3·25	1·75
468/72 *Set of 5*		11·00	4·75
MS473	111×85 mm. 1m.50, Black-backed Jackal (47×31 mm). P 13½×14	2·75	1·90

No. **MS**473 exists imperforate from stock dispersed by the liquidator of Format International Security Printers Ltd.

133 Scout Bugler

(Des G. Vasarhelyi. Litho Format)

1982 (5 Mar). 75th Anniv of Boy Scout Movement. T **133** and similar horiz designs. Multicoloured. P 13½.

474	6s. Type **133**	30	25
	a. Booklet pane. Nos. 474/8×2 and **MS**479	5·00	
475	30s. Scouts hiking	35	50
476	40s. Scout sketching	40	60
477	50s. Scout with flag	40	65
478	75s. Scouts saluting	45	80
474/8 *Set of 5*		1·75	2·50
MS479	117×92 mm. 1m.50, Lord Baden-Powell	1·00	2·00

Nos. 474/9 exist imperforate from stock dispersed by the liquidator of Format International Security Printers Ltd.

134 Jules Rimet Trophy with Footballers and Flags of 1930 Finalists (Argentina and Uruguay)

(Des G. Vasarhelyi. Litho Format)

1982 (14 Apr). World Cup Football Championship, Spain. T **134** and similar horiz designs showing World Football Cup with players and flags of countries in past finals (Nos. 480/90). Multicoloured. P 14½.

480	15s. Type **134**	25	25
	a. Sheetlet. Nos. 480/91	2·50	2·50
481	15s. Jules Rimet Trophy with Czechoslovakia and Italy, 1934	25	25
482	15s. Jules Rimet Trophy with Hungary and Italy, 1938	25	25
483	15s. Jules Rimet Trophy with Brazil and Uruguay, 1950	25	25

484	15s. Jules Rimet Trophy with Hungary and West Germany, 1954	25	25
485	15s. Jules Rimet Trophy with Sweden and Brazil, 1958	25	25
486	15s. Jules Rimet Trophy with Czechoslovakia and Brazil, 1962	25	25
487	15s. Jules Rimet Trophy with West Germany and England, 1966	25	25
488	15s. Jules Rimet Trophy with Italy and Brazil, 1970	25	25
489	15s. World Cup with Holland and West Germany, 1974	25	25
490	15s. World Cup with Holland and Argentina, 1978	25	25
491	15s. World Cup and map of World on footballs	25	25
480/91	*Set of* 12	2·50	2·50
MS492	118×93 mm. 1m.25, Bernabeu Stadium, Madrid (47×35 mm). P 13½	1·10	1·25

Nos. 480/91 were printed together, *se-tenant*, in sheetlets of 12.

Nos. 480/92 exist imperforate from stock dispersed by the liquidator of Format International Security Printers Ltd.

135 Portrait of George Washington

136 Lady Diana Spencer in Tetbury, May 1981

(Des G. Vasarhelyi. Litho Format)

1982 (7 June). 250th Birth Anniv of George Washington. T **135** and similar horiz designs. Multicoloured. P 14×13½.

493	6s. Type **135**	10	10
494	7s. Washington with step-children and dog	10	10
495	10s. Washington with Indian chief	15	10
496	25s. Washington with troops	25	30
497	40s. Washington arriving in New York	30	40
498	1m. Washington on parade	75	1·10
493/8	*Set of* 6	1·40	1·90
MS499	117×92 mm. 1m.25, Washington crossing the Delaware	1·00	1·00

No. **MS**499 exists imperforate from stock dispersed by the liquidator of Format International Security Printers Ltd.

1982 (14 June). As Nos. 437/50 but W w **14** (sideways on Nos. 500, 502/5 and 507). "1982" imprint date.

500	1s. Type **127**	20	75
501	2s. Speckled Pigeon (horiz)	20	75
502	3s. South African Crowned Crane	30	75
503	5s. Bokmakierie Shrike	30	55
504	6s. Cape Robin Chat	30	10
505	7s. Yellow Canary	30	10
506	10s. Red-billed Pintail (horiz)	30	10
507	25s. Malachite Kingfisher	80	30
508	40s. Yellow-tufted Malachite Sunbird (horiz)	1·00	45
509	60s. Cape Longclaw (horiz)	1·25	90
510	75s. Hoopoe (horiz)	1·50	90
511	1m. Red Bishop (horiz)	1·75	2·75
512	2m. Egyptian Goose (horiz)	1·75	5·50
513	5m. Lilac-breasted Roller (horiz)	2·25	12·00
500/13	*Set of* 14	11·00	23·00

Nos. 500/13 exist imperforate from stock dispersed by the liquidator of Format International Security Printers Ltd.

(Des Jennifer Toombs. Litho Format)

1982 (1 July). 21st Birthday of Princess of Wales. T **136** and similar vert designs. Multicoloured. W w **14**. P 13½.

514	30s. Lesotho coat of arms	50	50
	a. Perf 13½×14	40	50
515	50s. Type **136**	50	50
	a. Perf 13½×14	1·25	1·50
516	75s. Wedding picture at Buckingham Palace	60	80
	a. Perf 13½×14	1·00	1·40
517	1m. Formal portrait	80	1·25
	a. Perf 13½×14	1·40	1·75
514/17	*Set of* 4	2·25	2·75
514a/17a	*Set of* 4	3·50	4·75

Nos. 514/17 exist imperforate from stock dispersed by the liquidator of Format International Security Printers Ltd.

137 Mosotho reading Sesotho Bible

138 Birthday Greetings

(Des G. Vasarhelyi. Litho Format)

1982 (20 Aug). Centenary of Sesotho Bible. T **137** and similar multicoloured designs. P 14½.

518	6s. Type **137**	15	20
	a. Horiz strip of 3. Nos. 518/20	75	1·10
519	15s. Sesotho Bible and Virgin Mary holding infant Jesus	20	25
520	1m. Sesotho Bible and Cathedral (62×42 mm)	50	75
518/20	*Set of* 3	75	1·10

Nos. 518/20 were printed together, *se-tenant*, in horizontal strips of 3 throughout the sheet.

(Des G. Vasarhelyi. Litho Questa)

1982 (30 Sept). Birth of Prince William of Wales. T **138** and similar vert design. Multicoloured. P 14×13½.

521	6s. Type **138**	3·00	4·00
	a. Sheetlet. No. 521 and 522×5	5·50	
522	60s. Princess Diana and Prince William of Wales	60	1·00

Nos. 521/2 come from sheetlets of 6 containing one 6s. and five 60s. stamps.

139 "A Partridge in a Pear Tree"

(Litho Format)

1982 (1 Dec). Christmas. "The Twelve Days of Christmas". T **139** and similar horiz designs depicting Walt Disney cartoon characters. Multicoloured. P 11.

523	2s. Type **139**	10	10
	a. Horiz pair. Nos. 523/4	10	10
524	2s. "Two turtle doves"	10	10
525	3s. "Three French hens"	10	10
	a. Horiz pair. Nos. 525/6	10	10
526	3s. "Four calling birds"	10	10
527	4s. "Five golden rings"	10	10
	a. Horiz pair. Nos. 527/8	15	15
528	4s. "Six geese a-laying"	10	10
529	75s. "Seven swans a-swimming"	1·40	1·75
	a. Horiz pair. Nos. 529/30	2·75	3·50
530	75s. "Eight maids a-milking"	1·40	1·75
523/30	*Set of* 8	2·75	3·50
MS531	126×101 mm. 1m.50, "Nine ladies dancing, ten lords a-leaping, eleven pipers piping, twelve drummers drumming". P 13½	2·40	2·75

Nos. 523/4, 525/6, 527/8 and 529/30 were each printed in horizontal *se-tenant* pairs throughout the sheet.

140 *Lepista caffrorum*

(Des G. Vasarhelyi. Litho Format)

1983 (11 Jan). Fungi. T **140** and similar horiz designs. Multicoloured. P 14½.

532	10s. Type **140**	15	10
	a. Tête-bêche (vert pair)	30	30
	b. Booklet pane. Nos. 532/5	2·50	
	c. Booklet pane. Nos. 532/3	3·25	
533	30s. *Broomeia congregata*	30	40
	a. Tête-bêche (vert pair)	60	80
534	50s. *Afroboletus luteolus*	60	90
	a. Tête-bêche (vert pair)	1·10	1·75
535	75s. *Lentinus tuber-regium*	90	1·40
	a. Tête-bêche (vert pair)	1·75	2·75
532/5 *Set of 4*		1·75	2·50

Nos. 532/5 were each printed in sheets of 36 stamps plus 4 labels as the fourth horizontal row.

The stamps in horizontal rows two, six, eight and ten were inverted, forming vertical tête-bêche pairs.

Nos. 532/5 exist imperforate from stock dispersed by the liquidator of Format International Security Printers Ltd.

141 Ba-Leseli Dance

(Des J.W. Litho Format)

1983 (14 Mar). Commonwealth Day. T **141** and similar multicoloured designs. P 14½.

536	5s. Type **141**	10	10
537	30s. Tapestry weaving	15	30
538	60s. Queen Elizabeth II (vert)	25	65
539	75s. King Moshoeshoe II (vert)	30	80
536/9 *Set of 4*		70	1·60

Nos. 536/9 exist imperforate from stock dispersed by the liquidator of Format International Security Printers Ltd.

142 "Dancers in a Trance" (rock painting from Ntloana Tsoana)

(Des G. Drummond. Litho Format)

1983 (20 May). Rock Paintings. T **142** and similar multicoloured designs. P 14½.

540	6s. Type **142**	20	10
541	25s. "Baboons", Sehonghong	45	35
542	60s. "Hunters attacking Mountain Reedbuck", Makhetha	50	1·10
543	75s. "Eland", Lehaha la Likhomo	50	1·60
540/3 *Set of 4*		1·50	2·75
MS544	166×84 mm. Nos. 540/3 and 10s. "Cattle herding", Sehonghong (52×52 mm)	1·25	3·50

Nos. 540/4 exist imperforate from stock dispersed by the liquidator of Format International Security Printers Ltd.

143 Montgolfier Balloon, 1783

(Des J.W. Litho Format)

1983 (11 July). Bicentenary of Manned Flight. T **143** and similar multicoloured designs. P 14½.

545	7s. Type **143**	15	10
	a. Booklet pane. Nos. 545/8	2·75	
546	30s. Wright brothers and *Flyer I*	30	40
547	60s. First airmail flight	50	1·25
548	1m. Concorde	2·25	2·50
545/8 *Set of 4*		2·75	3·75
MS549	180×92 mm. Nos. 545/8 and 6s. Dornier Do-28D Skyservant of Lesotho Airways (60×60 mm)	2·75	2·75

Nos. 545/9 exist imperforate from stock dispersed by the liquidator of Format International Security Printers Ltd.

144 Rev. Eugene Casalis

(Des G. Vasarhelyi. Litho Questa)

1983 (5 Sept). 150th Anniv of Arrival of the French Missionaries. T **144** and similar horiz designs. Multicoloured. P 13½×14.

550	6s. Type **144**	10	10
	a. Tête-bêche (vert pair)	10	15
551	25s. The founding of Morija	10	10
	a. Tête-bêche (vert pair)	15	20
552	40s. Baptism of Libe	10	15
	a. Tête-bêche (vert pair)	20	30
553	75s. Map of Lesotho	20	25
	a. Tête-bêche (vert pair)	40	50
550/3 *Set of 4*		40	60

Nos. 550/3 were each issued in sheets of 20 containing two panes (2×5) separated by a vertical gutter. Within these sheets horizontal rows two and four are inverted forming tête-bêche vertical pairs.

145 Mickey Mouse and Pluto Greeted by Friends

(Litho Questa)

1983 (18 Oct). Christmas. T **145** and similar horiz designs showing Disney cartoon characters in scenes from "Old Christmas" (Washington Irving's sketchbook). Multicoloured. P 14×13½.

554	1s. Type **145**	10	10
555	2s. Donald Duck and Pluto	10	10
556	3s. Donald Duck with Huey, Dewey and Louie	10	10
557	4s. Goofy, Donald Duck and Mickey Mouse	10	10
558	5s. Goofy holding turkey, Donald Duck and Mickey Mouse	10	10
559	6s. Goofy and Mickey Mouse	10	10
560	75s. Donald and Daisy Duck	2·00	2·40
561	1m. Goofy and Clarabell	2·50	2·75
554/61 *Set of 8*		4·50	5·00
MS562	132×113 mm. 1m.75, Scrooge McDuck, Pluto and Donald Duck	3·25	4·50

146 *Danaus chrysippus*

(Des and litho Format)

1984 (20 Jan). Butterflies. T **146** and similar horiz designs. Multcoloured. P 14.

563	1s. Type **146**	30	60
564	2s. *Aeropetes tulbaghia*	30	60
565	3s. *Colotis evenina*	35	60
566	4s. *Precis oenone*	35	60
567	5s. *Precis hierta*	35	60
568	6s. *Catopsilia florella*	35	10
569	7s. *Phalanta phalantha*	35	10
570	10s. *Acraea stenobea*	40	10

571	15s. *Cynthia cardui*	75	10
572	20s. *Colotis subfasciatus*	75	10
573	30s. *Charaxes jasius*	75	30
574	50s. *Terias brigitta*	75	40
575	60s. *Pontia helice*	75	50
576	75s. *Colotis regina*	75	50
577	1m. *Hypolimnas misippus*	75	1·50
578	5m. *Papilio demodocus*	1·50	7·50
563/78	*Set of* 16	8·50	12·50

Nos. 563/78 exist imperforate and as progressive proofs from stock dispersed by the liquidator of Format International Security Printers Ltd.

147 "Thou Shalt not have Strange Gods before Me"

(Des G. Vasarhelyi. Litho Format)

1984 (30 Mar). Easter. The Ten Commandments. T **147** and similar vert designs. Multicoloured. P 13½×14.

579	20s. Type **147**	25	30
	a. Sheetlet. Nos. 579/88	2·25	2·75
580	20s. "Thou shalt not take the name of the Lord thy God in vain"	25	30
581	20s. "Remember thou keep holy the Lord's Day"	25	30
582	20s. "Honour thy father and mother"	25	30
583	20s. "Thou shalt not kill"	25	30
584	20s. "Thou shalt not commit adultery"	25	30
585	20s. "Thou shalt not steal"	25	30
586	20s. "Thou shalt not bear false witness against thy neighbour"	25	30
587	20s. "Thou shalt not covet thy neighbour's wife"	25	30
588	20s. Thou shalt not covet thy neighbour's goods"	25	30
579/88	*Set of* 10	2·25	2·75
MS589	102×73 mm. 1m.50, Moses with Tablets (45×28 mm). P 14	1·00	2·50

Nos. 579/88 were printed together in small sheets of 12 including 2 *se-tenant* stamp-size labels.

148 Torch Bearer

(Des G. Vasarhelyi. Litho Format)

1984 (3 May). Olympic Games, Los Angeles. T **148** and similar horiz designs. Multicoloured. P 13½×14.

590	10s. Type **148**	10	10
591	30s. Horse-riding	10	10
592	50s. Swimming	15	20
593	75s. Basketball	20	25
594	1m. Running	25	30
590/4	*Set of* 5	70	80
MS595	101×72 mm. 1m.50, Olympic Flame and flags.	1·25	2·75

Nos. 590/4 exist imperforate from stock dispersed by the liquidator of Format International Security Printers Ltd.

149 Sauropodomorph Footprints

(Des G. Drummond. Litho Format)

1984 (2 July). Prehistoric Footprints (2nd series). T **149** and similar horiz designs. Multicoloured. P 13½×14.

596	10s. Type **149**	30	30
597	30s. Lesothoasaurus footprints	40	1·00
598	50s. Footprint of carnivorous dinosaur	50	1·50
596/8	*Set of* 3	1·10	2·50

Nos. 596/8 exist imperforate from stock dispersed by the liquidator of Format International Security Printers Ltd.

150 Wells Fargo Coach, 1852

(Des G. Vasarhelyi. Litho Format)

1984 (5 Sept). "Ausipex" International Stamp Exhibition, Melbourne, and Bicentenary of First Mail Coach Run. T **150** and similar horiz designs. Multicoloured. P 14.

599	6s. Type **150**	10	10
	a. Sheetlet. Nos. 599×4 and No. 603	70	
600	7s. Basotho mail cart, circa 1900	10	10
	a. Sheetlet. No. 600×4 and No. 603	80	
601	10s. Bath mail coach, 1784	10	10
	a. Sheetlet. No. 601×4 and No. 603	90	
602	30s. Cobb coach, 1853	15	15
	a. Sheetlet. No. 602×4 and No. 603	1·00	
603	50s. Exhibition logo and Royal Exhibition Buildings, Melbourne (82×25 mm)	50	80
599/603	*Set of* 5	75	1·10
MS604	147×98 mm. 1m.75, G.B. Penny Black, Basutoland 1934 "OFFICIAL" optd 6d. and Western Australia 1854 4d. with frame inverted (82×25 mm)	2·25	3·75

In addition to the listed sheetlets, Nos. 599/602 also exist in separate sheets of 50. No. 603 only comes from the sheetlets.

Nos. 599/602 exist imperforate from stock dispersed by the liquidator of Format International Security Printers Ltd.

151 "The Orient Express" (1900)

(Des Walsall. Litho Format)

1984 (5 Nov). Railways of the World. T **151** and similar horiz designs. Multicoloured. P 14×13½.

605	6s. Type **151**	30	15
606	15s. Class 05 streamlined steam locomotive No. 001, Germany (1935)	30	30
607	30s. Caledonian Railway steam locomotive Cardean (1906)	35	60
608	60s. Atchison, Topeka & Santa Fe "Super Chief" express (1940)	40	1·75
609	1m. LNER "Flying Scotsman" (1934)	40	2·00
605/9	*Set of* 5	1·60	4·25
MS610	108×82 mm. 2m. South African Railways "The Blue Train" (1972)	1·00	2·50

No. 607 exists imperforate from stock dispersed by the liquidator of Format International Security Printers Ltd.

152 Eland Calf

153 Crown of Lesotho

(Des G. Drummond. Litho Format)

1984 (20 Dec). Baby Animals. T **152** and similar horiz designs. Multicoloured. P 14×13½ (1m.) or 15 (others).

611	15s. Type **152**	35	20
612	20s. Young Chacma Baboons	35	25
613	30s. Oribi calf	35	40
614	75s. Young Natal Red Hares	50	1·60
615	1m. Black-backed Jackal pups (46×27 mm)	50	2·00
611/15	*Set of 5*	1·75	4·00

No. 615 exists imperforate from stock dispersed by the liquidator of Format International Security Printers Ltd.

(Des G. Vasarhelyi. Litho Format)

1985 (30 Jan). Silver Jubilee of King Moshoeshoe II. T **153** and similar vert designs. Multicoloured. P 15.

616	6s. Type **153**	10	10
617	30s. King Moshoeshoe in 1960	20	30
618	75s. King Moshoeshoe in traditional dress, 1985	50	85
619	1m. King Moshoeshoe in uniform, 1985	70	1·25
616/19	*Set of 4*	1·25	2·25

154 Christ condemned to Death

(Des G. Vasarhelyi. Litho Format)

1985 (8 Mar). Easter. The Stations of the Cross. T **154** and similar vert designs. Multicoloured. P 11.

620	20s. Type **154**	25	35
	a. Sheetlet. Nos. 620/33	3·25	4·50
621	20s. Christ carrying the Cross	25	35
622	20s. Falling for the first time	25	35
623	20s. Christ meets Mary	25	35
624	20s. Simon of Cyrene helping to carry the Cross	25	35
625	20s. Veronica wiping the face of Christ	25	35
626	20s. Christ falling a second time	25	35
627	20s. Consoling the women of Jerusalem	25	35
628	20s. Falling for the third time	25	35
629	20s. Christ being stripped	25	35
630	20s. Christ nailed to the Cross	25	35
631	20s. Dying on the Cross	25	35
632	20s. Christ taken down from the Cross	25	35
633	20s. Christ being laid in the sepulchre	25	35
620/33	*Set of 14*	3·25	4·50
MS634	138×98 mm. 2m. "The Crucifixion" (Mathias Grünewald). P 13½×14	1·50	3·50

Nos. 620/33 were printed together, *se-tenant*, in a sheetlet of 14 stamps with one stamp-sized label which appears in the central position.

155 Duchess of York with Princess Elizabeth, 1931

(Des G. Vasarhelyi. Litho Format)

1985 (30 May). Life and Times of Queen Elizabeth the Queen Mother. T **155** and similar multicoloured designs. P 13½×14.

635	10s. Type **155**	25	10
636	30s. The Queen Mother in 1975	70	50
637	60s. Queen Mother with Queen Elizabeth and Princess Margaret, 1980	80	90
638	2m. Four generations of Royal Family at Prince Henry's christening, 1984	1·25	2·50
635/8	*Set of 4*	2·75	3·50
MS639	139×98 mm. 2m. Queen Elizabeth with the Princess of Wales and her children at Prince Henry's christening (37×50 mm)	2·25	2·75

156 B.M.W. "732i"

(Litho Format)

1985 (10 June). Century of Motoring. T **156** and similar multicoloured designs. P 14×13½.

640	6s. Type **156**	25	15
641	10s. Ford "Crown Victoria"	35	15
642	30s. Mercedes-Benz "500SE"	75	50
643	90s. Cadillac "Eldorado Biarritz"	1·50	2·50
644	2m. Rolls-Royce "Silver Spirit"	2·00	4·00
640/4	*Set of 5*	4·25	6·50
MS645	139×98 mm. 2m. Rolls-Royce "Silver Ghost Tourer", 1907 (37×50 mm). P 13½×14	4·00	6·00

Nos. 640/5 exist imperforate from stock dispersed by the liquidator of Format International Security Printers Ltd.

157 American Cliff Swallow

158 Two Youths Rock-climbing

(Litho Format)

1985 (5 Aug). Birth Bicentenary of John J. Audubon (ornithologist). T **157** and similar multicoloured designs showing original paintings. P 15.

646	5s. Type **157**	40	30
647	6s. Great Crested Grebe (horiz)	40	30
648	10s. Vesper Sparrow (horiz)	55	30
649	30s. Greenshank (horiz)	1·25	75
650	60s. Stilt Sandpiper (horiz)	1·75	2·75
651	2m. Glossy Ibis (horiz)	2·50	6·00
646/51	*Set of 6*	6·25	9·25

Nos. 646/51 were reissued in February 1986 in sheetlets containing five stamps and one label.

(Des Walsall. Litho Format)

1985 (26 Sept). International Youth Year and 75th Anniv of Girl Guide Movement. T **158** and similar vert designs. Multicoloured. P 15.

652	10s. Type **158**	20	10
653	30s. Young technician in hospital laboratory	50	40
654	75s. Three guides on parade	1·00	1·25
655	2m. Guide saluting	1·75	3·00
652/5	*Set of 4*	3·00	4·25
MS656	138×98 mm. 2m. "Olave, Lady Baden Powell" (Grace Wheatley) (37×50 mm). P 13½×14	2·40	2·75

159 UN (New York) 1951 1c. Definitive and UN Flag

(Des G. Vasarhelyi. Litho Format)

1985 (15 Oct). 40th Anniv of United Nations Organization. T **159** and similar designs. P 15.

657	10s. multicoloured	25	10
658	30s. multicoloured	60	35
659	50s. multicoloured	95	85
660	2m. black and bronze-green	5·00	6·50
657/60	*Set of 4*	6·25	7·00

Designs: Vert—30s. Ha Sofonia Earth Satellite Station; 2m. Maimonides (physician, philosopher and scholar). Horiz—50s. Lesotho Airways Fokker F.27 Friendship at Maseru Airport.

160 Cosmos

160a Mrs. Jumbo and Baby Dumbo

(Des D. Drummond. Litho Format)

1985 (11 Nov). Wild Flowers. T **160** and similar vert designs. Multicoloured. P 15.

661	6s. Type **160**	40	15
662	10s. Small Agapanthus	55	15
663	30s. Pink Witchweed	1·10	70
664	60s. Small Iris	1·50	2·00
665	90s. Wild Geranium or Cranesbill	1·75	3·00
666	1m. Large Spotted Orchid	3·00	5·00
661/6	*Set of 6*	7·50	10·00

(Des Walt Disney Productions. Litho Questa)

1985 (2 Dec). 150th Birth Anniv of Mark Twain. T **160a** and similar vert designs showing Walt Disney cartoon characters illustrating various Mark Twain quotations. Multicoloured. P 11.

667	6s. Type **160a**	50	15
668	50s. Uncle Scrooge and Goofy reading newspaper	1·50	1·00
669	90s. Winnie the Pooh, Tigger, Piglet and Owl	2·00	2·00
670	1m.50 Goofy at ship's wheel	3·00	3·00
667/70	*Set of 4*	6·25	5·50
MS671	127×102 mm. 1m.25, Mickey Mouse as astronaut. P 13½×14	4·75	3·75

No. 669 was printed in sheetlets of 8 stamps.

160b Donald Duck as the Tailor

161 Male Lammergeier on Watch

(Des Walt Disney Productions. Litho Format)

1985 (2 Dec). Birth Bicentenaries of Grimm Brothers (folklorists). T **160b** and similar vert designs showing Walt Disney cartoon characters in scenes from "The Wishing Table". Multicoloured. P 11.

672	10s. Type **160b**	50	20
673	60s. The second son (Dewey) with magic donkey and gold coins	1·50	1·50
674	75s. The eldest son (Huey) with wishing table laden with food	1·75	1·75
675	1m. The innkeeper stealing the third son's (Louie) magic cudgel	2·00	2·75
672/5	*Set of 4*	5·25	5·50
MS676	127×102 mm. 1m.50, The tailor and eldest son with wishing table. P 13½×14	4·75	5·50

No. 673 was printed in sheetlets of 8 stamps.

(Des G. Drummond. Litho Format)

1986 (20 Jan). Flora and Fauna of Lesotho. T **161** and similar vert designs. Multicoloured. P 15.

677	7s. Type **161**	1·75	65
678	9s. Prickly Pear	70	20
679	12s. Stapelia	70	20
680	15s. Pair of Lammergeiers	2·50	60
681	35s. Pig's Ears	1·10	60
682	50s. Male Lammergeier in flight	3·75	2·75
683	1m. Adult and juvenile Lammergeiers	3·75	4·75
684	2m. Columnar cereus	3·75	6·50
677/84	*Set of 8*	16·00	14·50
MS685	125×106 mm. 2m. Verreaux's Eagle	8·50	12·00

162 Two Players chasing ball

162a Galileo and 200-inch Hale telescope at Mt. Palomer Observatory, California

(Des Lori Anzalone. Litho Questa)

1986 (17 Mar). World Cup Football Championship, Mexico. T **162** and similar vert designs. Multicoloured. P 14.

686	35s. Type **162**	1·25	50
687	50s. Goalkeeper saving goal	1·75	1·25
688	1m. Three players chasing ball	3·00	2·75
689	2m. Two players competing for ball	5·00	5·00
686/9	*Set of 4*	10·00	8·50
MS690	104×74 mm. 3m. Player heading ball	9·00	8·50

(Des W. Hanson. Litho Questa)

1986 (5 Apr). Appearance of Halley's Comet. T **162a** and similar horiz designs. Multicoloured. P 14.

691	9s. Type **162a**	75	15
692	15s. Halley's Comet and "Pioneer Venus 2" spacecraft	90	20
693	70s. Halley's Comet of 684 A.D. (from Nuremberg Chronicle, 1493)	1·60	1·40
694	3m. Comet and landing of William the Conqueror, 1066	4·25	5·50
691/4	*Set of 4*	6·75	6·50
MS695	101×70 mm. 4m. Halley's Comet over Lesotho	6·50	7·00

Nos. 691/3 show the face value followed by "S". Examples of these stamps without this currency abbreviation were prepared, but not issued.

163 International Year of the Child Gold Coin

163a Princess Elizabeth in Pantomime

(Litho Format)

1986 (Apr). First Anniv of New Currency (1980). T **163** and similar horiz designs. Multicoloured. P 13½×14.

696	30s. Type **163**	4·00	6·50
	a. Horiz strip of 5. Nos. 696/700	18·00	
697	30s. Five maloti banknote	4·00	6·50
698	30s. Fifty lisente coin	4·00	6·50
699	30s. Ten maloti banknote	4·00	6·50
700	30s. One sente coin	4·00	6·50
696/700	*Set of 5*	18·00	29·00

Nos. 696/700 were printed together, *se-tenant*, in horizontal strips of 5 throughout the sheet.

These stamps were prepared in 1980, but were not issued at that time. Due to increased postal rates a severe shortage of 30s. stamps occurred in 1986 and Nos. 696/700 were sold for postal purposes from mid-April until early August.

(Des L. Nardo. Litho Questa)

1986 (21 Apr). 60th Birthday of Queen Elizabeth II. T **163a** and similar vert designs. P 14.

701	90s. black and yellow	50	60
702	1m. multicoloured	55	65
703	2m. multicoloured	90	1·40
701/3	*Set of 3*	1·75	2·40
MS704	119×85 mm. 4m. black and grey-brown	1·75	3·25

Designs:—1m. Queen at Windsor Horse Show, 1971; 2m. At Royal Festival Hall, 1971; 4m. Princess Elizabeth in 1934.

163b Statue of Liberty and Bela Bartok (composer)

(Des J. Iskowitz. Litho Questa)

1986 (5 May). Centenary of Statue of Liberty. T **163b** and similar horiz designs showing the Statue of Liberty and immigrants to the USA. Multicoloured. P 14.

705	15s. Type **163b**	85	30
706	35s. Felix Adler (philosopher)	85	30
707	1m. Victor Herbert (composer)	3·50	2·00
708	3m. David Niven (actor)	4·50	4·25
705/8 *Set of 4*		8·50	6·25
MS709	103×74 mm. 3m. Statue of Liberty (vert)	3·50	5·00

163c Mickey Mouse and Goofy as Japanese Mail Runners

(Des Walt Disney Productions. Litho Format)

1986 (25 May). "Ameripex" International Stamp Exhibition, Chicago. T **163c** and similar horiz designs showing Walt Disney cartoon characters delivering mail. Multicoloured. P 11.

710	15s. Type **163c**	80	20
711	35s. Mickey Mouse and Pluto with mail sledge	1·25	30
712	1m. Goofy as postman riding Harley Davidson motorcycle	2·50	2·75
713	2m. Donald Duck operating railway mailbag apparatus	2·75	4·00
710/13 *Set of 4*		6·50	6·50
MS714	127×101 mm. 4m. Goofy driving mail to aircraft. P 14×13½	6·50	7·00

Nos. 720a, 720bb, 721a, 721ca, 730ba. Occurs eleven times in the sheet of 40 on R. 1/5, 1/6, 1/8, 1/9, 2/6, 2/7, 2/8, 3/5, 4/4, 4/6 and 4/8 for Nos. 720a, 720bb and 730bc or R. 1/4, 2/4, 4/4, 5/4, 6/4, 7/1, 7/4, 9/1, 9/3, 10/1 and 10/2 for Nos. 721a and 721ca. No. 728a. Occurs thirteen times in the sheet of 49 on R. 6/2 to 7 and on all positions in Row 7.

1986 (6 June)–**88**. Various stamps surch.

(a) As T **164/7a** *by Lesotho Ads, Maseru*

(i) On Nos. 440, 447, 500/1, 506/7 and 509

715	9s. on 10s. Red-billed Pintail (horiz) (No. 506) (Type **164**)	4·00	1·25
	a. Surch on No. 443 ("1982" imprint date)	2·25	2·25
	b. Surch double	†	—
	c. Surch double, one inverted	†	—
716	15s. on 1s. Type **127** (No. 500) (22.8.86)	8·00	3·00
	a. Extra bar		
	b. Surch on No. 437 ("1982" imprint date)	£110	
	c. Surch on No. 437a	5·00	6·00
	ca. Extra bar		
	cb. Surch double		
717	15s. on 2s. Speckled Pigeon (horiz) (22.8.86)	4·00	4·50
	a. Surch double	60·00	
	b. Surch triple		
	c. Surch omitted (in horiz pair with normal)		
718	15s. on 5s. Bokmakierie Shrike ("1982" imprint date) (2.11.87)	3·00	35
	a. Surch double	50·00	
719	15s. on 60s. Cape Longclaw (horiz) (No. 509) (22.8.86)	20	10
	a. Surch on No. 446	60	30
720	35s. on 25s. Malachite Kingfisher (No. 507) (9.87)	19·00	22·00
	a. Small "s"	35·00	40·00
	b. Surch on No. 444	50·00	50·00
	ba. Surch double	£100	
	bb. Small "s"	£100	£100
	bc. Small "s"		
	bd. Surch omitted (in horiz pair) with normal		
721	35s. on 75s. Hoopoe (horiz) (No. 447) (Type **167**) (9.87)	22·00	16·00
	a. Small "s"	40·00	32·00
	b. Surch double	55·00	
	c. Surch on No. 510	£140	£120
	ca. Small "s"	£250	
721*d*	35s. on 75s. Hoopoe (horiz) (No. 447) (Type **167a**) (1.88)	75·00	

(ii) On Nos. 563/5, 567, 573 and 575/6

722	9s. on 30s. Charaxes jasius (Type **164**) (1.7.86)	15	10
	a. Surch with Type **165**	6·50	4·50
	ab. Surch double	†	—
	ac. Surch double (in horiz pair with normal)		
	ad. Surch omitted (in horiz pair with normal)	75·00	
	ae. Surch triple		
	b. Surch omitted (in horiz pair with misplaced surch)		
723	9s. on 60s. Pontia helice (Type **165**) (1.7.86)	3·25	4·00
	a. Surch double	50·00	
	b. Surch double, one inverted	50·00	
	c. Surch inverted		
	d. Surch triple		
724	15s. on 1s. Type **146** (25.6.86)	2·00	2·25
	a. Surch double		
	b. Surch omitted (in horiz pair with normal)		
725	15s. on 2s. Aeropetes tulbaghia (25.6.86)	20	20
726	15s. on 3s. Colotis evenina (25.6.86)	20	20
727	15s. on 5s. Precis hierta (14.8.87)	20	20
	a. Surch double	32·00	
	b. Surch omitted (in horiz pair with normal)	30·00	
728	35s. on 75s. Colotis regina (15.8.86)	35	35
	a. Small "s"	1·50	1·50

(b) As T **168/170** *by Epic Printers, Maseru*

(i) On Nos. 440 and 444

729	9s. on 5s. Bokmakierie Shrike ("1982" imprint date) (30.12.87)	75	20
	a. Long bars		
730	16s. on 25s. Malachite Kingfisher (No. 444) (3.88)	3·50	1·00
	a. Surch on No. 507	£250	
	b. Surch on No. 720	£100	
	ba. Small "s" in surch T **167**	£190	
731	35s. on 25s. Malachite Kingfisher (No. 444) (15.12.87)	2·25	60
	a. Surch on No. 507	13·00	10·00

(ii) On Nos. 566 and 569

732	20s. on 4s. *Precis oenone* (30.12.87)	20	10
	a. Surch double		
	b. Surch double, one inverted	12·00	9·00
	c. Surch triple		
733	40s. on 7s. *Phalanta phalantha* (30.12.87)	20	20

(iii) On No. 722

734	3s. on 9s. on 30s. *Charaxes jasius* (2.2.88)	1·50	1·50
	a. Surch Type **164**	†	—
	b. Additionally Surch 7s. (as No. 735)		
735	7s. on 9s. on 30s. *Charaxes jasius* (2.2.88)	1·75	1·50
715/35 *Set of 21*		65·00	55·00

Some examples of Nos. 722a and 723 show thicker figures due to the method used to construct the artwork for the surcharge.

Nos. 730b/ba show a 16s. surcharge as T **168** applied to stamps previously surcharged with T **167**.

170a Prince Andrew and Miss Sarah Ferguson

171 Basotho Pony and Rider

(Des D. Miller. Litho Questa)

1986 (23 July). Royal Wedding. T **170a** and similar vert designs. Multicoloured. P 14.

736	50s. Type **170a**	40	40
737	1m. Prince Andrew	70	80
738	3m. Prince Andrew piloting helicopter	2·75	2·25
736/8 *Set of 3*		3·50	3·00
MS739 88×88 mm. 4m. Prince Andrew and Miss Sarah Ferguson (different)		3·50	4·50

(Des B. Bundock. Litho Format)

1986 (3 Oct). 20th Anniv of Independence. T **171** and similar horiz designs. Multicoloured. P 15.

740	9s. Type **171**	40	10
741	15s. Basotho woman spinning mohair	40	15
742	35s. Crossing river by rowing boat	50	30
743	3m. Thaba Tseka Post Office	1·00	3·00
740/3 *Set of 4*		2·10	3·25
MS744 109×78 mm. 4m. King Moshoeshoe I		4·75	8·00

171a Chip n'Dale pulling Christmas Cracker

172 Rally car

(Des Walt Disney Co. Litho Format)

1986 (4 Nov). Christmas. T **171a** and similar vert designs showing Walt Disney cartoon characters. Multicoloured. P 11.

745	15s. Type **171a**	80	20
746	35s. Mickey and Minnie Mouse	1·10	30
747	1m. Pluto pulling Christmas taffy	1·90	2·75
748	2m. Aunt Matilda baking	2·25	4·00
745/8 *Set of 4*		5·50	6·50
MS749 126×102 mm. 5m. Huey and Dewey with gingerbread house. P 13½×14		5·50	7·00

(Litho Questa)

1987 (28 Apr). Roof of Africa Motor Rally. T **172** and similar vert designs. Multicoloured. P 14.

750	9s. Type **172**	30	10
751	15s. Motorcyclist	35	15
752	35s. Motorcyclist (different)	55	35
753	4m. Rally car (different)	3·00	5·00
750/3 Set of 4		3·75	5·00

173 Lawn Tennis

(Des Y. Berry. Litho Questa)

1987 (29 May). Olympic Games, Seoul (1988) (1st issue). T **173** and similar vert designs. Multicoloured. P 14.

754	9s. Type **173**	70	10
755	15s. Judo	70	15
756	20s. Athletics	75	20
757	35s. Boxing	85	30
758	1m. Diving	1·10	1·75
759	3m. Ten-pin bowling	2·75	5·50
754/9 *Set of 6*		6·25	7·25
MS760 Two sheets, each 75×105 mm. (a) 2m. Lawn tennis (different). (b) 4m. Football *Set of $1 sheets*		6·00	5·00

Nos. 754/60 incorrectly show the Lesotho flag with white field and emblem at top right.

Similar stamps, with face values of 5, 10, 25, 40, 50s., 3m.50 and a 4m. miniature sheet showing the correct flag with white field and emblem at top left, were placed on philatelic sale from 30 November 1987. They were not, however, according to the Lesotho Philatelic Bureau, sold through post offices and agencies for postal purposes (Price for set of 6 £3, *mint; miniature sheet* £2.75 *mint*).

See also Nos. 838/42.

174 Isaac Newton and Reflecting TelescopeIsaac Newton and Reflecting Telescope

(Des Mary Walters. Litho Format)

1987 (30 June). Great Scientific Discoveries. T **174** and similar horiz designs. Multicoloured. P 15.

761	5s. Type **174**	30	10
762	9s. Alexander Graham Bell and first telephone	30	15
763	75s. Robert Goddard and liquid fuel rocket	80	75
764	4m. Chuck Yeager and Bell XS-1 rocket plane	2·75	4·50
761/4 *Set of 4*		3·50	5·00
MS765 98×68 mm. 4m. "Mariner 10" spacecraft		2·75	3·00

175 Grey Rhebuck

(Des G. Drummond. Litho Format)

1987 (14 Aug). Flora and Fauna. T **175** and similar multicoloured designs. P 15.

766	5s. Type **175**	40	15
767	9s. Cape Clawless Otter	40	15
768	15s. Cape Grey Mongoose	55	20
769	20s. Free State Daisy (vert)	60	20
770	35s. River Bells (vert)	75	30
771	1m. Turkey Flower (vert)	1·75	2·50
772	2m. Sweet Briar (vert)	2·25	3·75
773	3m. Mountain Reedbuck	2·75	5·00
766/73 *Set of 8*		8·50	11·00
MS774 114×98 mm. (a) 2m. Pig-Lily (vert). (b) 4m. Cape Wildebeest. *Set of 2 sheets*		6·00	10·00

176 Scouts hiking

(Des Mary Walters. Litho Questa)

1987 (10 Sept). World Scout Jamboree, Australia. T **176** and similar vert designs. Multicoloured. P 14.

775	9s. Type **176**	60	20
776	15s. Scouts playing football	65	20
777	35s. Kangaroos	80	50
778	75s. Scout saluting	1·75	1·25
779	4m. Australian scout windsurfing	3·75	6·50
775/9 *Set of 5*		6·75	7·75
MS780 96×66 mm. 4m. Outline map and flag of Australia		3·25	4·00

177 Spotted Trunkfish and Columbus' Fleet

(Des I. MacLaury. Litho Questa)

1987 (14 Dec). 500th Anniv of Discovery of America by Columbus (1992). T **177** and similar horiz designs. Multicoloured. P 14.

781	9s. Type **177**	65	20
782	15s. Green Turtle and ships	80	20
783	35s. Columbus watching Common Dolphins from ship	1·00	40
784	5m. White-tailed Tropic Bird and fleet at sea	6·50	8·00
781/4	*Set of 4*	8·00	8·00
MS785	105×76 mm. 4m. Santa Maria and Cuban Amazon in flight	5·50	4·00

No. 782 is inscribed "Carribbean" in error.

178 "Madonna and Child" (detail)

(Litho Questa)

1987 (21 Dec). Christmas. T **178** and similar vert designs showing religious paintings by Raphael. Multicoloured. P 14.

786	9s. Type **178**	30	10
787	15s. "Marriage of the Virgin"	45	15
788	35s. "Coronation of the Virgin" (detail)	90	40
789	90s. "Madonna of the Chair"	2·00	3·50
786/9	*Set of 4*	3·25	3·75
MS790	75×100 mm. 3m. "Madonna and Child enthroned with Five Saints" (detail)	3·00	3·00

179 Lesser Pied Kingfisher

(Des G. Drummond. Litho Format)

1988 (5 Apr). Birds. T **179** and similar horiz designs. Multicoloured. "1988" imprint date, but no printer's imprint. P 15.

791	2s. Type **179**	20	30
792	3s. Three-banded Plover	20	30
793	5s. Spur-winged Goose	20	30
794	10s. Clapper Lark	20	20
795	12s. Red-eyed Bulbul	30	10
796	16s. Cape Weaver	30	10
797	20s. Paradise Sparrow ("Red-headed Finch")	30	10
798	30s. Mountain Chat	35	20
799	40s. Stonechat	40	20
800	55s. Pied Barbet	50	25
801	60s. Red-shouldered Glossy Starling	55	50
802	75s. Cape Sparrow	60	60
803	1m. Cattle Egret	60	80
804	3m. Giant Kingfisher	90	2·50
805	10m. Helmet Guineafowl	1·90	7·00
791/805	*Set of 15*	6·75	12·00

For these stamps showing Questa imprint at bottom left see Nos. 887/99.

40TH WEDDING ANNIVERSARY
H.M. QUEEN ELIZABETH II
H.R.H. THE DUKE OF EDINBURGH

(**180**)

1988 (3 May). Royal Ruby Wedding. Nos. 701/4 optd with T **180** in silver.

806	90s. black and yellow	90	65
807	1m. multicoloured	1·00	80
808	2m. multicoloured	1·75	1·40
806/8	*Set of 3*	3·25	2·50
MS809	119×85 mm. 4m. black and grey-brown	3·25	2·75

*Nos. 806/9 were not available in Lesotho until the middle of 1990.

181 Mickey Mouse and Goofy outside Presidential Palace, Helsinki

(Des Walt Disney Co. Litho Questa)

1988 (2 June). "Finlandia '88" International Stamp Exhibition, Helsinki. T **181** and similar horiz designs showing Walt Disney cartoon characters in Finland. Multicoloured. P 14×13½.

810	1s. Type **181**	10	10
811	2s. Goofy and Mickey Mouse in sauna	10	10
812	3s. Goofy and Mickey Mouse fishing in lake	10	10
813	4s. Mickey and Minnie Mouse and Finlandia Hall, Helsinki	10	10
814	5s. Mickey Mouse photographing Goofy at Sibelius Monument, Helsinki	10	10
815	10s. Mickey Mouse and Goofy pony trekking	10	10
816	3m. Goofy, Mickey and Minnie Mouse at Helsinki Olympic stadium	4·50	3·00
817	5m. Mickey Mouse and Goofy meeting Santa at Arctic Circle	5·50	4·00
810/17	*Set of 8*	9·50	6·75
MS818	Two sheets, each 127×102 mm. (a) 4m. Mickey Mouse and nephew as Lapps. (b) 4m. Daisy Duck, Goofy, Mickey and Minnie Mouse by fountain, Helsinki. *Set of 2 sheets*	5·50	7·00

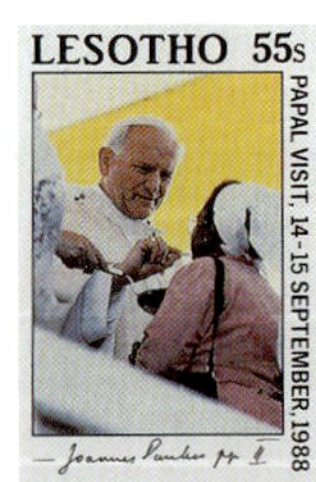

182 Pope John Paul II giving Communion

183 Large-toothed Rock Hyrax

(Litho Questa)

1988 (1 Sept). Visit of Pope John Paul II. T **182** and similar multicoloured designs. P 14.

819	55s. Type **182**	40	25
820	2m. Pope leading procession	1·25	1·50
821	3m. Pope at airport	1·75	2·00
822	4m. Pope John Paul II	2·25	2·75
819/22	*Set of 4*	5·00	6·00
MS823	98×79 mm. 5m. Archbishop Morapeli (horiz)	5·00	4·50

(Des L. Watkins. Litho B.D.T.)

1988 (13 Oct). Small Mammals of Lesotho. T **183** and similar vert designs. Multicoloured. P 14.

824	16s. Type **183**	55	15
825	40s. Ratel and Black-throated Honeyguide (bird)	2·00	55
826	75s. Small-spotted Genet	1·50	85
827	3m. Yellow Mongoose	3·25	5·50
824/7	*Set of 4*	6·50	6·25
MS828	110×78 mm. 4m. Meerkat	3·75	4·00

184 "Birth of Venus" (detail) (Botticelli)

(Litho Questa)

1988 (17 Oct). Famous Paintings. T **184** and similar vert designs. Multicoloured. P 13½×14.

829	15s. Type **184**	30	15
830	25s. "View of Toledo" (El Greco)	35	20
831	40s. "Maids of Honour" (detail) (Velasquez)	45	25
832	50s. "The Fifer (Manet)	55	30
833	55s. "Starry Night" (detail) (Van Gogh)	55	30
834	75s. "Prima Ballerina" (Degas)	70	70
835	2m. "Bridge over Water Lilies" (Monet)	1·75	2·25
836	3m. "Guernica" (detail) (Picasso)	1·75	2·75
829/36	*Set of 8*	5·75	6·25
MS837	Two sheets, each 110×95 mm. (a) 4m."The Presentation of the Virgin in the Temple" (Titian). (b) 4m. "The Miracle of the Newborn Infant" (Titian) *Set of 2 sheets*	4·00	4·50

185 Wrestling

(Des J. Martin. Litho B.D.T.)

1988 (11 Nov). Olympic Games, Seoul (2nd issue). T **185** and similar multicoloured designs. P 14.

838	12s. Type **185**	10	10
839	16s. Show jumping (vert)	10	10
840	55s. Shooting	20	30
841	3m.50 As 16s. (vert)	1·40	2·00
838/41	*Set of 4*	1·50	2·25
MS842	108×77 mm. 4m. Olympic flame (vert)	2·75	3·50

A similar set of three values and a miniature sheet, with fencing instead of show jumping on the 16s., exists, but was not issued, possibly because the 55s., 3m.50 and miniature sheet show the obsolete Lesotho flag.

186 Yannick Noah and Eiffel Tower, Paris

(Des J. McDaniels. Litho Questa)

1988 (18 Nov). 75th Anniv of International Tennis Federation. T **186** and similar multicoloured designs. P 14.

843	12s. Type **186**	60	25
844	20s. Rod Laver and Sydney Harbour Bridge and Opera House	1·75	30
845	30s. Ivan Lendl and Prague	65	25
846	65s. Jimmy Connors and Tokyo (vert)	80	40
847	1m. Arthur Ashe and Barcelona (vert)	1·25	60
848	1m.55 Althea Gibson and New York (vert)	1·25	90
849	2m. Chris Evert and Vienna (vert)	1·50	1·25
850	2m.40 Boris Becker and Houses of Parliament, London (vert)	1·75	1·75
851	3m. Martina Navratilova and Golden Gate Bridge, San Francisco	2·00	2·00
843/51	*Set of 9*	10·50	7·00
MS852	98×72 mm. 4m. Steffi Graf and Berlin	3·00	3·75

No. 844 is inscribed "SIDNEY" in error.

186a "The Averoldi Polyptych" (detail) (Titian)

(Litho Questa)

1988 (1 Dec). Christmas. 500th Birth Anniv of Titian (artist). T **186a** and similar multicoloured designs. P 13½×14.

853	12s. Type **186a**	20	10
854	20s. "Christ and the Adulteress" (detail)	20	10
855	35s. "Christ and the Adulteress" (different detail)	30	20
856	45s. "Angel of the Annunciation"	40	30
857	65s. "Saint Dominic"	55	50
858	1m. "The Vendramin Family" (detail)	75	80
859	2m. "Mary Magdalen"	1·25	1·75
860	3m. "The Tribute Money"	1·75	2·50
853/60	*Set of 8*	4·75	5·50
MS861	(a) 94×110 mm. 5m. "Mater Doloroso". P 13½×14. (b) 110×94 mm. 5m. "Christ and the Woman taken in Adultery" (horiz). P 14×13½ *Set of 2 sheets*	6·00	8·00

187 Pilatus PC-6 Turbo Porter

(Des K. Gromell. Litho Questa)

1989 (30 Jan). 125th Anniv of International Red Cross. Aircraft. T **187** and similar multicoloured designs. P 14.

862	12s. Type **187**	70	20
863	20s. Unloading medical supplies from Cessna 208 Caravan I	1·00	25
864	55s. de Havilland DHC-6 Twin Otter 200/300.	1·40	50
865	3m. Douglas DC-3	2·75	3·50
862/5	*Set of 4*	5·50	4·25
MS866	109×80 mm. 4m. Red Cross logo and Douglas DC-3 (vert)	7·00	4·00

187a "Dawn Mist at Mishima" (Hiroshige)

(Litho Questa)

1989 (19 June). Japanese Art. Paintings by Hiroshige. T **187a** and similar horiz designs. Multicoloured. P 14×13½.

867	12s. Type **187a**	30	10
868	16s. "Night Snow at Kambara"	35	10
869	20s. "Wayside Inn at Mariko Station"	35	10
870	35s. "Shower at Shono"	55	10
871	55s. "Snowfall on the Kisokaido near Oi"	65	40
872	1m. "Autumn Moon at Seba"	85	85
873	3m.20 "Evening Moon at Ryogoku Bridge"	2·00	3·00
874	5m. "Cherry Blossoms at Arashiyama"	2·25	3·75
867/74	*Set of 8*	6·50	7·50
MS875	Two sheets, each 102×76 mm. (a) 4m. "Listening to the Singing Insects at Dokanyama". (b) 4m. "Moonlight, Nagakubo" *Set of 2 sheets*	6·00	7·50

Nos. 867/74 were each printed in sheetlets of 10 containing two horizontal strips of 5 stamps separated by printed labels commemorating Emperor Hirohito.

188 Mickey Mouse as General

189 *Paxillus involutus*

(Des Walt Disney Company. Litho Questa)

1989 (10 July). "Philexfrance 89" International Stamp Exhibition, Paris. T **188** and similar multicoloured designs showing Walt Disneycartoon characters in French military uniforms of the Revolutionary period. P 13½×14.

876	1s. Type **188**	10	10
877	2s. Ludwig von Drake as infantryman	10	10
878	3s. Goofy as grenadier	10	10
879	4s. Horace Horsecollar as cavalryman	10	10
880	5s. Pete as hussar	10	10
881	10s. Donald Duck as marine	10	10
882	3m. Gyro Gearloose as National Guard	3·25	3·25
883	5m. Scrooge McDuck as admiral	4·00	4·25
876/83	*Set of 8*	6·75	7·00
MS884	Two sheets, each 127×102 mm. (a) 4m. Mickey and Minnie Mouse as King Louis XVI and Marie Antoinette with Goofy as a National Guard (*horiz*). P 14×13½. (b) 4m. Mickey Mouse as drummer. P 13½×14. *Set of 2 sheets*	7·50	9·00

No. 879 is inscribed "CALVARYMAN" in error.

(Litho Questa)

1989 (31 Aug)–**91**. As Nos. 793, 795/7 and 803/5, but "1989" imprint date and with printer's imprint at bottom left. P 14.

887	5s. Spur-winged Goose (18.1.90)	55	70
889	12s. Red-eyed Bulbul	60	15
890	16s. Cape Weaver (11.11.89)	60	15
891	20s. Paradise Sparrow ("Red-headed Finch") (2.12.89)	60	15
897	1m. Cattle Egret (1991)	1·75	1·10
898	3m. Giant Kingfisher (1991)	2·75	3·50
899	10m. Helmet Guineafowl (1991)	7·00	8·00
887/99	*Set of 7*	12·00	12·00

This issue is also known perforated 12, but there is no evidence that stamps in this perforation were used for postal purposes in Lesotho.

(Des S. Wood. Litho Questa)

1989 (8 Sept). Fungi. T **189** and similar vert designs. Multicoloured. P 14.

900	12s. Type **189**	20	10
901	16s. *Ganoderma applanatum*	20	15
902	55s. *Suillus granulatus*	45	35
903	5m. *Stereum hirsutum*	3·25	4·50
900/3	*Set of 4*	3·75	4·50
MS904	96×69 mm. 4m. *Scleroderma cepa* ("flavidum")	5·00	5·50

190 Sesotho Huts

191 Marsh Sandpiper

(Des S. Wood. Litho Questa)

1989 (18 Sept). Maloti Mountains. T **190** and similar vert designs. Multicoloured. P 14.

905	1m. Type **190**	70	1·00
	a. Horiz strip of 4. Nos. 905/8	2·50	3·50
906	1m. American Aloe and mountains	70	1·00
907	1m. River valley with waterfall	70	1·00
908	1m. Msotho tribesman on ledge	70	1·00
905/8	*Set of 4*	2·50	3·50
MS909	86×117 mm. 4m. Spiral Aloe	3·00	4·00

Nos. 905/8 were printed together, *se-tenant*, in horizontal strips of 4 throughout the sheet forming a composite design.

(Des Tracy Pedersen. Litho Questa)

1989 (18 Sept). Migrant Birds. T **191** and similar multicoloured designs. P 14.

910	12s. Type **191**	80	30
911	65s. Little Stint	1·50	70
912	1m. Ringed Plover	2·00	1·50
913	4m. Curlew Sandpiper	3·50	5·50
910/13	*Set of 4*	7·00	7·25
MS914	97×69 mm. 5m. Ruff (vert)	9·00	9·50

192 Launch of "Apollo 11"

193 English Penny Post Paid Mark, 1680

(Des G. Welker. Litho Questa)

1989 (6 Nov). 20th Anniv of First Manned Landing on Moon. T **192** and similar multicoloured designs. P 14.

915	12s. Type **192**	25	10
916	16s. Lunar module Eagle landing on Moon (horiz)	25	15
917	40s. Neil Armstrong leaving Eagle	45	25
918	55s. Edwin Aldrin on Moon (horiz)	50	30
919	1m. Aldrin performing scientific experiment (horiz)	85	85
920	2m. Eagle leaving Moon (horiz)	1·50	1·75
921	3m. Command module Columbia in Moon orbit (horiz)	2·00	2·25
922	4m. Command module on parachutes	2·50	2·75
915/22	*Set of 8*	7·50	7·50
MS923	81×111 mm. 5m. Astronaut on Moon	5·50	6·00

(Des U. Purins. Litho B.D.T)

1989 (17 Nov). "World Stamp Expo '89" International Stamp Exhibition, Washington (1st issue). Stamps and Postmarks. T **193** and similar horiz designs. P 14.

924	75s. brown-lake, black and stone	80	80
	a. Sheetlet. Nos. 924/32	6·50	6·50
925	75s. black, grey and rosine	80	80
926	75s. dull violet, black and cinnamon	80	80
927	75s. red-brown, black and cinnamon	80	80
928	75s. black and olive-yellow	80	80
929	75s. multicoloured	80	80
930	75s. black and bright brown-lilac	80	80
931	75s. black, bright carmine and pale brown	80	80
932	75s. brt carmine, black & greenish yellow	80	80
924/32	*Set of 9*	6·50	6·50

Designs:—No. 925, German postal seal and feather, 1807; 926, British Post Offices in Crete 1898 20pa. stamp; 927, Bermuda 1848 Perot 1d. provisional; 928, USA Pony Express cancellation, 1860; 929, Finland 1856 5k. stamp; 930, Fiji 1870 Fiji Times 1d. stamp, 1870; 931, Sweden newspaper wrapper handstamp, 1823; 932, Bhor 1879 ½a. stamp.

Nos. 924/32 were printed together, *se-tenant*, in sheetlets of 9.

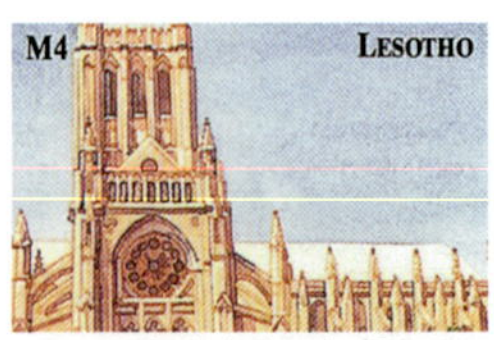

193a Cathedral Church of St. Peter and St. Paul, Washington

193b "The Immaculate Conception" (Valazquez)

(Des Design Element. Litho Questa)

1989 (17 Nov). "World Stamp Expo '89" International Stamp Exhibition, Washington (2nd issue). Sheet 78×61 mm. P 14.

MS933	**193a** 4m. multicoloured	2·50	3·00

(Litho Questa)

1989 (18 Dec). Christmas. Paintings by Velazquez. T **193b** and similar vert designs. Multicoloured. P 14.

No.	Description	Unused	Used
934	12s. Type **193b**	10	10
935	20s. "St. Anthony Abbot and St. Paul the Hermit"	15	10
936	35s. "St. Thomas the Apostle"	25	25
937	55s. "Christ in the House of Martha and Mary"	35	35
938	1m. "St. John writing The Apocalypse on Patmos"	60	75
939	3m. "The Virgin presenting the Chasuble to St. Ildephonsus"	1·60	2·25
940	4m. "The Adoration of the Magi"	2·00	2·75
934/40	*Set of 7*	4·50	6·00
MS941	71×96 mm. 5m. "The Coronation of the Virgin"	7·00	8·00

194 Scene from 1966 World Cup Final, England

(Des G. Vasarhelyi. Litho Questa)

1989 (27 Dec). World Cup Football Championship, Italy. T **194** and similar horiz designs showing scenes from past finals. Multicoloured. P 14.

No.	Description	Unused	Used
942	12s. Type **194**	50	10
943	16s. 1970 final, Mexico	50	15
944	55s. 1974 final, West Germany	1·00	40
945	5m. 1982 final, Spain	3·75	5·50
942/5	Set of 4	5·25	5·50
MS946	106×85 mm. 4m. Player's legs and symbolic football	6·00	7·00

16 s (**195**) — 16 s (**196**) — 16 s Long bars (R. 6/3) — 16 s (**196a**)

1990 (22 Feb)–**91**. Nos. 795, 798/9 and 889 surch with T **195**/**196a** by Lesotho Ads.

No.	Description	Unused	Used
947	16s. on 12s. Red-eyed Bulbul (No. 795) (T **195**)	8·00	1·50
948	16s. on 12s. Red-eyed Bulbul (No. 889) (T **196**)	2·25	20
	a. Surch inverted	40·00	
	b. Surch double	60·00	
	c. Long bars		
	d. Surch with Type **195**		
948e	16s. on 30s. Mountain Chat (No. 798) (T **196a**) (18.1.91)	75	15
	ea. Surch inverted		
	eb. Lower bar omitted	5·00	
948*f*	16s. on 40s. Stonechat (No. 799) (T **196a**) (18.1.91)	1·00	15
	fa. Lower bar omitted	5·00	
947/8f	*Set of 4*	11·00	1·75

The lower cancelling bar is frequently completely omitted from Type **196a** on R. 4/4, although on occasions traces of it do remain.

197 *Byblia anvatara*

198 *Satyrium princeps*

(Des L Nelson. Litho Questa)

1990 (26 Feb). Butterflies. T **197** and similar vert designs. Multicoloured. P 14.

No.	Description	Unused	Used
949	12s. Type **197**	80	15
950	16s. *Cynthia cardui*	90	15
951	55s. *Precis oenone*	1·40	40
952	65s. *Pseudacraea boisduvali*	1·40	65
953	1m. *Precis orithya*	2·25	1·25
954	2m. *Precis sophia*	3·25	2·50
955	3m. *Danaus chrysippus*	4·25	4·25
956	4m. *Druryia antimachus*	5·00	6·50
949/56	*Set of 8*	17·00	14·00
MS957	105×70 mm. 5m. *Papilio demodocus*	8·50	10·00

(Des B. Tear. Litho Questa)

1990 (12 Mar). "EXPO 90" International Garden and Greenery Exhibition, Osaka. Local Orchids. T **198** and similar horiz designs. Multicoloured. P 14.

No.	Description	Unused	Used
958	12s. Type **198**	55	15
959	16s. *Huttonaea pulchra*	60	15
960	55s. *Herschelia graminifolia*	1·25	30
961	1m. *Ansellia gigantea*	1·75	75
962	1m.55 *Polystachya pubescens*	2·00	1·75
963	2m.40 *Penthea filicornis*	2·00	2·25
964	3m. *Disperis capensis*	2·25	3·25
965	4m. *Disa uniflora*	3·00	4·00
958/65	*Set of 8*	12·00	11·50
MS966	95×68 mm. 5m. *Stenoglottis longifolia*	7·50	9·00

198a Lady Elizabeth Bowes-Lyon and Brother in Fancy Dress

199 King Moshoeshoe II and Prince Mohato wearing Seana-Marena Blankets

(Des Young Phillips Studio. Litho Questa)

1990 (5 July). 90th Birthday of Queen Elizabeth the Queen Mother. T **198a** and similar vert portraits, 1910–1919. P 14.

No.	Description	Unused	Used
967	1m.50 brownish black and bright magenta	1·25	1·25
	a. Strip of 3. Nos. 967/9	3·25	3·25
968	1m.50 brownish black and bright magenta	1·25	1·25
969	1m.50 brownish black and bright magenta	1·25	1·25
967/9	*Set of 3*	3·25	3·25
MS970	90×75 mm. 5m. dull orange-brown, brownish black and bright magenta	4·25	4·25

Designs:—No. 967, Type **198a**; 968, Lady Elizabeth Bowes-Lyon in evening dress; 969, Lady Elizabeth Bowes-Lyon wearing hat; **MS**970, Lady Elizabeth Bowes-Lyon as a child.

Nos. 967/9 were printed together, horizontally and vertically *se-tenant*, in sheetlets of 9 (3×3).

(Litho B.D.T.)

1990 (17 Aug). Traditional Blankets. T **199** and similar multicoloured designs. P 14.

No.	Description	Unused	Used
971	12s. Type **199**	10	10
972	16s. Prince Mohato wearing Seana-Marena blanket	10	10
973	1m. Pope John Paul II wearing Seana-Marena blanket	1·75	1·10
974	3m. Basotho horsemen wearing Matlama blankets	2·00	3·00
971/4	*Set of 4*	3·50	3·25
MS975	85×104 mm. 5m. Pope John Paul II wearing hat and Seana-Marena blanket (horiz)	4·50	4·75

200 Filling Truck at No. 1 Quarry

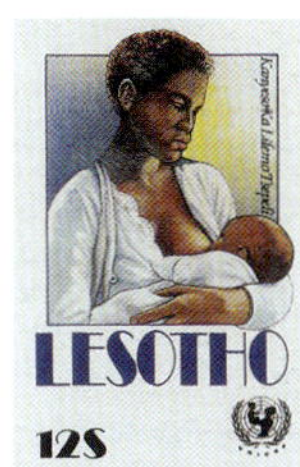

201 Mother breastfeeding Baby

(Litho B.D.T.)

1990 (24 Aug). Lesotho Highlands Water Project. T **200** and similar vert designs. Multicoloured. P 14.

No.	Description	Unused	Used
976	16s. Type **200**	1·00	10

977	20s. Tanker lorry on Pitseng–Malibamatso road	1·00	20
978	55s. Piers for Malibamatso Bridge	1·00	30
979	2m. Excavating Mphosong section of Pitseng–Malibamatso road	3·00	3·75
976/9	*Set of 4*	5·50	3·75
MS980	104×85 mm. 5m. Sinking blasting boreholes on Pitseng–Malibamatso road	7·00	8·00

(Litho Questa)

1990 (26 Oct). UNICEF Child Survival Campaign. T **201** and similar vert designs. Multicoloured. P 14.

981	12s. Type **201**	75	10
982	55s. Baby receiving oral rehydration therapy	1·25	45
983	1m. Weight monitoring	1·75	3·25
981/3	*Set of 3*	3·25	3·25

King Letsie III, November 1990–25 January 1995 (abdicated).

202 Men's Triple Jump

203 "Virgin and Child" (detail, Rubens)

(Des B. Grout. Litho Questa)

1990 (5 Nov). Olympic Games, Barcelona (1992). T **202** and similar multicoloured designs. P 14.

984	16s. Type **202**	70	10
985	55s. Men's 200 metres race	95	25
986	1m. Men's 5000 metres race	1·60	1·25
987	4m. Show jumping	4·25	6·00
984/7	*Set of 4*	6·75	6·75
MS988	100×70 mm. 5m. Olympic flame (horiz)	7·00	8·00

(Litho Questa)

1990 (5 Dec). Christmas. Paintings by Rubens. T **203** and similar vert designs. Multicoloured. P 13½×14.

989	12s. Type **203**	20	10
990	16s. "Adoration of the Magi" (detail)	20	10
991	55s. "Head of One of the Three Kings"	45	25
992	80s. "Adoration of the Magi" (different detail)	60	60
993	1m. "Virgin and Child" (different detail)	70	70
994	2m. "Adoration of the Magi" (different detail)	1·25	1·75
995	3m. "Virgin and Child" (different detail)	2·00	2·50
996	4m. "Adoration of the Magi" (different detail)	2·25	3·25
989/96	*Set of 8*	7·00	8·25
MS997	71×100 mm. 5m. "Assumption of the Virgin" (detail)	4·25	6·00

204 Mickey Mouse at Nagasaki Peace Park

(Des Walt Disney Company. Litho Questa)

1991 (10 June). "Phila Nippon '91" International Stamp Exhibition, Tokyo. T **204** and similar horiz designs showing Walt Disney cartoon characters in Japan. Multicoloured. P 14×13½.

998	20s. Type **204**	80	15
999	30s. Mickey Mouse on Kamakura Beach	85	20
1000	40s. Mickey and Donald Duck with Bunraku puppet	95	25
1001	50s. Mickey and Donald eating soba	1·00	35
1002	75s. Mickey and Minnie Mouse at tea house	1·40	70
1003	1m. Mickey running after "Hikari" express train	1·40	1·00
1004	3m. Mickey Mouse with deer at Todaiji Temple, Nara	3·25	3·50
1005	4m. Mickey and Minnie outside Imperial Palace	3·25	4·00
998/1005	*Set of 8*	11·50	9·00
MS1006	Two sheets, each 127×112 mm. (a) 5m. Mickey Mouse skiing; (b) 5m. Mickey and Minnie having a picnic *Set of 2 sheets*	8·00	8·50

205 Stewart Granger (*King Solomon's Mines*)

206 *Satyrus aello*

(Des R. Jung. Litho Questa)

1991 (20 June). Famous Films with African Themes. T **205** and similar vert designs. Multicoloured. P 14.

1007	12s. Type **205**	35	20
1008	16s. Johnny Weissmuller (*Tarzan the Ape Man*)	35	20
1009	30s. Clark Gable with Grace Kelly (*Mogambo*)	50	35
1010	55s. Sigourney Weaver and male gorilla (*Gorillas in the Mist*)	75	55
1011	70s. Humphrey Bogart and Katharine Hepburn (*The African Queen*)	90	80
1012	1m. John Wayne and capture of rhinoceros (*Hatari!*)	1·25	1·00
1013	2m. Meryl Streep and de Havilland DH.60G Gipsy Moth light aircraft (*Out of Africa*)	2·00	2·25
1014	4m. Arsenio Hall and Eddie Murphy (*Coming to America*)	2·75	3·50
1007/14	*Set of 8*	8·00	8·00
MS1015	108×77 mm. 5m. Elsa the lioness (*Born Free*).	3·75	4·50

(Des S. Heimann. Litho Cartor)

1991 (1 Aug)–**92**. Butterflies. T **206** and similar horiz designs. Multicoloured. P 14×13½.

A. Without imprint date

1016cA	2s. Type **206** (p 13½)	30	50
1017cA	3s. *Erebia medusa* (p 13½)	30	50
1018A	5s. *Melanargia galathea*	30	50
1019A	10s. *Erebia aethiops*	30	50
1020A	20s. *Coenonympha pamphilus*	20	10
	c. Perf 13½	35	30
1021A	25s. *Pyrameis atalanta*	35	30
1022A	30s. *Charaxes jasius*	40	30
	c. Perf 13½	40	30
1023A	40s. *Colias palaeno*	40	30
1024A	50s. *Colias Cliopatra*	45	40
1025A	60s. *Colias philodice*	60	60
1026A	70s. *Rhumni gonepterix*	75	75
1027cA	1m. *Colias caesonia* (p 13½)	75	75
1028A	2m. *Pyrameis cardui*	1·50	1·75
	c. Perf 13½	1·50	1·75
1029cA	3m. *Danaus chrysippus* (p 13½)	1·40	2·00
1030cA	10m. *Apatura iris* (p 13½)	4·50	7·00
1016cA/130cA	*Set of 15*	12·00	14·50

B. With imprint date ("1992") at foot (4.92)

1016B	2s. Type **206**	40	65
1017B	3s. *Erebia medusa*	40	65
1018B	5s. *Melanargia galathea*	40	50
1019B	10s. *Erebia aethiops*	40	50
1020B	20s. *Coenonympha pamphilus*	5·00	40
	c. Perf 13½	40	10
1021B	25s. *Pyrameis atalanta*	45	20
1022B	30s. *Charaxes jasius*	50	10
	c. Perf 13½	55	10
1023B	40s. *Colias palaeno*	55	10
1024B	50s. *Colias cliopatra*	55	10
1025B	60s. *Colias philodice*	60	30
1026B	70s. *Rhumni gonepterix*	65	10
1027B	1m. *Colias caesonio*	1·00	50
1028B	2m. *Pyrameis cardui*	2·00	1·25
1029B	3in. *Danaus chrysippus*	2·75	2·50
1030B	10m. *Apatura iris*	6·50	7·50
1016B/30B	*Set of 15*	16·00	13·00

207 Victim of Drug Abuse

208 Wattled Cranes

(Litho Cartor)

1991 (23 Sept). "Say No To Drugs" Campaign. P 13½×14.

1031	**207**	16s. multicoloured	2·00	60

(Litho Cartor)

1991 (10 Oct). Southern Africa Development Co-ordination Conference. Tourism Promotion. T **208** and similar horiz designs. Multicoloured. P 14×13½.

1032	12s. Type **208**	2·00	1·00
1033	16s. Butterfly on flowers	2·00	1·00
1034	25s. Zebra and tourist bus at Mukurub (former rock formation), Namibia	2·50	1·50
1032/4	*Set of 3*	6·00	3·25
MS1035	75×117 mm. 3m. Basotho women in ceremonial dress. P 13×12	4·00	5·00

209 De Gaulle in 1939

210 Prince and Princess of Wales

(Des D. Miller. Litho B.D.T.)

1991 (6 Dec). Birth Centenary of Charles de Gaulle (French statesman). T **209** and similar vert designs. P 14.

1036	20s. black and lake-brown	80	15
1037	40s. black and purple	1·00	1·25
1038	50s. black and yellow-olive	1·00	40
1039	60s. black and greenish blue	1·00	70
1040	4m. black and dull vermilion	3·50	4·50
1036/40	*Set of 5*	6·50	6·25

Designs:—40s. General De Gaulle as Free French leader; 50s. De Gaulle as provisional President of France, 1944–46; 60s. Charles de Gaulle in 1958; 4m. Pres. De Gaulle, 1969.

(Des D. Miller. Litho B.D.T.)

1991 (9 Dec). 10th Wedding Anniv of Prince and Princess of Wales. T **210** and similar horiz designs. Multicoloured. P 14.

1041	50s. Type **210**	1·50	25
1042	70s. Prince Charles at polo and Princess Diana holding Prince Henry	1·50	45
1043	1m. Prince Charles with Prince Henry and Princess Diana in evening dress	1·60	70
1044	3m. Prince William and Prince Henry in school uniform	2·25	3·00
1041/4	*Set of 4*	6·25	4·00
MS1045	68×91 mm. 4m. Portraits of Prince with Princess and sons	5·50	4·25

211 "St. Anne with Mary and the Child Jesus" (Dürer)

(Litho Walsall)

1991 (13 Dec). Christmas. Drawings by Albrecht Dürer. T **211** and similar vert designs. P 12.

1046	20s. black and bright magenta	60	10
1047	30s. black and new blue	75	20
1048	50s. black and yellowish green	90	25
1049	60s. black and vermilion	95	30
1050	70s. black and lemon	1·00	60
1051	1m. black and orange	1·25	1·10
1052	2m. black and bright purple	2·50	2·75
1053	4m. black and ultramarine	3·50	6·00
1046/53	*Set of 8*	9·50	10·00
MS1054	Two sheets, each 102×127 mm. (a) 5m. black and carmine-rose. (b) 5m. black and cobalt. P 14. *Set of 2 sheets*	6·00	7·50

Designs:—30s. "Mary on Grass Bench"; 50s. "Mary with Crown of Stars"; 60s. "Mary with Child beside Tree"; 70s. "Mary with Child beside Wall"; 1m. "Mary in Halo on Crescent Moon"; 2m. "Mary breastfeeding Child"; 4m. "Mary with Infant in Swaddling Clothes"; 5m. (No. **MS**1054a) "The Birth of Christ"; 5m. (No. **MS**1054b) "The Holy Family with Dragonfly".

212 Mickey Mouse and Pluto pinning the Tail on the Donkey

(Des Walt Disney Co. Litho Questa)

1991 (16 Dec). Children's Games. T **212** and similar vert designs showing Walt Disney cartoon characters. Multicoloured. P 13½×14.

1055	20s. Type **212**	65	15
1056	30s. Mickey playing mancala	70	20
1057	40s. Mickey rolling hoop	80	20
1058	50s. Minnie Mouse hula-hooping	90	25
1059	70s. Mickey and Pluto throwing a frisbee	1·25	75
1060	1m. Donald Duck with a diabolo	1·60	1·40
1061	2m. Donald's nephews playing marbles	2·50	3·00
1062	3m. Donald with Rubik's cube	3·00	4·00
1055/62	*Set of 8*	10·50	9·00
MS1063	Two sheets, each 127×112 mm. (a) 5m. Donald's and Mickey's nephews playing tug-of-war; (b) 5m. Mickey and Donald mock fighting. *Set of 2 sheets*	8·50	9·00

213 Lanner Falcon

214 Queen Elizabeth II and Cooking at a Mountain Homestead

(Des Tracy Pedersen. Litho Questa)

1992 (10 Feb). Birds. T **213** and similar vert designs. Multicoloured. P 14½×14.

1064	30s. Type **213**	75	60
	a. Sheetlet. Nos. 1064/83	13·50	11·00
1065	30s. Bateleur	75	60
1066	30s. Paradise Sparrow ("Red-headed Finch")	75	60
1067	30s. Lesser Striped Swallow	75	60
1068	30s. Alpine Swift	75	60
1069	30s. Didric Cuckoo	75	60
1070	30s. Yellow-tufted Malachite Sunbird	75	60
1071	30s. Burchell's Gonolek ("Crimson- breasted Shrike")	75	60
1072	30s. Pin-tailed Whydah	75	60
1073	30s. Lilac-breasted Roller	75	60
1074	30s. Little Black Bustard ("Korhaan")	75	60
1075	30s. Black-collared Barbet	75	60
1076	30s. Secretary Bird	75	60
1077	30s. Red-billed Quelea	75	60
1078	30s. Red Bishop	75	60
1079	30s. Ring-necked Dove	75	60
1080	30s. Yellow Canary	75	60
1081	30s. Cape Longclaw	75	60
1082	30s. Cordon-bleu ("Blue Waxbill")	75	60
1083	30s. Golden Bishop	75	60
1064/83 *Set of 20*		13·50	11·00

Nos. 1064/83 were printed together, *se-tenant*, as a sheetlet of 20 with the backgrounds forming a composite design.

(Des D. Miller. Litho Questa)

1992 (2 Mar). 40th Anniv of Queen Elizabeth II's Accession. T **214** and similar horiz designs. Multicoloured. P 14.

1084	20s. Type **214**	40	15
1085	30s. View of the Lowlands	40	20
1086	1m. Agaves and escarpment	1·25	65
1087	4m. Thaba-Bosiu	3·00	3·50
1084/7 *Set of 4*		4·50	4·00
MS1088 75×97 mm. 5m. Mountains at sunset		4·50	4·50

215 Minnie Mouse as Spanish Lady, 1540–1660

(Des Walt Disney Co. Litho Questa)

1992 (13 Apr). International Stamp Exhibitions. T **215** and similar vert designs showing Walt Disney cartoon characters. Multicoloured. P 13½×14.

(a) "Granada 92", Spain. Traditional Spanish Costumes

1089	20s. Type **215**	1·00	20
1090	50s. Mickey Mouse as Don Juan at Lepanto, 1571	1·25	40
1091	70s. Donald in Galician costume, 1880	1·50	70
1092	2m. Daisy Duck in Aragonese costume, 1880	3·00	3·75
1089/92 *Set of 4*		6·00	4·50
MS1093 127×112 mm. 5m. Goofy the Bullfighter		4·50	5·50

(b) "World Columbian Stamp Expo '92". Red Indian Life

1094	30s. Donald Duck making arrowheads	90	30
1095	40s. Goofy playing lacrosse	95	40
1096	1m. Mickey Mouse and Donald Duck planting corn	1·50	1·10
1097	3m. Minnie Mouse doing bead work	3·00	3·50
1094/7 *Set of 4*		5·75	4·75
MS1098 127×112 mm. 5m. Mickey paddling canoe		4·50	5·50

216 Stegosaurus

(Des D. Burkhart. Litho Questa)

1992 (9 June). Prehistoric Animals. T **216** and similar horiz designs. Multicoloured. P 14.

1099	20s. Type **216**	1·00	30
1100	30s. Ceratosaurus	1·10	35
1101	40s. Procompsognathus	1·40	45
1102	50s. Lesothosaurus	1·60	55
1103	70s. Plateosaurus	1·60	70
1104	1m. Gasosaurus	2·00	1·25
1105	2m. Massospondylus	2·50	3·25
1106	3m. Archaeopteryx	2·50	4·00
1099/106 *Set of 8*		12·00	9·75
MS1107 Two sheets, each 105×77 mm. (a) 5m. As 50s. (b) 5m. As 3m. *Set of 2 sheets*		11·00	10·00

217 Men's Discus

(Litho Questa)

1992 (5 Aug). Olympic Games, Albertville and Barcelona. T **217** and similar multicoloured designs. P 14.

1108	20s. Type **217**	20	15
1109	30s. Men's long jump	25	15
1110	40s. Women's 4×100 metres relay	30	25
1111	70s. Women's 100 metres	50	50
1112	1m. Men's parallel bars	70	70
1113	2m. Men's double luge (horiz)	1·40	1·75
1114	3m. Women's 30k cross-country skiing (horiz)	1·75	2·50
1115	4m. Men's biathlon	2·00	2·75
1108/15 *Set of 8*		6·50	7·75
MS1116 Two sheets, each 100×70 mm. (a) 5m. Women's figure skating. (b) 5m. Ice hockey (horiz). *Set of 2 sheets*		6·75	7·50

218 "Virgin and Child" (Sasaetta)

219 World Trade Centre, New York

(Litho Questa)

1992 (2 Nov). Christmas. Religious Paintings. T **218** and similar vert designs. Multicoloured. P 13½×14.

1117	20s. Type **218**	55	15
1118	30s. "Coronation of the Virgin" (Master of Bonastre)	65	20
1119	40s. "Virgin and Child" (Master of SS. Cosmas and Damian)	75	25
1120	70s. "The Virgin of Great Panagia" (detail) (12th-century Russian school)	1·25	55
1121	1m. "Madonna and Child" (Vincenzo Foppa)	1·75	1·10
1122	2m. "Madonna and Child" (School of Lippo Memmi)	2·50	2·75
1123	3m. "Virgin and Child" (Barnaba da Modena)	3·00	3·75
1124	4m. "Virgin and Child with Saints" (triptych) (Simonedei Crocifissi)	3·25	4·00
1117/24 *Set of 8*		12·00	11·50
MS1125 Two sheets, each 76×102 mm. (a) 5m. "Virgin and Child with Saints"(different detail) (Simone dei Crocifissi). (b) 5m. "Virgin and Child enthroned and surrounded by Angels" (Cimabue). *Set of 2 sheets*		10·00	12·00

(Des Kerri Schiff. Litho Questa)

1992 (17 Nov). Postage Stamp Mega Event, New York. Sheet 100×70 mm. P 14.
MS1126 **219** 5m. multicoloured .... 6·00 7·00

220 Baby Harp Seal (Earth Summit '92, Rio)

(Des L. Birmingham. Litho Questa)

1993 (8 Feb). Anniversaries and Events. T **220** and similar horiz designs. Multicoloured. P 14.

1127 20s. Type **220** .... 1·25 50
1128 30s. Giant Panda (Earth Summit '92, Rio) .... 1·75 50
1129 40s. Airship LZ-127 *Graf Zeppelin* over globe (75th death anniv of Count Ferdinand von Zeppelin) .... 1·60 50
1130 70s. Woman grinding maize (International Conference on Nutrition, Rome) 60 55
1131 4m. Lt. Robinson's Royal Aircraft Factory B.E 2C shooting down Schutte Lanz SL-11 airship (75th death anniv of Count Ferdinand von Zeppelin) .... 3·75 4·75
1132 5m. Valentina Tereshkova and "Vostok 6" (30th anniv of first woman in space) .... 3·75 4·75
1127/32 *Set of 6* .... 11·50 10·50
MS1133 Two sheets, each 100×70 mm. (a) 5m. Dr. Ronald McNair (Challenger astronaut) (International Space Year). (b) 5m. South African Crowned Crane (Earth Summit '92, Rio). *Set of 2 sheets* .... 10·00 10·00

221 "Orpheus and Eurydice" (detail) (Poussin)

222 Aloe

(Litho Walsall)

1993 (19 Mar). Bicentenary of the Louvre, Paris. T **221** and similar vert designs showing paintings. Multicoloured. P 12.

1134 70s. Type **221** 80 80
a. Sheetlet. Nos. 1134/41 .... 5·75 5·75
1135 70s. "Rape of the Sabine Women" (left detail) (Poussin) 80 80
1136 70s. "Rape of the Sabine Women" (right detail) (Poussin) 80 80
1137 70s. "The Death of Sapphira" (left detail) (Poussin) 80 80
1138 70s. "The Death of Sapphira" (right detail) (Poussin) 80 80
1139 70s. "Echo and Narcissus"(left detail) (Poussin).. 80 80
1140 70s. "Echo and Narcissus" (right detail) (Poussin) 80 80
1141 70s. "Self-portrait" (Poussin) 80 80
1134/41 *Set of 8* .... 5·75 5·75
MS1142 70×100 mm. 5m. "The Money Lender and his Wife" (57×89 mm) (Metsys). P 14½ .... 4·75 5·00

Nos. 1134/41 were printed together, *se-tenant*, in sheetlets of 8 stamps and one centre label.

(Des Mary Walters. Litho B.D.T.)

1993 (1 June). Flowers. T **222** and similar vert designs. Multicoloured. P 14.

1143 20s. Type **222** 40 10
1144 30s. Calla Lily 45 15
1145 40s. Bird of Paradise plant 45 15
1146 70s. Amaryllis 75 40
1147 1m. Agapanthus 90 60
1148 2m. Crinum .... 3·75 2·25
1149 4m. Watsonia .... 2·50 3·25
1150 5m. Gazania .... 2·50 3·50
1143/50 *Set of 8* .... 10·50 9·50
MS1151 Two sheets, each 98×67 mm. (a) 7m. Plumbago. (b) 7m. Desert Rose. *Set of 2 sheets* .... 8·00 8·50

223 *Precis westermanni*

(Des L. Nelson. Litho B.D.T.)

1993 (30 June). Butterflies. T **223** and similar horiz designs. Multicoloured. P 14.

1152 20s. Type **223** 40 15
1153 40s. *Precis sophia* 50 20
1154 70s. *Precis terea* 65 45
1155 1m. *Byblia acheloia* 75 75
1156 2m. *Papilio antimachus* .... 1·25 1·50
1157 5m. *Pseudacraea boisduvali* .... 1·75 3·00
1152/7 *Set of 6* .... 4·75 5·50
MS1158 Two sheets, each 96×62 mm. (a)7m. Precis oenone. (b) 7m. *Precis octavia*. *Set of 2 sheets* .... 7·00 7·00

No. 1157 is inscribed "*Pesudacraea boisduvali*" in error.

224 Queen Elizabeth II at Coronation (photograph by Cecil Beaton)

(Des Kerri Schiff. Litho Questa)

1993 (30 July). 40th Anniv of Coronation. T **224** and similar designs. P 13½×14.

1159 20s. multicoloured 90 90
a. Sheetlet. Nos. 1159/62×2 .... 12·00 12·00
1160 40s. multicoloured .... 1·25 1·25
1161 1m. black and bottle-green .... 1·60 1·60
1162 5m. multicoloured .... 3·50 3·50
1159/62 *Set of 4* .... 6·50 6·50
MS1163 70×100 mm. 7m. multicoloured (42½×28½ mm). P 14 .... 6·50 6·50

Designs: *Vert*—40s. St. Edward's Crown and Sceptre; 1m. Queen Elizabeth the Queen Mother; 5m. Queen Elizabeth II and family. Horiz—7m. "Conversation Piece at Royal Lodge, Windsor" (detail) (Sir James Gunn).

Nos. 1159/62 were printed in sheetlets of 8, containing two *se-tenant* blocks of 4.

225 East African Railways Vulcan Steam Locomotive, 1929

226 Court-house

(Des. G. Vasarhelyi. Litho B.D.T.)

1993 (31 Aug). African Railways. T **225** and similar horiz designs. Multicoloured. P 14.

1164 20s. Type **225** 85 25
1165 30s. Bayer-Garratt Class 15A steam locomotive, Zimbabwe Railways, 1952.. 95 30
1166 40s. Class (25) steam locomotive, South African Railways, 1953 .... 1·00 30
1167 70s. Class A 58 steam locomotive, East African Railways .... 1·50 60

1168 1m. Class 9E electric locomotives, South African Railways ... 1·60 85
1169 2m. Class 87 diesel-electric locomotive No. 8737, East African Railways, 1971 ... 2·00 1·75
1170 3m. Class 92 diesel locomotive, East African Railways, 1971 ... 2·25 2·50
1171 5m. Class 26 steam locomotive, No. 3450, South African Railways, 1982 ... 2·75 3·75
1164/71 *Set of 8* ... 11·50 9·25
MS1172 Two sheets, each 104×82 mm. (a) 7m. Class 6E electric locomotive, South African Railways, 1969. (b) 7m. Class 231-132BT steam locomotive, Algerian Railways, 1937. *Set of 2 sheets* ... 11·00 11·00

(Des V. Seatile Nkhomo. Litho Government Printer, Pretoria)

1993 (24 Sept). Traditional Houses. T **226** and similar horiz designs. Multicoloured. P 14×14½.
1173 20s. Type **226** ... 50 10
1174 30s. House with reed fence ... 55 15
1175 70s. Unmarried girls' house ... 1·00 40
1176 4m. Hut made from branches ... 3·50 5·00
1173/6 *Set of 4* ... 5·00 5·00
MS1177 81×69 mm. 4m. Decorated houses ... 4·00 4·50

227 Black and White Shorthair

(Des V. Seatile Nkhomo. Litho Government Printer, Pretoria)

1993 (29 Oct). Domestic Cats. T **227** and similar multicoloured designs. P 14.
1178 20s. Type **227** ... 75 25
1179 30s. Shorthair Tabby lying down ... 75 25
1180 70s. Head of Shorthair Tabby ... 1·00 40
1181 5m. Black and White Shorthair with Shorthair Tabby ... 3·00 4·00
1178/81 *Set of 4* ... 5·00 5·00
MS1182 113×89 mm. 5m. Shorthair Tabby with rat (vert) ... 4·25 4·50

228 Pluto in Chung Cheng Park, Keelung

229 Tseliso "Frisco" Khomari (Lesotho)

(Des Rosemary DeFiglio. Litho Questa)

1993 (15 Nov). "Taipei '93" Asian International Stamp Exhibition, Taiwan. T **228** and similar multicoloured designs showing Walt Disney cartoon characters in Taiwan. P 14×13½ (horiz) or 13½×14 (vert).
1183 20s. Type **228** ... 65 10
1184 30s. Donald Duck at Chiao-Tienkung Temple Festival ... 75 15
1185 40s. Goofy with lantern figures ... 85 20
1186 70s. Minnie Mouse shopping at temple festival ... 1·25 40
1187 1m. Daisy Duck at Queen's Head Rock, Yehliu (vert) ... 1·50 70
1188 1m.20 Mickey and Minnie at National Concert Hall (vert) ... 1·60 1·60
1189 2m. Donald at Chiang Kai-shek Memorial Hall (vert) ... 1·75 2·00
1190 2m.50 Donald and Daisy at the Grand Hotel, Taipei ... 2·00 2·75
1183/90 *Set of 8* ... 9·25 7·00
MS1191 Two sheets, each 128×102 mm. (a) 5m. Goofy over National Palace Museum, Taipei. (b) 6m. Mickey and Minnie at Presidential Palace Museum, Taipei (vert). *Set of 2 sheets* ... 8·50 8·50

(Des Rosemary DeFiglio. Litho Cartor)

1994 (1 Feb). World Cup Football Championship '94, U.S.A. T **229** and similar multicoloured designs. P 13½×14.
1192 20s. Type **229** ... 50 10
1193 30s. Thato "American Spoon" Mohale (Lesotho) ... 55 15
1194 40s. Jozic Davor (Yugoslavia) and Freddy Rincorn (Colombia) ... 65 20
1195 50s. Lefika "Mzee" Lekhotla (Lesotho) ... 70 25
1196 70s. Litsiso "House-on-fire" Khali (Lesotho) ... 85 55
1197 1m. Roger Milla (Cameroun) ... 1·00 85
1198 1m.20 David Platt (England) ... 1·50 2·00
1199 2m. Karl Heinz Rummenigge (Germany) and Soren Lerby (Denmark) ... 1·75 2·50
1192/9 *Set of 8* ... 6·75 6·00
MS1200 Two sheets, each 100×70 mm. (a) 6m. Klaus Lindenberger (Czechoslovakia). (b) 6m. Franco Baresi (Italy) and Ivan Hasek (Czechoslovakia) (horiz). P 13. *Set of 2 sheets* ... 9·00 9·00

230 King Letsie III signing the Oath of Office

231 Aquatic River Frog

(Litho Government Printer, Pretoria)

1994 (2 Apr). 1st Anniv of Restoration of Democracy. T **230** and similar multicoloured designs. P 14.
1201 20s. Type **230** ... 20 20
1202 30s. Parliament building (horiz) ... 25 20
1203 50s. Swearing-in of Dr. Ntsu Mokhehle as Prime Minister (horiz) ... 40 25
1204 70s. Maj-Gen (P.) Ramaema handing Instruments of Government to Dr. Ntsu Mokhehle (horiz) ... 70 45
1201/4 *Set of 4* ... 1·40 1·00

(Des V. Seatile Nkhomo (Nos. 1205/8), R. Rundo (No. **MS**1209). Litho Questa)

1994 (16 Aug). "Philakorea '94" International Stamp Exhibition, Seoul. Frogs and Toads. T **231** and similar multicoloured designs. P 14×14½.
1205 35s. Type **231** ... 25 10
1206 50s. Bubbling Kassina ... 35 15
1207 1m. Guttural Toad ... 60 60
1208 1m.50 Common River Frog ... 80 1·25
1205/8 *Set of 4* ... 1·75 1·90
MS1209 Two sheets, each 102×72 mm. (a) 5m. Jade frog (sculpture). (b) 5m. Black Spotted Frog and Oriental White Eye (bird) (*vert*). P 14. *Set of 2 sheets* ... 9·00 9·00

232 de Havilland DHC-6 Twin Otter and Emblem

(Des V. Seatile Nkhomo. Litho Goverment Printer, Pretoria)

1994 (17 Nov). 50th Anniv of International Civil Aviation Organization. T **232** and similar horiz designs. Multicoloured. P 14.
1210 35s. Type **232** ... 60 15
1211 50s. Fokker F.27 Friendship on runway ... 75 20
1212 1m. Fokker F.27 Friendship over Moshoeshoe I International Airport ... 1·25 80
1213 1m.50 Cessna light aircraft over mountains ... 1·60 2·00
1210/13 *Set of 4* ... 3·75 2·75

King Moshoeshoe II, 25 January 1995 (restored)–15 January 1996

20s =

(**233**)

234 *Tagetes minuta*

1995 (3 Mar). No. 1022Bc surch with T **233** by Mazenod Ptg Wks, Lesotho.

1214	20s. on 30s. *Charaxes jasius* (p13½)	1·50	75
	a. Perf 14×13½ (No. 1022B)	1·50	65

(Des V. Seatile Nkhomo. Litho Government Printer, Pretoria)

1995 (22 May). Medicinal Plants. T **234** and similar vert designs. Multicoloured. P 14.

1215	35s. Type **234**	35	10
1216	50s. *Plantago lanceolata*	40	15
1217	1m. *Amaranthus spinosus*	65	60
1218	1m.50 *Taraxacum officinale*	1·10	2·00
1215/18 *Set of 4*		2·25	2·50
MS1219	120×91 mm. 5m. *Datura stramonium*	2·50	3·25

235 Pius XII College, 1962

(Des Sumitra Talukdar (2m.), D. Ambrose (others). Litho Government Printer, Pretoria)

1995 (26 July). 50th Anniv of University Studies in Lesotho. T **235** and similar horiz designs. Multicoloured. P 14.

1220	35s. Type **235**	20	10
1221	50s. Campus, University of Basutoland, Bechuanaland and Swaziland, 1966	25	15
1222	70s. Campus, University of Botswana, Lesotho and Swaziland, 1970	35	15
1223	1m. Administration Block, University of Botswana, Lesotho andSwaziland, 1975	55	40
1224	1m.50 Administration Block, National University of Lesotho, 1988	75	1·10
1225	2m. Procession of Vice-Chancellors, National University of Lesotho, 1995	1·00	1·75
1220/5 *Set of 6*		2·75	3·25

236 Qiloane Pinnacle, Thaba-Bosiu

(Des M. Phakisi. Litho Government Printer, Pretoria)

1995 (28 Aug). 20th Anniv of World Tourism Organization. T **236** and similar multicoloured designs. P 14.

1226	35s. Type **236**	25	10
1227	50s. Ha Mohalenyane rock formation	30	15
1228	1m. Botsoela Falls (vert)	55	45
1229	1m.50 Backpackers in Makhaleng River Gorge	80	1·50
1226/9 *Set of 4*		1·75	2·00
MS1230	143×88 mm. 4m. Red Hot Pokers (38×57 mm)	2·25	3·00

No. **MS**1230, which is inscribed "RED HOT PORKERS" in error, was withdrawn in Lesotho on 12 September.

237 "Peace"

238 "Sutter's Gold" Rose

(Des V. Seatile Nkhomo. Litho Government Printer, Pretoria)

1995 (26 Sept). 50th Anniv of United Nations. T **237** and similar multicoloured designs. P 14.

1231	35s. Type **237**	30	10
1232	50s. "Justice" (scales)	40	20
1233	1m.50 "Reconciliation" (clasped hands) (horiz)	1·00	1·90
1231/3 *Set of 3*		1·50	2·00

(Des V. Seatile Nkhomo. Litho Government Printer, Pretoria)

1995 (1 Nov). Christmas. Roses. T **238** and similar vert designs. Multicoloured. P 14.

1234	35s. Type **238**	30	10
1235	50s. "Michele Meilland"	35	10
1236	1m. "J. Otto Thilow"	60	50
1237	2m. "Papa Meilland"	95	1·60
1234/7 *Set of 4*		2·00	2·00

King Letsie III. 15 January 1996 (restored)

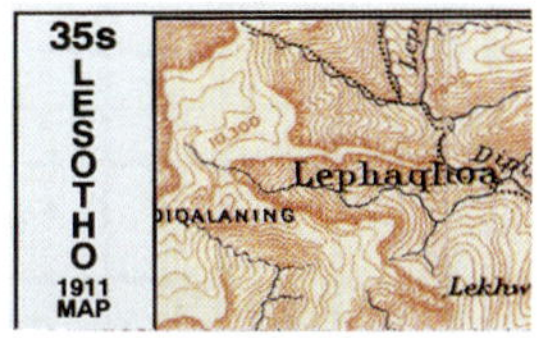

239 Part of 1911 Map showing Lephaqhoa

240 Adding Salt to Cooking Pot

(Des D.Ambrose. Litho Government Printer, Pretoria)

1996 (17 June). Completion of New Standard Map of Lesotho (1994). T **239** and similar horiz designs showing map sections of the Malibamatso Valley. Multicoloured. P 14.

(a) 1911 Map

1238	35s. Type **239**	40	40
	a. Sheetlet. Nos. 1238/47	3·50	3·50
1239	35s. Boritsa Tsuene	40	40
1240	35s. Molapo	40	40
1241	35s. Nkeu	40	40
1242	35s. Three rivers flowing east	40	40
1243	35s. Tibedi and Rafanyane	40	40
1244	35s. Two rivers flowing east	40	40
1245	35s. Madibatmatso River	40	40
1246	35s. Bokung River	40	40
1247	35s. Semena River	40	40

Nos. 1238/47, 1248/57 and 1258/67 were printed together, *se-tenant*, in sheetlets, of 10 (2×5) each forming composite designs.

Nos. 1238/67 were issued in conjunction with a schools campaign to promote use and understanding of maps.

(b) 1978 Map

1248	35s. Mountains and river valley	40	40
	a. Sheetlet. Nos. 1248/57	3·50	3·50
1249	35s. Pelaneng and Lepaqoa	40	40
1250	35s. Mamohau	40	40
1251	35s. Ha Lejone	40	40
1252	35s. Ha Thoora	40	40
1253	35s. Ha Mikia	40	40
1254	35s. Ha Kosetabole	40	40
1255	35s. Ha Seshote	40	40
1256	35s. Ha Rapooane	40	40
1257	35s. Bokong Ha Kennan	40	40

(c) 1994 Map

1258	35s. Mafika-Lisiu Pass	40	40
	a. Sheetlet. Nos. 1258/67	3·50	3·50
1259	35s. Ha Lesaoana	40	40
1260	35s. Ha Masaballa	40	40
1261	35s. Ha Nkisi	40	40
1262	35s. Ha Rafanyane	40	40
1263	35s. Laitsoka Pass	40	40
1264	35s. "Katse Reservoir"	40	40
1265	35s. Seshote	40	40
1266	35s. Sephareng	40	40
1267	35s. Katse Dam	40	40
1238/67 *Set of 30*		10·50	10·50

(Des V. Seatile Nkhomo. Litho Government Printer, Pretoria)

1996 (30 July). 50th Anniv of UNICEF. T **240** and similar multicoloured designs. P 14.

1268	35s. Type **240**	25	10
1269	50s. Herdboys with livestock (horiz)	35	20
1270	70s. Children in class (horiz)	45	20
1271	1m.50 Boys performing traditional dance (horiz)	90	1·50
1268/71 *Set of 4*		1·75	1·75

241 USA Basketball Team, 1936

(Des J. Puvillard. Litho Questa)

1996 (1 Aug). Olympic Games, Atlanta. Previous Gold Medal Winners. T **241** and similar multicoloured designs. P 14.

1272	1m. Type **241**	50	20
1273	1m.50 Brandenburg Gate and stadium, Berlin, 1936	50	30
1274	1m.50 Glen Morris (USA) (decathlon, 1936) (vert)	50	50
	a. Sheetlet. Nos. 1274/82	4·00	4·00
1275	1m.50 Saidi Aouita (Morocco) (5000m running, 1984) (vert)	50	50
1276	1m.50 Arnie Robinson (USA) (long jump, 1976) (vert)	50	50
1277	1m.50 Hans Woellke (Germany) (shotput, 1936) (vert)	50	50
1278	1m.50 Renate Stecher (Germany) (100m running, 1972) (vert)	50	50
1279	1m.50 Evelyn Ashford (USA) (100m running, 1984) (vert)	50	50
1280	1m.50 Willie Davenport (USA) (110m hurdles, 1968) (vert)	50	50
1281	1m.50 Bob Beamon (USA) (long jump, 1968) (vert)	50	50
1282	1m.50 Heidi Rosendhal (Germany) (long jump, 1972) (vert)	50	50
1283	2m. Jesse Owens (USA) (track and field, 1936) (vert)	65	70
1284	3m. Speed boat racing	85	1·00
1272/84	*Set of* 13	6·25	6·00
MS1285	Two sheets, each 110×80 mm. (a) 8m. Michael Gross (Germany) (swimming, 1984) (vert). (b) 8m. Kornelia Ender (Germany) (swimming, 1976) (vert). *Set of 2 sheets*	7·50	7·50

No. 1273 is inscribed "BRANDEBOURG GATE" in error.

No. 1274 incorrectly identifies Glen Morris as the gold medal winner in the 1936 long jump.

Nos. 1274/82 were printed together, *se-tenant*, in sheetlets of 9, the backgrounds forming a composite design.

242 Class WP Steam Locomotive (India)

243 Mothers' Union Member, Methodist Church

(Des G. Bibi. Litho Questa)

1996 (2 Sept). Trains of the World. T **242** and similar horiz designs. Multicoloured. P 14.

1286	1m.50 Type **242**	85	85
	a. Sheetlet. Nos. 1286/91	4·50	4·50
1287	1m.50 Canadian Pacific steam locomotive No. 2471 (Canada)	85	85
1288	1m.50 The "Caledonian" (Great Britain)	85	85
1289	1m.50 Steam locomotive William Mason (USA)	85	85
1290	1m.50 "Trans-Siberian Express" (Russia)	85	85
1291	1m.50 Steam train (Switzerland)	85	85
1292	1m.50 ETR 450 high speed train (Italy)	85	85
	a. Sheetlet. Nos. 1292/7	4·50	4·50
1293	1m.50 TGV express train (France)	85	85
1294	1m.50 XPT high speed train (Australia)	85	85
1295	1m.50 "Blue Train" (South Africa)	85	85
1296	1m.50 Intercity 225 express train (Great Britain)	85	85
1297	1m.50 "Hikari" express train (Japan)	85	85
1286/97	*Set of* 12	9·00	9·00
MS1298	Two sheets, each 98×68 mm. (a) 8m. Class 52 steam locomotive (Germany) (57×43 mm). (b) 8m. ICE high speed train (Germany) (57×43 mm). *Set of 2 sheets*	7·50	8·50

Nos. 1286/91 and 1292/7 were each printed together, *se-tenant*, in sheetlets of 6.

(Des V. Seatile Nkhomo. Litho Goverment Printer, Pretoria)

1996 (10 Dec). Christmas. Mothers' Unions. T **243** and similar vert designs. Multicoloured. P 14.

1299	35s. Type **243**	30	10
1300	50s. Roman Catholic Church	35	10
1301	1m. Lesotho Evangelical Church	65	40
1302	1m.50 Anglican Church	1·00	1·50
1299/1302	*Set of* 4	2·10	1·75

No. 1302 is inscribed "Anglian" in error.

244 Hand Clasp (Co-operation for Development)

245 Land Reclamation

(Des V. Seatile Nkhomo. Litho Government Printer, Pretoria)

1997 (21 Apr). 10th Anniv of Lesotho Highland Water Project (1996). T **244** and similar horiz designs. Multicoloured. P 14.

1303	35s. Type **244**	25	10
1304	50s. Bearded Vulture and rock painting (Nature and Heritage)	1·40	45
1305	1m. Malibamatso Bridge (Engineering)	70	55
1306	1m.50 Katse Valley in 1986 and 1996 (75×28 mm)	1·00	1·75
1303/6	*Set of* 4	3·00	2·50

No. 1305 is inscribed "Developement" in error.

(Des V. Seatile Nkhomo. Litho Government Printer, Pretoria)

1997 (30 June). Environment Protection. T **245** and similar vert designs. Multicoloured. P 14.

1307	35s. Type **245**	30	10
1308	50s. Throwing rubbish into bin	35	15
1309	1m. Hands holding globe and tree	65	40
1310	1m.20 Recycling symbol and rubbish	75	1·00
1311	1m.50 Collecting rain water	85	1·10
1307/11	*Set of* 5	2·50	2·50

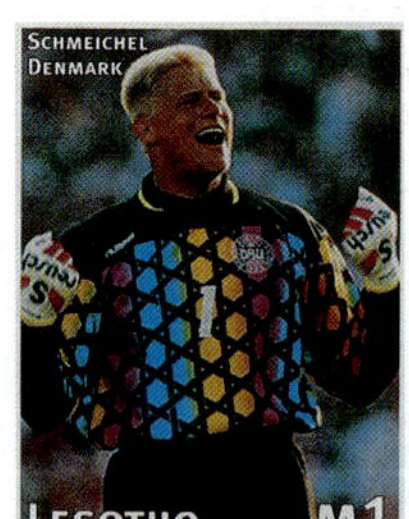

246 Schmeichel, Denmark

247 *Spalia spio*

(Litho Questa)

1997 (3 Nov). World Cup Football Championship, France (1998). T **246** and similar multicoloured designs. P 13½×14.

1312	1m. Type **246**	40	20
1313	1m.50 Bergkamp, Netherlands	55	55
1314	1m.50 Argentine players celebrating	55	55
	a. Sheetlet. Nos. 1314/19	3·00	3·00
1315	1m.50 Argentine and Dutch players competing for ball	55	55
1316	1m.50 Players heading ball	55	55
1317	1m.50 Goalkeeper deflecting ball	55	55
1318	1m.50 Goalmouth melee	55	55
1319	1m.50 Argentine player kicking ball	55	55
1320	2m. Southgate, England	70	70
1321	2m.50 Asprilla, Colombia	80	85
1322	3m. Gascoigne, England	90	95
1323	4m. Giggs, Wales	1·10	1·25
1312/23	*Set of* 12	7·00	7·00
MS1324	Two sheets, each 127×102 mm. (a) 8m. Littbarski, West Germany (horiz). P 14×13½. (b) 8m. Shearer, England. P 13½×14. *Set of 2 sheets*	6·50	7·00

Nos. 1314/19 were printed together, *se-tenant*, in sheetlets of 6 and show scenes from the Argentina v Netherlands final of 1978.

Although First Day Covers for Nos. 1312/24 are dated 31 October 1997, the stamps were not available from Lesotho post offices before 3 November.

(Des D. Burkhart. Litho Questa)

1997 (28 Nov). Butterflies. T **247** and similar horiz designs. Multicoloured. P 14.

1325	1m.50 Type **247**	60	60
	a. Sheetlet. Nos. 1325/33	4·75	4·75
1326	1m.50 *Leptotes pirithous*	60	60
1327	1m.50 *Acratea satis*	60	60
1328	1m.50 *Belenois aurota aurota*	60	60
1329	1m.50 *Spindasis natalensis*	60	60
1330	1m.50 *Torynesis orangica*	60	60
1331	1m.50 *Lepidochysops variabilis*	60	60
1332	1m.50 *Pinacopteryx eriphia*	60	60
1333	1m.50 *Anthene butleri livida*	60	60
1325/33 *Set of 9*		4·75	4·75
MS1334 Two sheets, each 106×76 mm. (a) 8m. *Bematistes aganice*. (b) 8m. *Papilio demodocus*. *Set of 2 sheets*		8·00	8·00

Nos. 1325/33 were printed together, *se-tenant*, in sheetlets of 9 with the backgrounds forming a composite design.

No. 1326 is inscribed "Cyclyrius pirithous", No. 1332 "Pinacopteryx eriphea" and No. **MS**1334(b) "Papalio demodocus", all in error.

248 Rock Paintings and Boy of Wales

(Des V. Seatile Nkhomo. Litho Government Printer, Pretoria)

1998 (30 Jan). 40th Anniv of Morija Museum and Archives. T **248** and similar multicoloured designs based on drawings by Frédéric Christol. P 14½ (with two elliptical holes on the horiz sides (45s. and 2m.) or on the vert sides (others)).

1335	35s. Type **248**	25	10
1336	45s. Hippopotamus and lower jaw bone (horiz)	40	20
1337	50s. Woman and cowhide skirt	30	20
1338	1m. Drum and "thomo" (musical bow)	40	40
1339	1m.50 Warrior with "khau" (gorget awarded for valour)	60	1·00
1340	2m. Herders with ox (horiz)	75	1·25
1335/40 *Set of 6*		2·40	2·75

249 Diana, Princess

(Litho Questa)

1998 (16 Mar). Diana, Princess of Wales Commemoration. T **249** and similar vert designs. Multicoloured. P 13½.

1341	3m. Type **249**	1·10	1·25
	a. Sheetlet. Nos. 1341/6	6·00	6·75
1342	3m. Wearing grey jacket	1·10	1·25
1343	3m. Wearing white polo-necked jumper	1·10	1·25
1344	3m. Wearing pearl necklace	1·10	1·25
1345	3m. Wearing white evening dress	1·10	1·25
1346	3m. Wearing pale blue jacket	1·10	1·25
1341/6 *Set of 6*		6·00	6·75
MS1347 70×100 mm. 9m. Accepting bouquet		6·50	6·50

Nos. 1341/6 were printed together, *se-tenant*, in sheetlets of 6.

250 Atitlan Grebe

251 Cape Vulture

(Des M. Leboeuf (Nos. 1368/76, **MS**1377d D. Burkhart (others). Litho Questa)

1998 (14 Apr). Fauna of the World. T **250** and similar multicoloured designs. P 14.

(a) Vert designs as T **250**

1348	1m. Type **250**	40	40
	a. Sheetlet. Nos. 1348/67	7·00	7·00
1349	1m. Cabot's Tragopan	40	40
1350	1m. Spider Monkey	40	40
1351	1m. Dibatag	40	40
1352	1m. Right Whale	40	40
1353	1m. Imperial Parrot	40	40
1354	1m. Cheetah	40	40
1355	1m. Brown-eared Pheasant	40	40
1356	1m. Leatherback Turtle	40	40
1357	1m. Imperial Woodpecker	40	40
1358	1m. Andean Condor	40	40
1359	1m. Barbary Deer	40	40
1360	1m. Grey Gentle Lemur	40	40
1361	1m. Cuban Parrot	40	40
1362	1m. Numbat	40	40
1363	1m. Short-tailed Albatross	40	40
1364	1m. Green Turtle	40	40
1365	1m. White Rhinoceros	40	40
1366	1m. Diademed Sifaka	40	40
1367	1m. Galapagos Penguin	40	40

P 13½×14

(b) Horiz designs, each 48×31 mm

1368	1m.50 Impala	55	55
	a. Sheetlet. Nos. 1368/76	4·50	4·50
1369	1m.50 Black Bear	55	55
1370	1m.50 American Buffalo	55	55
1371	1m.50 African Elephant	55	55
1372	1m.50 Kangaroo	55	55
1373	1m.50 Lion	55	55
1374	1m.50 Giant Panda	55	55
1375	1m.50 Tiger	55	55
1376	1m.50 Zebra	55	55
1348/76 *Set of 29*		11·50	11·50
MS1377 Four sheets, each 98×68 mm. (a) 8m. White-bellied Sunbird. P 14. (b) 8m. Golden-shouldered Parrot. P 14. (c) 8m. Snail Darter. P 14. (d) 8m. Monkey (47×31 mm). P 13½×14 *Set of 4 sheets*		10·00	10·00

Nos. 1348/67 and 1368/76 were each printed together, *se-tenant*, in sheetlets of 20 or 9.

(Des D. Burkhart. Litho Questa)

1998 (14 Apr). Endangered Species. Cape Vulture. T **251** and similar horiz designs. Multicoloured. P 14.

1378	1m. Type **251**	50	65
	a. Horiz strip of 4. Nos. 1378/81	1·75	
1379	1m. Looking towards ground	50	65
1380	1m. Looking over shoulder	50	65
1381	1m. Facing right	50	65
1378/81 *Set of 4*		1·75	2·40

Nos. 1378/81 were printed together, *se-tenant*, in horizontal strips of 4 throughout the sheet.

252 Siamese

(Des D. Burkhart. Litho Questa)

1998 (4 May). Cats of the World. T **252** and similar horiz designs. Multicoloured. P 14.

1382	70s. Type **252**	30	20
1383	1m. Chartreux	40	25
1384	2m. Korat	65	65

1385	2m. Japanese Bobtail	65	65
	a. Sheetlet. Nos. 1385/90	3·50	3·50
1386	2m. British White	65	65
1387	2m. Bengal	65	65
1388	2m. Abyssinian	65	65
1389	2m. Snowshoe	65	65
1390	2m. Scottish Fold	65	65
1391	2m. Maine Coon	65	65
	a. Sheetlet. Nos. 1391/6	3·50	3·50
1392	2m. Balinese	65	65
1393	2m. Persian	65	65
1394	2m. Javanese	65	65
1395	2m. Turkish Angora	65	65
1396	2m. Tiffany	65	65
1397	3m. Egyptian Mau	85	85
1398	4m. Bombay	95	1·10
1399	5m. Burmese	1·10	1·25
1382/99	*Set of* 18	11·00	11·00
MS1400	Two sheets, each 98×69 mm. (a) 8m. Tonkinese. (b) 8m. Singapura. *Set of 2 sheets*	6·50	7·00

Nos. 1385/90 and 1391/6 were each printed together, *se-tenant*, in sheetlets of 6 with the backgrounds forming composite designs.

253 *Laccaria laccata*

(Des Rina Lyamphe. Litho Questa)

1998 (2 June). Fungi of the World. T **253** and similar horiz designs. Multicoloured. P 14.

1401	70s. Type **253**	30	20
1402	1m. *Mutinus caninus*	40	40
1403	1m. *Hygrophorus psittacinus*	40	40
	a. Sheetlet. Nos. 1403/14	4·25	4·25
1404	1m. *Cortinarius obtusus*	40	40
1405	1m. *Volvariella bombycina*	40	40
1406	1m. *Cortinarius caerylescens*	40	40
1407	1m. *Laccaria amethystina*	40	40
1408	1m. *Tricholoma aurantium*	40	40
1409	1m. *Amanita excelsa* (spissa)	40	40
1410	1m. *Clavaria helvola*	40	40
1411	1m. Unidentified species (inscr "Cortinarius caerylescens")	40	40
1412	1m. *Russula queletii*	40	40
1413	1m. *Amanita phalloides*	40	40
1414	1m. *Lactarius deliciosus*	40	40
1415	1m.50 *Tricholoma lascivum*	55	55
1416	2m. *Clitocybe geotropa*	65	65
1417	3m. *Amanita excelsa*	85	90
1418	4m. *Red-capped Bolete*	95	1·10
1401/18	*Set of* 18	7·75	7·75
MS1419	Two sheets, each 98×68 mm. (a) 8m. *Amanita pantherina*. (b) 8m. *Boletus satanas*. *Set of 2 sheets*	5·50	6·50

Nos. 1403/14 were printed together, *se-tenant*, in sheetlets of 12.

Nos. 1406, 1407, 1414, 1416 and **MS**1419b are inscribed *"Continarius caerylescens", "Laccaria amethystea", "Lactarius delicious", "Clitocybe geotrapa"* and *"Boletys satanus"*, all in error.

254 Simba

(Des Zina Saunders (Nos. 1420/7, **MS**1437a), J. Iskowitz (others). Litho B.D.T.)

1998 (14 July). World Cinema. T **254** and similar multicoloured designs. P 14.

(a) Films about Africa

1420	2m. Type **254**	60	60
	a. Sheetlet. Nos. 1420/7	4·25	4·25
1421	2m. Call to Freedom	60	60
1422	2m. Cry the Beloved Country	60	60
1423	2m. King Solomon's Mines	60	60
1424	2m. Flame and the Fire	60	60
1425	2m. Cry Freedom	60	60
1426	2m. Bopha!	60	60
1427	2m. Zulu	60	60

(b) Japanese Film Stars

1428	2m. Takamine Hideko	60	60
	a. Sheetlet. Nos. 1428/36	4·75	4·75
1429	2m. James Shigeta	60	60
1430	2m. Miyoshi Umeki	60	60
1431	2m. May Ishimara	60	60
1432	2m. Sessue Hayakawa	60	60
1433	2m. Miiko Taka	60	60
1434	2m. Mori Masayuki	60	60
1435	2m. Hara Setsuko	60	60
1436	2m. Kyo Machiko	60	60
1420/36	*Set of* 17	9·25	9·25
MS1437	Two sheets. (a) 68×98 mm. 10m. Lion cubs from Born Free (horiz). (b) 70×100 mm. 10m. Toshiro Mifune *Set of 2 sheets*	6·50	7·00

Nos. 1420/7 and 1428/36 were each printed together, *se-tenant*, in sheetlets of 8 or 9, with the backgrounds forming composite designs.

No. 1423 is inscribed "KING SOLOMAN'S MINES" in error.

255 Ceresiosaurus

(Des R. Rundo. Litho B.D.T.)

1998 (10 Aug). Prehistoric Animals. T **255** and similar multicoloured designs. P 14.

1438	2m. Type **255**	60	60
	a. Sheetlet. Nos. 1438/46	4·75	4·75
1439	2m. Rhomaleosaurus	60	60
1440	2m. Anomalocaris	60	60
1441	2m. Mixosaurus	60	60
1442	2m. Stethacanthus	60	60
1443	2m. Dunklosteus	60	60
1444	2m. Tommotia	60	60
1445	2m. Sanctacaris	60	60
1446	2m. Ammonites	60	60
1447	2m. Rhamphorhynchus	60	60
	a. Sheetlet. Nos. 1447/55	4·75	4·75
1448	2m. Brachiosaurus	60	60
1449	2m. Mamenchisaurus hochuanensis	60	60
1450	2m. Ceratosaurus nasicornis	60	60
1451	2m. Archaeopteryx	60	60
1452	2m. Leaellynasaura amicagraphica	60	60
1453	2m. Chasmosaurus belli	60	60
1454	2m. Deinonychus and Pachyrhinosaurus	60	60
1455	2m. Deinonychus	60	60
1456	2m. Nyctosaurus	60	60
	a. Sheetlet. Nos. 1456/64	4·75	4·75
1457	2m. Volcanoes	60	60
1458	2m. Eudimorphodon	60	60
1459	2m. Apatosaurus	60	60
1460	2m. Peteinosaurus	60	60
1461	2m. Tropeognathus	60	60
1462	2m. Pteranodon ingens	60	60
1463	2m. Ornithodesmus	60	60
1464	2m. Wuerhosaurus	60	60
1438/64	*Set of* 27	14·50	14·50
MS1465	Three sheets, each 100×70 mm. (a) 10m. Coelophysis (vert). (b) 10m. Tyrannosaurus (vert). (c) 10m. Woolly Rhinoceros. *Set of 2 sheets*	8·50	10·00

Nos. 1438/46, 1447/55 and 1456/64 were each printed together, *se-tenant*, in sheetlets of 9 with the backgrounds forming composite designs.

256 Treefish

(Des D. Burkhart. Litho Questa)

1998 (15 Oct). Year of the Ocean. Fishes. T **256** and similar horiz designs. Multicoloured. P 14.

1466	1m. Type **256**	30	30
1467	1m. Tigerbarb	30	30
1468	1m. Bandtail Puffer	30	30
1469	1m. Cod	30	30
1470	1m.50 Clown Loach	45	45
1471	1m.50 Christy's Lyretail	45	45
1472	1m.50 Filefish	45	45
1473	1m.50 Sicklefin Killie	45	45
1474	2m. Brook Trout	55	55
1475	2m. Emerald Betta	55	55
1476	2m. Pacific Electric Ray	55	55
1477	2m. Bighead Searobin	55	55
1478	2m. Weakfish	55	55
	a. Sheetlet. Nos. 1478/85	4·00	4·00
1479	2m. Red Drum	55	55
1480	2m. Blue Marlin	55	55
1481	2m. Yellowfin Tuna	55	55
1482	2m. Barracuda	55	55
1483	2m. Striped Bass	55	55
1484	2m. White Shark	55	55
1485	2m. Permit	55	55
1486	2m. Purple Firefish	55	55
	a. Sheetlet. Nos. 1486/93	4·00	4·00
1487	2m. Harlequin Sweetlips	55	55
1488	2m. Clown Wrasse	55	55
1489	2m. Bicolour Angelfish	55	55
1490	2m. False Cleanerfish	55	55
1491	2m. Mandarinfish	55	55
1492	2m. Regal Tang	55	55
1493	2m. Clownfish	55	55
1494	2m. Bluegill	55	55
	a. Sheetlet. Nos. 1494/1501	4·00	4·00
1495	2m. Grayling	55	55
1496	2m. Walleye	55	55
1497	2m. Brown Trout	55	55
1498	2m. Atlantic Salmon	55	55
1499	2m. Northern Pike	55	55
1500	2m. Large-mouth Bass	55	55
1501	2m. Rainbow Trout	55	55
1502	2m. Platy Variatus	55	55
	a. Sheetlet. Nos. 1502/9	4·00	4·00
1503	2m. Archerfish	55	55
1504	2m. Clown Knifefish	55	55
1505	2m. Angelicus	55	55
1506	2m. Black Arowana	55	55
1507	2m. Spotted Scat	55	55
1508	2m. Kribensis	55	55
1509	2m. Golden Pheasant	55	55
1510	3m. Harlequin Tuskfish	80	80
1511	4m. Half-moon Angelfish	90	90
1512	5m. Spotted Trunkfish	1·10	1·10
1513	6m. Wolf Eel	1·40	1·50
1514	7m. Cherubfish	1·50	1·60
1466/1514	*Set of 49*	26·00	26·00
MS1515	Four sheets, each 98×73 mm. (a) 12m. Common Carp. (b) 12m. Sockeye Salmon. (c) 12m. Winter Flounder. (d) 12m. Horn Shark. *Set of 4 sheets*	10·00	11·00

Nos. 1470/3 show the face value as "M1.5".

Nos. 1478/85, 1486/93, 1494/1501 and 1502/9 were each printed together, *se-tenant*, in sheetlets of 8.

Distribution of Nos. 1466/1515 and possibly also Nos. 1516/18, was delayed by unrest in Maseru.

257 Crowning of King Letsie III

(Des V. Seatile Nkhomo. Litho Government Printer, Pretoria)

1998 (31 Oct). First Anniv of Coronation of King Letsie III. T **257** and similar horiz designs. Multicoloured. P 14.

1516	1m. Type **257**	65	65
	a. Horiz strip of 3. Nos. 1516/18	1·75	1·75
1517	1m. King saluting Basotho nation	65	65
1518	1m. King Letsie in profile	65	65
1516/18	*Set of 3*	1·75	1·75

Nos. 1516/18 were printed together, *se-tenant*, in horizontal strips of 3.

258 *Pelargonium sidiodes*

259 Japanese Akita

(Des Ina-Maria Harris. Litho Government Printer, Pretoria)

1998 (23 Nov). Flowers. T **258** and similar vert designs. Multicoloured. P 14.

1519	10s. Type **258**	10	50
1520	15s. *Aponogeton ranunculiflorus*	10	50
1521	20s. *Sebaea leiostyla*	10	50
1522	40s. *Sebaea grandis*	15	30
1523	50s. *Satyrium neglectum*	15	20
1524	60s. *Massonia jasminiflora*	20	20
1525	70s. *Ajuga ophrydis*	20	20
1526	80s. *Nemesia fruticans*	20	20
1527	1m. *Aloe broomii*	30	20
1528	2m. *Wahlenbergia androsacea*	45	30
1529	2m.50 *Phygelius capensis*	55	40
1530	3m. *Dianthus basuticus*	65	50
1531	4m.50 *Rhodohypoxis baurii*	90	90
1532	5m. *Turbina oblongata*	1·00	1·25
1533	6m. *Hibiscus microcarpus*	1·25	1·50
1534	10m. *Lobelia erinus* (Moraea stricta)	2·00	2·50
1519/34	*Set of 16*	7·50	9·00

(Des R. Francisco. Litho Questa)

1999 (18 May). Dogs. T **259** and similar horiz designs. Multicoloured. P 14.

1535	70s. Type **259**	40	20
1536	1m. Canaan dog	45	20
1537	2m. Husky ("ESKIMO DOG")	60	60
1538	2m. Cirneco dell' Etna	60	60
	a. Sheetlet. Nos. 1538/43	3·25	3·25
1539	2m. Afghan Hound	60	60
1540	2m. Finnish Spitz	60	60
1541	2m. Dalmatian	60	60
1542	2m. Basset Hound	60	60
1543	2m. Shar-pei	60	60
1544	2m. Boxer	60	60
	a. Sheetlet. Nos. 1544/9	3·25	3·25
1545	2m. Catalan Sheepdog	60	60
1546	2m. English Toy Spaniel	60	60
1547	2m. Greyhound	60	60
1548	2m. Keeshond	60	60
1549	2m. Bearded Collie	60	60
1550	4m.50 Norwegian Elkhound	1·50	1·60
1535/50	*Set of 16*	9·25	8·75
MS1551	Two sheets, each 98×69 mm. (a) 8m. Rough Collie. (b) 8m. Borzoi. *Set of 2 sheets*	6·50	6·50

Nos. 1538/43 and 1544/9 were each printed together, *se-tenant*, in sheetlets of 6 with the backgrounds forming composite designs.

260 Belted Kingfisher

261 *Cattleya dowiana*

(Des R. Rundo, Litho Questa)

1999 (28 June). Birds. T **260** and similar multicoloured designs. P 14.

1552	70s. Type **260**	60	20
1553	1m.50 Palm Cockatoo (vert)	85	45
1554	2m. Red-tailed Hawk	85	70
1555	2m. Evening Grosbeak	85	85
	a. Sheetlet. Nos. 1555/63	7·00	7·00
1556	2m. Lesser Blue-winged Pitta	85	85
1557	2m. Atlamira Oriole	85	85
1558	2m. Rose-breasted Grosbeak	85	85
1559	2m. Yellow Warbler	85	85
1560	2m. Akiapolaau	85	85
1561	2m. American Goldfinch	85	85
1562	2m. Northern Flicker	85	85
1563	2m. Western Tanager	85	85

1564	2m. Blue Jay (vert)	85	85
	a. Sheetlet. Nos. 1564/72	7·00	7·00
1565	2m. Northern Cardinal (vert)	85	85
1566	2m. Yellow-headed Blackbird (vert)	85	85
1567	2m. Red Crossbill (vert)	85	85
1568	2m. Cedar Waxwing (vert)	85	85
1569	2m. Vermilion Flycatcher (vert)	85	85
1570	2m. Pileated Woodpecker (vert)	85	85
1571	2m. Western Meadowlark (vert)	85	85
1572	2m. Kingfisher (vert)	85	85
1573	3m. Tufted Puffin	1·00	1·25
1574	4m. Reddish Egret	1·25	1·50
1575	5m. Hoatzin (vert)	1·25	1·75
1552/75	*Set of 24*	17·00	17·00

MS1576 Two sheets. (a) 76×106 mm. 8m. Great Egret. (b) 106×76 mm. 8m. Chestnut-flanked White Eye (Zosterops erythropleura) *Set of 2 sheets* .... 7·50 8·00

No. 1553 shows the face value as "M1.5".

Nos. 1555/63 and 1564/72 were each printed together, *se-tenant*, in sheetlets of 9 with the backgrounds forming composite designs.

(Des D. Burkhart. Litho Questa)

1999 (30 July). Orchids of the World. T **261** and similar vert designs. Multicoloured. P 14.

1577	1m.50 Type **261**	75	30
1578	2m. *Cochleanthes discolor*	75	75
	a. Sheetlet. Nos. 1578/86	6·00	6·00
1579	2m. *Cischweinfia dasyandra*	75	75
1580	2m. *Ceratostylis retisquama*	75	75
1581	2m. *Comparettia speciosa*	75	75
1582	2m. *Cryptostylis subulata*	75	75
1583	2m. *Cycnoches ventricosum*	75	75
1584	2m. *Dactylorhiza maculata*	75	75
1585	2m. *Cypripedium calceolus*	75	75
1586	2m. *Cymbidium finlaysonianum*	75	75
1587	2m. *Apasia epidendroides*	75	75
	a. Sheetlet. Nos. 1587/95	6·00	6·00
1588	2m. *Barkaria lindleyana*	75	75
1589	2m. *Bifrenaria tetragona*	75	75
1590	2m. *Bulbophyllum graveolens*	75	75
1591	2m. *Brassavola flagellaris*	75	75
1592	2m. *Bollea lawrenceana*	75	75
1593	2m. *Caladenia carnea*	75	75
1594	2m. *Catasetum macrocarpum*	75	75
1595	2m. *Cattleya aurantiaca*	75	75
1596	2m. *Dendrobium bellatulum*	75	75
	a. Sheetlet. Nos. 1596/1604	6·00	6·00
1597	2m. *Dendrobium trigonopus*	75	75
1598	2m. *Dimerandra emarginata*	75	75
1599	2m. *Dressleria eburnea*	75	75
1600	2m. *Dracula tubeana*	75	75
1601	2m. *Disa kirstenbosch*	75	75
1602	2m. *Encyclia alata*	75	75
1603	2m. *Epidendrum pseudepidendrum*	75	75
1604	2m. *Eriopsis biloba*	75	75
1605	3m. *Diurus behrii*	1·00	1·00
1606	4m. *Ancistrochilus rothchildianus*	1·25	1·25
1607	5m. *Aerangis curnowiana*	1·40	1·40
1608	7m. *Arachnis flos-aeris*	1·75	2·00
1609	8m. *Aspasia principissa*	1·75	2·25
1577/1609	*Set of 33*	24·00	24·00

MS1610 Four sheets, each 110×82 mm. (a) 10m. *Paphiopedilum tonsum*. (b) 10m. *Ansellia africana*. (c) 10m. *Laelia rubescens*. (d) 10m. *Ophrys apifera*. *Set of 4 sheets* .... 14·00 15·00

Nos. 1578/86, 1587/95 and 1596/1604 were each printed together, *se-tenant*, in sheetlets of 9.

No. 1583 was inscribed "Cycnoches ventricsum" in error.

262 "Austerity" Type Series 52 Steam Locomotive, Frankfurt, 1939

(Des B. Pevsner. Litho Questa)

1999 (16 Aug). "iBRA '99" International Stamp Exhibition, Nuremburg. Railway Locomotives. T **262** and similar horiz design. Multicoloured. P 14×14½.

1611	7m. Type **262**	2·00	2·00
1612	8m. Adler and Brandenburg Gate, Berlin, 1835	2·00	2·00

263 "View of Sumida River in Snow" (Hokusai)

264 African Boy

(Des R. Sauber. Litho Questa)

1999 (16 Aug). 150th Death Anniv of Katsushika Hokusai (Japanese artist). T **263** and similar multicoloured designs. P 14×13½.

1613	3m. Type **263**	75	75
	a. Sheetlet. Nos. 1613/18	4·00	4·00
1614	3m. "Two Carp"	75	75
1615	3m. "The Blind" (woman with eyes closed)	75	75
1616	3m. "The Blind" (woman with one eye open)	75	75
1617	3m. "Fishing by Torchlight"	75	75
1618	3m. "Whaling off the Goto Islands"	75	75
1619	3m. "Makamaro watching the Moon from a Hill"	75	75
	a. Sheetlet. Nos. 1619/24	4·00	4·00
1620	3m. "Peonies and Butterfly"	75	75
1621	3m. "The Blind" (old man with open eyes)	75	75
1622	3m. "The Blind" (old man with one eye open)	75	75
1623	3m. "People crossing an Arched Bridge" (four people on bridge)	75	75
1624	3m. "People crossing an Arched Bridge" (two people on bridge)	75	75
1613/24	*Set of 12*	8·00	8·00

MS1625 Two sheets, each 102×72 mm. (a) 10m. "Bellflower and Dragonfly" (*vert*). (b) 10m. "Moon above Yodo River and Osaka Castle" (*vert*). P 13½×14 *Set of 2 sheets* .... 5·50 6·00

Nos. 1613/18 and 1619/24 were each printed together, *se-tenant*, in sheetlets of 6.

(Des M. Harper. Litho Questa)

1999 (16 Aug). 10th Anniv of United Nations Rights of the Child Convention. T **264** and similar vert designs. Multicoloured. P 14.

1626	2m. Type **264**	85	90
	a. Sheetlet. Nos. 1626/8	2·25	3·40
1627	2m. Asian girl	85	90
1628	2m. European boy	85	90
1626/8	*Set of 3*	2·25	2·40

Nos. 1626/8 were printed together, *se-tenant*, in sheetlets of 3 with the backgrounds forming a composite design.

265 Mephistopheles appearing as Dog in Faust's study

(Des J. Iskowitz. Litho Questa)

1999 (16 Aug). 250th Birth Anniv of Johann von Goethe (German writer). T **265** and similar designs. P 14.

1629	6m. multicoloured	1·40	1·75
	a. Sheetlet. Nos. 1629/31	3·75	4·75
1630	6m. deep ultramarine, slate-lilac and black	1·40	1·75
1631	6m. multicoloured	1·40	1·75
1629/31	*Set of 3*	3·75	4·75

MS1632 76×106 mm. 12m. bright crimson, reddish violet and black .... 2·75 3·25

Designs: Horiz—No. 1629, Type **265**; 1630, Von Goethe and Von Schiller; 1631, Mephistopheles disguised as a dog scorching the Earth. Vert—No. **MS**1632, Mephistopheles.

Nos. 1629/31 were printed together, *se-tenant*, in sheetlets of 3 with enlarged illustrated margins.

No. 1629, in addition to the normal country name, shows "GUYANA" twice in violet across the centre of the design.

266 "Water Lily at Night" (Pan Tianshou)

(Litho Questa)

1999 (16 Aug). "China '99" International Stamp Exhibition, Beijing. Paintings of Pan Tianshou (Chinese artist). T **266** and similar multicoloured designs. P 13×13½.

1633	1m.50	Type **266**	40	50
		a. Sheetlet. Nos. 1633/42	3·50	4·50
1634	1m.50	"Hen and Chicks"	40	50
1635	1m.50	"Plum Blossom and Orchid"	40	50
1636	1m.50	"Plum Blossom and Banana Tree"	40	50
1637	1m.50	"Crane and Pine"	40	50
1638	1m.50	"Swallows"	40	50
1639	1m.50	"Eagle on the Pine" (bird looking up)	40	50
1640	1m.50	"Palm Tree"	40	50
1641	1m.50	"Eagle on the Pine" (bird looking down)	40	50
1642	1m.50	"Orchids"	40	50
1633/42		*Set of* 10	3·50	4·50
MS1643		138×105 mm. 6m. "Sponge Gourd" (51×39 mm); 6m. "Dragonfly" (51×39 mm). P 13	4·25	4·75

Nos. 1633/42 were printed together, *se-tenant*, in sheetlets of 10.

267 Queen Elizabeth, 1938

268 Chinese Soldier firing Rocket, 1150

(Litho Questa)

1999 (17 Aug). "Queen Elizabeth the Queen Mother's Century". T **267** and similar vert designs. P 14.

1644	5m.	black and gold	1·50	1·50
		a. Sheetlet. Nos. 1644/7	5·50	5·50
1645	5m.	multicoloured	1·50	1·50
1646	5m.	black and gold	1·50	1·50
1647	5m.	multicoloured	1·50	1·50
1644/7		*Set of* 4	5·50	5·50
MS1648		153×152 mm. 15m. multicoloured. P 13½×14.	3·75	4·00

Designs: (As Type **267**)—No. 1644 Type **267**; 1645, King George VI and Queen Elizabeth, 1948; 1646, Queen Mother wearing tiara, 1963; 1647, Queen Mother wearing blue hat, Canada, 1989. (37×50 mm)—No. **MS**1648, Queen Mother outside Clarence House.

Designs: (As Type **267**)—No. 1644 Type **267**; 1645, King George VI and Queen Elizabeth, 1948; 1646, Queen Mother wearing tiara, 1963; 1647, Queen Mother wearing blue hat, Canada, 1989. (37×50 mm)—No. **MS**1648, Queen Mother outside Clarence House.

Nos. 1644/7 were printed together, *se-tenant*, as a sheetlet of 4 stamps and a central label with inscribed and embossed margins.

No. **MS**1648 also shows the Royal Arms embossed in gold.

(Des L. Birmingham. Litho Cartor)

1999 (31 Dec). New Millennium. Events of Second Half of 12th Century. T **268** and similar multicoloured designs. P 12½.

1649	1m.50	Type **268**	60	60
		a. Sheetlet. Nos. 1649/65	9·00	9·00
1650	1m.50	Burmese temple guardian, 1150	60	60
1651	1m.50	Troubadour serenading Lady, 1150	60	60
1652	1m.50	Abbot Sager (advisor to French Kings), 1150	60	60
1653	1m.50	Pope Adrian IV, 1154	60	60
1654	1m.50	Henry II of England, 1154	60	60
1655	1m.50	Bust of Frederick Barbarossa, King of Germany and Holy Roman Emperor, 1155	60	60
1656	1m.50	Shogun Yoritomo of Japan, 1156	60	60
1657	1m.50	Count and Countess of Vaudemont (Crusader monument), 1165	60	60
1658	1m.50	Ibn Rushd (Arab translator), 1169	60	60
1659	1m.50	Archbishop Thomas a Becket, 1170	60	60
1660	1m.50	Leaning Tower of Pisa, 1174	60	60
1661	1m.50	Pivot windmill, 1180	60	60
1662	1m.50	Saladin (Saracen general), 1187	60	60
1663	1m.50	King Richard the Lionheart of England, 1189	60	60
1664	1m.50	Moai (statues), Easter Island, 1150 (59×39 mm)	60	60
1665	1m.50	Crusader, 1189	60	60
1649/65		*Set of* 17	9·00	9·00

Nos. 1649/65 were printed together, *se-tenant*, in sheetlets of 17 including a central label (59×39 mm) and inscribed left margin.

269 U.S.S. *New Jersey* (battleship)

270 King Letsie III and Miss Karabo Anne Motsoeneng

(Des F. Rivera. Litho Questa)

1999 (31 Dec). Maritime Development 1700–2000. T **269** and similar multicoloured designs. P 14.

1666	4m.	Type **269**	1·00	1·00
		a. Sheetlet. Nos. 1666/71	5·50	5·50
1667	4m.	*Aquila* (Italian aircraft carrier)	1·00	1·00
1668	4m.	*De Zeven Provincien* (Dutch cruiser)	1·00	1·00
1669	4m.	HMS *Formidable* (aircraft carrier)	1·00	1·00
1670	4m.	*Vittorio Veneto* (Italian cruiser)	1·00	1·00
1671	4m.	HMS *Hampshire* (destroyer)	1·00	1·00
1672	4m.	*France* (French liner)	1·00	1·00
		a. Sheetlet. Nos. 1672/7	5·50	5·50
1673	4m.	*Queen Elizabeth 2* (liner)	1·00	1·00
1674	4m.	*United States* (American liner)	1·00	1·00
1675	4m.	*Queen Elizabeth* (liner)	1·00	1·00
1676	4m.	*Michelangelo* (Italian liner)	1·00	1·00
1677	4m.	*Mauretania* (British liner)	1·00	1·00
1678	4m.	*Shearwater* (British hydrofoil ferry)	1·00	1·00
		a. Sheetlet. Nos. 1678/83	5·50	5·50
1679	4m.	British Class M submarine	1·00	1·00
1680	4m.	SRN 130 hovercraft	1·00	1·00
1681	4m.	Italian Second World War submarine	1·00	1·00
1682	4m.	SRN 3 hovercraft	1·00	1·00
1683	4m.	*Soucoupe Plongeante* (oceanographic submersible)	1·00	1·00
1684	4m.	*James Watt* (early steamship)	1·00	1·00
		a. Sheetlet. Nos. 1684/9	5·50	5·50
1685	4m.	*Savannah* (steam/sail ship), 1819	1·00	1·00
1686	4m.	*Amistad* (slave schooner)	1·00	1·00
1687	4m.	American Navy brig	1·00	1·00
1688	4m.	*Great Britain* (liner)	1·00	1·00
1689	4m.	*Sirius* (paddle steamer)	1·00	1·00
1666/89		*Set of* 24	22·00	22·00
MS1690		Four sheets, each 106×76 mm. (a) 15m. U.S.S. *Enterprise* (aircraft carrier) (vert); (b) 15m. *Titanic* (liner); (c) 15m. German U-boat; (d) 15m. *E. W. Morrison* (Great Lakes schooner) (vert) *Set of 4 sheets*	15·00	16·00

Nos. 1666/71, 1672/7, 1678/83 and 1684/9 were each printed together, *se-tenant*, in sheetlets of 6 with enlarged illustrated and inscribed top margins.

No. 1686 is wrongly described as "ARMISTAD" and No. 1687 "BRICK", both on the sheetlet margin.

(Des M. Friedman. Litho Questa)

2000 (18 Feb). Wedding of King Letsie III. T **270** and similar vert designs. Multicoloured. P 14.

1691 1m. Type **270** 75 75
a. Sheetlet. Nos. 1691/4 .... 2·75 2·75
1692 1m. Miss Karabo Anne Motsoeneng 75 75
1693 1m. King Letsie III 75 75
1694 1m. King Letsie III and Miss Karabo Motsoeneng in traditional dress 75 75
1691/4 *Set of 4* .... 2·75 2·75

Nos. 1691/4 were printed together, *se-tenant*, as a sheetlet of 4 stamps and a central label with enlarged illustrated margins.

271 "Apollo 18" and "Soyuz 19" docked in orbit

272 Gena Rowlands (actress), 1978

(Des G. Capasso. Litho B.D.T.)

2000 (12 June). 25th Anniv of "Apollo–Soyuz" Joint Project. T **271** and similar horiz designs. Multicoloured. P 14.

1695 8m. Type **271** .... 2·00 2·00
a. Sheetlet. Nos. 1695/7 .... 5·50 5·50
1696 8m. "Apollo 18" and docking module .... 2·00 2·00
1697 8m. "Soyuz 19" .... 2·00 2·00
1695/7 *Set of 3* .... 5·50 5·50
MS1698 106×76 mm. 15m. Docking module and "Soyuz 19" .... 4·00 4·50

Nos. 1695/7 were printed together, *se-tenant*, in sheetlets of 3 with enlarged illustrated and inscribed margins.

(Des R. Sauber. Litho B.D.T.)

2000 (12 June). 50th Anniv of Berlin Film Festival. T **272** and similar vert designs showing actors, directors and film scenes with awards. Multicoloured. P 14.

1699 6m. Type **272** .... 1·25 1·40
a. Sheetlet. Nos. 1699/704 .... 6·75 7·50
1700 6m. Vlastimil Brodsky (actor), 1975 .... 1·25 1·40
1701 6m. Carlos Saura (director), 1966 .... 1·25 1·40
1702 6m. Scene from *La Collectionneuse*, 1967 .... 1·25 1·40
1703 6m. Scene from *Le Depart*, 1967 .... 1·25 1·40
1704 6m. Scene from *Le Diable Probablement*, 1977 1·25 1·40
1699/1704 *Set of 6* .... 6·75 7·50
MS1705 97×103 mm. 15m. Scene from *Stammeheim*, 1986 .... 4·25 4·50

Nos. 1699/1704 were printed together, *se-tenant*, in sheetlets of 6 with an enlarged illustrated and inscribed left margin showing the Silver Berlin Bear Award.

No. 1704 is inscribed LE DIIABLE PROBABLEMENT" in error.

273 George Stephenson

274 Johann Sebastian Bach

(Des J. Iskowitz. Litho B.D.T.)

2000 (12 June). 175th Anniv of Stockton and Darlington Line (first public railway). T **273** and similar horiz designs. Multicoloured. P 14.

1706 8m. Type **273** .... 2·25 2·25
a. Sheetlet. Nos. 1706/8 .... 6·00 6·00
1707 8m. Stephenson's Patent Locomotive .... 2·25 2·25
1708 8m. Robert Stephenson's Britannia Tubular Bridge, Menai Straits .... 2·25 2·25
1706/8 *Set of 3* .... 6·00 6·00

Nos. 1706/8 were printed together, *se-tenant*, in sheetlets of 3 with an enlarged illustrated and inscribed right margin.

(Des R. Rundo. Litho B.D.T.)

2000 (12 June). 250th Death Anniv of Johann Sebastian Bach (German composer). Sheet 105×101 mm. P 14.

MS1709 **274** 15m. multicoloured .... 4·50 4·50

275 Albert Einstein

(Des R. Sauber. Litho B.D.T.)

2000 (12 June). Election of Albert Einstein (mathematical physicist) as Time Magazine "Man of the Century". Sheet 117×91 mm. P 14.

MS1710 **275** 15m. multicoloured .... 3·75 4·00

276 Ferdinand Zeppelin and LZ-127 *Graf Zeppelin*, 1928

(Des G. Capasso. Litho B.D.T.)

2000 (12 June). Centenary of First Zeppelin Flight. T **276** and similar horiz designs. Multicoloured. P 14.

1711 8m. Type **276** .... 2·00 2·00
a. Sheetlet. Nos. 1711/13 .... 5·50 5·50
1712 8m. LZ-130 *Graf Zeppelin* II, 1938 .... 2·00 2·00
1713 8m. LZ-10 *Schwaben*, 1911 .... 2·00 2·00
1711/13 *Set of 3* .... 5·50 5·50
MS1714 83×119 mm. 15m. LZ-130 *Graf Zeppelin*, 1938 (50×37 mm) .... 3·75 4·25

Nos. 1711/13 were printed together, *se-tenant*, in sheetlets of 3 with enlarged illustrated and inscribed margins.

277 Nedo Nadi (Italian fencer), 1920

278 Prince William in Evening Dress

(Litho B.D.T.)

2000 (12 June). Olympic Games, Sydney. T **277** and similar horiz designs. Multicoloured. P 14.

1715 6m. Type **277** .... 1·75 2·00
a. Sheetlet. Nos. 1715/18 .... 6·25 7·25
1716 6m. Swimming (butterfly stroke) .... 1·75 2·00
1717 6m. Aztec Stadium, Mexico City, 1968 .... 1·75 2·00
1718 6m. Ancient Greek boxing .... 1·75 2·00
1715/18 *Set of 4* .... 6·25 7·25

Nos. 1715/18 were printed together, *se-tenant*, in sheetlets of 4 (2×2), with the horizontal rows separated by a gutter margin showing Sydney Opera House and athlete with Olympic Torch.

(Litho Questa)

2000 (21 June). 18th Birthday of Prince William. T **278** and similar vert designs. Multicoloured. P 14.

1719 4m. Type **278** .... 1·40 1·40
a. Sheetlet. Nos. 1719/22 .... 5·00 5·00
1720 4m. Wearing coat and scarf .... 1·40 1·40
1721 4m. Wearing striped shirt and tie .... 1·40 1·40
1722 4m. Getting out of car .... 1·40 1·40
1719/22 *Set of 4* .... 5·00 5·00

MS1723 100×80 mm. 15m. Prince William (37×50 mm). P 13½×14 .... 4·50 4·50

Nos. 1719/22 were printed together, *se-tenant*, in sheetlets of 4 with illustrated margins.

279 Spotted-leaved Arum

280 Black Rhinoceros

(Des R. Matin. Litho Questa)

2000 (26 June). African Flowers. T **279** and similar multicoloured designs. P 14.

No.	Design	Unused	Used
1724	3m. Type **279**	85	85
	a. Sheetlet. Nos. 1724/9	4·50	4·50
1725	3m. Christmas Bells	85	85
1726	3m. Lady Monson	85	85
1727	3m. Wild Pomegranate	85	85
1728	3m. Blushing Bride	85	85
1729	3m. Bot River Protea	85	85
1730	3m. Drooping Agapanthus	85	85
	a. Sheetlet. Nos. 1730/5	4·50	4·50
1731	3m. Yellow Marsh Afrikander	85	85
1732	3m. Weak-stemmed Painted Lady	85	85
1733	3m. Impala Lily	85	85
1734	3m. Beatrice Watsonia	85	85
1735	3m. Pink Arum	85	85
1736	3m. Starry Gardenia	85	85
	a. Sheetlet. Nos. 1736/41	4·50	4·50
1737	3m. Pink Hibiscus	85	85
1738	3m. Dwarf Poker	85	85
1739	3m. Coast Kaffirboom	85	85
1740	3m. Rose Cockade	85	85
1741	3m. Pride of Table Mountain	85	85
1742	4m. Moore's Crinum	1·50	1·50
1743	5m. Flame Lily	1·50	1·50
1744	6m. Cape Clivia	1·60	1·60
1745	8m. True Sugarbush	1·75	2·00
1724/45	*Set of* 22	19·00	19·00

MS1746 Two sheets, each 107×77 mm. (a) 15m. Red Hairy Erika (horiz). (b) 15m. Green Arum *Set of 2 sheets* .... 9·00 11·00

Nos. 1724/9, 1730/5 and 1736/41 were each printed together, *se-tenant*, in sheetlets of 6, with the backgrounds forming composite designs.

No. 1733 is inscribed "LIly", No. 1736 "Gardenia thumbergii" and No. 1741 "Disa unoflora", all in error.

(Des H. Friedman. Litho Questa)

2000 (10 Aug). "The Stamp Show 2000" International Stamp Exhibition, London. Endangered Wildlife. T **280** and similar multicoloured designs. P 14.

No.	Design	Unused	Used
1747	4m. Type **280**	1·25	1·25
	a. Sheetlet. Nos. 1747/52	6·75	6·75
1748	4m. Leopard	1·25	1·25
1749	4m. Roseate Tern	1·25	1·25
1750	4m. Mountain Gorilla	1·25	1·25
1751	4m. Mountain Zebra	1·25	1·25
1752	4m. Zanzibar Red Colobus Monkey	1·25	1·25
1753	4m. Cholo Alethe	1·25	1·25
	a. Sheetlet. Nos. 1753/8	6·75	6·75
1754	4m. Temminck's Pangolin	1·25	1·25
1755	4m. Cheetah	1·25	1·25
1756	4m. African Elephant	1·25	1·25
1757	4m. Chimpanzee	1·25	1·25
1758	4m. Northern White Rhinoceros	1·25	1·25
1759	5m. Blue Wildebeest	1·25	1·25
	a. Sheetlet. Nos. 1759/62	5·00	5·00
1760	5m. Tree Hyrax	1·40	1·40
1761	5m. Red Lechwe	1·40	1·40
1762	5m. Eland	1·40	1·40
1747/62	*Set of* 16	18·00	18·00

MS1763 Two sheets, each 65×118 mm. (a) 15m. Dugong (vert). (b) 15m. West African Manatee (vert). *Set of 2 sheets* .... 9·00 11·00

Nos, 1747/52, 1753/8 and 1759/62 were each printed together, *se-tenant*, in sheetlets of 6 or 4 with the backgrounds forming composite designs and enlarged margins at top and bottom.

281 Cadillac Eldorado Seville (1960)

(Des F. Rivera. Litho Walsall)

2000 (1 Sept). Classic Cars. T **281** and similar multicoloured designs. P 14.

No.	Design	Unused	Used
1764	3m. Type **281**	90	90
	a. Sheetlet. Nos. 1764/9	4·75	4·75
1765	3m. Citroen DS (1955–75)	90	90
1766	3m. Ford Zephyr Zodiac MK II (1961)	90	90
1767	3m. MG TF (1945–55)	90	90
1768	3m. Porsche 356 (1949–65)	90	90
1769	3m. Ford Thunderbird (1955)	90	90
1770	3m. Cisitalia 202 Coupe (1948–52)	90	90
	a. Sheetlet. Nos. 1770/5	4·75	4·75
1771	3m. Dodge Viper (1990s)	90	90
1772	3m. TVR Vixen SI (1968–69)	90	90
1773	3m. Lotus 7 (1957–70)	90	90
1774	3m. Ferrari 275 GTB/4 (1964–68)	90	90
1775	3m. Pegasus – Touring Spider (1951–58)	90	90
1776	4m. Fiat Type O (1913)	90	90
	a. Sheetlet. Nos. 1776/81	4·75	4·75
1777	4m. Stutz Bearcat (1914)	90	90
1778	4m. French Leyat (1924)	90	90
1779	4m. Benz gasoline-driven Motorwagon (1886)	90	90
1780	4m. Isotta Fraschini Type 8A (1925)	90	90
1781	4m. Markus Motor Carriage (1887)	90	90
1782	4m. Morris Minor (1951)	90	90
	a. Sheetlet. Nos. 1782/7	4·75	4·75
1783	4m. Hispano-Suiza Type 68 (1935)	90	90
1784	4m. MG TC (1949)	90	90
1785	4m. Morgan 4/4 (1955)	90	90
1786	4m. Jaguar XK120 (1950)	90	90
1787	4m. Triumph 1800/2000 Roadster (1946–49)	90	90
1764/87	*Set of* 24	19·00	19·00

MS1788 Four sheets. (a) 110×85 mm. 15m. AC ACE (1953–63). (b) 110×85 mm. 15m. Morris Minor 1000 (1948–71). (c) 85×110 mm. 15m. Ferrari F40 (vert). (d) 110×85 mm. 15m. Bersey Electric Cab (1896). *Set of 4 sheets* .... 15·00 16·00

Nos. 1764/9, 1770/5, 1776/81 and 1782/7 were each printed together, *se-tenant*, in sheetlets of 6 with either enlarged illustrated top or bottom margins.

282 Basotho Warrior fighting "AIDS"

(Des V. Seatile Nkhomo. Litho Questa)

2001 (22 Jan). Anti-Aids Campaign. T **282** and similar horiz designs. Multicoloured. P 14.

No.	Design	Unused	Used
1789	70c. Type **282**	55	20
1790	1m. "Speed Kills So Does Aids"	80	30
1791	1m.50 Two women (vert)	1·25	1·25
1792	2m.10 "Even when you're off duty protect the nation" and symbols	1·50	1·75
1789/92	*Set of* 4	3·50	3·25

Nos. 1789/92 show the Aids emblem printed on the top (1m.50) or left sheet margin.

283 Great Orange Tip

(Des T. Wood. Litho Cartor)

2001 (30 Apr). Butterflies. T **283** and similar horiz designs. Multicoloured. P 13½.

No.	Design	Unused	Used
1793	70s. Type **283**	50	20
1794	1m. Red-banded Pereute	60	20
1795	1m.50 Sword Grass Brown	80	45

1796	2m. Striped Blue Crow	80	65
1797	2m. Orange-banded Sulphur	65	80
	a. Sheetlet. Nos. 1797/804	5·75	5·75
1798	2m. Large Wood Nymph	65	80
1799	2m. The Postman	65	80
1800	2m. Palmfly	65	80
1801	2m. Gulf Fritillary	65	80
1802	2m. Cairns Birdwing	65	80
1803	2m. Common Morpho	65	80
1804	2m. Common Dotted Border	65	80
1805	2m. African Migrant	65	80
	a. Sheetlet. Nos. 1805/12	5·75	5·75
1806	2m. Large Oak Blue	65	80
1807	2m. The Wanderer	65	80
1808	2m. Tiger Swallowtail	65	80
1809	2m. Union Jack	65	80
1810	2m. Saturn	65	80
1811	2m. Broad-bordered Grass Yellow	65	80
1812	2m. Hewitson's Uraneis	65	80
1813	3m. Bertoni's Antwren Bird	85	85
	a. Sheetlet. Nos. 1813/20	6·00	6·00
1814	3m. Chlorinde	85	85
1815	3m. Iolas Blue	85	85
1816	3m. Mocker Swallowtail	85	85
1817	3m. Common Indian Crow	85	85
1818	3m. Grecian Shoemaker	85	85
1819	3m. Small Flambeau	85	85
1820	3m. Orchid Swallowtail	85	85
1821	3m. Alfalfa Butterfly	85	85
1822	4m. Doris Butterfly	95	1·25
1793/822 *Set of 30*		20·00	19·00
MS1823	Two sheets, each 70×100 mm. (a) 15m. Forest Queen. (b) 15m. Crimson Tip. *Set of 2 sheets*	12·00	13·00

Nos. 1797/1804, 1805/12 and 1813/20 were each printed together, *se-tenant*, in sheetlets of 8 with the backgrounds forming composite designs.

284 Roman General and Soldiers from "Battle of Lepanto and Map of the World" (anon)

285 *Cortinarius violaceus*

(Litho Questa)

2001 (31 May). "Philanippon 01" International Stamp Exhibition, Tokyo. Paintings from Momoyama Era. T **284** and similar vert designs. Multicoloured. P 14 (5m.) or 13½×14 (others).

1824	1m.50 Type **284**	60	30
1825	2m. Pikemen and musketeers from "Battle of Lepanto and Map of the World"	90	40
1826	3m. Crane from "Birds and Flowers of the Four Seasons" (Kano Eitoku)	1·00	65
1827	4m. Travellers in the mountains from "Birds and Flowers of the Four Seasons"	1·00	1·00
1828	5m. "Portrait of a Lady" (24½×81½ mm)	1·00	1·00
	a. Sheetlet. Nos. 1828/32	4·50	4·50
1829	5m. "Honda Tadakatsu" (24½×81½ mm)	1·00	1·00
1830	5m. "Wife of Goto Tokujo" (24½×81½ mm)	1·00	1·00
1831	5m. "Emperor Go-Yozei (Kano Takanobu) (24½×81½ mm)	1·00	1·00
1832	5m. "Tenzuiin Hideyoshi's Mother, Hoshuku Sochin" (24½×81½ mm)	1·00	1·00
1833	6m. "Hosokawa Yusai" (Ishin Suden) (24½×81½ mm)	1·25	1·25
	a. Sleetlet. Nos. 1833/7	5·75	5·75
1834	6m. "Sen No Rikyu" (attr Hasegawa Tohaku) (24½×81½ mm)	1·25	1·25
1835	6m. "Oichi No Kata" (24½×81½ mm)	1·25	1·25
1836	6m. "Inaba Ittetsu" (attr Hasegawa Tohaku) (24½×81½ mm)	1·25	1·25
1837	6m. "Oda Nobunaga (Kokei Sochin) (24½×81½ mm)	1·25	1·25
1838	7m. "Viewing the Maples at Mount Takao"	1·50	2·00
1839	8m. "The Four Accomplishments" (Kaiho Yusho)	1·50	2·25
1824/39 *Set of 16*		16·00	16·00
MS1840	Two sheets. (a) 98×131 mm. 15m. "Tokugawa Ieyasu". (b) 114×134 mm. 15m. "Toyotomi Hideyoshi". *Set of 2 sheets*	9·50	11·00

Nos. 1828/32 and 1833/7 were each printed together, *se-tenant*, in sheetlets of 5 with inscribed top and bottom margins.

(Des Irina Lyampe. Litho B.D.T.)

2001 (29 June). "Belgica 2001" International Stamp Exhibition, Brussels. African Fungi. T **285** and similar multicoloured designs. P 14.

1841	3m. Type **285**	1·10	1·10
	a. Sheetlet. Nos. 1841/6	6·00	6·00
1842	3m. *Pleurocybella Porrigens*	1·10	1·10
1843	3m. *Collybia velutibes*	1·10	1·10
1844	3m. *Lentinellus cochleatus*	1·10	1·10
1845	3m. *Anthurua aseroiformis*	1·10	1·10
1846	3m. Caesar's Mushroom	1·10	1·10
1847	4m. *Cortinarius traganus*	1·10	1·10
	a. Sheetlet. Nos. 1847/52	6·00	6·00
1848	4m. *Peziza sarcosphaera*	1·10	1·10
1849	4m. *Russula emetica*	1·10	1·10
1850	4m. *Stropharia ambigua*	1·10	1·10
1851	4m. *Phologiotis helvelliodes*	1·10	1·10
1852	4m. *Clitocybe odora*	1·10	1·10
1853	5m. Golden False Pholiota	1·25	1·25
1854	5m. *Coprinus micaceus*	1·25	1·25
1855	5m. *Hygrophorus camarophyllus*	1·25	1·25
1856	5m. *Panaeolus campanulatus*	1·25	1·25
1841/56 *Set of 16*		16·00	16·00
MS1857	Two sheets, each 75×55 mm. (a). 15m. *Boletus parasiticus* (horiz). (b) 15m. *Hygrophorus hygrocybe conicus* (horiz). *Set of 2 sheets*	14·00	14·00

Nos. 1841/6 and 1847/52 were each printed together, *se-tenant*, in sheetlets of 6, with illustrated margins.

No. 1841 is inscribed "violaceys", No. 1842 "Pleyrocybella", No. 1844 "Cochleathus", No. 1852 "Clitoeybe" and No. 1856 "Panaelus companulatus", all in error.

286 "Woman with Baby in Sunset" (Leila Hall)

(Litho Questa)

2001 (20 Aug). Winners of United Nations Children's Art Competiton. T **286** and similar multicoloured designs. P. 14.

1858	70s. Type **286**	50	15
1859	1m. "Herdboy with Lamb" (Chambeli Ramathe)	65	30
1860	1m.50 "Girl with A.I.D.S. Ribbon" (Chambeli Ramathe) (vert)	1·00	1·00
1861	2m.10 "Satellite Dish and Map seen through Keyhole" (Mika Sejake) (vert)	1·25	1·50
1858/61 *Set of 4*		3·00	2·75

287 Black Kite

(Des K. Maja. Litho Questa)

2001 (1 Oct). Birds of Prey. T **287** and similar vert designs. Multicoloured. P 14.

1862	70s. Type **287**	55	30
1863	1m. Martial Eagle	70	35
1864	1m.50 Bateleur	90	80
1865	2m.10 African Goshawk	1·25	1·25
1866	2m.50 Bearded Vulture	1·25	1·50
1867	3m. Jackal Buzzard	1·40	1·75
1862/7 *Set of 6*		5·50	5·50

No. 1865 is inscribed "GASHAWK" in error.

288 Grass Owl

(Des R. Martin. Litho Questa)

2001 (15 Oct). Wildlife of Southern Africa. T **288** and similar multicoloured designs. P 14.

1868	1m. Type **288**	1·00	60
1869	2m.10 Klipspringer	1·00	70
1870	3m. Saddle-backed Jackal	1·25	80
1871	4m. Aardvark	1·25	1·25
	a. Sheetlet. Nos. 1871/6	6·75	6·75
1872	4m. Rock Kestrel	1·25	1·25
1873	4m. Black-footed Cat	1·25	1·25
1874	4m. Springhare	1·25	1·25
1875	4m. Aardwolf	1·25	1·25
1876	4m. Rock Hyrax	1·25	1·25
1877	4m. Damara Zebra	1·25	1·25
	a. Sheetlet. Nos. 1877/82	6·75	6·75
1878	4m. Bontebok	1·25	1·25
1879	4m. Eland	1·25	1·25
1880	4m. Lion	1·25	1·25
1881	4m. Saddled-backed Jackal	1·25	1·25
1882	4m. Yellow-billed Kite	1·25	1·25
1883	5m. Black Wildebeest	1·25	1·50
1868/83	*Set of* 16	17·00	16·00
MS1884	Two sheets, each 90×64 mm. (a). 15m. Black-shouldered Kite. (b) 15m. Caracal (vert). *Set of* 2 *sheets*	10·00	11·00

Nos. 1871/6 and 1877/82 were each printed together, *se-tenant*, in sheetlets of 6, with the backgrounds forming composite designs which continue onto the sheetlet margins.

289 Queen Elizabeth wearing Purple Coat

(Des D. Miller. Litho Questa)

2002 (3 June). Golden Jubilee. T **289** and similar square designs. Multicoloured. P 14½.

1885	8m. Type **289**	2·50	2·50
	a. Sheetlet. Nos. 1885/8	9·00	9·00
1886	8m. Queen Elizabeth with Duke of Edinburgh on launch	2·50	2·50
1887	8m. Queen Elizabeth with mayor	2·50	2·50
1888	8m. Duke of Edinburgh wearing sunglasses	2·50	2·50
1885/8	*Set of* 4	9·00	9·00
MS1889	76×108 mm. 20m. Queen Elizabeth inspecting R.A.F. guard of honour. P 14	6·50	7·00

Nos. 1885/8 were printed together, *se-tenant*, in sheetlets of 4, with an illustrated left margin.

290 Homer Wood (Rotary pioneer)

(Des R. Rundo. Litho Questa)

2002 (13 Aug). 25th Anniv of Rotary International in Lesotho. T **290** and similar multicoloured designs. P 14.

1890	8m. Type **290**	2·00	2·00
1891	10m. Paul Harris (founder of Rotary International)	2·25	2·25
MS1892	Two sheets. (a) 60×75 mm. 25m. Coloured globe and Rotary logo (horiz). *Set of* 2 *sheets*	12·00	14·00

No. 1890 is inscribed "HORNER" in error.

291 Machache

(Des H. Friedman. Litho Questa)

2002 (13 Aug). International Year of Mountains. T **291** and similar multicoloured designs showing Lesotho mountains. (except No. **MS**1897). P 14.

1893	8m. Type **291**	2·00	2·00
	a. Sheetlet. Nos. 1893/6	7·25	7·25
1894	8m. Thabana-li-Mèlè	2·00	2·00
1895	8m. Qiloane	2·00	2·00
1896	8m. Thaba-Bosiu	2·00	2·00
1893/6	*Set of* 6	7·25	7·25
MS1897	64×83 mm. 25m. The Matterhorn, Switzerland (vert)	7·50	8·50

Nos. 1893/6 were printed together, *se-tenant*, in sheetlets of 4 with enlarged illustrated left and bottom margins. No. **MS**1897 is inscribed "Mount Rainer" in error.

292 Boys with Calf, Lithabaneng

(Des M. Friedman. Litho Questa)

2002 (13 Aug). S.O.S. Children's Villages (Kinderdorf International). P 14.

1898	**292**	10m. multicoloured	2·75	3·00

293 Spiral Aloe

294 U.S. Flag as Statue of Liberty with Lesotho Flag)

(Des R. Rundo. Litho Questa)

2002 (13 Aug). UN Year of Eco Tourism. T **293** and similar multicoloured designs. P 14.

1899	6m. Type **293**	1·60	1·75
	a. Sheetlet. Nos. 1899/1904	8·50	8·50
1900	6m. *Anthrixia gerradii* (flower)	1·60	1·75
1901	6m. Horseman and Packhorse	1·60	1·75
1902	6m. Lion	1·60	1·75
1903	6m. Frog	1·60	1·75
1904	6m. Thatched building	1·60	1·75
1899/904	*Set of* 6	8·50	9·50
MS1905	77×83 mm. 20m. European Bee Eater (*vert*)	7·00	8·00

Nos. 1899/1904 were printed together, *se-tenant*, in sheetlets of 6 with an enlarged inscribed bottom margin.

(Des M. Friedman. Litho Questa)

2002 (13 Aug). "United We Stand". Support for Victims of 11 September 2001 Terrorist Attacks. P 14.

1906	**294**	7m. multicoloured	1·60	2·00

No. 1906 was printed in sheetlets of 4 with an illustrated left margin.

295 Sheet Bend Knot

(Des H. Friedman. Litho Questa)

2002 (13 Aug). 20th World Scout Jamboree, Thailand. T **295** and similar horiz designs. Multicolured. P 14.

1907	9m. Type **295**	2·00	2·25
	a. Sheetlet. Nos. 1907/10	7·25	8·00
1908	9m. Pup and forester tents	2·00	2·25
1909	9m. Scouts in canoe	2·00	2·25
1910	9m. Life-saving	2·00	2·25
1907/10	*Set of 4*	7·25	8·00
MS1911	75×59 mm. 25m. Scouts asleep in tent	7·00	8·00

Nos. 1907/10 were printed together, *se-tenant*, in sheetlets of 4 with enlarged illustrated left and top margins.

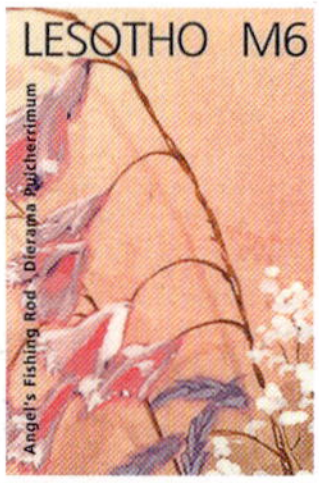

296 Angel's Fishing Rod (*Dierama pulcherrimum*)

(Des R. Rundo. Litho Walsall)

2003 (13 Jan). Flowers, Orchids and Insects. T **296** and similar multicoloured designs. P 14.

MS1912	100×180 mm. 6m. Type **296**; 6m. Marigold (*Calendula officinalis*); 6m. Dianthus "Joan's Blood", 6m. Mule Pink (*Dianthus plumarius*) ; 6m. Tiger Lily (*Lilium lancifolium*); 6m. *Clematis viticella* "Comtesse de Bouchaud"	8·50	9·00
MS1913	180×100 mm. 6m. Leaf Grasshopper (*Brochopeplus exalatus*); 6m. Golden-ringed Dragonfly (*Cordulegaster boltoni*); 6m. Weevel-hunting Wasp (*Cerceris arenaria*); 6m. European Grasshopper (*Oedipoda miniata*); 6m. Thread-waisted Wasp (*Ammophilia alberti*) 6m. Mantid (*Mantis Acontista*) (all horiz)	8·50	9·00
MS1914	95×103 mm. 6m. *Phragmipedium besseae*; 6m. *Cypripedium calceolus*; 6m. Cattleya "Louise Georgiana"; 6m. *Brassocattleya binosa*; 6m. *Laelia gouldiana*; 6m. *Paphiopedilum maudiae* "Alba"	8·50	9·00
MS1915	Three sheets. (a) 63×75 mm. 20m. Bleeding Heart (*Dicentra spectabilis*). (b) 75×63 mm. 20m. Orb Web Spider (*Argiope bruennichi*). (c) 75×63 mm. 20m. *Brassavola tuberculata*. *Set of 3 sheets*	16·00	18·00

297 Blèriot's Canard at Bagatelle, 1906

298 Prince William

(Des J. Iskowiz. Litho BDT)

2004 (17 May). Centenary of Powered Flight. T **297** and similar horiz designs. Multicolured. P 14.

MS1916	177×97 mm. 6m. Type **297**; 6m. Blèriot's Double-winged Libellule, 1907; 6m. Blèriot's No. VIII in Touy–Artenay cross-country flight, 1908; 6m. Blèriot's XII Test Flight, 1909	5·00	5·50
MS1917	66×97 mm. 15m. Louis Blériot's No. XI	4·00	4·25

(Des R. Rundo. Litho BDT)

2004 (17 May). 21st Birthday of Prince William. T **298** and similar vert designs. Multicoloured. P 14.

MS1918	77×148 mm. 8m. Type **298**; 8m. Wearing grey suit and tie; 8m. Wearing yellow polo shirt	6·50	7·00
MS1919	98×68 mm. 15m. Young Prince William	4·25	4·50

299 Queen Elizabeth II

300 *Acraea rabbaiae*

(Des R. Rundo. Litho BDT)

2004 (17 May). 50th Anniv (2003) of Coronation. T **299** and similar vert designs. Multicolured. P 14.

MS1920	148×85 mm. 8m. Wearing ivory suit and hat; 8m. Wearing royal uniform	6·50	7·00
MS1921	68×97 mm. 15m. Queen Elizabeth II	4·25	4·50

(Des R. Rundo. Litho BDT)

2004 (17 May). Butterflies. T **300** and similar horiz designs. Multicoloured. P 14.

1922	1m.50 Type **300**	80	40
1923	2m.10 *Alaena margaritacea*	1·00	55
1924	4m. *Bematistes aganice*	1·75	2·00
1925	6m. *Acraea quirina*	2·50	3·00
1922/5	*Set of 4*	5·50	5·50
MS1926	117×116 mm. 6m. *Bematistes excisa* (male) 6m. *Bematistes excisa* (female); 6m. *Bematistes epiprotea*; 6m. *Bematiste poggei*	8·50	9·00
MS1927	67×98 mm. 15m. *Acraea satis*	5·00	5·50

301 Secretary Bird

302 Bald Ibis

(Des R. Rundo. Litho BDT)

2004 (17 May). Birds. T **301** and similar vert designs. Multicoloured. P 14.

1928	1m.50 Type **301**	80	50
1929	2m.10 South African Crowned Crane ("Gray-crowned Crane")	1·00	70
1930	3m. Pied Avocet	1·50	1·50
1931	5m. Common Kestrel	2·00	2·50
1928/31	*Set of 14*	4·75	4·75
MS1932	108×136 mm. 6m. European Roller; 6m. European Cuckoo ("Common Cuckoo"); 6m. Great Spotted Cuckoo; 6m. Pel's Fishing Owl	9·50	11·00
MS1933	68×97 mm. 15m. Kori Bustard	5·00	5·50

(Des Irina Lyampe. Litho BDT)

2004 (17 May). Endangered Species. Bald Ibis. T **302** and similar horiz designs.

1934	3m. Type **302**	1·50	1·50
	a. Strip of 4. Nos. 1934/7	5·50	5·50
1935	3m. Bald Ibis at rest	1·50	1·50
1936	3m. Bald Ibis on nest	1·50	1·50
1937	3m. Bald Ibis in flight (facing right)	1·50	1·50
1934/7	*Set of 4*	5·50	5·50
MS1938	207×132 mm. Designs as Nos. 1934/6 and1937 (Bald Ibis facing left), each×2	10·00	11·00

Nos. 1934/7 were printed together, *se-tenant*, in horizontal and vertical strips of 4 in sheets of 16.

No. **MS**1938 contained two strips of four stamps separated by an enlarged illustrated gutter showing a Bald Ibis.

303 Cape Porcupine

(Litho BDT)

2004 (17 May). Animals. T **303** and similar multicoloured designs. P 14.

1939	1m. Type **303**	50	20
1940	1m.50 Brown rat	70	45
1941	2m.10 Springhare (vert)	90	70
1942	5m. South African galago (vert)	1·75	2·25
1939/42	*Set of 4*	3·50	3·25
MS1943	117×136 mm. 5m. Striped grass mouse; 5m. Greater galago; 5m. Ground pangolin; 5m. Banded mongoose	7·50	8·50
MS1944	68×98 mm. 15m. Egyptian rousette (vert)	4·50	5·00

304 *Sparaxis grandiflora*

(Litho BDT)

2004 (17 May). Flowers. T **304** and similar vert designs. Multicoloured. P 14.

1945	1m.50 Type **304**	70	30
1946	2m.10 *Agapanthus africanus*	90	65
1947	3m. *Protea linearis*	1·25	1·25
1948	5m. *Nerine cultivars*	1·75	2·25
1945/8	*Set of 4*	4·25	4·00
MS1949	104×117 mm. 5m. *Kniphofia uvaria*; 5m. *Amaryllis belladonna*; 5m. *Gazania Splendens*; 5m. *Erica coronata*	7·50	8·50
MS1950	68×98 mm. 15m. *Saintpaulia culitvars*	4·50	5·00

305 Qiloane Falls

2004 (17 May). International Year of Freshwater. T **305** and similar horiz designs. Multicoloured. Litho. P 14.

MS1951	85×167 mm. 8m. Type **305**; 8m. Halfway down Qiloane Falls; 8m. Base of Qiloane Falls	8·50	9·50
MS1952	118×84 mm. 15m. Orange River	4·50	5·00

306 Mokhoro (Round House and Cooking Hut)

(Des Makhabane C. Moshoeshoe. Litho BDT)

2005 (21 Feb). Basotho Houses. T **306** and similar horiz designs. Multicoloured. P 14.

1953	70s. Type **306**	40	15
1954	1m. Heisi (Rectangular house)	65	35
1955	1m.50 Typical homestead	90	70
1956	2m.10 Mathule (Round house with porch)	1·25	1·75
1953/6	*Set of 4*	2·75	2·75

No. 1953 is inscribed "70L" and No. 1956 "Mohlongoa-fat'se", both in error.

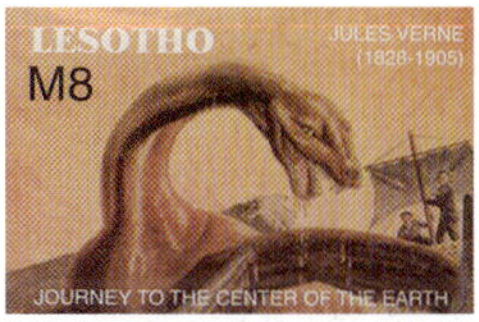

307 *Journey to the Centre of the Earth*

(Litho State Ptg Wks, Beijing)

2005 (22 Aug). Death Centenary of Jules Verne (writer). T **307** and similar multicoloured designs. P 13.

1957	8m. Type **307**	2·25	2·25
	a. Sheetlet. Nos. 1957/9	6·00	6·00
1958	8m. Jules Verne and "100 YEARS"	2·25	2·25
1959	8m. *20,000 Leagues under the Sea*	2·25	2·25
1957/9	*Set of 3*	6·00	6·00
MS1960	107×83 mm. 15m. Jules Verne (vert)	4·00	4·50

308 USS *Arizona* (battleship)

309 US Troops land on Omaha Beach

(Litho State Ptg Wks, Beijing)

2005 (22 Aug). 60th Anniv of Victory in Japan. T **308** and similar vert designs. Multicoloured. P 13.

1961	4m. Type **308**	1·60	1·60
	a. Sheetlet. Nos. 1961/5	7·25	7·25
1962	4m. Bunker at Chula Beach, Tinian Island	1·60	1·60
1963	4m. Flight crew of *Bockscar* (B-29 aircraft)	1·60	1·60
1964	4m. Men showing newspaper headline	1·60	1·60
1965	4m. Marker of second atomic bomb loading pit, Tinian Island	1·60	1·60
1961/5	*Set of 5*	7·25	7·25

Nos. 1961/5 were printed together, *se-tenant*, in sheetlets of five stamps with an enlarged, illustrated top margin.

(Litho State Ptg Wks, Beijing)

2005 (22 Aug). 60th Anniv of Victory in Europe. T **309** and similar vert designs. Multicoloured. P 13.

1966	4m. Type **309**	1·60	1·60
	a. Sheetlet. Nos. 1966/70	7·25	7·25
1967	4m. General George C. Marshall	1·60	1·60
1968	4m. Field Marshall Wilhelm Keitel	1·60	1·60
1969	4m. General Dwight D. Eisenhower and Lt. General George S. Patton	1·60	1·60
1970	4m. Soldiers searching through rubble	1·60	1·60
1966/70	*Set of 5*	7·25	7·25

Nos. 1966/70 were printed together, *se-tenant*, in sheetlets of five stamps with an enlarged, illustrated top margin.

310 Pope John Paul II

311 Albert Einstein

(Litho State Ptg Wks, Beijing)

2005 (22 Aug). Pope John Paul II Commemoration. P 13.

1971	**310** 10m. multicoloured	4·00	4·00

No. 1971 was printed in sheetlets of four stamps with an enlarged, illustrated left margin.

(Litho State Ptg Wks, Beijing)

2005 (22 Aug). 50th Death Anniv of Albert Einstein (physicist). T **311** and similar multicoloured designs. P 13.

1972	8m. Wearing glasses	2·25	2·25
	a. Sheetlet. Nos. 1972/4	6·00	6·00
1973	8m. With Nikola Tesla (inscr "Testa") and Charles Steinmetz	2·25	2·25
1974	8m. Type **311**	2·25	2·25
1972/4 *Set of 3*		6·00	6·00
MS1975	100×70 mm. 15m. On the cover of *Time* magazine (vert)	4·00	4·50

Nos. 1972/4 were printed together, *se-tenant*, in sheetlets of three stamps with an enlarged illustrated top margin.

312 Uruguay Football Team, 1930

(Litho State Ptg Wks, Beijing)

2005 (22 Aug). 75th Anniv of First World Cup Football Championship, Uruguay. T **312** and similar multicoloured designs. P 12.

1976	8m. Type **312**	2·25	2·25
	a. Sheetlet. Nos. 1976/8	6·00	6·00
1977	8m. Opposing players and referee	2·25	2·25
1978	8m. German team	2·25	2·25
1976/8 *Set of 3*		6·00	6·00
MS1979	105×70 mm. 15m. Bodo Illgner (Germany) (vert)	4·00	4·50

Nos. 1976/8 were printed together, *se-tenant*, in sheetlets of three stamps with illustrated and inscribed margins.

313 Child eating

314 Hans Christian Andersen (statue)

(Litho State Ptg Wks, Beijing)

2005 (22 Aug). Centenary of Rotary International. T **313** and similar vert designs. Multicoloured. P 13.

1980	8m. Type **313**	2·25	2·25
	a. Sheetlet. Nos. 1980/2	6·00	6·00
1981	8m. Classroom scene	2·25	2·25
1982	8m. Children	2·25	2·25
1980/2 *Set of 3*		6·00	6·00

Nos. 1980/2 were printed together, *se-tenant*, in sheetlets of three stamps with enlarged, illustrated and inscribed top and left margins.

(Litho State Ptg Wks, Beijing)

2005 (22 Aug). Birth Bicentenary of Hans Christian Andersen (writer). T **314** and similar vert designs. Multicoloured. P 13.

1983	8m. Type **314**	2·25	2·25
	a. Sheetlet. Nos. 1983/5	6·00	6·00
1984	8m. Former home of Hans Christian Andersen, Odense	2·25	2·25
1985	8m. "The Steadfast Tin Soldier"	2·25	2·25
1983/5 *Set of 3*		6·00	6·00
MS1986	75×82 mm. 15m. "The Little Mermaid"	4·00	4·50

Nos. 1983/5 were printed together, *se-tenant*, in sheetlets of three stamps with illustrated and inscribed margins.

315 HMS *Victory*

(Litho State Ptg Wks, Beijing)

2005 (22 Aug). Bicentenary of the Battle of Trafalgar. T **315** and similar horiz designs. Multicoloured. P 13.

1987	8m. Type **315**	3·50	3·00
	a. Sheetlet. Nos. 1987/90	12·50	11·00
1988	8m. Admiral Lord Horatio Nelson	3·50	3·00
1989	8m. Admiral Nelson fatally wounded	3·50	3·00
1990	8m. Ships engaged in battle	3·50	3·00
1987/90 *Set of 4*		12·50	11·00
MS1991	70×100 mm. 25m. Admiral Lord Horatio Nelson and crew (50×38 mm). P 12	13·00	13·00

Nos. 1987/90 were printed together, *se-tenant*, in sheetlets of four stamps with an enlarged, illustrated right margin.

316 Brownies

317 Herdboy riding Calf

(Litho BDT)

2005 (12 Dec). 80th Anniv of Lesotho Girl Guides Association. T **316** and similar multicoloured designs. P 14.

1992	70l. Type **316**	40	15
1993	1m. Procession of rangers and guides	60	30
1994	1m.50 Rangers recycling tin cans (vert)	90	80
1995	2m.10 Ranger and guides at Lesotho Girl Guides Headquarters	1·25	1·50
1992/5 *Set of 4*		2·75	2·50
MS1996	66×98 mm. 10m. Queen 'Mamohato Seeiso (patron 1966–2003)	3·50	4·00

(Des Vincent Seatile Nkhomo. Litho BDT)

2006 (13 Mar). Herdboys. T **317** and similar vert designs. Multicoloured. P 14.

1997	70l. Type **317**	30	10
1998	1m. Feeding cattle	50	25
1999	1m.50 Three herdboys playing morabaraba and grazing cattle	70	65
2000	2m. Carrying newborn lamb on shoulders	90	1·25
1997/2000 *Set of 4*		2·25	2·00
MS2001	95×65 mm. 10m. Herdboys dancing ndlamo and practicing stick fighting	3·50	4·00

318 Woman carrying Thatch Grass

319 Woven Grass Baskets and Broom

(Des Vincent Seatile Nkhomo. Litho BDT)

2006 (19 June). Head Carrying by Mosotho Women. T **318** and similar vert designs. Multicoloured. P 14.

2002	70l. Type **318**	30	10
2003	1m. Carrying iron cooking pot on head	50	25
2004	1m.50 Carrying clay water pot on head	70	65
2005	2m.10 Carrying basket of pumpkins and maize on head and baby on back	90	1·25
2002/5 *Set of 4*		2·25	2·00
MS2006	96×67 mm. 10m. Girl carrying basket of maize flour on head	3·50	4·00

(Des Roman Francisco. Litho Questa)

2006 (9 Oct). Handicrafts. T **319** and similar multicoloured designs. Litho. P 14.

2007	70l. Type **319**	30	10
2008	1m. Artist and tapestry (vert)	50	25
2009	1m.50 Calabash, clay pots and pipe	70	65
2010	2m.10 Horn, carved fish and bird	90	1·25

2007/10 *Set of 4* 2·25 2·00
MS2011 96×65 mm. 10m. Young girl wearing traditional headband and necklace of clay beads (vert) 3·50 4·00

320 *Spiranthes laciniata*

(Litho BDT)

2007 (20 Aug). Orchids of the World. T **320** and similar multicoloured designs. Litho. P 14.

2012 1m.50 Type **320** 70 50
2013 2m.10 *Triphora craigheadii* 90 70
2014 3m. *Arethusa bulbosa* 1·25 1·00
2015 6m. *Encyclia tampensis* 2·50 2·50
a. Sheetlet. Nos. 2015/18 9·00 9·00
2016 6m. *Prosthechea cochleata* 2·50 2·50
2017 6m. *Vanilla pompona* 2·50 2·50
2018 6m. *Cypripedium acaule* 2·50 2·50
2019 10m. *Calypso bulbosa* 3·75 4·50
2012/19 *Set of 8* 15·00 15·00
MS2020 Two sheets, each 98×68 mm (a) 15m. *Epidendrum radicans* (horiz). (b) 15m. *Vanilla barbellata* 11·00 12·00

Nos. 2015/19 were printed together, *se-tenant*, in sheetlets of four stamps with enlarged illustrated margins.

321 Crested Caracara

(Litho BDT)

2007 (20 Aug). Birds of the World. T **321** and similar vert designs. Multicoloured. P 14.

2021 1m. Type **321** 55 30
2022 1m.50 Wood stork 70 50
2023 2m.10 Tawny-shouldered blackbird 90 70
2024 6m. Great blue heron 2·50 2·50
a. Sheetlet. Nos. 2024/7 9·00 9·00
2025 6m. Anna's hummingbird 2·50 2·50
2026 6m. Grey Silky-flycatcher 2·50 2·50
2027 6m. Limpkin 2·50 2·50
2028 15m. Jabiru 5·50 6·25
2021/8 *Set of 8* 16·00 16·00
MS2029 Two sheets, each 68×97 mm. (a) 15m. Monk parakeet. (b) 15m. Western reef-heron 11·00 12·00

Nos. 2024/7 were printed together, *se-tenant*, in sheetlets of four stamps with enlarged illustrated margins.

322 *Mylothris erlangeri*

(Litho BDT)

2007 (20 Aug). Butterflies of Africa. T **322** and similar vert designs. Multicoloured. Litho. P 14.

2030 1m. Type **322** 55 30
2031 1m.50 *Papilio nireus* 70 50
2032 2m.10 *Acraea terpiscore* 90 70
2033 10m. *Salamis temora* 3·75 4·50
2030/3 *Set of 4* 5·50 5·50
MS2034 133×110 mm. 6m.×4 *Danaus chrysippus*; *Myrina silenus*; *Chrysiridia madagascariensis*; *Hypolimnas dexithea* 9·00 10·00
MS2035 Two sheets, each 103×72 mm. (a) 15m. *Amphicallia tigris*. (b) 15m. *Papiliodemodocus* 11·00 12·00

The stamps and margins of No. **MS**2034 form a composite background design showing flowers.

323 *Amanita pantherina*

(Litho BDT)

2007 (20 Aug). African Mushrooms. T **323** and similar vert designs. Multicoloured. P 14.

2036 1m. Type **323** 55 30
2037 1m.50 *Agaricus xanthodermus* 70 50
2038 2m.10 *Amanita rubescens* 90 70
2039 6m. *Amanita phalloides* 2·50 2·50
a. Sheetlet. Nos. 2039/42 9·00 9·00
2040 6m. *Amanita pantherina* 2·50 2·50
2041 6m. *Panaeolus papilionaceus* 2·50 2·50
2042 6m. *Amanita rubescens* (different) 2·50 2·50
2043 15m. *Amanita phalloides* (different) 5·50 6·25
2036/43 *Set of 8* 16·00 16·00
MS2044 Two sheets, each 103×73 mm. (a) 15m. *Amanita Panther*. (b) 15m. *Podaxis pistillaris* 11·00 12·00

Nos. 2039/42 were printed together, *se-tenant*, in sheetlets of four stamps with enlarged illustrated margins.

324 Rowing

2008 (18 Aug). Olympic Games, Beijing. T **324** and similar vert designs. Multicoloured. Litho. P 12.

2045 3m.50 Type **324** 1·10 1·25
a. Sheetlet. Nos. 2045/8 4·00 4·50
2046 3m.50 Softball 1·10 1·25
2047 3m.50 Wrestling 1·10 1·25
2048 3m.50 Volleyball 1·10 1·25
2045/8 *Set of 4* 4·00 4·50

Nos. 2045/8 were printed together, *se-tenant*, in sheetlets of four stamps with enlarged illustrated margins.

(Des Anja Denker. Litho Enschedé)

2010 (9 Apr). Third Joint Issue of Southern Africa Postal Operators Association Members. World Cup Football Championship, South Africa. Sheet 188×167 mm containing circular designs as T **258** of Botswana, each showing Zakumi mascot, different silhouettes of players on football and the national flag of a member country. Multicoloured. P 13½.

MS2049 5m.×9 Namibia; South Africa; Zimbabwe; Malawi; Swaziland; Botswana; Mauritius; Lesotho; Zambia 11·00 12·00

The stamps within **MS**2049 were each perforated in a circle contained within an outer perforated square.

Similar designs were issued by Botswana, Malawi, Mauritius, Namibia, South Africa, Swaziland, Zambia and Zimbabwe.

STAMP BOOKLETS

1981 (20 Apr). Multicoloured cover, 165×100 mm, showing Hoopoe (bird) on front and Lesotho village scene on back. Stapled.

SB1 4m.30 booklet containing 5s., 6s., 7s. and 25s. (Nos. 440, 441/2, 444) in blocks of 10 9·00

1981 (22 July). Royal Wedding. Multicoloured cover, 150×100 mm, showing Prince Charles and Lady Diana Spencer on front and Ba-Leseli dance on back. Stitched.

SB2	6m. booklet containing four different panes of 3 stamps and 1 label (Nos. 451a/b, 452a, 453a) ...	2·00
	a. Stapled ...	

1982 (5 Mar). 75th Anniv of Boy Scout Movement. Multicoloured cover, 170×98 mm, showing Lord Baden-Powell on front and Scout with flag on back. Pane attached by selvedge.

SB3	5m.52 booklet containing *se-tenant* pane of 10 stamps and one miniature sheet (No. 474a).......	5·00

1982 (14 Apr). World Cup Football Championship, Spain. Multicoloured cover, 170×102 mm, showing Championship emblems. Stamps attached by selvedge.

SB4	4m.85 booklet containing twenty-four 15s. (Nos. 480/91) in blocks of 12 and one miniature sheet (No. **MS**492)...	6·00

1982 (14 June). Multicoloured cover as No. SB1. Stapled.

SB5	4m.30 booklet containing 5s., 6s., 7s. and 25s. (Nos. 503/5, 507) in blocks of 10...	8·50

1983 (11 Jan). Fungi. Multicoloured cover, 155×80 mm, showing fungi on front and with biography of G. L. Vasarhelyi on back. Panes attached by selvedge.

SB6	3m.70 booklet containing two *se-tenant* panes of 4 stamps and 1 label (No. 532b) and one *se-tenant* pane of 2 stamps and 1 label (No. 532c)...	7·50

1983 (11 July). Bicentenary of Manned Flight. Multicoloured cover, 211×100 mm, showing Montgolfier balloon. Panes attached by selvedge.

SB7	4m. booklet containing *se-tenant* pane of 4 stamps and 1 label (No. 545a) and one miniature sheet (No. **MS**549) ...	5·25

OFFICIAL STAMPS

OFFICIAL

(O **1**)

1934 (Feb). Nos. 1/3 and 6 optd with Type O **1**, by Govt printer, Pretoria.

O1	**1**	½d. emerald...	£12000	£7000
O2		1d. scarlet...	£4000	£3250
O3		2d. bright purple...	£4500	£1000
O4		6d. orange-yellow...	£12000	£4750
O1/4 *Set of 4*...			£30000	£14000

Collectors are advised to buy these stamps only from reliable sources. They were not sold to the public.

300 of each value were supplied in January 1934 for use by the Secretariat in Maseru. Limited usage is recorded between 28 Feb 1934 and 8 June 1934. The issue was then withdrawn and the remainders destroyed. Only the following numbers appear to have been issued: ½d. 24, 1d. 34, 2d. 54, 6d. 27, from which a maximum of ten mint sets exist.

POSTAGE DUE STAMPS

D **1**

Normal

Large "d." (R. 9/6, 10/6)

(Typo D.L.R.)

1933 (1 Dec)–**52**. Ordinary paper. Wmk Mult Script CA. P 14.

D1	D **1**	1d. carmine...	2·75	13·00
		a. Scarlet (1938)...	50·00	55·00
		b. Chalk-surfaced paper. *Deep carmine* (24.10.51)...	1·75	6·50
		ba. Error. Crown missing, W **9***a*...	£325	
		bb. Error. St. Edward's Crown, W **9***b*.....	£130	
D2		2d. violet...	8·50	23·00
		a. Chalk-surfaced paper (6.11.52)........	30	22·00
		ab. Error. Crown missing, W **9***a*...	£350	
		ac. Error. St. Edward's Crown, W **9***b*.....	£140	
		ad. Large "d"...	7·50	
D1s/2s Perf "Specimen" *Set of 2*...			60·00	

D **2**

(Typo D.L.R.)

1956 (1 Dec). Wmk Mult Script CA. P 14.

D3	D **2**	1d. carmine...	30	3·00
D4		2d. deep reddish violet...	30	6·00

5c (I)　　**5c** (II)

1961 (14 Feb). Surch as T **24**, but without stop.

D5	D **2**	1c. on 1d. carmine...	10	35
D6		1c. on 2d. deep reddish violet...	10	1·25
D7		5c. on 2d. deep reddish violet (Type I)...	15	45
		a. Type II...	14·00	50·00
D5/7 *Set of 3*...			30	1·90

1961 (1 June). No. D2a surch as T **24** (without stop).

D8	D **1**	5c. on 2d. violet...	1·00	6·50
		a. Error. Missing Crown, W **9a**...	£1700	
		b. Error. St. Edward's Crown, W **9b**.....	£350	
		c. Large "d"...	19·00	

1964. As No. D3/4 but values in cents and W w **12** (sideways on 1c.).

D9	D **2**	1c. carmine...	4·00	23·00
D10		5c. deep reddish violet...	4·00	23·00

1966 (1 Nov). Nos. D9/10 optd as T **34** but smaller.

D11	D **2**	1c. carmine...	30	75
		a. "LSEOTHO" (R.4/7)...	29·00	
D12		5c. deep reddish violet...	30	90
		a. "LSEOTHO" (R.4/7)...	50·00	

No. D11 exists with the overprint centred near the foot of the stamp (just above "POSTAGE DUE") (*price* £50 *mint*). It is believed that this comes from a proof sheet which was issued in the normal way. It contains the "LSEOTHO" error, which only occurred in the first printing.

D **3**

D **4**

(Litho B.W.)

1967 (18 Apr). No wmk. P 13½.

D13	D **3**	1c. blue...	15	3·00
D14		2c. brown-rose...	15	3·50
D15		5c. emerald...	20	3·50
D13/15 *Set of 3*...			45	9·00

1976 (30 Nov). W **53** (sideways). P 13½.

D17	D **3**	2c. rose-red...	1·50	6·00
D18		5c. emerald...	1·75	6·00

(Des G. Vasarhelyi. Litho Format)

1986. No wmk. P 13×13½.

D19	D **4**	2s. light green...	20	1·25
D20		5s. new blue...	20	1·25
D21		25s. violet...	70	1·50
D19/21 *Set of 3*...			1·00	3·50

Nos. D19/21 exist imperforate from stock dispersed by the liquidator of Format International Security Printers Ltd.

POSTAL FISCAL

In July 1961 the 10s. stamp, T **9**, surcharged "R1 Revenue", was used for postage at one post office at least, but such usage was officially unauthorised.

Appendix

The following stamps have either been issued in excess of postal needs, or have not been made available to the public in reasonable quantities at face value. Miniature sheets, imperforate stamps etc., are excluded from this section.

1981–83. 15th Anniv of Independence. Classic Stamps of the World. 10m.×40, each embossed on gold foil.

Malawi
formerly Nyasaland

PRICES FOR STAMPS ON COVER TO 1945	
Nos. 1/9*a*	*from* × 15
Nos. 10/19	—
No. 20	*from* × 10
Nos. 21/6	*from* × 5
Nos. 27/31	—
Nos. 32/7	*from* × 6
Nos. 38/42	—
Nos. 43/7	*from* × 12
Nos. 48/52	—
No. 53	*from* × 15
No. 54	*from* × 2
No. 55	*from* × 4
Nos. 55*b*/7*a*	*from* × 7
Nos. 57*d*/63	*from* × 6
Nos. 64/71	—
Nos. 72/9	*from* × 5
Nos. 80/2	—
Nos. 83/95	*from* × 4
Nos. 96/9	—
Nos. 100/57	*from* × 2

By 1891 the territory west of Lake Nyasa was recognised as being under British protection and the southern, eastern and northern borders had been delineated with the Portuguese and German governments.

BRITISH CENTRAL AFRICA

A protectorate under the name "Nyassaland Districts" was declared on 14 May 1891, the title being changed to the "British Central Africa Protectorate" on 22 February 1893. Such a description had been in use for some time previously and the handwritten notice of 20 July 1891, announcing the introduction of postal services, described the area as "British Central Africa".

Until 1895 the British South Africa Company contributed to the revenues of the protectorate administration which, in return governed North-eastern Rhodesia. Stamps of the British South Africa Company overprinted "B.C.A.", in addition to use in British Central Africa, were issued to post offices at Fife, Fort Rosebery, Katwe, Johnston Falls, Rhodesia (later Kalungwisi) and Tanganyika (later Abercorn) in North-eastern Rhodesia from 1893 until 1899.

B.C.A. (1)

B.C.A. FOUR SHILLINGS. (2)

ONE PENNY. (3)

1891 (20 July)–**95**. Stamps of Rhodesia optd as T **1**. P 14, 14½.

1	**1**	1d. black	12·00	8·50
2	**4**	2d. sea-green and vermilion	12·00	4·00
		a. Bisected (1d.) (on cover) (1895)	†	£6500
3		4d. reddish chestnut and black	12·00	5·50
4	**1**	6d. ultramarine	55·00	20·00
5		6d. deep blue	15·00	8·00
6	**4**	8d. rose-lake and ultramarine	19·00	29·00
6*a*		8d. red and ultramarine	35·00	50·00
7	**1**	1s. grey-brown	24·00	17·00
8		2s. vermilion	40·00	55·00
9		2s.6d. grey-purple	70·00	90·00
9*a*		2s.6d. lilac	75·00	90·00
10	**4**	3s. brown and green (1895)	80·00	80·00
11		4s. grey-black and vermilion (2.93)	80·00	90·00
12	**1**	5s. orange-yellow	95·00	95·00
13		10s. deep green	£170	£200
14	**2**	£1 deep blue	£900	£650
15		£2 rose-red	£1100	
16		£5 sage-green	£1700	
17		£10 brown	£4000	£4750
1/14 *Set of* 13			£1400	£1200

The overprint varies on values up to 10s. Sets may be made with *thin* or *thick* letters.

Specialists have identified four separate settings; either of 30 (10×3) or 60 (10×6) impressions.

The bisected 2d, No. 2a, was authorised for use at Blantyre, Chiromo and Zomba in July and October 1895.

1892 (Aug)–**93**. Stamps of Rhodesia surch as T **2**.

18	**4**	3s. on 4s. grey-black and vermilion (10.93)	£350	£350
19	**1**	4s. on 5s. orange-yellow	90·00	90·00

1895. No. 2 surch at Cape Town with T **3**.

20	**4**	1d. on 2d. sea-green and vermilion	24·00	50·00
		a. Surch double	£9000	£6500

Specimens are known with double surcharge, without stop after "PENNY". These are from a trial printing made at Blantyre, but it is believed that they were not issued to the public (*Price* £550 *un.*).

5 Arms of the Protectorate

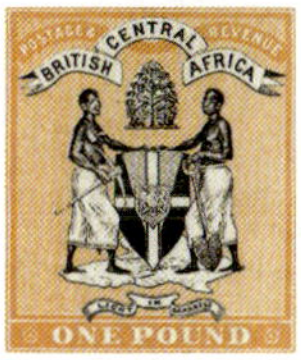

6 Arms of the Protectorate

(Des Sir Harry Johnston. Litho D.L.R.)

1895. No wmk. P 14.

21	**5**	1d. black	18·00	13·00
22		2d. black and green	40·00	12·00
23		4d. black and reddish buff	75·00	50·00
24		6d. black and blue	80·00	8·00
25		1s. black and rose	95·00	35·00
26	**6**	2s.6d. black and bright magenta	£300	£300
27		3s. black and yellow	£180	50·00
28		5s. black and olive	£225	£225
29		£1 black and yellow-orange	£1100	£450
30		£10 black and orange-vermilion	£6000	£4000
31		£25 black and blue-green	£12000	
21/8 *Set of* 8			£900	£600
21s/9s Optd "SPECIMEN" *Set of* 9			£400	

Cancellations inscribed "BRITISH CENTRAL AFRICA" within a double-circle and with the name of a town across the centre or at foot were intended for use on stamps presented for the payment of the hut tax. Such marks can be found in black, violet or blue and are without date. Stamps with such fiscal obliterations are of little value. Prices quoted are for postally used.

1896 (Feb). Wmk Crown CA (T **5**) or CC (sideways) (T **6**). P 14.

32	**5**	1d. black	3·25	8·00
		y. Wmk inverted and reversed	†	£550
33		2d. black and green	17·00	5·00
34		4d. black and orange-brown	27·00	17·00
35		6d. black and blue	40·00	13·00
36		1s. black and rose	40·00	22·00
37	**6**	2s.6d. black and magenta	£170	£140
38		3s. black and yellow	£150	60·00
39		5s. black and olive	£200	£200
40		£1 black and blue	£1000	£500
41		£10 black and orange	£8000	£4250
		s. Optd "SPECIMEN"	£190	
42		£25 black and green	£18000	
		s. Optd "SPECIMEN"	£350	
32/9 *Set of* 8			£600	£425
32s/40s Optd "SPECIMEN" *Set of* 9			£400	

7

8

(Typo D.L.R.)

1897 (Aug)–**1900**. T **7** (wmk Crown CA) and **8** (wmk Crown CC). P 14.

43	**7**	1d. black and ultramarine	3·25	1·25
		w. Wmk inverted	£170	£275
44		2d. black and yellow	2·00	2·00
45		4d. black and carmine	6·50	1·50
46		6d. black and green	55·00	4·25
47		1s. black and dull purple	11·00	7·00
48	**8**	2s.6d. black and ultramarine	80·00	42·00
49		3s. black and sea-green	£275	£300
50		4s. black and carmine	90·00	95·00
50*a*		10s. black and olive-green (1900)	£225	£250
51		£1 black and dull purple	£400	£180
52		£10 black and yellow	£6500	£2250
		s. Optd "SPECIMEN"	£225	
43/51 *Set of* 10			£1000	£800
43s/51s Optd "SPECIMEN" *Set of* 10			£325	

ONE

PENNY

(9)

10

1897 (31 Dec). No. 49 surch with T **9**, in red.

53	**8**	1d. on 3s. black and sea-green	9·00	13·00
		a. "PNNEY" (R. 4/2)	£7000	£5000
		b. "PENN"	£3500	£2750
		c. Surch double	£550	£950

No. 53b shows an albino impression of the "Y".

1898 (11 Mar). Imperf.

(a) Setting I. The vertical frame lines of the stamps cross the space between the two rows of the sheet

(i) With the initials "J.G." or "J.T.G." on the back in black ink

54	**10**	1d. vermilion and grey-blue	£1300	£1000
		a. Without the initials	£6000	
		b. Without the initials and centre inverted	£28000	

(ii) With a control number and letter or letters, printed in plain relief at the back

55	**10**	1d. vermilion and grey-blue	—	£700

(b) Setting II. The vertical frame lines do not cross the space between the rows except at the extreme ends of the sheet. Control as No. 55

55*b*	**10**	1d. vermilion and pale ultramarine	—	£130
		c. Control on face	—	£3250
		d. Centre omitted (vert pair with normal)	£14000	
56		1d. vermilion and deep ultramarine	—	£140
		a. Without Control at back	£5000	£180
		b. Control doubly impressed	—	£450

1898 (June). Setting II. Control as No. 55. P 12.

57	**10**	1d. vermilion and pale ultramarine	£4250	29·00
57*a*		1d. vermilion and deep ultramarine	—	40·00
		ab. Without Control at back	£2750	90·00
		ac. Two different Controls on back	—	£600
		ad. Control printed in black	£3750	

The two different settings of these stamps are each in 30 types, issued without gum.

1901. Wmk Crown CA. P 14.

57*d*	**7**	1d. dull purple and carmine-rose	2·50	50
57*e*		4d. dull purple and olive-green	8·50	11·00
58		6d. dull purple and brown	5·50	3·00
57d/8 *Set of 3*			15·00	13·00
57ds/8s Optd "SPECIMEN" *Set of 3*			70·00	

11

12

(Typo D.L.R.)

1903–04. T **11** (Wmk Crown CA) and **12** (Wmk Crown CC). P 14.

59	**11**	1d. grey and carmine	8·00	1·75
60		2d. dull and bright purple	3·50	1·00
61		4d. grey-green and black	2·50	9·00
62		6d. grey and reddish buff	3·75	2·00
		aw. Wmk inverted	£180	
62*b*		1s. grey and blue	4·75	13·00
63	**12**	2s.6d. grey-green and green	60·00	95·00
64		4s. dull and bright purple	85·00	85·00
		w. Wmk inverted	£1100	
65		10s. grey-green and black	£180	£250
66		£1 grey and carmine	£300	£190
67		£10 grey and blue	£6500	£4000
		s. Optd "SPECIMEN"	£450	
59/66 *Set of 9*			£600	£600
59s/66s Optd "SPECIMEN" *Set of 9*			£400	

1907. Chalk-surfaced paper. Wmk Mult Crown CA. P 14.

68	**11**	1d. grey and carmine	8·00	2·75
69		2d. dull and bright purple	£15000	
70		4d. grey-green and black	£15000	
71		6d. grey and reddish buff	38·00	50·00

Nos. 69/70 were prepared, but not issued in Nyasaland due to the Protectorate's name being changed. It is estimated that no more than a dozen examples of each remain in collectors' hands.

NYASALAND PROTECTORATE

The title of the Protectorate was changed again from 6 July 1907.

13

14

Serif on "G" (R. 4/5. All ptgs of £1 Duty plate)

(Typo D.L.R.)

1908 (22 July)–**11**. P 14.

(a) Wmk Crown CA. Chalk-surfaced paper

72	**13**	1s. black/*green*	3·50	15·00

(b) Wmk Mult Crown CA. Ordinary paper (½d., 1d.) or chalk-surfaced paper (others)

73	**13**	½d. green	1·75	2·25
74		1d. carmine	7·00	1·00
75		3d. purple/*yellow*	1·50	4·25
		w. Wmk inverted	£350	
76		4d. black and red/*yellow*	1·50	1·50
		w. Wmk inverted	£130	£160
77		6d. dull purple and bright purple	4·25	11·00
78	**14**	2s.6d. brownish black & carm-red/*blue*	65·00	95·00
		a. Brownish black and deep rose-red/pale blue (1911)	£225	£275
79		4s. carmine and black	95·00	£150
80		10s. green and red/*green*	£180	£275
81		£1 purple and black/*red*	£550	£650
		c. Serif on "G"	£2250	£2500
82		£10 purple and ultramarine	£9500	£6500
		s. Optd "SPECIMEN"	£950	
72/81 *Set of 10*			£800	£1100
72s/81s Optd "SPECIMEN" *Set of 10*			£550	

15

16

Break in scroll (R. 1/12)

Broken crown and scroll (R. 2/12)

Nick in top right scroll (R. 3/12)

Break in lines below left scroll (R. 4/9)

1913 (1 Apr)–**19**. Wmk Mult Crown CA. Ordinary paper (½d. to 2½d.) or chalk-surfaced paper (others). P 14.

No.	Type	Description	Unused	Used
83	**15**	½d. green	1·25	2·25
84		½d. blue-green (1918)	2·50	2·50
85		1d. carmine-red	2·50	2·00
86		1d. scarlet (1916)	4·00	1·00
87		2d. grey (1916)	5·50	1·00
88		2d. slate	13·00	3·75
89		2½d. bright blue	2·25	7·00
90		3d. purple/*yellow* (1914)	6·00	4·50
		a. On pale yellow	5·50	10·00
		w. Wmk inverted		
91		4d. black and red/*yellow* (*shades*)	2·00	2·50
		a. On pale yellow	6·50	8·50
92		6d. dull and bright purple	4·50	10·00
92*a*		6d. dull purple and bright violet	13·00	10·00
93		1s. black/*green*	1·75	8·50
		a. On blue-green, olive back	5·50	1·50
		aw. Wmk inverted	£160	£200
		b. On emerald back	4·50	6·50
		bs. Optd "SPECIMEN"	65·00	
94	**16**	2s.6d. black and red/*blue*	11·00	19·00
		a. Break in scroll	£200	
		b. Broken crown and scroll	£300	
		c. Nick in top right scroll	£225	£300
		f. Damaged leaf at bottom right	£250	
		h. "Bullet-holes" flaw	£475	
		x. Wmk reversed	†	£2000
95		4s. carmine and black	30·00	70·00
		a. Break in scroll	£300	
		b. Broken crown and scroll	£350	
		d. Nick in top right scroll	£300	
		f. Damaged leaf at bottom right	£325	
		h. "Bullet-holes" flaw	£475	
		i. Triangle flaw	£450	
96		10s. pale green and deep scarlet/*green*	£110	£130
		d. Nick in top right scroll	£500	
		e. Green and deep scarlet/green (1919)	£120	£160
		ea. Break in scroll	£550	
		eb. Broken crown and scroll	£550	
		ef. Damaged leaf at bottom right	£600	
		eh. "Bullet holes" flaw	£850	
98		£1 purple and black/*red*	£200	£150
		a. Break in scroll	£850	
		b. Broken crown and scroll	£850	
		c. Nick in top right scroll	£900	
		e. Break in lines below left scroll	£950	
		f. Damaged leaf at bottom right	£850	
		h. "Bullet holes" flaw	£1500	
		i. Serif on "G"	£950	£700
		w. Wmk inverted		
99		£10 purple and dull ultramarine	£7000	
		c. Nick in top right scroll	£9000	
		e. Purple and royal blue (1919)	£3500	£1700
		ea. Break in scroll	£6500	£3250
		eb. Broken crown and scroll	£6500	
		ef. Damaged leaf at bottom right	£7000	
		eh. "Bullet holes" flaw	£8000	
		s. Optd "SPECIMEN"	£550	
83/98 *Set of 12*			£350	£375
83s/98s Optd "SPECIMEN" *Set of 12*			£500	

For stamps overprinted "N.F." see TANZANIA.

Damaged leaf at bottom right (R. 5/6)

"Bullet holes" flaw (R. 5/2. March 1919 ptgs)

Triangle flaw (R. 3/5. March 1919 ptg of 4s.)

Break through scroll (R. 1/9)

Gash in fruit and leaf (R. 5/12)

Breaks in scrolls at right (R. 1/3)

Damaged crown (R. 4/1. 2s.6d. ptg of June 1924)

1921–30. Wmk Mult Script CA. Ordinary paper (½d. to 2d.) or chalk-surfaced paper (others). P 14.

100	**15**	½d. green	2·25	50
		w. Wmk inverted	—	£325
101		1d. carmine	2·50	50
102		1½d. orange	3·25	17·00
103		2d. grey	2·00	50
105		3d. purple/*pale yellow*	14·00	3·25
106		4d. black and red/*yellow*	4·00	11·00
107		6d. dull and bright purple	3·50	3·25
108		1s. black/*emerald* (1930)	11·00	4·50
109	**16**	2s. purple and blue/*blue* (1926)	18·00	12·00
		a. Break in scroll	£170	£160
		b. Broken crown and scroll	£170	£160
		d. Break through scroll (Oct 1933 ptg only)	£250	£250
		e. Break in lines below left scroll	£170	£160
		f. Damaged leaf at bottom right	£170	£160
		g. Gash in fruit and leaf (Oct 1933 ptg only)	45·00	26·00
		h. Breaks in scrolls at right (Oct 1933 ptg only)	£250	£250
110		2s.6d. black and red/*blue* (1924)	23·00	26·00
		a. Break in scroll	£190	£200
		b. Broken crown and scroll	£190	£200
		c. Nick in top right scroll	£190	£200
		d. Break through scroll (Oct 1933 ptg only)	£275	£275
		e. Break in lines below left scroll	£190	£200
		f. Damaged leaf at bottom right	£190	£200
		g. Gash in fruit and leaf (Oct 1933 ptg only)	£275	£275
		h. Breaks in scrolls at right (Oct 1933 ptg only)	£275	£275
		i. Damaged crown	£400	£400
111		4s. carmine and black (1927)	20·00	38·00
		a. Break in scroll	£200	
		b. Broken crown and scroll	£200	
		c. Nick in top right scroll	£200	
		e. Break in lines below left scroll	£200	
		f. Damaged leaf at bottom right	£200	
112		5s. green and red/*yellow* (1929)	50·00	85·00
		a. Break in scroll	£350	
		b. Broken crown and scroll	£350	
		c. Nick in top right scroll	£350	
		e. Break in lines below left scroll	£350	
		f. Damaged leaf at bottom right	£350	
113		10s. green and red/*pale emerald* (1926)	£110	£110
		a. Break in scroll	£500	£550
		b. Broken crown and scroll	£500	£550
		c. Nick in top right scroll	£500	£550
		e. Break in lines below left scroll	£500	£550
		f. Damaged leaf at bottom right	£500	£550
		g. *Green and scarlet/emerald* (1927)	£650	£800
		ga. Break in scroll	£1800	
		gb. Broken crown and scroll	£1800	
		ge. Break in lines below left scroll	£1800	
		gf. Damaged leaf at bottom right	£1800	
100/13 *Set of* 13			£225	£275
100s/13s Optd or Perf (1s., 5s.) "SPECIMEN" *Set of* 13			£475	

For illustrations of the other varieties on Nos. 109/13 see above Bermuda No. 51*b*.

17 King George V and Symbol of the Protectorate

(Des Major H. E. Green. Recess Waterlow)

1934 (June)–**35**. Wmk Mult Script CA. P 12½.

114	**17**	½d. green	75	1·25
115		1d. brown	75	75
116		1½d. carmine	75	3·00
117		2d. pale grey	80	1·25
118		3d. blue	3·00	1·75
119		4d. bright magenta (20.5.35)	4·50	3·50
120		6d. violet	2·50	50
121		9d. olive-bistre (20.5.35)	7·00	9·00
122		1s. black and orange	18·00	14·00
114/22 *Set of* 9			35·00	32·00
114s/22s Perf "SPECIMEN" *Set of* 9			£275	

17a Windsor Castle

Kite and vertical log (Plate "2A" R. 10/6)

Bird by turret (Plate "7" R. 1/5)

(Des H. Fleury. Recess Waterlow)

1935 (6 May). Silver Jubilee. Wmk Mult Script CA. P 11×12.

123	**17a**	1d. ultramarine and grey	1·00	2·00
		k. Kite and vertical log	£160	
		m. "Bird" by turret	£225	
124		2d. green and indigo	1·00	1·50
		m. "Bird" by turret	£225	
125		3d. brown and deep blue	8·50	20·00
		k. Kite and vertical log	£375	
126		1s. slate and purple	25·00	55·00
		k. Kite and vertical log	£450	£650
123/6 *Set of* 4			32·00	70·00
123s/6s Perf "SPECIMEN" *Set of* 4			£140	

17b King George VI and Queen Elizabeth

(Des D.L.R. Recess B.W.)

1937 (12 May). Coronation. Wmk Mult Script CA. P 11×11½.

127	**17b**	½d. green	30	2·25
128		1d. brown	50	1·50
129		2d. grey-black	50	3·25
127/9 *Set of 3*			1·10	6·25
127s/9s Perf "SPECIMEN" *Set of 3*			£120	

18 Symbol of the Protectorate

19

(T **18** recess Waterlow; T **19** typo D.L.R.)

1938 (1 Jan)–**44**. Chalk-surfaced paper (2s. to £1). P 12½ (T **18**) or 14 (T **19**).

(a) *Wmk Mult Script CA.*

130	**18**	½d. green	30	2·50
130*a*		½d. brown (12.12.42)	10	2·50
131		1d. brown	4·00	30
131*a*		1d. green (12.12.42)	30	2·25
132		1½d. carmine	7·50	6·50
132*a*		1½d. grey (12.12.42)	30	7·50
133		2d. grey	8·00	1·25
133*a*		2d. carmine (12.12.42)	30	1·75
134		3d. blue	1·00	1·50
135		4d. bright magenta	2·75	2·00
136		6d. violet	2·75	2·00
137		9d. olive-bistre	3·00	5·00
138		1s. black and orange	3·50	3·25
139	**19**	2s. purple and blue/*blue*	10·00	17·00
140		2s.6d. black and red/*blue*	14·00	19·00
141		5s. pale green and red/*yellow*	55·00	30·00
		a. Ordinary paper. *Green and red/ pale yellow* (3.44)	80·00	£140
142		10s. emerald and deep red/*pale green*	55·00	70·00
		a. Ordinary paper. *Bluish green and brown-red/pale green* (1.38)	£400	£400
		(b) *Wmk Mult Crown CA*		
143	**19**	£1 purple and black/*red*	48·00	45·00
		c. Serif on "G"	£950	£850
130/43 *Set of 18*			£190	£190
130s/43s Perf "SPECIMEN" *Set of 18*			£850	

No. 141a has a yellow surfacing often applied in horizontal lines giving the appearance of laid paper.

The printer's archives record the despatch of No. 142a to Nyasaland in January 1938, but no examples have been reported used before 1945. The paper coating on this printing varied considerably across the sheet. It is reported that some examples show a faint reaction to the silver test.

20 Lake Nyasa

21 King's African Rifles

22 Tea estate

23 Map of Nyasaland

24 Fishing Village

25 Tobacco

25a Badge of Nyasaland

(Recess B.W.)

1945 (1 Sept). T **20**/**25a** and similar designs. Wmk Mult Script CA (sideways on horiz designs). P 12.

144	**20**	½d. black and chocolate	50	10
145	**21**	1d. black and emerald	20	70
146	**22**	1½d. black and grey-green	30	50
147	**23**	2d. black and scarlet	1·50	85
148	**24**	3d. black and light blue	30	30
149	**25**	4d. black and claret	2·00	80
150	**22**	6d. black and violet	3·00	90
151	**20**	9d. black and olive	3·50	3·00
152	**23**	1s. indigo and deep green	3·75	20
153	**24**	2s. emerald and maroon	9·50	5·50
154	**25**	2s.6d. emerald and blue	9·50	7·00
155	**25a**	5s. purple and blue	7·00	6·50
156	**23**	10s. claret and emerald	20·00	18·00
157	**25a**	20s. scarlet and black	27·00	32·00
144/57 *Set of 14*			80·00	70·00
144s/57s Perf "SPECIMEN" *Set of 14*			£400	

(Des and recess D.L.R.)

1946 (16 Dec). Victory. Wmk Mult Script CA. P 13½×14.

158	1d. green	20	30
159	2d. red-orange	30	30
158s/9s Perf "SPECIMEN" *Set of 2*		£110	

26 Symbol of the Protectorate

(Recess B.W.)

1947 (20 Oct). Wmk Mult Script CA. P 12.

160	**26**	1d. red-brown and yellow-green	50	30
		a. Perf "SPECIMEN"	75·00	

26a King George VI and Queen Elizabeth

26b King george VI and Queen Elizabeth

(Des and photo Waterlow (T **26a**). Design recess; name typo B.W. (T **26b**))

1948 (15 Dec). Royal Silver Wedding. Wmk Mult Script CA.

161	**26a**	1d. green (p 14×15)	15	10
162	**26b**	10s. mauve (p 11½×11)	18·00	27·00

26c Hermes, Globe and Forms of Transport

26d Hemispheres, Jet-powered Vickers Viking Airliner and Steamer

26e Hermes and Globe

26f U.P.U. Monument

(Recess Waterlow (T **26c**, **26f**) or B.W. (T **25d**, **25e**))

1949 (21 Nov). 75th Anniv of U.P.U. Wmk Mult Script CA.

163	**26c**	1d. blue-green (p 13½×14)	30	20
		a. "A" of "CA" missing from wmk	£850	
164	**26d**	3d. greenish blue (p 11×11½)	2·25	4·25
165	**26e**	6d. purple (p 11×11½)	50	70
166	**26f**	1s. ultramarine (p 13½×14)	30	50
163/6 *Set of* 4			3·00	5·00

As on other examples of this variety, No. 163a shows traces of the left leg of the "A".

27 Arms in 1891 and 1951

(Des C. Twynam. Recess B.W.)

1951 (15 May). Diamond Jubilee of Protectorate. Wmk Mult Script CA. P 11×12.

167	**27**	2d. black and scarlet	1·25	1·50
168		3d. black and turquoise-blue	1·25	1·50
169		6d. black and violet	1·50	2·00
170		5s. black and indigo	5·00	7·00
167/70 *Set of* 4			8·00	11·00

28 Arms of Rhodesia and Nyasaland

28a Queen Elizabeth II

(Recess Waterlow)

1953 (30 May). Rhodes Centenary Exhibition. Wmk Mult Script CA. P 14×13½.

171	**28**	6d. violet	50	30

(Des and recess B.W.)

1953 (2 June). Coronation. Wmk Mult Script CA. P 13½×13.

172	**28a**	2d. black and brown-orange	70	80

29 Grading Cotton

(Recess B.W.)

1953 (1 Sept)–**54**. Designs previously used for King George VI issue, but with portrait of Queen Elizabeth II as in T **29**. Wmk Mult Script CA. P 12.

173	½d. black and chocolate	10	1·50
	a. Perf 12×12½ (8.3.54)	10	1·50
174	1d. brown and bright green	65	40
175	1½d. black and deep grey-green	20	1·90
176	2d. black and yellow-orange	85	30
	a. Perf 12×12½ (8.3.54)	40	30
177	2½d. green and black	20	50
178	3d. black and scarlet	30	20
179	4½d. black and light blue	40	40
180	6d. black and violet	1·00	1·50
	a. Perf 12×12½ (8.3.54)	2·00	1·00
181	9d. black and deep olive	1·00	2·50
182	1s. deep blue and slate-green	3·50	50
183	2s. deep green and brown-red	3·00	3·75
184	2s.6d. deep emerald and deep blue	4·00	6·00
185	5s. purple and Prussian blue	9·00	6·00
186	10s. carmine and deep emerald	7·50	19·00
187	20s. red and black	22·00	32·00
173a/87 *Set of* 15		38·00	65·00

Designs: Horiz—½d., 9d. Lake Nyasa; 1½d., 6d. Tea estate; 2d., 1s., 10s. Map of Nyasaland; 3d., 2s.6d. Tobacco; 5s., 20s. Badge of Nyasaland. Vert—1d. Symbol of the protectorate; 4½d., 2s. Fishing village.

Stamps perf 12×12½ come from sheets comb-perforated 11.8×12.25. They were also issued in coils of 480 stamps made up from sheets.

For issues between 1954 and 1963, see RHODESIA AND NYASALAND.

30

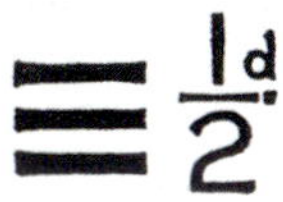

(**31**)

(Recess B.W.)

1963 (1 Nov). Revenue stamps optd "POSTAGE", as in T **30**, or additionally surch as T **31**. P 12.

188	½d. on 1d. greenish blue	30	30
189	1d. green	30	10
190	2d. scarlet	30	30
191	3d. blue	30	10
192	6d. brown-purple	30	10
193	9d. on 1s. cerise	40	25
194	1s. purple	45	10
195	2s.6d. black	1·25	2·75
196	5s. chocolate	3·25	2·00
197	10s. yellow-olive	5·50	8·50
	a. Greenish olive	17·00	18·00
198	£1 deep violet	5·50	8·50
188/98 *Set of* 11		16·00	20·00

32 Mother and Child

33 Chambo (fish)

34 Tea Industry

35 Nyala

(Des V. Whiteley. Photo Harrison)

1964 (1 Jan). Designs as T **32/5**. P 14½.

199	½d. reddish violet	10	30
200	1d. black and green	10	10
201	2d. light red-brown	10	10
202	3d. red-brown, yellow-green & bistre-brown	10	10
203	4d. indigo and orange-yellow	20	30

204	6d. purple, yellow-green and light blue	70	70
205	1s. brown, turquoise-blue and pale yellow	15	10
206	1s.3d. bronze-green and chestnut	3·75	10
207	2s.6d. brown and blue	3·25	50
208	5s. blue, green, yellow and black	1·50	1·75
209	10s. green, orange-brown and black	2·50	3·25
210	£1 deep reddish purple and yellow	7·00	14·00
199/210 *Set of* 12		17·00	19·00

Designs: As T **32/3**—2d. Zebu Bull; 3d. Groundnuts; 4d. Fishing. As T **34**—1s. Timber; 1s.3d. Turkish tobacco industry; 2s.6d. Cotton industry; 5s. Monkey Bay, Lake Nyasa; 10s. Forestry, Afzelia.

Nyasaland attained independence on 5 July 1964 when the country was renamed Malawi.

MALAWI

INDEPENDENT

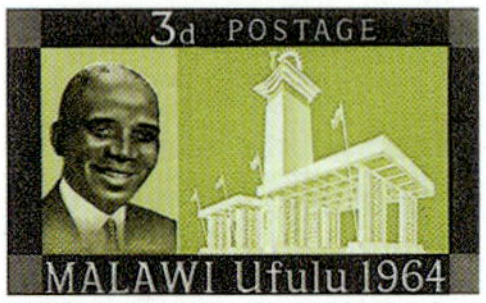

44 Dr. H. Banda (Prime Minister) and Independence Monument

(Des M. Goaman. Photo Harrison)

1964 (6 July). Independence. T **44** and similar horiz designs. P 14½.

211	3d. yellow-olive and deep sepia	10	10
212	6d. red, gold, blue, carmine and lake	10	10
213	1s.3d. red, green, black and bluish violet	45	10
214	2s.6d. multicoloured	45	1·25
	a. Blue omitted	£1800	
211/14 *Set of* 4		1·00	1·40

Designs:—6d. Banda and rising sun; 1s.3d. Banda and Malawi flag; 2s.6d. Banda and Malawi coat of arms.

Six examples of No. 214a are known from the top horizontal row of an otherwise normal sheet.

48 Tung Tree

49 Christmas Star and Globe

(Des V. Whiteley. Photo Harrison)

1964 (6 July)–**65**. As Nos. 199/210, but inscr "MALAWI" and T **48** (9d.). No wmk. P 14½.

215	½d. reddish violet	10	60
216	1d. black and green	10	10
217	2d. light red-brown	10	10
218	3d. red-brown, yellow-green & bistre-brown	15	10
219	4d. black and orange-yellow	85	15
220	6d. bluish violet, yellow-green and light blue	75	10
221	9d. bistre-brown, green and yellow	30	15
222	1s. brown, turquoise-blue and pale yellow	25	10
223	1s.3d. bronze-green and chestnut	50	60
224	2s.6d. brown and blue	1·10	1·00
225	5s. blue, green, yellow and sepia	65	3·25
225*a*	5s. blue, green, yellow and sepia (1.6.65)	10·00	1·00
226	10s. green, orange-brown and black	1·50	2·00
227	£1 deep reddish purple and yellow	6·00	5·50
215/27 *Set of* 14		20·00	13·00

No. 225*a* is inscribed "LAKE MALAWI" instead of "LAKE NYASA".

See also Nos. 252/62.

(Des V. Whiteley. Photo Harrison)

1964 (1 Dec). Christmas. P 14½.

228 **49**	3d. blue-green and gold	10	10
	a. Gold (star) omitted	£450	
229	6d. magenta and gold	10	10
230	1s.3d. reddish violet and gold	10	10
231	2s.6d. blue and gold	20	50
228/31 *Set of* 4		45	70
MS231*a* 83×126 mm. Nos. 228/31. Imperf		1·00	1·75

No. 228a comes from a sheet on which 41 examples had the gold colour omitted due to a paper fold.

50 Coins

1/6
═

(51)

(Des V. Whiteley. Photo Enschedé)

1965 (1 Mar). Malawi's First Coinage. Coins in black and silver. P 13½.

232 **50**	3d. green	10	10
233	9d. magenta	20	10
	a. Silver omitted		
234	1s.6d. purple	25	10
235	3s. blue	35	1·10
232/5 *Set of* 4		80	1·25
MS235*a* 126×104 mm. Nos. 232/5. Imperf		1·40	1·40

1965 (14 June). Nos. 223/4 surch as T **51**.

236	1s.6d. on 1s.3d. bronze-green and chestnut	10	10
237	3s. on 2s.6d. brown and blue	20	20

On No. 237 "3/-" occurs below the bars.

52 Chilembwe leading Rebels

(Des M. Goaman. Photo Harrison)

1965 (20 Aug). 50th Anniv of 1915 Rising. P 14×14½.

238 **52**	3d. violet and light olive-green	10	10
239	9d. olive-brown and red-orange	10	10
240	1s.6d. red-brown and grey-blue	15	10
241	3s. turquoise-green and slate-blue	20	25
238/41 *Set of* 4		40	60
MS241*a* 127×83 mm. Nos. 238/41		5·00	6·00

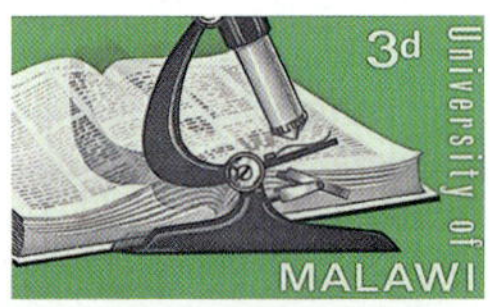

53 "Learning and Scholarship"

(Des H. E. Baxter. Photo Harrison)

1965 (6 Oct). Opening of Malawi University. P 14½.

242 **53**	3d. black and emerald	10	10
243	9d. black and magenta	10	10
244	1s.6d. black and reddish violet	10	10
245	3s. black and blue	15	40
242/5 *Set of* 4		30	50
MS246 127×84 mm. Nos. 242/5		2·50	2·50

54 *Papilio ophidicephalus*

(Des V. Whiteley. Photo Enschedé)

1966 (15 Feb). Malawi Butterflies. T **54** and similar horiz designs. Multicoloured. P 13½.

247	4d. Type **54**	80	10
248	9d. *Papilio desmondi (magdae)*	1·25	10
249	1s.6d. *Epamera handmani*	1·75	30
250	3s. *Amauris crawshayi*	2·75	6·00
247/50 *Set of* 4		6·00	6·00
MS251 130×100 mm. Nos. 247/50		17·00	11·00

55 Cockerels

56 Burley Tobacco

57 *Cyrestis camillus* (butterfly)

(New values des V. Whiteley (1s.6d.), M. Goaman (£2). Photo Harrison)

1966–67. As Nos. 215 etc. but W **55** (sideways on ½d., 2d.), and new values and designs (1s.6d., £2). P 14½.

No.	Type	Description		
252	–	½d. reddish violet (1.4.66)	10	10
253	–	1d. black and green (1.4.66)	15	10
254	–	2d. light red-brown (4.6.66)*	15	10
255	–	3d. red-brn, yell-grn & bis-brn (4.3.67)*	20	10
256	–	6d. bluish violet, yell-grn and lt bl (2.7.66)*	2·25	85
257	**48**	9d. bistre-brown, green and yell (5.12.66)*	2·00	10
258	–	1s. brown, turquoise-bl and pale yellow (1.4.66)	25	10
259	**56**	1s.6d. chocolate and yellow-grn (15.11.66)	55	10
260	–	5s. blue, green, yellow and sepia (6.10.66)*	8·50	4·00
261	–	10s. green, orange-brown and blk (6.10.66)*	20·00	26·00
262	**57**	£2 black, orange-yellow, pale yellow and slate-violet (7.9.66)	26·00	24·00
252/62		*Set of 11*	55·00	50·00

*These are local dates of issue. The Crown Agents, in London, did not distribute these printings until some time later.

No. 260 is inscribed "LAKE MALAWI".

The 2d. exists with both PVA gum and gum arabic.

58 British Central Africa 6d. Stamp of 1891

59 President Banda

(Des V. Whiteley. Photo Harrison)

1966 (4 May–10 June). 75th Anniv of Postal Services. W **55**. P 14½.

No.	Type	Description		
263	**58**	4d. grey-blue and yellow-green	10	10
264		9d. grey-blue and claret	15	10
265		1s.6d. grey-blue and reddish lilac	20	10
266		3s. grey-blue and new blue	30	70
263/6		*Set of 4*	60	80
MS267		83×127 mm. Nos. 263/6 (10 June)	5·00	3·25

REPUBLIC

(Des M. Goaman. Photo Harrison)

1966 (6 July). Republic Day. W **55**. P 14×14½.

No.	Type	Description		
268	**59**	4d. brown, silver and emerald	10	10
269		9d. brown, silver and magenta	10	10
270		1s.6d. brown, silver and violet	15	10
271		3s. brown, silver and blue	25	15
268/71		*Set of 4*	50	30
MS272		83×127 mm. Nos. 268/71	2·00	3·25

60 Bethlehem

(Des and photo Harrison)

1966 (12 Oct). Christmas. W **55**. P 14½.

No.	Type	Description		
273	**60**	4d. myrtle-green and gold	10	10
274		9d. brown-purple and gold	10	10
275		1s.6d. orange-red and gold	15	10
276		3s. blue and gold	40	80
273/6		*Set of 4*	65	1·00

61 *Ilala I*

(Des Mrs. H. Breggar. Photo Harrison)

1967 (4 Jan). Lake Malawi Steamers. T **61** and similar horiz designs. W **55**. P 14½.

277	4d. black, yellow and bright green	40	10
	a. Yellow omitted	†	£650
278	9d. black, yellow and magenta	45	10
279	1s.6d. black, red and violet	65	20
280	3s. black, red and bright blue	1·25	1·75
277/80	*Set of 4*	2·50	1·90

Designs:—9d. *Dove*; 1s.6d. *Chauncy Maples I* (wrongly inscr "Chauncey"); 3s. *Gwendolen*.

No. 277a occurs on first day covers from Blantyre.

62 Golden Mbuna (female)

(Des R. Granger Barrett. Photo Enschedé)

1967 (3 May). Lake Malawi Cichlids. T **62** and similar horiz designs. Multicoloured. W **55** (sideways). P 12½×12.

281	4d. Type **62**	30	10
282	9d. Scraper-mouthed Mbuna	45	10
283	1s.6d. Zebra Mbuna	60	25
	a. Imperf (pair)	£275	
284	3s. Orange Mbuna	1·25	2·00
	a. Imperf (pair)	£325	
281/4	*Set of 4*	2·40	2·25

63 Rising Sun and Gearwheel

(Des Jennifer Toombs. Litho D.L.R.)

1967 (5 July). Industrial Development. P 13½×13.

No.	Type	Description		
285	**63**	4d. black and emerald	10	10
286		9d. black and carmine	10	10
287		1s.6d. black and reddish violet	10	10

288		3s. black and bright blue	15	30
285/8 *Set of 4*			30	50
MS289 134×108 mm. Nos. 285/8			1·00	1·75

64 Mary and Joseph beside Crib

(Des Jennifer Toombs. Photo Harrison)

1967 (21 Nov–1 Dec). Christmas. W **55**. P 14×14½.

290	**64**	4d. royal blue and turquoise-green	10	10
291		9d. royal blue and light red	10	10
292		1s.6d. royal blue and yellow	10	10
293		3s. royal blue and new blue	15	30
290/3 *Set of 4*			30	50
MS294 114×100 mm. Nos. 290/3. Wmk sideways. P 14×13½ (1 Dec)			1·00	3·00

65 *Calotropis procera*

(Des G. Drummond. Litho D.L.R.)

1968 (24 Apr). Wild Flowers. T **65** and similar horiz designs. Multicoloured. W **55** (sideways). P 13½×13.

295		4d. Type **65**	15	10
296		9d. *Borreria dibrachiata*	15	10
297		1s.6d. *Hibiscus rhodanthus*	15	10
298		3s. *Bidens pinnatipartita*	20	95
295/8 *Set of 4*			60	1·10
MS299 135×91 mm. Nos. 295/8			1·25	3·25

66 Bagnall Steam Locomotive No. 1, *Thistle*

(Des R. Granger Barrett. Photo Harrison)

1968 (24 July). Malawi Locomotives. T **66** and similar horiz designs. W **55**. P 14×14½.

300		4d. grey-green, slate-blue and red	25	10
301		9d. red, slate-blue and myrtle-green	30	15
302		1s.6d. multicoloured	40	30
303		3s. multicoloured	70	3·00
300/3 *Set of 4*			1·50	3·00
MS304 120×88 mm. Nos. 300/3. P 14½			1·50	6·00

Designs:—9d. Class G steam locomotive No. 49; 1s.6d. Class "Zambesi" diesel locomotive No. 202; 3s. Diesel railcar No. DR1.

67 "The Nativity" (Piero della Francesca)

(Des and photo Harrison)

1968 (6 Nov). Christmas. Paintings. T **67** and similar horiz designs. Multicoloured. W **55** (sideways on 4d.). P 14×14½.

305		4d. Type **67**	10	10
306		9d. "The Adoration of the Shepherds" (Murillo)	10	10
307		1s.6d. "The Adoration of the Shepherds" (Reni)	10	10
308		3s. "Nativity with God the Father and Holy Ghost" (Pittoni)	15	15
305/8 *Set of 4*			30	30
MS309 115×101 mm. Nos. 305/8. P 14×13½			35	1·60

68 Scarlet-chested Sunbird

69 Nyasa Lovebird

70 Carmine Bee Eater

(Des V. Whiteley. Photo Harrison)

1968 (13 Nov). Birds. T **68/70** and similar designs. Multicoloured. W **55** (sideways on 1d. to 4d. and 3s. to £1). P 14½.

310		1d. Type **68**	15	50
311		2d. Violet Starling	30	20
312		3d. White-browed Robin Chat	30	10
313		4d. Red-billed Fire Finch	50	40
		a. Red omitted	†	—
314		6d. Type **69**	2·50	15
315		9d. Yellow-rumped Bishop	2·50	60
316		1s. Type **70**	1·00	15
317		1s.6d. Grey-headed Bush Shrike	5·00	8·00
318		2s. Paradise Whydah	5·00	8·00
319		3s. African Paradise Flycatcher	8·50	4·25
320		5s. Bateleur	6·00	4·25
321		10s. Saddle-bill Stork	4·50	7·50
322		£1 Purple Heron	8·00	18·00
323		£2 Knysna Turaco ("Livingstone's Loerie")	42·00	48·00
310/23 *Set of 14*			75·00	90·00

Sizes:—2d. to 4d. as T **68**; 9d. as T **69**; 1s.6d., 2s, £2 as T **70**; 3s. to £1 as T **70** but vertical.

No. 310 exists in coils, constructed from normal sheets.

An example of No. 313a is known used on local cover from Limbe in September 1970.

71 I.L.O. Emblem

(Des G. Drummond. Photo, emblem die-stamped Harrison)

1969 (5 Feb). 50th Anniv of the International Labour Organization. W **55** (sideways on No. **MS**328). P 14.

324	**71**	4d. gold and myrtle-green	10	10
325		9d. gold and chocolate	10	10
326		1s.6d. gold and blackish brown	10	10
327		3s. gold and indigo	15	15
324/7 *Set of 4*			30	30
MS328 127×89 mm. Nos. 324/7			1·00	4·75

72 White-fringed Ground Orchid

73 African Development Bank Emblem

(Des J.W. Litho B.W.)

1969 (9 July). Orchids of Malawi. T **72** and similar horiz designs. Multicoloured. W **55**. P 13½×13.

329	4d. Type **72**	15	10
330	9d. Red Ground orchid	20	10
331	1s.6d. Leopard Tree orchid	30	20
332	3s. Blue Ground orchid	60	2·00
329/32 *Set of 4*		1·10	2·00
MS333 118×86 mm. Nos. 329/32		1·10	3·75

(Des G. Vasarhelyi. Litho D.L.R.)

1969 (10 Sept). Fifth Anniv of African Development Bank. W **55**. P 14.

334 **73**	4d. yellow, yellow-ochre and chocolate	10	10
335	9d. yellow, yellow-ochre & myrtle-green	10	10
336	1s.6d. yellow, yell-ochre & blackish brn	10	10
337	3s. yellow, yellow-ochre and indigo	15	15
334/7 *Set of 4*		30	30
MS338 102×137 mm. Nos. 334/7		50	1·00

74 Dove over Bethlehem

(Des Jennifer Toombs. Photo Harrison)

1969 (5 Nov). Christmas. W **55**. P 14½×14.

339 **74**	2d. black and olive-yellow	10	10
340	4d. black and deep turquoise	10	10
341	9d. black and scarlet	10	10
342	1s.6d. black and deep bluish violet	10	10
343	3s. black and ultramarine	15	15
339/43 *Set of 5*		30	30
MS344 130×71 mm. Nos. 339/43		1·00	1·75
	a. Ultramarine (background of 3s.) omitted	£3750	

75 *Zonocerus elegans* (grasshopper)

(Des V. Whiteley. Litho Format)

1970 (4 Feb). Insects of Malawi. T **75** and similar vert designs. Multicoloured. W **55**. P 14.

345	4d. Type **75**	15	10
346	9d. *Mylabris dicincta* (beetle)	15	10
347	1s.6d. *Henosepilachna elaterii* (ladybird)	20	15
348	3s. *Sphodromantis speculabunda* (mantid)	35	1·10
345/8 *Set of 4*		75	1·25
MS349 86×137 mm. Nos. 345/8		1·25	2·50

Rand Easter Show
1970

(**76**)

1970 (18 Mar). Rand Easter Show. No. 317 optd with T **76**.

350	1s.6d. multicoloured	50	2·25

77 Runner

(Des J. Cooter. Litho B.W.)

1970 (3 June). Ninth British Commonwealth Games, Edinburgh. W **55**. P 13.

351 **77**	4d. royal blue and blue-green	10	10
352	9d. royal blue and carmine	10	10
353	1s.6d. royal blue and dull yellow	10	10
354	3s. royal blue and new blue	15	15
351/4 *Set of 4*		30	30
MS355 146×96 mm. Nos. 351/4		55	1·00

(New Currency, 100 tambalas = 1 kwacha)

10t

(**78**)

79 *Aegocera trimeni*

1970 (2 Sept). Decimal Currency. Nos. 316 and 318 surch as T **78**.

356	10t. on 1s. multicoloured	3·00	25
	a. Surch double	†	
357	20t. on 2s. multicoloured	3·00	4·50

(Des R. Granger Barrett. Litho B.W.)

1970 (30 Sept). Moths. T **79** and similar horiz designs. Multicoloured. W **55**. P 11×11½.

358	4d. Type **79**	20	10
359	9d. *Faidherbia bauhiniae*	30	10
360	1s.6d. *Parasa karschi*	50	20
361	3s. *Teracotona euprepia*	1·25	3·50
358/61 *Set of 4*		2·00	3·50
MS362 112×92 mm. Nos. 358/61		4·25	6·50

80 Mother and Child

30t
Special
United
Kingdom
Delivery
Service

(**81**)

(Des Brother W. Meyer. Litho J.W.)

1970 (4 Nov). Christmas. W **55** (sideways). P 14.

363 **80**	2d. black and light yellow	10	10
364	4d. black and emerald	10	10
365	9d. black and orange-red	10	10
366	1s.6d. black and light purple	10	10
367	3s. black and blue	15	15
363/7 *Set of 5*		30	30
MS368 166×100 mm. Nos. 363/7		1·00	2·50

1971 (8 Feb). No. 319 surch with T **81**.

369	30t. on 3s. multicoloured	50	2·25

No. 369 was issued for use on letters carried by an emergency airmail service from Malawi to Great Britain during the British postal strike. The fee of 30t. was to cover the charge for delivery by a private service, and ordinary stamps to pay the normal airmail fee had to be affixed as well.

The strike ended on 8 March, when private delivery services were withdrawn.

82 Decimal Coinage and Cockerel

(Des V. Whiteley. Litho Format)

1971 (15 Feb). Decimal Coinage. W **55** (sideways). P 14.

370 **82**	3t. multicoloured	15	10
371	8t. multicoloured	20	10
372	15t. multicoloured	25	20
373	30t. multicoloured	35	1·50
370/3 *Set of 4*		85	1·60
MS374 140×101 mm. Nos. 370/3		1·00	2·50

83 Greater Kudu

84 Eland

(Des and litho J.W.)

1971 (15 Feb)–**75**. Decimal Currency. Antelopes. Vert designs as T **83** (1t. to 8t.), or T **84** (others). Multicoloured. W **55** (sideways* on 1t. to 8t.). P 13½×14 (1t. to 8t.) or 14½ (others).

375	1t. Type **83**	10	10
	a. Coil stamp. P 14½×14	55	40
	b. Perf 14† (*wmk cockerel facing right*) (12.11.74)	45	1·75
376	2t. Nyala	15	15
	w. Wmk cockerel facing right (5.2.75)	30	40
377	3t. Mountain Reedbuck	20	50
	a. Perf 14† (*wmk cockerel facing right*) (12.11.74)	65	1·50
378	5t. Puku	40	1·25
	a. Perf 14† (*wmk cockerel facing right*) (12.11.74)	65	2·25
379	8t. Impala	45	1·00
380	10t. Type **84**	60	10
381	15t. Klipspringer	1·00	20
	w. Wmk inverted	†	£200
382	20t. Suni	1·50	90
383	30t. Roan Antelope	11·00	1·40
384	50t. Waterbuck	1·00	65
	w. Wmk inverted (9.5.73)	1·00	1·00
385	1k. Bushbuck	1·50	85
386	2k. Red Forest Duiker	2·75	1·50
387	4k. Common Duiker	21·00	24·00
375/87	*Set of* 13	38·00	29·00

*The normal sideways watermark shows the cockerel's head facing left *as seen from the back of the stamp.*

†These actually gauge 14.2×14 instead of 13.7×14 and are line-perforated; in blocks they can easily be distinguished as in alternate rows across the sheet the horizontal perfs have two holes where they cross the vertical perfs.

No. 387 is incorrectly inscr "Gray Duiker".

85 Christ on the Cross

87 *Holarrhena febrifuga*

(Des G. Drummond. Litho Questa)

1971 (7 Apr). Easter. Details from Painting "The Small Passion" by Dürer. T **85** and similar vert design. W **55**. P 13½.

388	3t. black and green	10	25
	a. Pair. Nos. 388/9	10	50
389	3t. black and green	10	25
390	8t. black and orange-red	10	25
	a. Pair. Nos. 390/1	15	50
391	8t. black and orange-red	10	25
392	15t. black and violet	15	30
	a. Pair. Nos. 392/3	30	60
393	15t. black and violet	15	30
394	30t. black and bright blue	20	45
	a. Pair. Nos. 394/5	40	90
395	30t. black and bright blue	20	45
388/95	*Set of* 8	85	2·25
MS396	Two sheets, each 95×145 mm (a) Nos. 388, 390, 392 and 394; (b) Nos. 389, 391, 393 and 395	1·50	4·00

Designs:—Nos. 388, 390, 392 and 394, Type **85**; Nos. 389, 391, 393 and 395, The Resurrection.

Nos. 388/9, 390/1, 392/3 and 394/5 were each printed together, *se-tenant*, in pairs throughout the sheet.

(Des G. Drummond. Litho J.W.)

1971 (14 July). Flowering Shrubs and Trees. T **87** and similar vert designs. Multicoloured. W **55**. P 14.

397	3t. Type **87**	10	10
398	8t. *Brachystegia spiciformis*	10	10
399	15t. *Securidaca longepedunculata*	15	15
400	30t. *Pterocarpus rotundifolius*	30	1·25
397/400	*Set of* 4	55	1·40
MS401	102×135 mm. Nos. 397/400	1·00	2·50

88 Drum Major

89 "Madonna and Child" (William Dyce)

(Des J.W. Litho Questa)

1971 (5 Oct). 50th Anniv of Malawi Police Force. W **55**. P 14×14½.

402	**88**	30t. multicoloured	65	1·50

(Des J. Cooter. Litho Format)

1971 (10 Nov). Christmas. T **89** and similar vert designs. Multicoloured. W **55**. P 14½.

403	3t. Type **89**	10	10
404	8t. "The Holy Family" (M. Schöngauer)	15	10
405	15t. "The Holy Family with St. John" (Raphael).	20	20
406	30t. "The Holy Family" (Bronzino)	50	1·40
403/6	*Set of* 4	85	1·50
MS407	101×139 mm. Nos. 403/6	1·10	2·75

90 Vickers Viscount 700

(Des R. Granger Barrett. Litho Questa)

1972 (9 Feb). Air. Malawi Aircraft. T **90** and similar horiz designs. Multicoloured. W **55** (sideways). P 13½.

408	3t. Type **90**	40	10
409	8t. Hawker Siddeley H.S.748	60	10
410	15t. Britten Norman Islander	85	30
411	30t. B.A.C. One Eleven	1·40	2·75
408/11	*Set of* 4	3·00	2·75
MS412	143×94 mm. Nos. 408/11	8·00	6·00

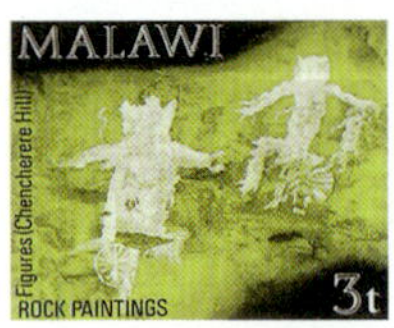

91 Figures (Chencherere Hill)

92 Boxing

(Des R. Granger Barrett. Litho Format)

1972 (10 May). Rock Paintings. T **91** and similar horiz designs. W **55** (sideways). P 13½.

413	3t. apple-green, grey-green and black	25	10
414	8t. red, grey and black	30	10
415	15t. multicoloured	35	30
416	30t. multicoloured	45	1·00
413/16	*Set of* 4	1·25	1·25
MS417	121×97 mm. Nos. 413/16. P 15	2·75	2·75

Designs:—8t. Lizard and cat (Chencherere Hill); 15t. Schematics (Diwa Hill); 30t. Sun through rain (Mikolongwe Hill).

(Des local artist. Litho Harrison)

1972 (9 Aug). Olympic Games, Munich. W **55** (sideways). P 14×14½.

418	**92**	3t. multicoloured	10	10
419		8t. multicoloured	15	10

420 15t. multicoloured 20 10
421 30t. multicoloured 35 45
418/21 *Set of 4* 70 55
MS422 110×92 mm. Nos. 418/21. P 14×13½ 1·25 1·75

93 Arms of Malawi

94 "Adoration of the Kings" (Orcagna)

(Des G. Drummond. Litho Questa)

1972 (20 Oct). Commonwealth Parliamentary Conference. W **55**. P 13½.
423 **93** 15t. multicoloured 30 35

(Des V. Whiteley. Litho Questa)

1972 (8 Nov). Christmas. T **94** and similar vert designs. Multicoloured. W **55**. P 14½×14.
424 3t. Type **94** 10 10
425 8t. "Madonna and Child Enthroned" (Florentine School) 10 10
426 15t. "Virgin and Child" (Crivelli) 20 10
427 30t. "Virgin and Child with St. Anne" (Flemish School) 45 70
424/7 *Set of 4* 70 80
MS428 95×121 mm. Nos. 424/7 1·10 2·00

"MALAWI". All issues from No. 429 onwards have a circumflex accent over the "W", to give the correct pronunciation of "Malavi".

95 *Charaxes bohemani*

(Des PAD Studio. Litho Questa)

1973 (7 Feb–5 Apr). Butterflies. T **95** and similar horiz designs. Multicoloured. W **55** (sideways). P 13½×14.
429 3t. Type **95** 50 10
430 8t. *Uranothauma crawshayi* 75 10
431 15t. *Charaxes acuminatus* 1·00 30
432 30t. *Amauris ansorgei* (inscr in error "EUPHAEDRA ZADDACHI") 4·00 8·50
433 30t. *Amauris ansorgei* (inscr corrected) (5 Apr) 5·50 8·50
429/33 *Set of 5* 10·50 16·00
MS434 145×95 mm. Nos. 429/32 7·00 12·00

96 Livingstone and Map

(Des J.W. Litho Format)

1973 (1 May). Death Centenary of David Livingstone (1st issue). W **55** (sideways). P 13½×14.
435 **96** 3t. multicoloured 10 10
436 8t. multicoloured 15 10
437 15t. multicoloured 20 10
438 30t. multicoloured 35 60
435/8 *Set of 4* 70 70
MS439 144×95 mm. Nos. 435/8 1·00 1·75

See also Nos. 450/**MS**451.

97 Thumb Dulcitone

(Des Jennifer Toombs. Litho Questa)

1973 (8 Aug). Musical Instruments. T **97** and similar multicoloured designs. W **55** (sideways on 8, 15t. and **MS**444). P 14.
440 3t. Type **97** 10 10
441 8t. Hand zither (*vert*) 15 10
442 15t. Hand drum (*vert*) 25 10
443 30t. One-stringed fiddle 45 60
440/3 *Set of 4* 85 65
MS444 120×103 mm. Nos. 440/3 2·75 2·00

98 The Magi

(Des J.W. Litho Format)

1973 (7 Nov). Christmas. W **55** (sideways). P 13½.
445 **98** 3t. greenish blue, dp lilac & dull ultram 10 10
446 8t. salmon-red, bluish lilac & red-brn 10 10
447 15t. reddish mve, greenish bl & dp mve 15 10
448 30t. orange-yell, bluish lilac & lt lake-brn 30 70
445/8 *Set of 4* 50 75
MS449 165×114 mm. Nos. 445/8 75 1·40

99 Stained-glass Window, Livingstonia Mission

(Des PAD Studio. Litho Questa)

1973 (12 Dec). Death Centenary of David Livingstone (2nd issue). W **55** (sideways). P 13½.
450 **99** 50t. multicoloured 45 1·25
MS451 71×77 mm. No. 450 80 1·60

100 Large-mouthed Black Bass

(Des Sylvia Goaman. Litho Questa)

1974 (20 Feb). 35th Anniv of Malawi Angling Society. T **100** and similar horiz designs. Multicoloured. W **55** (sideways). P 14.
452 3t. Type **100** 20 10
453 8t. Rainbow Trout 25 10
454 15t. Silver Alestes ("Lake Salmon") 40 20
455 30t. Tigerfish 70 1·90
452/5 *Set of 4* 1·40 2·00
MS456 169×93 mm. Nos. 452/5 2·50 3·00

101 U.P.U. Monument and Map of Africa

(Des J. Cooter. Litho J.W.)

1974 (24 Apr). Centenary of Universal Postal Union. W **55** (sideways). P 13½ (Nos. 460/**MS**461) or 14½×14 (others).

457	**101**	3t. green and ochre	10	10
		a. Perf 13½ (pair)	£300	
458		8t. red and ochre	10	10
459		15t. violet and ochre	15	10
460		30t. indigo and ochre	30	1·10
457/60 *Set of 4*			60	1·25
MS461 115×146 mm. Nos. 457/60			65	2·00
		a. Perf 14½×14	£550	£250

No. 457a comes from normal sheets and not No. **MS**461. It can also be identified as a marginal single.

102 Capital Hill, Lilongwe

(Des PAD Studio. Litho Questa)

1974 (3 July). Tenth Anniv of Independence. W **55** (sideways). P 14.

462	**102**	3t. multicoloured	10	10
463		8t. multicoloured	10	10
464		15t. multicoloured	10	10
465		30t. multicoloured	25	35
462/5 *Set of 4*			40	40
MS466 120×86 mm. Nos. 462/5			45	1·25

103 "Madonna of the Meadow" (Bellini)

104 Arms of Malawi

(Des Jennifer Toombs. Litho Enschedé)

1974 (4 Dec). Christmas. T **103** and similar horiz designs. Multicoloured. W **55** (sideways). P 13×13½.

467	3t. Type **103**	10	10
468	8t. "The Holy Family with Sts. John and Elizabeth" (Jordaens)	10	10
469	15t. "The Nativity" (Pieter de Grebber)	15	10
470	30t. "Adoration of the Shepherds" (Lorenzo di Credi)	30	50
467/70 *Set of 4*		50	50
MS471 163×107 mm. Nos. 467/70		60	1·50

(Des and litho Harrison)

1975 (1 Feb)–**84**. Coil stamps. W **55** (sideways). P 14½×14.

472	**104**	1t. deep blue	20	40
472*a*		5t. bright carmine (20.9.84)	65	2·25

105 African Snipe

106 Spur-winged Goose

(Des J.W. Litho Questa)

1975 (19 Feb). Birds. T **105/6** and similar multicoloured designs. W **55** (sideways on 2, 3, 8, 50t., 1k., 4k.). White, ordinary paper.

*(a) Size as T **105**. P 13½×14 (1, 5t.) or 14×13½ (others)*

473	1t. Type **105**	1·50	2·50
474	2t. Double-banded Sandgrouse	1·50	2·25
475	3t. Blue Quail	1·50	1·75
476	5t. Bare-throated Francolin	3·50	1·25
477	8t. Harlequin Quail	4·75	1·00

*(b) Size as T **106**. P 14*

478	10t. Type **106**	9·00	50
479	15t. Barrow's Bustard	3·75	3·75
480	20t. Comb Duck	1·00	2·25
481	30t. Helmet Guineafowl	1·25	70
482	50t. African Pigmy Goose	2·00	1·60
483	1k. Garganey	3·00	8·50
484	2k. White-faced Whistling Duck	17·00	18·00
485	4k. African Green Pigeon	13·00	16·00
473/85 *Set of 13*		55·00	55·00

See also Nos. 501/4.

107 M.V. *Mpasa*

108 *Habenaria splendens*

(Des R. Granger Barrett. Litho J.W.)

1975 (12 Mar). Ships of Lake Malawi (1st series). T **107** and similar horiz designs. Multicoloured. W **55** (sideways). P 13½.

486	3t. Type **107**	30	10
487	8t. M.V. *Ilala II*	40	10
488	15t. M.V. *Chauncy Maples II*	75	30
489	30t. M.V. *Nkwazi*	1·00	3·50
486/9 *Set of 4*		2·25	3·50
MS490 105×142 mm. Nos. 486/9. P 14		2·25	4·25

See also Nos. 728/32.

(Des Sylvia Goaman. Litho Questa)

1975 (6 June). Malawi Orchids. T **108** and similar vert designs. Multicoloured. W **55**. P 14.

491	3t. Type **108**	50	10
492	10t. *Eulophia cucullata*	60	10
493	20t. *Disa welwitschii*	90	25
494	40t. *Angraecum conchiferum*	1·25	2·25
491/4 *Set of 4*		2·75	2·40
MS495 127×111 mm. Nos. 491/4		7·00	8·50

109 Thick-tailed Bushbaby

10th ACP
Ministerial
Conference
1975

(**110**)

(Des R. Granger Barrett. Litho Walsall)

1975 (3 Sept). Malawi Animals. T **109** and similar vert designs. Multicoloured. W **55** (inverted). P 14.

496	3t. Type **109**	10	10
497	10t. Leopard	35	10
498	20t. Roan Antelope	55	35
499	40t. Common Zebra	1·00	3·25
496/9 *Set of 4*		1·75	3·50
MS500 88×130 mm. Nos. 496/9. W **55** (sideways)		2·50	3·50

1975 (1 Oct). As Nos. 473 etc, but no *wmk*. Toned, chalk-surfaced paper.

501	3t. Blue Quail	3·00	1·50
502	10t. Type **106**	2·00	1·50
503	15t. Barrow's Bustard	2·00	2·00

504 2k. White-faced Whistling Duck ... 5·00 11·00
501/4 *Set of 4* ... 11·00 13·00
Nos. 505/13 are vacant.

1975 (9 Dec). Tenth Africa, Caribbean and Pacific Ministerial Conference. No. 482 optd with T **110**.
514 50t. African Pygmy Goose ... 1·00 2·50

111 "A Castle with the Adoration of the Magi"

(Des PAD Studio. Litho J.W.)

1975 (12 Dec). Christmas. T **111** and similar horiz designs showing religious medallions. Multicoloured. W **55** (sideways). P 13×13½.
515 3t. Type **111** ... 10 10
516 10t. "The Nativity" ... 15 10
517 20t. "The Adoration of the Magi" ... 20 10
518 40t. "The Angel appearing to the Shepherds" ... 50 2·50
515/18 *Set of 4* ... 80 2·50
MS519 98×168 mm. Nos. 515/18. P 14 ... 1·50 3·75

112 Alexander Graham Bell

(Des C. Abbott. Litho Questa)

1976 (24 Mar). Centenary of the Telephone. W **55**. P 14.
520 **112** 3t. black and dull green ... 10 10
w. Wmk inverted ... 6·50
521 10t. black and magenta ... 10 10
522 20t. black and light reddish violet ... 20 10
523 40t. black and bright blue ... 50 1·40
520/3 *Set of 4* ... 80 1·50
MS524 137×114 mm. Nos. 520/3 ... 1·10 1·75

113 President Banda

114 Bagnall Diesel Shunter No. 100

(Des PAD Studio. Litho J.W.)

1976 (2 July). Tenth Anniv of the Republic. Multicoloured; frame colour given. W **55**. P 13.
525 **113** 3t. green ... 10 10
526 10t. magenta ... 10 10
527 20t. new blue ... 20 10
528 40t. dull ultramarine ... 50 1·40
525/8 *Set of 4* ... 80 1·50
MS529 102×112 mm. Nos. 524/8. P 13½ ... 1·00 2·50

(Des G. Drummond. Litho Questa)

1976 (1 Oct). Malawi Locomotives. T **114** and similar horiz designs. Multicoloured. W **55** (sideways). P 14½×14.
530 3t. Type **114** ... 40 15
531 10t. Class "Shire" diesel locomotive No. 503. ... 70 15
532 20t. Nippon Sharyo diesel-hydraulic locomotive No. 301 ... 1·40 45
533 40t. Hunslet diesel-hydraulic locomotive No. 110 ... 2·10 6·50
530/3 *Set of 4* ... 4·25 6·50
MS534 130×118 mm. Nos. 530/3 ... 4·25 7·00

Blantyre Mission Centenary 1876-1976

(**115**)

116 Child on Bed of Straw

1976 (22 Oct). Centenary of Blantyre Mission. Nos. 503 and 481 optd with T **115**.
535 15t. Barrow's Bustard ... 1·50 1·50
536 30t. Helmet Guineafowl ... 1·75 3·75

(Des Jennifer Toombs. Litho Walsall)

1976 (6 Dec). Christmas. W **55**. P 14.
537 **116** 3t. multicoloured ... 10 10
538 10t. multicoloured ... 10 10
539 20t. multicoloured ... 20 10
540 40t. multicoloured ... 40 60
537/40 *Set of 4* ... 70 70
MS541 135×95 mm. Nos. 537/40 ... 1·60 2·50

117 Man and Woman

118 Chileka Airport

(Des G. Hutchins. Litho Questa)

1977 (1 Apr). Handicrafts. T **117** and similar multicoloured designs showing wood-carvings. W **55** (sideways on 10 and 20t.). P 14.
542 4t. Type **117** ... 10 10
543 10t. Elephant (horiz) ... 15 10
544 20t. Rhino (horiz) ... 20 10
545 40t. Deer ... 50 70
542/5 *Set of 4* ... 80 80
MS546 153×112 mm. Nos. 542/5. Wmk sideways ... 1·50 2·75

(Des Harrison. Litho Walsall)

1977 (12 July). Transport. T **118** and similar horiz designs. Multicoloured. W **55** (sideways). P 14½×14.
547 4t. Type **118** ... 40 10
548 10t. Blantyre-Lilongwe Road ... 40 10
549 20t. M.V. *Ilala II* ... 1·00 35
550 40t. Blantyre-Nacala rail line ... 1·50 4·75
547/50 *Set of 4* ... 3·00 4·75
MS551 127×83 mm. Nos. 547/50 ... 3·00 4·75

119 Blue-grey Mbuna

120 "Madonna and Child with St. Catherine and the Blessed Stefano Maconi" (Borgognone)

(Des R. Granger Barrett. Litho J.W.)

1977 (4 Oct). Fish of Lake Malawi. T **119** and similar horiz designs. Multicoloured. P 13½.

A. No wmk

552A	4t. Type **119**	50	10
553A	10t. Livingston's Mbuna	60	10
554A	20t. Zebra Mbuna	1·40	45
555A	40t. Malawi Scale-eater	1·40	2·75
552A/5A *Set of 4*		3·50	3·00
MS556A 147×99 mm. Nos. 552A/5A. P 13		3·00	5·00

B. W **55** *(sideways)*

552B	4t. Type **119**	30	10
553B	10t. Livingston's Mbuna	50	20
554B	20t. Zebra Mbuna	£150	2·00
555B	40t. Malawi Scale-eater	1·50	1·25
MS556B 147×99 mm. Nos. 552B/5B. P 13		5·00	7·50

(Des G. Hutchins. Litho Enschedé)

1977 (21 Nov). Christmas. T **120** and similar vert designs. Multicoloured; frame colours given. No wmk. P 14×13½.

557	4t. deep blue-green	10	10
558	10t. light vermilion	15	10
559	20t. dull violet	25	10
560	40t. blue	60	1·50
557/60 *Set of 4*		1·00	1·60
MS561 150×116 mm. Nos. 557/60		2·50	3·00

Designs:—10t. "Madonna and Child with the Eternal Father and Angels" (Borgognone); 20t. Bottigella altarpiece (detail, Foppa); 40t. "Madonna of the Fountain" (van Eyck).

121 "Entry of Christ into Jerusalem" (Giotto)

122 Nyala

(Des G. Hutchins. Litho Cartor)

1978 (1 Mar). Easter. T **121** and similar vert designs showing paintings by Giotto. Multicoloured. P 12×12½.

562	4t. Type **121**	10	10
563	10t. "The Crucifixion"	15	10
564	20t. "Descent from the Cross"	30	10
565	40t. "Jesus appears before Mary"	50	55
562/5 *Set of 4*		90	70
MS566 150×99 mm. Nos. 562/5		1·90	2·40

(Des G. Hutchins. Litho Enschedé)

1978 (1 June). Endangered Species. T **122** and similar multicoloured designs. P 13½×13 (4, 40t.) or 13×13½ (others).

567	4t. Type **122**	2·75	10
568	10t. Lion (horiz)	7·50	40
569	20t. Common Zebra (horiz)	11·00	1·00
570	40t. Mountain Reedbuck	12·00	7·50
567/70 *Set of 4*		30·00	8·00
MS571 173×113 mm. Nos. 567/70		35·00	12·00

123 Malamulo Seventh Day Adventist Church

124 *Vanilla polylepis*

(Des and litho Walsall)

1978 (15 Nov). Christmas. Churches. T **123** and similar horiz designs. Multicoloured. W **55** (sideways). P 13½.

572	4t. Type **123**	10	10
573	10t. Likoma Cathedral	10	10
574	20t. St. Michael's and All Angels', Blantyre	20	10
575	40t. Zomba Catholic Cathedral	40	1·50
572/5 *Set of 4*		70	1·60
MS576 190×105 mm. Nos. 572/5		70	1·75

(Des G. Drummond. Litho J.W.)

1979 (2 Jan)–**82**. Orchids. Vert designs as T **124**. Multicoloured. W **55**. P 13½.

577	1t. Type **124**	50	40
578	2t. *Cirrhopetalum umbellatum*	50	40
	w. Wmk inverted	10·00	
579	5t. *Calanthe natalensis*	50	10
580	7t. *Ansellia gigantea*	50	60
581	8t. *Tridactyle bicaudata*	50	40
582	10t. *Acampe pachyglossa*	50	10
	w. Wmk inverted (14.6.82)	1·25	50
583	15t. *Eulophia quartiniana*	50	15
584	20t. *Cyrtorchis arcuata (variabilis)*	50	60
	w. Wmk inverted		
585	30t. *Eulophia tricristata*	1·25	30
586	50t. *Disa hamatopetala*	85	60
587	75t. *Cynorchis glandulosa*	2·00	6·50
588	1k. *Aerangis kotschyana*	1·60	1·75
589	1k.50 *Polystachya dendrobiiflora*	1·75	6·00
590	2k. *Disa ornithantha*	1·25	2·00
591	4k. *Cyrtorchis praetermissa*	1·50	5·00
577/91 *Set of 15*		12·50	22·00

125 Tsamba

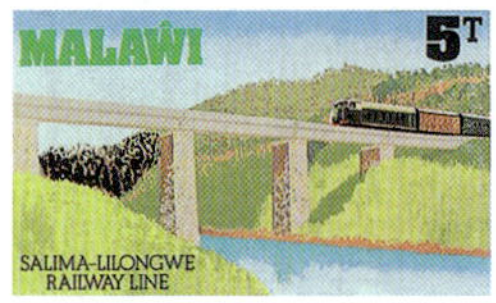

126 Train crossing Viaduct

(Des L. Curtis. Litho Questa)

1979 (21 Jan). National Tree Planting Day. T **125** and similar vert designs. Multicoloured. W **55**. P 13½.

592	5t. Type **125**	20	10
593	10t. Mulanje Cedar	25	10
594	20t. Mlombwa	40	20
595	40t. Mbawa	70	2·75
592/5 *Set of 4*		1·40	2·75
MS596 118×153 mm. Nos. 592/5		1·40	3·00

(Des J.W. Litho Questa)

1979 (17 Feb). Opening of Salima-Lilongwe Railway. T **126** and similar horiz designs. Multicoloured. W **55** (sideways) (5t.) or no wmk (others). P 14½.

597	5t. Type **126**	25	15
598	10t. Diesel railcar at station	40	15
599	20t. Diesel train rounding bend	60	30
600	40t. Diesel train passing through cutting	85	2·50
597/600 *Set of 4*		1·90	2·75
MS601 153×103 mm. Nos. 597/600. W **55** (sideways)		3·25	4·50

Examples of an unissued 4t. value as Type **126** and of a miniature sheet containing this 4t. value exist from supplies sent to Malawi before it was decided to increase the internal postage rate to 5t. (price single 4t. £130 on, 4t. in m/s £500).

127 Young Child

(Des BG Studio. Litho Questa)

1979 (10 July). International Year of the Child. T **127** and similar horiz designs showing young children. Multicoloured; background colours given. W **55** (sideways). P 13½.

602	5t. green	10	10
603	10t. red	10	10
604	20t. mauve	25	10
605	40t. blue	45	1·60
602/5 *Set of 4*		80	1·75

128 1964 3d. Independence Commemorative Stamp

(Des J.W. Litho Enschedé)

1979 (17 Sept). Death Centenary of Sir Rowland Hill. T **128** and similar horiz designs showing 1964 Independence commemorative stamps. Multicoloured. W **55** (sideways*). P 13×13½.

606	5t. Type **128**	10	10
607	10t. 6d. value	10	10
	w. Wmk cockerel facing right	3·25	
608	20t. 1s.3d. value	20	10
609	40t. 2s.6d. value	35	85
606/9	*Set of 4*	65	1·00
MS610	163×108 mm. Nos. 606/9	75	1·40

*The normal sideways watermark has the cockerel facing left, *as seen from the back of the stamp.*

129 River Landscape

130 Limbe Rotary Club Emblem

(Des BG Studio. Litho Format)

1979 (15 Nov). Christmas. T **129** and similar horiz designs showing landscapes. Multicoloured. W **55** (sideways). P 13½×14.

611	5t. Type **129**	10	10
612	10t. Sunset	10	10
613	20t. Forest and hill	25	15
614	40t. Plain and mountain	50	2·25
611/14	*Set of 4*	85	2·50

(Des L. Curtis. Litho J.W.)

1980 (23 Feb). 75th Anniv of Rotary International. T **130** and similar vert designs. W **55**. P 13½.

615	5t. multicoloured	10	10
616	10t. multicoloured	10	10
617	20t. multicoloured	30	15
618	40t. ultramarine and gold	75	2·25
615/18	*Set of 4*	1·10	2·25
MS619	105×144 mm. Nos. 615/18. P 14×14½	1·10	2·50

Designs:—10t. Blantyre Rotary Club pennant; 20t. Lilongwe Rotary Club pennant; 40t. Rotary International emblem.

131 Mangochi District Post Office

132 Agate Nodule

(Des C. Abbott. Litho Walsall)

1980 (6 May). "London 1980" International Stamp Exhibition. T **131** and similar horiz designs. W **55** (sideways). P 14½×14.

620	5t. black and blue-green	10	10
621	10t. black and vermilion	10	10
622	20t. black and violet	15	10
623	1k. black and deep blue	65	1·10
620/3	*Set of 4*	80	1·10
MS624	114×89 mm. Nos. 620/3	1·25	2·25

Designs:—10t. New Blantyre Sorting Office; 20t. Mail Transfer Hut, Walala; 1k. First Nyasaland Post Office, Chiromo.

(Des G. Drummond. Litho J.W.)

1980 (20 Aug). Gemstones. T **132** and similar vert designs. Multicoloured. W **55**. P 13.

625	5t. Type **132**	60	10
626	10t. Sunstone	80	10
627	20t. Smoky Quartz	1·40	30
628	1k. Kyanite crystal	3·50	6·00
625/8	*Set of 4*	5·75	6·00

133 Elephants

134 Suni

(Des C. Abbott. Litho J.W.)

1980 (10 Nov). Christmas. Children's Paintings. T **133** and similar horiz designs. Multicoloured. W **55** (sideways). P 13.

629	5t. Type **133**	40	10
630	10t. Flowers	30	10
631	20t. Class "Shire" diesel train	75	20
632	1k. Malachite Kingfisher	1·60	2·00
629/32	*Set of 4*	2·75	2·25

(Des G. Drummond. Litho Questa)

1981 (4 Feb). Wildlife. T **134** and similar horiz designs. Multicoloured. W **55** (sideways). P 14.

633	7t. Type **134**	15	10
634	10t. Blue Duiker	20	10
635	20t. African Buffalo	30	15
636	1k. Lichtenstein's Hartebeest	1·25	1·60
633/6	*Set of 4*	1·75	1·75

135 "Kanjedza II" Standard "A" Earth Station

(Des L. Curtis. Litho Harrison)

1981 (24 Apr). International Communications. T **135** and similar horiz designs. Multicoloured. W **55** (sideways). P 14½.

637	7t. Type **135**	10	10
638	10t. Blantyre International Gateway Exchange	15	10
639	20t. "Kanjedza I" standard "B" earth station	25	15
640	1k. "Satellite communications"	1·50	1·90
637/40	*Set of 4*	1·75	1·90
MS641	101×151 mm. Nos. 637/40	1·75	3·25

136 Maize

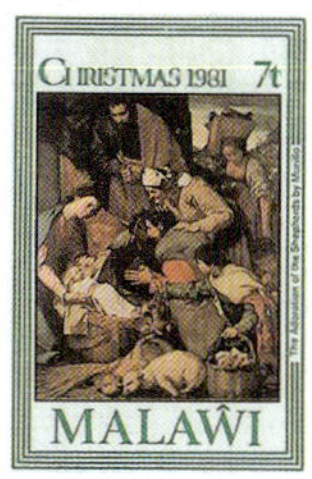

137 "The Adoration of the Shepherds" (Murillo)

(Des Jennifer Toombs. Litho Harrison)

1981 (11 Sept). World Food Day. Agricultural Produce. T **136** and similar horiz designs. Multicoloured. W **55** (sideways). P 14.

642	7t. Type **136**	15	10
643	10t. Rice	20	10
644	20t. Finger-millet	30	20
645	1k. Wheat	1·00	1·40
642/5	*Set of 4*	1·50	1·50

(Des BG Studio. Litho J.W.)

1981 (26 Nov). Christmas. Paintings. T **137** and similar multicoloured designs. W **55** (sideways on 10 and 20t.). P 13½×13 (7t., 1k.) or 13×13½ (others).

646 7t. Type **137** ... 20 10
647 10t. "The Holy Family" (Lippi) (*horiz*) ... 25 10
648 20t. "The Adoration of the Shepherds" (Louis le Nain) (*horiz*) ... 45 15
649 1k. "The Virgin and Child, St. John the Baptist and an Angel" (Paolo Morando) 1·10 2·25
646/9 *Set of* 4 ... 1·75 2·25

138 Impala Herd

(Des A. Theobald. Litho Harrison)

1982 (15 Mar). National Parks. Wildlife. T **138** and similar horiz designs. Multicoloured. W **55** (sideways). P 14½×14.

650 7t. Type **138** ... 20 10
651 10t. Lions ... 35 10
652 20t. Greater Kudu ... 50 20
653 1k. Greater Flamingoes ... 1·75 5·50
650/3 *Set of* 4 ... 2·50 5·50

139 Kamuzu Academy

(Des PAD Studio. Litho Questa)

1982 (1 July). Kamuzu Academy. T **139** and similar horiz designs showing buildings. W **55** (sideways). P 14½.

654 7t. multicoloured ... 15 10
655 20t. multicoloured ... 20 10
656 30t. multicoloured ... 30 45
657 1k. multicoloured ... 1·00 3·75
654/7 *Set of* 4 ... 1·50 4·00

(Des and litho Harrison)

1982 (8 Sept). World Cup Football Championship, Spain. T **140** and similar vert designs. Multicoloured. W **55**. P 14×15.

658 7t. Type **140** ... 75 25
659 20t. FIFA World Cup trophy ... 1·60 1·25
660 30t. Football stadium ... 1·90 3·25
658/60 *Set of* 3 ... 3·75 4·25
MS661 80×59 mm. 1k. Football ... 1·75 1·75

141 Blantyre War Memorial, St. Paul's Church

(Des W. Fenton. Litho Format)

1982 (5 Nov). Remembrance Day. T **141** and similar horiz designs. Multicoloured. W **55** (sideways). P 14½×14.

662 7t. Type **141** ... 10 10
663 20t. Zomba war memorial ... 15 10
664 30t. Chichiri war memorial ... 20 30
665 1k. Lilongwe war memorial ... 65 4·25
662/5 *Set of* 4 ... 1·00 4·25

142 Kwacha International Conference Centre

(Des Walsall. Litho Format)

1983 (14 Mar). Commonwealth Day. T **142** and similar horiz designs. Multicoloured. W **55** (sideways). P 14.

666 7t. Type **142** ... 10 10
667 20t. Tea-picking, Mulanje ... 20 10
668 30t. World map showing position of Malawi ... 25 30
669 1k. President Dr. H. Kamuzu Banda ... 60 1·50
666/9 *Set of* 4 ... 1·00 1·75

143 "Christ and St. Peter"

(Des C. Abbott. Litho Format)

1983 (4 Apr). 500th Birth Anniv of Raphael. Details from the cartoon for "The Miraculous Draught of Fishes" Tapestry. T **143** and similar multicoloured designs. W **55** (sideways on 30t.). P 14.

670 7t. Type **143** ... 25 10
671 20t. "Hauling in the Catch" ... 55 80
672 30t. "Fishing Village" (*horiz*) ... 60 2·50
670/2 *Set of* 3 ... 1·25 3·00
MS673 110×90 mm. 1k. "Apostle" ... 1·75 1·75

144 Pair by Lake

(Des N. Arlott. Litho Questa)

1983 (11 July). African Fish Eagle. T **144** and similar vert designs. Multicoloured. W **55**. P 14.

674 30t. Type **144** ... 1·60 2·00
a. Horiz strip of 5. Nos. 674/8 ... 7·00 9·00
675 30t. Making gull-like call ... 1·60 2·00
676 30t. Diving on prey ... 1·60 2·00
677 30t. Carrying fish ... 1·60 2·00
678 30t. Feeding on catch ... 1·60 2·00
674/8 *Set of* 5 ... 7·00 9·00

Nos. 674/8 were printed together, *se-tenant*, in horizontal strips of 5 throughout the sheet, the backgrounds of each design forming a composite picture of Lake Malawi.

145 Kamuzu International Airport

(Des A. Theobald. Litho Questa)

1983 (31 Aug). Bicentenary of Manned Flight. T **145** and similar horiz designs. Multicoloured. W **55** (sideways). P 14.

679 7t. Type **145** ... 10 10
680 20t. Kamuzu International Airport (*different*) ... 25 15
681 30t. B.A.C. One Eleven ... 40 45
682 1k. Short S.23 Empire "C" Class flying boat at Cape Maclear ... 1·10 2·75
679/82 *Set of* 4 ... 1·75 3·00
MS683 100×121 mm. Nos. 679/82 ... 2·00 4·00

146 *Clerodendrum myricoides*

(Des R. Reader. Litho J.W.)

1983 (1 Nov). Christmas. Flowers. T **146** and similar vert designs. Multicoloured. P 13 (20t.) or 14 (others).

684	7t. Type **146**	40	10
	a. Perf 13	20·00	
685	20t. *Gloriosa superba*	90	15
686	30t. *Gladiolus laxiflorus*	1·00	60
687	1k. *Aframomum angustifolium*	2·25	7·00
684/7 *Set of 4*		4·00	7·00

147 Golden Mbuna

(Des L. Curtis. Litho Harrison)

1984 (2 Jan). Fishes. T **147** and similar horiz designs. Multicoloured. W **55** (sideways). With imprint date. P 14½×14.

688	1t. Type **147**	30	1·00
689	2t. Malawi Eyebiter	30	1·00
690	5t. Blue Mbuna	30	1·00
691	7t. Lombardo's Mbuna	30	30
692	8t. Golden Zebra Mbuna	30	30
693	10t. Fairy Cichlid	30	10
694	15t. Crabro Mbuna	30	10
695	20t. Marbled Zebra Mbuna	30	10
696	30t. Sky-blue Mbuna	50	20
697	40t. Venustus Cichlid	60	30
698	50t. Thumbi Emperor Cichlid	2·50	3·25
699	75t. Purple Mbuna	3·00	5·50
700	1k. Zebra Mbuna	3·50	5·00
701	2k. Fairy Cichlid (*different*)	4·00	7·00
702	4k. Mbenje Emperor Cichlid	5·00	11·00
688/702 *Set of 15*		19·00	32·00

Imprint dates: "1984", Nos. 688/702; "1986", Nos. 688, 691/7.

148 Smith's Red Hare

149 Running

(Des Garden Studios. Litho Format)

1984 (2 Feb). Small Mammals. T **148** and similar horiz designs. Multicoloured. W **55** (sideways). P 14.

703	7t. Type **148**	20	10
704	20t. Gambian Sun Squirrel	35	50
705	30t. South African Hedgehog	35	1·10
706	1k. Large-spotted Genet	50	5·50
703/6 *Set of 4*		1·25	6·50

(Des C. Collins. Litho Harrison)

1984 (1 June). Olympic Games, Los Angeles. T **149** and similar vert designs. Multicoloured. W **55** (sideways). P 14.

707	7t. Type **149**	15	10
708	20t. Boxing	35	20
709	30t. Cycling	75	70
710	1k. Long jumping	1·00	4·00
707/10 *Set of 4*		2·00	4·50
MS711 90×128 mm. Nos. 707/10. Wmk upright		2·40	5·00

150 *Euphaedra neophron*

(Des and photo Courvoisier)

1984 (1 Aug). Butterflies. T **150** and similar vert designs. Granite paper. P 11½.

712	7t. multicoloured	75	30
713	20t. lemon, blackish brown and red	1·75	45
714	30t. multicoloured	2·00	1·10
715	1k. multicoloured	3·25	9·00
712/15 *Set of 4*		7·00	9·75

Designs:—20t. *Papilio dardanus*; 30t. *Antanartia schaeneia*; 1k. *Spindasis nyassae*.

151 "The Virgin and Child" (Duccio)

(Des C. Abbott. Litho Harrison)

1984 (22 Oct). Christmas. Religious Paintings. T **151** and similar vert designs. Multicoloured. W **55**. P 14½.

716	7t. Type **151**	45	10
717	20t. "Madonna and Child" (Raphael)	1·10	20
718	30t. "The Virgin and Child" (ascr to Lippi)	1·40	70
719	1k. "The Wilton Diptych"	2·50	8·00
716/19 *Set of 4*		5·00	8·00

152 *Leucopaxillus gracillimus*

(Des A. Jardine. Litho Harrison)

1985 (23 Jan). Fungi. T **152** and similar horiz designs. Multicoloured. W **55** (sideways). P 14½×14.

720	7t. Type **152**	1·00	30
721	20t. *Limacella guttata*	2·00	45
722	30t. *Termitomyces eurrhizus*	2·50	1·25
723	1k. *Cyptotrama aspratum* ("*Kerulina asprata*")	4·00	9·50
720/3 *Set of 4*		8·50	10·50

No. 720 is known with the country name and face value omitted, used.

153 Map showing Member States, and Lumberjack (Forestry)

(Des A. Theobald. Litho Harrison)

1985 (1 Apr). 5th Anniv of Southern African Development Coordination Conference. T **153** and similar horiz designs showing map and aspects of development. W **55** (sideways). P 14.

724	7t. black, yellowish green and pale green	75	10
725	15t. black, scarlet-vermilion & salmon pink	1·25	20

726	20t. blk, bright bluish violet & bright mauve	4·00	1·75
727	1k. black, bright blue and cobalt	4·50	10·00
724/7	*Set of 4*	9·50	11·00

Designs:—15t. Radio mast (Communications); 20t. Diesel locomotive (Transport); 1k. Trawler and net (Fishing).

154 M.V. *Ufulu*

155 Stierling's Woodpecker

(Des L. Curtis. Litho Cartor)

1985 (3 June). Ships of Lake Malawi (2nd series). T **154** and similar horiz designs. Multicoloured. W **55** (sideways). P 13½×13.

728	7t. Type **154**	90	10
729	15t. M.V. *Chauncy Maples II*	1·75	20
730	20t. M.V. *Mtendere*	2·25	65
731	1k. M.V. *Ilala II*	4·50	6·00
728/31	*Set of 4*	8·50	6·25
MS732	120×84 mm. Nos. 728/31. P 13×12	8·00	9·00

(Des M. Stringer. Litho Harrison)

1985 (1 Aug). Birth Bicentenary of John J. Audubon (ornithologist). T **155** and similar vert designs. Multicoloured. W **55**. P 14.

733	7t. Type **155**	1·00	30
734	15t. Lesser Seedcracker	1·75	30
735	20t. East Coast Akelat	1·75	65
736	1k. Boehm's Bee Eater	3·25	7·00
733/6	*Set of 4*	7·00	7·50
MS737	130×90 mm. Nos. 733/6. Wmk sideways	8·00	10·00

156 "The Virgin of Humility" (Jaime Serra)

(Photo Courvoisier)

1985 (14 Oct). Christmas. Nativity Paintings. T **156** and similar vert designs. Multicoloured. Granite paper. P 11½.

738	7t. Type **156**	30	10
739	15t. "The Adoration of the Magi" (Stefano da Zevio)	75	15
740	20t. "Madonna and Child" (Gerard van Honthorst)	85	25
741	1k. "Virgin of Zbraslav" (Master of Vissy Brod)	2·25	5·50
738/41	*Set of 4*	3·75	5·50

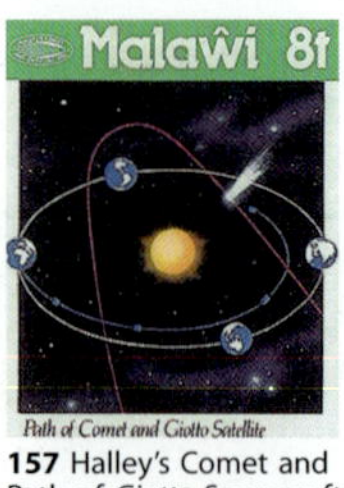

157 Halley's Comet and Path of *Giotto* Spacecraft

(Des N. Shewring. Litho Walsall)

1986 (10 Feb). Appearance of Halley's Comet. T **157** and similar vert designs. Multicoloured. W **55**. P 14½×14.

742	8t. Type **157**	60	10
743	15t. Halley's Comet above Earth	65	15
	w. Wmk inverted	1·00	
744	20t. Comet and dish aerial, Malawi	1·00	30
745	1k. *Giotto* spacecraft	2·00	6·50
742/5	*Set of 4*	3·75	6·50

158 Two Players competing for Ball

159 President Banda

(Des and photo Courvoisier)

1986 (26 May). World Cup Football Championship, Mexico. T **158** and similar horiz designs. Multicoloured. Granite paper. P 11½.

746	8t. Type **158**	70	10
747	15t. Goalkeeper saving goal	95	20
748	20t. Two players competing for ball (*different*)	1·10	35
749	1k. Player kicking ball	4·00	5·50
746/9	*Set of 4*	6·00	5·50
MS750	108×77 mm. Nos. 746/9	10·00	12·00

(Des and litho Harrison)

1986 (30 June). 20th Anniv of the Republic. T **159** and similar vert designs. Multicoloured. P 14.

751	8t. Type **159**	1·50	2·75
752	15t. National flag	80	15
753	20t. Malawi coat of arms	85	25
754	1k. Kamuzu International Airport and emblem of national airline	3·50	6·00
751/4	*Set of 4*	6·00	8·25

It is reported that No. 751 was withdrawn locally five days after issue.

160 "Virgin and Child" (Botticelli)

(Des and photo Courvoisier)

1986 (15 Dec). Christmas. T **160** and similar vert designs showing paintings. Multicoloured. Granite paper. P 11½.

755	8t. Type **160**	45	10
756	15t. "Adoration of the Shepherds" (Guido Reni)	80	15
757	20t. "Madonna of the Veil" (Carlo Dolci)	1·25	35
758	1k. "Adoration of the Magi" (Jean Bourdichon)	3·75	9·00
755/8	*Set of 4*	5·50	9·00

161 Wattled Crane

(Des W. Oliver. Litho Walsall)

1987 (16 Feb)–**88**. Endangered Species. Wattled Crane. T **161** and similar horiz designs. Multicoloured. P 14×14½.

*(a) W **55** (sideways)*

759	8t. Type **161**	1·50	40
760	15t. Two cranes	2·25	50
761	20t. Cranes at nest	2·25	80
762	75t. Crane in lake	4·50	12·00
759/62	*Set of 4*	9·50	12·50

*(b) W w **14** (sideways) (10.88)*

763	8t. Type **161**	4·00	2·00
764	15t. Two cranes	5·50	2·75
765	20t. Cranes at nest	6·00	3·25
766	75t. Cranes in lake	8·00	13·00
763/6 *Set of 4*		21·00	19·00

162 Bagnall Steam Locomotive No. 2, *Shamrock*

163 Hippopotamus grazing

(Des and litho Cartor)

1987 (25 May). Steam Locomotives. T **162** and similar horiz designs. Multicoloured. P 14×13½.

767	10t. Type **162**	2·00	45
768	25t. Class D steam locomotive No. 8, 1914	2·75	70
769	30t. Bagnall steam locomotive No. 1, *Thistle*	3·00	85
770	1k. Kitson steam locomotive, No. 6, 1903	6·00	13·00
767/70 *Set of 4*		12·50	13·50

(Des and photo Courvoisier)

1987 (24 Aug). Hippopotamus. T **163** and similar vert designs. Multicoloured. Granite paper. P 12½.

771	10t. Type **163**	1·50	40
772	25t. Hippopotami in water	2·25	50
773	30t. Female and calf in water	2·25	75
774	1k. Hippopotami and Cattle Egret	6·00	12·00
771/4 *Set of 4*		11·00	12·50
MS775 78×101 mm. Nos. 771/4		11·00	12·50

164 *Stathmostelma spectabile*

165 African and Staunton Knights

(Des and litho Harrison)

1987 (19 Oct). Christmas. Wild Flowers. T **164** and similar vert designs. Multicoloured. P 14.

776	10t. Type **164**	65	10
777	25t. *Pentanisia schweinfurthii*	1·50	25
778	30t. *Chironia krebsii*	1·75	55
779	1k. *Ochna macrocalyx*	3·00	9·50
776/9 *Set of 4*		6·25	9·50

(Des Jennifer Toombs. Litho Walsall)

1988 (8 Feb). Chess. T **165** and similar vert designs showing local and Staunton chess pieces. Multicoloured. W w **16**. P 14½×14.

780	15t. Type **165**	1·25	30
781	35t. Bishops	1·75	70
782	50t. Rooks	2·00	1·50
783	2k. Queens	6·00	12·00
780/3 *Set of 4*		10·00	13·00

166 High Jumping

167 Scrub Warbler

(Des and litho Harrison)

1988 (13 June). Olympic Games, Seoul. T **166** and similar vert designs. Multicoloured. P 14.

784	15t. Type **166**	30	10
785	35t. Javelin throwing	50	20
786	50t. Tennis	75	50
787	2k. Shot-putting	1·60	3·75
784/7 *Set of 4*		2·75	4·00
MS788 91×121 mm. Nos. 784/7		3·50	4·00

(Des N. Arlott (No. 804), Courvoisier (others). Litho Questa (No. 804) or photo Courvoisier (others))

1988 (25 July)–**95**. Birds. T **167** and similar vert designs. Multicoloured. W w **14** (sideways) (No. 804) or no wmk (others). Granite paper (1t. to 4k.). P 15×14½ (No. 804) or 11½ (others).

789	1t. Type **167**	50	1·50
790	2t. Yellow-throated Woodland Warbler	70	1·50
791	5t. Moustached Green Tinkerbird	70	1·50
792	7t. Waller's Red-winged Starling	70	1·50
793	8t. Oriole-Finch	70	1·50
794	10t. Starred Robin	2·75	1·50
795	15t. Bar-tailed Trogon	1·00	20
796	20t. Green-backed Twin-spot	70	20
797	30t. African Grey Cuckoo Shrike	70	20
798	40t. Black-fronted Bush Shrike	70	20
799	50t. White-tailed Crested Flycatcher	3·25	1·50
800	75t. Green Barbet	70	1·25
801	1k. Lemon Dove ("Cinnamon Dove")	70	1·25
802	2k. Silvery-cheeked Hornbill	1·00	1·60
803	4k. Crowned Eagle	1·25	2·50
804	10k. Anchieta's Sunbird (3.10.88)	12·00	14·00
804*a*	10k. As 10t. (1.10.95)	9·00	3·75
789/804*a* *Set of 17*		32·00	32·00

167a Rebuilt Royal Exchange, 1844

168 "Madonna in the Church" (Jan van Eyck)

(Des D. Miller (15t.), L. Curtis and D. Miller (35t.), A. Theobald and D. Miller (50t.), E. Nisbet and D. Miller (2k.). Litho B.D.T.)

1988 (24 Oct). 300th Anniv of Lloyd's of London. T **167a** and similar multicoloured designs. W w **14** (sideways on 35, 50t.). P 14.

805	15t. Type **167a**	30	10
806	35t. Opening ceremony, Nkula Falls Hydroelectric Power Station	70	20
807	50t. Air Malawi B.A.C. One Eleven airliner (*horiz*)	3·00	75
808	2k. *Seawise University* (formerly *Queen Elizabeth*) on fire, Hong Kong, 1972	7·00	5·00
805/8 *Set of 4*		10·00	5·50

(Des and litho Harrison)

1988 (28 Nov). Christmas. T **168** and similar vert designs showing paintings. Multicoloured. P 14.

809	15t. Type **168**	60	10
810	35t. "Virgin, Infant Jesus and St. Anna" (da Vinci)	90	25
811	50t. "Virgin and Angels" (Cimabue)	1·25	70
812	2k. "Virgin and Child" (Baldovinetti Apenio)	3·00	6·50
809/12 *Set of 4*		5·25	6·75

169 Robust Cichlid

(Des and litho Harrison)

1989 (10 Apr). 50th Anniv of Malawi Angling Society. T **169** and similar horiz designs. Multicoloured. P 14.

813	15t. Type **169**	60	20
814	35t. Small-scaled Minnow ("Mpasa")	1·10	35

815	50t. Large-scaled Yellowfish	1·50	1·40
816	2k. Tigerfish	4·00	9·50
813/16	*Set of 4*	6·50	10·50

170 Independence Arch, Blantyre

(Des and litho Harrison)

1989 (26 June). 25th Anniv of Independence. T **170** and similar horiz designs. Multicoloured. P 14.

817	15t. Type **170**	80	20
818	35t. Grain silos	1·50	35
819	50t. Capital Hill, Lilongwe	2·00	1·50
820	2k. Reserve Bank Headquarters	5·00	10·00
817/20	*Set of 4*	8·50	11·00

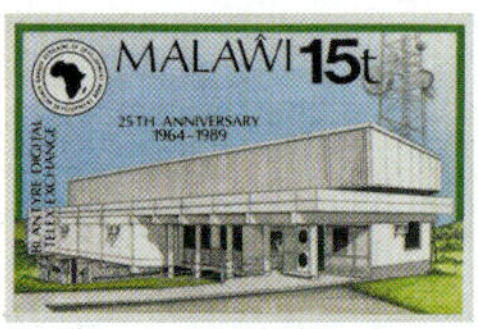

171 Blantyre Digital Telex Exchange

(Des and litho Harrison)

1989 (30 Oct). 25th Anniv of African Development Bank. T **171** and similar horiz designs. Multicoloured. P 14.

821	15t. Type **171**	80	20
822	40t. Dzalanyama steer	1·50	35
823	50t. Mikolongwe heifer	2·00	1·50
824	2k. Zebu bull	5·00	10·00
821/4	*Set of 4*	8·50	11·00

172 Rural House with Verandah

(Des and litho Harrison)

1989 (1 Dec). 25th Anniv of Malawi–United Nations Co-operation. T **172** and similar horiz designs. Multicoloured. P 14.

825	15t. Type **172**	80	20
826	40t. Rural house	1·50	35
827	50t. Traditional hut and modern houses	2·00	1·50
828	2k. Tea plantation	5·00	10·00
825/8	*Set of 4*	8·50	11·00

173 St. Michael and All Angels Church

(Des and litho Harrison)

1989 (15 Dec). Christmas. Churches of Malawi. T **173** and similar horiz designs. Multicoloured. P 14.

829	15t. Type **173**	80	20
830	40t. Catholic Cathedral, Limbe	1·50	35
831	50t. C.C.A.P. Church, Nkhoma	2·00	1·50
832	2k. Cathedral, Likoma Island	5·00	11·00
829/32	*Set of 4*	8·50	12·00

174 Ford "Sedan", 1915

(Des and litho Cartor)

1990 (2 Apr). Vintage Vehicles. T **174** and similar horiz designs. Multicoloured. P 14×13½.

833	15t. Type **174**	1·25	20
834	40t. Two-seater Ford, 1915	1·75	35
835	50t. Ford pick-up, 1915	2·00	1·50
836	2k. Chevrolet bus, 1930	5·00	11·00
833/6	*Set of 4*	9·00	12·00
MS837	120×85 mm. Nos. 833/6. P 13×12	15·00	15·00

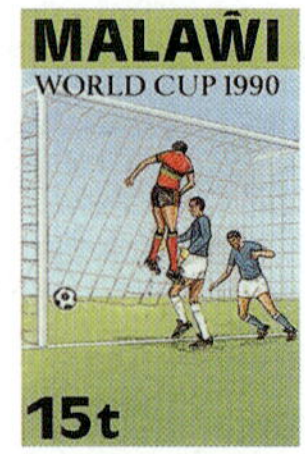

175 Player heading Ball into Net

(Des and litho Questa)

1990 (14 June). World Cup Football Championship, Italy. T **175** and similar vert designs. Multicoloured. P 14.

838	15t. Type **175**	1·00	20
839	40t. Player tackling	1·60	35
840	50t. Player scoring goal	2·00	1·50
841	2k. World Cup	5·50	11·00
838/41	*Set of 4*	9·00	12·00
MS842	88×118 mm. Nos. 838/41	11·00	13·00

176 Anniversary Emblem on Map

177 *Aerangis kotschyana*

(Des and litho Questa)

1990 (24 Aug). Tenth Anniv of Southern Africa Development Co-ordination Conference. T **176** and similar horiz designs. Multicoloured. P 14.

843	15t. Type **176**	1·00	20
844	40t. Tilapia	1·60	40
845	50t. Cedar plantation	2·00	1·50
846	2k. Male Nyala (antelope)	5·00	11·00
843/6	*Set of 4*	8·50	12·00
MS847	174×116 mm. Nos. 843/6	14·00	16·00

(Litho Cartor)

1990 (26 Nov). Orchids. T **177** and similar vert designs. Multicoloured. P 13½×14.

848	15t. Type **177**	1·75	25
849	40t. *Angraecum eburneum*	2·75	80
850	50t. *Aerangis luteo-alba rhodostica*	2·75	1·60
851	2k. *Cyrtorchis arcuata whytei*	6·50	12·00
848/51	*Set of 4*	12·50	13·00
MS852	85×120 mm. Nos. 848/51. P 12×13	15·00	15·00

178 "The Virgin and the Child Jesus" (Raphael)

179 Buffalo

(Litho Cartor)

1990 (7 Dec). Christmas. Paintings by Raphael. T **178** and similar vert designs. Multicoloured. P 13½×14.

853	15t. Type **178**	1·00	20
854	40t. "Transfiguration" (detail)	1·75	35
855	50t. "St. Catherine of Alexandrie" (detail)	1·75	90
856	2k. "Transfiguration"	5·50	12·00
853/6	*Set of* 4	9·00	12·00
MS857	85×120 mm. Nos. 853/6. P 12×13	14·00	16·00

(Litho Cartor)

1991 (23 Apr). Wildlife. T **179** and similar horiz designs. Multicoloured. P 14×13½.

858	20t. Type **179**	1·00	25
859	60t. Cheetah	2·25	1·00
860	75t. Greater Kudu	2·25	1·00
861	2k. Black Rhinoceros	9·00	11·00
858/61	*Set of* 4	13·00	12·00
MS862	120×85 mm. Nos. 858/61. P 13×12	13·00	15·00

180 Chiromo Post Office, 1891

181 Red Locust

(Litho Cartor)

1991 (2 July). Centenary of Postal Services. T **180** and similar horiz designs. Multicoloured. P 14×13½.

863	20t. Type **180**	1·25	20
864	60t. Re-constructed mail exchange hut at Walala	2·25	85
865	75t. Mangochi post office	2·25	95
866	2k. Satellite Earth station	8·00	12·00
863/6	*Set of* 4	12·50	12·50
MS867	119×83 mm. Nos. 863/6. P 13×12	12·00	14·00

(Litho Cartor)

1991 (26 Sept). Insects. T **181** and similar vert designs. Multicoloured. P 13½×14.

868	20t. Type **181**	1·00	25
869	60t. Weevil	2·25	1·10
870	75t. Cotton Stainer Bug	2·25	1·40
871	2k. Pollen Beetle	6·50	11·00
868/71	*Set of* 4	11·00	12·00

182 Child in Manger

183 Red Bishop

(Litho Cartor)

1991 (26 Nov). Christmas. T **182** and similar vert designs. Multicoloured. P 13½×14.

872	20t. Type **182**	80	20
873	60t. Adoration of the Kings and Shepherds	1·75	55
874	75t. Nativity	2·00	75
875	2k. Virgin and Child	4·75	12·00
872/5	*Set of* 4	8·50	12·00

(Des Jennifer Toombs. Litho Questa)

1992 (7 Apr). Birds. T **183** and similar horiz designs. Multicoloured. P 14.

876	75t. Type **183**	2·25	2·25
	a. Sheetlet. Nos. 876/95	40·00	
877	75t. Lesser Striped Swallow	2·25	2·25
878	75t. Long-crested Eagle	2·25	2·25
879	75t. Lilac-breasted Roller	2·25	2·25
880	75t. African Paradise Flycatcher	2·25	2·25
881	75t. White-fronted Bee Eater	2·25	2·25
882	75t. White-winged Black Tern	2·25	2·25
883	75t. African Fire Finch	2·25	2·25
884	75t. White-browed Robin Chat	2·25	2·25
885	75t. African Fish Eagle	2·25	2·25
886	75t. Malachite Kingfisher	2·25	2·25
887	75t. Lesser Masked Weaver	2·25	2·25
888	75t. Barn Owl	2·25	2·25
889	75t. Variable Sunbird	2·25	2·25
890	75t. Lesser Flamingo	2·25	2·25
891	75t. South African Crowned Crane	2·25	2·25
892	75t. African Pitta	2·25	2·25
893	75t. African Darter	2·25	2·25
894	75t. White-faced Whistling Duck	2·25	2·25
895	75t. African Pied Wagtail	2·25	2·25
876/95	*Set of* 20	40·00	40·00

Nos. 876/95 were printed together, *se-tenant*, as a sheetlet of 20, forming a composite design.

184 Long Jumping

185 "The Angel Gabriel" (detail, "The Annunciation") (Philippe de Champaigne)

(Des G. Vasarhelyi. Litho B.D.T.)

1992 (28 July). Olympic Games, Barcelona. T **184** and similar horiz designs. Multicoloured. P 13½.

896	20t. Type **184**	80	20
897	60t. High Jumping	1·25	60
898	75t. Javelin	1·50	90
899	2k. Running	3·50	7·00
896/9	*Set of* 4	6·25	8·00
MS900	110×100 mm. Nos. 896/9	6·50	9·00

(Des D. Miller. Litho Walsall)

1992 (9 Nov). Christmas. Religious Paintings. T **185** and similar vert designs. Multicoloured. P 14.

901	20t. Type **185**	70	20
902	75t. "Virgin and Child" (Bernandino Luini)	1·50	50
903	95t. "Virgin and Child" (Sassoferrato)	1·75	90
904	2k. "Virgin Mary" (detail, "The Annunciation") (De Champaigne)	4·50	9·00
901/4	*Set of* 4	7·50	9·50

186 "Voyager 2" passing Saturn

187 *Strychnos spinosa*

(Des A. Theobald. Litho Cartor)

1992 (7 Dec). International Space Year. T **186** and similar horiz designs. Multicoloured. P 13½.

905	20t. Type **186**	1·00	30
906	75t. Centre of galaxy	2·00	90
907	95t. Kanjedza II Standard A Earth Station	2·00	1·00
908	2k. Communications satellite	4·50	8·00
905/8	*Set of* 4	8·50	9·25

(Des Jennifer Toombs. Litho Cartor)

1993 (21 Mar). World Forestry Day. Indigenous Fruit Trees. T **187** and similar vert designs. Multicoloured. P 13½×14.

909	20t. Type **187**	70	20
910	75t. *Adansonia digitata*	1·50	80
911	95t. *Ximenia caffra*	1·60	1·00
912	2k. *Uapaca kirkiana*	3·25	6·50
909/12	*Set of* 4	6·25	7·75

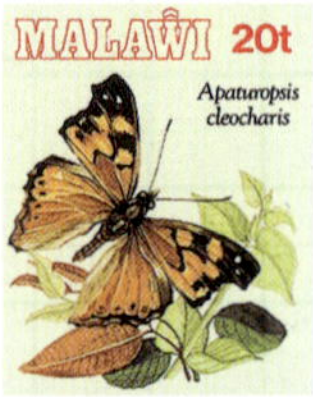

188 *Apaturopsis cleocharis*

189 The Holy Family

(Des Leta Marsden-Hugguis. Adapted D. Miller. Litho Cartor)

1993 (28 June). Butterflies. T **188** and similar vert designs. Multicoloured. P 13.

913	20t. Type **188**	90	30
914	75t. *Euryphura achlys*	1·75	85
915	95t. *Cooksonia aliciae*	2·00	1·25
916	2k. *Charaxes protoclea azota*	3·00	5·50
913/16	*Set of* 4	7·00	7·00

(Des G. Vasarhelyi. Photo Courvoisier)

1993 (30 Nov). Christmas. T **189** and similar vert designs. Multicoloured. Granite paper. P 11½.

917	20t. Type **189**	15	10
918	75t. Shepherds and star	30	20
919	95t. Three Kings	30	30
920	2k. Adoration of the Kings	75	2·50
917/20	*Set of* 4	1·40	2·75

190 Kentrosaurus

191 Socolofs Mbuna

(Des E. Kapitapita and R. Larson. Litho Cartor)

1993 (30 Dec). Prehistoric Animals. T **190** and similar horiz designs. Multicoloured. P 13.

921	20t. Type **190**	55	30
922	75t. Stegosaurus	90	90
923	95t. Sauropod	1·00	1·00
921/3	*Set of* 3	2·25	2·00
MS924	157×97 mm. 2k. Tyrannosaurus; 2k. Dilophosaurus; 2k. Brachiosaurus; 2k. Gallimimus; 2k. Triceratops; 2k. Velociraptor	11·00	12·00

(Des R. Watton. Litho Enschedé)

1994 (21 Mar). Fishes. T **191** and similar horiz designs. Multicoloured. P 14×15.

925	20t. Type **191**	25	10
926	75t. Golden Mbuna	60	30
927	95t. Lombardo's Mbuna	65	35
928	1k. Scraper-mouthed Mbuna	65	70
929	2k. Zebra Mbuna	1·40	2·25
930	4k. Elongate Mbuna	2·25	4·50
925/30	*Set of* 6	5·25	7·25

192 *Ilala II* (lake vessel)

193 "Virgin and Child" (detail) (Dürer)

(Des N. Shewring. Litho Enschedé)

1994 (19 Oct). Ships of Lake Malawi. T **192** and similar horiz designs. Multicoloured. P 13½×14.

931	20t. Type **192**	40	10
932	75t. *Ufulu* (tanker)	1·00	35
933	95t. *Pioneer* (steam launch)	1·10	40
934	2k. *Dove* (paddle-steamer)	1·75	3·00
931/4	*Set of* 4	3·75	3·50
MS935	85×51 mm. 5k. *Monteith* (lake vessel)	3·50	5·00

(Litho Courvoisier)

1994 (30 Nov). Christmas. Religious Paintings. T **193** and similar multicoloured designs. P 14½.

936	20t. Type **193**	60	10
937	75t. "Wise Men presenting Gifts" (Franco-Flemish Book of Hours)	1·10	15
938	95t. "The Nativity" (detail) (Fra Filippo Lippi) (horiz)	1·25	15
939	2k. "Nativity Scene with Wise Men" (Rogier van der Weyden) (horiz)	2·25	3·50
936/9	*Set of* 4	4·75	3·50

194 Pres. Bakili Muluzi (C.O.M.E.S.A. chairman, 1994–95)

195 Telecommunications Training

(Des and litho Courvoisier)

1995 (10 Apr). Establishment of C.O.M.E.S.A. (Common Market for Eastern and Southern African States). P 11½.

940	**194**	40t. multicoloured	15	10
941		1k.40 multicoloured	30	20
942		1k.80 multicoloured	30	55
943		2k. multicoloured	40	1·00
940/3		*Set of* 4	1·00	1·60

(Litho Courvoisier)

1995 (30 Oct). 50th Anniv of the United Nations. T **195** and similar horiz designs. Multicoloured. Granite paper. P 11½.

944	40t. Type **195**	50	10
945	1k.40 Village women collecting water	1·00	35
946	1k.80 Mt. Mulanje	1·10	1·25
947	2k. Villagers in field	1·25	2·00
944/7	*Set of* 4	3·50	3·25
MS948	123×77 mm. As Nos. 944/7, but ordinary paper	3·50	4·00

196 Teacher and Class

(Photo Courvoisier)

1995 (13 Nov). Christmas. T **196** and similar horiz designs. Multicoloured. Granite paper. P 11½.

949	40t. Type **196**	30	10
950	1k.40 Dispensing medicine	70	25
951	1k.80 Crowd at water pump	80	1·00
952	2k. Refugees on ferries	1·00	1·60
949/52	*Set of* 4	2·50	2·75

197 *Precis tugela*

198 Children's Party

(Des Leta Marsden-Hugguis. Photo Courvoisier)

1996 (5 Dec). Butterflies. T **197** and similar horiz designs. Multicoloured. Granite paper. P 11½.

953	60t. Type **197**	40	10
954	3k. *Papilio pelodorus*	90	45
955	4k. *Acrea acrita*	1·00	75
956	10k. *Melanitis leda*	2·25	3·50
953/6	*Set of 4*	4·00	4·25

(Des G. Vasarhelyi. Photo Courvoisier)

1996 (12 Dec). Christmas. T **198** and similar vert designs. Multicoloured. Granite paper. P 11½.

957	10t. Type **198**	50	25
958	20t. Nativity play	75	25
959	30t. Children wearing party hats	90	25
960	60t. Mother and child	1·50	2·25
957/60	*Set of 4*	3·25	2·75

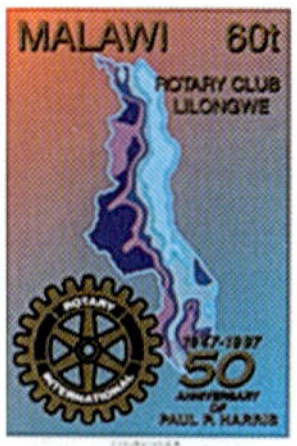

199 Map of Malawi

200 Mother and Child

(Des M. Brussow. Photo Courvoisier)

1997 (6 Oct). 50th Death Anniv of Paul Harris (founder of Rotary International). T **199** and similar vert designs. Multicoloured. Granite paper. P 11½.

961	60t. Type **199**	50	15
962	3k. African Fish Eagle	1·50	80
963	4k.40 Leopard	1·00	1·25
964	5k. Rotary International emblem	1·00	1·50
961/4	*Set of 4*	3·50	3·25

(Photo Courvoisier)

1997 (14 Oct). 50th Anniv of UNICEF. T **200** and similar horiz designs. Multicoloured. Granite paper. P 11½.

965	60t. Type **200**	30	10
966	3k. Children in class	65	35
967	4k.40 Boy with fish	1·25	1·50
968	5k. Nurse inoculating child	1·40	1·75
965/8	*Set of 4*	3·25	3·25

201 The Nativity

201a Diana, Princess of Wales

(Photo Courvoisier)

1997 (15 Dec). Christmas. T **201** and similar vert designs. Multicoloured. Granite paper. P 11½.

969	60t. Type **201**	30	10
970	3k. The Nativity (*different*)	60	30
971	4k.40 Adoration of the Magi	1·25	1·25
972	5k. The Holy Family	1·40	1·75
969/72	*Set of 4*	3·25	3·00

(Des D. Miller. Litho Questa)

1998 (30 Nov). Diana, Princess of Wales Commemoration. T **201a** and similar vert designs. Multicoloured. P 14½×14.

973	60t. Wearing red dress	20	10
974	6k. Wearing lilac jacket	40	35
975	7k. With headscarf	50	70
976	8k. Wearing blue evening dress	55	80
973/6	*Set of 4*	1·50	1·75
MS977	145×70 mm. Nos. 973/6	1·25	1·75

202 Tattooed Rock, Mwalawamphini, Cape Maclear

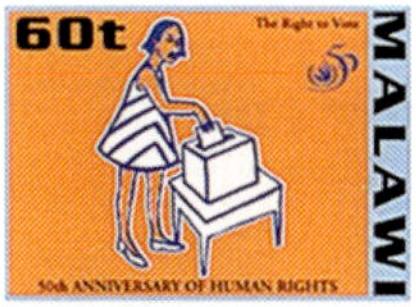

203 Woman voting

(Litho Oriental Press, Bahrain)

1998 (2 Dec). Monuments. T **202** and similar multicoloured designs. P 13½×13 (60t., 6k.) or 13×13½ (others).

978	60t. Type **202**	20	10
979	6k. War Memorial Tower, Zomba	70	65
980	7k. Mtengatenga Postal Hut, Walala (horiz)	85	1·00
981	8k. P.I.M. Church, Chiradzulu (horiz)	95	1·10
978/81	*Set of 4*	2·50	2·50

No. 978 is inscribed "tatooed" and No. 979 "Memoral", both in error.

(Litho Cartor)

1998 (10 Dec). 50th Anniv of Declaration of Human Rights. T **203** and similar horiz designs. Multicoloured. P 13×13½.

982	60t. Type **203**	25	10
983	6k. Books, pens and pencils ("Education")	70	65
984	7k. Man and woman on scales ("Justice")	85	1·00
985	8k. Person hugging house and land ("Property")	95	1·10
982/5	*Set of 4*	2·50	2·50

204 "Madonna and Child with Book"

(Photo Courvoisier)

1998 (15 Dec). Christmas. Religious Paintings. T **204** and similar vert designs. Multicoloured. P 11½.

986	60t. Type **204**	3·00	20
987	6k. Madonna and Child	14·00	1·75
988	7k. Angel	14·00	2·50
989	8k. Adoration of the Magi	14·00	3·00

205 "Madonna and Child"

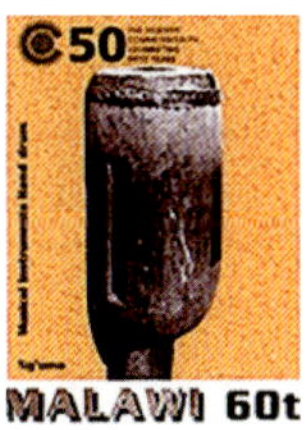

206 Ng'oma (hand drum)

(Photo Courvoisier)

1999 (13 Dec). Christmas. Religious Paintings. T **205** and similar vert designs. Multicoloured. P 11½.

990	60t. Type **205**	60	10
991	6k. "The Nativity"	1·75	55
992	7k. "Adoration of the Magi"	1·75	1·00
993	8k. "Flight into Egypt"	1·75	1·40
990/3	*Set of 4*	5·25	2·75

(Litho Cartor)

2000 (22 Feb). 50th Anniv of the Commonwealth. Musical Instruments. T **206** and similar vert designs. Multicoloured. P 13½.

994	60t. Type **206**	30	10
995	6k. Kaligo (single stringed fiddle)	70	55

996	7k. Kalimba (thumb dulcitone)	85	90
997	8k. Chisekese (rattle)	95	1·10
994/7	*Set of 4*	2·50	2·40

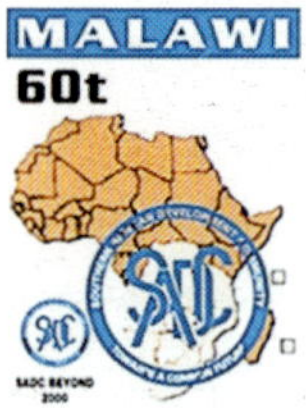

207 Map of Africa and S.A.D.C. Emblem

208 "Madonna and Child"

(Litho Cartor)

2000 (22 Feb). South African Development Community. T **207** and similar multicoloured designs. P 13½.

998	60t. Type **207**	40	10
999	6k. Bottles of Malambe fruit juice	65	55
1000	7k. *Ndunduma* (fisheries research ship) (horiz)	1·50	1·25
1001	8k. Class "Shire" diesel locomotive and goods train (horiz)	2·00	1·75
998/1001	*Set of 4*	4·00	3·25

(Photo Courvoisier)

2000 (12 Dec). Christmas. T **208** and similar vert designs showing religious paintings. Multicoloured. P 11½.

1002	5k. Type **208**	45	10
1003	18k. "Adoration of the Shepherds"	1·50	1·75
1004	20k. "Madonna and Child"	1·50	1·75
1002/4	*Set of 3*	3·00	3·25

209 *Euxanthe wakefieldi*

210 Puku

(Des Leta Huggins. Litho Oriental Press, Bahrain)

2002 (24 Oct). Butterflies. T **209** and similar vert designs. Multicoloured. P 14½×13½.

1005	1k. Type **209**	30	70
1006	2k. *Pseudacraea boisdurali*	30	70
1007	4k. *Catacroptera cloanthe*	30	70
1008	5k. *Myrina silenus ficedula*	50	30
1009	10k. *Cymothoe zombana*	70	60
1010	20k. *Charaxes castor*	1·00	1·00
1011	50k. *Charaxes pythoduras ventersi*	1·75	2·00
1012	100k. *Iolaus lalos*	3·00	4·00
1005/12	*Set of 8*	7·00	8·00

(Des Esther Ainspan. Litho Cartor)

2003 (10 Nov). Endangered Species. Puku (Kobus vardonii). T **210** and similar horiz designs. Multicoloured. P 13½.

1013	50k. Type **210**	1·50	2·00
	a. Strip of 4. Nos. 1013/16	5·50	7·00
1014	50k. Two males	1·50	2·00
1015	50k. Male and female	1·50	2·00
1016	50k. Herd	1·50	2·00
1013/16	*Set of 4*	5·50	7·00
MS1017	204×138 mm. Nos. 1013/16, each ×2	10·00	13·00

Nos. 1013/16 were printed together, *se-tenant*, in horizontal and vertical strips of 4 in sheetlets of 16.

211 Hoopoe (*Upupa epops*)

212 Vickers Vimy

(Des R. Rundo. Litho Cartor)

2003 (10 Nov). Fauna and Flora of Africa. T **211** and similar multicoloured designs. P 13½.

MS1018	118×137 mm. 50k. Type **211**; 50k. Grey Parrot (*Psittacus erithacus*); 50k. Bateleur (*Terathopius ecaudatus*); 50k. Martial Eagle (*Polemaetus bellicosus*); 50k. Masked Lovebird (*Agapornis personatus*); 50k. Pel's Fishing Owl (*Scotopelia peli*)	7·50	8·50
MS1019	113×138 mm. 50k. *Bebearia octogramma*; 50k. *Charaxes nobilis*; 50k. *Cymothoe beckeri*; 50k. *Salamis anteva*; 50k. *Charaxes xiphares*; 50k. *Bebearia arcadius Fabricius* (all horiz)	7·50	8·50
MS1020	137×117 mm. 50k. *Pleurotus ostreatus*; 50k. *Macrolepiota procera*; 50k. *Amanita vaginata*; 50k. *Cantharellus tubaeformis*; 50k. *Hydnum repandum*; 50k. *Trametes versicolor* (all horiz)	7·50	8·50
MS1021	95×135 mm. 50k. *Angraecum eburneum*; 50k. *Ancistrochilus rothschildianus*; 50k. *Angraecum infundibulare*; 50k. *Ansellia africana*; 50k. *Disa veitchii*; 50k. *Angraecum compactum*	7·50	8·50
MS1022	Four sheets. (a) 105×71 mm. 180k. Grey Heron (*Ardea cinerea*) (horiz). (b) 72×98 mm. 180k. *Carterocephalus palaemon* (horiz). (c) 68×94 mm. 180k. *Auricularia auricula*. (d) 93×66 mm. 180k. *Aerangis kotschyana* (horiz) *Set of 4 sheets*	13·00	15·00

(Des R. Rundo. Litho BDT)

2004 (6 Feb). Centenary of Powered Flight. T **212** and similar horiz designs. Multicoloured. P 14.

MS1023	174×97 mm. 75k. Type **212**; 75k. D.H.9A; 75k. Messerschmitt Bf; 75k. Mitsubishi A6M3	4·00	4·50
MS1024	96×67 mm. 180k. Fiat CR.2	3·00	3·25

213 Corvette Convertible (1965)

(Des T. Wood. Litho BDT)

2004 (6 Feb). 50th Anniv of the Corvette. T **213** and similar horiz designs. Multicoloured. P 14.

MS1025	116×156 mm. 75k. Type **213**; 75k. Corvette Stingray (1965); 75k. Corvette (1979); 75k. Corvette (1998)	4·00	4·50
MS1026	110×83 mm. 180k. Corvette (1998)	3·00	3·25

214 Cadillac Eldorado (1959)

215 Joop Zoetemelk (1980)

(Des T. Wood. Litho BDT)

2004 (6 Feb). Centenary of the Cadillac. T **214** and similar horiz designs. Multicoloured. P 14.

MS1027	116×156 mm. 75k. Type **214**; 75k. Cadillac Series 62 (1962); 75k. Cadillac Sedan DeVille (1961); 75k. Cadillac V-16 (1930)	4·00	4·50
MS1028	110×85 mm. 180k. Cadillac Eldorado (1954)	3·00	3·25

(Des R. Rundo. Litho BDT)

2004 (6 Feb). Centenary of Tour de France Cycle Race. T **215** and similar vert designs showing winners. Multicoloured. P 13½×13.

MS1029	157×96 mm. 75k. Type **215**; 75k. Bernard Hinault (1981); 75k. Bernard Hinault (1982); 75k. Laurent Fignon (1983)	5·00	5·50
MS1030	95×67 mm. 180k. Miguel Induráin (1991–5)	3·50	4·00

(Des Anja Denker)

2004 (11 Oct). First Joint Issue of Southern Africa Postal Operators Association Members. Sheet 170×95 mm. As T **227a** of Zambia. Multicoloured. P 14.

MS1031	15k. African Fish Eagle (Namibia); 15k. Two African fish eagles perched (Zimbabwe); 15k. Peregrine falcon (Angola); 15k. Cattle egret (Botswana); 15k. Purple-crested turaco ("Lourie") (Swaziland); 15k. Stanley ("Blue") crane (South Africa); 15k. Bar-tailed trogon (Malawi); 15k. Two African fish eagles in flight (Zambia)	4·50	5·00

The stamp depicting the bar-tailed trogon is not inscribed with the name of the country of which the bird is a national symbol. Miniature sheets of similar designs were also issued by Angola, Botswana, Namibia, South Africa, Swaziland, Zambia and Zimbabwe.

217 Boys in Classroom

(Litho Madras Security Printers, India)

2005 (25 July). Centenary of Rotary International. Sheet 150×131 mm containing T **217** and similar horiz designs. Multicoloured. P 13½.

MS1032	25k. Type **217**; 55k. Boy in wheelchair; 60k. Boys and teacher in classroom; 65k. Nurse and newborn baby in incubator	4·50	5·00

(Litho)

2007. Butterflies. Vert designs as Nos. 1008/12 and new values, all with 'PROTECT NATURE' emblem. Multicoloured. P 13½×12½.

1032*a*	5k. *Myrena silenus ficedula*	10	10
1032*b*	10k. *Cymothoe zombana*	20	15
1032*c*	20k. *Charaxes castor*	35	25
1032*d*	40k. *Papilio pelodorus*	60	60
1032*e*	50k. *Charaxes pythoduras ventersi*	70	70
1032*f*	65k. *Papilio pelodorus*	80	80
1032*g*	75k. *Acrea acrita*	1·00	1·00
1032*h*	100k. *Iolaus lalos*	1·10	1·10
1032*i*	105k. *Acrea acrita*	1·10	1·10
1032*j*	110k. *Euxanthe wakefieldi*	1·25	1·25
1032*k*	115k. *Pseudacraea boisdurali*	1·40	1·40
1032a/k	*Set of* 11	6·75	6·75

218 Handprint

2008 (19 Nov). UNICEF "STOP CHILD ABUSE". Day of the African Child. Multicoloured. Litho. P 13.

1033	40k. Type **218**	75	75
MS1034	141×160 mm. 40k. Type **218**	75	75

219 Black Rhinoceros (*Diceros bicornis*)

2009 (30 Sept). Endangered Animals of Malawi. T **219** and similar horiz designs. Multicoloured. Litho. P 11½×12 (**MS**1035) or 11½ (**MS**1036).

MS1035	100×110 mm. 65k.×4 Type **219**; Sable antelope (*Hippotragus niger*); Zebra (*Equus zebra*); African buffalo (*Syncerus caffer*)	2·75	2·75
MS1036	100×70 mm. 325k. Roan antelope (*Hippotragus equinus*)	2·25	2·25

220 Hippopotamus

2009 (30 Sept). Hippopotamuses of Malawi (*Hippopotamus amphibius*). T **220** and similar multlcoloured designs. Litho. P 11½×12 (**MS**1037) or 11½ (**MS**1038).

MS1037	120×100 mm. 105k.×4 Type **220**; Hippos laying in mud; Hippo standing; Two hippos in water	3·50	3·50
MS1038	100×71 mm. 325k. Hippos in water (vert)	2·25	2·25

221 Lion (*Panthera leo*)

2009 (30 Sept). Wildlife of Malawi. T **221** and similar horiz designs. Multicoloured. Litho. P 11½.

MS1039	145×110 mm. 110k.×6 Type **221**; Elephant shrew (*Macroscelides proboscideus*); Black-backed jackal (*Canis mesomelas*); Reedbuck (*Redunca redunca*); African elephant (*Loxodonta africana*); Warthog (*Phacochoerus africanus*)	8·00	8·00
MS1040	70×100 mm. 325k. Leopard (*Panthera pardus*)	2·25	2·25

222 Flock of Lovebirds

2009 (30 Sept). Endangered Species. Lilian's Lovebird (*Agapornis lilianae*). T **222** and similar horiz designs. Multicoloured. Litho. P 13½.

1041	115k. Type **222**	1·40	1·50
	a. Strip of 4. Nos. 1041/4	5·00	5·50
1042	115k. Six lovebirds perched on branches	1·40	1·50
1043	115k. Seven lovebirds in flight	1·40	1·50
1044	115k. Pair perched on branch and four others in flight	1·40	1·50
1041/4	*Set of* 4	5·00	5·50
MS1045	112×165 mm. Nos. 1041/4, each ×2	11·50	11·50

Nos. 1041/4 were printed together, *se-tenant*, as horizontal and vertical strips of four in sheetlets of 16 stamps. No. **MS**1045 contains two blocks of Nos. 1041/4 separated by an illustrated gutter.

223 Player, Football, Namibian Flag and Zakumi Mascot

(Des Anja Denker. Litho Enschedé)

2010 (20 Dec). Third Joint Issue of Southern Africa Postal Operators Association Members. World Cup Football Championship, South Africa. T **223** and similar circular designs, each showing Zakumi mascot, different silhouettes of players on football, and the national flag of a member country. Multicoloured. P 13½.

1046	105k. Type **223**	1·10	1·10
1047	105k. South Africa	1·10	1·10
1048	105k. Zimbabwe	1·10	1·10
1049	105k. Malawi	1·10	1·10
1050	105k. Swaziland	1·10	1·10

1051	105k. Botswana	1·10	1·10
1052	105k. Mauritius	1·10	1·10
1053	105k. Lesotho	1·10	1·10
1054	105k. Zambia	1·10	1·10
MS1055	188×167 mm. Nos. 1046/54	9·00	9·00

224 Crib Figures

(Litho)

2010 (20 Dec). Christmas. T **224** and similar horiz designs showing wooden crib figures. Multicoloured: colour of lower background given. P 13.

1056	**224**	65k. orange-red	80	80
1057		65k. Indian red	80	80
1058		65k. Royal blue	80	80
1059		65k. yellowish green	80	80

225 School, Clinic and Water Pump

(Litho)

2011 (18 Jan). 35th Anniv of EU Aid Projects in Malawi. T **225** and similar multicoloured design showing children's art. P 14.

1060	65k. Type **225**	80	80
1061	65k. '35' in circle of stars and family (vert)	80	80

STAMP BOOKLETS

1954 (1 Jan). Black on green cover, stitched (No. SB1) or buff cover, stapled (No. *SB2*). R.W. Gunson (Seeds) Ltd. advertisement on front.

SB1	2s.6d. booklet containing four ½d., 1d., and twelve 2d. (Nos. 173/4, 176), each in blocks of 4	29·00
SB2	5s. booklet containing eight ½d., 1d., 6d. and twelve 2d. (Nos. 173/4, 176, 180), each in blocks of 4	35·00

POSTAGE DUE STAMPS

D **1**

D **2**

(Typo D.L.R)

1950 (1 July). Wmk Mult Script CA. P 14.

D1	D **1**	1d. scarlet	4·00	32·00
D2		2d. ultramarine	18·00	32·00
D3		3d. green	17·00	6·00
D4		4d. purple	30·00	60·00
D5		6d. yellow-orange	42·00	£160
D1/5 *Set of 5*			£100	£250

(Litho Bradbury, Wilkinson)

1967 (1 Sept). W **55**. P 11½.

D6	D **2**	1d. carmine	15	4·50
D7		2d. sepia	20	4·50
D8		4d. reddish violet	25	4·75
D9		6d. blue	25	5·00
D10		8d. emerald	35	5·50
D11		1s. black	45	6·00
D6/11 *Set of 6*			1·50	27·00

1971 (15 Feb). As Nos. D6/11, but values in tambalas. W **55**. P 11½.

D12	D **2**	2t. greenish drab	30	5·00
D13		4t. bright mauve	50	3·00
D14		6t. royal blue	50	3·25
D15		8t. dull green	50	3·25
D16		10t. blackish brown	60	3·25
D12/16 *Set of 5*			2·25	16·00

(Litho Walsall)

1975–84. Design redrawn, with circumflex accent over "W" of "MALAWI". P 14.

*(a) W **55** (sideways)*

D17	D **2**	2t. chestnut (15.9.75)	1·25	6·50
D18		2t. brown (14.6.82)	60	4·00
D19		4t. deep mauve (14.6.82)	60	4·00
D20		6t. royal blue (9.84)	1·50	4·00
D21		8t. green (9.84)	1·50	4·00
D22		10t. black (14.6.82)	60	4·00
D17/22 *Set of 6*			5·50	24·00

(b) No wmk

D23	D **2**	2t. brown (19.10.77)	7·00	7·00
D24		4t. mauve (19.10.77)	7·00	7·00
D25		8t. green (15.12.78)	3·75	7·00
D26		10t. brownish grey (19.10.77)	7·00	7·00
D23/6 *Set of 4*			22·00	23·00

(Photo Harrison)

1989. As Nos. D17/26, but design redrawn smaller, 17×20½ mm instead of 17½×21 mm. No wmk. P 15×14.

D27	D **2**	2t. light brown	3·75	5·50
D28		4t. bright purple	3·75	5·50
D29		6t. bright blue	3·75	5·50
D31		10t. brownish black	3·75	5·50
D27/31 *Set of 4*			13·50	20·00

Mozambique

The Republic of Mozambique joined the Commonwealth on 2 November 1995.

(Currency. 100 centavos = 1 metical)

267 Child wearing Blue Cloak

268 Player scoring Goal

(Des F. Jofane. Litho State Printing Works, Maputo)

1995 (22 Nov). 20th Anniv of UNICEF in Mozambique. P 11½×11.

1417 **267** 5000m. multicoloured ... 1·00 1·00

(Des F. Jofane. Litho State Printing Works, Maputo)

1996 (5 Apr). Football. T **268** and similar horiz designs. Multicoloured. P 11×11½.

1418 1000m. Type **268** ... 35 35
1419 2000m. Goalkeeper holding ball ... 60 60
1420 4000m. Referee admonishing players ... 80 80
1421 6000m. Two players tackling for ball ... 1·10 1·10
1418/1421 *Set of* 4 ... 2·50 2·50

269 Mask

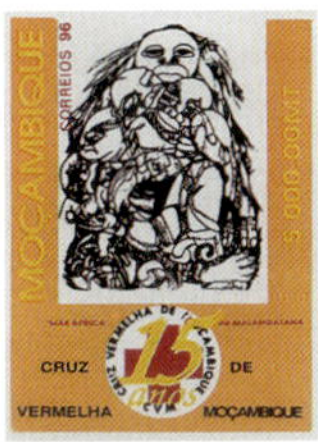

270 'Mae Africa' (De Malangatana)

(Litho State Printing Works, Maputo)

1996 (2 July). Local Masks. T **269** and similar horiz designs, showing different masks. P 11½×11.

1422 100m. Type **269** ... 35 35
1423 200m. multicoloured ... 60 60
1424 400m. multicoloured ... 80 80
1425 600m. multicoloured ... 1·10 1·10
1422/5 *Set of* 4 ... 2·50 2·50

(Litho State Printing Works, Maputo)

1996 (1 July). 15th Anniv Mozambique Red Cross. P 11½×11.

1426 **270** 5000m. multicoloured ... 1·00 1·00

271 African Elephant

272 Minefield

(Litho State Printing Works, Maputo)

1996 (3 Sept). Wild Animals. T **271** and similar vert. designs. Multicoloured. P 14×11.

1427 1000m. Type **271** ... 75 40
1428 2000m. White rhinoceros ... 1·00 75
1429 4000m. Leopard ... 1·25 1·00
1430 1000m. Pel's Fishing owl ... 2·00 1·50
1427/30 *Set of* 4 ... 4·50 3·25

(Litho State Printing Works, Maputo)

1996 (9 Nov). Land Mine Clearance Campaign. T **272** and similar vert designs. Multicoloured. P 11½×11.

1431 2000m. Type **272** ... 50 35
1432 6000m. Warning sign ... 1·25 65
1433 8000m. Soldier with mine detector ... 1·50 1·00
1434 10000m. Soldier lifting mine ... 2·25 1·50
1431/4 *Set of* 3 ... 5·00 3·00

273 City Street

274 5r. stamp of 1876 and Magnifying Glass

(Litho State Printing Works, Maputo)

1996 (16 Dec). "Keep the City Clean". P 11½×11.

1435 **273** 2000m. multicoloured ... 50 25

(Litho State Printing Works, Maputo)

1996 (16 Dec). 120th Anniv of Mozambique Stamps. P 11½×11.

1436 **274** 2000m. multicoloured ... 50 25

275 Mitumbui

275a Anhinga

(Litho State Printing Works, Maputo)

1997 (10 Apr). Local Boats. T **275** and similar horiz designs Multicoloured. P 11×11½.

1437 2000m. Type **275** ... 40 25
1438 6000m. Muterere ... 1·25 65
1439 8000m. Lancha ... 1·50 1·00
1440 10000m. Dhow ... 2·25 2·00
1437/40 *Set of* 4 ... 5·00 3·50

1997 (16 Apr). First AICEP (Association of Post Office and Telecommunications Operators of Portuguese Speaking Territories) Philatelic Conference, Sao Tome. Sheet 70×91 mm. Litho. P 11½×11.

MS1440*a* **275a** 5000m. multicoloured ... 12·00 12·00

276 Village Scene

277 *Enaretta conifere*

(Litho State Printing Works, Maputo)

1997 (1 June). International Children's Day. P 11×11½.

1441 **276** 2000m. multicoloured ... 50 25

(Litho State Printing Works, Maputo)

1997 (5 July). Beetles. T **277** and similar horiz designs. Multicoloured. P 11×11½.

1442 2000m. Type **277** ... 50 25
1443 6000m. *Zographus hieroglyphicus* ... 1·50 75
1444 8000m. *Tragiscochema bertolonii* ... 2·00 1·00
1445 10000m. *Tragocepthala ducalis* ... 2·75 1·50
1442/5 *Set of* 4 ... 6·00 3·00
MS1446 97×105 mm. Nos. 1442/5 ... 6·00 6·00

No **MS**1446 also commemorates the "LUBRAPEX 97" International Stamp Exhibition, Brazil.

278 Yellow-billed Stork

279 Abstract Patterns

(Litho State Printing Works, Maputo)

1997 (16 July). Aquatic Birds. similar multicoloured designs. P 11½×11 (vert) or 11×11½ (horiz).

1447	2000m. Type **278**	50	25
1448	4000m. Black-winged stilt	1·50	75
1449	8000m. Long-toed stint (horiz)	2·00	1·00
1450	10000m. Eastern white pelican	2·75	1·50
1447/50	*Set of 4*	6·00	6·00

(Des P. Barbosa. Litho State Printing Works, Maputo)

1997 (5 Sept). Centenary Joao Ferreira dos Santos Group. P 11×11½.

1451	**279**	2000m. multicoloured	1·00	5·00

280 Sun and Globe

281 Gandhi

(Litho State Printing Works, Maputo)

1997 (18 Sept). Protection of Ozone Layer. P 11½×11.

1452	**280**	2000m. multicoloured	30	25

1997 (2 Oct). 50th Anniv of Republic of India. Litho.

1453	**281**	2000m. multicoloured	1·00	40

282 Dove holding Olive Branch

284 Coelacanth

1997 (4 Oct). 5th Anniv of Peace Accord. Litho. P 11½×11.

1454	**282**	2000m. multicoloured	50	25

(Litho State Printing Works, Maputo)

1998 (22 May). 'EXPO 98' International Stamp exhibition, Lisbon. P 11×11½.

1463	**284**	2000m. multicoloured	1·00	50

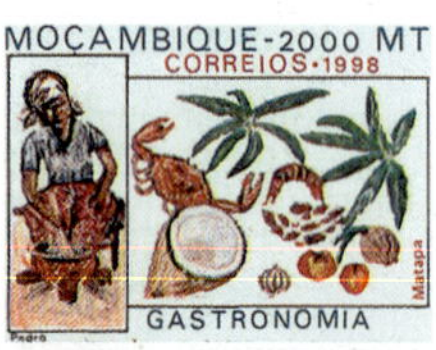

285 Woman with various Food Products

(**286**)

(Litho State Printing Works, Maputo)

1998 (1 Jun). Food Production. P 11×11½.

1464	**282**	2000m. multicoloured	60	30

1998. No. 1143 surch as T **286**.

1465	12500m. on 8m. Emerald	4·00	4·00

Between 1997–2000 numerous stamps from old stocks were provisionally surcharged to meet postal needs. Below is a table of values reported to date. Until the quantities in existence can be ascertained it is not possible to provide a valuation.

100m. on 10m. Ricinis communis (on 1981 Wild flowers)
500m. on 16m. Notobranchius zachovii (on 1984 freshwater fish)
2000m. on 1.00 Castor oil (1981)
2000m. on 12.50 Locomotive (1979 Locomotives)
2000m. on 12.50 Cocker spaniel (1979 Dogs)
2000m. on 12.50 Coconuts (1981)
3000m. on 4000m. Teacher (1998 Women's Day)
3000m. on 8000m. Traditional Dwelling (1998)
3000m. on 8000m. Using computer (1998 Women's Day)
3000m. on 15,000m. Traditional Dwelling
3000m. on 20,000m. Traditional Dwelling
3000m. on 30,000m. Traditional Dwelling
3000m. on 4000m. Teacher (1998 Women's Day)
4000m. on 12.50 Coconut (1981)
5000m on 10m. Ricinis communis (1981)
6000m. on 7.50 Ansellia gigantean (1981 flowers)
7500m. on 16m. 500m. banknote (1986 National Savings Campaign)
7500m. on 30m. 1000m. banknote (1986 National Savings Campaign)
10,000m. on 7.50 Palinurus delagoae (1981 crabs)
10,000m. on 12.50 Stapelia leendertsiae (1981 flowers)
10,000m. on 7.50 Ansellia gigantean (1981 flowers)
10,000m. on 50m. on 7.50 Ansellia gigantean previously surcharged
10,000m. on 12.50 Lusiosquilla maculata (1981 crabs)
10,000m. on 12.50 football player and Barcelona stadium (1981 Espana 82 World Cup Football)
12,500m. on 16m. Malachite (1987 Minerals)
17,000m. on 10m. Swimming (1991 Olympics Barcelona)
17,000m. on 50m. Roller hockey (1991 Olympics Barcelona)
17,000m. on 125m. Chinhambonine (1991 Fountains of Maputo)
17,000m. on 200m. Table tennis (1991 Olympics Barcelona)
17,000m. on 1,000m. Badminton (1991 Olympics Barcelona)
17,000m. on 10,000m. Traditional Dwellings

286a Breast Feeding

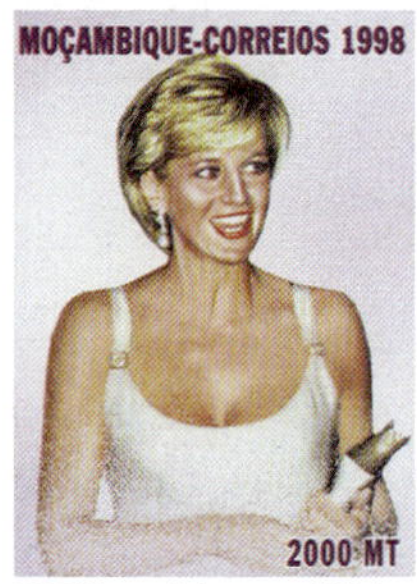

287 Diana, Princess of Wales

1998 (25 June). Mothers Day. T **286a** and similar vert designs. Multicoloured. Litho. P 11.

1466	2000m. Type **286a**	1·50	—
1467	4000m. Teacher	1·75	—
1468	8000m. Using computer	2·00	—
1469	10,000m. Woman in field	2·50	—
1466/1469	*Set of 4*	6·00	—

1998 (7 July). Diana, Princess of Wales Commemoration (1st issue). T **287** and similar vert designs. Multicoloured. Litho. P 13½.

MS1473 135×189 mm. 2000m. Type **287**; 2000m. Wearing tiara and white dress; 2000m. Wearing black V-neck dress; 2000m. Wearing blue sleeveless dress and choker; 2000m. With Indian woman and baby; 2000m. Wearing black halter-neck dress; 2000m. In RNLI uniform; 2000m. Wearing red dress; 2000m. Wearing Red Cross badge and protective vest 85 90

MS1474 135×189 mm. 5000m. Wearing red and white hat and pearl necklace; 5000m. Wearing pink check hat and dress; 5000m. Wearing red hat and red patterned dress; 5000m. Wearing blue hat and white jacket with blue edging; 5000m. Wearing red and black hat and red and white check jacket; 5000m. Wearing dark blue and white hat and white jacket with dark blue edging; 5000m. Wearing white and grey hat and white dress; 5000m. Turquoise and white hat and dress; 5000m. Wearing blue hat and blue jacket with flower brooch .... 2·20 2·30

MS1475 135×190 mm. 8000m. Wearing cream embroidered dress and bolero; 8000m. Wearing black dress and choker; 8000m. Wearing red dress; 8000m. Wearing red dress; 8000m. Wearing beige embroidered dress and bolero; 8000m. Wearing white dress and choker; 8000m. Wearing pale blue dress and pearl necklace; 8000m. Wearing dark blue dress; 8000m. Wearing white lace dress and carrying clutch bag .... 3·25 3·50

MS1476 Two sheets, each 130×100 mm. (a) 30000m. Wearing mauve dress (41×59 mm). (b) 30000m. With African child (41×59 mm). *Set of 2 sheets* .... 3·00 3·25

See also Nos. **MS**1506, **MS**1507, **MS**1593 and **MS**1594.

288 Breast Feeding

289 Mother Teresa

1998. Promotion of Breast Feeding. Litho.

1477	**288**	2000m. multicoloured	80	25

1998. Mother Teresa. Litho.

1478	**289**	2000m. multicoloured	80	25

290 Kudu

291 *Garcinia livingstonei*

1998 (9 Oct). 18th Anniv of PAPU. Litho. P 11×11½.

1479	**290**	2000m. multicoloured	80	30

1998 (9 Oct). Plants. Wild Fruit. T **291** and similar vert designs. Multicoloured. Litho. P 12½.

1480	2000m. Type **291**	1·50	—
1481	7500m. *Tabernaemontana elegans*	2·50	—
1482	12,500m. *Ximenia caffra*	3·00	—
1483	25,000m. *Syzygium guineense*	4·50	—
1480/1483	*Set of 4*	1·00	—
MS1484	50,000m. *Uapaca kirkiana*	1·00	—

292 Traditional Dwelling

296 Lucy (Lucille Ball) wearing Dark Brown Hat and Coat

1998. Traditional Dwellings. T **292** and similar horiz designs. Litho. P 11×11½.

1485	**292**	2000m. multicoloured		
1486		4000m. multicoloured		
1487		6000m. multicoloured		
1488		8000m. multicoloured		
1489		10,000m. multicoloured		
1490		15,000m. multicoloured		
1491		20,000m. multicoloured		
1492		30,000m. multicoloured		
1493		50,000m. multicoloured		
1494		100,000m. multicoloured		
1485/94		*Set of 10*	20·00	—

1999. Scenes from *I Love Lucy* (American TV comedy series). Two sheets containing T **296** and similar multicoloured design. Litho. P 13½.

MS1505 (a) 88×121 mm. 35000m. Type **296**; (b) 121×88 mm. 35000m. Lucy as ballet dancer .... 3·50 3·75

297 Diana, Princess of Wales

298 Joe Besser, Larry and Moe with Frying Pan

1999. Diana, Princess of Wales Commemoration (2nd issue). T **297** and similar vert designs. Multicoloured. Litho. P 14.

MS1506 165×170 mm. 6500m. Type **297** (violet and black); 6500m. In profile, looking left (light brown and black); 6500m. Wearing jacket and pearl necklace (chestnut and black); 6500m. Wearing round-collared dress (brown-olive and black); 6500m. Wearing hat with feathers (bright lilac and black); 6500m. Wearing white blouse with pointed collar, looking to left (purple-brown and black) .... 1·80 1·90

MS1507 165×170 mm. 6500m. Wearing large white collar (lilac and black); 6500m. Wearing hat (lilac and black); 6500m. Wearing white (purple-brown and black); 6500m. Wearing dress with narrow straps (light brown and black); 6500m. Wearing patterned blouse (violet and black); 6500m. In profile, with bouquet of flowers (brown-olive and black) .... 1·50 1·60

1999. Scenes from *The Three Stooges* (American TV comedy series). T **298** and similar horiz designs. Multicoloured. Litho. P 13½.

MS1508 174×140 mm. 5000m. Type **298**; 5000m. Shemp wearing trilby; 5000m. Moe and Larry putting pan on Joe Besser's head; 5000m. Moe with pipe; 5000m. Larry and Moe pouring drinks on Curly's head; 5000m. Larry wearing straw hat; 5000m. Joe Besser and Larry pulling Moe's tooth; 5000m. Curly wearing mauve shirt; 5000m. Shemp, Larry and Moe behind green sofa .... 2·20 2·30

MS1509 Two sheets, each 140×89 mm. (a) 35000m. Larry wearing pink shirt. (b) 35000m. Larry holding shovel. *Set of 2 sheets* .... 3·50 3·75

299 AE-AC "Blue Tiger", Germany

300 Betty Boop astride Motorcycle

1999 (12 Oct). Trains. T **299** and similar horiz designs. Multicoloured. Litho. P 14.

1510	2000m. Type **299**	10	15
1511	2500m. DB 218 locomotive, Germany	15	20
1512	3000m. Mt. Pilatus incline railway car, Switzerland	1·20	1·30
1513	3500m. Berlin underground railway train, Germany	1·80	1·90
1510/13	*Set of 4*	3·00	3·25

MS1514 162×219 mm. 2500m. DB V200 locomotive, Germany; 2500m. Union Pacific locomotive, USA; 2500m. Class 613 locomotive, Germany; 2500m. Canadian Pacific 4242 locomotive, Canada; 2500m. *Duchess of Hamilton* steam locomotive, Great Britain; 2500m. Pacific Delhi locomotive, India; 2500m. ISA locomotive, South Africa; 2500m. DR VT 18-16-07 locomotive, Germany; 2500m. DB-DE locomotive, Australia .... 1·20 1·30

MS1515 162×219 mm. 3000m. DB 218 locomotive, Germany; 3000m. QJ Class 2-10-2 steam locomotive, China; 3000m. 232 232.9 locomotive, Germany; 3000m. *Flying Scotsman* steam locomotive, Great Britain; 3000m. WR 360 CH locomotive, Germany; 3000m. Henschel 2-8.2 steam locomotive; 3000m. Santa Fe 39C locomotive (EUA); 3000m. Steam locomotive heading "Balkan Express", Greece; 3000m. DB 218 locomotive, Germany .... 1·20 1·30

MS1516 Two sheets, each 81×106 mm. (a) 25000m. German 2-8-2 steam locomotive. (b) 25000m. German DMU Talento Talbot Alamao locomotive. *Set of 2 sheets* .... 2·50 2·60

1999. Betty Boop (cartoon character). T **300** and similar vert designs. Multicoloured. Litho. P 13½.

MS1517 132×178 mm. 3500m. Type **300**; 3500m. Riding motorcycle, wearing purple top; 3500m. Wearing cap and light brown patterned top; 3500m. Astride motorcycle, wearing cap and jeans; 3500m. Looking through handlebars, wearing blue jacket and cap; 3500m. Riding motorcycle, wearing "Biker Betty" top; 3500m. With gasoline can, hitching lift; 3500m. Astride motorcycle, wearing bandana; 3500m. Astride motorcycle, wearing red jacket .... 1·80 1·90

MS1518 Two sheets, each 140×89 mm. (a) 35000m. Astride motorcycle, wearing red jacket. (b) 35000m. Sat beside motorcycle, with gasoline can. *Set of 2 sheets* .... 1·80 1·90

In 2000 various stamps overprinted "* 2000" surcharged have been reported. Until the quantities in existence can be ascertained it is not possible to provide a valuation.

2000m. on 12.50 Coconuts surcharge in blk & brn [-see prev 1998–2000 surch]
4000m. Traditional dwellings (1998)
4000m. on 12.50 Coconuts Surcharge in brown [-see prev 1998–2000 surch]
6000m. Traditional dwellings (1998)
6000m. on 7.50 Ansellia gigantea (1981 flowers)
8000m. Tragiscoschema bertoloma (1997 Lubrapex insects)
10,000m. Traditional Dwellings (1998)
15,000m. Traditional Dwellings (1998)

301 Chartreux

302 Pterandon

(Des R. Sauber. Litho Questa)

2000 (29 Mar). Cats and Dogs of the World. T **301** and similar vert designs. Multicoloured. P 14.

MS1519 148×186 mm. 4000m. Type **301**; 4000m. Australian mist; 4000m. Egyptian Mau; 4000m. Scottish fold; 4000m. Cornish Rex; 4000m. Abyssinian .... 1·20 1·30

MS1520 127×164 mm. 4000m. Himalayan; 4000m. Balinese; 4000m. Persian; 4000m. Turkish van; 4000m. Norwegian forest cat; 4000m. Maine coon .. 1·20 1·30

MS1521 155×222 mm. 4500m. Shetland sheepdog; 4500m. Basenji; 4500m. Poodle; 4500m. St. Bernard; 4500m. Shar pei; 4500m. Spinone .... 1·50 1·60

MS1522 153×218 mm. 4500m. Jack Russell terrier; 4500m. Schweizer laufhound; 4500m. Japanese spitz; 4500m. Australian shepherd dog; 4500m. Saluki; 4500m. Siberian husky .... 1·50 1·60

MS1523 Four sheet. (a) 75×105 mm. 25000m. Ragdoll. (b) 75×105 mm. 25000m. Siamese. (c) 70×100 mm. 25000m. Chow Chow (horiz). (d) 70×100 mm. 25000m. Border collie (horiz). *Set of 4 sheets* .... 6·00 6·00

(Des M. Servin. Litho Questa)

2000 (28 Apr). Dinosaurs. T **302** and similar horiz designs. Multicoloured. P 14.

MS1524 139×116 mm. 3000m. Type **302**; 3000m. Bothriospondylus; 3000m. Iguanodon (head); 3000m. Stegosaurus; 3000m. Nodosaurus; 3000m. Elaphrosaurus and Iguanodon (body); 3000m. Petrolacosaurus; 3000m. Procompsognathus; 3000m. Dimetrodon .... 1·40 1·50

MS1525 139×116 mm. 3000m. Plesiosaurus; 3000m. Ceresiosaurus; 3000m. Cryptoclidus; 3000m. Placochelys; 3000m. Plotosaurus; 3000m. Ictiosaurus; 3000m. Platecarpus; 3000m. Archelon; 3000m. Mosasaur .... 1·40 1·50

MS1526 Two sheets, each 110×85 mm. (a) 20000m. Tyrannosaurus rex. (b) 20000m. Honodus. *Set of 2 sheets* 2·00 2·10

303 *Palla ussheri*

304 Male and Female Blue Wildebeest

(Des T. Wood. Litho Questa)

2000 (28 Apr). Butterflies of the World. T **303** and similar multicoloured designs. P 14.

1527	2000m. Type **303**	10	10
1528	2500m. *Euschemon rafflesia*	15	20
1529	3000m. *Buttus philenor*	20	25
1530	3000m. *Hypolimnas bolina*	20	25
1531	3500m. *Lycorea cleobaea*	20	25
1532	4000m. *Dynastor napoleon*	20	25
1533	4500m. *Callimorpha dominula*	25	30
1534	5000m. *Pereute leucodrosime*	25	30
1527/34	*Set of 8*	1·40	1·50

MS1535 95×100 mm. 4500m. *Tisiphone abeone*; 4500m. *Pseudacraea boisduvali*; 4500m. *Mylothris chloris*; 4500m. *Papilio glaucus*; 4500m. *Mimacraea marshalli*; 4500m. *Gonepteryx Cleopatra* .... 1·20 1·30

MS1536 95×100 mm. 4500m. *Palla ussheri*; 4500m. *Hypolimnas salmacis*; 4500m. *Pereute leucodrosime*; 4500m. *Anteos clorinde*; 4500m. *Colias eurytheme*; 4500m. *Hebomoia glaucippe* .... 1·20 1·30

MS1537 95×100 mm. 4500m. *Thauria aliris*; 4500m. *Catocala ilia*; 4500m. *Colotis danae*; 4500m. *Agrias claudia*; 4500m. *Euploe core*; 4500m. *Scoptes alphaeus* (all horiz) .... 1·20 1·30

MS1538 95×100 mm. 4500m. *Phoebis philea*; 4500m. *Anteos clorinde*; 4500m. *Arhopala amantes*; 4500m. *Mesene phareus*; 4500m. *Euploea mulciber*; 4500m. *Heliconius ricini* (all horiz) .... 1·20 1·30

MS1539 141×112 mm. 4500m. *Euphaedra neophorn*; 4500m. *Catopsilia florella*; 4500m. *Charaxes bohemani*; 4500m. *Junonia orithya*; 4500m. *Colotis danae*; 4500m. *Eurytela dryope* .... 1·20 1·30

MS1540 141×112 mm. 4500m. *Papilio demodocus*; 4500m. *Kallimoides rumia*; 4500m. *Danaus chrysippus*; 4500m. *Palla ussheri*; 4500m. *Hypolimnas salmacis*; 4500m. *Zinina otis* .... 1·20 1·30

MS1541 Six sheets. (a) 85×110 mm. 20000m. *Papilio glaucus*. (b) 85×110 mm. 20000m. *Delias mysis* (horiz). (c) 85×110 mm. 20000m. *Mylothris cloris* (horiz). (d) 20000m. *Loxura atymnus* (horiz). (e) 70×100 mm. 20000m. *Hemiolaus coeculus* (horiz). (f) 73×103 mm. 20000m. *Euxanthe wakefieldii* (horiz). *Set of 6 sheets* ..... 6·00 6·25

(Des D. Burkhart. Litho Questa)

2000 (28 Apr). Endangered Species. Blue Wildebeest. T **304** and similar horiz designs. Multicoloured. Litho. P 14.

1542	6500m. Type **304**	30	35
	a. Block of 4. Nos. 1542/5	1·10	1·25
1543	6500m. Female and calf	30	35
1544	6500m. Lion catching Blue wildebeest	30	35
1545	6500m. Blue wildebeest	30	35
1542/5	*Set of 4*	1·10	1·25

Nos. 1542/5 were printed together, *se-tenant*, in blocks of 4 in sheetlets of 16 (4×4).

305 *Leptailerus several*

306 *Laetiocottleya*

(Des J. Iskowitz. Litho Questa)

2000 (28 Apr). Wild Cats of the World. T **305** and similar multicoloured designs. P 14.

MS1546 134×200 mm. 3000m. Type **305**; 3000m. *Panthera onca*; 3000m. *Panthera tigris corbetti*; 3000m. *Puma concolor*; 3000m. *Panthera leo persica*; 3000m. *Felis pardina*; 3000m. *Lepardus pardalia*; 3000m. *Acinonyx jubatus*; 3000m. *Felis wrangeli* .... 1·30 1·40

MS1547 134×200 mm. 3000m. *Felis silvestris grampia*; 3000m. *Felis ourata*; 3000m. *Panthera tigris tigris*; 3000m. *Panthera uncia*; 3000m. *Felis caracal*; 3000m. *Panthera pardus*; 3000m. *Panthera tigris amoyensis*; 3000m. *Panthera once*; 3000m. *Neofelis nabuluso* .... 1·30 1·40

MS1548 Two sheets. (a) 25000m. 85×110 mm. *Panthera tigris altaica*. (b) 110×85 mm. 25000m. *Panthera tigris* (horiz). *Set of 2 sheets* .... 2·50 2·60

(Des Irina Lyampe. Litho Questa)

2000 (28 Apr). Exotic Flowers. T **306** and similar multicoloured designs. P 14.

MS1549 137×105 mm. 3000m. Type **306**; 3000m. *Papaver orientale* and *Nomada* (wasp); 3000m. *Anemone blanda*; 3000m. *Ipoema alba* and hawkmoth; 3000m. *Phalaenopsis luma* and *Delta unguiculata* (wasp); 3000m. *Iris ensata* and Colorado Beetle; 3000m. *Bomarea caldasil* and *Coenagrion puella* (dragonfly); 3000m. Rosa "Raubritter" and *Bombus hortorum* (bumble bee); 3000m. Iris×daylily hybrid and fly .... 1·20 1·30

MS1550 137×105 mm. 3000m. *Lilium auratum* and *Tragocephala variegata* (beetle); 3000m. *Oncidim macianthum* and beetle; 3000m. *Dendrobium* and *Agelia petali* (beetle); 3000m. *Cobaea scandens*; 3000m. *Paphiopedium gilda* and *Cotalpa linegera scarabaedae*; 3000m. *Papaver nudicaule* and *Delta unduiculate* (wasp); 3000m. *Colocasia esculenta*; 3000m. *Carinatum tricolor* and butterfly; 3000m. *Phalaenopsis* and locust .... 1·20 1·30

MS1551 125×103 mm. 3500m. *Euanthe sanderiana* and *Teiratαenia surinama* (grasshopper); 3500m. *Torenia fourleri*; 3500m. Pansies and *Papilio polyxenes caterpillar*; 3500m. *Gladiolus* "Preludio"; 3500m. *Dendrobium primulinum* and beetle; 3500m. Clematis "Lasurstern" and carrion beetle; 3500m. *Helianthus annuus* and beetle; 3500m. *Jacinto Grana* (all vert) .... 1·60 1·70

MS1552 Four sheets, each 100×70 mm. (a) 20000m. *Viola×wittrockiana* (pansies). (b) 20000m. *Nelimbo nucifera*. (c) 20000m. *Gerbera jamesoni*. (d) 20000m. Daffodils and anemones *Set of 4 sheets* .... 4·00 4·25

311 Cycling

2000. Sports and Chess. T **311** and similar horiz designs. Multicoloured. Litho. P 13½.

MS1562 140×115 mm. 6500m. Type **311**; 6500m. Volleyball; 6500m. Boxing; 6500m. Weightlifting; 6500m. Fencing; 6500m. Judo .... 1·80 1·90

MS1563 140×115 mm. 9000m. Six chess pieces, including red queen and elephant carrying palanquin; 9000m. Six pieces, including ivory bishop and grey bishop; 9000m. Five knights; 9000m. Six rooks, including red elephant and sailing ship; 9000m. Six pawns; 9000m. Six pawns, including soldiers, flute player and spearholder .... 2·75 2·75

MS1564 140×115 mm. 9500m. Paul Morphy; 9500m. Mikhaïl Botvinnik; 9500m. Emanuel Lasker; 9500m. Wilhelm Steinitz; 9500m. José Raúl Capablanca; 9500m. Howard Staunton .... 2·75 2·75

MS1565 140×115 mm. 12500m. Cricket (batsmen and bowler); 12500m. Cricket (four batsmen and fielder); 12500m. Polo players on horseback and elephant polo; 12500m. Four galloping polo players; 12500m. Golf (two men); 12500m. Man and woman playing golf .... 3·50 3·75

MS1566 140×115 mm. 14000m. Two tennis players (woman with headband serving at right); 14000m. Table tennis (two men); 14000m. Table tennis (man with pink shirt and woman); 14000m. Three tennis players (two men at left); 14000m. Tennis players (man with cap at left); 14000m. Table tennis (man with red shirt and woman) .... 3·50 3·75

MS1567 Two sheets, each 110×87 mm. (a) 35000m. Garry Kasparov (chess champion) (50×35 mm). (b) 35000m. Table tennis (50×35 mm) *Set of 2 sheets* .... 3·75 4·00

2001. Nos. 896, 1468 and 1490/1 surch with *** and face value.

1567*a* 3000m. on 8000m. Using computer ....
1567*b* 3000m. on 15,000m. Traditional dwelling
1567*c* 3000m. on 20,000m. Traditional dwelling
1567*d* 5000m. on 10m. Castor oil ....

312 Threadfin Butterflyfish

313 Luis Figo

(Des G. Capasso (**MS**1568, **MS**1572a/b), Irina Lyampe (**MS**1569, **MS**1572c), T. Wood (**MS**1570/1, **MS**1572d/e). Litho Walsall)

2001 (8 Aug). Marine Life. T **312** and similar horiz designs. Multicoloured. P 14.

MS1568 162×177 mm. 4550m. Type **312**; 4550m. Common clownfish; 4550m. Regal tang; 4550m. Regal angelfish; 4550m. Copperbanded butterflyfish; 4550m. Blue-girdled angelfish; 4550m. Sharpnosed pufferfish; 4550m. Humbug damselfish; 4550m. Tailbar lionfish; 4550m. Forcepsfish; 4550m. Powder blue surgeonfish; 4550m. Moorish idol .... 2·00 2·10

MS1569 155×117 mm. 9500m. Oceanic whitetip shark; 9500m. Grey reef shark; 9500m. Tiger shark; 9500m. Silky shark; 9500m. Basking shark; 9500m. Epaulette shark .... 2·75 3·00

MS1570 117×131 mm. 9500m. Sperm whale; 9500m. Giant squid; 9500m. Killer whale; 9500m. Great white shark; 9500m. Manta ray; 9500m. Octopus .... 2·75 3·00

MS1571 117×131 mm. 9500m. Blue whale; 9500m. Dolphinfish; 9500m. Hammerhead shark; 9500m. Whale shark; 9500m. Leatherback turtle; 9500m. Porkfish .... 2·75 3·00

MS1572 Five sheets, each 85×57 mm. (a) 35000m. Wimple fish. (b) 35000m. Queen angelfish. (c) 35000m. Phryniehthys wedli. (d) 35000m. Bull shark. (e) 35000m. Spotted trunkfish. *Set of 5 sheets* .... 9·00 9·25

2001. European Football Championships, Belgium and The Netherlands (2000). T **313** and similar square designs. Multicoloured. Litho. P 13½×13.

MS1573 131×99 mm. 10000m. Type **313**; 10000m. Fernando Couto; 10000m. Luis Figo diving at ball; 10000m. Sergio Conceicao; 10000m. Nuno Gomes; 10000m. Rui Costa .... 3·00 3·25

MS1574 131×99 mm. 17000m. Nicolas Anelka; 17000m. Didier Deschamps; 17000m. Emmanuel Petit; 17000m. Thierry Henry; 17000m. Marcel Desailly; 17000m. Zinedine Zidane .... 5·25 5·50

314 Domenico Fivaranti (swimming)

315 Mikhail Botvinnik

2001. Olympic Games, Sydney (2000). T **314** and similar square designs. Multicoloured. Litho. P 13½×13.

MS1575 131×135 mm. 8500m. Type **314**; 8500m. Stacy Dragila (pole vault); 8500m. Pieter van den Hoogenband (swimming); 8500m. David O'Connor (three day eventing); 8500m. Venus Williams (tennis); 8500m. Maurice Greene (athletics); 8500m. Joy Fawcett (football); 8500m. Marion Jones (athletics); 8500m. Patricio Ormazabal and Jeff Agoos (football) .... 3·75 4·00

MS1576 131×135 mm. 10000m. Agnes Kovacs (swimming); 10000m. Youlia Rasksina (gymnastics); 10000m. Kong Linghui and Lui Guoliang (table tennis); 10000m. Nicolas Gill; 10000m. Anky van Grunsven (dressage); 10000m. Brian Olsen; 10000m. Wang Nan (table tennis); 10000m. Megan Quann (swimming); 10000m. Venus Williams (tennis) 6·25 6·50

MS1577 131×99 mm. 17000m. Vince Carter (basketball); 17000m. Blaine Wilson (gymnastics); 17000m. Steve Keir (handball); 17000m. Wen Xiao Wang and Chris Xu (table tennis); 17000m. Venus and Serena Williams (tennis); 17000m. Gu Jun and Ge Fei (table tennis) 5·25 5·50

MS1578 131×99 mm. 20000m. Clara Hughes (cycling); 20000m. Martina Hingis (tennis); 20000m. Otilla Badescu (table tennis); 20000m. Isabel Fernandez (judo); 20000m. Coralie Simmons (water polo). 20000m. Mia Hamm (football) 6·00 6·25

MS1579 131×99 mm. 28000m. Patrick Rafter (tennis); 28000m. Tadahiro Nomura (judo); 28000m. Seiko Iseki (table tennis); 28000m. Michael Dodge (cycling); 28000m. Ann Dow (water polo); 28000m. David Beckham (football) 8·25 8·50

MS1580 Six sheets, each 95×98 mm. (a) 50000m. Andre Agassi (tennis). (b) 50000m. Chang Jun Gao and Michelle Do (table tennis). (c) 50000m. Kong Linghui (table tennis). (d) 50000m. Michelle Do (table tennis); (e) 100000m. Michelle Do. (f) 100000m. Serena Williams (tennis). (g) 100000m. Christophe Legout and Damien Eldi (table tennis). *Set of 6 sheets* 12·00 12·50

2001. Chess Players. T **315** and similar square designs. Multicoloured. Litho. P 13½×13.

MS1581 131×135 mm. 10000m. Type **315**; 10000m. Garry Kasparov; 10000m. Wilhelm Steinitz; 10000m. Emanuel Lasker; 10000m. Paul Morphy; 10000m. Anatoly Karpov; 10000m. Tigran Petrossian; 10000m. Mikhail Tal; 10000m. José Raul Capablanca 4·00 4·25

MS1582 131×135 mm. 10000m. Judith Polgar (wearing maroon jumper); 10000m. Xie Jun; 10000m. Zsuza Polgar; 10000m. Nana Ioseliani; 10000m. Alisa Galliamova; 10000m. Judith Polgar (with head in hands); 10000m. Judith Polgar (wearing blouse); 10000m. Monica Calzetta; 10000m. Anjelina Belakovskaia 4·00 4·25

MS1583 Two sheets, each 96×100 mm. (a) 100000m. Garry Kasparov. (b) 100000m. Judith Polgar. *Set of 2 sheets* 5·00 5·25

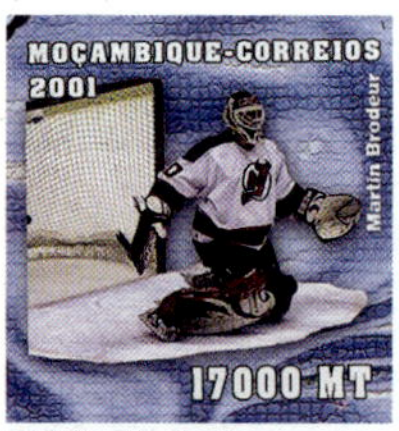

316 Martin Brodeur (ice hockey goalkeeper)

317 Skier

2001. Winter Olympic Games, Salt Lake City (2002). T **316** and similar square designs. Multicoloured. Litho. P 13½×13.

MS1584 131×99 mm. 17000m. Type **316**; 17000m. Svetlana Vysokova (speed skating); 17000m. Ray Bourque and Patrik Elias (ice hockey); 17000m. Rachel Belliveau (cross-country skiing); 17000m. Scott Gomez and Janne Laukkanen (ice hockey); 17000m. Sonja Nef (skiing) 5·00 5·25

MS1585 131×99 mm. 20000m. Rusty Smith (speed skating); 20000m. Sandra Schmirler (curling); Totmianina and Marinin (ice skating); 20000m. Brigitte Obermoser (skiing); 20000m. Roman Turek (ice hockey); 20000m. Jennifer Heil (skiing) 5·00 5·25

MS1586 131×99 mm. 28000m. Kovarikova and Novotny (skating); 28000m. Li Song (speed skating); 28000m. Armin Zoeggeler (bobsleigh); 28000m. Michael von Gruenigen (skiing); 28000m. Tami Bradley (skiing); 28000m. Chris Drury, Turner Stevenson and Greg de Vries (ice hockey) 8·00 8·25

MS1587 Three sheets, each 95×98 mm. (a) 50000m. Armin Zoggeler (toboggan). (b) 75000m. Tommy Salo. (c) 100000m. Jayne Torvill and Christopher Dean (ice dancing). *Set of 3 sheets* 10·00 10·50

(Litho BDT)

2002 (6 May). Winter Olympic Games, Salt Lake City, U.S.A (2nd issue). T **317** and similar multicoloured design. P 13½.

1588 10000m. Type **317** 50 55

1589 17000m. Skier upside down (vert) 85 90

318 Dhow

319 Princess Diana

(Litho BDT)

2002 (6 May). Ships. T **318** and similar multicoloured designs. P 13½.

MS1590 147×105 mm. 13500m. Type **318**; 13500m. Junk; 13500m. Galleon; 13500m. Schooner; 13500m. Full-rigged ship; 13500m. Barque 4·00 4·25

MS1591 147×105 mm. 13500m. Viking longboat; 13500m. Canoe; 13500m. Gondola; 13500m. Fishing boat; 13500m. Light boat; 13500m. Tug 4·00 4·25

MS1592 Two sheets. (a) 79×60 mm. 40000m. Aircraft carrier; (b) 60×80 mm. 40000m. Figurehead (vert). *Set of 2 sheets* 4·00 4·25

(Litho BDT)

2002 (6 May). Diana, Princess of Wales Commemoration (3rd issue). T **319** and similar vert designs. Multicoloured. P 13½.

MS1593 Three sheets each 132×135 mm. (a) 28000m. Type **319**; 28000m. Wearing feathered hat; 28000m. Wearing pearl necklace; 28000m. Wearing wide brimmed hat. (b) 28000m. Wearing blue top; 28000m. Wearing white top; 28000m. Looking right; 28000m. Holding bouquet. (c) 28000m. Wearing pink outfit; 28000m. Wearing black with drop earrings; 28000m. Looking straight ahead; 28000m. Wearing black and white outfit 12·00 12·50

MS1594 Three sheets each 81×112 mm. (a) 50000m. Wearing hat and wrap. (b) 50000m. With hand on chin; (c) 50000m. Wearing large stud earrings. *Set of 3 sheets* 7·50 8·00

320 Amerigo Vespucci

321 England World Cup Poster

(Litho BDT)

2002 (6 May). 500th Anniv (2001) of Amerigo Vespucci's Third Voyage. T **320** and similar multicoloured designs. P 13½.

MS1595 157×117 mm. 30000m. Type **320**; 30000m. Green parrot; 30000m. Homes on stilts and ship 4·50 4·75

MS1596 55×76 mm. 50000m. Outline of Brazil and ship's course 2·50 2·75

(Litho BDT)

2002 (6 May). World Cup Football Championship, Japan and South Korea. T **321** and similar multicoloured designs. P 13½.

MS1597 Two sheets each 153×175 mm. (a) 28000m. Type **321**; 28000m. Italian player; 28000m. Danish player (red strip); 28000m. Colombian player; 28000m. Munhak stadium (55×41 mm). (b) 28000m. Brazilian player; 28000m. Swedish poster; 28000m. Nigerian player; 28000m. Danish player (white strip); 28000m. Gwangju stadium (55×41 mm) 12·00 12·50

MS1598 Two sheets. (a) 53×73 mm. 50000m. Pelé (Brazilian player). (b) 73×53 mm. 50000m. Max Morlock (German player). *Set of 2 sheets* 5·00 5·25

322 Horse

323 Mount Binga, Mozambique

(Litho BDT)

2002 (6 May). Chinese New Year ("Year of the Horse"). T **322** and similar multicoloured designs. P 13½.

MS1599 68×58 mm. 11000m. Type **322**; 11000m. Purple and red horse; 11000m. Purple horse; 11000m. Orange and red horse ... 2·20 2·30

MS1600 100×70 mm. 22000m. Horse cantering (27×41 mm) ... 55 60

(Litho BDT)

2002 (6 May). International Year of Mountains. T **323** and similar horiz designs. Multicoloured. P 13½.

1601	17000m. Type **323**	85	90
1602	17000m. Mount Namuli, Mozambique	85	90

MS1603 160×98 mm. 17000m. Mount Kenya, Kenya; 17000m. Mount Cook, New Zealand; 17000m. Mount Ararat, Turkey; 17000m. Mount Paine, Chile; 17000m. Mount Everest, Nepal; 17000m. Mount Kilimanjaro, Tanzania ... 5·00 5·25

MS1604 72×51 mm. 50000m. Mount Zugspitze, Germany ... 2·50 3·00

324 *Papilio demoleus*

325 *Hemerocallis*

(Litho BDT)

2002 (17 June). Butterflies. T **324** and similar vert designs. Multicoloured. P 14.

1605	5000m. Type **324**	25	30
1606	10000m. *Euschemon rafflesia*	50	55
1607	17000m. *Liphyra brassolis*	85	90
1608	28000m. *Mimacraea marshalli*	1·40	1·50
1605/8	*Set of 4*	2·75	3·00

MS1609 Two sheets each 112×155 mm. (a) 10000m. Parides coon; 10000m. *Delias mysis*; 10000m. *Troides brookiana*; 10000m. *Syrmatia dorilas*; 10000m. *Danis danis*; 10000m. *Lycaena dispar*; 10000m. *Mesene phareus*; 10000m. *Kallima inachus*; 10000m. *Morpho rhetenor*. (b) 10000m. *Eurema brigitta*; 10000m. *Loxura atymunus*; 10000m. *Arhopala amantes*; 10000m. *Junonia coenia*; 10000m. *Eurides isabella*; 10000m. *Heliconius ricini*; 10000m. *Zipaetis xcylax* (scylax); 10000m. *Cepheuptychia cephus*; 10000m. *Philaethria dido*. *Set of 2 sheets* ... 9·00 9·25

MS1610 Two sheets each 106×81 mm. (a) 50000m. *Papilio cresphontes*. (b) 50000m. *Ornithoptera alexandrae*. *Set of 2 sheets* ... 5·00 5·25

(Litho BDT)

2002 (17 June). Flowers. T **325** and similar multicoloured designs. P 14.

MS1611 Three sheets. (a) 150×117 mm. 10000m. Type **325**; 10000m. *Nazcissys* (Narcissus); 10000m. Hybrid tea; 10000m. *Cayenne Capers*; 10000m. *Araceae*; 10000m. *Hymenocallis narcissiflora*; 10000m. *Hymenocallis*; 10000m. *Tulipa*; 10000m. *Lachenalia aloides* and *meconopsis poppies*. (b) 150×117 mm. 10000m. *Narcissus*; 10000m. *L. Bulbiferum var croceum*; 10000m. *Iris purpureobractea* and butterfly; 10000m. *Neomarica caerulea*; 10000m. *Peonia lactiflora*, *Primula chungensis* and *Viola cornuta*; 10000m. *Cayenne caper* and beetle; 10000m. *Iris purpureobractea*; 10000m. *Tuberous begonia cultivar*; 10000m. *Oriental hybrid lily*. (c) 108×160 mm. 10000m. *Viola jeannie*; 10000m. Sunflower; 10000m. *Momo botan*; 10000m. *Scho,buzgkia orchid*; 10000m. *Dahlia hybrid*; 10000m. *Sparaxis elegans harlequin*; 10000m. *Dianthus*; 10000m. *Tulipa saxatilis* and *camassia leichtlinii*; 10000m. Hybrid ("Hibrid"). *Set of 3 sheets* .. 13·00 13·50

326 *Tachymarptis melba*

327 *Creagrus furcatus*

(Litho BDT)

2002 (17 June). Birds. T **326** and similar multicoloured designs. P 14.

1612	5000m. Type **326**	25	30
1613	5000m. *Falco tinnunculus*	25	30
1614	10000m. *Ardea cinerea*	50	55
1615	10000m. *Pitta angolensis*	50	55
1616	17000m. *Corythaeola cristata*	85	90
1617	28000m. *Butastur rufipennis*	1·40	1·50
1612/7	*Set of 6*	3·50	3·75

MS1618 Two sheets each 116×116 mm. (a) 17000m. *Coracias garrulus*; 17000m. *Estrilda astrild*; 17000m. *Upupa epops*; 17000m. *Merops apiaster*; 17000m. *Ploceus Cucullatus*; 17000m. *Clamator glandarius*. (b) 17000m. *Psittacus erithacus*; 17000m. *Ficedula hypoleuca*; 17000m. *Tchagra senegala*; 17000m. *Oriolus oriolus*; 17000m. *Luscinia megarhynchos*; 17000m. *Halcyon malimbica* ... 10·00 10·50

MS1619 Four sheets. (a) 83×108 mm. 50000m. *Strix varia*. (b) 83×108 mm. 50000m. *Falco subbuteo*. (c) 83×108 mm. 50000m. *Butorides striatus*. (d) 108×83 mm. 50000m. *Actophilornis africana* (africanus) (horiz). *Set of 4 sheets* ... 10·00 10·50

The stamps in No. **MS**1618a/b were printed together, *se-tenant*, with the backgrounds forming composite designs.

(Litho BDT)

2002 (17 June). Sea Birds. T **327** and similar multicoloured designs. P 14.

1620	5000m. Type **327**	25	30
1621	10000m. *Larosterna inca*	50	55
1622	17000m. *Pelecanus crispus*	85	90
1623	28000m. *Morus bassanus*	1·20	1·50
1620/3	*Set of 4*	2·50	3·00

MS1624 110×162 mm. 10000m. *Phaethon aethereus*; 10000m. *Catharacta maccormicki*; 10000m. *Diomedea bulleri*; 10000m. *Puffinus iherminieri*; 10000m. *Oceanities oceanicus*; 10000m. *Pterodroma hasitata*; 10000m. *Fregata magnificens*; 10000m. *Sula nebouxii*; 10000m. *Uria aagle* ... 4·50 4·75

MS1625 Two sheets. (a) 98×68 mm. 50000m. *Spheniscus demersus*. (b) 97×68 mm. 50000m. *Rynchops niger* (horiz). *Set of 2 sheets* ... 5·00 5·25

The stamps in No. **MS**1624 were printed together, *se-tenant*, with the background forming a composite design.

328 Maine Coon Cat

329 Protosaurus

(Litho BDT)

2002 (17 June). Cats. T **328** and similar square designs. Multicoloured. P 13½.

MS1626 118×91 mm. 17000m. Type **328**; 17000m. Cornish Rex; 17000m. La Perm (Red Tabby); 17000m. Sphynx; 17000m. Siamese; 17000m. Persian ... 4·25 4·25

MS1627 66×96 mm. 50000m. Chestnut (Oriental Longhair) ... 2·50 2·75

(Litho BDT)

2002 (17 June). Dogs. Square designs as T **328**. Multicoloured. P 13½.

MS1628 118×91 mm. 17000m. Labrador; 17000m. Bulldog; 17000m. Cocker spaniel; 17000m. Golden retriever; 17000m. Boxer; 17000m. Bloodhound ... 5·00 5·25

MS1629 66×96 mm. 40000m. Basset hound ... 2·00 2·10

(Litho BDT)

2002 (17 June). Horses. Square designs as T **328**. Multicoloured. P 13½.

MS1630 118×91 mm. 17000m. Hanoverian; 17000m. Haflinger; 17000m. Nonius; 17000m. Belgian heavy draughts; 17000m. Australian-bred Arab; 17000m. Thoroughbred .... 5·00 5·25

MS1631 96×66 mm. 50000m. Two Don horses .... 2·50 2·75

(Litho BDT)

2002 (17 June). Prehistoric Animals. T **329** and similar multicoloured designs. P 14.

1632	5000m. Type **329**	25	30
1633	10000m. Psittacosaurus	50	55
1634	17000m. Torosaurus	85	90
1635	28000m. Triceratops	1·40	1·50
1632/5	*Set of 4*	2·75	3·00

MS1636 Two sheets each 180×135 mm. (a) 10000m. Diplodocus; 10000m. Pterosaurs; 10000m. Young diplodocus; 10000m. Afrovenator; 10000m. Parasarolophus; 10000m. Ramphorincus; 10000m. Lambeosaur; 10000m. Euoplocephalus; 10000m. Cynodont. (b) 10000m. Brachiosaur; 10000m. Monoclonius; 10000m. Homalocephale; 10000m. Pterodactyl; 10000m. Deinonychus; 10000m. Archaeopteryx; 10000m. Cretaceous landscape; 10000m. Hypsilophodon; 10000m. Lystrosaur .... 9·00 9·25

MS1637 Two sheets. (a) 100×68 mm. 50000m. Baryonyx. (b) 100×70 mm. 50000m. Styracosaurus (vert). *Set of 2 sheets* .... 5·00 5·25

The stamps in No. **MS**1636a/b were each printed together, *se-tenant*, plus labels, with the backgrounds forming composite designs.

330 *Heraclides cresphontes*

331 Scout Badge

(Litho BDT)

2002 (17 June). Woodland Fauna and Flora. T **330** and similar horiz designs. Multicoloured. P 14.

MS1638 Two sheets each 153×115 mm. (a) 10000m. Type **330**; 10000m. *Tyto alba*; 10000m. *Drocopus pileatus*; 10000m. *Archilochus colobris* (colubris) (Ruby-throated Hummingbird) and *Cypripedium parviflorum*; 10000m. *Vulpes vulpes*; 10000m. *Odocoileus virginianus*; 10000m. *Enallagma sp.*; 10000m. *Amanita muscaria*; 10000m. *Tamiasciurus hudsonicus*. (b) 10000m. *Pandion haliaetus*; 10000m. Flying squirrel; 10000m. Fox squirrel; 10000m. *Agelaius phoeniceus*; 10000m. *Papilio polyxenes*; 10000m. *Didelphus viginiana*; 10000m. *Hyla crucifer*; 10000m. Two *Odocoileus virginianus*; 10000m. *Procyon lotor* .... 9·00 9·25

The stamps in No. **MS**1638a/b were each printed together, *se-tenant*, with the backgrounds forming composite designs.

2002 (2 Sept). World Scout Congress. T **331** and similar multicoloured designs. Litho. P 13½.

MS1639 109×99 mm. 28000m. Type **331**; 28000m. 19th Jamboree badge; 28000m. Tiger mascot; 28000m. 20th Jamboree logo .... 5·50 5·75

MS1640 111×82 mm. 28000m. Scout (vert) .... 1·40 1·50

332 African Elephant

333 Lord Baden Powell

(Litho BDT)

2002 (20 Sept). Endangered Animals. African Elephant. T **332** and similar horiz designs. Multicoloured. P 13½.

1641	1900m. Type **332**	10	10
	a. Sheetlet. Nos. 1641/4	35	35
1642	1900m. Elephants at waterhole	10	10
1643	1900m. Elephant in swamp	10	10
1644	1900m. Elephant with calf	10	10
1641/4	*Set of 4*	35	35

MS1645 145×170 mm. Nos. 1641/4 plus four stamp-sized labels, each picturing Prince Bernhard or elephants 45 45

Nos. 1641/4 were printed together, *se-tenant*, as horizontal or vertical strips of 4, throughout sheetlets of 16.

2002 (28 Sept). World Scout Jamboree (2003). T **333** and similar vert designs showing Lord Baden Powell and plants or butterflies. Multicoloured. Litho. P 13½×13.

MS1646 Two sheets each 133×101 mm. (a) 17000m. Type **333**; 17000m. *Morpho Aega*; 17000m. *Prepona meander*; 17000m. *Charaxes bernardus*; 17000m. *Hypolimnas salmacis*; 17000m. *Morpho rhetenor*. (b) 17000m. Four mushrooms; 17000m. Two pink and white flowers; 17000m. Three orange mushrooms; 17000m. Five purple and red flowers; 17000m. Three brownish white mushrooms; 17000m. Two striped-petal flowers .... 10·00 10·50

MS1647 98×100 mm. 88000m. Lord Baden Powell with arms crossed .... 4·25 4·50

2002 (28 Sept). Aviation. Sheet 96×100 mm containing vert designs as T **333**. Multicoloured. Litho. P 13½×13.

MS1648 22000m. Antoine de Saint-Exupery; 22000m. Charles Lindbergh and *Spirit of St. Louis*; 22000m. Charles Lindbergh and light aircraft; 22000m. Concorde .... 2·30 2·40

2002 (28 Sept). Cinematic Personalities. Sheet 97×101 mm containing vert designs as T **333**. Multicoloured. Litho. P 13½×13.

MS1649 25000m. Charlie Chaplin; 25000m. Frank Sinatra; 25000m. Alfred Hitchcock; 25000m. Walt Disney ....

2002 (28 Sept). John Audubon (ornithologist) Commemoration. Vert designs as T **333**. Multicoloured. Litho. P 13½×13.

MS1650 97×101 mm. 33000m. John Audubon; 33000m. *Aix sponsa*; 33000m. *Toxostoma rufum* ("Toxastoma montanum") and *Ixoreus naevius*; 33000m. *Loxia Leucoptera* .... 3·25 3·50

MS1651 Two sheets each 97×101 mm. (a) 11000m. *Quiscalus quiscula*. (b) 11000m. *Columba leucocephala* ("Patagioenas leucocephala"). *Set of 2 sheets* 60 65

2002 (28 Sept). 40th Death Anniv of Marilyn Monroe. Vert designs as T **333**. Litho. P 13½×13.

MS1652 Two sheets each 133×101 mm. (a) 17000m. Looking at camera; 17000m. Wearing drop earrings; 17000m. Laughing; 17000m. Wearing choker; 17000m. Looking over shoulder; 17000m. Looking surprised. (b) 17000m. Wearing sleeveless top; 17000m. Looking over shoulder (different); 17000m. Beckoning with finger; 17000m. Wearing fur stole and drop earrings; 17000m. With arms folded; 17000m. Smiling with long hair. *Set of 2 sheets* .... 10·00 10·50

MS1653 Two sheets each 97×100 mm. (a) 88000m. Wearing crochet top. (b) 88000m. Wearing red top with pearls. *Set of 2 sheets* .... 4·50 4·75

2002 (28 Sept). Visits of Pope John Paul II. Vert designs as T **333**. Multicolored. Litho. P 13½×13.

MS1654 133×100 mm. 15000m. Pope John Paul II waving; 15000m. Wearing red robe; 15000m. Carrying Pastoral staff; 15000m. Wearing mitre; 15000m. Sitting in chair; 15000m. Looking left .... 4·75 5·00

MS1655 97×100 mm. 20000m. Princess Diana wearing poppy; 20000m. Princess Diana carrying bouquet; 20000m. The Pope looking down; 20000m. The Pope looking up .... 4·00 4·25

MS1656 Two sheets each 97×100 mm. (a) 88000m. Pope John Paul II. (b) 110000m. Mother Teresa. *Set of 2 sheets* .... 5·00 5·25

2002 (28 Sept). Egyptian Pharaohs. Vert designs as T **333**. Multicoloured. Litho. P 13½×13.

MS1657 Two sheets each 133×100 mm. (a) 15000m. Seti I; 15000m. Djedefre; 15000m. Smenkhkare; 15000m. Seti II; 15000m. Senusret III; 15000m. Tutankhamun. (b) 17000m. Netjenkhet Djoser; 17000m. Death mask of Tutankhamun (front); 17000m. Neferefre; 17000m. Amenhotep III; 17000m. Pepi I; 17000m. Amenmesses .... 7·25 7·50

MS1658 Three sheets each 98×100 mm. (a) 20000m. Amenhotep II; 20000m. Merenptah; 20000m. Amenophis IV; 20000m. Tuthmosis (stone). (b) 20000m. Nefertiti (profile); 20000m. Cleopatra VII; 20000m. Nefertari (facing left); 20000m. Nefertiti (front). (c) 20000m. Nefertari (facing right); 20000m. Death mask of Tutankhamun (from angle); 20000m. Tuthmosis (black and gold); Nefertiti (from angle). *Set of 3 sheets* .... 11·00 11·50

MS1659 Two sheets each 97×101 mm. (a) 110000m. Nefertiti. (b) 110000m. Tutankhamun. *Set of 2 sheets* 1·00 1·50

2002 (28 Sept). Nobel Prize Winners. Vert designs as T **333**. Multicoloured. Litho. P 13½×13.

MS1660 Two sheets each 133×100 mm. (a) 15000m. Henri ("Hemri") Dunant; 15000m. Theodore Roosevelt; 15000m. Albert Einstein; 15000m. Ernest Hemingway; 15000m. Thomas Nast; 15000m. Albert Camus. (b) 17000m. Albert Einstein with hands clasped; 17000m. Dalai Lama; 17000m. Winston Churchill; 17000m. Hideki Yukawa; 17000m. Albert Schweitzer; 17000m. Linus Pauling. *Set of 2 sheets* 8·25 8·25

Although included in the set, Thomas Nast was not the recipient of a Nobel Prize.

2002 (28 Sept). Robert Stephenson Commemoration. Vert designs as T **333**. Multicoloured. Litho. P 13½×13.

MS1661 97×100 mm. 25000m. Robert Stephenson (blue-black); 25000m. Early US steam locomotive; 25000m. Great Western Railway steam locomotive; 25000m. Early steam locomotive 5·00 5·50

MS1662 Two sheets each 97×101 mm. (a) 110000m. Robert Stephenson (dark sepia). (b) 110000m. Robert Stephenson (bronze-green). *Set of 2 sheets* 2·75 2·50

2002 (28 Sept). Explorers. Vert designs as T **333**. Multicoloured. Litho. P 13½×13.

MS1663 97×101 mm. 22000m. Vasco de Gama; 22000m. Ferdinand Magellan; 22000m. Christopher Columbus; 22000m. Amerigo Vespucci 1·10 1·20

MS1664 97×101 mm. 110000m. Vasco de Gama 5·50 5·75

2002 (28 Sept). Charles Darwin and Alexander Fleming Commemorations. Sheet 97×100 mm containing vert designs as T **333**. Multicoloured. Litho. P 13½×13.

MS1665 33000m. Charles Darwin and Byronosaurus; 33000m. Alexander Fleming and *Tricholoma terreum*; 33000m. Alexander Fleming and *Boletus edulis*; 33000m. Charles Darwin and Irratator 6·00 6·25

2002 (28 Sept). Composers. Vert designs as T **333**. Multicoloured. Litho. P 13½×13.

MS1666 97×101 mm. 5000m. Antonio Vivaldi; 5000m. Franz Liszt; 5000m. Ludwig van Beethoven; 5000m. Wolfgang Mozart 1·00 1·00

MS1667 97×101 mm. 88000m. Wolfgang Mozart at piano 2·20 2·30

2002 (28 Sept). 25th Death Anniv of Elvis Presley (entertainer). Vert designs as T **333**. Multicoloured. Litho. P 13½×13.

MS1668 133×101 mm. 15000m. Wearing jacket and tie; 15000m. Looking down in cable-knit sweater; 15000m. Wearing white shirt; 15000m. Wearing square checked shirt; 15000m. Reclining in cable-knit sweater; 15000m. Wearing hat 4·50 4·75

MS1669 97×100 mm. 110000m. Wearing blue jacket 5·50 5·75

2002 (28 Sept). Personalities. Vert designs as T **333**. Multicoloured. Litho. P 13½×13.

MS1670 Three sheets each 97×100 mm. (a) 20000m. Che Guevara; 20000m. Pope John Paul II; 20000m. Martin Luther King; 20000m. Mao Zedung. (b) 22000m. Dalai Lama; 22000m. Mother Teresa; 22000m. Pope John Paul II waving; 22000m. Mahatma Gandhi. (c) 33000m. Albert Schweitzer; 33000m. Claude Bernard; 33000m. Henri Dunant; 33000m. Raoul Follerau 10·00 10·50

2002 (28 Sept). Formula 1 Motor Sport. Sheet 97×100 mm containing vert designs as T **333**. Multicoloured. Litho. P 13½×13.

MS1671 20000m. Ayrton Senna; 20000m. Modern Formula 1 racing car; 20000m. Early Formula 1 racing car; 20000m. Juan Manuel Fangio 4·00 4·25

2002 (28 Sept). Birth Centenary of Victor Hugo (author). Sheet 97×101 mm containing vert design as T **333**. Multicoloured. Litho. P 13½×13.

MS1672 88000m. Victor Hugo 4·25 4·50

2002 (28 Sept). John F. Kennedy (President of USA 1961–3) Commemoration. Sheet 97×101 mm. Vert design as T **333**. Multicoloured. Litho. P 13½×13.

MS1673 88000m. John F. Kennedy 4·25 4·50

2002 (28 Sept). Political Leaders. Sheet 97×100 mm containing vert designs as T **333**. Multicoloured. Litho. P 13½×13.

MS1674 25000m. Winston Churchill; 25000m. John F. Kennedy; 25000m. Konrad Adenauer; 25000m. Charles de Gaulle 5·00 5·25

(Litho UAB Stamperija)

2002 (28 Sept). Haroun Tazieff (French vulcanologist and geologist) Commemoration. Sheet 97×100 mm containing vert designs as T **333**. Multicoloured. P 13½×13.

MS1675 25000m. Scipionyx and erupting volcano; 25000m. Beipiaosaurus and erupting volcano; 25000m. Haroun Tazieff wearing radiation suit and vanadinite rock; 25000m. Haroun Tazieff and adamite rock 5·00 5·25

(Litho UAB Stamperija)

2002 (28 Sept). Astronauts and Concorde. Vert designs as T **333**. Multicoloured. P 13½×13.

MS1676 133×101 mm. 17000m. Michael Collins; 17000m. Concorde taking off to right;17000m. John Glenn ("Genn"); 17000m. Concorde flying left; 17000m. Neil Armstrong; 17000m. Concorde taking off to left 4·75 5·00

MS1677 97×101 mm. 88000m. John Glenn 4·25 4·50

(Litho UAB Stamperija)

2002 (28 Sept). 180th Birth Anniv of Louis Pasteur (French Chemist). Sheet 97×101 mm containing vert designs as T **333**, each showing Louis Pasteur with a different breed of dog. Multicoloured. P 13½×13.

MS1678 25000m. Husky; 25000m. Weimaraner; 25000m. Wolfhound; 25000m. Springer spaniel 5·00 5·25

(Litho UAB Stamperija)

2002 (28 Sept). Fifth Death Anniv of Diana, Princess of Wales. Vert designs as T **333**. Multicoloured. Litho. P 13½×13.

MS1679 133×100 mm. 15000m. Diana and Pope John Paul II; 15000m. Wearing white halter-neck top; 15000m. Wearing red hat and spotted top; 15000m. Holding award; 15000m. Wearing deep purple dress; 15000m. Wearing blue dress and choker 4·75 5·00

MS1680 97×101 mm. 88000m. Wearing tiara 4·25 4·50

334 Ferdinand von Zeppelin

335 Mercedes (1906)

(Litho BDT)

2002 (18 Nov). Ferdinand von Zeppelin (inventor) Commemoration. T **334** and similar multicoloured designs. P 13½.

MS1681 Two sheets each 173×120 mm. (a) 28000m. Type **334**; 28000m. LZ 2 airship (1905); 28000m. LZ10 airship (1911); 28000m. LZ 1 airship (1900). (b) 28000m. LZ 1 airship over water; 28000m. LZ 2 airship over water; 28000m. LZ 10 airship over field of sheep; 28000m. Ferdinand von Zeppelin holding binoculars. *Set of 2 sheets* 10·00 10·50

MS1682 Two sheets. (a) 106×70 mm. 50000m. Ferdinand von Zeppelin wearing shirt and tie (vert). (b) 70×106 mm. 50000m. Ferdinand von Zeppelin wearing army uniform (vert). *Set of 2 sheets* 5·00 5·25

(Litho BDT)

2002 (18 Nov). Vintage Cars (1st series). Racing Cars. T **335** and similar horiz designs. Multicoloured. P 13½.

MS1683 Two sheets each 172×146 mm. (a) 13000m. Type **335**; 13000m. Morgan (1951); 13000m. Sunbeam (1912); 13000m. Sunbeam (1922); 13000m. Sunbeam Tiger (1925); 13000m. Austin 100 HP (1908). (b) 13000m. Bentley (1912); 13000m. Delage Grand Prix (1914); 13000m. Healey Silverstone (1949); 13000m. Duesenberg (1922); 13000m. Delage 1500cc Grand Prix; 13000m. Ferrari 375 F1 (1961). *Set of 2 sheets* 8·25 8·50

MS1684 Two sheets. (a) 100×70 mm. 40000m. Marmon Wasp (1911). (b) 70×100 mm. 40000m. Alfa Romeo (1931). *Set of 2 sheets* 8·00 8·25

336 Austin (1908)

337 Western Railway of France

(Litho BDT)

2002 (18 Nov). Vintage Cars (2nd series). T **336** and similar horiz designs. Multicoloured. P 13½.

MS1685 Two sheets each 165×102 mm. (a) 17000m. Type **336**; 17000m. Studebaker Coupe (1937): 17000m. Type 40GP Bugatti (1930); 17000m. Ford Model A Roadster (1931); 17000m. Alfa Romeo 2900B (1937); 17000m. Cord 812 (1937). (b) 17000m. Type **57** Bugatti Alalanta Coupe (1937); 17000m. Tucker Torpedo (1948); 17000m. Honda S 800M (1966); 17000m. Cisitalia 202 GT (1946): 17000m. Chevrolet Impala (1958); 17000m. Cadillac LaSalle Convertible (1934). *Set of 2 sheets* .... 10·00 10·50

MS1686 Two sheets each 92×60 mm. (a) 50000m. Mercedes Benz SSK (1928). (b) 50000m. Plymouth Fury (1957). *Set of 2 sheets* .... 4·75 5·00

(Litho BDT)

2002 (18 Nov). Trains. T **337** and similar multicoloured designs. P 13½.

MS1687 Three sheets each 161×114 mm. (a) 17000m. Type **337**; 17000m. Netherlands State Railway (bridge); 17000m. Great Indian Peninsula Railway; 17000m. Paris Orleans Railway; 17000m. Madras and Southern Mahratta Railway of India; 17000m. Netherlands State Railway. (b) 17000m. Great Southern Railway of Spain ; 17000m. Shantung Railway of China; 17000m. Shanghai-Nanking Railway of China; 17000m. Austrian State Railway; 17000m. Victorian Government Railways of Australia; 17000m. London and Northwestern Railways. (c) 17000m. London, Midland and Scottish Railway; 17000m. Great Northern Railway of Ireland; 17000m. Southern Railway of England; 17000m. Great Northern Railway of USA; 17000m. Chicago, Milwaukee, St. Paul and Pacific Railroad; 17000m. London and Northeastern Railway. *Set of 3 sheets* .... 12·00 12·50

MS1688 Two sheets each 98×67 mm. (a) 50000m. New York Central Lines (vert). (b) 50000m. London, Brighton and South Coast Railway (vert). *Set of 2 sheets* .... 4·75 5·00

337a Pote

337b Justino Chemane

337c Bauxite

(Litho State Printing Works, Maputo)

2002 (2 Dec). Pottery. T **337a** and similar vert designs. Multicoloured.

1688*a* 1000m. Pote ....
1688*b* 2000m. Chaleira ....
1688*c* 4000m. Tacas ....
1688*d* 5000m. Cantaro ....
1688*e* 17,000m. Panela ....
1688*f* 28,000m. Alguidar ....
1688*g* 50,000m. Jarra ....
1688*h* 1000,000m. Bihas ....

(Litho State Printing Works, Maputo)

2003 (11 July). Justino Chemane, composer of national anthem.

1688*i* **337b** 6000m. multicoloured ....

2004 (30 Apr). Minerals. T **337c** and similar vert designs. Multicoloured. Litho.

1688*j* 5000m. Bauxite ....
1688*k* 14,000m. Marble ....
1688*l* 19,000m. ....
1688*m* 33,000m. Gold ....

338 "October" (James Jacques Tissot)

339 National Flags, Buildings, Panda and Giraffe

2004 (17 June). Paintings. T **338** and similar vert designs. Multicoloured. Litho. P 13½×13.

1689/1694 6500m. ×6, Type **338**; "Seaside" (James Jacques Tissot); "The Bunch of Lilacs" (James Jacques Tissot); "The Traveller" (James Jacques Tissot); "Young Lady holding Japanese Objects" (James Jacques Tissot); "Young Lady in a Boat" (James Jacques Tissot) .... 1·80 1·90
a. Sheetlet. Nos. 1689/94 .... 1·80 1·90

1695/1700 6500m. ×6, "Portrait of Madame de Senonnes" (Jean Auguste Ingres); "The Virgin of the Host" (Jean Auguste Ingres); "Portrait of Countess D'Haussonville" (Jean Auguste Ingres); "Paolo and Francesca" (Jean Auguste Ingres); "Portrait of Baroness James de Rothschild" (Jean Auguste Ingres); "Portrait of Madame Moitessier Sitting" (Jean Auguste Ingres) .... 1·80 1·90
a. Sheetlet. Nos. 1695/1700 .... 1·80 1·90

1701/6 10000m. ×6, "The Promenade" (Pierre Auguste Renoir); "Alfred Sisley and His Wife" (Pierre Auguste Renoir); "Little Miss Romaine Lacaux" (Pierre Auguste Renoir); "In the Summer" (Pierre Auguste Renoir); "The Dancer" (Pierre Auguste Renoir); "Bouquet of Chrysanthemums" (Pierre Auguste Renoir) .... 3·00 3·25
a. Sheetlet. Nos. 1701/6 .... 3·00 3·25

1707/12 17000m. ×6, "Miss La La at the Circus Fernando" (Edgar Degas); "Portrait of Madame Dietz-Monnin" (Edgar Degas); "Woman Ironing" (Edgar Degas); "The Star" (Edgar Degas); "Cafe Concert Singer" (Edgar Degas); "The Dance Examination" (Edgar Degas) .... 3·00 3·25
a. Sheetlet. Nos. 1707/12 .... 3·00 3·25

MS1713 Three sheets, each 87×133 mm. (a) 6500m. As No. 1693. (b) "Madame Monet in Japanese Costume" (Claude Monet). (c) "Charlotte Dubourg" (Henri Fantin-Latour). *Set of 3 sheets* .... 3·50 3·75

Nos. 1689/94, 1695/1700, 1701/6 and 1707/12 were each printed together, *se-tenant*, in sheetlets of 6 stamps.

2005 (25 June). 30th Anniv of Diplomatic Relations between Mozambique and Republic of China. T **339** and similar vert design. Multicoloured. Litho.

1714 33,000m. Type **339** ....
a. Horiz pair. Nos. 1714/15 ....
1715 33,000m. Arms, Admiral Zheng He and building ....

Nos. 1714/15 were printed together, *se-tenant*, in horizontal pairs throughout the sheet.

340 Emblem and Transport

341 Trees

(Litho State Printing Works, Maputo)

2005 (11 Aug). 25th Anniv of Southern African Development Community.

1716 **340** 8000m. multicoloured ....

(Litho State Printing Works, Maputo)

2005 (31 Aug). Traditional African Medicine Day.

1717 **341** 8000m. multicoloured ....

342 Woman and Emblem

343 Telephone and Mast

(Litho State Printing Works, Maputo)

2005 (9 Oct). World Summit on the Information Society, Tunis.
1718 **342** 8000m. multicoloured

2005?. Nos. 1478, 1481/2, 1621/2 and 1688b surch with new value in black and silver (1724) or surch with * * and new value (others).
1719 3000m. on 2000m. Mother Teresa
1720 6000m. on 2000m. Chaleira (pottery)
1721 6000m. on 10000m. Larosterna inca
1722 8000m. on 17,000m. Pelecanus crispus
1723 33,000m. on 7500m. Tabernaemontana elegans
1724 33,000m. on 12,500m. Ximenia caffra

2006 (10 June). 25th Anniv of Mozambique Telecommunications Company (TDM). Litho.
1725 **343** 8000m. multicoloured

344 Pres. Armando Guebuza holding Gavel

345 Dam and Reservoir

2006 (9 Oct). Presidential Initiative against AIDS. T **344** and similar horiz designs. Multicoloured. Litho.
1726 8m. Type **344**
1727 16m. Pres. Guebuza behind microphones
1728 33m. With arm raised

2006. No. 1725 surch.
1729 33m. on 8000m. multicoloured

(Des F. Jofane. Litho)

2007 (26 Nov). Cahora Bassa Dam. T **345** and similar horiz designs. Multicoloured. P 11×11½.
1730 8m. Type **345** 50 50
1731 20m. Dignitaries shaking hands 1·25 1·25
1732 33m. Dam and flag of Mozambique 2·00 2·00
1730/2 *Set of 3* 3·75 3·75

346 Building

347 Emblems

2007 (Nov). 50th Anniv of the Reign of Aga Khan. Sheet containing T **346** and similar horiz designs. Multicoloured. Litho.
MS1733 8m. Type **346**; 20m. People on beach; 20m. People under shelter; 33m. Polana Serena Hotel; 33m. Students in classroom (30×40 mm) 7·00 7·00

2008 (10 Apr). Centenary of Minerva Central Publishers (bookshop and publishing house), Maputo. Litho.
1734 **347** 8m. multicoloured 50 50
1735 20m. multicoloured 1·25 1·25
1736 33m. multicoloured 2·00 2·00
1734/6 *Set of 3* 3·75 3·75

348 Emblem

349 Football

(Des F. Jofane. Litho)

2008 (25 July). 40th Anniv of Second Frelimo Party Congress, Matchedje. P 11×11½.
1737 **348** 8m. multicoloured 50 50

2008. Olympic Games, Beijing (1st issue). T **349** and similar vert designs. Multicoloured. P 13½×12½.
1738 8m. Type **349** 50 50
a. Sheetlet. Nos. 1738/41 2·00
1739 8m. Basketball 50 50
1740 8m. Swimming 50 50
1741 8m. Athletics 50 50
1738/41 *Set of 4* 2·00 2·00

Nos. 1738/41 were printed together, *se-tenant*, in sheetlets of four stamps.

8.00 MT

(**350**)

351 Bolo de milho (maize cake)

2008. Olympic Games, Beijing (2nd issue). Nos. 1738/41 surch as Type **350**.
1742 8m. Type **349** 50 50
a. Sheetlet. Nos. 1742/5 2·00
1743 8m. Basketball 50 50
1744 8m. Swimming 50 50
1745 8m. Athletics 50 50
1742/5 *Set of 4* 2·00 2·00

(Des F. Jofane. Litho)

2008 (9 Oct). Mozambique Gastronomy. T **351** and similar vert designs. Multicoloured. P 11½×11.
1746 8m. Type **351** 50 50
1747 20m. Mathapa com carangueio (cassava with crab, coconut and peanuts) 1·25 1·25
1748 33m. Quiabo com camarao (okra with prawns and coconut) 2·00 2·00
1746/8 *Set of 3* 3·75 3·75

352 Maria de Lurdes Mutola with Mozambique Flag

353 Eduardo Mondlane

2009 (21 Jan). Maria de Lurdes Mutola (800 metre gold medallist, 2000 Olympics).
1749 **352** 8m. multicoloured 50 50

2009 (20 June). Eduardo Chivambo Mondlane (President of Mozambique Liberation Front) Commemoration. P 11½×11.
1750 **353** 33m. black and bright scarlet 2·00 2·00

354 Roan Antelope

355 Two Football Players

2010 (30 Jan). Endangered Species. Roan Antelope (Hippotragus equinus). T **354** and similar horiz designs. Multicoloured. P 13×13½.

1751	33m. Type **354**		
	a. Strip of 4. Nos. 1751/4	5·50	5·50
	b. Block of 4. Nos. 1751/4	5·50	5·50
1752	33m. Adult and juvenile		
1753	33m. Two antelopes at waterhole		
1754	33m. Roan antelopes in savannah		
MS1755	83×63 mm. 175m. Roan antelope grazing	8·50	8·50

Nos. 1751/4 were printed together, *se-tenant*, as horizontal and vertical strips of four stamps in sheetlets of 16 stamps.

They were also printed together, *se-tenant*, in sheetlets of eight containing two blocks of four (No. 1751b) separated by a gutter.

2010 (31 Mar). World Cup Football, South Africa. Sheet containing T **355** and similar vert designs, each showing two football players. Multicoloured.

MS1756	33m.×4 Type **355**; Players wearing pink (left) and green (right shirts; Players wearing pale mauve (left) and pale blue (right) shirts; Players wearing pink shirt (left) or white (right)	6·00	6·00

356 Emblem

357 Emblem

(Des P. António. Litho)

2010 (14 Apr). 30th Anniv of LAM (Linhas Aéreas de Mocambique).

1757	**356**	8m. multicoloured	40	40
1758		20m. multicoloured	90	90
1759		33m. multicoloured	1·50	1·50
1757/9 *Set of 3*			2·75	2·75

(Des P. António. Litho)

2010 (10 Nov). 20th Anniv of AICEP.

1760	**357**	33m. multicoloured	50	50

358 Anniversary Emblem

(Des P. António. Litho)

2011 (28 Feb). 30th Anniv of TVM.

1761	**358**	66m. multicoloured	30	30
1762		92m. multicoloured	50	50

Appendix

The following issues for Mozambique have either been issued in excess of postal needs, or have not been made available to the public in reasonable quantities at face value. Miniature sheets, imperforate stamps etc are excluded from this section.

1999

Birds and Butterflies. 6000m.×6, 7500m.×6
Minerals. 12500m.×6
Dinosaurs. 9000m.×6
Animals. 6500×6
Mushrooms. 9500m.×6

2000

Formula 1 Drivers. 6500m.×6

2001

Artists. 5000m.×6. 10000m.×87, 12000m.×48, 15000m.×6, 17000m.×6, 28000m.×6
Painters. 28000m.×6
World Cup Football (2002). 5000m.×33, 8500m.×18, 12000m.×6, 17000m.×6, 20000m.×6, 28000m.×6

2002

Nelson Mandela. 20000m.×4
World of the Sea. 5000m.×6, 17000m.×146, 20000m.×6, 33000×6

2007

Wild Cats. 8m.×3, 33m.×3
Elephants. 8m.×3, 33m.×3
Lighthouses and Marine Mammals. 8m.×3, 33m.×3
Birds of Prey. 8m.×3, 33m.×3
Hummingbirds and Ochids. 8m.×3, 33m.×3
Bees. 8m.×3, 33m.×3
Butterflies. 8m.×3, 33m.×3
Crocodiles. 8m.×3, 33m.×3
Frogs. 8m.×3, 33m.×3
Dinosaurs. 8m.×3, 33m.×3
Cacti. 8m.×3, 33m.×3
Fruit. 8m.×3, 33m.×3
Minerals. 8m.×3, 33m.×3
Primates. 20m.×6
Lighthouses and Whales. 20m.×6
Owls. 20m.×6
Parrots. 20m.×6
Butterflies, Moths and Flowers. 20m.×6
Fish. 20m.×6
Marine Life. 20m.×6
Reptiles. 20m.×6
Turtles. 20m.×6
Snakes. 20m.×6
Dinosaurs. 20m.×6
Trees. 20m.×6
Orchids. 20m.×6
Minerals. 20m.×6

2009

Transport with Animals. 33m.×6
Two-wheeled Transport. 33m.×6
Vintage Cars. 33m.×6
Modern Cars. 33m.×6
Modern Electric Cars. 33m.×6
Ancient Sailing Vessels. 33m.×6
Ships and Maps. 33m.×6
Steam-powered Ships. 33m.×6
Warships. 33m.×12
Modern Ships. 33m.×6
Early Locomotives. 33m.×6
Locomotives. 33m.×18
High-speed Trains. 33m.×12
Pioneer Aircraft. 33m.×12
Airplanes. 33m.×6
Military Airplanes. 33m.×12
Supersonic Airplanes. 33m.×6
Fire Vehicles. 33m.×6
Ambulances. 33m.×6
Spacecraft. 33m.×12
Chinese New Year. Year of the Tiger (2010). 8m.×6
500th Death Anniv of Shen Chou (artist). 8m.×6
90th Birth Anniv of Pope John Paul II. 8m.×6
140th Birth Anniv of Mahatma Gandhi. 8m.×6
Chinese Film Stars. 8m.×6
60th Anniv of the People's Republic of China. 8m.×6
120th Birth Anniv of Charlie Chaplin (actor). 20m.×6
20th Death Anniv of Emperor Hirohito of Japan. 20m.×6
Pres. John F. Kennedy Commemoration. 20m.×6
Marilyn Monroe (actress) Commemoration. 20m.×6
Elvis Presley Commemoration. 20m.×6
Michael Jackson (singer) Commemoration. 20m.×6
Pope Benedict XVI. 20m.×6
Expo 2010, Shanghai. 20m.×6
Galileo Galilei (astronomer) Commemoration. 33m.×6
Johannes Kepler (astronomer) Commemoration. 33m.×6
250th Death Anniv of George Frideric Handel (composer). 33m.×6
250th Birth Anniv of William Kirby (entomologist). 33m.×6
240th Birth Anniv of Napoleon Bonaparte (emperor of France). 33m.×6
Death Bicentenary of Joseph Haydn (composer). 33m.×6
Birth Bicentenary of Charles Darwin (naturalist). 33m.×6
Birth Bicentenary of Louis Braille (inventor of Braille). 33m.×6
160th Death Anniv of Katsushika Hokusai (artist). 33m.×6
150th Death Anniv of Alexander von Humboldt (naturalist). 33m.×6
150th Birth Anniv of Georges-Pierre Seurat (artist). 33m.×6
Birth Centenary of Sir Peter Scott (founder of Worldwide Fund for Nature). 33m.×6
40th Anniv of the First Man on the Moon. 33m.×6
International Polar Year. 33m.×6

2010

Giraffes. 8m.x6
Wild Pigs. 8m.x6
Zebras. 8m.x6
Squirrels. 8m.x6
Elephants. 8m.x6
Peonies. 20m.x6
Tropical Birds and Plants. 20m.x6
Pigeons. 20m.x6
Rabbits and Hares. 20m.x6
Wild Dogs and Hyenas. 20m.x6
Wild Cats. 20m.x6
Aardvarks. 20m.x6
Bats. 20m.x6
Rhinos. 20m.x6
Antelopes and Gazelles. 20m.x6
Marine Birds. 33m.x6
Parrots. 33m.x6
Birds of Prey. 33m.x6
Hippos. 33m.x6
Pangolins. 33m.x6
Seals and Sea Lions. 33m.x6
Dolphins. 33m.x6
Whales. 33m.x6
Monkeys. 33m.x6
Orchids. 33m.x6
Volcanoes. 33m.x6
Global Warming. 33m.x6
World Cup Football Stadiums, South Africa. 8m.x6
Winter Olympic Gold Medallists, Vancouver. 20m.x12, 33m.x12
Table Tennis Players. 20m.x6, 33m.x6
Cyclists. 20m.x6, 33m.x6
Chess Players. 20m.x6, 33m.x6
Golfers. 33m.x6
Tennis Players. 33m.x6
Baseball Players. 33m.x6
Ice Hockey Players. 33m.x6
Judo. 33m.x6
Taekwondo. 33m.x6
Polo Players. 33m.x6
Horse Racing. 33m.x6
Dog Racing. 33m.x6
Rugby Players. 33m.x6
Football Players. 33m.x12
Lionel Messi (football player). 33m.x6
Roger Federer (tennis player). 33m.x6
Alberto Contador (cyclist). 33m.x6
Valentino Rossi (cyclist). 33m.x6
Prehistoric Art. 8m.x6
Architecture of the World. 20m.x24, 33m.x48
Paintings and Musums of the World. 20m.x6, 33m.x12
French Castles and Chateaux. 33m.x6
Bridges of the World. 33m.x6
335th Birth Anniv of Jan Vermeer 66m.x4
Animals from Ocean Park Zoo, Hong Kong. 16m.x8
19th Commonwealth Games, New Delhi. 16m.x8
Chinese New Year. Year of the Rabbit (2011). 16m.x6
400th Death Anniv of Michelangelo Merisi da Caravaggio (artist). 16m.x6, 92m.x2
Tony Curtis (actor) Commemoration. 16m.x6, 92m.x2
Explosion of Deepwater Horizon Oil Platform and Oil Spill, Gulf of Mexico. 16m.x6, 92m.x2
Christmas Paintings. 16m.x6, 92m.x2
90th Death Anniv of Amedeo Modigliani. 16m.x3, 66m.x3
30th Death Anniv of Alfred Hitchcock. 16m.x3, 33m.x3
50th Birth Anniv of Princess Diana. 16m.x3, 33m.x3
Witali Sewastianow (cosmonaut) Commemoration. 16m.x3, 33m.x3
70th Birthday of Pele (footballer). 16m.x3, 33m.x3
Engagement of Prince William and Miss Catherine Middleton. 16m.x3, 66m.x3

Namibia
formerly South West Africa

The stamps of Germany were used in the colony from July 1886 until the introduction of issues for GERMAN SOUTH-WEST AFRICA in May 1897. Following occupation by South African forces in 1914–15 the issues of SOUTH AFRICA were used, being replaced by the overprinted issues in 1923.

Walvis (or Walfish) Bay, the major anchorage on the South West Africa coast, was claimed by Great Britain as early as 1796. In 1878 the 430 sq mile area around the port, together with a number of offshore islands, was annexed to Cape Province, passing to the Union of South Africa in 1910.

Stamps of the Cape of Good Hope and South Africa were used at Walfish Bay, often cancelled with numeral obliterator 300, until the enclave was transferred to the South West Africa administration on 1 October 1922.

The Walfish Bay territory reverted to South Africa on 30 August 1977 and from that date the stamps of South Africa were, once again, in use.

PRICES FOR STAMPS ON COVER TO 1945

Nos.	1/40*a*	*from* × 6
Nos.	41/133	*from* × 2
Nos.	D1/5	*from* × 10
Nos.	D6/51	*from* × 20
Nos.	O1/4	*from* × 3
Nos.	O5/20	*from* × 15
No.	O21	*from* × 2
No.	O22	*from* × 15

INSCRIPTIONS. Most of the postage stamps up to No. 140 are inscribed alternately in English and Afrikaans throughout the sheets and the same applies to all the Official stamps and to Nos. D30/33.

PRICES for Nos. 1/140 are for unused horizontal pairs, used horizontal pairs or used singles (either inscr), *unless otherwise indicated.*

OVERPRINT SETTINGS. Between 1923 and 1928 the King George V definitives of South Africa, Types **2** and **3**, and the various postage due stamps were issued overprinted for use in South West Africa. A number of overprint settings were used:

- Setting I – Overprint Types **1** and **2** ("Zuid-West Afrika"). 14 mm between lines of overprint. See Nos. 1/12 and D1/9
- Setting II – As Setting I, but 10 mm between lines of overprint. See Nos. 13/15 and D10/13
- Setting III – Overprint Types **3** ("Zuidwest Afrika") and **4**. "South West" 14 mm long. "Zuidwest" 11 mm long. 14 mm between lines of overprint. See Nos. 16/27 and D14/17
- Setting IV – As Setting III, but "South West" 16 mm long, "Zuidwest" 12 mm long and 14 mm between lines of overprint. See Nos. 28 and D17*a*/20
- Setting V – As Setting IV, but 12 mm between lines of overprint. See Nos. D21/4
- Setting VI – As Setting IV, but 9½ mm between lines of overprint. See Nos. 29/40 and D25/32.

South West	**Zuid-West**
Africa.	**Afrika.**
(1)	(2)

1923 (1 Jan–17 June). Nos. 3/4, 6 and 9/17 of South Africa optd alternately with T **1** and **2** by typography.

(a) Setting I (14 mm between lines of opt)

		Un pair	Us pair	Us single
1	½d. green	2·50	9·00	1·00
	a. "Wes" for "West" (R. 20/8)	£100	£150	
	b. "Afr ica" (R. 20/2)	£130		
	c. Litho opt in shiny ink (17 June)	11·00	60·00	4·75
2	1d. rose-red	5·00	9·50	1·00
	a. Opt inverted	£500		
	b. "Wes" for "West" (R. 12/2)	£170		
	c. "Af.rica" for "Africa" (R. 20/6)	£170	£275	
	d. Opt double	£1000		
	e. "Afr ica" (R. 20/2)	£130		
	f. "Afrika" without stop (R. 17/8)	£350		
3	2d. dull purple	6·50	12·00	1·50
	a. Opt inverted	£700	£800	
	b. "Wes" for "West" (R. 20/8)	£275		
	c. Litho opt in shiny ink (30 Mar)	65·00	£140	10·00
4	3d. ultramarine	9·00	16·00	2·75
5	4d. orange-yellow and sage-green	15·00	48·00	4·00
	a. Litho opt in shiny ink (19 Apr)	38·00	70·00	8·00
6	6d. black and violet	8·00	48·00	4·00
	a. Litho opt in shiny ink (19 Apr)	32·00	80·00	7·50
7	1s. orange-yellow	18·00	50·00	5·00
	a. Litho opt in shiny ink (19 Apr)	60·00	£120	11·00
	b. "Afrika" without stop (R. 17/8)	£6000		
8	1s.3d. pale violet	38·00	60·00	5·50
	a. Opt inverted	£400		
	b. Litho opt in shiny ink (19 Apr)	80·00	£150	14·00
9	2s.6d. purple and green	70·00	£140	18·00
	a. Litho opt in shiny ink (19 Apr)	£140	£300	35·00
10	5s. purple and blue	£200	£375	50·00
11	10s. blue and olive-green	£1400	£2750	£400
12	£1 green and red	£750	£1900	£250
1/12 *Set of 12*		£2250	£4750	£650
1s/12s Optd "SPECIMEN" *Set of 12 singles*		£1500		

Nos. 1/12 were overprinted in complete sheets of 240 (4 panes 6×10).

No. 3b shows traces of a type spacer to the right of where the "t" should have been. This spacer is not visible on Nos. 1a and 2b.

Minor varieties, such as broken "t" in "West", were caused by worn type. Stamps showing one line of overprint only or with the lower line above the upper line due to overprint misplacement may also be found. All values exist showing a faint stop after "Afrika" on R. 17/8, but only examples of the 1d. and 1s. have been seen with it completely omitted.

(b) Setting II (10 mm between lines of opt) (31 Mar)

		Un pair	Us pair	Us single
13	5s. purple and blue	£150	£275	45·00
	a. "Afrika" without stop (R. 6/1)	£1200	£1400	£225
14	10s. blue and olive-green	£500	£850	£140
	a. "Afrika" without stop (R. 6/1)	£2500	£3000	£550
15	£1 green and red	£1000	£1400	£200
	a. "Afrika" without stop (R. 6/1)	£4500	£5500	£1000
13/15 *Set of 3*		£1500	£2250	£350

Nos. 13/15 were overprinted in separate panes of 60 (6×10).

Examples of most values are known showing a forged Windhoek postmark dated "30 SEP 24".

Zuidwest	**South West**
Afrika.	**Africa.**
(3)	(4)

1923 (15 July)–**26**. Nos. 3/4, 6 and 9/17 of South Africa optd as T **3** ("Zuidwest" in one word, without hyphen) and **4** alternately.

(a) Setting III ("South West" 14 mm long, "Zuidwest" 11 mm long, 14 mm between lines of opt)

		Un pair	Us pair	Us single
16	½d. green (5.9.24)	9·00	38·00	4·00
	a. "outh" for "South" (R. 1/1)	£1700		
17	1d. rose-red (28.9.23)	6·00	9·00	1·40
	a. "outh" for "South" (R. 1/1)	£1600		
18	2d. dull purple (28.9.23)	9·00	11·00	1·40
	a. Opt double	£1000		
19	3d. ultramarine	5·00	10·00	1·25
20	4d. orange-yellow and sage-green	6·00	21·00	2·75
	w. Wmk inverted	†	†	—
21	6d. black and violet (28.9.23)	12·00	45·00	5·00
22	1s. orange-yellow	12·00	45·00	5·00
23	1s.3d. pale violet	23·00	48·00	5·50
24	2s.6d. purple and green	45·00	90·00	10·00
25	5s. purple and blue	65·00	£140	18·00
26	10s. blue and olive-green	£160	£275	40·00
27	£1 green and red (28.9.23)	£325	£450	60·00
16/27 *Set of 12*		£600	£1100	£140

Nos. 16/27 were overprinted in complete sheets of 240 (4 panes 6×10).

Two sets may be made with this overprint, one with bold lettering, and the other from September 1924, with thinner lettering and smaller stops.

(b) Setting IV ("South West" 16 mm long, "Zuidwest" 12 mm long, 14 mm between lines of opt)

		Un pair	Us pair	Us single
28	2s.6d. purple and green (29.6.24)	85·00	£170	28·00

No. 28 was overprinted on two panes of 60 horizontally side by side.

(c) Setting VI ("South West" 16 mm long, "Zuidwest" 12 mm long, 9½ mm between lines of opt)

		Un pair	Us pair	Us single
29	½d. green (16.12.25)	7·00	40·00	5·00

30	1d. rose-red (9.12.24)	3·25	10·00	1·40
	a. Opt omitted (in pair with normal)	£1800		
31	2d. dull purple (9.12.24)	4·00	22·00	1·75
32	3d. ultramarine (31.1.26)	4·50	29·00	2·75
	a. Deep bright blue (20.4.26)	42·00	£100	12·00
33	4d. orge-yellow & sage-grn (9.12.24)	5·50	48·00	4·00
34	6d. black and violet (9.12.24)	9·50	48·00	5·00
35	1s. orange-yellow (9.12.24)	8·50	48·00	5·00
36	1s.3d. pale violet (9.12.24)	11·00	48·00	5·00
37	2s.6d. purple and green (9.12.24)	38·00	75·00	10·00
38	5s. purple and blue (31.1.26)	50·00	£120	14·00
39	10s. blue and olive-green (9.12.24)	90·00	£170	20·00
40	£1 green and red (9.1.26)	£275	£425	55·00
	a. Pale olive-green and red (8.11.26)	£275	£475	65·00
29/40 *Set of 12*		£450	£950	£120
35s, 39s/40 H/S "SPECIMEN" *Set of 3*		£500		

Nos. 29/40 were overprinted in complete sheets of 240 (4 panes of 6×10) with, initially, "South West Africa" 16½ mm long on the upper two panes and 16 mm long on the lower two. This order was subsequently reversed. For printings from 8 November 1926 all four panes showed the 16½ mm measurement. No. 40*a* only comes from this printing.

Examples of most values are known showing a forged Windhoek postmark dated "30 SEP 24".

Suidwes Afrika. (5) **South West Africa.** (6)

1926 (1 Jan–1 May). Nos. 30/2 of South Africa (Waterlow printings) optd with T **5** (on stamps inscr in Afrikaans) and **6** (on stamps inscr in English) sideways, alternately in black.

41	½d. black and green	4·25	9·00	1·00
42	1d. black and carmine	3·50	8·00	80
43	6d. green and orange (1 May)	23·00	50·00	7·00
41/3 *Set of 3*		27·00	60·00	8·00

SOUTH WEST AFRICA (7) **SUIDWES-AFRIKA** (8)

1926. No. 33 of South Africa, imperf optd.

*(a) With T **7** (English)*

			Single Stamps
44A	4d. grey-blue	75	3·00

*(b) With T **8** (Afrikaans)*

44B	4d. grey-blue	75	3·00

1927. As Nos. 41/3, but Afrikaans opt on stamp inscr in English and vice versa.

45	½d. black and green	2·00	9·00	1·00
	a. "Africa" without stop (R. 13/8)	£160		
46	1d. black and carmine	3·00	2·50	50
	a. "Africa" without stop (R. 13/8)	£300		
47	6d. green and orange	8·00	35·00	3·00
	a. "Africa" without stop (R. 13/8)	£180		
45/7 *Set of 3*		11·50	42·00	4·00

The overprints on Nos. 45/7 were applied to both the Waterlow and Pretoria printings of South Africa Nos. 30/2.

SOUTH WEST AFRICA (9) **S.W.A.** (10) **S.W.A.** (11)

1927. As No. 44A, but overprint T **9**.

			Single Stamps
48	4d. grey-blue	6·50	19·00
	s. Handstamped "SPECIMEN"	70·00	

1927 (Apr). Nos. 34/9 of South Africa optd alternately as T **5** and **6**, in blue, but with lines of overprint spaced 16 mm.

49	2d. grey and purple	4·75	16·00	1·75
50	3d. black and red	4·75	32·00	2·50
51	1s. brown and blue	15·00	32·00	4·00
52	2s.6d. green and brown	38·00	95·00	13·00
53	5s. black and green	75·00	£190	20·00
54	10s. blue and bistre-brown	65·00	£160	20·00
49/54 *Set of 6*		£180	£475	50·00
49s/51s, 54s H/S "SPECIMEN" *Set of 4*		£375		

A variety of Nos. 49, 50, 51 and 54 with spacing 16½ mm between lines of overprint, occurs in the third vertical row of each sheet.

1927. As No. 44, but perf 11½ by John Meinert Ltd, Windhoek.

*(a) Optd with T **7** (English)*

			Single Stamps
55A	4d. grey-blue	1·25	6·00
	a. Imperf between (pair)	38·00	85·00
	s. Handstamped "SPECIMEN"	70·00	

*(b) Optd with T **8** (Afrikaans)*

55B	4d. grey-blue	1·25	6·00
	a. Imperf between (pair)	40·00	85·00
	s. Handstamped "SPECIMEN"	70·00	

1927 (Aug)–**30**. Optd with T **10**.

(a) On Nos. 13 and 17a of South Africa

56	1s.3d. pale violet	1·25	6·50
	a. Without stop after "A" (R. 3/4)	£100	
	s. Handstamped "SPECIMEN"	75·00	
57	£1 pale olive-green and red	95·00	£160
	a. Without stop after "A" (R. 3/4)	£1600	£2500

(b) On Nos. 30/2 and 34/9 of South Africa

		Un pair	*Us pair*	*Us single*
58	½d. black and green	2·50	7·50	80
	a. Without stop after "A"	42·00	75·00	
	b. "S.W.A." opt above value	2·75	16·00	2·25
	c. As b, in vert pair, top stamp without opt	£550		
59	1d. black and carmine	1·25	3·75	55
	a. Without stop after "A"	40·00	75·00	
	b. "S.W.A." opt at top (30.4.30)	1·75	14·00	1·60
	c. As b, in vert pair, top stamp without opt	£600		
60	2d. grey and maroon	9·00	32·00	1·75
	c. Perf 14×13½	20·00	48·00	
	ca. Without stop after "A"	85·00	£140	
	cb. Opt double, one inverted	£750	£1000	
61	3d. black and red	5·00	26·00	3·25
	a. Without stop after "A"	75·00	£120	
	b. Perf 14×13½	12·00	48·00	
	ba. Without stop after "A"	90·00	£160	
	bb. Without stop after "W"	£170		
62	4d. brown (4.28)	12·00	45·00	7·00
	a. Without stop after "A"	90·00	£140	
	b. Perf 14×13½	35·00	65·00	
63	6d. green and orange	7·00	28·00	2·75
	a. Without stop after "A"	£120		
64	1s. brown and deep blue	10·00	48·00	5·00
	b. Perf 14×13½	60·00	90·00	
	ba. Without stop after "A"	£1500	£1800	£350
65	2s.6d. green and brown	42·00	85·00	12·00
	a. Without stop after "A"	£160	£275	
	b. Perf 14×13½	80·00	£140	
	ba. Without stop after "A"	£225	£350	
66	5s. black and green	60·00	£120	18·00
	a. Without stop after "A"	£250	£375	
	b. Perf 14×13½	£110	£180	
	ba. Without stop after "A"	£300	£450	
67	10s. bright blue and brown	£100	£200	28·00
	a. Without stop after "A"	£375	£600	
58/67 *Set of 10*		£225	£500	70·00
58s/61s, 63s/7s H/S "SPECIMEN" *Set of 9*		£600		

On the ½d., 1d. and 6d. the missing stop variety occurs three times on each sheet, R. 1/7, 13/4 and one position not yet identified. For the other values it comes on R. 2/3 of the right pane and, for the 2s.6d., 5s. and 10s., on R. 8/1 of the left pane.

The missing stop after "W" on the 3d. occurs on R. 10/5 of the right pane.

The overprint is normally found at the base of the ½d., 1d., 6d., 1s.3d. and £1 values and at the top of the remainder.

Examples of all values are known showing a forged Windhoek postmark dated "20 MAR 31".

1930–31. Nos. 42 and 43 of South Africa (rotogravure printing) optd with T **10**.

68	½d. black and green (1931)	15·00	38·00	3·50
69	1d. black and carmine	10·00	27·00	2·75

1930 (27 Nov–Dec). Air. Nos. 40/1 of South Africa optd.

*(a) As T **10***

		Un single	*Us single*
70	4d. green (*first printing*)	7·00	28·00
	a. No stop after "A" of "S.W.A."	70·00	£140
	b. Later printings	3·50	28·00
71	1s. orange (*first printing*)	70·00	£120
	a. No stop after "A" of "S.W.A."	£450	£650
	b. Later printings	5·00	50·00

First printing: Thick letters, blurred impression. Stops with rounded corners.

Later printings: Thinner letters, clear impression. Clean cut, square stops.

*(b) As T **11** (12.30)*

72	4d. green	1·25	6·00
	a. Opt double	£200	

	b. Opt inverted	£200		
73	1s. orange	2·50	15·00	
	a. Opt double	£500		

12 Kori Bustard

13 Cape Cross

14 Bogenfels

15 Windhoek

16 Waterberg

17 Luderitz Bay

18 Bush Scene

19 Elands

20 Mountain Zebra and Blue Wildebeests

21 Herero Huts

22 Welwitschia Plant

23 Okuwahaken Falls

24 Monoplane over Windhoek

25 Biplane over Windhoek

(Recess B.W.)

1931 (5 Mar). T **12** to **25** (inscr alternately in English and Afrikaans). W **9** of South Africa. P 14×13½.

(a) Postage

74	½d. black and emerald	3·00	2·50	10
75	1d. indigo and scarlet	2·25	2·50	10
76	2d. blue and brown	70	6·50	15
	w. Wmk inverted	£550		
77	3d. grey-blue and blue	70	4·50	15
78	4d. green and purple	1·50	7·00	20
79	6d. blue and brown	1·50	11·00	20
80	1s. chocolate and blue	3·00	15·00	25
81	1s.3d. violet and yellow	6·00	11·00	50
82	2s.6d. carmine and grey	23·00	24·00	1·75
83	5s. sage-green and red-brown	16·00	35·00	2·75
84	10s. red-brown and emerald	50·00	50·00	6·00
85	20s. lake and blue-green	75·00	80·00	10·00

(b) Air

86	3d. brown and blue	28·00	35·00	2·50
87	10d. black and purple-brown	50·00	85·00	7·00
74/87 *Set of 14*		£225	£300	28·00

Examples of most values are known showing a forged Windhoek postmark dated "20 MAR 31".

26

(Recess B.W.)

1935 (1 May). Silver Jubilee. Inscr bilingually. W **9** of South Africa. P 14×13½.

			Un single	*Us single*
88	**26**	1d. black and scarlet	1·00	25
89		2d. black and sepia	1·50	25
90		3d. black and blue	7·50	25·00
91		6d. black and purple	3·00	15·00
88/91 *Set of 4*			11·50	35·00

1935–36. Voortrekker Memorial Fund. Nos. 50/3 of South Africa optd with T **10**.

92	½d. +½d. black and green	1·50	5·50	75
	a. Opt inverted	£275		
93	1d. +½d. grey-black and pink	1·50	3·25	40
	a. Blurred "SOUTH AFRICA" and red "comet" flaw	55·00		
94	2d. +1d. grey-green and purple	5·50	6·00	80
	a. Without stop after "A"	£200	£225	
	b. Opt double	£225		
95	3d. +1½d. grey-green and blue	17·00	40·00	4·00
	a. Without stop after "A"	£250	£325	
92/5 *Set of 4*		23·00	50·00	5·50

27 Mail Train

28

Re-entry (R. 6/3)

(Recess B.W.)

1937 (1 Mar). W **9** of South Africa. P 14×13½.

96	**27**	1½d. purple-brown	28·00	4·25	35

(Recess B.W.)

1937 (12 May). Coronation. W **9** of South Africa (sideways). P 13½×14.

97	**28**	½d. black and emerald	40	15	10
98		1d. black and scarlet	40	15	10
99		1½d. black and orange	40	15	10
100		2d. black and brown	40	15	10
101		3d. black and blue	50	15	10
102		4d. black and purple	50	20	10
		a. Re-entry	19·00	19·00	
103		6d. black and yellow	50	3·25	20
104		1s. black and grey-black	55	3·50	25
97/104 *Set of 8*			3·25	7·00	65

On. No. 102a the frame and leaves at lower left are doubled. The stamp is inscribed in Afrikaans.

1938 (14 Dec). Voortrekker Centenary Memorial. Nos. 76/9 of South Africa optd as T **11**.

105	½d. +½d. blue and green	11·00	29·00	2·25
106	1d. +1d. blue and carmine	28·00	21·00	1·50
107	1½d. +1½d. chocolate and blue-green	29·00	35·00	3·25
108	3d. +3d. bright blue	50·00	95·00	8·50
105/8	*Set of 4*	£110	£160	14·00

1938 (14 Dec). Voortrekker Commemoration. Nos. 80/1 of South Africa optd as T **11**.

109	1d. blue and carmine	13·00	23·00	1·50
	a. Three bolts in wheel rim	70·00		
110	1½d. greenish blue and brown	19·00	28·00	2·00

1939 (17 July). 250th Anniv of Landing of Huguenots in South Africa and Huguenot Commemoration Fund. Nos. 82/4 of South Africa optd as T **11**.

111	½d. +½d. brown and green	14·00	16·00	1·25
112	1d. +1d. green and carmine	21·00	16·00	1·25
113	1½d. +1½d. blue-green and purple	35·00	16·00	1·25
111/13	*Set of 3*	65·00	42·00	3·25

SWA (29) **SWA** (30) **SWA** (31) **S W A** (32)

1941 (1 Oct)–**43**. War Effort. Nos. 88/96 of South Africa optd with T **29** or **30** (3d. and 1s.).

(a) Inscr alternately

114	½d. green (1.12.41)	75	5·50	30
	a. Blue-green (1942)	65	2·50	15
115	1d. carmine (1.11.41)	1·00	3·75	20
	a. "Stain" on uniform	19·00		
116	1½d. myrtle-green (21.1.42)	55	4·00	20
117	3d. blue	23·00	26·00	1·00
	a. Cigarette flaw	95·00		
118	4d. orange-brown	7·00	20·00	1·00
	a. Red-brown	18·00	28·00	3·00
119	6d. red-orange	7·50	9·00	50
120	1s.3d. olive-brown (15.1.43)	13·00	23·00	1·25

(b) Inscr bilingually

		Un single	*Us single*
121	2d. violet	50	1·75
122	1s. brown (17.11.41)	1·60	2·00
114/22	*Set of 7 pairs and 2 singles*	50·00	80·00

1943–44. War Effort (reduced sizes). Nos. 97/104 of South Africa, optd with T **29** (1½d. and 1s., No. 130), or T **31** (others).

(a) Inscr alternately

		Un unit	*Us unit*	*Us single*
123	½d. blue-green (T)	50	7·00	25
	a. Green	5·50	9·00	30
	b. Greenish blue	4·25	7·50	25
124	1d. carmine-red (T)	4·00	7·00	20
	a. Bright carmine	3·50	7·00	20
125	1½d. red-brown (P)	50	1·75	15
	a. Ear flap flaw	15·00		
126	2d. violet (P)	8·50	5·50	20
	a. Reddish violet	11·00	7·00	20
	b. Apostrophe flaw	55·00		
127	3d. blue (T)	3·25	22·00	65
128	6d. red-orange (P)	6·00	3·00	30
	a. Opt inverted	£650		
	(b) Inscr bilingually			
129	4d. slate-green (T)	2·00	23·00	70
	a. Opt inverted	£850	£550	60·00
130	1s. brown (opt T **29**) (P)	15·00	29·00	2·00
	a. Opt inverted	£700	£375	
	b. Opt T **31**(1944)	4·00	6·00	30
	c. Opt T **31** inverted	£600	£350	40·00
	d. "Bursting shell"	45·00		
	e. Smoking "L"	45·00		
123/30*b*	*Set of 8*	25·00	65·00	2·50

The "units" referred to above consist of pairs (P) or triplets (T).

No. 128 exists with another type of opt as Type **31**, but with broader "s", narrower "w" and more space between the letters.

1945. Victory. Nos. 108/10 of South Africa optd with T **30**.

131	1d. brown and carmine	25	75	10
	a. Opt inverted	£400	£425	
132	2d. slate-blue and violet	30	75	10
133	3d. deep blue and blue	1·50	1·75	10
131/3	*Set of 3*	1·75	3·00	20

1947 (17 Feb). Royal Visit. Nos. 111/13 of South Africa optd as T **31**, but 8½×2 mm.

134	1d. black and carmine	10	10	10
135	2d. violet	10	60	10
	a. "Bird" on "2"	8·00		
136	3d. blue	15	40	10
	a. "Black-eyed Princess"	9·50		
134/6	*Set of 3*	30	1·00	15

1948 (26 Apr). Royal Silver Wedding. No. 125 of South Africa, optd as T **31**, but 4×2 mm.

137	3d. blue and silver	1·00	35	10

1949 (1 Oct). 75th Anniv of U.P.U. Nos. 128/30 of South Africa optd as T **30**, but 13×4 mm.

138	½d. blue-green	75	2·25	25
139	1½d. brown-red	75	1·75	15
140	3d. bright blue	1·25	1·00	25
	a. Serif on "C"	55·00		
	b. "Lake" in East Africa	55·00		
138/40	*Set of 3*	2·50	4·50	60

1949 (1 Dec). Inauguration of Voortrekker Monument, Pretoria. Nos. 131/3 of South Africa optd with T **32**.

		Un single	*Us single*
141	1d. magenta	10	10
142	1½d. blue-green	10	10
143	3d. blue	15	60
141/3	*Set of 3*	30	70

1952 (14 Mar). Tercentenary of Landing of Van Riebeeck. Nos. 136/40 of South Africa optd as T **30**, but 8×3½ mm (1d., 4½d.) or 11×4 mm (others).

144	½d. brown-purple and olive-grey	10	50
145	1d. deep blue-green	10	10
146	2d. deep violet	50	10
	a. "Full Moon"	10·00	
	b. "Line through sails" (vert pair)	15·00	
147	4½d. blue	30	2·25
148	1s. brown	75	20
144/8	*Set of 5*	1·50	2·75

33 Queen Elizabeth II and *Catophracies Alexandri*

1953 (2 June). Coronation. T **33** and similar horiz designs. W **9** of South Africa. P 14.

149	1d. bright carmine	40	10
150	2d. deep bluish green	40	10
151	4d. magenta	50	30
152	6d. dull ultramarine	50	70
153	1s. deep orange-brown	65	20
149/53	*Set of 5*	2·25	1·25

Designs:—2d. *Bauhinia macrantha*, 4d. *Caralluma nebrownii*, 6d. *Gloriosa virescens*, 1s. *Rhigozum trieholotum*.

34 "Two Bucks" (rock painting)

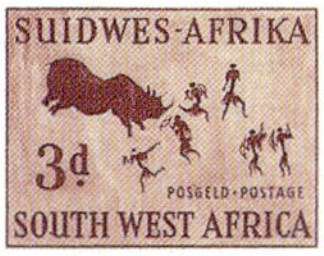

36 "Rhinoceros Hunt" (rock painting)

38 Karakul Lamb

39 Ovambo Woman blowing Horn

(Des O. Schroeder (1d. to 4d.), M. Vandenschen (4½d. to 10s.))

1954 (15 Nov). T **34**, **36**, **38/9** and similar designs. W **9** of South Africa (sideways* on vert designs). P 14.

154	1d. brown-red	30	10
	w. Wmk horns of springbok to right	16·00	11·00
155	2d. deep brown	35	10
156	3d. dull purple	1·25	10
157	4d. blackish olive	1·50	10
158	4½d. deep blue	70	40

159	6d. myrtle-green	70	70
	w. Wmk horns of springbok to right	80·00	38·00
160	1s. deep mauve	70	50
161	1s.3d. cerise	2·00	1·25
162	1s.6d. purple	2·00	50
163	2s.6d. bistre-brown	4·50	70
164	5s. deep bright blue	6·00	2·75
165	10s. deep myrtle-green	32·00	16·00
154/65 *Set of 12*		48·00	21·00

Designs: *Vert* (*as T* **34**)—2d. "White Lady" (rock painting). (*As T* **38**)—2s.6d. Lioness; 5s. Gemsbok; 10s. African Elephant. (*As T* **39**)—1s. Ovambo woman; 1s.3d. Herero woman 1s.6d. Ovambo girl. *Horiz* (*as T* **36**)—1d. "White Elephant and Giraffe (rock painting).

*The normal sideways watermark shows the horns of the springbok pointing left, *as seen from the back of the stamp.*

1960. As Nos. 154/7, 162, but W **102** of South Africa (sideways on vert designs). P 14.

166	1d. brown-red	55	2·25
167	2d. deep brown	70	2·25
168	3d. dull purple	1·40	5·50
169	4d. blackish olive	2·75	4·75
169*a*	6d. myrtle-green	£950	£475
170	1s.6d. purple	20·00	15·00
166/70 (ex 169*a*) *Set of 5*		23·00	27·00

(New Currency. 100 cents = 1 South African rand)

46 G.P.O. Windhoek

47 Finger Rock

48 Mounted Soldier Monument

49 Quivertree

50 S.W.A. House, Windhoek

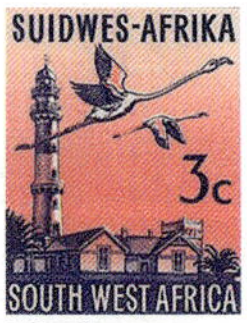

50a Greater Flamingoes and Swakopmund Lighthouse

51 Fishing Industry

52 Greater Flamingo

53 German Lutheran Church, Windhoek

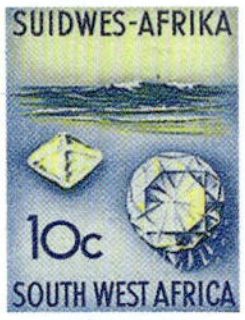

54 Diamond

55 Fort Namutoni

55a Hardap Dam

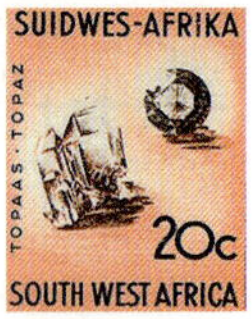

56 Topaz

57 Tourmaline

58 Heliodor

1961 (14 Feb)–**63**. Unsurfaced paper. W **102** of South Africa (sideways on vert designs). P 14.

171	**46**	½c. brown and pale blue	60	10
172	**47**	1c. sepia and reddish lilac	15	10
173	**48**	1½c. slate-violet and salmon	20	10
174	**49**	2c. deep green and yellow	75	1·40
175	**50**	2½c. red-brown and light blue	35	10
176	**50a**	3c. ultramarine and rose-red (1.10.62)	5·50	40
177	**51**	3½c. indigo and blue-green	1·00	15
178	**52**	5c. scarlet and grey-blue	8·00	10
179	**53**	7½c. sepia and pale lemon	70	15
180	**54**	10c. blue and greenish yellow	1·75	60
181	**55**	12½c. indigo and lemon	60	40
182	**55a**	15c. chocolate and light blue (16.3.63)	14·00	3·25
183	**56**	20c. brown and red-orange	4·00	30
184	**57**	50c. deep bluish green and yellow-orange	4·50	1·50
185	**58**	1r. yellow, maroon and blue	7·50	12·00
171/185 *Set of 15*			45·00	18·00

See also Nos. 186/91, 202/16 and 224/6.

1962–66. As No. 171, etc., but without watermark.

186	**46**	½c. brown and pale blue (8.62)	50	1·50
187	**48**	1½c. slate-violet and salmon (9.62)	5·00	45
188	**49**	2c. deep green and yellow (5.62)	3·50	3·50
189	**50**	2½c. red-brown and light blue (1964)	9·00	6·50
190	**51**	3½c. indigo and blue-green (1966)	10·00	3·75
191	**52**	5c. scarlet and grey-blue (9.62)	7·00	1·50
186/91 *Set of 6*			32·00	15·00

59 "Agricultural Development"

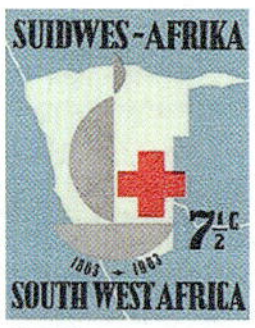

60 Centenary Emblem and Map

61 Centenary Emblem and part of Globe

1963 (16 Mar). Opening of Hardap Dam. W **102** of South Africa (sideways). P 14.

192	**59**	3c. chocolate and light green	30	15

1963 (30 Aug). Centenary of Red Cross. P 14.

193	**60**	7½c. red, black and light blue	4·00	5·00
194	**61**	15c. red, black and orange-brown	6·00	8·00

62 Interior of Assembly Hall

63 Calvin

1964 (14 May). Opening of Legislative Assembly Hall, Windhoek. W **102** of South Africa. P 14.

195	**62**	3c. ultramarine and salmon	50	30

1964 (1 Oct). 400th Death Anniv of Calvin (Protestant reformer). P 14.

196	**63**	2½c. brown-purple and gold	50	15
197		15c. deep bluish green and gold	2·25	3·75

64 Mail Runner of 1890

65 Kurt von Francois (founder)

(Des D. Aschenborn)

1965 (18 Oct). 75th Anniv of Windhoek. Chalk-surfaced paper. W **127** of South Africa (sideways). P 14.

198	**64**	3c. sepia and scarlet	50	15
199	**65**	15c. red-brown and blue-green	90	1·75

66 Dr. H. Vedder

1966 (4 July). 90th Birth Anniv, of Dr. H. Vedder (philosopher and writer). Chalk-surfaced paper. W **127** of South Africa (sideways). P 14.

200	**66**	3c. blackish green and salmon	30	15
201		15c. deep sepia and light blue	70	40

Nos. 200/1 exist on Swiss-made paper with *tête-bêche* watermark from a special printing made for use in presentation albums for delegates to the U.P.U. Congress in Tokyo in 1969, as supplies of the original Harrison paper were by then exhausted (*Set of 2 price* £22 *mint*).

1966–72. As 1961–66 but chalk-surfaced paper and W **127** of South Africa* (sideways† on vert designs).

202	**46**	½c. brown and pale blue (1967)	1·25	10
203	**47**	1c. sepia and light reddish lilac (1967)	1·50	10
		a. Grey-brown and lilac (9.72)	3·25	10
204	**48**	1½c. slate-violet and salmon (1968)	7·00	30
205	**49**	2c. deep bluish green and yellow	5·00	10
206	**50**	2½c. deep red-brown and light turquoise-blue	2·50	30
		a. Deep red-brown and pale blue (1967)	70	10
207	**50a**	3c. ultramarine and rose-red (1970)	8·50	1·75
208	**51**	3½c. indigo and blue-green (1967)	4·00	7·00
209	**50**	4c. deep red-brown and light turquoise-blue (1.4.71)	1·50	2·50
210	**52**	5c. scarlet and grey-blue (1968)	4·00	10
211	**53**	6c. sepia and greenish yellow (31.8.71)	8·00	9·50
212		7½c. sepia and pale lemon (1967)	3·50	30
		w. Wmk top of triangle to right	3·50	30
213	**55**	9c. indigo and greenish yellow (1.7.71)	10·00	12·00
214	**54**	10c. bright blue and greenish yellow (6.70)	18·00	2·50
		a. Whiter background** (9.72)	18·00	3·25
215	**55a**	15c. chocolate and light blue (1.72)	25·00	7·00
216	**56**	20c. brown and red-orange (1968)	18·00	1·75
202/16 *Set of 15*			£100	38·00

*The watermark in this issue is indistinct but the stamps can be distinguished from the stamps without watermark by their shades and the chalk-surfaced paper which is appreciably thicker and whiter. The 1 1½, 3 4 5, 6, 9 10 15 and 20c. are known only with the watermark *tête-bêche* but the ½c. and 2½c. exist with both forms, the remainder being as illustrated.

†The normal sideways watermark shows top of triangle pointing to left, *as seen from the back of the stamp.*

**No. 214a, printed from sheets, has a much whiter background around the value and behind "SOUTH WEST AFRICA" compared with No. 214, which was issued in coils only.

See also Nos. 224/6.

67 Camelthorn Tree

(Des D. Aschenborn (2½c., 3c.), Govt Printer, Pretoria (15c.))

1967 (6 Jan). Verwoerd Commemoration. Chalk-surfaced paper. T **67** and similar designs. W **127** of South Africa (sideways on vert designs). P 14.

217	2½c. black and emerald-green	15	10
218	3c. brown and new blue	15	10
219	15c. blackish brown and reddish purple	55	45
217/19 *Set of 3*		75	60

Designs: *Vert.*—3c. Waves breaking against rock; 15c. Dr. H. F. Verwoerd.

70 President Swart

71 President and Mrs. Swart

1968 (2 Jan). Swart Commemoration. Chalk-surfaced paper. W **127** of South Africa (*tête-bêche*, sideways). P 14×15.

220	**70**	3c. orange-red, black and turquoise-blue		
		G. Inscribed in German	35	20
		A. Inscribed in Afrikaans	35	20
		E. Inscribed in English	35	20
221	**71**	15c. red, blackish olive and dull green.		
		G. Inscribed in German	1·50	1·75
		A. Inscribed in Afrikaans	1·50	1·75
		E. Inscribed in English	1·50	1·75
		a. Red, brownish olive and bronze-green		
		G. Inscribed in German	3·00	3·25
		A. Inscribed in Afrikaans	3·00	3·25
		E. Inscribed in English	3·00	3·25
220/1 *Set of 2 values in strips of three*			5·00	5·50
Set of 6 singles			2·00	2·25

The three languages appear, *se-tenant*, both horizontally and vertically, throughout the sheet.

1970 (14 Feb). Water 70 Campaign. As Nos. 299/300 of South Africa, but without phosphor band and inscr "SWA".

222	2½c. green, bright blue and chocolate	50	30
223	3c. Prussian blue, royal blue and buff	50	30

72 G.P.O., Windhoek

1970–71. As Nos. 202 and 204/5 but "POSGELD INKOMSTE" omitted and larger figure of value as in T **72**. W **127** of South Africa (*tête-bêche*, sideways on 1½ and 2c.).

224	**72**	½c. brown and pale blue (6.70)	1·00	30
225	–	1½c. slate-violet and salmon (1.6.71)	15·00	18·00
226	–	2c. deep bluish green and lemon (11.70)	5·00	40
224/6 *Set of 3*			19·00	18·00

1970 (24 Aug). 150th Anniv of Bible Society of South Africa. As Nos. 301/2 of South Africa, but inscr "SWA".

228	2½c. multicoloured	75	10
229	12½c. gold, black and blue	3·50	4·50

No. 228 has a phosphor frame, probably added in error.

A mint example of No. 229 exists with a second, blind, impression of the die-stamped features.

1971 (31 May). "Interstex" Stamp Exhibition, Cape Town. As No. 303A of South Africa, but without phosphor frame and inscr "SWA".

230	5c. light greenish blue, black and pale yellow	3·25	1·50

1971 (31 May). Tenth Anniv of Antarctic Treaty. As No. 304 of South Africa, but without phosphor frame, and inscr "SWA".

231	12½c. blue-black, greenish blue and orange-red	18·00	15·00

1971 (31 May). Tenth Anniv of the South African Republic. As Nos. 305/6 of South Africa, but without phosphor frame, and inscr "SWA".

232	2c. pale flesh and brown-red	3·25	75
233	4c. green and black	3·25	75

1972 (19 Sept). Centenary of SPCA. As No. 312 of South Africa, but inscr "SWA".

234	5c. multicoloured	3·00	1·25

WATERMARK. All issues from this date are on unwatermarked paper.

(Lettering by E. de Jong)

1973 (1 May). Scenery. T **73** and similar multicoloured designs showing paintings by Adolph Jentsch. P 11½×12½ (10 and 15c.) or 12½×11½ (others).

235	2c. Type **73**	75	75
236	4c. "After the Rain"	85	1·00
237	5c. "Barren Country"	1·00	1·25
238	10c. "Schaap River" (vert)	1·25	1·75
239	15c. "Namib Desert" (vert)	2·25	3·25
235/9 *Set of 5*		5·50	7·25

1973 (28 May). As Nos. 207 but without wmk. Phosphorised paper.

240	**50a** 3c. ultramarine and rose-red	2·50	2·00

No. 240 is also distinguishable in that the lettering of "SOUTH WEST AFRICA" is whiter.

74 *Sarcocaulon rigidum*

75 *Euphorbia virosa*

(Des D. Findlay)

1973 (1 Sept)–**79**. Succulents. Various multicoloured designs as T **74/5**. Phosphorised glossy paper (original printing of all values) or ordinary paper (1, 2, 3, 4, 5, 9, 10, 15, 20, 30, 50c.).

*(a) As T **74**. P 12½*

241	1c. Type **74**	15	10
	a. Black (face value, etc.) omitted	£250	
242	2c. *Lapidaria margaretae*	1·00	75
	a. Perf 14×13½ (4.8.79)	20	10
243	3c. *Titanopsis schwantesii*	20	10
	a. Black (face value, etc.) omitted	80·00	
	b. Perf 14×13½ (8.8.79)	30	15
244	4c. *Lithops karasmontana*	25	10
245	5c. *Caralluma lugardii*	40	50
	a. Black (face value, etc.) omitted	£140	
	b. Perf 14×13½ (12.12.79)	50	20
246	6c. *Dinteranthus microspermus*	2·50	3·50
247	7c. *Conophytum gratum*	1·50	2·75
248	9c. *Huernia oculata*	1·00	2·50
249	10c. *Gasteria pillansii*	1·25	1·00
	a. Black (face value, etc.) omitted	£275	
	b. Perf 14×13½ (13.8.79)	40	30
250	14c. *Stapelia pedunculata*	2·00	3·00
251	15c. *Fenestraria aurantiaca*	65	30
252	20c. *Decabelone grandiflora*	5·00	3·50
253	25c. *Hoodia bainii*	5·00	3·00

*(b) As T **75**. P 11½×12½ (30c., 1r.) or 12½×11½ (50c.)*

254	30c. Type **75**	75	1·00
	a. Perf 13½×14 (27.12.79)	70	90
255	50c. *Pachypodium namaquanum* (vert)	1·00	2·50
	a. Perf 14×13½ (18.12.79)	75	1·25
256	1r. *Welwitschia bainesii*	1·00	5·00
241/56 *Set of 16*		22·00	26·00

1973 (1 Sept)–**80**. Coil stamps. As Nos. 241/2 and 245 but photo, colours changed. P 14.

257	1c. black and light mauve	70	75
	a. Chalk-surfaced paper (7.76)	1·00	40
	b. Imperf×perf 14. Chalk-surfaced paper (1980)	4·75	5·50
258	2c. black and yellow	50	50
	a. Chalk-surfaced paper (7.76?)	1·00	50
	b. Imperf×perf 14. Chalk-surfaced paper (1.79)	1·00	40
	ba. Yellow omitted		
	bb. Black omitted		
259	5c. black and light rose-red	1·75	1·25
	a. Imperf×perf 14. Chalk-surfaced paper (8.2.78)	1·00	1·00
257/9 *Set of 3*		2·75	2·25

Coils of Nos. 257b, 258b and 259a come with every fifth stamp numbered on the reverse.

76 Chat-shrike

77 Giraffe, Antelope and Spoor

(Des D. Findlay)

1974 (13 Feb). Rare Birds. T **76** and similar vert designs. Multicoloured. P 12½×11½.

260	4c. Type **76**	2·25	1·00
261	5c. Peach-faced Lovebirds	2·75	1·50
262	10c. Damaraland Rock Jumper	5·00	5·50
263	15c. Rüppell's Parrots	7·00	9·50
260/3 *Set of 4*		15·00	16·00

(Des O. Schröder)

1974 (10 Apr). Twyfelfontein Rock-engravings. T **77** and similar multicoloured designs. P 11½×12½ (15c.) or 12½ (others).

264	4c. Type **77**	1·00	50
265	5c. Elephant, hyena, antelope and spoor	1·00	80
	a. Black (value and "SWA") omitted	£1200	
266	15c. Kudu cow (38×21 mm)	4·00	6·50
264/6 *Set of 3*		5·50	7·00

78 Cut Diamond

(Des M. Barnett)

1974 (30 Sept). Diamond Mining. T **78** and similar vert design. Multicoloured. P 12½×11½.

267	10c. Type **78**	2·75	4·25
268	15c. Diagram of shore workings	2·75	4·25

79 Wagons and Map of the Trek

(Des K. Esterhuysen)

1974 (13 Nov). Centenary of Thirstland Trek. P 11½×12½.

269	**79** 4c. multicoloured	75	1·00

80 Peregrine Falcon

81 Kolmannskop (ghost town)

(Des D. Findlay)

1975 (19 Mar). Protected Birds of Prey. T **80** and similar vert designs. Multicoloured. P 12½×11½.

270	4c. Type **80**	1·50	1·25
271	5c. Verreaux's Eagle	1·50	1·75
272	10c. Martial Eagle	2·50	4·00
273	15c. Egyptian Vulture	3·50	6·00
270/3 *Set of 4*		8·00	11·50

(Des A. H. Barrett)

1975 (23 July). Historic Monuments. T **81** and similar horiz designs. Multicoloured. P 11½×12½.

274	5c. Type **81**	15	15
275	9c. "Martin Luther" (steam tractor)	30	65
276	15c. Kurt von François and Old Fort, Windhoek	50	75
274/6	*Set of 3*	85	1·40

82 "View of Lüderitz"

(Des J. Hoekstra)

1975 (15 Oct). Otto Schröder. T **82** and similar horiz designs showing his paintings. Multicoloured. P 11½×12½.

277	15c. Type **82**	30	60
	a. Block of 4. Nos. 277/80	1·10	2·25
278	15c. "View of Swakopmund"	30	60
279	15c. "Harbour Scene"	30	60
280	15c. "Quayside, Walvis Bay"	30	60
277/80	*Set of 4*	1·10	2·25
MS281	122×96 mm. Nos. 277/80	1·00	3·50

Nos. 277/80 were printed together, in *se-tenant* blocks of four within the sheet.

83 Elephants

(Des H. Pager)

1976 (31 Mar). Prehistoric Rock Paintings. T **83** and similar horiz designs. Multicoloured. P 11½×12½.

282	4c. Type **83**	30	15
283	10c. Rhinoceros	30	60
284	15c. Antelope	35	70
285	20c. Man with bow and arrow	40	1·00
282/5	*Set of 4*	1·25	2·20
MS286	121×95 mm. Nos. 282/5	1·25	3·50

84 Schwerinsburg

(Des H. Pager)

1976 (14 May). Castles. T **84** and similar horiz designs. Multicoloured. P 11½×12½.

287	10c. Type **84**	20	30
288	15c. Schloss Duwisib	30	50
289	20c. Heynitzburg	30	70
287/9	*Set of 3*	70	1·25

85 Large-toothed Rock Hyrax

(Des D. Findlay)

1976 (16 July). Fauna Conservation. T **85** and similar horiz designs. Multicoloured. P 11½×12½.

290	4c. Type **85**	20	15
291	10c. Kirk's Dik-Dik	40	60
292	15c. Kuhl's Tree Squirrel	60	1·50
290/2	*Set of 3*	1·10	2·00

86 The Augustineum, Windhoek

(Des H. Pager)

1976 (17 Sept). Modern Buildings. T **86** and similar horiz design. P 11½×12½.

293	15c. black and yellow	30	60
294	20c. black and light yellow	40	80

Design:—20c. Katutura Hospital, Windhoek.

87 Ovambo Water Canal System

(Des A. H. Barrett)

1976 (19 Nov). Water and Electricity Supply. T **87** and similar horiz design. Multicoloured. P 11½×12½.

295	15c. Type **87**	30	50
296	20c. Ruacana Falls Power Station	40	75

88 Coastline near Pomona

(Des A. H. Barrett)

1977 (29 Mar). Namib Desert. T **88** and similar horiz designs. Multicoloured. P 12½.

297	4c. Type **88**	15	15
298	10c. Bush and dunes, Sossusvlei	20	20
299	15c. Plain near Brandberg	35	35
300	20c. Dunes, Sperr Gebiet	40	40
297/300	*Set of 4*	1·00	1·00

89 Kraal

(Des A. H. Barrett)

1977 (15 July). The Ovambo People. T **89** and similar horiz designs. P 11½×12½.

301	4c. multicoloured	10	10
302	10c. black, dull orange and cinnamon	20	15
303	15c. multicoloured	25	20
304	20c. multicoloured	25	35
301/4	*Set of 4*	70	70

Designs—10c. Grain baskets; 15c. Pounding grain; 20c. Women in tribal dress.

90 Terminal Buildings

(Des H. Pager and A. H. Barrett)

1977 (22 Aug). J. G. Strijdom Airport, Windhoek. P 12½.

305	**90**	20c. multicoloured	40	30

91 Drostdy, Lüderitz

92 Side-winding Adder

(Des A. H. Barrett)

1977 (4 Nov). Historic Houses. T **91** and similar horiz designs. Multicoloured. P 12×12½.

306	5c. Type **91**	15	10
307	10c. Woermannhaus, Swakopmund	25	30
308	15c. Neu-Heusis, Windhoek	30	35
309	20c. Schmelenhaus, Bethanie	40	40
306/9	*Set of 4*	1·00	1·00
MS310	122×96 mm. Nos. 306/9	1·00	2·00

(Des D. Findlay)

1978 (6 Feb). Small Animals. T **92** and similar horiz designs Multicoloured. P 12½.

311	4c. Type **92**	15	10
312	10c. Grant's Desert Golden Mole	25	20
313	15c. Palmato Gecko	25	25
314	20c. Namaqua Chameleon	25	25
311/14	*Set of 4*	80	70

93 Ostrich Hunting

(Des A. H. Barrett)

1978 (14 Apr). The Bushmen. T **93** and similar horiz designs in light grey-brown, stone and black. P 12×12½.

315	4c. Type **93**	25	10
316	10c. Woman carrying ostrich eggs	25	20
317	15c. Hunters kindling fire	30	20
318	20c. Woman with musical instrument	30	30
315/18	*Set of 4*	1·00	70

94 Lutheran Church, Windhoek

ALGEMENE STEMREG
(**95**)

(Des A. H. Barrett)

1978 (16 June). Historic Churches. T **94** and similar horiz designs. P 12½.

319	4c. grey-black and cinnamon	10	10
320	10c. grey-black and ochre	15	20
321	15c. grey-black and light brown-rose	20	25
322	20c. grey-black and light grey-blue	30	35
319/22	*Set of 4*	65	80
MS323	125×90 mm. Nos. 319/22	75	1·75

Designs:—10c. Lutheran Church, Swakopmund; 15c. Rhenish Mission Church, Otjimbingwe; 20c. Rhenish Missionary Church, Keetmanshoop.

1978 (1 Nov). Universal Suffrage. Designs as Nos. 244/5, 249 and 251/3 optd with T **95** (or similar inscr in English or German).

324	4c. *Lithops karasmontana*		
	A. Opt in Afrikaans	10	10
	E. Opt in English	10	10
	G. Opt in German	10	10
325	5c. *Caralluma lugardii*		
	A. Opt in Afrikaans	10	10
	E. Opt in English	10	10
	G. Opt in German	10	10
326	10c. *Gasteria pillansii*		
	A. Opt in Afrikaans	10	10
	E. Opt in English	10	10
	G. Opt in German	10	10
327	15c. *Fenestraria aurantiaca*		
	A. Opt in Afrikaans	10	15
	E. Opt in English	10	15
	G. Opt in German	10	15
328	20c. *Decabelone grandiflora*		
	A. Opt in Afrikaans	10	15
	E. Opt in English	10	15
	G. Opt in German	10	15
329	25c. *Hoodia bainii*		
	A. Opt in Afrikaans	15	15
	E. Opt in English	15	15
	G. Opt in German	15	15
324/9	*Set of* 18 (6 strips of 3)	1·25	1·50

Nos. 324A/G, 325A/G, 326A/G, 327A/G, 328A/G and 329A/G were each printed together, *se-tenant*, in horizontal and vertical strips of 3 throughout the sheets.

96 Greater Flamingo

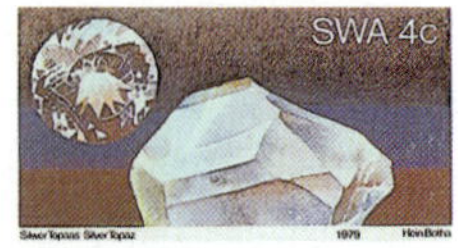

97 Silver Topaz

(Des D. Findlay)

1979 (5 Apr). Water Birds. T **96** and similar vert designs. Multicoloured. P 14.

330	4c. Type **96**	20	10
331	15c. White-breasted Cormorant	35	25
332	20c. Chestnut-banded Sand Plover	35	35
333	25c. Eastern White Pelican	35	40
330/3	*Set of 4*	1·10	1·00

(Des H. Botha)

1979 (26 Nov). Gemstones. T **97** and similar horiz designs. Multicoloured. P 14.

334	4c. Type **97**	30	10
335	15c. Aquamarine	65	35
336	20c. Malachite	70	45
337	25c. Amethyst	70	55
334/7	*Set of 4*	2·10	1·25

98 Killer Whale

99 Impala

(Des A. H. Barrett)

1980 (25 Mar). Whales. T **98** and similar multicoloured designs. P 14.

338	4c. Type **98**	20	15
339	5c. Humpback Whale (38×22 mm)	20	20
340	10c. Black Right Whale (38×22 mm)	30	30
341	15c. Sperm Whale (58×22 mm)	40	60
342	20c. Fin Whale (58×22 mm)	45	70
343	25c. Blue Whale (88×22 mm)	50	1·10
338/43	*Set of 6*	1·90	2·75
MS344	202×95 mm. Nos. 338/43	2·00	4·00

(Des P. Bosman)

1980 (25 June). 25th Anniv of Division of Nature Conservation and Tourism. Antelopes. T **99** and similar horiz designs. Multicoloured. P 14.

345	5c. Type **99**	15	10
346	10c. Topi	15	10
347	15c. Roan Antelope	25	15
348	20c. Sable Antelope	25	20
345/8	*Set of 4*	70	50

100 Black-backed Jackal

101 Meerkat

(Des Sheila Nowers (11, 12, 14, 16c.), P. Bosman (others))

1980 (1 Oct)–**89**. Wildlife. Multicoloured designs as T **100**. Ordinary paper. P 14.

349	1c. Type **100**	15	10
	a. Chalk-surfaced paper (11.6.85)	1·00	1·50
350	2c. Hunting Dog	15	10
	a. Chalk-surfaced paper (4.6.86)	1·25	1·75
351	3c. Brown Hyena	15	10

	a. Chalk-surfaced paper (10.2.88)	80	1·25
352	4c. Springbok	15	10
	a. Chalk-surfaced paper (29.7.87)	80	1·25
353	5c. Gemsbok	15	10
	a. Chalk-surfaced paper (11.6.85)	2·25	2·25
354	6c. Greater Kudu	15	10
	a. Chalk-surfaced paper (8.8.88)	2·50	2·75
355	7c. Mountain Zebra (horiz)	40	20
	a. Chalk-surfaced paper (19.3.86)	2·00	2·50
356	8c. Cape Porcupine (horiz)	20	10
	a. Chalk-surfaced paper (11.6.85)	2·25	2·50
357	9c. Ratel (horiz)	20	10
	a. Chalk-surfaced paper (10.2.88)	2·25	2·25
358	10c. Cheetah (horiz)	30	10
358*a*	11c. Blue Wildebeest (2.4.84)	40	30
358*b*	12c. African Buffalo (horiz) (1.4.85)	70	1·75
	ba. Booklet pane of 10 with margins all round (1.8.85)	5·50	
358*c*	14c. Caracal (horiz) (chalk-surfaced paper) (1.4.86)	3·50	2·25
359	15c. Hippopotamus (horiz)	30	10
	a. Chalk-surfaced paper (10.2.88)	80	1·25
359*b*	16c. Warthog (horiz) (chalk-surfaced paper) (1.4.87)	2·25	1·75
	ba. Ordinary paper (15.2.89)	3·75	3·75
360	20c. Eland (horiz)	30	10
	a. Chalk-surfaced paper (11.6.85)	80	1·50
361	25c. Black Rhinoceros (horiz)	50	20
	a. Chalk-surfaced paper (11.6.85)	80	1·50
362	30c. Lion (horiz)	50	20
	a. Chalk-surfaced paper (4.6.86)	1·75	2·50
363	50c. Giraffe	50	30
	a. Chalk-surfaced paper (21.4.88)	1·25	1·75
364	1r. Leopard	50	55
	a. Chalk-surfaced paper (4.6.86)	2·25	3·00
365	2r. African Elephant	50	90
	a. Chalk-surfaced paper (10.2.88)	3·00	3·25
349/65	*Set of 21*	10·50	8·50

Some printings of the 4, 15 and 25c. from 1983/4 were on phosphorescent paper. The same paper was used for printings of the 1, 2, 3, 8, 9, 10, 16c. (No. 359ba), 20, 30c. and 1r. during 1989. For $1.20 design as No. 359*b* see No. **MS**675 and for $1.30 as No. 358*c* see No. **MS**685.

(Des P. Bosman. Photo)

1980 (1 Oct). Coil stamps. Wildlife. Vert designs as T **101**. Imperf×perf 14.

366	1c. yellow-brown	20	20
367	2c. deep dull blue	20	20
368	5c. yellow-olive	30	30
366/8	*Set of 3*	65	65

Designs:—2c. Savanna Monkey; 5c. Chacma Baboon.

102 Von Bach

(Des A. H. Barrett)

1980 (25 Nov). Water Conservation. Dams. T **102** and similar horiz designs. Multicoloured. P 14.

369	5c. Type **102**	10	10
370	10c. Swakoppoort	15	10
371	15c. Naute	15	20
372	20c. Hardap	15	25
369/72	*Set of 4*	50	60

103 View of Fish River Canyon

104 *Aloe erinacea*

(Des A. H. Barrett)

1981 (20 Mar). Fish River Canyon. T **103** and similar horiz designs showing various views of canyon. P 14.

373	5c. multicoloured	10	10
374	15c. multicoloured	15	20
375	20c. multicoloured	20	25
376	25c. multicoloured	20	30
373/6	*Set of 4*	60	75

(Des D. Findlay)

1981 (14 Aug). Aloes. T **104** and similar vert designs. Multicoloured. P 14×13½.

377	5c. Type **104**	15	10
378	15c. *Aloe viridiflora*	25	25
379	20c. *Aloe pearsonii*	35	25
380	25c. *Aloe littoralis*	35	30
377/80	*Set of 4*	1·00	80

105 Paul Weiss-Haus

(Des A. H. Barrett)

1981 (16 Oct). Historic Buildings of Lüderitz. T **105** and similar horiz designs. Multicoloured. P 14.

381	5c. Type **105**	10	10
382	15c. Deutsche Afrika Bank	15	20
383	20c. Schroederhaus	20	30
384	25c. Altes Postamt	20	35
381/4	*Set of 4*	60	85
MS385	125×90 mm. Nos. 381/4	65	1·00

106 Salt Pan

107 Kalahari Starred Tortoise (*Psammobates oculifer*)

(Des A. H. Barrett)

1981 (4 Dec). Salt Industry. T **106** and similar horiz designs Multicoloured. P 14.

386	5c. Type **106**	10	10
387	15c. Dumping and washing	20	20
388	20c. Loading by conveyor	25	30
389	25c. Dispatch to refinery	30	35
386/9	*Set of 4*	75	85

(Des A. H. Barrett)

1982 (12 Mar). Tortoises. T **107** and similar horiz designs. Multicoloured. P 14.

390	5c. Type **107**	15	10
391	15c. Leopard Tortoise (*Geochelone pardalis*)	25	25
392	20c. Angulate Tortoise (*Chersina angulata*)	30	35
393	25c. Speckled Padloper (*Homopus signatus*)	40	45
390/3	*Set of 4*	1·00	1·00

108 Mythical Sea-monster

(Des Sheila Nowers)

1982 (28 May). Discoverers of South West Africa. (1st series). Bartolomeu Dias. T **108** and similar horiz designs. Multicoloured. P 14.

394	15c. Type **108**	20	20
395	20c. Bartolomeu Dias and map of Africa showing voyage	40	30
396	25c. Dias' caravel	65	40
397	30c. Dias erecting commemorative cross, Angra das Voltas, 25 July 1488	70	1·10
394/7	*Set of 4*	1·75	1·75

See also Nos. 455/8.

109 Brandberg

(Des A. H. Barrett)

1982 (3 Aug). Mountains of South West Africa. T **109** and similar horiz designs. Multicoloured. P 13½×14.

398	6c. Type **109**	10	10
399	15c. Omatako	20	20
400	20c. Die Nadel	25	30
401	25c. Spitzkuppe	30	35
398/401	*Set of 4*	75	85

110 Otjikaeva Head-dress of Herero Woman

(Des A. H. Barrett)

1982 (15 Oct). Traditional Head-dresses of South West Africa (1st series). T **110** and similar vert designs. Multicoloured. P 14.

402	6c. Type **110**	10	10
403	15c. Ekori head-dress of Himba	20	35
404	20c. Oshikoma hair-piece and iipando plaits of Ngandjera	25	45
405	25c. Omhatela head-dress of Kwanyama	25	60
402/5	*Set of 4*	70	1·25

See also Nos. 427/30.

111 Fort Vogelsang

112 Searching for Diamonds, Kolmanskop, 1908

(Des J. van Ellinckhuijzen)

1983 (16 Mar). Centenary of Lüderitz. T **111** and similar designs. P 14.

406	6c. brownish black and deep carmine-red	10	10
407	20c. brownish black and yellow-brown	15	20
408	25c. brownish black and chestnut	20	25
409	30c. brownish black and brown-purple	20	30
410	40c. brownish black and bright green	25	50
406/10	*Set of 5*	80	1·25

Designs: Vert (23×29 mm)—20c. Chief Joseph Fredericks; 30c. Heinrich Vogelsang (founder); 40c. Adolf Lüderitz (colonial promoter). Horiz (As T **111**)—25c. Angra Pequena.

(Des J. van Ellinckhuijzen)

1983 (8 June). 75th Anniv of Discovery of Diamonds. T **112** and similar designs. P 13½×14 (10, 20c.) or 14×13½ (others).

411	10c. deep brown and pale stone	15	15
412	20c. maroon and pale stone	30	40
413	25c. Prussian blue and pale stone	35	45
414	40c. brownish black and pale stone	55	85
411/14	*Set of 4*	1·25	1·75

Designs: Horiz (34×19 mm)—20c. Digging for diamonds, Kolmanskop, 1908. Vert (19×26 mm)—25c. Sir Ernest Oppenheimer (industrialist); 40c. August Stauch (prospector).

113 "Common Zebras drinking"

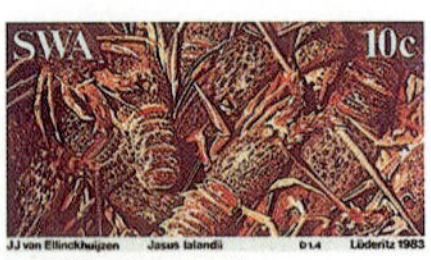

114 The Rock Lobster

(Des J. van Ellinckhuijzen)

1983 (1 Sept). Painters of South West Africa. T **113** and similar horiz designs. Multicoloured. P 13½×14.

415	10c. Type **113**	15	15
416	20c. "Rossing Mountain" (H. Henckert)	20	30
417	25c. "Stampeding African Buffalo" (F. Krampe)	20	35
418	40c. "Erongo Mountains" (J. Blatt)	30	55
415/18	*Set of 4*	75	1·25

(Des J. van Ellinckhuijzen)

1983 (23 Nov). Lobster Industry. T **114** and similar horiz designs Multicoloured. P 13½×14.

419	10c. Type **114**	15	15
420	20c. Mother ship and fishing dinghies	20	30
421	25c. Netting lobsters from dinghy	20	35
422	40c. Packing lobsters	30	55
419/22	*Set of 4*	75	1·25

115 Hohenzollern House

(Des A. H. Barrett)

1984 (8 Mar). Historic Buildings of Swakopmund. T **115** and similar horiz designs. P 14.

423	10c. grey-black and orange-brown	15	15
424	20c. grey-black and new blue	20	25
425	25c. grey-black and yellow-green	20	30
426	30c. grey-black and ochre	25	30
423/6	*Set of 4*	70	90

Designs:—20c. Railway Station; 25c. Imperial District Bureau; 30c. Ritterburg.

(Des A. H. Barrett)

1984 (25 May). Traditional Head-dresses of South West Africa (2nd series). Multicoloured designs as T **110.** P 14.

427	11c. Eendjushi head-dress of Kwambi	15	15
428	20c. Bushman woman	20	25
429	25c. Omulenda head-dress of Kwaluudhi	20	35
430	30c. Mbukushu women	20	35
427/30	*Set of 4*	70	1·00

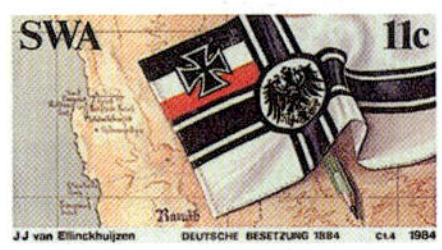

116 Map and German Flag

117 Sweet Thorn

(Des J. van Ellinckhuijzen)

1984 (7 Aug). Centenary of German Colonisation. T **116** and similar horiz designs. Multicoloured. P 14×14½.

431	11c. Type **116**	35	15
432	25c. Raising the German flag, 1884	65	50
433	30c. German Protectorate boundary marker	65	65
434	45c. Elizabeth and Leipzig (German corvettes)	1·40	2·00
431/4	*Set of 4*	2·75	3·00

(Des Eva-Maria Linsmayer)

1984 (22 Nov). Spring in South West Africa. T **117** and similar vert designs. Multicoloured. P 14.

435	11c. Type **117**	15	15
436	25c. Camel Thorn	20	35
437	30c. Hook Thorn	20	35
438	45c. Candle-pod Acacia	25	50
435/8	*Set of 4*	70	1·25

118 Head of Ostrich

(Des J. van Ellinckhuijzen)

1985 (15 Mar). Ostriches. T **118** and similar horiz designs. Multicoloured. P 14.

439	11c. Type **118**	40	10
440	25c. Ostrich on eggs	60	30
441	30c. Newly-hatched chick and eggs	70	50
442	50c. Mating dance	90	75
439/42	*Set of 4*	2·40	1·50

119 Kaiserstrasse

(Des A. H. Barrett)

1985 (6 June). Historic Buildings of Windhoek. T **119** and similar horiz designs. P 14.

443	12c. black and brown-ochre	15	10
444	25c. black and grey-olive	20	25
445	30c. black and brown	20	30
446	50c. black and yellow-brown	25	70
443/6	*Set of 4*	70	1·25

Designs:—25c. Turnhalle; 30c. Old Supreme Court Building; 50c. Railway Station.

120 Zwilling Locomotive

121 Lidumu-dumu (keyboard instrument)

(Des J. van Ellinckhuijzen)

1985 (2 Aug). Narrow-gauge Railway Locomotives. T **120** and similar horiz designs. Multicoloured. P 14.

447	12c. Type **120**	25	10
448	25c. Feldspur side-tank locomotive	45	25
449	30c. Jung and Henschel side-tank locomotive	40	35
450	50c. Henschel Hd locomotive	60	70
447/50	*Set of 4*	1·50	1·25

(Des J. van Ellinckhuijzen)

1985 (17 Oct). Traditional Musical Instruments. T **121** and similar horiz designs. Multicoloured. P 14.

451	12c. Type **121**	10	10
452	25c. Ngoma (drum)	15	20
453	30c. Okambulumbumbwa (stringed instrument)	20	25
454	50c. Gwashi (stringed instrument)	25	35
451/4	*Set of 4*	60	80

122 Erecting Commemorative Pillar at Cape Cross, 1486

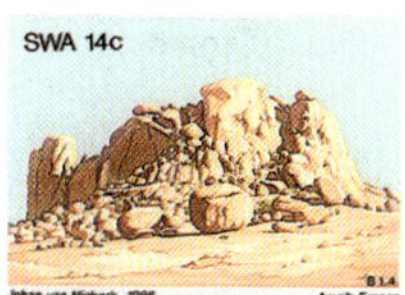

123 Ameib, Erongo Mountains

(Des J. van Ellinckhuijzen)

1986 (24 Jan). Discoverers of South West Africa (2nd series). Diogo Coa. T **122** and similar horiz designs. P 14.

455	12c. black, brownish grey and deep dull green	35	10
456	20c. black, brownish grey and pale red-brown	55	35
457	25c. black, brownish grey and dull blue	75	50
458	30c. black, brownish grey and dull reddish purple	80	85
455/8	*Set of 4*	2·25	1·60

Designs:—20c. Diogo Cao's coat of arms; 25c. Caravel; 30c. Diogo Cao.

(Des J. van Niekerk)

1986 (24 Apr). Rock Formations. T **123** and similar horiz designs Multicoloured. P 14.

459	14c. Type **123**	35	15
460	20c. Vingerklip, near Outjo	40	25
461	25c. Petrified sand dunes, Kuiseb River	45	40
462	30c. Orgelpfeifen, Twyfelfontein	50	55
459/62	*Set of 4*	1·50	1·25

PHILATELIC FOUNDATION MINIATURE SHEETS. These miniature sheets were issued by the Philatelic Foundation of Southern Africa and not the postal administration. They could be purchased by post or from a limited number of philatelic offices, mainly in South Africa, at a premium in aid of various national and international stamp exhibitions.

124 Model wearing Swakara Coat

125 Pirogue, Lake Liambezi

(Des J. van Ellinckhuijzen)

1986 (10 July). Karakul Industry. T **124** and similar vert designs. Multicoloured. P 14.

463	14c. Type **124**	15	15
464	20c. Weaving karakul wool carpet	25	30
465	25c. Flock of karakul ewes on Veld	25	45
466	30c. Karakul rams	30	60
463/6	*Set of 4*	85	1·40

The 30c. value exists as a Philatelic Foundation miniature sheet.

1986 (6 Nov). Life in the Caprivi Strip. T **125** and similar horiz designs. Multicoloured. P 14.

467	14c. Type **125**	30	15
468	20c. Ploughing with oxen	50	80
469	25c. Settlement in Eastern Caprivi	60	1·25
470	30c. Map of Caprivi Strip	1·00	2·00
467/70	*Set of 4*	2·25	3·75

126 "Gobabis Mission Station",1863

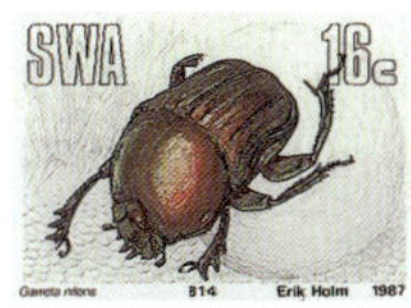

127 *Garreta nitens* (beetle)

1987 (19 Feb). Paintings by Thomas Baines. T **126** and similar horiz designs. Multicoloured. P 14.

471	14c. Type **126**	30	15
472	20c. "Outspan at Koobie", 1861	55	80
473	25c. "Outspan under Oomahaama Tree", 1862	70	1·50
474	30c. "Swakop River", 1861	80	2·25
471/4	*Set of 4*	2·10	4·25

The 25c. value exists as a Philatelic Foundation miniature sheet.

(Des E. Holm)

1987 (7 May). Useful Insects. T **127** and similar horiz designs Multicoloured. P 14.

475	16c. Type **127**	40	15
476	20c. *Alcimus stenurus* (fly)	60	80
477	25c. *Anthophora caerulea* (bee)	75	1·50
478	30c. *Hemiempusa capensis* (mantid)	1·10	2·00
475/8	*Set of 4*	2·50	4·00

128 Okaukuejo

(Des J. van Niekerk)

1987 (23 July). Tourist Camps. T **128** and similar horiz designs Multicoloured. P 14½×14.

479	16c. Type **128**	25	15
480	20c. Daan Viljoen	40	55
481	25c. Ai-Ais	45	1·25
482	30c. Hardap	50	1·40
479/82	*Set of 4*	1·40	3·00

129 Wreck of *Hope* (Dutch whaling schooner), 1804

130 Bartolomeu Dias

(Des Sheila Nowers)

1987 (15 Oct). Shipwrecks. T **129** and similar horiz designs Multicoloured. P 14.

483	16c. Type **129**	50	15
484	30c. *Tilly* (brig), 1885	75	80
485	40c. *Eduard Bohlen* (steamer), 1909	1·00	2·00
486	50c. *Dunedin Star* (liner), 1942	1·25	2·50
483/6	*Set of 4*	3·25	5·00

(Des Sheila Nowers)

1988 (7 Jan). 500th Anniv of Discovery of Cape of Good Hope by Bartolomeu Dias. T **130** and similar vert designs. Multicoloured. P 14.

487	16c. Type **130**	35	15
488	30c. Caravel	70	55
489	40c. Map of South West Africa, c. 1502	80	70
490	50c. King João II of Portugal	80	75
487/90	*Set of 4*	2·40	1·90

131 Sossusvlei

(Des J. van Niekerk)

1988 (3 Mar). Landmarks of South West Africa. T **131** and similar horiz designs. Multicoloured. P 14.

491	16c. Type **131**	30	15
492	30c. Sesriem Canyon	60	65
493	40c. Hoaruseb "clay castles"	70	1·25
494	50c. Hoba meteorite	80	1·50
491/4	*Set of 4*	2·25	3·25

132 First Postal Agency, Otyimbingue, 1888

133 Herero Chat

(Des H. Pulon)

1988 (7 July). Centenary of Postal Service in South West Africa. T **132** and similar horiz designs. Multicoloured. P 14.

495	16c. Type **132**	30	15
496	30c. Post Office, Windhoek, 1904	60	55
497	40c. Mail-runner and map	70	75
498	50c. Camel mail, 1904	80	1·00
495/8	*Set of 4*	2·25	2·25

The 50c. value exists as a Philatelic Foundation miniature sheet.

(Des G. Arnott)

1988 (3 Nov). Birds of South West Africa. T **133** and similar vert designs. Multicoloured. P 14.

499	16c. Type **133**	80	25
500	30c. Gray's Lark	1·25	80
501	40c. Rüppell's Bustard	1·40	1·25
502	50c. Monteiro's Hornbill	1·40	1·40
499/502	*Set of 4*	4·25	3·25

134 Dr. C. H. Hahn and Gross-Barmen Mission

135 Beech Commuter 1900

(Des H. Pulon)

1989 (16 Feb). Missionaries. T **134** and similar horiz designs Multicoloured. P 14.

503	16c. Type **134**	20	10
504	30c. Revd. J. G. Krönlein and Berseba Mission	35	60
505	40c. Revd. F. H. Kleinschmidt and Rehoboth Mission	40	70
506	50c. Revd. J. H. Schmelen and Bethanien Mission	40	85
503/6	*Set of 4*	1·25	2·00

(Des M. Botha)

1989 (18 May). 75th Anniv of Aviation in South West Africa. T **135** and similar horiz designs. Multicoloured. P 14.

507	18c. Type **135**	55	20
508	30c. Ryan Navion	90	60
509	40c. Junkers F-13	1·00	65
510	50c. Pfalz Otto biplane	1·25	85
507/10	*Set of 4*	3·25	2·10

The 50c. value exists as a Philatelic Foundation miniature sheet.

136 Barchan Dunes

(Des A. H. Barrett)

1989 (14 Aug). Namib Desert Sand Dunes. T **136** and similar horiz designs. Multicoloured. P 14.

511	18c. Barchan dunes	20	15
512	30c. Star dunes (36×20 mm)	30	40
513	40c. Transverse dunes	35	60
514	50c. Crescentic dunes (36×20 mm)	40	80
511/14	*Set of 4*	1·10	1·75

137 Ballot Box and Outline Map of South West Africa

1989 (24 Aug). South West Africa Constitutional Election. P 14.

515	**137**	18c. purple-brown and salmon	15	15
516		35c. deep grey-blue and pale emerald	25	40
517		45c. plum and lemon	35	60
518		60c. dull green and deep yellow- ochre	45	80
515/18		*Set of 4*	1·10	1·75

138 Gypsum

139 Oranjemund Alluvial Diamond Field

Type I

Type II

Two types of the 18c.
I Inscripbed "$K(H_3O)(UO_2)(SiO_4)$"
II Inscription corrected to "$K_2(UO_2)_2(SiO_3)_2(OH)_2SH_2O$"

(Des J. van Niekerk)

1989 (16 Nov)–**90**. Minerals. T **138/9** and similar multicoloured designs. Phosphorised paper (25c.) or chalk-surfaced paper (30, 35, 50c., 1r.). P 14.

No.	Description	Unused	Used
519	1c. Type **138**	15	30
520	2c. Fluorite	20	30
521	5c. Mimetite	30	30
522	7c. Cuprite	45	45
523	10c. Azurite	50	20
524	18c. Boltwoodite (inscr "$K(H_3O)(UO_2)(SiO_4)$")	70	10
	a. Formula corrected to "$K_2(UO_2)_2(SiO_3)_2(OH)_2SH_2O$" (25.10.90)	11·00	2·00
525	20c. Dioptase	75	15
526	25c. Type **139**	1·25	15
527	30c. Tsumeb lead and copper complex	1·00	20
528	35c. Rosh Pinah zinc mine	1·00	20
529	40c. Diamonds	1·25	30
530	45c. Wulfenite	1·00	30
531	50c. Uis tin mine	1·25	40
532	1r. Rössing uranium mine	1·75	1·00
533	2r. Gold	2·75	2·00
519/33	*Set of* 15	13·00	5·75

The 1, 2, 5, 7, 10, 18, 20, 40, 45c. and 2r. are vertical as T **138**, and the 25, 30, 35, 50c. and 1r. horizontal as T **139**.

140 Arrow Poison

(Des Eva-Maria Linsmayer)

1990 (1 Feb). Flora. T **140** and similar vert designs. Multicoloured. P 14.

No.	Description	Unused	Used
534	18c. Type **140**	20	10
535	35c. Baobab flower	35	40
536	45c. Sausage Tree flowers	40	50
537	60c. Devil's Claw	45	1·25
534/7	*Set of* 4	1·25	2·00

The 60c. value exists as a Philatelic Foundation miniature sheet.

NAMIBIA

South West Africa became independent, as Namibia, on 21 March 1990. The Walvis Bay Territory was ceded by South Africa to Namibia on 1 March 1994.

PRINTERS. The following stamps were printed in lithography by the Government Printer, Pretoria, South Africa.

141 Pres. Sam Nujoma, Map of Namibia and National Flag

142 Fish River Canyon

(Des T. Marais)

1990 (21 Mar). Independence. T **141** and similar multicoloured designs. P 14.

No.	Description	Unused	Used
538	18c. Type **141**	20	15
539	45c. Hands releasing dove and map of Namibia (vert)	50	75
540	60c. National flag and map of Africa	1·00	1·50
538/40	*Set of* 3	1·50	2·25

(Des J. van Ellinckhuijzen)

1990 (26 Apr). Namibia Landscapes. T **142** and similar horiz designs. Multicoloured. P 14.

No.	Description	Unused	Used
541	18c. Type **142**	25	20
542	35c. Quiver-tree forest, Keetmanshoop	50	35
543	45c. Tsaris Mountains	60	55
544	60c. Dolerite boulders, Keetmanshoop	70	65
541/4	*Set of* 4	1·90	1·60

The 60c. value exists as a Philatelic Foundation miniature sheet.

143 Stores on Kaiser Street, c. 1899

144 Maizefields

(Des J. van Ellinckhuijzen)

1990 (26 July). Centenary of Windhoek. T **143** and similar horiz designs. Multicoloured. P 14.

No.	Description	Unused	Used
545	18c. Type **143**	20	20
546	35c. Kaiser Street, 1990	30	35
547	45c. City Hall, 1914	40	65
548	60c. City Hall, 1990	50	1·00
545/8	*Set of* 4	1·25	2·00

1990 (11 Oct). Farming. T **144** and similar horiz designs. Multicoloured. P 14.

No.	Description	Unused	Used
549	20c. Type **144**	15	20
550	35c. Sanga bull	30	35
551	50c. Damara ram	40	45
552	65c. Irrigation in Okavango	50	60
549/52	*Set of* 4	1·25	1·40

145 Gypsum

146 Radiosonde Weather Balloon

(Des J. van Niekerk)

1991 (2 Jan). Minerals. Designs as Nos. 519/21 and 523/33, some with values changed, and new design (5r.), inscr "Namibia" as T **145**. Multicoloured. Chalk-surfaced paper (25, 30, 35, 50c., 1r.). P 14.

No.	Description	Unused	Used
553	1c. Type **145**	15	30
554	2c. Fluorite	25	30
555	5c. Mimetite	35	30
556	10c. Azurite	50	30
557	20c. Dioptase	65	10
558	25c. Type **139**	1·00	20
	a. Ordinary paper (14 June)	1·00	20
559	30c. Tsumeb lead and copper complex	85	20
560	35c. Rosh Pinah zinc mine	85	20
561	40c. Diamonds	1·50	25
562	50c. Uis tin mine	1·00	25
563	65c. Boltwoodite	90	35
564	1r. Rössing uranium mine	1·25	50
565	1r.50 Wulfenite	1·40	70
566	2r. Gold	2·00	1·10
567	5r. Willemite (vert as T 145)	3·00	2·75
553/67	*Set of* 15	14·00	7·00

Printings of the 5c. and 10c. in 1992 were on phosphorescent paper.

(Des L. Kriedemann)

1991 (1 Feb). Centenary of Weather Service. T **146** and similar horiz designs. Multicoloured. P 14.

No.	Description	Unused	Used
568	20c. Type **146**	20	20
569	35c. Sunshine recorder	35	30
570	50c. Measuring equipment	45	50
571	65c. Meteorological station, Gobabeb	50	60
568/71	*Set of* 4	1·40	1·40

147 Herd of Zebras

148 Karas Mountains

1991 (18 Apr). Endangered Species. Mountain Zebra. T **147** and similar horiz designs. Multicoloured. P 14.

572	20c. Type **147**	1·00	60
573	25c. Mare and foal	1·10	70
574	45c. Zebras and foal	1·50	1·75
575	60c. Two zebras	1·75	3·00
572/5 *Set of 4*		4·75	5·50

The 45c. value exists as a Philatelic Foundation miniature sheet.

(Des A. H. Barrett)

1991 (18 July). Mountains of Namibia. T **148** and similar horiz designs. Multicoloured. P 14.

576	20c. Type **148**	20	20
577	25c. Gamsberg Mountains	30	30
578	45c. Mount Brukkaros	45	70
579	60c. Erongo Mountains	65	1·00
576/9 *Set of 4*		1·50	2·00

149 Bernabe de la Bat Camp

150 Artist's Pallet

(Des J. van Niekerk)

1991 (24 Oct). Tourist Camps. T **149** and similar horiz designs Multicoloured. P 14.

580	20c. Type **149**	45	30
581	25c. Von Bach Dam Recreation Resort	55	45
582	45c. Gross Barmen Hot Springs	85	65
583	60c. Namutoni Rest Camp	1·00	1·00
580/3 *Set of 4*		2·50	2·25

(Des H. Pulon)

1992 (30 Jan). 21st Anniv of Windhoek Conservatoire. T **150** and similar horiz designs. Multicoloured. P 14.

584	20c. Type **150**	20	15
585	25c. French horn and cello	25	20
586	45c. Theatrical masks	50	60
587	60c. Ballet dancers	65	1·00
584/7 *Set of 4*		1·40	1·75

151 Mozambique Mouthbrooder

152 Old Jetty

(Des B. Jackson)

1992 (16 Apr). Freshwater Angling. T **151** and similar horiz designs. Multicoloured. P 14.

588	20c. Type **151**	40	20
589	25c. Large-mouthed Yellowfish	45	20
590	45c. Common Carp	85	50
591	60c. Sharp-toothed Catfish	95	65
588/91 *Set of 4*		2·40	1·40

The 45c. value exists as a Philatelic Foundation miniature sheet.

1992 (2 July). Centenary of Swakopmund. T **152** and similar horiz designs. Multicoloured. P 14.

592	20c. Type **152**	25	25
593	25c. Recreation centre	25	25
594	45c. State House and lighthouse	80	60
595	60c. Sea front	85	75
592/5 *Set of 4*		1·90	1·60
MS596 118×93 mm. Nos. 592/5		3·25	3·75

153 Running

154 Wrapping English Cucumbers

(Des B. Jackson)

1992 (24 July). Olympic Games, Barcelona. T **153** and similar horiz designs. Multicoloured. P 14.

597	20c. Type **153**	25	20
598	25c. Map of Namibia, Namibian flag and Olympic rings	30	20
599	45c. Swimming	50	40
600	60c. Olympic Stadium, Barcelona	65	55
597/600 *Set of 4*		1·50	1·25
MS601 115×75 mm. Nos. 597/600 (sold at 2r.)		2·25	3·00

1992 (10 Sept). Integration of the Disabled. T **154** and similar horiz designs. Multicoloured. P 14.

602	20c. Type **154**	20	15
603	25c. Weaving mats	20	15
604	45c. Spinning thread	40	30
605	60c. Preparing pot plants	55	50
602/5 *Set of 4*		1·25	1·00

155 Elephants in Desert

156 Herd of Simmentaler Cattle

(Des D. Murphy)

1993 (25 Feb). Namibia Nature Foundation. Rare and Endangered Species. T **155** and similar horiz designs. Multicoloured. P 14.

606	20c. Type **155**	60	20
607	25c. Sitatunga in swamp	30	20
608	45c. Black Rhinoceros	90	50
609	60c. Hunting Dogs	65	60
606/9 *Set of 4*		2·25	1·40
MS610 217×59 mm. Nos. 606/9 (sold at 2r.50)		3·75	3·50

(Des Carola Kronsbein-Goldbeck)

1993 (16 Apr). Centenary of Simmentaler Cattle in Namibia. T **156** and similar horiz designs. Multicoloured. P 14.

611	20c. Type **156**	30	10
612	25c. Cow and calf	30	15
613	45c. Bull	60	40
614	60c. Cattle on barge	85	75
611/14 *Set of 4*		1·90	1·25

The 45c. value exists as a Philatelic Foundation miniature sheet.

157 Sand Dunes, Sossusvlei

158 Smiling Child

(Des J. van Ellinckhuijzen)

1993 (4 June). Namib Desert Scenery. T **157** and similar horiz designs. Multicoloured. P 14.

615	30c. Type **157**	25	20
616	40c. Blutkuppe	25	20
617	65c. River Kuiseb, Homeb	40	45
618	85c. Desert landscape	60	65
615/18 *Set of 4*		1·40	1·40

(Des J. van Ellinckhuijzen)

1993 (6 Aug). S.O.S. Child Care in Namibia. T **158** and similar horiz designs. Multicoloured. P 14.

619	30c. Type **158**	20	20
620	40c. Family	25	20
621	65c. Modern house	45	55
622	85c. Young artist with mural	65	80
619/22 *Set of 4*		1·40	1·60

(New Currency.100 cents = 1 Namibia dollar)

159 *Charaxes jasius*

(Des A. Ainslie)

1993 (1 Oct). Butterflies. T **159** and similar vert designs. Multicoloured. P 14.

623	5c. Type **159**	20	40
624	10c. *Acraea anemosa*	20	40
625	20c. *Papilio nireus*	30	30
626	30c. *Junonia octavia*	30	10
627	40c. *Hypolimnus misippus*	30	10
628	50c. *Physcaeneura panda*	40	20
629	65c. *Charaxes candiope*	40	30
630	85c. *Junonia hierta*	50	40
631	90c. *Colotis cellmene*	50	40
632	$1 *Cacyreus dicksoni*	55	35
633	$2 *Charaxes bohemani*	80	80
634	$2.50 *Stugeta bowkeri*	1·00	1·10
635	$5 *Byblia anvatara*	1·50	1·75
623/35	*Set of* 13	6·25	6·00

For similar design inscribed "STANDARDISED MAIL" see No. 648. For 5c. and 50c. with elliptical perforations see Nos. 707/8.

160 White Seabream

(Des B. Jackson)

1994 (4 Feb). Coastal Angling. T **160** and similar horiz designs Multicoloured. P 14.

636	30c. Type **160**	25	25
637	40c. Kob	25	25
638	65c. West Coast Steenbras	40	40
639	85c. Galjoen	60	60
636/9	*Set of* 4	1·40	1·40
MS640	134×89 mm. Nos. 636/9 (sold at $2.50)	2·00	2·50

161 Container Ship at Wharf

162 *Adenolobus pechuelii*

(Des Liza van der Wal (85c.))

1994 (1 Mar). Incorporation of Walvis Bay Territory into Namibia. T **161** and similar vert designs. Multicoloured. P 14.

641	30c. Type **161**	40	30
642	65c. Aerial view of Walvis Bay	60	90
643	85c. Map of Namibia	95	1·40
641/3	*Set of* 3	1·75	2·40

(Des Auriol Batten)

1994 (8 Apr). Flowers. T **162** and similar vert designs. Multicoloured. P 14.

644	35c. Type **162**	25	25
645	40c. *Hibiscus elliottiae*	25	25
646	65c. *Pelargonium cortusifolium*	40	40
647	85c. *Hoodia macrantha*	50	60
644/7	*Set of* 4	1·25	1·40

1994 (8 Apr). Butterflies. Vert design as T **159**, but inscr "STANDARDISED MAIL". Multicoloured. P 14.

648	35c. Graphium antheus	40	20

No. 648 was initially sold at 35c., but this was subsequently increased to reflect changes in postal rates.

163 Yellow-billed Stork

164 Steam Railcar, 1908

(Des A. Barrett)

1994 (3 June). Storks. T **163** and similar vert designs. Multicoloured. P 14.

649	35c. Type **163**	60	30
650	40c. Abdim's Stork	60	40
651	80c. African Open-bill Stork	80	80
652	$1.10 White Stork	1·00	1·25
649/52	*Set of* 4	2·75	2·50

(Des H. Botha)

1994 (5 Aug). Steam Locomotives. T **164** and similar horiz designs. Multicoloured. P 14.

653	35c. Type **164**	45	30
654	70c. Krauss side-tank locomotive No. 106, 1904	70	50
655	80c. Class 24 locomotive, 1948	75	55
656	$1.10 Class 7C locomotive, 1914	1·10	80
653/6	*Set of* 4	2·75	1·90

The 80c. value exists as a Philatelic Foundation miniature sheet.

165 Cape Cross Locomotive No. 84 Prince Edward, 1895

166 National Arms

(Des H. Botha)

1995 (8 Mar). Centenary of Railways in Namibia. T **165** and similar horiz designs. Multicoloured. P 14.

657	35c. Type **165**	45	25
658	70c. Steam locomotive, German South West Africa	70	35
659	80c. South African Railways Class 8 steam locomotive	75	40
660	$1.10 Trans-Namib Class 33-400 diesel electric locomotive	1·10	55
657/60	*Set of* 4	2·75	1·40
MS661	101×94 mm. Nos. 657/60	2·75	2·50
	a. Optd "November 1995" on sheet margin (1 Nov)	3·25	3·00

(Des B. Wepener)

1995 (21 Mar). 5th Anniv of Independence. P 14.

662	**166** 35c. multicoloured	45	30

No. 662 is inscribed "STANDARDISED MAIL" and was initially sold for 35c., but this was subsequently increased to reflect changes in postal rates.

167 Living Tortoise and *Geochelone stromeri* (fossil)

168 Martii Rautanen and Church

(Des L. Kriedemann)

1995 (24 May). Fossils. T **167** and similar vert designs. Multicoloured. P 14.

663	40c. Type **167**	65	25
664	80c. Ward's Diamond Bird and *Diamantornis wardi* (fossil eggs)	1·00	70
665	90c. Hyraxes and *Prohyrax hendeyi* skull	1·10	1·00
666	$1.20 Crocodiles and *Crocodylus lloydi* skull	1·40	2·00
663/6	*Set of 4*	3·75	3·50

The 80c. value exists as a Philatelic Foundation miniature sheet.

(Des H. Pulon)

1995 (10 July). 125th Anniv of Finnish Missionaries in Namibia. T **168** and similar horiz designs. Multicoloured. P 14.

667	40c. Type **168**	25	20
668	80c. Albin Savola and hand printing press	50	50
669	90c. Karl Weikkolin and wagon	60	65
670	$1.20 Dr. Selma Rainio and Onandjokwe Hospital	85	95
667/70	*Set of 4*	2·00	2·10

169 Ivory Buttons

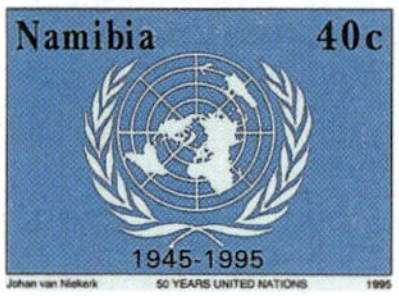

170 UN Flag

(Des H. Pulon)

1995 (16 Aug). Personal Ornaments. T **169** and similar vert designs. Multicoloured. P 14.

671	40c. Type **169**	20	20
672	80c. Conus shell pendant	45	45
673	90c. Cowrie shell headdress	55	55
674	$1.20 Shell button pendant	85	95
671/4	*Set of 4*	1·90	2·00

(Des Sheila Nowers)

1995 (1 Sept). "Singapore '95" International Stamp Exhibition. Sheet, 110×52 mm, containing design as No. 359*b* with altered face value and inscription. P 14.

MS675	$1.20 multicoloured	1·10	1·40

No. **MS**675 shows the exhibition emblem printed on the sheet margin.

(Des J. van Niekerk)

1995 (24 Oct). 50th Anniv of the United Nations. P 14.

676	**170** 40c. new blue and black	25	30

171 Bogenfels Arch

172 Sister Leoni Kreitmeier and Döbra Education and Training Centre

(Des Christine Marais. Litho Harrison)

1996 (1 Apr). Tourism. T **171** and similar horiz designs. Multicoloured. P 15×14.

677	45c. Type **171**	15	15
678	90c. Ruacana Falls	30	30
679	$1 Epupa Falls	30	30
680	$1.30 Herd of wild horses	35	50
677/80	*Set of 4*	1·00	1·10

No. 677 is inscribed "Standardised Mail" and was initially sold at 45c.

(Des J. van Niekerk. Litho Harrison)

1996 (27 May). Centenary of Catholic Missions in Namibia. T **172** and similar horiz designs. Multicoloured. P 15×14.

681	50c. Type **172**	20	20
682	95c. Father Johann Malinowski and Heirachabis Mission	30	40
683	$1 St. Mary's Cathedral, Windhoek	30	40
684	$1.30 Archbishop Joseph Gotthardt and early church, Ovamboland	35	80
681/4	*Set of 4*	1·00	1·60

(Des Sheila Nowers)

1996 (8 June). "CAPEX '96" International Stamp Exhibition, Toronto. Sheet, 105×45 mm, containing design similar to No. 358*c* with new face value and inscription. P 14½×14.

MS685	$1.30 multicoloured	1·00	1·40

173 Children and UNICEF Volunteer

(Des A. Ainslie. Litho Harrison)

1996 (14 June). 50th Anniv of UNICEF. T **173** and similar horiz design. Multicoloured. P 15×14.

686	50c. Type **173**	15	15
687	$1.30 Girls in school	60	60

No. 686 is inscribed "STANDARD POSTAGE" and was initially sold at 50c.

174 Boxing

175 Scorpius

(Des B. Jackson. Litho Harrison)

1996 (27 June). Centennial Olympic Games, Atlanta. T **174** and similar horiz designs. Multicoloured. P 15×14.

688	50c. Type **174**	15	15
689	90c. Cycling	50	40
690	$1 Swimming	30	40
691	$1.30 Running	30	55
688/91	*Set of 4*	1·10	1·40

No. 688 is inscribed "Standard Postage" and was initially sold at 50c.

(Des J. van Ellinckhuijzen. Litho Harrison)

1996 (12 Sept). Stars in the Namibian Sky. T **175** and similar horiz designs. Multicoloured. P 15×14.

692	50c. Type **175**	15	15
693	90c. Sagittarius	25	30
694	$1 Southern Cross	30	30
695	$1.30 Orion	40	50
692/5	*Set of 4*	1·00	1·10
MS696	100×80 mm. No. 694	1·50	1·75

No. 692 is inscribed "Standard Postage" and was initially sold at 50c.

For No. **MS**696 revalued to $3.50 see No. **MS**706.

176 Urn-shaped Pot

177 Khauxainas Ruins

(Des Sheila Nowers. Litho Harrison)

1996 (17 Oct). Early Pottery. T **176** and similar vert designs Multicoloured. P 14×15.

697	50c. Type **176**	15	15
698	90c. Decorated storage pot	30	40
699	$1 Reconstructed cooking pot	30	40
700	$1.30 Storage pot	35	70
697/700	*Set of 4*	1·00	1·50

No. 697 is inscribed "Standard Postage" and was initially sold at 50c.

(Des J. van Ellinckhuijzen. Litho Harrison)

1997 (6 Feb). Khauxainas Ruins. T **177** and similar horiz designs showing different views. P 15×14.

701	50c. multicoloured	35	20
702	$1 multicoloured	75	55
703	$1.10 multicoloured	85	75
704	$1.50 multicoloured	1·40	2·00
701/4	*Set of 4*	3·00	3·25

No. 701 is inscribed "Standard postage" and was initially sold at 50c.

178 Ox

179 Heinrich von Stephan

(Des J. van Ellinckhuijzen. Litho Harrison)

1997 (12 Feb). "HONG KONG '97" International Stamp Exhibition and Chinese New Year ("Year of the Ox"). Sheet 103×67 mm. P 15×14.

MS705	**178** $1.30 multicoloured	1·10	1·40

1997 (12 Feb). Support for Organised Philately. No. **MS**696 with margin additionally inscr "Reprint February 17 Sold in aid of organized Philately N$3.50".

MS706	$1 Southern Cross (sold at $3.50)	2·00	2·25

(Litho Harrison)

1997 (26 Mar). As Nos. 623 and 628, but P 14½ (with two elliptical holes on each vertical side).

707	5c. Type **159**	25	25
708	50c. Physcaeneura panda	1·00	75

(Des J. van Ellinckhuijzen. Litho Harrison)

1997 (8 Apr). Death Centenary of Heinrich von Stephan (founder of UPU). P 14×15.

709	**179** $2 multicoloured	1·25	1·40

180 Cinderella Waxbill

181 Helmet Guineafowl

(Des Julia Birkhead. Photo Harrison)

1997 (6 May). Waxbills. T **180** and similar horiz design. Multicoloured. P 14×14½ (with one elliptical hole on each horizontal side).

710	50c. Type **180**	25	30
	a. Booklet pane. Nos. 710/11, each×5	2·25	
711	60c. Black-cheeked Waxbill	25	30

Nos. 710/11 were only issued in $5.50 stamp booklets.

(Des Isabel van der Ploeg. Photo Enschedé)

1997 (6 May). Greetings Stamp. P 15×14.

712	**181** $1.20 multicoloured	1·00	1·00

For similar designs see Nos. 743/6.

182 Jackass Penguins calling

183 Caracal

(Des D. Thorpe. Litho Harrison)

1997 (15 May). Endangered Species. Jackass Penguin. T **182** and similar vert designs. Multicoloured. P 14×15.

713	50c. Type **182**	35	30
714	$1 Incubating egg	55	40
715	$1.10 Adult with chick	60	50
716	$1.50 Penguins swimming	75	60
713/16	*Set of 4*	1·90	1·50
MS717	101×92 mm. As Nos. 713/16, but without the WWF symbol (sold at $5)	1·90	1·50

No. 713 is inscribed "STANDARD POSTAGE" and was initially sold for 50c.

(Des Sheila Nowers. Litho Harrison)

1997 (12 June). Wildcats. T **183** and similar horiz designs Multicoloured. P 15×14.

718	50c. Type **183**	20	20
719	$1 *Felis lybica*	40	30
720	$1.10 *Serval*	50	40
721	$1.50 Black-footed Cat	60	55
718/21	*Set of 4*	1·50	1·25
MS722	100×80 mm. $5 As No. 721	2·00	2·25

No. 718 is inscribed "STANDARD POSTAGE" and was initially sold at 50c. No. **MS**722 was sold in aid of organised philately in Southern Africa.

184 *Catophractes alexandri*

185 Collecting Bag

(Des T. Breckwoldt (Nos. 723/7), Isabel van der Ploeg (others). Litho Enschedé)

1997 (27 June). Greeting Stamps. Flowers and Helmet Guineafowl. T **184** and similar horiz designs. Multicoloured. P 14×13½.

723	50c. Type **184**	30	30
	a. Booklet pane. Nos. 723/7, each ×2, and (10) labels	2·75	
724	50c. *Crinum paludosum*	30	30
725	50c. *Gloriosa superba*	30	30
726	50c. *Tribulus zeyheri*	30	30
727	50c. *Aptosimum pubescens*	30	30
728	50c. Helmet Guineafowl raising hat	30	30
	a. Booklet pane. Nos. 728/32, each ×2, and (10) labels	4·00	
729	50c. Holding bouquet	30	30
730	50c. Ill in bed	30	30
731	$1 With heart round neck	50	60
732	$1 With suitcase and backpack	50	60
723/32	*Set of 10*	3·00	3·25

These stamps only come from $5 (Nos. 723/7) or $7 (Nos. 728/32) stamp booklets where they occur in panes of 10 (5×2) with margins all round and greetings labels at top and bottom. Nos. 723/7 are inscribed "Standard Postage" and were initially sold at 50c. each.

(Des J. van Niekerk. Litho Harrison)

1997 (8 July). Basket Work. T **185** and similar vert designs. Multicoloured. P 14×15.

733	50c. Type **185**	20	20
734	90c. Powder basket	30	30
735	$1.20 Fruit basket	35	35
736	$2 Grain basket	70	75
733/6	*Set of 4*	1·40	1·40

186 Veterinary Association Coat of Arms

(Litho Harrison)

1997 (12 Sept). 50th Anniv of Namibian Veterinary Association. P 14×14½.

737	**186** $1.50 multicoloured	50	50
	a. Tête-bêche pair	1·00	1·00

No. 737 was issued in sheets of 10 containing one row of *tête-bêche* pairs.

187 Head of Triceratops

188 German South West Africa Postman

(Des J. van Ellinckhuijzen. Litho Enschedé)

1997 (27 Sept). Youth Philately. Dinosaurs. Sheet 82×56 mm. P 12½×13.

MS738 **187** $5 multicoloured ... 1·50 1·75

(Des J. Madisia. Litho Enschedé)

1997 (9 Oct). World Post Day. P 14×15.

739 **188** 50c. multicoloured ... 30 30

No. 739 is inscribed "STANDARD POSTAGE" and was initially sold at 50c.

189 False Mopane

190 Flame Lily

(Des Auriol Batten. Litho Enschedé)

1997 (10 Oct). Trees. T **189** and similar vert designs. Multicoloured. P 14×15.

740 50c. Type **189** ... 15 20

741 $1 Ana Tree ... 30 40

742 $1.10 Shepherd's Tree ... 35 55

743 $1.50 Kiaat ... 50 70

740/3 *Set of 4* ... 1·10 1·60

No. 740 is inscribed "STANDARD POSTAGE" and was initially sold at 50c.

(Des Isabel van der Ploeg. Litho Enschedé)

1997 (3 Nov). Christmas. Multicoloured designs as T **181** showing Helmet Guineafowl, each with festive frame. P 13×12½.

744 50c. Guineafowl facing right ... 20 20

745 $1 Guineafowl in grass ... 35 30

746 $1.10 Guineafowl on rock ... 35 40

747 $1.50 Guineafowl in desert ... 50 55

744/7 *Set of 4* ... 1·25 1·25

MS748 110×80 mm. $5 Helmet Guineafowl (*vert*). P 12½×13 ... 3·00 3·25

No. 744 is inscribed "standard postage" and was initially sold at 50c.

(Des D. Murphy. Litho Enschedé)

1997 (3 Nov). Flora and Fauna. T **190** and similar vert designs. Multicoloured.

(a) P 13½

749 5c. Type **190** ... 10 50

a. Perf 14×13½ ... 10 75

ab. Booklet pane. Nos. 749a/66a with margins all round ... 9·50

750 10c. Bushman Poison ... 10 50

a. Perf 14×13½ ... 10 75

751 20c. Camel's Foot ... 10 50

a. Perf 14×13½ ... 10 75

752 30c. Western Rhigozum ... 20 50

a. Perf 14×13½ ... 15 75

753 40c. Blue-cheeked Bee-eater ... 50 50

a. Perf 14×13½ ... 35 75

754 50c. Laughing Dove ... 50 20

a. Perf 14×13½ ... 35 45

755 50c. Peach-faced Lovebird ... 50 20

a. Perf 14×13½ ... 25 25

ab. Booklet pane. No. 755a ×10 with margins all round ... 2·25

756 60c. Lappet-faced Vulture ... 60 25

a. Perf 14×13½ ... 50 60

757 90c. Yellow-billed Hornbill ... 60 25

a. Perf 14×13½ ... 50 60

758 $1 Lilac-breasted Roller ... 60 30

a. Perf 14×13½ ... 50 60

759 $1.10 Hippopotamus ... 1·00 40

a. Perf 14×13½ ... 60 60

760 $1.20 Giraffe ... 1·00 40

a. Perf 14×13½ ... 70 60

761 $1.20 Leopard ... 70 30

a. Perf 14×13½ ... 35 35

ab. Booklet pane. No. 761a ×10 with margins all round ... 3·00

762 $1.50 Elephant ... 1·25 45

a. Perf 14×13½ ... 80 70

763 $2 Lion ... 75 45

a. Perf 14×13½ ... 60 85

764 $4 Buffalo ... 1·25 85

a. Perf 14×13½ ... 1·00 1·50

765 $5 Black Rhinoceros ... 2·00 1·25

a. Perf 14×13½ ... 1·50 2·25

766 $10 Cheetah ... 2·50 2·25

a. Perf 14×13½ ... 2·00 3·25

749/66 *Set of 18* ... 12·50 9·00

(b) Self-adhesive. P 12×12½

767 50c. As No. 755 ... 25 35

768 $1 As No. 758 ... 45 55

769 $1.20 As No. 761 ... 50 70

767/9 *Set of 3* ... 1·10 1·40

Nos. 755a and 767 are inscribed "standard postage" and were each initially sold at 50c., Nos. 761a and 769 are inscribed "postcard rate" and were each initially sold at $1.20.

Stamps perforated 14×13½ (13.8×13.3) come from the three booklets only. They show 20 teeth along the top and the bottom instead of the 19 on the sheet stamps (13.3).

191 John Muafangejo

192 Gabriel B. Taapopi

(Des J. van Ellinckhuijzen. Litho Harrison)

1997 (27 Nov). 10th Death Anniv of John Muafangejo (artist). P 14×15.

770 **191** 50c. multicoloured ... 60 50

No. 770 is inscribed "STANDARD POSTAGE" and was initially sold at 50c.

(Des J. van Ellinckhuijzen. Litho Enschedé)

1998 (15 Jan). Gabriel B. Taapopi (educator) Commemoration. P 14×15.

771 **192** 50c. silver and reddish brown ... 40 40

No. 771 is inscribed "STANDARD POSTAGE" and was sold for 50c.

193 Year of the Tiger

(Litho Enschedé)

1998 (19 Jan). International Stamp and Coin Exhibition 1997, Shanghai. Sheets, 165×125 mm or 97×85 mm, containing multicoloured designs as T **193**.

(a) Lunar New Year

MS772 165×125 mm. $2.50×6. Type **193**; Light green tiger and circular symbol; Yellow tiger and head symbol; Blue tiger and square symbol; Emerald tiger and square symbol; Mauve tiger and triangular symbol (61×29 mm). P13½×12½ ... 2·50 3·25

MS773 97×85 mm. $6 Symbolic tiger designs(71×40 mm). P 12½ ... 1·25 1·40

(b) Chinese Calendar

MS774 165×125 mm. $2.50×6. Various calendar symbols (24×80 mm). P 14×13½ ... 2·50 3·25

MS775 97×85 mm. $6 Soft toy tigers (71×36 mm). P 12½ ... 1·25 1·40

(c) 25th Anniv of Shanghai Communique

MS776 165×125 mm. $3.50×4. Pres. Nixon's visit to China, 1972; Vice Premier Deng Xiaoping's visit to U.S.A., 1979; Pres. Reagan's visit to China, 1984; Pres. Bush's visit to China, 1989 (61×32 mm). P 13½×12½ ... 2·00 3·00

MS777 97×85 mm. $6 China-U.S.A. Communique, 1972 (69×36 mm). P 14½×13 ... 1·25 1·40

(d) Pres. Deng Xiaoping's Project for Unification of China

MS778 165×125 mm. $3.50×4. Beijing as national capital; Return of Hong Kong; Return of Macao; Links with Taiwan (37×65 mm). P 14×13 ... 2·00 3·00

MS779 97×85 mm. $6 Reunified China (71×41 mm). P 12½ ... 1·25 1·40

(e) Return of Macao to China, 1999

MS780	Two sheets, each 165×120 mm. (a) $4.50×3 Carnival dragon and modern Macao (44×33 mm). P 13½. (b) $4.50×3 Ruins of St. Paul's Church, Macao (62×29 mm). P 13½×12½. *Set of 2 sheets*	3·00	5·50
MS781	Two sheets, each 97×85 mm. (a) $6 Carnival dragon and modern Macao (62×32 mm). P 13½×12½. (b) $6 Deng Xiaoping and ruins of St. Paul's Church, Macao (71×36 mm). P 12½. *Set of 2 sheets*	1·75	2·75

194 Leopard

(Des Sheila Nowers. Litho Enschedé)

1998 (26 Jan). Large Wild Cats. T **194** and similar horiz designs. Multicoloured. P 13×12½.

782	$1.20 Type **194**	60	25
783	$1.90 Lioness and cub	80	65
784	$2 Lion	80	1·00
785	$2.50 Cheetah	95	1·40
782/5	*Set of 4*	2·75	3·00
MS786	112×98 mm. Nos. 782/5	3·50	3·50

195 Narra Plant

(Des Christine Marais. Litho Enschedé)

1998 (9 Feb). Narra Cultivation. P 12½.

787	**195** $2.40 multicoloured	55	65

196 Collecting Rain Water

196a Princess Diana Wearing Protective Mask

(Des J. van Ellinckhuijzen. Litho Enschedé)

1998 (23 Mar). World Water Day. P 14×15.

788	**196** 50c. multicoloured	50	40

No. 788 is inscribed "STANDARD POSTAGE" and was initially sold at 50c. On 1 April 1998 the standard postage rate was increased to 55c.

(Des D. Miller. Litho Questa)

1998 (31 Mar). Diana, Princess of Wales Commemoration. Sheet, 145×70 mm, containing vert designs as T **196a**. Multicoloured. P 14½×14.

MS789	$1 Type **196a**; $1 Wearing Red Cross badge; $1 Wearing white shirt; $1 Comforting crippled child	1·60	1·75

197 White-faced Scops Owl

(Des H. Denker. Litho Enschedé)

1998 (1 Apr). Owls of Namibia. T **197** and similar multicoloured designs. P 13½×12½.

790	55c. Black-tailed Tree Rat (20×24 mm)	40	40
	a. Booklet pane. Nos. 790/4	3·75	
791	$1.50 Type **197**	90	95
792	$1.50 Barred Owl	90	95
793	$1.90 Spotted Eagle Owl	1·00	1·25
794	$1.90 Barn Owl (61×24 mm)	1·00	1·25
790/4	*Set of 5*	3·75	4·25

Nos. 790/4 were only issued in $7.35 stamp booklets. For miniature sheet containing $11 as No. 794 see No. **MS**850.

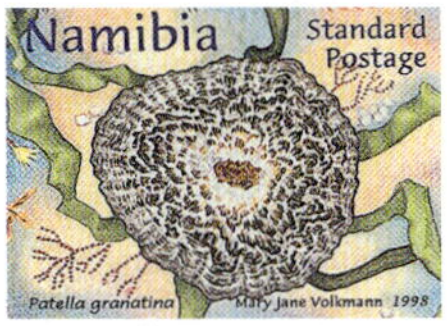

198 *Patella ganatina* (Limpet)

(Des Mary Volkmann. Litho Enschedé)

1998 (14 May). Shells. T **198** and similar horiz designs. Multicoloured. P 13×12½.

795	55c. Type **198**	30	10
796	$1.10 *Cymatium cutaceum africanum* (Triton)	65	30
797	$1.50 *Conus mozambicus* (Cone)	85	65
798	$6 *Venus verrucosa* (Venus Clam)	2·75	3·75
795/8	*Set of 4*	4·00	4·25
MS799	109×84 mm. Nos. 795/8	4·50	5·50

No. 795 is inscribed "Standard Postage" and was initially sold at 55c.

199 Underwater Diamond Excavator

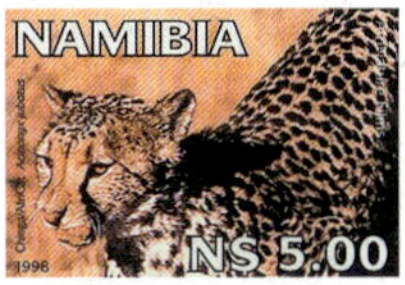

200 "Chinga" (cheetah)

(Des S. Williams. Litho Questa)

1998 (18 May). Marine Technology. Sheet 70×90 mm. P 14½×14.

MS800	**199** $2.50 multicoloured	2·50	2·50

(Litho Enschedé)

1998 (5 June). Wildlife Conservation. "Racing for Survival" (Olympic sprinter Frank Frederiks v cheetah). Sheet 108×80 mm. P 13.

MS801	**200** $5 multicoloured	1·75	2·25

201 Namibian Beach

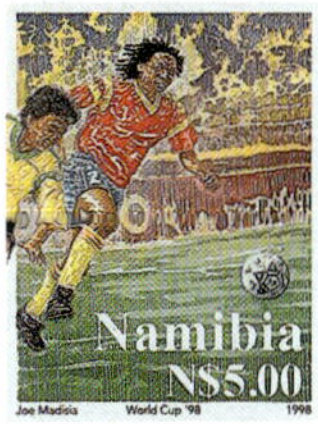

202 Two Footballers

(Litho Cartor)

1998 (5 June). World Environment Day. T **201** and similar horiz designs. Multicoloured. P 13×13½.

802	55c. Type **201**	20	10
803	$1.10 Okavango sunset	40	30
804	$1.50 Sossusvlei	55	60
805	$1.90 African Moringo tree	80	1·00
802/5	*Set of 4*	1·75	1·75

No. 802 is inscribed "STANDARD POSTAGE" and was initially sold at 55c.

(Des J. Madisia. Litho Enschedé)

1998 (15 June). World Cup Football Championship, France. Sheet 80×56 mm. P 14×13½.

MS806	**202** $5 multicoloured	1·25	1·75

203 Chacma Baboon

204 Carmine Bee-eater

(Des D. Murphy. Litho Cartor)

1998 (18 June). Animals with their Young. Sheet, 176×60 mm, containing T **203** and similar vert designs. P 13½×13.

MS807	$1.50 Type **203**; $1.50 Blue Wildebeest; $1.50 Meercat(suricate); $1.50 African Elephant; $1.50 Burchell's Zebra	1·75	2·50

(Des Mary Volkmann. Litho Cartor)

1998 (26 Sept). Wildlife of the Caprivi Strip. T **204** and similar multicoloured designs. P 12½.

808	60c. Type **204**	75	75
	a. Sheetlet. Nos. 808/17	6·75	6·75
809	60c. Sable Antelope (40×40 mm)	75	75
810	60c. Lechwe (40×40 mm)	75	75
811	60c. Woodland Waterberry	75	75
812	60c. Nile Monitor (40×40 mm)	75	75
813	60c. African Jacana	75	75
814	60c. African Fish Eagle	75	75
815	60c. Woodland Kingfisher	75	75
816	60c. Nile Crocodile (55×30 mm)	75	75
817	60c. Black Mamba (32×30 mm)	75	75
808/17	*Set of* 10	6·75	6·75

Nos. 808/17 were printed together, *se-tenant*, in sheetlets of 10 with the backgrounds forming a composite design.

205 Black Rhinoceros and Calf

(Des H. Denker. Litho Cartor)

1998 (20 Oct). "ILSAPEX '98" International Stamp Exhibition, Johannesburg. Sheet 103×68 mm. P 13.

MS818	**205** $5 multicoloured	1·75	2·25

206 Blue Whale

(Des Mary Butterfield. Litho Questa)

1998 (23 Oct). Whales of the Southern Oceans (joint issue with Norfolk Island and South Africa). Sheet 103×70 mm. P 13½×14.

MS819	**206** $5 multicoloured	1·75	2·25

207 Damara Dik-dik

(Des L. Voight. Litho Enschedé)

1999 (18 Jan). "Fun Stamps for Children". Animals. T **207** and similar multicoloured design. P 14×13½ ($1.80) or 13½×14 ($2.65).

820	$1.80 Type **207**	2·00	1·50
821	$2.65 Striped Tree Squirrel (26×36 mm)	3·50	3·00

208 Yoka perplexed

209 *Windhuk* (liner)

(Des J. van Ellinckhuijzen. Litho Enschedé)

1999 (1 Feb). "Yoka the Snake" (cartoon) (1st series). T **208** and similar multicoloured designs. Self-adhesive. P 5.

822	$1.60 Type **208**	35	40
	a. Booklet pane. Nos. 822/31	3·00	
823	$1.60 Yoka under attack (33×27 mm)	35	40
824	$1.60 Yoka caught on branch	35	40
825	$1.60 Yoka and wasps (33×27 mm)	35	40
826	$1.60 Yoka and footprint	35	40
827	$1.60 Yoka and tail of red and white snake	35	40
828	$1.60 Mouse hunt (33×27 mm)	35	40
829	$1.60 Snakes entwined	35	40
830	$1.60 Red and white snake singing	35	40
831	$1.60 Yoka sulking (33×27 mm)	35	40
822/31	*Set of* 10	3·00	3·50

Nos. 822/31 were only printed, *se-tenant*, in $16 stamp booklets on which the backing paper forms the cover.

See also Nos. **MS**835 and **MS**877.

(Litho German State Ptg Wks, Berlin)

1999 (18 Mar). *Windhuk* (liner) Commemoration. Sheet 110×90 mm. P 14.

MS832	**209** $5.50, multicoloured	1·50	2·00

210 Zögling Glider, 1928

211 Yoka the Snake with Toy Zebra

(Des D. Bagnall. Litho Cartor)

1999 (13 Apr). Gliding in Namibia. T **210** and similar horiz design. Multicoloured. P 13.

833	$1.60 Type **210**	40	50
834	$1.80 Schleicher glider, 1998	60	75

(Des J. van Ellinckhuijzen. Litho German State Ptg Wks, Berlin)

1999 (27 Apr). "iBRA '99" International Stamp Exhibition, Nuremberg. Sheet 110×84 mm. P 14.

MS835	**211** $5.50 multicoloured	1·25	1·75

212 Greater Kestrel

(Des H. Denker. Litho Cartor)

1999 (18 May). Birds of Prey. T **212** and similar horiz designs. Multicoloured. P 13½.

836	60c. Type **212**	60	35
837	$1.60 Common Kestrel ("Rock Kestrel")	1·10	80
838	$1.80 Red-headed Falcon	1·10	90
839	$2.65 Lanner Falcon	1·75	2·50
836/9	*Set of* 4	4·00	4·00

213 Wattled Crane

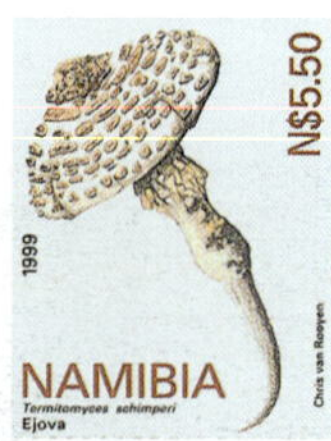

214 *Termitomyces schimperi* (fungus)

(Des C. van Rooyen. Litho Enschedé)

1999 (28 June). Wetland Birds. T **213** and similar horiz designs. Multicoloured. P 13×12½.

840	$1.60 Type **213**	1·00	65
841	$1.80 Variegated Sandgrouse ("Burchell's Sandgrouse")	1·10	85
842	$1.90 Pratincole	1·10	85
843	$2.65 Eastern White Pelican	1·75	2·25
840/3	*Set of 4*	4·50	4·25

(Des C. van Rooyen. Litho Enschedé)

1999 (2 July). "PhilexFrance '99" International Stamp Exhibition, Paris. Sheet 79×54 mm. P 14×13½.

MS844	**214** $5.50 multicoloured	1·75	2·25

215 *Eulophia hereroensis* (orchid)

216 Johanna Gertze

(Des Mary Volkmann. Litho and embossed Cartor)

1999 (21 Aug). "China '99" International Philatelic Exhibition, Beijing. Orchids. T **215** and similar diamond-shaped designs. Multicoloured. P 12½.

845	$1.60 Type **215**	80	65
846	$1.80 *Ansellia africana*	90	75
847	$2.65 *Eulophia leachii*	1·40	1·50
848	$3.90 *Eulophia speciosa*	2·00	2·25
845/8	*Set of 4*	4·50	4·75
MS849	72×72 mm. $5.50 *Eulophia walleri*	2·00	2·50

(Des H. Denker. Litho Cartor)

1999 (30 Sept). Winning entry in 5th Stamp World Cup, France. Sheet 120×67 mm design as No. 794, but with changed face value. Multicoloured. P 13½×12½.

MS850	$11 Barn Owl (61×24 mm)	7·00	7·00

(Des Inge Madlé. Litho Enschedé)

1999 (1 Oct). Johanna Gertze Commemoration. P 12½×13.

851	**216** $20 Indian red, flesh and bright new blue	4·00	5·00

217 Sunset over Namibia

(Des J. van Ellinckhuijzen. Litho Enschedé)

1999 (31 Dec)–**2002**. New Millennium. T **217** and similar multicoloured designs. P 13½.

852	$2.20 Type **217**	90	1·00
853	$2.40 Sunrise over Namibia (1.1.2000)	1·00	1·25
MS854	77×54 mm. $9 Globe (hologram) (37×44 mm). P 14×13½	3·00	3·50

218 South African Shelduck

standard postage

(**219**)

(Des P. Huebsch. Litho Enschedé)

2000 (18 Feb). Ducks of Namibia. T **218** and similar horiz designs. Multicoloured. P 13.

855	$2 Type **218**	90	60
856	$2.40 White-faced Whistling Duck	1·10	75
857	$3 Comb Duck ("Knobbilled duck")	1·40	1·25
858	$7 Cape Shoveler	3·00	4·00
855/8	*Set of 4*	5·75	6·00

No. 858 is inscribed "Cape shoveller" in error.

2000 (1 Mar). Nos. 749/52 optd as T **219**.

859	65c. on 5c. Type **190**	40	15
860	$1.80 on 30c Western Rhigozum	75	40
861	$3 on 10c. Bushman Poison	1·00	1·00
862	$6 on 20c. Camel's Foot	1·75	2·25
859/62	*Set of 4*	3·50	3·50

No. 859 was initially sold at 65c. The other surcharges show face values.

220 Namibian Children

(Des Saatchi and Saatchi. Litho Enschedé)

2000 (21 Mar). 10th Anniv of Independence. T **220** and similar square design. Multicoloured. P 13½×14.

863	65c. Type **220**	50	15
864	$3 Namibian flag	1·75	1·75

221 Actor playing Jesus wearing Crown of Thorns

(Des J. van Ellinckhuijzen. Litho Enschedé)

2000 (1 Apr). Easter Passion Play. T **221** and similar horiz design. Multicoloured. P 13½×14.

865	$2.10 Type **221**	70	70
866	$2.40 On the way to Calvary	80	80

222 Tenebrionid Beetle

(Des Mary Volkmann. Litho SNP Ausprint, Australia)

2000 (22 May). "The Stamp Show 2000" International Stamp Exhibition, London. Wildlife of Namibian Dunes. Sheet 165×73 mm containing T **222** and similar multicoloured designs. P 14½.

MS867	$2 Type **222**; $2 Namib Golden Mole; $2 Brown Hyena; $2 Shovel-snouted Lizard (49×30 mm); $2 Dune Lark (25×36 mm); $6 Namib Side-winding Adder (25×36 mm)	7·00	7·50

No. **MS**867 shows the dunes, animal tracks and vegetation highlighted in varnish and phosphor ink.

223 *Welwitschia mirabilis*

(Des H. Denker. Litho Enschedé)

2000 (21 June). *Welwitschia mirabilis* (prehistoric plant). T **223** and similar vert designs. Multicoloured. P 14×13½.

868 65c. Type **223** 40 20
869 $2.20 *Welwitschia mirabilis* from above .... 1·00 60
870 $3 Seed pods .... 1·40 1·40
871 $4 Flats covered by *Welwitschia mirabilis* plants .... 1·50 2·00
868/71 *Set of* 4 .... 3·75 3·75

No. 868 is inscribed "Standard inland mail" and was sold for 65c.

224 High Energy Stereoscopic System Telescopes

(Des K. van Ellinckhuijzen. Litho Enschedé)

2000 (7 July). High Energy Stereoscopic System Telescopes Project, Namibian Khomas Highlands. Sheet 100×70 mm. P 13½×14.

MS872 **224** $11 multicoloured .... 5·00 6·00

225 Jackal-berry Tree

(Des H. Denker. Litho Enschedé)

2000 (16 Aug). Trees with Nutritional Value. T **225** and similar horiz designs. Multicoloured. P 13½×14.

873 65c. Type **225** 45 25
874 $2 Sycamore Fig .... 1·00 80
875 $2.20 Bird Plum .... 1·10 85
876 $7 Marula .... 3·25 4·00
873/6 *Set of* 4 .... 5·25 5·50

No. 873 is inscribed "Standard inland mail" and was sold for 65c.

226 Yoka and Nero the Elephant

(Des K. van Ellinckhuijzen. Litho Enschedé)

2000 (1 Sept). "Yoka the Snake" (cartoon) (2nd series). Sheet 103×68 mm. P 13.

MS877 **226** $11 multicoloured .... 4·50 5·50

227 Striped Anemone

(Des Anja Denker. Litho Enschedé)

2001 (18 Apr). Sea Anemone. T **227** and similar vert designs. Multicoloured. P 13½.

878 (70c.) Type **227** 45 15
879 $2.45 Violet-spotted Anemone .... 1·00 70
880 $3.50 Knobbly Anemone .... 1·40 1·40
881 $6.60 False Plum Anemone .... 2·50 3·00
878/81 *Set of* 4 .... 4·75 4·75

No. 878 is inscribed "Standard inland mail" and was originally sold for 70c.

228 Cessna 210 Turbo Aircraft

(Des D. Bagnall. Litho Enschedé)

2001 (9 May). Civil Aviation. T **228** and similar horiz designs. Multicoloured. P 13½.

882 (70c.) Type **228** 70 25
883 $2.20 Douglas DC-6B airliner .... 1·50 70
884 $2.50 Pitts S2A bi-plane .... 1·50 80
885 $13.20 Bell 407 helicopter .... 5·75 6·50
882/5 *Set of* 4 .... 8·50 7·50

No. 882 is inscribed "Standard inland mail" and was originally sold for 70c.

229 Wood-burning Stove

(Des J. van Ellinckhuijzen. Litho Enschedé)

2001 (15 Aug). Renewable Energy Sources. T **229** and similar square designs. Multicoloured. P 13½×14.

886 ($1) Type **229** 70 70
a. Sheetlet. Nos. 886/95 .... 8·00 9·50
887 ($1) Biogas digester 70 70
888 ($1) Solar cooker 70 70
889 ($1) Re-cycled tyre 70 70
890 ($1) Solar water pump 70 70
891 $3.50 Solar panel above traditional hut .... 1·10 1·40
892 $3.50 Solar street light .... 1·10 1·40
893 $3.50 Solar panels on hospital building .... 1·10 1·40
894 $3.50 Solar telephone .... 1·10 1·40
895 $3.50 Wind pump .... 1·10 1·40
886/95 *Set of* 10 .... 8·00 9·50

Nos. 886/95 were printed together, *se-tenant*, in sheetlets of 10 with the backgrounds forming a composite design which extends onto the sheetlet margins Nos. 886/90 are inscribed "Standard Mail" and were originally sold for $1 each.

230 Ruppell's Parrot

231 Plaited Hair, Mbalantu

(Des H. Denker. Litho Cartor)

2001 (5 Sept). Flora and Fauna from the Central Highlands. T **230** and similar multicoloured designs. P 12½.

896 ($1) Type **230** 90 90
a. Sheetlet. Nos. 896/905 .... 9·75 11·00
897 ($1) Flap-necked Chameleon (40×30 mm) 90 90
898 ($1) Klipspringer (40×30 mm) 90 90
899 ($1) Rockrunner (40×30 mm) 90 90
900 ($1) Pangolin (40×40 mm) 90 90
901 $3.50 Camel Thorn (55×30 mm) .... 1·25 1·50
902 $3.50 Berg Aloe (40×30 mm) .... 1·25 1·50
903 $3.50 Kudu (40×40 mm) .... 1·25 1·50
904 $3.50 Rock Agama (40×40 mm) .... 1·25 1·50
905 $3.50 Armoured Ground Cricket (40×30 mm) .... 1·25 1·50
896/905 *Set of* 10 .... 9·75 11·00

Nos. 896/905 were printed together, *se-tenant*, in sheetlets of 10 with the backgrounds forming a composite design which extends onto the sheetlet margins. Nos. 896/900 are inscribed "Standard Mail" and were originally sold for $1 each.

(269)

2006 (20 June). Nos. 758 and 760 surch with T **269**.

1044	($3.30) on $1 Lilac-breasted roller	2·50	1·25
1045	($3.30) on $1.20 Giraffe	2·50	1·25

Nos. 1044/5 are surch "Postcard Rate" and were sold for $3.30 each.

270 Orange River in the Southern Namib

(Des Helge Denker. Litho Enschedé)

2006 (24 July). Perennial Rivers of Namibia. T **270** and similar multicoloured designs. P 13½ ($5.50) or 14×13½ (others).

1046	$3.10 Type **270**	1·50	60
1047	$5.50 Kunene River, northern Namib (24×58 mm)	2·00	1·50
1048	($19.90) Zambezi River and African fish eagle (90×25 mm)	6·50	8·00
1046/8	*Set of* 3	9·00	9·00

No. 1048 is inscribed "Registered Non Standard Mail" and sold for $19.90 each.

271 Construction of OMEG Railway Line

(Des Anja Denker. Litho Enschedé)

2006 (9 Aug). Centenary of OMEG Railway Line. T **271** and similar horiz designs. Multicoloured. P 15×14.

1049	$3.10 Type **271**	1·50	60
1050	$3.70 Henschel Class NG15 locomotive No. 41	1·75	90
1051	$5.50 Narrow gauge Class Jung tank locomotive No. 9 pulling iron ore train	2·50	3·25
1049/51	*Set of* 3	5·25	4·25

272 Centenary Emblem and Cheetah

273 Bullfrog (*Pyxicephalus adspersus*) and River

(Des H. Mupotsa. Litho Austrian State Ptg Wks, Vienna)

2006 (17 Nov). Centenary of Otjiwarongo. P 14.

1052	**272**	$1.90 multicoloured	1·00	1·00

No. 1052 was printed in sheetlets of ten with the two rows of five stamps separated by a horizontal central gutter.

(Des Helge Denker and Anja Denker. Litho Enschedé)

2007 (15 Feb). Biodiversity. T **273** and similar horiz designs. Multicoloured. P 14×13½.

1053	5c. Type **273**	10	10
1054	10c. Mesemb (*Namibia cinerea*) and desert landscape	10	10
1055	30c. Solifuge (*Ceroma inerme*) and seashore with shell, plover and seal	10	10
1056	40c. Jewel beetle (*Julodis egho*) and antelopes in desert	15	10
1057	60c. Compass jellyfish (*Chrysaora hysoscella*), turtle and seabirds	20	10
1058	($1.90) Web-footed gecko (*Palmatogecko rangei*) and sand dunes	60	20
1059	$2 Otjikoto tilapia (*Tilapia guinasana*)	70	30
1059a	$4.10 Thimblegrass (*Fingerhuthia africana*) (1.10.08)	1·00	45
1059b	$4.60 Bronze whaler shark (*Caracharhinus branchyurus*) (1.10.08)	1·10	50
1059c	$5.30 Deepsea red crab (*Chaceon mantae*) (1.10.08)	1·50	1·10
1060	$6 Milkbush (*Euphorbia damarana*) and zebras in desert	1·75	70
1061	($6) African hawk-eagle with prey and landscape with trees	1·75	70
1062	$10 Black-faced impala and sandy river-bed	2·50	1·50
1062a	$18.20 False ink cap (*Podaxis pistillaris*) (1.10.08)	1·80	1·90
1063	$25 Lichens (*Santessonia* and *Xanthorea*sp.) on seashore rocks	5·50	4·50
1064	$50 Baobab, elephant and antelopes in bushveldt	9·00	9·00
1053/64	*Set of* 16	25·00	19·00

No. 1062a was inscr 'Registered Mail' and originally sold for $18.20.

Nos. 1053/9, 1060/2 and 1063/4 were re-issued on November 2008 with PVA gum instead of gum arabic.

No. 1058 is inscr "Standard Mail" and sold for $1.90. No. 1061 is inscr "Non-Standard Mail" and sold for $6.

274 Caracal, Snake and Zebras, Otjovasandu Wilderness Area ("Conservation")

275 Red-billed Quelea

(Des Helge Denker)

2007 (22 Mar). Centenary of Etosha National Park. Multicoloured. P 14×13½.

(a) T **274** *and similar horiz designs. Litho and die-stamped Enschedé*

1065	($1.90) Type **274**	1·00	35
1066	$3.40 Lions, elephants and gemsbok, Okaukuejo Waterhole and Resort ("Tourism")	1·75	90
1067	($17.20) Researcher and elephant herd ("Anthrax Research")	7·00	8·00
1065/7	*Set of* 3	8·75	8·25

(b) T **275** *and similar multicoloured designs. Litho Enschedé*

MS1068 172×112 mm. ($2.25)×10 Gabar goshawk (29×29 mm); *Acacia tortillis* (umbrella thorn) (49×29 mm); Type **275**; Burchell's zebra; Elephant; Blue Wildebeest; *Salvadora persica* (mustard tree); *Anax tristis* (black emperor dragonfly) (39×40 mm); Springbok (39×40 mm); *Agama aculeata* (ground agama) (39×40 mm) 9·50 11·00

No. 1065 is inscr "Standard Mail" and sold for $1.90. No. 1067 is inscr "Inland Registered Mail Paid" and sold for $17.20. The stamps within **MS**1068 are all inscr "Postcard Rate", and the miniature sheet sold for $22.50. The stamps and margins of **MS**1068 form a composite design showing wildlife at the Salvadora Waterhole.

276 *Anax imperator* (blue emperor)

(Des Anja Denker. Litho Enschedé)

2007 (16 Apr). Dragonflies of Namibia. T **276** and similar horiz designs. Multicoloured. Litho. P 13×14.

No.	Description	Unused	Used
1069	($1.90) Type **276**	75	20
1070	$3.90 *Trithemis kirbyi ardens* (rock dropwing)	1·50	70
1071	$4.40 *Trithemis arteriosa* (red-veined dropwing)	1·60	2·00
1072	($6) *Trithemis stictica* (jaunty dropwing)	2·00	2·25
1069/72	*Set of* 4	5·25	4·75
MS1073	75×54 mm. $6 *Urothemis edwardsii* (blue basker)	2·00	2·50

No. 1069 is inscr "Standard Mail" and sold for $1.90.
No. 1072 is inscr "Non Standard Mail Paid" and sold for $6.

277 *Commiphora kraeuseliana*

(Des J. J. van Ellinckhuijzen. Litho Enschedé)

2007 (20 July). Commiphora (corkwood) Trees of Namibia. T **277** and similar horiz designs. Multicoloured. P 13½×14.

No.	Description	Unused	Used
1074	($1.90) Type **277**	70	20
1075	$3.40 *Commiphora wildii*	1·25	60
1076	$3.90 *Commiphora glaucescens*	1·50	90
1077	($6) *Commiphora dinteri*	2·50	3·00
1074/7	*Set of* 4	5·50	4·25

No. 1074 is inscr "Standard Mail" and sold for $1.90 No. 1077 is inscr "Non-standard Mail" and sold for $6.

278 *Cheiridopsis caroli-schmidtii*

(Des Anja Denker. Litho Enschedé)

2007 (31 Aug). Indigenous Flowers of Namibia. T **278** and similar horiz designs. Multicoloured. P 13½×14.

No.	Description	Unused	Used
1078	($1.90) Type **278**	70	20
1079	($6) *Namibia ponderosa*	2·25	2·25
1080	($17.20) *Fenestraria rhopalophylla*	6·50	7·50
1078/80	*Set of* 3	8·50	9·00

No. 1078 is inscr "STANDARD MAIL" and sold for $1.90 No. 1079 is inscr "NON-STANDARD MAIL" and sold for $6.

No. 1080 is inscr "INLAND REGISTERED MAIL PAID" and sold for $17.20.

Standard Mail ═ (279)

N$ 3.70 ═ (280)

N$ 4.20 ═ (281)

N$ 4.85 ═ (282)

Non Standard Mail ═ (283)

Registered Mail ═ (284)

2007 (1 Oct). Nos. 757, 760, 762 and 764 surch with Types **279/84**.

No.	Description	Unused	Used
1081	($2) on 90c. Yellow-billed hornbill	1·25	50
1082	($2) on $1.20 Giraffe	1·25	50
1083	($2) on $1.50 Elephant	1·25	50
1084	($2) on $4 Buffalo	1·25	50
1085	$3.70 on $1.20 Giraffe	1·75	1·00
1086	$4.20 on $1.20 Giraffe	2·25	1·75
1087	$4.85 on $1.20 Giraffe	2·25	1·75
1088	($6.50) on $1.20 Giraffe	2·75	2·50
1089	($16.45) on $1.20 Giraffe	7·00	8·00
1081/9	*Set of* 8	19·00	15·00

Nos. 1081/4 are surch 'Standard Mail' and sold for $2, No. 1088 is surch 'Non Standard Mail' and sold for $6.50 and No. 1089 is surch 'Registered Mail' and sold for $16.45.

285 Nyala (Malawi)

(Des Anja Denker. Litho Enschedé)

2007 (9 Oct). Second Joint Issue of Southern Africa Postal Operators Association Members. Sheet 135×170 mm containing T **285** and similar square designs showing national mammals of Association members. Multicoloured. P 14.

No.	Description	Unused	Used
MS1090	($2) Type **285**; ($2) Nyala (Zimbabwe); ($2) Burchell's zebra (Botswana); ($2) Oryx (Namibia); ($2) Buffalo (Zambia)	3·00	3·25
	a. Country inscr "NAMIBIA" and margin inscr "National Animals SECOND SAPOA JOINT ISSUE" in silver		

The stamps within **MS**1090 are all inscr "Standard mail".

Miniature sheets of similar designs were also issued by Botswana, Malawi, Zambia and Zimbabwe. Botswana and Zambia also issued sheet stamps.

286 Southern Masked-weaver (*Ploceus velatus*)

(Des Anja Denker. Litho Enschedé)

2008 (28 Feb). Weaver Birds of Namibia. T **286** and similar vert designs. Multicoloured. P 13½×14.

No.	Description	Unused	Used
1091	($2) Type **286**	60	20
1092	$3.70 Red-headed weaver (*Anaplectes rubriceps*)	1·00	35
1093	($3.90) White-browed sparrow-weaver (*Plocepasser mahali*)	1·00	35
1094	$4.20 Sociable weaver (*Philetarius socius*)	1·25	1·00
1095	($18.45) Thick-billed weaver (*Amblyospiza albifrons*)	6·00	7·50
1091/5	*Set of* 5	9·00	8·50

No. 1091 is inscr 'Standard Mail' and sold for $2, No. 1093 is inscr 'Postcard Rate' and sold for $3.90 and No. 1095 is inscr 'Inland Registered Mail Paid' and sold for $18.45.

287 *Euphorbia virosa*

287a I
Damaged "E" in "Euphorbia"

287b II
Redrawn (corrected) "E" in "Euphorbia"

(Des Anja Denker. Litho Enschedé)

2008 (3 Mar). Euphorbias of Namibia. T **287** and similar vert designs. Multicoloured. P 13½×14.

1096 ($3.90) Type **287** .... 1·00 25
1097 $6.45 *Euphorbia dregeana* .... 1·75 1·75
a. Type II (27.5.2008) .... 2·00 2·00
1098 ($22.95) *Euphorbia damarana* .... 5·00 6·50
1096/8 *Set of* 3 .... 7·00 7·75

No. 1096 is inscr 'Postcard Rate' and sold for $3.90 and No. 1098 is inscr 'Registered Non Standard Mail' and sold for $22.95.

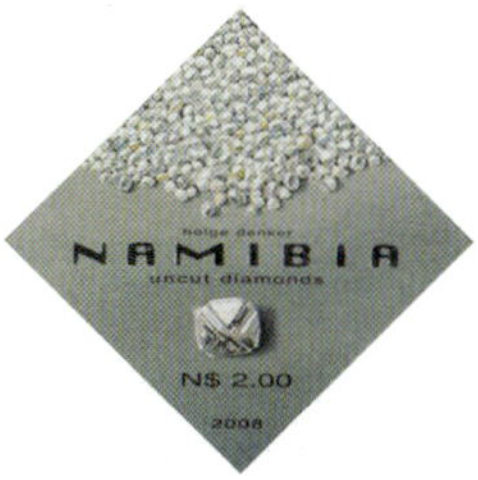

288 Uncut Diamonds

(Des Helge Denker. Litho Enschedé)

2008 (15 Apr). Centenary of the Discovery of Diamonds in Namibia. Sheet 128×91 mm containing T **288** and similar diamond-shaped designs. Multicoloured. P 14×13½.

MS1099 $2×4 Type **288**; Land mining; Marine mining; Diamond jewellery .... 3·00 3·00

No. **MS**1099 is an irregular diamond-shape with the top point missing. The stamps are printed in a block of four within the sheet, with the land mining and marine mining designs oriented with the top of the stamp facing left (land) or right (marine) within the block.

289 Herero

290 The Lion-Man

(Des Frans Nambinga. Litho Enschedé)

2008 (27 May). Traditional Houses of Namibia. T **289** and similar horiz designs. Multicoloured. P 14×13½.

1100 ($2) Type **289** 55 55
a. Sheetlet. Nos. 1100/5 .... 3·00 3·00
1101 ($2) Kavango 55 55
1102 ($2) Owambo 55 55
1103 ($2) Nama 55 55
1104 ($2) Caprivi 55 55
1105 ($2) San 55 55
1100/5 *Set of* 6 .... 3·00 3·00

Nos. 1100/5 are all inscr 'standard mail' and sold for $2 each. They were printed in *se-tenant* sheetlets of six stamps with enlarged illustrated margins.

(Des Marco Ruben Trinos Malto II. Litho Enschedé)

2008 (27 June). Petroglyphs at Twyfelfontein World Heritage Site. T **290** and similar vert designs. Multicoloured. Litho. P 13×13½.

1106 ($6.50) Type **290** .... 2·00 2·00
1107 ($6.50) The Giraffe and the Dancing Kudu .... 2·00 2·00
1108 ($6.50) The Elephant .... 2·00 2·00
1106/8 *Set of* 3 .... 5·50 5·50
MS1109 105×70 mm. (2r.)×3 As Nos. 1106/8 .... 2·00 2·00

Nos. 1106/8 were inscr 'Non Standard Mail' and sold for $6.50. The stamps within **MS**1109 were inscr "Standard Mail" and were valid for 2r. each.

293 Martial Eagle (*Polemaetus bellicosus*)

(Des Helge Denker. Litho Enschedé)

2009 (2 Feb). Eagles of Namibia. T **293** and similar horiz designs. Multicoloured. P 13×13½.

1118 $4.10 Type **293** .... 1·40 75
1119 ($4.30) Bateleur (*Terathopius ecaudatus*) .... 1·40 85
1120 $4.60 Verreaux's eagle (*Aquila verreauxii*) .... 1·50 95
1121 ($25.40) Tawny eagle (*Aquila rapax*) .... 6·50 8·00
1118/21 *Set of* 4 .... 9·75 9·50

No. 1119 was inscr "Postcard Rate" and sold for $4.30. No. 1121 was inscr "Registered Non-Standard Mail" and sold for $25.40.

294 Ox

(Des Anja Denker. Litho Enschedé)

2009 (10 Apr). Chinese New Year. Year of the Ox. P 14×13.

1122 **294** $2.20 multicoloured .... 1·00 55

295 Augur Buzzard (*Buteo augur*)

(Des Helge Denker. Litho Enschedé)

2009 (10 Apr). The Brandberg. Sheet 172×112 mm containing T **295** and similar multicoloured designs. P 14×13.

MS1123 (4r.30)×10 Type **295**; Numasfels peak (49×29 mm); Quiver tree (*Aloe dichotoma*) (39×29 mm); CMR beetle (*Mylabrisoculata*) (39×29 mm); Leopard (*Panthera pardus*) (39×29 mm); Kobas tree (*Cyphostemma curiorii*) (39×29 mm); Bokmakiri (*Telophorus zeylonus*) (39×29 mm); Jameson's red rock rabbit (*Pronolagus randensis*) (39×39 mm); Brandberg halfmens (*Euphorbia monteiri* ssp. *brandbergensis*) (39×39 mm); Jordan's girdled lizard (*Cordylus jordani*) (39×39 mm) .... 3·75 4·25

The stamps within **MS**1123 are all inscr "Postcard Rate", and the miniature sheet sold for $43.

The stamps and margins of **MS**1123 form a composite design showing wildlife in a view towards Wasserfallfläche and Numasfels.

296 Paul Graetz and his Team in their Special Vehicle, 1909

(Des J. J. van Ellinckhuijzen. Litho Enschedé)

2009 (1 May). Centenary of First Africa Crossing (from Dar es Salaam to Swakopmund) by Car. Sheet 67×56 mm. P 13½×14.

MS1124 **296** $7.10 multicoloured .... 1·75 2·00

297 Stallions fighting

(Des Anja Denker. Litho Enschedé)

2009 (3 July – 2 Nov). Wild Horses of Namibia. T **297** and similar horiz designs. Multicoloured. P 13½×14.

1124*a*	(4r.60)	Black stallion and chestnut mare with young horses (2 Nov)	1·00	50
1125	$5.30	Type **297**	1·25	50
1126	$8	Bay horses in a rocky landscape	1·75	1·00
1127	($20.40)	Chestnut stallion and mares with foal grazing	5·00	6·00
1125/7		*Set of* 4	8·00	7·00

No. 1124*a* was inscr 'Postcard Rate' and originally sold for 4r.60.

No. 1127 was inscr 'Inland Registered Mail Paid' and initially sold for $20.40 The rate increased to $22.20 from 1 October 2009.

298 Children as Centenary Emblem

(Des Anja Denker. Litho Southern Colour Print, New Zealand)

2009 (21 Aug). Centenary of DHPS (Deutsche Höhere Privatschule), Windhoek. Sheet 75×55 mm. P 13½.

MS1128 **298** $4.60 multicoloured .... 2·00 2·25

299 Festive Gecko (*Narudasia festiva*)

(Des Helge Denker. Litho Enschedé)

2009 (30 Sept). Geckos. T **299** and similar horiz designs. Multicoloured. P 14.

1129	$4.40	Type **299**	1·10	1·10
1130	$5	Koch's barking gecko (*Ptenopus kochi*)	1·25	1·25
1131	$6	Giant ground gecko (*Chondrodactylus angulifer namibensis*)	1·50	1·50
1132	$7.70	Velvety thick-toed gecko (*Pachydactylus bicolor*)	1·90	1·90
1133	($20.40)	Bradfield's namib day gecko (*Rhoptropus bradfieldi*)	5·25	5·25
1129/33		*Set of* 5	11·00	11·00

No. 1133 was inscr 'Registered Mail' and originally sold for $20.40.

300 Wattled Crane (*Grus carunculatus*)

(Des Anja Denker. Litho Cartor)

2010 (8 Feb). Endangered Species. T **300** and similar vert designs. Multicoloured. P 13½ ×13.

1134	($4.60)	Type **300**	2·50	2·50
		a. Sheetlet. Nos. 1134/43	22·00	22·00
1135	($4.60)	Gazania thermalis	2·50	2·50
1136	($4.60)	Leatherback turtle (*Dermochelys coriacea*) and jellyfish	2·50	2·50
1137	($4.60)	Giant quiver tree (*Aloe pillansii*)	2·50	2·50
1138	($4.60)	Cape vulture (*Gyps coprotheres*)	2·50	2·50
1139	($4.60)	White Namib toktokkie (*Cauricara eburnea*)	2·50	2·50
1140	($4.60)	Two cheetahs (*Acinonyx jubatus*)	2·50	2·50
1141	($4.60)	Hook-lipped rhinoceros (*Diceros bicornis*)	2·50	2·50
1142	($4.60)	Wild dog (*Lycaon pictus*)	2·50	2·50
1143	($4.60)	Nama-padloper tortoise (*Homopus solus*).	2·50	2·50
1134/43		*Set of* 10	22·00	22·00

Nos. 1134/43 were inscr 'Postcard Rate' and were initially valid for $4.60. Nos. 1134/43 were printed together, *se-tenant*, in sheetlets of nine with enlarged illustrated margins.

301 Map and Flag of Namibia

(Des Helge Denker. Litho Enschedé)

2010 (21 Mar). 20th Anniv of Independence. P 13½.

1144 **301** ($2.50) multicoloured .... 1·00 85

No. 1144 was inscr "Standard Mail" and originally sold for $2.50.

(Des Anja Denker. Litho Enschedé)

2010 (9 Apr). Third Joint Issue of Southern Africa Postal Operators Association Members. World Cup Football Championship, South Africa. Sheet 188×167 mm containing circular designs as T **258** of Botswana but with gold foil background, each showing Zakumi mascot, different silhouettes of players on football and the national flag of a member country. Multicoloured. P 13½.

MS1145 (4r.60)×9 Namibia; South Africa; Zimbabwe; Malawi; Swaziland; Botswana, Mauritius; Lesotho; Zambia .... 14·00 14·00

The stamps within **MS**1145 were each inscr 'postcard rate' and were originally valid for $4.60 each. They were each perforated in a circle contained within an outer perforated square.

Similar designs were issued by Botswana, Lesotho, Malawi, Mauritius, South Africa, Swaziland, Zambia and Zimbabwe.

302 Northern Black Korhaan (*Eupodotis afraoides*)

(Des Helge Denker. Litho Enschedé)

2010 (14 Apr). Bustards and Korhaans. T **302** and similar vert designs. Multicoloured. P 13×14.

1146	($4.60)	Type **302**	2·50	2·50
		a. Sheetlet. Nos. 1146/51	13·50	13·50
1147	($4.60)	Red-crested korhaan (*Eupodotis ruficrista*)	2·50	2·50
1148	($4.60)	Black-bellied bustard (*Eupodotis melanogaster*)	2·50	2·50
1149	($4.60)	Rüppell's korhaan (*Eupodotis rueppellii*)	2·50	2·50
1150	($4.60)	Ludwig's bustard (*Neotis ludwigii*)	2·50	2·50
1151	($4.60)	Kori bustard (*Ardeotis kori*)	2·50	2·50
1146/51		*Set of* 6	13·50	13·50

Nos. 1146/51 were all inscr 'postcard rate' and originally sold for $4.60 each. They were printed together, *se-tenant*, in sheetlets of six stamps with enlarged illustrated margins.

303 Swakopmund Lighthouse

304 Christuskirche, Windhoek

(Des Elgin Barh. Litho Austrian State Ptg Wks, Vienna)

2010 (18 June). Lighthouses. T **303** and similar vert designs. Multicoloured. P 13½.

1152 $4.40 Type **303** .... 2·00 1·25
1153 ($9.50) Diaz Point Lighthouse, Lüderitzbucht 4·00 4·00
1154 ($18.20) Pelican Point Lighthouse, Walvis Bay 7·00 8·00
1152/4 *Set of* 3 .... 11·50 12·00

No. 1153 was inscr 'Non Standard Mail' and originally sold for $9.50.
No. 1154 was inscr 'Registered Mail' and originally sold for $18.20.

(Des Anja Denker. Litho Austrian State Ptg Wks, Vienna)

2010 (6 Aug). Centenary of the Christuskirche, Windhoek. Sheet 76×56 mm. P 14.

MS1155 **304** $5 multicoloured .... 2·00 2·50

305 Stylised Figures and Globe

(Litho Enschedé)

2010 (18 Sept). World Standards Day. Sheet 75×55 mm. P 14×13½.

MS1156 **305** $5.30 multicoloured .... 2·00 2·50

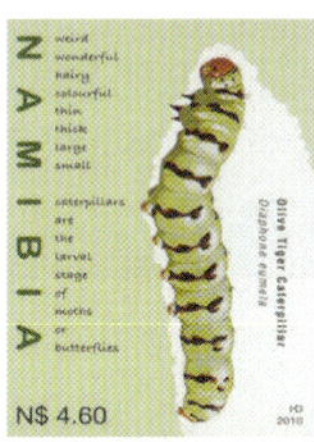

306 Olive Tiger Caterpillar (*Diaphone eumela*)

(Des Helge Denker. Litho Austrian State Ptg Wks, Vienna)

2010 (1 Oct). Caterpillars. T **306** and similar vert designs. Multicoloured. P 14.

1157 $4.60 Type **306** .... 2·00 1·75
1158 $5.30 African armyworms (*Spodoptera exempta*) .... 2·50 2·50
1159 $6.40 Wild Silk Caterpillar (*Gonometa postica*) .... 2·75 2·75
1160 ($29.40) Mopane caterpillar (*Imbrasia belina*).. 10·00 12·00
1157/60 *Set of* 4 .... 15·00 17·00

No. 1160 was inscr 'Registered Non-Standard Mail' and originally sold for $29.40.

307 Leopard (*Panthera pardus*)

(Des Anita Roux. Litho Enschedé)

2011 (28 Jan). The Big Five (animals). T **307** and similar multicoloured designs. P 14×13½ (horiz) or 13½×14 (vert).

1161 $4.60 Type **307** .... 1·50 1·75
1162 ($5) African elephant (*Loxodonta africana*) (vert) .... 2·25 2·25
1163 $5.30 Black rhino (*Diceros bicornis*) .... 2·25 2·25
1164 $6.40 African buffalo (*Syncerus caffer*) .... 2·25 2·50
1165 ($8.50) Lion (*Panthera leo*) (vert) .... 2·50 2·75
1161/5 *Set of* 5 .... 9·75 10·50

No. 1162 was inscr 'Postcard Rate' and originally sold for $5.
No. 1165 was inscr 'Non Standard Mail' and originally sold for $8.50.

308 Long Reed Frog (*Hyperolius nasutus*)

(Des Anja Denker. Litho Enschedé)

2011 (23 Mar). Frogs. Sheet 175×123 mm containing T **308** and similar horiz designs. Multicoloured. P 13×13½.

MS1166 ($5)×4 Type **308**; Bubbling kassina (*Kassina senegalensis*); Tandy's sand frog (*Tomopterna tandyi*); Angolan reed frog (*Hyperolius parallelus*) ...... 8·50 8·50

The stamps within **MS**1166 were all inscr 'Postcard Rate' and were originally valid for $5.

No. **MS**1166 was cut around in the shape of a giant bullfrog.

309 Eye and Desert Road

(Des Helge Denker. Litho. Lowe-Martin)

2011 (11 May). Decade of Action for Road Safety 2011-2020. Sheet 75×55 mm. P 13.

MS1167 **309** $5.30 multicoloured .... 1·50 1·50

The stamps and margins of **MS**1167 form a composite design showing rocks and ocean.

310 Cape Gannet (*Morus capensis*)

(Des Anja Denker. Litho Enschedé)

2011 (16 May). Endangered Marine Life. Sheet 172×112 mm containing T **310** and similar multicoloured designs. P 14×13.

MS1168 $4.60×8 Type **310**; Atlantic yellow-nosed albatross (*Thalassarche chlororhynchos*) (50×30 mm); African penguin (*Spheniscus demersus*) (40×30 mm); Southern right whale (*Eubalaena australis*) (40×30 mm); Bank cormorant (*Phalacrocorax neglectus*) (40×30 mm); Westcoast steenbras (fish) (*Lithognathus aureti*) (40×30 mm); Split-fan kelp (*Laminaria pallida*) (40×40 mm); Cape rock lobster (*Jasus lalandii*) (40×40 mm) .... 12·00 12·00

The stamps and margins of **MS**1168 form a composite design showing rocks and ocean.

311 *Aloe gariepensis*

312 Great Crested Grebe (*Podiceps cristatus*)

(Des Anja Denker. Litho Enschedé)

2011 (21 June). Aloes. T **311** and similar vert designs. Multicoloured. P 13½×14.

1169	($5) Type **311**	2·00	1·90
1170	($8.50) *Aloe variegata*	3·00	2·75
1171	($20.90) *Aloe striata* sp. *Karasbergensis*	6·00	7·00
1169/71	*Set of 3*	10·00	10·50

No. 1169 was inscr 'Postcard Rate' and originally sold for $5.
No. 1170 was inscr 'Non Standard Mail' and originally sold for $8.50.
No. 1171 was inscr 'Registered Mail' and originally sold for $20.90.

2011 (18 July). Grebes of Namibia. T **312** and similar multicoloured designs. P 13×13½ (vert) or 13½×13 (horiz).

1172	($2.70) Type **312**	1·00	85
1173	($2.70) Little grebe (*Tachybaptus ruficollis*)	1·00	85
1174	($20.90) Black-necked grebe (*Podiceps nigricollis*) (horiz)	6·00	7·00
1172/4	*Set of 3*	8·00	8·50

Nos. 1172/3 were each inscr 'Standard Mail' and originally sold for $2.70.
No. 1174 was inscr 'Inland Registered Mail' and initially sold for $20.90.

MACHINE LABELS

MACHINE LABELS. From 30 March 1988 gummed labels in the above design numbered "PT01", ranging in value from 1c. to 99r.99, were available from a machine located at the Windhoek Post Office. During1989 three further machines at Windhoek Ausspanplatz (PT02) (6 March), Swakopmund (PT03) (10 March and Keepmanshoop (PT04) (14 March) were added. Machines PT01/2 were withdrawn on 23 November 1990 and the other two followed four days later. A commemorative design, without code number, was used at the "OTYIMBINGUE" philatelic exhibition, Windhoek, between 7 and 9 July 1988.

STAMP BOOKLETS

B **1** Buffalo (Illustration further reduced. Actual size 125×74 mm)

1985 (1 Aug). Multicoloured cover as Type B **1**. Pane attached by selvedge.

SB1 1r.20 booklet containing pane of 10 12c. (No. 358ba) ... 5·50

1986 (1 Feb). Multicoloured cover as Type B **1** but smaller, 125×70 mm, showing herd of buffaloes. Pane attached by selvedge.

SB2 1r.20 booklet containing pane of 10 12c. (No. 358ba) 6·50

B **2**

1997 (1 Feb). Multicoloured cover as Type B **2**. Stamps attached by selvedge.

SB3 ($5) booklet containing block of 10 "STANDARDISED MAIL" (No. 648) ... 3·50

SB4 ($5) booklet containing two strips of 5 "STANDARDISED MAIL" (No. 662) ... 4·00

B **3**

1997 (6 May). Waxbills. Multicoloured cover as Type B **3**. Stamps attached by selvedge.

SB5 $5.50 booklet containing block of 10 (2×5) (No. 710a) 2·25

B **4** *Tribulus zeyheri* (Illustration further reduced. Actual size 132×80 mm)

1997 (27 June). Greetings Stamps. Multicoloured covers as Type B **4**. Panes attached by selvedge.

SB6 ($5) booklet containing pane of 10 (5×2) (No. 723a) (Type B 4) ... 2·75

SB7 $7 booklet containing pane of 10 (5×2) (No. 728a) (cover showing Helmet Guineafowl and chicks) 4·00

B **5** Peach-faced Lovebird

1997 (3 Nov). Flora and Fauna. Multicoloured covers as Type B **5**. Panes attached by selvedge.

SB8 ($5) booklet containing pane of 10 (5×2) (No. 755ab) (cover showing Peach-faced Lovebird) ... 2·25

SB9 ($12) booklet containing pane of 10 (5×2) (No. 761ab) (cover showing Leopard) ... 3·00

SB10 ($30.55) booklet containing pane of 18 (9×2) (No. 749ab) (cover showing animals and birds) ... 9·50

B **6** Eagle Owl

1998 (1 Apr). Owls of Namibia. Multicoloured cover as Type B **6**. Pane attached by selvedge.

SB11	$7.35 booklet containing *se-tenant* pane (No. 790a)...	3·75

B **7** Yoka the Snake

1999 (1 Feb). Yoka the Snake. Multicoloured cover as Type B **7**. Self-adhesive.

SB12	$16 booklet containing *se-tenant*pane (No. 822a).....	3·00

POSTAGE DUE STAMPS

PRICES for Nos. D1/39 are for unused horizontal pairs, used horizontal pairs and used singles.

1923 (1 Jan–July). Optd with T **1** and **2** alternately.

(a) Setting I (14 mm between lines of overprint)

(i) On Nos. D5/6 of Transvaal

		Un pair	*Us pair*	*Us single*
D1	5d. black and violet	4·00	55·00	11·00
	a. "Wes" for "West" (R. 8/6, 10/2 left pane)	£190		
	b. "Afrika" without stop (R. 6/1)	£130		
D2	6d. black and red-brown	17·00	50·00	11·00
	a. "Wes" for "West" (R. 10/2)	£450		
	b. "Afrika" without stop (R. 6/1, 7/2)	£275		
	c. 12 mm between lines of opt (R. 1/1)	£325		

(ii) On Nos. D3/4 and D6 of South Africa (De La Rue printing)

D3	2d. black and violet	42·00	55·00	10·00
	a. "Wes" for "West" (R. 10/2)	£325	£425	
	b. "Afrika" without stop (R. 6/1, 7/2)	£275		
D4	3d. black and blue	21·00	55·00	10·00
	a. "Wes" for "West" (R. 8/6, 10/2)	£200		
	b. "Africa" without stop (R. 9/1)	£350		
D5	6d. black and slate (20 Apr)	40·00	65·00	13·00
	a. "Wes" for "West" (R. 8/6)	£275		

(iii) On Nos. D 9/10, D11 and D14 of South Africa (Pretoria printings)

D6	½d. black and green (P 14)	6·00	30·00	5·50
	a. Opt inverted	£600		
	b. Opt double	£1400	£1600	
	c. "Wes" for "West" (R. 10/2)	£140		
	d. "Afrika" without stop (R. 6/1, 7/2)	£130		
D7	1d. black and rose (*roul*)	7·00	30·00	6·00
	a. "Wes" for "West" (R. 10/2)	£150	£350	
	b. "Afrika" without stop (R. 6/1)	£150		
	c. Imperf between (horiz pair)	£1800		
D8	1½d. black and yellow-brown (*roul*)	1·25	14·00	2·75
	a. "Wes" for "West" (R. 8/6, 10/2)	£100		
	b. "Afrika" without stop (R. 6/1)	£110		
D9	2d. black and violet (P 14) (21 June)	3·75	28·00	5·00
	a. "Wes" for "West" (R. 8/6)	£140		
	b. "Afrika" without stop (R. 6/1)	£170		

Nos. D1/9 were initially overprinted as separate panes of 60, but some values were later done as double panes of 120.

A variety of Nos. D1, D4/5 and D9 with 15 mm between the lines of overprint occurs on four positions in each pane from some printings.

(b) Setting II (10 mm between lines of overprint)

(i) On No. D5 of Transvaal

D10	5d. black and violet (20 Apr)	55·00	£180	

(ii) On Nos. D 3/4 of South Africa (De La Rue printing)

D11	2d. black and violet (20 Apr)	19·00	50·00	9·00
	a. "Afrika" without stop (R. 6/1)	£275		
D12	3d. black and blue (20 Apr)	7·50	28·00	5·50
	a. "Afrika" without stop (R. 6/1)	£130		

(iii) On No. D 9 of South Africa (Pretoria printing). Roul

D13	1d. black and rose (July)	£14000	—	£1600

1923 (30 July)–**26**. Optd as T **3** ("*Zuidwest*" in one word without hyphen) and **4**.

(a) Setting III ("South West" 14 mm long, "Zuidwest" 11 mm long and 14 mm between lines of overprint)

(i) On No. D6 of Transvaal

D14	6d. black and red-brown	21·00	90·00	20·00

(ii) On Nos. D 9 and D11/12 of South Africa (Pretoria printing)

D15	½d. black and green (P 14)	18·00	38·00	5·50
D16	1d. black and rose (*roul*)	9·50	38·00	5·50
D17	1d. black and rose (P 14) (2.8.23)	27·00	38·00	5·50

(b) Setting IV ("South West" 16 mm long, "Zuidwest" 12 mm long and 14 mm between lines of overprint)

(i) On No. D5 of Transvaal

D17*a*	5d. black and violet (1.7.24)	£800	£1200	

(ii) On Nos. D11/12 and D16 of South Africa (Pretoria printing). P 14

D18	½d. black and green (1.7.24)	7·50	35·00	5·50
D19	1d. black and rose (1.7.24)	8·50	30·00	5·50
D20	6d. black and slate (1.7.24)	2·25	42·00	9·00
	a. "Africa" without stop (R. 9/5)	£130	£325	

(c) Setting V (12 mm. between lines of overprint)

(i) On No. D5 of Transvaal

D21	5d. black and violet (6.8.24)	8·00	65·00	9·00

(ii) On No. D4 of South Africa (De La Rue printing)

D22	3d. black and blue (6.8.24)	16·00	50·00	11·00

(iii) On Nos. D11 and D13 of South Africa (Pretoria printing). P 14

D23	½d. black and green (6.8.24)	3·00	30·00	6·50
D24	1½d. black yellow-brown (6.8.24)	5·00	48·00	7·50

(d) Setting VI (9½ mm between lines of overprint)

(i) On No. D5 of Transvaal

D25	5d. black and violet (7.9.24)	2·75	21·00	3·50
	a. "Africa" without stop (R. 9/5)	85·00		

(ii) On No. D4 of South Africa (De La Rue printing)

D26	3d. black and blue (3.2.26)	10·00	65·00	11·00

(iii) On Nos. D11/16 of South Africa (Pretoria printing). P 14

D27	½d. black and green (1.3.26)	14·00	35·00	7·50
D28	1d. black and rose (16.3.25)	2·00	12·00	1·60
	a. "Africa" without stop (R. 9/5 right pane)	85·00		
D29	1½d. black yellow-brown (1.10.26)	4·50	35·00	6·50
	a. "Africa" without stop (R. 9/5 right pane)	95·00		
D30	2d. black and violet (7.9.24)	2·50	18·00	3·50
	a. "Africa" without stop (R. 9/5) right pane)	80·00		
D31	3d. black and blue (6.5.26)	4·50	19·00	3·75
	a. "Africa" without stop (R. 9/5) right pane)	90·00		
D32	6d. black and slate (1.10.26)	16·00	55·00	14·00
	a. "Africa" without stop (R. 9/5 right pane)	£180		
D27/32	*Set of 6*	38·00	£160	32·00

For Setting VI the overprint was applied to sheets of 120 (2 panes of 60) of the 1d., 3d. and 6d., and to individual panes of 60 for the other values. The two measurements of "South West", as detailed under No. 40, also occur on the postage dues. Nos. D25 and D31/2 show it 16 mm long, No. 27 16½ mm long and the other stamps can be found with either measurement. In addition to the complete panes the 16½ mm long "South West" also occurs on R. 2/4 in the 16 mm left pane for Nos. D28 and D30/2.

Suidwes	South West
Afrika.	Africa.
(D **1**)	(D **2**)

1927 (14 May–27 Sept). Optd as Types D **1** and D **2**, alternately, 12 mm between lines of overprint.

(a) On No. D5 of Transvaal

D33	5d. black and violet (27 Sept)	21·00	85·00	23·00

(b) On Nos. D13/16 of South Africa (Pretoria printing). P 14

D34	1½d. black and yellow-brown	1·00	21·00	3·50
D35	2d. black and pale violet (27 Sept)	4·75	18·00	3·25
	a. Black and deep violet	8·00	18·00	3·50
D37	3d. black and blue (27 Sept)	16·00	48·00	11·00
D38	6d. black and slate (27 Sept)	12·00	38·00	8·50

(c) On No. D18 of South Africa (Pretoria printing). P 14

D39	1d. black and carmine	1·00	12·00	2·25
D33/9 *Set of 6*		50·00	£200	45·00

No. D33 was overprinted in panes of 60 and the remainder as complete sheets of 120.

Examples of all values can be found with very small or very faint stops from various positions in the sheet.

1928–29. Optd with T **10**.

(a) On Nos. D15/16 of South Africa

		Un single	Us single
D40	3d. black and blue	1·50	17·00
	a. Without stop after "A" (R. 3/6)	42·00	
D41	6d. black and slate	6·00	32·00
	a. Without stop after "A" (R. 3/6)	£150	

(b) On Nos. D17/21 of South Africa

D42	½d. black and green	50	9·50
D43	1d. black and carmine	50	3·25
	a. Without stop after "A" (R. 3/6)	40·00	
D44	2d. black and mauve	50	4·50
	a. Without stop after "A" (R. 3/6)	55·00	
D45	3d. black and blue	2·25	26·00
D46	6d. black and slate	1·50	23·00
	a. Without stop after "A" (R. 3/6)	60·00	£200
D42/6 *Set of 5*		4·75	60·00

D **3**

D **4**

(Litho B.W.)

1931 (23 Feb). Inscribed bilingually. W **9** of South Africa. P 12.

D47	D **3**	½d. black and green	1·00	7·50
D48		1d. black and scarlet	1·00	1·25
D49		2d. black and violet	1·00	2·75
D50		3d. black and blue	4·25	13·00
D51		6d. black and slate	13·00	25·00
D47/51 *Set of 5*			18·00	45·00

PRINTER. The following issues have been printed by the South African Government Printer, Pretoria.

1959 (18 May). Centre typo; frame roto. W **9** of South Africa. P 15×14.

D52	D **4**	1d. black and scarlet	1·50	15·00
D53		2d. black and reddish violet	1·50	15·00
D54		3d. black and blue	1·50	15·00
D52/4 *Set of 3*			4·00	40·00

1960 (1 Dec). As Nos. D52 and D54 but *W* **102** of South Africa.

D55	1d. black and scarlet	1·50	3·00
D56	3d. black and blue	1·50	3·75

1961 (14 Feb). As Nos. D52 etc, but whole stamp roto, and value in cents. *W* **102** of South Africa.

D57	1c. black and blue-green	70	3·75
D58	2c. black and scarlet	70	3·75
D59	4c. black and reddish violet	70	6·00
D60	5c. black and light blue	1·00	4·25
D61	6c. black and green	1·25	6·50
D62	10c. black and yellow	4·00	9·00
D57/62 *Set of 6*		7·50	30·00

1972 (22 Mar). W **127** (sideways tête-bêche). Phosphorised chalk-surfaced paper. P 14×13½.

D63	D **5**	1c. emerald	75	5·00
D64		8c. ultramarine	3·00	8·50

The use of Postage Due stamps ceased in April 1975.

OFFICIAL STAMPS

OFFICIAL South West Africa.
(O **1**)

OFFISIEEL Suidwes Afrika.
(O **2**)

1926 (Dec). Nos. 30, 31, 6 and 32 of South Africa optd with Type O **1** on English stamp and O **2** on Afrikaans stamp alternately.

		Un pair	Us pair	Us single
O1	½d. black and green	90·00	£200	30·00
O2	1d. black and carmine	95·00	£200	30·00
O3	2d. dull purple	£225	£375	45·00
O4	6d. green and orange	£120	£225	30·00
O1/4 *Set of 4*		£475	£900	£120

OFFICIAL S.W.A.
(O **3**)

OFFISIEEL S.W.A.
(O **4**)

1929 (May). Nos. 30, 31, 32 and 34 of South Africa optd with Type O **3** on English stamp and O **4** on Afrikaans stamp.

O5	½d. black and green	1·00	17·00	2·75
O6	1d. black and carmine	1·00	17·00	2·75
	w. Wmk inverted	£375		
O7	2d. grey and purple	1·50	22·00	3·50
	a. Pair, one stamp without stop after "OFFICIAL"	6·50	50·00	
	b. Pair, one stamp without stop after "OFFISIEEL"	6·50	50·00	
	c. Pair, comprising a and b	17·00	95·00	
O8	6d. green and orange	2·00	20·00	3·75
O5/8 *Set of 4*		5·00	£701	11·50

Types O **3** and O **4** are normally spaced 17 mm between lines on all except the 2d. value, which is spaced 13 mm.

Except on No. O7, the words "OFFICIAL" or "OFFISIEEL" normally have no stops after them.

OFFICIAL S.W.A.
(O **5**)

OFFISIEEL S.W.A.
(O **6**)

OFFICIAL. S.W.A.
(O **7**)

OFFISIEEL. S.W.A.
(O **8**)

1929 (Aug). Nos. 30, 31 and 32 of South Africa optd with Types O **5** and O **6**, and No. 34 with Types O **7** and O **8**, languages to correspond.

O9	½d. black and green	75	16·00	2·75
O10	1d. black and carmine	1·00	17·00	2·75
O11	2d. grey and purple	1·00	17·00	3·25
	a. Pair, one stamp without stop after "OFFICIAL"	3·75	45·00	
	b. Pair, one stamp without stop after "OFFISIEEL"	3·75	45·00	
	c. Pair, comprising a and b	18·00	£100	
O12	6d. green and orange	2·50	27·00	6·50
O9/12 *Set of 4*		4·75	70·00	13·50

Examples of Nos. O1/12 are known showing forged Windhoek postmarks dated "30 SEP 24" or "20 MAR 31".

OFFICIAL
(O **9**)

OFFISIEEL
(O **10**)

1931. English stamp optd with Type O **9** and Afrikaans stamp with Type O **10** in red.

O13	**12**	½d. black and emerald	10·00	22·00	3·50
O14	**13**	1d. indigo and scarlet	1·00	19·00	3·50
O15	**14**	2d. blue and brown	2·25	10·00	2·25
O16	**17**	6d. blue and brown	4·00	14·00	3·25
O13/16 *Set of 4*			15·00	60·00	11·50

OFFICIAL (O 11) OFFISIEEL (O 12)

1938 (1 July). English stamp optd with Type O **11** and Afrikaans with Type O **12** in red.

O17	**27**	1½d. purple-brown	32·00	50·00	6·00

OFFICIAL (O 13) **OFFISIEEL** (O 14)

1945–50. English stamp optd with Type O **13**, and Afrikaans stamp with Type O **14** in red.

O18	**12**	½d. black and emerald	13·00	35·00	5·00
O19	**13**	1d. indigo and scarlet (1950)	14·00	20·00	3·25
		a. Opt double	£600		
O20	**27**	1½d. purple-brown	35·00	55·00	7·00
O21	**14**	2d. blue and brown (1947?)	£650	£800	£100
O22	**17**	6d. blue and brown	25·00	70·00	8·00
O18/20, O22 *Set of 4*			80·00	£160	21·00

OFFICIAL (O 15) **OFFISIEEL** (O 16)

1951 (16 Nov)–**52**. English stamp optd with Type O **15** and Afrikaans stamp with Type O **16**, in red.

O23	**12**	½d. black and emerald (1952)	18·00	24·00	4·50
		a. Opts transposed	†	£2500	
O24	**13**	1d. indigo and scarlet	5·00	22·00	2·00
		a. Opts transposed	£100	£250	
O25	**27**	1½d. purple-brown	25·00	32·00	5·00
		a. Opts transposed	75·00	95·00	
O26	**14**	2d. blue and brown	4·00	26·00	3·50
		a. Opts transposed	75·00	£250	
O27	**17**	6d. blue and brown	2·75	55·00	7·50
		a. Opts transposed	28·00	£170	
O23/7 *Set of 5*			50·00	£140	20·00

The above errors refer to stamps with the English overprint on Afrikaans stamp and *vice versa*.

The use of official stamps ceased in January 1955.

Rhodesia

Stamps of BECHUANALAND were used in Matabeleland on the runner post between Gubulawayo and Mafeking (Bechuanaland) from 9 August 1888 until 5 May 1894. Such stamps were cancelled "GUBULAWAYO" or by the barred oval "678" obliteration.

Between 27 June 1890 and 13 May 1892 external mail from Mashonaland sent via Bechuanaland was franked with that territory's stamps. A similar arrangement, using the stamps of MOZAMBIQUE existed for the route via Beira inaugurated on 29 August 1891. In both instances the stamps were cancelled by the post offices receiving the mail from Mashonaland. From 14 May until 31 July 1892 letters via Bechuanaland were franked with a combination of B.S.A Company and Bechuanaland issues.

Rhodesia joined the South African Postal Union on 1 August 1892 when its stamps became valid for international mail. Combination frankings with Mozambique stamps continued to be required until April 1894.

For the use of British Central Africa overprints in North-eastern Rhodesia from 1893 to 1899 see MALAWI.

PRICES FOR STAMPS ON COVER TO 1945

Nos.	1/7	*from* × 6
Nos.	8/13	—
Nos.	14/17	*from* × 2
Nos.	18/24	*from* × 10
Nos.	25/6	—
Nos.	27/8	*from* × 7
Nos.	29/35	*from* × 10
Nos.	36/7	—
Nos.	41/6	*from* × 6
Nos.	47/50	—
Nos.	51/3	*from* × 2
Nos.	58/64	*from* × 3
Nos.	66/72	*from* × 8
Nos.	73/4	—
Nos.	75/87	*from* × 6
Nos.	88/93*a*	—
Nos.	94/9	*from* × 3
Nos.	100/10	*from* × 5
Nos.	111/13*e*	—
Nos.	114/18	*from* × 7
Nos.	119/60*a*	*from* × 10
Nos.	160*b*/6*b*	—
Nos.	167/78	*from* × 6
Nos.	179/81*a*	—
Nos.	182/5*a*	*from* × 4
Nos.	186/208	*from* × 8
Nos.	209/41	*from* × 8
Nos.	242/54*a*	—
Nos.	255/77	*from* × 8
Nos.	278/9*c*	—
Nos.	280/1	*from* × 15
Nos.	282/310	*from* × 8
Nos.	311/22	—

A. ISSUES FOR THE BRITISH SOUTH AFRICA COMPANY TERRITORY

1

2

½d.

(3)

(Recess B.W.)

1892 (2 Jan*)–**93**. Thin wove paper. P 14, 14½.

1	1	1d. black	14·00	3·25
2		6d. ultramarine	55·00	26·00
3		6d. deep blue (1893)	40·00	3·75
4		1s. grey-brown	50·00	13·00
5		2s. vermilion	65·00	32·00
6		2s.6d. grey-purple	40·00	50·00
7		2s.6d. lilac (1893)	55·00	55·00
8		5s. orange-yellow	80·00	60·00
9		10s. deep green	£100	£100
10	2	£1 deep blue	£250	£150
11		£2 rose-red**	£500	£170
12		£5 sage-green	£1600	£450
13		£10 brown	£2750	£700
1/10 *Set of 8*			£550	£375

Great caution is needed in buying the high values in either used or unused condition, many stamps offered being revenue stamps cleaned and re-gummed or with forged postmarks.

*Printing of stamps in Types **1**, **2** and **4** commenced in 1890, although none were used for postal purposes before 2 January 1892 when the route to the East Coast was inaugurated.

**For later printings of the £2 see No. 74.

The following sheet watermarks are known on Nos. 1/26: (1) William Collins, Sons & Co's paper watermarked with the firm's monogram, and "PURE LINEN WOVE BANK" in double-lined capitals (1890 and 1891 ptgs). (2) As (1) with "EXTRA STRONG" and "139" added (1892 ptgs). (3) Paper by Wiggins Teape & Co, watermarked "W T & Co" in script letters in double-lined wavy border (1893 ptgs). (4) The same firm's paper, watermarked "1011" in double-lined figures (1894 ptgs except ½d.). (5) "WIGGINS TEAPE & CO LONDON" in double-lined block capitals (1894 ptg of No. 18). Many values can also be found on a slightly thicker paper without wmk, but single specimens are not easily distinguishable.

1892 (2 Jan). Nos. 2 and 4 surch as T **3**.

14	1	½d. on 6d. ultramarine	£140	£475
15		2d. on 6d. ultramarine	£170	£650
16		4d. on 6d. ultramarine	£190	£750
17		8d. on 1s. grey-brown	£200	£850
14/17 *Set of 4*			£650	£2500

Caution is needed in buying these surcharges as both forged surcharges and forged postmarks exist.

4

5 (Ends of scrolls behind legs of springboks)

(T **4**. Centre recess; value B.W.)

1892 (2 Jan)–**94**. Thin wove paper (wmks as note after No. 13). P 14, 14½.

18	4	½d. dull blue and vermilion	3·00	4·50
19		½d. deep blue and vermilion (1893)	3·50	6·50
20		2d. deep dull green and vermilion	19·00	5·50
21		3d. grey-black and green (8.92)	19·00	3·75
22		4d. chestnut and black	35·00	4·25
23		8d. rose-lake and ultramarine	18·00	19·00
24		8d. red and ultramarine (1892)	14·00	19·00
25		3s. brown and green (1894)	£170	90·00
26		4s. grey-black and vermilion (1893)	40·00	50·00
18/26 *Set of 7*			£275	£160

(Recess P.B. from the Bradbury, Wilkinson plates)

1895. Thick soft wove paper. P 12½.

27	4	2d. green and red	28·00	17·00
28		4d. yellow-brown and black	28·00	19·00
		a. Imperf (pair)	£1800	

(T **5**. Centre recess; value typo P.B.)

1896–97. Wove paper. P 14.

(a) Die I. Plates 1 and 2. Small dot to the right of the tail of the right-hand supporter in the coat of arms. Body of lion only partly shaded

29	5	1d. scarlet and emerald	20·00	4·50
		a. Carmine-red and emerald		
30		2d. brown and mauve	30·00	2·00
31		3d. chocolate and ultramarine	9·50	2·00
32		4d. ultramarine and mauve	55·00	
		a. Imperf between (pair)		
		b. Blue and mauve	35·00	22·00
33		6d. mauve and pink	80·00	24·00
34		8d. green and mauve/*buff*	13·00	60
		a. Imperf between (pair)		
		b. Imperf (pair)	£3750	
35		1s. green and blue	18·00	2·75
36		3s. green and mauve/*blue*	75·00	42·00
		a. Imperf (pair)	£9500	
37		4s. orange-red and blue/*green*	55·00	2·75
29/37 *Set of 9*			£300	90·00

(b) Die II. Plates 3 and 4. No dot. Body of lion heavily shaded all over

41	5	½d. slate and violet	4·50	3·25
42		1d. scarlet and emerald	8·50	4·50
43		2d. brown and mauve	19·00	7·00
44		4d. ultramarine and mauve	75·00	13·00
		a. Blue and mauve	17·00	50
46		6d. mauve and rose	14·00	75
47		2s. indigo and green/*buff*	40·00	10·00

48		2s.6d. brown and purple/*yellow*	85·00	55·00
49		5s. chestnut and emerald	55·00	10·00
50		10s. slate and vermilion/*rose*	£120	65·00
41/50 *Set of 9*			£325	£140

One Penny

(6)

THREE PENCE.

(7)

(Surch by Bulawayo Chronicle)

1896 (April–May). Matabele Rebellion provisionals. Surch with T **6** and **7**.

51	**6**	1d. on 3d. (No. 21)	£600	£750
		a. "P" in "Penny" inverted	£42000	
		b. "y" in "Penny" inverted		
52		1d. on 4s. (No. 26)	£300	£325
		a. "P" in "Penny" inverted	£32000	
		b. "y" in "Penny" inverted	£32000	
		c. Single bar through original value	£1100	£1200
53	**7**	3d. on 5s. (No. 8) (5.96)	£190	£250
		a. "R" in "THREE" inverted	£32000	
		b. "T" in "THREE" inverted	£42000	

Nos. 51 and 52 occur in two settings, one with 9¾ mm between value and upper bar, the other with 11 mm between value and upper bar.

BRITISH SOUTH AFRICA COMPANY.

(8)

9 (Ends of scrolls between legs of springboks)

1896 (22 May–Aug). Cape of Good Hope stamps optd by Argus Printing Co, Cape Town, with T **8**. Wmk Anchor (3d. wmk Crown CA). P 14.

58	**6**	½d. grey-black (No. 48*a*)	15·00	22·00
59	**17**	1d. rose-red (No. 58)	16·00	23·00
60	**6**	2d. deep bistre (No. 50*a*)	22·00	13·00
61		3d. pale claret (No. 40)	55·00	75·00
62		4d. blue (No. 51)	26·00	24·00
		a. "COMPANY," omitted	£9500	
63	**4**	6d. deep purple (No. 52*a*)	65·00	75·00
64	**6**	1s. yellow-ochre (No. 65) (Aug)	£140	£140
58/64 *Set of 7*			£300	£325

No. 62 also exists with "COMPANY" partially omitted. Examples with the word completely omitted, as No. 62a, are known from positions 1 to 6 of the setting.

Forgeries of this overprint show a narrow final "A" in "AFRICA" and have a rectangular full stop. On the genuine overprint both "As" are the same and the stop is oval.

(T **9**. Eng J. A. C. Harrison (vignette), Bain or Rapkin (£1) (frames). Recess Waterlow)

1897. P 13½ to 16.

66	**9**	½d. grey-black and purple	5·00	8·00
67		1d. scarlet and emerald	5·50	7·50
68		2d. brown and mauve	15·00	3·50
69		3d. brown-red and slate-blue	5·50	50
		a. Imperf between (vert pair)	£4000	
70		4d. ultramarine and claret	18·00	3·75
		a. Imperf between (horiz pair)	£15000	£15000
71		6d. dull purple and pink	12·00	3·50
72		8d. green and mauve/*buff*	19·00	50
		a. Imperf between (vert pair)	†	£3250
73		£1 black and red-brown/*green*	£375	£225

(T **2**. Recess Waterlow, from the Bradbury plate)

1897 (Jan). P 15.

74	**2**	£2 rosy red	£1700	£450

10

11

12

(Recess Waterlow)

1898–1908. P 13½ to 15½.

75	**10**	½d. dull bluish green	10·00	2·75
		a. *Yellow green* (1904)	4·25	2·75
		aa. Imperf vert (horiz pair)	£800	
		ab. Imperf (pair)	£850	
		ac. Imperf between (vert pair)	£1400	
76		½d. deep green (*shades*) (1908)	30·00	3·25
77		1d. rose (*shades*)	9·00	50
		a. Imperf (pair)	£700	£750
		b. Imperf between (vert pair)	£550	
		c. Imperf between (horiz pair)	—	£950
78		1d. red (*shades*) (1905)	8·50	50
		a. Imperf vert (horiz pair)	£400	£450
		ab. Imperf horiz (vert pair)	£1000	
		b. Imperf (pair)	£600	£600
		c. Imperf between (horiz pair)	£800	£500
		d. Imperf between (vert strip of 4)	£2250	
79		2d. brown	6·00	1·50
80		2½d. dull blue (*shades*)	13·00	1·50
		a. Imperf vert (horiz pair)	£950	£1100
		b. Grey-blue (*shades*) (1903)	15·00	1·50
81		3d. claret	11·00	80
		a. Imperf between (vert pair)	£700	
82		4d. olive	9·50	30
		a. Imperf between (vert pair)	£700	
83		6d. reddish purple	18·00	2·50
		a. Reddish mauve (1902)	22·00	6·50
84	**11**	1s. bistre	25·00	3·75
		a. Imperf between (vert pair)	£2750	
		ab. Imperf between (horiz pair)	£3250	
		b. Deep olive-bistre (1907)	£325	
		bc. Imperf (pair)	£2750	
		bd. Imperf between (horiz pair)	£4000	
		c. Bistre-brown (1908)	60·00	15·00
		d. Brownish yellow (1908)	25·00	9·50
85		2s.6d. bluish grey (11.06)	60·00	1·75
		a. Imperf between (vert pair)	£1100	£500
86		3s. deep violet (1902)	27·00	3·25
		a. Deep bluish violet (1908)	70·00	13·00
87		5s. brown-orange	55·00	17·00
88		7s.6d. black (11.01)	90·00	27·00
89		10s. grey-green	50·00	1·50
90	**12**	£1 greyish red-purple (p 15½) (7.01)	£375	£140
		a. Perf 14. *Blackish purple* (1902)	£600	£130
91		£2 brown (5.08)	£120	6·50
92		£5 deep blue (7.01)	£3250	£2500
93		£10 lilac (7.01)	£3250	£2250
93*a*		£20 yellow-bistre (1901?)	£15000	
75/90 *Set of 14*			£650	£170
80s/1s, 85s/6s, 88s/93s Perf "SPECIMEN" *Set of 10*			£900	

A £100 cherry-red, perf 13½, was ordered in June 1901, a number of mint, together with several examples showing fiscal cancellations being known.

13 Victoria Falls

RHODESIA.

(**14**)

(Recess Waterlow)

1905 (13 July). Visit of British Association and Opening of Victoria Falls Bridge. P 14½ to 15 (5d.), 14 (others).

94	**13**	1d. red	7·00	8·00
		a. Perf 14½ to 15	16·00	17·00
95		2½d. deep blue	15·00	9·50
		a. Perf 14½ to 15	24·00	17·00
96		5d. claret	30·00	55·00
		a. Perf 14	60·00	75·00
		sa. Optd "SPECIMEN"	£160	
97		1s. blue-green	35·00	50·00
		a. Imperf (pair)	£23000	
		b. Imperf between (horiz pair)	£30000	
		c. Imperf between (vert pair)	£32000	
		d. Imperf vert (horiz pair)	£24000	
		e. Perf 14½ to 15	—	£350
98		2s.6d. black	£110	£150
99		5s. violet	£100	40·00
		a. Perf 14½ to 15	£400	
94/9 *Set of 6*			£275	£275
94s/9s Optd or Perf (5d.) "SPECIMEN" *Set of 6*			£400	

1909 (15 Apr)–**12**. Optd as T **14**. P 13½ to 15.

100	**10**	½d. green to deep green	3·75	2·25
		a. No stop	70·00	40·00
		b. Yellow-green (1911)	38·00	28·00
101		1d. carmine-rose	7·50	1·25
		a. No stop	80·00	30·00

		b. Imperf between (horiz pair)	£450	
		c. Deep carmine-rose	7·50	1·25
		cd. Imperf between (horiz pair)	£450	
102		2d. brown	3·00	6·00
		a. No stop	£130	85·00
103		2½d. pale dull blue	1·75	80
		a. No stop	55·00	27·00
104		3d. claret	2·25	1·75
		a. No stop	£170	75·00
		b. Opt inverted	†	18·00
		c. Opt double	†	£1100
105		4d. olive	8·50	3·00
		a. No stop	85·00	65·00
		b. Opt inverted	†	15·00
106		6d. reddish purple	6·00	7·50
		a. No stop	75·00	
		b. Reddish mauve		
		c. Dull purple	20·00	7·50
		ca. No stop	£110	65·00
107	**11**	1s. bistre	24·00	
		a. No stop	£170	
		b. Bistre-brown		
		ba. No stop		
		c. Deep brownish bistre	11·00	7·50
		ca. No stop	95·00	55·00
108		2s.6d. bluish grey	26·00	11·00
		a. No stop	£120	65·00
		b. Opt inverted	†	22·00
109		3s. deep violet	21·00	11·00
110		5s. orange	42·00	60·00
		a. No stop	£140	£170
111		7s.6d. black	£100	26·00
112		10s. dull green	60·00	19·00
		a. No stop	£350	£200
113	**12**	£1 grey-purple	£190	95·00
		a. Vert pair, lower stamp without opt	£32000	
		b. Opt in violet	£375	£190
113*c*		£2 brown	£4000	£300
113*d*		£2 rosy brown (*bluish paper*) (P 14½×15) (1912)	£3250	£275
113*e*		£5 deep blue (*bluish paper*)	£7500	£4250
100/13 *Set of 14*			£425	£225
100s/13s Perf "SPECIMEN" *Set of 14*			£375	

In some values the no stop variety occurs on every stamp in a vertical row of a sheet, in other values only once in a sheet. Other varieties, such as no serif to the right of apex of "A", no serif to top of "E", etc., exist in some values.

No. 113a comes from a sheet with the overprint omitted from the bottom row.

(**15**)

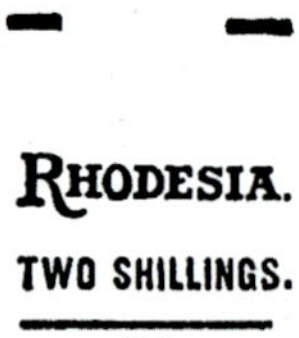

(**16**)

1909 (April)–**11**. Surch as T **15** and **16** (2s.) in black.

114	**10**	5d. on 6d. reddish purple	9·50	17·00
		a. Surcharge in violet	90·00	
		b. Reddish mauve		
		c. Dull purple	19·00	17·00
116	**11**	7½d. on 2s.6d. bluish grey	4·00	3·75
		a. Surcharge in violet	23·00	10·00
		ab. Surch double	†	£6500
117		10d. on 3s. deep violet	15·00	18·00
		a. Surcharge in violet	5·50	3·75
118		2s. on 5s. orange	12·00	7·50
114s/18s Perf "SPECIMEN" *Set of 4*			£180	

In the 7½d. and 10d. surcharges the bars are spaced as in T **16**.

17

18

(Recess Waterlow)

1910 (11 Nov)–**13**.

(a) P 14

119	**17**	½d. yellow-green	13·00	1·75
		a. Imperf between (horiz pair)	£24000	
120		½d. bluish green	25·00	4·25
		a. Imperf (pair)	£14000	£7000
121		½d. olive-green	38·00	4·75
122		½d. dull green	70·00	50·00
123		1d. bright carmine	29·00	3·75
		a. Imperf between (vert pair)	£20000	£13000
		b. Imperf between (horiz pair)		
124		1d. carmine-lake	70·00	3·50
125		1d. rose-red	32·00	3·25
126		2d. black and grey	55·00	11·00
127		2d. black-purple and slate-grey	£160	£750
128		2d. black and slate-grey	65·00	7·50
129		2d. black and slate	80·00	10·00
130		2d. black and grey-black	90·00	19·00
131		2½d. ultramarine	29·00	8·50
131*a*		2½d. bright ultramarine	24·00	8·50
132		2½d. dull blue	29·00	12·00
133		2½d. chalky blue	25·00	20·00
134		3d. purple and ochre	42·00	45·00
135		3d. purple and yellow-ochre	50·00	15·00
136		3d. magenta and yellow-ochre	£180	19·00
137		3d. violet and ochre	£130	85·00
138		4d. greenish black and orange	£100	£100
139		4d. brown-purple and orange	85·00	65·00
140		4d. black and orange	50·00	23·00
141		5d. purple-brown and olive-green	40·00	55·00
141*a*		5d. purple-brown and olive-yellow	40·00	60·00
		ab. Error. Purple-brown and ochre	£650	£150
143		5d. lake-brown and olive	£325	60·00
143*a*		5d. lake-brown and green (9.12)	£22000	£1600
144		6d. red-brown and mauve	50·00	45·00
145		6d. brown and purple	50·00	21·00
145*a*		6d. bright chestnut and mauve	£700	65·00
146		8d. black and purple	£5000	
147		8d. dull purple and purple	£180	£100
148		8d. greenish black and purple	£170	£100
149		10d. scarlet and reddish mauve	48·00	50·00
150		10d. carmine and deep purple	£650	60·00
151		1s. grey-black and deep blue-green	60·00	30·00
151*a*		1s. black and deep blue-green	£160	45·00
152		1s. black and pale blue-green	65·00	20·00
152*a*		1s. purple-black and blue-green	£250	70·00
153		2s. black and ultramarine	£100	75·00
154		2s. black and dull blue	£1200	85·00
154*a*		2s. purple-black and ultramarine	£3000	£225
155		2s.6d. black and lake	£350	£400
155*a*		2s.6d. black and crimson	£325	£275
156		2s.6d. sepia and deep crimson	£400	£350
156*a*		2s.6d. bistre-brown and crimson	£1100	£650
157		2s.6d. black and rose-carmine	£325	£375
158		3s. green and violet (*shades*)	£225	£190
158*a*		3s. bright green and magenta	£1200	£750
159		5s. vermilion and deep green	£325	£400
160		5s. scarlet and pale yellow-green	£300	£200
160*a*		5s. crimson and yellow-green	£275	£200
160*b*		7s.6d. carmine and pale blue	£650	£425
161		7s.6d. carmine and light blue	£850	£1100
162		7s.6d. carmine and bright blue	£2750	£1100
163		10s. deep myrtle and orange	£650	£300
164		10s. blue-green and orange	£425	£500
165		£1 carmine-red and bluish black	£1300	£700
166		£1 rose-scarlet and bluish black	£1300	£375
166*a*		£1 crimson and slate-black	£1700	£1400
		b. Error. Scarlet and reddish mauve	£10000	

(b) P 15

167	**17**	½d. blue-green	£300	13·00
168		½d. yellow-green	£350	11·00
169		½d. apple-green	£600	28·00
170		1d. carmine	£300	8·50
170*a*		1d. carmine-lake	£450	18·00
170*b*		1d. rose-carmine	£350	12·00
171		2d. black and grey-black	£900	40·00
171*a*		2d. black and grey	£900	40·00
171*b*		2d. black and slate	£1000	40·00
172		2½d. ultramarine (*shades*)	70·00	38·00
173		3d. purple and yellow-ochre	£7500	85·00
173*a*		3d. claret and pale yellow-ochre	£3250	70·00
174		4d. black and orange (*shades*)	60·00	70·00
175		5d. lake-brown and olive	£800	80·00
176		6d. brown and mauve	£900	60·00
177		1s. black and blue-green (*shades*)	£1200	55·00
178		2s. black and dull blue	£2250	£350
179		£1 red and black	£16000	£3000

(c) P 14×15 (½d., 3d., 1s.) or 15×14 (1d., 4d.)

179*a*	**17**	½d. yellow-green	†	£2750
179*b*		1d. carmine	†	£6000
180		3d. purple and ochre	£6500	£275
181		4d. black and orange	£450	
181*a*		1s. black and blue-green	£27000	£2500

(d) P 13½

182	**17**	½d. yellow-green	£300	50·00
182*a*		½d. green	£350	55·00
183		1d. bright carmine	£2000	48·00
184		2½d. ultramarine (*shades*)	38·00	70·00
185		8d. black and purple (*shades*)	60·00	£250
185*a*		8d. grey-purple and dull purple	£375	£450

119s/85s Optd "SPECIMEN." (all perf 14 except 2½d. and 8d. perf 13½) *Set of* 18 .... £3500

Plate varieties in T **17** are:—½d., double dot below "D" in right-hand value tablet (R. 3/9) (*from* £500 *un.* £350 *used*); 2d. to £1 excluding 2½d., straight stroke in Queen's right ear known as the "gash in ear" variety (R. 1/2) (*from* 3 *to* 5 *times normal*).

Stamps from the above and the next issue are known compound perf with 14 or 15 on one side only or on adjoining sides but we no longer list them.

Examples of some values are known with a forged registered Bulawayo postmark dated "JA 10 11".

(Recess Waterlow)

1913 (1 Sept)–**22**. No wmk.

(i) From single working plates

(a) P 14

186	**18**	½d. blue-green	10·00	2·25
187		½d. deep green	8·00	2·25
		a. Imperf horiz (vert pair)	£800	
		b. Imperf between (vert strip of 5)	£3500	
188		½d. yellow-green	19·00	2·25
		a. Imperf between (horiz pair)	£850	
188*b*		½d. dull green	12·00	2·25
		ba. Imperf vert (horiz pair)	£850	£850
		bb. Imperf between (horiz pair)	£1200	
189		½d. bright green	25·00	2·25
		a. Imperf between (vert pair)	£1500	
190		1d. rose-carmine	6·50	2·25
		a. Imperf between (horiz pair)	£950	£800
191		1d. carmine-red (*shades*)	10·00	2·50
		a. Imperf between (pair)	£1400	
192		1d. brown-red	4·00	3·00
193		1d. red	6·50	2·25
		a. Imperf between (horiz pair)	£900	
194		1d. scarlet	20·00	2·50
		a. Imperf between (horiz pair)	£1100	
195		1d. rose-red	10·00	2·25
		a. Imperf between (horiz pair)	£850	£850
		b. Imperf between (vert pair)	£2250	
196		1d. rosine	£500	20·00
197		1½d. brown-ochre (1919)	5·00	2·25
		a. Imperf between (horiz pair)	£750	£750
198		1½d. bistre-brown (1917)	5·50	2·25
		a. Imperf between (horiz pair)	£750	£750
199		1½d. drab-brown (1917)	6·50	2·25
		a. Imperf between (horiz pair)	£750	
		b. Imperf between (vert pair)	£2000	
200		2½d. deep blue	7·00	38·00
201		2½d. bright blue	7·00	32·00

(b) P 15

202	**18**	½d. blue-green	8·50	25·00
203		½d. green	14·00	20·00
204		1d. rose-red	£550	22·00
		a. Imperf between (horiz pair)	£16000	
205		1d. brown-red	5·50	8·50
206		1½d. bistre-brown (1919)	42·00	7·00
		a. Imperf between (horiz pair)	£22000	
206*b*		1½d. brown-ochre (1917)	48·00	12·00
207		2½d. deep blue	21·00	65·00
208		2½d. bright blue	16·00	60·00

(c) P 14×15

208*a*	**18**	½d. green	£7000	£200

(d) P 15×14

208*b*	**18**	½d. green	£7000	£350
208*c*		1½d. drab-brown		

(e) P 13½

208*d*	**18**	1d. red (1914)	†	£550

Die I Die II Die III

The remaining values were printed from double, i.e. head and duty, plates. There are at least four different head plates made from three different dies, which may be distinguished as follows:—

Die I. The King's left ear is neither shaded nor outlined; no outline to top of cap. Shank of anchor in cap badge is complete.

Die II. The ear is shaded all over, but has no outline. The top of the cap has a faint outline. Anchor as Die I.

Die III. The ear is shaded and outlined; a heavy continuous outline round the cap. Shank of anchor is broken just below the lowest line which crosses it.

(ii) Printed from double plates. Head Die I

(a) P 14

209	**18**	2d. black and grey	16·00	9·00
210		3d. black and yellow	85·00	20·00
211		4d. black and orange-red	10·00	35·00
212		5d. black and green	6·00	18·00
213		6d. black and mauve	£225	27·00
213*a*		8d. violet and green	£5000	
214		2s. black and brown	£130	95·00

(b) P 15

215	**18**	3d. black and yellow	7·50	24·00
216		4d. black and orange-red	£150	27·00
217		6d. black and mauve	9·00	10·00
217*a*		8d. violet and green	£19000	£22000
218		2s. black and brown	15·00	50·00

(iii) Head Die II

(a) P 14

219	**18**	2d. black and grey	18·00	7·50
220		2d. black and brownish grey	65·00	11·00
221		3d. black and deep yellow	45·00	10·00
222		3d. black and yellow	75·00	10·00
223		3d. black and buff	10·00	9·00
224		4d. black and orange-red	27·00	13·00
225		4d. black and deep orange-red	19·00	13·00
226		5d. black and grey-green	21·00	45·00
227		5d. black and bright green	20·00	45·00
228		6d. black and mauve	40·00	5·50
229		6d. black and purple	80·00	6·50
230		8d. violet and green	16·00	75·00
231		10d. blue and carmine-red	25·00	55·00
232		1s. black and greenish blue	60·00	55·00
233		1s. black and turquoise-blue	16·00	18·00
234		2s. black and brown	95·00	15·00
235		2s. black and yellow-brown	£350	40·00
236		2s.6d. indigo and grey-brown	70·00	50·00
236*a*		2s.6d. pale blue and brown	£1000	75·00
236*b*		3s. brown and blue	£110	£120
237		3s. chestnut and bright blue	£110	£150
238		5s. blue and yellow-green	£170	95·00
239		5s. blue and blue-green	80·00	85·00
240		7s.6d. blackish purple and slate-black	£300	£325
241		10s. crimson and yellow-green	£200	£350
242		£1 black and purple	£425	£600
243		£1 black and violet	£375	£600

(b) P 15

244	**18**	2d. black and grey	11·00	16·00
245		4d. black and deep orange-vermilion	£1100	£275
246		8d. violet and green	£190	£170
247		10d. blue and red	14·00	42·00
248		1s. black and greenish blue	70·00	20·00
249		2s.6d. indigo and grey-brown	48·00	90·00
250		3s. chocolate and blue	£700	£300
251		5s. blue and yellow-green	£180	£190
251*a*		5s. blue and blue-green	£1900	
252		7s.6d. blackish purple and slate-black	£150	£275
253		10s. red and green	£200	£375
		a. Frame double, one albino	£600	
254		£1 black and purple	£1400	£1400
254*a*		£1 black and deep purple	£3000	£2500

186s, 190s, 198s, 208s, 209s, 211s/12s, 215s, 217s/18s, 230s, 232s, 237s/8s, 240s/2s, 247s, 249s Optd "SPECIMEN" *Set of* 19 .... £3500

(iv) Head Die III (1919). Toned paper, yellowish gum

(a) P 14

255	**18**	2d. black and brownish grey	15·00	6·50
256		2d. black and grey-black	10·00	3·50
		a. Imperf between (horiz pair)	£5500	
		b. Imperf between (horiz strip of 3)	£13000	
		c. Imperf vert (horiz pair)	£5000	£5000
257		2d. black and grey	15·00	11·00
258		2d. black and sepia	60·00	11·00
259		3d. black and yellow	14·00	3·50
260		3d. black and ochre	16·00	4·00
261		4d. black and orange-red	19·00	9·50
262		4d. black and dull red	18·00	13·00
263		5d. black and pale green	9·00	42·00
		a. Imperf between (horiz strip of 3)	£30000	
264		5d. black and green	9·00	42·00
265		6d. black and reddish mauve	9·50	8·00
		a. Imperf between (horiz pair)	£22000	
266		6d. black and dull mauve	9·50	8·00
267		8d. mauve and dull blue-green	24·00	22·00
268		8d. mauve and greenish blue	22·00	70·00
		a. Imperf vert (horiz pair)	£13000	
269		10d. indigo and carmine	20·00	55·00
270		10d. blue and red	18·00	60·00
271		1s. black and greenish blue	13·00	16·00
272		1s. black and pale blue-green	9·00	11·00
272*a*		1s. black and light blue	14·00	20·00
272*b*		1s. black and green	80·00	50·00
273		2s. black and brown	18·00	18·00
		aa. Imperf between (vert pair)	†	£40000
273*a*		2s. black and yellow-brown	£3250	£160
274		2s.6d. dp ultramarine & grey-brn	48·00	70·00
274*a*		2s.6d. pale blue and pale bistre-brown (*shades*)	£120	75·00

274*b* 3s. chestnut and light blue £275 £180
275 5s. deep blue and blue-green (*shades*) £110 75·00
276 5s. blue & pale yell-grn (*shades*) £150 80·00
276*a* 7s.6d. maroon and slate-black £800 £1200
277 10s. carmine-lake and yellow-green £350 £250
278 £1 black and bright purple £475 £650
279 £1 black and deep purple £500 £650
279*a* £1 black and violet-indigo £600 £700
279*b* £1 black and deep violet £650 £700

(b) P 15

279*c* **18** 2d. black and brownish grey £5500 £400

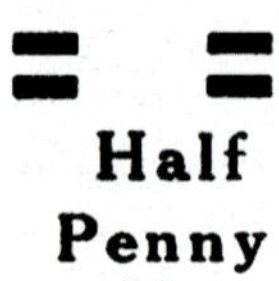

(19)

(20)

1917 (15 Aug). No. 190 surch at the Northern Rhodesian Administrative Press, Livingstone, with T **19**, in violet or violet-black.

280 **18** ½d. on 1d. rose-carmine (*shades*) 2·50 9·50
a. Surch inverted £1400 £1500
b. Letters "n n" spaced wider 11·00 35·00
c. Letters "n y" spaced wider 7·50 27·00

The setting was in two rows of 10 repeated three times in the sheet. The two colours of the surcharge occur on the same sheet.

1917 (22 Sept). No. 190 surch as T **20** (new setting with hyphen, and full stop after "Penny"), in deep violet.

281 **18** ½d. on 1d. rose-carmine (shades) 1·75 8·50

1922–24. New printings on white paper with clear white gum.

(i) Single working plates

(a) P 14

282 **18** ½d. dull green (1922) 5·50 8·50
a. Imperf between (vert pair) £2500 £1700
283 ½d. deep blue-green (1922) 5·50 9·00
284 1d. bright rose (1922) 10·00 7·00
285 1d. bright rose-scarlet (1923) 10·00 7·00
a. Imperf between (horiz pair) £1800
b. Imperf between (vert pair) £2250
286 1d. aniline red (8.24) (*toned paper*) 20·00 15·00
287 1½d. brown-ochre (1923) 9·50 7·50
a. Imperf between (vert pair) £2500 £1600

(b) P 15

288 **18** ½d. dull green (1923) 45·00
289 1d. bright rose-scarlet (1923) 48·00
290 1½d. brown-ochre (1923) 48·00

(ii) Double plates. Head Die III

(a) P 14

291 **18** 2d. black and grey-purple (1922) 11·00 7·50
292 2d. black and slate-purple (1923) 9·00 10·00
293 3d. black and yellow (1922) 13·00 35·00
294 4d. black and orange-vermilion (1922–3) 18·00 48·00
295 6d. jet-black and lilac (1922–3) 6·00 6·50
296 8d. mauve and pale blue-green (1922) 35·00 90·00
297 8d. violet and grey-green (1923) 45·00 85·00
298 10d. bright ultramarine and red (1922) 15·00 70·00
299 10d. bright ultramarine and carmine-red (1923) 24·00 70·00
300 1s. black and dull blue (1922–3) 12·00 18·00
a. Imperf between (horiz pair) £19000
b. Imperf between (vert pair) £22000
301 2s. black and brown (1922–3) 21·00 55·00
302 2s.6d. ultramarine and sepia (1922) 55·00 95·00
303 2s.6d. violet-blue and grey-brown (1923) 70·00 95·00
304 3s. red-brown and turquoise-blue (1922) £110 £150
305 3s. red-brown and grey-blue (1923) £130 £160
306 5s. bright ultramarine and emerald (1922) £130 £160
307 5s. deep blue and bright green (1923) £140 £160
308 7s.6d. brown-purple and slate (1922) £225 £350
309 10s. crimson and bright yellow-green (1922) £200 £250
310 10s. carmine and yellow-green (1923) £225 £300
311 £1 black and magenta (1922) £550 £750
311*a* £1 black and deep magenta (1923) £750 £950

(b) P 15 (1923)

312 **18** 2d. black and slate-purple 45·00
313 4d. black and orange-vermilion 48·00
314 6d. jet-black and lilac 65·00
315 8d. violet and grey-green 70·00
316 10d. bright ultramarine and carmine-red 80·00
317 1s. black and dull blue 90·00
318 2s. black and brown £130
319 2s.6d. violet-blue and grey-brown £140
320 3s. red-brown and grey-blue £180
321 5s. deep blue and bright green £300
322 £1 black and deep magenta £900

The 1922 printing shows the mesh of the paper very clearly through the gum. In the 1923 printing the gum is very smooth and the mesh of the paper is not so clearly seen. Where date is given as "(1922–23)" two printings were made, which do not differ sufficiently in colour to be listed separately.

Nos. 288/90 and 312/22 were never sent out to Rhodesia, but only issued in London. Any used copies could, therefore, only have been obtained by favour.

Southern Rhodesia, that part of the Company's territory south of the River Zambesi, became a self-governing colony on 1 October 1923. British South Africa Company rule continued in Northern Rhodesia until the administration was transferred to the Colonial Office on 1 April 1924.

The current stamps of Rhodesia, the Admiral series first issued in 1913, continued to be used in Southern Rhodesia until 1 April 1924 (invalidated 1 May 1924) and in Northern Rhodesia until 1 April 1925 (invalidated 30 September 1925).

For issues from 1924 to 1964 see Southern Rhodesia.

In October 1964 Southern Rhodesia was renamed Rhodesia.

Rhodesia & Nyasaland

Stamps for the Central Africa Federation of Northern and Southern Rhodesia and Nyasaland Protectorate.

1

2

3 Queen Elizabeth II

(Recess Waterlow)

1954 (1 July)–**56**. P 13½×14 (T **1**), 13½×13 (T **2**) or 14½×13½ (T **3**).

1	**1**	½d. orange-red	15	10
		a. Coil stamp. Perf 12½×14. *Reddish orange* (6.2.56)	30	2·00
2		1d. ultramarine	15	10
		a. Coil stamp. Perf 12½×14. *Deep blue* (9.55)	1·50	19·00
		ab. Ultramarine (1.10.55)	4·75	17·00
3		2d. bright green	15	10
3a		2½d. ochre (15.2.56)	6·50	10
4		3d. carmine-red	20	10
5		4d. red-brown	60	20
6		4½d. blue-green	30	1·50
7		6d. bright reddish purple	2·25	10
		a. Bright purple (5.5.56)	6·00	10
8		9d. violet	2·50	1·00
9		1s. grey-black	2·50	10
10	**2**	1s.3d. red-orange and ultramarine	4·75	40
11		2s. deep blue and yellow-brown	8·50	6·00
12		2s.6d. black and rose-red	8·00	2·25
13		5s. violet and olive-green	22·00	7·50
14	**3**	10s. dull blue-green and orange	22·00	9·50
15		£1 olive-green and lake	38·00	30·00
1/15 *Set of 16*			£110	50·00

Nos. 1a and 2a printed on rotary machines by subsidiary company, Imprimerie Belge de Securité, in Belgium.

4 de Havilland DH.106 Comet 1 over Victoria Falls

5 Livingstone and Victoria Falls

3d. Wing flaw (R. 3/3)

(Des J. E. Hughes (3d.), V. E. Horne (1s.). Recess Waterlow)

1955 (15 June). Centenary of Discovery of Victoria Falls. P 13½ (3d.) or 13 (1s.).

16	**4**	3d. ultramarine & dp turquoise-green	1·00	30
		a. Wing flaw	13·00	8·00
17	**5**	1s. purple and deep blue	55	70

6 Tea Picking

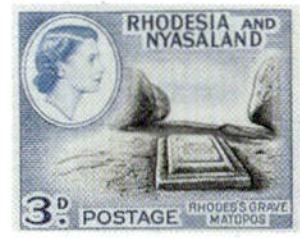

10 Rhodes's Grave

11 Lake Bangweulu

12a Rhodesian Railway Trains

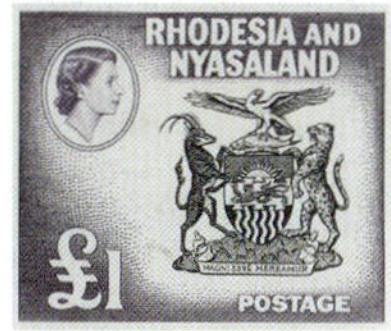

19 Federal Coat of Arms

(Des M. Kinsella (9d.). Recess Waterlow (½d., 1d., 2d., 1s.) until 1962, then D.L.R. (2½d., 4d., 6d., 9d., 2s., 2s.6d.) and B.W. (others))

1959 (12 Aug)–**62**. T **6**, **10/11**, **12a**, **19** and similar designs. P 13½×14 (½d., 1d., 2d.), 14½ (2½d., 4d., 6d., 9d., 2s., 2s.6d.), 14×13½ (3d.), 13½×13 (1s.), 14 (1s.3d.) or 11 (others).

18	½d. black and light emerald	1·25	2·00
	a. Coil stamp. Perf 12½×14	3·25	5·50
19	1d. carmine-red and black	30	10
	a. Coil stamp. Perf 12½×14	3·25	9·00
	ab. Carmine-red and grey-black	6·50	13·00
	ac. Carmine-red (centre) omitted	£250	
20	2d. violet and yellow-brown	2·50	50
21	2½d. purple and grey-blue	2·00	2·00
22	3d. black and blue	1·00	10
	a. Black (centre) omitted	£25000	
	b. Printed on the gummed side	£425	
23	4d. maroon and olive	1·50	10
24	6d. ultramarine and deep myrtle-green	2·75	10
24a	9d. orange-brown and reddish violet (15.5.62)	9·00	3·00
25	1s. light green and ultramarine	1·25	10
26	1s.3d. emerald and deep chocolate	3·00	10
27	2s. grey-green and carmine	4·00	60
28	2s.6d. light blue and yellow-brown	7·00	65
29	5s. deep chocolate and yellow-green	15·00	2·50
30	10s. olive-brown and rose-red	28·00	25·00
31	£1 black and deep violet	48·00	65·00
18/31 *Set of 15*		£110	90·00

Designs: *Vert* (*as T* **6**)—1d. V.H.F. mast; 2d. Copper mining; 2½d. Fairbridge Memorial. (*As T* **11**)—6d. Eastern Cataract, Victoria Falls. *Horiz* (*as T* **12a**)—1s. Tobacco; 1s.3d. Lake Nyasa; 2s. Chirundu Bridge; 2s.6d. Salisbury Airport. (*As T* **19**)—5s. Rhodes Statue; 10s. Mlanje.

Only three examples from two different sheets, all unused, are believed to exist of No. 22a, although further stamps from the same sheets can be found with the centre partially omitted.

20 Kariba Gorge, 1955

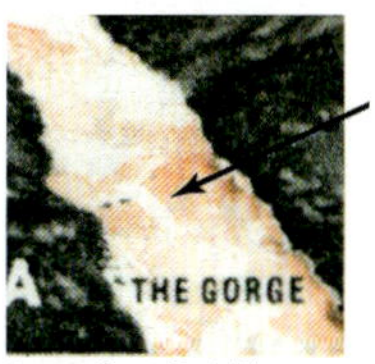

Gorge flaw (R. 4/6)

1s.3d. Ear-ring flaw (R. 1/4)

(Photo Harrison (3d., 6d.), D.L.R. (others))

1960 (17 May). Opening of Kariba Hydro-Electric Scheme. T **20** and similar horiz designs. P 14½×14 (3d., 6d.) or 13 (others).

32	3d. blackish green and red-orange	70	10

		a. Red-orange omitted	£5500	
		b. Gorge flaw	18·00	8·50
33		6d. brown and yellow-brown	70	20
34		1s. slate-blue and green	2·50	4·00
35		1s.3d. light blue and orange-brown	2·50	3·25
		aa. Ear-ring flaw	35·00	
		a. Blue and deep orange-brown	9·50	7·50
36		2s.6d. deep slate-purple and orange-red	3·50	8·50
37		5s. reddish violet and turquoise-blue	9·00	11·00
32/7 *Set of 6*			17·00	24·00

Designs:—6d. 330 kV power lines; 1s. Barrage wall; 1s.3d. Barrage and lake; 2s.6d. Interior of power station; 5s. Barrage wall and Queen Mother (top left).

No. 35aa. comes on the first shade only.

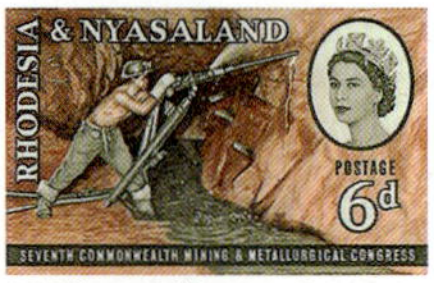

26 Miner Drilling

(Des V. Whiteley. Photo Harrison)

1961 (8 May). Seventh Commonwealth Mining and Metallurgical Congress. T **26** and similar horiz design. P 15×14.

38		6d. olive-green and orange-brown	65	20
39		1s.3d. black and light blue	65	80

Design:—1s.3d. Surface installations, Nchanga Mine.

Imperforate examples of the 6d. are believed to be printer's waste.

28 de Havilland DH.66 Hercules *City of Basra* on Rhodesian Airstrip

31 Tobacco Plant

1962 (6 Feb). 30th Anniv of First London-Rhodesia Airmail Service. T **28** and similar horiz designs. P 14½×14.

40		6d. bronze-green and vermilion	1·50	75
41		1s.3d. light blue, black and yellow	1·75	50
42		2s.6d. rose-red and deep violet	4·00	6·50
40/2 *Set of 3*			6·50	7·00

Designs:—1s.3d. Short S.23 flying boat *Canopus* taking off from Zambesi; 2s.6d. Hawker Siddeley Comet 4 at Salisbury airport.

(Des V. Whiteley. Photo Harrison)

1963 (18 Feb). World Tobacco Congress, Salisbury. T **31** and similar vert designs. P 14×14½.

43		3d. green and olive-brown	30	10
44		6d. green, brown and blue	40	35
45		1s.3d. chestnut and indigo	1·25	45
46		2s.6d. yellow and brown	1·50	3·25
43/6 *Set of 4*			3·00	3·75

Designs:—6d. Tobacco field; 1s.3d. Auction floor; 2s.6d. Cured tobacco.

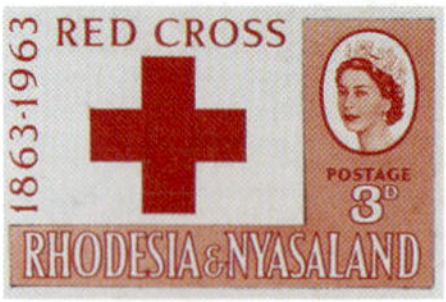

35 Red Cross Emblem

(Photo Harrison)

1963 (6 Aug). Red Cross Centenary. P 14½×14.

47	**35**	3d. red	1·25	10

36 African "Round Table" Emblem

(Des V. Whiteley. Photo Harrison)

1963 (11 Sept). World Council of Young Men's Service Clubs, Salisbury. P 14½×14.

48	**36**	6d. black, gold and yellow-green	75	1·50
49		1s.3d. black, gold, yellow-grn & lilac	1·00	1·25

STAMP BOOKLETS

1955 (1 Jan). Black on yellow cover. Stitched.

SB1	5s. booklet containing twelve ½d. and eighteen 1d. and 2d. (Nos. 1/3) in blocks of 6	35·00

1963 (4 Apr). Black on yellow cover. Stitched.

SB2	1s. booklet containing 3d. (No. 22) in block of 4	2·00

POSTAGE DUE STAMPS

After Federation in 1954 existing stocks of Postage Due Stamps from Northern Rhodesia, Nyasaland and Southern Rhodesia continued to be used and were sometimes distributed throughout the federation.

Increased postal rates in July 1956 and in 1959 led to the exhaustion of certain values, in particular the 1d., and various offices then used Rhodesia and Nyasaland postage issues for postage due purposes. There were isolated instances of such stamps being cancelled "POSTAGE DUE" from December 1956 onwards.

Some of these handstamps may have been applied at Bulawayo while others, in violet or black, originate from the Salisbury Delivery Room at Kingsway Post Office. Only the 1d. and 2d. (Nos. 2/3) are known with such handstamps. After mint examples began to appear the Postmaster General suppressed the use of the handstamps in August 1959.

D **1**

(Des E.W. Jones. Typo Federal Printing and Stationery Dept, Salisbury)

1961 (19 Apr). P 12½.

D1	D **1**	1d. vermilion	3·75	5·50
		a. Imperf between (horiz pair)	£650	£750
D2		2d. deep violet-blue	3·00	3·00
D3		4d. green	3·50	9·50
D4		6d. purple	4·50	7·50
		a. Imperf between (horiz pair)	£1800	
D1/4 *Set of 4*			13·00	23·00

The 2d. has a stop below the "D".

The stamps of the Federation were withdrawn on 19 February 1964 when all three constituent territories had resumed issuing their own stamps.

South Africa

South Africa as a nation, rather than a geographical term, came into being with the creation of the Union of South Africa on 31 May 1910.

The development, both political and philatelic, of the area is very complex and the method adopted by the catalogue is to first list, in alphabetical order, the various colonies and republics which formed this federation, followed by stamps for the Union of South Africa.

The section is divided as follows:

I. CAPE OF GOOD HOPE.
British Kaffraria. Mafeking Siege Stamps. Vryburg
II. GRIQUALAND WEST
III. NATAL
IV. NEW REPUBLIC
V. ORANGE FREE STATE.
Orange River Colony
VI. TRANSVAAL.
Pietersburg. Local British Occupation Issues
VII. ZULULAND
VIII. BRITISH ARMY FIELD OFFICES
DURING SOUTH AFRICAN WAR
IX. UNION OF SOUTH AFRICA
X. REPUBLIC OF SOUTH AFRICA

I. CAPE OF GOOD HOPE

PRICES FOR STAMPS ON COVER

Nos.	1/4	*from* × 4
Nos.	5/14	*from* × 3
Nos.	18/21	*from* × 5
No.	22	—
Nos.	23/6	*from* × 5
Nos.	27/31	*from* × 8
Nos.	32/3	*from* × 10
No.	34	*from* × 25
No.	35	*from* × 20
No.	36	*from* × 10
Nos.	37/8	*from* × 25
Nos.	39/45	*from* × 10
Nos.	46/7	*from* × 12
Nos.	48/54	*from* × 10
Nos.	55/6	*from* × 25
No.	57	*from* × 50
Nos.	58/69	*from* × 10
Nos.	70/8	*from* × 6

PRICES. Our prices for early Cape of Good Hope are for stamps in very fine condition. Exceptional copies are worth more, poorer copies considerably less.

1 Hope

2

(Des Charles Bell, Surveyor-General. Eng W. Humphrys. Recess P.B.)

1853 (1 Sept). W **2**. Imperf.

(a) Paper deeply blued

1	1	1d. pale brick-red	£4250	£375
		a. Deep brick-red	£5500	£400
		b. Wmk sideways	†	£475
2		4d. deep blue	£3000	£200
		a. Wmk sideways	£4000	£300

Plate proofs of the 4d. in a shade similar to the issued stamp exist on ungummed watermarked paper. (*Price* £350) The blueing on the reverse of these proofs is uneven giving a blotchy appearance.

(b) Paper slightly blued (blueing not pronounced at back)

3	1	1d. brick-red	£3250	£275
		a. Brown-red	£3500	£300
		b. Wmk sideways	†	£375
4		4d. deep blue	£1500	£1400
		a. Blue	£1600	£170
		b. Wmk sideways	†	£300

PERKINS BACON "CANCELLED". For notes on these handstamps showing "CANCELLED" between horizontal bars forming an oval, see Catalogue Introduction.

1855–63. W **2**.

(a) Imperf

5	1	1d. brick-red/*cream toned paper* (1857)	£5000	£900
		a. Rose (1858) (H/S "CANCELLED" in oval £20000)	£600	£225
		ab. Wmk sideways	—	£475
		b. Deep rose-red	£850	£275
		ba. Wmk sideways	—	£500
6		4d. deep blue/*white paper* (1855)	£900	75·00
		a. Blue (H/S "CANCELLED" in oval £20000)	£700	70·00
		b. Bisected (on cover)	†	£35000
		c. Wmk sideways	†	£225
7		6d. pale rose-lilac/*white paper* (18.2.58) (H/S "CANCELLED" in oval £16000)	£900	£250
		a. Wmk sideways	†	£1100
		b. Deep rose-lilac/white paper	£1800	£350
		c. Slate-lilac/blued paper (1862)	£4500	£450
		d. Slate-purple/blued paper (1863)	£4000	£1000
		e. Bisected (on cover)	†	—
8		1s. bright yellow-green/*white paper* (18.2.58) (H/S "CANCELLED" in oval £20000)	£3250	£250
		a. Wmk sideways	†	£1600
		b. Deep dark green (1859)	£375	£500

The method adopted for producing the plate of the 4d., 6d and 1s. stamps involved the use of two dies, so that there are two types of each of these values differing slightly in detail, but produced in equal numbers.

The 1d. value in dull rose on ungummed watermarked paper with the watermark sideways is a plate proof. (*Price* £325).

The 4d. is known bisected in 1858 and used with two other 4d. values to pay the inland registered fee. The 6d. is known bisected and used with 1d. for 4d. rate.

The paper of No. 5 is similar to that of Nos. 1/4, but is without the blueing. It is much thicker than the white paper used for later printings of the 1d. The evolution of the paper on these Cape of Good Hope stamps is similar to that of the line-engraved issues of Great Britain. Examples of the 6d. slate-lilac apparently on white paper have had the blueing washed out.

The 4d. value is known printed in black on white watermarked paper. Twelve authenticated copies have been recorded, the majority of which show cancellations or, at least, some indication that they have been used.

It was, at one time, believed that these stamps came from a small supply printed in black to mark the death of the Prince Consort, but references to examples can be found in the philatelic press before news of this event reached Cape Town.

It is now thought that these stamps represent proof sheets, possibly pressed into service during a shortage of stamps in 1861.

There is, however, no official confirmation of this theory. (*Price* £35000 *un*, £30000 *with obliteration*).

(b) Unofficially rouletted

9	1	1d. brick-red	†	£3000
10		4d. blue	†	£2250
11		6d. rose-lilac	†	£1500
12		1s. bright yellow-green	†	£3250
		a. Deep dark green	†	£3500

These rouletted stamps are best collected on cover.

3 Hope

(Local provisional (so-called "wood-block") issue. Engraved on steel by C. J. Roberts. Printed from stereotyped plates by Saul Solomon & Co, Cape Town)

1861 (Feb–Apr). Laid paper. Imperf.

13	3	1d. vermilion (27 February)	£16000	£2500
		a. Carmine (7 March)	£28000	£3250
		b. Brick-red (10 April)	£45000	£4500
		c. Error. Pale milky blue	£180000	£28000
		ca. Pale bright blue	—	£30000
14		4d. pale milky blue (23 February)	£24000	£1800
		aa. Retouch or repair to rt-hand corner	—	£7500

South Africa
SG O35

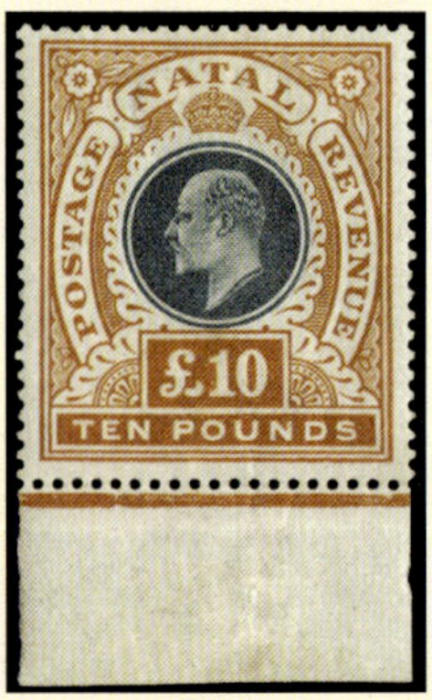

Natal
SG145

Cape of Good Hope
SG18/21
'SPECIMEN' (type D5)

		a. Pale grey-blue (March?)	£25000	£1800
		b. Pale bright blue (March?)	£25000	£2250
		ba. Retouch or repair to rt-hand corner	—	£7500
		c. Deep bright blue (12 April)	£110000	£4750
		d. Blue	£30000	£3250
		e. Error. Vermilion	£180000	£40000
		ea. Carmine	—	£95000
		f. Sideways *tête-bêche* (pair)	†	£160000

Nos. 13/14 were each issued in *tête-bêche* pairs normally joined at edges bearing the same inscription ("POSTAGE" against "POSTAGE", etc). No. 14f, of which only one used example is known, comes from the first printing and shows the right-hand stamp misplaced so that "FOUR PENCE" adjoins "POSTAGE".

Nos. 13*c*/*ca* and 14*e*/*ea* were caused by the inclusion of incorrect clichés in the plates of the 1d. or 4d. values.

Both values were officially reprinted in March 1883, on wove paper. The 1d. is in deep red, and the 4d. in a deeper blue than that of the deepest shade of the issued stamp.

Examples of the reprints have done postal duty, but their use thus was not intended. There are no reprints of the errors or of the retouched 4d.

Further reprints were made privately but with official permission, in 1940/41, in colours much deeper than those of any of the original printings, and on thick carton paper.

Examples of the 4d. are known unofficially rouletted.

Early in 1863, Perkins Bacon Ltd handed over the four plates used for printing the triangular Cape of Good Hope stamps to De La Rue & Co, Ltd, who made all the subsequent printings.

(Printed from the P.B. plates by D.L.R.)

1863–64. Imperf.

(a) W **2**

18	**1**	1d. deep carmine-red (1864)	£225	£250
		a. Wmk sideways	£425	£350
		b. Deep brown-red	£500	£275
		ba. Wmk sideways	£600	£325
		c. Brownish red	£500	£250
		ca. Wmk sideways	£600	£300
19		4d. deep blue (1864)	£200	90·00
		a. Blue	£225	£100
		b. Slate-blue	£2500	£500
		c. Steel-blue	£2250	£275
		d. Wmk sideways	£750	£250
20		6d. bright mauve (1864)	£325	£450
		a. Wmk sideways	†	£1600
21		1s. bright emerald-green	£475	£550
		a. Pale emerald-green	£1300	

(b) Wmk Crown CC (sideways)

22	**1**	1d. deep carmine-red	£24000	

No. 22 was a trial printing, and is only known unused.

Our prices for the 4d. blue are for stamps which are blue by comparison with the other listed shades. An exceptionally pale shade is recognised by specialists and is rare.

With the exception of the 4d., these stamps may be easily distinguished from those printed by Perkins Bacon by their colours, which are quite distinct.

The De La Rue stamps of all values are less clearly printed, the figure of Hope and the lettering of the inscriptions standing out less boldly, while the fine lines of the background appear blurred and broken when examined under a glass. The background as a whole often shows irregularity in the apparent depth of colour, due to wear of the plates.

For note regarding the two dies of the 4d., 6d., and 1s. values, see after No. 8.

All the triangular stamps were demonetised as from 1 October 1900.

4 "Hope" seated, with vine and ram. (With outer frame-line)

Four Pence.

(**5**)

(Des Charles Bell. Die engraved on steel and stamps typo by D.L.R.)

1864–77. With outer frame-line surrounding the design. Wmk Crown CC. P 14.

23	**4**	1d. carmine-red (5.65)	£110	32·00
		a. Rose-red	£100	30·00
		w. Wmk inverted	£375	£170
24		4d. pale blue (8.65)	£150	4·25
		a. Blue	£150	4·25
		b. Ultramarine	£325	55·00
		c. Deep blue (1872)	£200	4·50
		w. Wmk inverted	£500	£190
25		6d. pale lilac (before 21.3.64)	£160	26·00
		a. Deep lilac	£300	8·00
		b. Violet (to bright) (1877)	£180	1·50
		w. Wmk inverted	†	£375
26		1s. deep green (1.64)	£650	21·00
		a. Green	£170	4·50
		ax. Wmk reversed		
		b. Blue-green	£180	6·00
		w. Wmk inverted	£800	£200

The 1d. rose-red, 6d. lilac, and 1s. blue-green are known imperf, probably from proof sheets.

The 1d. and 4d. stamps of this issue may be found with side and/or top outer frame-lines missing, due to wear of the plates.

See also Nos. 44 and 52/3.

(Surch by Saul Solomon & Co, Cape Town)

1868 (17 Nov). No. 25a surch with T **5**.

27	**4**	4d. on 6d. deep lilac (R.)	£400	17·00
		a. "Peuce" for "Pence"	£2250	£700
		b. "Fonr" for "Four"	—	£700
		w. Wmk inverted	—	£400

Examples may also be found with bars omitted or at the top of the stamp, due to misplacement of the sheet.

The space between the words and bars varies from 12½ to 16 mm, stamps with spacing 15½ and 16 mm being rare. There were two printings, one of 120,000 in November 1868 and another of 1,000,000 in December. Stamps showing widest spacings are probably from the earlier printing.

6 (No outer frame-line)

(Die re-engraved. Typo D.L.R.)

1871–76. Outer frame-line removed. Wmk Crown CC. P 14.

28	**6**	½d. grey-black (*shades*) (12.75)	28·00	11·00
		w. Wmk inverted	—	£150
29		1d. carmine-red (*shades*) (2.72)	45·00	1·00
		w. Wmk inverted	£375	£160
30		4d. dull blue (*shades*) (12.76)	£140	75
		b. Ultramarine	£275	50·00
		w. Wmk inverted	£425	£120
31		5s. yellow-orange (25.8.71)	£425	20·00
		w. Wmk inverted	†	£400

The ½d., 1d. and 5s. are known imperf, probably from proof sheets.

See also Nos. 36, 39, 40/3, 48/51, 54, 61/2 and 64/8.

ONE PENNY (**7**)

THREE PENCE (**8**)

(Surch by Saul Solomon & Co, Cape Town)

1874–76. Nos. 25a and 26a surch with T **7**.

32	**4**	1d. on 6d. deep lilac (R.) (1.9.74)	£600	£120
		a. "E" of "PENNY" omitted	†	£1500
33		1d. on 1s. green (11.76)	£110	65·00

These provisionals are found with the bar only, either across the centre of the stamp or at top, with value only; or with value and bar close together, either at top or foot. Such varieties are due to misplacement of sheets during surcharging.

1879 (1 Nov). No. 30 surch with T **8**.

34	**6**	3d. on 4d. blue (R.)	£140	2·00
		a. "PENCB" for "PENCE"	£2500	£225
		b. "THE.EE" for "THREE"	£3000	£275
		c. Surch double	£11000	£3750
		d. Variety b. double		

The double surcharge must also have existed showing variety a. but only variety b. is known.

There are numerous minor varieties, including letters broken or out of alignment, due to defective printing and use of poor type.

The spacing between the bar and the words varies from 16½ to 18 mm.

THREEPENCE (**9**) **3** (**10**) **3** (**11**)

(Surch by D.L.R.)

1880 (Feb). Special printing of the 4d. in new colour, surch, with T **9**. Wmk Crown CC.

35	**6**	3d. on 4d. pale dull rose	90·00	2·75
		w. Wmk inverted	—	£300

A minor constant variety exists with foot of "P" in "PENCE" broken off, making the letter appear shorter.

1880 (1 July). Wmk Crown CC. P 14.

36	**6**	3d. pale dull rose	£275	32·00
		w. Wmk inverted	—	£400

(Surch by Saul Solomon & Co, Cape Town)

1880 (Aug). No. 36 surch.

37	**10**	"3" on 3d. pale dull rose	£110	1·75
		a. Surch inverted	£1300	40·00
		b. Vert pair. Nos. 37/8	£1400	£500
		w. Wmk inverted	—	£200
38	**11**	"3" on 3d. pale dull rose	£300	9·50
		a. Surch inverted	£11000	£950
		w. Wmk inverted	—	£550

The "3" (T **10**) is sometimes found broken. Vert pairs are known showing the two types of surcharge *se-tenant*, and vertical strips of three exist, the top stamp having surcharge T **10**, the middle stamp being without surcharge, and the lower stamp having surcharge T **11** (*Price for strip of 3 £4500 un.*).

1881 (Jan). Wmk Crown CC. P 14.

39	**6**	3d. pale claret	£180	4·00
		a. Deep claret	£150	3·75
		w. Wmk inverted		

This was a definite colour change made at the request of the Postmaster-General owing to the similarity between the colours of the 1d. stamp and the 3d. in pale dull rose. Imperf copies are probably from proof sheets.

Proofs of this value were printed in brown, on unwatermarked wove paper and imperf, but the colour was rejected as unsuitable.

1882 (July)–**83**. Wmk Crown CA. P 14.

40	**6**	½d. black (1.9.82)	35·00	3·00
		a. Grey-black	32·00	3·00
		w. Wmk inverted	—	£180
41		1d. rose-red	75·00	2·50
		a. Deep rose-red	75·00	2·50
		w. Wmk inverted	—	£225
42		2d. pale bistre (1.9.82)	£120	1·25
		a. Deep bistre	£130	1·25
		w. Wmk inverted	—	£225
43		3d. pale claret	9·50	1·50
		a. Deep claret	16·00	75
		aw. Wmk inverted		£140
44	**4**	6d. mauve (*to bright*) (8.82)	£120	80
45	**6**	5s. orange (8.83)	£850	£250

Imperf pairs of the ½d., 1d. and 2d. are known, probably from proof sheets.

One Half-penny.

(**12**)

(Surch by Saul Solomon & Co, Cape Town)

1882 (July). Nos. 39a and 43a surch with T **12**.

46	**6**	½d. on 3d. deep claret (Wmk CC)	£4250	£150
		a. Hyphen omitted	—	£3750
47		½d. on 3d. deep claret (Wmk CA)	45·00	5·00
		a. "p" in "penny" omitted	£2500	£800
		b. "y" in "penny" omitted	£1500	£700
		c. Hyphen omitted	£800	£350
		w. Wmk inverted	—	£400

Varieties also exist with broken and defective letters, and with the obliterating bar omitted or at the top of the stamp.

13 "Cabled Anchor"

1884–90. W **13**. P 14.

48	**6**	½d. black (1.86)	8·00	10
		a. Grey-black	8·00	10
		w. Wmk inverted	—	£475
49		1d. rose-red (12.85)	10·00	10
		a. Carmine-red	10·00	10
		w. Wmk inverted	—	£225
50		2d. pale bistre (12.84)	32·00	1·50
		a. Deep bistre	11·00	10
		w. Wmk inverted	—	£180
51		4d. blue (6.90)	19·00	50
		a. Deep blue	19·00	50
52	**4**	6d. reddish purple (12.84)	60·00	1·60
		a. Purple (shades)	16·00	20
		b. Bright mauve	13·00	50
		w. Wmk inverted	—	£375
53		1s. green (12.85)	£180	6·00
		a. Blue-green (1889)	£140	50
		w. Wmk inverted	—	£475
54	**6**	5s. orange (7.87)	£130	8·00
48/54 *Set of 7*			£300	8·50

All the above stamps are known in imperf pairs, probably from proof sheets.

For later shade and colour changes, etc., see Nos. 61, etc.

2½d

(**14**)

15

(Surch by D.L.R.)

1891 (Mar). Special printing of the 3d. in new colour, surch with T **14**.

55	**6**	2½d. on 3d. pale magenta	13·00	2·00
		a. Deep magenta	6·00	20
		b. "1" with horiz serif	75·00	32·00

No. 55b occurs on two stamps (Nos. 8 and 49) of the pane of 60.

Two types of "d" are found in the surcharge, one with square end to serif at top, and the other with pointed serif.

1892 (June). W **13**. P 14.

56	**15**	2½d. sage-green	18·00	10
		a. Olive-green	18·00	55

See also No. 63.

ONE PENNY.

(**16**)

(Surch by W. A. Richards & Sons, Cape Town)

1893 (Mar). Nos. 50/a surch with T **16**.

57	**6**	1d. on 2d. pale bistre	10·00	2·50
		a. Deep bistre	4·75	50
		b. No stop after "PENNY"	85·00	19·00
		c. Surch double	—	£475

No. 57b occurs on stamp No. 42 of the upper left-hand pane, and on No. 6 of the lower right-hand pane.

Minor varieties exist showing broken letters and letters out of alignment or widely spaced. Also with obliterating bar omitted, due to misplacement of the sheet during surcharging.

17 "Hope" standing. Table Bay in background

18 Table Mountain and Bay with Arms of the Colony

(Des Mr. Mountford. Typo D.L.R.)

1893 (Oct)–**1902**. W **13**. P 14.

58	**17**	½d. green (9.98)	6·50	20
59		1d. rose-red	9·00	2·25
		a. Carmine	2·50	10
		aw. Wmk inverted	†	£160
60		3d. magenta (3.02)	5·50	2·50

The 1d. is known in imperf pairs, probably from proof sheets.

1893–98. New colours, etc. W **13**. P 14.

61	**6**	½d. yellow-green (12.96)	1·50	50
		a. Green	2·75	50
62		2d. chocolate-brown (3.97)	2·50	2·25
63	**15**	2½d. pale ultramarine (3.96)	9·00	15
		a. Ultramarine	9·00	10
64	**6**	3d. bright magenta (9.98)	15·00	1·00
65		4d. sage-green (3.97)	8·00	3·50
66		1s. blue-green (12.93)	85·00	7·00
		a. Deep blue-green	£100	13·00
67		1s. yellow-ochre (5.96)	15·00	2·75
		w. Wmk inverted	†	—
68		5s. brown-orange (6.96)	£100	3·75
61/8 *Set of 8*			£200	19·00

(Des E. Sturman. Typo D.L.R.)

1900 (Jan). W **13**. P 14.

69	**18**	1d. carmine	6·00	10
		w. Wmk inverted	—	£160

19

20

21

22

23

24

25

26

27

(Typo D.L.R.)

1902 (Dec)–**04**. W **13**. P 14.

70	**19**	½d. green	2·50	10
71	**20**	1d. carmine	2·50	10
		w. Wmk inverted		
		y. Wmk inverted and reversed		
72	**21**	2d. brown (10.04)	18·00	80
		w. Wmk inverted		
73	**22**	2½d. ultramarine (3.04)	4·00	9·00
74	**23**	3d. magenta (4.03)	13·00	1·25
75	**24**	4d. olive-green (2.03)	16·00	65
76	**25**	6d. bright mauve (3.03)	24·00	30
77	**26**	1s. yellow-ochre	17·00	1·25
78	**27**	5s. brown-orange (2.03)	£130	24·00
70/8 *Set of 9*			£200	35·00

All values exist in imperf pairs, from proof sheets.

The ½d. exists from coils constructed from normal sheets for use in stamp machines introduced in 1911.

STAMP BOOKLET

1905 (Dec). Black on red cover. Stapled.

SB1	2s.7d. booklet containing thirty 1d. (No. 71) in blocks of 6	£2000

OFFICIAL STAMPS

The following stamps, punctured with a double triangle device, were used by the Stationery and Printed Forms Branch of the Cape of Good Hope Colonial Secretary's Department between 1904 and 1906. Later South Africa issues may have been similarly treated, but this has not been confirmed.

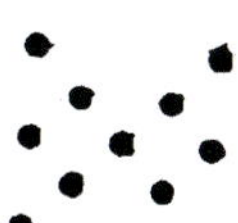
(O **1**)

1904. Various issues punctured as Type O **1**.

		(a) Nos. 50 and 52a	
O1	**6**	2d. pale bistre	27·00
O2	**4**	6d. purple	32·00
		(b) Nos. 58 and 60	
O3	**17**	½d. green	35·00
O4		3d. magenta	28·00
		(c) Nos. 62 and 64/5	
O5	**6**	2d. chocolate-brown	27·00
O6		3d. bright magenta	35·00
O7		4d. sage-green	35·00
		(d) No. 69	
O8	**18**	1d. carmine	25·00
		(e) Nos. 70/2 and 74/8	
O9	**19**	½d. green	35·00
O10	**20**	1d. carmine	20·00
O11	**21**	2d. brown	32·00
O12	**23**	3d. magenta	27·00
O13	**24**	4d. olive-green	28·00
O14	**25**	6d. bright mauve	30·00
O15	**26**	1s. yellow-ochre	38·00
O16	**27**	5s. brown-orange	85·00

Nos. O1/16 are only known used.

Cape of Good Hope became a province of the Union of South Africa on 31 May 1910.

BRITISH KAFFRARIA

The history of the Cape eastern frontier was punctuated by a series of armed conflicts with the native population, known as the Kaffir Wars. After a particularly violent outbreak in 1846 the Governor, Sir Harry Smith, advanced the line of the Cape frontier to the Keikama and Tyumie Rivers. In the area between the new frontier and the Kei River a buffer state, British Kaffraria, was established on 17 December 1847. This area was not annexed to the Cape, but was administered as a separate Crown dependency by the Governor of Cape Colony in his capacity as High Commissioner for South Africa.

The territory, with its administration based on King William's Town, used the stamps of the Cape of Good Hope from 1853 onwards, the mail being sent via Port Elizabeth or overland from the Cape. Covers from British Kaffraria franked with the triangular issues are rare.

The first postal marking known from British Kaffraria is the 1849 type octagonal numeral No 47 from Port Beaufort. Oval post-marks of the 1853 type were used at Alice, Aliwal North, Bedford, Fort Beaufort, King William's Town and Queenstown. In 1864 numeral cancellations were issued to all post offices within the Cape system and it is known that the following numbers were initially assigned to post towns in Kaffraria: 4 (King William's Town), 7 (Bedford), 11 (Queenstown), 29 (East London), 32 (Fort Beaufort), 38 (Aliwal North) and 104 (Cathcart).

It is believed that post offices may have also existed at Adelaide, Barkly East, Sterkstoom and Stutterheim, but, to date, no examples of handstamps or cancellations are known from them during the British Kaffraria period.

Following the decimation by famine of the Xhosa tribes in 1857 British Kaffraria was annexed to Cape Colony in 1865. The area eventually formed the basis of the Ciskei independent "homeland".

MAFEKING SIEGE STAMPS

PRICES FOR STAMPS ON COVER		
Nos.	1/16	*from* × 12
Nos.	17/18	*from* × 25
Nos.	19/20	*from* × 15
Nos.	21/2	*from* × 12

23 MARCH to 17 MAY 1900

There are numerous forgeries of the Mafeking overprints, many of which were brought home by soldiers returning from the Boer War.

MAFEKING,
3d.
BESIEGED.
(**1**)

MAFEKING
3d.
BESIEGED.
(**2**)

(Surcharged by Townsend & Co, Mafeking)

1900 (23 Mar–28 Apr). Various stamps surch as T **1** and **2**.

		*(a) Cape of Good Hope stamps surch as T **1** (23 Mar)*		
1	**6**	1d. on ½d. green	£275	80·00
2	**17**	1d. on ½d. green (24.3)	£325	£100
3		3d. on 1d. carmine	£275	65·00
4	**6**	6d. on 3d. magenta (24.3)	£40000	£300
5		1s. on 4d. sage-green (24.3)	£7500	£400

A variety in the setting of each value exists without comma after "MAFEKING".

		*(b) Nos. 59 and 61/3 of Bechuanaland Protectorate (previously optd on Great Britain) surch as T **1***		
6		1d. on ½d. vermilion (28.3)	£275	75·00
		a. Surch inverted	†	£7000
		b. Vert pair, surch *tête-bêche*	†	£35000
7		3d. on 1d. lilac (4.4)	£950	£120
		a. Surch double	†	£30000
8		6d. on 2d. green and carmine (6.4)	£2500	£100
9		6d. on 3d. purple/*yellow* (30.3)	£6500	£375
		a. Surch inverted	†	£38000
		b. Surch double		
		*(c) Nos. 12 and 35 of British Bechuanaland (4d. previously optd on Great Britain) surch as T **1***		
10		6d. on 3d. lilac and black (27.3)	£475	85·00
11		1s. on 4d. green and purple-brown (29.3)	£1600	95·00
		a. Surch double (both Type **1**)	†	£27000
		ab. Surch double (Type **1** and Type **2**)	£12000	£7000
		b. Surch treble	†	£27000
		c. Surch double, one inverted	†	£27000

(d) Nos. 61/2 and 65 of Bechuanaland Protectorate (previously optd on Great Britain) surch as T **2**

No.	Type	Description	Unused	Used
12		3d. on 1d. lilac (1 Apr)	£1000	95·00
		a. Surch double	†	£10000
13		6d. on 2d. green and carmine (1 Apr)	£1300	95·00
14		1s. on 6d. purple/*rose-red* (12 Apr)	£6500	£120

(e) Nos. 36/7 of British Bechuanaland (previously optd on Great Britain) surch as T **2**

No.	Type	Description	Unused	Used
15		1s. on 6d. purple/*rose-red* (28 Apr)	£30000	£800
16		2s. on 1s. green (13 Apr)	£13000	£550

On the stamps overprinted "BECHUANALAND PROTECTORATE" and "BRITISH BECHUANALAND" the local surcharge is so adjusted as not to overlap the original overprint.

Two used examples of British Bechuanaland No. 37 are known surcharged 2s. as T **1** but their status is uncertain. (*Price* £38000).

3 Cadet Sergt.-major Goodyear

4 General Baden-Powell

(Des Dr. W. A. Hayes (T **3**), Capt. H. Greener (T **4**))

1900 (6–11 Apr). Produced photographically by Dr. D. Taylor. Horiz laid paper with sheet wmk "OCEANA FINE". P 12.

(a) 18½ mm wide. (b) 21 mm wide

No.	Type	Description	Unused	Used
17	**3**	1d. pale blue/*blue* (7.4)	£1000	£300
18		1d. deep blue/*blue*	£1000	£300
19	**4**	3d. pale blue/*blue* (*a*)	£1400	£425
		a. Reversed design	£80000	£42000
20		3d. deep blue/*blue* (*a*)	£1400	£375
		a. Imperf between (horiz pair)	†	£85000
		b. Double print	†	£20000
21		3d. pale blue/*blue* (*b*) (10.4)	£10000	£950
		a. Vert laid paper	£15000	
22		3d. deep blue/*blue* (*b*) (10.4)	£12000	£1200

These stamps vary a great deal in colour from deep blue to pale grey.

No. 18 imperforate and without gum is believed to be a proof (*Price for unused pair* £22000).

No. 19a comes from a sheet of 12 printed in reverse of which ten, three mint and seven used, are known to have survived.

VRYBURG

PRICES FOR STAMPS ON COVER	
Nos. 1/4	*from* × 5
Nos. 11/12	*from* × 2

BOER OCCUPATION

Vryburg was occupied by Boer forces on 15 October 1899. Unoverprinted stamps of Transvaal were used initially. Nos. 1/4 were only available from 24 to 29 November. The Boers evacuated the town on 7 May 1900.

½ PENCE

Z.A.R.

(1)

1899 (24 Nov). Cape stamps surch as T **1** at the offices of De Stellalander. Surch 12 mm high on No. 3 and 10 mm on all other values.

No.	Type	Description	Unused	Used
1	**6**	½ PENCE green	£200	80·00
		a. Italic "Z"	£2000	£700
		b. Surch 12 mm high	£2000	£700
2	**17**	1 PENCE rose	£225	£100
		a. Italic "Z"	£2250	£800
		b. Surch 12 mm high	£2250	£800
		c. "I" for "1"	£1400	£500
3	**4**	2 PENCE on 6d. mauve	£2000	£500
		a. Italic "Z"	£13000	£4250
4	**15**	2½ PENCE on 2½d. blue	£1700	£425
		a. Italic "Z"	£13000	£4250
		b. Surch 12 mm high	£13000	£4250

The "2 PENCE" on 6d. shows the surcharge 12 mm high. It is possible that this was the first value surcharged as the remaining three show the height reduced to 10 mm with the exception of one position in the second vertical row of the setting. The italic "Z" occurs on one position in the sixth vertical row. It is believed that the setting was of 60 (6×10).

BRITISH REOCCUPATION

V. R. SPECIAL POST

(2)

1900 (16 May). Provisionals issued by the Military Authorities. Stamps of Transvaal handstamped with T **2**.

No.	Type	Description	Unused	Used
11	**30**	½d. green	—	£2500
11*a*		1d. rose-red (No. 206)		
12		1d. rose-red and green (No. 217)	£10000	£4500
13		2d. brown and green	†	£40000
14		2½d. dull blue and green	†	£40000

No. 11 is known used with double handstamp and Nos. 11/12 with the overprint reading downwards.

II. GRIQUALAND WEST

Griqualand West was situated to the North of Cape Colony, bounded on the north by what became British Bechuanaland and on the east by the Orange Free State.

The area was settled in the early nineteenth century by the Griqua tribal group, although many members of the tribe, including the paramount chief, migrated to Griqualand East (between Basutoland and the east coast of South Africa) in 1861–63. There was little European involvement in Griqualand West before 1866, but in that year the diamond fields along the Vaal River were discovered. Sovereignty was subsequently claimed by the Griqua Chief, the Orange Free State and the South African Republic (Transvaal). In 1871 the British authorities arbitrated in favour of the Griqua Chief who promptly ceded his territory to Great Britain. Griqualand West became a separate Crown Colony in January 1873.

During the initial stages of the prospecting boom, mail was passed via the Orange Free State, but a post office connected to the Cape Colony postal system was opened at Klip Drift (subsequently Barkly) in late 1870. Further offices at De Beer's New Rush (subsequently Kimberley), Douglas and Du Toit's Pan (subsequently Beaconsfield) were open by September 1873.

Cape of Good Hope stamps to the 5s. value were in use from October 1871, but those originating in Griqualand West can only be identified after the introduction of Barred Oval Diamond Numeral cancellations in 1873. Numbers known to have been issued in the territory are:

1 De Beers N.R. (New Rush) (subsequently Kimberley)
3 Junction R. & M. (Riet and Modder Rivers)
4 Barkly
6 or 9 Du Toit's Pan (subsequently Beaconsfield)
8 Langford (transferred to Douglas)
10 Thornhill

PRICES FOR STAMPS ON COVER. The stamps of Griqualand West are worth from ×10 the price quoted for used stamps, when on cover from the territory.

FORGED OVERPRINTS. Many stamps show forged overprints. Great care should be taken when purchasing the scarcer items.

***Stamps of the Cape of Good Hope,* Crown CC, perf 14, overprinted.**

1874 (Sept). No. 24*a* of Cape of Good Hope surch "1d." in red manuscript by the Kimberley postmaster.

No.	Description	Unused	Used
1	1d. on 4d. blue	£1700	£2500

G. W.

(1)

1877 (Mar). Nos. 29/30 of Cape of Good Hope optd with T **1**.

No.	Description	Unused	Used
2	1d. carmine-red	£650	95·00
	a. Opt double	†	£2750
3	4d. dull blue (R.)	£400	80·00
	w. Wmk inverted	£1300	£275

G (1a) **G** (2) **G** (3) **G** (4) **G** (5) **G** (6)

G (7) **G** (8) **G** (9) **G** (10) **G** (11)

G (12) ***G*** (13) ***G*** (14)

1877 (Mar)–**78**. Nos. 24*a*, 25*a*, 26*a* and 28/31 Cape of Good Hope optd with capital "G".

(a) First printing. Optd with T **1a/6** *and* **8** *in black (1d.) or red (others)*

4 ½d. grey-black
a. Opt Type **1a** 35·00 38·00
b. Opt Type **2** 80·00 95·00
c. Opt Type **3** 48·00 55·00
d. Opt Type **4** 80·00 95·00
e. Opt Type **5** 90·00 £110
f. Opt Type **6** 42·00 50·00
g. Opt Type **8** £700 £750

5 1d. carmine-red
a. Opt Type **1a** 35·00 24·00
b. Opt Type **2** 85·00 55·00
c. Opt Type **3** 48·00 35·00
d. Opt Type **4** 85·00 55·00
e. Opt Type **5** 95·00 70·00
f. Opt Type **6** 35·00 24·00
g. Opt Type **8** *

6 4d. blue (with frame-line) (No. 24*a*)
a. Opt Type **1a** £375 55·00
b. Opt Type **2** £900 £150
c. Opt Type **3** £600 80·00
d. Opt Type **4** £900 £150
e. Opt Type **5** £1000 £180
f. Opt Type **6** £450 75·00
g. Opt Type **8** £3000 £850

7 4d. dull blue (without frame-line) (No. 30)
a. Opt Type **1a** £300 38·00
b. Opt Type **2** £650 £100
c. Opt Type **3** £425 50·00
d. Opt Type **4** £650 £100
e. Opt Type **5** £700 £130
f. Opt Type **6** £400 45·00
g. Opt Type **8** £2500 £600

8 6d. deep lilac
a. Opt Type **1a** £200 42·00
b. Opt Type **2** £450 £110
c. Opt Type **3** £300 55·00
cw. Wmk inverted † £400
d. Opt Type **4** £450 £110
e. Opt Type **5** £550 £140
f. Opt Type **6** £275 55·00
g. Opt Type **8** £2250 £750

9 1s. green
a. Opt Type **1a** £250 35·00
ab. Opt inverted — £700
b. Opt Type **2** £550 85·00
ba. Opt inverted — £1100
c. Opt Type **3** £400 45·00
d. Opt Type **4** £550 85·00
da. Opt inverted — £1100
e. Opt Type **5** £650 £100
f. Opt Type **6** £375 42·00
fa. Opt inverted — £800
g. Opt Type **8** £3750 £750

10 5s. yellow-orange
a. Opt Type **1a** £850 42·00
b. Opt Type **2** £1400 95·00
c. Opt Type **3** £1100 55·00
cw. Wmk inverted † £900
d. Opt Type **4** £1400 95·00
dw. Wmk inverted † £1300
e. Opt Type **5** £2000 £120
f. Opt Type **6** £1000 48·00
fw. Wmk inverted † £1000
g. Opt Type **8** £3750 £900

*The 1d. with overprint Type **8** from this setting can only be distinguished from that of the second printing when *se-tenant* with overprint Type **3**.

Nos. 4/10 were overprinted by a setting of 120 covering two panes of 60 (6×10). This setting contained 41 examples of Type **1a**, 10 of Type **2**, 23 of Type **3**, 10 of Type **4**, 8 of Type **5**, 27 of Type **6** and 1 of Type **8**. Sub-types of Types **1a** and **2** exist. The single example of Type **8** occurs on R.7/4 of the right-hand pane.

It is believed that there may have been an additional setting used for the 5s. which was in considerable demand to cover the postage and registration on diamond consignments. It is also possible that single panes of this value and of the 1s. were overprinted using the right-hand half of the normal 120 setting.

(b) Second printing. Optd with T **6/14** *in black (1878)*

11 1d. carmine-red
a. Opt Type **6** *
b. Opt Type **7** 38·00 24·00
c. Opt Type **8** 85·00 42·00
d. Opt Type **9** 42·00 25·00
e. Opt Type **10** £100 80·00
f. Opt Type **11** 90·00 55·00
g. Opt Type **12** 90·00 70·00
h. Opt Type **13** £150 £110
i. Opt Type **14** £500 £350

12 4d. dull blue (without frame-line) (No. 30)
a. Opt Type **6** £450 80·00
b. Opt Type **7** £190 35·00
c. Opt Type **8** £425 70·00
d. Opt Type **9** £200 35·00
e. Opt Type **10** £500 95·00
f. Opt Type **11** £450 85·00
g. Opt Type **12** £450 85·00
h. Opt Type **13** £750 £150
i. Opt Type **14** £2250 £500

13 6d. deep lilac
a. Opt Type **6** £650 £120
b. Opt Type **7** £350 65·00
ba. Opt double
c. Opt Type **8** £600 £100
d. Opt Type **9** £400 75·00
da. Opt double — £1100
e. Opt Type **10** £750 £160
ea. Opt double — £1400
f. Opt Type **11** £650 £120
g. Opt Type **12** £650 £140
h. Opt Type **13** £950 £225
i. Opt Type **14** £2750 £700

*The 1d. with overprint Type **6** from this setting can only be distinguished from that of the first printing when *se-tenant* with Types **11**, **12** or **13**.

Nos. 11/13 were overprinted by another double-pane setting of 120 in which only Types **6** and **8** were repeated from that used for the first printing. The second printing setting contained 12 examples of Type **6**, 30 of Type **7**, 13 of Type **8**, 27 of Type **9**, 9 of Type **10**, 11 of Type **11**, 11 of Type **12**, 6 of Type **13** and 1 of Type **14**. Sub-types of Types **7** and **12** exist.

G G G
(15) **(16)** **(17)**

1878 (June). Nos. 24*a*, 25*a* and 28/30 of Cape of Good Hope optd with small capital "G", T **15/16**.

14 **15** ½d. grey-black (R.) 21·00 21·00
a. Opt inverted 23·00 23·00
b. Opt double 65·00 80·00
c. Opt double, both inverted £130 £150
d. Black opt £275 £150
da. Opt inverted £300
db. Opt double, one inverted in red £475
dc. Opt double, one inverted (Type **16**) in red £250

15 **16** ½d. grey-black (R.) 22·00 22·00
a. Opt inverted 22·00 23·00
b. Opt double £100 £100
c. Opt double, both inverted 85·00 95·00
d. Black opt 65·00 65·00
da. Opt inverted £140 95·00
db. Opt double, one inverted (Type **15**) in red £250

16 **15** 1d. carmine-red 22·00 16·00
a. Opt inverted 22·00 22·00
b. Opt double £275 70·00
c. Opt double, both inverted £275 90·00
d. Opt double, both inverted with one in red 50·00 55·00
e. Opt double, both inverted with one (Type **16**) in red

17 **16** 1d. carmine-red 22·00 17·00
a. Opt inverted £110 40·00
b. Opt double — £120
c. Opt double, both inverted — £150
d. Opt double, both inverted with one in red £110 £110

18 **15** 4d. blue (with frame-line) (No. 24*a*) — £200
19 **16** 4d. blue (with frame-line) (No. 24*a*) — £200
20 **15** 4d. dull blue (without frame-line) (No. 30) £180 40·00
a. Opt inverted £325 £110
b. Opt double — £300
c. Opt double, both inverted — £375
d. Red opt £450 £130
da. Opt inverted £500 £100

21 **16** 4d. dull blue (without frame-line) (No. 30) £200 20·00
a. Opt inverted £350 40·00
b. Opt double — £275
c. Opt double, both inverted — £350
d. Red opt — £110
da. Opt inverted £475 £110

22 **15** 6d. deep lilac £190 38·00
23 **16** 6d. deep lilac — 38·00

Nos. 14/23 were also overprinted using a double-pane setting of 120. Based on evidence from surviving ½d. and 1d. sheets all overprints in the left-hand pane were roman, Type **15**, and all those in the right-hand pane italic, Type **16**, except for R.1/6, 4/5, 6/6, 7/6, 8/6, 9/6 and 10/6 which were Type **15**. There is considerable evidence to suggest that after the ½d. value had been overprinted the setting was amended to show a Type **15**, instead of a Type **16**, on R.10/5 of the right-hand pane. Two strikes of the setting were required to overprint the sheets of 240 and it would appear that on many sheets the bottom two panes had the overprints inverted.

1879. Nos. 25*b*, 26*b* and 28/31 of Cape of Good Hope optd with small capital "G", T **17**.

24		½d. grey-black	25·00	9·00
		a. Opt double	£475	£300
25		1d. carmine-red	26·00	7·00
		a. Opt inverted	—	95·00
		b. Opt double	—	£150
		c. Opt treble	—	£275
		w. Wmk inverted	†	£350
26		4d. dull blue	50·00	7·00
		a. Opt double	—	£130
27		6d. violet	£190	11·00
		a. Opt inverted	—	45·00
		b. Opt double	£850	£190
28		1s. green	£180	7·50
		a. Opt double	£450	£100
29		5s. yellow-orange	£600	20·00
		a. Opt double	£800	£100
		b. Opt treble	—	£350

Nos. 24/9 were also overprinted using a setting of 120 which contained a number of minor type varieties.

Griqualand West was merged with Cape Colony in October 1880. The remaining stock of the overprinted stamps was returned from Kimberley to Cape Town and redistributed among various post offices in Cape Colony where they were used as ordinary Cape stamps.

III. NATAL

PRICES FOR STAMPS ON COVER

Nos.	1/7	*from* × 2
Nos.	9/25	*from* × 3
Nos.	26/56	*from* × 4
Nos.	57/8	—
Nos.	59/73	*from* × 5
Nos.	76/84	*from* × 4
Nos.	85/93	*from* × 3
Nos.	96/103	*from* × 6
Nos.	104/5	*from* × 5
Nos.	106/25	*from* × 6
Nos.	127/42	*from* × 4
Nos.	143/5*a*	—
Nos.	146/57	*from* × 4
No.	162	—
Nos.	165/71	*from* × 3
No.	F1	—
Nos.	O1/6	*from* × 10

1

2

3

4

5

(Embossed in plain relief on coloured wove paper)

1857 (26 May)–**61**. Imperf.

1	**1**	1d. blue (9.59)	—	£1200
2		1d. rose (1859)	—	£1800
3		1d. buff (1861)	—	£1100
4	**2**	3d. rose	—	£400
		a. *Tête-bêche* (pair)	—	£35000
5	**3**	6d. green	—	£1100
6	**4**	9d. blue	—	£7000
7	**5**	1s. buff	—	£5500

All the above have been reprinted more than once, and the early reprints of some values cannot always be distinguished with certainty from originals.

Stamps on surface-coloured paper with higher face values and perforated 12½ are fiscals.

NOTE. The value of the above stamps depends on their dimensions, and the clearness of the embossing, but our prices are for fine used.

PERKINS BACON "CANCELLED". For notes on these handstamps showing "CANCELLED" between horizontal bars forming an oval, see Catalogue Introduction.

6

7

(Eng C. H. Jeens. Recess P.B.)

1859–60. No wmk. P 14.

9	**6**	1d. rose-red (1860) (H/S "CANCELLED" in oval £13000)	£150	75·00
10		3d. blue	£190	50·00
		a. Imperf between (vert pair)	†	£10000

No. 10a is only known from a cover of 1867 franked with two such pairs.

The 3d. also exists with "CANCELLED" in oval, but no examples are believed to be in private hands.

1861. No wmk. Intermediate perf 14 to 16.

11	**6**	3d. blue	£275	65·00

1861–62. No wmk. Rough perf 14 to 16.

12	**6**	3d. blue	£140	38·00
		a. Imperf between (horiz pair)	£5000	
13		6d. grey (1862)	£225	65·00

1862. Wmk Small Star. Rough perf 14 to 16.

15	**6**	1d. rose-red	£160	65·00

The 1d. without watermark and the 3d. watermark Small Star, both imperforate, are proofs.

(Recess D.L.R.)

1863. Thick paper. No wmk. P 13.

18	**6**	1d. lake	£100	27·00
19		1d. carmine-red	£100	27·00

1863–65. Wmk Crown CC. P 12½.

20	**6**	1d. brown-red	£160	42·00
		y. Wmk inverted and reversed	—	£120
21		1d. rose	£100	35·00
		x. Wmk reversed	£100	35·00
22		1d. bright red	£110	40·00
		x. Wmk reversed	£110	40·00
23		6d. lilac	85·00	17·00
24		6d. violet	70·00	32·00
		x. Wmk reversed	70·00	32·00

The 1d. stamp in yellow and the 6d. in rose are both fiscals.

(Typo D.L.R.)

1867 (Apr). Wmk Crown CC. P 14.

25	**7**	1s. green	£225	42·00
		w. Wmk inverted	—	£325

Stamps as T **7** in purple-brown or deep blue are fiscals.

POSTAGE **(7a)**   **Postage.** **(7b)**   **Postage.** **(7c)**

Postage. **(7d)**   **POSTAGE.** **(7e)**

1869 (23 Aug). Optd horiz in Natal. No wmk (3d.), wmk Crown CC (others). P 14 or 14–16 (3d.), 12½ (1d., 6d) or 14 (1s.).

*(a) With T **7a** (tall capitals without stop)*

26	**6**	1d. rose	£500	95·00
		x. Wmk reversed	£475	85·00
27		1d. bright red	£450	90·00
		x. Wmk reversed	—	80·00
28		3d. blue (No. 10)	£3000	£750
28*a*		3d. blue (No. 11)	£900	£300

No.	Type	Description	Unused	Used
28*b*		3d. blue (No. 12)	£650	£100
29		6d. lilac	£700	80·00
30		6d. violet	£650	90·00
		x. Wmk reversed	£650	£100
31	**7**	1s. green	£16000	£1500
		(b) With T **7b** *(12¾ mm long)*		
32	**6**	1d. rose	£450	85·00
33		1d. bright red	£425	80·00
		a. Opt double	†	£1600
		x. Wmk reversed	£400	75·00
34		3d. blue (No. 10)	—	£400
34*a*		3d. blue (No. 11)	£800	£250
34*b*		3d. blue (No. 12)	£550	90·00
35		6d. lilac	£600	75·00
36		6d. violet	£500	90·00
		x. Wmk reversed	£500	90·00
37	**7**	1s. green	£13000	£1200
		(c) With T **7c** *(13¾ mm long)*		
38	**6**	1d. rose	£900	£250
39		1d. bright red	£950	£225
		x. Wmk reversed	—	£200
40		3d. blue (No. 10)		
40*a*		3d. blue (No. 11)	—	£900
40*b*		3d. blue (No. 12)	£2000	£450
41		6d. lilac	£2250	£180
42		6d. violet	£2000	£180
		x. Wmk reversed	—	£190
43	**7**	1s. green	—	£2500
		(d) With T **7d** *(14½ to 15½ mm long)*		
44	**6**	1d. rose	£800	£190
45		1d. bright red	£800	£170
46		3d. blue (No. 10)		
46*a*		3d. blue (No. 11)	—	£600
46*b*		3d. blue (No. 12)	—	£350
47		6d. lilac	—	£120
48		6d. violet	£1700	£110
49	**7**	1s. green	£25000	£1800
		(e) With T **7e** *(small capitals with stop)*		
50	**6**	1d. rose	£120	50·00
		x. Wmk reversed	£120	50·00
51		1d. bright red	£170	50·00
		x. Wmk reversed	£170	50·00
52		3d. blue (No. 10)	£350	85·00
53		3d. blue (No. 11)	£180	50·00
54		3d. blue (No. 12)	£200	50·00
		a. Opt double	†	£1300
54*b*		6d. lilac	£200	70·00
55		6d. violet	£170	55·00
		x. Wmk reversed	£170	60·00
56	**7**	1s. green	£275	75·00

It is believed that there were two settings of these overprints. The first setting, probably of 240, contained 60 examples of Type **7a**, 72 of Type **7b**, 20 of Type **7c**, 28 of Type **7d** and 60 of Type **7e**. The second, probably of 60 (6×10), contained Type **7e** only.

(**8**)

1870. No. 25 optd with T **8** by De La Rue.

No.	Type	Description	Unused	Used
57	**7**	1s. green (C.)	†	£6500
58		1s. green (Blk.)	†	£1400
		a. Opt double	†	£3250
59		1s. green (G.)	£120	10·00

For 1s. orange, see No. 108.

(**9**) (**10**) (**11**)

1870–73. Optd with T **9** by De La Rue. Wmk Crown CC. P 12½.

No.	Type	Description	Unused	Used
60	**6**	1d. bright red	95·00	13·00
		x. Wmk reversed	95·00	13·00
61		3d. bright blue (R.) (1872)	£100	13·00
		x. Wmk reversed	£100	13·00
62		6d. mauve (1873)	£190	35·00
		x. Wmk reversed	£225	

1873 (July). Fiscal stamp optd locally with T **10**. Wmk Crown CC. P 14.

No.	Type	Description	Unused	Used
63	**7**	1s. purple-brown	£325	26·00
		w. Wmk inverted	—	£375

1874 (Apr). No. 21 optd locally with T **11**.

No.	Type	Description	Unused	Used
65	**6**	1d. rose	£325	80·00
		a. Opt double		
		x. Wmk reversed	—	80·00

12

13

14

15

16

(Typo D.L.R.)

1874 (Jan)–**99**. Wmk Crown CC (sideways on 5s.). P 14.

No.	Type	Description	Unused	Used
66	**12**	1d. dull rose	35·00	5·50
67		1d. bright rose	35·00	5·50
68	**13**	3d. blue	£150	30·00
		a. Perf 14×12½	£1800	£850
69	**14**	4d. brown (1878)	£160	15·00
		aw. Wmk inverted	£425	£140
		b. Perf 12½	£325	70·00
70	**15**	6d. bright reddish violet	80·00	7·50
		w. Wmk inverted	†	£190
71	**16**	5s. maroon (1882)	£275	65·00
		a. Perf 15½×15 (1874)	£450	£100
72		5s. rose	£120	40·00
73		5s. carmine (1899)	95·00	35·00
		s. Handstamped "*SPECIMEN*"	£200	

(**17**)

(**18**)

1875–76. Wmk Crown CC. P 14 (1s.) or 12½ (others).

No.	Type	Description	Unused	Used
		(a) Optd locally with T **17**		
76	**6**	1d. rose	£150	60·00
		a. Opt double	£1400	£500
		x. Wmk reversed	£150	60·00
77		1d. bright red	£140	70·00
		x. Wmk reversed	£140	70·00
		(b) Optd locally with T **18** *(14½ mm long, without stop)*		
81	**6**	1d. rose (1876)	£110	75·00
		a. Opt inverted	£1400	£500
		x. Wmk reversed	£110	75·00
82		1d. yellow (1876)	80·00	80·00
		a. Opt double, one albino	£225	
		x. Wmk reversed	85·00	85·00
83		6d. violet (1876)	75·00	8·00
		a. Opt double	—	£700
		b. Opt inverted	£700	£150
		w. Wmk inverted	—	£130
		x. Wmk reversed	75·00	8·00
84	**7**	1s. green (1876)	£110	7·50
		a. Opt double	—	£325

TYPE 19. There are several varieties of this surcharge, of which T **19** is an example. They may be divided as follows:

(*a*) "½" 4½ mm high, "2" has straight foot.
(*b*) As last but "½" is 4 mm high.
(*c*) As last but "2" has curled foot.
(*d*) "½" 3½ mm. high, "2" has straight foot.
(*e*) As last but "2" has curled foot.
(*f*) As last but "2" smaller.

As the "½" and "HALF" were overprinted separately, they vary in relative position, and are frequently overlapping.

(**19**)

1877 (13 Feb). No. 66 surch locally as T **19**.

No.	Type	Description	Unused	Used
85	**12**	½d. on 1d. rose (*a*)	38·00	75·00
		a. "½" double		
86		½d. on 1d. rose (*b*)	£150	
87		½d. on 1d. rose (*c*)	£130	
88		½d. on 1d. rose (*d*)	75·00	£110
89		½d. on 1d. rose (*e*)	80·00	
90		½d. on 1d. rose (*f*)	90·00	

POSTAGE

Half-penny

(21)

23

ONE HALF-
PENNY.

(24)

1877 (7 Oct)–**79**. T **6** (wmk Crown CC. P 12½) surch locally as T **21**.

91		½d. on 1d. yellow	9·50	20·00
		a. Surch inverted	£275	£190
		b. Surch double	£250	£180
		c. Surch omitted (lower stamp, vertical pair)	£3500	£1600
		d. "POSTAGE" omitted (in pair with normal)	£2000	
		e. "S" of "POSTAGE" omitted (R. 8/3)	£250	£190
		f. "T" of "POSTAGE" omitted	£250	£250
		x. Wmk reversed	9·50	20·00
92		1d. on 6d. violet (10.10.77)	65·00	11·00
		a. "S" of "POSTAGE" omitted (R. 8/3)	£500	£150
		x. Wmk reversed	—	11·00
93		1d. on 6d. rose (12.2.79)	£120	50·00
		a. Surch inverted	£700	£325
		b. Surch double	—	£250
		c. Surch double, one inverted	£300	£200
		d. Surch four times	£500	£225
		e. "S" of "POSTAGE" omitted (R. 8/3)	£800	£300
		x. Wmk reversed	—	50·00

No. 93c. is known with one surcharge showing variety "S" of "POSTAGE" omitted.

Other minor varieties exist in these surcharges.

(Typo D.L.R.)

1880 (13 Oct). Wmk Crown CC. P 14.

96	**23**	½d. blue-green	23·00	28·00
		a. Imperf between (vert pair)		

1882 (20 Apr)–**89**. Wmk Crown CA. P 14.

97	**23**	½d. blue-green (23.4.84)	£100	16·00
		a. Dull green (10.4.85)	4·50	1·25
		aw. Wmk inverted	£275	
99	**12**	1d. rose (*shades*) (1.84)	5·00	25
		a. Carmine	5·50	35
		w. Wmk inverted	†	£190
100	**13**	3d. blue (23.4.84)	£130	17·00
101		3d. grey (11.89)	7·00	4·25
102	**14**	4d. brown	11·00	1·75
103	**15**	6d. mauve	8·50	2·25
		w. Wmk inverted	†	£150
97*a*/103 *Set of 6*			£150	24·00
97*a*s, 99*a*s, 101s/3s H/S *"SPECIMEN" Set of 5*			£325	

1885 (26 Jan). No. 99 surch locally with T **24**.

104	**12**	½d. on 1d. rose	19·00	11·00
		a. No hyphen after "HALF"	90·00	48·00

TWO PENCE

(25)

26

TWOPENCE
HALFPENNY

(27)

1886 (7 Jan). No. 101 surch with T **25** by D.L.R.

105	**13**	2d. on 3d. grey	26·00	5·50

(Typo D.L.R.)

1887 (Sept)–**89**. Wmk Crown CA. P 14.

106	**26**	2d. olive-green (Die I)	50·00	2·25
		a. Top left triangle detached	—	£250
		s. Optd "SPECIMEN"	90·00	
107		2d. olive-green (Die II) (1889)	5·00	1·40
		s. Handstamped *"SPECIMEN"*	75·00	

The differences between Dies I and II are shown in the introduction.

For illustration of "top left triangle detached" variety see above No. 21 of Antigua.

1888 (16 Mar). As No. 25, but colour changed and wmk Crown CA, optd with T **8** by D.L.R.

108	**7**	1s. orange (C.)	7·50	1·75
		a. Opt double	—	£1600
		s. Handstamped *"SPECIMEN"*	£110	

1891 (22 Apr). Surch locally with T **27**.

109	**14**	2½d. on 4d. brown	15·00	15·00
		a. "TWOPENGE"	60·00	
		b. "HALFPENN"	£250	£200
		c. Surch double	£275	£200
		d. Surch inverted	£425	£350
		s. Handstamped *"SPECIMEN"*	65·00	

(28)

POSTAGE.

Half-Penny

(29)

POSTAGE.

Varieties of long-tailed letters

(Typo D.L.R.)

1891 (June). Wmk Crown CA. P 14.

113	**28**	2½d. bright blue	8·50	1·50
		s. Handstamped *"SPECIMEN"*	70·00	

1895 (12 Mar). No. 24 surch locally with T **29** in carmine.

114	½d. on 6d. violet	2·50	8·50
	a. "Ealf-Penny"	23·00	55·00
	b. "Half-Pennv" and long "P"	23·00	55·00
	ba. "Half Pennv" and long "T" and "A"	23·00	55·00
	c. No stop after "POSTAGE" and long "P", "T" and "A"	23·00	55·00
	d. Long "P"	2·75	9·00
	e. Long "T"	2·75	9·00
	f. Long "A"	3·50	12·00
	g. Long "P" and "T"	2·75	9·00
	h. Long "P" and "A"	2·75	9·00
	i. Long "T" and "A"	3·25	10·00
	k. Long "P", "T" and "A"	3·25	12·00
	ka. Long "P", "T" and "A" with comma after "POSTAGE"	13·00	26·00
	l. Surch double	£275	
	la. Surch double, one vertical	£275	
	m. "POSTAGE" omitted	£1000	
	s. Handstamped *"SPECIMEN"*	60·00	
	x. Wmk reversed	2·50	8·50

The surcharge was applied as a setting of 60 (12×5) which contained seventeen normals, one each of Nos. 114a, 114b, 114ba, 114c, six of No. 114d, six of 114e, three of 114f, six of 114g, seven of 114h, five of No. 114i, four of No. 114k and two of No. 114ka.

HALF

(30)

31

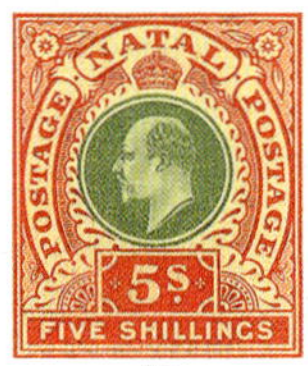

32

1895 (18 Mar). No. 99 surch locally with T **30**.

125	HALF on 1d. rose (*shades*)	3·00	2·25
	a. Surch double	£400	£400
	b. "H" with longer left limb	35·00	
	c. Pair, one without surcharge		
	s. Handstamped *"SPECIMEN"*	65·00	

No. 125b, in which the "A" also has a short right leg, occurs on the second, fourth, sixth etc., stamps of the first vertical column of the right-hand pane of the first printing only.

In the second printing what appears to be a broken "E" (with the top limb removed) was used instead of "L" in "HALF" on the last stamp in the sheet (*Price* £32). No. 125c also comes from this second printing.

(Typo D.L.R)

1902–03. Inscr "POSTAGE REVENUE". Wmk Crown CA. P 14.

127	**31**	½d. blue-green	4·50	50
128		1d. carmine	9·50	15
129		1½d. green and black	4·00	4·50
130		2d. red and olive-green	4·00	35
131		2½d. bright blue	1·75	5·00
132		3d. purple and grey	1·25	2·50
133		4d. carmine and cinnamon	7·50	23·00
134		5d. black and orange	3·25	3·50
		w. Wmk inverted	£180	£100
135		6d. green and brown-purple	3·25	4·25
136		1s. carmine and pale blue	4·25	4·50
137		2s. green and bright violet	50·00	9·00
138		2s.6d. purple	40·00	12·00
139		4s. deep rose and maize	80·00	80·00
127/39 *Set of 13*			£190	£130
127s/39s Optd "SPECIMEN" *Set of 13*			£190	

No. 139 exists imperforate and partly perforated, from a proof sheet.

(Typo D.L.R.)

1902. Wmk Crown CC. P 14.

140	**32**	5s. dull blue and rose	45·00	12·00
141		10s. deep rose and chocolate	90·00	32·00
142		£1 black and bright blue	£250	65·00
143		£1. 10s green and violet	£475	£110
		s. Optd "SPECIMEN"	90·00	

No.	Type	Description	Unused	Used
144		£5 mauve and black	£3750	£1000
		s. Optd "SPECIMEN"	£170	
145		£10 green and orange	£9000	£4500
		as. Optd "SPECIMEN"	£350	
145*b*		£20 red and green	£18000	£12000
		bs. Optd "SPECIMEN"	£400	
140s/2s Optd "SPECIMEN" *Set of* 3			£140	

USED HIGH VALUES. Collectors are warned against fiscally used high value Natal stamps with penmarks cleaned off and forged postmarks added.

1904–08. Chalk-surfaced paper (£1. 10s.). Wmk Mult Crown CA. P 14.

No.	Type	Description	Unused	Used
146	**31**	½d. blue-green	9·00	15
147		1d. rose-carmine	9·00	15
		a. Booklet pane of 6, one stamp optd "NOT FOR USE" (1907)	£400	
148		1d. deep carmine	12·00	30
		w. Wmk inverted	†	90·00
149		2d. red and olive-green	15·00	3·25
152		4d. carmine and cinnamon	2·75	1·25
153		5d. black and orange (1908)	4·25	4·00
155		1s. carmine and pale blue	85·00	7·00
156		2s. dull green and bright violet	65·00	48·00
157		2s.6d. purple	60·00	48·00
162	**32**	£1. 10s. brown-orange and deep purple (1908)	£1500	£2750
		s. Optd "SPECIMEN"	£275	
146/57 *Set of* 9			£225	£100

1908–09. Inscr "POSTAGE POSTAGE". Wmk Mult Crown CA. P 14.

No.	Type	Description	Unused	Used
165	**31**	6d. dull and bright purple	4·50	3·00
166		1s. black/*green*	6·00	3·00
167		2s. purple and bright blue/*blue*	15·00	3·00
168		2s.6d. black and red/*blue*	25·00	3·00
169	**32**	5s. green and red/*yellow*	26·00	38·00
170		10s. green and red/*green*	£100	£100
171		£1 purple and black/*red*	£375	£325
165/71 *Set of* 7			£500	£425
165s/71s Optd "SPECIMEN" *Set of* 7			£325	

STAMP BOOKLETS

1906. Black on red cover. Stapled.

SB1 2s.7d. booklet containing thirty 1d. (No. 147) in blocks of 6 ..... £2250

1907. Black on red cover. Stapled.

SB2 2s.6d. booklet containing thirty 1d. (No. 147) in blocks of 6 ..... £2250

The first or third stamp of the first pane in No. SB2 was overprinted "NOT FOR USE" (No. 147a), the additional penny being used to defray the cost of production.

FISCALS USED FOR POSTAGE

1869. Embossed on coloured wove, surfaced paper. P 12½.

F1 **1** 1d. yellow ..... 50·00 80·00

Examples of 1d. yellow and 6d. rose values as Type **6**, 1s. purple-brown as Type **7** and various values between 5s, and £10 in the design illustrated above are believed to exist postally used, but, as such use was not authorised, they are not now listed.

OFFICIAL STAMPS

OFFICIAL

(O **1**)

1904. T **31**, wmk Mult Crown CA, optd with Type O **1** by De La Rue. P 14.

No.	Description	Unused	Used
O1	½d. blue-green	3·00	35
O2	1d. carmine	9·00	1·00
O3	2d. red and olive-green	35·00	18·00
O4	3d. purple and grey	20·00	4·50
O5	6d. green and brown-purple	70·00	70·00
O6	1s. carmine and pale blue	£190	£225
O1/6 *Set of* 6		£300	£275

Nos. O4 and O5 were from special printings of the 3d. and 6d. stamps, which were not issued on wmk Mult Crown CA paper without opt.

The use of stamps overprinted as above was discontinued after 30 May 1907, although later use has been reported. Stamps perforated with the letters "N.G.R." were for use on Government Railways.

Natal became a province of the Union of South Africa on 31 May 1910.

IV. NEW REPUBLIC

During the unrest following the death of Cetshwayo, the Zulu king, in 1884, a group of Boers from the Transvaal offered their support to his son, Dinizulu. The price for this support was the cession of a sizeable portion of Zulu territory to an independent Boer republic. The New Republic, centred on Vryheid, was proclaimed on 16 August 1884 with the remaining Zulu territory becoming a protectorate of the new administration. The first reference to an organised postal service occurs in December 1884.

Alarmed by these developments the British authorities annexed the southernmost part of the land grant, around St. Lucia Bay, to prevent access to the Indian Ocean. The remainder of the New Republic was, however, recognised as independent on 22 October 1886. Zululand was annexed by the British on 22 May 1887.

Difficulties beset the New Republic, however, and its Volksraad voted for union with the South African Republic (Transvaal). The two republics united on 21 July 1888. In 1903 the territory of the former New Republic was transferred to Natal.

Mail from Vryheid in 1884–85 was franked with issues of Transvaal (for dispatches made via Utrecht) or Natal (for those sent via Dundee from August 1885 onwards). Issues of the New Republic were never accepted as internationally valid by these administrations so that all external mail continued to show Transvaal or Natal stamps used in combination with those of the republic.

PRICES FOR STAMPS ON COVER

No.	1	—
Nos.	2/5	*from* × 50
Nos.	6/25	—
Nos.	26/9	*from* × 50
Nos.	30/47	—
Nos.	48/50	*from* × 50
No.	51	—
Nos.	52/3	*from* × 50
Nos.	72/5	*from* × 50
Nos.	76/7b	—
Nos.	78/80	*from* × 50
Nos.	81/95	—

1

Printed with a rubber handstamp on paper bought in Europe and sent out ready gummed and perforated.

1886 (7 Jan)–**87**. Various dates indicating date of printing. P 11½.

A. Without Arms

(i) Yellow paper

No.	Type	Description	Unused	Used
1	**1**	1d. black (9.1.86)	—	£3000
2		1d. violet (9.1.86)	14·00	16·00
		a. "1d." omitted (in pair with normal) (24.4.86)	£2000	
3		2d. violet (9.1.86)	16·00	20·00
		a. "d" omitted (13.10.86)	£4000	
4		3d. violet (13.1.86)	38·00	45·00
		a. "d" omitted (13.10.86)	£4000	
		b. *Tête-bêche* (pair) (13.10.86)		
5		4d. violet (30.8.86)	60·00	
6		6d. violet (20.2.86)	50·00	55·00
		a. "6d." omitted (in pair with normal) (2.7.86)		
7		9d. violet (13.1.86)	90·00	
8		1s. violet (30.8.86)	80·00	
		a. "1s." omitted (in pair with normal) (6.9.86)		
9		1/s. violet (13.10.86)	£650	
10		1/6 violet (30.8.86)	85·00	
11		1s.6d. violet (13.1.86)	£450	
		a. *Tête-bêche* (pair) (6.9.86)		
		b. "d" omitted (13.10.86)	£110	
12		2s. violet (30.8.86)	45·00	
		a. *Tête-bêche* (pair) (6.9.86)	£750	
13		2/6 violet (13.1.86)	£150	
14		2s.6d. violet (1.86)	£120	
15		4/s. violet (17.1.87)	£500	
15*a*		4s. violet (17.1.87)		
16		5s. violet (1.86)	38·00	48·00
		a. "s" omitted (in pair with normal) (7.3.86)	£3000	
17		5/6 violet (20.2.86)	£180	

No.	Type	Description	Unused	Used
18		5s.6d. violet (13.1.86)	£300	
19		7/6 violet (13.1.86)	£190	
20		7s.6d. violet (24.5.86)	£120	
21		10s. violet (13.1.86)	£150	£160
		a. *Tête-bêche* (pair) (2.7.86)		
22		10s.6d. violet (1.86)	£180	
		a. "d" omitted (1.86)	£100	
23		13s. violet (24.11.86)	£475	
24		£1 violet (13.1.86)	£120	
		a. *Tête-bêche* (pair) (13.10.86)	£500	
25		30s. violet (13.1.86)	£110	
		a. *Tête-bêche* (pair) (24.11.86)	£500	

(ii) Blue granite paper

No.	Type	Description	Unused	Used
26	1	1d. violet (20.1.86)	19·00	21·00
		a. "d" omitted (24.11.86)	£500	
		b. "1" omitted (in pair with normal) (24.11.86)		
27		2d. violet (24.1.86)	16·00	18·00
		a. "d" omitted (24.4.86)	£1000	
		b. "2d." omitted (in pair with normal) (24.4.86)		
28		3d. violet (30.8.86)	30·00	30·00
		a. *Tête-bêche* (pair) (13.10.86)	£300	
29		4d. violet (24.5.86)	40·00	45·00
30		6d. violet (20.2.86)	65·00	65·00
		a. "6" omitted in pair with normal (24.5.86)	£2000	
31		9d. violet (6.9.86)	£110	
32		1s. violet (1.86)	35·00	40·00
		a. *Tête-bêche* (pair) (21.5.86)	£325	
		b. "1s." omitted (in pair with normal) (29.4.86)	£2000	
33		1s.6d. violet (2.7.86)	£100	
		a. *Tête-bêche* (pair) (6.9.86)	£550	
		b. "d" omitted (13.10.86)		
34		1/6 violet (6.9.86)	£150	
35		2s. violet (21.5.86)	£120	
		a. "2s." omitted (in pair with normal) (24.5.86)	£2000	
36		2s.6d. violet (19.8.86)	£150	
37		2/6 violet (19.8.86)	£180	
38		4/s. violet (17.1.87)	£375	
39		5/6 violet (13.1.86)	£250	
		a. "/" omitted (13.1.87)		
		b. "6" omitted	£2500	
40		5s.6d. violet (13.1.86)	£250	
41		7/6 violet (13.1.86)	£250	
41*a*		7s.6d. violet (13.1.86)	£300	
42		10s. violet (1.86)	£200	£200
		a. *Tête-bêche* (pair) (2.7.86)	£425	
		b. "s" omitted (13.1.86)		
43		10s.6d. violet (1.86)	£200	
		a. *Tête-bêche* (pair) (13.1.86)		
		b. "d" omitted (1.86)	£450	
44		12s. violet (13.1.86)	£325	
45		13s. violet (17.1.87)	£500	
46		£1 violet (13.1.86)	£300	
47		30s. violet (13.1.86)	£275	

B. With embossed Arms of New Republic

(i) Yellow paper

No.	Type	Description	Unused	Used
48	1	1d. violet (20.1.86)	16·00	18·00
		a. Arms inverted (20.1.86)	27·00	30·00
		b. Arms *tête-bêche* (pair) (14.4.86)	£100	£120
		c. *Tête-bêche* (pair) (3.11.86)	£800	
49		2d. violet (30.8.86)	20·00	22·00
		a. Arms inverted (24.11.86)	25·00	30·00
50		4d. violet (2.12.86)	60·00	60·00
		a. Arms inverted (12.86)	£100	70·00
		b. Arms *tête-bêche* (pair) (12.86)	£250	
51		6d. violet (2.12.86)	£250	

(ii) Blue granite paper

No.	Type	Description	Unused	Used
52	1	1d. violet (20.1.86)	21·00	21·00
		a. Arms inverted (10.2.86)	38·00	42·00
		b. Arms *tête-bêche* (pair) (3.11.86)	£500	
53		2d. violet (24.5.86)	21·00	21·00
		a. Arms inverted (30.8.86)	50·00	60·00
		b. Arms *tête-bêche* (pair) (2.12.86)	£500	£500

Stamps as Type **1** were produced as and when stocks were required, each printing including in its design the date on which it was prepared. The dates quoted above for Nos. 1/53 are those on which the various stamps first appeared. Details of the various printing dates are given below. From these dates it can be seen that some values share common printing dates, and, it is believed, that the different values were produced *se-tenant* within the same sheet, at least in some instances. A reported proof sheet in the Pretoria Postal Museum, on yellow paper and embossed, contains 4 examples of the 6d. value and 3 each of the 3d., 4d., 9d., 1s., 1/6, 2/-, 2/6, 3s., 4s., 5s., 5/6, 7/6, 10/-, 10/6, £1 and 30/-.

The date on No. 1 measures 17 mm; on all others it is 15 mm.

The significance, if any, of the two coloured papers and the use of the embossing machine have never been satisfactorily explained. Both the different papers and the embossing machine were introduced in January 1886, and occur throughout the period that the stamps with dates were used.

PRINTINGS

Date	*Paper*	*Face value*	*Cat No.*	*Unused*	*Used*
Jan 86	*Yellow*	5s.	16	38·00	48·00
		10s.6d.	22	£200	
		10s.6	22a	£150	
	Blue	1s.	32		
		10s.	42	£200	£200
		10s.6d.	43	£200	
		10s.6	43b	£500	
7 Jan 86	*Yellow*	10s.6d.	22	£180	
	Blue	10s.	42		
		10s.6d.	43	£475	
9 Jan 86	*Yellow*	1d. blk	1	†	£3000
		1d. vio	2	14·00	16·00
		2d.	3	40·00	50·00
13 Jan 86	*Yellow*	1d.	2	38·00	
		2d.	3	35·00	38·00
		3d.	4	75·00	
		9d	7	£200	
		1s.6d.	11	£450	
		2/6	13	£160	
		2s.6d.	14	£200	
		5s.6d.	18		
		7/6	19	£190	
		10s.	21		
		£1	24	£150	
		30s.	25	£150	
	Blue	5/6	39	£250	
		5s.6d.	40	£250	
		7/6	41	£250	
		7s.6d.	41*a*	£300	
		10s.	42	£400	
		10s.	42b		
		10s.6d.	43	£200	
		10s.6d.	43a		
		12s.	44	£325	
		£1	46	£300	
		30s.	47	£275	
20 Jan 86	*Yellow*	1d.	2		
	Blue	1d.	26	£250	
	Yellow, embossed	1d.	48	75·00	
		1d.	48a	£100	
	Blue, embossed	1d.	52	£130	
Jan 20 86	*Blue*	1d.	26	26·00	
	Yellow, embossed	1d.	48a		
	Blue, embossed	1d.	52	£120	
24 Jan 86	*Blue*	1d.	26	32·00	
		2d.	27	50·00	
10 Feb 86	*Yellow*	1d.	2		
	Yellow, embossed	1d.	48		
		1d.	48a	75·00	
	Blue, embossed	1d.	52	£130	
		1d.	52a	45·00	
20 Feb 86	*Yellow*	6d.	6		
		1s.6d.	11		
		2s.6d.	14	£130	
		5/6	17	£180	
		5s.6d.	18		
	Blue	6d.	30		
7 Mar 86	*Yellow*	1d.	2	£110	
		2/6	13		
		2s.6d.	14	£120	
		5s.	16	£200	90·00
		5s.	16a	£3000	
		5/6	17	£180	
		5s.6d.	18	£300	
	Blue	2d.	27	£100	
		6d.	30		
		1s.	32		
17 Mar 86	*Yellow*	1d.	2	£100	
	Yellow, embossed	1d.	48	50·00	
	Blue, embossed	1d.	52	£130	
		1d.	52a	£110	
26 Mar 86	*Blue, embossed*	1d.	52a	£130	
14 Apr 86	*Yellow*	1d.	2		
	Yellow, embossed	1d.	48	30·00	
		1d.	48a	60·00	
		1d.	48b	£100	£120
	Blue, embossed	1d.	52	50·00	
		1d.	52a		
24 Apr 86	*Yellow*	1d.	2	£100	
		1d.	2a	£2000	
		5s.	16		
	Blue	2d.	27	75·00	
		2d.	27a	£1000	
		2d.	27b		
29 Apr 86	*Blue*	1s.	32	£110	
		1s.	32b		
21 May 86	*Yellow*	6d.	6	£130	
	Blue	1d.	26	90·00	
		1s.	32	35·00	40·00
		1s.	32a	£325	
		1s.	32b	£1500	
		2s.	35	£275	

Date	Paper	Face value	Cat No.	Unused	Used
23 May 86	*Blue, embossed*	1d.	52a	£100	
24 May 86	*Yellow*	1d.	2	£100	
		2d.	3	£120	
		5s.	16	£100	
		7/6	19	£190	
		7s.6d.	20	£120	
	Blue	1d.	26	35·00	38·00
		2d.	27	£300	£300
		4d.	29	£100	
		6d.	30	£120	
		6d.	30a	£2000	
		1s.	32	£200	
		1s.	32b	£2000	
		2s.	35	£150	
		2s.	35a	£2000	
	Blue, embossed	2d.	53	£100	
26 May 86	*Yellow*	1d.	2		
	Blue	1d.	26	£110	
	Yellow, embossed	1d.	48	£250	
		1d.	48a	£100	
	Blue, embossed	1d.	52	£130	
		1d.	52a	50·00	55·00
28 May 86	*Yellow, embossed*	1d.	48	£150	
Jun 30 86	*Blue*	1d.	26	18·00	20·00
	Yellow, embossed	1d.	48	20·00	22·00
		1d.	48a	27·00	30·00
		1d.	48b	£200	£225
	Blue, embossed	1d.	52	48·00	42·00
2 Jul 86	*Yellow*	6d.	6	£200	
		6d.	6a		
		9d	7	£200	£200
		10s.	21		
		10s.	21a		
	Blue	1s.6d.	33	£100	
		10s.	42	£200	
		10s.	42a	£425	
		10s.6d.	43		
		10s.6d.	43b	£475	
3 Jul 86	*Blue*	10s.	42		
Jul 7 86	*Yellow*	1d.	2		
	Blue	1d.	26		
	Yellow, embossed	1d.	48	75·00	
		1d.	48a	£100	£100
	Blue, embossed	1d.	52	22·00	23·00
		1d.	52a	60·00	42·00
4 Aug 86	*Yellow*	1d.	2		
	Yellow, embossed	1d.	48	60·00	
	Blue, embossed	1d.	52	60·00	
		1d.	52a		
19 Aug 86	*Yellow*	2/6	13		
		2s.6d.	14	£140	
	Blue	2s.6d.	36	£150	
		2/6	37	£180	
30 Aug 86	*Yellow*	1d.	2	14·00	16·00
		2d.	3	75·00	
		3d.	4	80·00	
		4d.	5	60·00	
		6d.	6	£100	
		9d.	7	90·00	
		1s.	8	80·00	
		1/6	10	85·00	
		2s.	12	£100	
		2/6	13	£150	
	Blue	2d.	27	16·00	18·00
		3d.	28		
	Yellow, embossed	2d.	49	£100	
	Blue, embossed	2d.	53	45·00	
		2d.	53a	£110	
6 Sep 86	*Yellow*	1d.	2	£100	
		2d.	3	35·00	40·00
		3d.	4	42·00	
		4d.	5	60·00	
		6d.	6	80·00	
		9d.	7	85·00	
		1s.	8	£100	
		1s.	8a		
		1/6	10	£140	
		1s.6d.	11	£450	
		1s.6d.	11a		
		2s.	12	£100	
		2s.	12a	£750	
		2/6	13	£150	
		2s.6d.	14		
		5s.	16	£150	
		7s.6d.	20	£200	
		10s.	21	£150	
		£1	24	£140	
	Blue	6d.	30	65·00	65·00
		9d.	31	£110	
		1s.	32	75·00	
		1s.6d.	33	£140	
		1s.6d.	33a	£550	
		1/6	34		
		2s.6d.	36		
		2/6	37	£400	
		7s.6d.	41a	£300	
		10s.6d.	43		
13 Sep 86	*Yellow*	1d.	2		
	Yellow, embossed	1d.	48	75·00	
		1d.	48a	75·00	
	Blue, embossed	1d.	52	£100	
6 Oct 86	*Yellow*	1d.	2		
	Blue	1d.	26	90·00	
	Yellow, embossed	1d.	48	75·00	60·00
		1d.	48a		
	Blue, embossed	1d.	52	48·00	25·00
		1d.	52a	90·00	
13 Oct 86	*Yellow*	1d.	2	25·00	25·00
		2d.	3	25·00	30·00
		2d.	3a	£4000	
		3d.	4	38·00	45·00
		3d.	4a	£4000	
		3d.	4b		
		4d.	5	60·00	
		6d.	6	50·00	55·00
		9d.	7	90·00	
		1s.	8	£150	
		1/s	9	£650	
		1/6	10	£160	
		1s 6.	11b	£110	
		2s.	12	45·00	
		2/6	13	£160	
		5s.	16	75·00	
		10s.	21	£150	£160
		10s.6.	22a	£100	
		£1	24	£120	
		£1	24a	£500	
	Blue	2d.	27	16·00	18·00
		3d.	28	30·00	30·00
		3d.	28a	£300	
		4d.	29	40·00	45·00
		1s.	32	55·00	
		1s 6.	33b		
		1/6	34	£150	
		2s.	35	£120	
3 Nov 86	*Yellow*	1d.	2	40·00	
	Blue	1d.	26		
	Yellow, embossed	1d.	48	16·00	18·00
		1d.	48a	27·00	30·00
		1d.	48b	£100	£120
		1d.	48c	£800	
	Blue, embossed	1d.	52	21·00	
		1d.	52a	38·00	42·00
		1d.	52b	£500	
13 Nov 86	*Yellow*	1d.	2	£120	
24 Nov 86	*Yellow*	1d.	2	£100	
		2d.	3	16·00	20·00
		3d.	4	42·00	50·00
		1/6	10	£150	
		10s.	21	£200	
		13s.	23	£425	
		30s.	25	£110	
		30s.	25a	£500	
	Blue	1d.	26	40·00	30·00
		1d.	26a	£500	
		1d.	26b		
		2d.	27	50·00	
		2d.	27a		
		4d.	29	40·00	45·00
		6d.	30	75·00	75·00
		9d.	31	£120	
		1s.	32	£100	£110
		1/6	34	£200	
		2s.	35	£150	
		2s.	35a	£3000	
	Yellow, embossed	2d.	49	£160	
		2d.	49a		
26 Nov 86	*Yellow*	1/6	10	£150	
2 Dec 86	*Yellow*	1d.	2		
		2d.	3		
	Blue	2d.	27		
	Yellow, embossed	1d.	48	25·00	30·00
		1d.	48a	£160	
		2d.	49	20·00	22·00
		2d.	49a	25·00	30·00
		4d.	50	£150	
		6d.	51	£225	
	Blue, embossed	1d.	52	35·00	
		1d.	52a	£160	
		2d.	53	21·00	21·00
		2d.	53a	50·00	60·00
		2d.	53b	£500	£500
3 Dec 86	*Yellow, embossed*	6d.	51		
Dec 86	*Yellow*	6d.	6		
	Blue	4d.	29		
	Yellow, embossed	4d.	50	60·00	60·00
		4d.	50a	£100	70·00
		4d.	50b	£250	

Date	*Paper*	*Face value*	*Cat No.*	*Unused*	*Used*
		6d.	51	£225	
4 Jan 87	*Yellow*	1d.	2	£100	
		2d.	3	40·00	
		13s.	23	£475	
	Blue	1d.	26	19·00	21·00
		2d.	27	20·00	20·00
	Blue, embossed	2d.	53	45·00	
13 Jan 87	*Yellow*	7/6	19		
	Blue	5/6	39	£450	
		5/6	39a		
		7/6	41	£500	
17 Jan 87	*Yellow*	1d.	2	75·00	
		2d.	3	75·00	
		3d.	4	75·00	
		4/s.	15	£500	
		4s.	15*a*		
	Blue	1d.	26	80·00	
		4/s.	38	£375	
		13s.	45	£500	
		30s.	47	£275	
20 Jan 87	*Blue*	2d.	27	38·00	
	Yellow, embossed	2d.	49	55·00	
		2d.	49a	£140	
	Blue, embossed	2d.	53	45·00	
		2d.	53a	£100	
Jan 20 87	*Yellow, embossed*	1d.	48a	£400	

1887 (Jan–Mar). As T **1**, but without date. With embossed Arms.

(a) Blue granite paper

72	1d. violet	24·00	15·00
	b. Stamps *tête-bêche* (pair)	£475	
	c. Arms *tête-bêche* (pair)		
	d. Arms inverted	27·00	25·00
	e. Arms omitted	£120	£120
	f. Arms sideways		
73	2d. violet	12·00	12·00
	a. Stamps *tête-bêche* (pair)	£325	
	b. Arms inverted	28·00	28·00
	c. Arms omitted	£110	£100
	d. Arms *tête-bêche* (pair)		
74	3d. violet	24·00	24·00
	a. Stamps *tête-bêche* (pair)	£375	
	b. Arms *tête-bêche* (pair)		
	c. Arms inverted	50·00	50·00
75	4d. violet	19·00	19·00
	a. Stamps *tête-bêche* (pair)	£325	
	b. Arms *tête-bêche* (pair)	£275	
	c. Arms inverted	90·00	
76	6d. violet	24·00	25·00
	a. Arms inverted	90·00	
77	1/6 violet	35·00	30·00
	a. Arms inverted	£120	
	b. Arms *tête-bêche* (pair)	£400	
77*c*	2/6 violet	†	£800

(b) Yellow paper (March 1887)

78	2d. violet (*arms omitted*)	30·00	
79	3d. violet	20·00	21·00
	b. Stamps *tête-bêche* (pair)	£325	£375
	c. Arms *tête-bêche* (pair)	£200	
	d. Arms inverted	27·00	27·00
	e. Arms sideways	£300	
80	4d. violet	14·00	14·00
	a. Arms inverted	19·00	19·00
81	6d. violet	12·00	13·00
	a. Arms *tête-bêche* (pair)	£350	
	b. Arms inverted	45·00	45·00
	c. Arms omitted	80·00	
82	9d. violet	12·00	15·00
	a. Arms inverted	£200	
	b. Arms *tête-bêche* (pair)	£350	
83	1s. violet	14·00	14·00
	a. Arms inverted	70·00	
84	1/6 violet	35·00	28·00
85	2s. violet	21·00	22·00
	a. Arms inverted	55·00	50·00
	b. Arms omitted	£110	
86	2/6 violet	30·00	30·00
	a. Arms inverted	35·00	35·00
87	3s. violet	55·00	55·00
	a. Arms inverted	70·00	70·00
	b. Stamps *tête-bêche* (pair)	£475	
88	4s. violet	£325	
	a. Arms omitted		
88*b*	4/s violet	55·00	55·00
	ba. Arms omitted	£200	
89	5s. violet	50·00	50·00
	b. Arms inverted	—	£110
90	5/6 violet	18·00	21·00
91	7/6 violet	26·00	28·00
	a. Arms *tête-bêche* (pair)		
	b. Arms inverted	£100	
92	10s. violet	22·00	23·00
	b. Arms *tête-bêche* (pair)	£120	
	c. Arms inverted	28·00	
	d. Arms omitted	£100	55·00
93	10/6 violet	20·00	24·00
	b. Arms inverted	50·00	
94	£1 violet	65·00	70·00
	a. Stamps *tête-bêche* (pair)	£450	£500
	b. Arms inverted	70·00	
95	30s. violet	£150	

A £15 value as Nos. 78/95 exists, but is only known fiscally used (*Price* £4000).

Many values exist with double impressions of the handstamp.

New Republic united with the South African Republic (Transvaal) on 21 July 1888. In 1903 the territory of the former New Republic was transferred to Natal.

V. ORANGE FREE STATE

PRICES FOR STAMPS ON COVER

Nos.	1/9	*from* × 20
Nos.	10/13	*from* × 30
Nos.	18/19	*from* × 20
No.	20	—
Nos.	21/42	*from* × 40
Nos.	48/51	*from* × 25
Nos.	52/138	*from* × 10
Nos.	139/51	*from* × 7
Nos.	F1/17	—
Nos.	PF1/3	*from* × 20
No.	M1	*from* × 20

Supplies of Cape of Good Hope stamps were available at Bloemfontein and probably elsewhere in the Orange Free State, from mid-1856 onwards for use on mail to Cape Colony and beyond. Such arrangements continued after the introduction of Orange Free State stamps in 1868. It is not known if the dumb cancellations used on the few surviving covers were applied in the Free State or at Cape Town.

1

(Typo D.L.R.)

1868 (1 Jan)–**94**. P 14.

1	**1**	1d. pale brown	27·00	2·25
2		1d. red-brown	17·00	45
3		1d. deep brown	28·00	55
4		6d. pale rose (1868)	60·00	8·00
5		6d. rose (1871)	28·00	5·50
6		6d. rose-carmine (1891)	28·00	12·00
7		6d. bright carmine (1894)	16·00	2·00
8		1s. orange-buff	£100	6·50
9		1s. orange-yellow	60·00	1·50
		a. Double print	—	£3000

4	4	4	4
(**2**) (*a*)	(*b*)	(*c*)	(*d*)

1877. No. 5 surcharged T **2** (*a*) to (*d*).

10	**1**	4d. on 6d. rose (*a*)	£400	55·00
		a. Surch inverted	—	£550
		b. Surch double (*a* + *c*)		
		c. Surch double, one inverted (*a* + *c* inverted)	†	£3750
		d. Surch double, one inverted (*a* inverted + *c*)	†	£5000
11		4d. on 6d. rose (*b*)	£1300	£180
		a. Surch inverted	—	£1100
		b. Surch double (*b* + *d*)		
12		4d. on 6d. rose (*c*)	£200	32·00
		a. Surch inverted	—	£350
		b. Surch double		
13		4d. on 6d. rose (*d*)	£250	35·00
		a. Surch inverted	£1200	£375
		b. Surch double, one inverted (*d* + *c* inverted)	†	£3750

The setting of 60 comprised nine stamps as No. 10, four as No. 11, twenty-seven as No. 12 and twenty as No. 13.

1878 (July). P 14.

18	**1**	4d. pale blue	24·00	4·25
19		4d. ultramarine	4·00	3·50
20		5s. green	10·00	15·00

1d. 1d. 1d. 1d. 1d. 1d.
(**3**) (*a*) (*b*) (*c*) (*d*) (*e*) (*f*)

Type **3**: (*a*) Small "1" and "d." (*b*) Sloping serif. (*c*) Same size as (*b*), but "1" with straighter horizontal serif. (*d*) Taller "1" with horizontal serif and antique "d". (*e*) Same size as (*d*) but with sloping serif and thin line at foot. (*f*) as (*d*) but with Roman "d".

1881 (19 May). No. 20 surch T **3** (*a*) to (*f*) with heavy black bar cancelling the old value.
21 **1** 1d. on 5s. green (*a*) .... £110 26·00
22 1d. on 5s. green (*b*) .... 60·00 26·00
a. Surch inverted .... — £850
b. Surch double .... — £1200
23 1d. on 5s. green (*c*) .... £275 80·00
a. Surch inverted .... — £1300
b. Surch double .... — £1500
24 1d. on 5s. green (*d*) .... 90·00 26·00
a. Surch inverted £1800 £850
b. Surch double .... — £1200
25 1d. on 5s. green (*e*) £550 £250
a. Surch inverted .... † £2250
b. Surch double .... † £2250
26 1d. on 5s. green (*f*) .... 85·00 26·00
a. Surch inverted .... — £800
b. Surch double .... — £800

No. 21 was the first printing in one type only. Nos. 22 to 25 constitute the second printing about a year later, and are all found on the same sheet; and No. 26 the third printing of which about half have the stop raised.

Owing to defective printing, examples of Nos. 22 and 24/5 may be found with the obliterating bar at the top of the stamps or, from the top row, without the bar.

½d
(**4**)

1882 (Aug). No. 20 surch with T **4** and with a thin black line cancelling old value.
36 **1** ½d. on 5s. green .... 22·00 4·75
a. Surch double £425 £325
b. Surch inverted £1300 £800

3d 3d 3d 3d 3d
(**5**) (*a*) (*b*) (*c*) (*d*) (*e*)

1882. No. 19 surch with T **5** (*a*) to (*e*) with thin black line cancelling value.
38 **1** 3d. on 4d. ultramarine (*a*) .... 90·00 29·00
a. Surch double .... † £1200
39 3d. on 4d. ultramarine (*b*) .... 90·00 18·00
a. Surch double .... † £1200
40 3d. on 4d. ultramarine (*c*) .... 42·00 20·00
a. Surch double .... † £1200
41 3d. on 4d. ultramarine (*d*) .... 90·00 20·00
a. Surch double .... † £1200
42 3d. on 4d. ultramarine (*e*) .... £250 65·00
a. Surch double .... † £2750

Examples of Nos. 39 and 41/2 exist without the cancelling bar due to the misplacement of the surcharge.

1883–84. P 14.
48 **1** ½d. chestnut .... 5·50 50
49 2d. pale mauve .... 17·00 1·00
50 2d. bright mauve .... 19·00 30
51 3d. ultramarine .... 6·00 2·00

For 1d. purple, see No. 68.

2d 2d 2d
(**6**) (*a*) (*b*) (*c*)

1888 (Sept–Oct). No. 51 surch with T **6** (*a*), (*b*) or (*c*).
(a) Wide "2". (b) Narrow "2"
52 **1** 2d. on 3d. ultramarine (*a*) (Sept) .... 70·00 9·00
a. Surch inverted .... — £750
53 2d. on 3d. ultramarine (*b*) .... 50·00 2·00
a. Surch inverted .... — £300
b. "2" with curved foot (*c*) £1300 £500

1d 1d 1d
(**7**) (*a*) (*b*) (*c*)

1890 (Dec)–**91**. Nos. 51 and 19 surch with T **7** (*a*) to (*c*).
54 **1** 1d. on 3d. ultramarine (*a*) .... 8·50 60
a. Surch double .... 90·00 70·00
c. "1" and "d" wide apart £150 £110
d. Dropped "d" (Right pane R. 5/6) £160 £120
55 1d. on 3d. ultramarine (*b*) .... 23·00 2·75
a. Surch double £300 £275
57 1d. on 4d. ultramarine (*a*) .... 35·00 9·50
a. Surch double £150 £120
b. Surch double (*a* + *b*) £400
c. Surch triple .... — £2750
d. Raised "1" (Left pane R. 3/1) .... £150 60·00
58 1d. on 4d. ultramarine (*b*) .... 85·00 55·00
a. Surch double £425 £325
59 1d. on 4d. ultramarine (*c*) £1800 £500
a. Surch double ....

The settings of the 1d. on 3d. and on 4d. are not identical. The variety (*c*) does not exist on the 3d.

2½d. 2½d.▪
(**8**) Printer's quad after surcharge (Lower right pane No. 43)

1892 (Oct). No. 51 surch with T **8**.
67 **1** 2½d. on 3d. ultramarine .... 19·00 70
a. No stop after "d" .... 85·00 50·00
b. Printer's quad after surcharge .... 85·00 50·00

1894 (Sept). Colour changed. P 14.
68 **1** 1d. purple .... 4·00 30

½d ½d ½d
(**9**) (*a*) (*b*) (*c*)

½d ½d ½d ½d
(*d*) (*e*) (*f*) (*g*)

Types (*a*) and (*e*) differ from types (*b*) and (*f*) respectively, in the serifs of the "**1**", but owing to faulty overprinting this distinction is not always clearly to be seen.

1896 (Sept). No. 51 surch with T **9** (*a*) to (*g*).
69 **1** ½d. on 3d. ultramarine (*a*) .... 7·50 11·00
70 ½d. on 3d. ultramarine (*b*) .... 14·00 14·00
71 ½d. on 3d. ultramarine (*c*) .... 13·00 2·50
72 ½d. on 3d. ultramarine (*d*) .... 13·00 2·25
73 ½d. on 3d. ultramarine (*e*) .... 13·00 2·25
74 ½d. on 3d. ultramarine (*f*) .... 14·00 15·00
75 ½d. on 3d. ultramarine (*g*) .... 8·00 4·50
a. Surch double .... 13·00 10·00
b. Surch triple .... 70·00 70·00

The double and triple surcharges are often different types, but are always type (*g*), or in combination with type (*g*).

Double surcharges in the same type, but without the "d" and bar, also exist, probably from a trial sheet prepared by the printer. Both unused and used examples are known.

Halve
Penny.

(**10**) 2½
(**11**)

1896. No. 51 surch with T **10**.
77 **1** ½d. on 3d. ultramarine .... 1·00 50
(i) Errors in setting
78 **1** ½d. on 3d. (no stop) .... 18·00 29·00
79 ½d. on 3d. ("Peuny") .... 18·00 29·00
(ii) Surch inverted
81 **1** ½d. on 3d. .... 60·00 65·00
81*a* ½d. on 3d. (no stop) £2000
81*b* ½d. on 3d. ("Peuny") £1500
(iii) Surch double, one inverted
81*c* **1** ½d. on 3d. (Nos. 77 and 81) £180 £200
81*d* ½d. on 3d. (Nos. 77 and 81*a*) £800 £800
81*e* ½d. on 3d. (Nos. 77 and 81*b*) £900 £900
81*f* ½d. on 3d. (Nos. 81 and 78) £1500 £900
82 ½d. on 3d. (Nos. 81 and 79) .... — £900

Examples from the top horizontal row can be found without the bar due to the surcharge being misplaced.

Nos. 69 to 75 also exist surcharged as last but they are considered not to have been issued with authority (*Prices from £30 each, unused*).

1897 (1 Jan). No. 51 surch with T **11**. (a) As in illustration. (b) With Roman "1" and antique "2" in fraction.
83 **1** 2½d. on 3d. ultramarine (*a*) .... 9·00 80
83*a* 2½d. on 3d. ultramarine (*b*) .... £170 90·00

1897. P 14.
84 **1** ½d. yellow (March) .... 2·50 35

85 ½d. orange .... 2·50 35
87 1s. brown (Aug) .... 27·00 1·50

The 6d. blue was prepared for use in the Orange Free State, but had not been brought into use when the stamps were seized in Bloemfontein. A few have been seen without the "V.R.I." overprint but they were not authorized or available for postage (*Price* £60).

BRITISH OCCUPATION

31 (Level stops) (**32**) Thin "V" (Raised stops) (**33**) Thick "V"

Inserted "R"

(Surch by Curling & Co, Bloemfontein)

1900. T **1** surch as T **31/33** (2½d. on 3d. optd "V.R.I." only).

(a) First printings surch as T **31** *with stops level (March)*

101 ½d. on ½d. orange .... 4·00 5·00
a. No stop after "V" (R.10/3) .... 22·00 26·00
b. No stop after "I" (R.1/3) £160 £160
c. "½" omitted (R.7/5) £180 £180
d. "I" and stops after "I" and "R" omitted (R. 2/3) £225 £200
e. "V.R.I." omitted £170
f. Value omitted £110
g. Small "½" .... 55·00 55·00
h. Surch double £180
102 1d. on 1d. purple .... 2·50 1·25
a. Surch on 1d. deep brown (No. 3) £600 £400
b. No stop after "V" (R. 10/3) .... 16·00 15·00
c. No stop after "R" £160 £170
d. No stop after "I" £1000
e. "1" omitted (R. 7/5) £180 £190
f. "I" omitted (with stops present) £325 £325
g. "I" and stop after "R" omitted (R. 2/3) £250 £250
h. "V.R.I." omitted £160 £170
i. "d" omitted £325 £325
j. Value omitted .... 90·00 95·00
k. Inverted stop after "R" £225 £250
l. Wider space between "1" and "d" £100 £100
m. "V" and "R" close £160 £160
n. Pair, one without surch £475
o. "V" omitted £850
103 2d. on 2d. bright mauve .... 3·75 1·75
a. No stop after "V" (R. 10/3) .... 16·00 19·00
b. No stop after "R" £275 £275
c. No stop after "I" £275 £275
d. "V.R.I." omitted £300 £300
e. Value omitted £300
104 2½d. on 3d. ultramarine (*a*) .... 20·00 18·00
a. No stop after "V" (R. 10/3) .... 90·00 90·00
105 2½d. on 3d. ultramarine (*b*) £250 £250
106 3d. on 3d. ultramarine .... 3·00 3·50
a. No stop after "V" (R. 10/3) .... 21·00 23·00
b. Pair, one without surch £550
c. "V.R.I." omitted £250 £250
d. Value omitted £250 £250
107 4d. on 4d. ultramarine .... 10·00 17·00
a. No stop after "V" (R.10/3) .... 65·00 75·00
108 6d. on 6d. bright carmine .... 40·00 35·00
a. No stop after "V" (R. 10/3) £250 £275
b. "6" omitted (R. 7/5) £300 £300
109 6d. on 6d. blue .... 11·00 5·00
a. No stop after "V" (R. 10/3) .... 45·00 45·00
b. "6" omitted (R. 7/5) .... 80·00 85·00
c. "V.R.I." omitted £500 £300
110 1s. on 1s. brown .... 7·00 2·75
a. Surch on 1s. orange-yellow (No. 9) £3500 £2500
b. No stop after "V" (R. 10/3) .... 50·00 32·00
c. "1" omitted £130 £130
ca. "1" inserted by hand .... † £1000
d. "1" omitted and spaced stop after "s" £140 £150
e. "V.R.I." omitted £190 £190
f. Value omitted £190 £190
g. Raised stop after "s" .... 21·00 11·00
h. Wider space between "1" and "s" £150 £150
111 5s. on 5s. green .... 26·00 55·00
a. No stop after "V" (R. 10/3) £250 £300
b. "5" omitted £950 £1000
c. Inverted stop after "R" (R. 2/2) £700 £700
d. Wider space between "5" and "s" (R. 3/6) £130 £140
e. Value omitted £375 £400

All values are found with a rectangular, instead of an oval, stop after "R". Misplaced surcharges (upwards or sideways) occur.

No. 110ca shows the missing "1" replaced by a handstamp in a different type face.

On No. 111c the stop is near the top of the "R". On 111d there is a 2mm space between "5" and "s"; lesser displacements exist on other positions.

(b) Subsequent printings

(i) Surch as T **32**

112 ½d. on ½d. orange 30 20
a. Raised and level stops mixed .... 2·50 2·00
b. Pair, one with level stops .... 13·00 17·00
c. No stop after "V" .... 3·25 3·50
d. No stop after "I" .... 32·00 32·00
e. "V" omitted £550
f. Small "½" .... 17·00 19·00
g. As a, and small "½" .... 17·00 19·00
i. Space between "V" and "R" .... 22·00 24·00
j. Value omitted £120 £120
113 1d. on 1d. purple 30 20
a. Raised and level stops mixed .... 2·00 2·50
b. Pair, one with level stops .... 22·00 24·00
c. No stop after "V" .... 3·50 7·00
d. No stop after "R" .... 18·00 18·00
e. No stop after "I" .... 18·00 18·00
f. No stops after "V" and "I" £300
g. Surch inverted £375
h. Surch double £110 £100
i. Pair, one without surch £250
j. Short figure "1" £110 £110
k. Space between "V" and "R" .... 50·00 55·00
l. Space between "R" and "I" £120 £130
m. Space between "1" and "d" £190 £190
n. Inserted "R" £325 £325
o. Inserted "V" £700
p. Stamp doubly printed, one impression inverted £2500
114 2d. on 2d. bright mauve .... 2·25 30
a. Raised and level stops mixed .... 6·00 4·75
b. Pair, one with level stops .... 10·00 11·00
c. Surch inverted £325 £325
d. "1" raised .... 75·00 75·00
e. Pair, one without surch £325 £325
f. No stop after "V" £1000
g. No stop after "I" ....
115 2½d. on 3d. ultramarine (*a*) £200 £190
a. Raised and level stops mixed £600
116 2½d. on 3d. ultramarine (*b*) £1200
117 3d. on 3d. ultramarine 80 30
a. Raised and level stops mixed .... 7·50 7·50
b. Pair, one with level stops .... 20·00 21·00
c. No stop after "V" £140 £140
d. No stop after "R" £375 £450
e. "I" and stop omitted £400 £425
ea. "I" and stop inserted ....
f. Surch double £400
g. Surch double, one diagonal £375
h. Ditto, diagonal surch with mixed stops £6500
n. Inserted "R" ....
o. Space between "3" and "d" £140
118 4d. on 4d. ultramarine .... 3·00 3·75
a. Raised and level stops mixed .... 10·00 14·00
b. Pair, one with level stops .... 22·00 32·00
119 6d. on 6d. bright carmine .... 40·00 50·00
a. Raised and level stops mixed £140 £160
b. Pair, one with level stops £225 £300
120 6d. on 6d. blue 70 40
a. Raised and level stops mixed .... 8·50 9·00
b. Pair, one with level stops .... 21·00 25·00
c. No stop after "V" £500 £500
d. No stop after "R" £300
e. Value omitted £450
121 1s. on 1s. brown .... 7·50 45
a. Surch on 1s. orange-yellow (No. 9) £1300 £1300
b. Raised and level stops mixed .... 22·00 22·00
c. Pair, one with level stops .... 40·00 45·00
f. "s" omitted £250
g. "V.R.I." omitted £400
122 5s. on 5s. green .... 9·00 12·00
a. Raised and level stops mixed £325 £325
b. Pair, one with level stops £1000
c. Short top to "5" .... 60·00 70·00
s. Handstamped "SPECIMEN" .... 55·00

(ii) Surch as T **33**

123 ½d. on ½d. orange .... 6·00 3·75
124 1d. on 1d. purple .... 7·00 35
a. Inverted "1" for "I" .... 22·00 22·00
b. No stops after "R" and "I" .... 90·00 70·00
c. No stop after "R" .... 48·00 55·00
d. Surch double £325 £325
n. Inserted "R" £400 £400
p. Stamp doubly printed, one impression inverted £6500
125 2d. on 2d. bright mauve .... 16·00 14·00
a. Inverted "1" for "I" .... 30·00 32·00
126 2½d. on 3d. ultramarine (*a*) £650 £750

127		2½d. on 3d. ultramarine (*b*)	£3750	
128		3d. on 3d. ultramarine	7·50	14·00
		a. Inverted "1" for "I"	65·00	75·00
		b. Surch double	£550	
		ba. Surch double, one diagonal	£550	
129		6d. on 6d. bright carmine	£425	£425
130		6d. on 6d. blue	20·00	27·00
131		1s. on 1s. brown	29·00	9·50
132		5s. on 5s. green	60·00	48·00
		s. Handstamped "SPECIMEN"	£160	

Stamps with thick "V" occur in certain positions in *later* settings of the type with stops above the line (T **32**). *Earlier* settings with stops above the line have all stamps with thin "V".

Some confusion has previously been caused by the listing of certain varieties as though they occurred on stamps with thick "V" in fact they occur on stamps showing the normal thin "V", included in the settings which also contained the thick "V".

For a short period small blocks of unsurcharged Free State stamps could be handed in for surcharging so that varieties occur which are not found in the complete settings. Nos. 102a, 110a and 121a also occur from such stocks.

The inserted "R" variety occurs on positions 6 (T **32**) and 12 (T **33**) of the forme. The "R" of the original surcharge failed to print and the "R", but not the full stop, was added by the use of a handstamp. Traces of the original letter are often visible. The broken "V" flaw, also shown in the illustration, does not appear on No. 124n.

ORANGE RIVER COLONY

CROWN COLONY

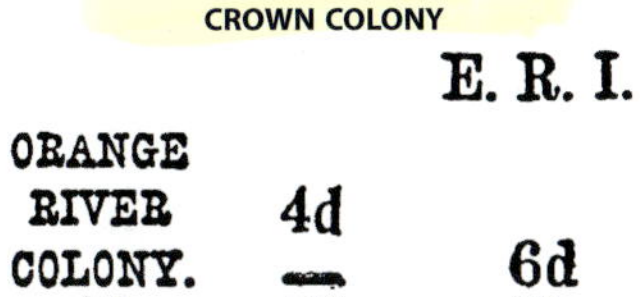

(**34**) (**35**) (**36**)

1900 (10 Aug)–**02**. Nos. 58, 59*a* and 63*a* of Cape of Good Hope (wmk Cabled Anchor. P 14) optd with T **34** by W. A. Richards and Sons, Cape Town.

133		½d. green (13.10.00)	50	10
		a. No stop	9·50	20·00
		b. Opt double	£650	£700
134		1d. carmine (May 1902)	2·00	10
		a. No stop	20·00	25·00
135		2½d. ultramarine	2·75	35
		a. No stop	75·00	75·00
133/5 *Set of 3*			4·75	50

In the ½d. and 2½d., the "no stop" after "COLONY" variety was the first stamp in the left lower pane. In the 1d. it is the twelfth stamp in the right lower pane on which the stop was present at the beginning of the printing but became damaged and soon failed to print.

1902 (14 Feb). Surch with T **35** by "Bloemfontein Express".

136		4d. on 6d. on 6d. blue (No. 120) (R.)	1·50	1·50
		a. No stop after "R"	38·00	50·00
		b. No stop after "I"	£1200	
		c. Surch on No. 130 (Thick "V")	2·00	6·50
		ca. Inverted "1" for "I"	6·50	17·00

1902 (Aug). Surch with T **36**.

137	**1**	6d. on 6d. blue	4·75	15·00
		a. Surch double, one inverted		
		b. Wide space between "6" and "d" (R. 4/2)	60·00	90·00

(**37**)

38 King Edward VII, Springbok and Gnu

1902 (Sept). Surch with T **37**.

138	**1**	1s. on 5s. green (O.)	9·00	22·00
		a. Thick "V"	15·00	45·00
		b. Short top to "5"	70·00	85·00
		c. Surch double	£1000	

(Typo D.L.R.)

1903 (3 Feb)–**04**. Wmk Crown CA. P 14.

139	**38**	½d. yellow-green (6.7.03)	9·00	2·00
		w. Wmk inverted	£190	95·00
140		1d. scarlet	6·50	10
		w. Wmk inverted	£190	75·00
141		2d. brown (6.7.03)	8·50	80
142		2½d. bright blue (6.7.03)	4·00	80
143		3d. mauve (6.7.03)	9·50	1·00
144		4d. scarlet and sage-green (6.7.03)	38·00	4·50
		a. "IOSTAGE" for "POSTAGE"	£950	£450
145		6d. scarlet and mauve (6.7.03)	8·50	1·00
146		1s. scarlet and bistre (6.7.03)	40·00	2·25
147		5s. blue and brown (31.10.04)	£100	27·00
139/47 *Set of 9*			£200	35·00
139s/47s Optd "SPECIMEN" *Set of 9*			£200	

No. 144a occurs on R. 10/2 of the upper left pane.

The 2d. exists from coils constructed from normal sheets for use in stamp machines introduced in 1911.

Several of the above values are found with the overprint "C.S.A.R.", in black, for use by the Central South African Railways. Examples also exist perforated "CSAR" or "NGR".

1905 (Nov)–**09**. Wmk Mult Crown CA. P 14.

148	**38**	½d. yellow-green (28.7.07)	13·00	75
149		1d. scarlet	9·50	30
150		4d. scarlet and sage-green (8.11.07)	4·50	4·25
		a. "IOSTAGE" for "POSTAGE"	£180	£160
151		1s. scarlet and bistre (2.09)	70·00	21·00
148/51 *Set of 4*			85·00	24·00

POSTCARD STAMPS

From 1889 onwards the Orange Free State Post Office sold postcards franked with adhesives as Type **1**, some subsequently surcharged, over which the State Arms had been overprinted.

There are five known dies of the Arms overprint which can be identified as follows:

(a) Shield without flags. Three cows (two lying down, one standing) at left. Point of shield complete.
(b) Shield with flags. Four cows (two lying down, two standing) at left (*illustrated*).
(c) Shield with flags. Three cows (one lying down, two standing) at left.
(d) Shield without flags. Three cows (one lying down, two standing) at left.
(e) Shield without flags. Three cows (two lying down, one standing) at left. Point of shield broken.

There are also other differences between the dies.

PRICES. Those in the left-hand column are for unused examples on complete postcard; those on the right for used examples off card. Examples used on postcard are worth more.

1889 (Feb). No. 2 (placed sideways on card) optd Shield Type (a).

P1	**1**	1d. red-brown	95·00	42·00
		a. Optd Shield Type (b)	35·00	8·00

1891 (Aug). No. 48 optd Shield Type (b).

P2	**1**	½d. chestnut	6·00	2·00
		a. Optd Shield Type (c)	14·00	4·50
		b. Optd Shield Type (d)	6·50	2·50
		c. Optd Shield Type (e)	15·00	5·50

1892 (June). No. 54 optd Shield Type (b).

P3	**1**	1d. on 3d. ultramarine	95·00	50·00
		a. Optd Shield Type (c)	16·00	3·50

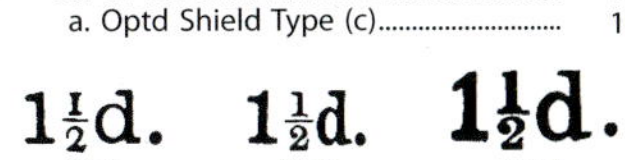

(P **1**) (P **2**) (P **3**)

1892 (Sept)–**95**. Nos. 50/1 optd Shield Type (b) or (d) (No. P6) and surch with Types P **1/3**.

P4	**1**	1½d. on 2d. bright mauve (Type P **1**) (11.92)	8·50	4·00
P5		1½d. on 2d. bright mauve (Type P **2**) (9.93)	6·50	2·00
		a. Surch inverted		
P6		1½d. on 2d. bright mauve (Type P **3**) (R.) (6.95)	14·00	4·75
P7		1½d. on 3d. ultramarine (Type P **1**)	8·00	2·50

No. P5a shows the stamp affixed to the card upside down with the surcharge correctly positioned in relation to the card.

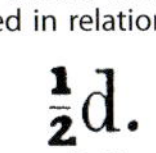

(P **4**)

1895 (Aug). No. 48 optd Shield Type (e) and surch with Type P4.

P8	**1**	½d. on ½d. chestnut	14·00	3·00

1½d. **1½d.**
(P **5**) (P **6**)

1895 (Dec)–**97**. No. 50 optd Shield Type (e) and surch with Types P **5/6**.

P9	**1**	1½d. on 2d. bright mauve (Type P **5**)	7·00	3·00
P10		1½d. on 2d. bright mauve (Type P **6**) (12.97)	8·00	3·50
P11		1½d. on 2d. bright mauve (as Type P **6**, but without stop) (12.97)	8·00	3·50

1897 (Mar). No. 85 optd Shield Type (d).

P12	**1**	½d. orange	14·00	2·00
		a. Optd Shield Type (e)	15·00	3·00

V.R.I.
(P **7**)

1900. Nos. P10/11 optd as T **31/2** or with Type P**7**.

P13	**1**	1½d. on 2d. bright mauve (No. P10) (T **31**)	30·00	6·00
P14		1½d. on 2d. bright mauve (No. P11) (T **31**)	30·00	6·00
P15		1½d. on 2d. bright mauve (No. P10) (T **32**)	30·00	6·00
P16		1½d. on 2d. bright mauve (No. P11) (T **32**)	30·00	6·00
P17		1½d. on 2d. bright mauve (No. P10) (Type P **7**)	42·00	11·00
P18		1½d. on 2d. bright mauve (No. P11) (Type P **7**)	42·00	11·00

POLICE FRANK STAMPS

The following frank stamps were issued to members of the Orange Free State Mounted Police ("Rijdende Dienst Macht") for use on official correspondence.

PF **1** (eight ornaments at left and right)

PF **2**

1896. P 12.

PF1	PF **1**	(–) Black	£225	£300

No. PF1 was printed in horizontal strips of 5 surrounded by wide margins.

1898. As Type PF **1**, but with nine ornaments at left and right. P 12.

PF2	(–) Black	£150	£200

No. PF2 was printed in blocks of 4 (2×2) surrounded by wide margins.

1899. P 12.

PF3	PF **2**	(–) Black/*yellow*	£130	£150
		a. No stop after "V"	£550	

No. PF3 was printed in sheets of 24 (6×4) with the edges of the sheet imperforate. It is believed that they were produced from a setting of 8 (2×4) repeated three times. No. PF3a occurs on R. 1/1 of the setting.

Examples of No. PF3 are known postmarked as late as 28 April 1900. The O.F.S. Mounted Police were disbanded by the British authorities at the end of the following month.

MILITARY FRANK STAMP

M **1**

(Typeset Curling & Co, Bloemfontein)

1899 (15 Oct). P 12.

M1	M **1**	(–) Black/*bistre-yellow*	24·00	55·00

Supplies of No. M1 were issued to members of the Orange Free State army on active service during the Second Boer War. To pass free through the O.F.S. fieldpost system, letters had to be franked with No. M1 or initialled by the appropriate unit commander. The franks were in use between October 1899 and February 1900.

No. M1 was printed in sheets of 20 (5×4) using a setting of five different types in a horizontal row. The colour in the paper runs in water.

Typeset forgeries can be identified by the appearance of 17 pearls, instead of the 16 of the originals, in the top and bottom frames. Forgeries produced by lithography omit the stops after "BRIEF" and "FRANKO".

FISCAL STAMPS USED FOR POSTAGE

The following were issued in December 1877 (Nos. F1 and F3 in 1882) and were authorised for postal use between 1882 and 1886.

F **1**

F **2**

F **3**

(Typo D.L.R.)

1882–86. P 14.

F1	F **1**	6d. pearl-grey	17·00	18·00
F2		6d. purple-brown	50·00	32·00
F3	F **2**	1s. purple-brown	20·00	21·00
F4		1s. pearl-grey	75·00	80·00
F5		1s.6d. blue	35·00	26·00
F6		2s. magenta	35·00	26·00
F7		3s. chestnut	40·00	75·00
F8		4s. grey		
F9		5s. rose	40·00	32·00
F10		6s. green	—	95·00
F11		7s. violet		
F12		10s. orange	90·00	50·00
F13	F **3**	£1 purple	£100	50·00
		a. "VRY-STAAT" (R. 1/5)		
F14		£2 red-brown	£120	£110
		a. "VRY-STAAT" (R. 1/5)		
F14*b*		£4 carmine		
		ba. "VRY-STAAT" (R. 1/5)		
F15		£5 green	£170	80·00
		a. "VRY-STAAT" (R. 1/5)		

Die proofs of Type F **3** showed a hyphen in error between "VRY" and "STAAT". This was removed from each impression on the plate before printing, but was missed on R. 1/5.

A fiscally used example of No. F2 exists showing "ZES PENCE" double, one inverted.

The 8s. yellow was prepared but we have no evidence of its use postally without surcharge Type F **4**.

ZES PENCE.
(F **4**)

1886. Surch with Type F **4**.

F16	F **2**	6d. on 4s. grey		
F17		6d. on 8s. yellow	£475	

Postage stamps overprinted for use as Telegraph stamps and used postally are omitted as it is impossible to say with certainty which stamps were genuinely used for postal purposes.

Orange Free State became a province of the Union of South Africa on 31 May 1910.

VI. TRANSVAAL

(*formerly* South African Republic)

From 1852 mail from the Transvaal was forwarded to the Cape of Good Hope, via the Orange Free State, by a post office at Potchefstroom. In 1859 the Volksraad voted to set up a regular postal service and arrangements were made for letters sent to the Cape and for overseas to be franked with Cape of Good Hope stamps.

The Potchefstroom postmaster placed his first order for these on 23 August 1859 and examples of all four triangular values are known postmarked there. From 1868 mail via the Orange Free State required franking with their issues also.

A similar arrangement covering mail sent overseas via Natal was in operation from 9 July 1873 until the first British Occupation. Such letters carried combinations of Transvaal stamps, paying the rate to Natal, and Natal issues for the overseas postage. Such Natal stamps were sold, but not postmarked, by Transvaal post offices.

PRICES FOR STAMPS ON COVER

Nos. 1/6 are rare used on cover.

Nos. 7/80	*from* × 20
Nos. 86/155	*from* × 3
Nos. 156/62	*from* × 6
Nos. 163/9	*from* × 5
Nos. 170/225	*from* × 10
Nos. 226/34	*from* × 20
Nos. 235/7	—
Nos. 238/43	*from* × 12
Nos. 244/55	*from* × 4
Nos. 256/7	*from* × 6
Nos. 258/9	—
Nos. 260/76	*from* × 20
Nos. F1/5	*from* × 5
Nos. D1/7	*from* × 20

The issues for Pietersburg, Lydenburg, Rustenburg, Schweizer Renecke and Wolmaransstad are very rare when on cover.

1 (Eagle with spread wings)

2

3

(Typo Adolph Otto, Gustrow, Mecklenburg-Schwerin)

1870 (1 May). Thin paper, clear and distinct impressions.

(a) Imperf

1	**1**	1d. brown-lake	£450	
		a. Orange-red	£600	£600
2		6d. bright ultramarine	£250	£250
		a. Pale ultramarine	£275	£275
3		1s. deep green	£750	£750
		a. *Tête-bêche* (pair)		

(b) Fine roulette, 15½ to 16

4	**1**	1d. brown-lake	£150	
		a. Brick-red	£130	
		b. Orange-red	£130	
		c. Vermilion	£130	
5		6d. bright ultramarine	£110	£110
		a. Pale ultramarine	£120	£120
6		1s. deep green	£250	£275
		a. Yellow-green	£190	£180
		b. Emerald-green	£150	£150

Examples of Nos. 1/6 may have been sold to dealers at some stage between their arrival in Transvaal during August 1869 and the sale of stamps to the public for postal purposes on 1 May 1870.

PLATES. The German printings of the 1d., 6d. and 1s. in Type **1** were from two pairs of plates, each pair printing sheets of 80 in two panes of five horizontal rows of eight.

One pair of plates, used for Nos. 4*a*, 4*c*, 5*a* and 6/*a*, produced stamps spaced 1¼ to 1½ mm apart with the rouletting close to the design on all four sides. The 1d. from these "narrow" plates shows a gap in the outer frame line at the bottom right-hand corner. The second pair, used for Nos. 1/3, 4, 4*b*, 5/*a* and 6*b*, had 2½ to 3½ mm between the stamps. These "wide" plates were sent to the Transvaal in 1869 and were used there to produce either single or double pane printings until 1883.

The 6d. and 1s. "wide" plates each had an inverted *cliché*. When printed these occurred on right-hand pane R. 4/1 of the 6d. and right-hand pane R. 1/1 of the 1s. These were never corrected and resulted in *tête-bêche* pairs of these values as late as 1883.

REPRINTS AND IMITATIONS. A number of unauthorised printings were made of these stamps by the German printer. Many of these can be identified by differences in the central arms, unusual colours or, in the case of the 1d., by an extra frame around the numeral tablets at top.

Genuine stamps always show the "D" of "EENDRAGT" higher than the remainder of the word, have no break in the border above "DR" and depict the flagstaff at bottom right, behind "MAGT", stopping short of the central shield. They also show the eagle's eye as a clear white circle. On the forgeries the eye is often blurred.

The most difficult of the reprints to detect is the 1s. yellow-green which was once regarded as genuine, but was subsequently identified, by J. N. Luff in *The Philatelic Record* 1911–12, as coming from an unauthorised plate of four. Stamps from this plate show either a white dot between "EEN" and "SHILLING" or a white flaw below the wagon pole.

(Typo M. J. Viljoen, Pretoria)

1870 (1 May–4 July).

I. Thin gummed paper from Germany. Impressions coarse and defective

(a) Imperf

8	**1**	1d. dull rose-red	£100	
		a. Reddish pink	85·00	
		b. Carmine-red	75·00	85·00
9		6d. dull ultramarine	£350	75·00
		a. *Tête-bêche* (pair)		

(b) Fine roulette, 15½ to 16

10	**1**	1d. carmine-red	£750	£300
11		6d. dull ultramarine	£225	£100
		a. Imperf between (vert pair)	£900	

(c) Wide roulette, 6½

12	**1**	1d. carmine-red	—	£1000

II. Thick, hard paper with thin yellow smooth gum (No. 15) or yellow streaky gum (others)

(a) Imperf

13	**1**	1d. pale rose-red	80·00	
		a. Carmine-red	80·00	90·00
14		1s. yellow-green	£140	£130
		a. *Tête-bêche* (pair)	£22000	
		b. Bisected (6d.) (on cover)	†	£2000

(b) Fine roulette, 15½ to 16

15	**1**	1d. carmine-red (24 May)	£100	
16		6d. ultramarine (10 May)	£120	£120
		a. *Tête-bêche* (pair)	£27000	£20000
17		1s. yellow-green	£700	£700

III. Medium paper, blotchy heavy printing and whitish gum. Fine roulette 15½ to 16 (4 July)

18	**1**	1d. rose-red	80·00	95·00
		a. Carmine-red	60·00	65·00
		b. Crimson. From over-inked plate	£150	£130
19		6d. ultramarine	£110	75·00
		a. *Tête-bêche* (pair)		
		b. Deep ultramarine. From over-inked plate	£475	£170
20		1s. deep green	£180	85·00
		a. From over-inked plate	£550	£180

The rouletting machine producing the wide 6½ gauge was not introduced until 1875.

Nos. 18*b*, 19*b* and 20a were printed from badly over-inked plates giving heavy blobby impressions.

(Typo J. P. Borrius, Potchefstroom)

1870 (Sept)–**71**. Stout paper, but with colour often showing through, whitish gum.

(a) Imperf

21	**1**	1d. black	£150	£130

(b) Fine roulette, 15½ to 16

22	**1**	1d. black	24·00	32·00
		a. Grey-black	24·00	32·00
23		6d. blackish blue (7.71)	£150	65·00
		a. Dull blue	£110	85·00

(Typo Adolph Otto, Gustrow, Mecklenburg-Schwerin)

1871 (July). Thin paper, clear and distinct impressions. Fine roulette, 15½ to 16.

24	**2**	3d. pale reddish lilac	80·00	90·00
		a. Deep lilac	95·00	£100
		b. Vert laid paper		

No. 24 and later printings in the Transvaal were produced from a pair of plates in the same format as the 1869 issue. All genuine stamps have a small dot on the left leg of the eagle.

Imperforate examples in the issued shade, without the dot on eagle's leg, had been previously supplied by the printer, probably as essays, but were not issued for postal purposes. (*Price* £550 *unused*). They also exist *tête-bêche* (*Price for un pair* £3250).

Imperforate and rouletted stamps in other colours are reprints.

(Typo J. P. Borrius, Potchefstroom)

1872–74. Fine roulette, 15½ to 16.

(a) Thin transparent paper

25	**1**	1d. black	£225	£650
26		1d. bright carmine	£180	60·00
27		6d. ultramarine	£140	48·00

28		1s. green	£160	65·00

(b) Thinnish opaque paper, clear printing (Dec 1872)

29	1	1d. reddish pink	75·00	45·00
		a. Carmine-red	75·00	45·00
30	2	3d. grey-lilac	£120	55·00
31	1	6d. ultramarine	75·00	32·00
		a. Pale ultramarine	85·00	35·00
32		1s. yellow-green	90·00	45·00
		a. Green	90·00	45·00
		aa. Bisected (6d.) (on cover)	†	£2000

(c) Thickish wove paper (1873–74)

33	1	1d. dull rose	£400	80·00
		a. Brownish rose	£500	£120
		b. Printed on both sides		
34		6d. milky blue	£160	55·00
		a. Deep dull blue	95·00	45·00
		aa. Imperf (pair)	£750	
		ab. Imperf between (horiz pair)	£800	
		ac. Wide roulette 6½		

(d) Very thick dense paper (1873–74)

35		1d. dull rose	£600	£140
		a. Brownish rose	£450	£120
36		6d. dull ultramarine	£200	70·00
		a. Bright ultramarine	£225	70·00
37		1s. yellow-green	£900	£700

(Typo P. Davis & Son, Pietermaritzburg)

1874 (Sept). P 12½.

(a) Thin transparent paper

38	1	1d. pale brick-red	£140	45·00
		a. Brownish red	£140	45·00
39		6d. deep blue	£180	65·00

(b) Thicker opaque paper

40	1	1d. pale red	£170	80·00
41		6d. blue	£170	60·00
		a. Imperf between (pair)		
		b. Deep blue	£170	60·00

(Typo Adolph Otto, Gustrow, Mecklenburg-Schwerin)

1874 (Oct). Thin smooth paper, clearly printed. Fine roulette 15½ to 16.

42	3	6d. bright ultramarine	65·00	26·00
		a. Bisected (3d.) (on cover)	†	£1500

Stamps in other shades of blue, brown or red, often on other types of paper, are reprints.

(Typo J. F. Celliers on behalf of Stamp Commission, Pretoria)

1875 (29 Apr)–**77**.

I. Very thin, soft opaque (semi-pelure) paper

(a) Imperf

43	1	1d. orange-red	£140	55·00
		a. Pin-perf	£800	£375
44	2	3d. lilac	£100	55·00
45	1	6d. blue	95·00	45·00
		a. Milky blue	£140	48·00
		aa. *Tête-bêche* (pair)	£16000	
		ab. Pin-perf	—	£375

(b) Fine roulette, 15½ to 16

46	1	1d. orange-red	£550	£150
47	2	3d. lilac	£600	£160
48	1	6d. blue	£550	£150

(c) Wide roulette, 6½

49	1	1d. orange-red	—	£225
50	2	3d. lilac	£750	£325
51	1	6d. blue	—	£160
		a. Bright blue	—	£160
		b. Milky blue	—	£160

II. Very thin, hard transparent (pelure) paper (1875–76)

(a) Imperf

52	1	1d. brownish red	65·00	35·00
		a. Orange-red	55·00	27·00
		b. Dull red	60·00	55·00
		ba. Pin-perf	£650	£400
53	2	3d. lilac	65·00	45·00
		a. Pin-perf	—	£425
		b. Deep lilac	75·00	45·00
54	1	6d. pale blue	65·00	55·00
		a. Blue	65·00	45·00
		ab. *Tête-bêche* (pair)		
		ac. Pin-perf	—	£375
		b. Deep blue	70·00	48·00

(b) Fine roulette 15½ to 16

55	1	1d. orange-red	£375	£130
		a. Brown-red	£375	£130
56	2	3d. lilac	£425	£140
57	1	6d. blue	£170	£100
		a. Deep blue	£170	£120

(c) Wide roulette, 6½

58	1	1d. orange-red	£1000	£200
		a. Bright red	—	£180
59	2	3d. lilac	£900	£250
60	1	6d. deep blue	£1000	£110

III. Stout hard-surfaced paper with smooth, nearly white, gum (1876)

(a) Imperf

61	1	1d. bright red	30·00	23·00
62	2	3d. lilac	£400	£130
63	1	6d. bright blue	£110	26·00
		a. *Tête-bêche* (pair)		
		b. Pale blue	£110	26·00
		c. Deep blue (deep brown gum)	65·00	22·00
		ca. *Tête-bêche* (pair)	—	£18000

(b) Fine roulette, 15½ to 16

64	1	1d. bright red	£425	£160
65	2	3d. lilac	£375	
66	1	6d. bright blue	£800	£110
		a. Deep blue (deep brown gum)	£650	£300

(c) Wide roulette, 6½

67	1	1d. bright red	£650	£160
68		6d. pale blue	—	£225
		a. Deep blue (deep brown gum)	£700	£275

IV. Coarse, soft white paper (1876–77)

(a) Imperf

69	1	1d. brick-red	£150	60·00
70		6d. deep blue	£225	£550
		a. Milky blue	£375	£110
71		1s. yellow-green	£450	£140
		a. Bisected (6d.) (on cover)	†	£1700

(b) Fine roulette, 15½ to 16

72	1	1d. brick-red	—	£400
73		6d. deep blue	—	£170
74		1s. yellow-green	£750	£375

(c) Wide roulette, 6½

75	1	1d. brick-red	—	£475
76		6d. deep blue	—	£1200
77		1s. yellow-green	—	£1300

(d) Fine × wide roulette

78	1	1d. brick-red	£750	£375

V. Hard, thick, coarse yellowish paper (1876–77)

79	1	1d. brick-red (imperf)	—	£400
80		1d. brick-red (*wide roulette*)	—	£500

The pin-perforated stamps have various gauges and were probably produced privately or by one or more post offices other than Pretoria.

On Nos. 63c/ca, 66*a* and 68*a* the brown gum used was so intense that it caused staining of the paper which is still visible on used examples.

See also Nos. 171/4.

FIRST BRITISH OCCUPATION

By 1876 conditions in the Transvaal had deteriorated and the country was faced by economic collapse, native wars and internal dissension. In early 1877 Sir Theophilus Shepstone, appointed Special Commissioner to the South African Republic by the British Government, arrived in Pretoria and on 12 April annexed the Transvaal with the acquiesence of at least part of the European population.

V. R. V. R.

TRANSVAAL. TRANSVAAL.

(4) (5)

T **4** is the normal overprint, but Setting I No. 11 (R. 2/3) has a wider-spaced overprint as T **5**.

1877 (Apr). Optd with T **4** in red.

(a) Imperf

86	2	3d. lilac (*semi-pelure*) (No. 44)	£1400	£325
		a. Opt Type **5**		
87		3d. lilac (*pelure*) (No. 53)	£1400	£200
		a. Opt Type **5**	£7500	£2500
		b. Opt on back	£3500	£3500
		c. Opt double, in red and in black	£6500	
88	1	6d. milky blue (No. 70)	£1700	£200
		a. Opt inverted	—	£5000
		b. Opt double	£4750	£1100
		c. Opt Type **5**	£8000	£3000
		d. Deep blue	—	£275
89		1s. yellow-green (No. 71)	£700	£200
		a. Bisected (6d.) (on cover)	†	£2000
		b. Opt inverted	—	£4500
		c. Opt Type **5**	£5000	£1500
		d. *Tête-bêche* (pair)		

(b) Fine roulette, 15½ to 16

90	2	3d. lilac (*pelure*) (No. 56)	—	£1600
91	1	6d. deep blue (No. 73)	—	£1700
92		1s. yellow-green (No. 74)	£18000	£750
		a. Opt Type **5**		

No.	Type	Description	Unused	Used
		(c) Wide roulette, 6½		
93	2	3d. lilac (*pelure*) (No. 59)	—	£2250
		a. Opt Type **5**		
94	1	6d. deep blue (No. 76)	—	£2250
		a. Opt Type **5**		
95		1s. yellow-green (No. 77)	£4000	£2000
		a. Opt inverted	—	£6000

Nos. 88a, 89b and 95a occurred on the inverted *cliché* of the basic stamps.

1877 (June). Optd with T **4** in black.

No.	Type	Description	Unused	Used
		I. Very thin, hard transparent (pelure) paper		
96	1	1d. orange-red (imperf) (No. 52*a*)	£300	£130
97		1d. orange-red (*fine roulette*) (No. 55)..	—	£1000
		II. Stout hard-surfaced paper with smooth, nearly white, gum		
98	1	1d. bright red (imperf) (No. 61)	32·00	25·00
		a. Opt inverted	£550	£500
		b. Opt Type **5**	£750	£800
99		1d. bright red (*fine roulette*) (No. 64)....	£200	55·00
		a. Opt inverted		
		b. Opt double	—	£1100
		c. Imperf between (horiz pair)	£850	
100		1d. bright red (*wide roulette*) (No. 67)..	£700	£200
100*a*		1d. bright red (*fine × wide roulette*) (No. 78)		
		III. New ptgs on coarse, soft white paper		
		(a) Imperf		
101	1	1d. brick-red (5.77)	32·00	25·00
		a. Opt double	—	£1200
		b. Opt Type **5**	£800	
102	2	3d. lilac	£110	50·00
		a. Opt inverted		
		b. Deep lilac	£180	90·00
103	1	6d. dull blue	£130	35·00
		a. Opt double	£3500	£2000
		b. Opt inverted	£1400	£180
		d. Opt Type **5**	—	£1100
		da. Opt Type **5** inverted		
		e. Blue (bright to deep)	£180	32·00
		ea. Bright blue, opt inverted	—	£500
		f. Pin-perf	—	£600
104		1s. yellow-green	£150	65·00
		a. Opt inverted	£1300	£250
		b. *Tête-bêche* (pair)	£22000	£22000
		c. Opt Type **5**	£5000	£1500
		d. Bisected (6d.) (on cover)	†	£1500
		(b) Fine roulette, 15½ to 16		
105	1	1d. brick-red	95·00	85·00
		a. Imperf horiz (vert strip of 3)		
		b. Imperf between (horiz pair)	†	£600
106	2	3d. lilac	£250	75·00
107	1	6d. dull blue	£300	65·00
		a. Opt inverted	—	£750
		b. Opt Type **5**	£5000	
108		1s. yellow-green	£325	£100
		a. Opt inverted	£1300	£500
		b. Opt Type **5**	—	£2750
		(c) Wide roulette, 6½		
109	1	1d. brick-red	£700	£160
		a. Opt Type **5**	—	£1100
110	2	3d. lilac	—	£800
111	1	6d. dull blue	—	£1300
		a. Opt inverted	—	£4250
112		1s. yellow-green	£550	£150
		a. Opt inverted	£1700	£650

1877 (31 Aug). Optd with T **4** in black.

No.	Type	Description	Unused	Used
113	1	6d. blue/*rose* (imperf)	£110	55·00
		a. Bisected (3d.) (on cover)		
		b. Opt inverted	£130	55·00
		c. *Tête-bêche* (pair)		
		d. Opt omitted	£3500	£2500
114		6d. blue/*rose* (*fine roulette*)	£275	75·00
		a. Opt inverted	£600	75·00
		b. *Tête-bêche* (pair)		
		c. Opt omitted		
		d. Bisected (3d.) (on cover)		
115		6d. blue/*rose* (*wide roulette*)		
		a. Opt inverted	—	£700
		b. Opt omitted		

Nos. 113/15 were overprinted from a setting of 40 which was applied upright to one pane in each sheet and inverted on the other.

(**6**)

(**7**)

1877 (28 Sept)–**79**. Optd with T **6** in black.

No.	Type	Description	Unused	Used
		(a) Imperf		
116	1	1d. red/*blue*	65·00	32·00
		a. "Transvral" (Right pane R. 2/3)	£5500	£2500
		b. Opt double	£4000	
		c. Opt inverted	£850	£425
		d. Opt omitted		
117		1d. red/*orange* (6.12.77)	28·00	22·00
		a. Pin-perf		
		b. Printed both sides		
		c. Opt double	£3500	
		d. Optd with Type **7** (15.4.78)	75·00	48·00
		e. Pair. Nos. 117 and 117d	£200	
118	2	3d. mauve/*buff* (24.10.77)	70·00	29·00
		a. Opt inverted	—	£750
		b. Pin-perf		
		c. Bisected (1½d) (on cover)	†	—
		d. Optd with Type **7** (15.4.78)	85·00	38·00
		da. Pin-perf	£750	£750
		e. Pair. Nos. 118 and 118d	£325	
119		3d. mauve/*green* (18.4.79)	£200	45·00
		a. Pin-perf		
		b. Opt inverted	—	£2000
		c. Opt double		
		d. Printed both sides	†	—
		e. Optd with Type **7**	£160	38·00
		ea. Opt inverted	—	£2000
		eb. Printed both sides	—	£1000
		f. Opt omitted	—	£3500
		g. Pair. Nos. 119 and 119e	£700	
120	1	6d. blue/*green* (27.11.77)	£120	40·00
		a. Deep blue/green	£130	42·00
		b. Broken "Y" for "V" in "V.R." (Left pane R. 3/7)	—	£750
		c. Small "v" in "Transvaal" (Left pane R. 5/2)	—	£750
		d. "V..R." (Right pane R. 3/4)	—	£750
		e. *Tête-bêche* (pair)	—	£19000
		f. Opt inverted	—	£1200
		g. Pin-perf		
		h. Bisected (3d.) (on cover)	†	—
121		6d. blue/*blue* (20.3.78)	80·00	29·00
		a. *Tête-bêche* (pair)		
		b. Opt inverted	—	£1200
		c. Opt omitted	—	£2250
		d. Opt double	—	£3250
		e. Pin-perf		
		f. Bisected (3d.) (on cover)	†	£850
		g. Optd with Type **7**	£160	32·00
		ga. *Tête-bêche* (pair)	£16000	
		gb. Opt inverted	—	£750
		gc. Bisected (3d.) (on cover)	†	—
		h. Pair. Nos. 121 and 121g	£500	
		(b) Fine roulette, 15½ to 16		
122	1	1d. red/*blue*	£120	40·00
		a. "Transvral" (Right pane R. 2/3)	—	£3000
123		1d. red/*orange* (6.12.77)	42·00	29·00
		a. Imperf between (pair)	£600	
		b. Optd with Type **7** (15.4.78)	£180	£130
		c. Pair. Nos. 123 and 123b	£475	
124	2	3d. mauve/*buff* (24.10.77)	£120	29·00
		a. Imperf horiz (vert pair)	£800	
		b. Opt inverted	—	£3000
		c. Optd with Type **7** (15.4.78)	£190	£120
		ca. Imperf between (pair)		
		d. Pair. Nos. 124 and 124c	£750	
125		3d. mauve/*green* (18.4.79)	£700	£160
		a. Optd with Type **7**	£700	£160
		b. Pair. Nos. 125 and 125a		
126	1	6d. blue/*green* (27.11.77)	£100	29·00
		a. "V..R" (Right pane R. 3/4)	—	£1200
		b. *Tête-bêche* (pair)		
		c. Opt inverted	—	£700
		d. Opt omitted	—	£4000
		e. Bisected (3d.) (on cover)	†	£750
127		6d. blue/*blue* (20.3.78)	£300	60·00
		a. Opt inverted	—	£950
		b. Opt omitted	—	£3500
		c. Imperf between (pair)		
		d. Bisected (3d.) (on cover)	†	£800
		e. Optd with Type **7**	£450	£120
		ea. Opt inverted	—	£1200
		(c) Wide roulette, 6¼		
128	1	1d. red/*orange* (15.4.78)	£300	£110
		a. Optd with Type **7**	—	£325
129	2	3d. mauve/*buff* (24.10.77)	—	£110
		a. Optd with Type **7** (15.4.78)	—	£375
130		3d. mauve/*green* (18.4.79)	£700	£300
		a. Optd with Type **7**	—	£325
131	1	6d. blue/*green* (27.11.77)	—	£1200
132		6d. blue/*blue* (20.3.78)	—	£325
		a. Opt inverted		
		b. Optd with Type **7**	—	£375
		ba. Opt inverted		

(d) Fine × wide roulette

No.	Type	Description	Unused	Used
132*c*	**1**	1d. red/*orange*	£750	

Nos. 116/32*c* were overprinted from various settings covering sheets of 80 or panes of 40 (8×5). Initially these settings contained Type **6** only, but from March 1878 settings also contained examples of Type **7**. Details of these mixed settings are as follows:

1d. red/*orange* (sheets of 80): all Type **6** except for 16 Type **7**.
3d. mauve/*buff* (panes of 40): 16 Type **7**.
3d. mauve/*green* (panes of 40): uncertain, some panes at least contained 27 Type **7**.
6d. blue/*blue* (sheets of 80): either 24 or 27 Type **7**.

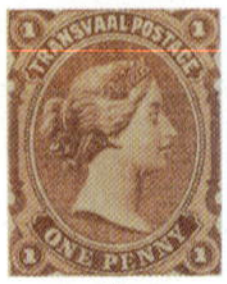

9

(Recess B.W.)

1878 (26 Aug)–**80**. P 14, 14½.

No.	Type	Description	Unused	Used
133	**9**	½d. vermilion (1.9.80)	27·00	90·00
134		1d. pale red-brown	17·00	5·50
		a. Brown-red	17·00	5·00
135		3d. dull rose (25 Nov)	23·00	8·00
		a. Claret	28·00	9·00
136		4d. sage-green	32·00	9·00
137		6d. olive-black (25 Nov)	15·00	8·00
		a. Black-brown	17·00	6·00
138		1s. green (25 Nov)	£140	48·00
139		2s. blue (25 Nov)	£225	85·00

The ½d. is printed on paper bearing the sheet watermark 'R TURNER/CHAFFORD MILLS' in double-lined block capitals. Other values are on unwatermarked paper.

The above prices are for examples perforated on all four sides. Stamps from margins of sheets, with perforations absent on one or two sides, can be supplied for about 30% less.

The used price quoted for No. 139 is for an example with telegraphic cancel, a 23.5 mm circular datestamp of Pretoria (or more rarely Heidelberg or Standerton). Postally used examples are worth much more.

1 Penny (10) 1 Penny (11) 1 Penny (12)

1 Penny (13) 1 Penny (14)

1 PENNY (15) *1 Penny* (16)

1879 (22 Apr). No. 137a surch with T **10** to **16** in black.

No.	Type	Description	Unused	Used
140	**10**	1d. on 6d.	95·00	45·00
		a. Surch in red	£300	£170
141	**11**	1d. on 6d.	£250	85·00
		a. Surch in red	£700	£375
142	**12**	1d. on 6d.	£250	85·00
		a. Surch in red	£700	£375
143	**13**	1d. on 6d.	£110	55·00
		a. Surch double		
		b. Surch in red	£350	£190
144	**14**	1d. on 6d.	£650	£170
		a. Surch in red	£6500	£1700
145	**15**	1d. on 6d.	55·00	25·00
		a. Surch in red	£180	85·00
146	**16**	1d. on 6d.	£225	80·00
		a. Surch in red	£650	£350

Nos. 140/6 were surcharged from a setting of 60 containing eleven examples of Type **10**, four of Type **11**, four of Type **12**, nine of Type **13**, two of Type **14** (although there may have been only one in the first two ptgs), twenty-five of Type **15** and five of Type **16**.

The red surcharges may have been produced first.

V. R. / Transvaal (16a)

V. R. / Transvaal — Small "T" (R. 2/8, 3/8, 4/8, 5/8 on right pane of 1d. and left pane of 3d.)

1879 (Aug–Sept). Optd with T **16a** in black.

(a) Imperf

No.	Type	Description	Unused	Used
147	**1**	1d. red/*yellow*	55·00	40·00
		a. Small "T"	£350	£225
		b. Red/orange	55·00	32·00
		ba. Small "T"	£300	£180
148	**2**	3d. mauve/*green* (Sept)	48·00	27·00
		a. Small "T"	£275	£110
149		3d. mauve/*blue* (Sept)	55·00	32·00
		a. Small "T"	£300	£100
		(b) Fine roulette 15½ to 16		
150	**1**	1d. red/*yellow*	£375	£225
		a. Small "T"	£1100	£700
		b. Red/orange	£800	£400
		ba. Small "T"	£2250	
151	**2**	3d. mauve/*green*	£800	£275
		a. Small "T"	—	£900
152		3d. mauve/*blue*	—	£200
		a. Small "T"	—	£700
		(c) Wide roulette 6½		
153	**1**	1d. red/*yellow*	£750	£700
		a. Small "T"		
		b. Red/orange	£1600	£1300
154	**2**	3d. mauve/*green*	£1100	£700
		a. Small "T"		
155		3d. mauve/*blue*	—	£800
		(d) Pin-perf about 17		
156	**1**	1d. red/*yellow*	—	£800
		a. Small "T"		
157	**2**	3d. mauve/*blue*	—	£1300

SECOND REPUBLIC

Following the first Boer War the independence of the South African Republic was recognised by the Convention of Pretoria from 8 August 1881.

Nos. 133/9 remained valid and some values were available for postage until 1885.

EEN PENNY

(17)

1882 (11 Aug). No. 136 surch with T **17**.

No.	Type	Description	Unused	Used
170	**9**	1d. on 4d. sage-green	20·00	7·00
		a. Surch inverted	£325	£200

Used examples of a similar, but larger, surcharge (width 20 mm) are known. These were previously considered to be forgeries, but it is now believed that some, at least, may represent a trial printing of the "EEN PENNY" surcharge.

(Typo J. F. Celliers)

1883 (20 Feb–3 Aug). Re-issue of T **1** and **2**. P 12.

No.	Type	Description	Unused	Used
171	**1**	1d. grey (*to* black) (5 Apr)	7·50	2·75
		a. Imperf vert (horiz pair)	£275	
		b. Imperf horiz (vert pair)	£550	£350
172	**2**	3d. grey-black (*to* black)/*rose*	30·00	7·00
		a. Bisected (1d.) (on cover)	†	£700
173		3d. pale red (7 May)	16·00	3·25
		a. Bisected (1d.) (on cover)	†	£700
		b. Imperf horiz (vert pair)	†	£1000
		c. Chestnut	30·00	6·00
		ca. Imperf between (horiz pair)	†	—
		d. Vermilion	30·00	6·50
174	**1**	1s. green (*to* deep) (3 Aug)	75·00	7·00
		a. Bisected (6d.) (on cover)	†	£500
		b. *Tête-bêche* (pair)	£1100	£160

Reprints are known of Nos. 172, 173, 173b and 173*c*. The paper of the first is *bright rose* in place of *dull rose*, and the impression is brownish black in place of grey-black to deep black. The reprints on white paper have the paper thinner than the originals, and the gum yellowish instead of white. The colour is a dull deep orange-red.

The used price quoted for No. 174b is for an example with telegraphic cancel. Postally used examples are worth much more. (See note below No. 139).

18

PERFORATIONS. Stamps perforated 11½×12 come from the first vertical row of sheets of the initial printing otherwise perforated 12½×12.

REPRINTS. Reprints of the general issues 1885–93, 1894–95, 1895–96 and 1896–97 exist in large quantities produced using the original plates from 1911 onwards. They cannot readily be distinguished from genuine originals except by comparison with used stamps, but the following general characteristics may be noted. The reprints are all perf 12½, large holes; the paper is whiter and thinner than that usually employed for the originals and their colours lack the lustre of those of the genuine stamps.

Forged surcharges have been made on these reprints.

(Des J. Vurtheim. Typo Enschedé)

1885 (13 Mar)–**93**. P 12½.

175	**18**	½d. grey (30.3.85)	2·00	10
		a. Perf 13½	7·50	1·50
		b. Perf 12½×12	3·25	10
		ba. Perf 11½×12	27·00	8·00
176		1d. carmine	1·75	10
		a. Perf 12½×12	1·75	10
		aa. Perf 11½×12	17·00	3·25
		b. Rose	1·50	10
		ba. Perf 12½×12	1·50	10
177		2d. brown-purple (P 12½×12) (9.85)	2·75	4·00
178		2d. olive-bistre (14.4.87)	2·50	10
		a. Perf 12½×12	4·25	10
179		2½d. mauve (*to* bright) (8.93)	3·50	55
180		3d. mauve (*to* bright)	3·75	2·50
		a. Perf 12½×12	8·00	2·00
		aa. Perf 11½×12	30·00	18·00
181		4d. bronze-green	5·00	1·50
		a. Perf 13½	10·00	2·00
		b. Perf 12½×12	16·00	1·50
		ba. Perf 11½×12	£200	80·00
182		6d. pale dull blue	4·00	3·50
		a. Perf 13½	6·50	1·75
		b. Perf 12½×12	8·00	60
		ba. Perf 11½×12		
183		1s. yellow-green	3·75	1·75
		a. Perf 13½	29·00	6·00
		b. Perf 12½×12	11·00	1·00
184		2s.6d. orange-buff (*to* buff) (2.12.85)	14·00	3·50
		a. Perf 12½×12	21·00	8·00
185		5s. slate (2.12.85)	8·50	6·00
		a. Perf 12½×12	40·00	9·50
186		10s. dull chestnut (2.12.85)	38·00	13·00
		a. Yellow-brown (1891)		
187		£5 deep green (3.92)*	£3250	£180
		s. Optd "Monster"	£150	

Singles of the 6d. pale dull blue imperforate have been reported used in 1893.

*Most examples of No. 187 on the market are either forgeries or reprints.

(19)

1885 (22 May–Aug). Surch with T **19**. Reading up or down.

188	**2**	½d. on 3d. (No. 173)	8·00	11·00
189	**1**	½d. on 1s. (No. 174) (Aug)	30·00	55·00
		a. *Tête-bêche* (pair)	£900	£375

Nos. 188/9 were surcharged by a setting of 40. After the left pane had been surcharged reading down, the sheets were turned so that the right pane had the surcharges reading up.

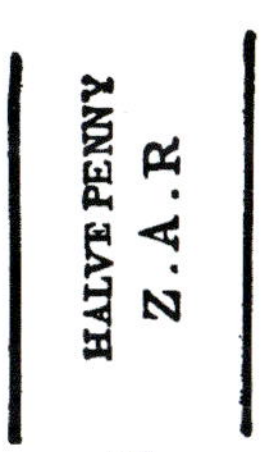

(20)

(21)

(22)

1885 (1 Sept). No. 137a surch with T **20/1** in red.

190	**9**	½d. on 6d. black-brown	80·00	£110
191		2d. on 6d. black-brown	11·00	16·00

1885 (28 Sept). No. 180a surch with T **22**.

192	**18**	½d. on 3d. mauve	7·50	7·50
		a. "PRNNY" (R. 6/6)	50·00	70·00
		b. 2nd "N" inverted (R. 3/8)	95·00	£110
		c. Perf 11½×12	17·00	17·00

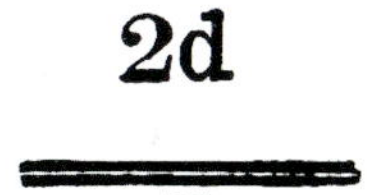

(23)

(24)

1887 (15 Jan). No. 180a surch with T **23/4**.

193	**18**	2d. on 3d. mauve (Type **23**)	11·00	10·00
		a. Surch double	—	£350
		b. Perf 11½×12	32·00	20·00
194		2d. on 3d. mauve (Type **24**)	2·25	4·50
		a. Surch double	£180	£180
		b. Perf 11½×12	9·00	14·00

Nos. 193/4 were surcharged from the same setting of 60 (10×6) which showed Type **24** on the top five horizontal rows and Type **23** on the sixth horizontal row.

(25)

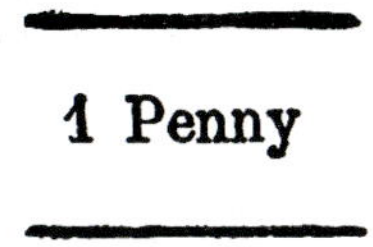

(26)

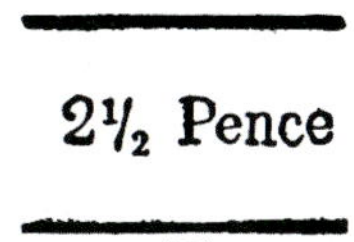

(27)

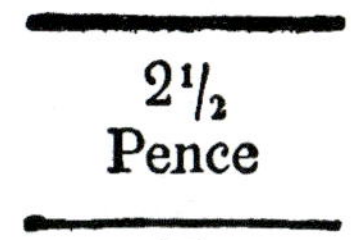

(28)

Two types of surcharge:

A. Vertical distance between bars 12½ mm.

B. Distance 13½ mm.

1893. T **18** surch. P 12½.

(a) In red

195	**25**	½d. on 2d. olive-bistre (A) (27 May)	80	2·75
		a. Surch inverted	2·50	3·25
		b. Surch Type B	1·50	3·50
		ba. Surch inverted	5·50	11·00

(b) In black

196	**25**	½d. on 2d. olive-bistre (A) (2 July)	1·00	2·75
		a. Surch inverted	4·50	5·00
		b. Extra surch on back inverted	£160	
		c. Surch Type B	1·75	3·50
		ca. Surch inverted	20·00	16·00
		cb. Extra surch on back inverted	£275	
197	**26**	1d. on 6d. blue (A) (26 Jan)	2·00	1·75
		a. Surch double	55·00	45·00
		b. Surch inverted	2·50	2·75
		c. Surch treble		
		d. Surch Type B	2·75	2·75
		da. Surch inverted	6·00	4·50
		db. Surch double	—	80·00
		e. Pair, one without surch	£250	
198	**27**	2½d. on 1s. green (A) (2 Jan)	2·75	6·50
		a. "2/½d" for "2½" (R. 1/10)	48·00	80·00
		b. Surch inverted	7·50	8·00
		ba. Surch inverted and "2/½d" for "2½"	£350	£300
		c. Extra surch on back inverted	£450	£450
		d. Surch double, one inverted	£700	
		e. Surch Type B	3·50	8·00
		ea. Surch inverted	9·50	18·00
199	**28**	2½d. on 1s. green (A) (24 June)	8·50	7·00
		a. Surch double	48·00	42·00
		b. Surch inverted	9·00	9·00
		c. Surch Type B	12·00	12·00
		ca. Surch double	80·00	90·00
		cb. Surch inverted	22·00	22·00

Surcharge Types **25/8** all show a similar setting of the horizontal bars at top and bottom. On horizontal rows 1 to 4 and 6, the bars are 12½ mm apart and on row 5 the distance is 13½ mm.

29 (Wagon with shafts)

30 (Wagon with pole)

1894 (July). P 12½.

200	**29**	½d. grey	1·75	75
201		1d. carmine	2·50	10

202		2d. olive-bistre	2·50	10
203		6d. pale dull blue	3·25	60
204		1s. yellow-green	17·00	22·00

For note *re* reprints, see below T **18**.

1895 (16 Mar)–**96**. P 12½.

205	**30**	½d. pearl-grey (1895)	1·50	10
		a. Lilac-grey	1·50	10
206		1d. rose-red	1·50	10
207		2d. olive-bistre (1895)	2·00	30
208		3d. mauve (1895)	3·00	1·00
209		4d. olive-black (1895)	3·25	80
210		6d. pale dull blue (1895)	3·25	1·00
211		1s. yellow-green (18.3.95)	4·00	1·50
212		5s. slate (1896)	18·00	32·00
212*a*		10s. pale chestnut (1896)	18·00	7·50
205s/8s, 211s Optd "Monster" *Set of 5*			£160	

For note *re* reprints, see below T **18**.

Halve
Penny

(**31**)

1d. 1d.

(**32**—Round dot) (**32*a***—Square dot)

1895 (July–Aug). Nos. 211 and 179 surch with T **31**/**2**.

213	**30**	½d. on 1s. green (R.)	1·75	25
		a. Surch spaced	3·25	2·00
		b. "Pennij" for "Penny" (R. 6/6)	60·00	70·00
		c. Surch inverted	5·00	4·50
		d. Surch double	65·00	90·00
214	**18**	1d. on 2½d. bright mauve (G.)	50	30
		a. Surch inverted	22·00	14·00
		b. Surch double	65·00	65·00
		c. Surch on back only	80·00	
		d. Surch Type **32*a***	1·75	1·75
		da. Surch inverted	65·00	
		e. Surch treble	£550	

The normal space between "Penny" and the bars is 3 mm. On No. 213a, which comes from the fifth horizontal row of the setting, this is increased to 4 mm. Copies may be found in which one or both of the bars have failed to print.

Type **32*a*** with square stop occurred on R. 3/3-4, 3/6-8, 4/4-5, 4/7-8, 4/10, 6/3, 6/7-8 and 6/10 of the setting of 60.

33

34

1895 (July). Fiscal stamp optd "POSTZEGEL". P 11½.

215	**33**	6d. bright rose (G.)	2·50	2·50
		a. Imperf between (pair)		
		b. Opt inverted		

(Litho The Press Printing and Publishing Works, Pretoria)

1895 (6 Sept). Introduction of Penny Postage. P 11.

215*c*	**34**	1d. red (pale *to* deep)	2·25	2·50
		ca. Imperf between (pair)	£140	£150
		cb. Imperf vert (horiz pair)		
		cc. Imperf (pair)		

1896–97. P 12½.

216	**30**	½d. green (1896)	1·25	10
217		1d. rose-red and green (1896)	1·25	10
218		2d. brown and green (2.97)	1·25	20
219		2½d. dull blue and green (6.96)	2·25	20
220		3d. purple and green (3.97)	2·50	2·50
221		4d. sage-green and green (3.97)	2·50	3·25
222		6d. lilac and green (11.96)	2·00	2·00
223		1s. ochre and green (3.96)	2·25	80
224		2s.6d. dull violet and green (6.96)	2·75	3·50

For note *re* reprints, see below T **18**.

SECOND BRITISH OCCUPATION

The Second Boer War began on 11 October 1899 and was concluded by the Peace of Vereeniging on 31 May 1902. Pretoria was occupied by the British on 5 June 1900 and a civilian postal service began operating thirteen days later.

FORGERIES. The forgeries of the "V.R.I." and "E.R.I." overprints most often met with can be recognised by the fact that the type used is perfect and the three stops are always in alignment with the bottom of the letters. In the genuine overprints, which were made from old type, it is impossible to find all three letters perfect and all three stops perfect and in exact alignment with the bottom of the letters.

V. R. I. (**35**) E. R. I. (**36**) E. R. I. Half Penny (**37**)

1900 (18 June). Optd with T **35**.

226	**30**	½d. green	30	60
		a. No stop after "V"	12·00	13·00
		b. No stop after "R"	9·00	10·00
		c. No stop after "I"	7·50	8·50
		d. Opt inverted	11·00	13·00
		e. Opt double		
		f. "V.I.R." (R. 4/4)	£800	
227		1d. rose-red and green	30	50
		a. No stop after "V"	12·00	13·00
		b. No stop after "R"	9·00	10·00
		c. No stop after "I"	6·00	7·00
		d. Opt inverted	11·00	18·00
		e. Opt double	75·00	90·00
		f. No stops after "R" and "I"	80·00	80·00
		g. Opt omitted (in pair with normal)	£300	
228		2d. brown and green	3·75	2·75
		a. No stop after "V"	30·00	32·00
		c. No stop after "I"	38·00	38·00
		d. Opt inverted	19·00	21·00
		e. Opt double		
		f. "V.I.R." (R. 4/4)	£800	£850
		g. Opt albino		
229		2½d. dull blue and green	1·00	2·75
		a. No stop after "V"	19·00	25·00
		b. No stop after "R"	45·00	60·00
		c. No stop after "I"	15·00	20·00
		d. Opt inverted	12·00	13·00
230		3d. purple and green	1·00	2·50
		a. No stop after "V"	23·00	29·00
		b. No stop after "R"	45·00	60·00
		c. No stop after "I"	30·00	42·00
		d. Opt inverted	75·00	85·00
231		4d. sage-green and green	3·25	3·25
		a. No stop after "V"	45·00	45·00
		b. No stop after "R"	60·00	60·00
		c. No stop after "I"	40·00	40·00
		d. Opt inverted	27·00	30·00
		f. "V.I.R." (R. 4/4)	£800	
232		6d. lilac and green	3·50	2·00
		a. No stop after "V"	24·00	24·00
		b. No stop after "R"	30·00	30·00
		c. No stop after "I"	30·00	30·00
		d. Opt inverted	30·00	35·00
233		1s. ochre and green	3·50	4·00
		a. No stop after "V"	24·00	27·00
		b. No stop after "R"	24·00	27·00
		c. No stop after "I"	45·00	50·00
		d. Opt inverted	40·00	45·00
		e. Opt double	80·00	90·00
234		2s.6d. dull violet and green	4·25	13·00
		a. No stop after "V"	45·00	
		b. No stop after "R"	85·00	
		c. No stop after "I"	—	£450
235		5s. slate	9·00	19·00
		a. No stop after "V"	£140	
236		10s. pale chestnut	11·00	22·00
		a. No stop after "V"	£120	
		c. No stop after "I"	£120	
237	**18**	£5 deep green*	£2000	£800
		a. No stop after "V"		
234s/7s Handstamped "SPECIMEN" *Set of 4*			£225	

*Many examples of No. 237 on the market are forgeries and the stamps should only be purchased if accompanied by a recent expert committee certificate.

The error "V.I.R." occurred on R. 4/4 in the first batch of stamps to be overprinted—a few sheets of the ½d., 2d. and 4d. The error was then corrected and stamps showing it are very rare. The corrected overprint shows the "I" dropped by 0.75mm. This variety is known on all values apart from the £5, but was later corrected.

A number of different settings were used to apply the overprint to Nos. 226/37. The missing stop varieties listed above developed during overprinting and occur on different positions in the various settings.

1901 (Jan)–**02**. Optd with T **36**.

238	**30**	½d. green	50	1·75
		a. Opt double		
239		1d. rose-red and green (20.3.01)	50	10
		a. "E." of opt omitted	80·00	
240		3d. purple and green (6.02)	2·25	4·00
241		4d. sage-green and green (6.02)	2·25	6·50
242		2s.6d. dull violet and green (10.02)	9·50	27·00

1901 (July). Surch with T **37**.

243	**30**	½d. on 2d. brown and green	65	1·25
		a. No stop after "E" (R. 4/6)	50·00	60·00

38 (POSTAGE REVENUE)

39 (POSTAGE POSTAGE)

(Typo D.L.R.)

1902 (1 Apr–17 Dec). Wmk Crown CA. P 14.

244	**38**	½d. black and bluish green	2·00	20
		w. Wmk inverted	£110	70·00
245		1d. black and carmine	1·25	15
		w. Wmk inverted	85·00	60·00
246		2d. black and purple	4·75	1·00
247		2½d. black and blue	11·00	1·25
		w. Wmk inverted	80·00	45·00
248		3d. black and sage-green (17.12.02)	10·00	80
249		4d. black and brown (17.12.02)	10·00	2·00
250		6d. black and orange-brown	4·25	1·25
251		1s. black and sage-green	15·00	19·00
252		2s. black and brown	55·00	65·00
253	**39**	2s.6d. magenta and black	16·00	16·00
254		5s. black and purple/*yellow*	30·00	40·00
255		10s. black and purple/*red*	65·00	42·00
244/55 *Set of* 12			£200	£170
244s/55s (*inc* 247ws) Optd "SPECIMEN" *Set of* 12			£170	

The colour of the "black" centres varies from brownish grey or grey to black.

1903 (1 Feb). Wmk Crown CA. P 14.

256	**39**	1s. grey-black and red-brown	14·00	4·50
257		2s. grey-black and yellow	17·00	18·00
258		£1 green and violet	£300	£170
259		£5 orange-brown and violet	£1500	£700
256s/9s Optd "SPECIMEN" *Set of* 4			£250	

1904–09. Ordinary paper. Wmk Mult Crown CA. P 14.

260	**38**	½d. black and bluish green	9·50	3·00
		w. Wmk inverted	£140	75·00
		y. Wmk inverted and reversed	£120	50·00
261		1d. black and carmine	8·00	1·00
262		2d. black and purple (*chalk-surfaced paper*) (1906)	17·00	2·00
263		2½d. black and blue (1905)	22·00	9·00
		aw. Wmk inverted	£120	80·00
		b. Chalk-surfaced paper	18·00	4·50
264		3d. black and sage-green (*chalk-surfaced paper*) (1906)	3·50	50
265		4d. black and brown (*chalk-surfaced paper*) (1906)	4·75	70
		w. Wmk inverted	£120	70·00
266		6d. black and orange (1905)	13·00	2·00
		a. Chalk-surfaced paper. *Black and brown-orange* (1906)	4·50	50
		w. Wmk inverted	£140	85·00
267	**39**	1s. black and red-brown (1905)	10·00	50
268		2s. black and yellow (1906)	25·00	11·00
269		2s.6d. magenta and black (1909)	50·00	9·50
270		5s. black and purple/*yellow*	27·00	1·50
271		10s. black and purple/*red* (1907)	75·00	3·50
272		£1 green and violet (1908)	£325	40·00
		a. Chalk-surfaced paper	£300	18·00
260/72a *Set of* 13			£500	50·00

There is considerable variation in the "black" centres as in the previous issue.

1905–09. Wmk Mult Crown CA. P 14.

273	**38**	½d. yellow-green	2·50	10
		a. Deep green (1908)	3·25	20
		w. Wmk inverted	£150	85·00
274		1d. scarlet	1·25	10
		aw. Wmk inverted	—	£275
		b. Wmk Cabled Anchor, T **13** of Cape of Good Hope	—	£325
275		2d. purple (1909)	3·50	60
276		2½d. bright blue (1909)	19·00	9·50
273/6 *Set of* 4			24·00	9·50
273s/6s Optd "SPECIMEN" *Set of* 4			90·00	

The monocoloured ½d. and 1d. are printed from new combined plates. These show a slight alteration in that the frame does not touch the crown.

1909. Prepared for use but not issued. Wmk Mult crown CA. P 14.

277s	**38**	2d. grey (optd "SPECIMEN")	£180

Although this stamp was distributed in " SPECIMEN" form by the UPU, the entire supply sent to Transvaal was destroyed.

The ½d., 1d. and 2d. exist from coils constructed from normal sheets for use in stamp machines introduced in 1911. These coils were originally joined horizontally but the 1d. was subsequently issued joined vertically.

Many of the King's Head stamps are found overprinted or perforated "C.S.A.R.", for use by the Central South African Railways.

STAMP BOOKLETS

1905 (July). Black on red cover showing arms. Stapled.

SB1	2s.7d. booklet containing thirty 1d. (No. 261) in blocks of 6	£2000

1905. Black on red cover. Stapled.

SB2	2s.7d. booklet containing thirty 1d. (No. 274) in blocks of 6	£2250

1909. Black on red cover. Stapled.

SB3	2s.6d. booklet containing ten ½d. (No. 273) in block of 6 and block of 4, and twenty-four 1d. (No. 274) in blocks of 6	£2750

Stocks of No. SB3 were supplied containing twelve examples of the ½d., it being intended that the postal clerks would remove two stamps before the booklets were sold. In some instances this did not occur.

POSTAL FISCAL STAMPS

1900–02. Fiscal stamps as in T **33**, but optd with T **35**. P 11½.

F1	1d. pale blue	—	45·00
F2	6d. dull carmine	—	65·00
F3	1s. olive-bistre	—	80·00
F4	1s.6d. brown	—	£100
F5	2s.6d. dull purple	—	£120

Nos. F1/5, previously listed as Nos. 1/5 of Volksrust, are fiscal issues which are known postally used from various Transvaal post offices between June 1900 and June 1902.

Other fiscal stamps are found apparently postally used, but these were used on telegrams not on postal matter.

POSTAGE DUE STAMPS

D **1**

Inverted "p" for "d" (Right pane R. 10/6)

(Typo D.L.R.)

1907. Wmk Mult Crown CA. P 14.

D1	D **1**	½d. black and blue-green	3·50	1·25
D2		1d. black and scarlet	4·00	85
D3		2d. brown-orange	5·50	1·25
D4		3d. black and blue	7·50	4·25
D5		5d. black and violet	2·50	12·00
		a. Inverted "p" for "d"	55·00	
D6		6d. black and red-brown	4·25	12·00
D7		1s. scarlet and black	14·00	8·50
D1/7 *Set of* 7			38·00	35·00

Transvaal became a province of the Union of South Africa on 31 May 1910.

PIETERSBURG

After the fall of Pretoria to the British in June 1900 the Transvaal government withdrew to the north of the country. Those post offices in areas not occupied by the British continued to function. The following stamps were then authorised by the State Secretary. Pietersburg itself was taken by British forces on 9 April.

PRICES. Genuinely used examples are very rare. Stamps cancelled by favour exist and are worth the same as the unused prices quoted.

The issued stamps are initialled by the Controller J. T. de V. Smit. All values exist without his signature and these come from claudesrine printings in excess of the official government print order. Unsigned stamps were not issued by the Post Office.

P 1

P 2

P 3

TYPES P **1/3.** Each value was printed in sheets of 24 (6×4) of which the first two horizontal rows were as Type P **1** (Large "P" in "POSTZEGEL" and large date), the third row as Type P **2** (Large "P" in "POSTZEGEL" and small date) and the fourth as Type P **3** (Small "P" in "POSTZEGEL" and small date).

(Type-set *De Zoutpansberg Wachter* Press, Pietersburg)

1901 (20 Mar (1d.)–3 Apr (others)).

A. Imperf

(a) Controller's initials in black

1	P **1**	½d. black/*green*	15·00
		e. Controller's initials omitted	95·00
2	P **2**	½d. black/*green*	45·00
		d. Controller's initials omitted	95·00
3	P **3**	½d. black/*green*	45·00
		d. Controller's initials omitted	95·00
4	P **1**	1d. black/*red*	3·50
5	P **2**	1d. black/*red*	5·50
6	P **3**	1d. black/*red*	7·00
7	P **1**	2d. black/*orange*	6·00
8	P **2**	2d. black/*orange*	14·00
9	P **3**	2d. black/*orange*	22·00
10	P **1**	4d. black/*blue*	5·50
11	P **2**	4d. black/*blue*	9·50
12	P **3**	4d. black/*blue*	32·00
13	P **1**	6d. black/*green*	9·50
14	P **2**	6d. black/*green*	15·00
15	P **3**	6d. black/*green*	40·00
16	P **1**	1s. black/*yellow*	8·00
17	P **2**	1s. black/*yellow*	14·00
18	P **3**	1s. black/*yellow*	25·00

(b) Controller's initials in red

19	P **1**	½d. black/*green*	15·00
20	P **2**	½d. black/*green*	35·00
21	P **3**	½d. black/*green*	40·00

B. P 11½

(a) Controller's initials in red

22	P **1**	½d. black/*green*	5·50
		c. Imperf vert (horiz pair)	95·00
23	P **2**	½d. black/*green*	17·00
		c. Imperf vert (horiz pair)	£120
24	P **3**	½d. black/*green*	12·00
		b. Imperf vert (horiz pair)	£120

(b) Controller's initials in black

25	P **1**	1d. black/*red*	2·00
		m. Imperf vert (horiz pair)	55·00
		n. Imperf between (vert pair: No. 25 + No. 26)	75·00
		o. Imperf horiz (vert pair)	55·00
26	P **2**	1d. black/*red*	2·75
		f. Imperf vert (horiz pair)	80·00
		g. Imperf horiz (vert pair: No. 26 + No.27)	60·00
27	P **3**	1d. black/*red*	4·00
		f. Imperf vert (horiz pair)	80·00
28	P **1**	2d. black/*orange*	5·50
29	P **2**	2d. black/*orange*	8·00
30	P **3**	2d. black/*orange*	14·00

For the ½d. the First printing had initials in red, those of the Second printing had them in black or red, and all of the Third were in red.

CONSTANT VARIETIES

½d. value

First printing

R.3/5	Centre figures "½" level	Imperf	(No. 20a)	70·00
		Perf	(No. 23d)	40·00
R.3/6	No stop after right "AFR"	Imperf	(No. 20b)	70·00
		Perf	(No. 23e)	40·00
R.4/6	Hyphen between right "AFR" and "REP"	Imperf	(No. 21a)	70·00
		Perf	(No. 24a)	40·00

Second printing—Imperf

R.1/1 & 4	Top left "½" inverted, no stop after right "AFR"	(No. 19c)	70·00
R.1/2	Top right "½" inverted	(No. 19d)	90·00
R.1/3	"⅓" at lower right	(No. 19e)	90·00
R.1/5	"POSTZFGEL"	(No. 19f)	90·00
R.1/6	Left spray inverted, "AFB" at right	(No. 19g)	90·00
R.2/1	"REB" at left, left side of inner frame 3 mm too high	(No. 19h)	90·00
R.2/2	"BEP" at left	(No. 19i)	90·00
R.2/3	"POSTZEOEL"	(No. 19j)	90·00
R.2/4	"AER" at right, left side of inner frame 2 mm too high	(No. 19k)	90·00
R.2/5	No stop after date	(No. 19l)	90·00
R.2/6	No stop after "PENNY"	(No. 19m)	
R.3/1	"⅓" at top left, "PE" of "PENNY" spaced	(No. 20c)	90·00
R.3/2	Right spray inverted	(No. 20d)	90·00
R.3/3	Top left "½" inverted	(No. 20e)	90·00
R.3/4	No stop after "Z" at left	(No. 20f)	
R.3/5	Centre figures "½" level	(No. 20g)	
R.3/6	"POSTZEGFL", no stop after right "AFR"	(No. 20h)	
R.4/3	"⅓" at top right	(No. 21b)	90·00
R.4/4	Lower left "½" inverted	(No. 21c)	90·00
R.4/5	"¼" at top left	(No. 21d)	90·00
R.4/6	Left spray inverted, "901" for "1901"	(No. 21e)	

Third printing

R.1/2	No stop after left "AFR"	Imperf	(No. 1a)	60·00
R.1/3	"⅓" at top left, no bar over lower right "½"	Imperf	(No. 1b)	60·00
R.1/6	No stop after date	Imperf	(No. 1c)	60·00
R.2/5	"BEP" at left, no stop after date	Imperf	(No. 1d)	60·00
R.3/3	"AFB" at left	Imperf	(No. 2a)	60·00
		Perf	(No. 23a)	
R.3/4	"POSTZEGEI"	Imperf	(No. 2b)	60·00
		Perf	(No. 23b)	
R.3/6	No bar over lower right "½"	Imperf	(No. 2c)	60·00
R.4/1	No stop after right "AFR"	Imperf	(No. 3a)	60·00
R.4/4	No stop after left "Z", no bar under top right "½"	Imperf	(No. 3b)	60·00
		Perf	(No. 23c)	
R.4/5	"POSTZECEL, AER" at left	Imperf	(No. 3c)	60·00

1d. value

First printing

R.1/2	First "1" in date dropped	Imperf	(No. 4l)	35·00
		Perf	(No. 25l)	22·00
R.3/6	No stop after right "AFR"	Imperf	(No. 5e)	35·00
		Perf	(No. 26e)	22·00
R.4/5	Dropped "P" in "PENNY"	Imperf	(No. 6e)	35·00
		Perf	(No. 27e)	22·00

Second printing

R.1/2	Inverted "1" at lower left, first "1" of date dropped	Imperf	(No. 4a)	35·00
		Perf	(No. 25a)	22·00
R.1/3	No bar under top left "1"	Imperf	(No. 4b)	35·00
		Perf	(No. 25b)	22·00
R.1/4	No bar over lower right "1"	Imperf	(No. 4c)	35·00
		Perf	(No. 25c)	22·00
R.1/5	"POSTZFGEL"	Imperf	(No. 4d)	35·00
		Perf	(No. 25d)	22·00
R.1/6	"AFB" at right	Imperf	(No. 4e)	35·00
		Perf	(No. 25e)	22·00
R.2/1	"REB" at left	Imperf	(No. 4f)	35·00
		Perf	(No. 25f)	22·00
R.2/2	"BEP" at left	Imperf	(No. 4g)	35·00
		Perf	(No. 25g)	22·00
R.2/3	"POSTZEOEL"	Imperf	(No. 4h)	35·00
		Perf	(No. 25h)	22·00
R.2/4	"AER" at right	Imperf	(No. 4i)	35·00
		Perf	(No. 25i)	22·00
R.2/5	No stop after date	Imperf	(No. 4j)	35·00
		Perf	(No. 25j)	22·00
R.2/6	No stop after "PENNY"	Imperf	(No. 4k)	35·00
		Perf	(No. 25k)	22·00
R.3/2	Right spray inverted	Imperf	(No. 5a)	35·00
		Perf	(No. 26a)	22·00
R.3/3	No bar over lower left "1"	Imperf	(No. 5b)	35·00
		Perf	(No. 26b)	22·00
R.3/4	No stop after left "Z"	Imperf	(No. 5c)	35·00

	.... Perf	(No. 26c)	22·00
R.3/6	"POSTZEGFL", no stop after right "AFR"		
	.... Imperf	(No. 5d)	35·00
	.... Perf	(No. 26d)	22·00
R.4/1	No stop after right "AFR"......... Imperf	(No. 6a)	35·00
	.... Perf	(No. 27a)	22·00
R.4/2 & 6	Left spray inverted..................		
	.... Imperf	(No. 6b)	22·00
	.... Perf	(No. 27b)	13·00
R.4/3	"POSTZEGEI"..................... Imperf	(No. 6c)	35·00
	.... Perf	(No. 27c)	22·00
R.4/4	No bar under top right "1"......... Imperf	(No. 6d)	35·00
	.... Perf	(No. 27d)	22·00

2d. value

First printing

R.1/2	First "1" in date dropped............ Imperf	(No. 7m)	45·00
	.... Perf	(No. 28a)	30·00
R.2/1	No stop after left "REP"............ Imperf	(No. 7n)	45·00
	.... Perf	(No. 28b)	30·00
R.3/6	No stop after right "AFR"............ Imperf	(No. 8f)	45·00
	.... Perf	(No. 29a)	30·00
R.4/1	Centre 2 wider, no stop after right "AFR"..................... Imperf	(No. 9a)	38·00
	.... Perf	(No. 30a)	30·00
R.4/2	Centre "2" wider..................... Imperf	(No. 9g)	45·00
	.... Perf	(No. 30b)	30·00
R.4/5	"P" in "PENCE" dropped............ Imperf	(No. 9h)	45·00
	.... Perf	(No. 30c)	30·00

Second printing—Imperf

R.1/1	"1" at lower right.....................	(No. 7a)	45·00
R.1/3	"PENNY" for "PENCE".....................	(No. 7d)	45·00
R.1/5	"POSTZFGEL".....................	(No. 7e)	45·00
R.1/6	"AFB" at right.....................	(No. 7f)	45·00
R.2/1	"REB" at left.....................	(No. 7g)	45·00
R.2/2	"AFB" at left.....................	(No. 7h)	45·00
R.2/3	"POSTZEOEL".....................	(No. 7i)	45·00
R.2/4	"AER" at right.....................	(No. 7j)	45·00
R.2/5	No stop after date (*occurs on third printing also*).....................	(No. 7k)	45·00
R.2/6	Vertical line after "POSTZEGEL"............	(No. 7l)	45·00
R.3/2	Right spray inverted.....................	(No. 8a)	45·00
R.3/3	No bar over lower left "2".....................	(No. 8b)	45·00
R.3/4	Centre "2" inverted, no stop after left "Z"	(No. 8c)	45·00
R.3/6	"POSTZEGFL", no stop after right "AFR".	(No. 8d)	45·00
R.4/1	Centre "2" wider, no stop after right "AFR" (*occurs on first and third printings also*).....	(No. 9a)	38·00
R.4/2	Centre "2" wider, left spray inverted......	(No. 9b)	45·00
R.4/3	"POSTZEGEI".....................	(No. 9c)	45·00
R.4/4	No bar under top right "2" (*occurs on third printing also*).....................	(No. 9d)	45·00
R.4/5	"1" at lower left, "P" in "PENCE" dropped.....................	(No. 9e)	45·00
R.4/6	Left spray inverted.....................	(No. 9f)	45·00

Third Printing

R. 1/2	No stop after left "AFR".....................
R. 1/3	No bar over lower right "2".....................
R. 1/5	"POSTZEGEI".....................
R. 2/1	No stop after left "REP".....................
R. 2/5	No stop after date.....................
R. 3/4	No stop after left "Z".....................
R. 3/5	"4" at lower right.....................
R. 4/1	Centre "2" wider, no stop after right "AFR"
R. 4/2	Centre "2" wider.....................
R. 4/4	No bar under upper right "2".....................
R. 4/5	"4" at upper left and "AER" at left...............

Varieties at R. 2/1, and R. 4/2 occur on the first and third printings, those on R. 2/5 and R. 4/4 on the second and third printings and that on R. 4/1 on all three printings.

4d. value

First printing

R.2/1	Left inner frame too high.....................	(No. 10k)	45·00
R.4/1–2	Centre "4" wider.....................	(No. 12g)	35·00
R.4/5	"P" in "PENCE" dropped.....................	(No. 12h)	45·00

Second printing

R.1/3	"PENNY" for "PENCE" (*on small part of printing*).....................	(No. 10c)	90·00
R.1/5	"POSTZFGEL".....................	(No. 10d)	45·00
R.1/6	"AFB" at right.....................	(No. 10e)	45·00
R.2/1	"REB" at left.....................	(No. 10f)	45·00
R.2/2	"AFB" at left.....................	(No. 10g)	45·00
R.2/3	"POSTZEOEL".....................	(No. 10h)	45·00
R.2/4	"AER" at right.....................	(No. 10i)	45·00
R.2/5	No stop after date.....................	(No. 10j)	45·00
R.3/2	Right spray inverted.....................	(No. 11a)	45·00
R.3/3	No bar over lower left "4" (*on small part of printing*).....................	(No. 11b)	90·00
R.3/4	No stop after left "Z".....................	(No. 11c)	45·00
R.3/6	"POSTZEGFL".....................	(No. 11d)	45·00
R.4/1	Centre "4" wider, no stop after right "AFR".	(No. 12a)	45·00
R.4/2	Centre "4" wider, left spray inverted......	(No. 12b)	45·00
R.4/3	"POSTZEGEI".....................	(No. 12c)	45·00
R.4/4	No bar under top right "4".....................	(No. 12d)	45·00
R.4/5	"P" in "PENCE" dropped.....................	(No. 12e)	45·00
R.4/6	Left spray inverted.....................	(No. 12f)	45·00

Varieties at R. 1/5, R. 2/1, R. 2/2, R. 2/3, R. 2/5, R. 3/4, R. 4/2 and R. 4/4 also occur on the third printing.

Third printing

R. 1/2	No stop after left "AFR".....................
R. 1/3	No bar over lower right "4".....................
R. 1/5	"POSTZFGEL".....................
R. 2/1	"REB" at left.....................
R. 2/2	"AFB" at left.....................
R. 2/3	"POSTZEOEL".....................
R. 2/4	"AER" at right.....................
R. 2/5	No stop after date.....................
R. 3/2	Right spray inverted.....................
R. 3/4	No stop after left "Z".....................
R. 3/5	"4" at lower right.....................
R. 3/6	"POSTZEGFL".....................
R. 4/1	Centre "4" wider.....................
R. 4/2	Centre "4" wider, left spray inverted.........
R. 4/4	No bar under upper right "4".....................
R. 4/5	"AER" at left and "P" in "PENCE" dropped.
R. 4/5	Left spray inverted.....................

The variety at R. 4/1 occurs on the first and third printings and those at R. 1/5, R. 2/1, R. 2/2, R. 2/3, R. 2/5, R. 3/4, R. 4/2 and R. 4/4 on the second and third printings.

6d. value

First printing

R.2/1	Left inner frame too high, no stop after left "REP".....................	(No. 13k)	55·00
R.4/1–2	Centre "6" wider.....................	(No. 15g)	40·00
R.4/5	"P" in "PENCE" dropped.....................	(No. 15h)	55·00

Second printing

R.1/3	"PENNY" for "PENCE" (*on small part of printing*).....................	(No. 13c)	£110
R.1/5	"POSTZFGEL".....................	(No. 13d)	55·00
R.1/6	"AFB" at right.....................	(No. 13e)	55·00
R.2/1	"REB" at left.....................	(No. 13f)	55·00
R.2/2	"AFB" at left.....................	(No. 13g)	55·00
R.2/3	"POSTZEOEL".....................	(No. 13h)	55·00
R.2/4	"AER" at right.....................	(No. 13i)	55·00
R.2/5	No stop after date.....................	(No. 13j)	55·00
R.3/2	Right spray inverted.....................	(No. 14a)	55·00
R.3/4	Centre "6" inverted, no stop after left "Z" (*on small part of printing*)............	(No. 14b)	£150
R.3/4	No stop after left "Z".....................	(No. 14c)	55·00
R.3/6	"POSTZEGFL".....................	(No. 14d)	55·00
R.4/1	Centre "6" wider, no stop after right "AFR".	(No. 15a)	55·00
R.4/2	Centre "6" wider, left spray inverted......	(No. 15b)	55·00
R.4/3	"POSTZEGEI".....................	(No. 15c)	55·00
R.4/4	No bar under top right "6".....................	(No. 15d)	55·00
R.4/5	"P" in "PENCE" dropped.....................	(No. 15e)	55·00
R.4/6	Left spray inverted.....................	(No. 15f)	55·00

Varieties at R. 1/5, R. 2/1, R. 2/2, R. 2/3, R. 2/5, R. 3/2, R. 3/4, R. 4/1, R. 4/2 and R. 4/4 also occur on the third printing.

Third printing

R. 1/2	No stop after left "AFR".....................
R. 1/3	No bar over lower right "6".....................
R. 1/5	"POSTZFGEL".....................
R. 1/6	"AFB" at right.....................
R. 2/1	"REB" at left.....................
R. 2/2	"AFB" at left.....................
R. 2/3	"POSTZEOEL".....................
R. 2/4	"AER" at right.....................
R. 2/5	No stop after date.....................
R. 3/2	Right spray inverted.....................
R. 3/4	No stop after left "Z".....................
R. 3/6	"POSTZEGFL".....................
R. 4/1	Centre "6" wider no stop after "AFR" at right.....................
R. 4/2	Centre "6" wider, left spray inverted.........
R. 4/3	"POSTZEGEI".....................
R. 4/4	No bar under upper right "6".....................
R. 4/5	"AER" at left, "P" in "PENCE" dropped.........
R. 4/6	Left spray inverted.....................

1s. value

R.1/2	No stop after left "AFR".....................	(No. 16a)	40·00
R.1/3	No bar over lower right "1".....................	(No. 16b)	40·00
R.2/5	No stop after date.....................	(No. 16c)	40·00

R.3/3	Centre "1" inverted (*on small part of printing*)	(No. 17a)	
R.3/4	"POSTZEGEI", no stop after left "Z"	(No. 17b)	40·00
R.4/1	No stop after right "AFR"	(No. 18a)	40·00
R.4/4	No bar under top right "1"	(No. 18b)	40·00
R.4/5	"AER" at left	(No. 18c)	40·00

LOCAL BRITISH OCCUPATION ISSUES DURING THE SOUTH AFRICAN WAR 1900–02

Stamps of the Transvaal Republic, unless otherwise stated, variously overprinted or surcharged.

LYDENBURG

Lydenburg was occupied by the British on 6 September 1900.

V.R.I.
3d.
(L **1**)

1900 (Sept). Nos. 215c and 217 surch as Type L **1**, others optd "V.R.I" only.

No.	Type	Description	Unused	Used
1	**30**	½d. green	£150	£150
2		1d. rose-red and green	£140	£130
2*a*	**34**	1d. on 1d. red		
3	**30**	2d. brown and green	£1300	£900
4		2½d. blue and green	£2250	£950
5		3d. on 1d. rose-red and green	£120	£100
6		3d. purple and green		
7		4d. sage-green and green	£3500	£950
8		6d. lilac and green	£3000	£900
9		1s. ochre and green	£4750	£3000

The above were cancelled by British Army postal service postmarks. These overprints with Transvaal cancellations are believed to be forgeries.

RUSTENBURG

British forces in Rustenburg, west of Pretoria, utilised Transvaal stamps, handstamped "V.R" on the command of Colonel Baden-Powell.

V.R.
(R **1**)

1900 (22 June). Handstamped with Type R **1** in violet.

No.	Type	Description	Unused	Used
1	**30**	½d. green	£160	£120
2		1d. rose-red and green	£120	90·00
3		2d. brown and green	£350	£140
4		2½d. blue and green	£200	£120
5		3d. purple and green	£275	£160
6		6d. lilac and green	£1300	£400
7		1s. ochre and green	£1800	£1000
8		2s.6d. dull violet and green	£9000	£4500
		a. Handstamp in black	†	£8000

Nos. 2 and 5 exist with the handstamp inverted.

SCHWEIZER RENECKE

BESIEGED
(SR **1**)

1900 (Sept). Handstamped with Type SR **1** in black, reading vert up or down.

(a) On stamps of Transvaal

No.	Type	Description	Unused	Used
1	**30**	½d. green	†	£275
2		1d. rose-red and green	†	£275
3		2d. brown and green	†	£375
4		6d. lilac and green	†	£1100

(b) On stamps of Cape of Good Hope

No.	Type	Description	Unused	Used
5	**17**	½d. green	†	£475
6		1d. carmine	†	£475

Schweizer Renecke, near the Bechuanaland border, was occupied by a British garrison from July 1900 to 9 January 1901. The British commander authorised the above stamps shortly after 19 August. All stamps were cancelled with the dated circular town postmark ("Schweizer Renecke, Z.A.R."), usually after having been stuck on paper before use. Unused, without the postmark, do not exist.

No. 4 exists with double handstamp.

WOLMARANSSTAD

A British party occupied this town in the south-west of the Transvaal from 15 June to 27 July 1900. Transvaal stamps, to a face value of £5. 2s.6d., were found at the local firm of Thos. Leask and Co. and surcharged as below. The first mail left on 24 June and the last on 21 July.

Cancelled — V-R-I. (L **3**)

Cancelled — V-R-I. (L **4**)

1900 (24 June). Optd with Type L **3**.

No.	Type	Description	Unused	Used
1	**30**	½d. green (B.)	£275	£400
		a. Opt inverted	£900	
		b. Opt in black		
1*c*		½d. on 1s. green (B.)		
2		1d. rose-red and green (B.)	£180	£300
		a. Opt in green	£1800	
		b. Opt in black		
3		2d. brown and green (B.)	£1800	£1800
		a. Opt in black	£3000	
4		2½d. blue and green (R.)	£1800	
		a. Opt in blue	£2750	£2750
		b. Opt in black		
5		3d. purple and green (B.)	£3000	£3250
6		4d. sage-green and green (B.)	£4000	£4500
7		6d. lilac and green (B.)	£4750	£5500
8		1s. ochre and green (B.)	—	£10000

The two lines of the overprint were handstamped separately. The ½d. exists with two impressions of the "Cancelled" handstamp, the 2½d. with two impressions of "V-R-I", one in red and one in blue and the 3d. with "Cancelled" in green and "V.R.I." in blue.

1900 (24 June). Optd with Type L **4**.

No.	Type	Description	Unused	Used
9	**34**	1d. red (B.)	£180	£325

The ½d., 1d. and 3d. in Type **30** are also known with this overprint.

VII. ZULULAND

Zululand remained an independent kingdom until annexed by Great Britain on 19 May 1887 when it was declared a Crown Colony.

The first European postal service was operated by a Natal postal agency at Eshowe opened in 1876 which cancelled Natal stamps with a "No. 56 P.O. Natal" postmark. The agency closed during the Zulu War of 1879 and did not re-open until 1885 when an Eshowe postmark was provided. "ZULULAND" was added to the cancellation in 1887 and stamps of Natal continued to be used until replaced by the overprinted series on 1 May 1888.

PRICES FOR STAMPS ON COVER		
Nos.	1/2	*from* × 100
Nos.	3/10	*from* × 20
No.	11	—
Nos.	12/16	*from* × 20
Nos.	20/3	*from* × 30
No.	24	*from* × 20
Nos.	25/6	*from* × 12
Nos.	27/9	—
No.	F1	*from* × 100

ZULULAND (**1**)

ZULULAND. (**2**)

1888 (1 May)–**93**.

(a) Nos. 173, 180, 197, 200/2, 205a, 207a/8, 209 and 211 of Great Britain (Queen Victoria) optd with T **1** *by D.L.R.*

No.	Description	Unused	Used
1	½d. vermilion (11.88)	6·00	2·75
2	1d. deep purple	28·00	5·00
3	2d. grey-green and carmine	24·00	45·00
4	2½d. purple/*blue* (9.91)	32·00	21·00
5	3d. purple/*yellow*	27·00	22·00
6	4d. green and deep brown	55·00	75·00
7	5d. dull purple and blue (3.93)	95·00	£120
	w. Wmk inverted	†	£1600
8	6d. purple/*rose-red*	19·00	17·00
9	9d. dull purple and blue (4.92)	£100	£110
10	1s. dull green (4.92)	£130	£150
11	5s. rose (4.92)	£650	£750
1/11	*Set of* 11	£1000	£1200
1s/11s	(*ex* 1d.) H/S "SPECIMEN" *Set of* 10	£650	

(b) No. 97a of Natal optd with T **2** *at Pietermaritzburg*

No.	Description	Unused	Used
12	½d. dull green (with stop) (7.88)	55·00	95·00
	a. Opt double	£1100	£1200
	d. Opt omitted (vert pair with normal)	£6500	
13	½d. dull green (without stop)	27·00	45·00

The T **2** opt has been extensively forged. Examples of No. 12 with opt inverted and No. 13 with opt double are now considered to be forgeries.

1893 (29 Nov*). T **15** of Natal optd with T **1** by D.L.R. (Wmk Crown CA. P 14).

No.	Description	Unused	Used
16	6d. dull purple	65·00	55·00

*Earliest known date of use. No. 16 was, apparently, originally supplied in 1889 for fiscal purposes.

3

4

1d. Shaved "Z" (R. 4/3 and R. 6/3)

(Typo D.L.R.)

1894 (18 Apr)–**96**. Wmk Crown CA. P 14.

20	**3**	½d. dull mauve and green	5·00	5·00
		w. Wmk inverted	£200	£250
21		1d. dull mauve and carmine	6·00	2·75
		a. Shaved "Z"	85·00	50·00
22		2½d. dull mauve and ultramarine	14·00	9·00
23		3d. dull mauve and olive-brown	8·00	3·00
24	**4**	6d. dull mauve and black	20·00	20·00
25		1s. green	48·00	38·00
26		2s.6d. green and black (2.96)	85·00	£100
27		4s. green and carmine	£140	£190
28		£1 purple/*red*	£500	£600
29		£5 purple and black/*red*	£4750	£1500
		s. Optd "SPECIMEN"	£450	
20/8 *Set of 9*			£750	£850
20s/8s Optd "SPECIMEN" *Set of 9*			£450	

Dangerous forgeries exist of the £1 and £5.

FISCAL STAMP USED FOR POSTAGE

ZULULAND

F **1**

1891 (5 May*). F **1**, Fiscal stamp of Natal optd with T **1**. Wmk Crown CA. P 14.

F1	1d. dull mauve	3·75	3·00
	a. Top left triangle detached	£190	£160
	s. Handstamped "*SPECIMEN*"	60·00	

*Earliest known date of postal use. A proclamation published in the *Natal Government Gazette* on 27 June 1891 authorised the use of this stamp for postal purposes, but it is clear from the wording that such use had already commenced.

For illustration of "top left triangle detached" variety see above No. 21 of Antigua.

Other values, 1s. to £20 as No. F1 exist apparently with postmarks, but, as these were never authorised for postal use, they are no longer listed.

Zululand was annexed to Natal on 31 December 1897 and its stamps were withdrawn from sale on 30 June 1898.

VIII. BRITISH ARMY FIELD OFFICES DURING SOUTH AFRICAN WAR, 1899–1902

Z 1

Z 2

Stamps of GREAT BRITAIN used by British Army Field Offices in South Africa cancelled as Types Z **1**, Z **2** or similar postmarks.

1881. Stamp of Queen Victoria.

Z1	1d. lilac (16 *dots*)	5·00

1883–84. Stamps of Queen Victoria.

Z1*a*	2s.6d lilac	£275
Z2	5s. rose	£325
Z2*a*	10s. ultramarine	£700

1887–92. Stamps of Queen Victoria.

Z3	½d. vermilion	6·00
Z4	1½d. dull purple and green	30·00
Z5	2d. grey-green and carmine	18·00
Z6	2½d. purple/*blue*	6·00
Z7	3d. purple/*yellow*	14·00
Z8	4d. green and brown	22·00
Z9	4½d. green and carmine	75·00
Z10	5d. dull purple and blue (Die II)	17·00
Z11	6d. purple/*rose-red*	14·00
Z12	9d. dull purple and blue	80·00
Z13	10d. dull purple and carmine	75·00
Z14	1s. dull green	£110
Z15	£1 green	£1000

1900. Stamps of Queen Victoria.

Z16	½d. blue-green	6·00
Z17	1s. green and carmine	£180

1902. Stamps of King Edward VII.

Z18	½d. blue-green	15·00
Z19	1d. scarlet	10·00
Z20	1½d. purple and green	70·00
Z21	2d. yellowish green and carmine-red	50·00
Z22	2½d. ultramarine	20·00
Z23	3d. purple/*orange-yellow*	60·00
Z24	4d. green and grey-brown	70·00
Z25	5d. dull purple and ultramarine	70·00
Z26	6d. pale dull purple	35·00
Z27	9d. dull purple and ultramarine	£120
Z28	10d. dull purple and carmine	£130
Z29	1s. dull green and carmine	90·00

ARMY OFFICIAL STAMPS

1896–1901. Stamps of Queen Victoria optd "ARMY OFFICIAL".

ZO1	½d. vermilion	£100
ZO2	½d. blue-green	£100
ZO3	1d. lilac (16 *dots*)	85·00
ZO4	6d. purple/*rose-red*	

IX. UNION OF SOUTH AFRICA

The provinces continued to use their existing issues until the introduction of Nos. 3/17. From 19 August 1910 the issues of any province were valid for use throughout the Union until they were demonetised on 31 December 1937.

PRICES FOR STAMPS ON COVER TO 1945		
Nos.	1/15	*from* × 4
Nos.	16/17	—
Nos.	18/21	*from* × 6
Nos.	26/32	*from* × 2
No.	33	*from* × 4
Nos.	34/110	*from* × 1
Nos.	D1/7	*from* × 4
Nos.	D8/33	*from* × 6
Nos.	O1/33	*from* × 4

1

(Des H. S. Wilkinson. Recess D.L.R.)

1910 (4 Nov). Opening of Union Parliament. Inscribed bilingually. Wmk Multiple Rosettes. P 14.

1	**1**	2½d. deep blue	3·00	1·75
		s. Handstamped "*Specimen.*"	£400	
2		2½d. blue	1·75	1·00

The deep blue shade is generally accompanied by a blueing of the paper.

2

3

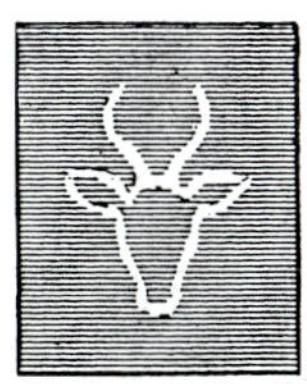
4 Springbok's Head

(Typo D.L.R.)

1913 (1 Sept)–**24**. Inscribed bilingually. W **4**.

(a) P 14

No.	Type	Description	Un	Used
3	**2**	½d. green	1·75	30
		a. Stamp doubly printed	£10000	
		b. Blue-green	2·00	20
		c. Yellow-green	2·50	80
		d. Printed on the gummed side	£800	
		w. Wmk inverted	2·00	80
4		1d. rose-red *(shades)*	1·75	10
		a. Carmine-red	2·25	10
		b. *Scarlet (shades)*	3·50	75
		c. Printed on the gummed side	£1000	
		w. Wmk inverted	2·50	70
5		1½d. chestnut *(shades)* (23.8.20)	80	10
		a. *Tête-bêche* (pair)	1·75	18·00
		b. Printed on the gummed side	£1100	
		c. Wmk sideways	†	£1500
		w. Wmk inverted	80	10
6	**3**	2d. dull purple	1·75	10
		a. Deep purple	2·50	10
		b. Printed on the gummed side	£1100	
		w. Wmk inverted	2·25	1·75
7		2½d. bright blue	3·75	1·00
		a. Deep blue	4·00	3·00
		w. Wmk inverted	£120	£120
8		3d. black and orange-red	12·00	30
		a. Black and dull orange-red	10·00	70
		w. Wmk inverted	20·00	8·50
9		3d. ultramarine *(shades)* (4.10.22)	3·75	1·25
		w. Wmk inverted	9·50	4·50
10		4d. orange-yellow and olive-green	9·00	75
		a. Orange-yellow and sage-green	6·50	55
		w. Wmk inverted	8·00	85
11		6d. black and violet	5·50	60
		a. Black and bright violet	9·50	1·25
		aw. Wmk inverted	16·00	9·50
12		1s. orange	10·00	60
		a. Orange-yellow	15·00	1·00
		w. Wmk inverted	20·00	1·50
13		1s.3d. violet *(shades)* (1.9.20)	11·00	6·00
		w. Wmk inverted	£130	£170
14		2s.6d. purple and green	55·00	1·50
15		5s. purple and blue	£110	8·50
		a. Reddish purple and light blue	£110	8·50
		w. Wmk inverted	£4750	£2750
16		10s. deep blue and olive-green	£180	7·50
		w. Wmk inverted	£4000	£1800
17		£1 green and red (7.16)	£600	£350
		a. Pale olive-green and red (1924)	£800	£1200
3/17 *Set of 15*			£900	£350
3s/8s, 10s/17s Optd or H/S (1½d. and 1s.3d. in violet, £1 in green) "SPECIMEN" *Set of 14*			£1400	

(b) Coil stamps. P 14×imperf

No.	Type	Description	Un	Used
18	**2**	½d. green	6·00	1·00
		w. Wmk inverted	£650	£325
19		1d. rose-red (13.2.14)	17·00	3·00
		a. Scarlet	22·00	8·50
		w. Wmk inverted	£650	£325
20		1½d. chestnut (15.11.20)	11·00	15·00
		w. Wmk inverted	†	—
21	**3**	2d. dull purple (7.10.21)	15·00	4·75
18/21 *Set of 4*			45·00	21·00

The 6d. exists with "Z" of "ZUID" wholly or partly missing at R. 8/3, lower right pane, due to wear of plate *(Price wholly missing, £95 un, £40 us)*.

5 de Havilland D.H.9 Biplane

(Eng A. J. Cooper. Litho *Cape Times* Ltd)

1925 (26 Feb). Air. Inscr bilingually. P 12.

No.	Type	Description	Un	Used
26	**5**	1d. carmine	5·00	12·00
27		3d. ultramarine	7·50	12·00
28		6d. magenta	11·00	14·00
29		9d. green	24·00	65·00
26/9 *Set of 4*			42·00	95·00

Beware of forgeries of all values perforated 11, 11½ or 13.

INSCRIPTIONS. From 1926 until 1951 most issues were inscribed in English and Afrikaans alternately throughout the sheets.

PRICES for Nos. 30/135 are for unused horizontal pairs, used horizontal pairs and used singles (either inscription), *unless otherwise indicated*. Vertical pairs are worth between 20% and 35% of the prices quoted for horizontal pairs.

6 Springbok

7 *Dromedaris* (Van Riebeeck's ship)

8 Orange Tree

9

(Typo Waterlow until 1927, thereafter Govt Printer, Pretoria)

1926 (2 Jan)–**27**. W **9**. P 14½×14.

No.	Type	Description	*Un pair*	*Used pair*	*Used single*
30	**6**	½d. black and green	2·50	3·25	10
		a. Missing "1" in "½"	£2000		
		b. Centre omitted (in pair with normal)	£2500		
		cw. Wmk inverted	4·75	6·00	20
		d. Frame printed double	£3250		
		e. Perf 13½×14 (1927)	85·00	85·00	4·00
		ea. *Tête-bêche* (pair)	£1200		
		ew. Wmk inverted	85·00	85·00	4·00
		f. Wmk sideways	—	£2250	
31	**7**	1d. black and carmine	1·50	50	10
		a. Imperf (vert pair)*	£700		
		b. Imperf 3 sides (vert pair)*	£700	£750	
		cw. Wmk inverted	5·50	2·25	20
		d. Perf 13½×14 (1927)	£110	80·00	4·00
		da. *Tête-bêche* (pair)	£1200		
		dw. Wmk inverted	£110	80·00	4·00
		e. Wmk sideways	£2250	£2000	
32	**8**	6d. green and orange (1.5.26)	42·00	48·00	1·50
		w. Wmk inverted	70·00	75·00	
30/2 *Set of 3*			42·00	48·00	1·50

No. 30a exists in Afrikaans only. Nos. 30e and 31d were only issued in booklets.

No. 30d occurred on the bottom left-hand corner of one sheet and included the bottom four stamps in the first vertical row and the bottom two in the second. As listed No. 30d shows the left-hand stamp with the frame completely double and the right-hand stamp with two-thirds of the frame double.

*Both Nos. 31a and 31b occur in blocks of four with the other vertical pair imperforate at left.

For ½d. with pale grey centre, see No. 126.

For rotogravure printing see Nos. 42, etc.

10 "Hope"

(Recess B.W.)

1926 (2 Jan). T **10**. Inscribed in English or Afrikaans. W **9** (upright or inverted in equal quantities).

No.	Description	*Single stamps*	
33	4d. grey-blue (English inscr) *(shades)*	1·75	1·25
	a. Inscr in Afrikaans	1·75	1·25

In this value the English and Afrikaans inscriptions are on separate sheets.

This stamp is known with private perforations or roulettes.

11 Union Buildings, Pretoria

12 Groot Schuur

12a A Native Kraal

13 Black and Blue Wildebeest

14 Ox-wagon inspanned

15 Ox-wagon outspanned

16 Cape Town and Table Bay

(Recess B.W.)

1927 (1 Mar)–**30**. W **9**. P 14.

			Un pair	*Used pair*	*Used single*
34	**11**	2d. grey and maroon	11·00	26·00	60
		aw. Wmk inverted	£700	£750	50·00
		b. Perf 14×13½ (2.30)	38·00	38·00	70
35	**12**	3d. black and red	15·00	27·00	60
		a. Perf 14×13½ (1930)	80·00	80·00	80
35*b*	**12a**	4d. brown (23.3.28)	30·00	50·00	1·00
		bw. Wmk inverted	£850	£800	50·00
		c. Perf 14×13½ (1930)	60·00	70·00	1·25
36	**13**	1s. brown and deep blue	30·00	55·00	1·00
		a. Perf 14×13½ (1930)	75·00	90·00	2·00
37	**14**	2s.6d. green and brown	£140	£400	17·00
		a. Perf 14×13½ (1930)	£375	£600	24·00
38	**15**	5s. black and green	£275	£750	35·00
		a. Perf 14×13½ (1930)	£475	£1000	42·00
39	**16**	10s. bright blue and brown	£180	£150	10·00
		a. Centre inverted (*single stamp*)	£16000		
		b. Perf 14×13½ (1930)	£250	£200	12·00
34/9 *Set of 7*			£600	£1300	55·00
34s/9s H/S "SPECIMEN" *Set of 7*			£1000		

17 de Havilland D.H.60 Cirrus Moth

(Typo Govt Ptg Wks, Pretoria)

1929 (16 Aug). Air. Inscribed bilingually. No wmk. P 14×13½.

			Un single	*Us single*
40	**17**	4d. green	5·00	1·75
41		1s. orange	12·00	13·00

PRINTER. All the following issues, except *where stated otherwise*, are printed by rotogravure (the design having either plain lines or a dotted screen) by the Government Printer, Pretoria.

I

II

The two types of the 1d. differ in the spacing of the horizontal lines in the side panels:—Type I close; Type II wide. The Afrikaans had the spacing of the words POSSEEL-INKOMSTE close in Type I and more widely spaced in Type II.

½d. "Cobweb" variety (retouch between horns) (Cyl. 1 R. 9/5)

½d. "Dollar" variety (Cyl. 2 R. 10/9)

2d. Airship flaw (Cyl 34 R. 9/4)

3d. Window flaw (R. 20/4 on all ptgs before 1937)

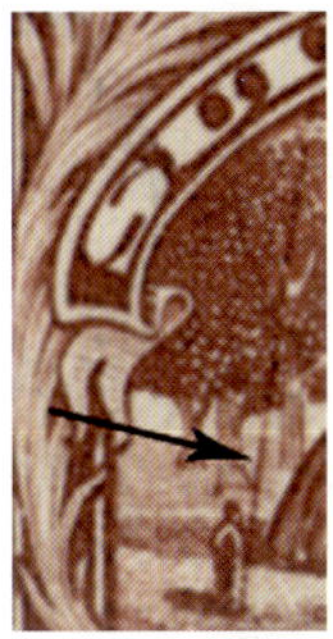

4d. Spear flaw (R. 9/2)

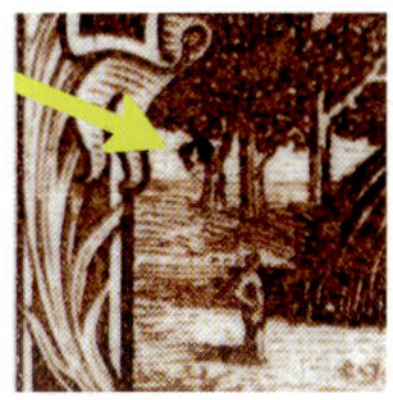

4d. "Monkey" in tree (R. 2/2)

1s. Twisted horn (Cyl 7020 R. 1/5)

1930–45. T **6** to **8** and **11** to **14** redrawn, "SUIDAFRIKA" (in one word) on Afrikaans stamps. W **9**. P 15×14 (½d., 1d., and 6d.) or 14.

		Un pair	*Used pair*	*Used single*
42	½d. black and green (5.30)	4·50	3·50	10
	a. Two English or two Afrikaans stamps *se-tenant* (vert strip of 4)	40·00		
	b. *Tête-bêche*	£1100		
	c. "Cobweb" variety	42·00		
	d. "Dollar" variety	42·00		
	w. Wmk inverted	4·50	3·50	10
43	1d. black and carmine (I) (4.30)	5·00	3·00	10
	a. *Tête-bêche*	£1200		
	b. Frame omitted (*single stamp*)	£475		
	cw. Wmk inverted	5·00	3·00	10
43*d*	1d. black and carmine (II) (8.32)	55·00	4·00	10
	dw. Wmk inverted	48·00	4·00	10
44	2d. slate-grey and lilac (4.31)	28·00	24·00	30
	a. *Tête-bêche*	£6500		
	bw. Wmk inverted	17·00	9·00	20
	bwa. Frame omitted (*single stamp*)	£4500	£5000	
	c. Airship flaw	£120	£130	

44*d*	2d. blue and violet (3.38)	£325	75·00	2·50
	da. Airship flaw	£850		
45	3d. black and red (11.31)	£100	£100	2·25
	aw. Wmk inverted	35·00	60·00	1·25
	b. Window flaw	£140		
45*c*	3d. blue (10.33)	23·00	7·00	20
	cw. Wmk inverted	6·00	6·00	10
	d. Window flaw	55·00		
	e. Centre omitted	£27000		
	f. Frame omitted (*single stamp*)	£13000		
46	4d. brown (19.11.32)	£225	£140	6·50
	aw. Wmk inverted	32·00	32·00	40
	b. Spear flaw	£150	£150	
46*c*	4d. brown (*shades*) (*again redrawn*) (1936)	3·75	2·75	10
	ca "Monkey" in tree	45·00		
	cw. Wmk inverted	13·00	9·50	10
47	6d. green and orange (*wmk inverted*) (13.5.31)	13·00	4·50	10
	w. Wmk upright (8.32)	50·00	18·00	10
48	1s. brown and deep blue (14.9.32)	£100	60·00	40
	aw. Wmk inverted	35·00	26·00	25
	b. Twisted horn flaw	£225	£275	
49	2s.6d. green & brown (*shades*) (24.12.32)	£110	£110	3·25
	aw. Wmk inverted	£200	£200	3·25
49*b*	2s.6d. blue and brown (1945)	26·00	15·00	20
42/9*b*	*Set of* 13	£500	£275	6·50

For similar designs with "SUID-AFRIKA" hyphenated, see Nos. 54 etc. and Nos. 114 etc.

Nos. 42/3, 43*d*/4 exist in coils.

No. 42a comes from the coil printing on the cylinder for which two horizontal rows were incorrectly etched so that two Afrikaans-inscribed stamps were followed by two English. This variety is normally without a coil join, although some examples do occur showing a repair join.

The 1d. (Type I) exists without watermark from a trial printing (*Price* £25 *un*).

Although it appears to be printed in one colour No. 45*c* was produced from vignette and frame cylinders in the same way as the bicoloured version. The clouds in the background, which are present on No. 45e, were printed from the frame cylinder.

Nos. 45b, 45d, 46b and 48b all occur on printings with either upright or inverted watermark. The price quoted is for the cheapest version in each instance.

The Rotogravure printings may be distinguished from the preceding Typographed and Recess printed issues by the following tests:—

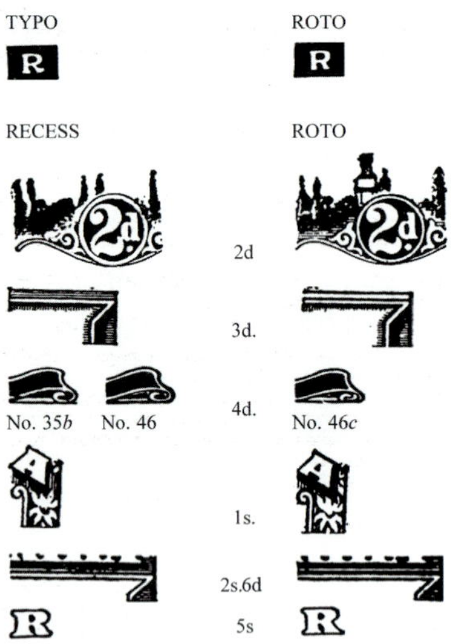

ROTOGRAVURE:

½d. 1d. and 6d. Leg of "R" in "AFR" ends squarely on the bottom line.
2d. The newly built War Memorial appears to the left of the value.
3d. Two fine lines have been removed from the top part of the frame.
4d. No. 46. The scroll is in solid colour.
No. 46*c*. The scroll is white with a crooked line running through it. (No. 35*b*. The scroll is shaded by the diagonal lines.)
1s. The shading of the last "A" partly covers the flower beneath.
2s.6d. The top line of the centre frame is thick and leaves only one white line between it and the name.
5s. (Nos. 64/*b*). The leg of the "R" is straight.
Rotogravure impressions are generally coarser.

18 Church of the Vow

19 "The Great Trek" (C. Michell)

20 A Voortrekker

21 Voortrekker Woman

1d. Blurred "SOUTH AFRICA" and red "comet" flaw (Cyls 6917/6922 R. 2/7)

(Des J. Prentice (½d., 2d., 3d.)

1933 (3 May)–**36**. Voortrekker Memorial Fund. W **9** (sideways). P 14.

50	**18**	½d. +½d. black and green (16.1.36)	4·00	7·00	50
51	**19**	1d. +½d. grey-black and pink	2·75	1·50	25
		a. Blurred "SOUTH AFRICA" and red "comet" flaw	55·00	60·00	
52	**20**	2d. +1d. grey-green and purple	4·00	4·00	55
53	**21**	3d. +1½d. grey-green and blue	6·50	5·00	70
50/3		*Set of* 4	15·00	16·00	1·75

22 Gold Mine

22a Groot Schuur

Dies of 6d.

I II III

23 Groot Constantia

1½d. Broken chimney and fainter headgear (Cyl 62 R. 11/6)

1½d. Flag on chimney at right (Cyl 62 R. 20/2)

6d. "Falling ladder" flaw (R. 5/10)

6. "Molehill" flaw (R. 20/11)

1933–48. "SUID-AFRIKA" (hyphenated) on Afrikaans stamps. W **9**. P 15×14 (½d., 1d. and 6d.) or 14 (others).

54	**6**	½d. grey and green (*wmk inverted*) (9.35)	5·00	2·25	10
		aw. Wmk upright (1936)	11·00	8·00	10
		b. Coil stamp. Perf 13½×14 (1935)	40·00	70·00	1·00
		bw. Wmk upright	40·00	70·00	1·00
		c. Booklet pane of 6 (with adverts on margins) (*wmk upright*)	30·00		
56	**7**	1d. grey and carmine (*shades*) (19.4.34)	1·75	2·25	10
		a. Imperf (pair) (*wmk inverted*)	£180		
		b. Frame omitted (*single stamp*)	£325		
		cw. Wmk inverted	1·75	2·25	10
		d. Coil stamp. Perf 13½×14 (1935)	42·00	65·00	1·40
		dw. Wmk inverted	42·00	65·00	1·40
		e. Booklet pane of 6 (with adverts on margins) (1935)	28·00		
		f. Booklet pane of 6 (with blank margins) (1937)	25·00		
		h. Booklet pane of 6 (with postal slogans on margins) (1948)	4·00		
		i. Grey & brt rose-carm (7.48)	70	2·25	10
57	**22**	1½d. green and bright gold (12.11.36)	4·50	2·50	10
		a. Shading omitted from mine dump (in pair with normal)	£250	£160	
		b. Broken chimney and faint headgear	24·00		
		c. Flag on chimney at right	24·00		
		dw. Wmk inverted	1·50	2·25	10
		e. Blue-green and dull gold (8.40)	7·00	3·25	10
58	**11**	2d. blue and violet (11.38)	75·00	42·00	75
58*a*		2d. grey and dull purple (5.41)	65·00	£100	1·50
59	**22a**	3d. ultramarine (2.40)	14·00	3·50	10
61	**8**	6d. green and vermilion (I) (10.37)	70·00	40·00	70
		a. "Falling ladder" flaw	£275	£300	
		b. "Molehill" flaw	£225	£225	
61*c*		6d. green and vermilion (II) (6.38)	42·00	1·00	10
61*d*		6d. green and red-orange (III) (11.46)	20·00	75	10
62	**13**	1s. brown and chalky blue (2.39) (*shades*)	55·00	18·00	20
		a. Frame omitted (*single stamp*)	£7000		
64	**15**	5s. black and green (10.33)	55·00	75·00	1·75
		aw. Wmk inverted	£120	£150	3·00
		b. Black and blue-green (9.44)	42·00	21·00	35
64*c*	**23**	10s. blue and sepia (*shades*) (8.39)	65·00	10·00	70
		ca. Blue and charcoal (1944)	45·00	5·50	30
54/9, 61*d*/64*ca* *Set of 10*			£300	£180	2·75

The ½d. and 1d. coil stamps may be found in blocks emanating from the residue of the large rolls which were cut into sheets and distributed to Post Offices.

Nos. 54 and 56 also exist in coils.

1d. Is printed from Type II. Frames of different sizes exist due to reductions made from time to time for the purpose of providing more space for the perforations.

3d. In No. 59 the frame is unscreened and composed of solid lines. Centre is diagonally screened. Scrolls above "3d." are clear lined, light in the middle and dark at sides.

6d. Die I. Green background lines faint. "SUID-AFRIKA" 16¼ mm long.

Die II. Green background lines heavy. "SUID-AFRIKA" 17 mm long. "S" near end of tablet. Scroll open.

Die III. Scroll closed up and design smaller (18×22 mm).

Single specimens of the 1933–48 issue inscribed in English may be distinguished from those of 1930–45 as follows:—

½d. and 1d. Centres in grey instead of varying intensities of black.
2d. The letters of "SOUTH AFRICA" are narrower and thinner.
3d. The trees are taller and the sky is without lines.
6d. The frame is vermilion.
1s. The frame is chalky blue.

For similar designs, but printed in screened rotogravure, see Nos. 114 to 122a.

BOOKLET PANES. Booklets issued in 1935 contained ½d. and 1d. stamps in panes with advertisements in the top and bottom margins and no margin at right (Nos. 54b and 56d). These were replaced in 1937 by editions showing blank margins on all four sides (Nos. 56e and 75ba). Following a period when the booklet panes were without margins a further 3s. booklet was issued in 1948 which had four margins on the panes and postal slogans at top and bottom (Nos. 56h, 87b and 114a).

24

JIPEX

1936
(24a)

"Cleft skull" flaw (R. 14/2)

Spots above head and behind neck (R. 12/5)

(Des J. Booysen)

1935 (1 May). Silver Jubilee. Inscr bilingually. W **9**. P 15×14.

No.	Type	Description	Un pair	Used pair	Used single
65	**24**	½d. black and blue-green	3·00	12·00	10
		a. "Cleft skull" flaw	8·50	25·00	
		b. Spots above head and behind neck	9·50	28·00	
66		1d. black and carmine	3·00	6·50	10
		a. "Cleft skull" flaw	8·50	18·00	
		b. Spots above head and behind neck	11·00	25·00	
67		3d. blue	15·00	55·00	2·25
		a. "Cleft skull" flaw	50·00	£120	
		b. Spots above head and behind neck	55·00	£130	
68		6d. green and orange	30·00	75·00	3·25
		a. "Cleft skull" flaw	80·00	£180	
		b. Spots above head and behind neck	85·00	£190	
65/8		*Set of 4*	45·00	£130	5·00

In stamps with English at top the ½d., 3d. and 6d. have "SILWER JUBILEUM" to left of portrait, and "POSTAGE REVENUE" or "POSTAGE" (3d. and 6d.) in left value tablet. In the 1d., "SILVER JUBILEE" is to the left of portrait. In alternate stamps the positions of English and Afrikaans inscriptions are reversed.

1936 (2 Nov). Johannesburg International Philatelic Exhibition. Optd with T **24a**. W **9** (inverted).

No.	Description	Un sheet	Us sheet
MS69	**6** ½d. grey and green (No. 54)	4·50	12·00
MS70	**7** 1d. grey and carmine (No. 56)	3·25	8·00

Issued each in miniature sheet of six stamps with marginal advertisements. Ten different arrangements of advertisements exist on the ½d. sheets, 21 different on the 1d.

25

1½d. "Mouse" flaw (R. 4/1)

(Des J. Prentice)

1937 (12 May). Coronation. W **9** (sideways*). P 14.

No.	Type	Description	Un pair	Used pair	Used single
71	**25**	½d. grey-black and blue-green	1·00	1·25	10
		w. Wmk horns pointing to left	1·00	1·25	10
72		1d. grey-black and carmine	1·00	1·00	10
		w. Wmk horns pointing to left	1·00	1·00	10
73		1½d. orange and greenish blue	1·00	80	10
		a. "Mouse" flaw	10·00		
		w. Wmk horns pointing to left	1·00	80	10
74		3d. ultramarine	1·50	3·00	10
		w. Wmk horns pointing to left	1·50	3·00	10
75		1s. red-brown and turquoise-blue	3·25	5·00	15
		a. Hyphen on Afrikaans stamp omitted (R. 2/13)	70·00	80·00	
		bw. Wmk horns pointing to left	3·25	5·00	15
71/5		*Set of 5*	7·00	10·00	40

*The normal sideways watermark shows the horns of the springbok pointing to the right, *as seen from the back of the stamp*.

No. 75a shows the hyphen completely omitted and the top of the "K" damaged. A less distinct flaw, on which part of the hyphen is still visible and with no damage to the "K", occurs on R. 4/17.

25a

½d. "Tick" flaw on ear and spot on nose (multipositive flaw (occurring in 1947) (R. 3/4 or 3/1 on some ptgs of No. 114))

1937–40. W **9**. P 15×14.

No.	Type	Description	Un pair	Used pair	Used single
75*c*	**25a**	½d. grey and green	11·00	2·50	10
		ca. Booklet pane of 6 (with blank margins) (1937)	60·00		
		cd. Grey and blue green (1940)	7·50	1·25	10
		ce. "Tick" flaw and spot on nose	70·00		

The lines of shading in T **25a** are all horizontal and thicker than in T **6**. In Nos. 75*c* and 75*cd* the design is composed of solid lines. For stamps with designs composed of dotted lines, see No. 114. Later printings of No. 75*cd* have a smaller design.

26 Voortrekker Ploughing

27 Wagon crossing Drakensberg

28 Signing of Dingaan–Retief Treaty

29 Voortrekker Monument

(Des W. Coetzer and J. Prentice)

1938 (14 Dec). Voortrekker Centenary Memorial Fund. W **9**. P 14 (Nos. 76/7) or 15×14 (others).

No.	Type	Description	Un pair	Used pair	Used single
76	**26**	½d. +½d. blue and green	18·00	5·50	40
77	**27**	1d. +1d. blue and carmine	22·00	5·50	40
78	**28**	1½d. +1½d. chocolate and blue-green	24·00	10·00	1·00
79	**29**	3d. +3d. bright blue	26·00	10·00	1·00
76/9		*Set of 4*	80·00	28·00	2·50

30 Wagon Wheel

31 Voortrekker Family

1d. Three bolts in wheel rim (R. 15/5)

(Des W. Coetzer and J. Prentice)

1938 (14 Dec). Voortrekker Commemoration. W **9**. P 15×14.

80	**30**	1d. blue and carmine	9·00	3·50	30
		a. Three bolts in wheel rim	50·00	27·00	
81	**31**	1½d. greenish blue and brown	11·00	3·50	30

32 Old Vicarage, Paarl, now a museum

33 Symbol of the Reformation

34 Huguenot Dwelling, Drakenstein Mountain Valley

(Des J. Prentice)

1939 (17 July). 250th Anniv of Huguenot Landing in South Africa and Huguenot Commemoration Fund. W **9**. P 14 (Nos. 82/3) or 15×14 (No. 84).

82	**32**	½d. +½d.brown and green	9·00	6·50	40
83	**33**	1d. +1d. green and carmine	15·00	7·00	40
84	**34**	1½d. +1½d. blue-green and purple	32·00	18·00	1·25
82/4 *Set of 3*			50·00	28·00	1·90

34a Gold Mine

1941 (Aug)–**48**. W **9** (sideways). P 14×15.

87	**34a**	1½d. blue-green and yellow-buff (*shades*)	3·50	1·50	10
		a. Yellow-buff (centre) omitted	£4500	£2250	
		b. Booklet pane of 6 (with postal slogans on margins) (1948)	9·00		

35 Infantry

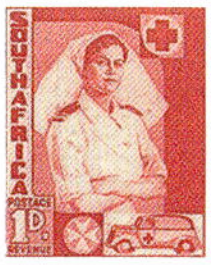

36 Nurse and Ambulance

37 Airman

38 Sailor, Destroyer and Lifebelts

39 Women's Auxiliary Services

40 Artillery

41 Electric Welding

42 Tank Corps

42a Signaller

1d. "Stain" on uniform (R. 14/11)

3d. "Cigarette" flaw (R. 18/2)

1941–46. War Effort. W **9** (sideways on 2d., 4d., 6d.). P 14 (2d., 4d., 6d.) or 15×14 (others).

(a) Inscr alternately

88	**35**	½d. green (19.11.41)	1·50	4·00	15
		a. Blue-green (7.42)	3·75	5·00	15
89	**36**	1d. carmine (3.10.41)	2·00	4·00	15
		a. "Stain" on uniform flaw	35·00		
90	**37**	1½d. myrtle-green (12.1.42)	1·50	4·00	15
91	**39**	3d. blue (1.8.41)	23·00	45·00	80
		a. "Cigarette" flaw	£110		
92	**40**	4d. orange-brown (20.8.41)	26·00	32·00	25
		a. Red-brown (6.42)	38·00	40·00	1·25
93	**41**	6d. red-orange (3.9.41)	12·00	15·00	20
94	**42a**	1s.3d. olive-brown (2.1.43)	17·00	13·00	25
		a. Blackish brown (5.46)	6·00	9·00	20

(b) Inscr bilingually

			Un single	*Us single*
95	**38**	2d. violet (15.9.41)	1·00	75
96	**42**	1s. brown (27.10.41)	3·75	1·00
88/96 *Set of 7 pairs and 2 singles*			70·00	£100

43 Infantry

44 Nurse

45 Airman

46 Sailor

47 Women's Auxiliary Services

48 Electric Welding

49 Heavy Gun in Concrete Turret

50 Tank Corps

Unit (*pair*)

Unit (*triplet*)

Ear Flap flaw (Cyl 43 R. 13/3)

Apostrophe flaw (Cyl 6931 R. 19/1) (later corrected)

Line on Cap (Cyl 39 R. 12/11)

1s. "Bursting Shell" (Cyl 46 R. 11/20)

1½d. Smoking "L" (Cyl 46 R. 8/2)

1942–44. War Effort. Reduced sizes. In pairs perf 14 (P) or strips of three, perf 15×14 (T), subdivided by roulette 6½. W **9** (sideways* on 3d., 4d. and 1s.).

		(a) Inscr alternately	*Un unit*	*Us unit*	*Us single*
97	**43**	½d. blue-green (T) (10.42)	2·00	1·50	10
		a. Green (3.43)	3·00	2·50	10
		b. Greenish blue (7.44)	2·00	2·25	10
		c. Roulette omitted	£1100	£900	
98	**44**	1d. carmine-red (T) (5.1.43)	1·50	1·50	10
		a. Bright carmine (3.44)	1·00	1·25	10
		b. Both roulettes omitted	£900	£900	
		ba. Left-hand roulette omitted	£1200		
99	**45**	1½d. red-brown (P) (9.42)	65	2·25	10
		a. Roulette 13 (8.42)	1·50	4·50	20
		b. Roulette omitted	£350	£375	
		c. Ear flap flaw	19·00		
100	**46**	2d. violet (P) (2.43)	90	2·00	10
		a. Reddish violet (6.43)	1·50	1·00	10
		b. Roulette omitted	£950	£850	
		c. Apostrophe flaw	70·00	75·00	
		d. Line on cap	70·00	75·00	
101	**47**	3d. blue (T) (10.42)	8·00	18·00	10
102	**48**	6d. red-orange (P) (10.42)	2·00	2·25	10
		(b) Inscr bilingually			
103	**49**	4d. slate-green (T) (10.42)	18·00	11·00	10
104	**50**	1s. brown (P) (11.42)	16·00	4·25	10
		a. "Bursting shell"	90·00		
		b. Smoking "L"	90·00		
97/104 *Set of 8*			42·00	38·00	65

*The sideways watermark shows springbok horns pointing to left on the 3d. and 1s., and to right on the 4d., *all as seen from the back of the stamp.*

52

53

1943. Coil stamps. Redrawn. In single colours with plain background. W **9**. P 15×14.

			Un pair	*Used pair*	*Used single*
105	**52**	½d. blue-green (18.2.43)	3·25	6·50	25
106	**53**	1d. carmine (9.43)	3·75	4·75	15

Quoted prices are for *vertical* pairs.

54 Union Buildings, Pretoria

1945–47. Redrawn. W **9**. P 14.

107	**54**	2d. slate and deep reddish violet (3.45)	20·00	2·50	10
		a. Slate and deep lilac (10.46)	20·00	6·00	20
		b. Slate and bright violet (1947)	4·25	10·00	20

In Nos. 107 to 107*b* the Union Buildings are shown at a different angle from Nos. 58 and 58*a*. Only the centre is screened i.e., composed of very small square dots of colour arranged in straight diagonal lines. For whole design screened and colours changed, see No. 116. No. 107*a*/*b* also show "2" of "2d." clear of white circle at top.

55 "Victory"

56 "Peace"

57 "Hope"

1945 (3 Dec). Victory. W **9**. P 14.

108	**55**	1d. brown and carmine	20	1·25	10
109	**56**	2d. slate-blue and violet	20	1·25	10
110	**57**	3d. deep blue and blue	20	1·50	10
108/10 *Set of 3*			55	3·50	25

58 King George VI

59 King George VI and Queen Elizabeth

60 Queen Elizabeth II as Princess, and Princess Margaret

"Bird" on "2" (Cyl 6912 R. 10/6)

3d. "Black-eyed Princess" (R. 19/2)

(Des J. Prentice)

1947 (17 Feb). Royal Visit. W **9**. P 15×14.

111	**58**	1d. black and carmine	10	35	10
112	**59**	2d. violet	15	60	10
		a. "Bird" on "2" flaw	5·00	7·50	
113	**60**	3d. blue	15	60	10
		a. "Black-eyed Princess"	6·50	10·00	
111/13 *Set of 3*			35	1·40	20

3d. "Flying saucer" flaw (Cyl 17 R. 17/2)

I

II 5s.

1947–54. "SUID-AFRIKA" hyphenated on Afrikaans stamps. Printed from new cylinders with design in screened rotogravure. W **9**. P 15×14 (½d., 1d. and 6d.) or 14 (others).

114	**25a**	½d. grey and green (frame only screened) (1947)	2·00	4·75	10
		a. Booklet pane of 6 (with postal slogans on margins) (1948)	3·50		
		b. "Tick" flaw and spot on nose	40·00		
		c. Entire design screened (2.49)	2·00	4·75	10
		ca. Booklet pane of 6 (with margin at right) (1951)	3·75		
		cb. "Tick" flaw and spot on nose	40·00		
115	**7**	1d. grey and carmine (1.9.50)	2·25	4·50	10
		a. Booklet pane of 6 (with margin at right) (1951)	4·25		
116	**54**	2d. slate-blue and purple (3.50)	5·50	15·00	50
117	**22a**	3d. dull blue (4.49)	3·75	7·00	10
117*a*		3d. blue (3.51)	4·25	6·00	10
		ab. "Flying saucer" flaw	70·00	70·00	
118	**12a**	4d. brown (22.8.52)	4·50	14·00	45
119	**8**	6d. green and red-orange (III) (1.50)	3·75	1·50	10
		a. Green and brown-orange (III) (1951)	3·25	1·25	10
120	**13**	1s. brown and chalky blue (1.50)	10·00	10·00	10
		a. Blackish brown and ultramarine (4.52)	15·00	17·00	20
121	**14**	2s.6d. green and brown (8.49)	10·00	30·00	1·00
122	**15**	5s. black and pale blue-green (I) (9.49)	45·00	80·00	2·00
122*a*		5s. black and deep yellow-green (II) (1.54)	50·00	£100	4·00
114/22 *Set of 9*			75·00	£130	3·50

In screened rotogravure the design is composed of very small squares of colour arranged in straight diagonal lines.

½d. Size 17¾×21¾ mm. Early printings have only the frame screened.

For the final printing of 114c, issued December 1951, the "Tick" flaw was removed, leaving a white "tick", but the spot on nose remained on R. 2/4.

1d. Size 18×22 mm. For smaller, redrawn design, see No. 135.

2d. For earlier issue with centre only screened, and in different colours, see Nos. 107/*a*.

3d. No. 117. Whole stamp screened with irregular grain. Scrolls above "3d." solid and toneless. Printed from two cylinders.

No. 117*a*. Whole stamp diagonally screened. Printed from one cylinder. Clouds more pronounced. Late printings were often in deep shades.

4d. Two groups of white leaves below name tablet and a clear white line down left and right sides of stamp.

61 Gold Mine

62 King George VI and Queen Elizabeth

1948 (1 Apr). Unit of four, perf 14, sub-divided by roulette 6½. W **9** (sideways).

			Un unit of 4	*Us unit*	*Used single*
124	**61**	1½d. blue-green and yellow-buff	2·50	5·50	10

(Des J. Booysen and J. Prentice)

1948 (26 Apr). Silver Wedding. W **9**. P 14.

			Un pair	*Used pair*	*Used single*
125	**62**	3d. blue and silver	50	1·25	10

(Typo Government Printer, Pretoria)

1948 (July). W **9**. P 14½×14.

126	**6**	½d. pale grey and blue-green	1·75	10·00	75

This was an economy printing made from the old plates of the 1926 issue for the purpose of using up a stock of cut paper. For the original printing in black and green, see No. 30.

63 *Wanderer* (emigrant ship) entering Durban

Extended rigging on mainmast (R. 14/2)

"Pennant" flaw (R. 17/5)

(Des J. Prentice)

1949 (2 May). Centenary of Arrival of British Settlers in Natal. W **9**. P 15×14.

127	**63**	1½d. claret	80	80	10
		a. Extended rigging	14·00	14·00	
		b. "Pennant" flaw	14·00	14·00	

64 Hermes

3d. Serif on "C" (R. 1/1)

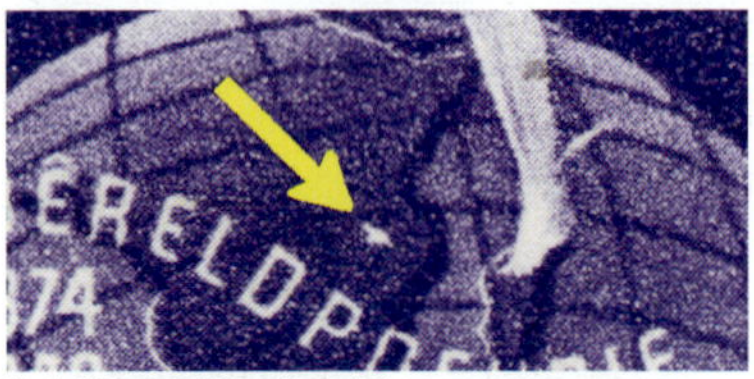

"Lake" in East Africa (R. 2/19)

(Des J. Booysen and J. Prentice)

1949 (1 Oct). 75th Anniv of Universal Postal Union. As T **64** inscr "UNIVERSAL POSTAL UNION" and "WERELDPOSUNIE" alternately. W **9** (sideways). P 14×15.

128	**64**	½d. blue-green	50	1·00	10
129		1½d. brown-red	50	1·00	10
130		3d. bright blue	60	1·00	10
		a. Serif on "C"	45·00		
		b. "Lake" in East Africa	45·00		
128/30 *Set of 3*			1·40	2·75	25

65 Wagons approaching Bingham's Berg

67 Bible, candle and Voortrekkers

66 Voortrekker Monument, Pretoria

68 Union Buildings, Pretoria

(Des W. Coetzer and J. Prentice)

1949 (1 Dec). Inauguration of Voortrekker Monument, Pretoria. T **65** and similar horiz designs. W **9**. P 15×14.

		Un single	*Us single*
131	1d. magenta	10	10
132	1½d. blue-green	10	10
133	3d. blue	15	15
131/3 *Set of 3*		30	30

Designs:—1½d. Voortrekker Monument, Pretoria; 3d. Bible, candle and Voortrekkers.

1950 (Apr)–**51**. W **9** (sideways). P 14×15.

			Un pair	*Used pair*	*Used single*
134	**68**	2d. blue and violet	40	1·00	10
		a. Booklet pane of 6 (with margin at right) (1951)	4·00		

1951 (22 Feb). As No. 115, but redrawn with the horizon clearly defined. Size reduced to 17¼×21¼ mm.

135	**7**	1d. grey and carmine	1·00	2·50	10

69 Seal and monogram

70 "Maria de la Quellerie" (D. Craey)

2d. "Full Moon" flaw under "R" of "AFRICA" (R. 6/3)

2d. Line through sails consists of a vertical line from near the top of the upper stamp, extending through the sails to the stamp below (pair comprising R. 11/2 and R. 12/12)

(Des Miss R. Reeves and J. Prentice (1d., 4½d.), Mrs. T. Campbell and J. Prentice (others))

1952 (14 Mar). Tercentenary of Landing of Van Riebeeck. T **69/70** and similar designs. W **9** (sideways on 1d. and 4½d.) P 14×15 (1d. and 4½d.) or 14×15 (others).

136	½d. brown-purple and olive-grey	10	10
137	1d. deep blue-green	10	10
138	2d. deep violet	50	10
	a. "Full Moon"	10·00	
	b. "Line through sails" (vert pair)	15·00	
139	4½d. blue	10	10
140	1s. brown	80	10
136/40	*Set of 5*	1·40	45

Designs: *Horiz*—2d. Arrival of Van Riebeeck's ships; 1s. "Landing at the Cape" (C. Davidson Bell). *Vert*—4½d. "Jan van Riebeeck" (D. Craey).

SATISE (**74**)   **SADIPU** (**75**)

76 Queen Elizabeth II

1952 (26 Mar). South African Tercentenary International Stamp Exhibition, Cape Town. No. 137 optd with T **74** and No. 138 with T **75**.

141	1d. deep blue-green	40	1·25
142	2d. deep violet	60	1·00

(Des H. Kumst)

1953 (3 June). Coronation. W **9** (sideways). P 14×15.

143	**76**	2d. deep violet-blue	40	10
		a. *Ultramarine*	40	10

77 1d. "Cape Triangular" Stamp

(Des H. Kumst)

1953 (1 Sept). Centenary of First Cape of Good Hope Stamp. T **77** and similar horiz design. W **9**. P 15×14.

144	1d. sepia and vermilion	10	10
145	4d. deep blue and light blue	50	20

Design:—4d. Four pence "Cape Triangular" stamp.

79 Merino Ram

80 Springbok

81 Aloes

(Des A. Hendriksz and J. Prentice (4½d.))

1953 (1 Oct). W **9**. P 14.

146	**79**	4½d. slate-purple and yellow	20	10
147	**80**	1s.3d. chocolate	1·50	10
148	**81**	1s.6d. vermilion and deep blue-green	60	35
146/8		*Set of 3*	2·10	45

82 Arms of Orange Free State and Scroll

(Des H. Kumst)

1954 (23 Feb). Centenary of Orange Free State. W **9**. P 15×14.

149	**82**	2d. sepia and pale vermilion	10	10
150		4½d. purple and slate	20	50

83 Warthog

92 Springbok

93 Gemsbok

(Des H. Kumst)

1954 (14 Oct). T **83**, **92/3** and similar designs. W **9** (sideways on large vert designs). P 15×14 (½d. to 2d.), 14 (others).

151	½d. deep blue-green	10	10
152	1d. brown-lake	10	10
153	1½d. sepia	10	10
154	2d. plum	10	10
155	3d. chocolate and turquoise-blue	1·00	10
156	4d. indigo and emerald	1·00	30
157	4½d. blue-black and grey-blue	60	1·00
158	6d. sepia and orange	50	10
159	1s. deep brown and pale chocolate	1·25	10
160	1s.3d. brown and bluish green	3·00	10
161	1s.6d. brown and rose	1·75	60
162	2s.6d. brown-black and apple-green	3·50	20
163	5s. black-brown and yellow-orange	8·00	1·60
164	10s. black and cobalt	13·00	4·50
151/64	*Set of 14*	30·00	7·50

Designs: *Vert* (*as T* **83**)—1d. Black Wildebeest; 1½d. Leopard; 2d. Mountain Zebra. (*As T* **93**)—3d. White Rhinoceros; 4d. African Elephant; 4½d. Hippopotamus; 1s. Greater Kudu; 2s.6d. Nyala; 5s. Giraffe; 10s. Sable Antelope. *Horiz* (*as T* **92**)—6d. Lion.

No. 152 exists in coils.

See also Nos. 170/7 and 185/97.

97 President Kruger

98 President M. Pretorius

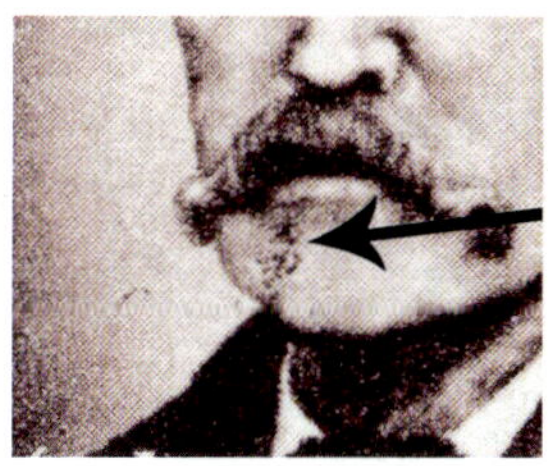

6d. "Scar" on chin (R. 1/7)

(Des H. Kumst)

1955 (21 Oct). Centenary of Pretoria. W **9** (sideways). P 14×15.

165	**97**	3d. slate-green	10	10
166	**98**	6d. maroon	10	30
		a. "Scar" on chin	8·00	

99 A. Pretorius, Church of the Vow and Flag

100 Settlers' Block-wagon and House

(Des H. Kumst)

1955 (1 Dec). Voortrekker Covenant Celebrations, Pietermaritzburg. W **9**. P 14.

			Un pair	Us pair	Us single
167	**99**	2d. blue and magenta	45	2·75	10

(Des H. Kumst)

1958 (1 July). Centenary of Arrival of German Settlers in South Africa. W **9**. P 14.

168	**100**	2d. chocolate and pale purple	10	10

101 Arms of the Academy

(Des H. Kumst)

1959 (1 May). 50th Anniv of the South African Academy of Science and Art, Pretoria. W **9**. P 15×14.

169	**101**	3d. deep blue and turquoise-blue	10	10
		a. Deep blue printing omitted	£4500	

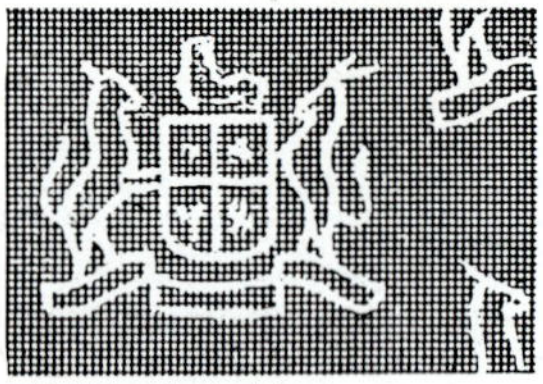

102 Union Coat of Arms

I II

1959–60. As Nos. 151/2, 155/6, 158/9 and 162/3, but W **102** (sideways on Nos. 172/3 and 175/7).

170	½d. deep greenish blue (12.60)	15	5·50
171	1d. brown-lake (I) (11.59)	10	10
	a. Redrawn. Type II (10.60)	20	10
172	3d. chocolate and turquoise-blue (9.59)	15	10
173	4d. indigo and emerald (1.60)	50	20
174	6d. sepia and orange (2.60)	70	2·00
175	1s. deep brown and pale chocolate (11.59)	7·00	80
176	2s.6d. brown-black and apple-green (12.59)	2·75	4·00
177	5s. black-brown and yellow-orange (10.60)	8·50	30·00
170/7 *Set of 8*		18·00	38·00

Nos. 171/a. In Type II "1d. Posgeld Postage" is more to the left in relation to "South Africa", with "1" almost central over "S" instead of to right as in Type I.

No. 171 exists in coils.

103 Globe and Antarctic Scene

(Des H. Kumst)

1959 (16 Nov). South African National Antarctic Expedition. W **102**. P 14×15.

178	**103**	3d. blue-green and orange	20	10

104 Union Flag

106 "Wheel of Progress"

(Des V. Ivanoff and H. Kumst (1s.), H. Kumst (others))

1960 (2 May). 50th Anniv of Union of South Africa. T **104**, **106** and similar designs. W **102** (sideways on 4d. and 6d.). P 14×15 (4d., 6d.) or 15×14 (others).

179	4d. orange-red and blue	30	10
180	6d. red, brown and light green	30	10
181	1s. deep blue and light yellow	30	10
182	1s. 6d. black and light blue	70	1·50
179/82 *Set of 4*		1·40	1·50

Designs: *Vert*—6d. Union Arms. *Horiz*—1s.6d. Union Festival emblem.

See also No. 190, 192/3.

108 Steam Locomotives *Natal* (1860) and Class 25 (1950s)

(Des V. Ivanoff)

1960 (2 May). Centenary of South African Railways. W **102**. P 15×14.

183	**108**	1s.3d. deep blue	1·10	30

109 Prime Ministers Botha, Smuts, Hertzog, Malan, Strijdom and Verwoerd

1960 (31 May). Union Day. W **102**. P 15×14.

184	**109**	3d. brown and pale brown	15	10
		a. Pale brown omitted*	£7500	

*This is due to a rectangular piece of paper adhering to the background cylinder, resulting in R.2/1 missing the colour completely and six adjoining stamps having it partially omitted. The item in block of eight is probably unique.

(New Currency. 100 cents= 1 rand)

1961 (14 Feb). As previous issues but with values in cents and rand. W **102** (sideways on 3½c., 7½c., 20c., 50c., 1r.). P 15×14 (½c., to 2½c., 10c.), 14×15 (3½c., 7½c.) or 14 (others).

185	½c. deep bluish green (as 151)	10	10
186	1c. brown-lake (as 152)	10	10
187	1½c. sepia (as 153)	10	10
188	2c. plum (as 154)	10	1·00
189	2½c. brown (as 184)	20	10
190	3½c. orange-red and blue (as 179)	15	2·25
191	5c. sepia and orange (as 158)	20	10
192	7½c. red, brown and light green (as 180)	20	3·00
193	10c. deep blue and light yellow (as 181)	40	60
194	12½c. brown and bluish green (as 160)	1·00	1·25
195	20c. brown and rose (as 161)	2·50	2·75
196	50c. black-brown and orange-yellow (as 163)	4·50	10·00
197	1r. black and cobalt (as 164)	14·00	24·00
185/97 *Set of 13*		21·00	40·00

X. REPUBLIC OF SOUTH AFRICA

OUTSIDE THE COMMONWEALTH

110 African Pygmy Kingfisher

111 Kafferboom Flower

112 Afrikander Bull

113 Pouring Gold

114 Groot Constantia

115 Burchell's Gonolek

116 Baobab Tree

117 Maize

118 Cape Town Castle Entrance

119 Protea

120 Secretary Bird

121 Cape Town Harbour

122 Strelitzia

Two types of ½c.:

I

II

Type I from sheets. Reeds indistinct.
Type II from coils. Reeds strengthened.

Three types of 1c.:

I

II

III

Type I. Lowest point of flower between "OS" of "POSTAGE". Right-hand petal over "E".
Type II. Flower has moved fractionally to the right so that lowest point is over "S" of "POSTAGE". Right-hand petal over "E .
Type III. Lowest point directly over "O". Right-hand petal over "G".

Two types of 2½c.

In Type I the lines of the building are quite faint. In Type II all lines of the building have been strengthened by re-engraving.

(Des Mrs. T. Campbell (½c., 3c., 1r.); Miss N. Desmond (1c.); De La Rue (2½c., 5c., 12½c.); H. L. Prager (50c.); Govt. Ptg Dept artist (others))

1961 (31 May)–**63**. Unsurfaced paper. W **102** (sideways* on ½c., 1½c., 2½c., 5c. to 20c.). P 14×15 (½c., 1½c.), 15×14 (1c.). or 14 (others).

198	**110**	½c. bright blue, carmine and brown (I)	10	10
		a. Perf 14 (3.63)	10	15
		b. Type II (coils) (18.5.63)	1·00	2·00
199	**111**	1c. red and olive-grey (I)	10	10
		a. Type II (1.62)	10	10
		b. Type III (coils) (5.63)	1·50	2·50
200	**112**	1½c. brown-lake and light purple	10	10
201	**113**	2c. ultramarine and yellow	2·00	10
202	**114**	2½c. violet and green (I)	15	10
		aw. Wmk top of arms to right	40	10
		b. Type II. *Dp violet & green* (9.61)	20	10
203	**115**	3c. red and deep blue	1·25	40
204	**116**	5c. yellow and greenish blue	30	10
205	**117**	7½c. yellow-brown and light green	60	10
206	**118**	10c. sepia and green	75	10
207	**119**	12½c. red, yellow and black-green	2·00	30
		a. Yellow omitted	£1200	
		b. Red omitted	£1800	
208	**120**	20c. turquoise-blue, carmine and brown orange	3·00	30
209	**121**	50c. black and bright blue	14·00	2·00
210	**122**	1r. orange, olive-green and light blue	7·00	2·00
198/210 *Set of* 13			26·00	4·50

*The normal sideways watermark shows the top of the arms to left, *as seen from the back of the stamp.*

1961–74 Definitives

Key to designs, perfs, watermarks, papers and phosphors

Value		*Type*	*Perf*	*W* **102** *Ordinary*	*No wmk Ordinary*	*W* **127** *Chalky*
½c.	**110**	(I)	14×15	198	—	—
		(I)	14	198a	—	—
		(II)	14×15	198b	—	—
1c.	**111**	(I)	15×14	199	211	—
		(II)		199a	211a	227
		(III)		199b	—	—
1½c.	**112**		14×15	200	—	228
2c.	**113**		14	201	212	229
2½c.	**114**	(I)	14	202	—	—
		(II)		202a	213/*a*	230/*a*
3c.	**115**		14	203	214	—
5c.	**116**		14	204	215	231
7½c.	**117**		14	205	216	232
10c.	**118**		14	206	217/*b*	233/*a*

Value	Type	Perf	W **102** Ordinary	No wmk Ordinary	W **127** Chalky
12½c.	**119**	14	207	—	—
20c.	**120**	14	208	218	234/a
50c.	**121**	14	209	219	235
1r.	**122**	14	210	—	236

Redrawn Designs

Value	Type		W **127** Upright or Tete-beche. Plain or phos	W **127** Tete-beche. Phos frame	No wmk. Phosphorised Glossy	Chalky
½c.	**130a**	14	238	—	—	—
		14×15	238b	—	—	—
		14	238c/d	—	—	—
1c.	**131**	15×14	239	—	—	—
		13½×14	239a	—	—	—
1½c.	**132**	14×15	240/b	284	—	—
		14×13½	240c	—	—	—
2c.	**133**	14	241/b	285/a	315a	—
		12½	—	—	315	315b
2½c.	**134**	14	242/a	286/a	—	—
3c.	**135**	14	243/a	287	—	—
		12½	—	—	316	316a
4c.	**134**	14	243b	288	—	—
5c.	**136**	14	244/a	289	318a	—
		12½	—	—	318	318b
6c.	**137**	14	—	290	—	—
		12½	—	—	—	319
7½c.	**137**	14	245	291	—	—
9c.	**139**	14	245a	292	—	—
		12½	—	—	320/a	—
10c.	**138**	14	246/a	293	321a	—
		12½	—	—	321	321b
12½c.	**139**	14	247/a	294	—	—
15c.	**140**	14	248	295	—	—
20c.	**141**	14	249/a	296/a	—	—
		12½	—	—	323	323a
50c.	**142**	14	250	—	—	—
		12½	—	—	324	324a
1r.	**143**	14	251	—	—	—
		12½	—	—	325	—

New Designs

			W **127** Upright or Tete-beche. Plain or phos	W **127** Tete-beche. Phos frame	No wmk. Phosphorised Glossy	Chalky
½c.	**168**	14×13½	276	282	—	—
		14×14½	276a	—	313	—
		14×15	—	282a	—	—
1c.	**169**	13½×14	277	283	—	—
		14	—	—	314	—
4c.	**182**	14	310/a	—	—	—
		12½	—	—	317/b	317c
15c.	**182a**	14	311	—	—	—
		12½	—	—	—	322

Although several of the stamps included in this table were issued after 1970 and are therefore not listed in this catalogue, the table has been shown here in full for the convenience of collectors

1961 (1 Aug)–**63**. As Nos. 199, 201/6 and 208/9 but without wmk.

211	**111**	1c. red and olive-grey (I)	10	30
		a. Type II (9.62)	70	55
212	**113**	2c. ultramarine and yellow (8.63)	8·00	1·50
213	**114**	2½c. deep violet and green (II)	20	20
		a. Violet and green (12.61)	20	10
214	**115**	3c. red and deep blue (10.61)	45	10
		a. Deep blue (face value, etc) omitted	£2000	
215	**116**	5c. yellow and greenish blue (12.61)	35	10
216	**117**	7½c. yellow-brown and light green (3.62)	60	15
217	**118**	10c. sepia and green (11.61)	60	50
		a. Sepia and emerald	50·00	18·00
		b. Sepia-brown and light green (7.63)	2·25	65
218	**120**	20c. turquoise-blue carmine and brown-orange (4.63)	8·00	2·75
219	**121**	50c. black and bright blue (8.62)	8·00	2·75
211/19 *Set of 9*			24·00	7·00

123 Blériot XI Monoplane and Boeing 707 Airliner over Table Mountain

124 Folk-dancers

1961 (1 Dec). 50th Anniv of First South African Aerial Post. W **102** (sideways). P 14×15.

220	**123**	3c. blue and red	50	10

(Des K. Esterhuysen)

1962 (1 Mar). 50th Anniv of Volkspele (folk-dancing) in South Africa. W **102** (sideways). P 14×15.

221	**124**	2½c. orange-red and brown	15	10

125 *The Chapman* (emigrant ship)

126 Red Disa (orchid), Castle Rock and Gardens

1962 (20 Aug). Unveiling of Precinct Stone, British Settlers Monument Grahamstown. W **102**. P 15×14.

222	**125**	2½c. turquoise-green and purple	50	10
223		12½c. blue and deep chocolate	1·75	1·25

(Des M. F. Stern)

1963 (14 Mar). 50th Anniv of Kirstenbosch Botanic Gardens, Cape Town. P 13½×14.

224	**126**	2½c. multicoloured	20	10
		a. Red (orchid, etc) omitted	£2500	£1500

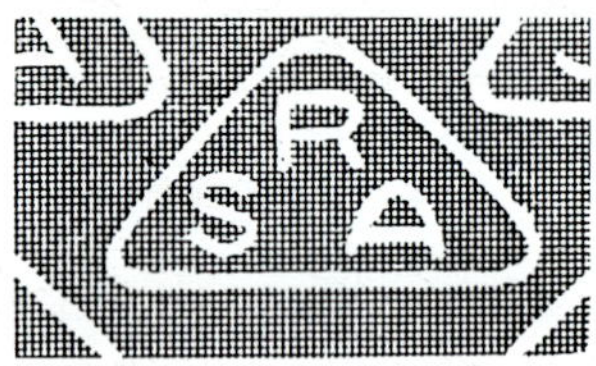

127 (normal version)

128 Centenary Emblem and Nurse

129 Centenary Emblem and Globe

1963 (30 Aug). Centenary of Red Cross. Chalk-surfaced paper. Wmk **127** (sideways on 2½c.). P 14×13½ (2½c.) or 15×14 (12½c.)

225	**128**	2½c. red, black and reddish purple	20	10
		w. Wmk reversed	3·25	1·75
226	**129**	12½c. red and indigo	1·75	1·00
		a. Red cross omitted	£2500	£1600

1963–67. As 1961–63 but chalk-surfaced paper and W **127** (sideways on 1½c., 2½c., (Nos. 230, 230aw) and 5c.), (sideways inverted on 2½c. (No. 230a), 7½c., 10c. and 20c.). P 15×14 (1c.) 14×15 (1½c.), or 14 (others).

227	**111**	1c. red and olive-grey (II) (9.63)	10	10
		w. Wmk reversed	65	65
228	**112**	1½c. brown-lake and light purple (1.67)	1·75	2·50
229	**113**	2c. ultramarine and yellow (11.64)	15	20
230	**114**	2½c. violet and green (I) (10.63)	10	10

		a. Bright reddish violet and emerald (II) (wmk sideways inverted) (3.66)	20	20
		aw. Wmk sideways	2·50	1·00
231	**116**	5c. yellow and greenish blue (9.66)	1·00	30
232	**117**	7½c. yellow-brown and bright green (23.2.66)	5·00	6·50
233	**118**	10c. sepia-brown and light emerald (9.64)	40	10
		a. Sepia-brown and green (1.67)	45	20
234	**120**	20c. turquoise-blue, carmine and brown orange (7.64)	1·00	1·50
		a. Deep turquoise-blue, carmine and flesh (20.7.65)	1·75	80
235	**121**	50c. black and ultramarine (4.66)	30·00	10·00
236	**122**	1r. orange, light green and pale blue (7.64)	48·00	48·00
227/36	*Set of* 10		80·00	60·00

In the 2½c. (No. 230*a*), 5c., 7½c., 10c. (Jan 1967 printing only) and 50c. the watermark is indistinct but they can easily be distinguished from the stamps without watermark by their shades and the chalk-surfaced paper which is appreciably thicker and whiter.

The normal sideways watermark shows the top of the triangle pointing left (*as seen from the back of the stamp*), i.e. sideways inverted. On Nos. 228, 230, 230aw and 231 the top of the triangle points to the right.

130 Assembly Building, Umtata

1963 (11 Dec). First Meeting of Transkei Legislative Assembly. Chalk-surfaced paper. W **127**. P 15×14.

237	**130**	2½c. sepia and light green	10	10
		a. Light green omitted	£2250	

130a African Pygmy Kingfisher

131 Kafferboom Flower

132 Afrikander Bull

133 Pouring Gold

134 Groot Constantia

135 Burchell's Gonolek

136 Baobab Tree

137 Maize

138 Cape Town Castle Entrance

139 Protea

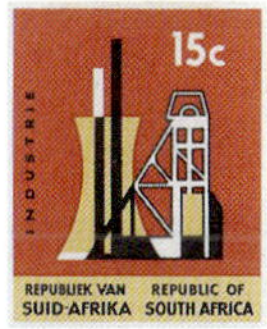

140 Industry

141 Secretary Bird

142 Cape Town Harbour

143 Strelitzia

(15c. des C. E. F. Skotnes)

Redrawn types.

½c. "½C" larger and REPUBLIEK VAN REPUBLIC OF" smaller.

3c. and 12½c. Inscriptions and figures of value larger.

Others. "SOUTH AFRICA" and SUID-AFRIKA larger and bolder. The differences vary in each design but are easy to see by comparing the position of the letters of the country name with "REPUBLIC OF" and "REPUBLIEK VAN".

1964–72. As 1961–63 but designs redrawn and new values (4c., 9c. and 15c.). Chalk-surfaced paper. W **127** (sideways on ½, 1½, 2½, 4, 5, 7½, 9, 10, 15 and 20c.). P 14×15 (1½c.), 15×14 (1c.) or 14 (others).

238	**130a**	½c. bright blue, carmine and brown (21.5.64)	10	10
		a. Imperf (pair)	£350	
		b. Perf 14×15. *Bright blue, carmine and yellow-brown* (6.7.67)	20	20
		c. Perf 14. *Bright blue, lake and yellow-brown* (3.68)	60	70
		d. Perf 14. *Bright blue, carmine lake and yellow-brown* (9.68)	30	10
239	**131**	1c. red and olive-grey (9.3.67)	10	10
		a. Perf 13½×14 (7.68)	30	10
240	**132**	1½c. dull red-brown and light purple (21.9.67)	15	10
		a. Purple-brown and light purple (1968)	15	10
		b. Bright red-brown and light purple (5.68)	15	10
		c. Perf 14×13½. *Red-brown and light purple* (14.8.69)	1·50	1·50
241	**133**	2c. ultramarine and yellow (8.1.68)	20	10
		a. Yellow omitted	£900	
		b. Blue and yellow (10.71)	70	10
242	**134**	2½c. violet and green (19.4.67)	20	10
		a. Reddish violet and green (8.67)	30	10
		w. Wmk top of RSA to left	£350	65·00
243	**135**	3c. red and deep blue (11.64)	30	10
		a. Brown-red and deep blue (3.72)	2·50	30
243*b*	**134**	4c. violet and green (10.71)	75	30
244	**136**	5c. orange-yellow and greenish blue (14.2.68)	40	10
		a. Lemon and deep greenish blue (10.71)	8·00	1·00
245	**137**	7½c. yellow-brown and bright green (26.7.67)	60	10
245*a*	**139**	9c. red, yellow and slate-green (2.72)	7·50	4·75
246	**138**	10c. sepia and green (10.6.68)	1·75	30
		a. Brown and pale green (7.68)	4·25	4·25
247	**139**	12½c. red, yellow and black-green (3.64)	1·00	40
		a. Red, pale yellow and blue-green (2.2.66)	2·75	40
248	**140**	15c. black, light olive-yellow and red-orange (1.3.67)	85	25
249	**141**	20c. turquoise-blue, carmine and brown-orange (2.68)	6·50	15
		a. Turquoise-blue, carmine and orange-buff (12.71)	7·00	1·50
250	**142**	50c. black and bright blue (17.6.68)	1·00	40
251	**143**	1r. orange, light green & lt bl (6.65)	1·00	1·00
		w. Wmk inverted		
238/51	*Set of* 16		19·00	6·75

*The normal sideways watermark shows the top of RSA to right *as seen from the back of the stamp*.

WATERMARK. Two forms of the watermark Type **127** exist in the above issue: the normal Type **127** (sometimes indistinct), and a very faint *tête-bêche* watermark, i.e. alternately facing up and down, which was introduced in mid 1967. As it is extremely difficult to distinguish these on single stamps we do not list it. The ½ (both perfs), 1, 2, 2½,

3, 15c. and 1r. are known in both forms, the 1½, 4, 5, 7½, 9, 10, 20 and 50c. only in the *tête-bêche* form and the 12½ c. Type **127** only.

GUM. The 2, 3, 5, 20, 50c. and 1r. exist with PVA gum as well as gum arabic.

PHOSPHORISED PAPER. From October 1971 onwards phosphor bands (see Nos. 282/96) gave way to phosphorised paper which cannot be distinguished from non-phosphor stamps without the aid of a lamp. For this reason we do not distinguish these printings in the above issue, but some are slightly different shades and all have PVA gum. The 4c. and 9c. are on phosphorised paper only and differ from Nos. 288 and 292 by the lack of phosphor bands.

145 "Springbok" Badge of Rugby Board

1964 (8 May). 75th Anniv of South African Rugby Board. Chalk-surfaced paper. T **145** and similar horiz design. W **127** (sideways on 2½c.). P 14×15 (2½c.) or 15×14 (12½c.)

252	2½c. yellow-brown and deep green	15	10
253	12½c. black and light yellow-green	2·00	2·25

Design:—12½c. Rugby footballer.

147 Calvin

1964 (10 July). 400th Death Anniv of Calvin (Protestant reformer). Chalk-surfaced paper. W **127** (sideways). P 14×13½.

254	**147**	2½c. cerise, violet and brown	10	10

148 Nurse's Lamp

149 Nurse holding Lamp

I. Screened base to lamp

II. Clear base to lamp

1964 (12 Oct). 50th Anniv of South African Nursing Association. Chalk-surfaced paper. W **127** (sideways on 2½c.). P 14×15 (2½ c.) or 15×14 (12½c.)

255	**148**	2½c. ultramarine and dull gold (Type I)	10	10
256		2½c. bright blue and yellow-gold (Type II)	30	10
		a. *Ultramarine and dull gold*	15	10
257	**149**	12½c. bright blue and gold	1·75	1·25
		a. Gold omitted	£2500	
255/7 *Set of 3*			1·75	1·25

150 I.T.U. Emblem and Satellites

1965 (17 May). I.T.U. Centenary. T **150** and similar horiz design. Chalk-surfaced paper. W **127**. P 15×14.

258	2½c. orange and blue	25	10
259	12½c. brown-purple and green	1·25	1·00

Design:—12½ c. I.T.U. emblem and symbols.

152 Pulpit in Groote Kerk, Cape Town

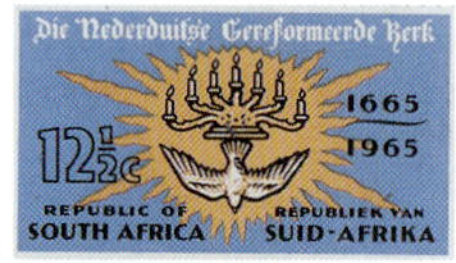

153 Church Emblem

1965 (21 Oct). Tercentenary of Nederduites Gereformeerde Kerk (Dutch Reformed Church) in South Africa. Chalk-surfaced paper. W **127** (sideways on 2½c., inverted on 12½c.). P 14×15 (2½c.) or 15×14 (12½c.).

260	**152**	2½c. brown and light yellow	15	10
261	**153**	12½c. black, light orange and blue	70	70

154 Diamond

155 Bird in flight

(Des C.E.F. Skotnes)

1966 (31 May). Fifth Anniv of Republic. T **154/5** and similar designs. Chalk-surfaced paper. W **127** (sideways on 1c., 3c.). P 14×13½ (1c.), 13½×14 (2½c.), 14×15 (3c.) or 15×14 (7½c.).

		Un pair	*Us pair*	*Us single*
262	1c. black, bluish green and olive-yellow	45	60	10
263	2½c. blue, deep blue and yellow-green	50	1·00	10
264	3c. red, greenish yellow and red-brown	1·25	1·75	10
265	7½c. blue, ultramarine and yellow	1·25	1·75	10
262/5 *Set of 4*		3·00	4·50	35

Designs: *Vert*—3c. Maize plants. *Horiz*—7½c. Mountain landscape.

Nos. 262/5 exsist on Swiss made paper with *tête bêche* watermark from special printing made for use in presentation albums for delegates to the U.P.U. Congress in Tokyo in 1969 as supplies of the original Harrison paper were by then exhausted (*Set of 4 pairs price £140 mint*).

158 Verwoerd and Union Buildings, Pretoria

(Des from portrait by Dr. Henkel)

1966 (6 Dec). Verwoerd Commemoration. T **158** and similar designs. Chalk-surfaced paper. W **127** (sideways on 3c.). P 14×15 (3c.) or 15×14 (others).

266	2½c. blackish brown and turquoise	10	10
267	3c. blackish brown and yellow-green	10	10
	a. Blackish brown (portrait) omitted	£5500	

268 12½ c. blackish brown and greenish blue........ 60 60
266/8 *Set of 3* 70 60

Designs: *Vert*—3c. "Dr. H.F. Verwoerd" (I. Henkel). *Horiz*—12½c. Verwoerd and map of South Africa.

161 "Martin Luther" (Cranach the Elder)

162 Wittenberg Church Door

1967 (31 Oct). 450th Anniv of Reformation. W **127** ((sideways), normal on 2½c., *tête-bêche* on 12½c.). P 14×15.

269 **161** 2½c. black and rose-red 10 10
270 **162** 12½c. black and yellow-orange .... 1·00 1·50

163 "Profile of Pres. Fouche" (I. Henkel)

164 Portrait of Pres. Fouche

1968 (10 Apr). Inauguration of President Fouche. W **127** (sideways). P 14×15.

271 **163** 2½c. chocolate and pale chocolate 10 10
272 **164** 12½c. deep blue and light blue .... 60 1·00

No. 272 also exists with the watermark *tête-bêche* (*Price un* £1; *used* £1.50).

165 Hertzog in 1902

1968 (21 Sept). Inauguration of General Hertzog Monument, Bloemfontein. T **165** and similar designs. W **127** (*tête-bêche* on 2½c., inverted on 3c., sideways on 12½c.). P 14×13½ (12½c.) or 13½×14 (others).

273 2½c. black, brown and olive-yellow 10 10
274 3c. black, red-brown, red-orange and yellow 15 10
275 12½c. red and yellow-orange .... 1·00 1·00
273/5 *Set of 3* .... 1·00 1·00

Designs: *Horiz*—3c. Hertzog in 1924. *Vert*—12½c. Hertzog Monument.

168 African Pygmy Kingfisher

169 Kafferboom Flower

1969. W **127** (*tête-bêche*, sideways on ½c.). P 14×13½ (½c.) or 13½×14 (1c.)

276 **168** ½c. new blue, carmine-red and yellow-ochre (1.69) 10 30
a. Coil. Perf 14×14½ (5.69) .... 1·75 3·50
277 **169** 1c. rose-red and olive-brown (1.69)..... 10 10

See also Nos. 282/3.

170 Springbok and Olympic Torch

171 Professor Barnard and Groote Schuur Hospital

1969 (15 Mar). South African Games, Bloemfontein. W **127** (*tête-bêche*, sideways). P 14×13½.

278 **170** 2½c. black, blue-black, red and sage-green 15 10
279 12½c. black, blue-black, red and cinnamon .... 70 1·00

1969 (7 July). World's First Heart Transplant and 47th South African Medical Association Congress. T **171** and similar horiz design. W **127** (*tête-bêche*). P 13½×14 (2½c.) or 15×14 (12½c.).

280 2½c. plum and rose-red 15 10
281 12½c. carmine-red and royal blue .... 1·25 1·40

Design:—12½c. Hands holding heart.

1969–72. As 1964–72 issue, Nos. 276/7, and new value (6c.), but with phosphor bands printed horizontally and vertically between the stamp designs, over the perforations, producing a frame effect. W **127** arranged *tête-bêche* (upright on 1, 2 and 3c., sideways on others). P 14×13½ (½, 1½c.), 13½×14 (1c.), or 14 (others).

282 **168** ½c. new blue, carmine-red and yellow-ochre (1.70) 15 70
a. Coil. Perf 14×15 (2.71) .... 3·50 4·75
w. Wmk reversed .... 65 1·25
283 **169** 1c. rose-red and olive-brown (12.69) .. 15 10
w. Wmk reversed 60 75
284 **132** 1½c. red-brown and light purple (12.69) 20 10
285 **133** 2c. ultramarine and yellow (11.69) .... 1·00 10
aa. Yellow omitted £1200
a. Deep ultramarine and yellow (8.70) 1·00 60
286 **134** 2½c. violet and green (1.70) 15 10
a. Purple and green (24.7.70) .... 1·75 10
w. Wmk reversed .... 20·00 17·00
287 **135** 3c. red and deep blue (30.9.69) .... 1·00 10
288 **134** 4c. violet and green (1.3.71) .... 40 1·25
289 **136** 5c. yellow and greenish blue (17.11.69) 60 10
290 **137** 6c. yellow-brown and bright green (3.5.71) 70 60
291 7½c. yellow-brown and bright green (17.11.69) .... 2·00 30
292 **139** 9c. red, yellow and black-green (17.5.71) .... 2·00 40
293 **138** 10c. brown and pale green (1.70) .... 1·00 10
294 **139** 12½c. red, yellow and black-green (2.5.70) .... 4·00 4·00
295 **140** 15c. black, light olive-yellow and red-orange (1.70) .... 1·00 1·75
296 **141** 20c. turquoise-blue, carmine and brown-orange 18.2.70) .... 8·00 2·75
a. Turquoise-blue, carmine and orange-buff (9.72) .... 11·00 2·25
282/96 *Set of 15* .... 20·00 10·00

No. 286 exists on normal RSA wmk as well as RSA *tête-bêche* wmk. The 1, 2, 2½, 3, 10, 15 and 20c. exist with PVA gum as well as gum arabic, but the 4, 6 and 9c. exist with PVA gum only. Stamps without watermark in these designs were issued between 1972 and 1974.

173 Mail Coach

174 Transvaal Stamp of 1869

1969 (6 Oct). Centenary of First Stamps of South African Republic (Transvaal). Phosphor bands on all four sides (2½c.). W **127** (*tête-bêche*, sideways on 12½c.). P 13½×14 (2½c.) or 14×13½ (12½c.)

297 **173** 2½c. yellow, indigo and yellow-brown... 15 10
298 **174** 12½c. emerald, gold and yellow-brown... 2·25 3·00

PHOSPHOR FRAME. Nos. 299/302 have phosphor applied on all four sides as a frame.

175 "Water 70" Emblem

177 "The Sower"

1970 (14 Feb). Water 70 Campaign. T **175** and similar design. W **127** (*tête-bêche* (sideways on 2½c.)). P 14×13½ (2½c.) or 13½×14 (3c.)

299 2½c. green, bright blue and chocolate 30 10
300 3c. Prussian blue, royal blue and buff 30 20

Design: *Horiz*—3c. Symbolic waves.

1970 (24 Aug). 150th Anniv of Bible Society of South Africa. T **177** and similar horiz design (gold die-stamped on 12½c.). W **127** (*tête-bêche*, sideways on 2½c.). P 14×13½ (2½c.) or 13½×14 (12½c.)

301 2½c. multicoloured 15 10
302 12½c. gold, black and blue .... 1·00 1·40

Design:—12½c. "Biblia" and open book.

178 J. G. Strijdom and Strijdom Tower

1971 (22 May). "Interstex" Stamp Exhibition, Cape Town. P 14×13½.

A. W **127** (sideways tête-bêche)

303A **178** 5c. light greenish blue, black and pale yellow 20 10

B. W **102** (sideways)

303B **178** 5c. light greenish blue, black and pale yellow .... 1·50 5·00

179 Map and Antarctic Landscape

1971 (22 May). Tenth Anniv of Antarctic Treaty. W **127** (*tête-bêche*). P 13½×14.

304 **179** 12½c. blue-black, greenish blue and orange-red .... 1·50 4·00

180 "Landing of British Settlers, 1820"

(T. Baines)

1971 (31 May). Tenth Anniv of the Republic of South Africa. T **180** and similar design. W **127** (*tête-bêche* sideways on 4c.). P 13½×14 (2c.) or 14×13½ (4c.).

305 2c. pale flesh and brown-red 15 20
w. Wmk reversed 80 80
306 4c. green and black 15 10
w. Wmk reversed .... 1·60 1·00

Design: *Vert*—4c. Presidents Steyn and Kruger and Treaty of Vereeniging Monument.

No. 306 exists with PVA gum as well as gum arabic.

PHOSPHORISED PAPER. All issues from here are on phosphorised paper unless otherwise stated.

181 View of Dam

(Des C. Bridgeford (4c.), C. Lindsay (others))

1972 (4 Mar). Opening of Hendrik Verwoerd Dam. T **181** and similar horiz designs. Multicoloured. W **127** (*tête-bêche*). P 13½×14.

307 4c. Type **181** 20 10
308 5c. Aerial view of Dam 25 10
309 10c. Dam and surrounding country (58×21 mm) .... 1·50 2·50
307/9 *Set of 3* .... 1·75 2·50

182 Sheep

182a Lamb

(Des K. Esterhuysen (4c.), H. Botha (15c.))

1972 (15 May). W **127** (*tête-bêche*). P 14.

310 **182** 4c. olive-brown, yellow, pale blue and slate-blue 30 10
a. yellow omitted £425
b. Grey-olive, yellow, bright blue and slate-blue (10.72) 30 10
311 **182a** 15c. pale stone, deep blue and dull blue .... 2·25 20

Other shades exist of the 4c.

See also Nos. 317 and 322.

183 Black and Siamese Cats

184 Transport and Industry

1972 (19 Sept). Centenary of Societies for the Prevention of Cruelty to Animals. W **127** (sideways *tête-bêche*). P 14×13½.

312 **183** 5c. multicoloured .... 1·25 10

1972–74. As Nos. 310/11 and 282 etc. but no wmk. Phosphorised, glossy paper. P 14×14½ (½c.). 14 (1c.) or 12½ (others).

313 **168** ½c. bright blue, scarlet and yellow-ochre (coil) (6.73) .... 15·00 17·00
314 **169** 1c. rose-red and olive-brown (1.74) 40 10
315 **133** 2c. blue and orange-yellow (11.72) 15 10
a. Perf 14. Deep ultramarine and orange-yellow (coil) (7.73) .... 11·00 14·00
b. Chalk-surfaced paper (17.7.74) .... 40 1·00
316 **135** 3c. scarlet and deep blue (8.5.73) 50 50
a. Chalk-surfaced paper (18.2.74) .... 1·25 1·50
317 **182** 4c. grey-blue, yellow, blue and bluish slate* (1.10.73) 30 40
a. Olive-sepia, yellow, azure and slate-blue (18.2.74) 60 40
b. Lavender-brown, pale yellow, blue and bluish slate* (26.7.74) 30 20
c. Chalk-surfaced paper* (22.8.74) 60 45
318 **136** 5c. orge-yell & greenish bl (4.10.73) .... 2·25 1·00
a. Perf 14. Yellow and light greenish blue (coil) (7.73) .... 12·00 14·00
b. Chalk-surfaced paper (5.74) .... 2·25 1·50
319 **137** 6c. yellow-brown and bright green (chalky paper) (22.7.74) .... 2·50 3·25
320 **139** 9c. red, yellow-green and green-black (6.73) .... 2·00 2·50

		a. Red, deep yellowish green and green-black (4.74)	3·00	1·50
321	138	10c. reddish brown & brt grn (8.5.73)	85	70
		a. Perf 14 (coil) (6.73)	14·00	17·00
		b. Chalk-surfaced paper (17.7.74)	1·50	1·25
322	182a	15c. pale stone, deep blue and dull blue (chalky paper) (4.9.74)	6·00	6·00
323	141	20c. turquoise-blue, rose-carmine and orange-buff (8.5.73)	3·25	1·00
		a. Chalk-surfaced paper (5.74)	5·00	80
324	142	50c. black and bright blue (6.73)	4·50	2·50
		a. Chalk-surfaced paper (22.7.74)	9·50	8·00
325	143	1r. orange, light green and light blue (8.10.73)	9·00	2·50
		a. Orange omitted	£2750	
313/25 *Set of* 13			42·00	32·00

*On these stamps the colours are known to vary within the sheet.

No. 314 also differs in that the central design has been moved down about 1 mm.

Nos. 317/c also differ from No. 310 by measuring 26¼×21 mm instead of 27¼×21¾ mm.

No. 325a exists on the bottom row of one sheet.

(Des J. Hoekstra (4c.), M. Barnett (others))

1973 (1 Feb). 50th Anniv of ESCOM (Electricity Supply Commission). T **184** and similar vert designs. Multicoloured. P 12×12½ (4c.) or 12½ (others).

326	4c. Type **184**	20	10
327	5c. Pylon (21×28 mm)	30	10
328	15c. Cooling Towers (21×28 mm)	3·00	3·50
326/8 *Set of* 3		3·25	3·50

185 University Coat of arms

187 C. J. Langenhoven

186 Rescuing Sailors

(Des P. de Wet (15c.), H. Meiring (others))

1973 (2 Apr). Centenary of University of South Africa. T **185** and similar designs. W **127** (*tête-bêche*) (5c.) or no wmk (others). P 12×12½ (5c.) or 12½ (others).

329	4c. multicoloured	20	10
330	5c. multicoloured	30	15
331	15c. black and gold	3·00	3·50
329/31 *Set of* 3		3·25	3·50

Designs: *Horiz* (37×21 mm)—5c. University Complex, Pretoria. Vert (As T **185**)—15c. Old University Building, Cape Town.

WATERMARK. All issues from this date are on unwatermarked paper, unless otherwise stated.

(Des M. Barnett)

1973 (2 June). Bicentenary of Rescue by Wolraad Woltemade. T **186** and similar horiz designs. P 11½×12½.

332	4c. light red-brown, light yellow-green and black	20	10
333	5c. yellow-olive, light yellow-green and black	40	10
334	15c. red-brown, light yellow-green and black	5·00	6·50
332/4 *Set of* 3		5·00	6·50

Designs:—5c. De Jonge Thomas foundering; 15c. De Jonge Thomas breaking up and sailors drowning.

(Des J. Mostert)

1973 (1 Aug). Birth Centenary of C. J. Langenhoven (politician and composer of national anthem). T **187** and similar designs. P 12½ (4 and 5c.) or 11½×12½ (15c.).

335	**187**	4c. multicoloured	25	10
336	–	5c. multicoloured	35	10
337	–	15c. multicoloured	3·50	5·00
335/7 *Set of* 3			5·00	5·00

Nos. 336/7 are as T **187** but with motifs rearranged. The 5c. is vert, 21×38 mm, and the 16c. is horiz, 38×21 mm.

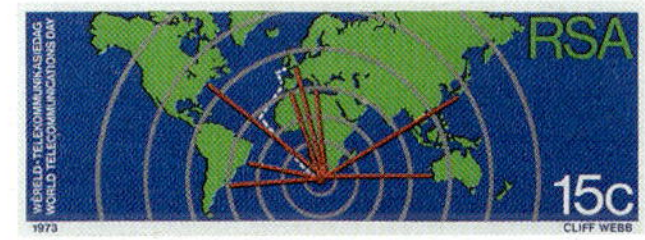

188 Communications Map

(Des C. Webb)

1973 (1 Oct). World Communications Day. P 12½.

(a) No wmk. Glossy paper

338	**188**	15c. multicoloured	50	1·40

(b) W **127** *(tête-bêche). Chalky paper*

339	**188**	15c. multicoloured	1·25	5·00

189 Restored Buildings

190 Burgerspond (obverse and reverse)

(Des W. Jordaan)

1974 (14 Mar). Restoration of Tulbagh. T **189** and similar multicoloured design. P 12½.

340	4c. Type **189**	15	10
341	5c. Restored Church Street (58×21 mm)	40	90

(Des P. de Wet. Litho)

1974 (6 Apr). Centenary of the Burgerspond (coin). P 12½×12.

342	**190**	9c. brown, orange-red and pale yellow-olive	60	1·00

191 Dr. Malan

192 Congress Emblem

(Des I. Henkel)

1974 (22 May). Birth Centenary of Dr. D. F. Malan (Prime Minister). P 12½×12.

343	**191**	4c. blue and light blue	20	10

(Des Ingrid Paul)

1974 (13 June). 15th World Sugar Congress, Durban. P 12×12½.

344	**192**	15c. deep ultramarine and silver	75	1·40

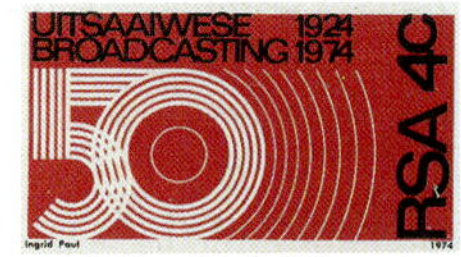

193 "50" and Radio Waves

(Des Ingrid Paul)

1974 (13 July). 50th Anniv of Broadcasting in South Africa. P 12×12½.

345	**193**	4c. red and black	10	10
		a. black omitted	£3500	

194 Monument Building

(Des G. Cunningham)

1974 (13 July). Inauguration of British Settlers' Monument, Grahamstown. P 12×12½.

346	**194**	5c. red and black	10	10

195 Stamps of the South African Provinces

(Des K. Esterhuysen)

1974 (9 Oct). Centenary of Universal Postal Union. P 12½.

347	**185**	15c. multicoloured	70	80

196 Iris

197 Bokmakierie Shrikes

(Des E. de Jong. Recess and photo)

1974 (20 Nov)–**76**. Multicoloured. Glossy paper (2, 3, 4, 6, 7, 30c. and 1r.) or chalk-surfaced paper (others,). P 12½ (1 to 25c.) or 12×12½ (others).

(a) Vert designs as T **196** *showing flowers, or horiz designs showing birds or fish*

348	1c. Type **196**	10	10
349	2c. Wild Heath	15	10
	a. Chalk-surfaced paper (2.75)	10	10
350	3c. Geranium	30	10
	a. Chalk-surfaced paper (deep claret background) (6.75)	10	10
	ab. Imperf (pair)	£120	
	ac. Brown-purple background (6.76)	10	10
351	4c. Arum Lily	30	10
	a. Chalk-surfaced paper (2.75)	10	10
	ab. Imperf (pair)	£120	
352	5c. Cape Gannet	20	10
353	6c. Galjoen (fish)	1·00	50
354	7c. Bontrok Seabream	25	10
355	9c. Dusky Batfish	30	75
356	10c. Moorish Idol	30	10
357	14c. Roman Seabream	30	10
358	15c. Greater Double-collared Sunbird	30	10
359	20c. Yellow-billed Hornbill	45	10
360	25c. Barberton Daisy	45	10

A used block of 4 and a single on cover of No. 351 have been seen with the yellow omitted.

(b) Horiz designs as T **197**

361	30c. Type **197**	7·00	70
362	50c. Stanley Cranes	1·00	35
363	1r. Bateleurs	4·00	3·25
348/63 *Set of* 16		14·00	5·50

1974 (20 Nov)–**76**. Coil stamps. As Nos. 348/9, 352 and 356 but photo, colours changed. Glossy paper. P 12½.

370	1c. reddish violet and pink	75	1·00
	a. Perf 14. Chalk-surfaced paper (12.75)	55	1·00
371	2c. bronze-green and yellow-ochre	80	60
	a. Chalk-surfaced paper (7.75)	1·40	1·00
	b. Perf 14. Chalk-surfaced paper (11.76?)	1·75	1·25
372	5c. black and light slate-blue	1·75	1·00
373	10c. deep violet-blue and light blue	6·00	8·50
	a. Perf 14. Chalk-surfaced paper (4.76)	5·50	6·50
370/3 *Set of* 4		8·50	10·00

198 Voortrekker Monument and Encampment

(Des J. Hoekstra)

1974 (6 Dec). 25th Anniv of Voortrekker Monument, Pretoria. P 12½.

374	**198**	4c. multicoloured	20	30

199 SASOL Complex

200 President Diederichs

(Des C. Webb)

1975 (26 Feb). 25th Anniv of SASOL (South African Coal, Oil and Gas Corporation Ltd). P 11½×12½.

375	**199**	15c. multicoloured	75	1·50

(Des J. L. Booysen. Recess (4c.) or photo (15c.))

1975 (19 Apr). Inauguration of the State President. P 12½×11½.

376	**200**	4c. agate and gold	10	10
377		15c. royal blue and gold	50	1·25

201 Jan Smuts

202 "Dutch East Indiaman, Table Bay"

(Des J. Hoekstra. Recess and photo)

1975 (24 May). Jan Smuts Commemoration. P 12½×11½.

378	**201**	4c. black and olive-black	10	10

(Des J. Hoekstra. Photo (Nos. 379/82) or litho (**MS**383))

1975 (18 June). Death Centenary of Thomas Baines (painter). T **202** and similar horiz designs. Multicoloured. P 11½×12½.

379	5c. Type **202**	15	10
380	9c. "Cradock, 1848"	15	15
381	15c. "Thirsty Flat, 1848"	25	25
382	30c. "Pretoria, 1874"	40	1·50
379/82 *Set of* 4		85	1·75
MS383 120×95 mm. Nos. 379/82		1·00	3·75

203 Gideon Malherbe's House, Paarl

(Des P. de Wet. Recess and photo)

1975 (14 Aug). Centenary of Genootskap van Regte Afrikaners (Afrikaner Language Movement). P 12½.

384	**203**	4c. multicoloured	10	10

204 "Automatic Sorting"

205 Title Page of Die Afrikaanse Patriot

(Des J. Sampson)

1975 (11 Sept). Postal Mechanisation. P 12½×11½.

385	**204**	4c. multicoloured	10	10

(Des K. Esterhuysen. Recess and photo (4c.). Des P. de Wet. Litho (5c.))

1975 (10 Oct). Inauguration of the Language Monument, Paarl. T **205** and similar vert design. P 12½×11½.

386 4c. black, pale stone and bright orange...... 10 10
387 5c. multicoloured 10 10

Design—5c. "Afrikaanse Taalmonument".

206 Table Mountain

(Des P. Bosman and J. Hoekstra. Litho)

1975 (13 Nov). Tourism. T **206** and similar horiz designs. Multicoloured. P 12½.

388 15c. Type **206** .... 1·50 2·75
a. Block of 4. Nos. 388/91 .... 6·00 10·00
ab. Yellow-orange and pale lemon ("RSA 15c") omitted.................................... £1600 £1100
389 15c. Johannesburg.................................... 1·50 2·75
390 15c. Cape Vineyards .... 1·50 2·75
391 15c. Lions in Kruger National Park.................... 1·50 2·75
388/91 *Set of 4*.................................... 6·00 10·00

Nos. 388/91 were printed together, *se-tenant*, in blocks of 4 throughout the sheet.

Nos. 388/91 were printed in six colours. At least two sheets, one of which was subsequently used to prepare official first day covers at Pretoria, had the final two colours, yellow-orange and pale lemon, omitted.

207 Globe and Satellites

(Des J. Hoekstra. Litho)

1975 (3 Dec). Satellite Communication. P 12½.

392 **207** 15c. multicoloured 30 30

208 Bowls

(**209**)

(Des J. Maskew. Litho)

1976. Sporting Commemorations. T **208** and similar vert designs. P 12½×11½.

393 15c. black and light sage-green (18.2)............ 20 1·00
394 15c. black and bright yellow-green (15.3)..... 50 1·25
395 15c. black and pale yellow-olive (16.8).......... 20 75
396 15c. black and apple-green (2.12).................. 50 1·00
393/6 *Set of 4* .... 1·25 3·50
MS397 161×109 mm. Nos. 393/6 (2.12)........................ 1·50 4·00

Designs:—No. 393, Type **208** (World Bowls Championships, Johannesburg); 394, Batsman (Centenary of Organised Cricket in South Africa); 395, Polo player; 396, Gary Player (golfer).

1976 (6 Apr). South Africa's Victory in World Bowls Championships. No. 393 optd with T **209** in gold.

398 **208** 15c. black and light sage-green.............. 30 1·00

210 "Picnic under a Baobab Tree"

(Des J. Hoekstra. Photo (4c.) or litho (others and **MS**403))

1976 (20 Apr). Birth Centenary of Erich Mayer (painter). T **210** and similar horiz designs. Multicoloured. P 11½×12½.

399 4c. Type **210** 15 10
a. Imperf (pair).................................... £1100
400 10c. "Foot of the Blaawberg"............................ 25 20
401 15c. "Harbeespoort Dam"................................ 30 90
402 20c. "Street scene, Doornfontein"..................... 40 1·25
399/402 *Set of 4*.................................... 1·00 2·25
MS403 121×95 mm. Nos. 399/402.................................... 1·25 4·00

211 Cheetah

212 "Emily Hobhouse" (H. Naude)

(Des P. Bosman. Photo (3c.) or litho (others))

1976 (5 June). World Environmental Day. T **211** and similar horiz designs. Multicoloured. P 11½×12½.

404 3c. Type **211** 15 10
405 10c. Black Rhinoceros.................................... 40 30
406 15c. Blesbok.................................... 40 40
407 20c. Mountain Zebra.................................... 45 75
404/7 *Set of 4* .... 1·25 1·40

(Des J. Hoekstra)

1976 (8 June). 50th Death Anniv of Emily Hobhouse (welfare worker). P 12½×11½.

408 **212** 4c. multicoloured.................................... 10 10

213 Dunrobin Castle (mail ship), 1876

214 Family with Globe

(Des K. Esterhuysen. Litho)

1976 (5 Oct). Ocean Mail Service Centenary. P 11½×12½.

409 **213** 10c. multicoloured .... 60 1·00
a. Imperf (horiz pair) £1100

(Des I. Ross)

1976 (6 Nov). Family Planning and Child Welfare. P 12½×11½.

410 **214** 4c. chestnut and light salmon................ 10 10

215 Glasses of wine

First "die" of Afrikaans inscription at left omitted (R. 1/2) on every third sheet

(Des H. Botha. Litho)

1977 (14 Feb). International Wine Symposium, Cape Town. P 12½×11½.

411	**215**	15c. multicoloured	40	1·25
		a. "die" omitted	16·00	22·00

216 Dr Jacob du Toit

(Des J. Hoekstra)

1977 (21 Feb). Birth Centenary of J. D. du Toit (theologian and poet). P 12½×11½.

412	**216**	4c. multicoloured	10	10

217 Palace of Justice

218 *Protea repens*

(Des H. Meiring)

1977 (18 May). Centenary of Transvaal Supreme Court. P 11½×12½.

413	**217**	4c. red-brown	10	10

(Des D. Findlay. Photo (1, 2, 3c. (No. 416), 4, 5, 8, 10 to 20c. (Nos. 425/a) and coil stamps) or litho (others))

1977 (27 May)–**82**. Vert designs as T **218** showing Proteas or other Succulents. Multicoloured.

(a) Sheet stamps. P 12½

414	1c. Type **218**	10	10
415	2c. *P punctata*	15	60
416	3c. *P neriifolia* (photo) (p 12½)	10	10
416*a*	3c. *P neriifolia* (litho) (p 14×13½) (1.10.79)	10	1·00
417	4c. *P longifolia*	10	10
	a. Imperf (pair)	£100	
418	5c. *P cynaroides*	10	10
	a. Perf 14×13½ (4.3.81)	10	10
	b. Imperf (pair)	£160	
419	6c. *P canaliculata*	35	1·25
	a. Black (face value and inscr at foot) omitted	90·00	
	b. Perf 14×13½ (25.10.79*)	60	1·40
420	7c. *P lorea*	25	1·25
	a. Emerald ("RSA") omitted	£120	
	b. Perf 14×13½ (19.9.80)	20	1·00
421	8c. *P mundii*	20	50
	a. Perf 14×13½ (10.7.81)	15	10
422	9c. *P roupelliae*	20	1·00
	a. Perf 14×13½ (22.12.78)	3·75	3·00
423	10c. *P aristata*	30	10
	a. Perf 14×13½ (12.1.82)	20	1·00
424	15c. *P eximia*	25	10
425	20c. *P magnifica* (photo)	30	10
	a. Perf 14×13½ (16.2.78)	60	1·25
425*b*	20c. *P magnifica* (litho) (p 14×13½) (24.5.82)	1·75	1·75
426	25c. *P grandiceps*	60	1·25
	a. Emerald ("RSA" and leaves) omitted	£190	
	b. Black (face value and inscr) omitted	£190	
	c. Perf 14×13½ (3.6.80)	40	1·00
427	30c. *P amplexicaulis*	45	10
	a. Perf 14×13½ (19.10.80)	60	75
428	50c. *Leucospermum cordifolium*	65	15
	a. Perf 14×13½ (9.10.80)	70	15
429	1r. *Paranomus reflexus*	70	1·00
	a. Perf 14×13½ (30.7.80)	50	1·00
430	2r. *Orothamnus zeyheri*	1·25	2·50
	a. Perf 14×13½ (22.5.81)	60	1·00

(b) Coil stamps. Imperf×perf 14

431	1c. *Leucadendron argenteum*	35	1·25
432	2c. *Mimetes cucullatus*	35	1·25
433	5c. *Serruria florida*	35	1·25
434	10c. *Leucadendron sessile*	35	1·25
414/34	*Set of 21*	5·50	11·00

*Sheets dated 15 August 1979.

There were two emerald plates used for the 7c.; one for the design and background and a second, common with other values in the issue, used to apply "RSA". No. 420a shows this second emerald plate omitted.

Later printings of the coil stamps come with every fifth stamp numbered on the back.

219 Gymnast

220 Metrication Symbol on Globe

(Des D. Cowie. Litho)

1977 (15 Aug). Eighth Congress of International Association of Physical Education and Sports for Girls and Women. P 12½×11½.

435	**219**	15c. black, salmon-red and yellow	30	75

(Des L. Wilsenach. Litho)

1977 (15 Sept). Metrication. P 12×12½.

436	**220**	15c. multicoloured	30	30

221 Atomic Diagram

(Des R. Sargent. Litho)

1977 (8 Oct). Uranium Development. P 12×12½.

437	**221**	15c. multicoloured	40	30

222 National Flag

(Des J. Hoekstra)

1977 (11 Nov). 50th Anniv of National Flag. P 12×12½.

438	**222**	5c. multicoloured	10	10

223 Walvis Bay, 1878

(Des A. H. Barrett. Litho)

1978 (10 Mar). Centenary of Annexation of Walvis Bay. P 12½.

439	**223**	15c. multicoloured	60	60

224 Dr. Andrew Murray

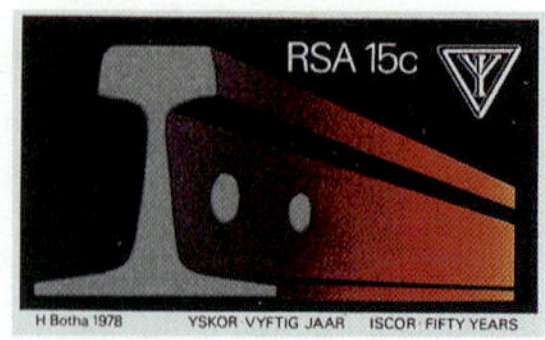

225 Steel Rail

(Des J. Hoekstra. Litho)

1978 (9 May). 150th Birth Anniv of Dr. Andrew Murray (church statesman). P 12½×12.

440	**224**	4c. multicoloured	10	10

(Des H. Botha, Litho)

1978 (5 June). 50th Anniv of I.S.C.O.R. (South African Iron and Steel Industrial Corporation). P 12½.

441	**225**	15c. multicoloured	30	30

226 Richards Bay

(Des A. H. Barrett. Litho)

1978 (31 July). Harbours. T **226** and similar horiz design. Multicoloured. P 12½.

442	15c. Type **226**	50	1·00
	a. Pair. Nos. 442/3	1·00	2·00
443	15c. Saldanhabaai	50	1·00

Nos. 442/3 were printed together, *se-tenant*, in horizontal and vertical pairs throughout the sheet.

227 "Shepherd's Lonely Dwelling, Riversdale"

(Des G. Mynhardt. Litho)

1978 (21 Aug). 125th Birth Anniv of J. E. A. Volschenk (painter). T **227** and similar horiz designs. Multicoloured. P 12½.

444	10c. Type **227**	15	20
445	15c. "Clouds and Sunshine, Laneberg Range, Riversdale"	20	30
446	20c. "At the Foot of the Mountain"	30	75
447	25c. "Evening on the Veldt"	35	1·40
444/7	*Set of 4*	90	2·50
MS448	124×90 mm. Nos. 444/7	1·25	4·00

228 Pres. B. J. Vorster

(Des A. H. Barrett. Litho)

1978 (10 Oct). Inauguration of President Vorster. P 14×13½.

449	**228**	4c. brown-purple and gold	70	20
		a. Perf 12½×12	10	10
450		15c. dull violet and gold	25	60

229 Golden Gate

(Des A. H. Barrett. Litho)

1978 (13 Nov). Tourism. T **229** and similar horiz designs. Multicoloured. P 12½.

451	10c. Type **229**	15	10
452	15c. Blyde River Canyon	25	35
453	20c. Amphitheatre, Drakensberg	40	1·10
454	25c. Cango Caves	55	1·50
451/4	*Set of 4*	1·25	2·75

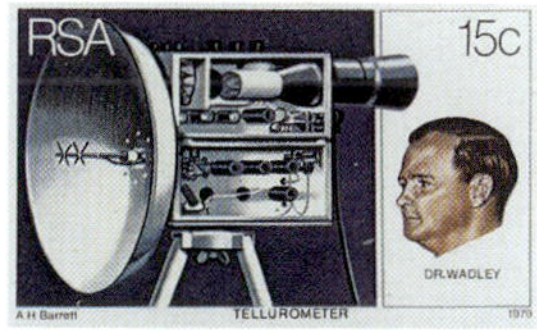

230 Dr. Wadley (inventor) and Tellurometer

(Des A. H. Barrett. Litho)

1979 (12 Feb). 25th Anniv of Tellurometer (radio distance measurer). P 12½.

455	**230**	15c. multicoloured	20	20

231 1929 4d. Airmail Stamp

(Des G. Mynhardt. Litho)

1979 (30 Mar). 50th Anniv of Stamp Production in South Africa. P 14.

456	**231**	15c. green, cream and slate	30	20

232 "Save Fuel"

(Des A. H. Barrett)

1979 (2 Apr). Fuel Conservation. P 12×12½.

457	**232**	4c. black and vermilion	25	65
		a. Pair. Nos. 457/8	50	1·50
458		4c. black and vermilion	25	65

No. 458 is as T **232** but has face value and country initials in bottom left-hand corner, and Afrikaans inscription above English.

Nos. 457/8 were printed together, *se-tenant*, in horizontal and vertical pairs throughout the sheet.

233 Isandlwana

(Des A. H. Barrett. Litho)

1979 (25 May). Centenary of Zulu War. T **233** and similar horiz designs in black and rose-red, showing drawings. P 14.

459	4c. Type **233**	20	10
460	15c. Ulundi	55	50
461	20c. Rorke's Drift	70	1·25
459/61	*Set of 3*	1·25	1·60
MS462	125×90 mm. Nos. 459/61. P 12½	1·75	3·50

234 "Health Care"

(Des J. Hoekstra. Litho)

1979 (19 June). Health Year. P 12½×12.

463	**234**	4c. multicoloured	10	10
		a. Perf 14×13½	30	30

235 Children looking at Candle

(Des G. Mynhardt. Litho)

1979 (13 Sept). 50th Anniv of Christmas Stamp Fund. P 14.

464	**235**	4c. multicoloured	10	10
		a. Gold (inscr) omitted		

236 University of Cape Town

237 "Gary Player"

(Des G. Mynhardt. Litho)

1979 (1 Oct). 50th Anniv of University of Cape Town. P 13½×14.

465	**236**	4c. multicoloured	20	30
		a. Perf 12×12½	15	15

(Des H. de Klerk. Litho)

1979 (4 Oct). "Rosafari 1979" World Rose Convention, Pretoria. T **237** and similar vert designs. Multicoloured. P 14×13½.

466	4c. Type **237**	15	10
467	15c. "Prof. Chris Barnard"	30	40
468	20c. "Southern Sun"	40	60
469	25c. "Soaring Wings"	40	85
466/9 *Set of 4*		1·10	1·75
MS470 100×125 mm. Nos. 466/9		1·10	2·50

238 University of Stellenbosch

239 F.A.K. Emblem

(Des A. H. Barrett. Litho)

1979 (8 Nov). 300th Anniv of Stellenbosch (oldest town in South Africa). T **238** and similar horiz design. Multicoloured. P 14.

471	4c. Type **238**	10	10
472	15c. Rhenish Church on the Braak	20	40

(Des J. Hoekstra)

1979 (18 Dec). 50th Anniv of F.A.K. (Federation of Afrikaans Cultural Societies). P 12½×12.

473	**239**	4c. multicoloured	10	15

240 "Still-life with Sweet Peas"

241 "Cullinan II"

(Des G. Mynhardt. Litho)

1980 (6 May). Paintings by Pieter Wenning. T **240** and similar multicoloured design. P 14×13½.

474	5c. Type **240**	10	10
475	25c. "House in the Suburbs, Cape Town" (44½×37 mm)	40	90
MS476 94×121 mm. Nos. 474/5		1·00	1·60

(Des A. H. Barrett. Litho)

1980 (12 May). World Diamond Congresses, Johannesburg. T **241** and similar vert design. Multicoloured. P 14.

477	15c. Type **241**	60	60
478	20c. "Cullinan I (Great Star of Africa)"	65	65

242 C. L. Leipoldt

243 University of Pretoria

(Des J. Hoekstra. Litho)

1980 (3 Sept). Birth Centenary of C. L. Leipoldt (poet). P 14×13½.

479	**242**	5c. multicoloured	10	10

(Des P. de Wet. Litho)

1980 (9 Oct). 50th Anniv of University of Pretoria. P 14×13½.

480	**243**	5c. multicoloured	10	10

244 "Marine with Shipping" (Willem van de Velde)

(Des G. Mynhardt. Litho)

1980 (3 Nov). Paintings from South African National Gallery, Cape Town. T **244** and similar multicoloured designs. P 14.

481	5c. Type **244**	15	10
482	10c. "Firetail and his Trainer" (George Stubbs)	20	25
483	15c. "Lavinia" (Thomas Gainsborough) (vert)	25	50
484	20c. "Classical Landscape" (Pieter Post)	30	80
481/4 *Set of 4*		80	1·50
MS485 126×90 mm. Nos. 481/4		1·00	1·75

245 Joubert, Kruger and M. Pretorius (Triumvirate Government)

246 Boers advancing up Amajuba Mountain

(Des A. H. Barrett. Litho)

1980 (15 Dec). Centenary of Paardekraal Monument (cairn commemorating formation of Boer Triumvirate Government). T **245** and similar multicoloured design. P 14×13½ (5c.) or 13½×14 (10c.).

486	5c. Type **245**	10	10
487	10c. Paardekraal Monument (vert)	20	90

(Des Diana Arbuthnot. Litho)

1981 (27 Feb). Centenary of Battle of Amajuba. T **246** and similar multicoloured design. P 13½×14 (5c.) or 14×13½ (15c.).

488	5c. Type **246**	20	10
489	15c. British troops defending hill (horiz)	40	90

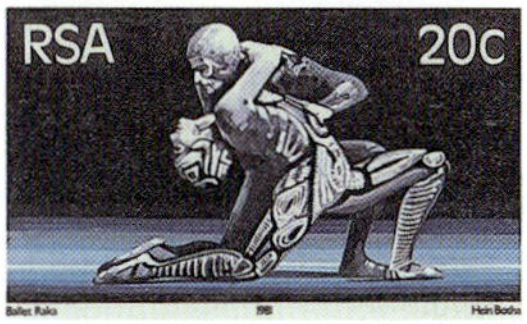

247 Ballet Raka

(Des H. Botha. Litho)

1981 (23 May). Opening of State Theatre, Pretoria. T **247** and similar horiz design. Multicoloured. P 14.

490	20c. Type **247**	25	30
491	25c. Opera Aida	40	35
MS492	110×90 mm. Nos. 490/1	65	70

248 Former Presidents C. R. Swart, J. J. Fouché, N. Diederichs and B. J. Vorster

(Des A. H. Barrett. Litho)

1981 (30 May). 20th Anniv of Republic. T **248** and similar design. P 14.

493	5c. black, grey-olive and bistre	15	10
494	15c. multicoloured	30	30

Design: (28×22 mm)—15c. President Marais Viljoen.

249 Girl with Hearing Aid

250 Microscope

251 *Calanthe natalensis*

(Des Mare Mouton. Litho)

1981 (12 June). Centenary of Institutes for Deaf and Blind, Worcester. T **249** and similar vert design. Multicoloured. P 13½×14.

495	5c. Type **249**	10	10
496	15c. Boy reading Braille	20	90

(Des N. Hanna. Litho)

1981 (10 July). 50th Anniv of National Cancer Association. P 13½×14.

497	**250**	5c. multicoloured	10	10

(Des Jeanette Stead. Litho)

1981 (11 Sept). Tenth World Orchid Conference, Durban. T **251** and similar vert designs. Multicoloured. P 14.

498	5c. Type **251**	10	10
499	15c. *Eulophia speciosa*	20	35
500	20c. *Disperis fanniniae*	20	75
501	25c. *Disa uniflora*	25	1·10
498/501	*Set of 4*	65	2·00
MS502	120×91 mm. Nos. 498/501	2·25	2·00

252 Voortrekkers in Uniform

253 Lord Baden-Powell

254 Dr. Robert Koch

(Des J. Hoekstra. Litho)

1981 (30 Sept). 50th Anniv of Voortrekker Movement (Afrikaans cultural youth organization). P 14.

503	**252**	5c. multicoloured	10	10

(Des J. Meyer. Litho)

1982 (22 Feb). 75th Anniv of Boy Scout Movement. P 13½×14.

504	**253**	15c. multicoloured	30	30

(Des J. Meyer. Litho)

1982 (24 Mar). Centenary of Discovery of Tubercle Bacillus by Dr. Robert Koch. P 13½×14.

505	**254**	20c. multicoloured	20	30

255 *Maria van Riebeeck* (submarine)

256 Old Provost, Grahamstown

(Des A. H. Barrett. Litho)

1982 (2 Apr). 25th Anniv of Simonstown as South African Navy Base. T **255** and similar horiz designs. Multicoloured. P 14.

506	8c. Type **255**	15	10
507	15c. Missile patrol vessel	20	30
508	20c. *Durban* (minesweeper)	25	60
509	25c. Harbour patrol boats	30	85
506/9	*Set of 4*	80	1·60
MS510	125×90 mm. Nos. 506/9	2·00	2·00

(Des A. H. Barrett. Recess (Nos. 511, 512b, 513, 514, 515a, 516a, 521, 522a, 524, 525, 526 and 527), photo (Nos. 528/31) or litho (others))

1982 (15 July)–**87**. South African Architecture. Designs as T **256**.

(a) Sheet stamps. P 14

511	1c. reddish brown (recess)	15	20
511*a*	1c. reddish brown (litho) (2.4.84)	30	30
	ab. Imperf (horiz pair)	35·00	
512	2c. yellow-olive (litho)	20	30
512*a*	2c. deep green (litho) (9.5.83)	1·00	30
512*b*	2c. bottle green (recess) (28.11.83)	10	20

512*c*	2c. bottle green (litho) (21.11.85)	1·25	1·00
513	3c. violet (recess)	30	85
513*a*	3c. violet (litho) (28.11.85)	1·75	1·50
514	4c. brown-olive (recess)	20	80
514*a*	4c. brown-olive (litho) (25.3.85)	1·25	1·50
515	5c. carmine (litho)	30	50
515*a*	5c. brown-purple (recess) (11.11.83)	10	25
	ab. Imperf (pair)	£110	
516	6c. deep blue-green (litho)	45	40
516*a*	6c. blackish green (recess) (9.8.84)	80	1·25
517	7c. dull yellowish green (litho)	30	1·50
518	8c. greenish blue (litho)	30	30
518*a*	8c. indigo (litho) (3.1.83)	40	10
519	9c. deep mauve (litho)	40	20
520	10c. Venetian red (litho)	40	1·00
520*a*	10c. purple-brown (litho) (26.1.83)	35	10
520*b*	11c. cerise (litho) (2.4.84)	40	1·00
520*c*	12c. deep violet-blue (litho) (1.4.85)	70	10
520*d*	14c. lake-brown (litho) (1.4.86)	2·25	10
521	15c. deep violet-blue (recess)	30	15
521*a*	16c. rosine (litho) (1.4.87)	1·00	1·75
522	20c. vermilion (litho)	65	30
522*a*	20c. brownish black (recess) (15.6.83)	80	10
522*b*	20c. brownish black (litho) (14.11.85)	1·50	15
523	25c. bistre (litho)	50	1·00
523*a*	25c. ochre (litho) (3.6.87)	2·75	1·40
524	30c. agate (recess)	50	30
524*a*	30c. reddish brown (litho) (12.3.86)	1·75	30
525	50c. deep turquoise-blue (recess)	50	70
	a. Deep slate-blue (18.3.83)	2·25	65
525*b*	50c. turquoise-blue (litho) (13.10.86)	3·00	30
526	1r. deep violet (recess)	50	15
526*a*	1r. deep violet (litho) (17.12.86)	1·50	60
527	2r. deep carmine (recess)	65	50
527*a*	2r. deep carmine (litho) (5.12.85)	1·25	50
511/27	*Set of 21 (one of each value)*	9·50	8·75

Designs: (28×20 mm)—2c. Tuynhuys, Cape Town; 3c. Appèlhof, Bloemfontein; 4c. Raadsaal, Pretoria; 5c. Cape Town Castle; 6c. Goewermentsgebou, Bloemfontein; 7c. Drostdy, Graaff-Reinet; 8c. Leeuwenhof, Cape Town; 9c. Libertas, Pretoria; 10c. City Hall, Pietermaritzburg; 11c. City Hall, Kimberley 12c. City Hall, Port Elizabeth; 14c. City Hall, Johannesburg; 15c. Matjesfontein; 16c. City Hall, Durban; 20c. Post Office, Durban; 25c. Melrose House, Pretoria. (45×28 mm)–30c. Old Legislative Assembly Building, Pietermaritzburg; 50c. Raadsaal, Bloemfontein; 1r. Houses of Parliament, Cape Town; 2r. Uniegebou, Pretoria.

For certain printings of Nos. 511/27*a* the design width of each stamp was reduced by a millimetre. Of the original set of 17 all showed "wide" designs with the exception of the 1r. Changes in design size occurred in subsequent printings so that Nos. 512*c*, 513, 521 and 524 can be found in both wide and narrow versions. Of the remainder Nos. 511*a*, 512*b*, 513*a*, 514*a*, 515*a*, 516*a*, 520*b/d*, 521*a*, 522*a/b*, 524*a*, 525a/*b*, 526 and 527*a* exist as "narrow" designs only.

(b) Coil stamps. P 14×imperf

528	1c. brown	30	1·25
529	2c. yellow-green	30	1·25
530	5c. lake-brown	30	1·25
531	10c. light brown	30	1·25
528/31	*Set of 4*	1·10	4·50

Designs: (28×20 mm)—1c. Drostdy, Swellendam; 2c. City Hall, East London; 5c. Head Post Office, Johannesburg; 10c. Morgenster, Somerset West.

257 Bradysaurus

258 Gough Island Base

(Des Sheila Nowers. Litho)

1982 (1 Dec). Karoo Fossils. T **257** and similar horiz designs. Multicoloured. P 14.

532	8c. Type **257**	30	10
533	15c. Lystrosaurus	35	60
534	20c. Euparkeria	40	75
535	25c. Thrinaxodon	45	90
532/5	*Set of 4*	1·50	2·10
MS536	107×95 mm. Nos. 532/5	1·50	3·25

(Des D. Thorpe. Litho)

1983 (19 Jan). Weather Stations. T **258** and similar horiz designs. Multicoloured. P 13½×14.

537	8c. Type **258**	20	10
538	20c. Marion Island base	30	45
539	25c. Taking meteorological readings	30	50
540	40c. Launching weather balloon, Sanae	40	90
537/40	*Set of 4*	1·10	1·75

259 Class S2 Krupp Locomotive, 1952

260 Rugby

(Des H. Botha. Litho)

1983 (27 Apr). Steam Railway Locomotives. T **259** and similar horiz designs. Multicoloured. P 14.

541	10c. Type **259**	30	10
542	20c. Class 16E Henschel express locomotive, 1935	50	70
543	25c. Class 6H locomotive, 1901	55	80
544	40c. Class 15F locomotive, 1939	65	1·50
541/4	*Set of 4*	1·75	2·75

(Des Sheila Nowers. Litho)

1983 (20 July). Sport in South Africa. T **260** and similar multicoloured designs. P 14.

545	10c. Type **260**	15	10
546	20c. Soccer (horiz)	20	30
547	25c. Yachting	25	50
548	40c. Horse-racing (horiz)	40	90
545/8	*Set of 4*	90	1·60

261 Plettenberg Bay

262 Thomas Pringle

(Des A. H. Barrett. Litho)

1983 (12 Oct). Tourism. Beaches. T **261** and similar horiz designs. Multicoloured. P 14.

549	10c. Type **261**	10	10
550	20c. Durban	20	30
551	25c. West coast	20	35
552	40c. Clifton	35	65
549/52	*Set of 4*	75	1·25
MS553	128×90 mm. Nos. 549/52	1·10	2·50

(Des J. van Ellinckhuijzen. Litho)

1984 (24 Feb). South African English Authors. T **262** and similar vert designs. P 14.

554	10c. olive-brown, yellow-brown and grey	10	10
555	20c. olive-brown, deep bluish green and grey	20	40
556	25c. olive-brown, deep brown-rose and grey	20	50
557	40c. olive-brown, olive-ochre and grey	35	85
554/7	*Set of 4*	75	1·75

Designs:—20c. Pauline Smith; 25c. Olive Schreiner; 40c. Sir Percy Fitzpatrick.

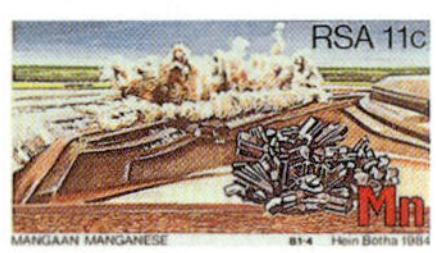

263 Manganese

(Des H. Botha. Litho)

1984 (8 June). Strategic Minerals. T **263** and similar horiz designs. Multicoloured. P 14.

558	11c. Type **263**	30	10
559	20c. Chromium	45	60
560	25c. Vanadium	50	80
561	30c. Titanium	60	90
558/61	*Set of 4*	1·75	2·25

264 Bloukrans River Bridge

(Des D. Bagnall. Litho)

1984 (24 Aug). South African Bridges. T **264** and similar horiz designs. Multicoloured. P 14.

No.	Description	Unused	Used
562	11c. Type **264**	25	10
563	25c. Durban four level interchange	40	60
564	30c. Mfolozi Railway Bridge	45	75
565	45c. Gouritz River bridge	55	1·40
562/5	*Set of 4*	1·50	2·50

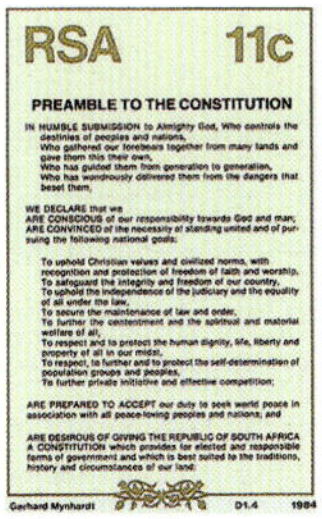

265 Preamble to the Constitution in Afrikaans

(Des G. Mynhardt. Litho)

1984 (3 Sept). New Constitution. T **265** and similar vert designs. P 14.

No.	Description	Unused	Used
566	11c. stone, black and bistre	70	1·25
	a. Horiz pair. Nos. 566/7	1·40	2·50
567	11c. stone, black and bistre	70	1·25
568	25c. stone, deep claret and bistre	45	50
569	30c. multicoloured	45	50
566/9	*Set of 4*	2·00	3·25

Designs:—No. 566, Preamble to the Constitution in English; 568, Last two lines of National Anthem; 569, South African coat of arms.

Nos. 566/7 were printed together, *se-tenant*, in horizontal pairs.

266 Pres. P. W. Botha

267 Pro Patria Medal

1984 (2 Nov). Inauguration of President Botha. Litho. P 14.

No.	Type	Description	Unused	Used
570	**266**	11c. multicoloured	30	10
571		25c. multicoloured	55	40

(Des B. Jackson. Litho)

1984 (9 Nov). Military Decorations. T **267** and similar vert designs. Multicoloured. P 14.

No.	Description	Unused	Used
572	11c. Type **267**	20	10
573	25c. De Wet Decoration	30	45
574	30c. John Chard Decoration	30	65
575	45c. Honoris Crux (Diamond) Decoration	35	1·00
572/5	*Set of 4*	1·00	2·10
MS576	71×116 mm. Nos. 572/5	1·00	3·00

268 "Reflections" (Frans Oerder)

269 Cape Parliament Building

1985 (22 Feb). Paintings by Frans Oerder. T **268** and similar horiz designs. Multicoloured. Litho. P 14.

No.	Description	Unused	Used
577	11c. Type **268**	20	15
578	25c. "Ladies in a Garden"	25	35
579	30c. "Still-life with Lobster"	25	45
580	50c. "Still-life with Marigolds"	40	70
577/80	*Set of 4*	1·00	1·50
MS581	129×74 mm. Nos. 577/80	1·25	3·00

(Des A. H. Barrett. Litho)

1985 (15 May). Centenary of Cape Parliament Building. T **269** and similar horiz designs. Multicoloured. P 14.

No.	Description	Unused	Used
582	12c. Type **269**	15	10
583	25c. Speaker's Chair	25	30
584	30c. "National Convention 1908–9" (Edward Roworth)	25	40
585	50c. Republic Parliamentary emblem	45	1·10
	a. Black (inscr and outline) omitted	£450	
582/5	*Set of 4*	1·00	2·25

270 Freesia

271 Sugar Bowl

(Des Sheila Nowers. Litho)

1985 (23 Aug). Floral Emigrants. T **270** and similar vert designs. Multicoloured. P 14.

No.	Description	Unused	Used
586	12c. Type **270**	15	10
587	25c. Nerine	25	30
588	30c. Ixia	25	45
589	50c. Gladiolus	40	1·25
586/9	*Set of 4*	1·00	1·90

(Des H. Botha. Litho)

1985 (5 Nov). Cape Silverware. T **271** and similar multicoloured designs. P 14.

No.	Description	Unused	Used
590	12c. Type **271**	20	10
591	25c. Teapot	30	30
592	30c. Loving cup (vert)	30	45
593	50c. Coffee pot (vert)	45	1·50
590/3	*Set of 4*	1·10	2·10

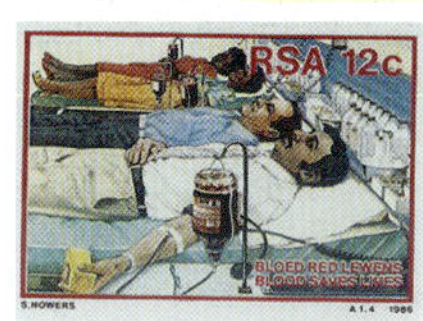

272 Blood Donor Session

273 National Flag

(Des Sheila Nowers. Litho)

1986 (20 Feb). Blood Donor Campaign. T **272** and similar horiz designs. Multicoloured. P 14.

No.	Description	Unused	Used
594	12c. Type **272**	45	10
	a. Black (inscriptions below design) omitted.	£300	
595	20c. Baby receiving blood transfusion	75	80
596	25c. Operation in progress	80	95
597	30c. Ambulanceman and accident victim	95	1·60
594/7	*Set of 4*	2·75	3·00

(Des J. Hoekstra. Litho)

1986 (30 May). 25th Anniv of Republic of South Africa. T **273** and similar horiz design. Multicoloured. P 14.

No.	Description	Unused	Used
598	14c. Type **273**	75	1·25
	a. Horiz pair. Nos. 598/9	1·50	2·50
599	14c. As Type **273**, but inscr "UNITY IS STRENGTH"	75	1·25

Nos. 598/9 were printed together, *se-tenant*, in horizontal pairs throughout the sheet.

274 Drostdyhof, Graaff-Reinet

(Des A. H. Barrett. Litho)

1986 (14 Aug). Restoration of Historic Buildings. T **274** and similar horiz designs. Multicoloured. P 14.

No.	Description	Unused	Used
600	14c. Type **274**	30	10
601	20c. Pilgrims Rest mining village	55	70

602	25c. Strapp's Store, Bethlehem	60	90
603	30c. Palmdene, Pietermaritzburg	75	1·40
600/3	*Set of 4*	2·00	2·75

PHILATELIC FOUNDATION MINIATURE SHEETS. These miniature sheets were issued by the Philatelic Foundation of Southern Africa and not the postal administration. They could be purchased by post or from a limited number of philatelic offices at a premium in aid of various national and international stamp exhibitions.

275 Von Brandis Square, Johannesburg, c. 1900

(Des J. van Niekerk. Litho)

1986 (25 Sept). Centenary of Johannesburg. T **275** and similar horiz designs. Multicoloured. P 14.

604	14c. Type **275**	35	10
605	20c. Gold mine (26×20 mm)	1·25	1·25
606	25c. Johannesburg skyline, 1986	1·00	1·60
607	30c. Gold bars (26×20 mm)	1·75	2·50
604/7	*Set of 4*	4·00	5·00

The 30c. value exists as a Philatelic Foundation miniature sheet.

276 Gordon's Rock, Paarlberg

(Des A. H. Barrett. Litho)

1986 (20 Nov). Rock Formations. T **276** and similar vert designs. Multicoloured. P 14.

608	14c. Type **276**	45	10
609	20c. The Column, Drakensberg	70	80
610	25c. Maltese Cross, Sederberge	75	1·00
611	30c. Bourke's Luck Potholes, Blyde River Gorge	85	1·75
608/11	*Set of 4*	2·50	3·25

277 *Cicindela regalis*

(Des E. Holm. Litho)

1987 (6 Mar). South African Beetles. T **277** and similar vert designs. Multicoloured. P 14.

612	14c. Type **277**	40	10
613	20c. *Trichostetha fascicularis*	55	60
614	25c. *Julodis viridipes*	65	90
615	30c. *Ceroplesis militaris*	75	2·00
612/15	*Set of 4*	2·10	3·25

278 Eland, Sebaaieni Cave

(Des H. Botha. Litho)

1987 (4 June). Rock Paintings. T **278** and similar horiz designs. Multicoloured. P 14.

616	16c. Type **278**	40	10
617	20c. Leaping lion, Clocolan	60	65
618	25c. Black Wildebeest, uMhlwazini Valley	75	90
619	30c. Bushman dance, Floukraal	80	1·75
616/19	*Set of 4*	2·25	3·00

279 Oude Pastorie, Paarl

(Des A. H. Barrett. Litho)

1987 (3 Sept). 300th Anniv of Paarl. T **279** and similar horiz designs. Multicoloured. P 14.

620	16c. Type **279**	20	10
621	20c. Grapevines	35	55
622	25c. Wagon-building	40	70
623	30c. KWV Cathedral Wine Cellar	45	1·50
620/3	*Set of 4*	1·25	2·50

The 30c. value exists as a Philatelic Foundation miniature sheet.

+10c

VLOEDRAMP
NATAL

(**280**)

281 "Belshazzar's Feast" (Rembrandt)

1987 (16 Nov). Natal Flood Relief Fund (1st issue). No. 521a surch as T **280** in Afrikaans or English.

624	16c.+10c. rosine (surch T 280)	30	80
	a. Pair. Nos. 624/5	60	1·60
625	16c.+10c. rosine (surch "NATAL FLOOD DISASTER")	30	80

Nos. 624/5 were surcharged together, *se-tenant*, in horizontal and vertical pairs throughout the sheet.

See also Nos. 629/30 and 635/6.

(Des Sheila Nowers. Litho)

1987 (19 Nov). The Bible Society of South Africa. T **281** and similar multicoloured designs. P 14.

626	16c. "The Bible" in 75 languages (54×34 mm)	35	10
627	30c. Type **281**	55	70
628	50c. "St. Matthew and the Angel" (Rembrandt) (vert)	85	1·90
626/8	*Set of 3*	1·60	2·40

A 40c. value, showing the inscription "The Word of God" in various languages, was prepared, but due to religious objections was recalled before issue, although examples are known to have been sold to the public at some smaller post offices (*Price* £450 *mint*, £550 *used*).

1987 (1 Dec). Natal Flood Relief Fund (2nd issue). No. 626 surch as T **280**, but larger (Afrikaans version 32 mm wide).

629	16c.+10c. multicoloured (surch "NATAL FLOOD DISASTER")	50	80
	a. Pair. Nos. 629/30	1·00	1·60
630	16c.+10c. multicoloured (surch as T **280**)	50	80

Nos. 629/30 were surcharged together, *se-tenant*, in horizontal and vertical pairs throughout the sheet. These stamps are known postmarked at Mooirivier on 25 November 1987.

282 Bartolomeu Dias and Cape of Good Hope

283 Huguenot Monument, Franschhoek

(Des Sheila Nowers. Litho)

1988 (3 Feb). 500th Anniv of Discovery of Cape of Good Hope by Bartolomeu Dias. T **282** and similar horiz designs. Multicoloured. P 14.

631	16c. Type **282**	60	10
632	30c. Kwaaihoek Monument	80	85
633	40c. Caravels	1·50	1·60
634	50c. Martellus map, c. 1489	1·90	2·50
631/4	*Set of 4*	4·25	4·50

The 50c. value exists as a Philatelic Foundation miniature sheet.

1988 (1 Mar). Natal Flood Relief Fund (3rd issue). No. 631 surch as T **280**, but larger (Afrikaans version 19 mm wide).

635	16c.+10c. multicoloured (surch as T **280**)	50	80
	a. Pair. Nos. 635/6	1·00	1·60
636	16c.+10c. multicoloured (surch "NATAL FLOOD DISASTER")	50	80

Nos. 635/6 were surcharged together, *se-tenant*, in horizontal and vertical pairs throughout the sheet.

(Des H. Botha. Litho)

1988 (13 Apr). 300th Anniv of Arrival of First French Huguenots at the Cape. T **283** and similar vert designs. Multicoloured. P 14.

637	16c. Type **283**	30	10
638	30c. Map of France showing Huguenot areas	85	80
639	40c. Title page of French/Dutch New Testament of 1672	85	1·25
640	50c. St. Bartholomew's Day Massacre, Paris, 1572	1·10	1·50
637/40	*Set of 4*	2·75	3·25

National Flood Disaster **+10c**

(284)

285 Pelican Point Lighthouse, Walvis Bay

1988 (13 Apr). National Flood Relief Fund. Nos. 637/40 surch as T **284** in English (E) or in Afrikaans ("Nasionale Vloedramp") (A).

641	16c.+10c. multicoloured (E)	40	65
	a. Pair. Nos. 641/2	80	1·25
642	16c.+10c. multicoloured (A)	40	65
643	30c.+10c. multicoloured (A)	55	75
	a. Pair. Nos. 643/4	1·10	1·50
644	30c.+10c. multicoloured (E)	55	75
645	40c.+10c. multicoloured (A)	60	90
	a. Pair. Nos. 645/6	1·10	1·75
646	40c.+10c. multicoloured (E)	60	90
647	50c.+10c. multicoloured (E)	70	1·25
	a. Pair. Nos. 647/8	1·40	2·50
648	50c.+10c. multicoloured (A)	70	1·25
641/8	*Set of 8*	4·00	6·25

The two versions of each surcharge were printed together, *se-tenant*, both horizontally and vertically, throughout the sheets.

(Des Sheila Nowers. Litho)

1988 (9 June). Lighthouses. T **285** and similar horiz designs. Multicoloured. P 14.

649	16c. Type **285**	70	10
650	30c. Green Point, Cape Town	90	70
651	40c. Cape Agulhas	1·10	1·25
652	50c. Umhlanga Rocks, Durban	1·50	1·75
649/52	*Set of 4*	3·75	3·50
MS653	132×112 mm. Nos. 649/52	5·00	4·50

286 *Huernia zebrina*

287 Map of Great Trek Routes

(Des H. Botha)

1988 (1 Sept)–**93**. Succulents. T **286** and similar horiz designs. Multicoloured.

(a) Sheet stamps. Litho. P 14

654	1c. Type **288**	10	50
	a. Coil strip. Nos. 654/7 and 662 (11.5.93)	50	
655	2c. *Euphorbia symmetrica*	10	50
656	5c. *Lithops dorotheae*	10	40
657	7c. *Gibbaeum nebrownii*	15	60
658	10c. *Didymaotus lapidiformis*	15	50
659	16c. *Vanheerdea divergens*	60	50
659*a*	18c. *Faucaria tigrina* (1.4.89)	50	10
660	20c. *Conophytum mundum*	80	10
660*a*	21c. *Gasteria armstrongii* (2.4.90)	40	10
661	25c. *Cheiridopsis peculiaris*	80	10
	a. Imperf (pair)	£180	
662	30c. *Tavaresia barklyi*	60	50
663	35c. *Dinteranthus witmotianus*	1·00	20
664	40c. *Frithia pulchra*	1·00	25
665	50c. *Lapidaria margaretae*	1·00	25
666	90c. *Dioscorea elephantipes*	1·25	45
667	1r. *Trichocaulon cactiforme*	1·00	50
668	2r. *Crassula columnaris*	1·25	90
668*a*	5r. *Anacampseros albissima* (1.3.90)	2·25	2·40
654/68a	*Set of 18*	12·00	7·75

(b) Coil stamps. Photo. P 14×imperf

669	1c. *Adromischus marianiae*	1·00	1·75
670	2c. *Titanopsis calcarea*	60	1·25
671	5c. *Dactylopsis digitata*	65	1·25
672	10c. *Pleiospilos bolusii*	70	1·25
669/72	*Set of 4*	2·75	5·00

Multi-value coil strip No. 654a was produced by the South African Post Office for use by a large direct mail marketing firm. Strips were also available from the Philatelic Service.

For similar design, but without face value and inscribed "Standardised mail" in English and Afrikaans, see No. 778.

(Des J. van Niekerk (16c.). Litho)

1988 (21 Nov). 150th Anniv of Great Trek. T **287** and similar multicoloured designs. P 14.

673	16c. Type **287**	75	10
674	30c. "Exodus" (tapestry by W. Coetzer) (56×20 mm)	1·00	90
675	40c. "Crossing the Drakensberg" (tapestry by W. Coetzer) (77×20 mm)	1·25	1·10
676	50c. "After the Service, Church of the Vow" (J. H. Pierneef) (horiz)	1·50	1·75
673/6	*Set of 4*	4·00	3·50

288 Coelacanth

(Des A. McBride. Litho)

1989 (9 Feb). 50th Anniv of Discovery of Coelacanth. T **288** and similar horiz designs. Multicoloured. P 14.

677	16c. Type **288**	75	15
678	30c. Prof J. L. B. Smith and Dr. M. Courtenay-Latimer examining Coelacanth	1·10	1·25
679	40c. J. L. B. Smith Institute of Ichthyology, Grahamstown	1·40	1·60
680	50c. Coelacanth and GEO midget submarine	1·50	2·25
677/80	*Set of 4*	4·25	4·75

The 50c. value exists as a Philatelic Foundation miniature sheet and also as a corporate miniature sheet, containing two examples, sponsored by Two Oceans Environmental Trust. See note above No. 822.

289 Man-made Desert

(Des D. Murphy. Litho)

1989 (3 May). National Grazing Strategy. T **289** and similar horiz designs. Multicoloured. P 14.

681	18c. Type **289**	40	15
682	30c. Formation of erosion gully	65	75
683	40c. Concrete barrage in gully	70	1·00

684	50c. Reclaimed veldt	80	1·40
681/4	*Set of 4*	2·25	3·00

290 South Africa v France Match, 1980

291 "Composition in Blue"

(Des B. Jackson. Litho)

1989 (22 June). Centenary of South African Rugby Board. T **290** and similar horiz designs. Multicoloured. P 14.

685	15c. Type **290**	80	15
686	30c. South Africa v Australia, 1963	1·25	90
687	40c. South Africa v New Zealand, 1937	1·50	1·60
688	50c. South Africa v British Isles, 1896	1·50	2·00
685/8	*Set of 4*	4·50	4·25

1989 (13 Aug). Paintings by Jacob Hendrik Pierneef . T **291** and similar horiz designs. Multicoloured. Litho. P 14.

689	18c. Type **291**	50	15
690	30c. "Zanzibar"	80	60
691	40c. "The Bushveld"	1·00	1·25
692	50c. "Cape Homestead"	1·10	1·75
689/92	*Set of 4*	3·00	3·50
MS693	114×86 mm. Nos. 689/92	2·25	2·75

292 Pres. F. W. de Klerk

293 Gas-drilling Rig, Mossel Bay

1989 (20 Sept). Inauguration of President F. W. de Klerk. T **292** and similar vert design. Multicoloured. Litho. P 14.

694	18c. Type **292**	50	15
695	45c. F. W. de Klerk (different)	75	1·40

(Des H. Botha. Litho)

1989 (19 Oct). Energy Sources. T **293** and similar horiz designs. Multicoloured. P 14×14½.

696	18c. Type **293**	40	10
697	30c. Coal to oil conversion plant	70	70
698	40c. Nuclear power station	80	85
699	50c. Thermal electric power station	90	1·25
696/9	*Set of 4*	2·50	2·50

294 Electric Goods Train and Map of Railway Route

295 Great Britain 1840 Penny Black

(Des A. H. Barrett. Litho)

1990 (15 Feb). Co-operation in Southern Africa. T **294** and similar horiz designs. Multicoloured. P 14½×14.

700	18c. Cahora Bassa Hydro-electric Scheme, Mozambique, and map of transmission lines (68×26 mm)	70	25
701	30c. Type **294**	90	70
702	40c. Projected dam on upper Orange River, Lesotho, and map of Highlands Water Project (68×26 mm)	1·10	1·10
703	50c. Cow, syringe, and outline map of Africa	1·40	1·25
700/3	*Set of 4*	3·75	3·00
MS704	136×78 mm. Nos. 700/3	3·25	2·75

1990 (12 May). National Stamp Day. T **295** and similar vert designs showing stamps. Multicoloured. Litho. P 14.

705	21c. Type **295**	40	55
	a. Horiz strip of 5. Nos. 705/9	1·75	2·50
706	21c. Cape of Good Hope 1853 4d. triangular pair	40	55
707	21c. Natal 1857 1s.40	50	55
708	21c. Orange Free State 1868 1s.40	50	55
709	21c. Transvaal 1869 1s.40	50	55
705/9	*Set of 5*	1·75	2·50

Nos. 705/9 were printed together, *se-tenant*, in horizontal strips of 5 throughout the sheet.

296 Knysna Turaco

297 Karoo Landscape near Britstown

(Des C. Finch-Davies. Litho)

1990 (2 Aug). Birds. T **296** and similar vert designs. Multicoloured. P 14.

710	21c. Type **296**	85	20
711	35c. Red-capped Robin Chat	1·25	80
712	40c. Rufous-naped Bush Lark	1·25	1·50
713	50c. Bokmakierie Shrike	1·50	2·00
710/13	*Set of 4*	4·25	4·00

The 50c. value exists as a Philatelic Foundation miniature sheet.

1990 (1 Nov). Tourism. T **297** and similar horiz designs. Multicoloured. Litho. P 14.

714	50c. Type **297**	1·25	1·75
	a. Block of 4. Nos. 714/17	4·50	6·00
715	50c. Camps Bay, Cape of Good Hope	1·25	1·75
716	50c. Giraffes in Kruger National Park	1·25	1·75
717	50c. Boschendal Vineyard, Drakenstein Mts.	1·25	1·75
714/17	*Set of 4*	4·50	6·00

Nos. 714/17 were printed together, *se-tenant*, in blocks of 4 throughout the sheet.

298 Woltemade Cross for Bravery

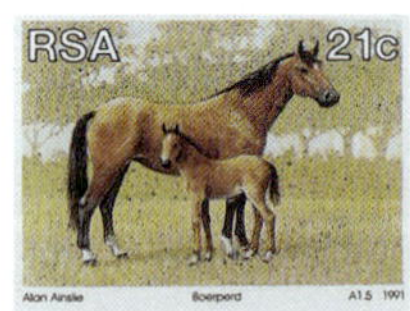

299 Boer Horses

(Des J. Hoekstra. Litho)

1990 (6 Dec). National Orders. T **298** and similar vert designs. Multicoloured. P 14.

718	21c. Type **298**	50	60
	a. Horiz strip of 5. Nos. 718/22	2·25	2·75
719	21c. Order of the Southern Cross	50	60
720	21c. Order of the Star of South Africa	50	60
721	21c. Order for Meritorious Service	50	60
722	21c. Order of Good Hope	50	60
718/22	*Set of 5*	2·25	2·75
MS723	143×70 mm. Nos. 718/22	2·25	2·75

Nos. 718/22 were printed together, *se-tenant*, in horizontal strips of 5 throughout the sheet.

(Des A. Ainslie. Litho)

1991 (12 Feb). Animal Breeding in South Africa. T **299** and similar horiz designs. Multicoloured. P 14.

724	21c. Type **299**	85	85
	a. Horiz strip of 5. Nos. 724/8	3·75	3·75
725	21c. Bonsmara bull	85	85
726	21c. Dorper sheep	85	85
727	21c. Ridgeback dogs	85	85
728	21c. Putterie racing pigeons	85	85
724/8	*Set of 5*	3·75	3·75

Nos. 724/8 were printed together, *se-tenant*, in horizontal strips of five throughout the sheet.

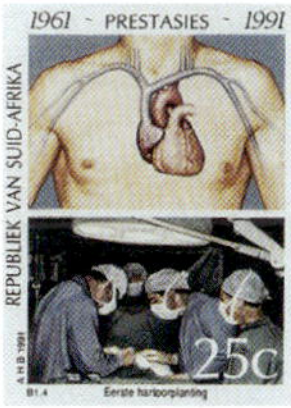

300 Diagram of Human Heart and Transplant Operation

301 State Registration of Nurses Act, 1891

(Des A. H. Barrett. Litho)

1991 (30 May). 30th Anniv of Republic. Scientific and Technological Achievements. T **300** and similar multicoloured designs. P 14.

729	25c. Type **300**	20	10
730	40c. Marimba Power Station (horiz)	35	35
731	50c. Dolos design breakwater (horiz)	45	45
732	60c. Western Deep Levels gold mine	60	60
729/32 *Set of 4*		1·40	1·40

The 60c. value exists as a Philatelic Foundation miniature sheet.

(Des T. Marais. Litho)

1991 (15 Aug). Centenary of State Registration for Nurses and Midwives. P 14.

733	**301**	60c. multicoloured	60	60

302 South Africa Post Office Ltd Emblem

303 Sir Arnold Theiler (veterinarian)

(Des Liza van der Wal. Litho)

1991 (1 Oct). Establishment of Post Office Ltd and Telekom Ltd. T **302** and similar horiz design. Multicoloured. P 14×14½.

734	27c. Type **302**	50	50
	a. Vert pair. Nos. 734/5	1·00	1·00
735	27c. Telekom SA Ltd emblem	50	50

Nos. 734/5 were printed together, *se-tenant*, in vertical pairs throughout the sheet.

(Des A. H. Barrett. Litho)

1991 (9 Oct). South African Scientists. T **303** and similar horiz designs. Multicoloured. P 14.

736	27c. Type **303**	45	15
737	45c. Sir Basil Schonland (physicist)	65	60
738	65c. Dr. Robert Broom (palaeontologist)	1·25	1·40
739	85c. Dr. Alex du Toit (geologist)	1·50	2·25
736/9 *Set of 4*		3·50	4·00

304 *Agulhas* (Antarctic research ship)

305 Soil Conservation

(Des Liza van der Wal (27c.), T. Marais (65c.). Litho)

1991 (5 Dec). 30th Anniv of Antarctic Treaty. T **304** and similar horiz design. Multicoloured. P 14.

740	27c. Type **304**	1·50	25
741	65c. Chart showing South African National Antarctic Expedition base	2·25	1·25

(Des J. van Niekerk. Litho)

1992 (6 Feb). Environmental Conservation. T **305** and similar horiz designs. Multicoloured. P 14×14½.

742	27c. Type **305**	50	15
743	65c. Water pollution	1·25	1·10
744	85c. Air pollution	1·50	1·50
742/4 *Set of 3*		3·00	2·50

The 65c. value exists as a Philatelic Foundation miniature sheet.

306 Dutch Fleet approaching Table Bay c. 1750

307 Queen Anne Settee.

(Des J. van Niekerk. Litho)

1992 (9 May). National Stamp Day. Cape of Good Hope Postal Stones. T **306** and similar horiz designs. Multicoloured. P 14.

745	35c. Type **306**	65	65
	a. Horiz strip of 5. Nos. 745/9	3·00	3·00
746	35c. Landing for water and provisions	65	65
747	35c. Discovering a postal stone	65	65
748	35c. Leaving letters under a stone	65	65
749	35c. Reading letters	65	65
745/9 *Set of 5*		3·00	3·00

Nos. 745/9 were printed together, *se-tenant*, in horizontal strips of 5 throughout the sheet.

1992 (9 July). Antique Cape Furniture. T **307** and similar multicoloured designs. Litho. P 14.

750	35c. Type **307**	55	60
	a. Sheetlet. Nos. 750/9	5·00	5·50
751	35c. Stinkwood settee, c. 1800	55	60
752	35c. Canopy bed, c. 1800 (vert)	55	60
753	35c.19 th-century rocking cradle	55	60
754	35c. Waterbutt, c. 1800 (vert)	55	60
755	35c. Flemish style cabinet, c. 1700 (vert)	55	60
756	35c. Armoire, c 1780 (vert)	55	60
757	35c. Late 17th-century church chair (vert)	55	60
758	35c. Tub chair, c. 1770 (vert)	55	60
759	35c. Bible desk, c. 1750 (vert)	55	60
750/9 *Set of 10*		5·00	5·50

Nos. 750/9 were printed together, *se-tenant*, as a sheetlet of 10.

308 Grand Prix Motor Racing

309 "Women's Monument" (Van Wouw)

(Des Liza van der Wal (35c. (No. 761)), C. Prinsloo (55c.), B. Jackson (70, 90c., 1r.05). Litho)

1992 (24 July). Sports. T **308** and similar horiz designs. Multicoloured. P 14×14½.

760	35c. Type **308**	30	25
761	35c. Football	30	25
762	55c. Total Paris–Cape Motor Rally	45	35
763	70c. Athletics	55	50
764	90c. Rugby	75	70
765	1r.05 Cricket	1·50	1·25
760/5 *Set of 6*		3·50	3·00
MS766 167×69 mm. Nos. 760/5		3·50	3·00

1992 (8 Oct). 130th Birth Anniv of Anton van Wouw (sculptor). T **309** and similar vert designs. Multicoloured. Litho. P 14.

767	35c. Type **309**	50	20
768	70c. "Sekupu Player"	90	60
769	90c. "The Hunter"	1·10	80
770	1r.05 "Postman Lehman"	1·25	1·00
767/70 *Set of 4*		3·25	2·40
MS771 96×149 mm. Nos. 767/70		2·75	2·40

310 Walvis Bay Harbour

1993 (28 Jan). South African Harbours. T **310** and similar horiz designs. Multicoloured. Litho. P 14.

772	35c. Type **310**	40	20
773	55c. East London	50	35
774	70c. Port Elizabeth	75	50
775	90c. Cape Town	95	75
776	1r.05 Durban	1·00	95
772/6 *Set of 5*		3·25	2·50
MS777 147×112 mm. Nos. 777/6		2·75	2·50

(Des H. Botha. Litho)

1993. Succulents. Design as T **286**, but inscr "Standardised mail" in English and Afrikaans. P 14.

778	– *Stapelia grandiflora*	60	10

No. 778 was sold at 45c.

311 Bristol "Boxkite", 1907

(Des D. Stahmer. Litho)

1993 (7 May). Aviation in South Africa. T **311** and similar horiz designs. Multicoloured. P 14.

779	45c. Type **311**	70	70
	a. Sheetlet. Nos. 779/803	16·00	16·00
780	45c. Voisin "Boxkite", 1909	70	70
781	45c. Bleriot XI, 1911	70	70
782	45c. Paterson No. 2 biplane, 1913	70	70
783	45c. Henri Farman H.F.27, 1915	70	70
784	45c. Royal Aircraft Factory B.E.2E., 1918	70	70
785	45c. Vickers Vimy *Silver Queen II*, 1920	70	70
786	45c. Royal Aircraft Factory S.E.5A.,1921	70	70
787	45c. Avro 504k, 1921	70	70
788	45c. Armstrong Whitworth A.W.(15) Atalanta, 1930	70	70
789	45c. de Havilland DH.66 Hercules, 1931	70	70
790	45c. Westland Wapiti, 1931	70	70
791	45c. Junkers F-13, 1932	70	70
792	45c. Handley Page H.P.42, 1933	70	70
793	45c. Junkers Ju 52/3m, 1934	70	70
794	45c. Junkers Ju 86, 1936	70	70
795	45c. Hawker Hartbees, 1936	70	70
796	45c. Short S.23 Empire "C" Class flying boat *Canopus*, 1937	70	70
797	45c. Miles Master II and Airspeed A.S.11 Oxford, (1940)	70	70
798	45c. North American AT-6 Harvard Mk IIa, (1942)	70	70
799	45c. Short S.26 Sunderland flying boat, 1945	70	70
800	45c. Avro Type 685 York, 1946	70	70
801	45c. Douglas DC-7B, 1955	70	70
802	45c. Sikorsky S-56c helicopter, 1956	70	70
803	45c. Boeing 707-344, 1959	70	70
779/803 *Set of 25*		16·00	16·00

Nos. 779/803 were printed together, *se-tenant*, in sheetlets of 25 (5×5). They were also available (in panes of 10) in booklets (SB24).

Nos. 779 and 803 exist as a Philatelic Foundation miniature sheet.

312 Table Mountain Ghost Frog

313 Dragoons carrying Mail between Cape Town and False Bay, 1803

Two types of species inscr:
I. Species name in Latin.
II. Species name in English.

Two types of "Standardised mail" stamp (No. 821):
III. Small rhinoceros. Inscr "DICEROS BICORNIS".
IV. Redrawn with larger rhinoceros. Inscr "BLACK RHINOCEROS".

60c. English Inscription superimposed over Latin (Pane B R. 8/8)

(Des D. Murphy. Litho)

1993 (3 Sept)–**97**. Endangered Fauna. T **312** and similar horiz designs. Multicoloured.

(a) Face values as T **312**

804	1c. Type **312** (I)	10	75
	a. Coil strip. Nos. 804, 805×2 and 808×2 (15.4.94)	65	
	b. Coil. Imperf×p 14 (1.9.95)	20	1·00
	ba. Coil strip. Nos. 804b, 805b×2, 806b and 810b (50c. stamp at right)	1·00	
	bb. Coil strip. As No. 804ba, but 50c. stamp in centre (1.12.95)	1·00	
	c. Type II (coil. Imperf×p 14) (1.8.96)	20	1·00
	ca. Coil strip. Nos. 804c, 805c×2, 807c and 811c	1·40	
805	2c. Smith's Dwarf Chameleon (I)	10	75
	b. Coil. Imperf×p 14 (1.9.95)	20	1·00
	c. Type II (coil. Imperf×p 14) (1.8.96)	20	1·00
806	5c. Giant Girdle-tailed Lizard (I)	10	40
	a. Coil strip. Nos. 806/7, each×2, and 808 (24.8.94)	50	
	b. Coil. Imperf×p 14 (2.95)	30	60
	ba. Coil strip. Nos. 806b×2, 807b×2 and 808b	2·00	
	c. Magenta omitted		
807	10c. Geometric Tortoise (I)	10	30
	b. Coil. Imperf×p 14 (2.95)	45	70
	c. Type II (coil. Imperf×p 14) (1.8.96)	45	70
808	20c. Southern African Hedgehog (I)	20	30
	b. Coil. Imperf×p 14 (2.95)	70	1·00
	c. Type II (25.6.97)	40	50
809	40c. Riverine Rabbit (I)	30	10
	c. Type II (27.3.97)	30	10
810	50c. Samango Monkey (I)	30	20
	b. Coil. Imperf×p 14 (1.9.95)	40	60
	c. Type II (1.7.97)	40	40
811	55c. Aardwolf (I)	30	10
	c. Type II (coil. Imperf×p 14) (1.8.96)	45	60
812	60c. Cape Hunting Dog (I)	50	20
	a. English inscription superimposed over Latin	25·00	
813	70c. Roan Antelope (I)	60	25
	c. Type II (19.5.97)	60	30
814	75c. African Striped Weasel (I)	50	20
815	80c. Kori Bustard (I)	1·50	25
815*a*	85c. Lemon-breasted Seedeater (I) (20.10.95)	1·50	25
816	90c. Jackass Penguin (I)	1·40	30
	a. Booklet pane. No. 816×10 with outer edges of pane imperf (1.12.95)	6·50	
	c. Type II (18.6.97)	1·75	30
817	1r. Wattled Crane (I)	1·50	30
	c. Type II (6.8.96)	1·50	30
818	2r. Blue Swallow (I)	1·75	55
	c. Type II (23.7.97)	1·75	55
819	5r. Martial Eagle (I)	2·25	1·40
	c. Type II (18.6.97)	2·25	1·40
820	10r. Bateleur (I)	3·25	2·10
804/20 *Set of 18*		14·00	8·00

(b) Inscr "Standardised mail" in English and Afrikaans (No. 821) or "Airmail postcard rate" (others)

821	(45c.) Black Rhinoceros (III)	60	25
	a. Booklet pane. No. 821×10 with outer edges of pane imperf (14.2.95)	5·50	
	b. Type IV (9.4.96)	60	35
	ba. Booklet pane. No. 821b×10 with outer edges of pane imperf	5·50	
821*c*	(1r.) White Rhinoceros (II) (8.5.96)	65	30
	c. Horiz strip of 5. Nos. 821*c/g*	3·00	
	cb. Pane. Nos. 821*c/g* plus 3 advertising and 2 airmail labels with margins all round	3·25	
	cc. Booklet pane. Nos. 821*c/g* plus 5 airmail labels with outer edges of pane imperf	3·25	
	cd. Booklet pane. Nos. 821*c/g* plus 5 Thulamela labels with outer edges of pane imperf (27.7.97)	3·25	
821*d*	(1r.) Buffalo (II) (8.5.96)	65	30
821*e*	(1r.) Lion (II) (8.5.96)	65	30
821*f*	(1r.) Leopard (II) (8.5.96)	65	30
821*g*	(1r.) African Elephant (II) (8.5.96)	65	30
821/*g* *Set of 6*		3·50	1·60

Multi-value coil strips Nos. 804a, 804ba/bb, 804ca, 806a and 806ba were produced by the South African Post Office for use by Reader's Digest. Strips were also available from the Philatelic Service and philatelic counters.

Nos. 804ba/bb and 804ca each include a label showing the Reader's Digest emblem at left. In each instance the right hand stamp (50c. on No. 804ba, 5c. on No. 804bb and 55c. on No. 804ca) is imperforate on three sides. No. 804ba originally had a black label, but was re-issued with a red label on 1 December 1995. No. 804bb had a blue label and No. 804ca a green one, but this was re-issued with an orange label on 11 November 1996.

No. 806ba occurs with both the left and right hand stamps (5c. and 20c.), or just the right hand stamp, imperforate on three sides.

No. 821 was initially sold at 45c. and No. 821b was only issued in stamp booklets, initially sold at 6r. The "Standardised mail" rate was increased to 50c. in August 1994, 60c. in April 1996, 70c. in August 1996, 1r. on 7 April 1997 and to 1r.10 on 14 April 1998.

Nos. 821*c/g*, which were each initially sold at 1r., were printed together, *se-tenant*, in sheets of 10 containing two horizontal strips of 5. No. 821b exists as a corporate miniature sheet sponsored by MILSET and commemorating the "ESI '97" Exhibition at Pretoria.No. 821*e* exists as a corporate miniature sheet sponsored by Coach House.

For stamps with elliptical perforations see Nos. 913/18 and for redrawn designs without frame and inscribed "South Africa" only see Nos. 1012a/49.

CORPORATE MINIATURE SHEETS. Such miniature sheets were introduced in 1996 and were produced for firms or other corporate bodies to use for advertising and publicity purposes. Each sponsor has to agree to purchase a minimum of 10,000 sheets with further supplies being placed on sale, at face value, by the South Africa Philatelic Bureau, philatelic counters and overseas agents.

(Des J. van Niekerk. Litho)

1993 (8 Oct). National Stamp Day. Early 19th-century Postal Services. T **313** and similar horiz designs. Multicoloured. P 14.

822	45c. Type **313**	30	25
823	65c. Ox wagon carrying Stellenbosch to Cape Town mail, 1803	45	50
824	85c. Khoi-Khoin mail runners from Stellenbosch, 1803	65	70
825	1r.05 Mounted postmen, 1804	80	90
822/5	*Set of* 4	2·00	2·10

314 Flowers from Namaqualand

1993 (12 Nov). Tourism. T **314** and similar horiz designs. Multicoloured. Litho. P 14.

826	85c. Type **314** (Afrikaans inscr)	65	85
	a. Horiz strip of 5. Nos. 826/30	3·00	3·75
827	85c. North Beach, Durban (English inscr)	65	85
828	85c. Lion (German inscr)	65	85
829	85c. "Appel Express" on Van Staden's Bridge (Dutch inscr)	65	85
830	85c. Gemsbok (antelope) (French inscr)	65	85
826/30	*Set of* 5	3·00	3·75

Nos. 826/30 were printed together, *se-tenant*, in horizontal strips of 5 thoughout the sheet.

315 Grapes and Packing Bench

(Des B. Jackson. Litho)

1994 (28 Jan). Export Fruits. T **315** and similar horiz designs. Multicoloured. P 14½×14.

831	85c. Type **315**	55	50
832	90c. Apple and picker	55	50
833	1r.05 Plum and fork-lift truck	65	60
834	1r.25 Orange and tractor with trailer	75	70
835	1r.40 Avocado and loading freighter	85	80
831/5	*Set of* 5	3·00	2·75

The 85c. value exists as a Philatelic Foundation miniature sheet.

316 "Children of Different Races"

(Nicole Davies)

1994 (8 Apr). Peace Campaign. Children's Paintings. T **316** and similar horiz designs. Multicoloured. Litho. P 14½×14.

836	45c. Type **316**	25	20
837	70c. "Dove and Tree" (Robynne Lawrie)	40	40
838	95c. "Children and Dove" (Batami Nothmann)	55	55
839	1r.15 "Multi-racial Crowd" (Karen Uys)	75	80
836/9	*Set of* 4	1·75	1·75

No. 839 exists as a corporate miniature sheet sponsored by I.G.P.C. and commemorating Chernobyl's Children charities.

317 Pres. Mandela

(Des Liza van der Wal (70c., 95c.). Litho)

1994 (10 May). Inauguration of President Nelson Mandela. T **317** and similar multicoloured designs. P 14×14½ (45c.) or 14½×14 (others).

840	45c. Type **317**	55	20
841	70c. South African national anthems	85	60
842	95c. New national flag	1·40	1·50
843	1r.15 Union Buildings, Pretoria	1·40	2·00
840/3	*Set of* 4	3·75	3·75

318 Tug *T. S. McEwen* towing *Winchester Castle* (liner), 1935

(Des Sheila Nowers. Litho)

1994 (13 May). Tugboats. T **318** and similar horiz designs. Multicoloured. P 14½×14.

844	45c. Type **318**	35	20
845	70c. Sir William Hoy with *Karanja* (liner), 1970	55	40
846	95c. Sir Charles Elliott and wreck of *Dunedin Star* (liner), 1942	70	55
847	1r.15 Eland and freighter at wharf, 1955	95	75
848	1r.35 *Pioneer* (paddle tug) and sailing ships, 1870	1·10	90
844/8	*Set of* 5	3·25	2·50
MS849	163×84 mm. Nos. 844/8	3·25	2·50

Commonwealth Member 1 June 1994.

319 "Mother hands out Work" (Emile du Toit)

1994 (1 July). International Year of the Family. Children's Paintings. T **319** and similar horiz designs. Multicoloured. Litho. P 14.

850	45c. Type **319**	50	55
	a. Vert strip of 5. Nos. 850/4	2·25	2·50
851	45c. "My Friends and I at Play" (Patrick Mackenzie)	50	55
852	45c. "Family Life" (Michelle du Pisani)	50	55
853	45c. "Sunday in Church" (Elizabeth Nel)	50	55
854	45c. "I visit my Brother in Hospital" (Zwelinzema Sam)	50	55
850/4	*Set of* 5	2·25	2·50

Nos. 850/4 were printed together, *se-tenant*, in vertical strips of 5 throughout the sheet.

320 Hands holding Invoice and Bulk Mail Envelope

(Des J. van Niekerk. Litho)

1994 (30 Sept). National Stamp Day. T **320** and similar horiz designs. Multicoloured. P 14.

855	50c. Type **320**	30	25
856	70c. Certified mail	40	40
857	95c. Registered mail	50	55
858	1r.15 Express Delivery mail	60	65
855/8	*Set of 4*	1·60	1·75

321 *Erica tenuifolia*

(Des J. van Niekerk. Litho)

1994 (18 Nov). Heathers. T **321** and similar vert designs. Multicoloured. P 14.

859	95c. Type **321**	65	70
	a. Horiz strip of 5. Nos. 859/63	3·00	3·25
860	95c. *Erica urna-viridis*	65	70
861	95c. *Erica decora*	65	70
862	95c. *Erica aristata*	65	70
863	95c. *Erica dichrus*	65	70
859/63	*Set of 5*	3·00	3·25

Nos. 859/63 were printed together, *se-tenant*, in horizontal strips of 5 throughout the sheet.

322 Warthogs (Eastern Transvaal) and Map

(Des A. Ainslie. Litho)

1995 (18 Jan). Tourism. T **322** and similar horiz designs, each including map. Multicoloured. P 14½×14.

(a) Face values as T **322**

864	50c. Type **322**	60	40
865	50c. Lost City Resort (North-West Province) (15 Feb)	60	40

(b) Inscr "Standardised mail" in English and Afrikaans

866	(60c.) White Rhinoceros and calf (Kwazulu/Natal) (28 April)	60	60
867	(60c.) Cape Town waterfront (Western Cape) (12 May)	60	40
868	(60c.) Baobab tree (Northern Transvaal) (30 June)	80	80
	a. Vert strip of 5. Nos. 868/72	3·50	3·50
869	(60c.) Highland Route (Free State) (30 June)	80	80
870	(60c.) Augrabies Falls (Northern Cape) (30 June)	80	80
871	(60c.) Herd of elephants, Addo National Park (Eastern Cape) (30 June)	80	80
872	(60c.) Union Buildings, Pretoria (Gauteng) (30 June)	80	80
864/72	*Set of 9*	5·75	5·00

Nos. 868/72 were printed together, *se-tenant*, in sheets of 10 containing two vertical *se-tenant* strips of 5.

No. 864 exists as a Philatelic Foundation miniature sheet.

No. 868 exists imperforate on three sides with a *se-tenant* stamp-size label as a corporate product sponsored by Coach House. The same value subsequently appeared as a corporate miniature sheet.

323 de Havilland D.H.9 Biplane and Cheetah D Jet Fighter

(Des Anne de Goede (50c.), A. H. Barrett (95c.). Litho)

1995 (1 Feb). Aviation Anniversaries. T **323** and similar horiz design. Multicoloured. P 14.

873	50c. Type **323** (75th anniv of South African Air Force)	1·00	40
874	95c. Vickers Vimy *Silver Queen II* (75th anniv of first Trans-African flight)	1·50	1·50

324 Player running with Ball and Silhouettes

1995 (25 May). World Cup Rugby Championship, South Africa. T **324** and similar multicoloured designs. Litho. P 14.

875	(60c.) Type **324**	30	25
	a. Perf 14×imperf (booklets)	35	35
	ab. Booklet pane. Nos. 875a/6a, each×5	3·25	
876	(60c.) Player running with ball and silhouettes (vert)	30	25
	a. Imperf×perf 14 (booklets)	35	35
	ab. Booklet pane. No. 876a×10	3·25	
877	1r.15 Player taking ball from scrum (68×26½ mm)	75	85
875/7	*Set of 3*	1·25	1·25
MS878	109×61 mm. No. 876	75	75

Nos. 875/6 are inscribed "STANDARD POSTAGE" in English and Afrikaans.

325 Rural Water Purification System

(Des J. van Niekerk. Litho)

1995 (15 June). 50th Anniv of CSIR (technological research organization). P 14.

879	**325** (60c.) multicoloured	45	45

No. 879 is inscribed "Standardised mail" in English and Afrikaans.

326 Player with Ball

327 Dr. John Gilchrist, South African Pilchards and *Africana* (oceanographic research ship)

1995 (28 June). South Africa's Victory in Rugby World Cup. T **326** and similar multicoloured design. Litho. P 14.

880	(60c.) Type **326**	40	50
881	(60c.) South African player holding trophy aloft (vert)	40	50

Nos. 880/1 are inscribed "STANDARD POSTAGE" in English and Afrikaans.

(Des D. Thorpe. Litho)

1995 (25 Aug). Centenary of Marine Science in South Africa. P 14.
882 **327** (60c.) multicoloured 30 30
No. 882 is inscribed "Standard Postage" in English and Afrikaans.

328 Singapore Lion

329 People building Flag Wall

(Des A. Ainslie. Litho)

1995 (1 Sept). "Singapore '95" International Stamp Exhibition. Sheet 71×55 mm. P 14.
MS883 **328** (60c.) multicoloured .... 1·25 1·75
No. **MS**883 is inscribed "STANDARD POSTAGE" in English and Afrikaans.
A second printing of No. **MS**883 included the date, "DEC 1995", on the sheet margin at bottom left.

1995 (16 Sept). Masakhane Campaign. Litho. P 14.
884 **329** (60c.) multicoloured (34×24 mm) 20 20
a. Booklet pane. No. 884×10 .... 2·00
884*b* (60c.) mult (26×20 mm) (1 Dec) 20 20
ba. Booklet pane. No. 884b×10 .... 2·00
Nos. 884 and 884*b* are inscribed "STANDARD POSTAGE" in English and Afrikaans.
No. 884*b* was only issued in 6r. stamp booklets.
Nos. 884a and 884ba show the three outer edges of the panes imperforate.

330 Papal Arms

331 Gandhi wearing Suit

1995 (16 Sept). Visit of Pope John Paul II. Litho. P 14.
885 **330** (60c.) multicoloured 65 30
No. 885 is inscribed "STANDARD POSTAGE" in English and Afrkaans.

(Des A. Ainslie. Litho)

1995 (2 Oct). India-South Africa Co-operation. 125th Birth Anniv of Mahatma Gandhi (1994). T **331** and similar vert design. P 14.
886 (60c.) deep violet .... 1·00 40
887 1r.40 bistre-brown .... 1·50 1·60
MS888 71×71 mm. No. 887 .... 1·40 1·60
Design:—1r.40, Gandhi wearing dhoti.
No. 886 is inscribed "STANDARD POSTAGE" in English and Afrikaans.
Stamps in similar designs were issued by India.
No. 886 exists as a corporate miniature sheet sponsored by Pradip Jain and commemorating the 50th anniversary of the Congress Alliance for a Democratic South Africa.

332 Traditional African Postman

(Des C. Emslie. Litho)

1995 (9 Oct). World Post Day. P 14.
889 **332** (60c.) multicoloured 30 30
No. 889 is inscribed "STANDARD POSTAGE" in English and Afrikaans.

No. 889 exists as a corporate miniature sheet sponsored by the South African Stamp Colour Catalogue.

(Des C. Emslie. Litho)

1995 (19 Oct). "Total Stampex '95" and "Ilsapex '98" Stamp Exhibitions. Sheet, 70×66 mm, containing T **332** and "ILSAPEX '98" logo. Imperf.
MS890 5r. multicoloured .... 2·00 2·50

333 "50" and UN Emblem

(Des C. Emslie (No. 891), A. Ainslie and F. Frescura (No. **MS**892). Litho)

1995 (24 Oct). 50th Annivs of United Nations and UNESCO T **333** and similar multicoloured design. P 14.
891 (60c.) Type **333** 30 30
MS892 101×78 mm. (60c.) Traditional village (30×47 mm) 30 45
Nos. 891/2 are inscribed "STANDARD POSTAGE" in English and Afrikaans.

334 *Afrivoluta pringlei*

335 Map of Africa and Player

(Des L. Kriedemann. Litho)

1995 (24 Nov). Sea Shells. T **334** and similar vert designs. Multicoloured. P 14½×14.
893 (60c.) Type **334** 40 40
a. Horiz strip of 5. Nos. 893/7 .... 1·75 1·75
894 (60c.) *Lyria Africana* 40 40
895 (60c.) *Marginella mosaica* 40 40
896 (60c.) *Conus pictus* 40 40
897 (60c.) *Gypreaea fultoni* 40 40
893/7 *Set of 5* .... 1·75 1·75
Nos. 893/7 were printed together, *se-tenant*, as horizontal strips of 5 in sheets of 10, each stamp being inscribed "STANDARD POSTAGE" in English and Afrikaans.
No. 893 is inscribed "priglei" in error.

(Des M. de Jong (Nos. 898/902), Z. Mashinini (No. **MS**903). Litho)

1996 (10 Jan). African Nations Football Championship, South Africa. T **335** and similar vert designs showing map and players. P 14½×14.
898 **335** (60c.) multicoloured ("RSA" in deep ultramarine) 55 60
a. Horiz strip of 5. Nos. 898/902 .... 2·50 2·75
899 (60c.) multicoloured ("RSA" in brown-ochre) 55 60
900 (60c.) multicoloured ("RSA" in bright scarlet) 55 60
901 (60c.) multicoloured ("RSA" in olive-grey) 55 60
902 (60c.) multicoloured ("RSA" in deep emerald) 55 60
898/902 *Set of 5* .... 2·50 2·75
MS903 75×55 mm. (60c.) mult (young player) 50 70
Nos. 898/902 were printed together, *se-tenant*, as horizontal strips of 5 in sheets of 10.
Nos. 898/903 are inscribed "STANDARD POSTAGE" in English and Afrikaans.

336 South African Player, Map and Trophy

(Des M. de Jong. Litho)

1996 (8 Feb). South Africa's Victory in African Nations Football Championship. P 14.

904	**336**	(60c.) multicoloured	40	30
		a. Football missing above date at bottom right (R. 1/2)	10·00	

No. 904 is inscribed "STANDARD POSTAGE" in English and Afrikaans. It is understood that No. 904a occurs on every tenth sheet.

337 Historical Buildings, Bloemfontein

338 Rat

(Des J. van Beukering. Litho)

1996. 50th Anniv of City of Bloemfontein. P 14.

905	**337**	(60c.) multicoloured	65	40

No. 905 is inscribed "Standard Postage" in English and Afrikaans.

(Des D. Murphy. Litho)

1996 (18 May). "CHINA '96" 9th Asian International Stamp Exhibition, Peking. Sheet 109×85 mm. P 14.

MS906	**338**	60c. multicoloured	70	80

339 "Man in a Donkey Cart"

(Gerard Sekoto)

1996 (1 June). Gerard Sekoto (artist) Commemoration. T **339** and similar multicoloured designs. Litho. P 14.

907	1r. Type **339**	30	30
908	2r. "Song of the Pick"	80	80
MS909	108×70 mm. 2r. "Yellow Houses, Sophiatown" (detail) (vert)	1·00	1·10

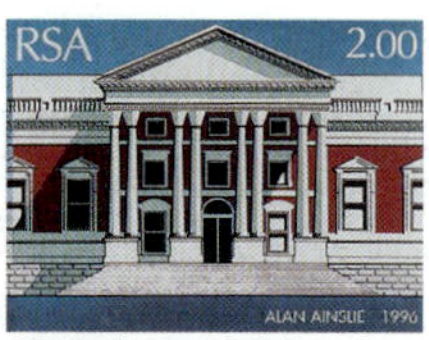

340 Parliament Building, Cape Town

341 Children playing

(Des A. Ainslie. Litho)

1996 (8 June). "CAPEX '96" International Stamp Exhibition, Toronto. Sheet 72×49 mm. P 14.

MS910	**340**	2r. multicoloured	1·00	1·10

1996 (8 June). Youth Day. Litho. P 14.

911	**341**	(60c.) multicoloured	30	20

No. 911 is inscribed "STANDARD POSTAGE" in English and Afrikaans.

342 Marathon Runners

(Des M. de Jong. Litho)

1996 (8 June). 75th Anniv of Comrades Marathon. P 14.

912	**342**	(60c.) multicoloured	30	20

No. 912 is inscribed "Standard postage" in English and Afrikaans.

(Des D. Murphy. Litho)

1996 (1–9 July). Endangered Fauna. As Nos. 808c, 810c, 812 (but with English inscr), 817c, 821b and new value (20r.) but P 14½ (20r.) or 14 (others), each with two elliptical holes on horizontal sides.

(a) Face values as T **312**

913	20c. Southern African Hedgehog (II) (28.5.97)	20	40
914	50c. Samango Monkey (II) (1.7.97)	30	20
915	60c. Cape Hunting Dog (II) (12.5.97)	40	15
916	1r. Wattled Crane (II) (11.6.97)	1·50	40
917	20r. Fish Eagle (II) (34×24 mm) (20.3.97)	6·50	5·00

(b) Inscr "Standardised mail" in English and Afrikaans

918	(60c.) Black Rhinoceros (IV)	1·00	40
913/18	*Set of 6*	9·00	6·00

The "Standardised mail" rate was increased to 70c. in August 1996, to 1r. on 7 April 1997 and to 1r.10 on 14 April 1998.

The printing of No. 918 issued on 1 July 1996 was shared between the Government Printer and Cape & Transvaal Printers.

343 Cycling

344 Constitutional Assembly Logo

(Des M. de Jong. Litho)

1996 (5 July). Olympic Games, Atlanta. T **343** and similar vert designs. Multicoloured. P 14.

919	(70c.) Type **343**	45	55
	a. Horiz strip of 5. Nos. 919/23	2·25	2·75
920	(70c.) Swimming	45	55
921	(70c.) Boxing	45	55
922	(70c.) Running	45	55
923	(70c.) Pole vaulting	45	55
924	(1r.40) South African Olympic emblem	45	55
919/24	*Set of 6*	2·50	3·00

Nos. 919/23, which are inscribed "STANDARD POSTAGE" in English and Afrikaans, were printed together in sheets of 10 containing two *se-tenant* horizontal strips of 5.

(Des M. de Jong. Litho)

1996 (1 Aug). New Democratic Constitution. P 14.

925	**344**	(70c.) myrtle-green, orange-red and black	30	30
		a. Horiz strip of 5. Nos. 925/9	1·25	1·25
926		(70c.) brt turquoise-blue, dp vio, & blk	30	30
927		(70c.) deep violet, orange-yellow and black	30	30
928		(70c.) ultramarine, scarlet and black	30	30
929		(70c.) scarlet, orange-yellow and black	30	30
925/9		*Set of 5*	1·25	1·25

Nos. 925/9 are inscribed "Standard Postage" in English and Afrikaans and were printed together, *se-tenant*, in horizontal strips of 5 throughout the sheet.

345 *Sea Pioneer* (bulk carrier)

346 "Xhosa Woman" (G. Pemba)

(Des E. Wale (No. 927), P. Bilas (others). Litho)

1996 (5 Aug). 50th Anniv of South African Merchant Marine. T **345** and similar horiz designs. Multicoloured. P 14.

930	(70c.) Type **345**	90	90
	a. Horiz pair. Nos. 930/1	1·75	1·75
931	(70c.) *Winterberg* (container ship)	90	90
932	1r.40 *Langkloof* (freighter)	1·50	1·75

a. Horiz pair. Nos. 932/3 ... 3·00 3·50
933 1r.40 *Vaal* (liner) ... 1·50 1·75
930/3 *Set of 4* ... 4·25 4·75
MS934 102×63 mm. 2r. *Constantine* (freighter) and tug (71×30 mm) (inscr "SOUTH AFRICAN MERCHANT MARINE 1946—1996" on top margin) .. 1·00 1·00

Nos. 930/1 are inscribed "Standard Postage" in English and Afrikaans.
Nos. 930/1 and 932/3 were printed together, *se-tenant*, in horizontal pairs throughout the sheets.
No. 931 exists as a corporate miniature sheet sponsored by Safmarine.
No. **MS**934 also comes with the top margin inscription replaced by "Safmarine" and logo.

1996 (9 Aug). National Women's Day. Litho. P 14.
935 **346** 70c. multicoloured ... 30 25

347 Postman delivering Letters

348 Candles and Holly

(Des J. van Niekerk. Litho)

1996 (9 Oct). World Post Day. P 14.
936 **347** 70c. multicoloured ... 30 25

(Des A. Ainslie. Litho)

1996 (9 Oct). Christmas. P 14.
937 **348** 70c. multicoloured ... 30 25
a. Booklet pane. No. 937×10 ... 3·00

No. 937a has the three outer edges of the pane imperforate.
No. 937 exists as a corporate miniature sheet sponsored by SANTA and sold at 2r. for charitable purposes.

349 "Liner Oranje at Cape Town" (E. Wale)

1996 (9 Oct). "Bloemfontein 150" National Stamp Show. Sheet 86×56 mm. Litho. P 14.
MS938 **349** 2r. multicoloured ... 1·50 1·50

350 Max Theiler (Medicine, 1951)

351 Early Motor Car

1996 (4 Nov). South African Nobel Laureates. T **350** and similar vert designs. Litho. P 14.
939 (70c.) dull violet and maroon ... 50 55
a. Sheetlet. Nos. 939/48 ... 4·50 5·00
940 (70c.) deep bluish green, maroon and dull violet ... 50 55
941 (70c.) maroon and dull violet ... 50 55
942 (70c.) deep bluish green, maroon and dull violet ... 50 55
943 (70c.) dull violet and maroon ... 50 55
944 (70c.) dull violet and maroon ... 50 55
945 (70c.) deep bluish green, maroon and dull violet ... 50 55
946 (70c.) maroon and dull violet ... 50 55
947 (70c.) deep bluish green, maroon and dull violet ... 50 55
948 (70c.) dull violet and maroon ... 50 55
939/48 *Set of 10* ... 4·50 5·00

Designs—No. 939, Type **350**; No. 940, Albert Luthuli (Peace, 1961); No. 941, Alfred Nobel; No. 942, Allan Cormack (Medicine, 1979); No. 943, Aaron Klug (Chemistry, 1982); No. 944, Desmond Tutu (Peace, 1984); No. 945, Nadine Gordimer (Literature, 1991); No. 946, Nobel Prizes symbol; No. 947, Nelson Mandela (Peace, 1993); No. 948, F. W. de Klerk (Peace, 1993).
Nos. 939/48, which are inscribed "Standard Postage" in English and Afrikaans, were printed together, *se-tenant*, in sheets of 10.
No. 941 exists as a corporate miniature sheet sponsored by AECI and celebrating the centenary of Modderfontein Industrial Complex.

(Des D. Bagnall. Litho)

1997 (4 Jan). Centenary of Motoring in South Africa. P 14.
949 **351** (70c.) multicoloured ... 1·00 35

No. 949 is inscribed "STANDARD POSTAGE" in English and Afrikaans.
No. 949 exists as a corporate minature sheet sponsored by Total.

352 Lion

353 Vegetables and Water Pump

(Des A. Ainslie. Litho)

1997 (12 Feb). "Hong Kong '97" International Stamp Exhibition. Sheet 82×68 mm. P 14 (with two elliptical holes on each vertical side).
MS950 **352** 3r. ultramarine, gold and rosine ... 1·40 1·40

(Des D. Murphy. Litho)

1997 (7 Mar). National Water Conservation. T **353** and similar horiz designs. Multicoloured. P 14 (with two elliptical holes at top or bottom).
951 (70c.) Type **353** ... 40 40
a. Booklet pane. Nos. 951/5, each ×2 ... 3·50
b. Perf 14 (without elliptical holes) (25 Mar) ... 40 40
ba. Booklet pane. Nos. 951b/5b each ×2 ... 3·50
952 (70c.) Flowers and watering can ... 40 40
b. Perf 14 (without elliptical holes) (25 Mar) ... 40 40
953 (70c.) Child in bath ... 40 40
b. Perf 14 (without elliptical holes) (25 Mar) ... 40 40
954 (70c.) Building tools ... 40 40
b. Perf 14 (without elliptical holes) (25 Mar) ... 40 40
955 (70c.) Water cart and stand pipe ... 40 40
b. Perf 14 (without elliptical holes) (25 Mar) ... 40 40
951/5 *Set of 5* ... 1·75 1·75

Nos. 951/5 and 951b/5b are inscribed "STANDARD POSTAGE" and were sold in 7r. stamp booklets containing Nos. 951a or 951ba.
Both booklet panes are imperforate on the three outer edges. On No. 951a the elliptical holes only occur on the horizontal line of perforations separating the two rows of stamps.
Like many other modern South African booklet panes Nos. 951a and 951ba were available to collectors as uncut booklet sheets. Imperf pairs come from these sheets.

354 S.A.S. *Umkomaas* (minesweeper)

355 Election Day Poster

(Des Sheila Nowers. Litho)

1997 (1 Apr). 75th Anniv of South African Navy. T **354** and similar horiz designs. Multicoloured. P 14 (with two elliptical holes on each vertical side).
956 (70c.) Type **354** ... 75 75
a. Block of 4. Nos. 956/9 ... 2·75 2·75
957 (70c.) S.A.S. *Emily Hobhouse* (submarine) and S.A.S. *President Steyn* (frigate) ... 75 75

958	(70c.) S.A.S. *Kobie Coetsee* (fast attack craft)	75	75
959	(70c.) S.A.S. *Protea* (hydrographic survey ship)	75	75
956/9	*Set of 4*	2·75	2·75

Nos. 956/9, which are inscribed "Standard Postage" in English and Afrikaans, were printed together, *se-tenant*, in blocks of 4 throughout the sheet.

(Des M. Maapola. Litho)

1997 (27 Apr). Freedom Day. T **355** and similar vert designs. Each black and red. P 14 (with two elliptical holes on each vertical side).

960	(1r.) Type **355**	40	40
	a. Horiz strip of 5. Nos. 960/4	1·75	1·75
961	(1r.) People queueing	40	40
962	(1r.) People registering	40	40
963	(1r.) Voting booth	40	40
964	(1r.) Woman placing vote in ballot box	40	40
960/4	*Set of 5*	1·75	1·75

Nos. 960/4, which are inscribed "STANDARD POSTAGE", were printed together, *se-tenant*, in horizontal strips of five throughout the sheet forming a composite design.

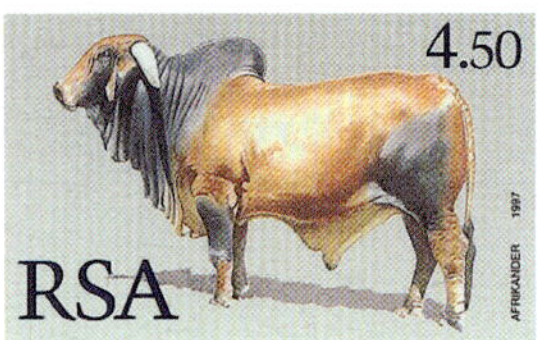

356 Brahman Bull

357 Zulu Baskets

(Des Leigh Voigt. Litho)

1997 (2 May). Chinese New Year ("Year of the Ox"). "SAPDA '97" Stamp Exhibition, Johannesburg. Sheet 107×61 mm. P 14.

MS965	**356**	4r.50 multicoloured	1·00	1·00

(Des D. Murphy. Litho Govt Printer (Nos. 966/75) or Questa (Nos. 966b/75b))

1997 (17 May). Year of Cultural Experiences. T **357** and similar vert designs. Multicoloured. P 14.

966	(1r.) Type **357**	40	40
	a. Sheetlet. Nos. 966/75	3·50	3·50
	b. Perf 14×15 (8 Dec)	40	40
	ba. Booklet pane. Nos. 966b/75b	3·50	
967	(1r.) Southern Sotho figure	40	40
	b. Perf 14×15 (8 Dec)	40	40
968	(1r.) South Ndebele figure	40	40
	b. Perf 14×15 (8 Dec)	40	40
969	(1r.) Venda door	40	40
	b. Perf 14×15 (8 Dec)	40	40
970	(1r.) Tsonga medicine gourd	40	40
	b. Perf 14×15 (8 Dec)	40	40
971	(1r.) Wooden pot, Northern Cape	40	40
	b. Perf 14×15 (8 Dec)	40	40
972	(1r.) Khoi walking stick	40	40
	b. Perf 14×15 (8 Dec)	40	40
973	(1r.) Tswana knife handle	40	40
	b. Perf 14×15 (8 Dec)	40	40
974	(1r.) Xhosa pipe	40	40
	b. Perf 14×15 (8 Dec)	40	40
975	(1r.) Swazi vessel	40	40
966/75	*Set of 10*	3·50	3·50

Nos. 966/75 which are inscribed "Standard Postage", were printed together, *se-tenant*, in sheetlets of 10 with illustrated left-hand margin.

The stamps printed by Questa, Nos. 966b/75b, show some designs redrawn and were only issued in 20r. stamp booklets.

358 Grocott's, Muirhead and Gowie Buildings, Grahamstown

359 White breasted Cormorant

(Des A. Ainslie. Litho)

1997 (29 May). "Pacific '97" International Stamp Exhibition, San Francisco. Sheet 94×49 mm. P 14.

MS976	**358**	5r. multicoloured	1·25	1·25

(Des Julia Birkhead and D. Murphy. Litho Govt Printer (Nos. 977/86) or Questa (Nos. 977b/86b))

1997 (5 June). World Environment Day. Waterbirds. T **359** and similar vert designs. Multicoloured. P 14.

977	(1r.) Type **359**	40	40
	a. Sheetlet. Nos. 977/86	3·50	3·50
	b. Perf 14×15 (8 Dec)	40	40
	ba. Booklet pane. Nos. 977b/86b	3·50	
978	(1r.) Hamerkop	40	40
	b. Perf 14×15 (8 Dec)	40	40
979	(1r.) Pied Kingfisher	40	40
	b. Perf 14×15 (8 Dec)	40	40
980	(1r.) Purple Heron	40	40
	b. Perf 14×15 (8 Dec)	40	40
981	(1r.) Black-headed Heron	40	40
	b. Perf 14×15 (8 Dec)	40	40
982	(1r.) Darter	40	40
	b. Perf 14×15 (8 Dec)	40	40
983	(1r.) Green-backed Heron	40	40
	b. Perf 14×15 (8 Dec)	40	40
984	(1r.) White-faced Duck	40	40
	b. Perf 14×15 (8 Dec)	40	40
985	(1r.) Saddle-billed Stork	40	40
	b. Perf 14×15 (8 Dec)	40	40
986	(1r.) Water Dikkop	40	40
	b. Perf 14×15 (8 Dec)	40	40
977/86	*Set of 10*	3·50	3·50

Nos. 977/86, are inscribed "STANDARD POSTAGE" and were printed together, *se-tenant*, in sheetlets of 10, with illustrated margin at left.

The stamps printed by Questa (Nos. 977b/86b) are in different shades and were only issued in 20r. stamp booklets.

No. 984 exists as a corporate miniature sheet sponsored by the "Junass" exhibition in aid of junior philately.

360 Double-headed Class 6E 1 Electric Locomotives

(Des A. Ainslie. Litho Govt Printer, Pretoria (Nos. 987/91) or Questa (Nos. 987b/91b))

1997 (1 Aug)–**98**. Inauguration of Revived Blue Train Service. T **360** and similar horiz designs. Multicoloured. P 14 (with four elliptical holes on each horizontal side).

987	(1r.20) Type **360**	90	90
	a. Vert strip of 5. Nos. 987/91	4·00	4·00
	b. Perf 15×14. One side phosphor band (11.98)	90	90
	ba. Booklet pane. Nos. 987b/91b, each×2	7·50	
988	(1r.20) Double-headed Class 6E 1 electric locomotives (different)	90	90
	b. Perf 15×14. One side phosphor band (11.98)	90	90
989	(1r.20) Double-headed Class 25NC steam locomotives	90	90
	b. Perf 15×14. One side phosphor band (11.98)	90	90
990	(1r.20) Double-headed Class 34,900 diesel locomotives on Modder River bridge	90	90
	b. Perf 15×14. One side phosphor band (11.98)	90	90
991	(1r.20) Double-headed Class 34 diesel locomotives and Baobab tree	90	90
	b. Perf 15×14. One side phosphor band (11.98)	90	90
987/91	*Set of 5*	4·00	4·00

Nos. 987/91, which are inscribed "AIRMAIL POSTCARD RATE" were printed together, *se-tenant*, in vertical strips of 5 throughout the sheets of 10. The rate for Airmail postcards increased to 1r.30 on 14 April 1998.

Nos. 987b/91b were only available from 13r. stamp booklets with the pane folded vertically down the centre. There are no elliptical holes in the perforations of these booklet stamps. No. 989b is inscr "HUTCHINSON" instead of "HUCHINSON" (989) and No. 991b is inscr "NORTHERN PROVINCE" instead of "NORTHERN TRANSVAAL" (991).

Nos. 987 and 989 exist in separate corporate miniature sheets sponsored by Harmers of London (No. 987) or Eastgate Universal Stamps and Coins Ltd (No. 989).

361 Nguni Breed

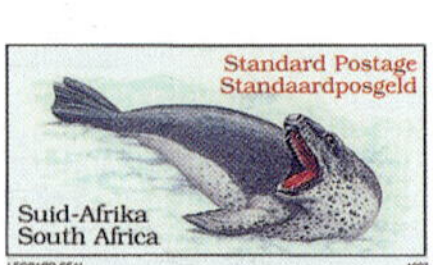

362 Leopard Seal

(Des D. Murphy. Litho)

1997 (10 Aug). Cattle Breeds. T **361** and similar horiz designs. Multicoloured. P 14½ (with two elliptical holes on each horizontal side).

992	(1r.) Type **361**	50	60
	a. Block of 4. Nos. 992/5	1·75	2·25
993	(1r.) Bonsmara	50	60
994	(1r.) Afrikander	50	60
995	(1r.) Drakensberger	50	60
992/5	*Set of* 4	1·75	2·25

Nos. 992/5 which are inscribed "Standard Postage" in English and Afrikaans, were printed together, *se-tenant*, in blocks of four throughout the sheet.

(Des D. Murphy. Litho)

1997 (27 Aug). Antarctic Fauna. T **362** and similar horiz designs. Multicoloured. P 14.

996	(1r.) Type **362**	50	25
997	1r.20 Antarctic Skua	90	50
998	1r.70 King Penguin	1·40	90
996/8	*Set of* 3	2·50	1·50

No. 996 is inscribed "Standard Postage" in English and Afrikaans. The Standard Postage rate increased to 1r.10 on 14 April 1998.

363 Enoch Sontonga and Verse from *Nkosi Sikelel'i Afrika*

(Des Thea Swanepoel and A. Ainslie. Litho)

1997 (24 Sept). Heritage Day. Centenary of *Nkosi Sikelel'i Afrika* (National Anthem). T **363** and similar horiz design. Multicoloured. P 14 (with two elliptical holes on each vertical side).

999	(1r.) Type **363**	50	50
	a. Horiz pair. Nos. 999/1000	1·00	1·00
1000	(1r.) As Type **363** but portrait at right	50	50

Nos. 999/1000, which are inscribed "Standard Postage", were printed together, *se-tenant*, in horizontal pairs throughout the sheet.

364 Horse-drawn Postcart delivering Mail

365 Modern Postbox

(Des D. Bagnall. Litho)

1997 (8 Oct). "Cape Town '97" National Stamp Show. Sheet 85×64 mm. P 14½×14.

MS1001	**364** 4r.50 multicoloured	1·50	1·50

(Des Thea Swanepoel. Litho)

1997 (9 Oct). World Post Day. Sheet, 108×69 mm. P 14 (with two elliptical holes on each vertical side).

MS1002	**365** (1r.) multicoloured	70	70

No. **MS**1002 is inscribed "STANDARD POSTAGE".

366 Bethlehem

1997 (3 Nov). Christmas. 50th Anniv of S.A.N.T.A. (South African National Tuberculosis Association). T **366** and similar vert designs showing charity labels. Multicoloured. Litho. P 14 (with two elliptical holes on each vertical side).

1003	(1r.) Type **366**	35	35
	a. Sheetlet. Nos. 1003/12	3·25	3·25
1004	(1r.) Cross of Lorraine and candles	35	35
1005	(1r.) Cross of Lorraine, angels and candles	35	35
1006	(1r.) Angel kneeling before Cross of Lorraine	35	35
1007	(1r.) Father Christmas carrying sack	35	35
1008	(1r.) Mary and Jesus	35	35
1009	(1r.) Christmas trees	35	35
1010	(1r.) Wise men on camels	35	35
1011	(1r.) Christmas bell	35	35
1012	(1r.) Child kneeling	35	35
1003/12	*Set of* 10	3·25	3·25

Nos. 1003/12 which are inscribed "STANDARD POSTAGE", were printed together, *se-tenant*, in sheetlets of 10, with illustrated left-hand margin.

367 Black Rhinoceros

(Des D. Murphy. Litho Cape & Transvaal Printers (No. 1029), Questa (1030p/4p, 1045/9) or Government Printer (others))

1997 (12 Dec)–**2000**. Endangered Fauna. (3rd series). Redrawn values as 1993–97 issue and new designs (Nos. 1030/4), all without frame or imprint and inscr "South Africa" only as in T **367**. Multicoloured.

(a) Designs as Nos. 806/20, and some new values, redrawn

(i) P 14½ (10r.), P. 14 (others)

1012*a*	5c. Giant Girdle-tailed Lizard (5.6.00)	30	50
1013	10c. Geometric Tortoise (5.2.98)	10	50
1014	20c. Southern African Hedgehog (19.3.98)	15	60
1015	30c. Spotted Hyena (13.3.98)	20	60
1016	40c. Riverine Rabbit (8.1.98)	30	60
1017	50c. Samango Monkey (23.3.98)	30	40
1018	60c. Cape Hunting Dog (29.8.98)	40	50
1019	70c. Roan Antelope (18.12.97)	40	50
1020	80c. Kori Bustard (16.3.98)	1·50	60
1021	90c. Jackass Penguin (19.12.97)	2·00	50
1022	1r. Wattled Crane (12.12.97)	1·50	45
1022*a*	1r.50 Tawny Eagle (20×37 mm) (5.6.00)	3·00	1·50
1023	2r. Blue Swallow (9.1.99)	1·75	45
1023*a*	2r.30 Cape Vulture (20×37 mm) (5.6.00)	3·00	2·00
1024	3r. Giraffe (24.3.98)	2·50	1·00
1025	5r. Martial Eagle (17.3.98)	2·50	1·40
1026	10r. Bateleur (34×24 mm) (28.8.98)	3·50	2·25

(ii) P 14 (2r.)or 14½ (20r.), both with two elliptical holes on each horizontal side

1027	2r. Blue Swallow (18.3.98)	1·50	45
1028	20r. Fish Eagle (34×24 mm) (26.8.98)	6·50	5·00
1012*a*/28	*Set of* 19	28·00	18·00

(b) Inscr "Standard Postage" (No. 1029) or "standard postage" (others)

(i) P 14

1029	(1r.) Black Rhinoceros (12.2.98)	60	60
	a. Booklet pane. No. 1029×10 with outer edges of pane imperf	5·50	
1030	(1r.10) Eland (vert) (18.5.98)	50	50
	a. Strip of 5. Nos. 1030/4	2·25	2·25
	p. With phosphor band (2.11.98)	60	70
	pa. Booklet pane. Nos. 1030p/4p, each ×2, with vertical edges of pane imperf	5·50	
1031	(1r.10) Greater Kudu (vert) (18.5.98)	50	50
	p. With phosphor band (2.11.98)	60	70
1032	(1r.10) Impala (vert) (18.5.98)	50	50
	p. With phosphor band (2.11.98)	60	70
1033	(1r.10) Waterbuck (vert) (18.5.98)	50	50
	p. With phosphor band (2.11.98)	60	70
1034	(1r.10) Blue Wildebeest (vert) (18.5.98)	50	50
	p. With phosphor band (2.11.98)	60	70

(ii). P 14 (with two elliptical holes on each vertical side)

1035	(1r.10) Eland (vert) (18.5.98)	50	60
	a. Booklet pane. Nos. 1035/9, each ×2 with outer edges of pane imperforate.	4·50	
1036	(1r.10) Greater Kudu (vert) (18.5.98)	50	60
1037	(1r.10) Impala (vert) (18.5.98)	50	60
1038	(1r.10) Waterbuck (vert) (18.5.98)	50	60
1039	(1r.10) Blue Wildebeest (vert) (18.5.98)	50	60

(c) Inscr "Airmail Postcard"

(i) P 14 (with two elliptical holes at top or bottom) (11.2.98)

1040	(1r.20) White Rhinoceros	90	1·00
	a. Booklet pane. Nos. 1040/4, each ×2, with outer edges of pane imperf	8·00	
1041	(1r.20) Buffalo	90	1·00
1042	(1r.20) Lion	90	1·00

1043 (1r.20) Leopard .... 90 1·00
1044 (1r.20) African Elephant .... 90 1·00
1040/4 *Set of 5* .... 4·00 4·50

(ii) P 14. With "L" shaped phosphor band (10.98)

1045 (1r.20) White Rhinoceros 75 90
a. Booklet pane. Nos. 1045/9, each ×2, with horiz edges of pane imperf .... 6·50
1046 (1r.20) Buffalo 75 90
1047 (1r.20) Lion 75 90
1048 (1r.20) Leopard 75 90
1049 (1r.20) African Elephant 75 90
1045/9 *Set of 5* .... 3·25 4·00

Nos. 1029, 1030p/4p and 1040/9 were only issued in booklets.

On pane No. 1040a the elliptical holes only occur on the horizontal line of perforations separating the two strips. Nos. 1035/9 were printed together, *se-tenant* both horizontally and vertically, as strips of 5 in sheets of 100.

The Questa printings (Nos. 1030p/4p and 1045/9) are redrawn with the inscriptions smaller.

Nos. 1030p/4p can be easily identified by the 3 mm (instead of 1½ mm) gap between "South Africa" and "standard postage".

On Nos. 1045/9 the gap between "South Africa" and "Airmail Postcard" is 5 mm instead of 4 mm (Nos. 1040/4). Both Questa printings show the phosphor as an "L" shaped band.

For self-adhesive versions of Nos. 1030/4 see Nos. 1075/9.

The Standard Postage and Airmail Postcard rates increased to 1r.10 and 1r.30 on 14 April 1998, to 1r.20 and 1r.70 on 1 April 1999, and to 1r.30 and 1r.90 on 1 April 2000.

368 Tiger (woodcut)

369 *Rescue 8* (lifeboat)

(Des Thea Swanepoel. Litho Questa)

1998 (28 Jan). Chinese New Year ("Year of the Tiger"). Sheet 67×85 mm. P 14×14½.
MS1051 **368** 5r. vermilion, black and deep green .... 1·50 1·50

(Des D. Bagnall. Litho)

1998 (11 Feb). 30th Anniv of National Sea Rescue Institute (1997). P 14 (with two elliptical holes on each horizontal side).
1052 **369** (1r.) multicoloured 65 30

370 Leopard

(Des J. Swanepoel. Litho)

1998 (1 May). "SAPDA '98" National Stamp Exhibition, Johannesburg. Sheet 64×84 mm. P 14×14½.
MS1053 **370** 5r. multicoloured .... 1·50 1·50

371 Football Player

(Des M. de Jong. Litho)

1998 (8 June). World Cup Football Championship, France. P 14.
1054 **371** (1r.10) multicoloured 60 30

No. 1054 is inscribed "STANDARD POSTAGE".

372 Stone Age Hand Axe

373 Pale Chanting Goshawk

(Des Sue Wickison. Litho Questa)

1998 (28 June). Early South African History. T **372** and similar vert designs. Multicoloured. Ordinary paper. Two phosphor bands. P 14×15.
1055 (1r.10) Type **372** 50 40
a. Sheetlet. Nos. 1055/64 .... 4·50 3·50
b. Booklet pane. Nos. 1055/64 .... 4·50
1056 (1r.10) Musuku (altar) 50 40
1057 (1r.10) San rock engravings 50 40
1058 (1r.10) Early Iron Age pot 50 40
1059 (1r.10) Khoekhoe pot 50 40
1060 (1r.10) Florisbad skull 50 40
1061 (1r.10) San rock painting 50 40
1062 (1r.10) Mapungubwe gold rhinoceros and pot 50 40
1063 (1r.10) Lydenburg Head (ceremonial mask) 50 40
1064 (1r.10) Taung skull 50 40
1055/64 *Set of 10* .... 4·50 3·50

Nos. 1055/64, which are inscribed "standard postage", were printed together, *se-tenant*, in sheetlets of 10 with illustrated left-hand margin and the top, bottom and right-hand margins perforated through.

No. 1055b has these three margins imperforate.

(Des C. van Rooyen. Litho Questa)

1998 (16 Aug). South African Raptors. T **373** and similar vert designs. Multicoloured. Ordinary paper. Two phosphor bands. P 14×15.
1065 (1r.10) Type **373** 60 50
a. Sheetlet. Nos. 1065/74 .... 5·50 4·50
b. Booklet pane. Nos. 1065/74 .... 5·00
1066 (1r.10) Augur Buzzard ("Jackal Buzzard") 60 50
1067 (1r.10) Lanner Falcon 60 50
1068 (1r.10) Lammergeier ("Bearded Vulture") 60 50
1069 (1r.10) Black Harrier 60 50
1070 (1r.10) Cape Vulture 60 50
1071 (1r.10) Bateleur 60 50
1072 (1r.10) Spotted Eagle Owl 60 50
1073 (1r.10) White-headed Vulture 60 50
1074 (1r.10) African Fish Eagle 60 50
1065/74 *Set of 10* .... 5·50 4·50

Nos. 1065/74, which are inscribed "standard postage" were printed together, *se-tenant*, in sheetlets of 10 with an illustrated left-hand margin and the top, bottom and right-hand margins perforated through.

No. 1065b has these three margins imperforate.

(Litho Pemara (Nos. 1075/9) or SNP Cambec (Nos. 1075a/9a, 1075b/9b))

1998 (18 Aug)–**99**. Endangered Fauna. Antelopes. Designs as Nos. 1030/4 but self-adhesive. Phosphor frame. P 13×12½.
1075 (1r.10) Eland (vert) 50 50
a. Phosphor frame at left and foot 50 60
ab. Booklet pane. Nos. 1075a/9a, each ×2 .. 4·00
b. Perf 11 (phosphor frame at left and foot) (12.99) 50 60
ba. Booklet pane. Nos. 1075b/9b, each ×2 . 4·00
1076 (1r.10) Greater Kudu (vert) 50 50
a. Phosphor frame at left and foot 50 60
b. Perf 11 (phosphor frame at left and foot) (12.99) 50 60
1077 (1r.10) Impala (vert) 50 50
a. Phosphor frame at left and foot 50 60
b. Perf 11 (phosphor frame at left and foot) (12.99) 50 60
1078 (1r.10) Waterbuck (vert) 50 50
a. Phosphor frame at left and foot 50 60
b. Perf 11 (phosphor frame at left and foot) (12.99) 50 60
1079 (1r.10) Blue Wildebeest (vert) 50 50
a. Phosphor frame at left and foot 50 60
b. Perf 11 (phosphor frame at left and foot) (12.99) 50 60
1075/9 *Set of 5* .... 2·25 2·25
1075a/9a *Set of 5* .... 2·25 2·75
1075b/9b *Set of 5* .... 2·25 2·75

The above are inscribed "standard postage" and were printed in rolls of 100 (Nos. 1075/9) with the surplus self-adhesive paper around each stamp removed or in booklets of 10 (Nos. 1075a/9a and 1075b/9b) with the surplus paper retained. The phosphor shows yellow under U.V. light. It forms a regular frame on Nos. 1075/9, but on Nos. 1075a/9a and 1075b/9b it is present at the left, following the outline of the antelope, and bottom only.

374 Shepherd's Tree

(Des Joan van Gogh. Litho Questa)

1998 (4 Sept). Trees. T **374** and similar horiz designs. Multicoloured. Ordinary paper. One side phosphor band. P 13½×14.

1080	(1r.10) Type **374**	70	70
	a. Block of 4. Nos. 1080/3	2·50	2·50
1081	(1r.10) Karee	70	70
1082	(1r.10) Baobab	70	70
1083	(1r.10) Umbrella Thorn	70	70
1080/3	*Set of 4*	2·50	2·50

Nos. 1080/3 are inscribed "Standard Postage" and were printed together, *se-tenant*, in sheets of 10, proving two blocks of 4 and a horizontal pair of Nos. 1080/1.

375 Sandstone Cliffs, Cape Point

(Des A. Ainslie. Litho Questa)

1998 (28 Sept). "Explore South Africa" (1st series). T **375** and similar horiz designs. Multicoloured. Ordinary paper. Two horiz phosphor bands. P 15×14.

(a) Western Cape

1084	(1r.30) Type **375**	90	70
	a. Booklet pane. Nos. 1084/8×2	8·00	70
1085	(1r.30) Robben Island	90	70
1086	(1r.30) Ostrich farming, Pinehurst Homestead	90	70
1087	(1r.30) Victoria and Alfred Waterfront, Capetown	90	70
1088	(1r.30) Homestead, Boschendal Wine Estate	90	70

Nos. 1084/8 and 1089/93, which are inscribed "AIRMAIL POSTCARD", were only available from separate 13r. stamp booklets, with the panes showing an illustrated margin at top, a small blank margin at foot and the vertical sides imperforate.

See also Nos. 1138/42.

(b) KwaZulu-Natal

1089	(1r.30) Drakensberg waterfall	90	70
	a. Booklet pane. Nos. 1089/93 ×2	8·00	
1090	(1r.30) Zulu women preparing food	90	70
1091	(1r.30) Pelicans and rhinoceros	90	70
1092	(1r.30) Rickshaw driver	90	70
1093	(1r.30) Indian dancers	90	70
1084/93	*Set of 10*	8·00	6·25

376 Angel

(Des Annamart Dednam. Litho Questa)

1998 (9 Oct). Christmas. T **376** and similar vert designs. Multicoloured. Ordinary paper. One side phosphor band. P 14×15.

1094	(1r.10) Type **376**	75	75
	a. Horiz strip of 5. Nos. 1094/8	3·25	3·25
1095	(1r.10) Christmas bell	75	75
1096	(1r.10) Present	75	75
1097	(1r.10) Christmas tree	75	75
1098	(1r.10) Star	75	75
1094/8	*Set of 5*	3·25	3·25

Nos. 1094/8 are inscribed "STANDARD POSTAGE" and were printed together, *se-tenant*, as horizontal strips of 5, in sheets of 10.

377 African Harrier Hawk

378 London Pictorial Essay, 1927

(Des C. van Rooyen. Litho Questa)

1998 (9 Oct). World Post Day. Sheet 67×85 mm. Ordinary paper. P 14×14½.

MS1099	**377** 5r. multicoloured	1·50	1·50

(Des Thea Swanepoel. Litho Questa)

1998 (20 Oct). "ILSAPEX '98" International Stamp Exhibition, Johannesburg. Sheet, 108×80 mm, containing T **378** and similar vert design. Ordinary paper. P 14½.

MS1100	5r. deep green, scarlet and cream (Type 378); 5r. black, deep green and cream (as Type **378**, but "SOUTH AFRICA" at top)	2·25	2·50

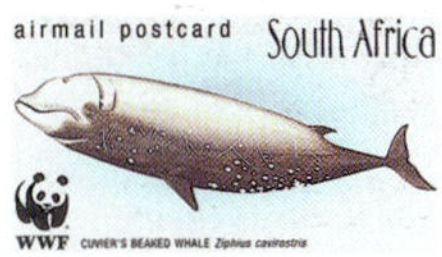

379 Cuvier's Beaked Whale

380 Emblem and Buildings

(Des C. Grant (Nos. 1101/4), M. Butterfield (No. **MS**1105). Litho Questa)

1998 (23 Oct). Endangered Species. Whales of the Southern Ocean. T **379** and similar horiz designs. Multicoloured. Ordinary paper. One side phosphor band. P 15×14.

1101	(1r.30) Type **379**	1·10	75
	a. Block of 4. Nos. 1101/4	4·00	2·75
1102	(1r.30) Minke Whale	1·10	75
1103	(1r.30) Bryde's Whale	1·10	75
1104	(1r.30) Pygmy Right Whale	1·10	75
1101/4	*Set of 4*	4·00	2·75
MS1105	103×68 mm. 5r. Blue Whale. No phosphor band. P 14	1·75	1·75

Nos. 1101/4 are inscribed "airmail postcard" and were printed together, *se-tenant*, in sheets of 10 providing two blocks of 4 and a horizontal pair of Nos. 1101/2.

Nos. 1101/4 were also issued on 18 August 1999 in a premium booklet, No. SP1, sold at 40r.

No. **MS**1105 forms part of joint issue with Namibia and Norfolk Island.

A corporate miniature sheet, sponsored by Clover SA for their centenary, showing an ice-cream van was issued on 15 November 1998.

(Des F. Frescura. Litho Questa)

1998 (9 Dec). 50th Anniv of Universal Declaration of Human Rights. Ordinary paper. One side phosphor band. P 14½.

1106	**380** (1r.10) multicoloured	1·00	35

No. 1106 is inscribed "Standard Postage".

381 Dennis Mail Van, 1913

(Des D. Bagnall. Litho Questa)

1999 (15 Feb). 125th Anniv of Universal Postal Union. T **381** and similar horiz designs. Multicoloured. Ordinary paper. U P U emblem and one side band in phosphor. P 13½×14.

1107	(1r.10) Type **381**	70	60
	a. Block of 4. Nos. 1107/10	2·50	2·25
1108	(1r.10) Ford V8 post van, 1935	70	60

1109	(1r.10) Mobile Post Office, 1937	70	60
1110	(1r.10) Trojan Post Office van, 1927	70	60
1107/10	*Set of 4*	2·50	2·25

Nos. 1107/10 are inscribed "Standard Postage", and were printed *se-tenant* in sheets of 10, providing two blocks of 4 and a horizontal pair of Nos. 1107/8.

382 Rabbit

(Des D. Murphy. Litho Questa)

1999 (16 Feb). Chinese New Year ("Year of the Rabbit"). Sheet 85×67 mm. Ordinary paper. P 14×13½.

MS1111 **382**	5r. multicoloured	1·50	1·50

383 *Discovery* (Scott)

(Des D. Bagnall. Litho Questa)

1999 (19 Mar). Famous Ships. T **383** and similar horiz designs. Multicoloured. Ordinary paper. One side phosphor band. P 13½×14.

1112	(1r.10) Type **383**	1·10	1·00
	a. Block of 4. Nos. 1112/15	4·00	3·50
1113	(1r.10) *Heemskerk* (Tasman)	1·10	1·00
1114	(1r.10) H.M.S. *Endeavour* (Cook)	1·10	1·00
1115	(1r.10) H.M.S. *Beagle* (Darwin)	1·10	1·00
1112/15	*Set of 4*	4·00	3·50

Nos. 1112/15 are inscribed "standard postage", and were printed *se-tenant* in sheets of 10, providing two blocks of 4 and a horizontal pair of Nos. 1112/13.

384 *Lawhill* (barque)

385 Traditional Nguni Love Token with AIDS Ribbon

(Des D. Bagnall. Litho Questa)

1999 (19 Mar). "Australia '99" International Stamp Exhibition, Melbourne. Sheet 65×85 mm. Ordinary paper. P 13½×14.

MS1116 **384**	5r. multicoloured	1·75	1·75

(Des Thea Swanepoel. Litho Questa)

1999 (1 Apr). AIDS Awareness Campaign. One side phosphor band. P 14½×14.

1117 **385**	(1r.20) multicoloured (bluish violet background)	65	65
	a. Booklet pane. Nos. 1117/18, each ×5	6·00	
1118	(1r.20) multicoloured (emerald background)	65	65

Nos. 1117/18 are inscribed "Standard Postage" and were printed *se-tenant* in 12r. stamp booklets containing No. 1117a which has the horizontal edges of the pane imperforate.

386 African Elephant

387 Class 19D Steam Locomotive, South African Railways

(Des C. van Rooyen. Litho)

1999 (27 Apr). "iBRA '99" International Stamp Exhibition, Nuremburg. Sheet 100×68 mm. Ordinary paper. P 14.

MS1119 **386**	5r. multicoloured	2·25	1·50

(Des H. Botha. Litho Questa)

1999 (30 Apr). "SAPDA '99" Stamp Show, Johannesburg. Sheet 100×75 mm. Ordinary paper. P 13½×14.

MS1120 **387**	5r. multicoloured	2·25	1·50

388 Nurse

389 President Thabo Mbeki

(Des Chenette Swart. Litho Questa)

1999 (1 May). Workers' Day. T **388** and similar vert designs. One side phosphor band. Multicoloured. P 14×15.

1121	(1r.20) Type **388**	60	60
	a. Sheetlet. Nos. 1121/30	5·50	5·50
1122	(1r.20) Cleaner with mop	60	60
1123	(1r.20) Forester with axe	60	60
1124	(1r.20) Farmer with spade	60	60
1125	(1r.20) Chef with sieve	60	60
1126	(1r.20) Fisherman with net	60	60
1127	(1r.20) Construction worker with scaffolding	60	60
1128	(1r.20) Miner with pick	60	60
1129	(1r.20) Postman with mail	60	60
1130	(1r.20) Road worker with pneumatic drill	60	60
1121/30	*Set of 10*	5·50	5·50

Nos. 1121/30 are inscribed "standard postage", and were printed together, *se-tenant*, in sheetlets of 10.

(Des Thea Swanepoel. Litho)

1999 (16 June). Inauguration of President Thabo Mbeki. P 14.

1131 **389**	(1r.20) multicoloured	1·00	45

No. 1131 is inscribed "standard postage".

390 Nelson Mandela in Mantle of Order

391 Actress with Drama Masks

(Des Sue Dickinson. Litho Questa)

1999 (23 June). 900th Anniv of Order of St. John of Jerusalem. Sheet 108×68 mm. Ordinary paper. P 14×14½.

MS1132	**390**	2r. multicoloured	1·25	1·25

(Des Thea Swanepoel. Litho)

1999 (29 June). 25th Anniv of Standard Bank National Arts Festival, Grahamstown. T **391** and similar vert designs. Multicoloured. P 14.

1133	(1r.20) Type **391**	70	70
	a. Horiz strip of 5. Nos. 1133/7	3·25	3·25
1134	(1r.20) Woman with roll of film	70	70
1135	(1r.20) Woman playing guitar	70	70
1136	(1r.20) Woman dancing	70	70
1137	(1r.20) Painter	70	70
1133/7	*Set of 5*	3·25	3·25

Nos. 1133/7 are inscribed "STANDARD POSTAGE" and were printed together, *se-tenant*, as horizontal strips of 5 in sheets of 10.

(Des A. Ainslie. Litho Questa)

1999 (6 Aug). "Explore South Africa" (2nd series). Mpumalanga and Northern Province. Horiz designs as T **375**. Multicoloured. One side phosphor band. P 15×14.

1138	(1r.70) Blyde River Canyon	1·10	1·10
	a. Booklet pane. Nos. 1138/42, each ×2	9·00	
1139	(1r.70) Lone Creek Falls, Sabie	1·10	1·10
1140	(1r.70) Ndebele women in traditional dress	1·10	1·10
1141	(1r.70) Pilgrim's Rest (historic town)	1·10	1·10
1142	(1r.70) Elephants, Kruger National Park	1·10	1·10
1138/42	*Set of 5*	5·00	5·00

Nos. 1138/42 are inscribed "AIRMAIL POSTCARD" and were only available from 17r. stamp booklets with the pane showing an illustrated margin at top, a small blank margin at foot and the vertical sides imperforate.

392 North Ndebele Wall Pattern

393 South African Rock Art Painting

(Des A. Ainslie. Litho Enschedé)

1999 (8 Aug). Traditional Wall Art. T **392** and similar square designs showing sections of wall art. Multicoloured. One side phosphor band. P 13½×14.

1143	(1r.20) Type **392**	60	60
	a. Sheetlet. Nos. 1143/52	5·50	5·50
1144	(1r.20) South Ndebele	60	60
1145	(1r.20) Swazi	60	60
1146	(1r.20) Venda	60	60
1147	(1r.20) South Sotho	60	60
1148	(1r.20) Xhosa	60	60
1149	(1r.20) North Sotho	60	60
1150	(1r.20) Tsonga	60	60
1151	(1r.20) Zulu	60	60
1152	(1r.20) Tswana	60	60
1143/52	*Set of 10*	5·50	5·50

Nos. 1143/52 are inscribed "STANDARD POSTAGE" and were printed together, *se-tenant*, in sheetlets of 10.

(Des A. Ainslie. Litho Enschedé)

1999 (21 Aug). China '99 International Stamp Exhibition, Beijing. Sheet 154×85 mm. P 14×13½.

MS1153	**393**	5r. multicoloured	1·75	1·75

394 *Strelitzia reginae* (flower)

395 Barn Swallow

(Des C. van Rooyen. Litho)

1999 (9 Sept). "JOPEX '99" National Stamp Exhibition, Johannesburg. Sheet 65×85 mm. Ordinary paper. P 14½.

MS1154	**394**	5r. multicoloured	1·75	1·75

(Des C. van Rooyen. Litho Enschedé)

1999 (4 Oct). Migratory Species of South Africa. T **395** and similar vert designs. Multicoloured. One side phosphor band. P 14×15.

1155	(1r.20) Type **395**	75	65
	a. Sheetlet. Nos. 1155/64	6·75	6·00
1156	(1r.20) Great White Shark	75	65
1157	(1r.20) Lesser Kestrel	75	65
1158	(1r.20) Common Dolphin	75	65
1159	(1r.20) European Bee-eater	75	65
1160	(1r.20) Loggerhead Turtle	75	65
1161	(1r.20) Curlew Sandpiper	75	65
1162	(1r.20) Wandering Albatross	75	65
1163	(1r.20) Springbok	75	65
1164	(1r.20) Lesser Flamingo	75	65
1155/64	*Set of 10*	6·75	6·00

Nos. 1155/64 are inscribed "Standard Postage" and were printed together, *se-tenant*, in sheetlets of 10 with an enlarged illustrated left margin.

Nos. 1155/64 were also issued in a premium booklet, No. SP2, sold at 29r.

396 Boers leaving for Commando

(Des H. Botha. Litho Questa)

1999 (11 Oct). Centenary of Anglo-Boer War (1st issue). T **396** and similar horiz design. Multicoloured. One phosphor band. P 13½×14.

1165	(1r.20) Type **396**	90	90
	a. Horiz pair. Nos. 1165/6	1·75	1·75
1166	(1r.20) British soldiers	90	90

Nos. 1165/6 were printed together, *se-tenant*, as horizontal pairs in sheets of 10.

Nos. 1165/6, 1203/4, 1343/4 and **MS**1384 were also issued on 1 May 2002 in a premium booklet, No SP4, sold at 45r. See also Nos. 1203/4, 1343/4 and **MS**1384.

397 Landscape

(Des Thea Swanepoel. Litho Enschedé)

2000 (1 Jan). New Millennium. P 13½×14.

1167	**397**	(1r.20) multicoloured	70	40

No. 1167 is inscribed "Standard Postage".

398 National Lottery Logo

(Des Thea Swanepoel. Litho Enschedé)

2000 (2 Mar). First National Lottery. P 13½×14.

1168	**398**	(1r.20) multicoloured	65	30

No. 1168 is inscribed "STANDARD POSTAGE".

399 Family inside Heart

(Des Chenette Swart. Litho Enschedé)

2000 (5 Apr). National Family Day. P 13.

1169	**399** (1r.30) multicoloured	65	30

No. 1169 is inscribed "Standard Postage".

400 Knysna Turaco ("Lourie")

(Des C. van Rooyen. Litho Enschedé)

2000 (22 May). "The Stamp Show 2000" International Stamp Exhibition, London. Sheet 108×68 mm. P 13½.

MS1170	**400** 4r.60 multicoloured	2·50	2·00

401 Banded Stream Frog

(Des C. van Rooyen. Litho Enschedé)

2000 (23 June). Frogs of South Africa. T **401** and similar horiz designs. Multicoloured. P 13½×14.

1171	1r.30 Type **401**	80	80
	a. Sheetlet. Nos. 1171/80	7·00	7·00
1172	1r.30 Yellow-striped Reed Frog	80	80
1173	1r.30 Natal Leaf-folding Frog	80	80
1174	1r.30 Paradise Toad	80	80
1175	1r.30 Table Mountain Ghost Frog	80	80
1176	1r.30 Banded Rubber Frog	80	80
1177	1r.30 Dwarf Grass Frog	80	80
1178	1r.30 Long-toed Tree Frog	80	80
1179	1r.30 Namaqua Rain Frog	80	80
1180	1r.30 Bubbling Kassina	80	80
1171/80	*Set of* 10	7·00	7·00

Nos. 1171/80 were printed together, *se-tenant*, in sheetlets of 10.

402 Forest Tree Frog

403 Stalked Bulbine

(Des C. van Rooyen. Litho Enschedé)

2000 (23 June). "JUNASS 2000" National Junior Stamp Show, Boksburg. Sheet 108×68 mm. P 13½.

MS1181	**402** 4r.60 multicoloured	2·25	2·25

(Des Joan van Gogh. Litho Enschedé)

2000 (1 Aug). Medicinal Plants. T **403** and similar vert designs. Multicoloured. P 14×13½.

1182	1r.30 Type **403**	70	70
	a. Horiz strip of 5. Nos. 1182/6	3·25	3·25
1183	1r.30 Wild Dagga	70	70
1184	1r.30 Wild Garlic	70	70
1185	1r.30 Pig?s Ear	70	70
1186	1r.30 Wild Ginger	70	70
1187	2r.30 Red Paintbrush	80	80
	a. Horiz strip of 5. Nos. 1187/91	3·50	3·50
1188	2r.30 Cancer Bush	80	80
1189	2r.30 Yellow Star	80	80
1190	2r.30 Bitter Aloe	80	80
1191	2r.30 Sour Fig	80	80
1182/91	*Set of* 10	6·75	6·75

Nos. 1182/6 and 1187/91 were each printed together, *se-tenant*, as horizontal strips of 5 in sheets of 10.

404 Athlete with South African Flag

405 Globe and Peace Doves

(Des Chenette Swart. Litho Enschedé)

2000 (1 Sept). Olympic Games, Sydney. T **404** and similar vert designs. Multicoloured. P 13½×14.

1192	1r.30 Type **404**	60	25
1193	1r.50 Elana Meyer (medal winner, 1992)	60	35
1194	2r.20 Joshua Thugwane (medal winner, 1996)	80	75
1195	2r.30 Olympic Rings and South African flag	95	80
1196	6r.30 Penny Heyns (medal winner, 1996)	1·75	2·75
1192/6	*Set of* 5	4·25	4·50

(Des Alet Swarts. Litho Enschedé)

2000 (19 Sept). United Nations International Year of Peace. P 13.

1197	**405** 1r.30 multicoloured	65	30

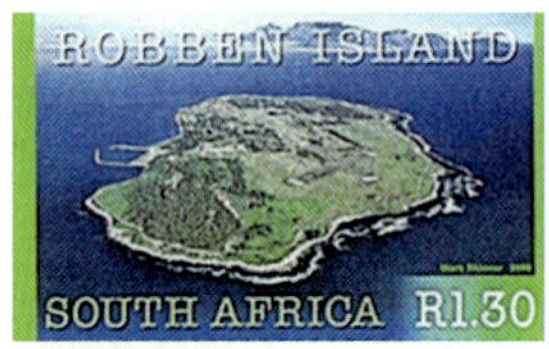

406 Robben Island

(Des Thea Swanepoel. Litho Enschedé)

2000 (22 Sept). UNESCO World Heritage Sites. T **406** and similar horiz designs. Multicoloured. P 13½×14.

1198	1r.30 Type **406**	75	55
1199	1r.30 Greater St. Lucia Wetland Park	75	55
1200	1r.30 Early skull from Sterkfontein	75	55
1198/1200	*Set of* 3	2·00	1·50

407 Dragon

408 Heart and Envelope

(Des M. Maas. Litho Enschedé)

2000 (9 Oct). Chinese New Year ("Year of the Dragon"). Sheet 85×65 mm. P 13.

MS1201	4r.60 multicoloured	1·50	1·50

(Des M. Maas. Litho Enschedé)

2000 (9 Oct)-**01**. World Post Day. P 13.

1202	**408** 1r.30 multicoloured	70	40
	a. Perf 13½×13 (22.1.01)	70	40

No. 1202 was originally printed in sheets of 10 (2×5). On 8 November 2000 it was re-issued as a sheet of 20 (4×5) with each stamp accompanied by a *se-tenant* half-size label depicting one of the cast from the Gladiators television series. Stamps from this sheet are perforated 13½×13 (No. 1202a). The sheets of 20 were originally sold at 35r. and stamps from them were not available at face value until 22 January 2001.

409 Sol Plaatje and Johanna Brandt

(Des H. Botha. Litho Enschedé) Centenary of Anglo-Boer War (2nd issue)

2000 (25 Oct). Authors. T **409** and similar horiz design. Multicoloured. P 13×14.

1203	1r.30 Type **409**	25	25
1204	4r.40 Arthur Conan Doyle and Winston Churchill	3·25	2·00

410 Palette Surgeonfish

411 The Rain Bull

(Des Joan van Gogh (1r.30), C. van Rooyen (others))

2000 (1 Nov). Flora and Fauna. T **410** and similar multicoloured designs.

(a) Litho Southern Colour Print or Questa (10, 20, 50, 70c., 5, 10, 20r. Questa (others). Phosphorised paper P 14½

1205	5c. Type **410**	10	50
1206	10c. Clown Surgeonfish ("Bluebanded Surgeon")	10	50
1207	20c. Regal Angelfish	10	50
1208	30c. Emperor Angelfish	10	50
1209	40c. Picasso Triggerfish ("Blackbar triggerfish")	15	50
1210	50c. Coral Hind ("Coral rockcod")	15	50
1211	60c. Powder-blue Surgeonfish	20	60
1212	70c. Thread-finned Butterflyfish	20	60
1213	80c. Long-horned Cowfish	20	60
1214	90c. Forceps Butterflyfish ("Longnose butterflyfish")	25	60
1215	1r. Two-spined Angelfish ("Coral Beauty")	30	60
1216	1r.30 Botterblom (vert)	45	60
	a. Horiz strip of 5. Nos. 1216/20	2·00	2·75
1217	1r.30 Blue Marguerite (vert)	45	60
1218	1r.30 Karoo Violet (vert)	45	60
1219	1r.30 Tree Pelargonium (vert)	45	60
1220	1r.30 Black-eyed Susy (vert)	45	60
1221	1r.40 Gold-banded Forester	75	40
1222	1r.50 Brenton Blue	85	50
1223	1r.90 Silver-barred Charaxes	1·25	1·00
1224	2r. Lilac-breasted Roller (vert)	1·50	1·00
1225	2r.30 Citrus Butterfly	1·75	1·25
1226	3r. Woodland Kingfisher (vert)	2·00	1·50
1227	5r. White-fronted Bee Eater (vert)	2·50	1·50
1228	6r.30 Narrow Blue-banded Swallowtail ("Green-banded swallowtail")	3·00	2·50
1229	10r. African Green Pigeon (vert)	4·50	4·00
1230	12r.60 False-dotted Border	5·00	5·00
1231	20r. Violet-crested Turaco ("Purple crested lourie") (vert)	7·50	7·50
1205/31	*Set of 27*	30·00	30·00

(b) Photo Enschedé. Designs as Nos. 1216/20, but smaller (20×25 mm). Self-adhesive. Phosphor frame. P 13×12½

1232	1r.30 As No. 1216 (inscr "Afrika Borwa")	70	90
	a. Booklet pane. Nos. 1232/41	6·25	8·25
	b. Perf 13½	70	80
	ba. Strip of 10. Nos. 1232b/41b	6·25	7·25
1233	1r.30 As No. 1216 (inscr "Afrika Dzonga")	70	90
	b. Perf 13½	70	80
1234	1r.30 As No. 1217 (inscr "Ningizimu Afrika")	70	90
	b. Perf 13½	70	80
1235	1r.30 As No. 1217 (inscr "Afrika Sewula")	70	90
	b. Perf 13½	70	80
1236	1r.30 As No. 1218 (inscr "Suid Afrika")	70	90
	b. Perf 13½	70	80
1237	1r.30 As No. 1218 (inscr "Afrika Borwa")	70	90
	b. Perf 13½	70	80
1238	1r.30 As No. 1219 (inscr "Afrika Tshipembe")	70	90
	b. Perf 13½	70	80
1239	1r.30 As No. 1219 (inscr "Ningizimu Afrika")	70	90
	b. Perf 13½	70	80
1240	1r.30 As No. 1220 (inscr "Afrika Borwa")	70	90
	b. Perf 13½	70	80
1241	1r.30 As No. 1220 (inscr "Mzantsi Afrika")	70	90
	b. Perf 13½	70	80
1232/41	*Set of 10*	6·25	8·25
1232b/41b	*Set of 10*	6·25	7·25

Designs from 5c. to 1r. show fish, 1r.30 flowers, 1r.40 to 1r.90, 2r.30, 6r.30 and 12r.60 butterflies and the 2, 3, 5, 10 and 20r. birds. For stamps perforated 13½×13 or 13×13½ see Nos. 1268/94.

. Nos. 1216/20 were printed together *se-tenant*, as horizontal strips of 5 throughout the sheets.

Nos. 1232/41 were only available in stamp booklets, No. SB60, in which the pane had imperforate edges so that Nos. 1232/3 are imperforate on two sides and the remainder on one side.

Nos. 1232b/41b come from coils containing all 10 designs in sequence with surplus self-adhesive paper around each stamp removed.

For similar designs inscribed "Standard Postage" see Nos. 1295/1314. See also Nos 1268/1314 and 1389/93.

(Des Siobhian Cuff (1r.50), Sophia Mazibuko (others). Litho Questa)

2001 (24 Jan). South African Myths and Legends. T **411** and similar vert designs. Multicoloured. P 13½.

1242	1r.30 Type **411**	50	25
1243	1r.50 The Grosvenor Treasure	55	30
1244	2r.20 Seven Magic Birds	70	45
1245	2r.30 The Hole in the Wall	75	55
1246	6r.30 Van Hunks and the Devil	1·60	2·25
1242/46	*Set of 5*	3·50	3·50

412 African Tree Snake

(Des M. Maas. Litho Questa)

2001 (1 Feb). Chinese New Year ("Year of the Snake") and "Hong Kong (2001)" Stamp Exhibition. Sheet 65×85 mm. P 14½×14.

MS1247	4r.60 multicoloured	1·75	1·75

413 Ernie Els (golf)

414 Elephant

(Des Liza van der Wal. Litho Questa)

2001 (28 Feb). South African Sporting Heroes. T **413** and similar horiz designs. Multicoloured. P 13½×14.

1248	1r.40 Type **413**	80	65
1249	1r.40 Lucas Radebe (soccer)	80	65
1250	1r.40 Francois Pienaar (rugby)	80	65
1251	1r.40 Terrence Parkin (swimming)	80	65
1252	1r.40 Rosina Magola (netball)	80	65
1253	1r.40 Hestrie Cloete (high-jumping)	80	65
1254	1r.40 Hezekiel Sepeng (athletics)	80	65
1255	1r.40 Jonty Rhodes (cricket)	80	65
	a. Perf 14½×14	80	65
1256	1r.40 Zanele Situ (paralympic javelin)	80	65
1257	1r.40 Vuyani Bungu (boxing)	80	65
1248/57	*Set of 10*	7·25	6·00

Nos. 1248/57 were each printed in sheets of 10 (2×5).

No. 1255a was printed in sheets of 15 (3×5) with each stamp accompanied by a *se-tenant* label showing a member of the South African cricket team.

(Des A. Ainslie. Litho Questa)

2001 (25 Apr)-**2005.** Wildlife. T **414** and similar horiz designs. Multicoloured. Phosphor frame. *(a) Designs 34×26 mm. P 14½.*

1258	(2r.10) Type **414**	1·10	1·10
	a. Pane. Nos. 1258/62, each ×2	9·00	9·00
1259	(2r.10) Lion	1·10	1·10
1260	(2r.10) Rhinoceros	1·10	1·10
1261	(2r.10) Leopard	1·10	1·10
1262	(2r.10) Buffalo	1·10	1·10
1258/62	*Set of 5*	5·00	5·00

(b) Designs 29×24 mm. Self-adhesive. P 11½×12

1263	(2r.10) Buffalo	75	1·00
	a. Booklet pane. Nos. 1263/7, each ×2	6·50	
	b. Perf 12½×12 (10.10.05)	75	1·00
	ba. Booklet pane. Nos. 1263/7, each ×2	6·50	
1264	(2r.10) Leopard	75	1·00
	b. Perf 12½×12 (10.10.05)	75	1·00

1265	(2r.10) Rhinoceros	75	1·00
	b. Perf 12½×12 (10.10.05)	75	1·00
1266	(2r.10) Lion	75	1·00
	b. Perf 12½×12 (10.10.05)	75	1·00
1267	(2r.10) Type **414**	75	1·00
	b. Perf 12½×12 (10.10.05)	75	1·00
1263/7 *Set of 5*		3·25	4·50

Nos. 1258/62 were printed together, *se-tenant*, in panes of 10 (5×2), either available separately or as part of a premium stamp booklet, No. SP3, sold at 49r.20.

All examples of No. 1262 are imperforate at right.

Nos. 1263/7 and 1263b/7b were only available *se-tenant*, in stamp booklets, Nos. SB62/a, which have the outer edges of the pane imperforate.

Nos. 1263/66 are imperforate at left or right and No. 1267 imperforate at foot and either at left or right.

Nos. 1258/67 are inscribed "AIRMAIL POSTCARD RATE" and were initially valid for 2r.10.

(Des Joan van Gogh (Nos. 1279/83, 1284a/e and 1295/1314), C. van Rooyen (others))

2001 (25 Apr)–**10**. Flora and Fauna (2nd series). Multicoloured designs as T **410**.

(a) Phosphorised paper. Litho Enschedé (Nos. 1270a, 1275a, 1284ac, 1294a), Southern Colour print (1284ae) or Cartor (others). P 13

1268	5c. Type **410** (2.10.02)	10	50
1269	10c. Clown surgeonfish ("Bluebanded Surgeon") (22.5.03)	15	50
1270	20c. Regal angelfish (23.9.03)	25	50
	a. Perf 14 (16.4.10)	50	50
1271	30c. Emperor angelfish (27.2.03)	30	50
1272	40c. Picasso triggerfish (23.9.03)	35	50
1273	50c. Coral Hind ("Coral rockcod") (7.6.02)	35	50
1274	60c. Powder-blue Surgeonfish (14.6.01)	40	40
1275	70c. Thread-finned butterflyfish (23.9.03)	40	40
	a. Perf 14 (16.4.10)	75	75
1276	80c. Long-horned cowfish (22.9.03)	40	40
1277	90c. Forceps butterflyfish ("Longnose butterflyfish") (27.2.03)	40	40
1278	1r. Two-spined angelfish ("Coral Beauty") (23.9.03)	45	40
1279	1r.40 Botterblom (vert)	50	55
	a. Horiz strip of 5. Nos. 1279/83	2·25	2·50
1280	1r.40 Blue Marguerite (vert)	50	55
1281	1r.40 Karoo Violet (vert)	50	55
1282	1r.40 Tree Pelargonium (vert)	50	55
1283	1r.40 Black-eyed Susy (vert)	50	55
1284	1r.60 Yellow Pansy Butterfly (16.6.01)	1·00	55
1284*a*	(1r.65) Botterblom (vert) (15.9.03)	2·75	3·00
	aa. Horiz strip of 5. Nos. 1284a/e	60	65
	ab. Perf 14 (1.2.10)	60	65
	ac. Horiz strip of 5. Nos. 1284ab/ea	2·75	3·00
	ad. Perf 14½ (24.2.10)	60	65
	ae. Horiz strip of 5. Nos. 1284ad/eb	2·75	3·00
1284*b*	(1r.65) Blue Marguerite (vert) (15.9.03)	60	65
	ba. Perf 14 (1.2.10)	60	65
	bb. Perf 14½ (24.2.10)	60	65
1284*c*	(1r.65) Karoo Violet (vert) (15.9.03)	60	65
	ca. Perf 14 (1.2.10)	60	65
	cb. Perf 14½ (24.2.10)	60	65
1284*d*	(1r.65) Tree Pelegonium (vert) (15.9.03)	60	65
	da. Perf 14 (1.2.10)	60	65
	db. Perf 14½ (24.2.10)	60	65
1284*e*	(1r.65) Black-eyed Susy (vert) (15.9.03)	60	65
	ea. Perf 14 (1.2.10)	60	65
	eb. Perf 14½ (24.2.10)	60	65
1285	1r.90 Large-spotted Acraea (16.6.01)	1·40	50
1286	2r. Lilac-breasted Roller (vert) (9.8.02)	1·50	50
1287	2r.10 Kopje Charaxes (16.6.01)	1·50	70
1288	2r.50 Common Grass-yellow (16.6.01)	1·60	70
1289	3r. Woodland Kingfisher (vert) (7.6.02)	2·00	75
1290	5r. White-fronted Bee-eater (vert) (7.6.02)	2·50	1·00
1291	7r. Southern Milkweed (16.6.01)	3·00	1·75
1292	10r. African Green Pigeon (vert) (1.10.01)	4·50	2·00
1293	14r. Lilac-tip (16.6.01)	6·00	4·50
1294	20r. Purple-crested Turaco ("Purplecrested lourie") (vert) (14.6.01)	7·50	6·00
	a. Perf 14 (16.4.10)	8·50	8·50
1268/94 *Set of 32*		40·00	27·00

(b) Photo Enschedé. Designs as Nos. 1279/83, but 20×25 mm and inscr "Standard Postage" instead of face value. Self-adhesive. Phosphor frame. P 13×12½

1295	(1r.40) As No. 1279 (inscr "Afrika Borwa")	45	55
	a. Booklet pane. Nos. 1295/1304	4·00	5·00
	b. Perf 13½	45	55
	ba. Strip of 10. Nos. 1295b/1304b	4·00	5·00
1296	(1r.40) As No. 1279 (inscr "Afrika Dzonga")	45	55
	b. Perf 13½	45	55
1297	(1r.40) As No. 1280 (inscr "Ningizimu Afrika")	45	55
	b. Perf 13½	45	55
1298	(1r.40) As No. 1280 (inscr "Afrika Sewula")	45	55
	b. Perf 13½	45	55
1299	(1r.40) As No. 1281 (inscr "Suid-Afrika")	45	55
	b. Perf 13½	45	55
1300	(1r.40) As No. 1281(inscr "Afrika Borwa")	45	55
	b. Perf 13½	45	55
1301	(1r.40) As No. 1282 (inscr "Afrika Tshipembe")	45	55
	b. Perf 13½	45	55
1302	(1r.40) As No. 1282 (inscr "Ningizimu Afrika")	45	55
	b. Perf 13½	45	55
1303	(1r.40) As No. 1283 (inscr "Afrika Borwa")	45	55
	b. Perf 13½	45	55
1304	(1r.40) As No. 1283 (inscr "Mzantsi Afrika")	45	55
	b. Perf 13½	45	55
1295/1304 *Set of 10*		4·00	5·00

(c) Litho Southern Colour Print, New Zealand. Designs as Nos. 1279/83, but 20×25 mm and inscr "Standard Postage" instead of face value. Self-adhesive. Phosphor frame. P 13½×13

1305	(1r.40) As No. 1279 (inscr "Afrika Borwa") (30.5.01)	45	55
	a. Strip of 10. Nos. 1305/14	4·00	5·00
	b. Perf 13×12½	45	55
	ba. Booklet pane. Nos. 1305b/14b	4·00	5·00
1306	(1r.40) As No. 1279 (inscr "Afrika Dzonga") (30.5.01)	45	55
	b. Perf 13×12½	45	55
1307	(1r.40) As No. 1280 (inscr "Ningizimu Afrika") (30.5.01)	45	55
	b. Perf 13×12½	45	55
1308	(1r.40) As No. 1280 (inscr "Afrika Sewula") (30.5.01)	45	55
	b. Perf 13×12½	45	55
1309	(1r.40) As No. 1281 (inscr "Suid-Afrika") (30.5.01)	45	55
	b. Perf 13×12½	45	55
1310	(1r.40) As No. 1281 (inscr "Afrika Borwa") (30.5.01)	45	55
	b. Perf 13×12½	45	55
1311	(1r.40) As No. 1282 (inscr "Afrika Tshipembe") (30.5.01)	45	55
	b. Perf 13×12½	45	55
1312	(1r.40) As No. 1282 (inscr "Ningizimu Afrika") (30.5.01)	45	55
	b. Perf 13×12½	45	55
1313	(1r.40) As No. 1283 (inscr "Afrika Borwa") (30.5.01)	45	55
	b. Perf 13×12½	45	55
1314	(1r.40) As No. 1283 (inscr "Mzantsi Afrika") (30.5.01)	45	55
	b. Perf 13×12½	45	55
1305/14 *Set of 10*		4·00	5·00

Nos. 1279/83 and 1284/a/e were each printed together, *se-tenant*, in horizontal strips of 5 throughout the sheets.

Nos. 1284a/e, are inscribed "Standard Postage" and were initially sold for 1r.65 each.

Nos. 1284, 1285, 1287/8, 1291 and 1293 show butterflies.

Nos. 1295/1304 were only available in stamp booklets, No. SB63, in which examples of No. 1295 are imperforate at top and left, No. 1296 at bottom and left and the remainder at top or bottom. The stamps are inscribed "Standard Postage" and were initially valid for 1r.40.

Nos. 1295b/1304b and 1305/14 come from coils containing all 10 designs in sequence with the surplus self-adhesive paper around each stamp removed.

Nos. 1305b/14b were only available in booklets, Nos. SB64/b with the surplus paper retained.

415 Gemsbok

416 Adult holding Child's Hand

(Des Karen Odiam. Litho Cartor)

2001 (12 May). Kgalagadi Transfrontier Wildlife Park. Joint Issue with Botswana. T **415** and similar multicoloured designs. Two phosphor bands. P 13.

1315	1r.40 Type **415**	45	25
1316	2r.50 Cheetah	75	55
1317	2r.90 Sociable Weaver (bird)	1·25	1·25
1318	3r.60 Meercat	1·25	1·50
1315/1318 *Set of 4*		3·25	3·25
MS1319	114×78 mm. Nos. 1316/17	1·75	1·75

(Des Mimi van Vuuren. Litho Questa)

2001 (16 May). "no excuse for child abuse" Campaign. P 13½.

1320	**416**	1r.40 multicoloured	50	55

No. 1320 was printed in sheets of ten with the stamps arranged as two diagonal crosses.

417 Victims of Soweto Uprising

418 Cape Horsehoe Bat

(Des L. Moagi after photograph by S. Nzima. Litho Questa)

2001 (16 June). 25th Anniv of Soweto Uprising. P 14×13½.

1321	**417**	1r.40 multicoloured	50	35

(Des Annemarie Wessels. Photo Questa)

2001 (22 June). Bats of South Africa. T **418** and similar multicoloured designs. L-shaped phosphor band. Self-adhesive. Die-cut. P 11½.

1322	1r.40 Type **418**	35	45
	a. Sheetlet. Nos. 1322/31	3·25	4·00
1323	1r.40 Welwitsch's Hairy Bat	35	45
1324	1r.40 Schreiber's Long-fingered Bat	35	45
1325	1r.40 Wahlberg's Epauletted Fruit Bat	35	45
1326	1r.40 Short-eared Trident Bat	35	45
1327	1r.40 Common Slit-faced Bat	35	45
1328	1r.40 Egyptian Fruit Bat	35	45
1329	1r.40 Egyptian Free-tailed Bat (vert)	35	45
1330	1r.40 De Winton's Long-eared Bat	35	45
1331	1r.40 Large-eared Free-tailed Bat	35	45
1322/21	*Set of* 10	3·25	4·00

Nos. 1322/31 were printed together, *se-tenant*, in sheetlets of 10 with the background forming a composite design. Descriptions of the various species are printed on the reverse of the backing paper. The phosphor band shows greenish yellow under U.V. light and the sheetlet inscription glows in the dark.

419 Conference logo

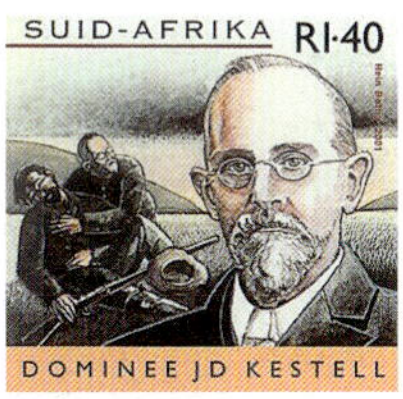

420 Dominee J. D. Kestell

(Des A. Nothling. Litho Enschedé)

2001 (7 Aug). Third U.N. World Conference Against Rascism, Durban. T **419** and similar vert designs. L-shaped phosphor band. P 14×13½.

1332	**419**	1r.40 mult (inscr as in T 419)	30	40
		a. Sheetlet. Nos. 1332/41	2·75	3·50
1333		1r.40 mult (inscr "ningizimu afrika" and "kubeketelelana" at foot)	30	40
1334		1r.40 mult (inscr "suid-afrika")	30	40
1335		1r.40 mult (inscr "afrika tshipembe")	30	40
1336		1r.40 mult (inscr "afrika borwa" and kutlwisiso" at foot)	30	40
1337		1r.40 mult (inscr "afrika dzonga")	30	40
1338		1r.40 mult (inscr "afrika sewula")	30	40
1339		1r.40 mult (inscr "?afrika borwa" and "kgothlelelo" at foot)	30	40
1340		1r.40 mult (inscr "ningizimu afrika" and "ukubekezelelana)	30	40
1341		1r.40 mult (inscr "mzantsi afrika")	30	40
1342		2r.40 mult (logo and South Africans)	50	60
1332/42		*Set of* 11	3·25	4·25

Nos. 1332/41 were printed together, *se-tenant*, in sheetlets of 10.
The phosphor appears as greenish yellow under U.V. light.

(Des H. Botha. Litho Enschedé)

2001 (21 Aug). Centenerary of Anglo-Boer War (3rd issue.) Angels of Mercy. T **420** and similar horiz designs. Multicoloured. Shaped phosphor band. P 13½.

1343	1r.40 Type **420**	75	25
1344	3r. Captain Thomas Crean V.C., R.A.M.C.	1·25	1·25

The phosphor appears as greenish yellow under U.V. light.

421 Boere Concertina

(Des Siobhan Cuff. Litho and die-samped Enschedé)

2001 (23 Aug). Musical Instruments. T **421** and similar horiz designs. Multicoloured. P 13½×14.

1345	1r.40 Type **421**	40	25
1346	1r.90 Trumpet	50	45
1347	2r.50 Electric guitar	60	55
1348	3r. African drum	70	75
1349	7r. Cello	1·60	2·25
1345/9	*Set of* 5	3·50	3·75

422 Field of Flowers, Namaqualand

(Des Thea Swanepoel. Litho Enschedé)

2001 (6 Sept). Natural Wonders of South Africa. T **422** and similar horiz designs. Multicoloured. L-shaped phosphor band. P 13½.

1350	(2r.10) Type **422**	70	70
1351	(2r.10) Cango Caves	70	70
1352	(2r.10) Richtersveld Desert	70	70
1353	(2r.10) Rocks on West Coast	70	70
1354	(2r.10) Snow covered mountains near Elliot	70	70
1355	(2r.10) Table Mountain	70	70
1356	(2r.10) Tsitsikamma Forest	70	70
1357	(2r.10) Augrabies Watefall	70	70
1358	(2r.10) Cape Mountain Zebra	70	70
1359	(2r.10) Vineyards, Stellenbosch	70	70
1350/59	*Set of* 10	6·25	6·25

Nos. 1350/9 are inscribed "Airmail Postcard Rate" and were initially valid at 2r.10 each.

423 Tree of Life decorated with Christmas Lights

424 Frame

(Des Siobhan Cuff. Litho Enschedé)

2001 (1 Oct). Christmas. T **423** and similar square design. Multicoloured L-shaped phosphor band. P 13½.

1360	2r. Type **423**	50	35
1361	3r. Angel	60	50

(Des S. Cuff. Litho Enschedé)

2001 (1 Oct). Greeting Stamps. Self-adhesive. L-shaped phosphor band. Die-cut. P 9.

1362	**424**	(1r.40) multicoloured	60	40
		a. Double-sided sheetlet. No. 1362 ×10	5·00	

No. 1362 is inscribed "Standard Postage" and was initially valid for 1r.40.

No. 1362 was printed in double-sided sheetlets of 10 (5 stamps each side) together with a selection of 20 self-adhesive labels, which were intended to be applied to the space in the centre of the frame. The surplus self-adhesive paper around the stamps and labels was retained.

425 Class Volvo 60 Yacht

(Des H. Botha. Litho Enschedé)

2001 (23 Oct). Volvo Round the World Ocean Race. T **425** and similar multicoloured design. L-shaped phosphor band. P 13.

1363 1r.40 Type **425** .... 1·00 45
MS1364 55×85 mm. 6r. Volvo yacht (horiz). P 14×13½. 1·25 1·25

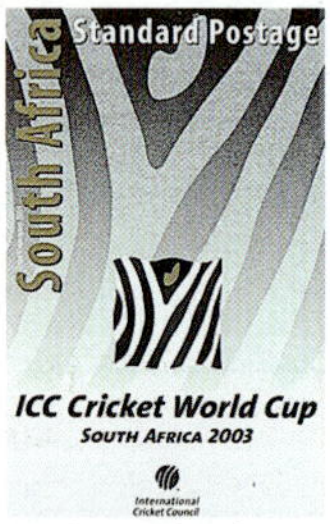

426 International Cricket Council Logo

(Des Thea Swanepoel. Litho Questa)

2001 (1 Nov). Cricket World Cup (2003) (1st issue). L-shaped phosphor band. P 14×13½.

1365 **426** (1r.40) black, gold and silver........ 1·50 65

No. 1365 is inscribed "Standard Postage" and was initially valid for 1r.40. See also Nos. 1389/94 and **MS**1418.

427 Horse's Head

(Des Anna-Marié Bands. Litho Questa)

2001 (2 Nov). Chinese New Year ("Year of the Horse"). Circular sheet 85 mm in diameter. L-shaped phosphor band. P 14×13½.

1366 **427** 6r. multicoloured........ 2·00 2·00

428 Scalloped Hammerhead Sharks

(Des Sheila Cooper)

2001 (2 Nov). Marine Life. T **428** and similar multicoloured designs. Photo. L-shaped phosphor band. Self-adhesive. Die-cut. P 13.

1367 1r.40 Type **428** 55 55
a. Sheetlet. Nos. 1367/76........ 5·00 5·00
1368 1r.40 Loggerhead Turtle (vert)........ 55 55
1369 1r.40 Clown Triggerfish (vert)........ 55 55
1370 1r.40 Cape Fur Seals (vert)........ 55 55
1371 1r.40 Bottlenosed Dolphins........ 55 55
1372 1r.40 Crowned Seahorses (vert)........ 55 55
1373 1r.40 Blue-spotted Ribbontail Ray (vert)........ 55 55
1374 1r.40 Moorish Idols........ 55 55
1375 1r.40 Octopus........ 55 55
1376 1r.40 Coral Rock Cod........ 55 55
1367/76 *Set of* 10........ 5·00 5·00

Nos. 1367/76 were printed together *se-tenant* in sheetlets of 10 with the background forming a composite design. Descriptions of the various species are printed on the reverse of the backing paper.

429 Child laughing

(Des P. Sibanda (No. 1380), 8 Seconds (others). Litho Enschedé)

2002 (17 Apr). World Summit for Sustainable Development, Johannesburg (1st issue). T **429** and similar multicoloured designs.

(a) PVA gum. P 14×13½ (Nos. 1377/9) or 13½×14 (1380)

1377 (1r.50) Type **429**........ 40 40
a. Sheetlet. No. 1377×4 and Nos. 1378/9 both ×3........ 4·25 4·25
1378 (1r.50) Globe in rainforest........ 50 50
1379 (1r.50) Trees in sunset........ 50 50
1380 (1r.50) Globe and South African landmarks (48×30 mm)........ 1·00 1·00
1377/80 *Set of* 4........ 2·25 2·25

Nos. 1377/9 were printed together, *se-tenant*, in sheetlets of 10.

Nos. 1377/9 and 1381/3 were each inscribed "Standard postage" and sold for 1r.50.

See also Nos. 1386/8.

(b) Designs 20×25 mm. Self-adhesive. P 12½×13 (25 Aug)

1381 (1r.50) Type **429**........ 45 50
a. Booklet Pane. Nos. 1381×4 and 1382/3, each ×3........ 4·50 5·00
1382 (1r.50) As No. 1378........ 55 60
1383 (1r.50) As No. 1379........ 55 60
1381/3 *Set of* 3........ 1·40 1·50

Nos. 1381/3 were only available in stamp booklets, No. SB65, in which the pane was imperforate on one side (Nos. 1381/3) or on two adjacent sides (Nos. 1381 and 1383).

430 Earl Kitchener

(Des H. Botha. Litho Enschedé)

2002 (17 May). Centenary of Anglo-Boer War (4th issue). Treaty of Vereeniging. Sheet, 105×65 mm, containing T **430** and similar square design. Multicoloured. L-shaped phosphor band. P 13½.

MS1384 1r.50 Type **430**; 3r.30 Boer representative signing Treaty........ 1·00 1·00

No. **MS**1381 was accompanied by a limited edition stamp booklet containing examples of Nos. 1165/6, 1203/4, 1343/4, in panes of two, and **MS**1381 together with two postal stationery postcards reproducing the design of No. 1344. This booklet, No. SP1, was only avalable from philatelic outlets initially at 45r., a premium of 11r.50 over the face value of the contents.

431 African Union Logo

(Des A. Notling. Litho)

2002 (25 June). First African Union Summit, Durban. P 13½ (and around stamp).

1385	**431**	1r.50 multicoloured	1·00	55

432 Water, Sanitation and Energy

(Des Michelle Casanova. Litho Cartor)

2002 (25 Aug). World Summit on Sustainable Development (2nd issue). T **432** and similar horiz designs. Multicoloured. P 13½×13.

1386	(1r.50) Type **432**	40	30
1387	(3r.) Child with hands raised to globe (Enviroment)	70	70
1388	(3r.30) Hands holding seedling (Food)	85	1·00
1386/8	*Set of 3*	1·75	1·75

No. 1386 is inscribed "standard postage", No. 1387 "airmail postcard rate" and No. 1388 "international letter rate". The stamps were initially sold at the values quoted above.

(Des C. van Rooyen. Litho Cartor)

2002 (20 Sept). Flora and Fauna (3rd series). Moths. Horiz designs as T **410**. P 13.

1389	1r.80 Emperor Moth	60	35
1390	2r.20 Peach Moth	70	50
1391	2r.80 Snouted Tiger Moth	80	65
1392	9r. False Tiger Moth	2·50	2·75
1393	16r. Moon Moth	4·50	5·00
1389/93	*Set of 5*	8·25	8·25

The inscriptions on Nos. 1390 and 1392 have been transposed. The 2r.20 actually shows the False Tiger Moth and the 9r. shows the Peach Moth.

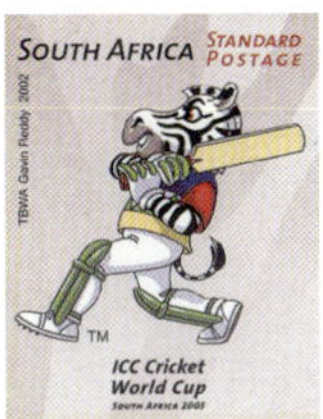

433 "Dazzler" Mascot Striking Ball

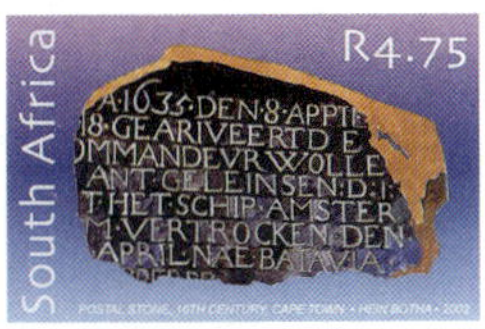

434 Postal Stone

(Des TBWA Gavin Reddy Litho Enschedé)

2002 (23 Sept - 21 Dec) Cricket World Cup (2003) (2nd issue). T **433** and similar vert designs showing "Dazzler" zebra mascot. Multicoloured. L-shaped phosphor bands. P 12½×13.

1394	(1r.50) Type **433**	50	50
1395	(1r.50) Bowler (after releasing ball)	50	50
1396	(1r.50) Fielder (1 Nov)	50	50
1397	(1r.50) Batsman (on one knee) (1 Nov)	50	50
1398	(1r.50) Bowler (running with ball) (21 Dec)	50	50
1399	(1r.50) Batsman preparing to strike ball (21 Dec)	50	50
1394/9	*Set of 6*	2·75	2·75

Nos. 1394/9×2 were each printed in sheets of six.

(Des H. Botha. Litho)

2002 (9 Oct). World Post Day. Sheet 105×65 mm. Phosphorised paper. P 13½.

MS1400	**434**	4r.75 multicoloured	1·25	1·25

435 Steve Biko

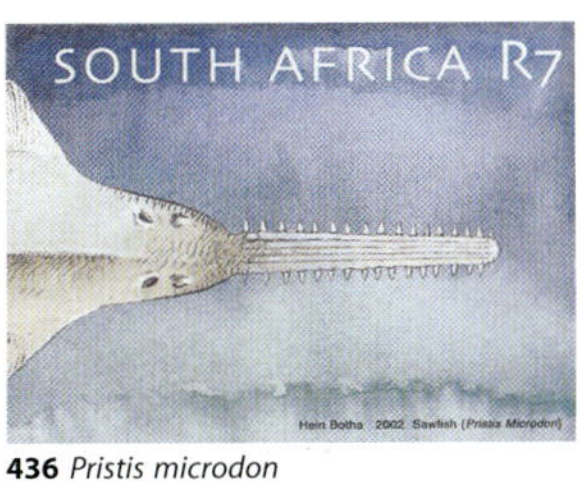

436 *Pristis microdon*

(Des Thea Swanepoel. Litho)

2002 (9 Oct). 25th Death Anniv of Steve Biko (anti-apartheid campaigner). Sheet 105×65 mm. Phosphorised paper. P 14½.

MS1401	**435**	4r.75 black, deep rose-red and cinnamon	1·25	1·25

(Des H. Botha. Litho)

2002 (23 Oct). "Algoapex" (**MS**1402) and "JUNASS" (**MS**1403) National Stamp Show. Sawfish. Two sheets containing horiz designs as T **436**. Multicoloured. Phosphorised Paper. P 14×13½.

MS1402	104×65 mm. 7r. Type **436**	1·75	1·90
MS1403	106×65 mm. 7r. Pristis pectinata	1·75	1·90

437 Stylized Goat

438 "The Tree of Life"

(Des Siobhan Cuff. Litho)

2002 (1 Nov). Chinese New Year ("Year of the Goat"). Star-shaped sheet 105×105 mm. Phosphorised paper. P 14½.

MS1404	**437**	7r. multicoloured	1·75	2·00

(Des H. Nesbit. Litho)

2002 (13 Nov). Christmas. T **438** and similar vert design showing stained glass. Multicoloured. Phosphorised paper. P 14×15.

1405	1r.50 Type **438**	40	15
1406	3r. "The Totem"	85	1·10

Nos. 1405/6 were each printed in sheets of 10 with the top row containing two stamps and two stamp-size labels at left and right. The sheets have enlarged illustrated top margins.

439 Man wearing Sunglasses

440 Total Eclipse

(Des P. Sibanda. Litho)

2002 (29 Nov). AIDS Prevention. Self-adhesive booklet stamps. T **439** and similar vert designs. Multicoloured. Phosphor frame. P 11½×12.

1407	(1r.50) Type **439**	50	55
	a. Booklet pane. Nos. 1407/16	4·50	5·00
1408	(1r.50) Woman with AIDS ribbon on headband	50	55
1409	(1r.50) Woman wearing sunglasses and hat	50	55
1410	(1r.50) Hand holding purple candle and "STOP"	50	55
1411	(1r.50) Woman's face and "AIDS"	50	55
1412	(1r.50) Man holding purple candle and "Be safe"	50	55
1413	(1r.50) Hand touching AIDS ribbon and green candle	50	55
1414	(1r.50) Raised palm of hand and "AIDS"	50	55
1415	(1r.50) Woman's face in glass jar	50	55
1416	(1r.50) Hand catching anti-HIV drugs and AIDS ribbon in heart	50	55
1407/16	*Set of 10*	4·50	5·00

Nos. 1407/16 are inscribed "Standard Postage" and were intially valid for 1r.50. They form a composite design and come from booklet No. SB66. Booklet pane No. 1407a was imperforate at top, bottom and left so that stamps are imperforate on one side (Nos. 1408/11 and 1413/16) or two adjacent sides (Nos. 1407, 1412).

(Des Thea Swanepoel. Litho)

2002 (4 Dec). Total Solar Eclipse, 4 December 2002. Sheet 105×65 mm. Phosphorised paper. P 14½.

MS1417	**440**	4r.75 black, yellow-orange and orange-red	1·25	1·50

441 Traditional Thatched Huts

(Des G. Reddy from paintings by G. Ndaba, D. Sibisi, J. Durno, B. Baqwa and V. Khumalo. Litho)

2003 (28 Feb). Cricket World Cup (3rd issue). South Africa Scenes. T **441** and similar horiz designs. Multicoloured. Phosphorised paper. P 14.

MS1418 174×90 mm. (1r.50) Type **441**; (1r.50) Man wearing brimmed hat on horse; (1r.50) Four cricketers and settlement houses; (1r.50) Passengers inside bus and on roof; (1r.50) Woman and baby; (1r.50) Double-decker bus .... 2·00 2·50

Stamps from **MS**1418 are inscribed "STANDARD POSTAGE" and were initially valid for 1r.50 each.

442 Chris Hani

443 Women carrying Water Drums

2003 (27 Apr). 10th Death Anniv of Chris Hani (former Secretary-General of South African Communist Party). Sheet 105×65 mm. Litho. Phosphorised paper. P 14½×15.

MS1419 **442** (1r.65) reddish brown and vermilion ... 60 75

No. **MS**1419 is inscribed "Standard Postage" and was initially valid for 1r.50.

(Des J. Lion. Litho)

2003 (16 May). Life in Informal Settlements. T **443** and similar vert designs. Multicoloured. Phosphor frame. P 14×13½.

1420	(1r.65) Type **443**	40	50
	a. Sheetlet. Nos. 1420/9	3·50	4·50
1421	(1r.65) Boy playing musical instrument	40	50
1422	(1r.65) Workman laying road	40	50
1423	(1r.65) Seamstress	40	50
1424	(1r.65) Two schoolchildren	40	50
1425	(1r.65) Shopkeeper with customer	40	50
1426	(1r.65) Shoemakers	40	50
1427	(1r.65) Woman wearing green hat	40	50
1428	(1r.65) Teanager leaning on tyre	40	50
1429	(1r.65) Mother and child	40	50
1420/9	*Set of 10*	3·50	4·50

Nos. 1420/9 were printed together, *se-tenant*, in sheetlets of 10. They are inscribed "STANDARD POSTAGE" and were initially valid for 1r.65 each.

444 Outline Map of Africa

(Des Thea Swanepoel. Litho)

2003 (25 May). Africa Day. Sheet 105×65 mm. Phosphorised paper. P 14½×15.

MS1430 **444** 11r.71 multicoloured .... 2·50 3·00

445 Oliver Tambo

(Des Thea Swanepoel. Litho)

2003 (29 May). 10th Death Anniv of Oliver Tambo. Sheet 105×65 mm. Phosphorised paper. P 14½×15.

MS1431 **445** (1r.65) multicoloured .... 70 1·00

No. **MS**1431 is inscribed "Standard Postage" and was initially valid for 1r.65.

446 Salsa Dancers

(Des Siobhan Buff. Litho Enschedé)

2003 (23 July). Dances. T **446** and similar horiz designs. Multicoloured. L-shaped phosphor bands. P 13½×14.

1432	1r.65 Type **446**	55	25
1433	2r.20 Rumba	70	45
1434	2r.80 Waltz	85	85
1435	3r.30 Foxtrot	1·00	1·40
1436	3r.80 Tango	1·40	1·75
1432/6	*Set of 5*	4·00	4·25

447 African Dog

448 Robert Mangaliso Sobukwe

(Des Ellena Schmitz. Litho DLR)

2003 (1 Aug). Dogs. Sheet 100×100 mm. containing T **447** and similar square designs. Multicoloured. L-shaped phosphor bands. P 14½.

MS1437 (1r.65) Type **447**; (1r.65) Rhodesian Ridgeback; (1r.65) Boerboel; (1r.65) Basenji .... 2·50 2·50

The stamps of No. **MS**1437 were each inscribed "standard postage" and sold for 1r.65.

(Des Thea Swanepoel. Litho)

2003 (24 Sept). 25th Anniv of Robert Mangaliso Sobukwe (nationalist leader and founder of the Pan Africanist Congress). Sheet 105×65 mm. P 14½×15.

MS1438 **448** 11r.71 multicoloured .... 3·25 3·50

449 Walter Max Ulyate Sisulu

450 Shaka

(Des Thea Swanepoel. Litho)

2003 (24 Sept). Walter Max Ulyate Sisulu (political activist and member of the African National Congress) Commemoration. Sheet 105×65 mm. P 14½×15.
MS1439 **449** 11r.71 muticoloured .... 3·25 3·50

(Des H. Botha. Litho Cartor)

2003 (24 Sept). Shaka (Warrior King of the Zulu) Commemoration. Phosphorised paper. P 13×13½.
1440 **450** (3r.) multicoloured .... 1·25 1·25
No. 1440 was printed in sheets of 10 with an enlarged, illustrated top margin. Each stamp was inscribed "Airmail Postcard" and sold for 3r.

451 Football Supporter and Globe

(Des L. Wyman. Litho)

2003 (26 Sept). World Cup Football Bid. T **451** and similar horiz design. Multicoloured. Phosphorised paper. P 15×14½.
1441 (3r.80) Type **451** .... 1·00 1·00
1442 (4r.25) Supporter and children playing football .... 1·10 1·40
Nos. 1441/2 were each printed in sheets of 10.
No. 1441 was inscribed "International Airmail Rate Small Letter" and sold for 3r.80.
No. 1442 was inscribed "B4 Domestic Large" and sold for for 4r.25.

452 Stamp of Fortune and Post Office Logos and Cars

(Des Thea Swanepoel. Litho)

2003 (29 Sept). Television and Post Office Joint Issue. P 14½×14.
1443 **452** (1r.65) multicoloured 50 35
No. 1443 was inscribed "Standard Postage" and sold for 1r.65.

453 Shongweni Dam Kwa-Zulu

(Des Rachel Joubert. Litho)

2003 (9 Oct). Engineering and Postal Communication. Sheet 90×143 mm containing T **453** and similar multicoloured designs. P 14×14½.
MS1444 (3r.30) Type **453**; (3r.30) Kimberly Microwave Tower (30×48 mm); (3r.30) Northern Cape Legislature (30×24 mm); (3r.30) Community Bridge, Limpopo (30×24 mm); (3r.30) Durban Westville Interchange (30×48 mm); (3r.30) Nelson Mandela Bridge, Gauteng (60×24 mm) .... 5·50 6·00

(Des Rachel Joubert. Litho)

2003 (19 Oct). 22nd PIARC World Road Congress. As No. **MS**1444 but inscr "XXIInd PIARC WORLD ROAD CONGRESS" on top margin, "CONNECTING THE WORLD" on bottom margin. Additional road agency logos are added to the left and right margins and the plate numbers, barcodes and SAICE logos are omitted. Sheet 90×143 mm containing T **453** and similar multicoloured designs. P 14×14½.
MS1444*a* (3r.30) Type **453**; (3r.30) Kimberly Microwave Tower (30×48 mm); (3r.30) Northern Cape Legislature (30×24 mm); (3r.30) Community Bridge, Limpopo (30×24 mm); (3r.30) Durban Westville Interchange (30×48 mm); (3r.30) Nelson Mandela Bridge, Gauteng (60×24 mm) .... 6·00 6·50

454 Pot created by Afrikania Job Creation Project

455 "Hope"

(Des Thea Swanepoel. Litho Cartor)

2003 (16 Oct). 10th Anniv of Diplomatic Relations with India. Sheet 105×65 mm. P 14½×15.
MS1445 **454** 3r.36 multicoloured .... 1·50 1·75

(Des Thea Swanepoel. Litho)

2003 (23 Oct). 150th Anniv of the Cape Triangular Stamp. As T **10** but with face value as T **455**. Phosphorised paper. P 12½.
1446 **455** (1r.65) grey-blue .... 1·00 1·00
a. Tête bêche pair .... 2·00 2·00
No. 1446 was issued in sheetlets of 4 containing two *tête-bêche* pairs.

456 Joseph with Mary on Donkey

457 Star

(Des Thea Swanepoel and Annemarie Wessels. Litho)

2003 (3 Nov). Christmas.

(a) Horiz designs as T **456**. *Multicoloured. Phosphorised paper. P 14*

1447 (1r.65) Type **456** 75 75
a. *se-tenant* strip of 5 .... 3·25 3·25
1448 (1r.65) Angels 75 75
1449 (1r.65) Three Wise Men 75 75
1450 (1r.65) Mary and Jesus 75 75
1451 (1r.65) Dove carrying holly 75 75
1447/51 *Set of 5* .... 3·25 3·25

(b) Vert design as T **457**. *Multicoloured. Phosphorised paper. P 14½×15*

1452 3r.80 Type **457** .... 1·50 1·50
Nos. 1447/51 were issued in sheets of 10 comprising two strips of five stamps. Each was inscribed "Standard Postage" and sold for 1r.65.

458 African Elephant

(Des A. Ainslie. Litho)

2003 (9 Dec). 10th Anniv of Diplomatic Relations with Thailand. T **458** and similar horiz design. Multicoloured. P 14½×14.
1453 3r.35 Type **458** .... 2·50 2·00
a. Horiz pair. Nos. 1453/4 .... 5·00 4·00
1454 3r.35 Indian Elephant .... 2·50 2·00
Nos. 1453/4 were printed together, *se-tenant*, in horizontal pairs within sheets of 10.

459 Paterson Biplane

460 Monkey

(Des H. Botha. Litho)

2003 (17 Dec). Centenery of Powered Flight. T **459** and similar horiz designs. Multicoloured. P 14.

1455	(1r.65) Type **459**	70	70
	a. Sheetlet of 10. Nos. 1455/64	6·25	6·25
1456	(1r.65) *Silver Queen* Vickers Vimy	70	70
1457	(1r.65) Wapiti	70	70
1458	(1r.65) de Havilland D.H.9	70	70
1459	(1r.65) Junkers Ju 52/53	70	70
1460	(1r.65) Sikorsky S-55	70	70
1461	(1r.65) Boeing 707	70	70
1462	(1r.65) Rooivalk	70	70
1463	(1r.65) SUNSAT Micro satellite	70	70
1464	(1r.65) Mark Shuttleworth (astronaut)	70	70
1455/64 *Set of* 10		6·25	6·25

Nos. 1455/64 were printed together, *se-tenant*, in sheets of 10. The stamps were each inscribed "Standard Postage" and sold for 1r.65.

(Des D. Murphy. Litho Enschedé)

2004 (27 Feb). Chinese New Year ("Year of the Monkey"). Sheet 105×65 mm. L-shaped phosphor bands. P 14×13½.

MS1465	**460** 11r.70 multicoloured	4·00	4·50

461 Patrol Sign and Pedestrian

(Des Rachel Joubert. Litho Enschedé)

2004 (24 Mar). "Drive Alive" Road Safety Campaign. T **461** and similar horiz designs. Multicoloured. L-shaped phosphor bands. P 13½×14.

1466	(1r.65) Type **461**	1·50	1·10
	a. Sheetlet. Nos. 1466/70, each ×2	12·00	
1467	(1r.65) Slippery road sign and alcohol	1·50	1·10
1468	(1r.65) Service sign and car in disrepair	1·50	1·10
1469	(1r.65) Slow lorry Sign and steering wheel	1·50	1·10
1470	(1r.65) Danger sign and sleeping driver	1·50	1·10
1466/70 *Set of* 5		6·75	5·00

Nos. 1466/7 were printed together, *se-tenant*, in sheetlets of 10 (2×5) stamps. They were inscribed "Standard Postage" and initially sold for 1r.65.

462 Dove and Outline of Africa

(Des P. Sibanda. Litho Cartor)

2004 (27 Apr). 10th Anniv of Democracy. T **462** and similar horiz designs. Multicoloured. Phosphorised paper. P 13½.

1471	(1r.65) Type **462**	1·00	1·00
	a. Sheetlet. Nos. 1471/5, each ×2	8·00	
1472	(1r.65) Voters	1·00	1·00
1473	(1r.65) Accessing services (water, electricity)	1·00	1·00
1474	(1r.65) Sports supporters	1·00	1·00
1475	(1r.65) Traditional arts and crafts	1·00	1·00
1471/5 *Set of* 5		4·50	4·50

Nos. 1471/5 were printed together, *se-tenant*, in sheetlets of 10 (2×5) stamps. They were inscribed "Standard Postage" and initially sold for 1r.65.

463 Slave Lodge, Cape Town

464 Abstract Footballer

(Des Anne-Marie Wessels. Litho Cartor)

2004 (1 May). The Legacy of Slaves. T **463** and similar horiz designs. Multicoloured. Phosphorised paper. P 13½.

1476	(1r.70) Type **463**	70	70
	a. Sheetlet. Nos. 1476/81	3·75	3·75
1477	(1r.70) First book written in Arabic and Afrikaans	70	70
1478	(1r.70) Stinkwood Tulback chair and Jonkmans cupboard	70	70
1479	(1r.70) Traditional food	70	70
1480	(1r.70) Labourers on sugar cane farm	70	70
1481	(1r.70) Miners	70	70
1476/81 *Set of* 6		3·75	3·75

Nos. 1476/81 were printed together, *se-tenant*, in sheetlets of 6. They were inscribed "Standard Postage" and initially sold for 1r.70.

(Des Thea Swanepoel. Litho)

2004 (15 May). Centenary of FIFA (Fédération Internationale de Football Association). Sheet 105×65 mm. P 14½×15.

MS1482	**464** 4r.35 multicoloured	1·50	2·00

465 Penguins (Enviromental Helpers)

(Des J. Mocke. Litho Enschedé)

2004 (9 Aug). Volunteers. T **465** and similar horiz designs. Multicoloured. L-shaped phosphor bands. P 13½×14.

1483	(1r.70) Type **465**	90	90
	a. Sheetlet. Nos. 1483/92	8·00	8·00
1484	(1r.70) Volunteer assisting elderly person (Caring for the elderly)	90	90
1485	(1r.70) Child with building blocks (Education)	90	90
1486	(1r.70) Paramedics (Medical and ambulance services)	90	90
1487	(1r.70) Life guards (Surf life saving)	90	90
1488	(1r.70) Volunteer with dogs (Helping abandoned pets)	90	90
1489	(1r.70) Child in cot (Caring for orphans)	90	90
1490	(1r.70) Rescuing someone from fire (Fire fighters)	90	90
1491	(1r.70) Group gardening (Community gardens)	90	90
1492	(1r.70) Blind person and volunteer recording tape (Tape aids for the blind)	90	90
1483/92 *Set of* 10		8·00	8·00

Nos. 1483/92 were printed together, *se-tenant*, in sheetlets of 10. Each was inscribed "Standard Postage" and sold for 1r.70.

466 Archery

467 Cape Sugarbird

(Des Saskia van Wyk. Litho Enschedé)

2004 (13 Aug). Sport. T **466** and similar vert designs. Multicolured. L-shaped phosphor bands. P 14×13½.

1493	(1r.70) Type **466**	90	90
	a. Sheetlet. Nos. 1493/1502	8·00	8·00
1494	(1r.70) Sprinting	90	90
1495	(1r.70) Show jumping	90	90
1496	(1r.70) Cycling	90	90
1497	(1r.70) Gymnastics	90	90
1498	(1r.70) Canoeing	90	90
1499	(1r.70) Football	90	90
1500	(1r.70) Swimming	90	90
1501	(1r.70) Boxing	90	90
1502	(1r.70) Tennis	90	90
1493/502 *Set of* 10		8·00	8·00

Nos. 1493/1502 were printed together, *se-tenant*, in sheetlets of 10. Each was inscribed "Standard Postage" and sold for 1r.70.

(Des Annamé Boshoff. Litho Southern Colour Print, New Zealand)

2004 (1 Sept). Ecology of Table Mountain. Sheet 172×233 mm containing T **467** and similar multicoloured designs. Self-adhesive. L-shaped phosphor bands. P 9×9½ (vert) or 9½×9.

MS1503 (4r.) Type **467**; (4r.) Dark Opal butterflies (horiz); (4r.); King Protea (flower) (horiz); (4r.) Cape Rock Hyrax (horiz); (4r.) Cuckoo Wasp (horiz); (4r.) Ghost Frog (horiz); (4r.) Cockroaches (horiz); (4r.) Staavia dodii (flower); (4r.) Spotted Skaapsteker (snake) (horiz); (4r.) Duvalia immaculata (horiz)......... 11·00 12·00

The backing paper of No. **MS**1503 is inscribed with details of all the species depicted on the stamps.

The stamps in No. **MS**1503 were each inscribed "International Airmail Rate Small Letter" and sold for 4r.

468 Children sharing Letters

(Des J. Lion. Litho Southern Colour Print, New Zealand)

2004 (23 Sept). Universal Postal Union Congress, Romania. Phosphorised paper. P 14.

1504	**468**	3r.45 multicoloured	1·00	1·25

No. 1504 was inscribed "Airmail Postcard" and sold for 3r.45.

469 Virgin "Hodigitria"

(Des Thea Swanepoel. Litho Enschedé)

2004 (1 Oct). Christmas. T **469** and similar vert design. Multicoloured. L-shaped phosphor bands. P 14×13½.

1505	(1r.70) Type **469**	50	15
1506	(4r.) Christ Pantocrator (Almighty)	1·25	1·25

No. 1505 was inscribed "Standard Postage" and initially sold for 1r.70.

No. 1506 was inscribed "International Airmail Letter" and initially sold for 4r.

470 Stylised Dove

(Des H. Botha. Litho Enschedé)

2004 (9 Oct). World Post Day. L-shaped phosphor bands. P 13½×14.

MS1507	**470**	12r.50 multicoloured	3·25	3·75

(Des Anja Denker. Litho Enschedé)

2004 (11 Oct). First Joint Issue of Southern Africa Postal Operators Association Members. Sheet 170×95 mm containing hexagonal designs as T **233** of Botswana showing national birds of Association members. Multicoloured. P 14.

MS1508 12r.50 African Fish Eagle (Namibia); 12r.50 Two African Fish Eagles perched (Zimbabwe); 12r.50 Peregrine Falcon (Angola); 12r.50 Cattle Egret (Botswana); 12r.50 Purple-crested Turaco ("Lourie") (Swaziland); 12r.50 Stanley ("Blue") Crane (South Africa); 12r.50 Bar-tailed Trogon (Malawi) (inscribed "apaloderma vittatum"); 12r.50 Two African Fish Eagles in flight (Zambia)............ 20·00 22·00

The stamp depicting the Bar-tailed Trogon is not inscribed with the country of which the bird is a national symbol. Minature sheets of similar designs were also issued by Namibia, Zimbabwe, Angola, Botswana, Swaziland, Malawi, and Zambia.

471 South African Large Telescope

472 South African Police Service Badge

(Des Anne-Marie Wessels. Litho Enschedé)

2004 (11 Nov). South African Large Telescope. T **471** and similar vert designs. Multicoloured. L-shaped phosphor bands. P 14×13½.

1509	4r. Type **471**	95	1·00
	a. Sheetlet. Nos. 1509/13, each ×2	8·00	
1510	4r. Cross-section of observatory	95	1·00
1511	4r. View of the Southern Cross	95	1·00
1512	4r. Telescope	95	1·00
1513	4r. Telescope inside observatory	95	1·00
1509/13	*Set of* 5	4·25	4·50

Nos. 1509/13 were printed together, *se-tenant*, in sheetlets of 10 (2×5) stamps.

(Des SAPS Graphic Unit (1514,1522), Reáldi Marx (1515,1517/18,1521,1523), Jacqueline van Marie (1516), Rinie Voges (1519) and Joannie Ras (1520). Litho Southern Colour Print, New Zealand)

2004 (23 Nov). South African Police Service (SAPS). T **472** and similar vert designs. Self-adhesive. Multicoloured. L-shaped phosphor bands. P 13½×12½.

1514	1r.70 Type **472**	90	90
	a. Sheetlet. Nos. 1514/23	8·00	8·00
1515	1r.70 Handcuffed hands and drugs (Fight Against Drugs)	90	90
1516	1r.70 Police Helicopter (SAPS Air Wing)	90	90
1517	1r.70 Microscope (Fingerprint and Forensic Science Units)	90	90
1518	1r.70 Parachutists (Special Task Force)	90	90
1519	1r.70 Child and officer (Family Violence, Child Protection and Sexual Offences Unit)	90	90
1520	1r.70 Officers and map (Sector Policing)	90	90
1521	1r.70 Three police officers (The Dignified Blue)	90	90
1522	1r.70 Officer on horse (SAPS Mounted Unit)	90	90
1523	1r.70 Officer and police dog (SAPS Dog Unit)	90	90
1514/23	*Set of* 10	8·00	8·00

Nos. 1514/23 were printed, *se-tenant*, together in sheetlets of 10 with a brief description of the individual units inscribed on the backing paper behind the corresponding stamp. They were each inscribed **"Standard Postage"** and initially sold for 1r.70.

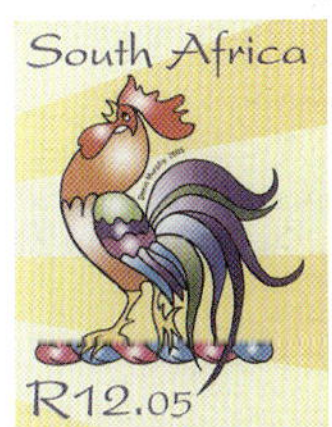

473 Rooster

474 Immunising Children

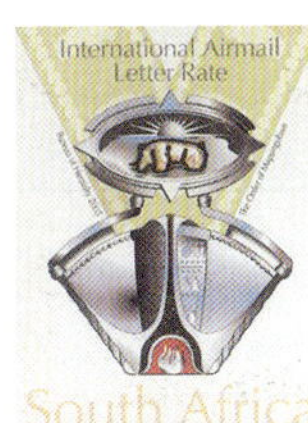

475 The Order of Mapungubwe

(Des Denis Murphy. Litho Southern Colour Print, Dunedin)

2005 (9 Feb). Chinese New Year ("Year of the Rooster"). Sheet 105×65 mm. Phosphorised paper. P 14½.

MS1524	**473**	12r.50 multicoloured	4·50	4·50

(Des Joe Hlongwane. Litho Southern Colour Print, Dunedin)

2005 (23 Feb). Centenary of Rotary International (humanitarian organisation). T **474** and similar horiz designs. L-shaped phosphor bands. P 14.

1525	(4r.) Type **474**	1·25	1·25
	a. Horiz pair. Nos. 1525/6	2·50	2·50
1526	(4r.) Computer and metal work	1·25	1·25

(Des Bureau of Heraldry. Litho and embossed Southern Colour Print, Dunedin)

2005 (26 Apr). National Orders of South Africa. T **475** and similar vert designs. Multicoloured. Phosphorised paper. P 14½.

1527	(4r.25) Type **475**	1·40	1·40
	a. Sheetlet. Nos. 1527/32	7·50	7·50
1528	(4r.25) The Order of Mendi for Bravery	1·40	1·40
1529	(4r.25) The Order of the Baobab	1·40	1·40
1530	(4r.25) The Order of Luthuli	1·40	1·40
1531	(4r.25) The Order of Ikhamanga	1·40	1·40
1532	(4r.25) The Order of the Companions of O R Tambo	1·40	1·40
1527/32	*Set of* 6	7·50	7·50

Nos. 1527/32 were printed together, *se-tenant*, in sheetlets of 6 stamps. Each was inscribed "International Airmail Letter Rate" and initially sold for 4r.25.

476 "Boland Winter" (Erik Laubscher)

(Litho Southern Colour Print, New Zealand)

2005 (6 May). Landscape Paintings. T **476** and similar horiz designs. Multicoloured. Phosphorised paper. P 14½.

1533	(3r.65) Type **476**	1·25	1·40
	a. Sheetlet. Nos. 1533/42	11·00	12·00
1534	(3r.65) "Table Mountain" (Maggie Laubser)	1·25	1·40
1535	(3r.65) "Fishermen Drawing Nets" (Walter Battiss)	1·25	1·40
1536	(3r.65) "Oh South Africa, you've turned my world completely upside down" (Lallitha Jawahirilal)	1·25	1·40
1537	(3r.65) "Untitled" (Lucky Sibiya)	1·25	1·40
1538	(3r.65) "Untitled" (Sophie Masiza)	1·25	1·40
1539	(3r.65) "Azibuye Emasisweni" (Trevor Makhoba)	1·25	1·40
1540	(3r.65) "Kontantwinkel Riebeeck-Wes" (John Kramer)	1·25	1·40
1541	(3r.65) "Houses in the Hills" (Gladys Mgudlandlu)	1·25	1·40
1542	(3r.65) "Sequence City" (Usha Seejarim)	1·25	1·40
1533/42	*Set of* 10	11·00	12·00

Nos. 1533/42 were printed together, *se-tenant*, in sheetlets of 10 stamps. Each was inscribed "International Airmail Postcard Rate" and initially sold for 3r.65.

477 Sunrise over the Gariep and "Freedom Charter" Reversed

478 Honeyguide's Revenge (Isi Ndebele)

(Des Thea Swanepoel. Litho Southern Colour Print, Dunedin)

2005 (24 June). 50th Anniv of the Freedom Charter. Sheet, 105×65 mm, containing T **477** and similar horiz design. Multicoloured. L-shaped phosphor bands. P 14½.

MS1543	(1r.77) Type **477**; (1r.77) Sunrise over the Gariep, "Freedom Charter" and "50"	2·50	2·75

The stamps of **MS**1543 form a panoramic design. Both were inscribed "Standard Postage" and sold for 1r.77.

(Des Hein Botha. Litho Southern Colour Print, Dunedin)

2005 (1 July). Folklore and Legends. T **478** and similar horiz designs. Multicoloured. L-shaped phosphor bands. P 14½.

1544	(3r.75) Type **478**	1·25	1·40
	a. Sheetlet. Nos. 1544/53	11·00	12·00
1545	(3r.75) How Ostrich got his Long Neck (Sesotho)	1·25	1·40
1546	(3r.75) How Serval got his Spots (Setswana)	1·25	1·40
1547	(3r.75) How Zebra got his Stripes (Isi Zulu)	1·25	1·40
1548	(3r.75) Jackal the Tiger Eater (Cape Malay)	1·25	1·40
1549	(3r.75) Jackal and Wolf (Afrikaans)	1·25	1·40
1550	(3r.75) King Lion and King Eagle (Isi Xhosa)	1·25	1·40
1551	(3r.75) Mantis and the Moon (San)	1·25	1·40
1552	(3r.75) Words as Sweet as Honey (Tshi Venda)	1·25	1·40
1553	(3r.75) When Lion could Fly (Ancient Khoenkhoen languages)	1·25	1·40
1544/53	*Set of* 10	11·00	12·00

Nos. 1544/53 were printed together, *se-tenant*, in sheetlets of ten stamps. Each was inscribed "B5" and sold initially for 3r.75.

479 Albert Einstein and Satellite

480 Lesser Bushbaby

(Des Rachel Ackermann. Litho Southern Colour Print, Dunedin)

2005 (7 July). Year of Physics. L-shaped phosphor bands. P 14½.

1554	**479** (3r.65) multicoloured	1·00	1·00

No. 1554 was inscribed "Airmail Postcard Rate" and initially sold for 3r.65.

(Des Chris van Rooyen. Litho Southern Colour Print, Dunedin)

2005 (15 July). JUNASS (2005). Small Indigenous Animals. Sheet, 145×90 mm, containing T **480** and similar multicoloured designs. L-shaped phosphor bands. P 14.

MS1555	(1r.77) Type **480**; (1r.77) Riverine Rabbit (24×30 mm); (1r.77) African Wildcat (49×30 mm); (1r.77) Steenbok (49×30 mm); (1r.77) Cape Fox (24×30 mm); (1r.77) Yellow Mongoose	5·00	5·00

The stamps of No. **MS**1555 were each inscribed "Standard Postage" and initially sold for 1r.77.

481 Hedgehog Spider

(Des Hein Botha. Litho Southern Colour Print, Dunedin)

2005 (30 July). Spiders. Sheet, 233×172 mm, containing T **481** and similar multicoloured designs. L-shaped phosphor bands. Self-adhesive. Die-cut perf 9½.

MS1556	(1r.77)×10, Type **481**; Golden orb-web spider; Lynx spider; Black button spider; Ladybird spider; Flower crab spider; Rain spider; Horn Baboon spider; Trap door spider; Spotted crab spider	7·00	7·50

The backing paper of No. **MS**1556 is inscribed with details of all the species depicted on the stamps. The stamps in No. **MS**1556 were each inscribed "Standard Postage" and sold for 1r.77. No. **MS**1556 was originally due to be released 30 July 2004 and the stamps show "2004" imprint date.

482 Wave

483 Christmas Tree, Candle and Heart

(Des Sulet Schulze. Litho Southern Colour Print, Dunedin)

2005 (26 Sept). Renewable Energy Sources. T **482** and similar vert designs. Multicoloured. L-shaped phosphor bands. P 14.

1557	(1r.77) Type **482**	60	60
1558	(3r.65) Wind	1·10	1·25
1559	(4r.25) Sun	1·25	1·50
1557/9	*Set of 3*	2·75	3·00

Nos. 1557/9 were inscribed "Standard Postage", "International Airmail Postcard" and "International Airmail Letter" and sold for 1r.77, 3r.65 and 4r.25, respectively.

(Des Peter Sibanda. Litho Southern Colour Print, New Zealand)

2005 (3 Oct). Christmas. T **483** and similar vert design showing wire and bead work decorations. Multicoloured. L-shaped phosphor bands. P 14×14½.

1560	(1r.77) Type **483**	70	25
1561	(4r.25) Angel and dove	1·25	1·25

No. 1560 was inscribed "Standard Postage" and sold at 1r.77.

No. 1561 was inscribed "International Airmail Letter" and sold at 4r.25.

484 "Hallo!" (Afrikaans)

(Litho Southern Colour Print, New Zealand)

2005 (7 Oct). World Post Day. T **484** and similar horiz designs showing South African flag and "Hello" in South African languages. Multicoloured. L-shaped phosphor bands. P 14½×15.

1562	(3r.65) Type **484**	1·10	1·25
	a. Sheetlet. Nos. 1562/9	8·00	9·00
1563	(3r.65) "Hi!" (English)	1·10	1·25
1564	(3r.65) "Sawubona" (IsiZulu and Siswati)	1·10	1·25
1565	(3r.65) "Ndi Masiari!" (Tshivenda)	1·10	1·25
1566	(3r.65) "Lotjha!" (IsiNdebele)	1·10	1·25
1567	(3r.65) "Avuxeni" (Xitsonga)	1·10	1·25
1568	(3r.65) "Dumela" (Northern Sotho)	1·10	1·25
1569	(3r.65) "Molo!" (IsiXhosa)	1·10	1·25
1562/9	*Set of 8*	8·00	9·00

Nos. 1562/9 were printed together, *se-tenant*, in sheetlets of eight stamps. Each stamp was inscribed "Airmail Postcard Rate" and sold at 3r.65.

485 "Hello" embossed in Braille

(Des Saskia van Wyk. Litho and embossing Southern Colour Print)

2005 (13 Oct). Prevention of Blindness. L-shaped phosphor bands. P 14½×14.

1570	**485** (1r.77) multicoloured	1·00	65

No. 1570 was inscribed "STANDARD POSTAGE" and sold at 1r.77.

486 Labrador Guide Dog

(Des Annemarie Wessels. Litho Cartor)

2006 (27 Jan). Chinese New Year ("Year of the Dog"). Sheet 125×65 mm. Phosphorised paper. P 13.

MS1571	(3r.75) Type **486**; (3r.75) Customs sniffer spaniel; (3r.75) Border collie chasing birds away from airport	4·75	4·75

The stamps within No. **MS**1571 were inscribed "B5" and the miniature sheet was sold for 11r.25.

487 San Dancers (from Linton panel, Iziko South African Museum)

488 Lion

(Litho Cartor)

2006 (15 Feb). Rock Art in South Africa. T **487** and similar horiz designs. Multicoloured. Phosphorised paper. P 13½×13.

1572	(1r.77) Type **487**	1·10	1·10
	a. Horiz strip of 5. Nos. 1572/6	5·00	5·00
1573	(1r.77) Mountain reedbuck (South African Museum of Rock Art)	1·10	1·10
1574	(1r.77) San ritual specialist (South African Museum of Rock Art)	1·10	1·10
1575	(1r.77) Rhinoceros (Wildebeest Kuil)	1·10	1·10
1576	(1r.77) Eland (Game Pass)	1·10	1·10
1572/6	*Set of 5*	5·00	5·00

Nos. 1572/6 were printed together, *se-tenant*, in horizontal strips of five in sheetlets of 10 (2×5) stamps. They were inscribed "Standard Postage" and sold for 1r.77 each.

(Litho Cartor)

2006 (24 Feb). Wildlife "The Big Five". Self-adhesive booklet stamps. T **488** and similar vert designs. Multicoloured. L-shaped phosphor bands. Die-cut.

1577	(3r.65) Type **488**	1·50	1·75
	a. Booklet pane. Nos. 1577/81, each ×2	13·00	
1578	(3r.65) Buffalo	1·50	1·75
1579	(3r.65) Elephant	1·50	1·75
1580	(3r.65) Black rhinoceros	1·50	1·75
1581	(3r.65) Leopard	1·50	1·75
1577/81	*Set of 5*	6·50	8·00

Nos. 1577/81 are inscribed "Airmail Postcard" and were initially valid for 3r.65 each. These stamps have straight edges on two adjacent sides (Type **488**) or at either top or bottom (others), with the remaining sides having wavy edges (simulating perforations).

489 Children riding Bicycles to School

490 Red Cross MBB BO105 Eurocopter

(Des Jerry Lion. Litho Enschedé)

2006 (6 Mar). Velo Mondial Conference, Cape Town. L-shaped phosphor bands. P 13½×14.

1582	**489** (4r.25) multicoloured	2·00	1·25

No. 1582 is inscribed "International Airmail Letter" and was sold for 4r.25.

(Des Hein Botha. Litho Cartor)

2006 (2 May). Medical Outreach to Rural Areas. T **490** and similar multicoloured designs. Phosphorised paper. P 13½.

1583	(1r.85) Type **490**	1·75	1·75
	a. Sheetlet. Nos. 1583/8	9·50	9·50
1584	(1r.85) Clasped hands (24×30 mm)	1·75	1·75
1585	(1r.85) Red Cross Pilatus PC12 aircraft (48×30 mm)	1·75	1·75
1586	(1r.85) eRanger motorcycle ambulance (24×30 mm)	1·75	1·75
1587	(1r.85) Phelophepa Health Care Train (71×29 mm)	1·75	1·75
1588	(1r.85) St. John's ambulance (24×30 mm)	1·75	1·75
1583/8	*Set of 6*	9·50	9·50

Nos. 1583/8 were printed together, *se-tenant*, in sheetlets of six stamps. They were inscribed "STANDARD POSTAGE" and sold for 1r.85 each.

491 Bhambatha ka Mancinza Zondi and Mome Gorge

(Des Denis Murphy. Litho Enschedé)

2006 (9 June). Centenary of the Bhambatha Rebellion. L-shaped phosphor bands. P 14×13½.

1589	**491** (1r.85) multicoloured	65	40

No. 1589 is inscribed "Standard Postage" and was sold for 1r.85.

492 Nursing Sister with Child

493 African Wild Dog standing on Football

(Des Tobie Beele. Litho Enschedé)

2006 (18 June). 50th Anniv of the Red Cross War Memorial Children's Hospital. L-shaped phosphor bands. P 14×13½ (1r.85) or 13½×14 (4r.40).

1590	(1r.85) Type **492**	75	25
1591	(4r.40) Hospital building (horiz)	1·75	2·00

No. 1590 has L-shaped phosphor bands at the right of the stamp, extending along the foot and halfway up the right-hand side. No. 1591 has L-shaped phosphor bands at left.

No. 1590 is inscribed "STANDARD POSTAGE" and was sold for 1r.85. No. 1591 is inscribed "INTERNATIONAL LETTER" and was sold for 4r.40.

(Des Michelle Beukes. Litho Southern Colour Print, New Zealand)

2006 (7 July). World Cup Football, South Africa, 2010. Sheet 105×65 mm. L-shaped phosphor band. P 14½.

MS1592	**493** (4r.40) multicoloured	1·75	2·00

No. **MS**1592 has L-shaped phosphor bands at right, extending along the foot and right-hand side of the stamp. No. **MS**1592 is inscribed "International Airmail Letter" and was sold for 4r.40.

494 Sophia Williams, Rahima Moosa, Helen Joseph and Lillian Ngoyi leading March

(Des Thea Swanepoel. Litho Enschedé)

2006 (9 Aug). 50th Anniv of the Women?s March to the Union Buildings, Pretoria. Sheet 105×65 mm. L-shaped phosphor bands. P 15×14½.

MS1593	**494** (3r.75) multicoloured	1·10	1·40

No. **MS**1593 has inverted L-shaped phosphor bands extending along the top and left-hand side of the stamp. No. **MS**1593 is inscribed "B5" and was sold for 3r.75.

495 *Clivia nobilis*

496 Buffalo

(Des Gillian Condy. Litho Cartor)

2006 (6 Sept). Clivias. T **495** and similar vert designs. Multicoloured. Phosphorised paper. P 13½.

1594	(1r.85) Type **495**	70	70
	a. Sheetlet. Nos. 1594/9	3·75	3·75
1595	(1r.85) *Clivia miniata*	70	70
1596	(1r.85) *Clivia gardenia*	70	70
1597	(1r.85) *Clivia caulescens*	70	70
1598	(1r.85) *Clivia mirabilis*	70	70
1599	(1r.85) *Clivia robusta*	70	70
1594/9	*Set of 6*	3·75	3·75

Nos. 1594/9 were printed together, *se-tenant*, in sheetlets of six stamps. They were inscribed "Standard Postage" and sold for 1r.85 each.

(Des Hantie Engelbrecht and Johan Schutte. Litho and die-stamped Enschedé)

2006 (15 Sept). Animal Tracks–"Stories in the Sand". T **496** and similar horiz designs. Multicoloured. L-shaped phosphor bands. P 14×13½.

1600	(1r.85) Type **496**	1·10	1·10
	a. Sheetlet. Nos. 1600/9	10·00	10·00
1601	(1r.85) Giraffe	1·10	1·10
1602	(1r.85) Elephant	1·10	1·10
1603	(1r.85) Spotted hyena	1·10	1·10
1604	(1r.85) Blue Wildebeest	1·10	1·10
1605	(1r.85) Leopard	1·10	1·10
1606	(1r.85) Hippopotamus	1·10	1·10
1607	(1r.85) Warthog	1·10	1·10
1608	(1r.85) Black rhinoceros	1·10	1·10
1609	(1r.85) Burchell's zebra	1·10	1·10
1600/9	*Set of 10*	10·00	10·00

Nos. 1600/9 were printed together, *se-tenant*, in sheetlets of ten stamps.

Nos. 1600/9 have inverted L-shaped phosphor bands extending along the top and right-hand side of the stamps.

Nos. 1600, 1602, 1604, 1606 and 1608 are inscribed "STANDARD POSTAGE", and Nos. 1601, 1603, 1605, 1607 and 1609 "standard postage". They were all sold for 1r.85.

497 Springbok

498 Climber ("Collect Stamps Start an Adventure")

(Des Dr. Jack. Litho Cartor)

2006 (2 Oct). Christmas. "Jungle Bells". T **497** and similar vert designs. Multicoloured. Phosphorised paper. P 13½×13.

1610	(1r.85) Type **497**	75	75
	a. Horiz strip of 5. Nos. 1610/14	3·25	3·25
1611	(1r.85) Warthog	75	75
1612	(1r.85) Zebra	75	75
1613	(1r.85) Hippopotamus	75	75
1614	(1r.85) King Lion as Father Christmas in donkey cart	75	75
1615	(4r.40) King Lion wearing Santa hat	1·75	1·75
1610/15	*Set of 6*	5·00	5·00

Nos. 1610/14 were printed together, *se-tenant*, in horizontal strips of five stamps throughout the sheet, each strip forming a composite design showing Springbok, Warthog, Zebra and Hippopotamus pulling Father Christmas in donkey cart.

Nos. 1610/14 are inscribed "Standard Postage" and sold for 1r.85.

No. 1615 is inscribed "International Airmail Letter" and sold for 4r.40.

(Des Hein Botha. Litho Cartor)

2006 (9 Oct). World Post Day. T **498** and similar horiz designs. Multicoloured. Phosphorised paper. P 13½×13.

1616	(1r.85) Type **498**	75	80
	a. Horiz strip of 5. Nos. 1616/20	3·25	3·50
1617	(1r.85) "Be Cool Collect Stamps"	75	80
1618	(1r.85) Reader ("Learn More Collect Stamps")	75	80
1619	(1r.85) "Have Fun Collect Stamps"	75	80
1620	(1r.85) Traveller with suitcase ("Travel the World Collect Stamps")	75	80
1616/20	*Set of 5*	3·25	3·50

Nos. 1616/20 were printed together, *se-tenant*, in horizontal strips of five in sheetlets of 10 (2×5) stamps. They were inscribed "STANDARD POSTAGE" and sold for 1.85 reach.

499 *Paranthropus robustus*

(Des François Durand. Litho Enschedé)

2006 (10 Nov). Origin of Humankind. Sheet 182×126 mm containing T **499** and similar vert designs. Multicoloured. L-shaped phosphor bands. Self-adhesive. Die-cut perf 11½×12.

MS1621	(3r.80)×4, Type **499**; *Australopithecus africanus; Homo heidelbergensis; Homo ergaster*	4·75	5·50

The stamps in **MS**1621 were each inscribed "Airmail Postcard" and sold for 3r.80 each.

They all have inverted L-shaped phosphor bands which extend along the top and left of Type **499** and *Australophithecus africanus*, and along the top and right of *Homoheidelbergensis* and *Homo ergaster*.

500 Barn Owl

501 Elephant

(Des Chris van Rooyen. Litho Southern Colour Print, New Zealand)

2007 (3 Aug). South African Owls. T **500** and similar vert designs. Multicoloured. L-shaped phosphor bands. P 14½.

1622	(4r.64) Type **500**	2·25	2·25
	a. Horiz strip of 5. Nos. 1622/6	10·00	10·00
1623	(4r.64) Cape eagle-owl	2·25	2·25
1624	(4r.64) African barred owlet	2·25	2·25
1625	(4r.64) Verreaux's eagle owl	2·25	2·25
1626	(4r.64) Pel's fishing owl	2·25	2·25
1622/6	*Set of 5*	10·00	10·00

Nos. 1622/6 were printed together, *se-tenant*, in horizontal strips of five in sheetlets of 10 (2×5) stamps. They were inscribed 'International Letter' and sold for 4r.64 each.

(Des Pawel Kot. Litho Cartor)

2007 (17 Aug). Wildlife 'The Big Five'. Self-adhesive booklet stamps. T **501** and similar horiz designs. Multicoloured. L-shaped phosphor bands. Die-cut.

1627	(4r.01) Type **501**	1·40	1·60
	a. Booklet pane. Nos. 1627/31, each ×2	12·00	
1628	(4r.01) Leopard	1·40	1·60
1629	(4r.01) Buffalo	1·40	1·60
1630	(4r.01) Lion	1·40	1·60
1631	(4r.01) Black rhinoceros	1·40	1·60
1627/31	*Set of 5*	6·25	7·25

Nos. 1627/31 are inscribed 'AIRMAIL POSTCARD' and sold for 4r.01 each.

These stamps have straight edges on two adjacent sides (Type **501**) or at either left or right side (others), with the remaining sides having wavy edges (simulating perforations).

502 Scout Salute

503 Pig

(Des Annemarie Wessels. Litho Southern Colour Print, New Zealand)

2007 (22 Aug). Centenary of World Scouting. Sheet 105×65 mm containing T **502** and similar vert design. Multicoloured. L-shaped phosphor bands. P 14½.

MS1632	(3r.90) ×2 Type **502**; Scout emblem	1·90	2·25

The two stamps within **MS**1632 were each inscribed 'B5'. The miniature sheet was sold for 7r.80.

(Des Annemarie Wessels. Litho and embossed Southern Colour Print, New Zealand)

2007 (7 Sept). Chinese New Year ('Year of the Pig'). Sheet 105×80 mm. L shaped phosphor band. P 14½.

MS1633	**503** (4r.70) multicoloured	2·25	2·25

No. **MS**1633 is inscr 'B4' and sold for 4r.70.

The stamp within **MS**1633 has reversed L-shaped phosphor bands which extend along the right and bottom.

504 First Telephone Exchange in South Africa, Port Elizabeth, 1882

505 Emblem

(Des Thea Clemons. Litho Southern Colour Print, New Zealand)

2007 (9 Oct). World Post Day. Phosphorised paper. P 14.

1634	**504** (3r.90) multicoloured	1·50	1·00

No. 1634 is inscr 'B5' and sold for 3r.90.

(Des Thea Clemons. Litho Enschedé)

2007 (9 Oct). 24th UPU Congress, Nairobi, Kenya. Sheet 105×65 mm. L-shaped phosphor band. P 14.

MS1635	**505** (4r.64) multicoloured	1·10	1·40

No. **MS**1635 is inscr 'INTERNATIONAL AIRMAIL SMALL LETTER' and sold for 4r.64.

506 Cheetah

(Des Denis Murphy. Litho Southern Colour Print (No. 1637a) or Enschedé (others))

2007 (19 Oct)-**09**. Flora and Fauna (4th series). T **506** and similar horiz design. Multicoloured. L-shaped phosphor bands. P 14.

1636	(3r.90) Type **506**	1·25	1·25
1637	(4r.89) Ostrich	2·00	2·00
	a. Perf 14½ (3.9.09)	2·50	2·50

No. 1636 is inscr 'B5 Domestic Medium' and sold for 3r.90.

No. 1637 is inscr 'Domestic Large' and 'B4' and sold for 4r.89 On No. 1636 the L-shaped phosphor bands are reversed and extend along the right and bottom of the stamp.

507 King Penguins

508 Mosterts Mill, Cape Town

(Des Tobie Beele. Litho Southern Colour Print, New Zealand)

2007 (31 Oct). International Polar and Heliophysical Year. Sheet 145×90 mm containing T **507** and similar multicoloured designs. L-shaped phosphor bands. P 14.

MS1638	(1r.93)×6 Type **507**; SANAE IV Base (72×30 mm); Wandering albatross (24×60 mm); Adélie penguins; Orca whale (48×30 mm); Weddell seal	4·75	4·75

The stamps within **MS**1638 form a composite design. They are all inscr 'Standard Postage' and were sold for 1r.93 each.

The L-shaped phosphor bands are at top and right on the right-hand (Wandering albatross) stamp in the miniature sheet and at top and left on the others.

(Des Robin Howard Kearney. Litho Southern Colour Print, New Zealand)

2007 (9 Nov). Mills of South Africa. T **508** and similar horiz designs. Multicoloured. Inverted L-shaped phosphor bands. P 14½.

1639	(2r.32) Type **508**	1·75	1·75
	a. Vert strip of 5. Nos. 1639/43	8·00	8·00
1640	(2r.32) La Cotte Watermill, Franschhoek, Western Cape	1·75	1·75
1641	(2r.32) Witpoort Watermill, Stoffberg, Mpumalanga	1·75	1·75
1642	(2r.32) Dwars Rivier Watermill, Cederberg, Western Cape	1·75	1·75
1643	(2r.32) Colesberg Horse Mill, Colesberg, Northern Cape	1·75	1·75
1639/43	*Set of* 5	8·00	8·00

Nos. 1639/43 were printed together, *se-tenant*, in vertical strips of five in sheetlets of 10 (2×5) stamps. They were inscr 'International Letter' and sold for 4r.64 each.

The inverted L-shaped phosphor bands on Nos. 1639/43 extend along the top and left of the stamps.

509 Raised Hands and Bouncing Football

510 *Dane*

(Des Tamarin Skead. Litho Southern Colour Print, New Zealand)

2007 (23 Nov). World Cup Football, South Africa, 2010 (2nd issue). Sheet 105×65 mm. L-shaped phosphor band. P 13½.

MS1644	**509** (4r.64) multicoloured	2·00	2·00

No. **MS**1644 is inscr 'INTERNATIONAL AIRMAIL SMALL LETTER' and sold for 4r.64.

(Des Peter Bilas. Litho Southern Colour Print, New Zealand)

2007 (5 Dec). Ships of the Union Castle Line. T **510** and similar horiz designs. Multicoloured. Inverted L-shaped phosphor bands. P 14½.

1645	(4r.01) Type **510**	1·75	1·75
	a. Vert strip of 5. Nos. 1645/9	8·00	8·00
1646	(4r.01) *Kildonan Castle*	1·75	1·75
1647	(4r.01) *SA Vaal*	1·75	1·75
1648	(4r.01) *Edinburgh Castle*	1·75	1·75
1649	(4r.01) *Windsor Castle*	1·75	1·75
1645/9	*Set of* 5	8·00	8·00

Nos. 1645/9 were printed together, *se-tenant*, in vertical strips of five in sheetlets of 10 (2×5) stamps. They are inscr 'International Postcard' and sold for 4r.01 each.

The inverted L-shaped phosphor bands on Nos. 1645/9 extend along the top and left of the stamps.

511 Assembly Logo

512 Flags of South Africa and China

(Des Thea Clemons. Litho Enschedé)

2008 (13 Apr). 118th Inter-Parliamentary Union Assembly, Cape Town. Inverted L-shaped phosphor band. P 14.

1650	**511** (2r.05) multicoloured	1·50	1·25

No. 1650 is inscr 'STANDARD POSTAGE' and was sold for 2r.05.

The inverted L-shaped phosphor band extends along the top and left of the stamp.

(Litho Enschedé)

2008 (24 Apr). 10th Anniv of Diplomatic Relations between South Africa and China. Sheet 105×65 mm. Inverted L-shaped phosphor bands. P 14.

MS1651	(2r.05) Type **512**; (4r.64) Flags of South Africa and China	1·25	1·75

The stamps within **MS**1651 are inscribed 'Standard Postage' (value 2r.05) and 'International Airmail Small Letter' (value 4r.64).

They have inverted L-shaped phosphor bands which extend along the top and right of both stamps.

513 Constitutional Court

(Litho Enschedé)

2008 (25 June). Architecture of the Constitutional Court of South Africa, Johannesburg. T **513** and similar multicoloured designs. L-shaped phosphor bands. P 14×13½.

1652	(2r.05) Type **513**	85	90
	a. Sheetlet. Nos. 1652/61	7·50	8·00
1653	(2r.05) Corner of building (30×30 mm)	85	90
1654	(2r.05) Courtyard	85	90
1655	(2r.05) Interior of building (30×30 mm)	85	90
1656	(2r.05) Glass tower (90×30 mm)	85	90
1657	(2r.05) Court buildings lit at dusk (30×30 mm)	85	90
1658	(2r.05) Column and spotlights (30×30 mm)	85	90
1659	(2r.05) Inscriptions on exterior wall (30×30 mm)	50	50
1660	(2r.05) Screen (30×30 mm)	85	90
1661	(2r.05) Court buildings on street corner	85	90
1652/61	*Set of* 10	7·50	8·00

Nos. 1652/61 were printed together, *se-tenant*, in sheetlets of ten stamps. They were inscr 'STANDARD POSTAGE' and sold for 2r.05 each.

514 Heelwalkers (Mantophasmatodea) (discovered 2002)

(Des Ellena Schmitz. Litho Enschedé)

2008 (4 July). International Entomology Conference (ICE), Durban. L-shaped phosphor band. P 14×13½.

1662	**514** (4r.20) multicoloured	1·75	1·50

No. 1662 is inscr 'Airmail Postcard' and was sold for 4r.20.

515 Nelson Mandela

(Des Halden Krog (**MS**1663a) or Cyril Coetzee (**MS**1663b)

2008 (15 July). 90th Birthday of Nelson Mandela. Two sheets, each 77×105 mm, containing T **515** and similar vert design. Multicoloured. L-shaped phosphor bands. P 14.

MS1663	(a) (2r.05) Type **515**; (b) (4r.90) Nelson Mandela (seated in armchair, wearing blue shirt)	1·75	2·25

No. **MS**1663 (a) was inscr 'Standard Postage' and sold for 2r.05. No. **MS**1663 (b) was inscr 'International Airmail Small Letter' and sold for 4r.90.

516 Southern Ground-Hornbill

(Litho Enschedé)

2008 (1 Aug). South African Big Five of Birds. T **516** and similar vert designs. Multicoloured. L-shaped phosphor bands. P 13½.

1664	(4r.90) Type **516**	1·75	1·75
	a. Horiz strip of 5. Nos. 1664/8	8·00	8·00
1665	(4r.90) Kori bustard	1·75	1·75
1666	(4r.90) Common ostrich	1·75	1·75
1667	(4r.90) Blue crane	1·75	1·75
1668	(4r.90) Bearded vulture	1·75	1·75
1664/8	*Set of 5*	8·00	8·00

Nos. 1664/8 were printed together, *se-tenant*, as horizontal strips of five stamps in sheetlets of ten. They were inscr 'International Airmail Small Letter' and sold for 4r.90 each.

517 Common Bokbaaivygie (*Dorotheanthus bellidiformis*)

(Des Denis Murphy. Litho Enschedé)

2008 (22 Aug). Flowers of Namaqualand. T **517** and similar horiz designs. Multicoloured. L-shaped phosphor bands. Self-adhesive. Die-cut.

1669	(4r.20) Type **517**	1·00	1·10
	a. Sheetlet. Nos. 1669/78	9·00	10·00
1670	(4r.20) Bokkeveld pride (*Geissorhiza splendidissima*)	1·00	1·10
1671	(4r.20) Springbok painted petals (*Lapeirousia silenoides*)	1·00	1·10
1672	(4r.20) White-eyed duiker-root (*Grielum humifusum*)	1·00	1·10
1673	(4r.20) Namaqualand daisy (*Dimorphotheca sinuata*)	1·00	1·10
1674	(4r.20) Satin boneseed (*Osteospermum pinnatum*)	1·00	1·10
1675	(4r.20) Karoo gazania (*Gazania rigida*)	1·00	1·10
1676	(4r.20) Harlequin hesperantha (*Hesperantha vaginata*)	1·00	1·10
1677	(4r.20) Showy sunflax (*Heliophila coronopifolia*)	1·00	1·10
1678	(4r.20) Red-eye sorrel (*Oxalis callosa*)	1·00	1·10
1669/78	*Set of 10*	9·00	10·00

Nos. 1669/78 were printed together, *se-tenant*, in sheetlets of ten stamps, all inscr 'Airmail Postcard' and sold for 4r.20 each. The left hand side of each stamp is cut around the flower, and the backing paper is divided into rectangles by rouletting.

Nos. 1669/78 have reversed L-shaped phosphor bands which extend along the right side of the stamp and part way along the bottom.

Nos. 1669/78 all have a wild flower scent contained in microscopic cells printed on the stamps using silkscreen.

518 Celebration

519 Young Woman running

(Des Jerry Lion. Litho)

2008 (5 Sept). World Cup Football, South Africa, 2010 (3rd issue). Sheet 105×65 mm. L-shaped phosphor bands. P 13½×14.

MS1679	**518** (4r.30) multicoloured	1·25	1·50

No. **MS**1679 is inscr 'AIRMAIL SOUTHERN AFRICA SMALL LETTER' and was sold for 3r.70.

(Des Thea Clemons. Litho Enschedé)

2008 (6 Sept). 30th Anniv of Alma Ata Declaration on Primary Health Care. Sheet 105×65 mm. L-shaped phosphor bands. P 13½×14.

MS1680	**519** (2r.05) multicoloured	1·00	1·00

No **MS**1680 is inscr 'Standard Postage' and was sold for 2r.05.

520 The Eastern Buttress and Devil's Tooth

(Litho Enschedé)

2008 (23 Sept). Drakensberg Park. T **520** and similar horiz designs. Multicoloured. L-shaped phosphor bands. P 13.

1681	(4r.90) Type **520**	1·25	1·25
	a. Sheetlet. Nos. 1681/4	4·50	4·50
1682	(4r.90) The Eastern Buttress seen from the Sentinel	1·25	1·25
1683	(4r.90) Amphitheatre seen from the Royal Natal National Park	1·25	1·25
1684	(4r.90) The Sentinel and the Amphitheatre	1·25	1·25
1681/4	*Set of 4*	4·50	4·50

Nos. 1681/4 were printed together, *se-tenant*, in sheetlets of four stamps, all inscr 'International Airmail Small Letter' and valid for 4r.90 each.

521 Main Building at Onderstepoort

(Des Rachel-Mari Ackermann. Litho Enschedé)

2008 (8 Oct). Centenary of Veterinary Research Laboratory, Onderstepoort. Sheet 105×65 mm. L-shaped phosphor band. P 13½×13.

MS1685	**521** (2r.05) multicoloured	1·10	1·10

No. **MS**1685 was inscr 'Standard Postage' and sold for 2r.05.

522 Aberdeen Post Office, Eastern Cape

523 Elephant

(Des Annemarie Wessels. Litho Enschedé)

2008 (9 Oct). World Post Day. South African Post Office Buildings. T **522** and similar vert designs. Multicoloured. Inverted L-shaped phosphor bands. P 13×13½.

1686	(2r.05) Type **522**	65	75
	a. Horiz strip of 5. Nos. 1686/90	3·00	3·25
1687	(2r.05) West Bank Post Office, East London, Eastern Cape	65	75
1688	(2r.05) Main Post Office, Durban	65	75
1689	(2r.05) Church Square Post Office, Pretoria	65	75
1690	(2r.05) Frankfort Post Office, Free State	65	75
1686/90	*Set of 5*	3·00	3·25

Nos. 1686/90 were printed together, *se-tenant*, as horizontal strips of five stamps in sheetlets of ten. They were inscr 'Standard Postage' and sold for 2r.05 each.

Nos. 1686/90 have inverted L-shaped phosphor bands which extend along the top and right of each stamp.

(Des Dr. Jack. Litho Southern Colour Print, New Zealand)

2008 (14 Nov). Wildlife. 'The Big Five' in Cartoons. Self-adhesive booklet stamps. T **523** and similar horiz designs. Multicoloured. L-shaped phosphor bands. P 12×12½.

1691	(4r.20) Type **523**	1·25	1·50
	a. Booklet pane. Nos. 1691/5, each ×2	9·00	12·00
1692	(4r.20) Lion	1·25	1·50
1693	(4r.20) Leopard	1·25	1·50
1694	(4r.20) Buffalo	1·25	1·50
1695	(4r.20) Rhinoceros	1·25	1·50
1691/5	*Set of 5*	4·75	6·50

Nos. 1691/5 were inscribed 'Airmail Postcard' and were valid for 4r.20 each.

Nos. 1691/5 have L-shaped phosphor bands which extend along the top and left of each stamp.

524 Early S.A.A. /S.A.L. Captain's Cap Badge and Uniform Insignia

525 Rose 'Johannesburg Sun'

(Des Hein Botha. Litho (Nos. 1696/701 also embossed) Enschedé)

2009 (30 Jan). 75th Anniv of South African Airways. T **524** and similar square designs showing Captain's cap badges and uniform insignia or aircraft tail fins. Multicoloured. Inverted L-shaped phosphor bands (Nos. 1696/701) or phosphor over parts of design (Nos. 1702/7). P 13.

1696	(2r.05) Type **524**	75	75
	a. Sheetlet. Nos. 1696/1701	4·00	4·00
1697	(2r.05) 'Flying springbok' and crown badge and pilot's wings, 1948	75	75
1698	(2r.05) 'Flying springbok' and arms of new South African Republic badge and arms wings, 1961	75	75
1699	(2r.05) 'Flying springbok' (facing right) badge and wings with shield, 1980s	75	75
1700	(2r.05) Flying springbok on blue shield badge and arms, 1991	75	75
1701	(2r.05) Flag emblem badge and arms, 1997	75	75
1702	(4r.90) Junkers Ju 53/3m, 1934–40	1·25	1·25
	a. Sheetlet. Nos. 1702/7	6·50	6·50
1703	(4r.90) Douglas DC-4, 1946–57	1·25	1·25
1704	(4r.90) Boeing 707, 1960–82	1·25	1·25
1705	(4r.90) Boeing 747, 1971–2008	1·25	1·25
1706	(4r.90) Airbus A300, 1976–2001	1·25	1·25
1707	(4r.90) Boeing 747, 1971–2008	1·25	1·25
1696/1707	*Set of 12*	10·50	10·50

Nos. 1696/1701 and 1702/7 were printed together, *se-tenant*, in separate sheetlets of six stamps. Nos. 1696/1701 were each inscr 'STANDARD POSTAGE' and initially sold for 2r.05 each.

Nos. 1702/7 were each inscr 'INTERNATIONAL AIRMAIL SMALL LETTER' and initially sold for 5r.60 each.

(Des Jeanlé Casarin. Litho Southern Colour Print, New Zealand)

2009 (13 Feb). 'All You Need is Love'. Sheet 167×187 mm containing T **525** and similar circular designs. Multicoloured. Phosphor frame. Self-adhesive. Die-cut perf 10½.

MS1708	(2r.25)×10 Type 525×2; 'Rina Hugo'×2; 'Beauty from Within'×2; 'Cotlands Rose'×2; 'Bewitched'×2	5·75	6·50

The stamps within **MS**1708 were all inscr 'Standard Postage'. The sheet was originally sold for 22r.50.

The backing paper of **MS**1708 is divided by lines of rouletting.

526 Sooty Albatross (*Phoebetria palpebrata*)

(Des Annemarie Wessels. Litho Enschedé)

2009 (2 Mar). Preserve the Polar Regions and Glaciers. Sheet 120×79 mm containing T **526** and similar horiz design. Multicoloured. L-shaped phosphor bands. P 13×13½.

MS1709	(2r.25) Type **526**; (5r.40) Jellyfish (*Dipulmaris*)	3·00	3·00

The stamps within **MS**1709 were inscr 'Standard Postage' and 'International Small Letter'. The miniature sheet was sold for 7r.65. The L-shaped phosphor bands extend along the top and right of each stamp.

527 President Motlanthe

(Des Thea Clemons. Litho Southern Colour Print, New Zealand)

2009 (19 Mar). President Kgalema Motlanthe. L-shaped phosphor bands.

1710	**527** (2r.05) multicoloured	1·00	60

No. 1710 was inscr 'STANDARD POSTAGE' and initially sold for 2r.05.

No. 1710 has L-shaped phosphor bands which extend along the top and left of the stamp.

528 Ergonomics in the Office

(Des Peter Sibanda. Litho Enschedé)

2009 (20 Mar). Occupational Health. T **528** and similar horiz designs. Multicoloured. P 13½×13.

1711	(2r.25) Type **528**	85	85
	a. Vert strip of 5. Nos. 1711/15	3·75	3·75
1712	(2r.25) Hearing test ('Medical surveillance')	85	85
1713	(2r.25) Firefighters ('Personal protective equipment')	85	85
1714	(2r.25) Inside a workshop ('Ensure a safe work place')	85	85
1715	(2r.25) Teaching safe method of lifting ('Training in the work place')	85	85
1711/15	*Set of 5*	3·75	3·75

Nos. 1711/15 were printed together, *se-tenant*, as vertical strips of five stamps in sheetlets of ten. They were inscr 'STANDARD POSTAGE' and originally sold for 2r.25 each.

529 The Benefit of the Doubt 2 (tapestry by Marlene Dumas), 2000

(Litho Southern Colour Print, New Zealand)

2009 (5 June). Artwork in the Constitutional Court. T **529** and similar multicoloured designs. L-shaped phosphor bands. P 14½.

1716	(2r.25) Type **530**	60	60
	a. Sheetlet. Nos. 1716/25	5·50	5·50
1717	(2r.25) Forgotten Family 1 (Penny Siopis), 1996 (51×35 mm)	60	60
1718	(2r.25) Bass Player (Dumile Feni)	60	60
1719	(2r.25) Head (William Kentridge), 1993	60	60
1720	(2r.25) Hotel with Landscape (Robert Hodgins), 1996 (51×35 mm)	60	60
1721	(2r.25) Hotlands 3 (Andrew Verster), 1993 (26×71 mm)	60	60
1722	(2r.25) Discussion (tapestry by Willie Bester), 1994 (51×35 mm)	60	60
1723	(2r.25) The Smoker (Gerard Sekoto), 1993 (51×35 mm)	60	60
1724	(2r.25) Tethered Monkey (Albert Adams)	60	60
1725	(2r.25) The Man Who Sang and the Woman Who Kept Silent 3 (Judith Mason)	60	60
1716/25	*Set of 10*	5·50	5·50

Nos. 1716/25, all inscr 'STANDARD POSTAGE', were printed together, *se-tenant*, in sheetlets of ten stamps, sold for 22r.50 per sheetlet.

The phosphor bands on Nos. 1716/25 extend along the top and right of each stamp.

530 Football Fan blowing Vuvuzela

(Des Rex Zimmer. Litho Enschedé)

2009 (14 June). World Cup Football, South Africa (2010) (4th issue). Sheet 105×65 mm. L-shaped phosphor band. P 13×13½.

MS1726 **530** (5r.40) multicoloured ... 2·75 2·75

No. **MS**1726 was inscr 'INTERNATIONAL AIRMAIL SMALL LETTER' and initially sold for 5r.40.

The phosphor bands on No. **MS**1726 extend along the top and right of the stamp.

531 Sugilite

(Des Sean Beukes. Litho Enschedé)

2009 (10 July). South African Gemstones. Sheet 120×70 mm containing T **531** and similar diamond-shaped designs. Multicoloured. L-shaped phosphor bands. P 13½.

MS1727 (4r.60)×4 Type **531**; Garnet; Jasper; Rodochrosite ... 7·00 7·00

The stamps within **MS**1727 were all inscr 'AIRMAIL POSTCARD' and were originally sold for 4r.60 each.

532 Jackass Penguin (*Spheniscus demersus*)

(Des Tobie Beele. Litho Southern Colour Print, New Zealand)

2009 (3 Aug). Sea and Coastal Birds of South Africa. T **532** and similar vert designs. Multicoloured. L-shaped phosphor bands. P 14½.

1728 (5r.40) Type **532** ... 2·25 2·25
a. Horiz strip of 5. Nos. 1728/32 ... 10·00 10·00
1729 (5r.40) Black oystercatcher (*Haematopus bachmani*) ... 2·25 2·25
1730 (5r.40) Common cape gannet (*Morus capensis*) ... 2·25 2·25
1731 (5r.40) Cape cormorant (*Phalacrocorax capensis*) ... 2·25 2·25
1732 (5r.40) Black backed seagull (*Larus dominicanus*) ... 2·25 2·25
1728/32 *Set of 5* ... 10·00 10·00

Nos. 1728/32 were printed together, *se-tenant*, as horizontal strips of five stamps in sheetlets of ten. They were inscr 'International Airmail Small Letter' and originally sold for 5r.40 each.

533 Gold Bowl

(Des Denis Murphy. Litho Southern Colour Print, New Zealand)

2009 (23 Sept). Mapungubwe Cultural Landscape. T **533** and similar horiz designs. Multicoloured. Inverted L-shaped phosphor bands. P 14½.

1733 (5r.40) Type **533** ... 1·50 1·50
a. Horiz strip of 5. Nos. 1733/7 ... 6·75 6·75
1734 (5r.40) Large and small bowls with spouts ... 1·50 1·50
1735 (5r.40) Gold rhinoceros ... 1·50 1·50
1736 (5r.40) Shallow terracotta bowl ... 1·50 1·50
1737 (5r.40) Gold scepter ... 1·50 1·50
1733/7 *Set of 5* ... 6·75 6·75

Nos. 1733/7 were printed together, *se-tenant*, as horizontal strips of five stamps in sheetlets of ten. They were inscr 'INTERNATIONAL SMALL LETTER' and originally sold for 5r.40 each.

The inverted L-shaped phosphor bands on Nos. 1733/7 extend along the top and right of each stamp.

534 First South African Stamp (1910 Opening of Union Parliament 2½d.)

535 Solomon Kalushi Mahlangu

(Des Thea Clemons. Litho Enschedé)

2009 (9 Oct). Joburg 1999 International Stamp Show, Johannesburg. Two sheets, each 105×65 mm, containing T **534** and similar vert design. Multicoloured. Inverted L-shaped phosphor bands. P 13½.

MS1738 (2r.25) Type **534** ... 1·10 1·10
MS1739 (5r.40) Exhibition logo (Nelson Mandela Bridge, Johannesburg) ... 2·50 2·50

No. **MS**1738 was inscr 'Standard Postage' and originally sold for 2r.25.

No. **MS**1739 was inscr 'INTERNATIONAL SMALL LETTER' and originally sold for 5r.40.

The inverted L-shaped phosphor bands on the stamps within **MS**1738/9 extend along the top and right of each stamp.

(Des Thea Clemons. Litho Cartor)

2009 (15 Oct). 30th Death Anniv of Solomon Kalushi Mahlangu. Sheet 105×65 mm. Inverted L-shaped phosphor bands. P 13×13½.

MS1740 **535** (2r.25) multicoloured ... 1·00 1·00

No. **MS**1740 was inscr 'Standard Postage' and originally sold for 2r.25.

The inverted L-shaped phosphor bands on the stamp within **MS**1740 extend along the top and right of the stamp.

536 Afrovenator

(Des Chantelle Basson. Litho Cartor)

2009 (2 Nov). Dinosaurs. Sheet 234×172 mm containing T **536** and similar multicoloured designs. Phosphor background. P 13.

MS1741 (4r.60)×10 Type **536**; Afrovenator skeleton; Heterodontosaurus (vert); Heterodontosaurus skeleton (vert); Ouranosaurus; Ouranosaurus skeleton; Jobaria (vert); Jobaria skeleton (vert); Suchomimus (vert); Suchomimus skeleton (vert) ... 13·00 13·00

The stamps within **MS**1741 were each inscr 'International Airmail Postcard' and sold for 4r.60 each. The stamps within **MS**1741 are printed using anaglyphs, stereo images that create a 3-D effect when seen through special glasses.

537 President Jacob Zuma

(Des Thea Clemons. Litho Cartor)

2009 (10 Nov). Inauguration of President Jacob Zuma. Phosphor background. P 13.

1742 **537** (2r.25) multicoloured ... 1·00 60

No. 1742 was inscr 'Standard Postage' and originally sold for 2r.25.

538 Human Figures and Cellphone

(Des Rozanne Backhouse. Litho)

2010 (18 Jan). Bridging the Digital Divide. Sheet 120×80 mm containing T **538** and similar multicoloured designs. Phosphor bands. P 14.

MS1743 (4r.05)×5 Type **538**; Cellphones, letters and buildings (28×28 mm); Postbox with computer code (parallelogram 28×40 mm); Open envelope with letter from university (triangle 80×40 mm) (p 13½ at top left only); Computer and rural village (triangle 80×40 mm) .... 5·00 6·00

The stamps within **MS**1743 were each inscr 'SOUHERN AFRICA SMALL LETTER' and sold for 4r.05 each.

The triangular stamps have phosphor bands at left and right, the square stamp has phosphor bands at top and right, and the parallelogram has phosphor bands at top and left of the stamp.

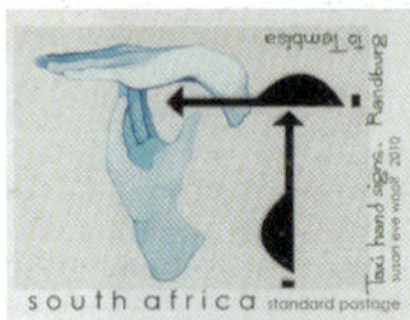

539 Randburg to Tembisa

(Des Susan Eve Woolf. Litho and thermography)

2010 (29 Jan). Taxi Hand Signs. T **539** and similar horiz designs. Multicoloured. Inverted L-shaped phosphor bands. P 13½×13.

1744	(2r.25) Type **539**	75	75
	a. Sheetlet. Nos. 1744/53	6·50	6·50
1745	(2r.25) Tembisa to Sebenza	75	75
1746	(2r.25) Turffontein to Mulbarton	75	75
1747	(2r.25) Gauteng to Johannesburg CBD	75	75
1748	(2r.25) Germiston to Katlehong	75	75
1749	(2r.25) Johannesburg to Sandton	75	75
1750	(2r.25) Alexandra to Randburg	75	75
1751	(2r.25) Emdeni to Highgate	75	75
1752	(2r.25) Local to the area	75	75
1753	(2r.25) Johannesburg to Phola Park	75	75
1744/53	*Set of* 10	6·50	6·50

Nos. 1744/53 were all inscr 'standard postage' and sold for 2r.25 each. They were printed with raised designs so that blind people could learn the signals, and contain traces of powdered limestone.

Nos. 1744/53 were printed together, *se-tenant*, in sheetlets of ten stamps.

The inverted L-shaped phosphor bands on Nos. 1744/53 extend along the top and right of each stamp.

540 Fish in Net and Beached Boat

(Des Jacoline Naudé. Litho)

2010 (19 Feb). The Life of Fisher Folk. T **540** and similar horiz designs. Multicoloured. Inverted L-shaped phosphor bands. P 13½×13.

1754	(5r.40) Type **540**	1·25	1·25
	a. Sheetlet. Nos. 1754/63	11·00	11·00
1755	(5r.40) Three fishermen launching boat	1·25	1·25
1756	(5r.40) Fisherman's cottage and setting sun	1·25	1·25
1757	(5r.40) Two fishermen sat on stern of beached boat	1·25	1·25
1758	(5r.40) Five fishermen walking away from beached boat	1·25	1·25
1759	(5r.40) Fishing village	1·25	1·25
1760	(5r.40) Cottage and two fishermen sat on stern of beached boat	1·25	1·25
1761	(5r.40) Angler and beached boat	1·25	1·25
1762	(5r.40) Fish, cottages and beached boat JEA 4JR	1·25	1·25
1763	(5r.40) Old man and rack of drying fish	1·25	1·25
1754/63	*Set of* 10	11·00	11·00

Nos. 1754/63 were all inscr 'international airmail small letter' and sold for 5r.40 each.

Nos. 1754/63 were printed together, *se-tenant*, in sheetlets of ten, each sheetlet cut around in the shape of a fish.

The inverted L-shaped phosphor bands on Nos. 1754/63 extend along the top and right of each stamp.

541 Giant African Mantis (*Sphodromantis viridis*) and Common Lionfish (*Pterois miles*)

(Des Tyrone Patrick. Litho)

2010 (12 Mar). International Year of Biodiversity. Sheet 126×91 mm containing T **541** and similar horiz designs. Multicoloured. Inverted L-shaped phosphor bands. P 13½.

MS1764 (15r.85)×4 Type **541**; Black rhinoceros (*Diceros bicornis*) and red-billed oxpecker (*Buphagus erythrorhynchus*); Common chameleon (*Chamaeleo chamaeleon*) and African reed frog (*Hyperolius argus*); Lilac-breasted roller (*Coracias caudatus*) and baobab tree (*Adansonia digitata*) .... 17·00 18·00

The stamps within **MS**1764 were all inscr 'SMALL REGISTERED LETTER' and originally sold for 15r.85 each.

The inverted L-shaped phosphor bands on the stamps within **MS**1764 extend along the top and right of each stamp.

542 Player, Football, Namibian Flag and Zakumi Mascot

543 Elephant

(Des Anja Denker. Litho Enschedé)

2010 (9 Apr). Third Joint Issue of Southern Africa Postal Operators Association Members. World Cup Football Championship, South Africa (5th issue). Sheet 188×167 mm containing T **542** and similar circular designs, each showing Zakumi mascot, different silhouettes of players on football, and the national flag of a member country. P 13½.

MS1765 5r.75×9 Type **542**; South Africa; Zimbabwe; Malawi; Swaziland; Botswana; Mauritius; Lesotho; Zambia .... 17·00 17·00

The stamps within **MS**1765 were each perforated in a circle contained within an outer perforated square.

Similar miniature sheets were issued by Botswana, Lesotho, Malawi, Mauritius, Namibia, Swaziland, Zambia and Zimbabwe.

2010 (5 May). Wildlife. "The Big Five". Self-adhesive booklet stamps. T **543** and similar vert designs. Multicoloured. Litho. L-shaped phosphor bands. Die-cut perf 12½×12.

1766	(4r.90) Type **543**	1·75	1·90
	a. Booklet pane. Nos. 1766/70, each ×2	15·00	
1767	(4r.90) Lion	1·75	1·90
1768	(4r.90) Buffalo	1·75	1·90
1769	(4r.90) Leopard	1·75	1·90
1770	(4r.90) Rhinoceros	1·75	1·90
1766/70	*Set of* 5	8·00	8·50

Nos. 1766/70 were inscribed 'AIRMAIL POSTCARD' and originally sold for 4r.90 each. These stamps have straight edges at top and left (Type **543**) or at either top or bottom (others).

544 'Number Four' (Old Fort Prison Complex)

(Litho Enschedé)

2010 (28 May). History of Constitution Hill. T **544** and similar multicoloured designs. Inverted L-shaped phosphor bands. P 13½.

1771	2r.40 Type **544**	80	80
	a. Sheetlet. Nos. 1771/80	6·50	6·50
1772	2r.40 Atrium of the women's jail (24×40 mm)	80	80
1773	2r.40 The Awaiting Trial Block, 1954	80	80
1774	2r.40 Flogging frame in cell no. 3	80	80
1775	2r.40 Remaining stairwells of the Awaiting Trial Block (24×40 mm)	80	80
1776	2r.40 Cells in the Fort (24×40 mm)	80	80
1777	2r.40 Isolation cells in Number Four (24×81 mm)	80	80
1778	2r.40 The Guard House in front of the isolation cells (24×40 mm)	80	80
1779	2r.40 Entrance to The Fort	80	80
1780	2r.40 The Ramparts (96×40 mm)	80	80
1771/80 *Set of 9*		6·50	6·50

Nos. 1771/80 were printed together, *se-tenant*, in sheetlets of nine stamps with a central label giving descriptions of the stamps.

545 Zakumi Mascot holding Football

(Des Thea Clemons. Litho Enschedé)

2010 (11 June). World Cup Football Championship, South Africa (6th issue). T **545** and similar vert designs showing Zakumi mascot. Multicoloured. L-shaped phosphor bands. Die-cut.

1781	2r.40 Type **545**	90	90
1782	2r.40 Zakumi about to kick ball	90	90
1783	2r.40 Zakumi holding South African flag	90	90
1784	2r.40 Zakumi kicking ball	90	90
1785	2r.40 Zakumi with arms raised in triumph	90	90
1781/5 *Set of 5*		4·50	4·50

Nos. 1781/5 are die-cut around the design.

Nos. 1781/5 were printed in sheetlets of 10 containing two horizontal strips of the five designs.

The backing paper is divided into rectangles by lines of rouletting.

546 Official World Cup 2010 Emblem

(Des Thea Clemons. Litho Southern Colour Print, New Zealand)

2010 (11 June). World Cup Football Championship, South Africa (7th issue). T **546** and similar circular designs. Multicoloured. Circular phosphor bands. Die-cut wavy edge.

MS1786 Circular 125×125 mm. 4r.90×6 Type **546**×2; Jabulami (official match ball)×2; World Cup trophy×2 ... 8·50 8·50

547 Tank Engine *Natal*, 1860

(Des Hein Botha. Litho Enschedé)

2010 (25 June). 150th Anniv of South African Railways. T **547** and similar horiz designs. Multicoloured. Inverted L-shaped phosphor bands. P 13½×13.

1787	2r.40 Type **547**	95	95
	a. Sheetlet. Nos. 1787/96	8·50	8·50
1788	2r.40 Class NGG 16 Garratt steam locomotive, 1937	95	95
1789	2r.40 Class 24 steam locomotive pulling Outeniqua Choo-Tjoe train, 1948	95	95
1790	2r.40 Class 25 steam locomotive, 1953	95	95
1791	2r.40 Class GMA/M Garratt steam locomotive, 1954	95	95
1792	2r.40 Class 35 Co-Co diesel-electric locomotive, 1974	95	95
1793	2r.40 Class 9E Co-Co 50KV ac electric locomotive, 1978	95	95
1794	2r.40 Class 26 steam locomotive, No. 3450 *Red Devil*, 1981	95	95
1795	2r.40 Class 19E Bo-Bo dual voltage electric locomotive, 2009	95	95
1796	2r.40 Gautrain Electrostar Bo-bo, 2010	95	95
1787/96 *Set of 10*		8·50	8·50

Nos. 1787/96 were printed together, *se-tenant*, in sheetlets of ten stamps.

The inverted L-shaped phosphor bands on Nos. 1787/96 extend along the top and right of each stamp.

548 Nelson Mandela Bay Stadium, Port Elizabeth

(Des Thea Clemons. Litho Cartor)

2010 (19 July). South African Sports Stadiums. T **548** and similar horiz designs. Multicoloured. Phosphorised paper. P 13½×13.

1797	2r.40 Type **548**	80	80
	a. Sheetlet. Nos. 1797/806	7·25	7·25
1798	2r.40 Ellis Park Stadium, Johannesburg	80	80
1799	2r.40 Free State Stadium, Bloemfontein	80	80
1800	2r.40 Cape Town Stadium	80	80
1801	2r.40 Moses Mabhida Stadium, Durban	80	80
1802	2r.40 Loftus Versfeld Stadium, Tshwane/ Pretoria	80	80
1803	2r.40 Peter Mokaba Stadium, Polokwane	80	80
1804	2r.40 Mbombela Stadium, Nelspruit	80	80
1805	2r.40 Soccer City Stadium, Johannesburg	80	80
1806	2r.40 Royal Bafokeng Stadium, Rustenburg	80	80
1797/1806 *Set of 10*		7·25	7·25

Nos. 1797/806 were printed together, *se-tenant*, in sheetlets of ten stamps.

549 Blue Korhaan (*Eupodotis caerulescens*)

550 Namaqua Chameleon (*Chamaeleo namaquensis*)

(Des André Olwage. Litho Enschedé)

2010 (6 Aug). Grassland Birds of South Africa. T **549** and similar vert designs. Multicoloured. L-shaped phosphor bands. P 13.

1807	5r.75 Type **549**	2·25	2·25
	a. Horiz strip of 5. Nos. 1807/11	10·00	10·00
1808	5r.75 Buff-streaked chat (*Oenanthe bifasciata*)	2·25	2·25
1809	5r.75 White-bellied korhaan (*Eupodotis cafra*)	2·25	2·25
1810	5r.75 White winged flufftail (*Sarothrura ayresi*)	2·25	2·25
1811	5r.75 Yellow-breasted pipit (*Anthus chloris*)	2·25	2·25
1870/11 *Set of 5*		10·00	10·00

Nos. 1807/11 were printed together, *se-tenant*, as horizontal strips of five stamps in sheetlets of ten.

(Des Jolinidi Ferreira. Litho)

2010 (23 Sept). Richtersveld Cultural and Botanical Landscape. T **550** and similar horiz designs. Multicoloured. P 13½×13.

1812	2r.40 Type **550**	1·00	1·00
	a. Horiz strip of 5. Nos. 1812/16	4·50	4·50
1813	2r.40 Namaqua sandgrouse (*Pterocles namaqua*)	1·00	1·00
1814	2r.40 Bastard quiver tree (*Aloe pilansii*)	1·00	1·00
1815	2r.40 Nama woman	1·00	1·00
1816	2r.40 Grey rhebok (*Pelea carpreolus*)	1·00	1·00
1812/16 *Set of 5*		4·50	4·50

Nos. 1812/16 were printed together, *se-tenant*, as horizontal strips of five stamps in sheetlets of ten.

551 1910 2½d. Blue (first South African stamp)

(Des Thea Clemons. Litho)

2010 (9 Oct). World Post Day. 'Celebrating Printing Techniques on South African Stamps'. T **551** and similar multicoloured designs. Inverted L-shaped phosphor bands (at top and right). P 13½.

1817 (2r.40) Type **551** 80 80
a. Sheetlet. Nos. 1817/28 8·50 8·50
1818 (2r.40) 1930 1s. Black and blue wildebeest stamp (first rotogravure stamp) 80 80
1819 (2r.40) 1929 4d. de Havilland DH.60 Cirrus Moth airmail stamp (first letterpress stamp by Government Printing Works). 80 80
1820 (2r.40) 2009 75th anniv of South African Airways standard postage stamp (first stamp embossed and printed with gold foil) 80 80
1821 (2r.40) 1974 Centenary of the Burgerspond Coin 9c. stamp (first litho stamp) (30×60 mm) 80 80
1822 (2r.40) 1963 50th anniv of Kirstenbosch Botanic Gardens 2½c. stamp (first stamp produced using process colour) (60×30 mm) 80 80
1823 (2r.40) 1970 150th anniv of Bible Society 12½c. stamp (first stamp with gold foil) (60×30 mm) 80 80
1824 (2r.40) 2005 Prevention of blindness standard postage stamp (first Braille stamp) (60×30 mm) 80 80
1825 (2r.40) 2008 Karoo gazania airmail postcard stamp (Flowers of Namaqualand first stamps printed with fragrance) (60×30 mm) 80 80
1826 (2r.40) 1997 Tswana knife handle standard postage stamp (Year of Cultural Experiences first superlitho stamps in world) (30×60 mm) 80 80
1827 (2r.40) 2009 Suchomimus International airmail postcard stamp (Dinosaurs first 3D effect stamps) 80 80
1828 (2r.40) 1974 25th anniv of Voortrekker Monument 4c. stamp (first intaglio stamp) (90×30 mm) 80 80
1817/28 *Set of 12* 8·50 8·50

Nos. 1817/28 were all inscr 'Standard Postage' and originally sold for 2r.40 each.

The face values on the original stamps have been digitally obscured.

Nos. 1817/28 were printed together, *se-tenant*, in sheetlets of 12 stamps.

552 Ladybird

(Des Thea Clemons. Litho)

2010 (27 Oct)–**11** (18 Feb). South African Beadwork. T **552** and similar multicoloured designs. Phosphorised paper. P 14½.

(a) Ordinary gum. Phosphorised paper. P 14½.

1829 5c. Type **552** 10 10
1830 10c. Dove 10 10
1831 20c. Llama 15 15
1832 30c. Cell phone 15 15
1833 40c. Hammerhead bird 15 15
1834 50c. Aeroplane 20 20
1835 60c. Angel 20 20
1836 70c. Nguni cow 25 25
1837 80c. Boxer 25 25
1838 90c. Zebra 30 30
1839 1r. Miner 30 30
1840 2r. Tsonga fertility figure 55 55
1841 (2r.40) Zulu neckpiece (vert) 60 60
a. Horiz strip of 5. Nos. 1841/5 2·75 2·75
1842 (2r.40) Ndebele neckpiece (vert) 60 60
1843 (2r.40) Xhosa neckpiece (vert) 60 60
1844 (2r.40) Swazi neckpiece (vert) 60 60
1845 (2r.40) Tsonga love token pin (vert) 60 60
1846 3r. Ndebele married woman's apron 60 60
1847 (4r.80) Tsonga neckpiece 1·25 1·25
1848 (4r.90) Zulu neckpieces 1·25 1·25
1849 5r. Mfengu tobacco bag 1·40 1·40
1850 (5r.40) Bhaca neckpiece (blue, white, green, yellow and black beads) 1·75 1·75
1851 (6r.) Bhaca neckpiece (blue, red and white beads) 2·25 2·25
1852 10r. South Sotho ceremonial whisk 2·75 2·75
1853 (Registered letter small) Bhaca neckpiece (yellow, red, blue and white beads) 3·25 3·25
1854 (Registered letter medium) Venda beadwork pin 3·25 3·25
1855 20r. Zulu neckpiece made of lion claws 5·50 5·50
1829/55 *Set of 26* 26·00 26·00

(b) Self-adhesive booklet stamps

1856 (2r.40) As No. 1841 60 60
a. Booklet pane. Nos. 1856/60, each ×2 6·00
b. Booklet pane. Nos. 1856/60, each ×20 60·00
1857 (2r.40) As No. 1842 60 60
1858 (2r.40) As No. 1843 60 60
1859 (2r.40) As No. 1844 60 60
1860 (2r.40) As No. 1845 60 60
1861 (4r.80) As No. 1847 but vert 1·25 1·25
a. Booklet pane. No. 1861×10 12·00
b. Booklet pane. No. 1861×50 60·00
1862 (6r.) As No. 1851 but vert 2·25 2·25
a. Booklet pane. No. 1862 ×10 22·00
b. Booklet pane. No. 1862 ×50 £100
1856/62 *Set of 7* 6·50 6·50

Nos. 1841/5 were inscr 'Standard Postage' and originally sold for 2r.40 each.

Nos. 1841/5 were printed together, *se-tenant*, in horizontal strips of five throughout the sheet.

No. 1847 was inscr 'B5' and originally sold for 4r.80.

No. 1848 was inscr 'Airmail Postcard' and originally sold for 4r.90.

No. 1850 was inscr 'International Small Letter' and originally sold for 5r.40.

No. 1851 was inscr 'B4' and originally sold for 6r.

Nos. 1856/8 are left for self-adhesive booklet stamps not yet received.

Nos. 1859/65 are left for possible additions to this definitive series.

553 Arms, 1910–30

(Des Thea Clemons. Litho Jhai British Security Printing Co. Ltd, Thailand)

2010 (29 Oct). Centenary of South Africa. Sheet 130×70 mm containing T **553** and similar square designs showing the coats of arms of South Africa from 1910 to 2010. 'All-over' phosphor. Multicoloured. P 13½.

MS1866 (2r.40)×4 Type **553**; Arms 1930–32 (on green base); Arms 1932–2000 (on green base, motto 'EX' 'UNITATE' 'VIRES' in three separate folds of scroll); Current coat of arms (shield with human figures, elephant tusks and secretary bird) 2·50 2·50

The stamps within **MS**1866 were all inscr 'Standard Postage' and were originally valid for 2r.40 each.

554 'First SA film that won an Academy Award® for Best Foreign Language Film of the Year'

(Des Thea Clemons. Litho)

2010 (5 Nov). South African Quiz. T **554** and similar horiz designs showing quiz questions with the answers obliterated by scratch off gold ink. Multicoloured. L-shaped phosphor bands. P 13½×13.

1867 4r.90 Type **554** 1·00 1·00
a. Sheetlet. Nos. 1867/76 9·00 9·00

1868	4r.90 'Number of UNESCO World Heritage Sites in SA'	1·00	1·00
1869	4r.90 'Which SA invention has been to the moon?'	1·00	1·00
1870	4r.90 'Which fish is known as a living fossil?'	1·00	1·00
1871	4r.90 'Indian spiritual and political leader whose career started in SA'	1·00	1·00
1872	4r.90 'When were SA's gold and diamond deposits formed?'	1·00	1·00
1873	4r.90 'Animal used by Dr Chris Barnard in trials preceding the first heart transplant'	1·00	1·00
1874	4r.90 'Telescope strong enough to see candle-light on the moon'	1·00	1·00
1875	4r.90 'The largest bird in the world occurring in SA'	1·00	1·00
1876	4r.90 'Where in SA was gold first mined?'	1·00	1·00
1867/76	*Set of* 10	9·00	9·00

Nos. 1867/76 were printed together, *se-tenant*, in sheetlets of ten stamps.

555 African Wild Cat (*Felis silvestris*)

(Des Annemarie Wessels. Litho Enschedé)

2011 (4 Feb). Small African Wild Cats. T **555** and similar multicoloured designs. Phosphorised paper. P 13½.

1877	(4r.30) Type **555**	1·25	1·25
	a. Sheetlet. Nos. 1877/81, each ×2	10·00	
1878	(4r.30) Serval (*Leptailarus serval*) (30×30 mm)	1·25	1·25
1879	(4r.30) Caracal (*Caracal caracal*) (30×30 mm)	1·25	1·25
1880	(4r.30) Black-footed cat (*Felis nigripes*) (30×30 mm)	1·25	1·25
1881	(4r.30) African golden cat (*Profelis aurata*) (30×30 mm)	1·25	1·25
1877/81	*Set of* 5	5·50	5·50

Nos. 1877/81 were all inscr 'Africa Airmail' and were originally valid for 4r.30 each.

Nos. 1877/81 were printed together, *se-tenant*, in sheetlets of ten stamps containing two of each design, No. 1877 at left of the sheetlet and Nos. 1878/81 in two blocks of four.

No. 1877 was perforated around the cat's head which is contained within an outer perforated square which continued the design.

556 Engineering Sumbandilasat

(Des Thea Clemons. Litho Enschedé)

2011 (1 Apr). Sumbandilasat (South African micro-satellite). T **556** and similar multicoloured designs. 'All-over' phosphor. P 13½×13 (horiz) or 13×13½ (vert).

1882	(2r.50) Type **556** (University of Stellenbosch)	75	75
	a. Sheetlet. Nos. 1882/6, each ×2	6·50	6·50
1883	(2r.50) Sumbandilasat in orbit	75	75
1884	(2r.50) 12m S-band antenna at Hartebeeshoek (satellite tracking)	75	75
1885	(2r.50) Soyuz 2.1b rocket on launch platform, Baikonur Cosmodrome, Kazakhstan (launch of Sumbandilasat), 2009	75	75
1886	(2r.50) Sumbandilasat (vert)	75	75
1882/6	*Set of* 5	3·25	3·25

Nos. 1882/6 were inscr 'STANDARD POSTAGE' and were orignally valid for 2r.50.

Nos. 1882/6 were printed together in sheetlets of ten stamps containing two of each design.

557 Opening Words of Preamble to the Constitution

(Des Muano Mainganye. Litho Cartor)

2011 (23 May). Honouring the Constitution. Sheet 105×75 mm. P 13.

MS1887	557 2r.50 multicoloured	1·00	1·00

558 //gwasi

559 Green Twinspot *Mandingoa nitidula*

(Des Hein Botha. Litho Cartor)

2011 (30 June). Rare Musical Instruments. T **558** and similar horiz designs. P 13.

1888	6r. Type **558**	1·50	1·50
	a. Sheetlet. Nos. 1888/97	12·00	12·00
1889	6r. Ramkie	1·50	1·50
1890	6r. Sansa	1·50	1·50
1891	6r. Drums	1·50	1·50
1892	6r. Bullroarer	1·50	1·50
1893	6r. Horns	1·50	1·50
1894	6r. Flute	1·50	1·50
1895	6r. Xylophone	1·50	1·50
1896	6r. Rattles	1·50	1·50
1897	6r. Bows	1·50	1·50
1888/97	*Set of* 10	12·00	12·00

Nos. 1888/97 were printed together, *se-tenant*, in sheetlets of ten.

(Des André Olwage. Litho Enschedé)

2011 (15 July). Forest Birds of South Africa. T **559** and similar vert designs. Multicoloured. P 13×13½.

1898	6r. Type **559**	1·50	1·50
	a Horiz strip of 5. Nos. 1898/902	7·50	7·50
1899	6r. Olive bush-shrike (*Telophorus olivaceus*)	1·50	1·50
1900	6r. Cape parrot (*Poicephalus robustus*)	1·50	1·50
1901	6r. Knysna turaco (*Tauraco corythaix*)	1·50	1·50
1902	6r. African crowned eagle (*Stephanoaetus coronatus*)	1·50	1·50
1898/902	*Set of* 5	7·50	7·50

560 Spinach

561 Springbok Emblem (1906-33)

(Des Will Lourens. Litho Cartor)

2011 (12 Aug). Green Earth Healthy Garden. Sheet 155×82 mm containing T **560** and similar square designs. Multicoloured. P 13.

MS1903	(6r.25)×6 Type **560**; Tomatoes; Beetroot; Carrots; Cabbage; Butternut squash	9·00	9·00

The stamps within **MS**1903 were all inscr 'B4' and were originally valid for 6r.25.

2011 (19 Aug). Evolution of the Springbok Emblem. T **561** and similar vert designs showing the springbok emblem of the South African national rugby team. Multicoloured. P 14½.

1904 (6r.) Type **561** ... 1·50 1·50
a. Sheetlet. Nos. 1904/13 ... 12·00 12·00
1905 (6r.) South African Rugby Board badge, 1935–72 ... 1·50 1·50
1906 (6r.) Springbok emblem, 1937–62 ... 1·50 1·50
1907 (6r.) Springbok emblem, 1963–4 ... 1·50 1·50
1908 (6r.) Springbok emblem, 1965–89 ... 1·50 1·50
1909 (6r.) South African Rugby Union badge, 1966–91 ... 1·50 1·50
1910 (6r.) Springbok emblem, 1992–5 ... 1·50 1·50
1911 (6r.) Springbok emblem, 1996–2003 ... 1·50 1·50
1912 (6r.) Springbok emblem, 2004–8 ... 1·50 1·50
1913 (6r.) Springbok emblem, 2009–1 ... 1·50 1·50
1904/13 *Set of* 10 ... 12·00 12·00

Nos. 1904/13 were printed together, *se-tenant*, in sheetlets of ten stamps.

MACHINE LABELS

From 14 August (1986) gummed labels in the above design, ranging in value from 1c. to 99r.99, were available from an experimental machine at Sunnyside Post Office in Pretoria. The machine was moved to the "Johannesburg 100" exhibition from 6 to 11 October 1986 and was then reinstalled at Sunnyside on 17 October 1986. Further machines were introduced subsequently and each can be identified by a code number, between P.001 and P.034, at right. Commemorative labels were subsequently available at "PAARL 300" (1987), "PIETERMARITZBURG 150" (1988), "WANDERERS 101" (1989), "STAMPS 150" (1990), "CAPE TOWN 1991", "PRETORIA 92", eTHEKWINI (Durban 1993) and "BENONI '94" stamp exhibitions.

A new series of machine labels, with nine different designs showing province landscapes, was introduced on 20 October 1998 with operational values from 1r.10 upwards. Sets showing other face values from 10c. to 20r. were available against special order.

STAMP BOOKLETS

1913. Black on red cover. With "UNION OF SOUTH AFRICA" at top and "UNIE VAN ZUID AFRIKA" at foot. Stapled.

SB1 2s.6d. booklet containing twelve ½d. and twenty-four 1d. (Nos. 3/4) in blocks of 6 ... £6000

1913–20. Black on red cover with "UNION OF SOUTH AFRICA" and "UNIE VAN ZUID AFRIKA" both at top. Stapled.

SB2 2s.6d. booklet containing twelve ½d. and twenty-four 1d. (Nos. 3/4) in blocks of 6 ... £6000
a. Black on pink cover (1920) ... £6000

1921. Black on salmon-pink cover with "UNION OF SOUTH AFRICA" and "UNIE VAN ZUID AFRIKA" either side of arms and telegraph rates beneath. Stapled.

SB3 3s. booklet containing twelve ½d., 1d. and 1½d. (Nos. 3/5) in blocks of 6 ... £475

1922. Black on salmon-pink cover as No. SB3 surch. Stapled.

SB4 3s.6d. on 3s. booklet containing twelve ½d., 1d. and 2d. (Nos. 3/4, 6) in blocks of 6 ... £1100

1926. Black on salmon-pink cover as No. SB3. Stitched.

SB5 2s.6d. booklet containing twelve ½d. and twenty-four 1d. (Nos. 30/1) ... £2500

1927. Black on salmon-pink cover as No. SB3, but inscr "Union of South Africa" and "Unie van Suidafrika". Stitched.

SB6 2s.6d. booklet containing twelve ½d. and twenty-four 1d. (Nos. 30e, 31d) ... £6000

1930. Black on pink cover as No. SB6, but with advertisement at foot instead of telegraph rates. Stitched.

SB7 2s.6d. booklet containing twelve ½d. and twenty-four 1d. (Nos. 42/3) in blocks of 6 ... £2250

1931. Black on pink cover. Smaller inscr and advertisement on front cover. Stitched.

SB8 3s. booklet containing twelve 1d. (No. 43) in blocks of 6 and twelve 2d. (No. 44) in blocks of 4 £2250

1935. Black on lemon cover. Advertisement on front cover. Stitched.

SB9 2s.6d. booklet containing two panes of six ½d. (No. 54c) and four panes of six 1d. (No. 56e), all with adverts on margins ... £300

1937. Black on lemon cover. Advertisement on front cover. Stitched.

SB10 2s.6d. booklet containing two panes of six ½d. (No. 75ca) and four panes of six 1d. (No. 56f), all with blank margins ... £650

1937. Machine vended booklets. Red cover. Stitched.

SB11 6d. booklet containing four ½d. and 1d. (Nos. 75*c*, 56) in pairs ... 7·00

1938. Machine vended booklets. Blue cover. Stitched.

SB12 3d. booklet containing ½d. and 1d. (Nos. 75*c*, 56), each in pair ... 40·00

1938. Black on buff cover. Union arms at top left with advertisement at foot. Stitched.

SB13 2s.6d. booklet containing twelve ½d. and twenty-four 1d. (Nos. 75*c*, 56) in blocks of 6 ... £700

1939. Black on buff cover. Union arms centred at top with advertisement at foot. Stitched.

SB14 2s.6d. booklet containing twelve ½d. and twenty-four 1d. (Nos. 75*c*, 56) in blocks of 6 ... £700

1939–40. Green on buff cover. Union arms centred at top with large advertisement at bottom left. Stitched.

SB15 2s.6d. booklet containing twelve ½d. and twenty-four 1d. (Nos. 75*c*, 56) in blocks of 6 ... £2500
a. Blue on buff cover (1940) ... £150

1941. Blue on buff cover as No. SB15. Stitched.

SB17 2s.6d. booklet containing twelve ½d. and 1d. (Nos. 75*c*, 56) in blocks of 6 and 1½d. (No. 57) in block of 4 £170

1948. Black on buff cover. With advertisement. Stitched.

SB18 3s. booklet containing two panes of six ½d., 1d. and 1½d. (Nos. 114a, 56h, 87b), all with postal slogans on margins, and pane of air mail labels 32·00

1951. Black on buff cover. Stitched.

SB19 3s.6d. booklet containing two panes of six ½d., 1d. and 2d. (Nos. 114ca, 115a, 134a), each with margins at right ... 13·00

B **1** City Hall, Durban

1987 (16 Nov). ?88 Flood Relief Fund. Multicoloured covers as Type B **1**. Stamps attached by selvedge.

SB20 2r.60 booklet (cover Type B 1) containing 16c.+10c. (Nos. 624/5) in block of 10 ... 9·00
SB21 2r.60 booklet (cover, 139×85 mm, showing Bible) containing 16c.+10c. (Nos. 629/30) in block of 10 (1.12.87) ... 9·00
SB22 2r.60 booklet (cover showing Bartolomeu Dias) containing 16c.+10c. (Nos. 635/6) in block of 10 (1.3.88) ... 9·00
SB23 2r.60 booklet (cover, 125×90 mm, showing Huguenot Monument, Franschhoek) containing ten 16c.+10c. (Nos. 641/2) in block of 10 (13.4.88)... 7·50

B **2** Stamp No. 787

1993 (7 May). Aviation in South Africa. Multicoloured cover as Type B **2**. Stamps attached by selvedge.

SB24 4r.50 booklet containing 45c. (Nos. 779/803) in block of 10 (back cover information in greybox) .... 16·00
a. ditto. (back cover information in red box) .... 16·00

Five versions of No. SB24/a exist showing different combinations of Nos. 779/803, *se-tenant* in panes of 10 (2×5). The Philatelic Bureau sold the booklets in sets of ten, each pane being numbered at foot.

Two versions of SB24 exist; with and without postage rate information on the inside front cover.

1993 (3 Sept). Endangered Fauna. Multicoloured cover as Type B **2** but showing No. 821. Stamps attached by selvedge.

SB25 4r.50 booklet containing "Standardised mail" stamp (No. 821) in block of 10 .... 5·50

B **3** Lioness and Cubs Drinking (Illustration further reduced. Actual size 142×64 mm)

1993 (12 Nov). Tourism. Multicoloured covers as Type B **3**. Stamps attached by selvedge. Five different cover designs: (a) Type B **3** (b) Luxury hotel (c) Table Mountain (d) Blue Train (e) Field of flowers.

SB26 8r.50 booklet containing 85c. (Nos. 826/30) in block of 10 (any cover) .... 7·50
Set of 5 different cover designs .... 35·00

B **4**

1995. Endangered Fauna. Ultramarine and bright scarlet cover as Type B **4**. Stamps attached by selvedge with outer edges of pane imperf.

SB27 (4r.50) booklet containing pane of 10 "Standardised mail" stamps (No. 821a) .... 5·50
a. Containing booklet pane No. 821ba (9.4.96) ... 5·50

No. SB27 as initially sold at 4r.50 which was increased to 5r. on 30 September 1994, to 6r. on 1 April 1995 and to 7r. in August 1996.

1995 (Mar). Tourism. Booklet No. SB26 with additional label inscr "FOR OVERSEAS POSTCARDS ONLY USE 1×85 c+1×5c = 90c.".

SB28 9r. booklet containing 85c. (Nos. 826/30 in block of 10 plus 5c. (No. 806) in strip of 10) (any cover) .... 14·00
a. With 5c. (No. 656) in block of 10 (5×2) .... 14·00
b. With 5c. (No. 806) in block of 10 (5×2) .... 14·00

1995 (Apr). Tourism. Booklet No. SB24 with additional label inscr "FOR OVERSEAS POSTCARDS ONLY USE 2×45c Stamps = 90c".

SB29 4r.50 booklet containing 45c. (Nos. 799/803) in block of 10 .... 14·00

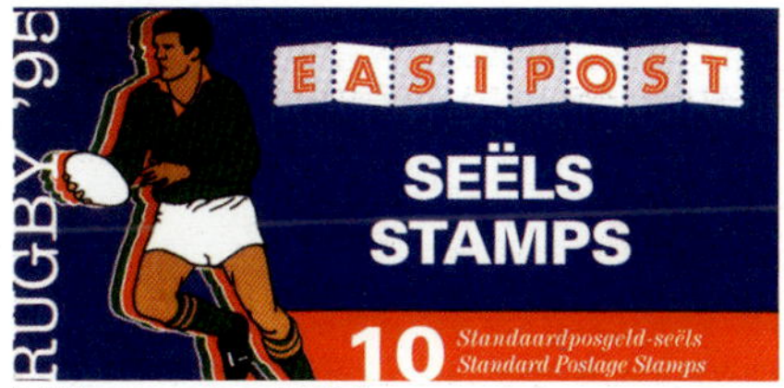

B **5** Player running with Ball

1995 (25 May). World Cup Rugby Championship, South Africa. Multicoloured cover as Type B **5**. Stamps attached by selvedge.

SB30 (6r.) booklet containing pane of 10 "STANDARDISED POSTAGE" stamps (No. 875ab) .... 3·25

SB31 (6r.) booklet containing pane of 10 "STANDARDISED POSTAGE" stamps (No. 876ab) .... 3·25

1995 (16 Sept). Masakhane Campaign. Bright scarlet and bright ultramarine covers as Type B **4**. Stamps attached by selvedge.

SB32 (6r.) booklet containing pane of ten "STANDARD POSTAGE" stamps (No. 884a) .... 2·00

SB33 (6r.) booklet containing pane of ten "STANDARD POSTAGE" stamps (No. 884ba) (1 Dec) .... 2·00

B **6** Jackass Penguin

1995 (1 Dec). Endangered Fauna. Multicoloured cover as Type B **6**. Stamps attached by selvedge.

SB34 9r. booklet containing pane of ten 90c. (No. 816a) 6·50

B **7** Lion

1996 (8 May). Tourism. Multicoloured cover as Type B **7**. Stamps attached by selvedge.

SB35 (5r.) booklet containing pane of 5 "Airmail postcard rate" stamps and five labels (No. 821cc) .... 3·25
a. As No. SB35, but with additional tab and hole at right (Dec) .... 3·25

B **8** Drummer and Decorations

1996 (9 Oct). Christmas. Multicoloured cover as Type B **8**. Stamps attached by selvedge.

SB36 7r. booklet containing pane of ten 70c. (No. 937a) 3·00

1996 (Nov). "Indaba '96" Tourism Exhibition, Durban. Multicoloured cover as Type B **7**, but 210×75 mm with inscr at right. Stamps affixed by selvedge.

SB37 (5r.) booklet containing pane of 5 "Airmail postcard rate" stamps, 3 advertising and 2 airmail labels (No. 821cb) .... 3·25

B **9** Landscape and Sunflower (Illustration reduced. Actual size 135×55 mm)

1997 (7–5 March). National Water Conservation. Multicoloured cover as Type B **9**. Pane attached by selvedge.

SB38 7r. booklet containing pane of ten 70c. (No. 951a) .... 3·50
 a. Containing booklet pane No. 951ba (25 Mar)... 3·50

B **10** Black Rhinoceros (Illustration reduced. Actual size 135×55 mm)

1997 (1 May). Endangered Fauna. Multicoloured cover as Type B **10**. "ILSAPEX 98" advertisement on the back. Stamps attached by selvedge.

SB39 10r. booklet containing 1r. (No. 817) in block of 10 12·00

1997 (June). Endangered Fauna. Multicoloured cover as Type B **10**. "ILSAPEX '98" advertisement on the back. Stamps attached by selvedge.

SB40 (10r.) booklet containing pane of 10 "Standardised mail" stamps (No. 821ba)........ 5·50
 a. Human Rights Commission advertisement on back (Nov)........ 5·50

B **11** Man holding Spear (Illustration reduced. Actual size 135×55 mm)

1997 (27 July). Thulamela National Heritage Site. Multicoloured cover as Type B **11**. Pane attached by selvedge.

SB41 ($6) booklet containing pane of 5 and 5 commemorative labels (No. 821cd) .... 3·25

B **12** Cultural Artefacts (Illustration reduced. Actual size 185×90 mm)

1997 (8 Dec). Year of Cultural Experiences. Multicoloured cover as Type B **12**. Booklet contains text and illustrations on left-hand margins of panes and on interleaving pages. Stitched.

SB42 (20r.) booklet containing two panes of 10 "Standard Postage" stamps (No. 966ba) .... 6·50

B **13** Egyptian Geese (Illustration reduced. Actual size 185×90 mm)

1997 (8 Dec). World Environment Day. Waterbirds. Multicoloured cover as Type B **13**. Booklet contains text and illustrations on left-hand margins of panes and on interleaving pages. Stitched.

SB43 (20r.) booklet containing two panes of 10 "STANDARD POSTAGE" stamps (No. 977ba)........ 6·50

1998 (11 Feb). Tourism. Multicoloured cover as Type B **10** showing lioness and inscr "10 AIRMAIL POSTCARD STAMPS". Stamps attached by selvedge.

SB44 (12r.) booklet containing pane of 10 "Airmail Postcard" stamps (No. 1040a)........ 8·00

B **15** Technology at Work (Illustration reduced. Actual size 135×55 mm)

1998 (12 Feb). Year of Science and Technology. Multicoloured cover as Type B **15**. Stamps attached by selvedge.

SB45 (10r.) booklet containing pane of 10 "Standard Postage" stamps (No. 1029a)........ 5·50

B **16** Sable Antelope

1998 (18 May). Centenary of Kruger National Park. Multicoloured cover as Type B **16**. Pane attached by selvedge.

SB46 (11r.) booklet containing pane of 10 "standard postage" stamps (No. 1035a) .... 4·50

B **17** Lydenburg Heads (Illustration reduced. Actual size 185×92 mm)

1998 (28 June). Early South African History. Multicoloured cover as Type B **17**. Booklet contains text and illustrations on left-hand margins of panes and on interleaving pages. Stitched.

SB47 (22r.) booklet containing two panes of 10 "standard postage" stamps (No. 1055b) and two pre-paid postcards........ 8·00

B **18** Cape Vultures (Illustration reduced. Actual size 185×92 mm)

1998 (16 Aug). South African Raptors. Multicoloured cover as Type B **18**. Booklet contains text and illustrations on left-hand margins of panes and on interleaving pages. Stitched.

SB48 (27r.) booklet containing two panes of 10 "standard postage" stamps (No. 1065b) and two pre-paid postcards........ 9·00

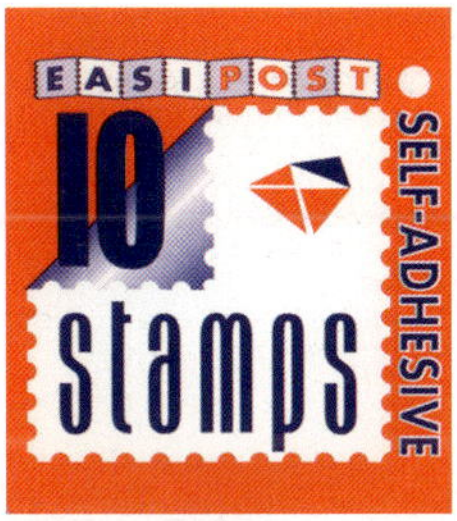

B **19**

1998 (18 Aug)–**99**. Endangered Fauna. Ultramarine and scarlet cover as Type B **19**. Self-adhesive.

SB49 (11r.) booklet containing pane of 10 "standard postage" stamps (No. 1075ab) (P 13×12½) .... 4·00
a. Containing pane No. 1075ba (P 11) (12.99) .... 4·00

B **20** Table Mountain

1998 (28 Sept). Explore South Africa. Multicoloured covers as Type B **20**. Stamps attached by selvedge.

SB50 (13r.) booklet containing pane of 10 Western Cape "AIRMAIL POSTCARD" stamps (No. 1084a) .... 8·00

SB51 (13r.) booklet containing pane of 10 KwaZulu-Natal "AIRMAIL POSTCARD" stamps (No. 1089a) (cover shows a rickshaw driver) .... 8·00

A limited edition booklet containing a sheet of ten of Nos. 1101/4 was only available at the "Ilsapex" Stamp Exhibition, Johannesburg, from 20 to 25 October 1998.

1998 (Oct). Tourism. Multicoloured cover as No. SB44 (lioness), but smaller, 110×47 mm with no hole at right. Stamps attached by selvedge.

SB52 12r. booklet containing pane of 10 "Airmail Postcard" stamps (No. 1045a) .... 6·50

B **21** Rhinoceros (from Beschryving van de Kaap de Goede Hoop, Peter Kolbe, 1727) (Illustration reduced. Actual size 138×55 mm)

1998 (18 Nov). AIDS Awareness. Multicoloured cover as Type B **21**. Stamps attached by selvedge.

SB53 (11r.) booklet containing "Standardised mail" (1r.10) (No. 821b) in block of 10 .... 7·50
a. Cover 110×55 mm without hang-sell hole at right. Containing No. 821 in block of 10 .... 7·50

The inside and back covers are printed with text and illustrations offering advice and telephone helpline numbers on AIDS. No. SB52a was adapted for use in supermarket dispensers.

B **22** The Blue Train

1998 (Nov). Inauguration of Revived Blue Train Service. Multicoloured cover as Type B **22**. Stamps attached by selvedge.

SB54 (13r.) booklet containing pane of 10 (1r.30) (No. 987ba) .... 7·50

B **23** Antelopes

1998 (2 Nov). Centenary of Kruger National Park. Multicoloured cover as Type B **23**. Pane attached by selvedge.

SB55 (11r.) booklet containing pane of 10 (standard postage) stamps (No. 1030pa) .... 5·50

B **24** Couple with AIDS Ribbon

1999 (1 Apr). AIDS Awareness Campaign. Multicoloured cover as Type B **24**. Stamps attached by selvedge.

SB56 (12r.) booklet containing pane of 10 "Standard Postage" stamps (No. 1117a) .... 6·00

1999 (6 Aug). "Explore South Africa" (2nd series). Mpumalanga and Northern Province. Multicoloured cover as Type B **20** showing Pilgrim's Rest (historic town). Stamps attached by selvedge.

SB57 17r. booklet containing pane of 10 "Airmail Postcard" stamps (No. 1138a) .... 9·00

NEW INFORMATION

The editor is always interested to correspond with people who have new information that will improve or correct this catalogue

B **27** Tree Pelargonium

2000 (1 Nov). Flowers. Multicoloured cover as Type B **27**. Self-adhesive.

SB60 13r. booklet containing pane of 10 1r.30 stamps (No. 1232a) .... 6·25

B **29** Lion

2001 (25 Apr)–**05**. Wildlife. Multicoloured cover as Type B **29** Self-adhesive.

SB62 (21r.) booklet containing pane of ten (2r.10) stamps (No. 1263a) .... 6·50

a. With changed telephone number, email address and website address on back cover (10.10.05) (No. 1263ba) .... 6·50

No. SB62 was re-issued on 12.10.2003 dated 10.12 on inside cover. No. SB62a is dated 2005.10.10 on the inside back cover.

2001 (25 Apr). Flowers. Multicoloured cover as Type B **27**, but showing Blue Marguerite. Self-adhesive.

SB63 (14r.) booklet containing pane of ten (1r.40) stamps (No. 1295a) .... 4·00

2001 (30 May). Flowers. Multicoloured cover as Type B **27** but showing Blue Marguerite. Self-adhesive.

SB64 (14r.) booklet containg ten (1r.40) stamps (No. 1305ba) .... 4·00

a. Institue for the Blind logo omitted from the back cover (19.8.02) .... 6·00

b. As above but with second fax number on back cover (5.5.03) .... 7·00

These booklets are dated as follows on inside back covers: SB64 2001.05.30, SB64a 2002.8.19, SB64b 2003.05.05 or 2004.02.09.

B **30** "People, planet and prosperity"

2002 (25 Aug). World Summit on Sustainable Development. Multicoloured cover as Type B **30**. Self-adhesive.

SB65 (15r.) booklet containing pane of ten (1r.50) stamps (No. 1381a) .... 4·50

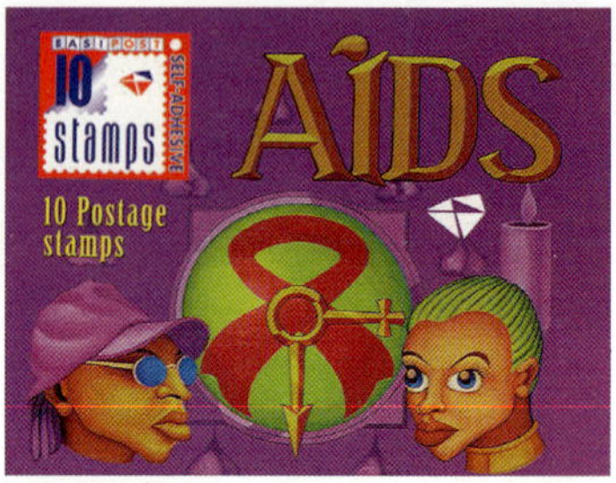

B **31** AIDS Ribbon

2002 (1 Dec). AIDS Prevention. Multicoloured cover as Type B **31**. Self-adhesive.

SB66 (15r.) booklet containing pane of ten (1r.50) stamps (No. 1407a) .... 4·50

B **32** Elephant

2006 (24 Feb). Wildlife "The Big Five". Multicoloured cover as Type B **32**. Self-adhesive.

SB67 (36r.50) booklet containing pane of ten (3r.65) stamps (No. 1577a) .... 13·00

B **33** Leopard (Illustration reduced. Actual size 75×61 mm)

2007 (17 Aug). Wildlife 'The Big Five'. Multicoloured cover as Type B **33**. Self-adhesive.

SB68 (40r.10) booklet containing pane of ten (4r.01) stamps (No. 1627a) .... 12·00

B **34** 'The Big Five' (Illustration reduced. Actual size 75×60 mm)

2008 (14 Nov). Wildlife. 'The Big Five' in Cartoons. Multicoloured cover as Type B **34**. Self-adhesive.

SB69 (42r.) booklet containing pane of ten (4r.20) stamps (No. 1691a) .... 9·00

B **35** Elephant

2010 (5 May). Wildlife. 'The Big Five'. Multicoloured cover as Type B **35**. Self-adhesive.

SB70 (49r.) booklet containing pane of ten (4r.90) stamps (No. 1766a) .... 15·00

B **35** Mfengu Love-Token Necklace, c. 1940

2011 (Feb). South African Beadwork. Multicoloured covers as Type B **36**. Self-adhesive.

SB71 (24r.) booklet containing pane of ten (2r.40) stamps (No. 1856a) (Type B **36**) (75×60 mm) .... 6·00

SB72 (48r.) booklet containing pane of ten (4r.80) stamps (No. 1861a) (cover 75×60 mm showing Tsonga neckpiece) .... 12·00

SB73 (48r.) booklet containing pane of ten (4r.80) stamps (No. 1861a) (cover 75×60 mm showing Tsonga neckpiece) .... 22·00

SB74 (240r.) booklet containing pane of 100 (2r.40) stamps (No. 1856b) (cover 210×105 mm as Type B **36**) 60·00

SB75 (240r.) booklet containing pane of 50 (4r.80) stamps (No. 1861b) (cover 210×105 mm showing Tsonga neckpiece)) .... 60·00

SB76 (300r.) booklet containing pane of 50 (6r.) stamps (No. 1862b) (cover 210×105 mm showing Bhaca neckpiece) £100

PREMIUM BOOKLETS

The following booklets were sold at a premium over the face value of the stamps. All are stitched and have text and illustrations on interleaving pages.

A Nelson Mandela booklet issued on 26 November 2001 contained ten Airmail Postcard Rate stamps (face value 21r.), but was sold for 45r.

P **1** Tail of Blue Whale (Illustration reduced. Actual size 190×90 mm)

1999 (18 Aug). Whales of the Southern Oceans. Multicoloured cover as Type P **1**. Stitched.

SP1 (B) 40r. booklet containing twenty "airmail postcard" (1r.70) stamps (Nos. 1101/4) in sheets of 10 plus two postal stationery postcards .... 9·00

Face value 37r.40.

P **2** Blue Marlin (Illustration reduced. Actual size 185×92 mm)

1999 (4 Oct). Migratory Species of South Africa. Multicoloured cover as Type P **2**. Stitched.

SP2 29r. booklet containing twenty "Standard Postage" stamps (Nos. 1155/64) in sheetlets of 10 plus two postal stationery postcards .... 10·00

Face value 26r.40.

P **3** Wildlife (Illustration reduced. Actual size 187×92 mm)

2001 (25 Apr). Wildlife. Multicoloured cover as Type P **3**. Stitched.

SP3 49r.20 booklet containing two panes of ten (2r.10) stamps (No. 1258a) plus two postal stationery postcards .... 10·00

Face value 46r.20.

P **4** (Illustration reduced. Actual size 185×91 mm)

2002 (17 May). Centenary of the Anglo-Boer War. Multicoloured cover as Type P **4**.

SP4 45r. booklet containing three panes of 2 stamps (Nos. 1165/6, 1203/4 and 1343/4) and minature sheet (No. **MS**1384) together with two postal stationery postcards reproducing the design of No. 1344 .... 11·00

No. SP4 was only available from philatelic outlets initially at 45r., a premium of 11r.50 over the face value of the contents.

POSTAGE DUE STAMPS

D **1**

(A) (B)

(Typo D.L.R.)

1914–22. Inscribed bilingually. Lettering as A. W **4**. P 14.

			Un single	*Used single*
D1	D **1**	½d. black and green (19.3.15)	2·25	3·75
D2		1d. black and scarlet (19.3.15)	2·25	15
		a. Black ptd double	£2000	
		w. Wmk inverted	£110	£120
D3		2d. black and reddish violet (12.12.14)	6·50	50
		a. Black and bright violet (1922)	7·00	60
		w. Wmk inverted	£160	
D4		3d. black and bright blue (2.2.15)	2·25	60
		w. Wmk inverted	45·00	65·00
D5		5d. black and sepia (19.3.15)	4·00	35·00
D6		6d. black and slate (19.3.15)	7·00	35·00
D7		1s. red and black (19.3.15)	60·00	£170
D1/7 *Set of 7*			75·00	£200

There are interesting minor varieties in some of the above values, e.g. ½d. to 3d., thick downstroke to "d"; 1d., short serif to "1"; raised "d"; 2d., forward point of "2" blunted; 3d., raised "d"; very thick "d".

(Litho Govt Printer, Pretoria)

1922. Lettering as A. No wmk. Rouletted.

D8	D **1**	½d. black and bright green (6.6.22)	2·00	16·00
D9		1d. black and rose-red (3.10.22)	1·00	1·25
D10		1½d. black and yellow-brown (3.6.22)	1·25	1·75
D8/10 *Set of 3*			3·75	17·00

(Litho Govt Printer, Pretoria)

1922–26. Type D **1** redrawn. Lettering as B. P 14.

D11		½d. black and green (1.8.22)	80	1·75
D12		1d. black and rose (16.5.23)	90	15
D13		1½d. black and yellow-brown (12.1.24)	1·00	1·25
D14		2d. black and pale violet (16.5.23)	1·00	70
		a. Imperf (pair)	£325	£425
		b. Black and deep violet	15·00	1·00
D15		3d. black and blue (3.7.26)	8·00	22·00
D16		6d. black and slate (9.23)	12·00	2·00
D11/16 *Set of 6*			21·00	25·00

The locally printed stamps, perf 14, differ both in border design and in figures of value from the rouletted stamps. All values except the 3d. and 6d. are known with closed "G" in "POSTAGE" usually referred to as the "POSTADE" variety. This was corrected in later printings.

D **2**

D **3**

D **4**

Blunt "2" (R. 3/6, 8/6)

(Typo Pretoria)

1927–28. Inscribed bilingually. No wmk. P 13½×14.

D17	D **2**	½d. black and green	1·00	3·25
		a. Blunt "2"	11·00	
D18		1d. black and carmine	1·25	30
D19		2d. black and mauve	1·25	30
		a. Black and purple	20·00	80
D20		3d. black and blue	8·50	24·00
D21		6d. black and slate	21·00	3·50
D17/21 *Set of 5*			30·00	28·00

On Nos. D20 and D21 there is no dot below "d".

1932–42. Type D **2** redrawn. W **9**. P 15×14.

(a) Frame roto, value typo

D22		½d. black and blue-green (1934)	2·75	1·75
		w. Wmk inverted	2·50	1·75
D23		2d. black and deep purple (10.4.33)	19·00	2·50
		w. Wmk inverted	19·00	2·50

(b) Whole stamp roto

D25		1d. black and carmine (wmk inverted) (3.34)	2·50	10
D26		2d. black and deep purple (10.39)	42·00	10
		a. Thick (double) "2d." (R. 5/6, R. 18/2)	£425	35·00
		w. Wmk inverted	42·00	50
D27		3d. black and Prussian blue (3.8.32)	25·00	9·00
D28		3d. deep blue and blue (wmk inverted) (1935)	7·00	30
		a. Indigo and milky blue (wmk inverted) (1942)	85·00	3·25
		w. Wmk upright	60·00	3·00
D29		6d. green and brown-ochre (wmk inverted) (7.6.33)	25·00	3·50
		a. Green and bright orange (wmk inverted) (1938)	16·00	2·25
D22/9a *Set of 7*			£100	14·00

In No. D26 the value is screened, whereas in No. D23 the black of the value is solid.

1943–44. Inscr bilingually. Roto. W **9**. In units of three, perf 15×14 subdivided by roulette 6½.

			Un unit	*Us unit*	*Us single*
D30	D **3**	½d. blue-green (1944)	19·00	60·00	40
D31		1d. carmine	10·00	5·50	10
D32		2d. dull violet	6·50	11·00	15
		a. Bright violet	16·00	50·00	65
D33		3d. indigo	55·00	70·00	1·25
D30/3 *Set of 4*			80·00	£130	1·90

Split "D" (R. 7/5 on every fourth sheet)

1948–49. New figure of value and capital "D". Whole stamp roto. W **9**. P 15×14.

D34	D **4**	½d. black and blue-green	6·00	14·00
D35		1d. black and carmine	18·00	5·50
D36		2d. black and violet (1949)	18·00	9·50
		a. Thick (double) "2D." (R. 15/5-6, R. 16/5-6)	85·00	40·00
D37		3d. deep blue and blue	15·00	17·00
		a. Split "D"	£300	£300
D38		6d. green and bright orange (1949)	25·00	8·00
D34/8 *Set of 5*			75·00	48·00

1950–58. As Type D **4**, but "SUID-AFRIKA" hyphenated. Whole stamp roto. W **9**. P 15×14.

D39		1d. black and carmine (5.50)	70	30
D40		2d. black and violet (4.51)	50	20
		a. Thick (double) "2D." (R. 15/5-6, R. 16/5-6)	8·00	10·00
		b. Black and reddish violet (12.52)	1·00	1·00
		ba. Thick (double) "2D."	11·00	14·00
		bb. Black (value) omitted	£4000	
D41		3d. deep blue and blue (5.50)	4·50	2·50
		a. Split "D"	£120	80·00
D42		4d. deep myrtle-green and emerald (2.58)	12·00	15·00
D43		6d. green and bright orange (3.50)	7·00	9·00
D44		1s. black-brown and purple-brown (2.58)	12·00	15·00
D39/44 *Set of 6*			32·00	38·00

No. D40bb occurs in horizontal pair with a normal.

D **5**

D **6** Afrikaans at top

D **7** English at top

1961 (14 Feb). Values in cents as Type D **5**. Whole stamp roto. W **102**. P 15×14.

D45		1c. black and carmine	20	3·75
D46		2c. black and violet	35	3·75
D47		4c. deep myrtle-green and emerald	80	8·50
D48		5c. deep blue and blue	1·75	8·50
D49		6c. green and orange-red	5·00	8·50
D50		10c. sepia and brown-lake	6·00	10·00
D45/50 *Set of 6*			13·00	38·00

1961 (31 May)–**69**. Roto. W **102**. P 15×14.

D51	D **6**	1c. black and carmine	40	60
D52	D **7**	1c. black and carmine (6.62)	40	3·75
D53		2c. black and deep reddish violet	40	55
D54	D **6**	4c. deep myrtle-green and light emerald*	2·25	2·25
D54*a*	D **7**	4c. deep myrtle-green and light emerald (6.69)*	12·00	23·00
D55		5c. deep blue and grey-blue	2·00	4·25
D56		5c. black and grey-blue (6.62)	1·25	4·50
D57	D **6**	6c. deep green and red-orange	8·00	4·75
D58	D **7**	10c. sepia and purple-brown	2·25	1·40
D51/8 *Set of 9*			26·00	40·00

1967 (1 Dec)–**71**. Roto. W **127** (*tête-bêche*)*. P 15×14.

D59	D **6**	1c. black and carmine	20	55
D60	D **7**	1c. black and carmine	20	30
D61	D **6**	2c. black and deep reddish violet	30	2·00
D62	D **7**	2c. black and deep reddish violet	30	2·00
D62*b*		4c. deep myrtle-green and emerald (6.69)*	35·00	32·00
D62*c*	D **6**	4c. deep myrtle-green and emerald (6.69)*	£350	£350
D63		4c. black and pale green (4.71)	32·00	38·00
D64	D **7**	4c. black and pale green (4.71)	32·00	38·00
D65	D **6**	5c. black and deep blue	50	1·00
D66	D **7**	5c. black and deep blue	50	50
D67	D **6**	6c. green and orange-red (1968)	3·50	11·00
D68	D **7**	6c. green and orange-red (1968)	3·50	11·00
D69	D **6**	10c. black and purple-brown	1·00	3·50
		a. *Black and brown-lake* (12.69)	1·00	2·75
D70	D **7**	10c. black and purple-brown	1·00	3·50

a. Black and brown-lake (12.69) 1·00 2·75
D59/70*a except* D62*b/c Set of* 12 70·00 95·00

Nos. D59/70 were printed in two panes, one with inscriptions as Type D **6** and the other as Type D **7**.

*Nos. D54*a*, D62*b/c* and further supplies of D54 were part of a printing released in June 1969. Most sheets were printed on paper with the Arms watermark, but some were printed on RSA paper with the watermark upright and faint. Of these many were spoilt, but a few sheets were issued in Types D 7 and D 6, the latter being very scarce.

1971 Roto. W **127** (*tête-bêche*). P 14

D71	D **6**	2c. black and deep reddish violet	24·00	7·00
D72	D **7**	2c. black and dep reddish violet	24·00	7·00
D74		4c. deep myrtle-green and light emerald	45·00	40·00
D71/4 *Set of* 3			85·00	48·00

Nos. D71/4 were also printed in double panes as Nos. D59/70. Although the 4c., as Type D **6** must have been printed it has not been possible to confirm that any were actually issued.

D **8**

1972 (22 Mar). English at right (1, 4 and 8c.) or at left (others). W **127** (sideways *tête beché*). Chalk-surfaced paper (4c. to 10c.). P 14×13½.

D75	D **8**	1c. deep yellowish green	50	2·25
D76		2c. bright orange	70	30
D77		4c. plum	1·75	3·50
D78		6c. chrome-yellow	1·75	4·75
D79		8c. ultramarine	2·00	5·00
D80		10c. bright scarlet	6·00	7·50
D75/80 *Set of* 6			11·50	23·00

The 6c. also exists on phosphorised paper.

The printing of Postage Due Stamps ceased in 1978. Isolated examples are known used as late as 1980.

OFFICIAL STAMPS

(O **1**) (O **2**)

(Approximate measurements of the space between the two lines of overprint are quoted in millimetres, either in the set headings or after individual listings)

1926 (1 Dec). Optd with Type O **1** (reading upwards with stops and 12½ mm between lines of opt).

(a) On 1913 issue (No. 6)

O1	**3**	2d. purple	22·00	1·75

(b) On 1926 issue (Nos. 30/2)

			Un pair	Us pair	Us single
O2	**6**	½d. black and green	9·00	21·00	1·50
O3	**7**	1d. black and carmine	4·00	8·00	50
O4	**8**	6d. green and orange	£550	75·00	10·00
		w. Wmk inverted	£1500	£475	32·00

The overprint occurs on both the London and Pretoria printings of Nos. 30/2. For the lower two values the overprinted London printings are scarcer than the Pretoria, but for the 6d. the ratio is reversed.

1928–30. Nos. 32 and 34 optd as Type O **1** (reading upwards without stops).

O5	**11**	2d. grey and maroon (P 14) (17½ *mm*)	6·00	23·00	2·00
		a. Lines of opt 19 mm apart (1929)	7·00	24·00	2·00
		ab. On No. 34a (P 14×13½) (1930)	65·00	70·00	5·50
O6	**8**	6d. green and orange (11½–12 *mm*)	22·00	50·00	2·75

1929–31. Optd with Type O **2**.

(a) On 1926 (Typo) issue (Nos. 30/2) (13½–15 mm between lines of opt)

O7	**6**	½d. black and green	2·75	4·50	35
		a. Stop after "OFFISIEEL" on English inscr stamp (1930)	45·00	55·00	3·25
		b. Ditto, but on Afrikaans inscr stamp (1930)	60·00	70·00	3·25
O8	**7**	1d. black and carmine	3·00	7·00	45
O9	**8**	6d. green and orange	7·00	40·00	3·25
		a. Stop after "OFFICIAL" on English inscr stamp (1930)	85·00	£160	10·00
		b. Ditto, but on Afrikaans inscr stamp (1930)	90·00	£170	12·00

(b) On 1927 (Recess) issue (Nos. 36a/7) (17½–19 mm between lines of opt)

O10	**13**	1s. brown and deep blue (1931)	42·00	95·00	9·50
		a. Stop after "OFFICIAL" on Afrikaans inscr stamp (R. 10/1, 10/7)	£140	£275	
		b. Lines of opt 20½–21 mm apart	£750		
O11	**14**	2s.6d. green and brown (1931)	70·00	£170	19·00
		a. Stop after "OFFICIAL" on Afrikaans inscr stamp (R. 10/1)	£325	£650	
O7/11 *Set of* 5			£110	£275	29·00

The "stop" varieties for the ½d., and 6d. occur on R. 5/3, 5/11, 8/12, 15/3, 15/11, 18/12 with English inscriptions and R. 9/10, 9/12, 19/10, 19/12 with Afrikaans on the 1930 overprinting only.

The 1932 printing of the 2s.6d. did not include No. O11a.

1930–47. Nos. 42/4 and 47/9 ("SUIDAFRIKA" in one word) optd with Type O **2**.

O12	**6**	½d. black and green (9½–12½ *mm*) (1931)	2·25	5·00	40
		a. Stop after "OFFISIEEL" on English inscr stamp	42·00	65·00	4·00
		b. Ditto, but on Afrikaans inscr stamp	28·00	55·00	3·50
		c. "Cobweb" variety	48·00		
		d. "Dollar" variety	45·00		
		e. Opt double	£425		
		f. Opt double, one inverted	£500		
		w. Wmk inverted (1934)	6·00	10·00	60
O13	**7**	1d. black and carmine (I) (12½–14 *mm*)	4·50	7·00	55
		a. Stop after "OFFISIEEL" on English inscr stamp	55·00	75·00	4·00
		b. Ditto, but on Afrikaans inscr stamp	38·00	60·00	3·50
		cw. Wmk inverted (1931)	4·50	7·00	55
		d. On Type II (No. 43d) (12½–13½ *mm*) (1933)	17·00	9·00	90
		da. Opt double	£275	£375	
O14	**11**	2d. slate-grey and lilac (20½–22½ *mm*) (1931)	6·50	11·00	1·50
		w. Wmk inverted (1934)	95·00	£130	8·00
O15		2d. blue and violet (20½–22½ *mm*) (1938)	£160	£100	9·00
		a. Airship flaw			
O16	**8**	6d. green and orange (12½–13½ *mm*) (*wmk inverted*) (1931)	6·50	8·50	85
		a. Stop after "OFFISIEEL" on English inscr stamp	£100	£120	6·50
		b. Ditto, but on Afrikaans inscr stamp	85·00	95·00	5·50
		c. "OFFISIEEL" reading upwards (R. 17/12, 18/12, 19/12, 20/12) (1933)	£1000		
		w. Wmk upright (1935)	85·00	£110	7·00
O17	**13**	1s. brown and deep blue (19 *mm*) (*wmk inverted*) (1932)	55·00	90·00	8·50
		a. Twisted horn flaw	£375		
		b. Lines of opt 21 mm apart (*wmk inverted*) (1933)	70·00	£100	7·50
		ba. Twisted horn flaw	£375		
		bw. Wmk upright (1936)	85·00	£150	10·00
O18	**14**	2s.6d. green and brown (17½–18½ *mm*) (1933)	85·00	£150	15·00
		a. Lines of opt 21 mm apart (1934)	60·00	75·00	8·50
		aw. Wmk inverted (1937)	£500	£550	
O19		2s.6d. blue and brown (19–20.5 *mm*) (1946)	55·00	£100	6·50
		a. Diaeresis over second "E" of "OFFISIEEL" on Afrikaans and English inscr stamps (1946)	£2000	£2500	
		b. Ditto, but on Afrikaans inscr stamp only	£1200	£1300	
		c. Ditto, but on English inscr stamp only	£1200	£1300	

The stop varieties for the ½d., 1d. and 6d. occur on R. 9/10, 9/12, 19/10, 19/12 with English inscriptions and R. 5/3, 5/11, 8/12, 15/3, 15/11, 18/12 with Afrikaans on the 1930 and 1931 overprintings only.

(O 3)

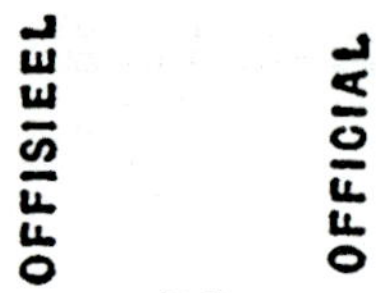

(O 4)

1935–49. Nos. 54, 56/8, 61/2 and 64*b*/*ca* ("SUID-AFRIKA" hyphenated) optd.

(a) With Type O **2** *(reading downwards with "OFFICIAL" at right)*

O20	**6**	½d. grey and green (12½ *mm*) (*wmk inverted*) (1936)	45·00	55·00	2·00
		w. Wmk upright (1937)	9·50	32·00	1·75
O21	**7**	1d. grey and carmine (11½–13 *mm*) (*wmk inverted*)	6·50	9·00	35
		aa. Pair, one stamp "OFFICIAL OFFICIAL"	†	£3000	—
		aw. Wmk upright (1937)	5·50	3·00	20
		b. Grey and bright rose-carmine (No. 56*i*) (1949)	4·00	5·00	30
O22	**22**	1½d. green and bright gold (20 *mm*) (*wmk inverted*) (1937)	50·00	35·00	1·75
		ab. Broken chimney and faint headgear			
		ac. Flag on chimney at right..			
		aw. Wmk upright (1939)	32·00	24·00	1·00
		b. Blue-green and dull gold (No. 57*e*) (1941)	50·00	11·00	1·10
O23	**11**	2d. blue and violet (20 *mm*) (1939)	£150	48·00	2·25
O24	**8**	6d. green and vermilion (I) (11½–13 *mm*) (1937)	85·00	55·00	3·75
		a. "Falling ladder" flaw	£900	£600	
		b. "Molehill" flaw	£800	£500	
		c. Die II (No. 61*c*) (1938)	14·00	10·00	1·25
		d. Die III *Green and red-orange* (No. 61*d*) (11.47)	4·00	8·50	85
O25		1s. brown and chalky blue (18.5–20 *mm*) (*shades*) (1939)	80·00	50·00	2·25
		a. Diaeresis over second "E" of "OFFISIEEL" on Afrikaans and English inscr stamps (1946)	£3000	£2000	
		b. Ditto, but on Afrikaans inscr stamp only	£1600	£1100	
		c. Ditto, but on English inscr stamp only	£1600	£1100	
O26	**15**	5s. black and blue-green (20 *mm*) (6.48)	65·00	£160	13·00
O27	**23**	10s. blue and blackish brown (No. 64*ca*) (20 *mm*) (6.48)	£110	£275	23·00

(b) With Type O **3** *(reading downwards with "OFFICIAL" at left and 18–19 mm between lines of opt)*

O28	**15**	5s. black and blue-green (1940)	£120	£140	12·00
O29	**23**	10s. blue and sepia (1940)	£500	£500	38·00

(c) With Type O **4** *(reading upwards with "OFFICIAL" at right and 18½ mm between lines of opt*

O30	**11**	2d. grey and dull purple (No. 58*a*) (1941)	11·00	35·00	2·25

Nos. O19a/c and O25a/c first appeared in a 1946 overprinting where the variety occurs on R. 1/5 (Afrikaans) and R. 1/6 (English). A setting of 60 (6×10) was applied to the top halves of the sheets only. The same setting was used for a printing of the 2d. value, applied twice to each sheet of 120, resulting in O36a. The diaeresis variety reappeared in the November 1947 printing of the 1s. and 2s.6d. values in position R. 6/2 on the Afrikaans stamp and R. 6/3 on the English stamp.

Horizontal rows of 6 of the 1s. exist with "OFFICIAL" twice on the first stamp and "OFFISIEEL" twice on the last stamp. Such rows are believed to come from two half sheets which were overprinted in 1947, but not placed into normal stock (*Price for row of 6, £2750, unused*).

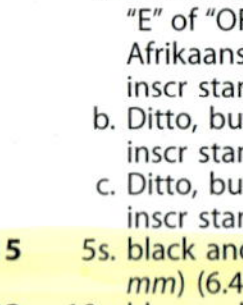

(O 5)

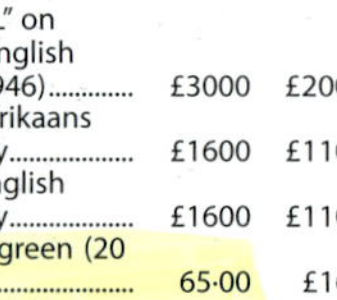

(O 6)

1937–44. No. 75c (redrawn design) optd.

(a) With Type O **2** *(reading downwards with "OFFICIAL" at right and 11–12½ mm between lines of opt)*

O31	**25a**	½d. grey and green	25·00	25·00	1·50
		a. Grey and blue-green (No. 75*cd*) (1944)	4·00	11·00	60

(b) With Type O **5** *(reading up and down with "OFFICIAL" at left and diaeresis over the second "E" of "OFFISIEEL". 10 mm between lines of opt)*

O32	**25a**	½d. grey and blue-green (No. 75*cd*) (1944)	50·00	30·00	2·00

1944–50. Nos. 87 and 134 optd.

(a) With Type O **2** *(reading downwards with "OFFICIAL" at right)*

O33	**34a**	1½d. blue-green and yellow-buff (14½ *mm*)	2·50	10·00	80
		a. With diaeresis over second "E" of "OFFISIEEL"	£700	£375	30·00
		b. Lines of opt 16½ mm apart (6.48)	2·25	12·00	60

(b) With Type O **6** *(reading upwards with "OFFICIAL" at left and 16 mm between lines of opt)*

O34	**34a**	1½d. blue-green and yellow-buff (1949)	85·00	85·00	4·00
O35	**68**	2d. blue and violet (1950)	£3750	£4250	£275

Two different formes were used to overprint Type **34a** between 1944 and 1946. The first, applied to the left halves of sheets only, had a diaeresis over the second "E" of "OFFISIEEL" on all positions of the setting, except for R. 1/2, 2/2, 3/2 and 8/1. The second form, from which the majority of the stamps came, was applied twice to overprint complete sheets, had no diaeresis.

Examples of T**34a** overprinted with Type O2 *horizontally* exist, but their status is unclear. (*Price £900, unused pair*).

1947 (Nov)–**49.** No. 107*a* optd with Type O **2** (reading downwards with "OFFICIAL" at right and 20 mm between lines of opt).

O36	**54**	2d. slate and deep lilac	5·50	24·00	1·90
		a. With diaeresis over second "E" of "OFFISIEEL" (R. 1/5-6, 11/5-6)	£550	£800	
		b. Slate and bright violet (No. 107*b*) (1949)	8·50	16·00	1·60

1949–50. Nos. 114 and 120 optd with Type O **2** (reading downwards with "OFFICIAL" at right).

O37	**25a**	½d. grey and green (11 *mm*)	5·00	12·00	1·00
		a. "Tick" flaw and spot on nose	65·00		
		b. Entire design screened (No. 114c)	5·50	12·00	1·00
		c. "Tick" flaw and spot on nose	65·00		
O38	**13**	1s. brown and chalky blue (17½–18½ *mm*) (1950)	11·00	28·00	2·50

(O 7)

1950 (June)–**54.** Optd as Type O **7** using stereo blocks measuring either 10 (½d., 1d., 6d.), 14½ (1½d., 2d.) or 19 mm (others) between the lines of opt.

O39	**25a**	½d. grey and green (No. 114c) (6.51)	70	1·50	15
O41	**7**	1d. grey and bright rose-carmine (No. 56*i*)	1·00	6·00	50
O42		1d. grey and carmine (No. 115) (3.51)	1·00	3·25	20
O43		1d. grey and carmine (No. 135) (6.52)	1·25	2·00	20
O44	**34a**	1½d. blue-green and yellow-buff (No. 87) (3.51)	2·75	4·50	30
O45	**68**	2d. blue and violet (No. 134)	1·00	2·00	20
		a. Opt inverted	£1100		
O46	**8**	6d. green and red-orange (No. 119)	1·50	4·00	35
		a. Green and brown-orange (No. 119*a*) (6.51)	1·75	3·50	35
O47	**13**	1s. brown and chalky blue (No. 120)	5·50	18·00	2·00
		a. Blackish brown and ultram (No. 120*a*) (2.53)	£170	£190	18·00
O48	**14**	2s.6d. green and brown (No. 121)	8·50	35·00	3·50
O49	**15**	5s. black and blue-green (No. 64*a*) (3.51)	£180	£120	9·00
O50		5s. black and pale blue-green (I) (No. 122) (2.53)	70·00	95·00	6·50
		a. Black and deep yellow-green (II) (No. 122*a*) (1.54)	75·00	£100	9·00
O51	**23**	10s. blue and charcoal (No. 64*ca*)	80·00	£250	22·00

The use of the official stamps ceased in January 1955.

XI. BOPHUTHATSWANA

The Tswana Territory Authority was established by South Africa in 1968, and was granted internal self-government in 1972 under the Bantu Homelands Constitution Act. Bophuthatswana became fully independent on 6 December 1977. This independence did not receive international political recognition, but the stamps were accepted as valid on international mail.

PRINTERS. All the following stamps were printed in lithography by the South African Government Printer, Pretoria.

1 Hands releasing Dove

2 African Buffalo (totem of Malete and Hwaduba tribes)

(Des A. H. Barrett)

1977 (6 Dec). Independence. T **1** and similar horiz designs. Multicoloured. P 12½.

1	4c. Type **1**	25	25
2	10c. Leopard (national emblem)	50	40
3	15c. Coat of arms	75	1·00
4	20c. National flag	1·25	1·40
1/4	*Set of 4*	2·50	2·75

(Des A. H. Barrett)

1977 (6 Dec)–**82**. Tribal Totems. T **2** and similar horiz designs. Multicoloured. P 12½.

5	1c. Type **2**	20	20
	a. Perf 14 (15.4.81)	15	20
6	2c. Bush Pig (Kolobeng)	20	20
	a. Perf 14 (21.6.82)	25	20
7	3c. Chacma Baboon (Hurutshe and Tlharo)	30	20
	a. Perf 14 (18.8.82)	15	20
8	4c. Leopard (national emblem)	3·00	1·25
	a. Perf 14 (6.7.79)	20	10
9	5c. Crocodile (Kwena and Fokeng)	1·00	50
	a. Perf 14 (25.1.80)	20	
10	6c. Savanna Monkey (Kgatla)	20	10
11	7c. Lion (Taung)	1·40	60
	a. Perf 14 (18.12.79)	30	15
12	8c. Spotted Hyena (Phiring)	35	15
	a. Perf 14 (2.2.82)	20	15
13	9c. Cape Porcupine (Rokologadi)	20	15
14	10c. Aardvark (Tlokwa)	20	10
	a. Perf 14 (21.6.82)	20	10
15	15c. Tilapia (fish) (Tlhaping)	1·00	15
16	20c. Hunting Dog (Tlhalerwa)	25	20
17	25c. Common Duiker (Mfatlha)	30	30
18	30c. African Elephant (Tlhako, Tloung and Pô)	1·00	35
19	50c. Python (Nogeng)	50	40
20	1r. Hippopotamus (Kubung)	1·00	1·00
21	2r. Greater Kudu (Rolong)	70	1·50
5/21	*Set of 17* (cheapest)	6·00	4·75

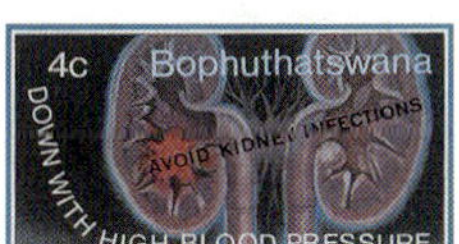

3 Infected Kidney

(Des A. H. Barrett)

1978 (4 Apr). World Hypertension Month. T **3** and similar horiz designs. Multicoloured. P 12×12½.

22	4c. Type **3**	50	25
23	10c. Heart and spoon of salt	70	70
24	15c. Spoon reflecting skull, knife and fork	1·25	1·25
22/4	*Set of 3*	2·25	2·00

4 Skull behind Wheel of Car

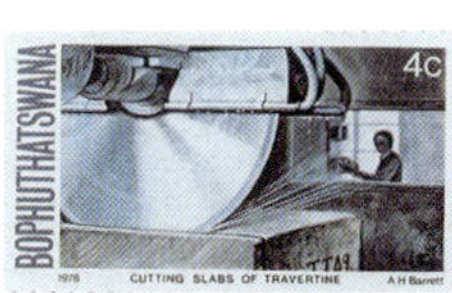

5 Cutting Slabs of Travertine

1978 (12 July). Road Safety. T **4** and similar horiz designs. Multicoloured. P 12×12½.

25	4c. Type **4**	70	40
26	10c. Child knocked off tricycle	90	80
27	15c. Pedestrian stepping in front of car	1·00	1·10
28	20c. Cyclist ignoring stop sign	1·40	1·75
25/8	*Set of 4*	3·50	3·50

(Des A. H. Barrett)

1978 (3 Oct). Semi-precious Stones. T **5** and similar horiz designs. Multicoloured. P 12×12½.

29	4c. Type **5**	65	25
30	10c. Polishing travertine	1·25	85
31	15c. Sorting semi-precious stones	1·50	1·25
32	20c. Factory at Taung	2·25	1·60
29/32	*Set of 4*	5·00	3·50

6 Wright *Flyer 1*

(Des A. H. Barrett)

1978 (1 Dec). 75th Anniv of First Powered Flight by Wright Brothers. T **6** and similar horiz design. P 12½.

33	10c. black, deep grey-blue and brown-red	1·00	1·00
34	15c. black, deep grey-blue and brown-red	1·40	1·50

Design:—15c. Orville and Wilbur Wright.

7 Pres. Lucas M. Mangope

8 Drying Germinated Wheat Sorghum

(Des A. H. Barrett)

1978 (6 Dec). First Anniv of Independence. T **7** and similar vert design. Multicoloured. P 12½.

35	4c. Type **7**	25	20
36	15c. Full face portrait of President	75	60

(Des A. H. Barrett)

1979 (28 Feb). Sorghum Beer-making. T **8** and similar horiz designs. Multicoloured. P 13½×14.

37	4c. Type **8**	20	20
38	15c. Cooking the ground grain	50	70
39	20c. Sieving the liquid	60	75
40	25c. Drinking the beer	65	1·00
37/40	*Set of 4*	1·75	2·40

9 Kallie Knoetze

10 Emblem and Drawing by Hendrick (South Africa) Sebapo of Local Fable

1979 (2 June). Knoetze-Tate Boxing Match. T **9** and similar horiz design. Multicoloured. P 13½×14.

41	15c. Type **9**	55	75
	a. Pair. Nos. 41/2	1·10	1·50
42	15c. John Tate (USA)	55	75

Nos. 41/2 were printed together, *se-tenant*, in pairs throughout the sheet.

1979 (7 June). International Year of the Child. Children's Drawings of Local Fables. T **10** and similar horiz designs. Multicoloured. P 14.

43	4c. Type **10**	20	20
44	15c. Family with animals (Daisy Morapedi)	25	25
45	20c. Man's head and landscape (Peter Tladi)	35	35
46	25c. Old man, boy and donkey (Hendrick Sebapo)	45	60
43/6	*Set of 4*	1·10	1·40

11 Miner and Molten Platinum

(Des B. Sargent)

1979 (15 Aug). Platinum Industry. T **11** and similar horiz designs. P 13½×14.

47	4c. multicoloured	25	10
48	15c. multicoloured	35	30
49	20c. multicoloured	45	45
50	25c. black, grey and deep grey	60	65
47/50 *Set of 4*		1·50	1·40

Designs:—15c. Platinum granules and industrial use; 20c. Telecommunications satellite; 25c. Jewellery.

12 Cattle

(Des A. H. Barrett)

1979 (25 Oct). Agriculture. T **12** and similar horiz designs. Multicoloured. P 13½×14.

51	5c. Type **12**	20	20
52	15c. Picking cotton	25	25
53	20c. Scientist examining maize	30	30
54	25c. Catch of fish	35	35
51/4 *Set of 4*		1·00	1·00

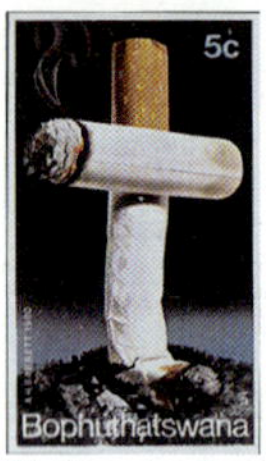

13 Cigarettes forming Cross

14 *Landolphia capensis*

(Des A. H. Barrett)

1980 (5 Mar). Anti-smoking Campaign. P 14×13½.

55	**13**	5c. multicoloured	40	20

(Des. D. Findlay)

1980 (4 June). Edible Wild Fruits. T **14** and similar vert designs. Multi coloured. P 14×13½.

56	5c. Type **14**	15	15
57	10c. *Vangueria infausta*	30	30
58	15c. *Bequaertiodendron magalismontanum*	40	40
59	20c. *Sclerocarya caffra*	55	55
56/9 *Set of 4*		1·25	1·25

15 Pied Babbler

(Des D. Findlay)

1980 (10 Sept). Birds. T **15** and similar vert designs. Multicoloured. P 14×13½.

60	5c. Type **15**	25	20
61	10c. Carmine Bee Eater	35	35
62	15c. Shaft-tailed Whydah	50	60
63	20c. Meyer's Parrot	55	65
60/3 *Set of 4*		1·50	1·60

16 Sun City Hotel

17 Deaf Child

(Des P. Roos and G. Mynhardt)

1980 (5 Dec). Tourism. Sun City. T **16** and similar horiz designs. Multicoloured. P 13½×14.

64	5c. Type **16**	10	15
65	10c. Gary Player Country Club	40	30
66	15c. Casino	45	50
67	20c. Extravaganza	50	70
64/7 *Set of 4*		1·25	1·50

(Des H. Botha)

1981 (30 Jan). International Year of Disabled Persons. T **17** and similar vert designs. Multicoloured. P 14×13½.

68	5c. Type **17**	15	10
69	15c. Blind child	30	20
70	20c. Archer in wheelchair	45	35
71	25c. Tuberculosis x-ray	60	60
68/71 *Set of 4*		1·40	1·10

18 "Behold the Lamb of God..."

19 Siemens and Halske Wall Telephone, 1885

(Des J. Meyer)

1981 (1 Apr). Easter. T **18** and similar horiz designs. Multicoloured. P 13½×14.

72	5c. Type **18**	10	10
73	15c. Bread ("I am the bread of life")	25	25
74	20c. Shepherd ("I am the good shepherd...")	35	35
75	25c. Wheatfield ("Unless a grain of wheat falls into the earth and dies...")	45	45
72/5 *Set of 4*		1·00	1·00

(Des J. Hoekstra)

1981 (31 July). History of the Telephone (1st series). T **19** and similar vert designs. Multicoloured. P 14×13½.

76	5c. Type **19**	10	10
77	15c. Ericsson telephone, 1895	25	25
78	20c. Hasler telephone, 1900	35	35
79	25c. Mix and Genest wall telephone, 1904	45	45
76/9 *Set of 4*		1·00	1·00

See also Nos. 92/5, 108/11 and 146/9.

20 *Themeda triandra*

21 Boy Scout

22 Jesus arriving at Bethany (John 12:1)

(Des D. Findlay)

1981 (25 Nov). Indigenous Grasses (1st series). T **20** and similar vert designs. Multicoloured. P 14×13½.

80	5c. Type **20**	10	10
81	15c. *Rhynchelytrum repens*	20	25
82	20c. *Eragrostis capensis*	20	30
83	25c. *Monocymbium ceresiiforme*	30	45
80/3	*Set of 4*	70	1·00

See also Nos. 116/19.

(Des Sheila Nowers)

1982 (29 Jan). 75th Anniv of Boy Scout Movement. T **21** and similar vert designs. Multicoloured. P 14×13½.

84	5c. Type **21**	15	10
85	15c. Mafeking siege stamps	30	35
86	20c. Original cadet	30	40
87	25c. Lord Baden-Powell	35	45
84/7	*Set of 4*	1·00	1·10

(Des J. Meyer)

1982 (1 Apr). Easter. Palm Sunday. T **22** and similar vert designs. Multicoloured. P 14×13½.

88	15c. Type **22**	25	25
89	20c. Jesus sending disciples for donkey (Matthew 21:1,2)	25	30
90	25c. Disciples taking donkey (Mark 11:5,6)	30	40
91	30c. Disciples with donkey and foal (Matthew 21:7)	30	45
	Set of 4	1·00	1·25

23 Ericsson Telephone

24 Old Parliament Building 1878

(Des J. Hoekstra)

1982 (3 Sept). History of the Telephone (2nd series). T **23** and similar vert designs. Multicoloured. P 14.

92	8c. Type **23**	15	10
93	15c. Ericsson telephone, 1885	20	20
94	20c. Ericsson telephone, 1893	20	20
95	25c. Siemens and Halske telephone, 1898	30	30
92/5	*Set of 4*	75	70

(Des A. H. Barrett)

1982 (12 Dec). Fifth Anniv of Independence. T **24** and similar horiz designs. Multicoloured. P 13½×14.

96	8c. Type **24**	10	10
97	15c. New government offices	20	20
98	20c. University, Mmabatho	25	25
99	25c. Civic Centre, Mmabatho	30	30
96/9	*Set of 4*	75	75

25 White Rhinoceros

(Des P. Bosman)

1983 (5 Jan). Pilanesberg Nature Reserve. T **25** and similar horiz designs. Multicoloured. P 13½×14.

100	8c. Type **25**	30	10
101	20c. Common Zebras	40	30
102	25c. Sable Antelope	40	35
103	40c. Hartebeest	60	60
100/3	*Set of 4*	1·50	1·10

26 Disciples bringing Donkeys to Jesus (Matthew 21:7)

27 Kori Bustard

(Des Sheila Nowers)

1983 (30 Mar). Easter. Palm Sunday. T **26** and similar horiz designs. Multicoloured. P 14×13½.

104	8c. Type **26**	10	10
105	20c. Jesus stroking colt (Mark 11:7)	30	30
106	25c. Jesus enters Jerusalem on donkey (Matthew 21:8)	35	35
107	40c. Crowd welcoming Jesus (Mark 11:9)	60	60
104/7	*Set of 4*	1·10	1·10

(Des I. Ellithorne)

1983 (22 June). History of the Telephone (3rd series). Vert designs as T **19**. Multicoloured. P 14×13½.

108	10c. A.T.M. table telephone, c. 1920	15	10
109	20c. A/S Elektrisk wall telephone, c. 1900	25	30
110	25c. Ericsson wall telephone, c. 1900	30	35
111	40c. Ericsson wall telephone, c. 1900 (different)	40	60
108/11d	*Set of 4*	1·00	1·25

(Des D. Finlay)

1983 (14 Sept). Birds of the Veld. T **27** and similar vert designs. Multicoloured. P 14.

112	10c. Type **27**	30	20
113	20c. Little Black Bustard ("Black Korhaan")	45	45
114	25c. Crested Bustard ("Red-crested Korhaan")	55	55
115	40c. Barrow's Bustard ("Stanley Bustard")	70	80
112/15	*Set of 4*	1·75	1·75

(Des D. Findlay)

1984 (20 Jan). Indigenous Grasses (2nd series). Vert designs as T **20**. Multicoloured. P 14½×14.

116	10c. *Panicum maximum*	15	10
117	20c. *Hyparrhenia dregeana*	20	20
118	25c. *Cenchrus ciliaris*	25	35
119	40c. *Urochloa brachyura*	50	70
116/19	*Set of 4*	1·00	1·25

28 Money-lenders in the Temple (Mark 11:11)

29 Car Upholstery, Ga-Rankuwa

(Des J. van Niekerk)

1984 (23 Mar). Easter. T **28** and similar horiz designs. Multicoloured. P 14½×14.

120	10c. Type **28**	15	10
121	20c. Jesus driving the money-lenders from the Temple (Mark 11:15)	25	20

122	25c. Jesus and fig tree (Matthew 21:19)	30	35
123	40c. The withering of the fig tree (Matthew 21:19)	40	70
120/3	*Set of 4*	1·00	1·25

(Des A. H. Barrett)

1984 (2 Apr)–**94**. Industries. T **29** and similar horiz designs. Multicoloured. Chalk-surfaced paper (except Nos. 134/5). P 14.

124	1c. Textile mill (25.10.85)	10	10
	a. Ordinary paper (18.7.94)	30	30
125	2c. Sewing sacks, Selosesha (25.10.85)	10	10
	a. Ordinary paper (5.6.92)	30	30
126	3c. Ceramic tiles, Babelegi (25.10.85)	10	10
127	4c. Sheepskin car seat covers (25.10.85)	10	10
	a. Ordinary paper (3.7.92)	30	30
128	5c. Crossbow manufacture (25.10.85)	15	10
	a. Ordinary paper (16.11.92)	30	30
129	6c. Automobile parts, Babelegi (25.10.85)	15	10
	a. Ordinary paper (26.6.92)	30	30
130	7c. Hosiery, Babelegi (25.10.85)	15	10
	a. Ordinary paper (26.6.92)	30	30
131	8c. Specialised bicycle factory, Babelegi (25.10.85)	30	10
132	9c. Lawn mower assembly line (25.10.85)	30	15
133	10c. Dress factory, Thaba 'Nchu (25.10.85)	20	10
134	11c. Molten platinum (ordinary paper)	60	20
135	12c. Type **29** (1.4.85) (ordinary paper)	40	15
	a. Chalk-surfaced paper (5.12.85)	40	15
136	14c. Maize mill, Mafeking (1.4.86)	50	15
137	15c. Plastic bags, Babelegi (25.10.85)	25	15
	a. Ordinary paper (3.7.92)	1·25	70
137*b*	16c. Brick factory, Mmabatho (1.4.87)	60	15
137*c*	18c. Cutlery manufacturing, Mogwase (3.7.89)	60	15
138	20c. Men's clothing, Babelegi (25.10.85)	25	15
	a. Ordinary paper (26.6.92)	1·40	75
138*b*	21c. Welding bus chassis (3.8.90)	50	50
	ba. Strip of five. Nos. 138b/f	2·25	2·25
138*c*	21c. Fitting engine to bus chassis (3.8.90)	50	50
138*d*	21c. Bus body construction (3.8.90)	50	50
138*e*	21c. Spraying and finishing bus (3.8.90)	50	50
138*f*	21c. Finished buses (3.8.90)	50	50
139	25c. Chromium plating pram parts (25.10.85)	30	20
	a. Ordinary paper (24.1.92)	60	30
140	30c. Spray painting metal beds (25.10.85)	40	25
	a. Ordinary paper (1.2.89)	75	50
141	50c. Milk processing plant (25.10.85)	50	40
	a. Ordinary paper (1.2.89)	85	75
142	1r. Modern printing works (25.10.85)	60	75
143	2r. Industrial complex, Babelegi (25.10.85)	1·00	2·50
124/43	*Set of 27*	9·00	7·50

Nos. 138*b/f* were printed together, *se-tenant*, in strips of five throughout the sheet.

(Des I. Ellithorne)

1984 (20 July). History of the Telephone (4th series). Vert designs as T **19**. Multicoloured. P 14.

146	11c. Schuchhardt table telephone, 1905	15	10
147	20c. Siemens wall telephone, 1925	25	20
148	25c. Ericsson table telephone, 1900	30	30
149	30c. Oki table telephone, 1930	40	50
146/9	*Set of 4*	1·00	1·00

30 Yellow-throated Plated Lizard

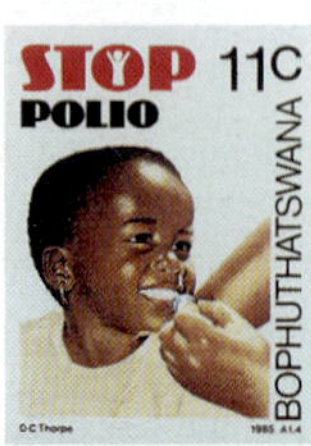

31 Giving Oral Vaccine against Polio

(Des Sheila Nowers)

1984 (25 Sept). Lizards. T **30** and similar horiz designs. Multicoloured. P 14×14½.

150	11c. Type **30**	20	10
151	25c. Transvaal Girdled Lizard	25	30
152	30c. Ocellated Sand Lizard	25	40
153	45c. Bibron's Thick-toed Gecko	40	60
150/3	*Set of 4*	1·00	1·25

(Des D. Thorpe)

1985 (25 Jan). Health. T **31** and similar vert designs. Multicoloured. P 14.

154	11c. Type **31**	40	10
155	25c. Vaccinating against measles	50	30
156	30c. Examining child for diphtheria	55	40
157	50c. Examining child for whooping cough	80	90
154/7	*Set of 4*	2·00	1·50

32 Chief Montshiwa Ratshidi of Barolong boo

33 The Sick flock to Jesus in the Temple (Matthew 21:14)

(Des A. H. Barrett)

1985 (11 Mar). Centenary of Mafeking. T **32** and similar vert design. P 14½×14.

158	11c. black, grey and orange	20	10
159	25c. black, grey and dull violet-blue	40	30

Design:—25c. Sir Charles Warren.

(Des J. van Niekerk)

1985 (2 Apr). Easter. T **33** and similar horiz designs. Multicoloured. P 14.

160	12c. Type **33**	20	10
161	25c. Jesus cures the sick (Matthew 21:14)	30	20
162	30c. Children praising Jesus (Matthew 21:15)	35	30
163	50c. Community leaders discussing Jesus's acceptance of praise (Matthew 21:15,16)	50	60
160/3	*Set of 4*	1·25	1·10

34 *Faurea saligna* and Planting Sapling

35 Jesus at the House of Mary and Martha, Bethany (John 12:2)

(Des B. Jackson)

1985 (4 July). Tree Conservation. T **34** and similar vert designs. Multicoloured. P 14.

164	12c. Type **34**	20	10
165	25c. *Boscia albitrunca* and Kudu	25	20
166	30c. *Erythrina lysistemon* and Mariqua Sunbird	35	30
167	50c. *Bequaertiondendron magalismontanum* and bee	55	50
164/7	*Set of 4*	1·25	1·00

(Des J. van Niekerk)

1986 (6 Mar). Easter. T **35** and similar horiz designs. Multicoloured. P 14½×14.

168	12c. Type **35**	25	10
169	20c. Mary anointing Jesus's feet (John 12:3)	30	20
170	25c. Mary drying Jesus's feet with her hair (John 12:3)	35	25
171	30c. Disciple condemns Mary for anointing Jesus's head with oil (Matthew 26:7)	45	50
168/71	*Set of 4*	1·25	1·00

PHILATELIC FOUNDATION MINIATURE SHEETS. These miniature sheets were issued by the Philatelic Foundation of Southern Africa and not by the postal administration. They could be purchased by post or from a limited number of philatelic offices at a premium in aid of various national and international stamp exhibitions.

36 "Wesleyan Mission Station and Residence of Moroka, Chief of the Barolong, 1834" (C. D. Bell)

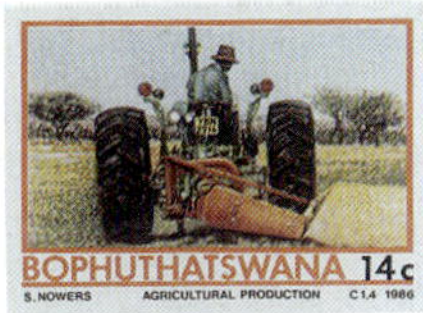

37 Farmer using Tractor (agricultural development)

1986 (15 May). Paintings of Thaba 'Nchu. T **36** and similar horiz designs. Multicoloured. P 14×14½.

172	14c. Type **36**	40	15
173	20c. "James Archbell's Congregation, 1834" (Charles Davidson Bell)	60	60
174	25c. "Mission Station at Thaba 'Nchu, 1850" (Thomas Baines)	65	80
172/4	*Set of 3*	1·50	1·40

The 25c. value exists as a Philatelic Foundation miniature sheet.

(Des Sheila Nowers)

1986 (6 Aug). Temisano Development Project. T **37** and similar horiz designs. Multicoloured. P 14.

175	14c. Type **37**	20	10
176	20c. Children at school (community development)	30	20
177	25c. Repairing engine (training)	35	30
178	30c. Grain elevator (secondary industries)	50	50
175/8	*Set of 4*	1·25	1·00

38 Stewardesses and Cessna Citation II of B.O.P. Airways

39 Netball

(Des R. Smith)

1986 (16 Oct). B.O.P. Airways. T **38** and similar horiz designs. Multicoloured. P 14.

179	14c. Type **38**	25	10
180	20c. Passengers disembarking from Boeing 707	40	20
181	25c. Mmabatho International Airport	50	35
182	30c. B.O.P. Airways Cessna Citation II	60	50
179/82	*Set of 4*	1·60	1·10

(Des B. Jackson)

1987 (22 Jan). Sports. T **39** and similar vert designs. Multicoloured. P 14×14½.

183	14c. Type **39**	20	15
184	20c. Tennis	30	30
185	25c. Football	30	30
186	30c. Athletics	45	50
183/6	*Set of 4*	1·10	1·10

40 *Berkheya zeyheri*

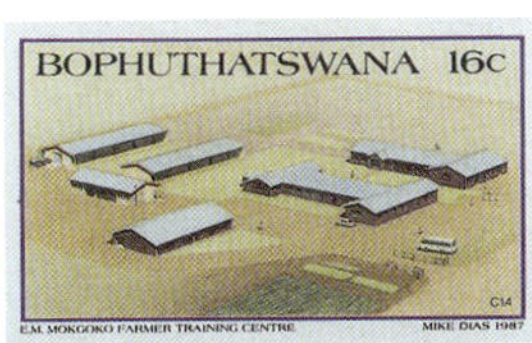

41 E. M. Mokgoko Farmer Training Centre

(Des Jeanette Stead)

1987 (23 Apr). Wild Flowers. T **40** and similar vert designs. Multicoloured. P 14×14½.

187	16c. Type **40**	25	15
188	20c. *Plumbago auriculata*	35	35
189	25c. *Pterodiscus speciosus*	35	35
190	30c. *Gazania krebsiana*	40	50
187/90	*Set of 4*	1·25	1·25

The 25c. value exists as a Philatelic Foundation miniature sheet.

(Des E. Dias)

1987 (6 Aug). Tertiary Education. T **41** and similar horiz designs. Multicoloured. P 14½×14.

191	16c. Type **41**	20	15
192	20c. Main lecture block, University of Bophuthatswana	30	35
193	25c. Manpower Centre	30	35
194	30c. Hotel Training School	30	50
191/4	*Set of 4*	1·00	1·25

42 Posts

43 Jesus entering Jerusalem on Donkey (John 12:12-14)

(Des J. van Niekerk)

1987 (4 Dec). Tenth Anniv of Independence. Communications. T **42** and similar horiz designs. Multicoloured. P 14½×14.

195	16c. Type **42**	25	15
196	30c. Telephone	35	35
197	40c. Radio	35	35
198	50c. Television	40	50
195/8	*Set of 4*	1·25	1·25

(Des J. van Niekerk)

1988 (31 Mar). Easter. T **43** and similar horiz designs. Multicoloured. P 14½×14.

199	16c. Type **43**	25	15
200	30c. Judas negotiating with chief priests (Mark 14:10-11)	35	35
201	40c. Jesus washing the disciples feet (John 13:5)	35	35
202	50c. Jesus handing bread to Judas (John 13:26)	40	50
199/202	*Set of 4*	1·25	1·25

44 Environment Education

(Des A. H. Barrett)

1988 (23 June). National Parks Board. T **44** and similar horiz designs. Multicoloured. P 14½×14.

203	16c. Type **44**	25	15
204	30c. Rhinoceros (Conservation)	40	40
205	40c. Catering workers	40	40
206	50c. Cheetahs (Tourism)	55	65
203/6	*Set of 4*	1·40	1·40

The 50c. value exists as a Philatelic Foundation miniature sheet.

45 Sunflowers

(Des A. H. Barrett)

1988 (15 Sept). Crops. T **45** and similar horiz designs. Multicoloured. P 14½×14.

207	16c. Type **45**	25	15

208	30c. Peanuts	35	35
209	40c. Cotton	45	45
210	50c. Cabbages	60	60
207/10	*Set of 4*	1·50	1·40

46 Ngotwane Dam

47 The Last Supper (Matthew 26:26)

(Des Estelle Marais)

1988 (17 Nov). Dams. T **46** and similar horiz designs. Multicoloured. P 14½×14.

211	16c. Type **46**	30	20
212	30c. Groothoek dam	50	50
213	40c. Sehujwane dam	50	50
214	50c. Molatedi dam	70	70
211/14	*Set of 4*	1·75	1·75

(Des J. van Niekerk)

1989 (9 Mar). Easter. T **47** and similar horiz designs. Multicoloured. P 14½×14.

215	16c. Type **47**	40	20
216	30c. Jesus praying in Garden of Gethsemane (Matthew 26.39)	60	55
217	40c. Judas kissing Jesus (Mark 14:45)	70	70
218	50c. Peter severing ear of High Priest's slave (John 18:10)	85	1·00
215/18	*Set of 4*	2·25	2·25

48 Cock (Thembi Atong)

49 Black-shouldered Kite

1989 (11 May). Children's Art. T **48** and similar horiz designs depicting winning entries in National Children's Day Art Competition. Multicoloured. P 14½×14.

219	18c. Type **48**	30	20
220	30c. Traditional thatched hut (Muhammad Mahri)	40	40
221	40c. Airplane, telephone wires and houses (Tshepo Mashokwi)	45	45
222	50c. City scene (Miles Brown)	50	60
219/22	*Set of 4*	1·50	1·50

1989 (1 Sept). Birds of Prey. T **49** and similar vert designs showing paintings by Claude Finch-Davies. Multicoloured. P 14×14½.

223	18c. Type **49**	1·25	30
224	30c. Pale Chanting Goshawk	1·40	75
225	40c. Lesser Kestrel	1·60	1·10
226	50c. Short-toed Eagle	1·75	1·50
223/6	*Set of 4*	5·50	3·25

The 50c. value exists as a Philatelic Foundation miniature sheet.

50 Bilobial House

51 Early Learning Schemes

(Des A. George)

1989 (28 Nov). Traditional Houses. T **50** and similar horiz designs. Multicoloured. P 14½×14.

227	18c. Type **50**	25	20
228	30c. House with courtyards at front and side	35	35
229	40c. House with conical roof	35	35
230	50c. House with rounded roof	40	50
227/30	*Set of 4*	1·25	1·25

(Des D. McLean)

1990 (11 Jan). Community Services. T **51** and similar horiz designs. Multicoloured. P 14.

231	18c. Type **51**	25	20
232	30c. Clinics	35	35
233	40c. Libraries	35	35
234	50c. Hospitals	40	45
231/4	*Set of 4*	1·25	1·25

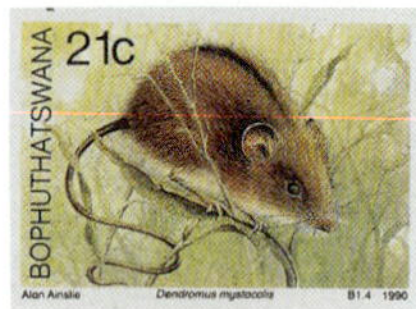

52 Lesser Climbing Mouse

53 Variegated Sandgrouse

(Des A. Ainslie)

1990 (11 Apr). Small Mammals. T **52** and similar horiz designs. Multicoloured. P 14.

235	21c. Type **52**	30	20
236	30c. Zorilla	40	40
237	40c. Transvaal Elephant Shrew	60	60
238	50c. Large-toothed Rock Hyrax	80	85
235/8	*Set of 4*	1·90	1·90

The 50c. value exists as a Philatelic Foundation miniature sheet.

1990 (12 July). Sandgrouse. T **53** and similar horiz designs showing paintings by Claude Finch-Davies. Multicoloured. P 14×14½.

239	21c. Type **53**	90	30
240	35c. Double-banded Sandgrouse	1·10	75
241	40c. Namaqua Sandgrouse	1·10	90
242	50c. Yellow-throated Sandgrouse	1·40	1·40
239/42	*Set of 4*	4·00	3·00

54 Basketry

55 Sud Aviation SE 3130 Alouette III Helicopter

(Des Sheila Nowers)

1990 (4 Oct). Traditional Crafts. T **54** and similar vert designs. Multicoloured. P 14½.

243	21c. Type **54**	40	20
244	35c. Tanning	60	60
245	40c. Beer making	60	65
246	50c. Pottery	65	75
243/6	*Set of 4*	2·00	2·00

1990 (12 Dec). Bophuthatswana Air Force. T **55** and similar horiz designs. Multicoloured. P 14½×14.

247	21c. Type **55**	1·40	1·10
	a. Horiz strip of 5. No. 247/51	6·25	5·00
248	21c. MBB-Kawasaki Bk-117 helicopter	1·40	1·10
249	21c. Pilatus PC-7 Turbo Trainer	1·40	1·10
250	21c. Pilatus PC-6 Turbo Porter	1·40	1·10
251	21c. CASA C-212 Aviocar	1·40	1·10
247/51	*Set of 5*	6·25	5·00

Nos. 247/51 were printed together, *se-tenant*, in horizontal strips of 5 throughout the sheet.

56 Wild Custard Apple

57 Arrest of Jesus (Mark 14:46)

(Des Gillian Condy)

1991 (24 Jan). Edible Wild Fruit. T **56** and similar vert designs. Multicoloured. P 14×14½.

252	21c. Type **56**	50	25
253	35c. Spine-leaved Monkey Orange	65	70
254	40c. Sycamore Fig	70	75
255	50c. Kei Apple	85	95
252/5 *Set of 4*		2·40	2·40

(Des J. van Niekerk)

1991 (21 Mar). Easter. T **57** and similar horiz designs. Multicoloured. P 14½×14.

256	21c. Type **57**	45	25
257	35c. First trial by the Sanhedrin (Mark 14:53)	60	55
258	40c. Assault and derision of Jesus after sentence (Mark 14:65)	70	70
259	50c. Servant girl recognizing Peter (Mark 14:67)	75	90
256/9 *Set of 4*		2·25	2·25

58 Class 7A Locomotive

59 Caneiro Chart, 1502 No. 350, 1897

(Des C. Becker)

1991 (4 July). Steam Locomotives. T **58** and similar horiz designs. Multicoloured. P 14.

260	25c. Class 6A locomotive No. 194 with trucks and caboose, 1897 (71×25 mm).	95	55
261	40c. Type **58**	1·25	85
262	50c. Double-boiler Class 6Z locomotives pulling Cecil Rhode's funeral train (71×25 mm)	1·40	1·25
263	60c. Class 8 locomotive at Mafeking station, 1904	1·50	1·75
260/3 *Set of 4*		4·50	4·00

The 60c. value exists as a Philatelic Foundation miniature sheet. See also Nos. 293/6.

(Des C. Becker (25, 40c.), T. Marais (others))

1991 (12 Sept). Old Maps (1st series). T **59** and similar vert designs. Multicoloured. P 14×14½.

264	25c. Type **59**	1·10	40
265	40c. Cantino Chart, 1502	1·50	95
266	50c. Giovanni Contarini's map, 1506	1·75	1·40
267	60c. Martin Waldseemuller's map, 1507	1·75	1·90
264/7 *Set of 4*		5·50	4·25

See also Nos. 268/71 and 297/300.

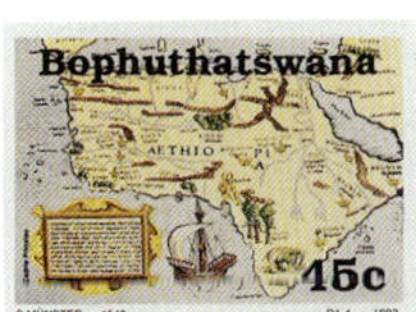

60 Fracanzano Map, 1508

61 Delivery of Jesus to Pilate (Mark 15:1)

(Des Liza van der Wal)

1992 (9 Jan). Old Maps (2nd series). T **60** and similar horiz designs. Multicoloured. P 14½×14.

268	27c. Type **60**	1·10	40
269	45c. Martin Waldseemuller's map (from edition of Ptolemy), 1513	1·50	95
270	65c. Section of Waldseemuller's woodcut Carta Marina Navigatora Portugallan Navigationes, 1516	1·75	1·50
271	85c. Map from Laurent Fries's Geographia, 1522	1·75	2·00
268/71 *Set of 4*		5·50	4·25

(Des J. van Niekerk)

1992 (1 Apr). Easter. T **61** and similar horiz designs. Multicoloured. P 14½×14.

272	27c. Type **61**	25	20
273	45c. Scourging of Jesus (Mark 15:15)	40	40
274	65c. Placing crown of thorns on Jesus's head (Mark 15:17-18)	50	70
275	85c. Soldiers mocking Jesus (Mark 15:19)	60	90
272/5 *Set of 4*		1·60	2·00

62 Sweet Thorn

63 View of Palace across Lake

(Des Gillian Coady)

1992 (18 June). Acacia Trees. T **62** and similar horiz designs. Multicoloured. P 14½×14.

276	35c. Type **62**	30	25
277	70c. Camel Thorn	50	60
278	90c. Umbrella Thorn	60	80
279	1r.05 Black Thorn	70	1·00
276/9 *Set of 4*		1·90	2·40

The 70c. value exists as a Philatelic Foundation miniature sheet.

1992 (19 Nov). The Lost City Complex, Sun City. T **63** and similar horiz designs. Multicoloured. P 14×14½.

280	35c. Type **63**	40	45
	a. Horiz strip of 5. Nos. 280/4	1·75	2·00
281	35c. Palace façade 35	40	45
282	35c. Palace porte cochère	40	45
283	35c. Palace lobby	40	45
284	35c. Tusk Bar, Palace	40	45
280/4 *Set of 5*		1·75	2·00

Nos. 280/4 were printed together, *se-tenant*, in horizontal strips of 5 throughout the sheet.

64 Light Sussex

65 Pilate offering to release Barabbas (Luke 23:25)

(Des M. Ginn)

1993 (12 Feb). Chickens. T **64** and similar horiz designs. Multicoloured. P 14½×14.

285	35c. Type **64**	40	25
286	70c. Rhode Island Red	55	50
287	90c. Brown Leghorn	60	80
288	1r.05 White Leghorn	70	1·10
285/8 *Set of 4*		2·00	2·50

The 70c. value exists as a Philatelic Foundation miniature sheet.

(Des J. van Niekerk)

1993 (5 Mar). Easter. T **65** and similar horiz designs. Multicoloured. P 14½×14.

289	35c. Type **65**	60	30
290	70c. Jesus falling under cross (John 19:17)	95	75
291	90c. Simon of Cyrene carrying cross (Mark 15:21)	1·25	1·25
292	1r.05 Jesus being nailed to cross (Mark 15:23)	1·40	1·75
289/92 *Set of 4*		3·75	3·50

66 Mafeking Locomotive Shed, 1933

(Des C. Becker)

1993 (18 June). Steam Locomotives (2nd series). T **66** and similar multicoloured designs. P 14.

293	45c. Type **66**	65	55
294	65c. Rhodesian Railways steam locomotive No. 5, 1901 (34×25 mm)	75	65
295	85c. Class 16B locomotive pulling "White Train" during Prince George's visit, 1934	95	95

296	1r.05 Class 19D locomotive, 1938 (34×25 mm)	1·25	1·40
293/6 *Set of 4*		3·25	3·25
MS297 127×113 mm. Nos. 293/6		2·75	3·25

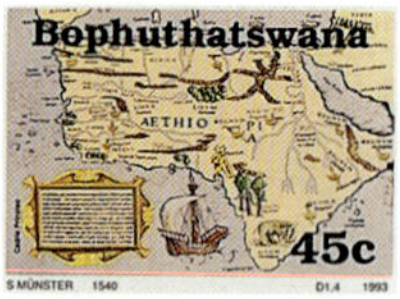

67 Sebastian Minister's Map (from edition of Ptolemy), 1540

68 Crucifixion (Luke 23:33)

(Des C. Prinsloo)

1993 (20 Aug). Old Maps (3rd series). T **67** and similar horiz designs. Multicoloured. P 14½×14.

298	45c. Type **67**	50	50
299	65c. Jacopo Gastaldi's map, 1564	65	65
300	85c. Map from Mercator's Atlas, 1595	75	90
301	1r.05 Map from Ortelius's Theatrum Orbis Terrarum, 1570	90	1·25
298/301 *Set of 4*		2·50	3·50

(Des J. van Niekerk)

1994 (25 Mar). Easter. T **68** and similar horiz designs. Multicoloured. P 14½×14.

302	35c. Type **68**	65	45
303	65c. Soldiers and Jews mocking Jesus (Luke 23:35-36)	95	80
304	85c. Soldier offering Jesus vinegar (Luke 23:36)	1·10	1·25
305	1r.05 Jesus on cross and charge notice (Luke 23:38)	1·60	1·75
302/5 *Set of 4*		3·75	3·75

Bophuthatswana was reincorporated into the Republic of South Africa on 27 April 1994.

The postal service continued to operate, using South African stamps, until 1 April 1996 when it was integrated with that of the Republic.

XII. CISKEI

The Ciskei Territorial Authority was established in 1961 and autonomous government was granted in 1972 under the Bantu Homelands Constitution Act. Ciskei became fully independent on 4 December 1981. This independence did not receive international political recognition, but the stamps were accepted as valid on international mail.

PRINTERS. All the following stamps were printed in lithography by the South African Government Printer, Pretoria.

1 Dr. Lennox Sebe, Chief Minister

2 Knysna Turaco

(Des A. H. Barrett)

1981 (4 Dec). Independence. T **1** and similar vert designs. Multicoloured. P 14.

1	5c. Type **1**	10	10
2	15c. Coat of arms	20	15
3	20c. Flag	30	30
4	25c. Mace	35	25
1/4 *Set of 4*		80	75

(Des D. Findlay)

1981 (4 Dec)–**90**. Birds. T **2** and similar vert designs. Multicoloured. P 14.

5	1c. Type **2**	20	30
6	2c. Cape Wagtail	20	30
7	3c. White-browed Coucal	50	30
8	4c. Yellow-tufted Malachite Sunbird	20	25
9	5c. Stanley Crane	20	20
10	6c. African Red-winged Starling	20	25
11	7c. Giant Kingfisher	20	25
12	8c. Hadada Ibis	30	15
13	9c. Black Cuckoo	30	15
14	10c. Black-collared Barbet	30	15
14*a*	11c. African Black-headed Oriole (2.4.84)	55	45
14*b*	12c. Malachite Kingfisher (1.4.85)	1·10	45
14*c*	14c. Hoopoe (1.4.86)	1·50	45
15	15c. African Fish Eagle	30	30
15*a*	16c. Cape Puff-back Flycatcher (1.4.87)	1·00	30
15*b*	18c. Long-tailed Whydah (3.7.89)	1·50	45
16	20c. Cape Longclaw	40	30
16*a*	21c. Lemon Dove (3.7.90)	2·50	1·25
17	25c. Cape Dikkop	30	30
18	30c. African Green Pigeon	40	40
19	50c. Cape Parrot	60	60
20	1r. Narina Trogon	90	1·25
21	2r. Cape Eagle Owl	1·75	2·50
5/21 *Set of 23*		14·00	10·00

3 Cecilia Makiwane (first Xhosa nurse)

4 Boom Sprayer

(Des A. H. Barrett)

1982 (30 Apr). Nursing. T **3** and similar multicoloured designs. P 14×13½ (vert) or 13½×14 (horiz).

22	8c. Type **3**	15	10
23	15c. Operating theatre	30	30
24	20c. Matron lighting nurse's lamp (horiz)	40	40
25	25c. Nurses and patient (horiz)	50	50
22/5 *Set of 4*		1·25	1·10

(Des A. H. Barrett)

1982 (20 Aug). Pineapple Industry. T **4** and similar horiz designs. Multicoloured. P 13½×14.

26	8c. Type **4**	10	10
27	15c. Harvesting	20	25
28	20c. Despatch to cannery	25	30
29	30c. Packing for local market	30	35
26/9 *Set of 4*		75	85

5 Brown Hare

6 Assegai

1982 (29 Oct). Small Mammals. T **5** and similar horiz designs. Multicoloured. P 13½×14.

30	8c. Type **5**	15	15
31	15c. Cape Fox	25	25
32	20c. Cape Ground Squirrel	30	30
33	25c. Caracal	40	40
30/3 *Set of 4*		1·00	1·00

(Des D. Findlay)

1983 (2 Feb). Trees (1st series). T **6** and similar vert designs. Multicoloured. P 14×13½.

34	8c. Cabbage Tree	15	10
35	20c. Type **6**	30	30
36	25c. Cape Chestnut	35	35
37	40c. Outeniqua Yellowwood	50	55
34/7 *Set of 4*		1·10	1·10

See also Nos. 52/5.

7 Dusky Shark

8 Lovedale

(Des Sheila Nowers)

1983 (13 Apr). Sharks. T **7** and similar horiz designs. Multicoloured. P 14.

38	8c. Type **7**	15	15
39	20c. Sand Tiger ("Ragged-tooth Shark")	30	30
40	25c. Tiger Shark (57×21 mm)	35	35
41	30c. Scalloped Hammerhead (57×21 mm)	40	40
42	40c. Great White Shark (57×21 mm)	50	50
38/42	*Set of* 5	1·50	1·50

(Des A. H. Barrett)

1983 (6 July). Educational Institutions. T **8** and similar horiz designs. P 14.

43	10c. stone, light brown and black	10	10
44	20c. pale stone, olive-sepia and black	20	20
45	25c. pale cinnamon, Venetian red and black	25	25
46	40c. cinnamon, pinkish brown and black	40	45
43/6	*Set of* 4	80	85

Designs:—20c. Fort Hare; 25c. Healdtown; 40c. Lennox Sebe.

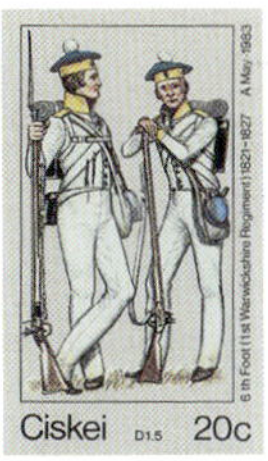

9 White Drill Uniform

10 Sandprawn

(Des A. May)

1983 (28 Sept). British Military Uniforms (1st series). 6th (Warwickshire) Regiment of Foot, 1821–27. T **9** and similar vert designs. Multicoloured. P 14.

47	20c. Type **9**	30	40
	a. Horiz strip of 5. Nos. 47/51	1·40	1·75
48	20c. Light Company privates	30	40
49	20c. Grenadier Company sergeants	30	40
50	20c. Officers in undress blue frock-coats	30	40
51	20c. Officer and field officer in parade order	30	40
47/51	*Set of* 5	1·40	1·75

Nos. 47/51 were printed together, *se-tenant*, in horizontal strips of 5 throughout the sheet. See also Nos. 64/8 and 95/8.

(Des D. Findlay)

1984 (6 Jan). Trees (2nd series). Vert designs as T **6**. Multicoloured. P 14.

52	10c. *Rhus chirindensis*	15	15
53	20c. *Phoenix reclinata*	25	35
54	25c. *Ptaeroxylon obliquum*	30	40
55	40c. *Apodytes dimidiata*	40	55
52/5	*Set of* 4	1·00	1·25

(Des D. Thorpe)

1984 (12 Apr). Fish-bait. T **10** and similar horiz designs. Multicoloured. P 14×14½.

56	11c. Type **10**	20	15
57	20c. Coral Worm	30	30
58	25c. Bloodworm	35	35
59	30c. Red-bait	40	40
56/9	*Set of* 4	1·10	1·10

11 Banded Sand Martin

(Des Sheila Nowers)

1984 (17 Aug). Migratory Birds. T **11** and similar horiz designs. Multicoloured. P 14½×14.

60	11c. Type **11**	25	20
61	25c. House Martin	50	50
62	30c. Greater Striped Swallow	60	60
63	45c. Barn Swallow ("European Swallow")	80	85
60/3	*Set of* 4	1·90	1·90

(Des A. May)

1984 (26 Oct). British Military Uniforms (2nd series). Cape Mounted Rifles. Vert designs as T **9**. Multicoloured. P 14.

64	25c. (1) Trooper in field and sergeant in undress uniforms, 1830	35	45
	a. Horiz strip of 5. Nos. 64/8	1·60	2·00
65	25c. (2) Trooper and sergeant in full dress, 1835	35	45
66	25c. (3) Officers in undress, 1830	35	45
67	25c. (4) Officers in full dress, 1827–34	35	45
68	25c. (5) Officers in full dress, 1834	35	45
64/8	*Set of* 5	1·60	2·00

Nos. 64/8 were printed together, *se-tenant*, in horizontal strips of 5 throughout the sheet. Each stamp is inscribed at the foot with a number from "D1.5" to "D5.5". The first number is given in brackets in the listing to aid identification.

12 White Steenbras

13 Brownies holding Handmade Doll

(Des D. Thorpe)

1985 (7 Mar). Coastal Angling. T **12** and similar horiz designs. Multicoloured. P 14.

69	11c. Type **12**	15	15
70	25c. Bronze Seabream	25	30
71	30c. Kob	30	45
72	50c. Spotted Grunt	40	80
69/72	*Set of* 4	1·00	1·50

(Des Sheila Nowers)

1985 (3 May). International Youth Year. 75th Anniv of Girl Guide Movement. T **13** and similar horiz designs. Multicoloured. P 14½×14.

73	12c. Type **13**	15	15
74	25c. Rangers planting trees	25	25
75	30c. Guides with flag	30	30
76	50c. Guides building fire	60	65
73/6	*Set of* 4	1·10	1·10

14 Furniture making

(Des B. Jackson)

1985 (8 Aug). Small Businesses. T **14** and similar horiz designs. Multicoloured. P 14.

77	12c. Type **14**	15	10
78	25c. Dressmaking	25	30
79	30c. Welding	25	30
80	50c. Basketry	45	65
77/80	*Set of* 4	1·00	1·25

15 *Antelope*

(Des R. Reynolds)

1985 (15 Nov). Sail Troopships. T **15** and similar horiz designs. Multicoloured. P 14.

81	12c. Type **15**	20	15
82	25c. *Pilot*	45	45

83	30c. *Salisbury*	45	45
84	50c. *Olive Branch*	80	85
81/4	*Set of 4*	1·75	1·75

16 Earth showing East Africa

17 Fifer in Winter Africa Dress

(Des J. van Ellinckhuijzen)

1986 (20 Mar). Appearance of Halley's Comet. T **16** and similar vert designs. Multicoloured. P 14.

85	12c. (1) Earth showing South America	60	70
	a. Sheetlet. Nos. 85/94	5·50	6·50
86	12c. (2) Type **16**	60	70
87	12c. (3) Stars and Moon	60	70
88	12c. (4) Moon and Milky Way	60	70
89	12c. (5) Milky Way and stars	60	70
90	12c. (6) Earth showing Australia	60	70
91	12c. (7) Earth and meteor	60	70
92	12c. (8) Meteor, Moon and comet tail	60	70
93	12c. (9) Comet head and Moon	60	70
94	12c. (10) Sun	60	70
85/94	*Set of 10*	5·50	6·50

Nos. 85/94 were printed together, *se-tenant*, in sheetlets of 10 forming a composite design of the southern skies in April. Each stamp is inscribed with a number from "A1-10" to "A10-10". The first number is given in brackets in the listing to aid identification.

PHILATELIC FOUNDATION MINIATURE SHEETS. These miniature sheets were issued by the Philatelic Foundation of Southern Africa and not by the postal administration. They could be purchased by post or from a limited number of philatelic offices at a premium in aid of various national and international stamp exhibitions.

(Des A. May)

1986 (12 June). British Military Uniforms (3rd series). 98th Regiment of Foot. T **17** and similar vert designs. Multicoloured. P 14.

95	14c. Type **17**	20	15
96	20c. Private in summer dress	30	30
97	25c. Grenadier in full summer dress	35	35
98	30c. Sergeant-major in full winter dress	50	50
95/8	*Set of 4*	1·25	1·10

The 30c. value exists as a Philatelic Foundation miniature sheet.

18 Welding Bicycle Frame

(Des J. van Niekerk)

1986 (18 Sept). Bicycle Factory, Dimbaza. T **18** and similar horiz designs. Multicoloured. P 14½×14.

99	14c. Type **18**	20	15
100	20c. Spray-painting frame	30	30
101	25c. Installing wheel-spokes	35	35
102	30c. Final assembly	50	50
99/102	*Set of 4*	1·25	1·10

19 President Dr. Lennox Sebe

(Des J. van Niekerk)

1986 (4 Dec). Fifth Anniv of Independence. T **19** and similar horiz designs. Multicoloured. P 14×14½.

103	14c. Type **19**	15	15
104	20c. National Shrine, Ntaba kaNdoda	20	20
105	25c. Legislative Assembly, Bisho	20	35
106	30c. Automatic telephone exchange, Bisho	25	50
103/6	*Set of 4*	70	1·10

20 *Boletus edulis*

21 Nkone Cow and Calf

(Des H. Botha)

1987 (19 Mar). Edible Mushrooms. T **20** and similar vert designs. Multicoloured. P 14×14½.

107	14c. Type **20**	20	15
108	20c. *Macrolepiota zeyheri*	25	30
109	25c. *Termitomyces sp*	30	40
110	30c. *Russula capensis*	35	55
107/10	*Set of 4*	1·00	1·25

The 20c. value exists as a Philatelic Foundation miniature sheet.

(Des D. Murphy)

1987 (18 June). Nkone Cattle. T **21** and similar horiz designs. Multicoloured. P 14½×14.

111	16c. Type **21**	20	15
112	20c. Nkone cow	25	30
113	25c. Nkone bull	30	35
114	30c. Herd of Nkone	40	55
111/14	*Set of 4*	1·00	1·25

22 Wire Windmill

23 Seven Birds

(Des A. H. Barrett)

1987 (17 Sept). Homemade Toys. T **22** and similar multicoloured designs. P 14×14½ (*vert*) or 14½×14 (*horiz*).

115	16c. Type **22**	20	15
116	20c. Rag doll	25	30
117	25c. Clay horse (*horiz*)	30	35
118	30c. Wire car (*horiz*)	40	55
115/18	*Set of 4*	1·00	1·25

(Des J. van Niekerk)

1987 (6 Nov). Folklore (1st series). Sikulume. T **23** and similar horiz designs. Multicoloured. P 14½×14.

119	16c. Type **23**	20	15
120	20c. Cannibals chasing Sikulume	25	30
121	25c. Sikulume attacking the inabulele	30	35
122	30c. Chief Mangangezulu chasing Sikulume and his bride	40	55
119/22	*Set of 4*	1·00	1·25

See also Nos. 127/36, 153/6 and 161/4.

24 Bush Lily (*Clivia nobilis*)

25 Numbakatali crying and Second Wife feeding Crows

(Des A. Batten)

1988 (17 Mar). Protected Flowers. T **24** and similar vert designs. Multicoloured. P 14×14½.

123	16c. Type **24**	15	15
124	30c. Harebell (*Dierama pulcherrimum*)	25	35
125	40c. Butterfly Iris (*Moraea reticulata*)	30	40
126	50c. Vlei Lily (*Crinum campanulatum*)	50	65
123/6 *Set of 4*		1·10	1·40

The 50c. value exists as a Philatelic Foundation miniature sheet.

(Des J. van Niekerk)

1988 (27 May). Folklore (2nd series). Mbulukazi. T **25** and similar horiz designs. Multicoloured. P 14×14½.

127	16c. Type **25**	25	30
	a. Sheetlet. Nos. 127/36	2·25	2·75
128	16c. Numbakatali telling doves of her childlessness	25	30
129	16c. Numbakatali finding children in earthenware jars	25	30
130	16c. Broad Breast sees Mbulukazi and brother at river	25	30
131	16c. Broad Breast asking to marry Mbulukazi	25	30
132	16c. Broad Breast and his two wives, Mbulukazi and her half-sister Mahlunguluza	25	30
133	16c. Mahlunguluza pushing Mbulukazi from precipice to her death	25	30
134	16c. Mbulukazi's ox tearing down Mahlunguluza's hut	25	30
135	16c. Ox licking Mbulukazi back to life	25	30
136	16c. Mahlunguluza being sent back to her father in disgrace	25	30
127/36 *Set of 10*		2·25	2·75

Nos. 127/36 were printed together, *se-tenant*, in sheetlets of 10.

26 Oranges and Grafted Rootstocks in Nursery

27 *Amanita phalloides*

(Des B. Jackson)

1988 (29 Sept). Citrus Farming. T **26** and similar horiz designs. Multicoloured. P 14×14½.

137	16c. Type **26**	15	15
138	30c. Lemons and marching rootstock onto mature tree	30	40
139	40c. Tangerines and fruit being hand picked	40	50
140	50c. Oranges and fruit being graded	50	65
137/40 *Set of 4*		1·25	1·50

(Des H. Botha)

1988 (1 Dec). Poisonous Fungi. T **27** and similar vert designs. Multicoloured. P 14×14½.

141	16c. Type **27**	50	30
142	30c. *Chlorophyllum molybdites*	70	75
143	40c. *Amanita muscaria*	80	1·10
144	50c. *Amanita pantherina*	85	1·25
141/4 *Set of 4*		2·50	3·00

28 Kat River Dam

29 Taking Eggs from Rainbow Trout

(Des Sheila Nowers)

1989 (2 Mar). Dams. T **28** and similar horiz designs. Multicoloured. P 14½×14.

145	16c. Type **28**	35	25
146	30c. Cata Dam	55	50
147	40c. Binfield Park Dam	65	65
148	50c. Sandile Dam	70	80
145/8 *Set of 4*		2·00	2·00

(Des B. Kent)

1989 (8 June). Trout Hatcheries. T **29** and similar horiz designs. Multicoloured. P 14½×14.

149	18c. Type **29**	25	15
150	30c. Fertilized eyed trout ova and alevins	45	45
151	40c. Five-week-old fingerlings	55	55
152	50c. Adult male	60	65
149/52 *Set of 4*		1·75	1·60

The 50c. value exists as a Philatelic Foundation miniature sheet.

30 Lion and Little Jackal killing Eland

(Des J. van Niekerk)

1989 (21 Sept). Folklore (3rd series). Little Jackal and the Lion. T **30** and similar horiz designs. Multicoloured. P 14½×14.

153	18c. Type **30**	15	15
154	30c. Little Jackal's children carrying meat to clifftop home	30	35
155	40c. Little Jackal pretending to be trapped	30	40
156	50c. Lion falling down cliff face	35	50
153/6 *Set of 4*		1·00	1·25

31 Cape Horse-cart

(Des J. Huntly)

1989 (7 Dec). Animal-drawn Transport. T **31** and similar horiz designs. Multicoloured. P 14×14½.

157	18c. Type **31**	20	15
158	30c. Jubilee spider	35	35
159	40c. Ballantine half-tent ox-drawn wagon	40	40
160	50c. Voortrekker wagon	45	50
157/60 *Set of 4*		1·25	1·25

32 Mpunzikazi offering Food to Five Heads

33 Handweaving on Loom

(Des J. van Niekerk)

1990 (15 Mar). Folklore (4th series). The Story of Makanda Mahlanu (Five Heads). T **32** and similar horiz designs. Multicoloured. P 14½×14.

161	18c. Type **32**	15	15
162	30c. Five Heads killing Mpunzikazi with his tail	30	35
163	40c. Mpunzanyana offering food to Five Heads	30	40
164	50c. Five Heads transformed into a man	35	50
161/4 *Set of 4*		1·00	1·25

(Des I. Ellithorne)

1990 (14 June). Handmade Carpets. T **33** and similar vert designs. Multicoloured. P 14×14½.

165	21c. Type **33**	20	20
166	35c. Spinning	40	50
167	40c. Dyeing yarn	55	70
168	50c. Knotting carpet	55	70
165/8 *Set of 4*		1·50	1·90

The 50c. value exists as a Philatelic Foundation miniature sheet.

34 Wooden Beam Plough, 1855

35 Prickly Pear Vendor

(Des J. Huntly)

1990 (6 Sept). Ploughs. T **34** and similar horiz designs. Multicoloured. P 14½×14.

169	21c. Type **34**	20	20
170	35c. Triple disc plough, 1895	30	40
171	40c. Reversible disc plough, 1895	35	50
172	50c. "Het Volk" double furrow plough, 1910	40	65
169/72	*Set of* 4	1·10	1·60

(Des A. H. Barrett)

1990 (29 Nov). Prickly Pear. T **35** and similar horiz designs. Multicoloured. P 14½×14.

173	21c. Type **35**	30	20
174	35c. Prickly pear bushes	50	50
175	40c. Whole and opened fruits	60	60
176	50c. Bushes in bloom	70	80
173/6	*Set of* 4	1·90	1·90

36 African Marsh Owl

37 São Bras (now Mossel Bay) on Map, 1500

(Des D. Finlay)

1991 (7 Feb). Owls. T **36** and similar vert designs. Multicoloured. P 14×14½.

177	21c. Type **36**	1·10	40
178	35c. African Scops Owl	1·40	80
179	40c. Barn Owl	1·75	1·00
180	50c. African Wood Owl	1·90	1·40
177/80	*Set of* 4	5·50	3·25

The 50c. value exists as a Philatelic Foundation miniature sheet.

(Des J. van Niekerk)

1991 (11 May). Stamp Day. D'Ataide's Letter of 1501. T **37** and similar horiz designs. Multicoloured. P 14×14½.

181	25c. Type **37**	70	70
	a. Horiz strip of 5. Nos. 181/5	3·25	3·25
182	25c. Bartolomeo Dias's ship foundering off Cabo Tormentoso (now Cape of Good Hope) during voyage to India, 1500	70	70
183	25c. Captain Pedro d'Ataide landing at So Bras, 1501	70	70
184	25c. D'Ataide leaving letter relating death of Dias on tree	70	70
185	25c. Captain Joao da Nova finding letter, 1501	70	70
181/5	*Set of* 5	3·25	3·25

Nos. 181/5 were printed together, *se-tenant*, in horizontal strips of 5 throughout the sheet. The inscriptions at the foot of Nos. 181 and 182 are transposed.

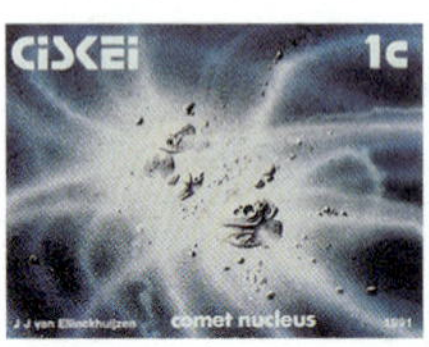

38 Comet Nucleus

39 Fort Armstrong and Xhosa Warrior

(Des J. van Ellinckhuijzen)

1991 (1 Aug). The Solar System. T **38** and similar horiz designs. Multicoloured. P 14.

186	1c. Type **38**	20	15
187	2c. Trojan asteroids	20	15
188	5c. Meteoroids	20	15
189	7c. Pluto	30	15
190	10c. Neptune	30	15
191	20c. Uranus	50	20
192	25c. Saturn	60	20
193	30c. Jupiter	65	30
194	35c. Planetoids in asteroid belt	65	40
195	40c. Mars	80	50
196	50c. The Moon	80	70
197	60c. Earth	80	80
198	1r. Venus	1·00	1·25
199	2r. Mercury	1·60	2·00
200	5r. The Sun	2·25	3·25
186/200	*Set of* 15	10·00	10·00
MS201	197×93 mm. Nos. 186/200	10·00	10·00

(Des D. Bagnall)

1991 (7 Nov). 19th-century Frontier Forts. T **39** and similar horiz designs. Multicoloured. P 14×14½.

202	27c. Type **39**	30	30
203	45c. Keiskamma Hoek Post and Sir George Grey (governor of Cape Colony, 1854–58)	45	55
204	65c. Fort Hare and Xhosa Chief Sandile	55	70
205	85c. Peddie Cavalry Barracks and cavalryman	75	1·25
202/5	*Set of* 4	1·90	2·50

40 *Cumulonimbus*

41 "Intelsat VI" Communications Satellite

(Des J. Meyer)

1992 (19 Mar). Cloud Formations. T **40** and similar vert designs. Multicoloured. P 14.

206	27c. Type **40**	40	25
207	45c. *Altocumulus*	55	65
208	65c. *Cirrus*	65	80
209	85c. *Cumulus*	75	1·10
206/9	*Set of* 4	2·10	2·50

(Des J. van Ellinckhuijzen)

1992 (4 June). International Space Year. Satellites over Southern Africa. T **41** and similar horiz designs. Multicoloured. P 14.

210	35c. Type **41**	40	25
211	70c. "G P S Navstar" (navigation)	80	80
212	90c. "Meteosat" (meteorology)	1·10	1·10
213	1r.05 "Landsat VI" (Earth resources survey)	1·25	1·40
210/13	*Set of* 4	3·25	3·25

The 70c. value exists as a Philatelic Foundation miniature sheet.

42 Universal Disc-harrow, 1914

43 Mpekweni Sun Marine Resort

(Des J. Huntly)

1992 (20 Aug). Agricultural Tools. T **42** and similar horiz designs. Multicoloured. P 14.

214	35c. Type **42**	40	25
215	70c. Clod crusher and pulveriser, 1914	80	70
216	90c. Self-dump hay rake, 1910	1·10	95
217	1r.05 McCormick hay tedder, 1900	1·10	1·10
214/17	*Set of* 4	3·00	2·75

1992 (5 Nov). Hotels. T **43** and similar horiz designs. Multicoloured. P 14.

218	35c. Type **43**	40	25
219	70c. Katberg Protea Hotel	80	80
220	90c. Fish River Sun Hotel	1·10	1·10
221	1r.05 Amatola Sun Hotel, Amatole Mountains	1·10	1·25
218/21	*Set of* 4	3·00	3·00

44 Vasco da Gama, São Gabriel and Voyage round Cape of Good Hope, 1497

45 Canary

(Des J. van Niekerk)

1993 (19 May). Navigators. T **44** and similar horiz designs. Multicoloured. P 14.

222	45c. Type **44**	65	30
223	65c. James Cook, H.M.S. *Endeavour* and first voyage, 1768–71	1·10	75
224	85c. Ferdinand Magellan, *Vitoria* and circumnavigation, 1519	1·25	90
225	90c. Sir Francis Drake, *Golden Hind* and circumnavigation, 1577–80	1·25	95
226	1r.05 Abel Tasman, Heemskerk and discovery of Tasmania, 1642	1·40	1·25
222/6	*Set of 5*	5·00	3·75

The ship on No. 222 is wrongly inscribed "San Gabriel", that on No. 224 "Victoria" and that on No. 226 "Heemskerck".

(Des J. Steyn (65c.), M. Goetz (85c.))

1993 (16 July). Cage Birds. T **45** and similar vert designs. Multicoloured. P 14.

227	45c. Type **45**	45	30
228	65c. Budgerigar	70	60
229	85c. Peach-faced Lovebirds	90	80
230	90c. Cockatiel	95	85
231	1r.05 Gouldian Finch	1·00	1·10
227/31	*Set of 5*	3·50	3·25

The 85c. value exists as a Philatelic Foundation miniature sheet.

46 Goshen Church (Moravian Mission), Whittlesea

(Des C. Meijer)

1993 (17 Sept). Churches and Missions. T **46** and similar horiz designs. P 14½×14.

232	45c. stone, black and scarlet	35	20
233	65c. azure, black and scarlet	60	60
234	85c. cinnamon, black and scarlet	80	80
235	1r.05 pale olive-yellow, black and scarlet	90	1·00
232/5	*Set of 4*	2·40	2·40

Designs:—65c. Kamastone Mission Church; 85c. Richie Thompson Memorial Church (Hertzog Mission), nr. Seymour; 1r.05, Bryce Ross Memorial Church (Pirie Mission), nr. Dimbaza.

47 Jointed Cactus

(Des Auriol Batten)

1993 (5 Nov). Invader Plants. T **47** and similar vert designs. Multicoloured. P 14.

236	45c. Type **47**	40	30
237	65c. Thorn Apple	70	60
238	85c. Coffee Weed	90	80
239	1r.05 Poisonous Wild Tobacco	1·00	1·00
236/9	*Set of 4*	2·75	2·40
MS240	98×125 mm. Nos. 236/9	2·75	2·75

48 *Losna* (steamer near Fish River), 1921

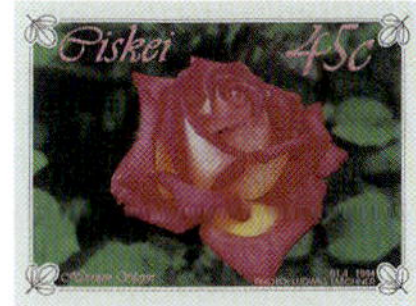

49 "Herman Steyn"

(Des Sheila Nowers)

1994 (18 Feb). Shipwrecks. T **48** and similar horiz designs. Multicoloured. P 14.

241	45c. Type **48**	75	30
242	65c. *Catherine* (barque) (Waterloo Bay), 1846	1·25	60
243	85c. *Bennebroek* (East Indiaman) (near Mtana River), 1713	1·40	90
244	1r.05 *São João Baptista* (galleon) (between Fish and Kei Rivers), 1622	1·50	1·25
241/4	*Set of 4*	4·50	2·75

1994 (15 Apr). Hybrid Roses. T **49** and similar horiz designs. Multicoloured. P 14.

245	45c. Type **49**	40	30
246	70c. "Esther Geldenhuys"	65	60
247	95c. "Margaret Wasserfall"	90	80
248	1r.15 "Professor Fred Ziady"	1·00	1·00
245/8	*Set of 4*	2·75	2·75
MS249	149×114 mm. Nos. 245/8	3·00	3·00

Ciskei was reincorporated into the Republic of South Africa on 27 April 1994. Its postal service continued to operate, using South African stamps, until 1 April 1996 when it was integrated with that of the Republic.

XIII. TRANSKEI

The Natives Land Act of 1913 laid down that Transkei should be reserved entirely for Black ownership and occupation. In 1963 Transkei was granted internal self-government by the South African Parliament and subsequently the Republic of Transkei was established, on 26 October 1976, as the first of the independent "black homelands". This independence did not receive international political recognition, but the stamps were accepted as valid on international mail.

PRINTERS. All the following stamps were printed in lithography by the South African Government Printer, Pretoria.

1 Lubisi Dam

2 K. D. Matanzima

(Des A. H. Barrett)

1976 (26 Oct)–**83**. Transkei Scenes and Occupations. T **1** and similar horiz designs. Multicoloured. P 12×12½.

1	1c. Type **1**	10	10
	a. Perf 14 (28.3.83)	30	20
2	2c. Soil cultivation	10	10
	a. Perf 14 (5.7.82)	15	10
3	3c. Threshing sorghum	15	10
	a. Perf 14 (6.7.82)	15	10
4	4c. Transkei matron	1·25	15
	a. Perf 14 (15.11.79)	15	10
5	5c. Grinding maize	1·25	15
	a. Perf 14 (8.4.80)	15	10
6	6c. Cutting Phormium tenax	15	10
	a. Perf 14 (8.7.82)	15	10
7	7c. Herd-boy	40	10
8	8c. Felling timber	20	10
	a. Perf 14 (20.1.82)	35	15
9	9c. Agricultural schooling	15	15
	a. Perf 14 (13.7.82)	25	25
10	10c. Tea picking	30	15
	a. Perf 14 (11.8.80)	20	15
11	15c. Carrying wood	40	25
	a. Perf 14 (16.10.81)	30	15
12	20c. Weaving industry	40	20
	a. Perf 14 (15.10.80)	35	15
13	25c. Cattle	45	25
	a. Perf 14 (26.10.81)	60	50
14	30c. Sledge transportation	60	50

	a. Perf 14 (13.8.80)	60	45
15	50c. Coat of arms and map	1·25	50
	a. Perf 14 (13.11.81)	60	60
16	1r. Administration building, Umtata	50	1·25
17	2r. The Bunga (Parliamentary building), Umtata	75	2·25
1/17	*Set of 17* (cheapest)	4·50	5·25

1976 (26 Oct). Independence. T **2** and similar vert designs. Multicoloured. P 12½.

18	4c. Type **2**	15	15
19	10c. Flag and mace	35	25
20	15c. K. D. Matanzima, Paramount Chief (different)	40	55
21	20c. Coat of arms	50	70
18/21	*Set of 4*	1·25	1·50

3 Beech 100 King Air of Transkei Airways

4 Artemisia afra

(Des A. H. Barrett)

1977 (11 Feb). Transkei Airways' Inaugural Flight. T **3** and similar horiz design. Multicoloured. P 12×12½.

22	4c. Type **3**	25	15
23	15c. Beech 100 King Air of Transkei Airways landing at Matanzima airport and on ground	75	85

(Des D. Findlay)

1977 (16 May). Medicinal Plants (1st series). T **4** and similar vert designs. Multicoloured. P 12½×12.

24	4c. Type **4**	15	10
25	10c. *Bulbine natalensis*	45	45
26	15c. *Melianthus major*	55	65
27	20c. *Cotyledon orbiculata*	65	90
24/7	*Set of 4*	1·60	1·75

See also Nos. 88/91.

5 Disc Jockey

6 Blind Basket Weaver

(Des A. H. Barrett)

1977 (26 Oct). First Anniv of Transkei Radio. T **5** and similar horiz design. Multicoloured. P 12×12½.

28	4c. Type **5**	15	10
29	15c. Announcer	60	60

(Des A. H. Barrett)

1977 (18 Nov). Help for the Blind. T **6** and similar vert designs. P 12½×12.

30	4c. black, grey-lilac and gold	15	10
31	15c. black, drab and gold	35	35
32	20c. black, pinkish brown and gold	75	80
30/2	*Set of 3*	1·10	1·10

Designs:—15c. Hands reading braille; 20c. Blind woman spinning.

7 Men's Carved Pipes

(Des A. H. Barrett)

1978 (1 Mar). Carved Pipes. T **7** and similar horiz designs. Multicoloured. P 12×12½.

33	4c. Type **7**	10	10
34	10c. Two men's pipes	15	15
35	15c. Multi-bowled men's pipes	25	40
36	20c. Woman's pipe and witch-doctor's pipe	30	50
33/6	*Set of 4*	70	1·00

8 Angora Goat

9 *Carissa bispinosa*

(Des A. H. Barrett)

1978 (9 June). Weaving Industry. T **8** and similar horiz designs. Multicoloured. P 12×12½.

37	4c. Type **8**	10	10
38	10c. Spinning mohair	15	15
39	15c. Dyeing mohair	20	25
40	20c. Weaving mohair rug	30	40
37/40	*Set of 4*	65	80

(Des D. Findlay)

1978 (25 Sept). Edible Wild Fruits. T **9** and similar vert designs. Multicoloured. P 12½×12.

41	4c. Type **9**	10	10
42	10c. *Dovyalis caffra*	15	15
43	15c. *Harpephyllum caffrum*	25	40
44	20c. *Syzygium cordatum*	30	60
41/4	*Set of 4*	70	1·10

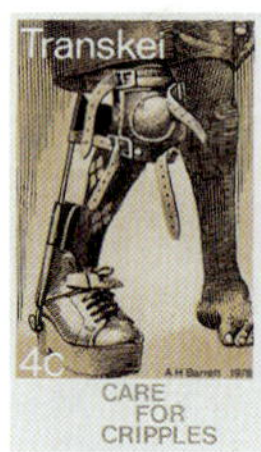

10 Calipers

11 Chi Cha Youth

(Des A. H. Barrett)

1978 (30 Nov). Care of Cripples. T **10** and similar vert designs. P 12½×12.

45	4c. black, pale brown and gold	10	10
46	10c. black, grey and gold	25	25
47	15c. black, olive-yellow and gold	40	50
45/7	*Set of 3*	65	75

Designs:—10c. Child in wheelchair; 15c. Nurse examining child's leg.

1979 (3 Jan). Abakwetha (coming-of-age ceremony of Xhosa males). T **11** and similar horiz designs. Multicoloured. P 12½.

48	4c. Type **11**	10	10
49	10c. Youths in three-month seclusion	15	20
50	15c. Umtshilo dance	25	35
51	20c. Burning of seclusion hut at end of final ceremony	35	45
48/51	*Set of 4*	75	1·00

12 President K. D. Matanzima

14 Magwa Falls

13 Windpump

1979 (20 Feb). Inauguration of Second State President. P 14×13½.

52	**12**	4c. brown-red and gold	15	10
53		15c. deep olive and gold	50	45

(Des K. De Beer)

1979 (13 Mar). Water Resources. T **13** and similar multicoloured designs. P 14.

54	4c. Type **13**	15	10
55	10c. Woman ladling water into jar	20	25
56	15c. Indwe River Dam (*horiz*)	35	55
57	20c. Ncora Dam (*horiz*)	40	70
54/7	*Set of 4*	1·00	1·40

(Des A. H. Barrett)

1979 (4 Sept). Waterfalls. T **14** and similar multicoloured designs. P 14×13½ (vert) or 13½×14 (horiz).

58	4c. Type **14**	15	10
59	10c. Bawa Falls	20	25
60	15c. Waterfall Bluff (horiz)	35	55
61	20c. Tsitsa Falls (horiz)	40	70
58/61	*Set of 4*	1·00	1·40

15 Expectant Mother pouring Milk

16 Black Gnat (dry fly)

(Des A. H. Barrett)

1979 (3 Dec). Child Health. T **15** and similar vert designs. Multicoloured. P 14×13½.

62	5c. Type **15**	15	10
63	15c. Mother breast-feeding baby	45	45
64	20c. Immunising child	60	65
62/4	*Set of 3*	1·10	1·10

(Des A. H. Barrett)

1980 (15 Jan). Fishing Flies (1st series). T **16** and similar horiz designs. Multicoloured. P 14.

65	5c. Type **16**	25	35
	a. Strip of 5. Nos. 65/9	1·10	1·60
66	5c. Zug Bug (nymph)	25	35
67	5c. March Brown (wet fly)	25	35
68	5c. Durham Ranger (salmon fly)	25	35
69	5c. Colonel Bates (streamer)	25	35
65/9	*Set of 5*	1·10	1·60

Nos. 65/9 were printed together, *se-tenant*, in strips of 5, both horizontally and vertically, within the sheet. See also Nos. 83/7, 99/103, 116/20 and 133/7.

17 Rotary Emblem

18 *Encephalartos altensteinii*

19 Red-chested Cuckoo

(Des G. Mynhardt and H. De Klerk)

1980 (22 Feb). 75th Anniv of Rotary International. P 14×13½.

70	**17**	15c. bright blue and gold	35	30

(Des D. Findlay)

1980 (30 Apr). Cycads. T **18** and similar vert designs. Multicoloured. P 14×13½.

71	5c. Type **18**	15	10
72	10c. *Encephalartos princeps*	20	25
73	15c. *Encephalartos villosus*	25	40
74	20c. *Encephalartos friderici-guilielmi*	30	55
71/4	*Set of 4*	80	1·10

(Des D. Findlay)

1980 (30 July). Birds. T **19** and similar vert designs. Multicoloured. P 14×13½.

75	5c. Type **19**	20	10
76	10c. Cape Puff-back Flycatcher	35	25
77	15c. South African Crowned Crane	50	60
78	20c. Spectacled Weaver	55	70
75/8	*Set of 4*	1·40	1·50

20 Hole in the Wall

(Des A. H. Barrett)

1980 (29 Oct). Tourism. T **20** and similar horiz designs. Multicoloured. P 14.

79	5c. Type **20**	15	10
80	10c. Port St. Johns	20	25
81	15c. The Citadel (rock)	25	40
82	20c. The Archway (rock)	30	55
79/82	*Set of 4*	80	1·10

(Des A. H. Barrett)

1981 (15 Jan). Fishing Flies (2nd series). Horiz designs as T **16**. Multicoloured. P 14.

83	10c. Kent's Lightning (streamer)	25	25
	a. Strip of 5. Nos. 83/7	1·10	1·10
84	10c. Wickham's Fancy (dry fly)	25	25
85	10c. Jock Scott (wet fly)	25	25
86	10c. Green Highlander (salmon fly)	25	25
87	10c. Tan Nymph	25	25
83/7	*Set of 5*	1·10	1·10

Nos. 83/7 were printed together, *se-tenant*, in strips of 5, both horizontally and vertically, within the sheet.

(Des D. Findlay)

1981 (15 Apr). Medicinal Plants (2nd series). Vert designs as T **4**. Multicoloured. P 14×13½.

88	5c. *Leonotis leonurus*	15	10
89	15c. *Euphorbia bupleurifolia*	20	30
90	20c. *Pelargonium reniforme*	20	35
91	25c. *Hibiscus trionum*	20	40
88/91	*Set of 4*	70	1·00

21 Eyamakhwenkwe

(Des A. H. Barrett)

1981 (28 Aug). Xhosa Women's Headdresses. T **21** and similar horiz designs. Multicoloured. P 14.

92	5c. Type **21**	10	10
93	15c. Eyabafana	20	35
94	20c. Umfazana	25	45
95	25c. Ixhegokazi	30	55
92/5	*Set of 4*	80	1·25
MS96	126×91 mm. Nos. 92/5	1·00	1·25

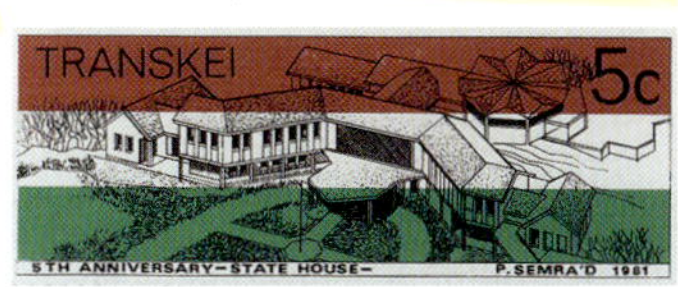

22 State House, Umtata

(Des P. Semra'd)

1981 (26 Oct). Fifth Anniv of Independence. T **22** and similar horiz design. P 14.

97	5c. black, lake-brown and emerald	15	10
98	15c. black, lake-brown and emerald	45	30

Design:—15c. University of Transkei.

(Des A. H. Barrett)

1982 (6 Jan). Fishing Flies (3rd series). Horiz designs as T **16**. Multicoloured. P 14.

99	10c. Blue Charm	25	30
	a. Strip of 5. Nos. 99/103	1·10	1·40
100	10c. Royal Coachman	25	30
101	10c. Light Spruce	25	30
102	10c. Montana Nymph	25	30
103	10c. Butcher	25	30
99/103 *Set of 5*		1·10	1·40

Nos. 99/103 were printed together, *se-tenant*, in strips of 5, both horizontally and vertically, within the sheet.

23 Cub Scout

24 Hippocrates

(Des H. Botha)

1982 (14 May). 75th Anniv of Boy Scout Movement. T **23** and similar vert designs. Multicoloured. P 14.

104	8c. Type **23**	15	10
105	10c. Scout planting tree	15	10
106	20c. Scout on raft	25	30
107	25c. Scout with dog	25	30
104/7 *Set of 4*		70	70

(Des J. Meyer)

1982 (5 Oct). Celebrities of Medicine (1st series). T **24** and similar vert designs. Multicoloured. P 14.

108	15c. Type **24**	20	20
109	20c. Antonie van Leeuwenhoek	25	30
110	25c. William Harvey	30	40
111	30c. Joseph Lister	35	45
108/11 *Set of 4*		1·00	1·25

See also Nos. 125/8, 160/3, 176/9, 249/52, 273/6, 281/4 and 305/8.

25 City Hall

(Des A. H. Barrett)

1982 (10 Nov). Centenary of Umtata. T **25** and similar horiz designs. Multicoloured. P 13½×14.

112	8c. Type **25**	10	10
113	15c. The Bunga	15	15
114	20c. Botha Sigcau Building	20	20
115	25c. Palace of Justice and K. D. Matanzima Building	25	30
112/15 *Set of 4*		65	65

(Des A. H. Barrett)

1983 (2 Mar). Fishing Flies (4th series). Horiz designs as T **16**. Multicoloured. P 14.

116	20c. Alexandra	25	30
	a. Strip of 5. Nos. 116/20	1·10	1·40
117	20c. Kent's Marbled Sedge	25	30
118	20c. White Marabou	25	30
119	20c. Mayfly Nymph	25	30
120	20c. Silver Wilkinson	25	30
116/20 *Set of 5*		1·10	1·40

Nos. 116/20 were printed together, *se-tenant*, in strips of 5, both horizontally and vertically, within the sheet.

26 Hotel Complex, Mzamba

(Des A. H. Barrett)

1983 (25 May). Wildcoast Holiday Complex, Mzamba. T **26** and similar horiz designs. Multicoloured. P 14.

121	10c. Type **26**	15	15
122	20c. Beach scene	25	25
123	25c. Casino	35	35
124	40c. Carousel	50	50
121/4 *Set of 4*		1·10	1·10

(Des J. Meyer)

1983 (17 Aug). Celebrities of Medicine (2nd series). Vert designs as T **24**. Multicoloured. P 14.

125	10c. Edward Jenner	15	15
126	20c. Gregor Mendel	25	30
127	25c. Louis Pasteur	30	35
128	40c. Florence Nightingale	40	55
125/8 *Set of 4*		1·00	1·25

27 Lady Frere Post Office

(Des A. H. Barrett)

1983 (9 Nov). Transkei Post Offices (1st series). T **27** and similar horiz designs. Multicoloured. P 14.

129	10c. Type **27**	15	15
130	20c. Idutywa	20	30
131	25c. Lusikisiki	20	35
132	40c. Cala	30	55
129/32 *Set of 4*		75	1·25

See also Nos. 156/9.

(Des A. H. Barrett)

1984 (10 Feb). Fishing Flies (5th series). Horiz designs as T **16**. Multicoloured. P 14.

133	20c. Silver Grey	35	45
	a. Strip of 5. Nos. 133/7	1·60	2·00
134	20c. Ginger Quill	35	45
135	20c. Hardy's Favourite	35	45
136	20c. March Brown	35	45
137	20c. Kent's Spectrum Mohawk	35	45
133/7 *Set of 5*		1·60	2·00

Nos. 133/7 were printed together, *se-tenant*, in strips of 5, both horizontally and vertically, within the sheet.

28 Amagqira

29 Soil Erosion by Overgrazing

(Des A. H. Barrett)

1984 (2 Apr)–**91**. Xhosa Culture. T **28** and similar horiz designs. Multicoloured. Ordinary paper. P 14.

138	1c. Type **28** (6.7.84)	20	10
	a. Chalk-surfaced paper (7.1.91)	30	10
139	2c. Horsemen (6.7.84)	20	10
140	3c. Mat making (6.7.84)	20	10
141	4c. hosa dancers (6.7.84)	20	10
142	5c. Shopping with donkeys (6.7.84)	20	10
143	6c. Young musicians (6.7.84)	30	15
144	7c. Fingo brides (6.7.84)	30	20
145	8c. Tasting the beer (6.7.84)	30	20
146	9c. Thinning the maize (6.7.84)	30	30
147	10c. Dancing demonstration (6.7.84)	30	15
148	11c. Water from the river	30	15
148*a*	12c. Preparing a meal (1.4.85)	30	15
148*b*	14c. Weeding mealies (chalk- surfaced paper) (1.4.86)	30	20
149	15c. National sport: stick fighting (6.7.84)	20	20
149*a*	16c. Morning pasture (chalk-surfaced paper) (1.4.87)	30	20
150	20c. Abakhwetha dance (6.7.84)	30	25

150*a* 21c. Building of initiation hut (chalk surfaced paper) (3.7.90) ..... 2·00 20
151 25c. Tribesman singing (6.7.84) 30 25
152 30c. Jovial matrons (6.7.84) 30 35
153 50c. Pipe making (6.7.84) 35 60
154 1r. Intonjane (6.7.84) ..... 50 1·10
155 2r. Abakhwetha (6.7.84) ..... 70 2·00
138/55 *Set of 22* ..... 7·50 6·50

(Des A. H. Barrett)

1984 (11 May). Transkei Post Offices (2nd series). Horiz designs as T **27**. Multicoloured. P 14.

156 11c. Umzimkulu 15 15
157 20c. Mount Fletcher 20 25
158 25c. Qumbu 20 25
159 30c. Umtata 30 50
156/9 *Set of 4* ..... 75 1·00

(Des J. Meyer)

1984 (12 Oct). Celebrities of Medicine (3rd series). Vert designs as T **24**. Multicoloured. P 14.

160 11c. Nicholas of Cusa 15 15
161 25c. William Morton 25 25
162 30c. Wilhelm Röntgen 30 40
163 45c. Karl Landsteiner 40 60
160/3 *Set of 4* ..... 1·00 1·25

(Des A. H. Barrett)

1985 (7 Feb). Soil Conservation. T **29** and similar horiz designs showing restoration of eroded landscape. Multicoloured. P 14½×14.

164 11c. Type **29** 15 15
165 25c. Removal of stock and construction of walls as sediment collectors 25 25
166 30c. Regeneration of vegetation 30 40
167 50c. Cattle grazing in lush landscape 40 60
164/7 *Set of 4* ..... 1·00 1·25

30 Tsitsa Bridge

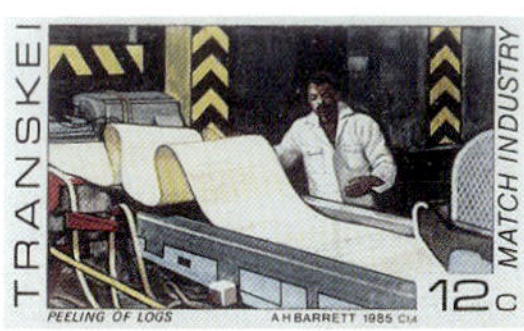

31 Veneer-peeling Machine

(Des D. Bagnall)

1985 (18 Apr). Bridges. T **30** and similar horiz designs. Multicoloured. P 14.

168 12c. Type **30** 20 15
169 25c. White Kei Railway Bridge 25 25
170 30c. Mitchell Bridge 35 35
171 50c. Umzimvubu Bridge 55 60
168/71 *Set of 4* ..... 1·25 1·25

(Des A. H. Barrett)

1985 (25 July). Match Industry, Butterworth. T **31** and similar horiz designs. Multicoloured. P 14½×14.

172 12c. Type **31** 10 15
173 25c. Cutting wood to match-size 15 25
174 30c. Dipping splints in chemical to form match heads 20 35
175 50c. Boxing matches 35 65
172/5 *Set of 4* ..... 70 1·25

(Des J. Meyer)

1985 (20 Sept). Celebrities of Medicine (4th series). Vert designs as T **24**. Multicoloured. P 14.

176 12c. Andreas Vesalius 20 15
177 25c. Marcello Malpighi 30 40
178 30c. Francois Magendie 35 45
179 50c. William Stewart Halsted 50 70
176/9 *Set of 4* ..... 1·25 1·50

32 Early Street Scene

33 *Aloe ferox*

(Des A. H. Barren)

1986 (6 Feb). Historic Port St. Johns. T **32** and similar horiz designs. Multicoloured. P 14½×14.

180 12c. Type **32** 20 15
181 20c. Umzimvubu (coaster) anchored at old jetty 45 45
182 25c. Wagons off-loading maize at jetty 50 50
183 30c. View of town at end of 19th century 50 55
180/3 *Set of 4* ..... 1·50 1·50
MS1841 30×94 mm. Nos. 180/3 ..... 1·50 1·50

PHILATELIC FOUNDATION MINIATURE SHEETS. These miniature sheets were issued by the Philatelic Foundation of Southern Africa and not the postal administration. They could be purchased by post or from a limited number of philatelic offices at a premium in aid of various national and international stamp exhibitions.

(Des D. Findlay)

1986 (1 May). Aloes. T **33** and similar vert designs. Multicoloured. P 14½×14.

185 14c. Type **33** 20 15
186 20c. *Aloe arborescens* 30 30
187 25c. *Aloe maculata* 35 35
188 30c. *Aloe ecklonis* 45 45
185/8 *Set of 4* ..... 1·10 1·10

The 30c. value exists as a Philatelic Foundation miniature sheet.

34 First Falls Station, Umtata River

35 Prime Minister George Matanzima

(Des R. Smith)

1986 (24 July). Hydro-electric Power Stations. T **34** and similar horiz designs. Multicoloured. P 14½×14.

189 14c. Type **34** 20 15
190 20c. Second Falls, Umtata River 25 25
191 25c. Ncora, Qumanco River 40 40
192 30c. Collywobbles, Mbashe River 50 50
189/92 *Set of 4* ..... 1·25 1·10

(Des J. van Niekerk)

1986 (26 Oct). Tenth Anniv of Independence. T **35** and similar horiz designs. Multicoloured. P 14½×14.

193 14c. Type **35** 15 15
194 20c. Technical College, Umtata 25 30
195 25c. University of Transkei, Umtata 30 40
196 30c. Palace of Justice, Umtata 40 50
193/6 *Set of 4* ..... 1·00 1·10

36 Piper PA-23 Apache 235 *Ulundi* flying through Clouds

37 Pondo Girl

(Des H. Botha)

1987 (5 Feb). Tenth Anniv of Transkei Airways Corporation. T **36** and similar horiz designs. Multicoloured. P 14½×14.

197	14c. Type **36**	20	15
198	20c. Tail fin of Ulundi	30	30
199	25c. Beech 100 King Air	40	40
200	30c. Control tower, K. D. Matanzima Airport	55	60
197/200	*Set of 4*	1·25	1·25

(Des A. H. Barrett)

1987 (22 May). Transkei Beadwork. T **37** and similar vert designs. Multicoloured. P 14×14½.

201	16c. Type **37**	15	15
202	20c. Bomvana woman	25	30
203	25c. Xessibe woman	35	40
204	30c. Xhosa man	40	60
201/4	*Set of 4*	1·00	1·25

The 25c. value exists as a Philatelic Foundation miniature sheet.

38 *Latrodectus indistinctus*

39 Common Black Pigs

(Des Liza van der Wal (16, 30c.), T. Marais (others))

1987 (27 Aug). Spiders. T **38** and similar vert designs. Multicoloured. P 14×14½.

205	16c. Type **38**	15	15
206	20c. *Nephila pilipes*	25	30
207	25c. *Lycosidae sp*	30	40
208	30c. *Argiope nigrovittata*	40	55
205/8	*Set of 4*	1·00	1·25

(Des B. Jackson)

1987 (22 Oct). Domestic Animals. T **39** and similar horiz designs. Multicoloured. P 14×14½.

209	16c. Type **39**	15	15
210	30c. Goats	20	30
211	40c. Merino sheep	30	50
212	50c. Cattle	45	65
209/12	*Set of 4*	1·00	1·40

40 *Plocamium corallorhiza*

(Des D. Thorpe)

1988 (18 Feb). Seaweed. T **40** and similar vert designs. Multicoloured. P 14×14½.

213	16c. Type **40**	15	15
214	30c. *Gelidium amanzii*	25	30
215	40c. *Ecklonia biruncinata*	30	40
216	50c. *Halimeda cuneata*	40	55
213/16	*Set of 4*	1·00	1·25

41 Spinning

(Des B. Jackson)

1988 (5 May). Blanket Factory, Butterworth. T **41** and similar horiz designs. Multicoloured. P 14½×14.

217	16c. Type **41**	10	10
218	30c. Warping	20	20
219	40c. Weaving	25	35
220	50c. Raising the nap	30	45
217/20	*Set of 4*	75	1·00

42 Map showing Wreck Site

43 Small-spotted Cat

(Des Sheila Nowers)

1988 (4 Aug). 206th Anniv of Shipwreck of Grosvenor (East Indiaman). T **42** and similar horiz designs. Multicoloured. P 14½×14.

221	16c. Type **42**	40	20
222	30c. "The Wreck of the Grosvenor" (R. Smirks)	50	50
223	40c. Dirk hilt, divider and coins from wreck.	55	55
224	50c. "African Hospitality" (G. Morland)	60	70
221/4	*Set of 4*	1·90	1·75

The 50c. value exists as a Philatelic Foundation miniature sheet.

(Des D. Murphy)

1988 (20 Oct). Endangered Animals. T **43** and similar horiz designs. Multicoloured. P 14½×14.

225	16c. Type **43**	60	30
226	30c. Blue Duiker	70	60
227	40c. Oribi	85	75
228	50c. Hunting Dog	1·25	1·00
225/8	*Set of 4*	3·00	2·40

44 Class 14 CRB Steam Locomotives

45 Mat, Baskets and Jar

(Des D. Hall-Green)

1989 (19 Jan). Trains. T **44** and similar multicoloured designs. P 14×14½ (horiz) or 14½×14 (vert).

229	16c. Type **44**	20	20
230	30c. Class 14 CRB locomotive and passenger train at Toleni Halt	40	40
231	40c. Double-headed steam train on Great Kei River Bridge (vert)	60	70
232	50c. Double-headed steam train in Kei Valley (vert)	65	80
229/32	*Set of 4*	1·75	1·90

The 50c. value exists as a Philatelic Foundation miniature sheet.

(Des Sheila Nowers)

1989 (20 Apr). Basketry. T **45** and similar horiz designs. Multicoloured. P 14½×14.

233	18c. Type **45**	20	15
234	30c. Basket and jar	30	30
235	40c. Jars and bag	40	50
236	50c. Dish and jars	55	75
233/6	*Set of 4*	1·25	1·50

46 Chub Mackerel

47 Broom Cluster Fig

(Des D. Thorpe)

1989 (20 July). Seafood. T **46** and similar horiz designs. Multicoloured. P 14½×14.

237	18c. Type **46**	55	15
238	30c. Squid	70	50

239	40c. Perna or Brown Mussels	85	70
240	50c. Rock Lobster	1·00	1·00
237/40	*Set of 4*	2·75	2·10

(Des B. Jackson)

1989 (5 Oct). Trees. T **47** and similar horiz designs. Multicoloured. P 14×14½.

241	18c. Type **47**	50	20
242	30c. Natal Fig	75	55
243	40c. Broad-leaved Coral	85	85
244	50c. Cabbage Tree	1·10	1·25
241/4	*Set of 4*	2·75	2·50

48 *Ginkgo koningensis*

(Des L. Kriedemann)

1990 (18 Jan). Plant Fossils. T **48** and similar horiz designs. Multicoloured. P 14.

245	18c. Type **48**	80	25
246	30c. *Pseudoctenis spatulata*	1·10	80
247	40c. *Rissikia media*	1·25	1·10
248	50c. *Taeniopteris anavolans*	1·40	1·50
245/8	*Set of 4*	4·00	3·25

49 Aretaeus (discoverer of diabetes)

(Des A. McBride)

1990 (29 Mar). Celebrities of Medicine (5th series). Diabetes Research. T **49** and similar vert designs. Multicoloured. P 14×14½.

249	18c. Type **49**	70	20
250	30c. Claude Bernard (discovered sugar formation by liver)	1·10	70
251	40c. Oscar Minkowski (discovered pancreas removal caused diabetes)	1·25	90
252	50c. Frederick Banting (discoverer of insulin)	1·40	1·25
249/52	*Set of 4*	4·00	2·75

50 Diviner dancing to Drum

51 Soldier Lily

(Des A. H. Barrett)

1990 (28 June). Diviners. T **50** and similar vert designs. Multicoloured. P 14×14½.

253	21c. Type **50**	50	20
254	35c. Lecturing Imichetywa (novitiates)	70	70
255	40c. Neophyte initiation	80	90
256	50c. Diviner's induction ceremony	95	1·40
253/6	*Set of 4*	2·75	3·00

The 50c. value exists as a Philatelic Foundation miniature sheet.

(Des A. Batten)

1990 (20 Sept). Flowers. T **51** and similar vert designs. Multicoloured. P 14.

257	21c. Type **51**	65	20
258	35c. *Disa crassicornis*	90	65
259	40c. Christmas Bells	1·00	90
260	50c. Port St. John's Creeper	1·25	1·40
257/60	*Set of 4*	3·50	2·75

52 Pink Ink Plant

53 Common Dolphin

(Des A. Batten)

1991 (10 Jan). Parasitic Plants. T **52** and similar vert designs. Multicoloured. P 14×14½.

261	21c. Type **52**	60	20
262	35c. White Harveya	90	70
263	40c. *Alectra sessiliflora*	1·00	1·10
264	50c. *Hydnora africana*	1·25	1·50
261/4	*Set of 4*	3·25	3·25

(Des D. Thorpe)

1991 (4 Apr). Dolphins. T **53** and similar horiz designs. Multicoloured. P 14½×14.

265	25c. Type **53**	1·00	25
266	40c. Bottle-nosed Dolphin	1·40	85
267	50c. Humpbacked Dolphin	1·60	1·25
268	60c. Risso's Dolphin	1·60	1·60
265/8	*Set of 4*	4·75	3·50

54 South African Crowned Crane

55 Emil von Behring and Shibasaburo Kitasako (diphtheria)

(Des A. Ainslie)

1991 (20 June). Endangered Birds. T **54** and similar vert designs. Multicoloured. P 14×14½.

269	25c. Type **54**	65	30
270	40c. Cape Vulture	1·00	85
271	50c. Wattled Crane	1·10	1·10
272	60c. Egyptian Vulture	1·25	1·40
269/72	*Set of 4*	3·50	3·25

The 60c. value exists as a Philatelic Foundation miniature sheet.

(Des J. van Niekerk)

1991 (26 Sept). Celebrities of Medicine (6th series). Vaccine Development. T **55** and similar horiz designs. Multicoloured. P 14×14½.

273	25c. Type **55**	1·00	25
274	40c. Camille Guérin and Albert Calmette (tuberculosis)	1·50	90
275	50c. Jonas Salk (poliomyelitis)	1·75	1·25
276	60c. John Enders (measles)	1·75	1·50
273/6	*Set of 4*	5·50	3·50

56 *Eulophia speciosa*

57 Thomas Weller (researcher into infectious viruses)

(Des A. Batten)

1992 (20 Feb). Orchids. T **56** and similar vert designs. Multicoloured. P 14.

277	27c. Type **56**	25	20
278	45c. *Satyrium sphaerocarpum*	40	40
279	65c. *Disa scullyi*	60	70
280	85c. *Disa tysonii*	80	1·00
277/80	*Set of 4*	1·90	2·10

(Des J. van Niekerk)

1992 (1 Apr). Celebrities of Medicine (7th series). T **57** and similar horiz designs. Multicoloured. P 14.

281	27c. Type **57**	75	25
282	45c. Ignaz Semmelweis	1·10	80
283	65c. Sir James Simpson	1·50	1·25
284	85c. René Laënnec	1·75	1·60
281/4	*Set of 4*	4·50	3·50

58 Red-billed Pintail

59 *Pseudomelania sutherlandi* (gastropod)

1992 (16 July). Waterfowl. T **58** and similar horiz designs. Multicoloured. P 14.

285	35c. Type **58**	60	60
	a. Pair. Nos. 285/6	1·10	1·10
286	35c. Hottentot Teal	60	60
287	70c. Maccoa Duck	90	90
	a. Pair. Nos. 287/8	1·75	1·75
288	70c. White-backed Duck	90	90
289	90c. African Black Duck	1·10	1·10
	a. Pair. Nos. 289/90	2·10	2·10
290	90c. Egyptian Goose	1·10	1·10
291	1r.05 Cape Shoveler	1·40	1·40
	a. Pair. Nos. 291/2	2·75	2·75
292	1r.05 Cape Teal	1·40	1·40
285/92	*Set of 8*	7·25	7·25

The two designs of each value were printed together, *se-tenant*, in pairs within the sheets.

No. 287 exists as a Philatelic Foundation miniature sheet.

(Des L. Kriedemann)

1992 (17 Sept). Marine Fossils. T **59** and similar horiz designs. Multicoloured. P 14.

293	35c. Type **59**	1·10	35
294	70c. *Gaudryceras denseplicatum* (ammonite)	1·50	1·10
295	90c. *Neithea quinquecostata* (bivalve)	1·60	1·50
296	1r.05 *Pugilina acuticarinatus* (gastropod)	1·75	1·60
293/6	*Set of 4*	5·50	4·00

60 Papillon

61 Fabrosaurus

(Des D. Murphy)

1993 (12 Feb). Dogs. T **60** and similar horiz designs. Multicoloured. P 14.

297	35c. Type **60**	60	30
298	70c. Pekinese	90	90
299	90c. Chihuahua	1·10	1·25
300	1r.05 Dachshund	1·40	1·60
297/300	*Set of 4*	3·50	3·50

The 70c. value exists as a Philatelic Foundation miniature sheet.

(Des L. Kriedemann)

1993 (18 June). Prehistoric Animals. T **61** and similar horiz designs. Multicoloured. P 14.

301	45c. Type **61**	1·10	40
302	65c. Diictodon	1·50	1·10
303	85c. Chasmatosaurus	1·75	1·60
304	1r.05 Rubidgea	1·75	1·75
301/4	*Set of 4*	5·50	4·25

62 Sir Alexander Fleming and Howard Florey

63 Laughing Doves

(Des J. van Niekerk)

1993 (20 Aug). Celebrities of Medicine (8th series). T **62** and similar horiz designs. Multicoloured. P 14.

305	45c. Type **62**	70	40
306	65c. Alexis Carrel	1·10	1·10
307	85c. James Lind	1·25	1·50
308	1r.05 Santiago Ramón y Cajal	1·40	1·60
305/8	*Set of 4*	4·00	4·25

(Des Julia Birkhead)

1993 (15 Oct). Doves. T **63** and similar horiz designs. Multicoloured. P 14.

309	45c. Type **63**	60	40
310	65c. Tambourine Doves	90	90
311	85c. Emerald-spotted Wood Doves	1·25	1·25
312	1r.05 Namaqua Doves	1·50	1·60
309/12	*Set of 4*	3·75	3·75
MS313	92×83 mm. Nos. 309/12	3·75	3·75

64 *Clan Lindsay* (steamer) on rocks, Mazeppa Bay, 1898

(Des J. van Niekerk)

1994 (18 Mar). Shipwrecks. T **64** and similar horiz designs. Multicoloured. P 14.

314	45c. Type **64**	1·25	60
315	65c. *Horizon* (freighter) on rocks near River Mngazi, 1967	1·60	1·25
316	85c. *Oceanos* (pleasure cruiser) sinking near Coffee Bay, 1991	1·90	1·60
317	1r.05 *Forresbank* (freighter) on fire near River Mtakatye, 1958	1·90	1·90
314/17	*Set of 4*	6·00	4·75

The 85c. value exists as a Philatelic Foundation miniature sheet.

Transkei was reincorporated into the Republic of South Africa on 27 April 1994. Its postal service continued to operate, using South African stamps, until 1 April 1996 when it was integrated with that of the Republic.

XIV. VENDA

The Venda Territory Authority was established in 1969 and was granted internal self-government on 1 February 1973 under the Bantu Homelands Constitution Act. Venda became fully independent on 13 September 1979. This independence did not receive international political recognition, but the stamps were accepted as valid on international mail.

PRINTERS. All the following stamps were printed in lithography by the South African Government Printer, Pretoria.

1 Flag and Mace

2 *Tecomaria capensis*

(Des A. H. Barrett)

1979 (13 Sept). Independence. T **1** and similar horiz designs. Multicoloured. P 14.

1	4c. Type **1**	20	20
2	15c. Government Buildings, Thohoyandou	25	40

3	20c. Chief Minister P. R. Mphephu	30	60
4	25c. Coat of arms	45	90
1/4	*Set of 4*	1·10	1·90

(Des D. Findlay)

1979 (13 Sept)–**85**. Flowers. T **2** and similar vert designs. Multicoloured. P 14 (11, 12c.) or 12½ (others).

5	1c. Type **2**	40	10
	a. Perf 14 (30.4.82)	10	10
6	2c. *Catophractes alexandri*	30	15
	a. Perf 14 (6.5.81)	20	15
7	3c. *Tricliceras lungipedunculatum*	30	10
	a. Perf 14 (18.8.82)	30	15
8	4c. *Dissotis princeps*	30	10
9	5c. *Gerbera jamesonii*	1·75	45
	a. Perf 14 (15.1.80)	30	10
10	6c. *Hibiscus mastersianus*	15	10
11	7c. *Nymphaea caerulea*	20	10
12	8c. *Crinum lagardiae*	45	25
	a. Perf 14 (27.1.82)	30	15
13	9c. *Xerophyta retinervis*	20	15
14	10c. *Hypoxis angustifolia*	40	25
	a. Perf 14 (4.3.83)	1·25	15
14*b*	11c. *Combretum microphyllum* (2.4.84)	55	15
14*c*	12c. *Clivia caulescens* (1.4.85)	30	15
15	15c. *Pycnostachys urticifolia*	30	15
16	20c. *Zantedeschia jucunda*	75	15
17	25c. *Leonotis mollis*	2·00	1·00
	a. Perf 14 (22.1.80)	50	40
18	30c. *Littonia modesta*	40	30
19	50c. *Protea caffra*	40	40
	a. Perf 14 (17.2.84)	1·40	1·25
20	1r. *Adenium multiflorum*	75	85
21	2r. *Strelitzia caudata*	1·25	2·00
5/21	*Set of 19* (cheapest)	7·00	10·00

3 Man drinking Beer

4 Tea Plants in Nursery

(Des A. H. Barrett)

1980 (13 Feb). Wood Carvings. T **3** and similar multicoloured designs. P 14.

22	5c. Type **3**	15	15
23	10c. Frying mealies in gourd	25	25
24	15c. King Nebuchadnezzar (horiz)	40	40
25	20c. Python squeezing woman to death (horiz)	50	60
22/5	*Set of 4*	1·10	1·25

(Des A. H. Barrett)

1980 (14 May). Tea Cultivation. T **4** and similar horiz designs. Multicoloured. P 14.

26	5c. Type **4**	15	10
27	10c. Tea pluckers	20	20
28	15c. Withering in the factory	35	35
29	20c. Cut, twist, curl unit	40	45
26/9	*Set of 4*	1·00	1·00

5 Young Banana Plants

6 *Precis tugela*

(Des A. H. Barrett)

1980 (13 Aug). Banana Cultivation. T **5** and similar horiz designs. Multicoloured. P 14.

30	5c. Type **5**	15	10
31	10c. Cutting "hands"	25	25
32	15c. Sorting and dividing into clusters	30	30
33	20c. Packing	40	45
30/3	*Set of 4*	1·00	1·00

(Des D. Findlay)

1980 (13 Nov). Butterflies. T **6** and similar vert designs. Multicoloured. P 14.

34	5c. Type **6**	20	15
35	10c. *Charaxes bohemani*	30	40
36	15c. *Catacroptera cloanthe*	40	55
37	20c. *Papilio dardanus*	50	70
34/7	*Set of 4*	1·25	1·60

7 Collared Sunbird

8 Nwanedi Dam

(Des J. Hoekstra)

1981 (16 Feb). Sunbirds. T **7** and similar vert designs. Multicoloured. P 14.

38	5c. Type **7**	20	15
39	15c. Mariqua Sunbird	30	40
40	20c. Southern White-bellied Sunbird	35	45
41	25c. Scarlet-chested Sunbird	35	55
38/41	*Set of 4*	1·10	1·40

(Des A. H. Barrett)

1981 (6 May). Lakes and Waterfalls. T **8** and similar horiz designs. Multicoloured. P 14.

42	5c. Type **8**	15	10
43	15c. Mahovhohovho Falls	30	30
44	20c. Phiphidi Falls	35	35
45	25c. Lake Fundudzi	35	40
42/5	*Set of 4*	1·00	1·00

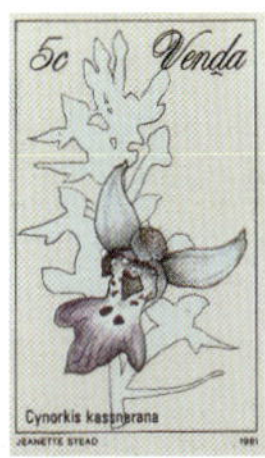

9 *Cynorkis kassnerana*

10 Mbila

(Des Jeannette Stead)

1981 (11 Sept). Orchids. T **9** and similar vert designs. Multicoloured. P 14.

46	5c. Type **9**	15	10
47	15c. *Eulophia fridericii*	30	35
48	20c. *Bonatea densiflora*	35	45
49	25c. *Mystacidium brayboniae*	35	55
46/9	*Set of 4*	1·00	1·25
MS50	96×120 mm. Nos. 46/9	1·25	1·40

(Des J. Hoekstra)

1981 (13 Nov). Musical Instruments. T **10** and similar horiz designs. P 14.

51	5c. yellow-orange and black	10	10
52	15c. red-orange and black	25	25
53	20c. orange-brown and black	30	35
54	25c. brown-ochre and black	30	35
51/4	*Set of 4*	80	90

Designs:—15c. Phalaphala; 20c. Tshizambi; 25c. Ngoma.

11 Gathering Sisal

(Des B. Ashton)

1982 (26 Feb). Sisal Cultivation. T **11** and similar horiz designs. Multicoloured. P 13½×14.

55	5c. Type **11**	10	10

56	10c. Drying	20	20
57	20c. Grading	30	35
58	25c. Baling	30	40
55/8	*Set of 4*	80	90

12 Bison Petrograph, Altamira, Spain

(Des H. Botha)

1982 (15 June). History of Writing (1st series). T **12** and similar horiz designs. Multicoloured. P 14.

59	8c. Type **12**	15	10
60	15c. Petroglyph, Eastern California	30	30
61	20c. Pictograph script (Sumerian tablet)	40	40
62	25c. Bushman burial stone, Humansdorp	45	45
59/62	*Set of 4*	1·10	1·10

No. 59 is inscribed "AHAMIRA" in error. See also Nos. 75/8, 87/90, 107/10, 139/42, 171/4 and 203/6.

13 *Euphorbia ingens*

14 *Rana angolensis*

(Des D. Findlay)

1982 (17 Sept). Indigenous Trees (1st series). T **13** and similar horiz designs. Multicoloured. P 14.

63	8c. Type **13**	15	10
64	15c. *Pterocarpus angolensis*	25	30
65	20c. *Ficus ingens*	30	40
66	25c. *Adansonia digitata*	40	55
63/6	*Set of 4*	1·00	1·25

See also Nos. 79/82, 95/8 and 227/30.

(Des A. H. Barrett)

1982 (26 Nov). Frogs. T **14** and similar horiz designs. Multicoloured. P 14.

67	8c. Type **14**	15	10
68	15c. *Chiromantis xerampelina*	25	30
69	20c. *Leptopelis sp*	30	40
70	25c. *Ptychadena anchietae*	40	55
67/70	*Set of 4*	1·00	1·25

15 European Bee Eater

(Des Sheila Nowers)

1983 (16 Feb). Migratory Birds (1st series). T **15** and similar horiz designs. Multicoloured. P 14.

71	8c. Type **15**	25	15
72	20c. Tawny Eagle ("Steppe Eagle")	50	65
73	25c. Violet Starling ("Plum-coloured Starling")	60	75
74	40c. Abdim's Stork ("White-bellied Stork")	90	1·50
71/4	*Set of 4*	2·00	2·75

See also Nos. 91/4.

(Des H. Botha)

1983 (11 May). History of Writing (2nd series). Multicoloured designs as T **12**, but vert. Multicoloured. P 14.

75	10c. Indus Valley script	15	10
76	20c. Sumerian cuneiform	20	25
77	25c. Egyptian hieroglyphics	25	30
78	40c. Chinese handscroll	50	70
75/8	*Set of 4*	1·00	1·25

(Des D. Findlay)

1983 (3 Aug). Indigenous Trees (2nd series). Horiz designs as T **13**. Multicoloured. P 14.

79	10c. *Gardenia spatulifolia*	15	10
80	20c. *Hyphaene natalensis*	25	30
81	25c. *Albizia adianthifolia*	30	40
82	40c. *Sesamothamnus lugardii*	40	60
79/82	*Set of 4*	1·00	1·25

16 Avocado

17 African Paradise Flycatcher

(Des B. Jackson)

1983 (26 Oct). Subtropical Fruit. T **16** and similar horiz designs. Multicoloured. P 14.

83	10c. Type **16**	15	10
84	20c. Mango	25	30
85	25c. Papaya	30	40
86	40c. Litchi	40	60
83/6	*Set of 4*	1·00	1·25

(Des H. Botha)

1984 (17 Feb). History of Writing (3rd series). Horiz designs as T **12**. Multicoloured. P 14×14½.

87	10c. Evolution of cuneiform sign	15	10
88	20c. Evolution of Chinese character	25	30
89	25c. Development of Cretan hieroglyphics	30	40
90	40c. Development of Egyptian hieroglyphics	40	60
87/90	*Set of 4*	1·00	1·25

(Des Sheila Nowers)

1984 (26 Apr). Migratory Birds (2nd series). T **17** and similar vert designs. Multicoloured. P 14½×14.

91	11c. White Stork	30	20
92	20c. Type **17**	50	50
93	25c. Black Kite ("Yellow-billed Kite")	60	60
94	30c. Wood Sandpiper	70	85
91/4	*Set of 4*	1·90	1·90

(Des D. Findlay)

1984 (21 June). Indigenous Trees (3rd series). Horiz designs as T **13**. Multicoloured. P 14.

95	11c. Afzelia quanzensis	15	10
96	20c. Peltophorum, africanum	25	30
97	25c. Gyrocarpus americanus	30	40
98	30c. Acacia sieberana	40	55
95/8	*Set of 4*	1·00	1·25

18 Dzata Ruins, Nzhelele Valley

19 White-browed Robin Chat

(Des B. Jackson)

1984 (13 Sept). Fifth Anniv of Independence. T **18** and similar horiz designs. Multicoloured. P 14.

99	11c. Type **18**	15	10
100	25c. Traditional hut	25	30
101	30c. Sub-economical house	30	35
102	45c. Modern home	45	65
99/102	*Set of 4*	1·00	1·25

(Des Sheila Nowers)

1985 (10 Jan). Songbirds. T **19** and similar vert designs. Multicoloured. P 14½×14.

103	11c. Type **19** (inscr "Heuglin's Robin")	25	20
104	25c. Black-collared Barbet	35	40

105	30c. African Black-headed Oriole	40	50
106	50c. Kurrichane Thrush	60	80
103/6	*Set of 4*	1·40	1·75

(Des H. Botha)

1985 (21 Mar). History of Writing (4th series). Horiz designs as T **12**. Multicoloured. P 14.

107	11c. Southern Arabic characters	15	10
108	25c. Phoenician characters	25	30
109	30c. Aramaic characters	30	40
110	50c. Canaanite characters	50	75
107/10	*Set of 4*	1·10	1·40

20 Transvaal Red Milkwood

21 *Pellaea dura*

(Des Sheila Nowers)

1985 (21 June). Food from the Veld (1st series). T **20** and similar vert designs. Multicoloured. P 14.

111	12c. Type **20**	15	10
112	25c. Buffalo Thorn	25	30
113	30c. Wild Water Melon	30	35
114	50c. Brown Ivory	40	60
111/14	*Set of 4*	1·00	1·25

See also Nos. 163/6.

(Des D. Findlay)

1985 (5 Sept). Ferns. T **21** and similar vert designs. Multicoloured. P 14.

115	12c. Type **21**	15	10
116	25c. *Actiniopteris radiata*	25	25
117	30c. *Adiantum hispidulum*	30	35
118	50c. *Polypodium polypodioides*	40	65
115/18	*Set of 4*	1·00	1·25

22 Three-lined Grass Snake

23 Etruscan Dish

1986 (16 Jan)–**93**. Reptiles. T **22** and similar horiz designs. Multicoloured. Chalk-surfaced paper. P 14.

119	1c. Type **22**	10	10
	a. Ordinary paper (29.5.89)	30	30
120	2c. Mole Snake	10	10
	a. Ordinary paper (29.5.89)	40	40
121	3c. Ornate Scrub Lizard	10	10
122	4c. Puff Adder	10	10
123	5c. Three-lined Skink	10	10
	a. Ordinary paper (12.7.93)	40	40
124	6c. Egyptian Cobra	15	10
125	7c. Blue-tailed Kopje Skink	15	10
126	8c. Spotted Bush Snake	20	20
	a. Ordinary paper (12.7.93)	40	40
127	9c. Yellow-throated Plated Lizard	20	20
128	10c. Northern Lined Shovelsnout	20	20
	a. Ordinary paper (20.7.93)	40	40
129	14c. Transvaal Flat Lizard (1.4.86)	1·25	20
130	15c. Soutpansberg Lizard	30	20
	a. Ordinary paper (13.9.89)	40	40
131	16c. Iguana Water Leguan (1.4.87)	60	20
132	18c. Black Mamba (ordinary paper) (3.7.89)	75	20
133	20c. Transvaal Flat Gecko	30	20
	a. Ordinary paper (17.9.90)	1·25	70
133	21c. Flap-necked Chameleon (ordinary paper) (3.8.90)	75	20
134	25c. Longtailed Garter Snake	40	30
135	30c. Tigroid Thick-toed Gecko	40	35
	a. Ordinary paper (4.9.92)	75	75
136	50c. Cape File Snake	40	50
137	1r. Soutpansberg Girdled Lizard	55	1·00
	a. Ordinary paper (9.7.90)	2·25	2·25
138	2r. African Python	70	2·00
	a. Ordinary paper (27.1.89)	3·75	3·75
119/38	*Set of 21*	7·00	6·00

(Des H. Botha)

1986 (10 Apr). History of Writing (5th series). T **23** and similar vert designs. Multicoloured. P 14×14½.

139	14c. Type **23**	15	10
140	20c. Greek inscription, AD70	30	30
141	25c. Roman inscription	40	40
142	30c. Cyrillic inscription (Byzantine mosaic)	55	60
139/42	*Set of 4*	1·25	1·25

24 Planting Pine Seedlings

(Des B. Jackson)

1986 (26 June). Forestry. T **24** and similar horiz designs. Multicoloured. P 14.

143	14c. Type **24**	20	15
144	20c. Mule hauling logs	30	30
145	25c. Off-loading logs at sawmill	40	40
146	30c. Using timber in construction	55	60
143/6	*Set of 4*	1·25	1·25

PHILATELIC FOUNDATION MINIATURE SHEETS. These miniature sheets were issued by the Philatelic Foundation of Southern Africa and not the postal administration. They could be purchased by post or from a limited number of philatelic offices at a premium in aid of various national and international stamp exhibitions.

25 Maxwell, 1910

26 Comb Duck

(Des A. H. Barrett)

1986 (4 Sept). FIVA International Veteran Car Rally. T **25** and similar horiz designs. Multicoloured. P 14½×14.

147	14c. Type **25**	20	15
148	20c. Bentley 4½ l., 1929	30	30
149	25c. Plymouth Coupé, 1933	40	40
150	30c. Mercedes Benz 220, 1958	55	60
147/50	*Set of 4*	1·25	1·25

The 30c. value exists as a Philatelic Foundation miniature sheet.

(Des A. H. Barrett)

1987 (8 Jan). Waterfowl. T **26** and similar multicoloured designs. P 14×14½ (vert) or 14½×14 (horiz).

151	14c. Type **26**	1·00	40
152	20c. White-faced Whistling Duck	1·10	70
153	25c. Spur-winged Goose (horiz)	1·25	90
154	30c. Egyptian Goose (horiz)	1·40	1·25
151/4	*Set of 4*	4·25	3·00

The 25c. value exists as a Philatelic Foundation miniature sheet.

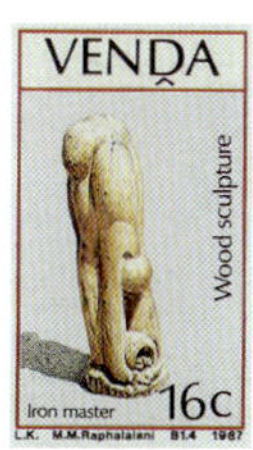

27 "Iron Master"

28 Tigerfish

(Des L. Kriedemann)

1987 (9 Apr). Wood Sculptures by Meshack Matamela Raphalalani. T **27** and similar vert designs. Multicoloured. P 14½×14.

155	16c. Type **27**	15	15
156	20c. "Distant Drums"	25	25
157	25c. "Sunrise"	30	30
158	30c. "Obedience"	40	40
155/8	*Set of 4*	1·00	1·00

(Des D. Thorpe)

1987 (2 July). Freshwater Fish. T **28** and similar horiz designs. Multicoloured. P 14×14½.

159	16c. Type **28**	25	20
160	20c. Barred Minnow	35	35
161	25c. Mozambique Mouthbrooder	45	45
162	30c. Sharp-toothed Catfish	55	60
159/62	*Set of 4*	1·40	1·40

29 Cross-berry

30 Picking Berries

(Des Sheila Nowers)

1987 (2 Oct). Food from the Veld (2nd series). T **29** and similar vert designs. Multicoloured. P 14×14½.

163	16c. Type **29**	20	15
164	30c. Wild Date Palm	30	30
165	40c. Tree Fuchsia	40	40
166	50c. Wild Cucumber	50	55
163/6	*Set of 4*	1·25	1·25

(Des B. Jackson)

1988 (21 Jan). Coffee Industry. T **30** and similar horiz designs. Multicoloured. P 14½×14.

167	16c. Type **30**	20	20
168	30c. Weighing bags of berries	30	30
169	40c. Drying beans in sun	35	35
170	50c. Roasting graded beans	45	45
167/70	*Set of 4*	1·10	1·10

31 "Universal Love" in Chinese

(Des H. Botha)

1988 (28 Apr). History of Writing (6th series). T **31** and similar horiz designs. P 14½×14.

171	16c. stone, black and bright scarlet	20	20
172	30c. stone, black and bright scarlet	25	35
173	40c. stone, black and deep rose-red	35	45
174	50c. black and gold	45	60
	a. Gold omitted		
171/4	*Set of 4*	1·10	1·40

Designs:—30c. "Picture of a lion on a stone" in Devanagari (Indian script); 40c. "Information" in Russian; 50c. "Peace be upon you" in Thuluth (Arabic script).

32 College

(Des L. Kriedemann)

1988 (18 Aug). Fifth Anniv of Shayandima Nurses' Training College. T **32** and similar horiz designs. Multicoloured. P 14½×14.

175	16c. Type **32**	20	15
176	30c. Students using microscope	30	35
177	40c. Anatomy class	35	40
178	50c. Clinical training	40	50
175/8	*Set of 4*	1·10	1·25

33 "Fetching Water"

34 Ndongwana (clay bowls)

1988 (6 Oct). Watercolours by Kenneth Thabo. T **33** and similar horiz designs. Multicoloured. P 14½×14.

179	16c. Type **33**	20	15
180	30c. "Grinding Maize"	30	35
181	40c. "Offering Food"	35	40
182	50c. "Kindling the Fire"	40	50
179/82	*Set of 4*	1·10	1·25

The 50c. value exists as a Philatelic Foundation miniature sheet.

(Des L. Kriedemann)

1989 (5 Jan). Traditional Kitchenware. T **34** and similar horiz designs. Multicoloured. P 14½×14.

183	16c. Type **34**	15	20
184	30c. Ndilo (wooden porridge bowls)	25	30
185	40c. Mufaro (basket with lid)	30	40
186	50c. Muthatha (dish woven from ilala palm)	40	45
183/6	*Set of 4*	1·00	1·25

35 Domba

36 Southern Ground Hornbill

(Des K. Thabo)

1989 (5 Apr). Traditional Dances. T **35** and similar horiz designs. Multicoloured. P 14½×14.

187	18c. Type **35**	15	20
188	30c. Tshinzerere	25	30
189	40c. Malende	30	40
190	50c. Malombo	40	45
187/90	*Set of 4*	1·00	1·25

(Des M. Enslin)

1989 (27 June). Endangered Birds. T **36** and similar vert designs. Multicoloured. P 14½×14.

191	18c. Type **36**	80	30
192	30c. Lappet-faced Vulture	1·10	70
193	40c. Bateleur	1·40	90
194	50c. Martial Eagle	1·60	1·25
191/4	*Set of 4*	4·50	2·75

The 50c. value exists as a Philatelic Foundation miniature sheet.

37 Pres. Gota F. N. Ravele

38 Lion

(Des A. H. Barrett)

1989 (13 Sept). Tenth Anniv of Independence. T **37** and similar horiz designs. Multicoloured. P 14½×14.

195	18c. Type **37**	20	20
196	30c. Presidential offices	30	30
197	40c. President's residence	40	40
198	50c. Thohoyandou Sports Stadium	45	45
195/8	*Set of 4*	1·25	1·25

(Des D. Murphy)

1990 (1 Mar). Nwanedi National Park. T **38** and similar vert designs. Multicoloured. P 14×14½.

199	18c. Type **38**	40	25
200	30c. Common Zebra	70	55
201	40c. Cheetah	75	65
202	50c. White Rhinoceros	1·50	1·25
199/202	*Set of 4*	3·00	2·40

The 50c. value exists as a Philatelic Foundation miniature sheet.

39 Calligraphy

40 *Aloe globuligemma*

(Des H. Botha)

1990 (23 May). History of Writing (7th series). T **39** and similar vert designs. P 14½×14.

203	21c. black and grey	20	15
204	30c. black and reddish brown	40	40
205	40c. black and yellowish green	50	50
206	50c. blue, new blue and black	60	65
203/6	*Set of 4*	1·50	1·50

Designs:—30c. Part of score for Beethoven's Moonlight Sonata; 40c. Characters from personal computer; 50c. Television picture of message transmitted into outer space from Arecibo 1000 radio telescope.

(Des G. Marx)

1990 (23 Aug). Aloes. T **40** and similar vert designs. Multicoloured. P 14½×14.

207	21c. Type **40**	30	25
208	35c. *Aloe aculeata*	50	50
209	40c. *Aloe lutescens*	60	70
210	50c. *Aloe angelica*	70	90
207/10	*Set of 4*	1·90	2·10

41 *Pseudacraea boisduvalii*

42 Cape Puff-back Flycatchers

(Des E. Forbes)

1990 (15 Nov). Butterflies. T **41** and similar vert designs. Multicoloured. P 14×14½.

211	21c. Type **41**	70	40
212	35c. *Papilio nireus*	1·00	75
213	40c. *Charaxes jasius*	1·10	1·00
214	50c. *Aeropetes tulbaghia*	1·25	1·25
211/14	*Set of 4*	3·50	3·00

1991 (7 Mar). Birds. T **42** and similar horiz designs showing paintings by Claude Finch-Davies. Multicoloured. P 14½×14.

215	21c. Type **42**	50	40
216	35c. Red-capped Robin Chat	75	80
217	40c. Collared Seabirds	85	1·00
218	50c. Yellow-streaked Greenbul	1·10	1·40
215/18	*Set of 4*	2·75	3·25

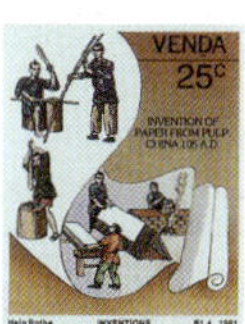

43 Paper made from Pulp

44 Venda Sun Hotel Complex, Thohoyandou

(Des H. Botha)

1991 (6 June). Inventions (1st series). T **43** and similar vert designs. Multicoloured. P 14½×14.

219	25c. Type **43**	55	35
220	40c. Magnetic compass	1·00	75
221	50c. Abacus	1·10	1·00
222	60c. Gunpowder	1·75	1·25
219/22	*Set of 4*	4·00	3·00

The 60c. value exists as a Philatelic Foundation miniature sheet. See also Nos. 239/42 and 259/62.

1991 (29 Aug). Tourism. T **44** and similar horiz designs. Multicoloured. P 14½×14.

223	25c. Type **44**	55	35
224	40c. Mphephu Resort	85	75
225	50c. Sagole Spa	95	95
226	60c. Luphephe-Nwanedi Resort	1·00	1·25
223/6	*Set of 4*	3·00	3·00

(Des D. Findlay)

1991 (21 Nov). Indigenous Trees (4th series). Horiz designs as T **13**. Multicoloured. P 14½×14.

227	27c. Fever Tree	60	35
228	45c. Transvaal Beech	1·00	75
229	65c. Transvaal Wild Banana	1·10	1·10
230	85c. Sausage Tree	1·40	1·50
227/30	*Set of 4*	3·50	3·25

45 Setting the Web

46 *Apis mellifera*

1992 (5 Mar). Clothing Factory. T **45** and similar horiz designs. Multicoloured. P 14.

231	27c. Type **45**	45	25
232	45c. Knitting	60	55
233	65c. Making up garment	90	1·00
234	85c. Inspection of finished product	1·25	1·50
231/4	*Set of 4*	2·75	3·00

(Des A. Ainslie)

1992 (21 May). Bees. T **46** and similar horiz designs. Multicoloured. P 14.

235	35c. Type **46**	70	40
236	70c. *Anthidium cordiforme*	1·10	90
237	90c. *Megachile frontalis*	1·50	1·25
238	1r.05 *Xylocopa caffra*	1·60	1·40
235/8	*Set of 4*	4·50	3·50

The 70c. value exists as a Philatelic Foundation miniature sheet.

47 Egyptian Plough

(Des H. Botha)

1992 (13 Aug). Inventions (2nd series). T **47** and similar horiz designs. Multicoloured. P 14.

239	35c. Type **47**	60	40
240	70c. Early wheel, Mesopotamia	1·00	90
241	90c. Making bricks, Egypt	1·40	1·25
242	1r.05 Early Egyptian sailing ship	1·50	1·40
239/42	*Set of 4*	4·00	3·50

48 Nile Crocodile

(Des A. Ainslie)

1992 (15 Oct). Crocodile Farming. T **48** and similar horiz designs. Multicoloured. P 14½×14.

243	35c. Type **48**	85	40

244	70c. Egg laying	1·40	1·00
245	90c. Eggs hatching	1·60	1·60
246	1r.05 Mother carrying young	1·75	1·90
243/6	*Set of 4*	5·00	4·50

49 Burmese

50 Green Heron

(Des Sheila Nowers)

1993 (19 May). Domestic Cats. T **49** and similar horiz designs. Multicoloured. P 14.

247	45c. Type **49**	1·00	45
248	65c. Tabby	1·40	1·00
249	85c. Siamese	1·60	1·40
250	1r.05 Persian	1·75	1·75
247/50	*Set of 4*	5·25	4·25

The 65c. value exists as a Philatelic Foundation miniature sheet.

(Des Priscilla Henley)

1993 (16 July). Herons. T **50** and similar horiz designs. Multicoloured. P 14.

251	45c. Type **50**	80	50
252	65c. Black-crowned Night Heron	1·10	95
253	85c. Purple Heron	1·40	1·40
254	1r.05 Black-headed Heron	1·60	1·90
251/4	*Set of 4*	4·50	4·25
MS255	86×132 mm. Nos. 251/4	4·50	4·75

51 Punching out Sole Lining

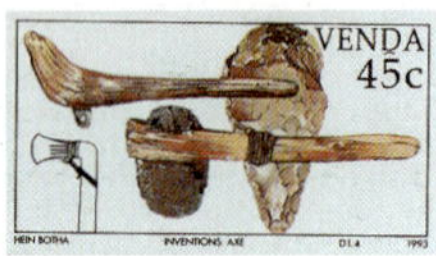

52 Axes

1993 (17 Sept). Shoe Factory. T **51** and similar horiz designs. Multicoloured. P 14×14½.

256	45c. Type **51**	25	20
257	65c. Shaping heel	45	50
258	85c. Joining the upper to inner sole	60	75
259	1r.05 Forming sole	70	1·25
256/9	*Set of 4*	1·75	2·40

(Des H. Botha)

1993 (5 Nov). Inventions (3rd series). T **52** and similar horiz designs. Multicoloured. P 14.

260	45c. Type **52**	30	35
261	65c. Armour	55	65
262	85c. Arches	75	85
263	1r.05 Pont du Gard aqueduct	85	1·25
260/3	*Set of 4*	2·25	2·75

53 Cocker Spaniel

54 Savanna Monkey

(Des D. Murphy)

1994 (14 Jan). Dogs. T **53** and similar horiz designs. Multicoloured. P 14.

264	45c. Type **53**	90	50
265	65c. Maltese	1·25	1·00
266	85c. Scottish Terrier	1·50	1·50
267	1r.05 Miniature Schnauzer	1·90	2·00
264/7	*Set of 4*	5·00	4·50

The 85c. value exists as a Philatelic Foundation miniature sheet.

(Des A. Ainslie)

1994 (4 Mar). Monkeys. T **54** and similar horiz designs. Multicoloured. P 14½×14.

268	45c. Type **54**	75	55
269	65c. Lesser Bushbaby	1·00	1·00
270	85c. Diademed Monkey	1·25	1·50
271	1r.05 Thick-tailed Bushbaby	1·50	2·00
268/71	*Set of 4*	4·00	4·50
MS272	119×70 mm. Nos. 268/71	4·00	4·50

55 Red-shouldered Glossy Starlings

(Des Julia Birkhead)

1994 (29 Apr). Starlings. T **55** and similar horiz designs. Multicoloured. P 14.

273	45c. Type **55**	1·00	65
274	70c. Violet Starlings	1·50	1·50
275	95c. African Red-winged Starlings	1·75	1·90
276	1r.15 Wattled Starlings	2·00	2·25
273/6	*Set of 4*	5·75	5·75

Venda was reincorporated into the Republic of South Africa on 27 April 1994. Its postal service continued to operate, using South African stamps, until 1 April 1996 when it was integrated with that of the Republic.

Swaziland

PRICES FOR STAMPS ON COVER TO 1945

Nos.	1/10	*from* × 40
Nos.	11/20	*from* × 4
Nos.	21/4	*from* × 5
Nos.	25/7	*from* × 10
Nos.	28/38	*from* × 4
Nos.	39/41	*from* × 5
Nos.	D1/2	*from* × 30

TRIPARTITE GOVERNMENT

Following internal unrest and problems caused by the multitude of commercial concessions granted by the Swazi king the British and Transvaal governments intervened during 1889 to establish a tripartite administration under which the country was controlled by their representatives, acting with the agent of the Swazi king.

The Pretoria government had previously purchased the concession to run the postal service and, on the establishment of the tripartite administration, provided overprinted Transvaal stamps for use from a post office at Embekelweni and later at Bremersdorp and Darkton.

Swazieland
(**1**)

1889 (18 Oct)–**90**. Stamps of Transvaal (South African Republic) optd with T **1**, in black.

(a) P 12½×12

1	**18**	1d. carmine	22·00	22·00
		a. Opt inverted	£700	£650
2		2d. olive-bistre	85·00	32·00
		a. Opt inverted	—	£1400
		b. "Swazielan"	£1100	£650
		c. "Swazielan" inverted		
3		1s. green	15·00	13·00
		a. Opt inverted	£800	£475

(b) P 12½

4	**18**	½d. grey	9·00	22·00
		a. Opt inverted	£950	£750
		b. "Swazielan"	£1800	£1000
		c. "Swazielan" inverted	—	£7000
5		2d. olive-bistre	27·00	16·00
		a. Opt inverted	£950	£450
		b. "Swazielan"	£475	£400
		c. "Swazielan" inverted	£7000	£4750
6		6d. blue	35·00	55·00
7		2s.6d. buff (20.10.90)	£325	£400
8		5s. slate-blue (20.10.90)	£170	£250
		a. Opt inverted	£1900	£3000
		b. "Swazielan"	£4500	
		c. "Swazielan" inverted		
9		10s. dull chestnut (20.10.90)	£6500	£4000

The "Swazielan" variety occurs on R. 6/1 in each sheet of certain printings.

A printing of the ½d, 1d., 2d. and 10s. yellow-brown with stop after "Swazieland" was made in July 1894, but such stamps were not issued.

It is possible that the dates quoted above were those on which the overprinting took place in Pretoria and that the stamps were issued slightly later in Swaziland itself.

1892 (Aug). Optd in carmine. P 12½.

10	**18**	½d. grey	7·50	16·00
		a. Opt inverted	£500	
		b. Opt double	£475	£475
		c. Pair, one without opt	—	£2000

No. 10 was overprinted in Pretoria during August 1892 when Swaziland was under quarantine due to smallpox. It is unlikely that it saw much postal use before all the overprints were withdrawn, although cancelled-to-order examples are plentiful.

It appears likely that no further supplies of stamps overprinted "Swazieland" were provided by Pretoria after December 1892, although stocks held at post offices were used up. The overprinted stamps were declared to be invalid from 7 November 1894. They were replaced by unoverprinted issues of the Transvaal (South African Republic).

Stamps of TRANSVAAL (SOUTH AFRICAN REPUBLIC) used in Swaziland between December 1892 and January 1900.

1885–93. (Nos. 175/87).

Z1	½d. grey	42·00
Z2	1d. carmine	42·00
Z3	2d. olive-bistre	22·00
Z4	2½d. mauve	45·00
Z5	3d. mauve	45·00
Z6	4d. bronze-green	45·00
Z9	2s.6d. orange-buff	

1893. (Nos. 195/9).

Z10	½d. on 2d. olive-bistre (Type A surch in red)	
	a. Surch Type B	
Z11	½d. on 2d. olive-bistre (Type A surch in black)	
Z12	1d. on 6d. blue (Type A surch)	50·00
	a. Surch Type B	60·00
Z13	2½d. on 1s. green ("2½ Pence" in one line) (Type A surch)	50·00
	a. Surch Type B	60·00

1894. (Nos. 200/4).

Z16	1d. carmine	42·00
Z17	2d. olive-bistre	42·00

1895–96. (Nos. 205/12*a*).

Z20	½d. pearl-grey	42·00
Z21	1d. rose-red	22·00
Z22	2d. olive-bistre	22·00
Z25	6d. pale dull blue	42·00

1895. (Nos. 213/14).

Z27	½d. on 1s. green	

1895. Introduction of Penny Postage (No. 215b).

Z29	1d. red	65·00

1896–97. (Nos. 216/24).

Z30	½d. green	42·00
Z31	1d. rose-red and green	22·00
Z33	2½d. dull blue and green	45·00
Z35	4d. sage-green and green	42·00
Z36	6d. lilac and green	42·00
Z37	1s. ochre and green	85·00

Prices are for clear and fairly complete postmarks. Examples dated in 1892 and 1893 are worth a premium. For list of post offices open during this period see boxed note below. Most known examples are from Bremersdorp (squared circle inscr "SWAZIEL" later replaced by "Z.A.R." or c.d.s.) or Darkton (c.d.s.).

Shortly after the outbreak of the Boer War in 1899 the Transvaal administration withdrew from Swaziland, although the post office at Darkton, which was on the border, was still operating in early 1900. There was, however, no further organised postal service in Swaziland until the country became a British Protectorate in March 1902. From that date, until the introduction of the 1933 definitives, the stamps of Transvaal and subsequently South Africa were in use.

The following post offices or postal agencies existed in Swaziland before 1933. Dates given are those on which it is generally accepted that the offices were first opened. Some were subsequently closed before the end of the period.

Bremersdorp (1890)	Mankaiana (1913)
Darkton (1891)	Mbabane (*previously* Embabaan) (1905)
Dwaleni (1918)	M'dimba (1898)
Embabaan (1895)	Mhlotsheni (1910)
Embekelweni (1889)	Mooihoek (1918)
Ezulweni (1910)	Motshane (1929)
Forbes Reef (1906)	Nomahasha (1904)
Goedgegun (1925)	Nsoko (1927)
Hlatikulu (1903)	Piggs Peak (1899)
Hluti (1912)	Sandhlan (1903)
Ivy (1912)	Sicunusa (1913)
Kubuta (1926)	Stegi (1910)
Mahamba (1899)	Umkwakweni (1898)
Malkerns (1914)	White Umbuluzi (1925)
Malomba (1928)	

BRITISH PROTECTORATE

2 King George V

3 King George VI

(Des Rev. C. C. Tugman. Recess D.L.R.)

1933 (3 Jan). Wmk Mult Script CA. P 14.

11	**2**	½d. green	30	30
12		1d. carmine	30	20
13		2d. brown	30	45
14		3d. blue	45	3·00
15		4d. orange	3·00	3·50
16		6d. bright purple	1·25	1·00
17		1s. olive	1·50	2·75

No.	Description	Un	Us
18	2s.6d. bright violet	15·00	22·00
19	5s. grey	32·00	50·00
20	10s. sepia	£110	£150
11/20 *Set of* 10		£150	£200
11s/20s Perf "SPECIMEN" *Set of* 10		£275	

The ½d, 1d., 2d. and 6d. values exist overprinted "OFFICIAL", but authority for their use was withdrawn before any were actually used. However, some stamps had already been issued to the Secretariat staff before instructions were received to invalidate their use (*Price* £27000 *per set un*).

1935 (4 May). Silver Jubilee. As Nos. 111/14 of Botswana, but ptd by B.W. P 11×12.

No.	Description	Un	Us
21	1d. deep blue and scarlet	50	1·50
	a. Extra flagstaff	£300	£375
	b. Short extra flagstaff	£475	
	c. Lightning conductor	£475	
	d. Flagstaff on right-hand turret	£130	
	e. Double flagstaff	£130	
22	2d. ultramarine and grey-black	2·00	2·75
	a. Extra flagstaff	£140	£200
	b. Short extra flagstaff	£160	£225
	c. Lightning conductor	£140	£200
23	3d. brown and deep blue	1·00	8·50
	a. Extra flagstaff	95·00	£250
	b. Short extra flagstaff	£130	£250
	c. Lightning conductor	£110	£250
24	6d. slate and purple	3·00	5·50
	a. Extra flagstaff	£120	£200
	b. Short extra flagstaff	£140	
	c. Lightning conductor	£150	
21/4 *Set of* 4		6·00	16·00
21s/4s Perf "SPECIMEN" *Set of* 4		£120	

For illustrations of plate varieties see above No. 111 of Botswana.

1937 (12 May). Coronation. As Nos. 115/17 of Botswana. P 11×11½.

No.	Description	Un	Us
25	1d. carmine	50	2·50
26	2d. yellow-brown	50	25
27	3d. blue	50	75
25/7 *Set of* 3		1·40	3·25
25s/7s Perf "SPECIMEN" *Set of* 3		£110	

(Recess D.L.R.)

1938 (1 Apr)–**54**. Wmk Mult Script CA. P 13½×13.

No.	Type	Description	Un	Us
28	**3**	½d. green	2·50	1·25
		a. Perf 13½×14 (1.43)	30	2·75
		b. Perf 13½×14. *Bronze-green* (2.50)	3·00	10·00
29		1d. rose-red	2·75	1·25
		a. Perf 13½×14 (1.43)	1·00	1·75
30		1½d. light blue	4·50	75
		a. Perf 14 (1941)	2·75	1·00
		b. Perf 13½×14 (1.43)	30	1·00
		ba. Printed on the gummed side	£4000	
31		2d. yellow-brown	2·50	1·25
		a. Perf 13½×14 (1.43)	40	50
32		3d. ultramarine	11·00	1·75
		a. Deep blue (10.38)	17·00	1·75
		b. Perf 13½×14 *Ultramarine* (1.43)	8·00	10·00
		c. Perf 13½×14 *Light ultram* (10.46)	24·00	23·00
		d. Perf 13½×14 *Deep blue* (10.47)	15·00	12·00
33		4d. orange	10·00	2·50
		a. Perf 13½×14 (1.43)	65	1·40
34		6d. deep magenta	22·00	2·75
		a. Perf 13½×14 (1.43)	5·50	4·50
		b. Perf 13½×14. *Reddish purple (shades)* (7.44)	4·50	1·50
		c. Perf 13½×14. *Claret* (13.10.54)	9·00	8·50
35		1s. brown-olive	22·00	2·00
		a. Perf 13½×14 (1.43)	1·25	65
36		2s.6d. bright violet	28·00	4·25
		a. Perf 13½×14. *Violet* (1.43)	24·00	4·50
		b. Perf 13½×14. *Reddish violet* (10.47)	22·00	15·00
37		5s. grey	65·00	18·00
		a. Perf 13½×14. *Slate* (1.43)	55·00	55·00
		b. Perf 13½×14. *Grey* (5.44)	45·00	18·00
38		10s. sepia	75·00	7·00
		a. Perf 13½×14 (1.43)	9·00	6·50
28/38a *Set of* 11			80·00	35·00
28s/38s Perf "SPECIMEN" *Set of* 11			£275	

The above perforations vary slightly from stamp to stamp, but the average measurements are respectively: 13.3×13.2 comb (13½×13), 14.2 line (14) and 13.3×13.8 comb (13½×14).

Swaziland
(4)

1945 (3 Dec). Victory. Nos. 108/10 of South Africa optd with T **4**.

No.	Description	Un pair	Us pair	Us single
39	1d. brown and carmine	65	80	10
40	2d. slate-blue and violet	65	80	10
41	3d. deep blue and blue	65	2·50	20
39/41 *Set of* 3		1·75	3·75	35

1947 (17 Feb). Royal Visit. As Nos. 132/5 of Botswana.

No.	Description	Un	Us
42	1d. scarlet	10	10
43	2d. green	10	10
44	3d. ultramarine	10	10
45	1s. mauve	10	10
42/5 *Set of* 4		35	35
42s/5s Perf "SPECIMEN" *Set of* 4		£130	

1948 (1 Dec). Royal Silver Wedding. As Nos. 136/7 of Botswana.

No.	Description	Un	Us
46	1½d. ultramarine	50	1·00
47	10s. purple-brown	40·00	45·00

1949 (10 Oct). 75th Anniv of U.P.U. As Nos. 138/41 of Botswana.

No.	Description	Un	Us
48	1½d. blue	15	20
	a. "A" of "CA" missing from wmk		
49	3d. deep blue	2·00	3·75
50	6d. magenta	30	70
51	1s. olive	30	3·00
	a. "A" of "CA" missing from wmk	£1000	
48/51 *Set of* 4		2·25	7·00

1953 (3 June). Coronation. As No. 142 of Botswana.

No.	Description	Un	Us
52	2d. black and yellow-brown	20	20

5 Havelock Asbestos Mine

7 Swazi Married Woman

(Recess B.W.)

1956 (2 July). T **5**, **7** and similar designs. Wmk Mult Script CA. P 13×13½ (horiz) or 13½×13 (vert).

No.	Type	Description	Un	Us
53	**5**	½d. black and orange	30	10
54	–	1d. black and emerald	10	10
55	**7**	2d. black and brown	30	10
56	–	3d. black and rose-red	20	10
57	–	4½d. black and deep bright blue	60	10
58	–	6d. black and magenta	2·75	10
59	**5**	1s. black and deep olive	20	10
60	–	1s.3d. black and sepia	3·50	4·75
61	–	2s.6d. emerald and carmine-red	2·50	3·00
62	–	5s. deep lilac and slate-black	10·00	7·00
63	**7**	10s. black and deep lilac	22·00	20·00
64	–	£1 black and turquoise-blue	60·00	38·00
53/64 *Set of* 12			90·00	65·00

Designs: *Horiz*—1d., 2s.6d. A Highveld view; *Vert*—3d., 1s.3d. Swazi courting couple; 4½d., 5s. Swazi warrior in ceremonial dress, 6d., £1. Greater Kudu.

(New Currency. 100 cents = 1 rand)

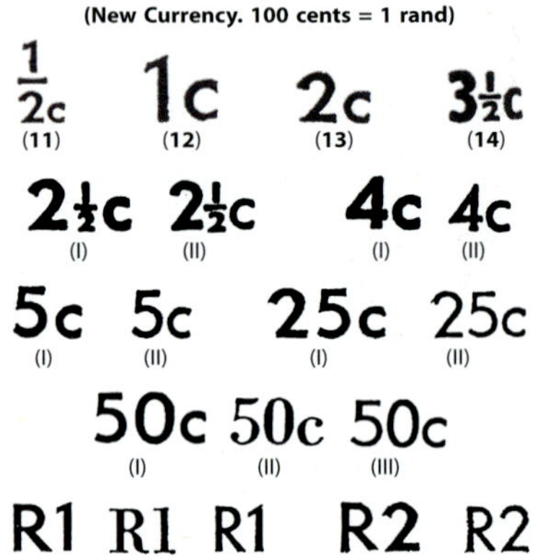

1961 (14 Feb). Nos. 53/64 surch as T **11** to **14**.

No.	Description	Un	Us
65	½c. on ½d.	3·25	5·50
	a. Surch inverted	£1200	
66	1c. on 1d.	10	2·25
	a. Surch double*	£1300	
67	2c. on 2d.	10	2·50
68	2½c. on 2d.	10	1·25
69	2½c. on 3d. (Type I)	10	10
	a. Type II	10	15
70	3½c. on 2d. (May)	10	1·25

71	4c. on 4½d. (Type I)	10	10
	a. Type II	20	10
72	5c. on 6d. (Type I)	20	10
	a. Type II	10	20
73	10c. on 1s.	35·00	6·50
	a. Surch double*	£1400	
74	25c. on 2s.6d. (Type I)	30	1·00
	a. Type II (central)	85	1·25
	b. Type II (bottom left)	£350	£425
75	50c. on 5s. (Type I)	30	1·00
	a. Type II	8·00	2·50
	b. Type III	£600	£750
76	1r. on 10s. (Type I)	1·50	1·25
	a. Type II	3·00	6·00
	b. Type III	70·00	£100
77	2r. on £1 (Type I)	16·00	16·00
	a. Type II (middle left)	11·00	17·00
	b. Type II (bottom)	80·00	£160
65/77a *Set of 13*		45·00	35·00

*On both Nos. 66a and 73a the second surcharge falls across the horizontal perforations.

No. 74b has the thin Type II surcharge at bottom left, in similar position to the thicker Type I, No. 74, with which it should not be confused.

No. 77b has the surcharge centrally placed at bottom. No. 77a has it at middle left, above "KUDU".

No. 66 with surcharge central (instead of bottom left) and No. 75a bottom left (instead of middle left) are believed to be from trial sheets released with the normal stocks. They do not represent separate printings. (No. 66 *price* £45 *un*, No. 75a *price* £150 *un*.).

(Recess B.W.)

1961. As 1956 issue, but with values in cents and rands. Wmk Mult Script CA. P 13×13½ (horiz) or 13½×13 (vert).

78	½c. black and orange (as ½d.) (14.2)	10	1·25
79	1c. black and emerald (as 1d.) (14.2)	10	10
80	2c. black and brown (as 2d.) (10.9)	10	2·50
81	2½c. black and rose-red (as 3d.) (14.2)	15	10
82	4c. black and deep bright blue (as 4½d.) (10.9)	15	1·50
83	5c. black and magenta (as 6d.) (10.9)	1·25	15
84	10c. black and deep olive (as 1s.) (14.2)	15	10
85	12½c. black and sepia (as 1s 3d.) (14.2)	1·25	70
86	25c. emerald and carmine-red (as 2s 6d.) (1.8)	4·50	6·00
87	50c. deep lilac and slate-black (as 5s.) (10.9)	4·50	2·25
88	1r. black and deep lilac (as 10s.) (10.9)	11·00	14·00
89	2r. black and turquoise-blue (as £1) (1.8)	18·00	12·00
78/89 *Set of 12*		35·00	35·00

15 Swazi Shields

16 Battle Axe

(Des Mrs. C. Hughes. Photo Enschedé)

1962 (24 Apr)–**66**. Various designs as T **15/16**. W w **12**. P 14×13 (horiz) or 13×14 (vert).

90	½c. black, brown and yellow-brown	10	10
	a. Brown omitted	£475	
	w. Wmk inverted	25·00	18·00
91	1c. yellow-orange and black	10	10
	w. Wmk inverted	1·75	2·00
92	2c. deep bluish green, black and yellow-olive	10	1·75
	w. Wmk inverted	32·00	32·00
93	2½c. black and vermilion	10	10
	a. Black and dull red (5.66)	2·00	25
	w. Wmk inverted	2·50	2·00
94	3½c. yellow-green and deep grey	10	40
	w. Wmk inverted	9·00	7·50
95	4c. black and turquoise-green	10	10
	a. Black and deep turquoise-green (5.66)	2·75	20
	w. Wmk inverted	9·00	7·50
96	5c. black, red and orange-red	1·50	10
	w. Wmk inverted	11·00	7·50
97	7½c. deep brown and buff	2·00	60
	a. Blackish brown and yellowish buff (5.66)	6·50	4·25
	w. Wmk inverted	12·00	10·00
98	10c. black and light blue	5·00	25
	w. Wmk inverted	50·00	38·00
99	12½c. carmine and grey-olive	2·25	3·50
	w. Wmk inverted		
100	15c. black and bright purple	1·50	1·50
101	20c. black and green	40	1·00
	w. Wmk inverted	—	£200
102	25c. black and bright blue	50	1·00
	w. Wmk inverted	38·00	35·00
103	50c. black and rose-red	19·00	6·00
	w. Wmk inverted	—	£200
104	1r. emerald and ochre	2·75	2·50
105	2r. carmine-red and ultramarine	21·00	12·00
90/105 *Set of 16*		50·00	27·00

Designs: *Vert*—2c. Forestry; 2½c. Ceremonial headdress; 3½c. Musical instrument; 4c. Irrigation; 5c. Long-tailed Whydah; 7½c. Rock paintings; 10c. Secretary Bird; 12½c. Pink Arum; 15c. Swazi married woman; 20c. Malaria control; 25c. Swazi warrior; 1r. Aloes. *Horiz*—50c. Southern Ground Hornbill; 2r. Msinsi in flower.

1963 (4 June). Freedom from Hunger. As No. 182 of Botswana.

106	15c. reddish violet	50	15

1963 (2 Sept). Red Cross Centenary. As Nos. 183/4 of Botswana.

107	2½c. red and black	30	10
108	15c. red and blue	70	90

31 Goods Train and Map of Swaziland Railway

(Des R. A. H. Street. Recess B.W.)

1964 (5 Nov). Opening of Swaziland Railway. W w **12**. P 11½.

109	**31**	2½c. emerald-green and purple	55	10
110		3½c. turquoise-blue and deep yellow-olive	55	1·00
111		15c. red-orange and deep chocolate	70	70
112		25c. olive-yellow and deep ultramarine	85	80
109/12 *Set of 4*			2·40	2·25

1965 (17 May). I.T.U. Centenary. As Nos. 190/1 of Botswana.

113	2½c. light blue and bistre	15	10
114	15c. bright purple and rose	35	20

1965 (25 Oct). International Co-operation Year. As Nos. 192/3 of Botswana.

115	½c. reddish purple and turquoise-green	10	10
116	15c. deep bluish green and lavender	40	20

1966 (24 Jan). Churchill Commemoration. As Nos. 194/7 of Botswana.

117	½c. new blue	10	2·50
118	2½c. deep green	25	10
119	15c. brown	55	25
	w. Wmk inverted	75·00	55·00
120	25c. bluish violet	80	1·00
117/20 *Set of 4*		1·50	3·50

32 Education

32 Science

32 Culture

1966 (1 Dec). 20th Anniv of U.N.E.S.C.O. Ww **12** (sideways) P 14.

121	**31a**	2½c. slate-violet, red, yellow and orange	15	10
122	**31b**	7½c. orange-yellow, violet and deep olive	45	60
123	**31c**	15c. black, bright purple and orange	80	1·25
121/3		*Set of* 3	1·25	1·75

PROTECTED STATE

32 King Sobhuza II and Map

33 King Sobhuza II

(Des and photo Harrison)

1967 (25 Apr). Protected State. W w **12** (sideways on horiz designs). P 14½.

124	**32**	2½c. multicoloured	10	10
125	**33**	7½c. multicoloured	15	15
126	**32**	15c. multicoloured	20	30
127	**33**	25c. multicoloured	25	40
124/7		*Set of* 4	65	80

34 Students and University

(Des V. Whiteley. Photo Harrison)

1967 (7 Sept). First Conferment of University Degrees. P 14×14½.

128	**34**	2½c. sepia, ultramarine and light yellow-orange	10	10
129		7½c. sepia, ultramarine and light greenish blue	15	15
130		15c. sepia, ultramarine and rose	25	30
131		25c. sepia, ultramarine and light violet	30	35
128/31		*Set of* 4	65	75

35 Incwala Ceremony

36 Reed Dance

(Des Mrs. G. Ellison. Photo Harrison)

1968 (5 Jan). Traditional Customs. P 14.

132	**35**	3c. silver, vermilion and black	10	10
133	**36**	10c. silver, light brown, orange and black	10	10
134	**35**	15c. gold, vermilion and black	15	20
135	**36**	25c. gold, light brown, orange and black	15	20
132/5		*Set of* 4	40	50

3c

(**37**)

38 Cattle Ploughing

1968 (1 May). No. 96 surch with T **37**.

136	3c. on 5c. black, red and orange-red	1·50	10
	w. Wmk inverted	7·50	2·00

INDEPENDENT

(Des Mrs. G. Ellison. Photo Enschedé)

1968 (6 Sept). Independence. T **38** and similar horiz designs. W w **12** (sideways). P 14×12½.

137	3c. multicoloured	10	10
	a. Imperf (pair)	£160	
138	4½c. multicoloured	10	45
	a. Imperf (pair)	£160	
139	17½c. yellow, green, black and gold	15	70
140	25c. slate, black and gold	45	90
137/40	*Set of* 4	65	1·75
MS141	180×162 mm. Nos. 137/40 each×5	14·00	23·00
	a. Error Imperf	£1600	

Designs:—4½c. Overhead cable carrying asbestos; 17½c. Cutting sugar cane; 25c. Iron ore mining and railway map.

Nos. 137/40 were printed in sheets of 50, but also in miniature sheets of 20 (4×5) containing *se-tenant* strips of each value.

INDEPENDENCE
1968

(**42**)

1968 (6 Sept). Nos. 90/105 optd as T **42**, and No. 93 additionally surch 3c., by Enschedé.

(a) Wmk upright

142	½c. black, brown and yellow-brown	10	10
	a. Brown omitted	£400	
	b. Albino opt	42·00	
143	1c. yellow-orange and black	10	10
	w. Wmk inverted	45·00	40·00
144	2c. deep bluish green, black and yellow-olive	10	10
	w. Wmk inverted	—	38·00
145	2½c. black and vermilion	75	1·40
	a. Black and dull red	2·75	10
	w. Wmk inverted	38·00	32·00
146	3c. on 2½c. black and vermilion	10	10
	a. Black and dull red	10	10
	w. Wmk inverted	40·00	32·00
147	3½c. yellow-green and deep grey	15	10
	w. Wmk inverted	42·00	35·00
148	4c. black and turquoise-green	10	10
	a. Black and deep turquoise-green	25	15
	b. Black and pale turquoise-green	20	1·50
149	5c. black, red and orange-red	4·25	10
	w. Wmk inverted	55·00	40·00
150	7½c. deep brown and buff	60	10
151	10c. black and light blue	4·50	10
152	12½c. carmine and grey-olive	25	1·00
	w. Wmk inverted	2·00	3·00
153	15c. black and bright purple	25	1·25
154	20c. black and green	75	2·00
155	25c. black and bright blue	35	1·25
156	50c. black and rose-red	6·00	4·00
157	1r. emerald and ochre	2·00	4·50
158	2r. carmine-red and ultramarine	4·00	9·00

(b) Wmk sideways

159	50c. black and rose-red	3·50	8·50
160	2r. carmine-red and ultramarine	8·00	5·00
142/60	*Set of* 19	32·00	35·00

The 2½c., 3½c., 5c., 12½c., 50c. (No. 156) and 2r. (No. 158) exist with gum arabic only, the 1c., 2c., 3c., 4c., and 15c. with both gum arabic and PVA gum and the remainder with PVA gum only.

43 Cape Porcupine

(Des and litho D.L.R.)

1969 (1 Aug)–**75**. T **43** and similar designs showing animals. Multicoloured. W w **12** (sideways on 3c., 3½c., 1r., 2r.). P 13×13½ (3, 3½c.), 12½×13 (1, 2r.) or 13×12½ (others).

161	½c. Caracal	10	10
162	1c. Type **43**	10	10
163	2c. Crocodile	20	10
	aw. Wmk inverted	4·00	
	b. Perf 12½×12 (29.9.75)	3·25	5·50
164	3c. Lion	1·00	10
165	3½c. African Elephant	75	10
166	5c. Bush Pig	30	10
167	7½c. Impala	35	10
168	10c. Charmer Baboon	45	10
169	12½c. Ratel	70	4·00
170	15c. Leopard	1·25	70
171	20c. Blue Wildebeest	95	60
172	25c. White Rhinoceros	1·40	1·75
	w. Wmk inverted	3·50	

173		50c. Common Zebra	1·50	3·25
174		1r. Waterbuck (*vert*)	3·00	6·50
175		2r. Giraffe (*vert*)	8·00	11·00
161/75 *Set of* 15			17·00	25·00

Nos. 161/73 are horizontal as Type **43** but the 3c. and 3½c. are larger, 35×24½ mm.

No. 163b was printed by the D.L.R. works in Bogota, Colombia.

Nos. 174 and 175 were reissued in new currency and No. 164 with Ww **12** upright in 1975.

44 King Sobhuza II and Flags

45 King Sobhuza II, U.N. Building and Emblem

(Des D.L.R. Litho P.B.)

1969 (24 Sept). Admission of Swaziland to the United Nations. W w **12** (sideways). P 13½.

176	**44**	3c. multicoloured	10	10
177	**45**	7½c. multicoloured	15	10
178	**44**	12½c. multicoloured	25	10
179	**45**	25c. multicoloured	40	40
176/9 *Set of* 4			75	55

46 Athlete, Shield and Spears

47 *Bauhinia galpinii*

(Des L. Curtis. Litho Format)

1970 (16 July). Ninth Commonwealth Games, Edinburgh. T **46** and similar vert designs. Multicoloured. W w **12**. P 14.

180		3c. Type **46**	10	10
181		7½c. Runner	20	10
182		12½c. Hurdler	25	10
183		25c. Procession of Swaziland competitors	35	40
180/3 *Set of* 4			75	55

(Des L. Curtis from "Wild Flowers of Natal" by Dr. W. G. Wright. Litho Questa)

1971 (1 Feb). Flowers. T **47** and similar vert designs. Multicoloured. W w **12**. P 14½.

184		3c. Type **47**	20	10
185		10c. *Crocosmia aurea*	20	10
186		15c. *Gloriosa superba*	30	25
187		25c. *Watsonia densiflora*	40	1·25
184/7 *Set of* 4			1·00	1·50

48 King Sobhuza II in Ceremonial Dress

49 UNICEF emblem

(Des L. Curtis. Litho Format)

1971 (22 Dec). Golden Jubilee of Accession of King Sobhuza II. T **48** and similar vert designs. Multicoloured. W w **12**. P 14.

188		3c. Type **48**	10	10
		w. Wmk inverted	50	
189		3½c. Sobhuza II in medallion	10	10
190		7½c. Sobhuza II attending Incwala ceremony	15	10
191		25c. Sobhuza II and aides at opening of Parliament	30	35
		w. Wmk inverted	70	
188/91 *Set of* 4			45	40

(Des Sylvia Goaman. Litho J.W.)

1972 (17 Apr). 25th Anniv of UNICEF. W w **12** (sideways). P 13½.

192	**49**	15c. black and bright lilac	15	20
193	–	25c. black and yellow-olive	20	80

The 25c. value is as T **49**, but the inscription is rearranged.

50 Local Dancers

(Des G. Drummond. Litho Questa)

1972 (11 Sept). Tourism. T **50** and similar horiz designs. Multicoloured. W w **12**. P 13½×14.

194		3½c. Type **50**	10	10
195		7½c. Swazi beehive hut	15	15
196		15c. Ezulwini Valley	20	50
197		25c. Fishing, Usutu River	65	1·25
194/7 *Set of* 4			1·00	1·75

51 Spraying Mosquitoes

(Des PAD Studio. Litho Questa)

1973 (21 May). 25th Anniv of WHO. T **51** and similar horiz design. Multicoloured. W w **12**. P 14.

198		3½c. Type **51**	20	10
199		7½c. Anti-malaria vaccination	40	80

52 Mining

(Des G. Drummond. Litho Questa)

1973 (21 June). Natural Resources. T **52** and similar horiz designs. Multicoloured. W w **12**. P 13½.

200		3½c. Type **52**	55	10
201		7½c. Cattle	25	15
202		15c. Water	30	20
203		25c. Rice	35	50
200/3 *Set of* 4			1·25	80

53 Coat of Arms

(Des J.W. Litho Walsall)

1973 (7 Sept). Fifth Anniv of Independence. T **53** and similar horiz designs. Multicoloured (except 3c.). W w **12**. P 14.

204		3c. Type **53** (salmon and black)	10	10
205		10c. King Sobhuza II saluting	15	10
206		15c. Parliament Buildings	30	75
207		25c. National Somhlolo Stadium	40	1·60
204/7 *Set of* 4			80	2·25

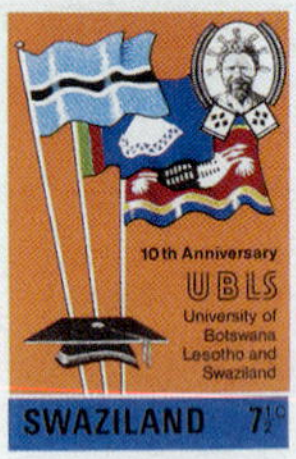

54 Flags and Mortarboard

55 King Sobhuza as College Student

(Des P. Powell. Litho Format)

1974 (29 Mar). Tenth Anniv of University of Botswana, Lesotho and Swaziland. T **54** and similar vert designs. Multicoloured. W w **12** (sideways). P 14.

208	7½c. Type **54**	20	10
209	12½c. University campus	25	10
210	15c. Map of Southern Africa	30	20
211	25c. University badge	40	35
208/11	*Set of* 4	1·00	60

(Des Mary Nelson; adapted PAD Studio. Litho Enschedé)

1974 (22 July). 75th Birthday of King Sobhuza II. T **55** and similar vert designs. Multicoloured. W w **12**. P 13×10½.

212	3c. Type **55**	10	10
213	9c. King Sobhuza in middle-age	10	10
214	50c. King Sobhuza at 75 years of age	70	60
212/14	*Set of* 3	80	60

56 New Post Office, Lobamba

(Des R. Granger Barrett. Litho Questa)

1974 (9 Oct). Centenary of Universal Postal Union. T **56** and similar horiz designs. Multicoloured. W w **12** (sideways). P 14.

215	4c. Type **56**	10	10
216	10c. Mbabane Temporary Post Office, 1902	15	15
217	15c. Carrying mail by cableway	30	50
218	25c. Mule-drawn mail-coach	40	70
215/18	*Set of* 4	80	1·25

(New Currency. 100 cents = 1 lilangeni (plural emalangeni))

1975 (2 Jan). New currency. As Nos. 174/5 but inscr in emalangeni. W w **12** (upright). P 12½×13.

219	1e. Waterbuck	50	2·00
220	2e. Giraffe	1·10	4·00
	w. Wmk inverted	75·00	

57 Umcwasho

58 Control Tower, Matsapa Airport Ceremony

(Des PAD Studio. Litho Kynoch Press)

1975 (20 Mar). Swazi Youth. T **57** and similar multicoloured designs. W w **12** (sideways on 3, 10 and 25c.). P 14.

221	3c. Type **57**	10	10
222	10c. Butimba (hunting party)	15	10
223	15c. Lusekwane (sacred shrub) (*horiz*)	40	40
224	25c. Goina Regiment	60	70
221/4	*Set of* 4	1·10	1·10

(Des V. Whiteley Studio. Litho Questa)

1975 (18 Aug). Tenth Anniv of Internal Air Service. T **58** and similar horiz designs. Multicoloured. W w **14** (sideways). P 14.

225	4c. Type **58**	30	10
226	5c. Fire engine	70	20
227	15c. Douglas DC-3	1·25	1·40
228	25c. Hawker Siddeley H.S.748	2·00	2·00
225/8	Set of 4	3·75	3·25

(Litho De La Rue, Bogota, Colombia).

1975 (29 Sept). As No. 164 but W w **12** upright.

229	3c. Lion	5·00	6·00

(59)

61 African Black-headed Oriole

1975 (15 Nov). Nos. 167 and 169 surch as T **59**.

230	3c. on 7½c. Impala	75	1·00
231	6c. on 12½c. Ratel	1·50	2·00

(Des Mary-Jane Rostami. Litho Questa)

1975 (22 Dec). International Women's Year. T **60** and similar designs. W w **14** (sideways on 4 and 5c.). P 14.

232	4c. light bluish grey, black and light bright blue	10	10
233	5c. multicoloured	10	10
234	15c. multicoloured	30	60
235	25c. multicoloured	50	90
232/5	*Set of* 4	80	1·50

Designs: *Horiz*—5c. Queen Labotsibeni. *Vert*—15c. Craftswoman; 25c. "Women in Service".

61 African Black-headed Oriole

(Des C. Abbott. Litho Questa)

1976 (2 Jan)–**78**. Birds. T **61** and similar multicoloured designs. W w **14** (sideways on 1c., 3c., 2e.). Chalk-surfaced paper. P 14.

236	1c. Type **61**	75	2·50
237	2c. African Green Pigeon (*vert*)	80	2·50
238	3c. Green-winged Pytilia	1·00	1·00
239	4c. Violet Starling (*vert*)	80	15
	aw. Wmk inverted	†	2·00
	b. Ordinary paper (31.7.78)	1·50	40
240	5c. Black-headed Heron (*vert*)	90	1·75
241	6c. Stonechat (*vert*)	1·50	2·50
242	7c. Chorister Robin Chat (*vert*)	1·40	2·75
243	10c. Four-coloured Bush-shrike (*vert*)	1·50	1·75
244	15c. Black-collared Barbet (*vert*)	2·25	55
245	20c. Grey Heron (*vert*)	3·25	2·00
246	25c. Giant Kingfisher (*vert*)	3·50	2·00
247	30c. Verreaux's Eagle (*vert*)	3·50	2·50
248	50c. Red Bishop (*vert*)	2·25	1·75
	a. Ordinary paper (31.7.78)	90	1·00
249	1e. Pin-tailed Whydah (*vert*)	2·50	2·75
	a. Ordinary paper (31.7.78)	1·40	2·50
250	2e. Lilac-breasted Roller	4·50	5·00
	a. Ordinary paper (31.7.78)	1·50	5·00
236/50a	*Set of* 15	21·00	27·00

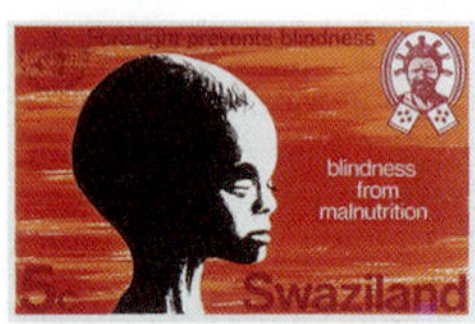

62 Blindness from Malnutrition

(Des Jennifer Toombs. Litho Questa)

1976 (15 June). Prevention of Blindness. T **62** and similar horiz designs. Multicoloured. W w **14** (sideways). P 14.

251	5c. Type **62**	20	10

252	10c. Infected retina	25	20
253	20c. Blindness from trachoma	45	85
254	25c. Medicines	50	1·10
251/4 *Set of 4*		1·60	2·00

63 Marathon

(Des PAD Studio. Litho Walsall)

1976 (17 July). Olympic Games, Montreal. T **63** and similar vert designs. Multicoloured. W w **14** (inverted). P 14.

255	5c. Type **63**	15	10
256	6c. Boxing	20	10
257	20c. Football	45	45
258	25c. Olympic torch and flame	55	65
255/8 *Set of 4*		1·25	65

64 Footballer Shooting

(Des J.W. Litho Questa)

1976 (13 Sept). FIFA Membership. T **64** and similar vert designs. Multicoloured. W w **14**. P 14.

259	4c. Type **64**	20	10
260	6c. Heading	20	10
261	20c. Goalkeeping	50	25
262	25c. Player about to shoot	50	30
259/62 *Set of 4*		1·25	60

65 Alexander Graham Bell and Telephone

(Des J.W. Litho Walsall)

1976 (22 Nov). Telephone Centenary. T **65** and similar horiz designs. W w **14** (sideways). P 14.

263	4c. multicoloured	10	10
264	5c. multicoloured	10	10
265	10c. multicoloured	10	10
266	15c. multicoloured	20	20
267	20c. multicoloured	25	30
263/7 *Set of 5*		70	55

Nos. 264/7 are as T **65**, but show different telephones.

66 Queen Elizabeth II and King Sobhuza II

(Des Walsall. Litho Questa)

1977 (7 Feb). Silver Jubilee. T **66** and similar horiz designs. Multicoloured. W w **14** (sideways). P 13½.

268	20c. Type **66**	15	15
269	25c. Coronation Coach at Admiralty Arch	15	15
270	50c. Queen in coach	20	40
268/70 *Set of 3*		45	65

67 Matsapa College

68 Animals and Hunters

(Des J. Cooter. Litho Questa)

1977 (2 May). 50th Anniv of Police Training. T **67** and similar multicoloured designs. W w **14** (upright on 20c., sideways on others). P 14.

271	5c. Type **67**	10	10
272	10c. Uniformed police and land rover	50	30
273	20c. Police badge (*vert*)	70	1·10
274	25c. Dog handling	1·25	1·75
271/4 *Set of 4*		2·25	2·75

(Des BG Studio. Litho Questa)

1977 (8 Aug). Rock Paintings. T **68** and similar horiz designs. Multicoloured. W w **14** (sideways*). P 14.

275	5c. Type **68**	30	10
276	10c. Four dancers in a procession	35	20
277	15c. Man with cattle	50	25
278	20c. Four dancers	55	35
275/8 *Set of 4*		1·50	80
MS279 103×124 mm. Nos. 275/8		2·00	2·75
	w. Wmk Crown to right of CA	6·00	

*The normal sideways watermark shows Crown to left of CA, as seen from the back of the stamp.

69 Timber, Highveld Region

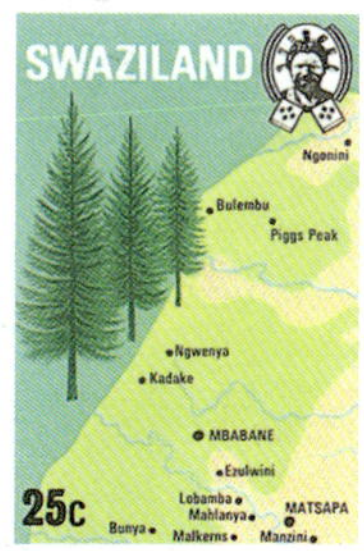

70 Timber, Highveld Region

(Des L. Curtis. Litho D.L.R.)

1977 (17 Oct). Maps of the Regions. T **69** and similar horiz designs. Multicoloured. W w **14** (sideways). P 13½.

280	5c. Type **69**	50	10
281	10c. Pineapple, Middleveld	60	10
282	15c. Orange and Lemon, Lowveld	80	65
283	20c. Cattle, Lubombo region	95	95
280/3 *Set of 4*		2·50	1·60
MS284 87×103 mm. Four 25c. designs as T **70**, together forming a composite map of Swaziland		1·40	1·60

71 Cabbage Tree

(Des Jennifer Toombs. Litho Walsall)

1978 (12 Jan). Trees of Swaziland. T **71** and similar horiz designs. Multicoloured (except 5c.). W w **14** (sideways). P 13½.

285	5c. Type **71** (apple-green, ochre and black)	15	15
286	10c. Marula	20	10

287	20c. Kiaat	45	1·25
288	25c. Lucky bean-tree	55	1·40
285/8	*Set of 4*	1·25	2·75

72 Rural Electrification at Lobamba

(Des G. Drummond. Litho Questa)

1978 (6 Mar). Hydro-electric Power. T **72** and similar horiz designs. W w **14** (sideways). P 13½.

289	5c. black and buff	10	15
290	10c. black and light green	15	15
291	20c. black and pale blue	25	40
292	25c. black and magenta	30	50
289/92	*Set of 4*	70	1·10

Designs:—10c. Edwaleni Power Station; 20c. Switchgear, Magudza Power Station; 25c. Turbine Hall, Edwaleni.

73 Elephant

(Des C. Abbott. Litho Questa)

1978 (2 June). 25th Anniv of Coronation. T **73** and similar vert designs. P 15.

293	25c. chalky blue, black and sage-green	15	25
	a. Sheetlet. Nos. 293/5×2	75	
294	25c. multicoloured	15	25
295	25c. chalky blue, black and sage-green	15	25
293/5	*Set of 3*	40	65

Designs:—No. 293, Queen's Lion; 294, Queen Elizabeth II; 295, Type **73**.

Nos. 293/5 were printed together in small sheets of 6, containing two *se-tenant* strips of 3, with horizontal gutter margin between.

74 Clay Pots

(Des C. Abbott. Litho Questa)

1978 (24 July). Handicrafts (1st series). T **74** and similar horiz designs. Multicoloured. W w **14** (sideways). P 13½×14.

296	5c. Type **74**	10	10
297	10c. Basketwork	10	10
298	20c. Wooden utensils	15	15
299	30c. Wooden pot	25	30
296/9	*Set of 4*	50	50

See also Nos. 310/13.

75 Defence Force

(Des BG Studio. Litho Questa)

1978 (6 Sept). 10th Anniv of Independence. T **75** and similar horiz designs. Multicoloured. W w **14** (sideways). P 14.

300	4c. Type **75**	15	10
301	6c. The King's Regiment	15	10
302	10c. Tinkabi tractor (agricultural development)	15	10
303	15c. Water-pipe laying (self-help scheme)	25	10
304	25c. Sebenta adult literacy scheme	30	25
305	50c. Fire emergency service	1·25	50
300/5	*Set of 6*	2·00	85

76 Archangel Gabriel appearing before Shepherds

77 Prospecting at Phophonyane

(Des V. Whiteley Studio. Litho Harrison)

1978 (12 Dec). Christmas. T **76** and similar horiz designs. Multicoloured. W w **14**. P 14½×14.

306	5c. Type **76**	10	10
307	10c. Three Wise Men paying homage to infant Jesus	15	10
308	15c. Archangel Gabriel warning Joseph	20	10
309	25c. Flight into Egypt	25	30
306/9	*Set of 4*	60	45

(Des C. Abbott. Litho Walsall)

1979 (10 Jan). Handicrafts (2nd series). Horiz designs as T **74**. Multicoloured. W w **14** (sideways). P 13½.

310	5c. Sisal bowls	10	10
311	15c. Pottery	15	10
312	20c. Basketwork	20	15
313	30c. Hide shield	30	20
310/13	*Set of 4*	60	45

(Des L. Curtis. Litho Questa)

1979 (27 Mar). Centenary of Discovery of Gold in Swaziland. T **77** and similar vert designs. W w **14**. P 14.

314	5c. gold and deep ultramarine	25	10
315	15c. gold and deep brown	45	20
316	25c. gold and deep green	65	35
317	50c. gold and carmine-red	90	2·00
314/17	*Set of 4*	2·00	2·40

Designs:—15c. Early 3-stamp battery mill; 25c. Cyanide tanks at Piggs Peak; 50c. Pouring off molten gold.

78 "Girls at the Piano"

(Des BG Studio. Litho Questa)

1979 (8 May). International Year of the Child. Paintings by Renoir. T **78** and similar horiz designs. Multicoloured. W w **14** (sideways). P 13½.

318	5c. Type **78**	10	10
319	15c. Madame Charpentier and her Children"	25	10
320	25c. "Girls picking Flowers"	35	15
321	50c. "Girl with Watering Can"	70	55
318/21	*Set of 4*	1·25	70
MS322	123×135 mm. Nos. 318/21	1·25	1·75

79 1933 1d. Carmine Stamp and Sir Rowland Hill

(Des J.W. Litho Walsall)

1979 (17 July). Death Centenary of Sir Rowland Hill. T **79** and similar horiz designs showing stamps and portrait of Sir Rowland Hill. Multicoloured. W w **14** (sideways*). P 14½×14.

323	10c. 1945 3d. Victory commemorative	15	10
324	20c. Type **79**	25	25
325	25c. 1968 25c. Independence commemorative	25	30
	w. Wmk Crown to right of CA	7·50	
323/5 *Set of 3*		60	60
MS326	115×90 mm. 50c. 1956 6d. Great Kudu Antelope definitive	75	85

*The normal sideways watermark shows Crown to left of CA, as seen from the back of of the stamp.

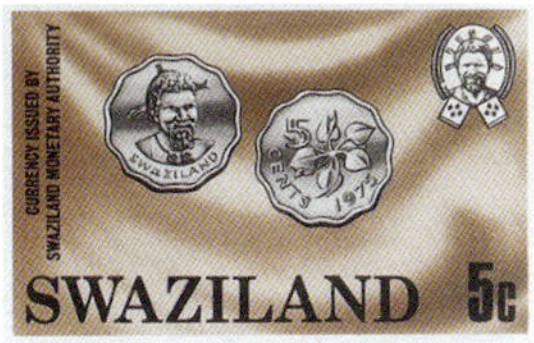

80 Obverse and Reverse of 5 Cents

(Des G. Hutchins. Litho Walsall)

1979 (6 Sept). Coins. T **80** and similar horiz designs. W w **14** (sideways). P 13½.

327	5c. black and light brown	15	10
328	10c. black and new blue	20	10
329	20c. black and yellowish green	35	20
330	50c. black and yellow-orange	50	50
331	1e. black and cerise	75	1·00
327/31 *Set of 5*		1·75	1·60

Designs:—10c. Obverse and reverse of 10 cents; 20c. Obverse and reverse of 20 cents; 50c. Reverse of 50 cents; 1c. Reverse of 1 lilangeni.

81 Big Bend Post Office

(Des J. Cooter. Litho Questa)

1979 (22 Nov). Post Office Anniversaries. T **81** and similar designs. W w **14** (sideways on 5, 20 and 50c.). P 13½.

332	5c. multicoloured	10	10
333	15c. multicoloured	15	10
334	20c. black, sage-green and magenta	20	15
335	50c. multicoloured	40	60
332/5 *Set of 4*		70	80

Designs and commemorations: *Horiz*—5c. Type **81** (25th anniversary of Posts and Telecommunications Services); 20c. 1949 75th anniversary of UPU 1s. commemorative stamp (10th anniversary of UPU membership); 50c. 1974 centenary of UPU 25c. commemorative stamp (10th anniversary of UPU membership). *Vert*—15c. Microwave antenna, Mount Ntondozi (25th anniversary of Posts and Telecommunications Services).

82 Map of Swaziland

83 Brunsvigia radulosa

(Des BG Studio. Litho Walsall)

1980 (23 Feb). 75th Anniv of Rotary International. T **82** and similar vert designs in gold and bright blue. W w **14**. P 13½.

336	5c. Type **82**	25	10
337	15c. Vitreous cutter and optical illuminator	45	10
338	50c. Scroll	50	55
339	1e. Rotary Headquarters, Evanston, U.S.A.	85	1·25
336/9 Set of 4		1·90	1·75

(Des BG Studio. Litho Secura, Singapore)

1980 (28 Apr)–**83**. Flowers. Multicoloured designs as T **83**.

A. Without imprint date below design. P 13½

340A	1c. Type **83**	10	10
341A	2c. *Aloe suprafoliata*	10	10
342A	3c. *Haemanthus magnificus*	10	10
	c. Perf 12	3·00	3·25
343A	4c. *Aloe marlothii*	10	10
	c. Perf 12	5·00	4·25
344A	5c. *Dicoma zeyheri*	10	10
	c. Perf 12	4·00	4·25
345A	6c. *Aloe kniphofioides*	15	30
346A	7c. *Cyrtanthus bicolor*	10	10
347A	10c. *Eucomis autumnalis*	20	10
348A	15c. *Leucospermum gerrardii*	15	10
	c. Perf 12		
349A	20c. *Haemanthus multiflorus*	30	25
350A	30c. *Acridocarpus natalitius*	20	20
351A	50c. *Adenium swazicum*	20	30
352A	1e. *Protea simplex*	35	60
353A	2e. *Calodendrum capense*	80	1·25
354A	5e. *Gladiolus ecklonii*	1·10	3·00
340A/54A *Set of 15*		3·50	5·50

B. With "1983" imprint date. P 12 (12.83)

340B	1c. Type **83**	1·00	1·50
341B	2c. *Aloe suprafoliata*	1·00	1·50
343B	4c. *Aloe marlothii*	1·50	1·50
345B	6c. *Aloe kniphofioides*	1·75	2·25
347B	10c. *Eucomis autumnalis*	2·00	1·25
349B	20c. *Haemanthus multiflorus*	2·25	2·00
340B/9B *Set of 6*		8·50	9·00

84 Mail Runner

(Des A. Theobald. Litho Walsall)

1980 (6 May). "London 1980" International Stamp Exhibition. T **84** and similar horiz designs. Multicoloured. W w **14** (sideways*). P 14.

355	10c. Type **84**	15	10
356	20c. Post Office mail truck	25	15
	w. Wmk Crown to right of CA	6·50	
357	25c. Mail sorting office	30	20
358	50c. Ropeway conveying mail at Bulembu	70	70
355/8 *Set of 4*		1·25	1·00

*The normal sideways watermark shows Crown to left of CA, as seen from the back of the stamp.

85 Scaly

(Des and litho Walsall)

1980 (25 Aug). River Fishes. T **85** and similar horiz designs. Multicoloured. W w **14** (sideways). P 13½.

359	5c. Type **85**	25	10
360	10c. Silver Catfish ("Silver Barbel")	25	10
361	15c. Tiger Fish	40	15
362	30c. Brown Squeaker	50	30
363	1e. Red-breasted Tilapia ("Bream")	60	1·40
359/63 *Set of 5*		1·75	1·75

86 Oribi

(Des G. Drummond. Litho Harrison)

1980 (1 Oct). Wildlife Conservation. T **86** and similar multicoloured designs. W w **14** (sideways on 5 and 50c.). P 14.

364	5c. Type **86**	15	10
365	10c. Nile Crocodile (*vert*)	30	10
366	50c. Temminck's Ground Pangolin	50	70
367	1e. Leopard (*vert*)	1·25	1·50
364/7 *Set of 4*		2·00	2·00

87 Public Bus Service

(Des G. Hutchins. Litho Format)

1981 (5 Jan). Transport. T **87** and similar horiz designs. Multicoloured. (sideways). W w **14** P 14½.

368	5c. Type **87**	10	10
369	25c. Royal Swazi National Airways	25	15
370	30c. Swaziland United Transport	30	20
371	1e. Swaziland Railway	1·25	1·75
368/71 *Set of 4*		1·60	2·00

88 Mantenga Falls

89 Prince Charles on Hike

(Des L. Curtis. Litho Format)

1981 (16 Mar). Tourism. T **88** and similar horiz designs. Multicoloured. W w **14**(sideways). P 14.

372	5c. Type **88**	10	10
373	15c. Mananga Yacht Club	15	10
374	30c. White Rhinoceros in Mlilwane Game Sanctuary	60	30
375	1e. Roulette wheel, playing cards and dice ("casinos")	80	1·60
372/5 *Set of 4*		1·50	1·90

(Des J.W. Litho Walsall)

1981 (21 July). Royal Wedding. T **89** and similar vert designs. Multicoloured. W w **14**. P 14.

376	10c. Wedding bouquet from Swaziland	10	10
377	25c. Type **89**	15	10
378	1e. Prince Charles and Lady Diana Spencer	40	70
376/8 *Set of 3*		60	75

90 Installation of King Sobhuza II, 22 December 1921

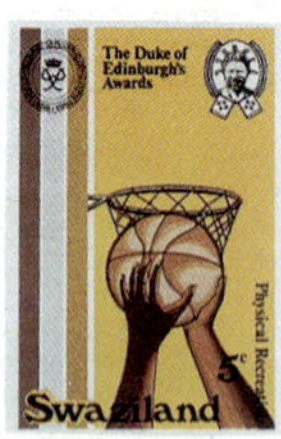

91 "Physical " Recreation

(Des J.W. Litho Harrison)

1981 (24 Aug). Diamond Jubilee of King Sobhuza II. T **90** and similar horiz designs. Multicoloured. W w **14** (sideways). P 14½.

379	5c. Type **90**	10	10
380	10c. Royal visit, 1947	10	10
381	15c. King Sobhuza II and Coronation of Queen Elizabeth II, 1953	15	15
382	25c. King Sobhuza taking Royal Salute, Independence, 1968	15	15
383	30c. King Sobuza in youth	20	20
384	1e. King Sobhuza and Parliament Buildings	50	90
379/84 *Set of 6*		1·00	1·40

(Des BG Studio. Litho Questa)

1981 (5 Nov). 25th Anniv of Duke of Edinburgh Award Scheme. T **91** and similar vert designs. Multicoloured. W w **14**. P 14.

385	5c. Type **91**	10	10
386	20c. "Expeditions"	20	10
387	50c. "Skills"	35	25
388	1e. Duke of Edinburgh in ceremonial dress	50	80
385/8 *Set of 4*		1·00	1·00

92 Disabled Person in Wheelchair

(Des and litho Walsall)

1981 (16 Dec). International Year of Disabled Persons. T **92** and similar multicoloured designs. W w **14** (sideways on 5c. and 1c.). P 14×14½ (5c., 1c.) or 14½×14 (others).

389	5c. Type **92**	30	10
390	15c. Teacher with disabled child (*vert*)	50	15
391	25c. Disabled craftsman (*vert*)	75	20
392	1e. Disabled driver in invalid carriage	2·25	2·75
389/92 *Set of 4*		3·50	3·00

93 Papilio demodocus

94 Man holding a Flower, after discarding Cigarettes

(Des I. Loe. Litho Rosenbaum Bros, Vienna)

1982 (6 Jan). Butterflies. T **93** and similar horiz designs. Multicoloured. W w **14** (sideways*). P 14.

393	5c. Type **93**	50	10
	w. Wmk Crown to left of CA	1·75	
394	10c. Charaxes candiope	50	10
	w. Wmk Crown to right of CA	2·75	
395	50c. Papilio nireus	1·50	85
	w. Wmk Crown to right of CA		
396	1e. Terias desjardinsii	2·00	2·00
	w. Wmk Crown to left of CA		
393/6 *Set of 4*		4·00	2·75

*The normal sideways watermark shows Crown to left of CA on 10c., 50c. and to right on the other values, all as seen from the back of the stamp.

(Des PAD Studio. Litho Format)

1982 (27 Apr). Pan-African Conference on Smoking and Health. T **94** and similar vert design. Multicoloured. W w **14**. P 14.

397	5c. Type **94**	50	85
398	10c. Smoker and non-smoker climbing stairs	60	90

95 Male Fishing Owl

(Des G. Drummond. Litho J.W.)

1982 (16 June). Wildlife Conservation (1st series). Pel's Fishing Owl. T **95** and similar vert designs. Multicoloured. W w **14**. P 13½×13.

399	35c. Type **95**	8·00	4·00
	a. Horiz strip of 5. Nos. 399/403	35·00	18·00
400	35c. Female Fishing Owl at nest	8·00	4·00
401	35c. Pair of Fishing Owls	8·00	4·00
402	35c. Fishing Owl, nest and egg	8·00	4·00
403	35c. Adult Fishing Owl with youngster	8·00	4·00
399/403	*Set of 5*	35·00	18·00

Nos. 399/403 were printed together, *se-tenant*, in horizontal and vertical strips of 5 throughout the sheet.

See also Nos. 425/9 and Nos. 448/52.

96 Swaziland Coat of Arms

(Des C. Abbott. Litho W. S. Cowells Ltd)

1982 (1 July). 21st Birthday of Princess of Wales. T **96** and similar vert designs. Multicoloured. W w **14**. P 14½.

404	5c. Type **96**	10	10
	w. Wmk inverted	42·00	
405	20c. Princess leaving Eastleigh Airport, Southampton, August 1981	80	10
406	50c. Bride at Buckingham Palace	60	30
407	1e. Formal portrait	1·50	85
	w. Wmk inverted	80·00	
404/7	*Set of 4*	2·75	1·25

97 Irrigation

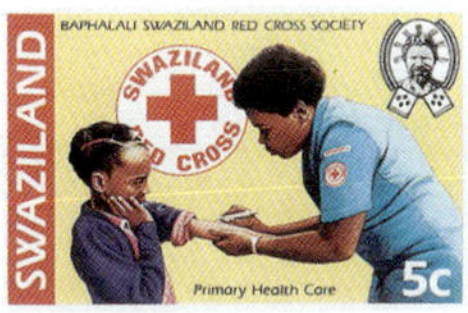

98 Nurse with Child

(Des G. Hutchins. Litho Walsall)

1982 (1 Sept). Sugar Industry. T **97** and similar horiz designs. Multicoloured. W w **14** (sideways). P 14×14½.

408	5c. Type **97**	10	10
409	20c. Harvesting	25	15
410	30c. Mhlume mills	35	25
411	1e. Sugar transportation by train	1·00	2·00
408/11	*Set of 4*	1·50	2·25

(Des L. Curtis. Litho Questa)

1982 (9 Nov). Swaziland Red Cross Society (Baphaladi). T **98** and similar horiz designs. Multicoloured. W w **14** (sideways). P 14.

412	5c. Type **98**	10	10
413	20c. Juniors carrying stretcher	25	15
414	50c. Disaster relief	55	75
415	1e. Henri Dunant (founder of Red Cross)	1·25	2·50
412/15	*Set of 4*	1·90	3·00

99 Taking the Oath

(Des B. Melton. Litho Format)

1982 (6 Dec). 75th Anniv of Boy Scout Movement. T **99** and similar horiz designs. Multicoloured. W w **14** (sideways*). P 14×13½.

416	5c. Type **99**	10	10
417	10c. Hiking and exploration	15	10
418	25c. Community development	30	30
	w. Wmk Crown to right of CA	11·00	
419	75c. Lord Baden-Powell	1·00	1·25
	w. Wmk Crown to right of CA	11·00	
416/19	*Set of 4*	1·40	1·60
MS420	107×109 mm. 1e. World scout badge	1·00	1·40

*The normal sideways watermark shows Crown to left of CA, as seen from the back of the stamp.

100 Satellite View of Earth

(Des A. Theobald. Litho Harrison)

1983 (14 Mar). Commonwealth Day. T **100** and similar multicoloured designs. W w **14** (sideways on 50c., 1c.). P 14.

421	6c. Type **100**	10	10
422	10c. King Sobhuza II	10	10
423	50c. Swazi woman and beehive huts (*horiz*)	35	55
424	1e. Spraying sugar crops (*horiz*)	70	1·00
421/4	*Set of 4*	1·10	1·50

(Des G. Drummond. Litho J.W.)

1983 (16 May). Wildlife Conservation (2nd series). Lammergeier. Vert designs as T **95**. Multicoloured. W w **14**. P 13½×13.

425	35c. Adult male	2·50	2·50
	a. Horiz strip of 5. Nos. 425/9	11·00	11·00
426	35c. Pair	2·50	2·50
427	35c. Nest and egg	2·50	2·50
428	35c. Female at nest	2·50	2·50
429	35c. Adult bird with fledgling	2·50	2·50
425/9	*Set of 5*	11·00	11·00

Nos. 425/9 were printed together, *se-tenant*, in horizontal strips of 5 throughout the sheet.

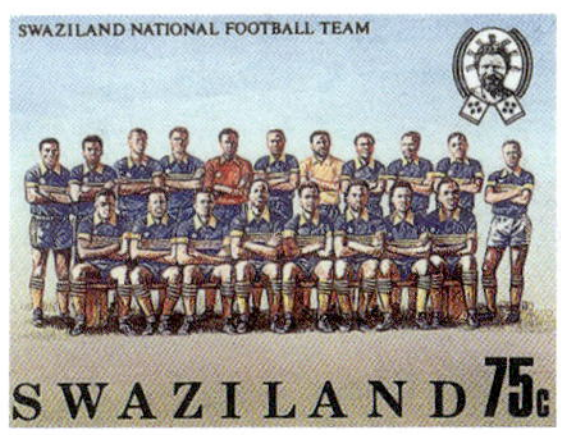

101 Swaziland National Football Team

102 Montgolfier Balloon

(Des G. Vasarhelyi. Litho Format)

1983 (20 Aug). Tour of Swaziland by English Football Clubs. Three sheets, 101×72 mm, each containing one 75c. stamp as T **101**. Multicoloured. W w **14** (sideways). P 13½.

MS430	75c. Type **101**; 75c. Tottenham Hotspur; 75c. Manchester United *Set of 3 sheets*	1·50	3·00

(Des. D. Hartley-Marjoram. Litho Format)

1983 (22 Aug). Bicentenary of Manned Flight. T **102** and similar multicoloured designs. W w **14** (sideways on 10c. to 50c.). P 14.

431	5c. Type **102**	10	10
432	10c. Wright brothers' *Flyer I* (*horiz*)	15	10
433	25c. Fokker F.28 Fellowship (*horiz*)	35	35
434	50c. Bell XS-1 (*horiz*)	85	65
431/4	*Set of 4*	1·25	1·00
MS435	73×73 mm. 1e. Space shuttle Columbia	1·00	1·40

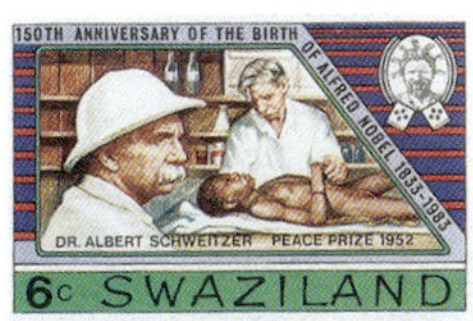

103 Dr. Albert Schweitzer (Peace Prize, 1952)

(Des G. Vasarhelyi. Litho Harrison)

1983 (21 Oct). 150th Birth Anniv of Alfred Nobel. T **103** and similar horiz designs. Multicoloured. W w **14** (sideways). P 14.

436	6c. Type **103**	2·75	80
437	10c. Dag Hammarskjöld (Peace Prize, 1961)	85	15
438	50c. Albert Einstein (Physics Prize, 1921)	3·75	2·25
439	1e. Alfred Nobel	3·75	4·50
436/9	*Set of 4*	10·00	7·00

104 Maize

(Des Jennifer Toombs. Litho Harrison)

1983 (29 Nov). World Food Day. T **104** and similar horiz designs. Multicoloured. W w **14** (sideways). P 14.

440	6c. Type **104**	25	10
441	10c. Rice	25	10
442	50c. Cattle herding	1·00	1·00
443	1e. Ploughing	1·60	3·00
440/3	*Set of 4*	2·75	3·75

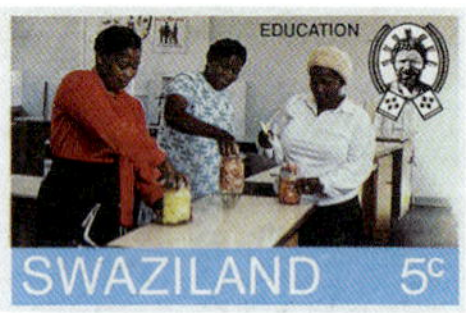

105 Women's College

(Des C. Abbott. Litho Format)

1984 (12 Mar). Education. T **105** and similar horiz designs. Multicoloured. W w **14** (sideways). P 14.

444	5c. Type **105**	10	10
445	15c. Technical Training School	15	15
446	50c. University	35	60
447	1e. Primary school	65	1·10
444/7	*Set of 4*	1·10	1·75

106 Male on Ledge

(Des G. Drummond. Litho J.W.)

1984 (18 May). Wildlife Conservation. (3rd series) Bald Ibis. T **106** and similar vert designs. Multicoloured. W w **14**. P 13½×13.

448	35c. Type **106**	3·00	3·00
	a. Horiz strip of 5. Nos. 448/52	13·50	13·50
449	35c. Male and female	3·00	3·00
450	35c. Bird and egg	3·00	3·00
451	35c. Female on nest of eggs	3·00	3·00
452	35c. Adult and fledgling	3·00	3·00
448/52	*Set of 5*	13·50	13·50

Nos. 448/52 were printed together, *se-tenant*, in horizontal strips of 5 throughout the sheet.

107 Mule-drawn Passenger Coach

(Des A. Theobald. Litho Walsall)

1984 (15 June). Universal Postal Union Congress, Hamburg. T **107** and similar horiz designs. Multicoloured. W w **14** (sideways). P 14½.

453	7c. Type **107**	30	15
454	15c. Ox-drawn post wagon	45	15
455	50c. Mule-drawn mail coach	90	1·00
456	1e. Bristol to London mail coach	1·40	2·00
453/6	*Set of 4*	2·75	3·00

108 Running

(Des Harrison. Litho Walsall)

1984 (27 July). Olympic Games, Los Angeles. T **108** and similar horiz designs. Multicoloured. W w **14** (sideways). P 14.

457	7c. Type **108**	15	15
458	10c. Swimming	15	15
459	50c. Shooting	60	1·00
460	1e. Boxing	1·10	2·00
457/60	*Set of 4*	1·75	3·00
MS461	100×70 mm. Nos. 457/60	3·25	5·50

109 Suillus bovinus

(Des J. Spencer. Litho Format)

1984 (19 Sept). Fungi. T **109** and similar multicoloured designs. W w **14** (sideways on 10c., 1c.). P 14.

462	10c. Type **109**	1·25	30
463	15c. *Langermannia gigantea (vert)*	2·00	55
	w. Wmk inverted	10·00	
464	50c. *Trametes versicolor* ("Coriolus versicolor") *(vert)*	2·25	2·75
465	1e. *Boletus edulis*	2·50	5·25
462/5	*Set of 4*	7·25	8·00

110 King Sobhuza opening Railway, 1964

(**111**)

(Des W. Fenton. Litho Walsall)

1984 (5 Nov). 20th Anniv of Swaziland Railways. T **110** and similar horiz designs. Multicoloured. W w **14** (sideways). P 14.

466	10c. Type **110**	30	15
467	25c. Type 15A locomotive at Siweni Yard	55	40
468	30c. Container loading, Matsapha Station	55	40
469	1e. Locomotive No. 268 leaving Alto Tunnel	1·25	2·75
466/9	*Set of 4*	2·40	3·25
MS470	144×74 mm. Nos. 466/9	2·75	6·00

1984 (15 Dec). Nos. 340B, 341A, 342A, 343A, 345B and 346A surch as T **111**.

471	10c. on 4c. *Aloe marlothii*	50·00	
	a. Surch on No. (343Ac)	35	10
	b. Surch on No. (343B)	4·75	4·75
472	15c. on 7c. *Cyrtanthus bicolor*	40	20
473	20c. on 3c. *Haemanthus magnificus*	35	15
	a. Surch on No. (342Ac)	4·75	4·75
474	25c. on 6c. *Aloe kniphofioides*	40	20
	a. Surch triple	†	
	b. Surch double		
475	30c. on 1c. Type **83**	50	20
	a. Surch omitted (horiz pair with normal)	£375	
476	30c. on 2c. *Aloe suprafoliata*	2·75	4·25
	a. Surch on No. 341B	4·75	4·75
	ab. Surch omitted (horiz pair) with normal	4·75	5·50
471a/6	*Set of 6*	4·25	4·50

112 Rotary International Logo and Map of World

113 Male Ground Hornbill

(Des G. Vasarhelyi. Litho Questa)

1985 (23 Feb). 80th Anniv of Rotary International. T **112** and similar horiz designs. Multicoloured. W w **14** (sideways). P 14.

477	10c. Type **112**	75	10
478	15c. Teacher and handicapped children	1·00	20
479	50c. Youth exchange	1·25	1·50
480	1e. Nurse and children	3·00	4·50
477/80 *Set of 4*		5·50	5·75

(Des G. Drummond. Litho Harrison)

1985 (15 May). Birth Bicentenary of John J. Audubon (ornithologist). Southern Ground Hornbills. T **113** and similar vert designs. Multicoloured. W w **14**. P 14.

481	25c. Type **113**	2·25	3·25
	a. Horiz strip of 5. Nos. 481/5	10·00	14·00
482	25c. Male and female Ground Hornbills	2·25	3·25
483	25c. Female at nest	2·25	3·25
484	25c. Ground Hornbill in nest, and egg	2·25	3·25
485	25c. Adult and fledgling	2·25	3·25
481/5 *Set of 5*		10·00	14·00

Nos. 481/5 were printed together, *se-tenant*, in horizontal strips of 5 throughout the sheet.

114 The Queen Mother in 1975

115 Buick "Tourer"

(Des A. Theobald (2e.), C. Abbott (others). Litho Questa)

1985 (7 June). Life and Times of Queen Elizabeth the Queen Mother. T **114** and similar vert designs. Multicoloured. W w **16**. P 14½×14.

486	10c. The Queen Mother in South Africa, 1947	40	10
487	15c. With the Queen and Princess Margaret, 1985 (from photo by Norman Parkinson)	40	10
488	50c. Type **114**	1·10	1·10
489	1e. With Prince Henry at his christening (from photo by Lord Snowdon)	1·40	2·50
486/9 *Set of 4*		3·00	3·50
MS490 91×73 mm. 2c. Greeting Prince Andrew. Wmk sideways		3·00	1·75

(Des D. Hartley. Litho Walsall)

1985 (16 Sept). Century of Motoring. T **115** and similar horiz designs. Multicoloured. (sideways). W w **14** P 14.

491	10c. Type **115**	50	10
492	15c. Four cylinder Rover	70	25
493	50c. De Dion Bouton	1·75	2·00
494	1e. "Model T" Ford	2·25	4·00
491/4 *Set of 4*		4·75	5·75

116 Youths building Bridge over Ravine

(Des Vrein Barlocher. Litho Format)

1985 (2 Dec). International Youth Year (10, 50c.), and 75th Anniv of Girl Guide Movement (others). T **116** and similar horiz designs. Multicoloured. W w **16** (sideways*). P 14.

495	10c. Type **116**	25	10
496	20c. Girl Guides in camp	30	20
	w. Wmk Crown to right of CA		
497	50c. Youth making model from sticks	60	1·25
498	1e. Guides collecting brushwood	80	2·25
495/8 *Set of 4*		1·75	3·50

*The normal sideways watermark shows Crown to left of CA, as seen from the back of the stamp.

117 Halley's Comet over Swaziland

117a Christening of Princess Anne, 1950

(Des Jennifer Toombs. Litho B.D.T.)

1986 (27 Feb). Appearance of Halley's Comet. W w **14** (sideways). P 14.

499	**117** 1e.50 multicoloured	2·75	4·00

(Des A. Theobald. Litho Format)

1986 (21 Apr). 60th Birthday of Queen Elizabeth II. Vert designs as T **117a**. Multicoloured. W w **16**. P 14×14½.

500	10c. Type **117a**	10	10
501	30c. On Palace balcony after wedding of Prince and Princess of Wales, 1981	15	25
502	45c. Royal visit to Swaziland, 1947	15	30
503	1e. At Windsor Polo Ground, 1984	30	70
504	2e. At Crown Agents Head Office, London, 1983	60	1·40
500/4 *Set of 5*		1·10	2·50

118 King Mswati III

119 Emblems of Round Table and Project Orbis (eye disease campaign)

(Des L. Curtis. Litho Walsall)

1986 (25 Apr). Coronation of King Mswati III. T **118** and similar designs. W w **16** (sideways on 20c. to 2c.). P 14½×14 (10c.) or 14×14½ (others).

505	10c. black and gold	35	25
506	20c. multicoloured	70	30
507	25c. multicoloured	80	35
508	30c. multicoloured	90	50
509	40c. multicoloured	3·25	2·00
510	2e. multicoloured	4·00	9·00
505/10 *Set of 6*		9·00	11·00

Designs: *Horiz*—20c. Prince with King Sobhuza II at Incwala ceremony; 25c. At primary school; 30c. At school in England; 40c. Inspecting guard of honour at Matsapha Airport; 2e. Dancing the Simemo.

(Des M. Kesson, adapted G. Vasarhelyi. Litho Walsall)

1986 (6 Oct). 50th Anniv of Round Table Organization. T **119** and similar vert designs showing branch emblems. Multicoloured. W w **16**. P 14.

511	15c. Type **119**	30	10
512	25c. Ehlanzeni 51	40	20
513	55c. Mbabane 30	85	70
514	70c. Bulembu 54	1·10	1·75
515	2e. Manzini 44	2·00	4·50
511/15 *Set of 5*		4·25	6·50

120 *Precis hierta*

(Des I. Loe. Litho Questa)

1987 (17 Mar). Butterflies (1st series). T **120** and similar horiz designs. Multicoloured. P 14.

516	10c. Type **120**	55	1·50
517	15c. *Hamanumida daedalus*	65	1·25
518	20c. *Charaxes boueti*	65	1·25
519	25c. *Abantis paradisea*	65	1·75
520	30c. *Acraea anemosa*	65	1·00
521	35c. *Graphium leonidas*	65	1·00
522	45c. *Graphium antheus*	70	2·00
523	50c. *Precis orithya*	70	1·25
524	55c. *Pinacopteryx eriphia*	70	1·25
525	70c. *Precis octavia*	80	1·40
526	1e. *Mylothris chloris*	1·00	3·00
527	5e. *Colotis regina*	85	1·50
528	10e. *Spindasis natalensis*	1·10	2·25
516/28	*Set of* 13	8·75	18·00

For these designs, and similar 5c., with different portrait of King Mswati III see Nos. 606/17.

121 Two White Rhinoceroses

(Des Doreen McGuinness. Litho Questa)

1987 (1 July). White Rhinoceros. T **121** and similar horiz designs. Multicoloured. W w **16** (sideways). P 14½.

529	15c. Type **121**	3·00	55
530	25c. Female and calf	3·50	1·00
531	45c. Rhinoceros charging	5·00	3·50
532	70c. Rhinoceros wallowing	7·25	8·50
529/32	*Set of* 4	17·00	12·00

122 Hybrid Tea Rose "Blue Moon"

(Des Josephine Martin. Litho Questa)

1987 (19 Oct). Garden Flowers. T **122** and similar vert designs. Multicoloured. W w **16**. P 14½.

533	15c. Type **122**	1·25	20
534	35c. Rambler Rose "Dense du fen"	2·25	80
535	55c. Pompon Dahlia "Odin"	2·50	1·50
536	2e. *Lilium davidii var. willmottiae*	7·00	12·00
533/6	*Set of* 4	11·50	13·00

40TH WEDDING ANNIVERSARY

122a

1987 (9 Dec). Royal Ruby Wedding. Nos. 501/4 optd with T **122a** in silver.

537	30c. On Palace balcony after wedding of Prince and Princess of Wales, 1981	40	20
538	45c. Royal visit to Swaziland, 1947	50	30
539	1e. At Windsor Polo Ground, 1984	85	1·75
540	2e. At Crown Agents Head Office, London, 1983	1·25	3·25
537/40	*Set of* 4	2·75	5·00

123 *Zabalius aridus* (grasshopper)

(Des I. Loe. Litho Questa)

1988 (14 Mar). Insects. T **123** and similar horiz designs. Multicoloured. W w **16** (sideways). P 14.

541	15c. Type **123**	1·40	15
542	55c. *Callidea bohemani* (shieldbug)	2·75	85
543	1e. *Phymateus viridipes* (grasshopper)	4·75	4·75
544	2e. *Nomadacris septemfasciata* (locust)	7·50	9·50
541/4	*Set of* 4	15·00	14·00

124 Athlete with Swazi Flag and Olympic Stadium

(Des C. Abbott. Litho Format)

1988 (22 Aug). Olympic Games, Seoul. T **124** and similar horiz designs. Multicoloured. W w **16** (sideways). P 14.

545	15c. Type **124**	1·25	10
546	35c. Taekwondo	1·75	45
547	1e. Boxing	2·25	2·50
548	2e. Tennis	3·75	5·50
545/8	*Set of* 4	8·00	7·75

125 Savanna Monkey ("Green Monkey")

126 Dr. David Hynd (founder of Swazi Red Cross)

(Des I. Lee. Litho Questa)

1989 (16 Jan). Small Mammals. T **125** and similar horiz designs. Multicoloured. W w **16** (sideways). P 14.

549	35c. Type **125**	2·00	30
550	55c. Large-toothed Rock Hyrax ("Rock Dassie")	2·50	75
551	1e. Zorilla	4·25	4·50
552	2e. African Wild Cat	7·50	10·00
549/52	*Set of* 4	14·50	14·00

(Des T. Chance. Litho Security Printers (M), Malaysia)

1989 (21 Sept). 125th Anniv of International Red Cross. T **126** and similar horiz designs. Multicoloured. W w **14** (sideways*). P 12.

553	15c. Type **126**	25	15
554	60c. First aid training	60	40
555	1e. Sigombeni Clinic	1·00	1·50
556	2e. Refugee camp	1·50	3·00
	w. Wmk Crown to right of CA		
553/6	*Set of* 4	3·00	4·50

*The normal sideways watermark shows Crown to left of CA, as seen from the back of the stamp.

127 King Mswati III with Prince of Wales, 1987

128 Manzini to Mahamba Road

(Des L. Curtis. Litho Harrison)

1989 (15 Nov). 21st Birthday of King Mswati III. T **127** and similar horiz designs. Multicoloured. P 14×14½.

557	15c. Type **127**	10	10
558	60c. King with Pope John Paul II, 1988	30	35
559	1e. Introduction of Crown Prince to people, 1983	50	55
560	2e. King Mswati III and Queen Mother	95	1·00
557/60	*Set of* 4	1·60	1·75

(Des A. Theobald. Litho Questa)

1989 (18 Dec). 25th Anniv of African Development Bank. T **128** and similar horiz designs. Multicoloured. W w **16** (sideways). P 14×14½.

561	15c. Type **128**	10	10
562	60c. Microwave Radio Receiver, Mbabane	30	40
563	1e. Mbabane Government Hospital	50	1·10
564	2e. Ezulwini Power Station switchyard	95	2·25
561/4	*Set of* 4	1·60	3·50

129 International Priority Mail Van

(Des G. Vasarhelyi. Litho Security Printers (M), Malaysia)

1990 (3 May). "Stamp World London 90" International Stamp Exhibition. T **129** and similar horiz designs. Multicoloured. W w **14** (sideways). P 12½.

565	15c. Type **129**	15	10
566	60c. Facsimile Service operators	40	40
567	1e. Rural post office	75	1·00
568	2e. Ezulwini Earth Station switchyard	1·40	2·50
565/8	*Set of* 4	2·40	3·50
MS569	105×85 mm. 2e. Mail runner. Wmk upright	5·50	6·00

No. **MS**569 also commemorates the 150th anniversary of the Penny Black.

129a Queen Mother

129b King George VI and Queen Elizabeth visiting Civil Resettlement Unit, Hatfield House

(Des D. Miller. Litho Questa)

1990 (4 Aug). 90th Birthday of Queen Elizabeth the Queen Mother. W w **16**. P 14×15 (75c.) or 14½ (4c.).

570	**129a**	75c. multicoloured	50	50
571	**129b**	4e. brownish black and deep turquoise-green	2·25	3·50

130 Pictorial Teaching

131 Rural Water Supply

(Des D. Aryeequaye. Litho Questa)

1990 (21 Sept). International Literacy Year. T **130** and similar horiz designs. Multicoloured. W w **14** (sideways). P 14.

572	15c. Type **130**	10	10
573	75c. Rural class	45	45
574	1e. Modern teaching methods	60	1·00
575	2e. Presentation of certificates	1·10	2·00
572/5	*Set of* 4	2·00	3·25

(Des D. Aryeequaye. Litho Cartor)

1990 (10 Dec). 40th Anniv of United Nations Development Programme. "Helping People to Help Themselves". T **131** and similar vert designs. Multicoloured. W w **14**. P 13½×14.

576	60c. Type **131**	35	35
577	1e. Seed multiplication project	60	1·10
578	2e. Low-cost housing project	1·25	2·25
576/8	*Set of* 3	2·00	3·25

(**132**)

133 Lobamba Hot Spring

1990 (17 Dec). Nos. 519/20, 522 and 524 surch as T **132**.

579	10c. on 25c. *Abantis paradisea*	30	30
580	15c. on 30c. *Acraea anemosa*	40	40
580*a*	15c. on 45c. *Graphium antheus*	17·00	17·00
581	20c. on 45c. *Graphium antheus*	40	40
582	40c. on 55c. *Pinacopteryx eriphia*	55	55

(Des D. Aryeequaye. Litho Harrison)

1991 (11 Feb). National Heritage. T **133** and similar horiz designs. Multicoloured. W **77** of Brunei (sideways). P 14½.

583	15c. Type **133**	40	10
584	60c. Sibebe Rock	1·50	45
585	1e. Jolobela Falls	2·00	2·00
586	2e. Mantjolo Sacred Pool	2·50	3·50
583/6	*Set of* 4	5·75	5·50
MS587	80×60 mm. 2e. Usushwana River. P 14	5·50	6·50

134 King Mswati III making Speech

(Des D. Aryeequaye. Litho Cartor)

1991 (24 Apr). 5th Anniv of King Mswati III's Coronation. T **134** and similar horiz designs. Multicoloured. W w **14** (sideways). P 14×13½.

588	15c. Type **134**	50	10
589	75c. Butimba Royal Hunt	1·40	60
590	1e. King and visiting school friends from Sherborne, 1986	1·75	2·00
591	2e. King opening Parliament	2·50	3·50
588/91	*Set of* 4	5·50	5·50

134a Prince Philip

135 *Xerophyta retinervis*

(Des D. Miller. Litho Questa)

1991 (17 June). 65th Birthday of Queen Elizabeth II and 70th Birthday of Prince Philip. Vert designs as T **134a**. Multicoloured. W w **16** (sideways). P 14½×14.

592	1e. Prince Philip	1·75	2·25
	a. Horiz pair. Nos. 592/3 separated by label	3·75	4·50
593	2e. Queen Elizabeth II	2·00	2·25

Nos. 592/3 were printed together *se-tenant*, in sheetlets of 10 (2×5) with designs alternating and the vertical rows separated by inscribed labels.

(Des D. Aryeequaye. Litho Questa)

1991 (30 Sept). Indigenous Flowers. T **135** and similar vert designs. Multicoloured. W w **14** (sideways). P 14.

594	15c. Type **135**	50	10
595	75c. *Bauhinia galpinii*	1·25	80
596	1e. *Dombeya rotundifolia*	1·50	1·75
597	2e. *Kigelia africana*	2·25	3·50
594/7	*Set of 4*	5·00	5·50

136 Father Christmas

137 Lubombo Flat Lizard arriving with Gifts

(Des D. Aryeequaye. Litho Cartor)

1991 (18 Dec). Christmas. T **136** and similar vert designs. Multicoloured. W w **14**. P 13½.

598	20c. Type **136**	15	10
599	70c. Singing carols	65	50
600	1e. Priest reading from Bible	80	1·25
601	2e. The Nativity	1·50	2·50
598/601	*Set of 4*	2·75	4·00

(Des D. Aryeequaye. Litho Cartor)

1992 (25 Feb). Reptiles (1st series). T **137** and similar horiz designs. Multicoloured. W w **14** (sideways). P 13½.

602	20c. Type **137**	90	20
603	70c. Natal Hinged Tortoise	2·25	1·50
604	1e. Swazi Thick-toed Gecko	2·75	2·75
605	2e. Nile Monitor	3·75	5·50
602/5	*Set of 4*	8·75	9·00

See also Nos. 658/61.

138 *Precis hierta*

139 Missionaries visiting King Sobhuza II and Queen Lomawa

Two types of 55c. stamp (No. 615):
I. "Closed" letter c in 55c. "1991" imprint date
II. Redrawn design with "2000" imprint date
There are a number of other differences in the redrawn design.

(Des I. Loe. Litho Questa)

1992 (26 Aug). Butterflies (2nd series). Designs as Nos. 516/26 and new value (5c.) showing different portrait of King Mswati III as in T **138**. Multicoloured. Without imprint date (5c.) or with "1991" imprint date below design (others). P 14.

606	5c. *Colotis antevippe*	10	50
607	10c. Type **138**	15	50
608	15c. *Hamanumida daedalus*	15	50
609	20c. *Charaxes boueti*	20	50
610	25c. *Abantis paradisea*	20	30
611	30c. *Acraea anemosa*	20	30
612	35c. *Graphium leonidas*	20	30
613	45c. *Graphium antheus*	25	30
614	50c. *Precis orithya*	25	30
	a. Type II (2000)	5·00	1·00
615	55c. *Pinacopteryx eriphia*	25	30
616	70c. *Precis octavia*	60	40
617	1e. *Mylothris chloris*	70	90
618	5e. *Colotis regina*(2000)	15·00	5·00
619	10e. *Spindasis natalersis*(2000)	15·00	7·00
606/19	*Set of 14*	30·00	16·00

Nos. 606/17 are all on chalk-surfaced paper.

(Des D. Aryeequaye. Litho Cartor)

1992 (16 Dec). Centenary of Evangelical Alliance Missions. T **139** and similar vert design. Multicoloured. P 13½×14.

620	20c. Type **139**	50	10
621	1e. Pioneer missionaries	2·50	3·25

140 Calabashes

(Des D. Aryeequaye. Litho Cartor)

1993 (18 Mar). Archaeological and Contemporary Artifacts. T **140** and similar vert designs. Multicoloured. P 13½×14.

622	20c. Type **140**	45	10
623	70c. Contemporary cooking pot	1·10	85
624	1e. Wooden bowl and containers	1·50	1·75
625	2e. Quern for grinding seeds	2·50	3·50
622/5	*Set of 4*	5·00	5·50

141 King Mswati III as Baby

(Des D. Aryeequaye. Litho Cartor)

1993 (6 Sept). 25th Birthday of King Mswati III and 25th Anniv of Independence. T **141** and similar vert designs. Multicoloured. P 13½×14.

626	25c. Type **141**	25	10
627	40c. King Mswati III addressing meeting	35	20
628	1e. King Sobhuza II receiving Instrument of Independence	90	1·50
629	2e. King Mswati III delivering Coronation speech	1·60	3·00
626/9	*Set of 4*	2·75	4·25

142 Male and Female Common Waxbills

143 Classroom and Practical Training

(Des D. Aryeequaye. Litho Cartor)

1993 (25 Nov). Common Waxbill. T **142** and similar vert designs. Multicoloured. P 13½.

630	25c. Type **142**	40	20
631	40c. Waxbill and eggs in nest	55	25
632	1e. Waxbill on nest	1·25	1·50
633	2e. Waxbill feeding chicks	2·00	2·75
630/3	*Set of 4*	3·75	4·25

(Des D. Aryeequaye. Litho Cartor)

1994 (22 Feb). 25th Anniv of U.S. Peace Corps in Swaziland. T **143** and similar vert designs. Multicoloured. P 13½.

634	25c. Type **143**	40	10
635	40c. Rural water supply	55	20

636	1e. Americans and Swazis in traditional costumes	2·00	2·00
637	2e. Swazi-American co-operation	2·25	3·25
634/7 *Set of 4*		4·75	5·00

144 Agaricus arvensis

145 Emblem and Fokker 100 on Runway

(Des D. Aryeequaye. Litho Cartor)

1994 (15 Sept). Fungi. T **144** and similar vert designs. Multicoloured. P 13½×14.

638	30c. Type **144**	1·25	50
639	40c. Boletus edulis	1·25	50
640	1e. Russula virescens	2·50	1·75
641	2e. Armillaria mellea	3·50	4·00
638/41 *Set of 4*		7·50	6·00

(Des D. Aryeequaye. Litho Walsall)

1994 (30 Nov). 50th Anniv of International Civil Aviation Organization. T **145** and similar horiz designs. Multicoloured. P 14.

642	30c. Type **145**	50	10
643	40c. Control tower and dish aerial	55	20
644	1e. Crash tenders	1·25	1·50
645	2e. Air traffic controllers	1·75	2·75
642/5 *Set of 4*		3·50	4·00

146 Wooden Bowls

147 Harvesting Maize

(Des D. Aryeequaye. Litho Cartor)

1995 (7 Apr). Handicrafts. T **146** and similar vert designs. Multicoloured. P 13½×14.

646	35c. Type **146**	45	20
647	50c. Chicken nests	65	35
648	1e. Leather crafts	1·00	1·25
649	2e. Wood carvings	1·75	2·50
646/9 *Set of 4*		3·50	3·75

(Des D. Aryeequaye. Litho Cartor)

1995 (5 June). 50th Anniv of Food and Agriculture Organization. T **147** and similar vert designs. Multicoloured. P 13½.

650	35c. Type **147**	30	20
651	50c. Planting vegetables	45	35
652	1e. Herd of cattle	75	1·00
653	2e. Harvesting sorghum	1·25	2·00
650/3 *Set of 4*		2·50	3·25

148 Knysna Turaco

149 Waterberry

(Des D. Aryeequaye. Litho Cartor)

1995 (27 Sept). Turacos ("Louries"). T **148** and simlar horiz designs. Multicoloured. P 13½×13.

654	35c. Type **148**	40	30
655	50c. Knysna Turaco in flight	55	45
656	1e. Violet-crested Turaco	80	1·00
657	2e. Livingstone's Turaco	1·25	2·00
654/7 *Set of 4*		2·75	3·25

(Des D. Aryeequaye. Litho Cartor)

1996 (17 Jan). Reptiles (2nd series). Horiz designs as T **137** with King's portrait at right. Multicoloured. P 13½×13.

658	35c. Chameleon	70	20
659	50c. Rock Monitor	80	35
660	1e. African Python	1·40	1·60
661	2e. Tree Agama	2·00	3·00
658/61 *Set of 4*		4·50	4·75

(Des D. Aryeequaye. Litho Cartor)

1996 (23 Apr). Trees. T **149** and similar vert designs. Multicoloured. P 13×13½.

662	40c. Type **149**	25	15
663	60c. Sycamore Fig	30	20
664	1e. Stem Fruit	50	80
665	2e. Wild Medlar	90	1·60
662/5 *Set of 4*		1·75	2·50

150 Mahamba Methodist Church

(Des D. Aryeequaye. Litho Cartor)

1996 (26 Aug). Historic Monuments. T **150** and similar horiz designs. Multicoloured. P 13½×13.

666	40c. Type **150**	50	15
667	60c. Colonial Secretariat, Mbabane	65	20
668	1e. King Sobhuza II Monument, Lobamba..	1·10	1·40
669	2e. First High Court Building, Hlatikulu	1·75	2·75
666/9 *Set of 4*		3·50	4·00

151 Children in Class

(Litho Enschedé)

1996 (31 Dec). 50th Anniv of UNICEF. T **151** and similar multicoloured designs. P 13½×14 (40c.) or 14×13½ (others).

670	40c. Type **151**	25	15
671	60c. Child being inoculated (*vert*)	35	20
672	1e. Child on crutches (*vert*)	60	90
673	2e. Mother and children (*vert*)	1·00	2·00
670/3 *Set of 4*		2·00	3·00

152 Klipspringer

(Litho Enschedé)

1997 (22 Sept). Mammals. T **152** and similar multicoloured designs. P 14×13½ (*vert*) or 13½×14 (*horiz*).

674	50c. Type **152**	30	20
675	70c. Grey Duiker	35	30
676	1e. Antbear (*horiz*)	50	70
677	2e. Cape Clawless Otter (*horiz*)	80	1·60
674/7 *Set of 4*		1·75	2·50

153 Umgaco Costume

154 Olive Toad

(Litho Cartor)

1997 (1 Dec). Traditional Costumes. T **153** and similar vert designs. Multicoloured. P 13×13½.

678	50c. Type **153**	25	15
679	70c. Sigeja cloak	35	25
680	1e. Umdada kilt	55	65
681	2e. Ligcebesha costume	90	1·40
678/81	*Set of* 4	1·90	2·25

(Des K. Addai-Yinkah. Litho Enschedé)

1998 (1 June). Amphibians. T **154** and similar horiz designs. Multicoloured. P 14½×14.

682	55c. Type **154**	35	15
683	75c. African Bullfrog	45	30
684	1e. Water Lily Frog	70	90
685	2e. Bushveld Rain Frog	1·25	1·90
682/5	*Set of* 4	2·50	3·00

155 Aerial View of King Sobhuza II Memorial Park

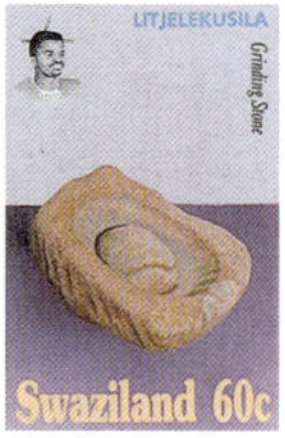

156 Grinding Stone

(Des K. Addai-Yinkah. Litho Enschedé)

1998 (3 Sept). 30th Anniv of Independence and 30th Birthday of King Mswati III. T **155** and similar multicoloured designs. P 14×13½ (75c.) or 13½×14 (others).

686	55c. Type **155**	40	15
687	75c. King Mswati III taking oath (*vert*)	50	25
688	1e. King Mswati delivering speech	75	90
689	2e. King Sobhuza II receiving Instrument of Independence	1·40	2·00
686/9	*Set of* 4	2·75	3·00

(Des D. Aryeequaye. Litho Cartor)

1999 (17 May). Local Culinary Utensils. T **156** and similar vert designs. Multicoloured. Two phosphor bands. P 13½.

690	60c. Type **156**	35	15
691	75c. Stirring sticks	40	20
692	80c. Clay pot	40	25
693	95c. Swazi spoons	55	45
694	1e.75 Beer cups	1·00	1·40
695	2e.40 Mortar and pestle	1·40	2·00
690/5	*Set of* 6	3·75	4·00

157 Internet Service

158 Lion and Lioness

(Des K. Addai-Yinkah. Litho Cartor)

1999 (9 Oct). 125th Anniv of Universal Postal Union. T **157** and similar multicoloured designs. Two phosphor bands. P 13½.

696	60c. Type **157**	35	15
697	80c. Cellular phone service	45	25
698	1e. Two post vans exchanging mail (*horiz*)	1·75	1·50
699	2e.40 Training school (*horiz*)	2·00	2·50
696/9	*Set of* 4	4·00	4·00

(Des K. Addai-Yinkah. Litho Cartor)

2000 (3 July). Wildlife. T **158** and similar multicoloured designs. Two phosphor bands. P 13½.

700	65c. Type **158**	55	20
701	90c. Leopard (*horiz*)	75	35
702	1e.50 Rhinoceros (*horiz*)	3·00	1·75
703	2e.50 Buffalo	2·25	3·00
700/3	*Set of* 4	6·00	4·75

159 Oribi with Young

160 Fighting Forest Fires

(Des A. Robinson. Litho Questa)

2001 (1 Feb). Endangered Species. Antelopes. T **159** and similar horiz designs. Multicoloured. W w **14** (sideways). P 14.

704	65c. Type **159**	45	25
	a. Strip of 4. Nos. 704/7	3·75	4·00
705	90c. Oribi Buck	70	40
706	1e.50 Young Klipspringers	1·25	1·50
707	2e.50 Male and female Klipspringers	1·75	2·25
704/7	*Set of* 4	3·75	4·00

Nos. 704/7 were printed in separate sheets of 50 (two panes 5×5) or in sheets of 16 (4×4) containing the four designs *se-tenant*, both horizontally and vertically. The sheets of 16 have illustrated margins.

(Des K. Addai-Yinkah. Litho Questa)

2001 (30 July). Enviromental Protection. T **160** and similar horiz designs. Multicoloured. P 14.

708	70c. Type **160**	50	20
709	95c. Tree planting	65	25
710	2e.05 Construction of Maguga Dam	1·40	1·75
711	2e.80 Building embankment	1·75	2·25
708/11	*Set of* 4	3·75	4·00

160a Princess Elizabeth, Prince Philip and Children, 1951

(Des A. Robinson. Litho Questa)

2002 (6 Feb). Golden Jubilee. W w **14** (sideways). P 14½.

712	70c. agate, violet and gold	65	10
713	95c. multicoloured	85	25
714	2e.05 agate, violet and gold	1·40	1·50
715	2e.80 multicoloured	1·75	2·00
712/15	*Set of* 4	4·25	3·50
MS716	16×95 mm. Nos. 712/15 and 22e.50, multicoloured. P 13½ (22e.50) or 14½ (others)	6·00	7·00

Designs: *Horiz*—70c. Type **160a**; 95c. Queen Elizebeth in blue and white beret; 2e.05 Queen Elizabeth in evening dress; 2e.80 Queen Elizabeth on visit to Norway, 2001. Vert (38×51 mm)—22e.50 Queen Elizabeth after Annigoni.

Designs as Nos. 712/15 in No. **MS**716 omit the gold frame around each stamp and the "Golden Jubilee 1952–2002" inscription.

161 Swazi Village

162 Sitolotolo (mouth organ)

(Des P. Dlamini. Litho Enschedé)

2002 (23 Dec). Tourism. T **161** and similar multicoloured designs. P 13½.

717	75c. Type **161**	20	10
718	1e.05 King Mswati and lions (*vert*)	30	20
719	2e.05 Crocodile	1·25	1·50
720	2e.80 Ostrich with young	1·75	2·25
717/20 *Set of 4*		3·25	3·50

(Des P. Dlamini. Litho Enschedé)

2003 (12 Aug). Musical Instruments. T **162** and similar multicoloured designs. P 14.

721	80c. Type **162**	30	20
722	1e.05 Emafahlawane (rattles) (*horiz*)	40	25
723	2e.35 Impalampala (Kudu horn trumpet) (*horiz*)	85	1·25
724	2e.80 Makhoyane (chordphone)	1·10	1·60
721/4 *Set of 4*		2·40	3·00

163 Community Health Worker

164 King Mswati III with AIDS Patient and outline of Africa

(Des P. Dlamini. Litho Enschedé)

2004 (9 Mar). AIDS Awareness Campaign. T **163** and similar multicoloured designs. P 13½×14 (*horiz*) or 14×13½ (*vert*).

725	85c. Type **163**	50	20
726	1e.10 Care and Voluntary Councelling and Testing Centre	60	30
727	2e.45 Testing Blood (*vert*)	1·40	1·40
728	3e.45 Nurse giving injection and sterilizer (*vert*)	1·75	2·25
725/8 *Set of 4*		3·75	3·75

(Des P. Dlamini. Litho Enschedé)

2004 (14 June). Global 2003 Smart Partnership Movement. T **164** and similar multicoloured designs. P 13½.

729	85c. Type **164**	35	20
730	1e.10 Outline of Africa and Logos (*horiz*)	45	25
731	2e.45 Stylized people holding globe	95	1·25
732	3e.35 King Mswati III and speaker	1·10	1·60
729/32 *Set of 4*		2·50	3·00

(Des Anja Denker. Litho Enschedé)

2004 (11 Oct). First Joint Issue of Southern Africa Postal Operators Association Members. Hexagonal designs as T **233** of Botswana showing national birds of Association members. Multicoloured. P 14.

733	85c. Purple-crested turaco ("Lourie") (Swaziland)	70	50
734	1e.10 Stanley ("Blue") crane (South Africa)	70	50
735	1e.35 Cattle egret (Botswana)	75	60
736	1e.90 Two African fish eagles perched (Zimbabwe)	1·40	1·10
737	2e. African fish eagle (Namibia)	1·40	1·10
738	2e.45 Bar-tailed trogon (Malawi) (inscribed "apaloderma vittatum")	1·50	1·50
739	3e. Two African fish eagles in flight (Zambia)	1·75	2·00
740	3e.35 Peregrine falcon (Angola)	1·90	2·50
733/40 *Set of 8*		9·00	9·00
MS741	170×95 mm. Nos. 733/40	9·00	10·00

The stamp depicting the bar-tailed trogon is not inscribed with the country of which the bird is a national symbol. Miniature sheets in similar designs were also issued by Namibia, Zimbabwe, Angola, Botswana, South Africa, Malawi and Zambia.

165 School Child under Car and Children by Road

(Des P. Dlamini. Litho Enschedé)

2005 (25 Jan). Road Safety Council. T **165** and similar horiz designs. Multicoloured. P 13½×14.

742	85c. Type **165**	50	35
743	1e.10 Fire rescue team pulling injured man from car	50	35
744	2e.45 Pedestrians and car approaching stop sign	80	1·10
745	3e.35 Bus and road safety officials	1·10	1·50
742/5 *Set of 4*		2·75	3·00

166 Black Mamba

166a Pope John Paul II

(Litho Enschedé)

2005 (5 Apr). Snakes. T **166** and similar horiz designs. Multicoloured. P 13½×14.

746	85c. Type **166**	30	15
747	1e.10 Python	40	30
748	2e.45 Boomslang	80	1·10
749	3e.35 Puff adder	1·10	1·50
747/9 *Set of 4*		2·40	2·75

(Des Andrew Robinson. Litho BDT)

2005 (18 Aug). Pope John Paul II Commemoration. W w **14** (inverted). P 14.

750	**166a** 4e.50 multicoloured	1·75	1·90

No. 750 was printed in sheetlets of eight stamps with an enlarged, illustrated right margin.

167 *Schistocerca solitaria*

(Des P. Dlamini. Litho Enschedé)

2005 (11 Oct). Locusts and Grasshoppers. T **167** and similar horiz designs. Multicoloured. P 13½×14.

751	85c. Type **167**	50	20
752	1e.10 *Nomadacris septemfasciata* (red locust)	60	35
753	2e.45 *Schistocerca gregaria flaviventris* (South African desert locust)	1·50	1·75
754	3e.35 *Locusta migratoria migratoroides* (African migratory locust)	2·00	2·50
751/4 *Set of 4*		4·25	4·25

168 Ntombi Tfwala (1983–)

(Des P. Dlamini. Litho Enschedé)

2006 (10 Jan). Queen Mothers of Swaziland. T **168** and similar vert designs. Multicoloured. P 14×13½.

755	85c. Type **168**	50	20
756	1e.10 Dzeliwe Shongwe (1980–3)	60	35
757	2e. Lomawa Ndwandwe (1921–38)	1·25	1·00
758	2e.45 Labotsibeni Mdluli (1895–1921)	1·50	1·75
759	3e.35 Tibati Nkambule (1881–95)	2·00	2·50
755/9 *Set of 5*		5·25	5·25

169 Mgubudla Falls, Northern

170 *Cussonia spicata* (common cabbage tree)

(Des P. Dlamini. Litho Austrian State Ptg Wks, Vienna)

2006 (26 Sept). Waterfalls. T **169** and similar multicoloured designs. P 14.

760	90c. Type **169**	60	25
761	1e.15 Phophonyane Falls, Phophonyane Nature Reserve	70	35
762	1e.40 Mantenga Falls, Mantenga Nature Reserve (*horiz*)	95	70
763	2e. Malolotja Falls, Malolotja Nature Reserve	1·40	1·10
764	2e.55 Mabhudlweni Falls, Mhlosheni, Shiselweni	1·75	2·00
765	3e.50 Manzamnyama Falls, Mdzimba Mountains (*horiz*)	2·50	2·75
760/5	*Set of 5*	7·00	6·50

(Des P. Dlamini. Litho Enschedé)

2007 (23 Jan). Trees. T **170** and similar horiz designs. Multicoloured. P 13½×14.

766	70c. Type **170**	30	20
767	85c. *Ficus sur* (broom cluster fig)	30	20
768	90c. *Acacia nilotica* (scented thorn)	35	25
769	1e.05 *Trichlia emetica* (Natal mahogany)	40	25
770	1e.15 *Sclerocarya birrea* (marula)	45	30
771	1e.40 *Bequaertiodendron megalismontanum* (stem fruit)	50	35
772	2e. *Acacia xanthophloea* (fever tree)	65	50
773	2e.40 *Erythrina latissima* (large-leaved coral tree)	70	60
774	2e.55 *Pterocarpus angolensis* (African teak)	75	65
775	3e.50 *Berchemia zeyheri* (red ivory)	95	85
776	5e. *Erythrina lysistemon* (common coral tree)	1·40	1·50
777	10e. *Pappea capensis* (jacket-plum)	2·75	3·00
778	20e. *Kigelia africana* (sausage tree)	5·00	6·00
766/78	*Set of 13*	13·00	13·00

171 District Office/Post Office, Manzini, 1920s

2007 (8 May). Postal History. T **171** and similar multicoloured designs. Litho. P 14.

779	90c. Type **171**	55	20
780	1e.15 Ox-wagon transferring post, 1880s–90s	65	35
781	2e. Bremersdorp Post Office, 1893	1·25	1·00
782	2e.55 Mail runner (*vert*)	1·60	1·75
783	3e.50 Temporary post office, Mbabane, 1902.	2·25	2·75
779/83	*Set of 4*	5·75	5·50

172 Nsangwini Rock Art

(Des P. Dlamini. Litho Enschedé)

2008 (22 Jan). Community Based Tourism. T **172** and similar horiz designs. Multicoloured. P 13½×14.

784	1e. Type **172**	60	20
785	1e.20 Mahamba Gorge Lodge	70	35
786	2e.70 Shewula Mountain Camp	1·50	1·75
787	3e.70 Khopho Camp, Ngwempisi trails	2·25	2·50
784/7	*Set of 5*	4·50	4·25

173 Inkhonyane

2008 (27 May). 'Swazi Finery' (traditional dress). T **173** and similar multicoloured designs. Litho. P 13½×14.

788	1e. Type **173**	60	30
789	2e.70 Beaded necklace (horiz)	1·50	1·75
790	3e.70 Anklets (horiz)	2·25	2·50
788/90	*Set of 3*	4·00	4·00

174 Steam Locomotive and Airliner ('Transport Infrastructure')

(Des P. Dlamini. Litho Enschedé)

2008 (28 Oct). 40th Anniv of Independence and 40th Birthday of King Mswati III. T **174** and similar multicoloured designs. P 13×13½ (horiz) or 13½×13 (vert).

791	1e. Type **174**	40	30
792	1e.05 King Mswati III receives new Swaziland constitution, 26 July 2005 (vert)	45	35
793	1e.30 Maguga Dam	50	40
794	1e.60 Maidens at reed dance (vert)	60	55
795	2e.15 One lilangeni note (First Lilangeni Currency, 1974)	50	50
796	2e.40 Nurse with boy ('Health and Social welfare')	70	80
797	2e.75 Boy using computer ('?Information Communication Technology')	75	1·00
798	2e.90 King Mswati III's 40th birthday	1·25	1·50
799	3e.95 King Subhuza declaring independence, 1968 (vert)	1·90	2·50
791/9	*Set of 9*	6·25	7·00

POSTAGE DUE STAMPS

D 1

(D **2**)

D **3**

(Typo D.L.R.)

1933 (23 Jan)–**57**. Wmk Mult Script CA. P 14.

D1	D **1**	1d. carmine	1·00	15·00
		a. Chalk-surfaced paper. *Dp carmine* (24.10.51)	20	20·00
		ac. Error. St Edward's Crown, W **9***b*	£375	
D2		2d. pale violet	3·50	32·00
		a. Chalk-surfaced paper (22.2.57)	6·00	48·00
		ab. Large "d"	55·00	
D1/2		Perf "Specimen" *Set of 2*	60·00	

For illustrations of No. D2ab see above No. D1 of Basutoland.

1961 (8 Feb). No. 55 surch with Type D **2**.

D3	**7**	2d. on 2d.	1·25	2·75

Another 2d. on 2d. Postage Due, with small surcharge as Type D **5**, was produced *after the currency change*, to meet the philatelic demand (*Price* 15*p unused*).

(Typo D.L.R.)

1961 (14 Feb). Chalk-surfaced paper. Wmk Mult Script CA. P 14.

D4	D **3**	1c. carmine	15	1·10
D5		2c. violet	15	1·10
D6		5c. green	20	1·10
D4/6		*Set of 3*	45	3·00

Postage Due
1c
(D **4**)

Postage Due
1c
(D **5**)

1961. No. 55 surcharged. A. As Type D **4**. (14 Feb).

D7	**7**	1c. on 2d.	1·25	2·50
D8		2c. on 2d.	1·25	2·50
D9		5c. on 2d.	2·25	2·50
D7/9 *Set of* 3			4·25	6·75

B. As Type D **5**. (Date?)

D10	**7**	1c. on 2d.	70	3·25
D11		2c. on 2d.	50	2·75
D12		5c. on 2d.	90	2·25
D10/12 *Set of* 3			1·90	7·50

D **6**

(Des and litho B.W.)

1971 (1 Feb). Size 18×23 mm. W w **12**. P 11½.

D13	D **6**	1c. bright rose-red	65	3·50
D14		2c. purple	75	3·50
D15		5c. dull green	1·00	4·00
D13/15 *Set of* 3			2·25	10·00

1977 (17 Jan). Size 18×23 mm. (sideways). W w **14**. P 11½.

D16	D **6**	1c. rose-red	85	3·50
D17		2c. purple	1·10	4·00
D18		5c. dull green	1·75	4·50
D16/18 *Set of* 3			3·25	11·00

(Litho Harrison)

1978 (20 Apr)–**85**. Size 17½×21 mm. W w **14**. P 15×14.

D19	D **6**	1c. carmine	30	1·75
D19*a*		1c. brown-red (13.3.85)	3·25	4·50
D20		2c. purple	30	1·50
D21		5c. blue-green	30	1·50
D19/21 *Set of* 4			3·75	8·25

(Litho Harrison)

1991 (17 July). Size 17½×21 mm. With imprint date. W w **14** (sideways) . P 15×14.

D23	D **6**	2c. purple	10	35
D24		5c. bright blue-green	10	35
D25		10c. pale greenish blue	15	35
D26		25c. red-brown	20	35
D23/6 *Set of* 4			40	1·25

Zambia
formerly Northern Rhodesia

The north-eastern and north-western provinces of Rhodesia, previously administered by the British South Africa Company, became a Crown Colony on 1 April 1924.

The current stamps of Rhodesia (the "Admiral" design first issued in 1913) remained in use until 31 March 1925 and continued to be valid for postal purposes until 30 September of that year.

PRICES FOR STAMPS ON COVER TO 1945		
Nos.	1/21	*from* × 2
Nos.	22/4	*from* × 5
Nos.	25/45	*from* × 2
Nos.	D1/4	*from* × 15

1

2

(Des W. Fairweather. Eng J. A. C. Harrison. Recess Waterlow)

1925 (1 April)–**29**. Wmk Mult Script CA. P 12½.

1	**1**	½d. green	1·75	80
2		1d. brown	1·75	10
3		1½d. carmine-red	3·50	30
4		2d. yellow-brown	3·75	10
5		3d. ultramarine	3·75	1·25
6		4d. violet	6·50	50
7		6d. slate-grey	6·50	40
8		8d. rose-purple	6·50	55·00
9		10d. olive-green	6·50	50·00
10	**2**	1s. yellow-brown and black	3·75	1·75
11		2s. brown and ultramarine	23·00	32·00
12		2s.6d. black and green	24·00	15·00
13		3s. violet and blue (1929)	32·00	23·00
14		5s. slate-grey and violet	45·00	19·00
15		7s.6d. rose-purple and black	£130	£225
16		10s. green and black	85·00	85·00
17		20s. carmine-red and rose-purple	£200	£250
1/17 *Set of 17*			£550	£700
1s/17s Optd or Perf (3s.) "SPECIMEN" *Set of 17*			£900	

A used example of the 4d. exists imperforate between the stamp and a fragment of another below it.

Diagonal line by turret (Plate 2A R. 10/1 and 10/2)

Dot to left of chapel (Plate 2B R. 8/3)

Dot by flagstaff (Plate 4 R. 8/4)

Dash by turret (Plate 4/ R. 3/6)

1935 (6 May). Silver Jubilee. As Nos. 123/6 of Malawi. P 13½×14.

18	1d. light blue and olive-green	1·50	1·50
	f. Diagonal line by turret	90·00	95·00
	g. Dot to left of chapel	£225	
	h. Dot by flagstaff	£150	£170
	i. Dash by turret	£160	£180
19	2d. green and indigo	2·25	2·75
	f. Diagonal line by turret	£110	£130
	g. Dot to left of chapel	£180	£200
20	3d. brown and deep blue	4·00	9·00
	f. Diagonal line by turret	£170	£250
	g. Dot to left of chapel	£300	£400
21	6d. slate and purple	8·00	1·75
	a. Frame printed double, one albino	£2500	£2750
	h. Dot by flagstaff	£400	£225
18/21 *Set of 4*		14·00	13·50
18s/21s Perf "SPECIMEN" *Set of 4*		£170	

THERN_RHODE

Hyphen between "NORTHERN" and "RHODESIA" (R. 9/6)

1937 (12 May). Coronation. As Nos. 127/9 Malawi. P 11×11½.

22	1½d. carmine	30	50
23	2d. buff	40	50
24	3d. blue	60	1·25
	a. Hyphen flaw	£350	
22/4 *Set of 3*		1·10	2·00
22s/4s Perf "SPECIMEN" *Set of 3*		£140	

3

4

"Tick bird" flaw (Pl 1 R. 7/1 of ptgs from Sept 1938 onwards)

(Recess Waterlow)

1938 (1 Mar)–**52**. Wmk Mult Script CA. P 12½.

25	**3**	½d. green	10	10
		a. "C" of "CA" missing from wmk	£2000	
26		½d. chocolate (15.11.51)	2·00	1·50
		a. Perf 12½×14 (22.10.52)	1·40	6·00
27		1d. brown	20	20
		a. Chocolate (1948)	1·75	1·00
28		1d. green (15.11.51)	1·00	2·00
29		1½d. carmine-red	50·00	75
		a. Imperf between (horiz pair)	£22000	
		b. "Tick bird" flaw	£6000	£425
30		1½d. yellow-brown (10.1.41)	30	10
		b. "Tick bird" flaw	£150	55·00
31		2d. yellow-brown	50·00	1·75
32		2d. carmine-red (10.1.41)	1·50	50
33		2d. purple (1.12.51)	45	1·50
34		3d. ultramarine	50	30
35		3d. scarlet (1.12.51)	50	3·00
36		4d. dull violet	40	40
37		4½d. blue (5.5.52)	2·75	10·00
38		6d. grey	40	10
39		9d. violet (5.5.52)	2·75	9·50
40	**4**	1s. yellow-brown and black	4·00	60
41		2s.6d. black and green	10·00	6·00
42		3s. violet and blue	22·00	16·00
43		5s. grey and dull violet	22·00	16·00
44		10s. green and black	27·00	27·00
45		20s. carmine-red and rose-purple	65·00	70·00
25/45 *Set of 21*			£225	£150
25s/45s Perf "SPECIMEN" *Set of 15*			£500	

Nos. 26a and 28 exist in coils, constructed from normal sheets.

1946 (26 Nov). Victory. As Nos. 158/9 of Malawi. P 13½×14.

No.		Description	Unused	Used
46		1½d. red-orange	1·00	1·50
		a. Perf 13½	14·00	12·00
47		2d. carmine	10	50
46s/7s		Perf "SPECIMEN" *Set of 2*	£120	

The decimal perforation gauge for Nos. 46/7 is 13.7×14.1 and for No. 46a 13.7×13.4.

1948 (1 Dec). Royal Silver Wedding. As Nos. 161/2 of Malawi, but 20s. ptd entirely in recess.

No.		Description	Unused	Used
48		1½d. orange	30	10
49		20s. brown-lake	65·00	70·00

1949 (10 Oct). 75th Anniv of U.P.U. As Nos. 163/6 of Malawi.

No.		Description	Unused	Used
50		2d. carmine	20	75
51		3d. deep blue	2·00	3·00
52		6d. grey	1·00	2·00
53		1s. red-orange	75	1·50
50/3		*Set of 4*	3·50	6·50

5 Cecil Rhodes and Victoria Falls

(Recess D.L.R.)

1953 (30 May). Birth Centenary of Cecil Rhodes. Wmk Mult Script CA. P 12×11½.

No.	Type	Description	Unused	Used
54	5	½d. brown	55	1·50
55		1d. green	45	1·50
56		2d. mauve	60	30
57		4½d. blue	45	3·50
58		1s. orange and black	1·00	4·75
54/8		*Set of 5*	2·75	10·50

1953 (30 May). Rhodes Centenary Exhibition. As No. 171 of Malawi.

No.	Type	Description	Unused	Used
59	6	6d. violet	70	1·25

1953 (2 June). Coronation. As No. 172 of Malawi but des and eng B.W. Recess D.L.R.

No.		Description	Unused	Used
60		1½d. black and yellow-orange	70	20

7

8

(Recess Waterlow)

1953 (15 Sept). Wmk Mult Script CA. P 12½×14 (pence values) or 12½×13½ (shilling values).

No.	Type	Description	Unused	Used
61	7	½d. deep brown	65	10
62		1d. bluish green	65	10
63		1½d. orange-brown	1·25	10
64		2d. reddish purple	1·25	10
65		3d. scarlet	80	10
66		4d. slate-lilac	1·25	2·00
67		4½d. deep blue	1·50	4·25
68		6d. grey-black	1·25	10
		w. Wmk inverted	£3750	£3250
69		9d. violet	1·25	4·25
70	8	1s. orange-brown and black	70	10
71		2s.6d. black and green	13·00	8·00
72		5s. grey and dull purple	14·00	14·00
73		10s. green and black	11·00	32·00
74		20s. rose-red and rose-purple	29·00	38·00
61/74		*Set of 14*	70·00	90·00

For issues from 1954 to 1963, see RHODESIA AND NYASALAND.

9 Arms

10 Arms

(Photo Harrison)

1963 (10 Dec). Arms black, orange and blue; portrait and inscriptions black; background colours below. P 14½ (T **9**) or 13½×13 (T **10**).

No.	Type	Description	Unused	Used
75	9	½d. bright violet	70	1·25
		a. Value omitted	£1100	
		b. Orange (eagle) omitted	£1300	
76		1d. light blue	1·50	10
		a. Value omitted	12·00	
77		2d. brown	70	10
78		3d. yellow	75	10
		a. Value omitted	£110	
		b. Value and orange (eagle) omitted	£275	
		c. Eagle printed double	£3500	
		d. Orange (eagle) omitted	£1200	
79		4d. green	70	30
		a. Value omitted	£120	
80		6d. light olive-green	1·00	10
		a. Value omitted	£800	
81		9d. yellow-brown	70	1·60
		a. Value omitted	£600	
		b. Value and orange (eagle) omitted	£550	
82		1s. slate-purple	50	10
83		1s.3d. bright purple	2·25	10
84	10	2s. orange	2·50	5·00
85		2s.6d. lake-brown	2·50	2·25
86		5s. magenta	10·00	8·50
		a. Value omitted	£2500	
87		10s. bright magenta	16·00	21·00
88		20s. blue	20·00	38·00
		a. Value omitted	£1100	
75/88		*Set of 14*	55·00	70·00

Nos. 75/6 exist in coils, constructed from normal sheets.

ZAMBIA

INDEPENDENT

11 Pres. Kaunda and Victoria Falls

12 College of Further Education, Lusaka

(Des M. Goaman (3d., 6d.), Gabriel Ellison (1s.3d.). Photo Harrison)

1964 (24 Oct). Independence. T **11/12** and similar vert design. P 13½×11½ (6d.) or 14½×13½ (others).

No.		Description	Unused	Used
91		3d. sepia, yellow-green and blue	10	10
92		6d. deep violet and yellow	15	20
93		1s.3d. red, black, sepia and orange	20	25
91/3		*Set of 3*	40	50

Design:—1s.3d. Barotse dancer.

14 Maize-Farmer and Silo

15 Health—Radiographer

21 Fishing at Mpulungu

22 Tobacco Worker

(Des Gabriel Ellison. Photo Harrison)

1964 (24 Oct). T **14/15**, **21/2** and similar designs. P 14½ (½d. to 4d.), 14½×13½ (1s.3d., 2s. and £1) or 13½×14½ (others).

No.		Description	Unused	Used
94		½d. red, black and yellow-green	10	1·50
95		1d. brown, black and bright blue	10	10
96		2d. red, deep brown and orange	10	10
97		3d. black and red	10	10
98		4d. black, brown and orange	15	10

99	6d. orange, deep brown & deep bluish green	30	10
100	9d. carmine, black and bright blue	15	10
101	1s. black, yellow-bistre and blue	15	10
102	1s.3d. light red, yellow, black and blue	20	10
103	2s. bright blue, black, deep brown & orange	25	30
104	2s.6d. black and orange-yellow	1·00	35
105	5s. black, yellow and green	1·00	1·00
106	10s. black and orange	4·50	3·75
107	£1 black, brown, yellow and red	2·00	5·50
94/107	*Set of 14*	9·00	11·50

Designs: *Vert* (*as T* **15**)—2d. Chinyau dancer; 3d. Cotton-picking. (*As T* **22**)—2s. Tonga basket-making; £1 Makishi dancer. *Horiz* (*as T* **14**)—4d. Angoni bull. (As T **21**)—6d. Communications, old and new; 9d. Zambezi sawmills and Redwood flower; 2s.6d. Luangwa Game Reserve; 5s. Education—student; 10s. Copper mining.

Nos. 94/5 and 97 exist in coils, constructed from normal sheets.

28 I.T.U. Emblem and Symbols

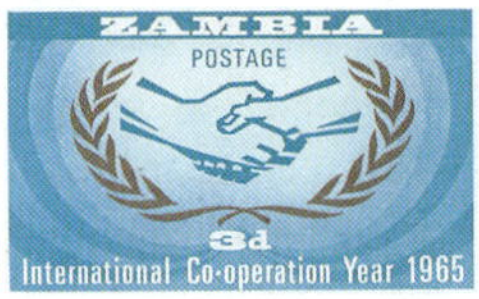

29 I.C.Y. Emblem

(Photo Harrison)

1965 (26 July). I.T.U. Centenary. P 14×14½.

108	**28**	6d. light reddish violet and gold	15	10
109		2s.6d. brownish grey and gold	85	1·50

(Photo Harrison)

1965 (26 July). International Co-operation Year. P 14½.

110	**29**	3d. turquoise and gold	15	10
111		1s.3d. ultramarine and gold	35	45

30 State House, Lusaka

34 W.H.O. Building and U.N. Flag

(Des Gabriel Ellison. Photo Harrison)

1965 (18 Oct). First Anniv of Independence. T **30** and similar multicoloured designs. No wmk. P 13½×14½ (3d.), 14×13½ (6d.) or 13½×14 (others).

112	3d. Type **30**	10	10
113	6d. Fireworks, Independence Stadium	10	10
	a. Bright purple (fireworks) omitted	£150	
114	1s.3d. Clematopsis (*vert*)	15	10
115	2s.6d. *Tithonia diversifolia* (*vert*)	30	1·25
112/15	*Set of 4*	50	1·25

(Des M. Goaman. Photo Harrison)

1966 (18 May). Inauguration of W.H.O. Headquarters, Geneva. P 14½.

116	**34**	3d. lake-brown, gold and new blue	40	10
		a. Gold omitted	£120	
117		1s.3d. gold, new blue & deep bluish vio.	1·10	95

35 Proposed University Building

36 National Assembly Building

(Des Gabriel Ellison. Photo Harrison)

1966 (12 July). Opening of Zambia University. P 14½.

118	**35**	3d. blue-green and copper-bronze	10	10
119		1s.3d. reddish violet and copper-bronze.	20	10

The building shown on Type **35** was never built.

(Des Gabriel Ellison. Photo Harrison)

1967 (2 May). Inauguration of National Assembly Building. P 14½.

120	**36**	3d. black and copper-bronze	10	10
121		6d. olive-green and copper-bronze	10	10

37 Airport Scene

(Des Gabriel Ellison. Photo Harrison)

1967 (2 Oct). Opening of Lusaka International Airport. P 13½×14½.

122	**37**	6d. violet-blue and copper-bronze	15	10
123		2s.6d. brown and copper-bronze	60	1·00

38 Youth Service Badge

39 "Co-operative Farming"

(Des Gabriel Ellison. Photo Harrison)

1967 (23 Oct). National Development. T **38/9** and similar designs. P 13½×14½ (6d., 1s.6d.) or 14½×13½ (others).

124	4d. black, red and gold	10	10
125	6d. black, gold and violet-blue	10	10
126	9d. black, grey-blue and silver	15	50
127	1s. multicoloured	50	10
128	1s.6d. multicoloured	70	2·25
124/8	*Set of 5*	1·40	2·75

Designs: *Vert*—9d. "Communications"; 1s. Coalfields. *Horiz*—1s.6d. Road link with Tanzania.

(New Currency. 100 ngwee = 1 kwacha)

43 Lusaka Cathedral

44 Baobab Tree

52 Chokwe Dancer

53 Kafue Railway Bridge

(Des Gabriel Ellison. Photo Harrison)

1968 (16 Jan). Decimal Currency. T **43/4**, **52/3** and similar designs. P 13½×14½ (1, 3, 15, 50n.) or 14½×13½ (others).

129	1n. multicoloured	10	10
	a. Copper-bronze (including value) omitted	£160	
	b. Ultramarine (windows) omitted	£180	
130	2n. multicoloured	10	10
131	3n. multicoloured	10	10
132	5n. bistre-brown and copper-bronze	10	10
133	8n. multicoloured	15	10
	a. Copper-bronze (background) omitted		
	b. Blue (of costumes) omitted	£140	

134	10n. multicoloured	35	10
135	15n. multicoloured	2·75	10
136	20n. multicoloured	4·75	10
137	25n. multicoloured	25	10
138	50n. chocolate, red-orange & copper-bronze	30	15
139	1k. royal blue and copper-bronze	6·00	20
140	2k. black and copper-bronze	1·75	1·25
129/40	*Set of* 12	15·00	1·75

Designs: *Horiz* (*as T* **43**)—3n. Zambia Airways BAC One-Eleven. (*As T* **53**)—15n. *Imbrasia zambesina* (moth); 2k. Eland. *Vert* (*as T* **44**)—5n. National Museum, Livingstone; 8n. Vimbuza dancer; 10n. Tobacco picking. (*As T* **52**)—20n. South African Crowned Cranes; 25n. Angoni warrior.

All values exist with PVA gum as well as gum arabic.

Nos. 129/30 and 132 exist in coils, constructed from normal sheets.

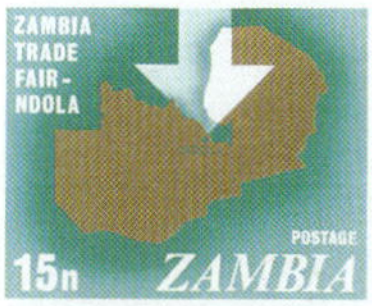

55 Ndola on Outline of Zambia

56 Human Rights Emblem and Heads

(Des Gabriel Ellison. Photo Harrison)

1968 (29 June). Trade Fair, Ndola. P 14.

141	**55**	15n. green and gold	10	10

(Des Gabriel Ellison. Photo and die-stamped (gold emblem) Harrison)

1968 (23 Oct). Human Rights Year. P 14.

142	**56**	3n. deep blue, pale violet and gold	10	10

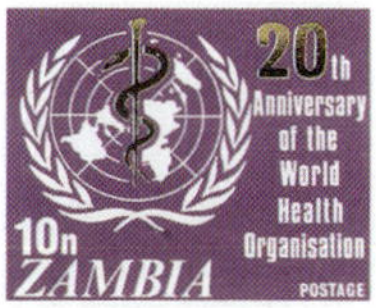

57 W.H.O. Emblem

58 Group of Children

(Des Gabriel Ellison. Photo and die-stamped (gold staff and "20") Harrison)

1968 (23 Oct). 20th Anniv of World Health Organization. P 14.

143	**57**	10n. gold and bluish violet	10	10

(Des Gabriel Ellison. Photo and die-stamped (gold children) Harrison)

1968 (23 Oct). 22nd Anniv of UNICEF. P 14.

144	**58**	25n. black, gold and ultramarine	15	70

59 Copper Miner

61 Zambia outlined on Map of Africa

(Des Gabriel Ellison. Photo Harrison)

1969 (18 June). 50th Anniv of International Labour Organization. T **59** and similar design. P 14½×13½ (3n.) or 13½×14½ (25n.).

145	3n. copper-bronze and deep violet	25	10
146	25n. pale yell copper-bronze & blackish brn	1·00	1·00

Design: *Horiz*—25n. Poling a furnace.

A used example of No. 145 exists with the copper-bronze omitted.

(Des Gabriel Ellison. Photo Harrison)

1969 (23 Oct). International African Tourist Year. T **61** and similar multicoloured designs. P 14×14½ (5n., 25n.) or 14½×14 (others).

147	5n. Type **61**	10	10
148	10n. Waterbuck (*horiz*)	15	10
149	15n. Kasaba Bay Golden Perch (*horiz*)	35	40
150	25n. Carmine Bee Eater	1·00	1·75
147/50	*Set of* 4	1·40	2·00

65 Satellite "Nimbus 3" orbiting the Earth

66 Woman collecting Water from Well

(Des Gabriel Ellison. Litho Enschedé)

1970 (23 Mar). World Meteorological Day. P 13×10½.

151	**65**	15n. multicoloured	20	50

(Des V. Whiteley (from local designs). Litho B.W.)

1970 (4 July). Preventive Medicine. T **66** and similar vert designs. P 13½×12.

152	3n. multicoloured	15	10
153	15n. multicoloured	30	30
154	25n. greenish blue, rosine and sepia	65	70
152/4	*Set of* 3	1·00	1·00

Designs:—15n. Child on scales; 25n. Child being immunized.

67 "Masks" (mural by Gabriel Ellison)

(Des Gabriel Ellison. Litho Harrison)

1970 (8 Sept). Conference of Non-Aligned Nations. P 14×14½.

155	**67**	15n. multicoloured	30	30

68 Ceremonial Axe

(Des Gabriel Ellison. Litho D.L.R.)

1970 (30 Nov). Traditional Crafts. T **68** and similar multicoloured designs. P 13½ (15n.), 12½ (25n.) or 14 (others).

156	3n. Type **68**	10	10
157	5n. Clay Smoking-Pipe Bowl	10	10
158	15n. Makishi Mask (30×47 *mm*)	25	30
159	25n. Kuomboka Ceremony (72×19 *mm*)	40	1·00
156/9	*Set of* 4	75	1·40
MS160	133×83 mm. Nos. 156/9. Imperf	6·00	13·00

69 Dag Hammarskjöld and U.N. General Assembly

(Des J.W. Litho Questa)

1971 (18 Sept). Tenth Death Anniv of Dag Hammarskjöld. T **69** and similar horiz designs, each with portrait of Hammarskjöld. Multicoloured. P 13½.

161	4n. Type **69**	10	10
162	10n. Tail of aircraft	15	10
163	15n. Dove of Peace	15	25
164	25n. Memorial tablet	30	1·75
161/4	*Set of* 4	55	2·00

70 Red-breasted Tilapia

71 North African Crested Porcupine

(Des G. Drummond. Litho J.W.)

1971 (10 Dec). Fish. T **70** and similar horiz designs. Multicoloured. P 13½.

165	4n. Type **70**	30	10
166	10n. Long-finned Tilapia ("Green-headed Bream")	50	40
167	15n. Tigerfish	60	2·50
165/7	*Set of* 3	1·25	2·75

(Des and litho J.W.)

1972 (15 Mar). Conservation Year (1st issue). T **71** and similar multicoloured designs. P 13½.

168	4n. Cheetah (58×21 *mm*)	15	25
169	10n. Lechwe (58×21 *mm*)	20	60
170	15n. Type **71**	25	85
171	25n. African Elephant	1·25	3·00
168/71	*Set of* 4	1·75	4·25

(Des and litho J.W.)

1972 (30 June). Conservation Year (2nd issue). Designs similar to T **71**. Multicoloured. P 13½.

172	4n. Soil conservation	15	20
173	10n. Forestry	15	30
174	15n. Water (58×21 *mm*)	20	80
175	25n. Maize (58×21 *mm*)	45	1·60
172/5	*Set of* 4	85	2·50

72 Giraffe and Common Zebra

(Des and litho J.W.)

1972 (30 June). National Parks. Sheet 114×140 mm containing T **72** and similar vert designs. Multicoloured. P 13½.

MS176 10n. (×4) Type **72**; Black Rhinoceros; Hippopotamus and Common Panther; Lion ... 6·50 12·00

Each design includes part of a map showing Zambian National Parks, the four forming a composite design.

73 Zambian Flowers

(Des and litho J.W.)

1972 (22 Sept). Conservation Year (3rd issue). T **73** and similar horiz designs. Multicoloured. P 13½.

177	4n. Type **73**	30	30
178	10n. *Papilio demodocus* (butterfly)	80	80
179	15n. *Apis mellifera* (bees)	85	1·40
180	25n. *Nomadacris septemfasciata* (locusts)	1·25	2·25
177/80	*Set of* 4	2·75	4·25

74 Mary and Joseph

(Des V. Whiteley. Litho Questa)

1972 (1 Dec). Christmas. T **74** and similar horiz designs. Multicoloured. P 14.

181	4n. Type **74**	10	10
182	9n. Mary, Joseph and Jesus	10	10
183	15n. Mary, Jesus and the shepherds	10	10
184	25n. The Three Wise Men	20	40
181/4	*Set of* 4	35	50

75 Oudenodon and Rubidgea

(Des Gabriel Ellison; adapted J.W. Litho Questa)

1973 (1 Feb). Zambian Prehistoric Animals. T **75** and similar horiz designs. Multicoloured. P 14×13½ (4n.) or 13½×14 (others).

185	4n. Type **75**	85	85
186	9n. Broken Hill Man	90	90
187	10n. Zambiasaurus	1·00	1·50
188	15n. *Luangwa drysdalli*	1·10	2·00
189	25n. Glossopteris	1·25	3·00
185/9	*Set of* 5	4·50	7·50

Nos. 186/9 are smaller, 38×21 mm.

76 "Dr. Livingstone, I Presume"

(Des J.W. Litho Format)

1973 (1 May). Death Centenary of Dr. Livingstone. T **76** and similar horiz designs. Multicoloured. P 13½.

190	3n. Type **76**	15	15
191	4n. Scripture Lesson	15	15
192	9n. Victoria Falls	30	40
193	10n. Scattering slavers	20	45
194	15n. Healing the sick	30	1·60
195	25n. Burial place of Livingstone's heart	30	2·75
190/5	*Set of* 6	1·25	5·00

77 Parliamentary Mace

(Des Gabriel Ellison. Litho Questa)

1973 (24 Sept). Third Commonwealth Conference of Speakers and Presiding Officers, Lusaka. P 13½.

196	**77**	9n. multicoloured	35	55
197		15n. multicoloured	40	1·10
198		25n. multicoloured	50	1·50
196/8 *Set of* 3			1·10	2·75

78 Inoculation

79 U.N.I.P. Flag

(Des Gabriel Ellison. Litho Questa)

1973 (16 Oct). 25th Anniv of W.H.O. T **78** and similar multicoloured designs. P 14.

199	4n. Mother washing baby (*vert*)	42·00	23·00
200	9n. Nurse weighing baby (*vert*)	45	2·25
201	10n. Type **78**	50	3·00
202	15n. Child eating meal	90	5·00
199/202 *Set of* 4		42·00	30·00

Only a small quantity of No. 199 was produced, and most examples were issued to post offices for local use.

(Des Gabriel Ellison. Litho Questa)

1973 (13 Dec). 1st Anniv of Second Republic. T **79** and similar vert designs. Multicoloured. P 14×13½.

203	4n. Type **79**	7·00	7·00
204	9n. Freedom House	30	1·50
205	10n. Army band	30	2·00
206	15n. "Celebrations" (dancers)	50	3·25
207	25n. Presidential chair	75	5·00
203/7 *Set of* 5		8·00	17·00

80 President Kaunda at Mulungushi

(Des Gabriel Ellison. Litho Harrison)

1974 (28 Apr). President Kaunda's 50th Birthday. T **80** and similar horiz designs. Multicoloured. P 14½×14 (4n.) or 14×14½ (others).

208	4n. Type **80**	40	40
209	9n. President's former residence	20	20
210	15n. President holding Independence flame	50	1·25
208/10 *Set of* 3		1·00	1·75

81 Nakambala Sugar Estate

(Des G. Vasarhelyi. Litho Questa)

1974 (23 Oct). Tenth Anniv of Independence. T **81** and similar horiz designs. Multicoloured. P 13½.

211	3n. Type **81**	15	10
212	4n. Local market	15	10
213	9n. Kapiri glass factory	20	10
214	10n. Kafue hydro-electric scheme	25	10
215	15n. Kafue Railway Bridge	50	95
216	25n. Non-aligned Conference, Lusaka, 1970	60	1·25
211/16 *Set of* 6		1·60	2·25
MS217 141×105 mm. 15n. (×4) Academic Education; Teacher Training College; Technical Education; Zambia University		5·00	8·50

82 Mobile Post-van

(Des Gabriel Ellison. Litho Format)

1974 (15 Nov). Centenary of Universal Postal Union. T **82** and similar horiz designs. Multicoloured. P 13½.

218	4n. Type **82**	20	15
219	9n. Hawker Siddeley H.S.748 airplane on tarmac	30	30
220	10n. Chipata Post Office	30	40
221	15n. Modern training centre	45	1·75
218/21 *Set of* 4		1·10	2·40

83 Dish Aerial

(Des Gabriel Ellison. Litho Questa)

1974 (16 Dec). Opening of Mwembeshi Earth Station (21 October). T **83** and similar horiz designs. Multicoloured. P 13½.

222	4n. Type **83**	25	20
223	9n. View at dawn	35	30
224	15n. View at dusk	40	70
225	25n. Aerial view	50	1·50
222/5 *Set of* 4		1·40	2·40

84 Black Rhinoceros and Calf

85 Independence Monument

(Des Gabriel Ellison. Litho J.W.)

1975 (3 Jan). T **84/5** and similar horiz designs. Multicoloured.

(a) Size as T **84**. *P 13½×14.*

226	1n. Type **84**	75	1·00
227	2n. Helmet Guineafowl	75	1·00
228	3n. National Dancing Troupe	15	1·00
229	4n. African Fish Eagle	1·00	10
230	5n. Knife-edge Bridge	1·00	1·00
231	8n. Sitatunga (antelope)	1·00	75
232	9n. African Elephant, Kasaba Bay	1·25	70
233	10n. Temminck's Ground Pangolin	20	10

(b) Size as T **85**. *P 13.*

234	15n. Type **85**	30	10
	a. Magenta omitted	£1500	
235	20n. Harvesting groundnuts	85	1·25
236	25n. Tobacco-growing	1·25	1·50
237	50n. Flying-Doctor service	3·25	2·50
238	1k. Lady Ross's Turaco	4·50	1·75
239	2k. Village scene	3·00	6·00
226/39 *Set of* 14		17·00	17·00

No. 234a shows much of the design in yellow-green due to the omission of the magenta which was used as an overlay on other colours.

Nos. 226/7 exist in coils, constructed from normal sheets.

86 Map of Namibia

87 Erection of Sprinkler Irrigation

(Des PAD Studio. Litho Questa)

1975 (26 Aug). Namibia Day. P 13½.

240	**86**	4n. green and light yellow-green	15	20
241		9n. steel-blue and light turquoise-green	20	30
242		15n. orange-yellow and greenish yellow	30	75
243		25n. orange and light orange	45	1·50
240/3 *Set of 4*			1·00	2·50

(Des and litho J. W.)

1975 (16 Dec). Silver Jubilee of the International Commission on Irrigation and Drainage. T **87** and similar horiz designs. Multicoloured. P 13.

244	4n. Type **87**	15	20
245	9n. Sprinkler irrigation (*different*)	30	50
246	15n. Furrow irrigation	65	1·50
244/6 *Set of 3*		1·00	2·00

88 Mutondo

(Des A. Chimfwembe. Litho J.W.)

1976 (22 Mar). World Forestry Day. T **88** and similar horiz designs showing trees. Multicoloured. P 13.

247	3n. Type **88**	15	10
248	4n. Mukunyu	15	10
249	9n. Mukusi	25	25
250	10n. Mopane	25	25
251	15n. Musuku	45	1·40
252	25n. Mukwa	55	2·00
247/52 *Set of 6*		1·60	3·75

89 Passenger Train

(Des A. Chimfwembe. Litho J.W.)

1976 (10 Dec). Opening of Tanzania-Zambia Railway. T **89** and similar horiz designs. Multicoloured. P 13½ (**MS**257) or 13 (others).

253	4n. Type **89**	30	30
254	9n. Copper exports	45	55
255	15n. Machinery imports	70	95
256	25n. Goods train	1·10	1·75
253/6 *Set of 4*		2·25	3·25
MS257 140×106 mm. 10n. Clearing bush; 15n. Laying track; 20n. Railway workers; 25n. Completed track		3·00	4·00

90 Kayowe Dance

(Des BG Studio. Litho Questa)

1977 (18 Jan). Second World Black and African Festival of Arts and Culture, Nigeria. T **90** and similar horiz designs. Multicoloured. P 13½.

258	4n. Type **90**	15	10
259	9n. Lilombola dance	15	15
260	15n. Initiation ceremony	30	40
261	25n. Munkhwele dance	55	1·00
258/61 *Set of 4*		1·00	1·50

91 Grimwood's Longclaw

(Des Gabriel Ellison. Litho Questa)

1977 (1 July). Birds of Zambia. T **91** and similar vert designs. Multicoloured. P 14½.

262	4n. Type **91**	40	10
263	9n. Shelley's Sunbird	55	50
264	10n. Black-cheeked Lovebird	55	50
265	15n. Locust Finch	1·00	1·75
266	20n. Black-chinned Tinkerbird	1·10	2·25
267	25n. Chaplin's Barbet	1·10	2·75
262/7 *Set of 6*		4·25	7·00

92 Girls with Building Blocks

(Des Gabriel Ellison. Litho Questa)

1977 (20 Oct). Decade for Action to Combat Racism and Racial Discrimination. T **92** and similar horiz designs. Multicoloured. P 14×14½.

268	4n. Type **92**	15	10
269	9n. Women dancing	20	20
270	15n. Girls with dove	30	1·00
268/70 *Set of 3*		60	1·10

93 Angels and Shepherds

(Des Gabriel Ellison. Litho J.W.)

1977 (20 Dec). Christmas. T **93** and similar horiz designs. Multicoloured. P 14.

271	4n. Type **93**	10	10
272	9n. The Holy Family	10	10
273	10n. The Magi	10	15
274	15n. Jesus presented to Simeon	20	1·00
271/4 *Set of 4*		45	1·25

94 African Elephant and Road Check

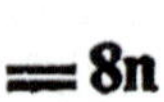

(**95**)

(Des Gabriel Ellison. Litho Questa)

1978 (1 Aug). Anti-Poaching Campaign. T **94** and similar horiz designs. Multicoloured. P 14×14½.

275	8n. Type **94**	45	20
276	18n. Lechwe and canoe patrol	30	65
277	28n. Warthog and Bell 206 JetRanger helicopter	75	1·10
278	32n. Cheetah and game guard patrol	75	1·50
275/8 *Set of 4*		2·00	3·00

1979 (15 Mar). Nos. 228, 232, 234 and 236 surch as T **95**.

279	8n. on 9n. African Elephant, Kasaba Bay	70	10
	a. Surch inverted	50·00	
280	10n. on 3n. National Dancing Troupe	10	10
	a. Surch inverted	50·00	
	b. Surch omitted (in pair with normal)		
281	18n. on 25n. Tobacco-growing	15	15
	a. Surch inverted		
282	28n. on 15n. Type **85**	20	25
	a. Surch inverted	8·00	
	b. Albino surch		
279/82 *Set of 4*		1·00	55

No. 280b was caused by a corner paper fold.

96 Kayowe Dance

97 "Kalulu and the Tug of War"

(Des Gabriel Ellison. Litho Questa)

1979 (1 Aug). Commonwealth Summit Conference, Lusaka. T **96** and similar horiz designs. Multicoloured. P 14.

283	18n. Type **96**	15	25
284	32n. Kutambala dance	20	40
285	42n. Chitwansombo drummers	20	60
286	58n. Lilombola dance	25	80
283/6 *Set of 4*		70	1·90

(Des Gabriel Ellison. Litho Questa)

1979 (21 Sept). International Year of the Child. Illustrations from Childrens Books. T **97** and similar vert designs. Multicoloured. P 14.

287	18n. Type **97**	25	30
288	32n. "Why the Zebra has no Horns"	30	55
289	42n. "How the Tortoise got his Shell"	35	85
290	58n. "Kalulu and the Lion"	45	1·00
287/90 *Set of 4*		1·00	2·40
MS291 90×120 mm. Nos. 287/90		1·25	2·25

98 Children of Different Races holding Anti-Apartheid Emblem

99 Sir Rowland Hill and 2s. Definitive Stamp of 1964

(Des Gabriel Ellison. Litho Questa)

1979 (13 Nov). International Anti-Apartheid Year. T **98** and similar horse designs showing children of different races together. Multicoloured. P 14½.

292	18n. Type **98**	15	25
293	32n. Children with toy car	25	40
294	42n. Young children with butterfly	35	70
295	58n. Children with microscope	50	1·00
292/5 *Set of 4*		1·10	2·10

(Des Gabriel Ellison. Litho Format)

1979 (20 Dec). Death Centenary of Sir Rowland Hill. T **99** and similar horiz designs. Multicoloured. P 14½.

296	18n. Type **99**	15	25
297	32n. Sir Rowland Hill and mailman	20	55
298	42n. Sir Rowland Hill and Northern Rhodesia 1963 ½d. definitive stamp	20	70
299	58n. Sir Rowland Hill and mail-carrying oxwaggon	20	1·10
296/9 *Set of 4*		65	2·40
MS300 112×89 mm. Nos. 296/9		1·00	2·50

LONDON 1980

(**100**)

101 Rotary Anniversary Emblem

1980 (16 May). "London 1980" International Stamp Exhibition. Nos. 296/300 optd with T **100**.

301	18n. Type **99**	25	40
302	32n. Sir Rowland Hill and mailman	30	60
303	42n. Sir Rowland Hill and Northern Rhodesia 1963 ½d. definitive stamp	40	75
304	58n. Sir Rowland Hill and mail-carrying oxwaggon	60	90
301/4 *Set of 4*		1·40	2·40
MS305 112×89 mm. Nos. 301/4		2·50	3·75

(Des J.W. Litho Questa)

1980 (18 June). 75th Anniv of Rotary International. P 14.

306	**101** 8n. multicoloured	10	10
307	32n. multicoloured	30	40
308	42n. multicoloured	35	50
309	58n. multicoloured	45	80
306/9 *Set of 4*		1·00	1·60
MS310 115×89 mm. Nos. 306/9		1·50	2·25

102 Running

(Des Gabriel Ellison. Litho J.W.)

1980 (19 July). Olympic Games, Moscow. T **102** and similar horiz designs. Multicoloured. P 13.

311	18n. Type **102**	20	25
312	32n. Boxing	30	45
313	42n. Football	40	80
314	58n. Swimming	50	1·25
311/14 *Set of 4*		1·25	2·50
MS315 142×144 mm. Nos. 311/14. P 14		2·50	3·25

103 *Euphaedra zaddachi*

104 Zambia Coat of Arms

(Des Gabriel Ellison. Litho Questa)

1980 (27 Aug). Butterflies. T **103** and similar horiz designs. Multicoloured. P 14.

316	18n. Type **103**	15	15
317	32n. *Aphnaeus questiauxi*	25	40
318	42n. *Abantis zambesiaca*	40	90
319	58n. *Spindasis modesta*	60	1·75
316/19 *Set of 4*		1·25	2·75
MS320 114×86 mm. Nos. 316/19		4·25	3·25

(Des Gabriel Ellison. Litho Format)

1980 (Sept). 26th Commonwealth Parliamentary Association Conference, Lusaka. P 14.

321	**104** 18n. multicoloured	15	25
322	32n. multicoloured	25	45
323	42n. multicoloured	30	75
324	58n. multicoloured	40	1·50
321/4 *Set of 4*		1·00	2·75

105 Nativity and St. Francis of Assisi (stained glass window, Ndola Church)

(Des Gabriel Ellison. Litho Questa)

1980 (3 Nov). 50th Anniv of Catholic Church on the Copperbelt. P 13½.

No.	Type	Description	Unused	Used
325	**105**	8n. multicoloured	10	10
326		28n. multicoloured	30	70
327		32n. multicoloured	30	70
328		42n. multicoloured	45	1·50
325/8		*Set of* 4	1·00	2·75

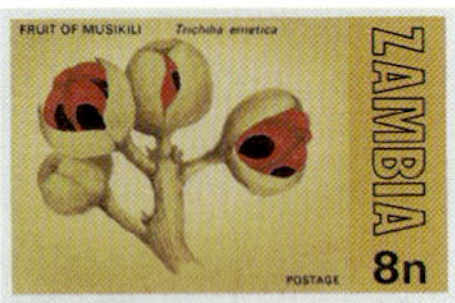

106 Musikili

(Des Gabriel Ellison. Litho Questa)

1981 (21 Mar). World Forestry Day. Seedpods. T **106** and similar horiz designs. Multicoloured. P 14.

No.	Description	Unused	Used
329	8n. Type **106**	10	10
330	18n. Mupapa	20	45
331	28n. Mulunguti	25	90
332	32n. Mulama	25	1·40
329/32	*Set of* 4	70	2·50

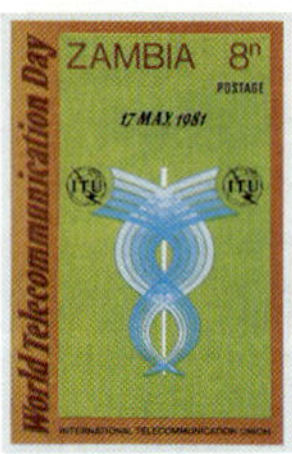

107 I.T.U. Emblem

108 Mask Maker

(Des J.W. Litho Format)

1981 (15 May). World Telecommunications and Health Day. T **107** and similar vert design. Multicoloured. P 14½.

No.	Description	Unused	Used
333	8n. Type **107**	20	10
334	18n. W.H.O. emblems	25	35
335	28n. Type **107**	30	70
336	32n. As 18n.	35	85
333/6	*Set of* 4	1·00	1·75

Nos. 333/6 exist imperforate from stock dispersed by the liquidator of Format International Security Printers Ltd.

(Des Gabriel Ellison. Litho Harrison)

1981 (2 June)–**83**. Multicoloured designs as T **108**. P 14×13½ (50n., 75n., 1k., 2k.) or 14½ (others).

No.	Description	Unused	Used
337	1n. Type **108**	10	10
338	2n. Blacksmith	10	10
339	5n. Pottery making	10	10
340	8n. Straw-basket fishing	10	10
341	10n. Thatching	10	10
342	12n. Mushroom picking (17.2.83)	3·00	1·75
343	18n. Millet grinding on stone	30	10
344	28n. Royal Barge paddler (11.11.81)	75	10
345	30n. Makishi tightrope dancer (11.11.81)	50	10
346	35n. Tonga Ila granary and house (11.11.81)	55	10
347	42n. Cattle herding (11.11.81)	55	1·75
348	50n. Traditional healer (38×26 mm) (11.11.81)	75	10
349	75n. Women carrying water (38×26 mm) (17.2.83)	55	60
350	1k. Pounding maize (38×26 mm) (17.2.83)	55	60
351	2k. Pipe-smoking, Gwembe Valley Belle (38×26 mm)	55	60
337/51	*Set of* 15	7·75	5·25

Nos. 338/9 and 341 exist in coils, constructed from normal sheets.

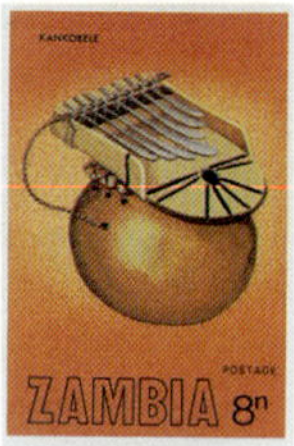

109 Kankobele

110 Banded Ironstone

(Des Gabriel Ellison. Litho Format)

1981 (30 Sept*). Traditional Musical Instruments. T **109** and similar vert designs. Multicoloured. P 15.

No.	Description	Unused	Used
356	8n. Type **109**	20	10
357	18n. Inshingili	25	55
358	28n. Ilimba	30	1·50
359	32n. Bango	35	1·75
356/9	*Set of* 4	1·00	3·50

*It has been reported that the Ndola Philatelic Bureau inadvertently sold some of these stamps some days earlier, and that cancelled-to-order examples exist postmarked 14 or 15 September.

Nos. 356 and 358/9 exist imperforate from stock dispersed by the liquidator of Format International Security Printers Ltd.

(Des Gabriel Ellison. Litho Questa)

1982 (5 Jan). Minerals (1st series). T **110** and similar vert designs. Multicoloured. P 14.

No.	Description	Unused	Used
360	8n. Type **110**	1·00	10
361	18n. Cobaltocalcite	2·00	80
362	28n. Amazonite	2·75	2·25
363	32n. Tourmaline	3·00	2·75
364	42n. Uranium ore	3·25	4·00
360/4	*Set of* 5	11·00	9·00

See also Nos. 370/4.

111 Zambian Scouts

(Des Gabriel Ellison. Litho Questa)

1982 (30 Mar). 75th Anniv of Boy Scout Movement. T **111** and similar horiz designs. Multicoloured. P 14.

No.	Description	Unused	Used
365	8n. Type **111**	20	10
366	18n. Lord Baden-Powell and Victoria Falls	60	40
367	28n. African Buffalo and Zambian Scout patrol pennant	60	50
368	1k. African Fish Eagle and Zambian Conservation badge	1·40	4·50
365/8	*Set of* 4	2·50	5·00
MS369	105×78 mm. Nos. 365/8	2·50	5·00

(Des Gabriel Ellison. Litho Questa)

1982 (1 July). Minerals (2nd series). Vert designs as T **110**. Multicoloured. P 14.

No.	Description	Unused	Used
370	8n. Bornite	95	10
371	18n. Chalcopyrite	2·25	90
372	28n. Malachite	2·75	3·00
373	32n. Azurite	2·75	3·00
374	42n. Vanadinite	3·25	4·25
370/4	*Set of* 5	11·00	10·00

112 Drilling Rig, 1926

(Des Gabriel Ellison. Litho Harrison)

1983 (26 Jan). Early Steam Engines. T **112** and similar horiz designs. Multicoloured. P 14×14½.

375	8n. Type **112**	45	20
376	18n. Fowler road locomotive, 1900	55	80
377	28n. Borsig ploughing engine, 1925	1·00	2·50
378	32n. Rhodesian Railways 7th Class steam locomotive, 1900	1·25	2·75
375/8	*Set of 4*	3·00	5·50

113 Cotton Picking

114 *Eulophia cucullata*

(Des Gabriel Ellison. Litho Harrison)

1983 (10 Mar). Commonwealth Day. T **113** and similar horiz designs. Multicoloured. P 14×13½.

379	12n. Type **113**	20	10
380	18n. Mining	40	30
381	28n. Ritual pot and traditional dances	30	50
382	1k. Violet-crested Turaco and Victoria Falls	2·75	5·50
379/82	*Set of 4*	3·25	5·75

(Des Gabriel Ellison. Litho Questa)

1983 (26 May). Wild Flowers. T **114** and similar vert designs. Multicoloured. P 14.

383	12n. Type **114**	20	10
384	28n. *Kigelia africana*	25	40
385	35n. *Protea gaguedi*	30	80
386	50n. *Leonotis nepetifolia*	50	2·25
383/6	*Set of 4*	1·10	3·25
MS387	141×71 mm. Nos. 383/6. P 12	1·00	3·50

115 Giraffe

(Des Gabriel Ellison. Litho Harrison)

1983 (21 July). Zambia Wildlife. T **115** and similar horiz designs. Multicoloured. P 14×13½.

388	12n. Type **115**	70	10
	a. Orange-brown and brown (inscr and face value) omitted	£500	
389	28n. Blue Wildebeest	75	70
390	35n. Lechwe	80	90
391	1k. Yellow-backed Duiker	1·25	4·25
388/91	*Set of 4*	3·25	5·25

116 Tigerfish

117 The Annunciation

(Des Gabriel Ellison. Litho J.W.)

1983 (29 Sept). Zambian Fish. T **116** and similar horiz designs. Multicoloured. P 14.

392	12n. Type **116**	35	15
393	28n. Silver Catfish	50	70
394	35n. Large-spotted Squeaker	60	1·75
395	38n. Red-breasted Tilapia	60	1·75
392/5	*Set of 4*	1·90	4·00

(Des Gabriel Ellison. Litho J.W.)

1983 (12 Dec). Christmas. T **117** and similar vert designs. Multicoloured. P 14.

396	12n. Type **117**	15	10
397	28n. The Shepherds	30	40
398	35n. Three Kings	40	1·25
399	38n. Flight into Egypt	45	1·75
396/9	*Set of 4*	1·10	3·25

118 Boeing 737

(Des Gabriel Ellison. Litho Harrison)

1984 (26 Jan). Air Transport. T **118** and similar horiz designs. Multicoloured. P 14×13½.

400	12n. Type **118**	25	10
401	28n. de Havilland D.H.C.2. Beaver	45	40
402	35n. Short S.45A Solent 3 flying boat	55	70
403	1k. de Havilland D.H.66 Hercules *City of Basra*	1·00	3·25
400/3	*Set of 4*	2·00	4·00

119 Receiving Flowers

(Des and litho J.W.)

1984 (28 Apr). 60th Birthday of President Kaunda. T **119** and similar multicoloured designs. P 14½×14 (12n., 60n.) or 14×14½ (others).

404	12n. Type **119**	20	10
405	28n. Swearing-in ceremony (*vert*)	25	40
406	60n. Planting cherry tree	50	2·25
407	1k. Opening of 5th National Assembly (*vert*)	65	3·25
404/7	*Set of 4*	1·40	5·50

120 Football

(Des Gabriel Ellison. Litho Format)

1984 (18 July). Olympic Games Los Angeles. T **120** and similar vert designs. Multicoloured. P 14½×14.

408	12n. Type **120**	25	10
409	28n. Running	30	50
410	35n. Hurdling	40	80
411	50n. Boxing	45	1·75
408/11	*Set of 4*	1·25	2·75

121 Gaboon Viper

(Des Gabriel Ellison. Litho Harrison)

1984 (5 Sept). Reptiles. T **121** and similar horiz designs. Multicoloured. P 14.

412	12n. Type **121**	20	10
413	28n. Chameleon	40	50
414	35n. Nile Crocodile	50	70

415	1k. Blue-headed Agama	1·00	2·75
412/15	*Set of 4*	1·90	3·50
MS416	120×101 mm. Nos. 412/15	2·00	4·00

122 Pres Kaunda and Mulungushi Rock

123 *Amanita flarnmeola*

(Des Gabriel Ellison. Litho Harrison)

1984 (22 Oct). 26th Anniv of United National Independence Party (12n.) and 20th Anniv of Independence (others) (1st issue). T **122** and similar horiz designs. Multicoloured. P 14.

417	12n. Type **122**	20	10
418	28n. Freedom Statue	30	50
419	1k. Pres Kaunda and agricultural produce ("Lima Programme")	75	3·00
417/19	*Set of 3*	1·10	3·25

See also Nos. 438/40.

(Des Gabriel Ellison. Litho J.W.)

1984 (12 Dec). Fungi. T **123** and similar vert designs. Multicoloured. P 14×14½.

420	12n. Type **123**	60	30
421	28n. *Amanita zambiana*	75	90
422	32n. *Termitomyces letestui*	75	1·50
423	75n. *Cantharellus miniatescens*	1·00	1·00
420/3	*Set of 4*	2·75	2·75

K5

(**124**)

1985 (5 Mar). No. 237 surch with T **124**.

424	5k. on 50n. Flying-doctor service	1·75	3·50

125 Chacma Baboon

(Des Gabriel Ellison. Litho Harrison)

1985 (25 Apr). Zambian Primates. T **125** and similar horiz designs. Multicoloured. P 14.

425	12n. Type **125**	45	10
426	20n. Diademed Monkey	60	40
427	45n. Diademed Monkey (*different*)	90	1·25
428	1k. Savanna Monkey	1·50	4·50
425/8	*Set of 4*	3·00	5·75

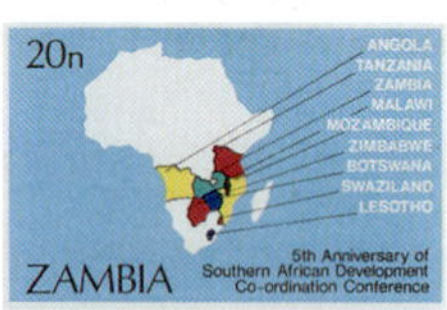

126 Map showing S.A.D.C.C. Member States

(Des Gabriel Ellison. Litho Harrison)

1985 (9 July). 5th Anniv of Southern African Development Co-ordination Conference. T **126** and similar horiz designs. P 14.

429	20n. multicoloured	75	15
430	45n. black, new blue and pale blue	1·75	1·10
431	1k. multicoloured	2·00	3·75
429/31	*Set of 3*	4·00	4·50

Designs:—45n. Mining; 1k. Flags of member states and Mulungushi Hall.

127 The Queen Mother in 1980

(Des and litho Harrison)

1985 (2 Aug). Life and Times of Queen Elizabeth the Queen Mother. T **127** and similar designs. P 14.

432	25n. multicoloured	10	10
433	45n. deep violet-blue and gold	10	15
434	55n. deep violet-blue and gold	15	25
435	5k. multicoloured	1·25	2·75
432/5	*Set of 4*	1·40	3·00

Designs: *Vert*—45n. The Queen Mother at Clarence House, 1963. *Horiz*—55n. With the Queen and Princess Margaret, 1980; 5k. At Prince Henry's christening, 1984.

20n

(**128**)

129 Postman and Lusaka Post Office, 1958

1985 (12 Sept–25 Nov). Nos. 340 and 342 surch as T **128** in chestnut (20n.) or greenish blue (25n.).

436	20n. on 12n. Mushroom picking	2·75	1·00
	a. Horiz pair, one without surch	£500	
437	25n. on 8n. Straw-basket fishing (25.11)	1·00	65

1985 (23 Oct). 26th Anniv of United National Independence Party (No. 438) and 20th Anniv of Independence (others) (2nd issue). Designs as Nos. 417/19 but larger, 55×34 mm, embossed on gold foil. P 10.

438	5k. Type **122**	1·25	2·25
439	5k. Freedom Statue	1·25	2·25
440	5k. Pres Kaunda and agricultural produce ("Lima Programme")	1·25	2·25
438/40	*Set of 3*	3·25	6·00

(Des Gabriel Ellison. Litho J.W.)

1985 (12 Dec). 10th Anniv of Posts and Telecommunication Corporation. T **129** and similar horiz designs. Multicoloured. P 13×12½.

441	20n. Type **129**	40	10
442	45n. Postman and Livingstone Post Office, 1950	65	25
443	55n. Postman and Kalomo Post Office, 1902	75	70
444	5k. Africa Trans-Continental Telegraph Line under construction, 1900	2·00	6·00
441/4	*Set of 4*	3·50	6·25

130 Boy in Maize Field

131 *Mylabris tricolor*

(Des Gabriel Ellison. Litho Harrison)

1985 (19 Dec). 40th Anniv of United Nations Organization. T **130** and similar vert designs. P 14.

445	20n. multicoloured	25	10
446	45n. black, new blue and brownish black	40	20
447	1k. multicoloured	75	2·00

448	2k. multicoloured	1·10	3·00
445/8	*Set of 4*	2·25	4·75

Designs:—45n. Logo and "40"; 1k. President Kaunda addressing U.N. General Assembly, 1970; 2k. Signing of U.N. Charter, San Francisco, 1945.

(Des Gabriel Ellison. Litho Harrison)

1986 (20 Mar). Beetles. T **131** and similar horiz designs. Multicoloured. P 14.

449	35n. Type **131**	15	10
450	1k. *Phasgonocnema melanianthe*	20	20
451	1k.70 *Amaurodes passerinii*	30	50
452	5k. *Ranzania petersiana*	85	2·00
449/52	*Set of 4*	1·40	2·50

131a Princess Elizabeth at Flower Ball, Savoy Hotel, 1951

(Des A. Theobald. Litho Format)

1986 (21 Apr). 60th Birthday of Queen Elizabeth II. Vert designs as T **131a**. Multicoloured. W w **16**. P 14×14½ (1k.95) or 14×13½ (others).

453	35n. Type **131a**	10	10
	a. Perf 14×14½	1·00	
454	1k.25 With Prince Andrew, Lusaka Airport, 1979	15	20
	a. Perf 14×14½	6·00	6·00
455	1k.70 With President Kaunda	15	25
	a. Perf 14×14½	10·00	
456	1k.95 In Luxembourg, 1976	15	30
457	5k. At Crown Agents Head Office, London, 1983	25	85
453/7	*Set of 5*	65	1·50

131b Prince Andrew and Miss Sarah Ferguson

(Des D. Miller. Litho Questa)

1986 (23 July). Royal Wedding. Square designs as T **131b**. Multicoloured. W w **16**. P 14.

458	1k.70	30	35
459	5k. Prince Andrew in Zambia, 1979	80	1·40

132 Goalkeeper saving Goal

133 Sculpture of Edmond Halley by Henry Pegram

(Des Gabriel Ellison. Litho Mardon Printers Ltd, Zimbabwe)

1986 (30 July). World Cup Football Championship, Mexico. T **132** and similar vert designs. Multicoloured. P 14½.

460	35n. Type **132**	85	15
461	1k.25 Player kicking ball	2·00	1·40
462	1k.70 Two players competing for ball	2·25	1·90
463	5k. Player scoring goal	3·25	6·00
460/3	*Set of 4*	7·50	8·50

(Des Jennifer Toombs. Litho Mardon Printers Ltd, Zimbabwe)

1986 (6 Aug). Appearance of Halley's Comet. T **133** and similar horiz designs. P 14½.

464	1k.25 multicoloured	1·00	55
465	1k.70 multicoloured	1·25	85
466	2k. multicoloured	1·75	1·75
467	5k. light blue and blue-black	3·50	6·50
464/7	*Set of 4*	6·75	8·75

Designs:—1k.70, Giotto spacecraft approaching nucleus of Comet; 2k. Studying Halley's Comet in 1682 and 1986; 5k. Part of Halley's chart of southern sky.

134 The Nativity

135 Diesel Train in Kasama Cutting

(Des and litho Harrison)

1986 (15 Dec). Christmas. Children's Paintings. T **134** and similar horiz designs. Multicoloured. P 14.

468	35n. Type **134**	50	10
469	1k.25 The Visit of the Three Kings	1·75	75
470	1k.60 The Holy Family with Shepherd and King	1·90	1·50
471	5k. Angel and Christmas Tree	4·00	7·50
468/71	*Set of 4*	7·25	9·00

(Des G. Vasarhelyi. Litho Questa)

1986 (22 Dec). 10th Anniv of Tanzania-Zambia Railway. T **135** and similar horiz designs. Multicoloured. P 14.

472	35n. Type **135**	25	10
473	1k.25 Passenger train leaving Tunnel No. 21	35	50
474	1k.70 Train between Tunnels Nos. 6 and 7	35	70
475	5k. Trains near Mpika Station	70	3·00
472/5	*Set of 4*	1·50	3·75

136 President Kaunda and Graduate

137 Arms of Kitwe

(Litho Harrison)

1987 (27 Jan). 20th Anniv of University of Zambia. T **136** and similar multicoloured designs. P 14.

476	35n. Type **136**	25	10
477	1k.25 University Badge (*vert*)	55	60
478	1k.60 University Statue	60	1·00
479	5k. President Kaunda laying foundation stone (*vert*)	2·00	6·50
476/9	*Set of 4*	3·00	7·50

(Litho Harrison)

1987 (26 Mar). Arms of Zambian Towns. T **137** and similar vert designs. Multicoloured. P 14.

480	35n. Type **137**	10	10
481	1k.25 Ndola	15	20
482	1k.70 Lusaka	20	25
483	20k. Livingstone	3·50	7·50
480/3	*Set of 4*	3·50	7·50

138 Chestnut-headed Crake

139 Look-out Tree, Livingstone

Two types of surcharge for 20n., 75n:

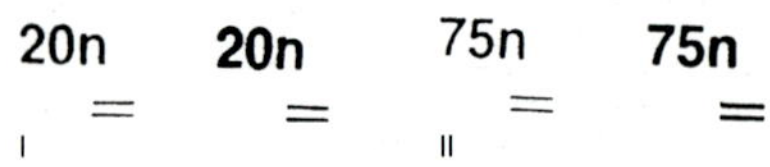

(I Surch by Format in Great Britain)

(II Surch in Zambia)

(Des Gabriel Ellison. Litho Questa)

1987 (16 Apr)–**88**. Birds (1st series). T **138** and similar vert designs, some additionally surch as T **128**. Multicoloured. P 11×13 (5n. to 40n., 75n., 1k.65) or 14 (others).

484 5n. Cloud-scraping Cisticola (8.10.87) 10 10
485 10n. White-winged Starling (8.10.87) 10 10
486 20n. on 1n. Yellow Swamp Warbler (I) (10.3.88) 30 50
a. Surch Type II 20 20
b. Surch omitted 35·00
487 25n. Type **138** 2·50 1·00
488 30n. Red-fronted Barbet ("Miombo Pied Barbet") (8.10.87) 20 10
489 35n. Black and Rufous Swallow 2·50 2·25
490 40n. Wattled Crane (8.10.87) 20 10
491 50n. Red-throated Heron ("Slaty Egret") (8.10.87) 20 10
492 75n. on 2n. Olive-flanked Robin Chat (I) (10.3.88) 30 1·40
a. Surch Type II 30 60
b. Surch omitted 35·00
493 1k. Bradfield's Hornbill 2·75 40
494 1k.25 Boulton's Puff-back Flycatcher ("Margaret's Batis") 2·50 3·00
495 1k.60 Anchieta's Sunbird 2·50 1·50
496 1k.65 on 30n. Red-fronted Barbet (10.3.88) 30 1·75
497 1k.70 Boehm's Bee Eater 2·50 3·00
498 1k.95 Perrin's Bush Shrike 2·50 2·25
499 2k. Whale-headed Stork ("Shoebill") (8.10.87) 35 35
500 5k. Taita Falcon 3·00 80
501 10k. on 50n. Red-throated Heron (10.3.88) 1·10 2·50
502 20k. on 2k. Whale-headed Stork (10.3.88) 1·25 3·75
484/502 *Set of 19* 22·00 21·00

Nos. 491, 493/5 and 497/502 are larger, size 24×39 mm.

It was not intended that the 1n. and 2n. should be issued without surcharge, but it is believed examples were placed on sale with the surcharged versions in error. C-t-o examples without surcharge cancelled 10 March 1988 also exist.

No. 502 is surcharged "K 20" only. For "K 20-00" surcharge see No. 594.

For further surcharges see Nos. 587/95, and for different designs see Nos. 625/38.

(Litho Questa)

1987 (30 June). Tourism. T **139** and similar horiz designs. Multicoloured. P 14.

503 35n. Type **139** 30 15
504 1k.25 Rafting on Zambezi 45 25
505 1k.70 Tourists photographing lions, Luangwa Valley 1·75 90
506 10k. Eastern White Pelicans 8·50 11·00
503/6 *Set of 4* 10·00 11·00

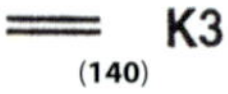

(**140**)

141 de Havilland D.H.C.2 Beaver

1987 (14 Sept). Various stamps surch as T **140**.

(a) On Nos. 432/5 in gold

507 **127** 3k. on 25n. multicoloured 1·00 1·00
508 – 6k. on 45n. deep violet-blue and gold 2·00 2·00
509 – 10k. on 55n. deep violet-blue and gold 2·50 2·75
510 – 20k. on 5k. multicoloured 5·00 7·50

(b) On Nos. 453/7

511 3k. on 35n. Princess Elizabeth at Flower Ball, Savoy Hotel, 1951 55 65
512 4k. on 1k.25 With Prince Andrew, Lusaka Airport, 1979 65 75
513 6k. on 1k.70 With President Kaunda 1·00 1·25
514 10k. on 1k.95 In Luxembourg, 1976 1·60 2·25
515 20k. on 5k. At Crown Agents Head Office, London, 1983 4·00 5·50

(c) On Nos. 460/3

516 3k. on 35n. Type **132** 1·00 1·00
517 6k. on 1k.25 Player kicking ball 2·00 2·00
518 10k. on 1k.70 Two players competing for ball 2·50 2·75
519 20k. on 5k. Player scoring goal 5·00 7·50

(d) On Nos. 464/7 in gold

520 **133** 3k. on 1k.25 multicoloured 2·00 1·25
a. Surch omitted (in horiz pair with normal) 80·00
521 – 6k. on 1k.70 multicoloured 2·75 2·25
522 – 10k. on 2k. multicoloured 4·00 5·00
523 – 20k. on 15k. light blue and blue-black 7·50 10·00
507/23 *Set of 17* 40·00 50·00

(Des and litho Questa)

1987 (21 Sept). 20th Anniv of Zambia Airways. T **141** and similar horiz designs showing aircraft. Multicoloured. P 14.

524 35c. Type **141** 85 10
525 1k.70 Douglas DC-10 2·00 70
526 5k. Douglas DC-3 4·25 3·75
527 10k. Boeing 707 6·50 8·00
524/7 *Set of 4* 12·00 11·00

142 Friesian/Holstein Cow

143 Mpoloto Ne Mikobango

(Des Gabriel Ellison. Litho Format)

1987 (1 Oct). 40th Anniv of Food and Agriculture Organization. T **142** and similar horiz designs. Multicoloured. P 14½×15.

528 35n. Type **142** 15 10
529 1k.25 Simmental bull 30 25
530 1k.70 Sussex bull 30 30
531 20k. Brahman bull 1·25 3·25
528/31 *Set of 4* 1·75 3·50

Nos. 528/31 exist imperforate from stock dispersed by the liquidator of Format International Security Printers Ltd.

(Litho Format)

1987 (3 Nov). People of Zambia. T **143** and similar vert designs. Multicoloured. P 12½.

532 35n. Type **143** 15 10
533 1k.25 Zintaka 25 25
534 1k.70 Mufuluhi 30 30
535 10k. Ntebwe 80 1·75
536 20k. Kubangwa Aa Mbulunga 1·25 3·50
532/6 *Set of 5* 2·50 5·50

Nos. 532/6 exist imperforate from stock dispersed by the liquidator of Format International Printers Ltd.

144 Black Lechwe at Waterhole

145 Cassava Roots

(Des Gabriel Ellison. Litho Questa)

1987 (21 Dec). Black Lechwe. T **144** and similar multicoloured designs. P 14.

537 50n. Type **144** 75 10
538 2k. Black Lechwe resting by pool (*horiz*) 2·00 40
539 2k.50 Running through water (*horiz*) 2·00 80
540 10k. Watching for danger 5·00 7·00
537/40 *Set of 4* 8·75 7·50

MS541 Two sheets, each 105×74 mm. (a) 20k. Caracal (predator). (b) 20k. Cheetah (predator) *Set of 2 sheets* 15·00 13·00

(Des Gabriel Ellison. Litho Questa)

1988 (20 May). International Fund for Agricultural Development. T **145** and similar horiz designs. Multicoloured. P 14.

542	50n. Type **145**	15	10
543	2k.50 Fishing	70	50
544	2k.85 Farmer and cattle	75	55
545	10k. Picking coffee beans	1·50	2·50
542/5	*Set of 4*	2·75	3·25

146 Breastfeeding

147 Asbestos Cement

(Des Gabriel Ellison. Litho Format)

1988 (12 Sept). UNICEF Child Survival Campaign. T **146** and similar vert designs. Multicoloured. P 12½.

546	50n. Type **146**	20	10
547	2k. Growth monitoring	60	30
548	2k.85 Immunization	70	70
549	10k. Oral rehydration	1·40	3·25
546/9	*Set of 4*	2·50	4·00

Nos. 546/9 exist imperforate from stock dispersed by the liquidator of Format International Security Printers Ltd.

(Des Gabriel Ellison. Litho Format)

1988 (10 Oct). Preferential Trade Area Fair. T **147** and similar vert designs. Multicoloured. P 12½.

550	50n. Type **147**	15	10
551	2k.35 Textiles	25	30
552	2k.50 Tea	25	40
553	10k. Poultry	90	3·00
550/3	*Set of 4*	1·40	3·50

Nos. 550/3 exist imperforate from stock dispersed by the liquidator of Format International Security Printers Ltd.

148 Emergency Food Distribution

149 Aardvark

(Des Gabriel Ellison. Litho Questa)

1988 (20 Oct). 125th Anniv of International Red Cross. T **148** and similar horiz designs. Multicoloured. P 14.

554	50n. Type **148**	25	10
555	2k.50 Giving first aid	60	60
556	2k.85 Practising bandaging	65	85
557	10k. Henri Dunant (founder)	1·75	4·00
554/7	*Set of 4*	3·00	5·00

(Des Gabriel Ellison. Litho Questa)

1988 (5 Dec). Endangered Species of Zambia. T **149** and similar horiz designs. Multicoloured. P 14.

558	50n. Type **149**	25	10
559	2k. Temminck's Ground Pangolin	50	40
560	2k.85 Hunting Dog	70	75
561	20k. Black Rhinoceros and calf	8·00	7·75
558/61	*Set of 4*	8·50	8·00

150 Boxing

151 Red Toad

(Des Gabriel Ellison. Litho Questa)

1988 (30 Dec). Olympic Games, Seoul. T **150** and similar horiz designs. Multicoloured. P 14.

562	50n. Type **150**	15	10
563	2k. Athletics	35	40
564	2k.50 Hurdling	40	70
565	20k. Football	3·25	6·50
562/5	*Set of 4*	3·75	7·00

MS566 Two sheets, each 97×72 mm. (a) 30k. Tennis. (b) 30k. Karate *Set of 2 sheets* 8·00 11·00
c. As **MS**566b but imperf

(Des Gabriel Ellison. Litho Format)

1989 (25 Jan). Frogs and Toads. T **151** and similar horiz designs. Multicoloured. P 12½.

567	50n. Type **151**	15	10
568	2k.50 Puddle Frog	50	50
569	2k.85 Marbled Reed Frog	55	75
570	10k. Young Reed Frogs	1·60	3·75
567/70	*Set of 4*	2·50	4·50

Nos. 567/70 exist imperforate from stock dispersed by the liquidator of Format International Security Printers Ltd.

152 Common Slit-faced Bat

153 Pope John Paul II and Map of Zambia

(Des Gabriel Ellison. Litho Format)

1989 (22 Mar). Bats. T **152** and similar horiz designs. Multicoloured. P 12½.

571	50n. Type **152**	20	10
572	2k.50 Little Free-tailed Bat	55	55
573	2k.85 Hildebrandt's Horseshoe Bat	65	75
574	10k. Peters' Epauletted Fruit Bat	1·75	4·00
571/4	*Set of 4*	2·75	4·75

Nos. 571/4 exist imperforate from stock dispersed by the liquidator of Format International Security Printers Ltd.

(Des and litho Harrison)

1989 (2 May). Visit of Pope John Paul II. T **153** and similar vert designs each with inset portrait. Multicoloured. P 12½.

575	50n. Type **153**	1·00	35
576	6k.85 Peace dove with olive branch	3·00	3·00
577	7k.85 Papal arms	3·50	3·50
578	10k. Victoria Falls	6·00	4·75
575/8	*Set of 4*	12·00	10·50

K19.50 = (**154**)

K20.00 = (**155**)

1989 (1 July–1 Nov). Various stamps surch.

(a) Nos. 339, 341/3, 345/6, 349 and 351 surch as T **154** (1k.20, 19k.50, 20k.50) or as T **155** (others)

579	1k.20 on 35n. Tonga Ila granary and house (Br.) (1 Nov)	20	15
580	3k.75 on 5n. Pottery making	30	20
581	8k.11 on 10n. Thatching	50	50
582	9k. on 30n. Makishi tightrope dancer	50	50
583	10k. on 75n. Women carrying water (38×26 mm)	50	50
584	18k.50 on 2k. Pipe-smoking Gwembe Valley belle (38×26 mm)	1·00	1·75
585	19k.50 on 12n. Mushroom picking (Br.) (1 Nov)	3·50	3·25
	a. Two stops between "K19" and "50" (R.8/1)	45·00	
586	20k.50 on 18n. Millet grinding on stone (V.) (1 Nov)	1·25	2·50

(b) Nos. 484, 489, 493/5 and 497/500 surch as T **155**

587	70n. on 35n. Black and Rufous Swallow	1·00	15
	a. Bars printed twice	†	—
588	3k. on 5n. Cloud-scraping Cisticola	1·00	30
589	8k. on 1k.25 Boulton's Puff-back Fly-catcher	1·25	60
590	9k.90 on 1k.70 Boehm's Bee Eater	1·75	80
591	10k.40 on 1k.60 Anchieta's Sunbird	1·75	90
	a. Error. Surch on 1k.95, Perrin's Bush Shrike (No. 498)	£150	
592	12k.50 on 1k. Bradfield's Hornbill	1·25	1·25
593	15k. on 1k.95 Perrin's Bush Shrike	1·25	2·00
594	20k. on 2k. Whale-headed Stork	1·75	2·75
595	20k.35 on 5k. Taita Falcon	2·25	2·75
579/95	*Set of 17*	19·00	19·00

No. 587a shows a second pair of bars applied by typography, the original surcharge in lithography being misplaced. One example of this error includes an extraneous "7".

No. 594 shows the surcharge as "K20-00". The previously listed 20k. on 2k., No. 502, is surcharged "K20" only.

156 *Parinari curatellifolia*

157 *Lamarckiana* sp

(Des Gabriel Ellison. Litho Questa)

1989 (26 July). Edible Fruits. T **156** and similar vert designs. Multicoloured. P 14½.

596	50n. Type **156**	15	10
597	6k.50 *Uapaca kirkiana*	1·25	1·50
598	6k.85 Wild Fig	1·25	2·00
599	10k. Bottle Palm	2·25	3·25
596/9	*Set of 4*	4·50	6·25

(Des Gabriel Ellison. Litho Cartor)

1989 (8 Nov). Grasshoppers. T **157** and similar horiz designs. Multicoloured. P 14×13½.

600	70n. Type **157**	20	10
601	10k.40 *Dictyophorus* sp	1·75	1·75
602	12k.50 *Cymatomera* sp	2·00	2·50
603	15k. *Phymateus iris*	2·50	4·50
600/3	*Set of 4*	5·75	8·00

158 Fireball

159 Postvan, Postman on Bicycle and Main Post Office, Lusaka

(Des Gabriel Ellison. Litho National Printing & Packaging, Zimbabwe)

1989 (6 Dec). Christmas. Flowers. T **158** and similar vert designs. Multicoloured. P 14½.

604	70n. Type **158**	15	10
605	10k.40 Flame Lily	1·25	1·25
606	12k.50 Foxglove Lily	1·75	1·75
607	20k. Vlei Lily	2·75	4·75
604/7	*Set of 4*	5·50	7·00

(Des D. Miller. Litho Questa)

1990 (2 May). "Stamp World London 90" International Stamp Exhibition. T **159** and similar horiz designs. Multicoloured. P 14.

608	1k.20 Type **159**	30	10
609	19k.50 Zambia 1980 18n. butterflies stamp	2·75	2·75
610	20k.50 Rhodesia and Nyasaland 1962 9d. and Northern Rhodesia 1925 ½d. stamps	2·75	2·75
611	50k. 1840 Penny Black and Maltese Cross cancellation)	5·00	7·00
608/11	*Set of 4*	9·75	11·50

160 Footballer and Ball

161 Road Tanker

(Des R. Vigurs. Litho Questa)

1990 (7 July). World Cup Football Championship, Italy. T **160** and similar vert designs showing football scenes. P 14.

612	1k.20 multicoloured	10	10
613	18k.50 multicoloured	2·00	2·50
614	19k.50 multicoloured	2·00	2·50
615	20k.50 multicoloured	2·00	2·50
612/15	*Set of 4*	5·50	6·50
MS616	100×73 mm. 50k. multicoloured	10·00	12·00

No. **MS**616 also exists imperforate from a limited printing.

(Litho Harrison)

1990 (23 July). 10th Anniv of Southern African Development Co-ordination Conference. T **161** and similar horiz designs, each showing map of Southern Africa. Multicoloured. P 12½.

617	1k.20 Type **161**	30	10
618	19k.50 Telecommunications	2·00	2·50
619	20k.50 "Regional Co-operation"	2·00	2·50
620	50k. Transporting coal by cable	8·00	9·50
617/20	*Set of 4*	11·00	13·50

162 Irrigation

163 The Bird and the Snake

(Des Gabriel Ellison. Litho Questa)

1990 (23 Oct). 26th Anniv of Independence. T **162** and similar horiz designs. Multicoloured. P 14.

621	1k.20 Type **162**	10	10
622	19k.50 Shoe factory	1·10	1·40
623	20k.50 Mwembeshi II satellite earth station	1·25	1·60
624	50k. "Mother and Child" (statue)	2·50	4·25
621/4	*Set of 4*	4·50	6·50

(Des Gabriel Ellison. Litho Questa)

1990 (30 Oct)–**91**. Birds (2nd series). Vert designs as T **138**. Multicoloured. P 11×13 (10, 15, 30, 50n., 1k., 1k.20, 2k., 3k., 5k.) or 14 (others).

625	10n. Livingstone's Flycatcher	1·25	1·00
626	15n. Bar-winged Weaver	1·25	1·00
627	30n. Purple-throated Cuckoo Shrike	1·25	1·00
628	50n. Retz's Red-billed Helmet Shrike	1·25	1·25
629	50n. As 10n. (7.5.91)	1·75	1·25
630	1k. As 15n. (7.5.91)	1·40	1·00
631	1k.20 Bronze-naped Pigeon	1·25	20
632	2k. As 30n. (7.5.91)	1·40	70
633	3k. As 50n. (No. 628) (7.5.91)	1·40	70
634	5k. As 1k.20 (7.5.91)	3·00	70
635	15k. Corncrake	1·25	40
636	20k. Dickinson's Kestrel (7.5.91)	2·25	1·50
637	20k.50 As 20k.	1·25	1·25
638	50k. Barrow's Bustard ("Denham's Bustard")	1·25	1·50
625/38	*Set of 14*	19·00	12·00

Nos. 635/8 are larger, size 23×39 mm.

(Des Gabriel Ellison. Litho Questa)

1991 (11 Jan). International Literacy Year. Folklore. T **163** and similar vert designs. Multicoloured. P 14.

639	1k.20 Type **163**	50	20
640	18k.50 Kalulu and the Leopard	2·75	3·25
641	19k.50 The Mouse and the Lion	2·75	3·25
642	20k.50 Kalulu and the Hippopotamus	3·25	3·25
639/42	*Set of 4*	8·25	9·00

164 Genet

K2

(165)

(Des Gabriel Ellison. Litho Questa)

1991 (25 Jan). Small Carnivores. T **164** and similar horiz designs. Multicoloured. P 14.

643	1k.20 Type **164**	50	15
644	18k.50 Civet	3·25	3·75
645	19k.50 Serval	3·25	3·75
646	20k.50 African Wild Cat	3·25	3·75
643/6	*Set of* 4	9·25	10·00

1991 (4 Mar). Nos. 441/4 surch with T **165**.

647	2k. on 20n. Type **129**	12·00	5·50
648	2k. on 45n. Postman and Livingstone Post Office, 1950	12·00	5·50
649	2k. on 55n. Postman and Kalomo Post Office, 1902	12·00	5·50
650	2k. on 5k. African Trans-Continental Telegraph Line under construction, 1900	12·00	5·50
647/50	*Set of* 4	45·00	20·00

166 Woman Cooking

(Des A. Mwansa and Daniela Schepp. Litho Cartor)

1991 (28 June). Soya Promotion Campaign. T **166** and similar vert designs. Multicoloured. P 13½.

651	1k. Type **166**	10	10
652	2k. Soya bean and field	10	10
653	5k. Mother feeding child	30	15
654	20k. Healthy and malnourished children	1·50	2·00
655	50k. President Kaunda holding child	2·50	3·50
651/5	*Set of* 5	4·00	5·25

1991 (5 July). Various stamps surch as T **165**.

656	**130**	2k. on 20n. multicoloured	32·00	5·00
657	**127**	2k. on 25n. multicoloured (Gold)	90·00	5·00
658	–	2k. on 28n. multicoloured (No. 344)	35·00	5·00
659	–	2k. on 28n. multicoloured (No. 393)	45·00	5·00
660	–	2k. on 28n. multicoloured (No. 401)	£250	5·00
661	–	2k. on 28n. multicoloured (No. 418)	—	5·00
662	–	2k. on 32n. multicoloured (No. 422)	27·00	5·00
663	–	2k. on 35n. multicoloured (No. 453)	—	5·00
664	**134**	2k. on 35n. multicoloured	75·00	5·00
665	**137**	2k. on 35n. multicoloured	42·00	5·00
666	–	2k. on 45n. multicoloured (No. 427)	42·00	5·00
667	–	2k. on 45n. black, new blue and pale blue (No. 430)	60·00	5·00
668	–	2k. on 45n. deep violet-blue and gold (No. 433)	90·00	5·00
669	–	2k. on 45n. black, new blue & brownish black (No. 446) (Gold+Blk.)	45·00	5·00
670	–	2k. on 1k.60 multicoloured (No. 470)	75·00	5·00
671	–	2k. on 1k.70 multicoloured (No. 451)	45·00	5·00
672	–	2k. on 1k.70 multicoloured (No. 482)	—	5·00
673	–	2k. on 5k. multicoloured (No. 435)	15·00	5·00
674	–	2k. on 5k. multicoloured (No. 452)	15·00	5·00
675	–	2k. on 6k.50 multicoloured (No. 597)	42·00	5·00
676	–	2k. on 6k.85 multicoloured (No. 576)	60·00	5·00
677	–	2k. on 6k.85 multicoloured (No. 598)	16·00	5·00
678	–	2k. on 7k.85 multicoloured (No. 577)	£100	5·00

The surcharge for No. 669 shows "K2" in gold and the bars in black over gold.

167 Chilubula Church near Kasama

(Des Gabriel Ellison. Litho Cartor)

1991 (18 July). 500th Birth Anniv of St. Ignatius Loyola. T **167** and similar vert designs. Multicoloured. P 13½.

679	1k. Type **167**	10	10
680	2k. Chikuni Church near Monze	15	15
681	20k. Bishop Joseph du Pont	2·75	2·75
682	50k. Saint Ignatius Loyola	4·50	6·50
679/82	*Set of* 4	6·75	8·50

168 *Adansonia digitata*

169 *Disa hamatopetala*

(Des Gabriel Ellison. Litho Cartor)

1991 (28 Nov). Flowering Trees. T **168** and similar horiz designs. Multicoloured. P 13½.

683	1k. Type **168**	20	10
684	2k. *Dichrostachys cinerea*	30	15
685	10k. *Stereospermum kunthianum*	1·75	1·40
686	30k. *Azana garckeana*	3·25	4·50
683/6	*Set of* 4	5·00	5·50

No. 685 is inscribed "Sterospermum" in error.

168a Queen's House

(Des D. Miller. Litho Cartor)

1992 (6 Feb). 40th Anniv of Queen Elizabeth II's Accession. Horiz designs as T **168a**. Multicoloured. W w **14** (sideways). P 13½.

687	4k. Type **168a**	10	10
688	32k. Traditional village	1·00	70
689	35k. Fishermen hauling nets	1·00	90
690	38k. Three portraits of Queen Elizabeth	1·25	1·25
691	50k. Queen Elizabeth II	1·60	2·75
687/91	*Set of* 5	4·50	5·00

(Des Gabriel Ellison. Litho Cartor)

1992 (28 Feb). Orchids. T **169** and similar vert designs. Multicoloured. P 13½.

692	1k. Type **169**	50	15
693	2k. *Eulophia paivaeana*	50	20
694	5k. *Eulophia quartiniana*	85	40
695	20k. *Aerangis verdickii*	3·50	5·00
692/5	*Set of* 4	4·75	5·25

170 Kasinja Mask

171 Bushbuck

(Des Gabriel Ellison. Litho Cartor)

1992 (10 Mar). Tribal Masks. T **170** and similar vert designs. Multicoloured. P 13½.

696	1k. Type **170**	25	30
697	2k. Chizaluke	30	30
698	10k. Mwanapweu	1·25	70
699	30k. Maliya	3·00	4·75
696/9	*Set of* 4	4·25	5·50

(Des Gabriel Ellison. Litho Questa)

1992 (14 Sept). Antelopes. T **171** and similar horiz designs. Multicoloured. P 14.

700	4k. Type **171**	25	60

701	40k. Eland	1·25	60
702	45k. Roan Antelope	1·25	60
703	100k. Sable Antelope	2·25	5·50
700/3	*Set of* 4	4·50	6·50

172 de Havilland D.H.66 Hercules *City of Basra*

(Des Gabriel Ellison. Litho Questa)

1992 (24 Nov). 60th Anniv of Airmail Service. T **172** and similar horiz designs. Multicoloured. P 14.

704	4k. Type **172**	50	50
705	40k. Vickers Super VC-10	2·25	1·00
706	45k. Short S.45A Solent 3 flying boat *Severn*	2·25	1·00
707	100k. Douglas DC-10	3·75	6·50
704/7	*Set of* 4	8·00	8·00

173 Wise Men with Gifts

174 Hurdling

(Litho Questa)

1992 (23 Dec). Christmas. T **173** and similar horiz designs. Multicoloured. P 14.

708	10k. Type **173**	30	10
709	80k. Nativity	2·00	2·00
710	90k. Angelic choir	2·25	2·50
711	100k. Angel and shepherds	2·25	3·00
708/11	*Set of* 4	6·00	6·75
MS712	209×57 mm. Nos. 708/11	10·00	12·00

(Des R. Vigurs. Litho Questa)

1992 (28 Dec). Olympic Games, Barcelona. T **174** and similar vert designs. Multicoloured. P 14.

713	10k. Type **174**	25	10
714	40k. Boxing	65	40
715	80k. Judo	1·40	2·25
716	100k. Cycling	3·75	4·00
713/16	*Set of* 4	5·50	6·00

175 Nkundalila Falls

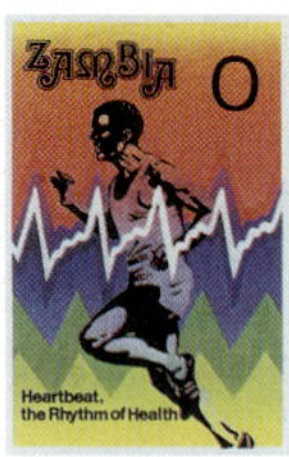

176 Athlete and Cardiograph

(Des Gabriel Ellison. Litho Cartor)

1993 (30 Sept). Waterfalls. T **175** and similar horiz designs. Multicoloured. P 13½.

717	50k. Type **175**	60	20
718	200k. Chishimba Falls	1·50	1·50
719	250k. Chipoma Falls	1·75	1·90
720	300k. Lumangwe Falls	1·90	2·25
717/20	*Set of* 4	5·25	5·25

(Litho National Printing & Packaging, Zimbabwe)

1993 (20 Oct). Heartbeat Campaign. T **176** and similar vert design. Multicoloured. P 14½.

721	(O) Type **176**	1·00	55
722	(P) Heart and cardiograph	1·00	55

These stamps were initially sold at 50k. (No. 721) for ordinary post and 80k. (No. 722) for priority mail. These face values were increased to reflect postage rates increases. See note below Nos. 723/38.

177 Bronze Sunbird

178 Tiger Snake

(Des Gabriel Ellison. Litho Cartor)

1994 (30 May). Sunbirds. T **177** and similar horiz designs. Multicoloured. P 13.

(a) Face values as T **177**

723	20k. Type **177**	45	1·00
724	50k. Violet-backed Sunbird	55	50
725	100k. Scarlet-chested Sunbird	80	10
726	150k. Bannerman's Sunbird	1·00	10
727	200k. Oustalet's White-bellied Sunbird	1·00	10
728	250k. Anchieta's Sunbird ("Red and Blue Sunbird")	1·00	20
729	300k. Olive Sunbird	1·25	40
730	350k. Green-headed Sunbird	1·25	40
731	400k. Red-tufted Malachite Sunbird	1·25	50
732	500k. Variable Sunbird	1·25	50
733	800k. Coppery Sunbird	1·50	1·75
734	1000k. Orange-tufted Sunbird	1·75	2·00
735	1500k. Amethyst Sunbird ("Black Sunbird")	2·00	3·00
736	2000k. Green-throated Sunbird	2·25	3·50

(b) Face values shown as capital letters

737	(O) Mariqua Sunbird ("Marico Sunbird")	1·25	55
738	(P) Eastern Double-collared Sunbird	1·25	55
723/38	*Set of* 16	18·00	13·50

Nos. 737/8 were initially sold at 50k. for ordinary post (No. 737) and 80k. for priority mail (No. 738). These rates were increased to 100k. for ordinary post and 150k. for priority mail on 20 June 1994. On 1 March 1995 the difference between the two rates was abolished and both "O" and "P" stamps were sold at 500k. This was reduced to 400k. each on 1 April 1995, but the rate reverted to 500k. on 8 February 1996.

(Litho Questa)

1994 (28 Sept). Snakes. T **178** and similar vert designs. Multicoloured. P 14.

739	50k. Type **178**	60	10
740	200k. Egyptian Cobra	1·75	65
741	300k. African Python	2·00	1·75
742	500k. Green Mamba	2·50	4·00
739/42	*Set of* 4	6·25	6·00

179 Women working on Road

(Des Gabriel Ellison. Litho Questa)

1995 (3 Apr). 75th Anniv of International Labour Organization. T **179** and similar horiz design. Multicoloured. P 14.

743	100k. Type **179**	50	20
744	450k. Women making cement blocks	2·00	2·75

180 Angel playing Kalimba and Flowers

181 Anniversary Emblem, Rainbow and Map

(Des Gabriel Ellison. Litho Walsall)

1995 (29 Aug). Christmas (1994). T **180** and similar diamond-shaped designs. Multicoloured. P 14×14½.

745	100k. Type **180**	45	15
746	300k. Angel at prayer and animals	1·00	60
747	450k. Angel with flute and birds	1·60	2·00
748	500k. Angel with drum and Baobab trees	1·75	2·25
745/8	*Set of 4*	4·25	4·50

(Photo Courvoisier)

1995 (30 Dec). 50th Anniv of United Nations. Granite paper. P 11½.

749	**181** 700k. multicoloured	2·25	3·25

182 David Livingstone (missionary) and Memorial

183 Saddle-bill Stork

(Des Gabriel Ellison. Litho Questa)

1996 (21 Feb). Monuments. T **182** and similar vert designs. Multicoloured. P 14.

750	100k. Type **182**	30	10
751	300k. Mbereshi Mission	80	60
752	450k. Von Lettow-Vorbeck Monument	1·40	2·00
753	500k. Niamkolo Church	1·50	2·00
750/3	*Set of 4*	3·50	4·25

(Des Gabriel Ellison. Litllo Walsall)

1996 (27 Nov). Endangered Species. Birds. T **183** and similar horiz designs. Multicoloured. P 14×14½.

754	200k. Type **183**	40	20
755	300k. Black-cheeked Lovebird	55	35
756	500k. Pair of Black-cheeked Lovebirds	75	85
757	900k. Saddle-bill Stork and chicks	1·00	2·00
754/7	*Set of 4*	2·40	3·00
MS758	120×90 mm. Nos. 754/7	75·00	75·00

O

═══

(**184**)

1996 (18 Dec). Christmas. Nos. 709/10 surch as T **184**.

759	(O) on 90k. Angelic Choir	50	15
760	900k. on 80k. Nativity	2·50	3·50

No. 759 was sold at 500k., which was the minimum local postage rate for ordinary post.

185 *Precis octavia sesamus*

(Des Gabriel Ellison. Litho Questa)

1997 (8 Aug). Butterflies and Moths. T **185** and similar vert designs. Multicoloured. P 14.

761	300k. Type **185**	1·50	30
762	500k. *Argema mimosae*	1·75	40
763	700k. *Imbrasia dione*	2·50	2·75
764	900k. *Papilio ophidicephalus cotterell*	4·00	4·50
761/4	*Set of 4*	8·75	7·00
MS765	85×120 mm. As Nos. 761/4, but each with face value of 900k.	15·00	16·00

═══ O

(**186**)

187 Verreaux's Eagle Owl

1997 (19 Sept). Nos. 688/90 surch as T **186**.

766	(O) on 32k. Traditional village	2·50	55
767	500k. on 35k. Fishermen hauling nets	2·50	70
768	900k. on 38k. Three portraits of Queen Elizabeth	5·00	5·50
766/8	*Set of 3*	9·00	6·00

No. 766 was sold at 500k. which was the minimum local postage rate for ordinary post.

(Des Gabriel Ellison. Litho Walsall)

1997 (18 Dec). Owls of Zambia. T **187** and similar vert designs. Multicoloured. P 14.

769	300k. Type **187**	1·25	50
770	500k. Pel's Fishing Owl	2·25	60
771	700k. Barn Owl	3·00	2·75
772	900k. Spotted Eagle Owl	4·00	4·50
769/72	*Set of 4*	9·50	7·50
MS773	128×85 mm. As Nos. 769/72, but each with face value of 900k.	10·00	11·00

188 Gandhi as Law Student, London, 1888

189 Dove and Map of Zambia

1998 (30 Jan). 50th Death Anniv of Mahatma Gandhi. T **188** and similar multicoloured designs. Litho. P 13½.

774	250k. Type **188**	1·50	80
775	(O) Gandhi at Red Fort, Delhi	2·50	1·50
776	500k. Gandhi with Nehru, 1946 (*horiz*)	2·50	1·50
777	900k. Gandhi at prayer	4·00	4·50
774/7	*Set of 4*	9·50	7·50
MS778	70×100 mm. 2000k. At Second Round Table Conference, London, 1931	7·00	8·00

No. 775 was sold at 500k. which was the minimum local postage rate for ordinary post.

(Des Gabriel Ellison. Litho Questa)

1998 (14 July). 18th Anniv of Pan African Postal Union. T **189** and similar horiz designs. P 14½.

779	(O) multicoloured	1·50	55
780	500k. multicoloured	1·50	55
781	900k. black, vermilion and reddish orange	2·00	2·75
779/81	*Set of 3*	4·50	3·50

Designs:—500k. Lechwe at Kafue Flats; 900k. Dove with "18th" note in beak.

No. 779 was sold at 500k. which was the minimum local postage rate for ordinary post.

190 Traveller and Dog ("Luchele nganga")

191 "U20C" Diesel-electric Locomotive, 1967

(Des Gabriel Ellison. Litho Cartor)

1998 (2 Dec). Christmas. Traditional Stories. T **190** and similar vert design. Multicoloured. P 14.

782 300k. Type **190** ... 1·25 30
783 500k. Man feeding crocodile ("Kasuli") ... 1·50 70
MS784 111×70 mm. 2000k. Type **190**; 2000k. As 500k. ... 7·00 8·00

The example of Type **190** in No. **MS**784 omits the vertical inscription at right.

(Des Gabriel Ellison. Litho Questa)

1999 (1 Feb). Trains. T **191** and similar horiz designs. Multicoloured. P 14½×15.

785 (O) Type **191** ... 60 30
786 800k. Beyer-Garratt Class 15A No. 401 steam locomotive, 1950 ... 1·50 1·75
787 800k. Class 7 No. 70 steam locomotive, 1900 1·50 1·75
788 900k. Class 20 No. 708 steam locomotive, 1954 ... 1·50 1·75
789 900k. H.P. diesel-electric railcar, 1966 ... 1·50 1·75
785/9 *Set of 5* ... 6·00 6·50
MS790 112×85 mm. 1000k. Class 7 No. 955 steam locomotive, 1892 ... 2·00 3·00

No. 785 was sold at 500k. which was the minimum local postage rate for ordinary post.

K500

(**192**)

1999 (1 June). No. 743 surch with T **192**.

791 500k. on 100k. Type **179** ... 4·00 1·25

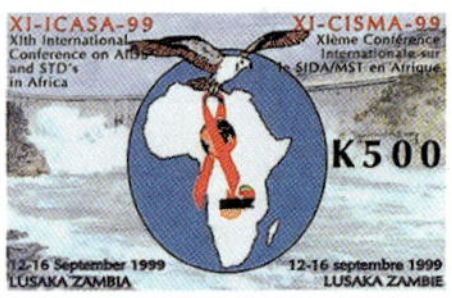

193 Conference Emblem and Dam

194 Blacksmith Plover

(Des Gabriel Ellison. Litho Walsall)

1999 (20 Aug). 11th International Conference on AIDS and STDs in Africa, Lusaka. T **193** and similar horiz design. Multicoloured. P 14.

792 500k. Type **193** ... 1·75 50
793 900k. Conference emblem and Victoria Falls.. 2·50 2·75

(Des Gabriel Ellison. Litho Questa)

1999 (20 Dec). Water Birds. T **194** and similar horiz designs. Multicoloured. *P 14½. A. Without imprint date.*

794A 50k. Type **194** ... 15 30
795A 100k. Sacred Ibis ... 25 30
796A 200k. Purple Swamphen ("Purple Gallinule"). 35 35
797A 250k. Purple Heron ... 40 40
798A 300k. Glossy Ibis ... 40 40
799A 400k. Marabou Stork ... 50 50
800A 450k. African Spoonbill ... 50 50
801A 500k. Peters's Finfoot ("African Finfoot") ... 50 20
802A (O) Comb Duck ("Knob-billed Duck") ... 50 20
803A 600k. African Darter ... 50 20
804A 700k. African Skimmer ... 3·00 65
805A 800k. Spur-winged Goose ... 50 35
806A 900k. Hammerkop ... 50 35
807A 1000k. Eastern White Pelican ... 3·00 2·00
808A 1500k. Black-winged Stilt ... 4·00 3·25
809A 2000k. Black-crowned Night Heron ... 1·00 1·25
794A/809A *Set of 16* ... 14·00 10·00

No. 794A is inscribed "Sarkidiomis melamotos" and No. 805A "Plectroterus gambensis", both in error.

B. With imprint date "2000" at foot (19.3.01)

802B (O) Comb Duck ("Knob-billed Duck") ... 1·00 40
810B (A) Blacksmith Plover ... 1·25 40
811B (B) Sacred Ibis ... 1·25 65
812B (C) Purple Swamphen ("Purple Gallinule").. 1·25 65
802B/12B *Set of 4* ... 4·25 1·90

No. 802A was initially sold at 500k. which was the minimum local postage rate for ordinary post.

Nos. 802B and 810B/12B were initially sold at 1000k., 1500k., 1700k. and 1800k. respectively.

K700

(**195**)

K1,200

(**196**)

2000 (11 Apr). No. 750 surch with T **195**.

813 700k. on 100k. Type **182** ... 5·00 1·75

2000 (5 July). Nos. 774 and 776 surch as T **196** by Mission Press.

814 1200k. on 250k. Type **188** ... 6·00 4·00
815 1500k. on 500k. Gandhi with Nehru, 1946 (*horiz*) ... 6·00 4·50

No. 775 was re-issued with Nos. 814/15 and sold at 700k.
The original face value on No. 815 is cancelled by two thin bars.

197 Map of Africa showing COMESA Member States

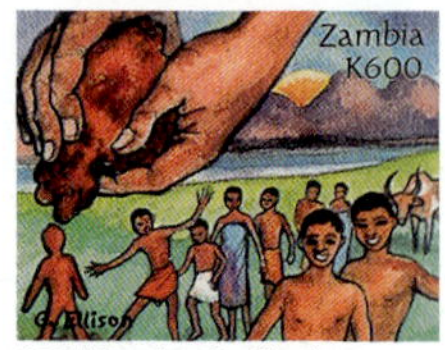

198 "Creation in Clay"

(Des Mrs. G. Ellison. Litho Questa)

2000 (31 Oct). Common Market for Eastern and Southern Africa (COMESA). T **197** and similar horiz designs. Multicoloured. P 14½.

816 600k. Type **197** ... 1·25 45
817 700k. Truck crossing free trade border ... 1·50 80
818 1000k. Exchange of money and sale of goods at border ... 1·75 2·00
816/18 *Set of 3* ... 4·00 3·00

(Des Mrs. G. Ellison. Litho Questa)

2000 (10 Nov). African Legends of Creation. T **198** and similar horiz designs. Multicoloured. P 14×14½.

819 600k. Type **198** ... 75 25
820 1000k. "The Chameleon and the Lizard" ... 1·25 1·00
821 1400k. "Why the Stones do not Die" ... 1·50 2·00
819/21 *Set of 3* ... 3·25 3·00
MS822 128×125 mm. As Nos. 819/21, but with brown borders, each ×3 ... 6·50 8·00
MS823 90×70 mm. 3500k. "The Rooster in the Sky" ... 4·50 5·50

199 Feeding Refugee Children

200 African Buffalo

2001 (13 Mar). 50th Anniv of United Nations High Commissioner for Refugees. T **199** and similar horiz design. Multicoloured. Litho. P 14.

824 700k. Type **199** ... 65 40
825 1500k. Refugees fleeing from conflict ... 1·25 2·00

(Des R. Rundo. Litho Cartor)

2001 (30 Mar). Animals of Africa. T **200** and similar multicoloured designs. P 13½.

826 500k. Type **200** ... 45 15
827 1000k. Cheetah (*vert*) ... 70 60
828 2000k. African Elephant ... 2·25 2·00
829 3200k. Ruffed Lemur (*vert*) ... 2·25 2·75
826/9 *Set of 4* ... 5·00 5·00
MS830 145×78 mm. 2000k. Cheetah; 2000k. Three adult and one young Impala; 2000k. Four adult Impala; 2000k. Warthog; 2000k. Two Lionesses; 2000k. Four Lionesses ... 5·50 6·50
MS831 74×165 mm. 2000k. Crimson-breasted Shrike; 2000k. European Bee Eater("Common Bee Eater"); 2000k. Blue Monkey; 2000k. Chimpanzee; 2000k. Lesser Bushbaby; 2000k. Small-spotted Genet (*all vert*). 5·50 6·50

MS832 145×78 mm. 2000k. Defussa Waterbuck; 2000k. Crowned Crane; 2000k. Hartebeest; 2000k. Pygmy Hippopotamus; 2000k. White Rhinoceros; 2000k. Giant Forest Hog .... 5·50 6·50
MS833 Three sheets, each 85×62 mm. (a) 6000k. African Elephant. (b) 6000k. Grevy's Zebra. (c) 6000k. Black Rhinoceros *Set of 2 sheets* .... 7·50 8·50

201 Woman watching Eclipse

202 "Sanjo Kantaro II and Ichikawa Monnosuke I, 1720s" (Okumura Masanobu)

(Des H. Methorst. Litho Questa)

2001 (1 June). Solar Eclipse of 21 June 2001. T **201** and similar vert designs. Multicoloured. P 13½×14.

834	1000k. Type **201**	60	30
835	1500k. Stylised bird	80	70
836	1700k. Chameleon on branch	90	1·40
837	1800k. Hand holding spear and elephant	90	1·40
838	2200k. Man with spear watching eclipse	1·10	1·75
834/8	*Set of 5*	4·00	5·00

(Litho BDT)

2001 (4 July). "Philanippon '01" International Stamp Exhibition, Tokyo. Japanese Art. T **202** and similar multicoloured (except No. 841) designs. P 14.

839	500k. Type **202**	30	35
840	500k. "Nakamura Senya as Toknatsu" (Torii Kiyomasu I)	30	35
841	1000k. "Standing Figure of a Woman" (Torii Kiyomasu I) (black, grey-green and reddish brown)	55	80
842	1000k. "Sanjo Kantaro and Ichikawa Monosuke, c. 1730" (Masanobu)	55	80
843	1500k. "Ono no Komachii?" (Masanobu)	80	1·10
844	1800k. "Dog bringing a Love Letter" (Shigenaga)	90	1·40
839/44	*Set of 6*	3·00	4·25

MS845 140×94 mm. 3200k. "Nakamura Kumetaro I" (Shunsho); 3200k. "Actor in Female Role" (Kiyomasu I); 3200k. "Segawa Kikunojo leaning on Sugoroku Board" (Kiyomasu I); 3200k. "Ichikawa Gennosuke as a Wakashu" (Kiyomasu I) .... 4·50 5·50
MS846 140×94 mm. 3200k. "Nakamura Matsue as a Cat Woman" (Shunsho); 3200k. "Sanjo Kantaro with Branch of Bamboo" (Kiyomasu I); 3200k. "Yamashika Kinsaku I as Peddler" (Torii Kiyomasu I); 3200k. "Portrait of an Actor" (Shunsho) .... 4·50 5·50
MS847 Two sheets. (a) 6000k. "Akashi of the Tamaya" (Hishikawa Ryukoku). (b) 6000k. "Events of Year in the Floating World" (Moroshige) (*horiz*) *Set of 2 sheets* .... 4·50 5·50

203 President Chiluba receiving Master's Degree, Warwick University

204 Children playing

(Litho Questa)

2001 (9 July). Frederick Chiluba (President of Zambia, 1991–2002). T **203** and similar multicoloured designs. P 14.

848	1000k. Type **203**	60	30
849	1500k. President Chiluba signing affidavit for second term of office, 1996	85	85
850	1700k. President after PHI Housing Empowerment of the people (*horiz*)	1·25	1·50
848/50	*Set of 3*	2·40	2·40

MS851 73×98 mm. 6000k. President receiving Master's Degree .... 3·00 4·00

(Litho Questa)

2001 (30 July). SOS Children's Villages (Kinderdorf International). P 14.

852	**204** 2500k. multicoloured	1·50	2·00

205 Princess Victoria as Young Girl

205a Mae Tse-tung as Student, 1918

(Des S. Stines. Litho Questa)

2001 (30 July). Death Centenary of Queen Victoria. T **205** and similar vert designs. Multicoloured. P 14.

MS853 2000k. Type **205**; 2000k. Queen Victoria as widow; 2000k. With baby daughter; 2000k. With Prince Albert; 2000k. After being crowned Empress of India, 1876; 2000k. Princess Victoria as teenager. 2·75 3·25
MS854 93×126 mm. 7000k. Young Queen Victoria .... 1·90 2·00

(Des R. Sauber. Litho Questa)

2001 (30 July). 25th Death Anniv of Mao Tse-tung (Chinese leader). T **205a** and similar vert designs. Multicoloured. P 13½×14.

MS855 177×183 mm. 3200k. Type **205a**; 3200k. Mao in 1945; 3200k. As guerrilla leader, 1937 .... 2·75 3·25
MS856 132×128 mm. 4000k. Writing .... 1·00 1·50

205b "The Promenade at Argenteuil"

(Litho Questa)

2001 (30 July). 75th Death Anniv of Claude-Oscar Monet (French artist). T **205b** and similar multicoloured designs. P 14×13½ (*horiz*) or 13½×14 (*vert*).

MS857 136×177 mm. 1500k. Type **205b**; 1500k. "View of the Argenteuil Plain from the Sannois Hills"; 1500k. "The Seine at Argenteuil"; 1500k. "The Basin at Argenteuil" .... 2·00 2·50
MS858 137×110 mm. 6000k. "Rouen Cathedral, Portal, Overcast Weather" (*vert*) .... 2·00 2·50

206 Princess Elizabeth as Baby

206a Benjamin Luxon as Falstaff

(Des R. Sauber. Litho Questa)

2001 (30 July). 75th Birthday of Queen Elizabeth II. T **206** and similar vert designs. Multicoloured. P 14.

MS859 157×175 mm. 4000k. Type **206**; 4000k. Princess Elizabeth as schoolgirl; 4000k. As young girl in garden; 4000k. In Women's Army Auxilliary Unit uniform, *c.* 1942 ... 3·50 4·00

MS860 79×109 mm. 8000k. Queen Elizabeth II as young woman (42×56 *mm*) ... 2·25 2·50

(Des R. Sauber. Litho Questa)

2001 (30 July). Death Centenary of Giuseppe Verdi (Italian composer). T **206a** and similar vert designs showing scenes from *Falstaff* (opera). Multicoloured. P 14.

MS861 160×180 mm. 4000k. Type **206a**; 4000k. Benjamin Luxon as Falstaff (in red and gold); 4000k. Paul Plishka as Falstaff; 4000k. Anne Collin as Mistress Quickly ... 6·00 6·00

MS862 79×109 mm. 8000k. 19th-century poster for *Falstaff* ... 3·00 3·00

207 HMS *Tabard*, 1946

208 LZ-1, 1900

(Des J. Larsen. Litho Questa)

2001 (30 July). Centenary of Royal Navy Submarine Service. Submarines. T **207** and similar multicoloured designs. P 14.

MS863 2000k. Type **207**; 2000k. HMS *Opossum*, 1963; 2000k. HMS *Unicorn*, 1992; 2000k. HMS *Churchill*, 1968; 2000k. HMS *Victorious*, 1992; 2000k. HMS *Triumph*, 1982 ... 6·00 7·00

MS864 101×78 mm. 6000k. Lieut-Commander Wanklyn (VC) and crew of HMS *Upholder*, 1941 (*vert*) ... 3·25 3·50

(Des G. Capaso. Litho Questa)

2001 (30 July). Zeppelins. T **208** and similar horiz designs. Multicoloured. P 14.

MS865 145×132 mm. 2000k. Type **208**; 2000k. Parseval PL25, 1915; 2000k LZ-3, 1906; 2000k. Baldwin, 1908; 2000k. LZ-129 *Hindenburg*, 1936; 2000k. *Norge*, 1926 ... 4·50 5·50

208a US Flag around Statue of Liberty and Zambian Flag

209 Norman Borlaug (USA, 1970)

(Des M. Friedman. Litho Cartor)

2002 (11 Feb). "United We Stand". Support for Victims of 11 September 2001 Terrorist Attacks. P 13½.

866 **208a** 3200k. multicoloured ... 1·00 1·50

No. 866 was printed in sheetlets of 4 with enlarged illustrated left-hand margins.

(Des R. Sauber. Litho Questa)

2002 (11 Feb). Centenary of Nobel Prizes. T **209** and similar vert designs. Multicoloured. P 14.

MS867 146×210 mm. 2000k. Type **209**; 2000k. Lester B. Pearson (Canada, 1957); 2000k. International Red Cross (1944); 2000k. Anwar Sadat (Egypt, 1978); 2000k. Georges Pire (Belgium, 1958); 2000k. Linus Pauling (USA, 1962) ... 4·00 5·00

MS868 146×210 mm. 2000k. Seamus Heaney (Ireland, 1995); 2000k. Toni Morrison (USA, 1993); 2000k. Günter Grass (Germany, 1999); 2000k. Wislawa Szymborska (Poland, 1996); 2000k. Dario Fo (Italy, 1997); 2000k. Jose Saramango (Portugal, 1998) ... 4·00 5·00

MS869 146×210 mm. 2000k. Isaac Bashevis Singer (USA, 1978); 2000k. Gao Xingjian (China, 2000); 2000k. Claude Simon (France, 1985); 2000k. Naguib Mahfouz (Egypt, 1988); 2000k. Camilo Jose Cela (Spain, 1989); 2000k. Czeslaw Milosz (USA, 1980) ... 4·00 5·00

MS870 Three sheets, each 106×128 mm. (a) 6000k. George Marshall (Peace, USA, 1953). (b) 6000k. Gerard Debreu (Economics, USA, 1983). (c) 6000k. Robert Fogel (Economics, USA, 1993) *Set of 3 sheets* ... 5·00 6·00

No. **MS**868 shows recipients of Nobel Peace Prizes and Nos. **MS**869/70 Literature prize winners.

210 Horse-taming Figurines, Tang Dynasty

(Des D. Kwok. Litho Cartor)

2002 (18 Feb). Chinese New Year ("Year of the Horse"). *Sheet* 108×76 *mm*. P 13½.

MS871 **210** 5000k. multicoloured ... 1·40 1·75

211 Ferenc Puskas (Hungary)

K500

(**212**)

(Des G. Bibby. Litho Questa)

2002 (26 Feb). World Cup Football Championship, Japan and Korea (2002). T **211** and similar multicoloured designs. P 14.

MS872 142×164 mm. 2000k. Type **211**; 2000k. Official poster of 1962 World Cup, Chile; 2000k. Spanish player; 2000k. England player; 2000k. Player and Jeonju World Cup Stadium, Korea (57×42 *mm*) ... 2·00 2·75

MS873 142×164 mm. 2000k. Official poster of 1954 World Cup, Switzerland; 2000k. Stanley Matthews (England); 2000k. Scotland player; 2000k. Belgian player; 2000k. Player and Daejeon World Cup Stadium, Korea (57×42 *mm*) ... 3·00 3·75

MS874 Two sheets, each 70×100 mm. (a) 8000k. Bryan Robson (England) scoring goal against France, 1982 (42×57 *mm*). (b) 8000k. Salenko (Russia) scoring goal against Cameroon, 1994 (57×42 *mm*) *Set of 2 sheets* ... 4·50 5·50

2002 (1 July). *Nos.* 724, 739, 743 and 745 surch as T **212**.

875	250k. on 50k. Type **178**	40	20
876	300k. on 50k. Violet-backed Sunbird	50	20
877	500k. on 100k. Type **179**	65	20
878	1000k. on 100k. Type **180**	1·25	60
875/8	*Set of 4*	2·50	1·10

No. 877 differs from No. 791 by having a different typeface for the **K500** and shorter bars.

212a Queen Elizabeth II disembarking from Plane

212b Ice Hockey

(Litho Questa)

2002 (15 July). Golden Jubilee. T **212a** and similar square designs. Multicoloured. P 14½.

MS879	132×100 mm. 3200k. Type **212a**; 3200k. Queen wearing pink blouse; 3200k. With Prince Edward; 3200k. Wearing tiara	4·00	5·00
MS880	76×108 mm. 7500k. With Duke of Edinburgh in library	2·50	3·00

(Litho Cartor)

2002 (13 July). Winter Olympic Games, Salt Lake City. T **212b** and similar horiz design. Multicoloured. P 13½.

881	1000k. Type **212b**	1·00	55
882	3200k. Cross-country skier	1·75	2·00

212c Scout Troop hiking

(Des H. Friedman. Litho Questa)

2002 (31 July). 20th World Scout Jamboree, Thailand. T **212c** and similar multicoloured designs. P 14.

MS883	153×115 mm. 3200k. Type **212c**; 3200k. Knot tying; 3200k. Archery; 3200k. Fire-making	4·00	5·00
MS884	58×76 mm. 8000k. Scout by campfire (*vert*)	2·75	3·25

212d Mount Whitney, USA

(Des H. Friedman. Litho Questa)

2002 (31 July). International Year of Mountains. T **212d** and similar horiz designs. Multicoloured. P 14.

MS885	151×109 mm. 1500k. Type **212d**; 1500k. Aconcagua, Argentina/Chile border; 1500k. Mönch, Switzerland; 1500k. Mount Ararat, Turkey	2·50	3·00
MS886	74×56 mm. 9000k. Mount Everest, Nepal/China border	3·50	4·00

213 White-fronted Bee Eater

214 Camelsfoot (*Bauhinia galpinii*)

2002 (12 Aug)–**03**. Birds of Zambia. T **213** and similar horiz designs. Multicoloured.

(a) Litho Questa. Size 35×28 mm. P 14

887	700k. Type **213**	45	30
888	1200k. Blue-cheeked Bee Eater	1·50	1·25
889	1400k. Boehm's Bee Eater	1·50	1·50
890	1500k. Little Bee Eater	1·60	1·60
887/90	*Set of 4*	4·50	4·25

(b) Litho BDT. Size 25×21 mm. P 13×13½

891	1000k. Type **213** (26.12.03)	1·25	65
892	1200k. Little Bee Eater (26.12.03)	1·50	1·25
893	1500k. Blue-cheeked Bee Eater (26.12.03)	1·50	1·50
894	1800k. Boehm's Bee Eater (26.12.03)	1·75	2·00
891/4	*Set of 4*	5·50	4·75

(Litho Walsall)

2002 (9 Sept). Flowers, Butterflies and Mushrooms of Zambia. T **214** and similar horiz designs. Multicoloured. P 14.

MS895	120×120 mm. 2500k. Type **214**; 2500k. Christmas Bells (*Sandersonia aurantiaca*); 2500k. Impala Lily (*Adenium obesum*); 2500k. Everlasting (*Helichrysum ecklonis*); 2500k. *Anomatheca grandiflora*; 2500k. Soldier Lily (*Cyrtanthus obliquus*)	5·00	6·00
MS896	120×120 mm. 2500k. False Monarch (*Mimicraea marshalli*); 2500k. Golden Piper (*Eurytera dryope*); 2500k. Blue Pansy (*Junonia orithya*); 2500k. Christmas Treeacraea (*Acraea anemosa*); 2500k. Grass Yellow (*Eurema brigitta*); 2500k. Gold-spotted Sylph (*Metisella metis*)	5·00	6·00
MS897	120×120 mm. 2500k. Copper Trumpet (*Clitocybe olearia*); 2500k. King Bolete (*Boletus edulis*); 2500k. Death Cap (*Amanita phalloides*); 2500k. Fly Agaric (*Amanita muscaria*); 2500k. Chantarelle (*Cantharellus cibarius*); 2500k. Deadly Fiber Cap (*Inocybe erubescens*)	5·00	6·00
MS898	Three sheets, each 100×70 mm. (a) 8000k. Arum Lily (*Zantedeschia aethiopica*). (b) 8000k. African Monarch (*Danaus chrysippus*). (c) 8000k. Stump Brittle-head (*Psathyrella piluliformis*) *Set of 3 sheets*	8·50	9·50

215 Queen Elizabeth II

216 Prince William

2003 (19 May). 50th Anniv of Coronation. T **215** and similar vert designs. Multicoloured. Litho. P 14.

MS899	156×93 mm. 5000k. Type **215**; 5000k. Wearing tiara and smiling; 5000k Wearing fuchsia hat and outfit	3·50	4·00
MS900	76×106 mm. 10000k. Wearing floral hat and outfit	3·00	4·00

2003 (19 May). 21st Birthday of Prince William. T **216** and similar vert designs. Multicoloured. Litho. P 14.

MS901	157×104 mm. 5000k. Type **216**; 5000k. As young boy; 5000k. Wearing yellow polo neck shirt..	3·50	4·00
MS902	68×98 mm. 10000k. Wearing cream round neck jumper and laughing	3·00	4·00

(217)

(218)

(219)

2003 (26 June). Nos. 754/7 surch as T **217**.

903	1000k. on 200k. Type **183**	25·00	12·00
904	1000k. on 300k. Black-cheeked Lovebird	25·00	12·00
905	1000k. on 500k. Pair of Black-cheeked Lovebirds	25·00	12·00
906	1000k. on 900k. Saddle-bill Stork and chicks	25·00	12·00
903/6	*Set of 4*	90·00	45·00

2003 (26 June). Nos. 739/42 surch as T **218**.

907	1700k. on 50k. Type **178**	2·25	2·50
908	1700k. on 200k. Egyptian Cobra	2·25	2·50
909	1700k. on 300k. African Python	2·25	2·50
910	1700k. on 500k. Green Mamba	2·25	2·50
907/10	*Set of 4*	8·00	9·00

2003 (26 June). Nos. 717/20 surch as T **219**.

911	1800k. on 50k. Type **175**	2·25	2·50
912	1800k. on 200k. Chishimba Falls	2·25	2·50
913	1800k. on 250k. Chipoma Falls	2·25	2·50
914	1800k. on 300k. Lumangwe Falls	2·25	2·50
911/14	*Set of 4*	8·00	9·00

(220)

(221)

(222)

(223)

2003 (26 June). Nos. 750/3 surch as T **220**.

915	2200k. on 100k. Type **182**	2·50	2·75
916	2200k. on 300k. Mbereshi Mission	2·50	2·75
917	2200k. on 450k. Von Lettow-Vorteck Monument	2·50	2·75
918	2200k. on 500k. Niamkolo Church	2·50	2·75

2003 (26 June). No. 779 surch as T **221**, No. 780 surch as T **222** and No. 781 surch as T **223**.

919	2500k. on (O) Type **189**	2·75	3·00
920	2500k. on 500k. Lechwe at Kafue Flats	2·75	3·00
921	2500k. on 900k. Dove with "18th" note in beak	2·75	3·00
	a. Surch inverted	10·00	
919/21	*Set of 3*	7·50	8·00

224 Cabora Bassa Dam

2003 (30 July). United Nations International Year of Freshwater. T **224** and similar vert designs. Multicoloured. Litho. P 13½.

MS922 (a) 147×85 mm. 5000k.×3, Type **224**; Lake Kariba; Mana Pools National Park. (b) 97×67 mm. 10000k. Victoria Falls *Set of 2 sheets* ... 7·00 8·00

225 Triplane Avro 547A

2003 (30 July). Centenary of Powered Flight. Planes of A. V. Roe. T **225** and similar horiz designs. Multicoloured. Litho. P 14.

923	4000k. Type **225**	1·90	2·25
	a. Sheetlet. Nos. 923/6	7·00	8·00
924	4000k. 504O with floats	1·90	2·25
925	4000k. Avro 584 Avocet	1·90	2·25
926	4000k. Avro 504M	1·90	2·25
923/6	*Set of 4*	7·00	8·00
MS927	106×76 mm. 9000k. Avro No. 621 Tutor Replica	4·75	5·50

Nos. 923/6 were printed together, *se-tenant*, in sheetlets of 4 with an enlarged illustrated top margin.

No. 925 is inscribed 'Avrocet' in error.

226 Stylised Ram

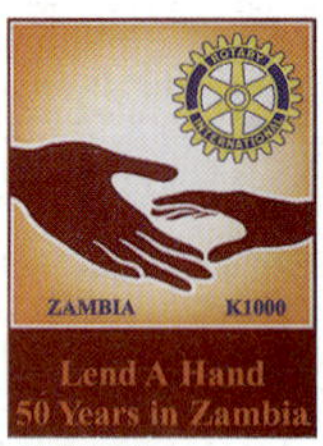

227 Hands

2003 (30 July). Chinese New Year ("Year of the Ram"). T **226** and similar vert designs. Litho. P 13½.

928/31	**226**	3200k.×4, yellow-green, dull orange and blackish green; mauve, dull orange and ultramarine; dull orange and brown-lake; bright violet, rose and dull orange	5·50	6·50
		a. Block of 4. Nos. 928/31	5·50	6·50

Nos. 928/31 were printed together, *se-tenant*, in blocks of 4 stamps.

2003 (21 Nov). 50th Anniv of Rotary International (humanitarian organisation). T **227** and similar vert design. Litho. P 13.

932	1000k. multicoloured	1·25	1·00
933	1200k. orange-red, lemon and ultramarine	1·50	1·50

Designs—No. 932, Type 227; No. 933, Rotary International emblem.

227a Two African Fish Eagles Perched (Zimbabwe)

228 Vimbuza Dancer

(Des Anja Denkar. Litho Enschedé)

2004 (11 Oct). First Joint Issue of Southern Africa Postal Operators Association Members. Sheet 170×95 mm containing hexagonal designs as T **227a** showing national birds of Association members. Multicoloured. P 14.

MS934 500k. Type **227a**; 750k. Cattle Egret (Botswana); 1000k. Two African Fish Eagles in flight (Zambia); 1100k. Peregrine Falcon (Angola); 1500k. Bar-tailed Trogon (Malawi) (inscribed "apaloderma vittatum"); 1700k. African Fish Eagle (Namibia); 1800k. Purple-crested Turaco ("Lourie") (Swaziland); 2200k. Stanley ("Blue") Crane (South Africa) ... 8·00 9·00

The stamp depicting the Bar–tailed Trogon is not inscribed with the country of which the bird is a national symbol.

Miniature sheets of similar designs were also issued by Namibia, Zimbabwe, Angola, Botswana, Swaziland, Malawi and South Africa.

(Des G. Ellison. Litho Cartor)

2004 (23 Oct). 40th Anniv of Independence. T **228** and similar horiz designs. Multicoloured. P 13.

935	1500k. Type **228**	85	50
936	1800k. Kayowe dancer	90	60
937	2700k. Ngoma dancer	1·40	1·75
938	3300k. Ukishi Dancer	1·75	2·25
935/8	*Set of 4*	4·50	4·50

K1000

(**229**)

2004 (28 Dec). No. 749 surch as T **229**.

939	1000k. on 700k. Type **181**	1·75	70
	a. Surch inverted	12·00	

230 *Fornasinius russus*

231 *Disa uniflora* (orange)

(Litho BDT)

2005 (27 June). Beetles. T **230** and similar vert designs. Multicoloured. P 14.

940	1500k. Type **230**	75	50
941	2250k. *Macrorhina*	1·40	1·75
942	2250k. *Goliathus giganteus*	1·40	1·75
943	2700k. *Chelorrhina polyphemus*	1·75	2·25
940/3	*Set of 4*	4·75	5·50
MS944	145×125 mm. 3300k.×4, *Sternotomis virescens* and *Sternotomis cava*; *Cicindela regalis*; *Goliathus meleagris*; *Mecosasms explanta*	8·50	10·00
MS945	66×98 mm. 10000k. *Meloid*	6·50	8·00

(Litho BDT)

2005 (27 June). Orchids. T **231** and similar vert designs. Multicoloured. P 14.

946	1500k. Type **231**	1·50	1·50
947	1500k. *Disa draconis*	1·50	1·50
948	1500k. *Disa uniflora* (red petals)	1·50	1·50
949	2700k. *Phalaenopsis penetrate*	2·75	3·25
946/9	*Set of 4*	6·50	7·00

MS950	145×125 mm. 3300k.×4, *Ansellia africana* (yellow petals); *Ansellia africana* (speckled petals); *Cattelya lueddemanniana*; *Laelia tenebrosa*	8·50	9·50
MS951	72×102 mm. 10000k. Cymbidium	7·50	8·50

232 *Acinonyx jubatus*

(Litho BDT)

2005 (27 June). Mammals. T **232** and similar multicoloured designs. P 14.

952	2250k. Type **232**	2·00	2·25
953	2250k. *Giraffa camelopardalis*	2·00	2·25
954	2250k. *Phacochoerus aethiopicus*	2·00	2·25
955	2700k. *Syncerus caffer*	2·25	2·50
952/5	*Set of 4*	7·50	8·25
MS956	145×125 mm. 3300k.×4, *Panthera pardus* (*vert*); *Pan troglodytes* (*vert*); *Lycaon pictus* (*vert*); *Equus burchelli* (*vert*)	8·00	9·00
MS957	67×96 mm. 10000k. *Diceros bicornis* (*vert*)	9·00	9·50

233 *Morpho portis nymphalidae*

234 Bishop Paul Lungu

2005 (27 June). Butterflies and Moths. T **233** and similar vert designs. Multicoloured. P 14.

958	2250k. Type **233**	2·00	2·00
959	2250k. *Ropalo ceres*	2·00	2·00
960	2250k. *Phyllocnistis citrella*	2·00	2·00
961	2700k. *H. misippus*	2·50	2·50
958/61	*Set of 4*	7·75	7·75
MS962	144×125 mm. 3300k.×4, *Colotis evippe*; *Papilio lormieri*; *Papilio dardanus*; *Papilio zalmoxis*	9·00	10·00
MS963	72×106 mm. 10000k. *Epiphora albida druce*	8·00	9·00

(Des G. Ellison. Litho Enschedé)

2005 (25 June). Centenary of the Jesuits in Zambia. T **234** and similar horiz designs. Multicoloured. P 13½×13.

964	1500k. Type **234**	1·60	1·10
965	2550k. Father Torrend, Kasisi Church	2·25	2·75
966	2700k. Father Moreau, Chikuni Church	2·75	3·25
967	3300k. Saint Ignatius Loyola	3·00	3·50
964/7	*Set of 4*	8·75	9·50
MS968	102×75 mm. Nos. 964/7	8·75	10·00

235 Dag Hammarskjold

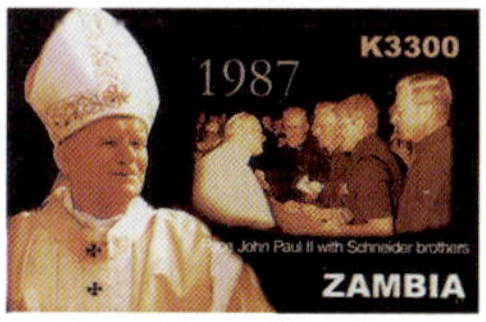

236 Pope John Paul II with Schneider Brothers

(Des G. Ellison. Litho Enschedé)

2005 (27 July). Birth Centenary of Dag Hammarskjold (Swedish diplomat, Secretary of UN and winner of Nobel Peace Prize, 1961). T **235** and similar horiz design. P 13½.

969	**235** 1500k. dull ultramarine background	1·60	1·10
970	2700k. turquoise-green background	2·75	3·50
MS971	108×80 mm. Nos. 969/70		

2005 (22 Aug). Pope John Paul II Commemoration. T **236** and similar multicoloured designs. Litho. P 13.

972	3300k. With Sri Chinmoy	4·00	4·00
	a. Sheetlet. Nos. 972/5	14·50	14·50
973	3300k. With boy and dove	4·00	4·00
974	3300k. Type **236**	4·00	4·00
975	3300k. Visiting Ukraine	4·00	4·00
976	7000k. With Jimmy Carter	9·00	9·00
972/7	*Set of 5*	22·00	22·00

Nos. 972/5 were printed together, *se-tenant*, in sheetlets of four stamps with an enlarged, illustrated right margin. No. 974 was also available as a single stamp in sheets of 18.

No. 976 was printed in sheetlets of four stamps with an enlarged, illustrated left margin.

237 Southern Railways "King Arthur" Class

2005 (22 Aug). Bicentenary of Steam Locomotives. T **237** and similar horiz designs. Multicoloured. Litho. P 13.

977/85	1700k.×9 Type **237**; Berkshire at Kaiman's Bridge; Indian Railways WT Class suburban tank steam locomotive; Steel cylinder ("railway builders"); Railway carriage under construction; New locomotive in factory; New train in factory; New railway carriage in factory; New steam locomotive in factory	12·00	14·00
	a. Sheetlet. Nos. 977/85	12·00	14·00
986/94	1700k.×9 Great Western Railway Hall Class; Argentinian 15B class; Mallet metre gauge steam locomotive, East Germany; Track repairs; Overhead cable repairs; Maintaining signals from mobile crane; Ground crew, two overhead crews and vehicle; Maintainance crew; Working on tracks	12·00	14·00
	a. Sheetlet. Nos. 986/94	12·00	14·00
995/1003	1700k.×9 British Rail Class 4MT; South African Railways Class 12A; Cubansugar plantation steam locomotive; LNER A4 Pacific (in wooded cutting); LNER A4 Pacific (in city); GWR City of Truro; British Railways HST Intercity 125; Eurostar; LNER A3 *Flying Scotsman*	12·00	14·00
	a. Sheetlet. Nos. 995/1003	12·00	14·00
1004/7	4200k.×4 Chinese Class KF; Indian Class WP; Irish 800 Class; French 241A Class	12·00	14·00
	a. Sheetlet. Nos. 1004/7	12·00	14·00
MS1008	Four sheets, each 100×70 mm. (a) 8000k. Finnish Class Hv2. (b) 8000k. Interior of Orient Express. (c) 8000k. Edinburgh to London Intercity train. (d) 8000k. Bernina Express	26·00	28·00

Nos. 977/85, 986/94, 995/1003 and 1004/7 were each printed together, *se-tenant*, in sheetlets of nine or four stamps with enlarged illustrated top margins.

238 David Livingstone and Victoria Falls

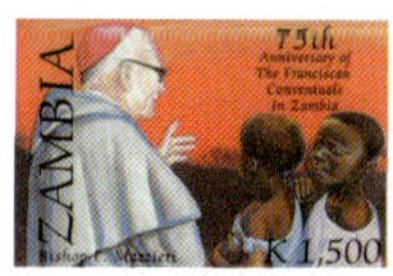

239 Bishop Mazzieri with Boys

2006 (20 Jan). 150th Anniv of Discovery of Victoria Falls by David Livingstone (explorer). T **238** and similar horiz design. Multicoloured. Litho. P 13×13½.

1009	1500k. Type **238**	2·00	1·10
1010	2700k. David Livingstone and steam train on Rail Bridge	4·00	4·50

(Des Simona Pierpaoli (1500k.) or G. Ellison (others). Litho Enschedé)

2006 (8 July). 75th Anniv of the Franciscan Conventuals in Zambia. T **239** and similar horiz designs. Multicoloured. P 13½×13.

1011	1500k. Type **239**	1·60	1·10
1012	2250k. "Sister Moon"	2·25	2·50
1013	2700k. "Brother Sun"	2·75	3·25

1014 3300k. "Sister Water" 3·00 3·75
1011/14 *Set of 4* 8·75 9·50

2006 (8 Aug). 80th Birthday of Queen Elizabeth II. Vert designs as T **159** of St. Kitts. Multicoloured. Litho. P 13½.

1015 3200k. Wearing diadem, c. 1955 4·00 4·00
a. Sheetlet. Nos. 1015/18 14·50 14·50
1016 3200k. Queen Elizabeth, c. 1955 4·00 4·00
1017 3200k. Princess Elizabeth 4·00 4·00
1018 3200k. With baby Princess Anne 4·00 4·00
1015/18 *Set of 4* 14·50 14·50
MS1019 120×120 mm. 6500k. Wearing green hat and coat, c. 2000 8·00 8·50

Nos. 1015/18 were printed together, *se-tenant*, in sheetlets of four stamps with enlarged illustrated margins.

240 Lord Robert Baden-Powell (founder)

2006 (8 Aug). Centenary (2007) of World Scouting. T **240** and similar multicoloured design. Litho. P 13½.

1020 3200k. Type **240** 4·00 4·00
a. Sheetlet. Nos. 1020/3 14·50 14·50
1021 3200k. As Type **240** (yellow-orange and lemon background) 4·00 4·00
1022 3200k. As Type **240** (pale blue and new blue background) 4·00 4·00
1023 3200k. As Type **240** (yellow-green and bright green background) 4·00 4·00
1020/23 *Set of 4* 14·50 14·50
MS1024 110×80 mm. 6500k. Lord Baden-Powell and scout emblem (*horiz*) 8·00 8·50

Nos. 1020/3 were printed together, *se-tenant*, in sheetlets of four stamps with enlarged illustrated margins.

K3,300

K1,500

(241) **(242)**

2007 (19 Mar). Nos. 889 and 892 surch with T **241/2**.

1025 1500k. on 1200k. Little bee-eater (No. 892) 3·00 1·60
1026 3300k. on 1400k Boehm's bee-eater (No. 889) 6·00 3·75
a. Surch inverted

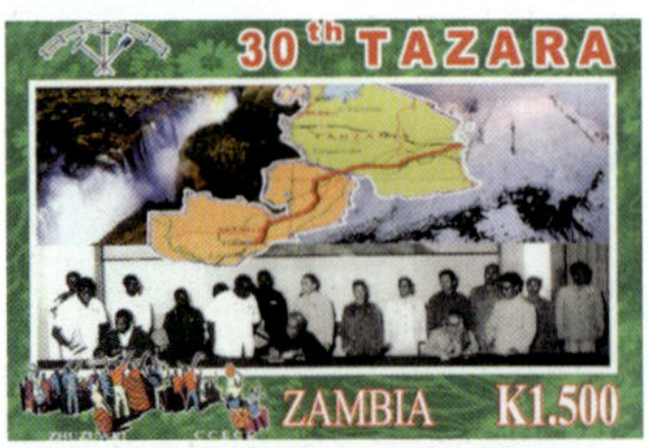

243 Signatories, Map, Victoria Falls and Mount Kilimanjaro

2007 (28 May). 30th Anniv of TAZARA Railways (2006). T **243** and similar horiz designs. Multicoloured. Litho. P 12.

1027 1500k. Type **243** 2·25 2·25
a. Sheetlet. Nos. 1027/31 12·00 12·00
1028 1500k. Kenneth Kaunda (Zambian President) and Julius Nyerere (Tanzanian Prime Minister) at inauguration, 1975 2·25 2·25
1029 1500k. TAZARA Headquarters, Dar-es-Salaam, Tanzania 2·25 2·25
1030 1500k. New Kapiri Mposhi railway station 2·25 2·25
1031 1500k. Train on viaduct 2·25 2·25
1032 1500k. Train on river bridge 2·25 2·25
1027/32 *Set of 6* 12·00 12·00

Nos. 1028/32 were printed together, *se-tenant*, in sheetlets of six stamps.

Stamps in similar designs were issued by Tanzania.

K 1,850

(244)

245 Bat-eared Fox

2007 (31 May). No. 723 surch with T **244**.

1033 1850k. on 20k. Type **177** 3·50 4·00

(Des Gabriel Ellison. Litho)

2007 (29 June). Animals of Zambia. T **245** and similar horiz designs. Multicoloured. P 13½.

1034 1500k. Type **245** 1·75 1·00
1035 2250k. Spotted hyaena 2·75 2·75
1036 2700k. Aardwolf 3·25 3·50
1037 3300k. Side-striped jackal 4·25 4·75
1034/7 *Set of 4* 11·00 11·00
MS1038 143×110 mm. Nos. 1034/7 11·00 12·00

(Des Anja Denker. Litho Enschedé)

2007 (9 Oct). Second Joint Issue of Southern Africa Postal Operators Association Members. Square designs as T **236** of Zimbabwe showing national mammals of association members. Multicoloured. P 14.

1039 1500k. Buffalo (Zambia) 1·75 1·00
1040 1800k. Nyala (Malawi) 2·00 2·00
1041 2250k. Nyala (Zimbabwe) 2·75 2·75
1042 2700k. Burchell's zebra (Botswana) 3·25 3·50
1043 3300k. Oryx (Namibia) 4·25 4·75
1039/43 *Set of 5* 8·50 9·00
MS1044 135×170 mm. Nos. 1039/43 13·00 14·00

Miniature sheets of similar designs were also issued by Botswana, Malawi, Nambia and Zimbabwe. Botswana also issued sheet stamps.

246 Football

2008 (8 June). Olympic Games, Beijing. T **246** and similar vert designs. Multicoloured. Litho. P 12.

1045 2000k. Type **246** 2·10 2·25
a. Sheetlet. Nos. 1045/8 7·50 8·00
1046 2000k. Hurdles 2·10 2·25
1047 2000k. Boxing 2·10 2·25
1048 2000k. Swimming 2·10 2·25
1045/8 *Set of 4* 7·50 8·00

Nos. 1045/8 were printed together, *se-tenant*, in sheetlets of four stamps with enlarged illustrated margins.

247 Greater Kudu Males fighting

(Des Owen Bell. Litho)

2008 (30 June). Endangered Species. Greater Kudu (Tragelaphus strepsiceros). T **247** and similar horiz designs. Multicoloured. P 13½.

1049	3000k. Type **247**	3·00	3·25
	a. Horiz strip of 4. Nos. 1049/52	11·00	11·50
1050	3000k. Female with suckling calf	3·00	3·25
1051	3000k. Male drinking	3·00	3·25
1052	3000k. Head of female	3·00	3·25
1049/52	*Set of 4*	11·00	11·50
MS1053	115×168 mm. Nos. 1049/52, each ×2	17·00	19·00

Nos. 1049/52 were printed together, *se-tenant*, in horizontal strips of four stamps in sheetlets of 16.

The stamps within **MS**1053 are arranged in two blocks of four separated by a horizontal gutter.

K1500

(**248**)

2008 (22 July). No. 821 surch with T **248**.

1054	1500k. on 1400k. 'Why the Stones do not Die'	4·00	3·50

K1500

(**249**)

2009 (17 Feb). No. 933 surch with T **249**.

1055	1500k. on 1200k. orange-red, lemon and ultramarine	1·75	1·75

250 Peonies

2009 (10 Apr). China 2009 World Stamp Exhibition, Luoyang. Litho. P 13.

1056	**250** 2000k. multicoloured	2·25	2·50

No. 1056 was printed in sheetlets of eight stamps.

K1,500

(**251**)

K3,300

(**252**)

2009 (29 May). Nos. 894 and 1035 surch with T **251/2**.

1057	1500k. on 1800k. Boehm's bee-eater	2·25	1·75
1058	3300k. on 2250k. Spotted hyaena	3·75	4·00

K 3,500

(**253**)

K 4,050

K3,800

(**254**)

(**255**)

K 4,950

(**256**)

2009 (1 Dec). Nos. 937, 969, 1010 and 1036 surch with T **253/6**.

1059	3500k. on 2700k. Type **235**	2·50	2·50
1060	3800k. on 2700k. Ngoma dancer	2·50	2·50
1061	4050k. on 2700k. David Livingstone and steam train on Rail Bridge	2·50	2·50
	a. Surch inverted		
1062	4950k. on 2700k. Aardwolf	2·50	2·50
1059/62	*Set of 4*	9·00	9·00

(Des Anja Denker. Litho Enschedé)

2010 (9 Apr). Third Joint Issue of Southern Africa Postal Operators Association Members. World Cup Football Championship, South Africa. Circular designs as T **542** of South Africa, each showing Zakumi mascot, different silhouettes of players on football, and the national flag of a member country. P 13½.

1063	2500k. Zambia	1·40	1·50
1064	4050k. Namibia	2·00	2·25
1065	4950k. South Africa	2·40	2·50
1063/5	*Set of 3*	5·25	5·50
MS1066	188×167 mm. 900k. Lesotho; 1000k. Mauritius; 2050k. Botswana; 2250k. Zimbabwe; 2500k. As No. 1063; 3500k. Malawi; 3800k. Swaziland; 4050k. As No. 1064; 4950k. As No. 1065	6·75	6·75

Nos. 1063/5 and the stamps within **MS**1066 were each perforated in a circle contained within an outer perforated square.

Stamps from **MS**1066 have a shiny gold background; the sheet stamps have a matt background.

It has been reported that these stamps were received in Zambia in early August and not put on sale until mid-August 2010, but the first day covers are dated 9 April 2010.

Similar miniature sheets were issued by Botswana, Lesotho, Malawi, Mauritius, Namibia, South Africa, Swaziland and Zimbabwe.

K2.500 B

(**257**)

2010 (12 Nov). No. 811B surch with T **257**.

1067	2500k. on (B) Sacred ibis	3·25	3·25

STAMP BOOKLETS

B **1**

1964. Black on blue cover as Type *B* **1**. Stitched.

SB1	1s. booklet containing 3d. (No. 78) in block of 4	16·00

B 2

1968. Black on buff covers as Type *B* **2** (No. SB2), or size 82×58 mm (No. SB3). Stitched.

SB2	20n. booklet containing eight 1n. and four 3n. (Nos. 129, 131) in blocks of 4	4·25
SB3	30n. booklet containing twelve 1n. and six 3n. (Nos. 129, 131) in blocks of 6	4·25

B 3

1970 (26 Aug). Black on green cover as Type *B* **3** (No. SB4) or black on rose cover, size 82×58 mm (No. SB5). Stitched.

SB4	20n. booklet containing eight 1n. and four 3n. (Nos. 129, 131) in blocks of 4	6·00
SB5	30n. booklet containing twelve 1n. and six 3n. (Nos. 129, 131) in blocks of 6	6·00

B 4

1976. Black on green cover as Type *B* **4**, (No. SB6), or black on blue cover, size 101×54 mm (No. SB7). Stitched.

SB6	44n. booklet containing four 3n. and eight 4n. (Nos. 228/9) in blocks of 4	11·00
SB7	78n. booklet containing 4n. and 9n. (Nos. 229, 232), each in block of 6	12·00

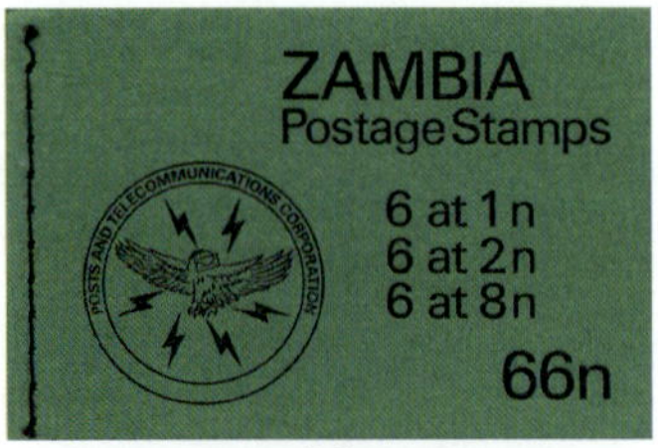

B 5

1981 (2 June). Black on emerald (No. SB8) or orange (No. SB9) covers as Type *B* **5**. Stitched.

SB8	66n. booklet containing 1n., 2n. and 8n. (Nos. 337/8, 340), each in block of 6	5·00
SB9	1k.08 booklet containing 8n. and 10n. (Nos. 340/1), each in block of 6	6·00

POSTAGE DUE STAMPS

D 1

D 2

(Typo D.L.R.)

1929 (June)–**52**. Wmk Mult Script CA. Ordinary paper. P 14.

D1	D **1**	1d. grey-black	2·50	2·50
		a. Chalk-surfaced paper. Blk (22.1.52)	28·00	85·00
		ab. Error. St. Edward's Crown, W**9***b*	£4500	
D2		2d. grey-black	5·50	3·00
D3		3d. grey-black	3·00	26·00
		a. Chalk-surfaced paper. Blk (22.1.52)	8·00	75·00
		ab. Error. Crown missing, W**9***a*	£550	
		ac. Error. St. Edward's Crown, W**9***b*	£350	
D4		4d. grey-black	9·50	38·00
D1/4 *Set of 4*			18·00	60·00
D1s/4s Perf "Specimen" *Set of 4*			£160	

The 2d. is known bisected and used as a 1d. at Luanshya or Nkana on various dates between 1937 and 1951 and on understamped letters from South Africa at Chingola in May 1950 (*Price on cover* £550).

Following the increase in the internal letter rate from 1½d. to 2d. on 1 July 1953 stocks of postage due stamps at Mkushi became exhausted. As an emergency measure the sub-postmaster was authorised to surcharge examples of Nos. 28 and 55 "POSTAGE DUE (or "postage due") 1d." in red by typewriter. Examples properly used on cover between 6 July and 15 September 1953 are of considerable scarcity (*Price on cover* £2250). No unused examples exist.

(Des D. Smith. Litho Govt Ptr, Lusaka)

1963 (10 Dec). P 12½.

D5	D **2**	1d. orange	2·75	5·00
D6		2d. deep blue	2·75	4·25
D7		3d. lake	2·75	7·00
D8		4d. ultramarine	2·75	12·00
D9		6d. purple	9·00	9·50
D10		1s. light emerald	10·00	27·00
		a. Imperf (vert pair)	£275	
		b. Block of four imperf horiz and imperf between vert	£1200	
D5/10 *Set of 6*			27·00	60·00

In all values the stamps in the right-hand vertical row of the sheet are imperforate on the right.

D 3

(Des D. Smith. Litho Govt Printer, Lusaka)

1964 (24 Oct). P 12½.

D11	D **3**	1d. orange	35	2·50
D12		2d. deep blue	35	2·50
D13		3d. lake	45	1·75
D14		4d. ultramarine	45	2·25
D15		6d. purple	45	2·25
D16		1s. light emerald	55	4·25
D11/16 *Set of 6*			2·25	14·00

In all values the left-hand vertical row of the sheet is imperf at left and the bottom horizontal row is imperf at foot. The above were crudely perforated, resulting in variations in the sizes of the stamps.

The above were withdrawn on 15 January 1968 and thereafter decimal currency postage stamps were used for postage due purposes with appropriate cancellations.

Appendix

The following stamps have either been issued in excess of postal needs, or have not been made available to the public in reasonable quantities at face value. Miniature sheets, imperforate stamps etc., are excluded from this section.

1984

Olympic Games, Los Angeles. 90n.×5, each embossed on gold foil.

1987

Classic Cars. 1k.50×25, each embossed on gold foil.

The following issues are reported by the Zambia Postal Services Corporation as being available from Philatelic Counters only. Some isolated examples have been reported on commercial mail.

1997

Disney's Chinese New Year. 250k., 400k., 500k.×7, 600k., 750k., 1000k.
Endangered Species. 500k.×6 1000k.×6
Trains of the World. 200k., 300k., 500k.×7, 900k., 1000k., 1500k.
Golden Wedding of Queen Elizabeth II and Prince Philip. 500k.×6
50th Death Anniv of Paul P. Harris (founder of Rotary International). 1000k.
"Pacific '97" International Stamp Exhibition, San Francisco. Death Centenary of Heinrich von Stephan (founder of the U.P.U) 1000k.×3
Christmas. Religious Paintings. 50k.×2, 100k.×2, 500k., 1000k.

1998

Diana, Princess of Wales Commemoration. 500k.×6, 700k.×6
Flowers. 500k.×13
Chinese New Year ("Year of the Tiger"). 700k.×4
Indian Landmarks. 900k.×3
Indian Art. 700k.×4
World Cup Football Championship, France. 450k.×8, 500k.×16
Muhammed Ali (boxing champion). 500k.×6
Parrots. Lories and Cockatoos. 500k.×6, 1000k.×6
Mushrooms. 250k.×2, 450k.×2, 500k.×2, 900k.×14, 1000k.×2
Cars. 300k., 500k., 900k.×13, 1000k.

1999

Lunar New Year ("Year of the Rabbit"). 700k.×4
Orchids. 100k.×2, 500k.×2, 900k.×18, 1000k.×2
"China '99" International Stamp Exhibition, Beijing. Hang Dagian Paintings. 500k.×10
"Queen Elizabeth the Queen Mother's Century". 2000k.×4
Prehistoric Animals. 50k., 100k., 500k., 900k.×19, 1000k., 1800k.
Fauna and Flora. 50k., 100k., 500k.×5, 700k.×36, 900k., 1000k., 1800k.
250th Birth Anniv of Johann von Goethe (German writer). 2000k.×3
Royal Wedding. 500k., 900k., 1000k.
"iBra'99" International Stamp Exhibition. Nuremberg. 1000k., 3200k.
Cats and Dogs. 50k., 100k.×2, 500k.×2, 900k.×2, 1000k.×25
Princess Diana Photomosaic. 1000k.×8
New Millennium. Events of Second Half of 20th Century. 500k.×18

2000

Butterflies. 400k., 450k., 500k., 800k., 900k., 1000k.×13, 1500k.×12
"The Stamp Show 2000" International Stamp Exhibition, London. Orchids. 1500k.×22

Popes of the Millennium. 1500k.×12
Birds of the World. 400k., 500k., 600k., 700k., 800k., 1000k.×10., 1200k.×10, 1400k.×10, 1500k.×25, 2000k., 3000k.

Zimbabwe

formerly Southern Rhodesia

PRICES FOR STAMPS ON COVER TO 1945
Nos. 1/61 *from* × 2

SELF-GOVERNMENT

The southern part of Rhodesia, previously administered by the British South Africa Company, was annexed by the British Government and granted the status of a self-governing colony from 1 October 1923.

The existing stamps of Rhodesia (the "Admiral" design first issued in 1913) remained in use until 31 March 1924 and continued to be valid for postal purposes until 30 April of that year.

1

2 King George V

3 Victoria Falls

(Recess Waterlow)

1924 (1 Apr)–**29**. P 14.

No.	Type	Description	Unused	Used
1	1	½d. blue-green	3·25	10
		a. Imperf between (horiz pair)	£950	£1100
		b. Imperf between (vert pair)	£950	£1100
		c. Imperf vert (horiz pair)	£1100	
2		1d. bright rose	1·75	10
		a. Imperf between (horiz pair)	£850	£950
		b. Imperf between (vert pair)	£1500	
		c. Perf 12½ (coil) (1929)	2·75	80·00
3		1½d. bistre-brown	3·00	80
		a. Imperf between (horiz pair)	£11000	
		b. Imperf between (vert pair)	£6500	
		c. Printed double, one albino	£375	
4		2d. black and purple-grey	4·50	1·50
		a. Imperf between (horiz pair)	£13000	
5		3d. blue	3·50	4·00
6		4d. black and orange-red	3·25	2·75
7		6d. black and mauve	2·50	6·00
		a. Imperf between (horiz pair)	£38000	
8		8d. purple and pale green	11·00	48·00
		a. Frame double, one albino	£500	
9		10d. blue and rose	16·00	50·00
10		1s. black and light blue	6·00	9·00
11		1s.6d. black and yellow	19·00	32·00
12		2s. black and brown	17·00	17·00
13		2s.6d. blue and sepia	30·00	60·00
14		5s. blue and blue-green	75·00	£160
1/14 *Set of 14*			£180	£350

Prices for "imperf between" varieties are for adjacent stamps from the same pane and not for those separated by wide gutter margins between vertical or horizontal pairs, which come from the junction of two panes.

(T **2** recess by B.W.; T **3** typo by Waterlow)

1931 (1 April)–**37**. T **2** (line perf 12 unless otherwise stated and **3** (comb perf 15×14). (The 11½ perf is comb.).

No.	Type	Description	Unused	Used
15	2	½d. green	1·50	1·00
		a. Perf 11½ (1933)	65	20
		b. Perf 14 (1935)	1·60	30
16		1d. scarlet	1·00	70
		a. Perf 11½ (1933)	2·25	20
		b. Perf 14 (1935)	50	20
16*c*		1½d. chocolate (3.3.33)	55·00	38·00
		d. Perf 11½ (1.4.32)	2·50	80
17	3	2d. black and sepia	5·50	1·40
18		3d. deep ultramarine	10·00	11·00
19	2	4d. black and vermilion	1·25	1·50
		a. Perf 11½ (1935)	18·00	5·00
		b. Perf 14 (10.37)	32·00	60·00
20		6d. black and magenta	2·25	3·00
		a. Perf 11½ (1933)	15·00	1·50
		b. Perf 14 (1936)	7·00	1·50
21		8d. violet and olive-green	1·75	3·25
		a. Perf 11½ (1934)	17·00	32·00
21*b*		9d. vermilion and olive-green (1.9.34)	6·50	10·00
22		10d. blue and scarlet	7·00	2·25
		a. Perf 11½ (1933)	6·00	13·00
23		1s. black and greenish blue	2·00	2·50
		a. Perf 11½ (1935)	£120	50·00
		b. Perf 14 (10.37)	£225	£160
24		1s.6d. black and orange-yellow	10·00	22·00
		a. Perf 11½ (1936)	60·00	£130
25		2s. black and brown	24·00	7·00
		a. Perf 11½ (1933)	35·00	32·00
26		2s.6d. blue and drab	42·00	35·00
		a. Perf 11½ (1933)	28·00	45·00
27		5s. blue and blue-green	50·00	50·00
		a. Printed on gummed side	£7500	
15/27 *Set of 15*			£140	£130

No. 16*c* was only issued in booklets.

PRINTERS. All stamps from Types **4** to **29** were recess-printed by Waterlow and Sons, Ltd, London, except where otherwise stated.

4

1932 (1 May). P 12½.

No.	Type	Description	Unused	Used
29	4	2d. green and chocolate	7·50	1·25
30		3d. deep ultramarine	7·50	2·00
		a. Imperf horiz (vert pair)	£10000	£13000
		b. Imperf between (vert pair)	£28000	

5 Victoria Falls

6 Victoria Falls and Railway Bridge

1935 (6 May). Silver Jubilee. P 11×12.

No.	Type	Description	Unused	Used
31	5	1d. olive and rose-carmine	4·50	3·25
32		2d. emerald and sepia	7·50	8·50
33		3d. violet and deep blue	5·50	11·00
34		6d. black and purple	11·00	23·00
31/4 *Set of 4*			26·00	42·00

1935–41. Inscr "POSTAGE AND REVENUE".

No.	Type	Description	Unused	Used
35	4	2d. green and chocolate (P 12½)	5·00	16·00
		a. Perf 14 (1941)	2·50	10
35*b*		3d. deep blue (P 14) (1938)	4·00	1·25

1937 (12 May). Coronation. P 12½.

No.	Type	Description	Unused	Used
36	6	1d. olive and rose-carmine	60	1·25
37		2d. emerald and sepia	60	1·75
38		3d. violet and blue	3·25	9·50
39		6d. black and purple	1·75	4·00
36/9 *Set of 4*			5·50	15·00

1937 (25 Nov). P 14.

No.	Type	Description	Unused	Used
40	7	½d. green	50	10
41		1d. scarlet	50	10
42		1½d. red-brown	1·00	30
43		4d. red-orange	1·50	10
44		6d. grey-black	1·50	50
45		8d. emerald-green	2·00	4·00
46		9d. pale blue	1·50	1·00
47		10d. purple	3·00	3·25
48		1s. black and blue-green	3·50	10
		a. Frame double, one albino	£3000	
49		1s.6d. black and orange-yellow	14·00	2·75
50		2s. black and brown	23·00	75
51		2s.6d. ultramarine and purple	12·00	8·00
52		5s. blue and blue-green	18·00	3·50
40/52 *Set of 13*			70·00	22·00

Nos. 40/1 exist in coils, constructed from normal sheets.

On No. 48a the frame appears blurred and over-inked.

7 King George VI

8 British South Africa Co's Arms

9 Fort Salisbury, 1890

10 Cecil John Rhodes (after S. P. Kendrick)

11 Fort Victoria

12 Rhodes makes peace

13 Victoria Falls Bridge

14 Statue of Sir Charles Coghlan

15 Lobengula's Kraal and Govt House, Salisbury

Recut shirt collar (R. 6/1)

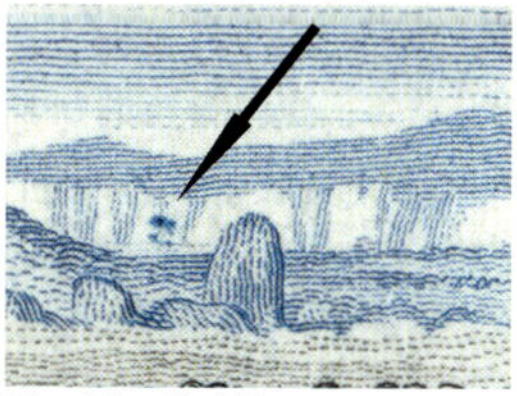

"Cave" flaw (R. 6/6)

(Des Mrs. L. E. Curtis (½d., 1d., 1½d., 3d.), Mrs I. Mount (others))

1940 (3 June). British South Africa Company's Golden Jubilee. T **8/15**. P 14.

53	½d. slate-violet and green	10	65
54	1d. violet-blue and scarlet	10	10
55	1½d. black and red-brown	15	80
	a. Recut shirt collar	25·00	45·00
56	2d. green and bright violet	30	70
57	3d. black and blue	30	1·50
	a. Cave flaw	60·00	£100
58	4d. green and brown	2·25	3·50
59	6d. chocolate and green	2·00	3·50
60	1s. blue and green	2·50	2·00
53/60	*Set of 8*	7·00	11·50

16 Mounted Pioneer

Hat brim retouch (Pl 1B R. 1/8)

Line under saddlebag (Pl 1A R. 6/10)

(Roto South African Govt Printer, Pretoria)

1943 (1 Nov). 50th Anniv of Occupation of Matabeleland. W **9** of South Africa (Mult Springbok) sideways. P 14.

61	**16**	2d. brown and green	20	1·75
		a. Hat brim retouch	24·00	30·00
		b. Line under saddlebag	24·00	30·00

17 Queen Elizabeth II when Princess and Princess Margaret

18 King George VI and Queen Elizabeth

1947 (1 Apr). Royal Visit. T **17/18**. P 14.

62	½d. black and green	30	60
63	1d. black and scarlet	30	60

19 Queen Elizabeth

20 King George VI

21 Queen Elizabeth II when Princess

22 Princess Margaret

Damage to right-hand frame (R. 1/10)

23 Queen Victoria, Arms and King George VI

1947 (8 May). Victory. P 14.

64	**19**	1d. carmine	10	15
65	**20**	2d. slate	10	15
		a. Double print	£2750	
		b. Damaged frame	£200	
66	**21**	3d. blue	85	1·90
67	**22**	6d. orange	30	1·40
64/7 *Set of 4*			1·25	3·25

(Recess B.W.)

1949 (10 Oct). 75th Anniv of U.P.U. As Nos. 138/1414 of Botswana.

68a	2d. slate-green	70	25
69	3d. blue	80	4·25

1950 (12 Sept). Diamond Jubilee of Southern Rhodesia. P 14.

70	**23**	2d. green and brown	1·00	1·75

24 "Medical Services"

(Des A. R. Winter (2d.), Mrs. J. M. Enalim (others))

1953 (15 Apr). Birth Centenary of Cecil Rhodes. T **24** and similar horiz designs. P 14.

71	½d. pale blue and sepia	15	2·25
72	1d. chestnut and blue-green	15	10
73	2d. grey-green and violet	15	10
74	4½d. deep blue-green and deep ultramarine	75	2·75
75	1s. black and red-brown	3·00	1·75
71/5 *Set of 5*		3·75	6·00

Designs:—1d. "Agriculture"; 2d. "Building"; 4½d. "Water Supplies"; 1s. "Transport".

No. 74 also commemorates the Diamond Jubilee of Matabeleland.

1953 (30 May). Rhodes Centenary Exhibition, Bulawayo. As No. 171 of Nyasaland, but without watermark.

76	6d. violet	30	75

30 Queen Elizabeth II

(Recess D.L.R.)

1953 (1 June). Coronation. P 12×12½.

77	**30**	2s.6d. carmine	6·00	6·00

31 Sable Antelope

32 Tobacco planter

33 Rhodes's Grave

34 Farm Worker

35 Flame Lily

36 Victoria Falls

37 Baobab tree

38 Lion

39 Zimbabwe Ruins

40 Birchenough Bridge

41 Kariba Gorge

42 Basket Maker

43 Balancing Rocks

44 Coat of Arms

(Recess, centre typo (4d.), B.W.)

1953 (31 Aug). T **31**/**44**. P 13½×14 (2d., 6d., 5s.), 14 (10s., £1) or 14×13½ (others).

78	½d. grey-green and claret	30	50
79	1d. green and brown	30	10
80	2d. deep chestnut and reddish violet	30	10
81	3d. chocolate and rose-red	55	2·75
82	4d. red, green and indigo	3·50	30
83	4½d. black and deep bright blue	2·50	4·00
84	6d. brown-olive and deep turquoise-green	4·25	1·50
85	9d. deep blue and reddish brown	4·00	4·00
86	1s. reddish violet and light blue	1·75	10
87	2s. purple and scarlet	15·00	6·50
88	2s.6d. yellow-olive and orange-brown	8·00	8·50
89	5s. yellow-brown and deep green	10·00	9·50
90	10s. red-brown and olive	17·00	25·00
91	£1 rose-red and black	19·00	32·00
78/91 *Set of 14*		75·00	85·00

For issues from 1954 to 1963 see under RHODESIA AND NYASALAND.

45 Maize

50 Flame Lily

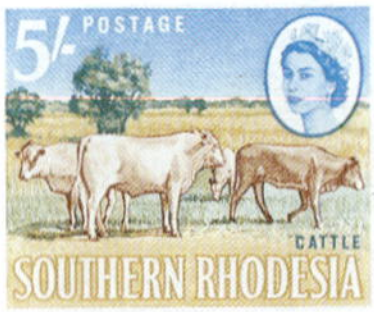

56 Cattle

58 Coat of Arms

2s. Large white dot over "IA" of "RHODESIA" (R. 5/8)

10s. A large coloured flaw on the small guinea fowl gives the appearance of an extra feather (R. 2/2)

(Des V. Whiteley. Photo Harrison)

1964 (19 Feb). T **45**, **50**, **56**, **58** and similar horiz designs. P 14½ (½d. to 4d.), 13½×13 (6d. to 2s.6d.) or 14½×14 (others).

92	½d. yellow, yellow-green and light blue	20	2·50
93	1d. reddish violet and yellow-ochre	15	10
	a. Reddish violet omitted	£3250	
94	2d. yellow and deep violet	60	10
95	3d. chocolate and pale blue	20	10
96	4d. yellow-orange and deep green	30	10
97	6d. carmine-red, yellow and deep dull green	40	10
98	9d. red-brown, yellow and olive-green	2·75	1·50
99	1s. blue-green and ochre	3·75	30
	a. Blue-green (Queen and emeralds) omitted	£4000	
100	1s.3d. red, violet and yellow-green	3·00	10
101	2s. blue and ochre	2·50	3·50
	a. Dot over "IA"	22·00	
102	2s.6d. ultramarine and vermilion	4·00	1·00
	a. Vermilion omitted	£4500	
	b. Ultramarine omitted	£13000	
103	5s. light brown, bistre-yellow and light blue	3·50	2·50
104	10s. black, yellow-ochre, light blue and carmine-red	11·00	8·50
	a. Extra "feather"	26·00	40·00
105	£1 brown, yellow-green, buff and salmon-pink	8·00	20·00
92/105 *Set of* 14		35·00	35·00

Designs: (*As T* **45**)—1d. African Buffalo; 2d. Tobacco; 3d. Greater Kudu; 4d. Citrus. (*As T* **50**)—9d. Ansellia Orchid; 1s. Emeralds; 1s.3d. Aloe; 2s. Lake Kyle; 2s.6d. Tigerfish. (*As T* **56**)—10s. Helmet Guineafowl.

Nos. 92 and 93 exist in coils constructed from normal sheets.

Nos. 102a and 102b occur on different sheets and involve one or two vertical rows of stamps in each instance. They were caused by the printing press being stopped and then restarted. Three such sheets showing No. 102a have been reported.

See also Nos. 359/72 of Rhodesia.

In October 1964 Southern Rhodesia was renamed Rhodesia.

In October 1964 Southern Rhodesia was renamed Rhodesia.

RHODESIA

59 "Telecommunications"

(Des V. Whiteley. Photo Harrison)

1965 (17 May). I.T.U. Centenary. P 14½.

351	**59**	6d. violet and light yellow-olive	1·50	40
352		1s.3d. violet and lilac	1·50	40
353		2s.6d. violet and light brown	3·50	4·50
351/3 *Set of* 3			6·00	4·75

60 Bangala Dam

63 Sir Winston Churchill, Quill, Sword and Houses of Parliament

(Des V. Whiteley. Photo Harrison)

1965 (19 July). Water Conservation. T **60** and similar vert designs. Multicoloured. P 14.

354	3d. Type **60**	30	10
355	4d. Irrigation canal	1·25	1·25
356	2s.6d. Cutting sugar cane	2·25	3·50
354/6 *Set of* 3		3·50	4·25

(Des H. Baxter. Photo Harrison)

1965 (16 Aug). Churchill Commemoration. P 14½.

357	**63**	1s.3d. black and bright blue	70	35

UNILATERAL DECLARATION OF INDEPENDENCE

Independence was declared by Rhodesia on 11 November 1965 but this was not recognised by the British Government. Following a conference in London during 1979 it was agreed that the British Government should resume control, pending elections to he held in February 1980.

After the elections Rhodesia became an independent republic within the Commonwealth on 18 April 1980, as ZIMBABWE.

64 Coat of Arms

(Des Col. C. R. Dickenson. Litho Mardon Printers, Salisbury)

1965 (8 Dec). "Independence". P 11.

358	**64**	2s.6d. multicoloured	15	15
		a. Imperf (pair)	£900	

INDEPENDENCE
11th November
1965

INDEPENDENCE
11th November 1965
(65)

5/-
(66)

1966 (17 Jan).

(*a*) *Nos. 92/105 optd with T* **65** *or larger (5s. to £1) by Mardon Printers, Salisbury*

359	½d. yellow, yellow-green and light blue	10	10
	a. Pair, one stamp without opt	£6500	
360	1d. reddish violet and yellow-ochre	10	10
361	2d. yellow and deep violet	10	10
362	3d. chocolate and pale blue	10	10

No.	Description	Unused	Used
363	4d. yellow-orange and deep green	15	10
364	6d. carmine-red, yellow & deep dull green	15	10
	a. Vetical strip of 6, bottom three stamps without opt	£4000	
365	9d. red-brown, yellow and olive-green	30	10
	a. Opt double	£700	
366	1s. blue-green and ochre	40	10
	a. Opt double	£700	
	b. Vertical strip of 6, bottom three stamps without opt	£4000	
367	1s.3d. red, violet and yellow-green	50	50
368	2s. blue and ochre	60	3·25
	a. Dot over '1A'	12·00	
369	2s.6d. ultramarine and vermilion	60	1·00
370	5s. light brown, bistre-yellow & light blue	2·00	5·50
	a. Opt double	£750	
371	10s. black, yellow-ochre, lt blue & carm-red	5·00	2·25
	a. Extra "feather"	30·00	
372	£1 brown, yell-green, buff & salmon-pink	1·25	2·25

(b) No. 357 surch with T **66**

No.	Description	Unused	Used
373	5s. on 1s.3d. black and bright blue (R.)	5·00	12·00
	a. "5/-" omitted		
359/73	*Set of 15*	15·00	24·00

Owing to the existence of forgeries, the errors should only be purchased when accompanied by a certificate of genuineness. Unique pairs of the 1d and 3d exist with the overprint omitted from one stamp, but both are defective. Other overprint errors exist from the clandestine use of the original settings.

67 Emeralds

(Des V. Whiteley. Photo Harrison)

1966 (9 Feb). As Nos. 92/105, but inscr "RHODESIA" as T **67**. Some designs and colours changed. P 14½ (1d. to 4d.), 13½×13 (6d. to 2s.6d) or 14½×14 (5s. to £1).

No.	Type	Description	Unused	Used
374	–	1d. reddish violet and yellow-ochre	10	10
375	–	2d. yellow-orange and dp grn (as No. 96)	10	10
		a. Yellow-orange omitted	£2500	
376	–	3d. chocolate and pale blue	10	10
		a. Chocolate omitted	£5000	
		b. Pale blue omitted	£3750	
377	**67**	4d. emerald and sepia	1·75	10
378	**50**	6d. carmine-red, yellow & dp dull green	15	10
379	–	9d. yellow and deep violet (as No. 94)	60	20
380	**45**	1s. yellow, yellow-green and light blue	15	10
381	–	1s.3d. blue and ochre (as No. 101)	25	15
		a. Ochre omitted	£3250	
382	–	1s.6d. red-brn, yell & ol-grn (as No. 98)	2·25	25
383	–	2s. red, violet and yell-grn (as No. 100)	60	80
384	–	2s.6d. blue, vermilion & turquoise-blue	1·50	20
385	**56**	5s. light brown, bistre-yellow & lt blue	1·00	90
386	–	10s. black, yell-ochre, lt blue & carm-red	4·25	3·50
387	**58**	£1 brown, yell-grn, buff & salmon-pink	3·25	7·00
374/87		*Set of 14*	14·00	12·00

Nos. 379/80 are in larger format, as T **50**.

No. 374 exists in coils constructed from normal sheets. Coil-vending machines were withdrawn from service in 1967.

No. 375a occured on single rows from two separate sheets, No. 376a in the bottom row of a sheet, No. 376b in the top two rows of a sheet and No. 381a in the third vertical row on two sheets.

For stamps printed by lithography, see Nos. 397/407.

PRINTERS. All the following stamps were printed by lithography by Mardon Printers, Salisbury.

68 Zeederberg Coach, *circa* 1895

(Des V. Whiteley (Nos. 388/90))

1966 (2 May). 28th Congress of Southern Africa Philatelic Federation ("Rhopex"). T **68** and similar horiz designs. P 14½.

No.	Description	Unused	Used
388	3d. multicoloured	15	10
389	9d. grey-buff, sepia and grey-green	15	20
390	1s.6d. pale blue and black	25	30
391	2s.6d. salmon-pink, pale dull grn & blk	30	55
388/91	*Set of 4*	7·50	13·00
MS392	126×84 mm. Nos. 388/91 (*toned paper*)	75	1·00
	a. White paper	5·00	11·00

Designs:—9d. Sir Rowland Hill; 1s.6d. The Penny Black; 2s.6d. Rhodesian stamp of 1892 (No. 12).

The 3d., 2s.6d. and minature sheet exist imperforate from sheets prepared for presentation purposes.

69 de Havilland D.H.89 Dragon Rapide (1946)

1966 (1 June). 20th Anniv of Central African Airways. T **69** and similar horiz designs. P 14½×14.

No.	Description	Unused	Used
393	6d. black, blue, yellow and green	1·00	35
394	1s.3d. blue, yellow-orange, black and green	1·00	40
395	2s.6d. black, blue, yellow and green	1·50	1·50
396	5s. black and blue	2·00	4·50
393/6	*Set of 4*	5·00	6·00

Aircraft:—1s.3d. Douglas DC-3 (1953); 2s.6d. Vickers Viscount 748 *Matopos* (1956); 5s. B.A.C. One Eleven 200.

The 6d., 2s.6d. and 5s. values exist imperforate from sheets prepared for presentation purposes.

1966–69. As Nos. 374/87 but litho. P 14½ (1d. to 2s.) or 14½×14 (others).

No.	Description	Unused	Used
397	1d. reddish violet and yellow-ochre (*shades*) (2.6.66)	15	10
398	2d. orange and green (1.11.67)	85	65
399	3d. chocolate-brn & pale grnsh bl (29.1.68)	1·50	10
400	4d. emerald, bistre-brown & drab (21.9.66)	65	10
401	6d. carmine-red, yell & ol-grey (1.11.66)	60	50
402	9d. yellow and light violet (20.11.67)	50	10
403	1s.3d. blue and ochre (1.11.66)	1·50	30
404	2s. dull red, violet & sage-green (18.7.66)	1·50	4·00
405	5s. yellow-brown, deep bistre-yellow and light blue (25.6.66)	2·00	5·00
406	10s. black, buff, lt bl & carm-red (10.8.66)	8·00	14·00
407	£1 pale brown, yellow-green, brown-ochre and salmon (10.8.66)	8·00	18·00
397/407	*Set of 11*	22·00	38·00

In addition to the change in printing process from photogravure to lithography and the difference in perforation in the 6d. to 2s. values (14½ instead of 13½×13) and shade variations, the oval portrait frame is larger (and in some values thicker) in the 1d. to 2s., and in the 1s.3d. the Queen's head is also larger.

Trial printings, made in June 1966, exist of the 5s., 10s. and £1 values on a slightly thinner paper. These are rare.

The 1d., 3d. and 5s. values exist imperforate from sheets prepared for presentation purposes.

70 Kudu

1967–68. Dual Currency Issue. As Nos. 376, 380 and 382/4 but value in decimal currency in addition as in T **70**. P 14½. White gum (No. 408) or cream gum (others).

No.	Description	Unused	Used
408	3d./2½c. chocolate-brown and pale greenish blue (15.3.67)	50	15
409	1s./10c. yell, grn & greenish bl (1.11.67)	50	25
410	1s.6d./15c. red-brown, yellow and yellow-green (11.3.68)	4·75	70
411	2s./20c. dull red, viol and sage-grn (11.3.68)	3·25	4·00
412	2s.6d./25c. ultramarine-blue, vermilion and bright turquoise-blue (9.12.68)	20·00	26·00
408/12	*Set of 5*	26·00	28·00

71 Dr. Jameson (administrator)

(Des from painting by F. M. Bennett)

1967 (17 May). Famous Rhodesians (1st issue) and 50th Death Anniv of Dr. Jameson. P 14½.

413	**71**	1s.6d. multicoloured	20	35

See also Nos. 426, 430, 457, 458, 469, 480, 488 and 513.

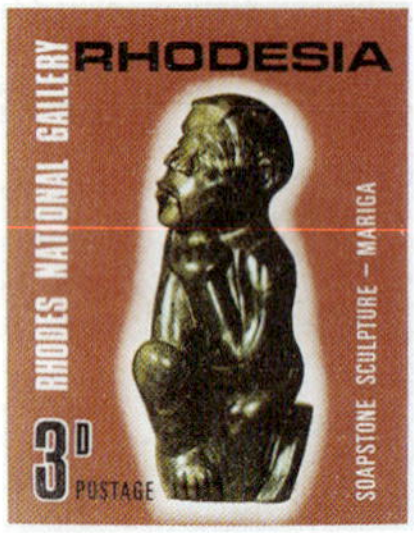

72 Soapstone Sculpture (Joram Mariga)

1967 (12 July). Tenth Anniv of Opening of Rhodes National Gallery. T **72** and similar vert designs. P 14½×14 (3d., 9d.) or 14 (others).

414	3d. reddish chestnut, yellow-olive and black	10	10
415	9d. lt greenish blue, dp olive-brown & black	20	20
	a. Perf 13½	5·50	15·00
416	1s.3d. multicoloured	20	25
417	2s.6d. multicoloured	25	60
414/17	*Set of 4*	65	1·00

Designs: 9d. "The Burgher of Calais" (detail, Rodin); 1s.3d. "The Knight" (stamp design wrongly inscr) (Roberto Crippa); 2s.6d. "John the Baptist" (M. Tossini).

73 Baobab Tree

1967 (6 Sept). Nature Conservation. T **73** and similar designs. P 14½.

418	4d. light brown and black	10	20
419	4d. yellow-olive and black	25	20
420	4d. deep grey and black	25	20
421	4d. yellow-orange and black	10	20
418/21	*Set of 4*	60	70

Designs: *Horiz*—No. 418, Type **73**; 419, White Rhinoceros; 420, African Elephants. *Vert*—No. 421, Wild Gladiolus.

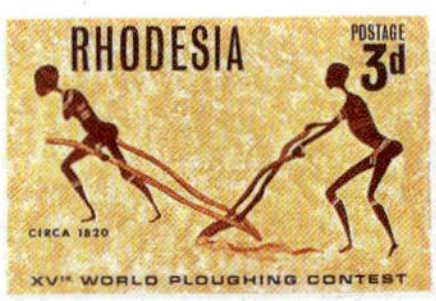

74 Wooden Hand Plough

(Des Rose Martin)

1968 (26 Apr). 15th World Ploughing Contest, Norton, Rhodesia. T **74** and similar horiz designs. P 14½.

422	3d. pale orange, orange-verm & lake-brown	10	10
423	9d. multicoloured	15	20
424	1s.6d. multicoloured	20	55
425	2s.6d. multicoloured	20	75
422/5	*Set of 4*	60	1·40

Designs: 9d. Early wheel plough; 1s.6d. Steam powered tractor, and ploughs; 2s.6d. Modern tractor, and plough.

75 Alfred Beit (national benefactor)

(Des from painting by A. Haywood)

1968 (15 July). Famous Rhodesians (2nd issue). P 14½.

426	**75**	1s.6d. pale orange, black and brown	20	30

76 Raising the Flag, Bulawayo, 1893

(Des Rose Martin)

1968 (4 Nov). 75th Anniv of Matabeleland. T **76** and similar vert designs. P 14½.

427	3d. pale orange, red-orange and black	15	10
428	9d. multicoloured	15	20
429	1s.6d. pale turquoise-green, deep emerald and blackish green	20	60
427/9	*Set of 3*	45	80

Designs:—9d. View and coat of arms of Bulawayo; 1s.6d. Allan Wilson (combatant in the Matabele War).

77 Sir William Henry Milton (administrator)

(Des from painting by S. Kendrick)

1969 (15 Jan). Famous Rhodesians (3rd issue). P 14½.

430	**77**	1s.6d. multicoloured	40	55

78 2 ft Gauge Steam Locomotive No. 15, 1897

(Des Rose Martin)

1969 (22 May). 70th Anniv of Opening of Beira-Salisbury Railway. T **78** and similar horiz designs showing locomotives. Multicoloured. P 14½.

431	3d. Type **78**	30	10
432	9d. 7th Class steam locomotive No. 43, 1903	50	40
433	1s.6d. Beyer Peacock 15th Class steam locomotive No. 413, 1951	60	75
434	2s.6d. Class DE2 diesel-electric locomotive No. 1203, 1955	1·00	3·00
431/4	*Set of 4*	2·25	3·75

79 Low Level Bridge

(Des Rose Martin)

1969 (18 Sept). Bridges of Rhodesia. T **79** and similar horiz designs. Multicoloured. P 14½.

435	3d. Type **79**	20	10
436	9d. Mpudzi bridge	40	20
437	1s.6d. Umniati bridge	60	60
438	2s.6d. Birchenough bridge	80	1·25
435/8	*Set of 4*	1·75	1·90

(New Currency. 100 cents = 1 dollar)

80 Harvesting Wheat

81 Devil's Cataract, Victoria Falls

(Des from colour-transparencies (3, 6c.), Rose Martin (others))

1970 (17 Feb)–**73**. Decimal Currency. T **80/1** and similar horiz designs. P 14½.

439	1c. multicoloured	10	10
	a. Booklet pane of 4	30	
440	2c. multicoloured	10	10
441	2½c. multicoloured	10	10
	a. Booklet pane of 4	35	
441*c*	3c. multicoloured (1.1.73)	1·25	10
	ca. Booklet pane of 4	4·50	
442	3½c. multicoloured	10	10
	a. Booklet pane of 4	65	
442*b*	4c. multicoloured (1.1.73)	1·75	1·00
	ba. Booklet pane of 4	6·00	
443	5c. multicoloured	15	10
443*b*	6c. multicoloured (1.1.73)	4·00	3·75
443*c*	7½c. multicoloured (1.1.73)	7·00	60
444	8c. multicoloured	75	20
445	10c. multicoloured	60	10
446	12½c. multicoloured	1·50	10
446*a*	14c. multicoloured (1.1.73)	12·00	70
447	15c. multicoloured	1·25	15
448	20c. multicoloured	1·00	15
449	25c. multicoloured	4·00	60
450	50c. turquoise and ultramarine	1·25	55
451	$1 multicoloured	4·75	2·00
452	$2 multicoloured	8·50	15·00
439/52 *Set of* 19		45·00	23·00

Designs: *Size as T* **80**—2c. Pouring molten metal; 2½c. Zimbabwe Ruins; 3c. Articulated lorry; 3½c. and 4c. Statute of Cecil Rhodes; 5c. Mine headgear. *Size as T* **81**—6c. Hydrofoil *Seaflight*; 7½c. As 8c.; 10c. Yachting on Lake McIlwaine; 12½c. Hippopotamus in river; 14c. and 15c. Kariba Dam; 20c. Irrigation canal. *As T* **80/1** *but larger* (31×26 *mm*)—25c. Bateleurs; 50c. Radar antenna and Vickers Viscount 810; $1 "Air Rescue"; $2 Rhodesian flag.

Booklet panes Nos. 439a, 441a, 441ca, 442a and 442ba have margins all round.

82 Despatch Rider, *circa* 1890

83 Mother Patrick (Dominican nurse and teacher)

(Des Rose Martin)

1970 (1 July). Inauguration of Posts and Telecommunications Corporation. T **82** and similar horiz designs. Multicoloured. P 14½.

453	2½c. Type **82**	30	10
454	3½c. Loading mail at Salisbury airport	40	50
455	15c. Constructing telegraph line, *circa* 1890	45	1·25
456	25c. Telephone and modern telecommunications equipment	50	2·00
453/6 *Set of* 4		1·50	3·50

(Des Rose Martin from photograph)

1970 (16 Nov). Famous Rhodesians (4th issue). P 14½.

457	**83**	15c. multicoloured	60	50

84 Frederick Courteney Selous (big-game hunter, explorer and pioneer)

(Des from painting by L. C. Dickinson)

1971 (1 Mar). Famous Rhodesians (5th issue). P 14½.

458	**84**	15c. multicoloured	40	70

85 Hoopoe

86 Porphyritic Granite

(Des from photographs by Peter Ginn)

1971 (1 June). Birds of Rhodesia (1st series). T **85** and similar multicoloured designs. P 14½.

459	2c. Type **85**	35	20
460	2½c. Half-collared Kingfisher (*horiz*)	35	10
461	5c. Golden-breasted Bunting	50	15
462	7½c. Carmine Bee Eater	60	15
463	8c. Red-eyed Bulbul	60	20
464	25c. Senegal Wattled Plover (*horiz*)	1·00	1·25
459/64 *Set of* 6		3·00	2·00

See also Nos. 537/42.

(Des from photographs by University of Rhodesia and Dept of Geological Survey)

1971 (30 Aug). "Granite 71" Geological Symposium. T **86** and similar vert designs. Multicoloured. P 14.

465	2½c. Type **86**	30	10
466	7½c. Muscovite mica seen through microscope	40	15
467	15c. Granite seen through microscope	65	35
468	25c. Geological map of Rhodesia	65	1·25
465/8 *Set of* 4		1·75	1·60

87 Dr. Robert Moffat (missionary)

1972 (14 Feb). Famous Rhodesians (6th issue). P 14½.

469	**87**	13c. multicoloured	50	75

88 Bird ("Be Airwise")

89 "The Three Kings"

(Des C. Lawton)

1972 (17 July). "Prevent Pollution". T **88** and similar horiz designs. Multicoloured. P 14½.

470	2½c. Type **88**	15	10
471	3½c. Antelope ("Be Countrywise")	15	20
472	7c. Fish ("Be Waterwise")	15	30
473	13c. City ("Be Citywise")	20	55
470/3 *Set of* 4		60	1·00

1972 (28 Aug). "Rhophil '72". As Nos. 439a, 441a and 442a with commemorative inscr in margins. Each 66×78 mm.

MS474 1c. multicoloured	1·10	2·00
MS475 2½c. multicoloured	1·10	2·00
MS476 3½c. multicoloured	1·10	2·00
MS474/6 *Set of* 3 sheets	3·00	5·50

(Des Rose Martin)

1972 (18 Oct). Christmas. P 14.

477	**89**	2c. multicoloured	10	10
478		5c. multicoloured	15	20
479		13c. multicoloured	30	55
477/9 *Set of* 3			50	75

90 Dr. David Livingstone

91 W.M.O. Emblem

1973 (2 Apr). Famous Rhodesians (7th issue). P 14.

480	**90**	14c. multicoloured	50	75

(Des S. J. Ivey)

1973 (2 July). I.M.O./W.M.O. Centenary. P 14.

481	**91**	3c. multicoloured	10	10
482		14c. multicoloured	30	15
483		25c. multicoloured	40	75
481/3 *Set of 3*			70	90

92 Arms of Rhodesia

1973 (10 Oct). 50th Anniv of Responsible Government. P 14.

484	**92**	2½c. multicoloured	10	10
485		4c. multicoloured	15	10
486		7½c. multicoloured	20	15
487		14c. multicoloured	35	1·00
484/7 *Set of 4*			70	1·10

93 George Pauling (construction engineer)

(Des P. Birch)

1974 (15 May). Famous Rhodesians (8th issue). P 14.

488	**93**	14c. multicoloured	50	1·25

94 Greater Kudu

95 Thunbergia

96 *Charaxes varanes*

(Des J. Huntly)

1974 (14 Aug)–**76**. Various vert designs as T **94/6**. Multicoloured. P 14½ (1 to 14c.) or 14 (others).

(a) Antelopes. Size as T **94**

489	1c. Type **94**	10	10
490	2½c. Eland	75	10
	a. Booklet pane of 4	2·75	
491	3c. Roan Antelope	10	10
	a. Booklet pane of 4	70	
492	4c. Reedbuck	20	10
	a. Booklet pane of 4	1·00	
493	5c. Bushbuck	20	60

(b) Wild Flowers. Size as T **95**

494	6c. Type **95**	20	10
495	7½c. Flame Lily	50	20
496	8c. As 7½c. (1.7.76)	20	10
497	10c. Devil Thorn	20	10
498	12c. Hibiscus (1.7.76)	40	2·00
499	12½c. Pink Sabi Star	1·00	35
500	14c. Wild Pimpernel	1·00	35
501	15c. As 12½c. (1.7.76)	40	75
502	16c. As 14c. (1.7.76)	40	30

(c) Butterflies. Size as T **96**

503	20c. Type **96**	1·00	35
504	24c. *Precis hierta* (s sp *cebrene*) (1.7.76)	40	40
505	25c. As 24c.	1·50	1·50
506	50c. *Colotis regina*	40	60
507	$1 *Graphium antheus*	40	60
508	$2 *Hamanumida daedalus*	40	75
489/508 *Set of 20*		8·75	8·50

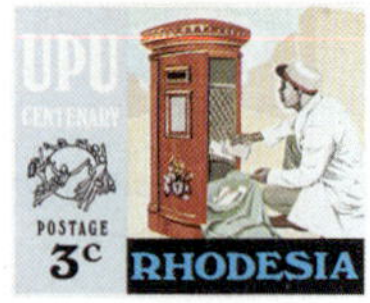

97 Collecting Mail

98 Thomas Baines (artist)

(Des M. Chase)

1974 (20 Nov). Centenary of Universal Postal Union. T **97** and similar horiz designs. Multicoloured. P 14.

509	3c. Type **97**	15	10
510	4c. Sorting mail	15	10
511	7½c. Mail delivery	20	20
512	14c. Weighing parcel	30	90
509/12 *Set of 4*		70	1·10

(Des from self-portrait)

1975 (12 Feb). Famous Rhodesians (9th issue). P 14.

513	**98**	14c. multicoloured	50	60

99 *Euphorbia confinalis*

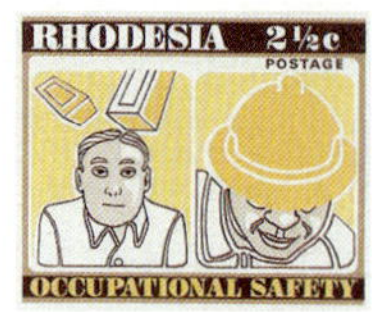

100 Prevention of Head Injuries

(Des Nancy Abrey)

1975 (16 July). International Succulent Congress, Salisbury ("Aloe '75"). T **99** and similar vert designs. Multicoloured. P 14½.

514	2½c. Type **99**	10	10
515	3c. *Aloe excelsa*	10	10
516	4c. *Hoodia lugardii*	10	10
517	7½c. *Aloe ortholopha*	15	10
518	14c. *Aloe musapana*	30	10
519	25c. *Aloe saponaria*	50	2·00
514/19 *Set of 6*		1·10	2·25

(Des Val Bond)

1975 (15 Oct). Occupational Safety. T **100** and similar horiz designs. Multicoloured. P 14.

520	2½c. Type **100**	10	10
521	4c. Bandaged hand and gloved hand	15	10
522	7½c. Broken glass and eye	15	15
523	14c. Blind man and welder with protective mask	20	55
520/3 *Set of 4*		50	80

101 Telephones, 1876 and 1976

8c

(**102**)

(Des M. Chase)

1976 (10 Mar). Telephone Centenary. T **101** and similar vert design. P 14.

524	3c. grey-black and pale blue	10	10
525	14c. brownish black and light stone	20	55

Design:—14c. Alexander Graham Bell.

1976 (1 July). Nos. 495, 500 and 505 surch as T **102**.

No.	Description	Mint	Used
526	8c. on 7½c. Flame Lily	15	15
	a. Surch double, one albino		
527	16c. on 14c. Wild Pimpernel	15	15
528	24c. on 25c. *Precis hierta* (s sp *cebrene*)	20	80
526/8	*Set of 3*	45	1·00

103 Roan Antelope

(Des N. Pedersen)

1976 (21 July). Vulnerable Wildlife. T **103** and similar horiz designs. Multicoloured. P 14.

No.	Description	Mint	Used
529	4c. Type **103**	10	10
530	6c. Brown Hyena	15	60
531	8c. Hunting Dog	15	10
532	16c. Cheetah	20	35
529/32	*Set of 4*	55	1·00

104 Msasa

(Des Nancy Abrey)

1976 (17 Nov). Trees of Rhodesia. T **104** and similar vert designs. Multicoloured. P 14.

No.	Description	Mint	Used
533	4c. Type **104**	10	10
534	6c. Red Mahogany	10	10
535	8c. Mukwa	15	10
536	16c. Rhodesian Teak	20	55
533/6	*Set of 4*	50	75

105 Common Bulbul

(Des B. Finch)

1977 (16 Mar). Birds of Rhodesia (2nd series). T **105** and similar vert designs. Multicoloured. P 14.

No.	Description	Mint	Used
537	3c. Type **105**	15	10
538	4c. Yellow-mantled Whydah	15	10
539	6c. Cape Longclaw	20	60
540	8c. Eastern Long-tailed Shrike	20	35
541	16c. Lesser Blue-eared Glossy Starling	25	60
542	24c. Green Wood Hoopoe	30	1·10
537/42	*Set of 6*	1·10	2·50

106 "Lake Kyle" (Joan Evans)

1977 (20 July). Landscape Paintings. T **106** and similar horiz designs. Multicoloured. P 14.

No.	Description	Mint	Used
543	3c. Type **106**	10	10
544	4c. "Chimanimani Mountains" (Joan Evans)	10	10
545	6c. "Rocks near Bonsor Reef" (Alice Balfour)	10	30
546	8c. "A Dwala near Devil's Pass" (Alice Balfour)	10	10
547	16c. "Zimbabwe" (Alice Balfour)	15	30
548	24c. "Victoria Falls" (Thomas Baines)	25	60
543/8	*Set of 6*	70	1·25

107 Virgin and Child

108 Fair Spire

(Des Dianne Deudney)

1977 (16 Nov). Christmas. P 14.

No.	Type	Description	Mint	Used
549	**107**	3c. multicoloured	10	10
550		6c. multicoloured	10	20
551		8c. multicoloured	10	10
552		16c. multicoloured	15	30
549/52		*Set of 4*	40	65

1978 (15 Mar). Trade Fair Rhodesia, Bulawayo. T **108** and similar vert design. Multicoloured. P 14.

No.	Description	Mint	Used
553	4c. Type **108**	10	10
554	8c. Fair Spire (*different*)	15	25

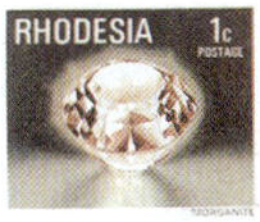

109 Morganite

110 White Rhinoceros

111 Odzani Falls

(Des N. Pedersen (1 to 17c.), D. Myles (21c. to $20))

1978 (16 Aug). Multicoloured.

(a) Horiz designs as T **109** *showing gemstones.* P 14½.

No.	Description	Mint	Used
555	1c. Type **109**	10	10
556	3c. Amethyst	10	10
557	4c. Garnet	10	10
558	5c. Citrine	10	10
559	7c. Blue Topaz	10	10

(b) Horiz designs as T **110** *showing wild animals.* P 14½.

No.	Description	Mint	Used
560	9c. Type **110**	15	10
561	11c. Lion	10	20
562	13c. Warthog	10	1·25
563	15c. Giraffe	15	20
564	17c. Common Zebra	15	10

(c) Horiz designs as T **111** *showing waterfalls.* P 14

No.	Description	Mint	Used
565	21c. Type **111**	15	40
566	25c. Goba Falls	15	15
567	30c. Inyangombi Falls	15	15
568	$1 Bridal Veil Falls	20	35
569	$2 Victoria Falls	30	60
555/69	*Set of 15*	1·60	3·25

112 Wright Flyer I

(Des C. Herbert)

1978 (18 Oct). 75th Anniv of Powered Flight. T **112** and similar horiz designs. Multicoloured. P 14.

570	4c. Type **112**	10	10
571	5c. Bleriot XI	10	10
572	7c. Vickers Vimy *Silver Queen II*	10	10
573	9c. Armstrong Whitworth A.W.15 Atlanta	10	10
574	17c. Vickers Viking 1B *Zambezi*	10	10
575	25c. Boeing 720B	15	50
570/5 *Set of 6*		50	75

ZIMBABWE

REPUBLIC

Rhodesia became independent under majority rule on 18 April 1980 and was renamed Zimbabwe.

PRINTERS. All stamps of Zimbabwe were printed in lithography by Mardon Printers (Pvt) Ltd, subsequently (from Nos. 724/7) National Printing and Packaging, Harare, *unless otherwise stated.*

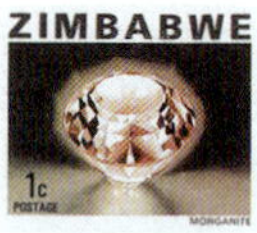

113 Morganite

114 Rotary Anniversary Emblem

1980 (18 Apr)–**83**. As Nos. 555/69 and new value (40c.), all inscr "ZIMBABWE" as in T **113**.

576	1c. Type **113**	10	30
577	3c. Amethyst	15	30
578	4c. Garnet	15	10
	a. Imperf (pair)	£120	
579	5c. Citrine	15	10
580	7c. Blue Topaz	15	10
581	9c. White Rhinoceros	15	10
582	11c. Lion	15	15
583	13c. Warthog	15	15
584	15c. Giraffe	15	20
585	17c. Common Zebra	15	20
586	21c. Odzani Falls	15	25
587	25c. Goba Falls	15	30
588	30c. Inyangombi Falls	15	50
588*a*	40c. Bundi Falls (14.3.83)	2·50	4·00
589	$1 Bridal Veil Falls	20	1·50
590	$2 Victoria Falls	35	3·00
576/90 *Set of 16*		4·25	10·00

1980 (18 June). 75th Anniv of Rotary International. P 14½.

591 **114**	4c. multicoloured	10	10
592	13c. multicoloured	15	20
593	21c. multicoloured	20	35
594	25c. multicoloured	20	60
591/4 *Set of 4*		50	1·10
MS595 140×84 mm. Nos. 591/4		75	1·60

115 Olympic Rings

(Des Nancy Abrey)

1980 (19 July). Olympic Games, Moscow. P 14½.

596 **115**	17c. multicoloured	30	40

116 Gatooma Post Office, 1912

(Des Mortimer Tiley and Partners Ltd)

1980 (17 Oct). 75th Anniv of Post Office Savings Bank. T **116** and similar horiz designs. P 14.

597	5c. black and yellow-brown	10	10
598	7c. black and red-orange	10	10
599	9c. black and olive-yellow	10	10
600	17c. black and light blue	25	25
597/600 *Set of 4*		40	40
MS601 125×84 mm. Nos. 597/600		55	1·25

Designs:—7c. Salisbury Post Office, 1912; 9c. Umtali Post Office, 1901; 17c. Bulawayo Post Office, 1895.

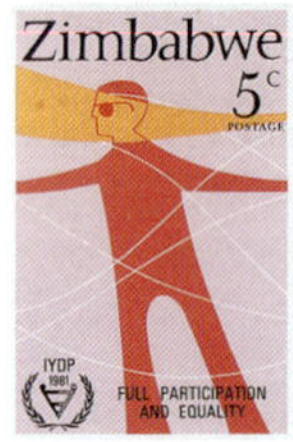

117 Stylized Blind Person

118 Msasa

(Des Rose Martin)

1981 (23 Sept). International Year of Disabled Persons. T **117** and similar vert designs showing stylized figures. Multicoloured. P 14.

602	5c. Type **117**	10	10
603	7c. Deaf person	10	10
604	11c. Person with one leg	15	10
605	17c. Person with one arm	20	25
602/5 *Set of 4*		50	50

(Des Nancy Abrey)

1981 (4 Dec). National Tree Day. T **118** and similar vert designs. Multicoloured. P 14½.

606	5c. Type **118**	10	10
607	7c. Mopane	10	10
608	21c. Flat-crowned Acacia	20	25
609	30c. Pod Mahogany	25	45
606/9 *Set of 4*		60	80

119 Painting from Gwamgwadza Cave, Mtoko Area

1982 (17 Mar). Rock Paintings. T **119** and similar horiz designs showing paintings from various locations. Multicoloured. P 14½.

610	9c. Type **119**	15	10
611	11c. Epworth Mission, near Harare	15	10
612	17c. Diana's Vow, near Harare	20	15
613	21c. Gwamgwadza Cave, Mtoko Area (*different*)	25	15
614	25c. Mucheka Cave, Msana Communal Land	35	50
615	30c. Chinzwini Shelter, Chiredzi Area	25	70
610/15 *Set of 6*		1·25	1·50

120 Scout Emblem

121 Dr. Robert Koch

(Des Rose Martin)

1982 (21 July). 75th Anniv of Boy Scout Movement. T **120** and similar vert designs. Multicoloured. P 14½×14.

616	9c. Type **120**	15	10
617	11c. Scouts around campfire	15	10
618	21c. Scouts map-reading	20	35
619	30c. Lord Baden-Powell	25	65
616/19 *Set of 4*		70	1·10

(Des Rose Martin)

1982 (17 Nov). Centenary of Dr. Robert Koch's Discovery of Tubercle Bacillus. T **121** and similar horiz design. P 14.

620	11c. salmon, black and greenish grey	40	10
621	30c. multicoloured	60	1·50

Design:—30c. Man looking through microscope.

122 "Wing Woman" (Henry Mudzengerere)

123 Traditional Ploughing Team (moving right)

1983 (14 Mar). Commonwealth Day. Sculptures. T **122** and similar multicoloured designs. P 14.

622	9c. Type **122**	10	10
623	11c. "Telling Secrets" (Joseph Ndandarika) (*horiz*)	10	10
624	30c. "Hornbill Man" (John Takawira) (*horiz*)	15	15
625	$1 "The Chief" (Nicholas Mukomberanwa)	40	1·25
622/5	*Set of 4*	65	1·40

(Des Rose Martin)

1983 (13 May). 30th World Ploughing Contest, Zimbabwe. T **123** and similar horiz designs. Multicoloured. P 14.

626	21c. Type **123**	15	25
	a. Horiz pair. Nos. 626/7	30	50
627	21c. Traditional ploughing team (moving left)	15	25
628	30c. Tractor ploughing	20	35
	a. Horiz pair. Nos. 628/9	40	70
629	30c. Modern plough	20	35
626/9	*Set of 4*	65	1·10

The two designs of each value were issued in horizontal *se-tenant* pairs, forming composite designs throughout the sheets.

124 Postman on Cycle

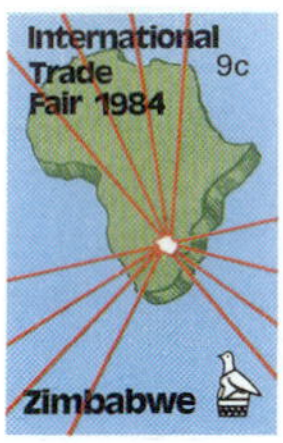

125 Map of Africa showing Zimbabwe

(Des R. Phillips)

1983 (12 Oct). World Communications Year. T **124** and similar multicoloured designs. P 14.

630	9c. Type **124**	20	10
631	11c. Aircraft controller directing airliner	20	10
632	15c. Switchboard operator	20	20
633	17c. Printing works	20	20
634	21c. Road transport (*horiz*)	35	40
635	30c. Rail transport (*horiz*)	45	1·00
630/5	*Set of 6*	1·40	1·75

(Des Bunty Woods and Nancy Abrey)

1984 (11 Apr). Zimbabwe International Trade Fair. T **125** and similar vert designs. Multicoloured. P 14½.

636	9c. Type **125**	10	10
637	11c. Globe	15	10
638	30c. Zimbabwe flag and Trade Fair logo	45	50
636/8	*Set of 3*	65	60

126 Cycling

(Des Vivienne Fick (11c.), Joanna Hogg (21c.), Blessing Chikoore (30c.), Wayne Gubb (40c.))

1984 (18 July). Olympic Games, Los Angeles. Children's Pictures. T **126** and similar horiz designs. Multicoloured. P 14½.

639	11c. Type **126**	40	15
640	21c. Swimming	20	20
641	30c. Running	25	55
642	40c. Hurdling	25	1·10
639/42	*Set of 4*	1·00	1·75

127 Liberation Heroes

128 African Fish Eagle

(Des N. Pearce (11c.), J. Akester (others))

1984 (8 Aug). Heroes' Days. T **127** and similar multicoloured designs showing various aspects of Heroes' Acre. P 14½.

643	9c. Type **127**	15	10
644	11c. Symbolic tower and flame (*vert*)	15	10
645	17c. Bronze sculpture (*vert*)	20	30
646	30c. Section of bronze mural	30	70
643/6	*Set of 4*	70	1·00

(Des B. Finch)

1984 (10 Oct). Birds of Prey. T **128** and similar vert designs. Multicoloured. P 14½.

647	9c. Type **128**	25	15
648	11c. Long-crested Eagle	25	15
649	13c. Bateleur	30	30
650	17c. Verreaux's Eagle	35	20
651	21c. Martial Eagle	45	35
652	30c. Bonelli's Eagle	65	1·00
647/52	*Set of 6*	2·00	1·90

129 9th Class Locomotive No. 86

130 "Intelsat V" Telecommunications Satellite

(Des G. Cameron)

1985 (15 May). "Zimbabwe Steam Safaris". Railway Locomotives. T **129** and similar horiz designs. Multicoloured. P 14½.

653	9c. Type **129**	30	15
654	11c. 12th Class locomotive No. 190	30	15
655	17c. 15th Class Beyer-Garratt locomotive No. 424 *Isilwane*	45	20
656	30c. 20th Class Garrett locomotive No. 726 *Gwaai*	90	1·25
653/6	*Set of 4*	1·75	1·60

1985 (8 July). Earth Satellite Station, Mazowe. T **130** and similar multicoloured design. P 14½×14 (26c.) or 14½ (57c.).

657	26c. Type **130**	40	25
658	57c. Earth Satellite Station, Mazowe (65×25 mm)	1·00	2·50

131 Tobacco

(Des Rose Rigden)

1985 (21 Aug)–**88**. National Infrastructure. T **131** and similar horiz designs. Multicoloured. P 14½.

659	1c. Type **131**	10	10
	a. Perf 14	28·00	1·50

660	3c. Maize	10	10
	a. Perf 14	10·00	1·50
661	4c. Cotton	15	10
	a. Perf 14	40·00	1·50
662	5c. Tea	50	10
	a. Perf 14	40·00	1·50
663	10c. Cattle	30	10
	a. Perf 14	20·00	1·50
664	11c. Birchenough Bridge	75	10
665	12c. Ore stamp mill	1·25	10
666	13c. Gold pouring	2·75	15
	a. Perf 14	20·00	3·00
667	15c. Dragline coal mining	2·25	15
	a. Perf 14	40·00	3·00
668	17c. Uncut amethyst	2·75	1·25
669	18c. Electric locomotive	2·25	2·75
670	20c. Kariba Dam	1·50	30
	a. Perf 14	20·00	3·00
671	23c. Elephants at water hole	4·25	45
672	25c. Sunset over Zambezi	65	30
	a. Perf 14	20·00	4·00
673	26c. Baobab tree	65	20
674	30c. Ruins of Great Zimbabwe	75	70
675	35c. Traditional dancing	60	30
676	45c. Village women crushing maize	1·00	40
677	57c. Woodcarving	75	70
678	$1 Playing Mbira (musical instrument)	1·25	90
	a. Perf 14	—	20·00
679	$2 Mule-drawn Scotch cart	2·00	3·00
680	$5 Zimbabwe coat-of-arms	2·25	4·50
659/80 *Set of 22*		26·00	15·00

The stamps perforated 14 date from the introduction of a new perforating head in 1988.

132 Chief Mutapa Gatsi Rusere and 17th-century Seal

133 Computer Operator

(Des C. Herbert)

1985 (18 Sept). 50th Anniv of National Archives. T **132** and similar horiz designs. Multicoloured. P 14½.

681	12c. Type **132**	20	15
682	18c. Chief Lobengula, seal and 1888 Treaty	25	40
683	26c. Exhibition gallery	35	45
684	35c. National Archives building	45	75
681/4 *Set of 4*		1·10	1·60

(Des C. Herbert)

1985 (13 Nov). United Nations Decade for Women. T **133** and similar horiz designs. Multicoloured. P 14½.

685	10c. Type **133**	20	10
686	17c. Nurse giving injection	30	20
687	26c. Woman student	60	1·40
685/7 *Set of 3*		1·00	1·50

134 Harare Conference Centre

(Des C. Herbert)

1986 (29 Jan). Harare International Conference Centre. T **134** and similar horiz design. Multicoloured. P 14½.

688	26c. Type **134**	40	20
689	35c. Interior of conference hall	70	90

135 Grain Storage Silo

136 *Bunaeopsis jacksoni*

(Des C. Herbert)

1986 (1 Apr). 6th Anniv of Southern African Development Co-ordination Conference. T **135** and similar horiz designs. Multicoloured. P 14½.

690	12c. Type **135**	55	20
691	18c. Rhinoceros and hawk at sunset	2·50	1·25
692	26c. Map showing S.A.D.C.C. member states, and Boeing 737	2·50	1·50
693	35c. Map and national flags of S.A.D.C.C. members	2·75	2·00
690/3 *Set of 4*		7·50	4·50

1986 (18 June). Moths of Zimbabwe. T **136** and similar horiz designs. Multicoloured. P 14½×14.

694	12c. Type **136**	35	20
695	18c. *Deilephila nerii*	50	45
696	26c. *Bunaeopsis zaddachi*	55	60
697	35c. *Heniocha apollonia*	80	2·75
694/7 *Set of 4*		2·00	3·50

137 Victoria Falls

(Des C. Herbert)

1986 (26 Aug). 8th Non-Aligned Summit Conference. T **137** and similar horiz design. Multicoloured. P 14½×14 (26c.) or 14½ ($1).

698	26c. Type **137**	75	30
699	$1 Ruins of Great Zimbabwe (62×24 *mm*)	1·50	4·50

138 Sopwith Motorcycle (1921)

(Des G. Cameron)

1986 (8 Oct). Centenary of Motoring. T **138** and similar horiz designs. Multicoloured. P 14½.

700	10c. Type **138**	20	10
701	12c. Gladiator motor car (1902)	20	10
702	17c. Douglas motorcycle (1920)	30	10
703	26c. Ford "Model A" (1930)	40	15
704	35c. Schacht motor car (1909)	55	1·00
705	40c. Benz three-wheeled car (1886)	80	1·50
700/5 *Set of 6*		2·25	2·50

139 Growth Monitoring

140 Barred Owlet

(Des Barbara Chalk)

1987 (11 Feb). Child Survival Campaign. T **139** and similar vert designs. Multicoloured. P 14×14½.

706	12c. Type **139**	75	1·25
	a. Block of 4. Nos. 706/9	2·75	4·50
707	12c. Breast-feeding	75	1·25
708	12c. Oral rehydration therapy	75	1·25
709	12c. Immunization	75	1·25
706/9 *Set of 4*		2·75	4·50

Nos. 706/9 were printed together, *se-tenant*, in blocks of four throughout the sheet.

(Des B. Finch)

1987 (15 Apr). Owls (1st series). T **140** and similar vert designs. Multicoloured. P 14½.

710	12c. Type **140**	2·00	30
711	18c. Pearl-spotted Owlet	2·50	70

712	26c. White-faced Scops Owl	3·00	70
713	35c. African Scops Owl	4·00	2·50
710/13	*Set of 4*	10·50	3·75

See also Nos. 850/3 and 988/91.

141 Brownie, Guide and Ranger saluting ("Commitment")

142 Common Grey Duiker

(Des Barbara Connelly)

1987 (24 June). 75th Anniv of Girl Guides' Association of Zimbabwe. T **141** and similar horiz designs. Multicoloured. P 14½.

714	15c. Type **141**	40	15
715	23c. Guides preparing meal over campfire ("Adventure")	55	20
716	35c. Guide teaching villagers to read ("Service")	70	30
717	$1 Handshake and globe ("International Friendship")	1·50	2·50
714/17	*Set of 4*	2·75	2·75

(Des Patricia Wilson)

1987 (7 Oct). Duikers of Africa Survey. T **142** and similar horiz designs each showing duiker and distribution map. Multicoloured. P 14½×14.

718	15c. Type **142**	45	15
719	23c. Zebra Duiker	55	20
720	25c. Yellow-backed Duiker	55	70
721	30c. Blue Duiker	60	90
722	35c. Jentink's Duiker	60	1·00
723	38c. Red Duiker	75	1·50
718/23	*Set of 6*	3·25	4·00

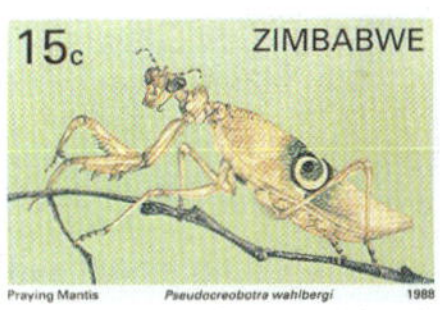

143 *Pseudocreobotra wahlberghi* (mantid)

144 "Cockerel" (Arthur Azevedo)

(Des Janet Duff)

1988 (12 Jan). Insects. T **143** and similar horiz designs. Multicoloured. P 14½.

724	15c. Type **143**	70	15
725	23c. *Dicranorrhina derbyana* (beetle)	85	30
726	35c. *Dictyophorus spumans* (grasshopper)	1·10	85
727	45c. *Chalcocoris rutilus* (bug)	1·40	2·00
724/7	*Set of 4*	3·50	3·00

1988 (14 Apr). 30th Anniv of National Gallery of Zimbabwe. T **144** and similar multicoloured designs showing painting (38c.) or sculptures (others). P 14×14½ (vert) or 14½×14 (horiz).

728	15c. Type **144**	20	10
729	23c. "Man into Hippo" (Bernard Matemera)	30	20
730	30c. "Spirit Python" (Henry Munyaradzi)	35	30
731	35c. "Spirit Bird carrying People" (Thomas Mukarobgwa) (*horiz*)	35	30
732	38c. "The Song of the Herd Boy" (George Nene) (*horiz*)	35	40
733	45c. "War Victim" (Joseph Muzondo) (*horiz*)	40	50
728/33	*Set of 6*	1·75	1·60

145 *Aloe cameronii var. bondana*

146 White-faced Whistling Duck

(Des Nancy Abrey)

1988 (14 July). Aloes. T **145** and similar vert designs. Multicoloured. P 14½.

734	15c. Type **145**	30	10
735	23c. *Orbeopsis caudata*	45	20
736	25c. *Euphorbia wildii*	45	35
737	30c. *Euphorbia fortissima*	50	45
738	35c. *Aloe aculeata*	50	55
739	38c. *Huernia zebrina*	60	70
734/9	*Set of 6*	2·50	2·00

(Des B. Finch and C. Herbert)

1988 (6 Oct). Wild Ducks and Geese of Zimbabwe. T **146** and similar horiz designs. Multicoloured. P 14½×14.

740	15c. Type **146**	75	20
741	23c. African Pygmy Goose	85	20
742	30c. Hottentot Teal	95	85
743	35c. Comb Duck ("Knob-billed Duck")	1·10	1·25
744	38c. White-backed Duck	1·10	1·50
745	45c. Maccoa Duck	1·60	2·75
740/5	*Set of 6*	5·75	6·00

147 O'Shaughnessy's Banded Gecko

148 Spotted Leaved Arum-Lily

1989 (10 Jan). Geckos. T **147** and similar horiz designs. Multicoloured. P 14½.

746	15c. Type **147**	80	15
747	23c. Tiger Rock Gecko	95	40
748	35c. Tasman's Gecko	1·50	1·25
749	45c. Bibron's Gecko	1·75	2·00
746/9	*Set of 4*	4·50	3·50

1989 (12 Apr). Wild Flowers. T **148** and similar vert designs. Multicoloured. P 14½.

750	15c. Type **148**	50	10
751	23c. Grassland Vlei-lily	60	25
752	30c. Manica Protea	65	40
753	35c. Flame Lily	75	40
754	38c. Poppy Hibiscus	80	55
755	45c. Blue Sesbania	90	65
750/5	*Set of 6*	3·75	2·00

149 Red-breasted Tilapia

150 Black Rhinoceros

(Des C. Herbert)

1989 (12 July). Fish (1st series). T **149** and similar horiz designs. Multicoloured. P 14½.

756	15c. Type **149**	50	15
757	23c. Chessa	70	25
758	30c. Eastern Bottlenose	75	50
759	35c. Vundu	75	50
760	38c. Large-mouthed Black Bass	80	80
761	45c. Lesser Tigerfish	1·00	1·50
756/61	*Set of 6*	4·00	3·25

See also Nos. 864/9.

1989 (10 Oct). Endangered Species. T **150** and similar horiz designs. Multicoloured. P 14½×14.

762	15c. Type **150**	1·25	40
763	23c. Cheetah	1·25	45
764	30c. Wild Dog	1·40	90
765	35c. Pangolin	1·40	1·25
766	38c. Brown Hyena	1·50	2·00
767	45c. Roan Antelope	1·60	2·25
762/7	*Set of 6*	7·50	6·50

151 Giant Tigerfish

152 Headrest

153 Bicycles

(Des Janet Duff (1 to 9c.), Rose Rigden (15 to 30c.), Nancy Abrey (33c. to $2))

1990 (2 Jan). Multicoloured.

(a) Horiz designs as T **151** showing wildlife. P 14

768	1c. Type **151**	30	20
	a. Perf 14½	1·00	10
769	2c. Helmet Guineafowl	1·00	20
	a. Perf 14½	1·50	20
770	3c. Scrub Hare	20	20
	a. Perf 14½	1·00	10
771	4c. Temminck's Ground Pangolin	40	20
	a. Perf 14½	75	10
772	5c. Greater Kudu	40	20
	a. Perf 14½	1·00	10
	b. Imperf (pair)	£160	
773	9c. Black Rhinoceros	1·75	30
	a. Perf 14½	1·75	30

(b) Horiz designs as T **152** showing cultural artifacts. P 14½×14

774	15c. Type **152**	40	20
775	20c. Hand axe and adze	20	20
776	23c. Gourd and water pot	20	20
777	25c. Snuff container	20	20
778	26c. Winnowing tray and basket	70	30
779	30c. Grinding stone	30	30

(c) Horiz designs as T **153** showing transport. P 14½

780	33c. Type **153**	1·75	30
781	35c. Buses	2·00	40
782	38c. Diesel train	2·50	40
783	45c. Mail motorcycle and trailer	1·75	40
784	$1 Air Zimbabwe Boeing 737 airliner	2·75	90
785	$2 Lorry	2·00	1·60
768/85	*Set of 18*	17·00	6·00

154 Pres. Mugabe and Joshua Nkomo at Signing of Unity Accord, 1987

155 Runhare House, 1986

(Adapted Nancy Abrey)

1990 (17 Apr). 10th Anniv of Independence. T **154** and similar horiz designs. Multicoloured. P 14½×14.

786	15c. Type **154**	45	10
787	23c. Conference Centre, Harare	50	20
788	30c. Children in class	55	40
789	35c. Intelsat aerial, Mazowe Earth Satellite Station	65	70
790	38c. National Sports Stadium	65	80
791	45c. Maize field	1·00	1·40
786/91	*Set of 6*	3·50	3·25

1990 (11 July). Centenary of the City of Harare. T **155** and similar horiz designs. Multicoloured. P 14½.

792	15c. Type **155**	30	10
793	23c. Market Hall, 1894	50	20
794	30c. Charter House, 1959	55	35
795	35c. Supreme Court, 1927	60	80
796	38c. Standard Chartered Bank, 1911	60	90
797	45c. The Town House, 1933	80	1·40
792/7	*Set of 6*	3·00	3·25

156 Speaker's Mace

157 Small-spotted Genet

1990 (17 Sept). 36th Commonwealth Parliamentary Conference, Harare. T **156** and similar vert design. Multicoloured. P 14½.

798	35c. Type **156**	50	25
799	$1 Speaker's chair	1·25	2·00

(Des Barbara Chalk)

1991 (15 Jan). Small Mammals. T **157** and similar horiz designs. Multicoloured. P 14½×14.

800	15c. Type **157**	1·00	20
801	23c. Red Squirrel	1·10	30
802	35c. Night-ape	1·60	1·25
803	45c. Bat-eared Fox	2·25	2·25
800/3	*Set of 4*	5·50	3·50

158 Hosho (rattles)

159 Snot-apple

(Des R. Pletts)

1991 (16 Apr). Traditional Musical Instruments. T **158** and similar vert designs. Multicoloured. P 14½.

804	15c. Type **158**	50	10
805	23c. Mbira (thumb piano)	55	15
806	30c. Ngororombe (pan pipes)	60	40
807	35c. Chipendani (mouth bow)	70	70
808	38c. Marimba (xylophone)	70	80
809	45c. Ngoma (drum)	80	1·10
804/9	*Set of 6*	3·50	2·75

(Des Barbara Chalk)

1991 (17 July). Wild Fruits (1st series). T **159** and similar vert designs. Multicoloured. P 14×14½.

810	20c. Type **159**	55	10
811	39c. Marula	55	30
812	51c. Mobola Plum	65	80
813	60c. Water Berry	75	85
814	65c. Northern Dwaba Berry	80	85
815	77c. Mahobohobo	90	1·10
810/15	*Set of 6*	3·75	3·50

See also Nos. 1038/43.

160 Bridal Veil Falls

161 Lion

(Des R. Jeffrey)

1991 (16 Oct). Commonwealth Heads of Government Meeting, Harare. T **160** and similar vert designs. Multicoloured. P 14½.

816	20c. Type **160**	80	15
817	39c. Meeting logo	65	35
818	51c. Chinhoyi Caves	1·50	75
819	60c. Kariba Dam	1·50	1·00
820	65c. Victoria Falls	1·75	1·25

821 77c. Balancing rocks 2·00 1·50
816/21 *Set of 6* 7·50 4·50

(Des R. Pletts)

1992 (8 Jan). Wildlife Conservation. Big Cats. T **161** and similar horiz designs. Multicoloured. P 14½×14.

822 20c. Type **161** 90 15
823 39c. Leopard 1·60 40
824 60c. Cheetah 2·25 1·75
825 77c. Serval 2·50 2·00
822/5 *Set of 4* 6·50 3·75

162 *Amanita zambiana*

163 Common Bulbul

(Des R. Pletts)

1992 (8 Apr). Edible Mushrooms. T **162** and similar vert designs. Multicoloured. P 14×14½.

826 20c. Type **162** 40 15
827 39c. *Boletus edulis* 55 30
828 51c. *Termitomyces* sp 60 60
829 60c. *Cantharellus densifolius* 70 80
830 65c. *Cantharellus longisporus* 75 85
831 77c. *Cantharellus cibarius* 1·00 1·50
826/31 *Set of 6* 3·50 3·75

(Des R. Pletts)

1992 (7 July). Birds. T **163** and similar vert designs. Multicoloured. P 14½.

832 25c. Type **163** 80 15
833 59c. Fiscal Shrike 1·10 45
834 77c. Forktailed Drongo 1·25 80
835 90c. Cardinal Woodpecker 1·40 95
836 98c. Yellow-billed Hornbill 1·40 95
837 $1.16 Crested Francolin 1·50 1·40
832/7 *Set of 6* 6·75 4·25

164 *Charaxes jasius*

165 Uranium

(Des R. Pletts)

1992 (15 Oct). Butterflies. T **164** and similar horiz designs. Multicoloured. P 14½×14.

838 25c. Type **164** 1·10 20
839 59c. *Eronia leda* 1·75 75
840 77c. *Princeps ophidicephalus* 1·90 1·25
841 90c. *Junonia oenone* 2·50 1·75
842 98c. *Danaus chrysippus* 2·50 1·90
843 $1.16 *Junonia octavia* 2·75 2·25
838/43 *Set of 6* 11·00 7·25

(Des R. Jeffrey)

1993 (12 Jan). Minerals. T **165** and similar horiz designs. Multicoloured. P 14½×14.

844 25c. Type **165** 1·60 20
845 59c. Chrome 2·25 55
846 77c. Copper 2·75 1·00
847 90c. Coal 3·00 1·50
848 98c. Gold 3·00 1·75
849 $1.16 Emerald 3·25 2·25
844/9 *Set of 6* 14·00 6·50

(Des B. Finch)

1993 (6 Apr). Owls (2nd series). Vert designs as T **140**. Multicoloured. P 14½.

850 25c. African Wood Owl 2·75 50
851 59c. Pel's Fishing Owl 3·75 1·10
852 90c. Spotted Eagle Owl 4·75 4·50
853 $1.16 Verreaux's Eagle Owl ("Giant Eagle Owl") 5·50 6·50
850/3 *Set of 4* 15·00 11·50

166 Hadyana (relish pot)

167 *Polystachya dendrobiflora*

(Des Dianne Deudney)

1993 (13 July). Household Pottery. T **166** and similar horiz designs. Multicoloured. P 14½×14.

854 25c. Type **166** 65 10
855 59c. Chirongo (water jar) 80 30
856 77c. Mbiya (relish bowl) 90 60
857 90c. Pfuko (water jar) 1·00 85
858 98c. Tsaya (cooking pot) 1·10 85
859 $1.16 Gate (beer pot) 1·25 1·00
854/9 *Set of 6* 5·25 3·25

(Des Paula Ware)

1993 (12 Oct). Orchids. T **167** and similar vert designs. Multicoloured. P 14×14½.

860 35c. Type **167** 1·25 20
861 $1 *Diaphananthe subsimplex* 2·25 75
862 $1.50 *Ansellia gigantea* 3·00 1·90
863 $1.95 *Vanilla polyepis* 3·25 2·50
860/3 *Set of 4* 8·75 4·75

(Des C. Herbert)

1994 (20 Jan). Fish (2nd series). Horiz designs as T **149**. Multicoloured. P 14½.

864 35c. Manyame Labeo ("Hunyani Salmon") 50 10
865 $1 Sharp-toothed Catfish ("Barbel") 80 30
866 $1.30 Rainbow Trout 90 65
867 $1.50 African Mottled Eel 95 70
868 $1.65 Common Carp 1·00 85
869 $1.95 Nembwe ("Robustus Bream") 1·10 1·00
864/9 *Set of 6* 4·75 3·25

168 City Hall, 1940

(Des Janet Duff)

1994 (5 Apr). Centenary of Bulawayo. T **168** and similar horiz designs. Multicoloured. P 14½.

870 35c. Type **168** 15 10
871 80c. Cresta Churchill Hotel, 1974 30 20
872 $1.15 High Court, 1938 40 40
873 $1.75 Douslin House, 1902 50 70
874 $1.95 Goldfields Building, 1895 60 90
875 $2.30 Parkade Centre, 1975 85 1·25
870/5 *Set of 6* 2·50 3·00

169 Strelitzia

(Des Dianne Deudney)

1994 (12 July). Export Flowers. T **169** and similar vert designs. Multicoloured. P 14½.

876 35c. Type **169** 40 10
877 80c. Protea 70 25
878 $1.15 Phlox 85 60
879 $1.75 Chrysanthemum 95 1·40

880	$1.95 Ullum	1·25	2·25
881	$2.30 Rose	1·50	2·75
876/81	*Set of 6*	5·00	6·50

170 The Annunciation

(Des Paula Ware)

1994 (11 Oct). Christmas. T **170** and similar vert designs. Multicoloured. P 14½.

882	35c. Type **170**	30	10
883	80c. Journey to Bethlehem	55	15
884	$1.15 The Nativity	70	40
885	$1.75 Shepherds	1·00	1·50
886	$1.95 Wise Men	1·10	1·90
887	$2.30 Mary and Jesus	2·50	2·50
882/7	*Set of 6*	5·50	6·00

171 Harvesting Maize

(Des R. Pletts (1c. to 4c.), C. Herbert (5c. on 50c.), D. Hobert (70c. to $10))

1995 (17 Jan)–**96**. Zimbabwe Culture. T **171** and similar horiz designs. Multicoloured. P 14.

888	1c. Type **171**	10	60
889	2c. Loading sugar cane	10	60
890	3c. Sunflowers	10	60
891	4c. Sorghum	10	60
892	5c. Miners	1·25	45
893	10c. Drilling for gold	1·75	50
894	20c. Opencast coal mining, Wankie	2·00	50
895	30c. Chrome smelting, Kwekwe	2·00	30
896	40c. Opencast iron extraction, Redcliff	2·00	20
896*a*	45c. Underground mining team (3.6.96)	2·00	20
897	50c. Gold smelting	2·00	20
898	70c. Bogie Clock Tower, Gweru	30	20
899	80c. Masvingo Watchtower	30	20
900	$1 Hanging Tree, Harare	30	25
901	$2 Cecil House, Harare	40	55
902	$5 The Toposcope, Harare	50	1·00
903	$10 Paper House, Kwekwe	70	1·50
888/903	*Set of 17*	14·00	7·75

172 Spider-hunting Wasp

173 Football

(Des Janet Duff)

1995 (4 Apr). Insects. T **172** and similar horiz designs. Multicoloured. P 14½.

904	35c. Type **172**	60	10
905	$1.15 Emperor Dragonfly	1·40	55
906	$1.75 Foxy Charaxes (butterfly)	2·25	2·75
907	$2.30 Antlion	2·75	3·50
904/7	*Set of 4*	6·25	6·25

(Des Paula Ware)

1995 (11 July). 6th All-Africa Games, Harare. T **173** and similar vert designs, each showing sport within map of Africa. Multicoloured. P 14×14½.

908	35c. Type **173**	40	10
909	80c. Running	50	20
910	$1.15 Boxing	55	30
911	$1.75 Swimming	80	1·00
912	$1.95 Hockey	3·50	3·25
913	$2.30 Volleyball	1·75	3·25
908/13	*Set of 6*	6·75	7·25

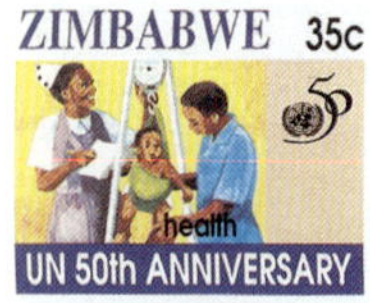

174 Weighing Baby (Health)

175 Fernandoa Tree

(Des Jane Debney)

1995 (17 Oct). 50th Anniv of United Nations. T **174** and similar horiz designs. Multicoloured. P 14½×14.

914	35c. Type **174**	15	10
915	$1.15 Women at pump (Environment)	30	35
916	$1.75 Workers on lorry (Food Distribution)	50	80
917	$2.30 Teacher and children (Education)	60	1·60
914/17	*Set of 4*	1·40	2·50

(Des Janet Duff)

1996 (24 Jan). Indigenous Flowering Trees. T **175** and similar vert designs. Multicoloured. P 14½.

918	45c. Type **175**	30	10
919	$1 Round Leaf Mukwa	50	20
920	$1.50 Luckybean Tree	70	60
921	$2.20 Winter Cassia	85	1·00
922	$2.50 Sausage Tree	90	1·40
923	$3 Sweet Thorn	1·00	1·75
918/23	*Set of 6*	3·75	4·50

176 Mazvikadei Dam

(Des R. Pletts)

1996 (9 Apr). Dams of Zimbabwe. T **176** and similar horiz designs. Multicoloured. P 14½.

924	45c. Type **176**	15	10
925	$1.50 Mutirikwi Dam	45	40
926	$2.20 Ncema Dam	65	90
927	$3 Odzani Dam	75	1·40
924/7	*Set of 4*	1·75	2·50

177 Matusadonha National Park at Sunset

178 Carved Frog

(Des Paula Ware)

1996 (18 July). Scenic Views. T **177** and similar horiz designs. Multicoloured. P 14½.

928	45c. Type **177**	15	10
929	$1.50 Juliasdale rocky outcrop	45	40
930	$2.20 Honde Valley	75	1·00
931	$3 Finger Rocks at Morgenster Mission	85	1·60
928/31	*Set of 4*	2·00	2·75

(Des M. Nyoni)

1996 (15 Oct). Animal Wood Carvings. T **178** and similar horiz designs. Multicoloured. P 14½×14.

932	45c. Type **178**	15	10
933	$1.50 Tortoise	30	20
934	$1.70 Kudu	35	40
935	$2.20 Chimpanzee	50	80
936	$2.50 Porcupine	55	90
937	$3 Rhinoceros	60	1·10
932/7	*Set of 6*	2·25	3·25

179 Mashona Cow

180 Cycad

(Des R. Pletts)

1997 (7 Jan). Cattle Breeds. T **179** and similar horiz designs. Multicoloured. P 14½.

938	45c. Type **179**	35	10
939	$1.50 Tuli cow	65	25
940	$2.20 Nkoni bull	85	1·00
941	$3 Brahman bull	1·25	1·75
938/41	*Set of 4*	2·75	2·75

(Des Paula Ware)

1997 (15 Apr). 10th Meeting of Convention on International Trade in Endangered Species Members, Harare. T **180** and similar horiz designs. Multicoloured. P 14½.

942	45c. Type **180**	10	10
943	$1.50 Peregrine Falcon	1·25	65
944	$1.70 Temminck's Ground Pangolin	30	60
945	$2.20 Black Rhinoceros	1·25	1·50
946	$2.50 African Elephant	1·25	1·50
947	$3 Python	70	1·60
942/7	*Set of 6*	4·25	5·50

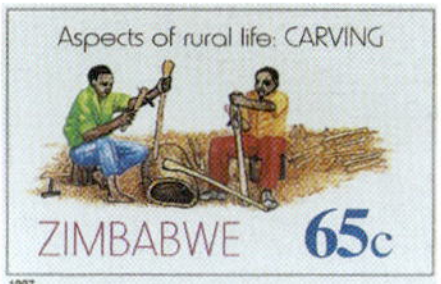

181 Wood Carving

182 Passenger Coach No. 1826

(Des Dianne Deudney)

1997 (22 July). Rural Life. T **181** and similar horiz designs. Multicoloured. P 14½.

948	65c. Type **181**	15	10
949	$1 Winnowing	15	10
950	$2.40 Dancing	25	35
951	$2.50 Ploughing	25	35
952	$3.10 Stamping cereals	30	50
953	$4.20 Fetching water	45	70
948/53	*Set of 6*	1·40	1·90

(Des Janet Duff)

1997 (28 Oct). Centenary of Zimbabwe Railways. T **182** and similar horiz designs. Multicoloured. P 14½.

954	65c. Type **182**	20	15
955	$1 Class 12 steam locomotive No. 257	20	15
956	$2.40 Class 16A steam locomotive No. 605	25	35
957	$2.50 Class EL 1 electric locomotive No. 4107	25	35
958	$3.10 Steam locomotive No. 7 *Jack Tar*	30	50
959	$4.20 Class DE 2 diesel-electric locomotive No. 1211	40	70
954/9	*Set of 6*	1·40	2·00

183 Aardwolf

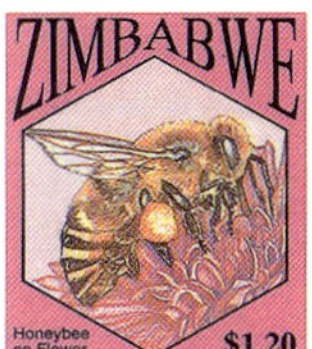

184 Honeybee on Flower

(Des C. Herbert)

1998 (20 Jan). Lesser Known Animals of Zimbabwe. T **183** and similar horiz designs. Multicoloured. P 14½.

960	65c. Type **183**	20	10
961	$2.40 Large Grey Mongoose	25	30
962	$3.10 Clawless Otter	30	55
963	$4.20 Antbear	35	80
960/3	*Set of 4*	1·00	1·60

(Des Jan Desmond and Gaye Dixon)

1998 (14 Apr). Bees and Bee-keeping. T **184** and similar vert designs. Multicoloured. P 14×14½.

964	$1.20 Type **184**	30	10
965	$4.10 Queen, worker and drone	35	35
966	$4.70 Queen and retinue	35	35
967	$5.60 Rural bee-keeper	45	50
968	$7.40 Commercial bee-keepers	65	80
969	$9.90 Products of the hive	85	1·10
964/9	*Set of 6*	2·75	3·00

185 Fossil Fish

186 Yellow-bellied Sunbird

(Des Janet Duff)

1998 (21 July). Fossils. T **185** and similar horiz designs. Multicoloured. P 14½×14.

970	$1.20 Type **185**	80	10
971	$5.60 Allosaurus footprints	1·10	70
972	$7.40 Left foot of Massospondylus	1·25	1·10
973	$9.90 Fossil wood	1·50	1·75
970/3	*Set of 4*	4·25	3·25

(Des Paula Ware)

1998 (20 Oct). Birds. T **186** and similar vert designs. Multicoloured. P 14×14½.

974	$1.20 Type **186**	50	15
975	$4.10 Lesser Blue-eared Starling	70	35
976	$4.70 Grey-headed Kingfisher ("Grey hooded Kingfisher")	70	45
977	$5.60 Miombo Grey Tit	75	75
978	$7.40 Chirinda Apalis	85	1·00
979	$9.90 Swynnerton's Robin	95	1·40
974/9	*Set of 6*	4·00	3·75

187 Philatelic Counter

(Des Paula Ware)

1999 (19 Jan). 125th Anniv of Universal Postal Union. T **187** and similar horiz designs. Multicoloured. P 14½×14.

980	$1.20 Type **187**	20	10
981	$5.60 Postman delivering letters	55	25
982	$7.40 19th-century runner, motorcycle and truck	1·75	70
983	$9.90 Harare Central Sorting Office	60	80
980/3	*Set of 4*	2·75	1·70

188 Serval

(Des D. Herbert)

1999 (16 Mar). Cats. T **188** and similar vert designs. Multicoloured. P 14×14½.

984	$1.20 Type **188**	30	10
985	$5.60 Cheetah	65	45
986	$7.40 Caracal	80	90
987	$9.90 Leopard	1·25	1·60
984/7	*Set of 4*	2·75	2·75

(Des B. Finch and C. Herbert)

1999 (8 June). Owls (3rd series). Vert designs as T **140**. Multicoloured. P 14½.

988	$1.20 Cape Eagle Owl	1·10	35
989	$5.60 Grass Owl	1·75	90
990	$7.40 Barn Owl	2·25	2·25
991	$9.90 Marsh Owl	2·50	2·75
988/91	*Set of 4*	7·00	5·50

189 Canoe Safari

190 Family Reunion

(Des Janet Duff)

1999 (10 Aug). Tourism in Zimbabwe. T **189** and similar horiz designs. Multicoloured. P 14½×14.

992	$2 Type **189**	15	15
993	$6.70 Rock climbing	50	40
994	$7.70 Flying microlight	55	50
995	$9.10 White water rafting	70	70
996	$12 Mountain scenery	80	1·10
997	$16 Game watching	1·10	1·75
992/7	*Set of 6*	3·50	4·25

No. 997 is inscribed "Game Veiwing" in error.

(Des Margaret Tredgold)

1999 (12 Oct). Christmas. T **190** and similar vert designs. Multicoloured. P 14×14½.

998	$2 Type **190**	20	10
999	$6.70 Elephants around Christmas tree	30	25
1000	$7.70 Children and dog with balloons	30	25
1001	$9.10 Flame Lily	40	35
1002	$12 Madonna and Child	55	85
1003	$16 The Nativity	65	1·10
998/1003	*Set of 6*	2·25	2·50

191 Nyala

192 Basketball

(Des C. Herbert, Paula Ware and R. Pletts)

2000 (25 Jan). Fauna, Industry and Development. T **191** and similar horiz designs. Multicoloured. P 14½.

1004	1c. Type **191**	10	20
1005	10c. Building development	10	20
1006	30c. Timber yard	10	20
1007	50c. Tobacco auction	10	20
1008	70c. Central Sorting Office, Harare	10	30
1009	80c. Harare New International Airport	50	30
1010	$1 Westgate Shopping Complex	10	20
1011	$2 Nile Crocodile	50	30
1012	$3 Pungwe River Water Project	20	30
1013	$4 Zebra	50	30
1014	$5 Mining	65	35
1015	$7 National University of Science and Technology	20	35
1016	$10 Ostrich	1·00	40
1017	$15 Cape Parrot	1·00	60
1018	$20 Leather products	60	80
1019	$30 Lilac-breasted Roller	1·50	1·00
1020	$50 Victoria Falls	1·60	1·60
1021	$100 Mukorsi Dam, Tokwe River	2·25	3·00
1021*a*	($100) Bateleur (24.6.03)	50	30
1021*b*	$500 Goliath Heron (24.6.03)	1·00	75
1021*c*	$1000 White Rhinoceros (24.6.03)	2·50	1·75
1021*d*	$5000 Cheetah (24.6.03)	1·50	2·00
1004/21	*Set of 18*	15·00	14·00

No. 1021*a* is inscribed "Standard Postage" and was initially sold at $100.

(Des B. Place)

2000 (25 Apr). Sporting Activities. T **192** and similar vert designs. Multicoloured. P 14×14½.

1022	$2 Type **192**	15	10
1023	$6.70 Tennis	40	35
1024	$7.70 Netball	40	45
1025	$9.10 Weightlifting	40	50
1026	$12 Taekwondo	55	65
1027	$16 Diving	65	75
1022/7	*Set of 6*	2·25	2·50

193 Dr. Joshua Nkomo

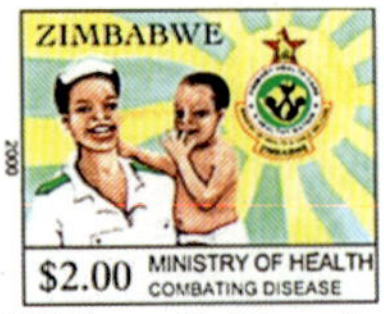

194 Nurse with Baby and Ministry of Health Logo

(Des C. Herbert)

2000 (27 June). First Death Anniv of Dr. Joshua Nkomo (nationalist leader). T **193** and similar vert design. Multicoloured. P 14×14½.

1028	$2 Type **193**	15	10
1029	$9.10 Nkomo in traditional costume	40	50
1030	$12 Type **193**	55	65
1031	$16 As $9.10	65	90
1028/31	*Set of 4*	1·60	1·90

(Des Gaye Dixon)

2000 (18 July). Health Promotion Campaign. T **194** and similar horiz designs. Multicoloured. P 14.

1032	$2 Type **194**	15	10
1033	$6.70 Boy with football and anti-tuberculosis emblem	30	30
1034	$7.70 Couple with baby and "New Start" logo	35	30
1035	$9.10 Health technician in motorcycle and Riders for Health badge	60	50
1036	$12 Ribbon emblem on map and Ministry of Health logo	65	70
1037	$16 Fisherman and Rotary International emblem	70	80
1032/7	*Set of 6*	2·50	2·40

195 Masawu Fruit

196 Boeing 737-200

(Des R. Pletts)

2000 (24 Oct). Wild Fruits (2nd series). T **195** and similar vert designs. Multicoloured. P 14.

1038	$2 Type **195**	15	10
1039	$6.70 Spiny Monkey Orange	30	30
1040	$7.70 Bird Plum	30	35
1041	$9.10 Shakama Plum	40	45
1042	$12 Wild Medlar	60	65
1043	$16 Wild Custard Apple	65	75
1038/43	*Set of 6*	2·25	2·25

(Des C. Herbert)

2001 (30 Jan). Aircraft. T **196** and similar horiz designs. Multicoloured. P 14½.

1044	$8 Type **196**	50	25
1045	$12 BAe Hawk MK 60	65	70
1046	$14 Hawker Hunter FGA-9	75	85
1047	$16 Cessna/Reims F-337	85	70
1048	$21 Aerospatiale Alouette III helicopter	95	1·10
1049	$28 Boeing 767-200ER	1·40	1·75
1044/9	*Set of 6*	4·50	4·50

197 Prominences (solar gas outbursts) during Total Solar Eclipse

198 "The Hare who rode Horseback"

(Des C. Herbert)

2001 (24 Apr). Total Solar Eclipse, 21 June 2001. T **197** and similar horiz designs. Multicoloured. P 14½ (No. 1052) or 14 (others).

1050	$8 Type **197**	55	25
1051	$21 Path of eclipse over Southern Africa	1·25	1·40
1052	$28 Phases of total solar eclipse (62×22 *mm*)	1·40	1·75
1050/2	*Set of 3*	3·00	3·00

(Des Lady Margaret Tredgold)

2001 (24 July). African Folk Tales. T **198** and similar vert designs. Multicoloured. P 14.

1053	$8 Type **198**	35	25
1054	$12 "The Hippo who lost his Hair"	45	35
1055	$13 "The Lion who was saved by a Mouse"	45	40
1056	$16 "The Bush Fowl who wakes the Sun"	60	50
1057	$21 "The Chameleon who came too Late"	85	90
1058	$28 "The Tortoise who collected Wisdom"	1·10	1·40
1053/8	*Set of 6*	3·50	3·50
MS1059	126×105 mm. Nos. 1053/8	3·50	3·50

199 Entrance, Heroes Acre Memorial, Harare

(Des C. Herbert)

2001 (7 Aug). 21st Anniv of Independence. Heroes Acre Memorial, Harare. T **199** and similar horiz designs. Multicoloured. P 14.

1060	$8 Type **199**	40	25
1061	$16 Statue of Unknown Soldier	60	45
1062	$21 Obelisk	80	1·00
1063	$28 Aerial view	1·10	1·40
1060/3	*Set of 4*	2·50	2·75

200 "Three Faces" (N. Mguni) (national winner)

2001 (16 Oct). U.N. Dialogue Among Civilisations. T **200** and similar vert design. Multicoloured. P 14×14½.

1064	$8 Type **200**	75	25
1065	$21 "Children encircling globe" (Urska Golob) (international winner)	1·75	2·00

201 *Charaxes bohemani* (butterfly)

202 Knitting and Crochet Work

(Des Lady Margaret Tredgold)

2001 (6 Dec). Butterflies (2nd series). T **201** and similar horiz designs. Multicoloured. P 14.

1066	$12 Type **201**	75	35
1067	$20 *Vanessa cardui*	1·00	70
1068	$25 *Precis oenone cebrene*	1·25	90
1069	$30 *Euphaedra neophron*	1·40	1·40
1070	$35 *Iolaus silas* (female)	1·60	1·60
1071	$45 *Acrea aglanice*	1·90	2·25
1066/71	*Set of 6*	7·25	6·50
MS1072	140×95 mm. Nos. 1066/71	7·25	8·00

(Des B. Place)

2002 (22 Jan). Local Crafts. T **202** and similar horiz designs. Multicoloured. P 14.

1073	$12 Type **202**	45	35
1074	$20 Art and design	60	55
1075	$25 Baskets	70	70
1076	$30 Pottery	80	90
1077	$35 Woodcarving	90	1·10
1078	$45 Sculpture	1·25	1·40
1073/8	*Set of 6*	4·25	4·50

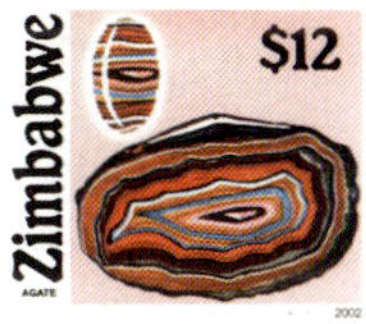

203 Agate

204 "Two Girls arm-in-arm" (Tazivei Makwavarara)

(Des C. Herbert)

2002 (23 Apr). Gemstones. T **203** and similar horiz designs. Multicoloured. P 14.

1079	$12 Type **203**	1·00	35
1080	$25 Aquamarine	1·50	1·00
1081	$35 Diamond	1·90	1·90
1082	$45 Emerald	2·25	2·50
1079/82	*Set of 4*	6·00	5·25

2002 (4 June). 5th Anniv of Childline in Zimbabwe. T **204** and similar horiz designs. Multicoloured. P 14.

1083	$12 Type **204**	75	35
1084	$25 "Girl using telephone" (Ashley Elkington)	1·25	90
1085	$35 "Teddy bear" (Goldine Hobbs)	1·60	1·75
1086	$45 "Hand holding telephone" (Admire Kacheche)	2·00	2·50
1083/6	*Set of 4*	5·00	5·00

205 Sally Mugabe

206 "Mail Runner and Local Post Office" (Agreement Ngwenya)

(Des C. Herbert)

2002 (6 Aug). 10th Death Anniv of Sally Mugabe (wife of President). T **205** and similar vert design. Multicoloured. P 14.

1087	$20 Type **205**	70	55
1088	$50 Mrs. Mugabe in black and white dress	1·50	1·75
1089	$70 Type **205**	1·90	2·25
1090	$90 As $50	2·50	3·00
1087/90	*Set of 4*	6·00	6·75

(Des C. Herbert)

2002 (8 Oct). "Technology Today" School Design Competition Winners. T **206** and similar horiz design. Multicoloured. P 14.

1091	$20 Type **206**	1·00	55
1092	$70 "Mail runner and Airliner" (Kudzai Chikomo)	3·25	3·50

207 *Dissotis princes*

208 Society Logo

(Des Lady Margaret Tredgold)

2002 (22 Oct). Wild Flowers (2nd series). T **207** and similar horiz designs. Multicoloured. P 14.

1093	$20 Type **207**	80	55
1094	$35 *Leonotis nepetifolia*	1·25	90
1095	$40 *Hibiscus vitifolius*	1·40	1·25

1096	$50 *Boophane disticha*	1·60	1·60
1097	$70 *Pycnostachys urticifolia*	2·00	2·50
1098	$90 *Gloriosa superba*	2·75	4·25
1093/8	*Set of 6*	8·75	10·00
MS1099	120×105 mm. Nos. 1093/8	9·00	10·00

(Des Josie Jones)

2003 (28 Jan). 50th Anniv of History Society of Zimbabwe. T **208** and similar vert designs. Multicoloured. P 14×14½.

1100	$30 Type **208**	60	15
1101	$80 Books and scroll (Historical Evidence)	1·50	90
1102	$110 Oral traditions	1·75	2·25
1103	$140 Old buildings	2·00	2·75
1100/3	*Set of 4*	5·25	5·50

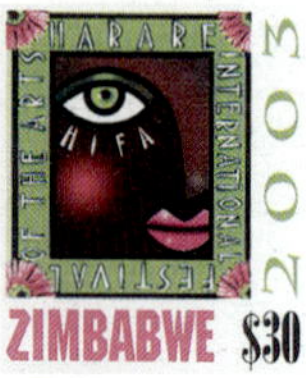

209 Logo

210 Baboon Spider (*Genus harpactira*)

(Des Jacqui Taylor)

2003 (22 Apr). Harare International Festival of the Arts. T **209** and similar vert designs. Multicoloured. P 14×14½.

1104	$30 Type **209**	25	10
1105	$80 Green logo and pink daisy	65	45
1106	$110 Eye logo and three pink daisies	85	85
1107	$140 Pink logo with pink and orange daisies	1·10	1·40
1104/7	*Set of 4*	2·50	2·50

(Des D. Herbert)

2003 (30 July). Spiders of Zimbabwe. T **210** and similar horiz designs. Multicoloured. P 14½.

1108	$150 Type **210**	30	15
1109	$200 Rain Spider (*Genus palystes*)	30	15
1110	$600 Black Button (Widow) Spider (*Latrodectus renivulvatus*)	75	30
1111	$900 Wolf Spider (*Lycosidae*)	1·10	1·10
1112	$1250 Violin Spider (*Loxoscelidae*)	1·25	1·60
1113	$1600 Wall Spider (*Selenopidae*)	1·50	2·00
1108/13	*Set of 6*	4·75	4·75
MS1114	159×98 mm. Nos. 1108/13	4·75	5·50

211 Woman Graduate with Briefcase and Hoe (Tamuka Makuluni)

212 Wild Verbena

(Des C. Herbert)

2003 (14 Oct). Empowerment of Women. T **211** and similar vert design showing winning entries from national stamp design competition. Multicoloured. P 14½.

1115	$300 Type **211**	50	15
1116	$2100 Woman graduate with friend (Chloe Edwards)	2·25	2·50

(Des Lady Margaret Tredgold)

2003 (28 Oct). Endangered Medicinal Herbs of Zimbabwe. T **212** and similar vert designs. Multicoloured. P 14×14½.

1117	$200 Type **212**	30	10
1118	$500 Pimpernel	70	20
1119	$1000 African Arrowroot	1·25	70
1120	$3000 Bird Pepper	2·50	2·75
1121	$4200 Wild Garlic	3·00	3·50
1122	$5400 Cleome	3·50	4·25
1117/22	*Set of 6*	10·00	10·50
MS1123	116×116 mm. Nos. 1117/22	10·00	11·00

213 Environment Africa Emblem

(Des Kerry-Lee Rogers)

2004 (17 Feb). Environment Africa. T **213** and similar vert designs. P 14×14½.

1124	$500 yellowish green	70	20
1125	$3000 multicoloured	2·50	2·25
1126	$4200 royal blue, cobalt and black	3·00	3·25
1127	$5400 black, orange-yellow and emerald	3·50	4·25
1124/7	*Set of 4*	8·75	9·00

Designs:—$3000 Sondela emblem; $4200 Water Africa emblem; $5400 Tree Africa emblem.

214 Independence Medal

(Des C. Herbert)

2004 (6 Apr). Medals. T **214** and similar vert designs. Multicoloured. P 14½.

1128	$1500 Type **214**	35	10
1129	$9000 Bronze Cross of Zimbabwe	2·20	2·20
1130	$13000 Silver Cross of Zimbabwe	3·25	3·50
1131	$16500 Gold Cross of Zimbabwe	4·00	4·25
1128/31	*Set of 4*	9·00	9·00

215 Aloe ballii

(Des Lady Margaret Tredgold)

2004 (20 July). Aloes. T **215** and similar vert designs. Multicoloured. P 14×14½.

1132	$1500 Type **215**	35	10
1133	$3000 *Aloe rhodesiana*	75	20
1134	$9000 *Aloe greatheadii*	2·20	2·10
1135	$10000 *Aloe ortholopha*	2·50	2·75
1136	$13000 *Aloe inyangensis*	3·25	3·75
1137	$16500 *Aloe arborescens*	4·00	4·75
1132/7	*Set of 6*	12·00	12·00
MS1138	120×106 mm. Nos. 1132/7	13·00	13·00

216 Simon Vengai Muzenda

(Des G. Mahaka)

2004 (20 Sept). First Death Anniv of Simon Vengai Muzenda (Co-Vice Pres.). T **216** and similar vert designs. Multicoloured. P 14×14½.

1139	**216**	$2300 red background	65	30
1140		$12000 greenish yellow background	2·00	2·00
1141		$17000 light green background	2·50	2·50
1142		$22000 olive-grey background	3·75	4·50
1139/42		*Set of 4*	8·00	8·50

(Des Anja Denker. Litho Enchedé)

2004 (11 Oct). First Joint Issue of Southern Africa Postal Operators Association Members. Sheet 170×95 mm containing hexagonal designs as T **227a** of Zambia showing national birds of Association members. Multicoloured. P 14.

MS1143 $500 African fish eagles in flight (Zimbabwe); $1000 Purple-crested turaco ('lourie') (Swaziland); $2300 African fish eagles perched on tree (Zimbabwe); $3000 Stanley ('Blue') crane (South Africa); $5000 Cattle egret (Botswana); $9000 Peregrine falcon (Angola); $12000 Bar-tailed trogon (Malawi) (inscr 'apaloderma vittatum'); $17000 African fish eagles perched and in flight (Namibia).... 35·00 35·00

The stamp depicting the bar-tailed trogon is not inscribed with the country of which the bird is a national symbol.

Miniature sheets of similar designs were also issued by Angola, Botswana, Malawi, Namibia, South Africa, Swaziland and Zambia.

217 Butterfly (Kingston Chigidhani)

2004 (26 Oct). "Conservation Practices in Zimbabwe" Stamp Design Competition. Winning Stamps from the Junior and Open Categories. T **217** and similar horiz design. P 14½×14.

1144	$4600 Type **217**	1·90	2·00
1145	$33500 Hands "protecting" wildlife (Kudzai Chikomo)	3·50	4·50

218 Black-collared Barbet

(Des C. Herbert)

2005 (8 Feb). Birds of Zimbabwe (1st series). T **218** and similar horiz designs. Multicoloured. P 14½.

1146	$500 Type **218**	50	75
1147	$5000 Grey-headed bush shrike	1·00	50
1148	(Z) Red-headed weaver	1·25	55
1149	$10000 Golden-breasted bunting	1·25	70
1150	$20000 Cut-throat weaver ("cut-throat finch")	1·75	1·25
1151	(A) Cabanis's yellow bunting ("Cabanis's bunting")	2·00	1·50
1152	(E) Miombo double-collared sunbird	2·00	1·50
1153	(R) Levaillant's barbet ("Crested barbet")	2·50	2·75
1154	$50000 White-browed robin chat ("Heuglin's robin")	5·00	6·00
1155	$100000 Giant kingfisher	8·00	9·00
1146/55	*Set of 10*	23·00	22·00

Nos. 1148 and 1151/3 were all inscribed "STANDARD POSTAGE" and were initially sold for $6900, $30000, $40000 or $50000 respectively.

See also Nos. 1215/**MS**1225.

219 Cirrus

(Des C. Herbert)

2005 (26 Apr). Cloud Formations.T **219** and similar horiz designs. Multicoloured. P 14½.

1156	$6900 Type **219**	85	40
1157	$13800 Nimbo-stratus	1·75	80
1158	$30000 Alto cumulus	3·75	4·50
1159	$40000 Cumulo-nimbus	4·75	5·50
1156/9	*Set of 4*	10·00	10·00

220 Banded Egyptian Cobra

221 Josiah Tongogara (nationalist)

(Des C. Herbert)

2005 (12 July). Snakes of Zimbabwe. T **220** and similar horiz designs. Multicoloured. P 14½×14.

1160	$6900 Type **220**	1·00	40
1161	$13800 Puff adder	1·50	70
1162	$20000 Boomslang	2·00	1·50
1163	$25000 Moçambique spitting cobra	2·50	2·50
1164	$30000 Gaboon viper	2·50	3·50
1165	$40000 Black mamba	3·50	4·50
1160/5	*Set of 6*	12·00	12·00
MS1166	140×102 mm. Nos. 1160/5	12·00	13·00

(Des G. Mahaka)

2005 (4 Aug). Commemorations (1st series). T **221** and similar vert designs. Multicoloured. P 14×14½.

1167	$6900 Type **221**	70	40
1168	$13800 Herbert Chitepo (nationalist)	1·00	70
1169	$30000 Bernard Chidzero (former Chief Minister)	2·00	2·25
1170	$50000 Moven Mahachi (Minister of Defence 1990–2001)	3·00	3·25
1167/70	*Set of 4*	6·00	6·00

See also Nos. 1192/5, 1230/33, 1262/5, and 1284/8 and 1318/21.

222 Great Zimbabwe and Soapstone Bird Sculpture

223 Man working in Fields and Woman looking after AIDS Patient

(Des C. Herbert)

2005 (6 Oct). World Heritage Sites of Zimbabwe. T **222** and similar horiz designs. Multicoloured. P 14½.

1171	(Z) Type **222**	60	30
1172	$15500 Wall patterns, Khami ruins	1·00	65
1173	$52000 Elephant eating apple ring acacia, Mana Pools National Park	6·00	6·00
1174	$62000 Victoria Falls	6·00	6·50
1171/4	*Set of 4*	12·00	12·00
MS1175	118×101 mm. Nos. 1171/4	12·00	13·00

(Des John Ndlovu ($18000) or Chengetai Nyika ($80000)

2005 (1 Dec). Anti-HIV and AIDS Campaign. T **223** and similar horiz design showing winning entries in stamp design competition. Multicoloured. P 14½×14.

1176	$18000 Type **223**	1·50	1·00
1177	$80000 Children looking after AIDS patient and boy teaching	5·50	6·00

224 Field Mushroom, Cep, *Cantharellus longisporus*

225 Pope John Paul II

(Des Lady Margaret Tredgold)

2006 (17 Jan). African Dishes. T **224** and similar vert designs. Multicoloured. P 14×14½.

1178	$25000 Type **224**	1·25	50
1179	$35000 Rapoko, maize and sorghum (grains)	75	50
1180	$50000 Pumpkin, watermelon and spiny cucumber	90	65
1181	$150000 Jackal berry, wild loquat, marula, numnum, kei apple and bush orange (wild fruits)	2·25	2·25
1182	$250000 Bramble, okra, bird peppers, wild hibiscus, rosella (herbs) and mopane worms (caterpillars)	4·00	4·50
1183	$300000 Sweet potato, cassava and ground nuts	4·00	4·50
1178/83 *Set of 6*		12·00	11·50
MS1183 114×104 mm. Nos. 1177/83			

(Des G. Mahaka)

2006 (9 Feb). Pope John Paul II Commemoration. T **225** and similar vert design. Multicoloured. P 14×14½.

1185	$25000 Type **225**	2·00	75
1186	$250000 Pope with crozier and mitre	8·00	9·00
MS1187 101×77 mm. Nos. 1184/5		10·00	10·00

226 Water Tap

227 Leopold Takawira (nationalist)

(Des Joan Soriano)

2006 (25 Apr). Water Conservation and Useage in Zimbabwe. T **226** and similar vert designs. Multicoloured. P 14×14½.

1188	$30000 Type **226**	50	25
1189	$225000 Irrigation channel and crops	2·25	1·50
1190	$375000 Lionesses drinking	3·00	3·50
1191	$450000 Sluice gates at Kariba Dam	3·25	3·75
1188/91 *Set of 4*		8·00	8·00

(Des G. Mahaka)

2006 (25 July). Commemorations (2nd series). T **227** and similar vert designs. Multicoloured. P 14×14½.

1192	$60000 Type **227**	60	35
1193	$350000 Simon Mazorodze (Deputy Minister of Health, 1980–1)	1·50	1·50
1194	$500000 Herbert Ushewokunze (Transport Minister, 1984–8)	2·00	2·50
1195	$650000 Tichafa Parirenyatwa (nationalist)	2·50	3·00
1192/5 *Set of 4*		6·00	6·50

228 Mpudzi River Bridge

229 Ancient Hut (Freddy Tembo)

(Des C. Herbert)

2006 (24 Oct). Bridges of Zimbabwe. T **228** and similar horiz designs. Multicoloured. P 14½×14.

1196	(Z) Type **228**	70	35
1197	$450 Victoria Falls Bridge over Zambezi River seen from No. 2 Gorge	1·60	55
1198	$600 Limpopo River Railway Bridge, Beitbridge	2·25	1·75
1199	$750 Otto Beit Suspension Bridge over Zambezi River, Chirundu	2·75	3·00
1200	$800 Lake Kariba Barrage Road Bridge	2·75	3·00
1201	$1000 Birchenough Save River Bridge	3·25	4·50
1196/1201 *Set of 4*		12·00	12·00
MS1202 140×103 mm. Nos. 1196/201		12·00	13·00

No. 1196 is inscribed "Standard Postage" and was originally sold for $100.

2006 (24 Oct). National Huts. T **229** and similar horiz design showing winning entries in postage stamp design competition. Multicoloured. P 14½×14.

1203	$100 Type **229**	50	25
1204	$800 Ancient, modern and future huts (Elisha Homera)	4·50	4·75
MS1205 104×74 mm. Nos. 1203/4		5·00	6·00

PRINTER: The following stamps were printed in lithography by Natprint of Harare.

230 *Ziziphuus Mauritania*

231 Scout Badge on Ruins of Great Zimbabwe

(Des Lucia Marisamhuka)

2006 (1 Dec). Trees of the Year. T **230** and similar vert designs. Multicoloured. P 14×14½.

1206	$150 Type **230**	60	35
1207	$600 *Schlerochra birrea* (marula)	2·00	1·50
1208	$750 *Jatropha carcus*	2·75	3·00
1209	$1000 *Uaparca kirkiana*	3·25	4·00
1206/9 *Set of 4*		7·75	8·00
MS1210 103×110 mm. Nos. 1206/9		7·75	8·50

(Des Boy Scouts Association of Zimbabwe and Lucia Marisamhuka)

2007 (20 Feb). Centenary of Scouting. T **231** and similar vert designs. Multicoloured. P 14×14½.

1211	$400 Type **231**	70	35
1212	$1500 Scout badge on Zimbabwe flag	2·50	1·50
1213	$2000 Peace doves and bird sculpture from Great Zimbabwe	3·50	3·75
1214	$2500 Scout badge on map of Africa	4·50	5·50
1211/4 *Set of 4*		10·00	10·00

2007 (20 Feb). Birds of Zimbabwe (2nd series). Horiz designs as T **218**. Multicoloured. P 14½.

1215	$50 Hoopoe	25	40
1216	$100 Cattle egret	30	40
1217	$500 Malachite Kingfisher	40	20
1218	$1000 Little bee-eater	50	30
1219	$2000 Purplecrested lourie	70	40
1220	$5000 Purple gallinule	1·00	70
1221	$10000 African jacana	2·00	1·25
1222	$20000 Ground hornbill	4·00	3·00
1223	$50000 Gorgeous bush shrike	8·00	8·50
1224	$100000 Secretary bird	11·00	12·00
1215/24 *Set of 10*		25·00	24·00
MS1225 154×87 mm. Nos. 1215/24		25·00	26·00

232 Mbuya Nehanda (resistance leader)

233 Jason Ziyaphapha Moyo and Reserve Bank of Zimbabwe

(Des Joan Soriano)

2007 (10 July). 'Women creating Zimbabwe'. T **232** and similar horiz designs. Multicoloured. P 14½.

1226	$7500 Type **232**	70	50
1227	$29000 Lozikeyi (senior wife) and Lobengula's court	2·00	2·00
1228	$35000 Mother Patrick (missionary)	2·25	2·75
1229	$45000 Amai Sally Mugabe and Chinyaradzo Children's Home, Harare	2·75	3·25
1226/9 *Set of 4*		4·00	7·75

(Des Lucia Marisamhuka)

2007 (9 Aug). Commemorations (3rd series). T **233** and similar vert designs. Multicoloured. P 14×14½.

1230	(Z) Type **233**	60	20
1231	(A) Maurice Nyagumbo	1·25	70

1232	(E)	Guy Clutton-Brock	2·00	2·00
1233	(R)	Chief Rekayi Tangwena	3·25	3·75
1230/3 *Set of 4*			6·25	6·00

No. 1230 was for domestic postage of letters weighing up to 20 grams.

Nos. 1231/3 were for letters weighing up to 10 grams to Africa (A), Europe (E) and rest of the World (R).

234 *Salamis parhassus* (mother-of-pearl)

235 Healthy Young Boy studying (John Ndhlovu)

(Des Lady Margaret Tredgold)

2007 (18 Sept). Butterflies (3rd series). T **234** and similar vert designs. Multicoloured. P 14×14½.

1234	(Z)	Type **234**	75	35
1235	(A)	*Papilio demodocus* (citrus swallowtail)	1·25	70
1236	(E)	*Anthocharis cardamines* (orange tip)	1·75	1·75
1237	(R)	*Charaxes bohemani* (blue charaxes)	2·50	2·75
1238	$50000	*Colotis danae* (crimson tip)	3·50	3·75
1239	$100000	*Cynthia cardui* (painted lady)	6·00	6·50
MS1240 125×104 mm. Nos. 1234/9			15·00	15·00

(Litho Natprint, Harare)

2007 (9 Oct). 'For Every Child Life in All its Fullness'. T **235** and similar vert design showing winning entries in postage stamp design competition. Multicoloured. P 14×14½.

1241	(Z)	Type **235**	75	30
1242	$100000	Mother feeding baby (Fungai Madzima)	4·75	5·50
MS1243 90×75 mm. Nos. 1241/2			5·50	6·00

236 African Buffalo (Zambia)

(Des Anja Denker. Litho and die-stamped Enschedé)

2007 (9 Oct). Second Joint Issue of Southern Africa Postal Operators Association Members. T **236** and similar square designs showing national animals of Association Members. Multicoloured. P 14.

1244	Z	Type **236**	75	35
1245	A	Nyala (pair) (Malawi)	1·50	75
1246	$100000	Nyala (Zimbabwe)	2·25	2·25
1247	E	Burchell's zebra (Botswana)	2·25	2·50
1248	R	Oryx (Namibia)	2·75	3·25
1244/8 *Set of 5*			8·50	8·25
MS1249 133×170 mm. Nos. 1244/8			10·00	10·00

237 Heart

(Des Darren Herbert. Litho Natprint, Harare)

2008 (24 Jan). Valentine?s Day. T **237** and similar vert designs. Multicoloured. P 14×14½.

1250	Z	Type **237**	75	35
1251	A	Cupid	1·25	75
1252	E	Heart-shaped valentine cards	1·50	1·75
1253	R	Red rose	2·00	2·50
1250/3 *Set of 4*			5·00	4·75
MS1254 89×114 mm. Nos. 1250/3			5·00	5·50

No. 1250, initially sold at $25000, was for domestic postage of letters weighing up to 20 grams.

Nos. 1251/3 were initially sold at $100000 (A), $170000 (E) and $240000 (R). They were for letters weighing up to 10 grams to Africa, Europe and rest of the world.

238 Striped Mouse (*Rhabdomys pumilio*)

(Des Joan Soriano. Litho Natprint, Harare)

2008 (24 Apr). Rats and Mice of Zimbabwe. T **238** and similar horiz designs. Multicoloured. P 14½.

1255	Z	Type **238**	70	35
1256	A	Water rat (*Dasymys incomtus*)	1·00	70
1257	E	Angoni vlei rat (*Otomys angoniensis*)	1·50	1·50
1258	R	Woodland dormouse (*Graphiurus (claviglis) murinus*)	2·50	2·50
1259	$5000000	Bushveld gerbil (*Tatera leucogaster*)	3·00	3·25
1260	$10000000	Namaqua rock mouse (*Aethomys namaquensis*)	5·00	5·50
1255/60 *Set of 6*				
MS1261 125×125 mm. Nos. 1255/60			12·00	12·00

No. 1255, initially sold at $550,000, was for domestic postage of letters weighing up to 20 grams.

Nos. 1256/8 were initially sold at $1,900,000 (A), $3,150,000 (E) and $4,600,000 (R). They were for letters weighing up to 10 grams to Africa, Europe and rest of the world.

239 Johanna Nkomo

240 The Water Cube

(Des Lucia Marisamhuka. Litho Natprint, Harare)

2008 (5 Aug). Commemorations (4th series). T **239** and similar vert designs. Multicoloured. P 14×14½.

1262	Z	Type **239**	75	35
1263	A	Ruth Lottie Nomonde Chinamano	1·25	75
1264	E	Swithun Tachiona Mombeshora	1·50	1·75
1265	R	Willie Dzawanda Musarurwa	2·00	2·75
1262/5 *Set of 4*			5·00	5·00

No. 1262, initially sold at $250m, was for domestic postage of letters weighing up to 20 grams.

Nos. 1263/5 were initially sold at $50bn (A), $90bn (E) or $110bn (R). They were for letters weighing up to 10 grams to Africa, Europe and rest of the world.

Litho

2009 (20 Jan). Olympic Games, beijing. T240 and horiz simlar designs. Multicoloured. P 14

1266	(Z)	Type **240**	1·00	60
1267	(A)	Bird's Nest Stadium	1·75	1·50
1268	(E)	The Olympic Pool	2·75	2·75
1269	(R)	Zimbabwe flag	3·00	3·25
1266/9 *Set of 4*			8·00	7·50

241 *Countryside* (James Jali), 2000

(Des Joan Soriano. Litho Natprint, Harare)

2009 (21 Apr). Contemporary Paintings by Zimbabwean Artists. T **241** and similar horiz designs. Multicoloured. P 14.

1270	(Zs)	Type **241**	85	50
1271	(Zb)	*Cardoor Scape* (Cosmos Shiridzinomwa), 2008	85	50

1272	(A) *Mountains* (George Churu), 1996	1·50	1·50
1273	(A) *Barn* (Hilary Kashiri), 1998	1·50	1·50
1274	(E) *Backyard* 1 (Freddy Tauro), 2007	1·75	2·00
1275	(R) *X in the Land* (Admire Kamudzengere), 2008	2·25	2·75
1270/5 *Set of* 6		8·00	8·00
MS1276 127×129mm. Nos1270/5		10·00	10·00

242 Leopard (*Panthera pardus*)

243 Vitalis Musungwa Gava Zvinavashe

(Des Lucia Marisamhuka. Litho Natprint, Harare)

2009 (23 June). ?The Big Five?. T **242** and similar horiz designs. Multicoloured. P 14.

1277	(Zb) Type **242**	1·00	60
1278	(Zs) Black rhinoceros (*Diceros bicornis*)	1·50	1·00
1279	(A) African buffalo (*Synceros caffer*)	1·75	1·50
1280	(A) Lion (*Panthera leo*)	1·75	1·50
1281	(E) African elephant (*Loxodonta africana*)	2·75	2·75
1282	(R) 'The Big Five'	3·00	3·25
1277/82 *Set of* 6		10·50	10·50
MS1283 126×127mm. Nos. 1277/82		12·00	12·00

2009 (4 Aug). Commemorations (5th series). T **243** and similar vert designs. Multicoloured. Litho. P 14.

1284	(Zb) Type **243**	60	35
1285	(Zs) Garikayi Hlomayi Settled Magadzire	75	60
1286	(A) George Bodzo Nyandoro	1·00	1·00
1287	(E) Border Madzibaba Gezi	1·50	1·50
1288	(R) Seugeant Masotsha Ndlovu	1·75	2·00
1284/8 *Set of* 5		5·00	5·00

Nos. 1284/5 were for domestic postage.

Nos. 1286/8 were for letters weighing up to 10 grams to Africa, Europe and rest of the world.

244 Santa Barbara's Catholic Church, Kariba Heights

(Des Cindy Stamps. Litho Natprint, Zimbabwe)

2009 (15 Dec). Christmas. Contemporary Rural Churches in Zimbabwe. T **244** and similar horiz designs. Multicoloured. P 14.

1289	(Z) Type **244**	75	20
1290	(A) Catholic Church, Regina Coeli	1·25	80
1291	(E) Elim Evangelical Church, Katerere	1·50	1·50
1292	(R) Free Presbyterian Church, Mbuma	2·00	2·50
1289/92 *Set of* 4		5·00	4·50
MS1293 125×101mm. Nos. 1289/92		8·00	8·00

No. 1289 was for domestic postage.

Nos. 1290/2 were for letters weighing up to 10 grams to Africa, Europe and rest of the world. .

245 Map of Zimbabwe enclosing National Flag, Animals and Kariba Dam (Fredy Tembo)

(Des Lucia Marisamhuka. Litho Natprint, Zimbabwe)

2010 (19 Jan). 'Zimbabwe Africa's Paradise'. T **245** and similar horiz designs showing winning entries in postage stamp design competition. Multicoloured. P 14.

1294	(Z) Type **245**	1·25	60
1295	(A) Torch illuminating boatman, elephant and rhino (Munashe M. Patsanza)	2·00	1·50
1296	(E) Map of Africa and footballs enclosing Zimbabwe scenes (Methembe Dhlamini)	2·25	2·50
1297	(R) Victoria Falls, lion, walls of Great Zimbabwe, Zimbabwe bird and flower (Kudzai Chikomo)	2·75	3·00
1294/7 *Set of* 4		7·50	7·00
MS1298 125×100mm. Nos. 1294/7		9·00	9·00

No. 1294 was for domestic postage.

Nos. 1295/7 were for letters weighing up to 10 grams to Africa, Europe and rest of the world.

2010 (9 Apr). Third Joint Issue of Southern Africa Postal Operators Association Members. World Cup Football Championship, South Africa. Circular designs as T **542** of South Africa, each showing Zakumi mascot, different silhouettes of players on football, and the national flag of a member country. Multicoloured. P 13½.

1299	10c. Namibia	15	15
1300	15c. South Africa	20	20
1301	25c. Zimbabwe	40	30
1302	(Z) Botswana	40	30
1303	50c. Malawi	75	75
1304	(A) Mauritius	1·10	1·10
1305	75c. Swaziland	1·10	1·10
1306	(E) Lesotho	1·10	1·10
1307	(R) Zambia	1·50	2·00
1299/1307 *Set of* 9		6·00	6·25
MS1308 189×167 mm. As Nos. 1299/307 but gold foil background		9·00	9·00

Nos. 1299/307 and the stamps within MS1308 were each perforated in a circle contained within an outer perforated square.

Stamps from **MS**1308 have a shiny gold background; the sheet stamps have a matt background.

Nos. 1299/301, 1303 and 1305 were donominated in US dollars.

Nos. 1302, 1304 and 1306/7 were originally sold at 25c. (Z), 50c. (A), 75c. (E) and $1 (R). No. 1302 was for domestic postage of letters weighing up to 20 grams. Nos. 1304 and 1306/7 were for letters weighing up to 10 grams to Africa, Europe and rest of the world.

Similar designs were issued by Botswana, Lesotho, Malawi, Mauritius, Namibia, South Africa, Swaziland and Zambia.

246 Joseph Wilfred Msika

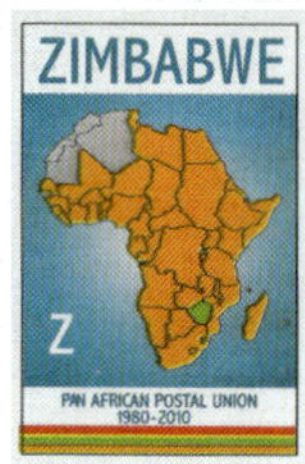

247 Map of Africa showing PAPU Countries

(Des Lucia Marisamhuka. Litho Natprint)

2010 (27 July). First Death Anniv of Joseph Wilfred Msika (Vice President 1999–2009). T **246** and similar vert design. Multicoloured. P 14.

1309	(Z) Type **246**	90	45
1310	(A) As Type **246** (grey background)	1·40	1·10
1311	(E) Joseph Msika (wearing hat) (red background)	1·40	1·40
1312	(R) As No. 1311 (green background)	1·75	2·00
1309/12 *Set of* 4		5·00	4·50

Nos. 1309/12 were originally sold at 25c. (Z), 50c. (A), 75c. (E) and $1 (R). No. 1309 was for domestic postage of letters weighing up to 20 grams. Nos. 1310/12 were for letters weighing up to 10 grams to Africa, Europe and rest of the world.

(Des Joan Soriano. Litho Natprint)

2010 (28 Dec). 30th Anniv of the Pan-African Postal Union. P 14.

1313	**247**	(Z) multicoloured	1·00	55

No. 1313 was inscr 'Z' and was originally valid for 25c. It was for domestic postage of letters weighing up to 20 grams.

248 Harare Railway Station

249 Tarcissius Malan George Silundika

(Des Fredy Tembo. Litho Natprint, Zimbabwe)

1999 (26 May). Railway Stations of Zimbabwe. T **248** and similar horiz designs. Multicoloured. P 14.

1314	25c. Type **248**	1·00	75
1315	30c. Kadoma	1·00	75
1316	85c. Bulawayo	2·25	2·50
1317	$1 Mutare	2·25	2·50
1314/17	*Set of* 4	6·00	6·00

2011 (27 July). Commemorations (6th series). T **249** and similar vert designs. Multicoloured. P 14

1318	25c. Type **249**	1·00	75
1319	30c. Julia Zvobgo	1·00	75
1320	85c. Ariston Maguranyanga Chambati	2·25	2·50
1321	$1 Joseph Luke Culverwell	2·25	2·50
1318/21	*Set of* 4	6·00	6·00

MACHINE LABELS

From 24 October 1985 gummed labels in the above design varying in value from 1c. to $99.99 were available from four automatic machines located at the Philatelic Bureau and at post offices in Bulawayo, Gwelo and Harare. Two further machines were installed at Harare offices in 1985–86, but by this time the Bureau machine had ceased to function. Paper showing an overall pattern of rhinoceroses appeared briefly in 1991, but it is reported that most machines were withdrawn by the end of March that year, although that at Bulawayo continued in use until at least May 1993.

STAMP BOOKLETS

1928 (1 Jan). Black on blue cover. Stitched.

SB1 2s.6d. booklet containing twelve ½d. and twenty-four 1d. (Nos. 1/2) in blocks of 6 .... £4500

1931. Black on blue cover. Stitched.

SB2 2s.6d. booklet containing twelve ½d. and twenty-four 1d. (Nos. 15/16) in blocks of 6 .... £5500

1933 (3 Mar). Black on red cover, size 69×53 mm. Stitched.

SB3 3s. booklet containing twelve ½d., 1d. and 1½d. (Nos. 15, 16, 16c) in blocks of 6 .... £3500

The 1½d. postage rate was reduced to 1d. eight weeks after No. SB3 was issued. Postal officials were instructed to detach the 1½d. panes and use them for other purposes. The remaining stocks of the booklet were then sold for 1s.6d.

1938 (Oct)–**45**. Black on yellow cover. Stitched.

SB4 2s.6d. booklet containing twenty-four ½d. and eighteen 1d. (Nos. 40/1) in blocks of 6 with postage rates on inside front cover £300

a. Label with new rates affixed to inside front cover (1945) £325

b. Inside front cover blank £325

No. SB4b was issued sometime between 1945 and 1949.

1954 (Jan). Black on yellow cover, size 71×54 mm. Stitched.

SB5 2s.6d. booklet containing twelve ½d. and twenty-four 1d. (Nos. 78/9) in blocks of 6 .... 70·00

1964 (19 Feb). Black on orange cover, size 57×45 mm. Stitched.

SB6 1s. booklet containing 3d. (No. 95) in block of 4 .... 3·25

1967 (Feb). Black on orange cover, size 57×45 mm. Stitched.

SB7 1s. booklet containing 3d. (No. 376) in block of 4 .... 3·75

Although not issued in Rhodesia until February 1967, No. SB7 was released in London in June 1966.

1968 (21 Dec). Black on yellow cover, size 51×94 mm. Stapled.

SB8 5s. booklet containing twelve 1d. and 3d., and six 2d. (Nos. 397/9) in blocks of 6 .... 18·00

1970 (17 Feb). Red on yellow cover. Stapled.

SB9 46c. booklet containing twelve 1c., eight 2½c. and four 3½c. in panes of 4 (Nos. 439a, 441a, 442a) .... 5·00

1972 (10 Apr). Green on yellow cover. Stapled.

SB10 48c. booklet containing eight 1c. and sixteen 2½c. in panes of 4 (Nos. 439a, 441a) .... 13·00

1973 (7 May). Blue on yellow cover. Stapled.

SB11 50c. booklet containing four 2½c. and 4c., and eight 3c. in panes of 4 (Nos. 441a, 441ca, 442ba) .... 18·00

1974 (14 Aug). White on blue cover. Stapled.

SB12 50c. booklet containing four 2½c. and 4c., and eight 3c. in panes of 4 (Nos. 490a, 491a, 492a) .... 6·00

POSTAGE DUE STAMPS

SOUTHERN

RHODESIA

(D **1**)

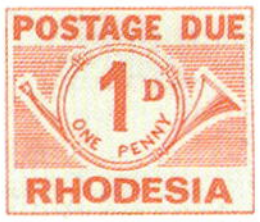

D **2**

1951 (1 Oct). Postage Due stamps of Great Britain optd with Type D **1**.

D1	D **1** 1½d. emerald (No. D27)		3·25	18·00
D2	1d. violet-blue (No. D36)		3·00	2·00
D3	2d. agate (No. D29)		2·50	1·75
D4	3d. violet (No. D30)		2·75	3·25
D5	4d. blue (No. D38)		1·75	3·50
D6	4d. dull grey-green (No. D31)		£250	£650
D7	1s. deep blue (No. D33)		2·50	5·00
D1/5, 7	*Set of* 6		14·00	27·00

No. D6 is reported to have been issued to Fort Victoria and Gwelo main post offices only.

(Typo Printing and Stationery Dept, Salisbury)

1965 (17 June). Roul 9.

D8	D **2** 1d. orange-red (*roul* 5)	50	12·00
	a. Roul 9	4·50	12·00
D9	2d. deep blue	40	8·00
D10	4d. green	50	8·00
D11	6d. plum	50	6·00
D8/11	*Set of* 4	1·75	30·00

The 2d. has a stop below the "D".

D **3** Zimbabwe Bird (soapstone sculpture)

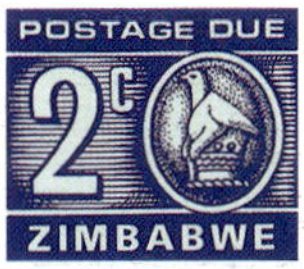

D **4** Zimbabwe Bird (soapstone sculpture)

(Litho Mardon Printers, Salisbury)

1966 (15 Dec). P 14½.

D12	D **3** 1d. red	60	3·25
D13	2d. bluish violet	75	1·75
D14	4d. pale green	75	4·00
D15	6d. reddish violet	75	1·50
D16	1s. red-brown	75	1·50
D17	2s. black	1·00	5·00
D12/17	*Set of* 6	4·25	15·00

1970 (17 Feb)–**73**. Decimal Currency. As Type D **3**, but larger (26×22½ mm). P 14½.

D18	D **3** 1c. bright green	75	1·25
D19	2c. ultramarine	75	60
	a. Printed on the gummed side	65·00	
D20	5c. bright reddish violet	1·25	1·75
D21	6c. pale lemon (7.5.73)	6·00	4·00
D22	10c. cerise	1·25	4·00
D18/22	*Set of* 5	9·00	10·50

1980. P 14½.

D23	D **4** 1c. bright green	20	1·25
D24	2c. ultramarine	20	1·25
D25	5c. bright reddish violet	25	1·25
	a. Imperf (pair)	90·00	
D26	6c. pale lemon	30	2·00
D27	10c. cerise	40	2·50
D23/7	*Set of* 5	1·25	7·50

D **5**

(D **6**)

1985 (21 Aug). P 14½.

D28	D **5** 1c. yellow-orange	35	1·25
D29	2c. magenta	35	1·25
D30	6c. blue-green	70	1·50
D31	10c. orange-brown	80	1·50

D32		13c. new blue	80	1·50
D28/32 *Set of 5*			2·75	6·25

1990 (2 Jan). No. D27 surch with Type D **6**.

D33	D **4**	25c. . on 10c cerise	3·00	3·00

No. D33 is reported to have been issued to the main post offices at Bulawayo, Gweru, Harare and Mutare.

D **7**

D **8** Bird Carving

1995 (17 Jan). P 14½.

D34	D **7**	1c. lemon	10	80
D35		2c. yellow-orange	10	80
D36		5c. mauve	10	80
D37		10c. pale blue	15	80
D38		25c. bright reddish violet	20	60
D39		40c. bright blue-green	30	70
D40		60c. red-orange	45	80
D41		$1 brown	55	1·00
D34/41 *Set of 8*			1·75	5·75

2000 (25 Jan). P 14½.

D42	D **8**	1c. black and light green	10	65
D43		10c. black and new blue	10	65
D44		50c. black and orange-brown	15	65
D45		$1 black and red	20	65
D46		$2 black and lemon	30	70
D47		$5 black and bright mauve	50	80
D48		$10 black and orange-red	90	1·25
D42/8 *Set of 7*			2·10	4·75

Est 1856

STANLEY GIBBONS

Dear Catalogue User,

As a collector and Stanley Gibbons catalogue user for many years myself, I am only too aware of the need to provide you with the information you seek in an accurate, timely and easily accessible manner. Naturally, I have my own views on where changes could be made, but one thing I learned long ago is that we all have different opinions and requirements.

I would therefore be most grateful if you would complete the form overleaf and return it to me. Please contact Lorraine Holcombe (lholcombe@stanleygibbons.co.uk) if you would like to be emailed the questionnaire.

Very many thanks for your help.

Yours sincerely,

Hugh Jefferies,
Editor.

Questionnaire

2011 Southern & Central Africa Catalogue

1. Level of detail
   Do you feel that the level of detail in this catalogue is:
   a. too specialised O
   b. about right O
   c. inadequate O

2. Frequency of issue
   How often would you purchase a new edition of this catalogue?
   a. Annually O
   b. Every two years O
   c. Every three to five years O
   d. Less frequently O

3. Design and Quality
   How would you describe the layout and appearance of this catalogue?
   a. Excellent O
   b. Good O
   c. Adequate O
   d. Poor O

4. How important to you are the prices given in the catalogue:
   a. Important O
   b. Quite important O
   c. Of little interest O
   d. Of no interest O

5. Would you be interested in an online version of this catalogue?
   a. Yes O
   b. No O

6. Do you like the 'layflat binding'?
   a. Yes O
   b. No O

7. What changes would you suggest to improve the catalogue? E.g. Which other features would you like to see included?
   ....
   ....
   ....
   ....

8. Which of the SG Great Britain Specialised catalogues do you buy?
   ....
   ....
   ....
   ....

9. Would you like us to let you know when the next edition of this catalogue is due to be published?
   a. Yes O
   b. No O

   If so please give your contact details below.
   Name: ....
   Address: ....
   ....
   ....
   ....
   Email: ....
   Telephone: ....

10. Which other Stanley Gibbons Catalogues are you interested in?
    a. ....
    b. ....
    c. ....

Many thanks for your comments.

Please complete and return it to: Hugh Jefferies (Catalogue Editor)
Stanley Gibbons Limited, 7 Parkside, Ringwood, Hampshire BH24 3SH, United Kingdom
or email: lholcombe@stanleygibbons.co.uk to request a soft copy

2011 Southern & Central Africa Catalogue

From Stanley Gibbons, THE WORLD'S LARGEST STAMP STOCK

Priority order form – Four easy ways to order

Phone: 020 7836 8444 Overseas: +44 (0)20 7836 8444

Fax: 020 7557 4499 Overseas: +44 (0)20 7557 4499

Email: lmourne@stanleygibbons.co.uk

Post: Lesley Mourne, Stamp Mail Order Department, Stanley Gibbons Ltd, 399 Strand, London, WC2R 0LX, England

Customer Details

Account Number ....

Name ....

Address ....

....

Postcode .... Country ....

Email ....

Tel No. .... Fax No. ....

Payment details

Registered Postage & Packing £3.60

○ Please find my cheque/postal order enclosed for £..

Please make cheques payable to Stanley Gibbons Ltd.

Cheques must be in £ sterling and drawn on a UK bank

○ Please debit my credit card for £.. in full payment.

○ Mastercard ○ VISA ○ Diners ○ AMEX ○ Switch

Card Number

CVC Number Issue No (Switch)

Start Date (Switch & Amex) / Expiry Date /

Signature .... Date ....

2011 Southern & Central Africa Stamp Catalogue

From Stanley Gibbons, THE WORLD'S LARGEST STAMP STOCK

Condition (mint/UM/used)	Country	SG No.	Description	Price	Office use only
			POSTAGE & PACKING	£3.60	
			GRAND TOTAL		

Minimum price. The minimum catalogue price quoted in 10p. For individual stamps, prices between 10p and 95p are provided as a guide for catalogue users. The lowest price charged for individual stamps or sets purchased from Stanley Gibbons Ltd is £1.

Please complete payment, name and address details overleaf